CPI™

Manual
THIRD EDITION
2002 PRINTING

Harrison G. Gough, Ph.D.

Pamela Bradley, Ph.D.

CALIFORNIA PSYCHOLOGICAL INVENTORY™

CPP, Inc.
800-624-1765
www.cpp.com

ISBN: 978-0-89106-034-5

Printed in the United States of America.
19 18   17 16 15 14 13 12 11

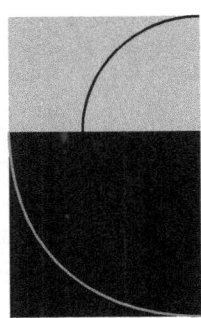

Contents

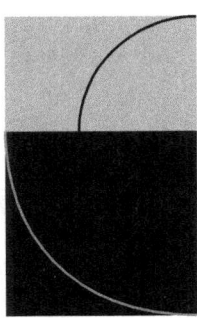

Acknowledgments

Acknowledgments for the 1996 Manual

First of all, we want to thank our spouses, Kathryn and Marlon, for their loving support and infinite patience in helping us to carry work on the manual through to completion. It is time now to return to a more normal existence.

Since the appearance of the previous manual in 1987, a great deal of new and important research has been published. For this reason alone, a new manual is needed. Another important reason for preparing a new manual was the passage in 1990 of the Americans with Disabilities Act. This Act made it illegal to ask about both psychological and physical disabilities in preemployment testing. Guidelines issued by the Equal Employment Opportunity Commission also prohibited inquiry that could be deemed invasive or prejudicial. At least some of the items in the inventory seemed to be contraindicated by these criteria.

In 1993, under the leadership of Tom Prehn of CPP, Inc., a survey of psychological and other experts was conducted, seeking advice on CPI™ items that might be interdicted according to the ADA and EEOC stipulations. We want to thank Tom for his guidance in these matters, and also the following individuals whose advice was so generously given: Wayne Cascio, Sandra Davis, George Domino, Lorraine Eyde, David Freeman, Linda Gottfredson, Leaetta Hough, Allen Hammer, Loring McAllister, Robert McHenry, Pierre Meyer, Robert Most, Richard Rees, Michael Roberts, and Heinz Werner.

In the fall of 1993, a smaller group, consisting of the two of us plus Tom, Robert Devine, Pete Meyer, Robert Most, Mike Roberts, and Diane Silver, went over every item in Form 462 of the CPI to determine which ones had to be dropped. Our goal, of course, was to retain as many items as possible, so as to maintain equivalence between the new version and Form 462. These deliberations led to the elimination of 28 items.

Early in 1994, we began the long and arduous process of reanalyzing CPI archival data at the item level for items to substitute in each scale for any that had been deleted. Insofar as possible, we wanted to keep normative statistics and profile configurations for Form 434 similar to those for Form 462. Another task at this time was the computation of the new interpretive data provided in the several appendices for this manual. Writing on the new manual began in 1995, in the expectation that the work would be completed by the end of the year; but in spite of our best intentions, it took another nine months to finish the task. We hope the final product will be judged worthy of the time and effort so many people have invested in it.

A few words should be said about the archival research files on which the manual is based. In the mid-1950s, a first collection of such material was initiated, with the help and guidance of Quintin Welch, at that time the computer consultant for the Institute of Personality Assessment and Research in Berkeley. In the mid-1960s, Susan Hopkin took his post and continued in charge of the CPI research files until the late 1970s. In addition to her constant surveillance of the data bank for accuracy and completeness, Susan carried out hundreds of analyses, many of which eventuated in journal papers and other publications. In the late 1970s, Daniel S. Weiss assumed responsibility for these functions, and in the early 1980s, Kevin Lanning became principal analyst. During Kevin's tenure, the first computerized interpretive narrative for the CPI was written, and then programmed by Kevin. In addition, the analyses on which the 1987 manual was based were almost entirely carried out by him. In the mid-1980s, Pamela Bradley took on these responsibilities. The analyses reported in this new manual come from her work. Looking into the future, Pamela will continue her stewardship of the archival research files from this point on.

A considerable portion of the research data for the CPI has come from assessments and other projects at the Institute in Berkeley. We are grateful to our present and past colleagues at IPAR who were kind enough to furnish such information to us, most importantly Frank Barron, Jack Block, Kenneth Craik, Richard Crutchfield, Wallace Hall, Ravenna Helson, and Donald MacKinnon. The act-frequency data reported extensively in chapter 5 were generously made available by David Buss.

Extracting staff ratings, life history interview protocols, and other materials from the files for each assessment was often quite difficult. In fact, it never could have been done without the help of Wallace Hall. We think of him as the magician of the research files, and cannot count the number of times he found things feared lost forever, or detected errors in our records that had escaped the attention of everyone else.

We have also been helped immeasurably by individuals at CPP, Inc., first and foremost Robert Devine. His buoyant optimism saw us through several crises, and his perceptive editorial critiques of our manuscript have been extraordinarily helpful. We also want to thank Joseph Duval and his staff of computer experts for programming the new Gough and McAllister interpretive narratives, Lorene Lederer and Mark Ong for their contributions to design, and Lorin Letendre for providing the wherewithal that made our work possible.

Harrison G. Gough
Pebble Beach, California
Pamela Bradley
Oakland, California
September 1996

Acknowledgments for the 1987 Administrator's Guide

As a (somewhat) young psychologist 28 years ago, I reviewed Carl Rogers' personality adjustment inventory for children in the *Fifth Mental Measurements Yearbook.* I commended Rogers for his insights into the psychology of adjustment, but scolded him for the fact that his manual had gone 25 years without a revision. Little did I think then that for my own *California Psychological Inventory*™, more than 30 years would elapse before publication of a new edition. One assumes early on that changes in a test will be easy to make; but as experience accrues, as criticisms accumulate, and as new potentialities of the instrument initially unforeseen become visible, the task of revision looms up as ever more formidable. So, in spite of my good intentions in 1956 for rather regular modifications of the CPI, it has taken all this time to prepare the present new version.

I hope that the changes made will prove to be good ones, and that persons who have used the CPI over the years will find this new edition an improvement on the old. I am a firm believer in the utilitarian criterion of worth, and value deeply the reactions and judgments of those who make serious use of the inventory. Responses to this new edition will be helpful in laying a good foundation for the next version of the test, which certainly should take less than 30 years to develop.

An enormous amount of work by others has gone into the assembling of material and data for this volume. In maintaining the research archives and conducting computer analyses, four individuals in particular have made major contributions: Susan Hopkin, Kevin Lanning, Daniel Weiss, and Quintin Welch. In addition, Kevin Lanning did all of the programming for the computerized narrative report. Statistical advice and clarification of problematic issues have come from Jack Block, Eliezir Karni, and Howard Terry. From the writings and comments on the CPI of George Domino, Mario Fioravanti, Francis Gendre, Lewis Goldberg, Malcolm Gynther, Robert Hogan, Benjamin Kleinmuntz, Renato Lazzari, Loring McAllister, Edwin Megargee, Pierre Meyer, David Rodgers, and George Welsh, I have learned a great deal. They will recognize many of their ideas in the new *Guide.*

My colleagues and students at the Institute of Personality Assessment and Research at Berkeley have provided data, support, and counsel at every stage. I especially want to thank the following persons: Frank Barron, Pamela Bradley, Alice Brilmayer, Jane Brooks, Kendall Bryant, David Buss, Lillian Cartwright, Kenneth Craik, George DeVos, Linda Dunn, Nickolaus Feimer, Wallace Hall, Ravenna Helson, Georgina La Russa, Peter Lifton, Georgine Marrott, Gerald Mendelsohn, Geraldine Moane, Daniel Ozer, Carolyn Phinney, John Searles, Avril Thorne, Ansfried Weinert, Paul Werner, and Paul Wink.

Important data files were made available to me by Dean Allen, David Buss, Marvin Dunnette, Robert Hogan, Joseph Horn, Keith Jacoby, Penelope Kegel-Flom, and Mary Adele Monson. New scales, either used directly in the current version of the inventory, or as benchmarks for the development of other scales, were drawn from the work of Donald Baucom, Charles Dicken, Leonard Goodstein, Robert Hogan, William Kurtines, Allan Leventhal, Robert Nichols, Richard Schnell, and William Schrader.

At CPP, Inc., the help of Robert Most on every feature of this new edition of the CPI has been generous and invaluable. John D. Black and Lorin Letendre have also given constant support and insightful counsel.

Finally, for the help and gentle nurturance of my wife Kathryn, I shall be forever grateful. I am sure she has heard every sentence of text in the *Guide* read aloud, while the two of us struggled for clarity of meaning and at least a semblance of grace in expression. Her share of whatever merit the *Guide* may possess is substantial.

My thoughts now turn to the future, as I await the results from new analyses, new applications, and new critiques. The inventory has shown a certain utility in the past; may it show even greater value in the future.

Harrison G. Gough
Pebble Beach, California
April 1987

Acknowledgments for the 1957 CPI™ Manual

Many persons have contributed to the development of the *California Psychological Inventory.* To list them all would be an impossibility. A special acknowledgment is due Dr. Starke R. Hathaway, whose work on the assessment of clinical and psychiatric variable served as a direct inspiration and background for the present effort. I am indebted to him and to the publishers of the *Minnesota Multiphasic Personality Inventory* for permitting items from the MMPI to be included in the *California Psychological Inventory.*

For direct collaboration on the development of scales included in the CPI, I am grateful to Dr. Herbert McClosky and Dr. Paul E. Meehl (the Dominance and Responsibility scales), to Dr. Donald R. Peterson (the Socialization scale), and to Dr. R. Nevitt Sanford (the Flexibility scale). I should also like to thank many colleagues and associates at the University of California Institute of Personality Assessment and Research who have worked so unstintingly on this project over the past six years, particularly Mrs. Eleanor Blanchard and Mrs. Mary Gibbons.

Harrison G. Gough
Berkeley, California
December 1956

Introduction

Purposes

The primary purpose of Form 434 of the CPI is the same as that of earlier versions, Form 480 (Gough, 1957) and Form 462 (Gough, 1987), namely, to furnish information to the interpreter from which a veridical (true-to-life) and useful picture may be drawn of the person taking the test. The portrait should be recognizable as accurate by friends and acquaintances, and should also provide a good starting point for predicting future behavior and for understanding prior actions. For the psychologist or other professional who interprets the profile, nomothetic and statistical information will be helpful, but nothing can substitute for the training and intuitive skills of the interpreter. For this reason, case studies of individuals are essential. Fortunately, there are excellent sources of this kind of material, including McAllister's (1996) interpretational guide, the book by Meyer and Davis (1992) on using the CPI in industrial and organizational psychology, Groth-Marnat's (1996) handbook on assessment, Craig's (1999) book on clinical interpretation, and case analyses relevant to specific criteria such as creativity (Gough, 1992), prejudice (Gough & Bradley, 1993), and career planning (Gough, 1995).

To put this in another way, the goal of the inventory is to assess individuals by means of variables and concepts that ordinary people use in their daily lives to understand, classify, and predict their own behavior and that of others. The patterns and configurations among such variables depict, and correspond to, the uniqueness of all individuals. The task of the interpreter is to synthesize the evidence provided by the scales of the inventory, and the configurations of these scales, into a totality that can meaningfully represent each person tested. The everyday variables for which the inventory is scaled (for example, dominance, sociability, self-control, and flexibility) may be thought of as *folk concepts*— that is, concepts that arise from and are linked to the processes of interpersonal life, and that are to be found everywhere that humans congregate into groups and establish societal functions.

Folk concepts of this kind constitute an attractive way to assess personal dispositions, because of their hypothesized universality, their relevance to the daily demands of the social nexus, and their emergence and survival over long periods of time in the natural language. This is not to deny, of course, that other and also worthwhile descriptive and analytic systems for the understanding of personality can be posited. Furthermore, techniques of measurement based on these other conceptual models are to be welcomed. In psychological assessment, it is a distinct advantage to have a range of tools available, each deriving from its own logic and theoretical roots. The professional user of such tools can then pick and choose those that are more helpful and accurate in the particular setting in which assessment is to be carried out.

Five Axioms

Psychologists and others who may use the CPI should be aware of the basic principles governing its construction and validation. There are five fundamental postulates or axioms (Gough, 1995). These axioms will be briefly described below, and then later, as appropriate, redescribed in expanded ways.

Axiom 1. This axiom is addressed to the query, "What attributes of personality will be assessed?" The answer is that the scales of the CPI are based on folk concepts. These are everyday constructs about personality that all people, everywhere, make use of to comprehend their own behavior and the behavior of others.

Axiom 2. Axiom two may be termed the *open system* axiom. It pertains to the question, "How many scales will the system include?" The guiding principle is that a sufficient number of scales will be included so that any consequential, recurring form of interpersonal behavior can be forecast, either from a single scale (the rare case), or from a combination of two, three, or sometimes four scales (the usual case). If an important criterion turns out to be unpredictable from the present set of scales, a new measure may be added to the system. If a scale now in the set seldom or never plays a part in this enterprise, it may be dropped. Since the CPI was first constructed, scales have been added and dropped in accordance with this axiom.

Axiom 3. This axiom may be called the *instrumental* axiom. It relates to the question, "What are the intentions of each scale?" In personality assessment, there are two major answers to this query. One, called here the *definitional approach*, views scales from the standpoint of trait measurement and seeks to develop scales having maximal internal consistency, minimal correlations with each other, and correct placement in a factor analytic matrix.

The instrumental approach, on the other hand, specifies two, and only two, criteria for each scale: (a) to predict with reasonable accuracy what people will say and do in defined situations, and (b) to identify people who will be described in meaningful and differentiated ways by those who know them well. Extended discussion of these instrumental/pragmatic objectives may be found in a number of prior reports (Gough, 1968a, 1987, 1989).

Axiom 4. This principle may be called the *topographical* axiom. It deals with the question, "How shall the scales be related to each other?" The axiom states that the inventory's scales should correlate with each other in the same direction and to the same degree as do the concepts as used by ordinary people in their everyday lives. The goal, in other words, is not orthogonality, or psychometric independence.

Axiom 5. This axiom may be called the *intensification of measurement* axiom, and provides an answer to the question, "Should measurement be restricted to single, key dimensions, or should facets within those dimensions be separately scaled?" For the CPI, major themes (such as introversion/extraversion) are assessed by a family of intercorrelated measures indicative of nuances and subtleties in the way in which the general disposition is manifested. For example, the first sector of the profile sheet contains seven scales depicting different but related ways in which self-assurance, poise, and participative dispositions are expressed. The second sector also has seven scales, each indicative of a facet in the realm of intrapersonal values and self-regulation.

Composition of Form 434

Form 434 of the CPI contains 434 items, 28 fewer than in the previous Form 462 of the inventory. The 28 items dropped from Form 462 include those contraindicated by the 1991 Americans with Disabilities Act, items possibly in conflict with fair employment practices legislation or that might violate rights of privacy, and a few items that an appreciable number of persons taking the test have found objectionable. Examples are, "I have never done any heavy drinking" and "I am troubled by attacks of nausea and vomiting" (ADA proscriptions), "I feel sure there is only one true religion" (privacy considerations), and "I like tall women" (objectionable item).

Scores on the 20 folk scales are printed in the computer reports in profile form, as derived from samples of 3,000 men and 3,000 women, and from the total sample of 6,000 persons. So as to maintain comparability of patterns of scores between Form 462 and Form 434, scales in Form 434 have been kept at the same length as in Form 462. For instance, if two items from a Form 462 scale were dropped, then two other items from among the 434 retained items were substituted in the scale. The three vector scales (see chapter 2 for a discussion of the three-vector model) are now reported in both raw and standard scores, and in a graphic display depicting lifestyle and level of self-realization.

A question sometimes asked about the CPI and about other inventories is, "What determines its length, and the number of items?" One of the determinants is the number of variables to be assessed, and the number of items needed for valid appraisals. Axioms 1 and 2 for the CPI specify folk concepts as the domain of measurement, and the need for something in the neighborhood of 20 such dimensions to permit prediction and conceptualization of all or nearly all consequential and recurring forms of interpersonal behavior. For true-false items, it takes from 25 to 30 items as a minimum to produce a sufficient range of scores for making differential predictions, which for 20 scales would mean from 500 to 600 items, if no overlap was allowed. However, because of a small amount of overlap among items in the scales, the total can be kept at 434. Inventories that are longer and inventories that are shorter are cited in Appendix C. For example, the original MMPI had 566 items and the present MMPI-2 has 567. The MMPI for adolescents has 478 items. *Jackson's Personality Research Form*, Form BB, has 440 items; the *Omnibus Personality Inventory* has 385 items; the *Guilford-Zimmerman Temperament Survey* has 300 items; and the NEO-AC has 240 items. In each instance, there is a proportionality between length and the number of variables that are scaled. A rule of thumb is that the narrower the scope of the inventory the fewer the items, and the broader or more encompassing the scope the larger the number.

Table 1.1 presents the 20 folk and 3 vector scales, their length, the number of new items in their Form 434 versions, and correlations between the scales as scored on Form 462 and as scored now on Form 434. In addition, means and standard deviations are given for the prior (old) scoring of the scales and the current (new) scoring, as computed on the contemporary profile norm samples of 3,000 persons of each sex. The means and standard deviations reported in the 1987 *CPI Administrator's Guide* for these scales were based on the prior norm samples of 1,000 of each sex, of course, and hence are different from the figures appearing in Table 1.1.

Correlations between the 462-item and 434-item versions of the 23 scales varied from a low of .96 (for both sexes, on the Sa and Wb scales), to an obvious high of 1.00 for the six scales scored the same way on both forms. These coefficients suggest that prior research findings for the CPI can be safely generalized to the 434-item form. Differences between scale means, for males, ranged from 0 to 1.11 (Wb), with an overall mean of 0.24. For females, the range was from 0 to 1.50 (Well-being), with a mean of 0.29. The differences on Wb can be attributed to the fact that seven items referring to disabilities were removed, with seven different items substituted. The generally low magnitude of differences in raw score means suggest that comparability of the scales has been maintained. The new profile sheets are, of course, based on the new norms.

In addition to the folk and vector scales carried over from Form 462, 13 special purpose or research scales are provided for use in designated settings and at the discretion of the examiner. Eight of these were also included in the manual for Form 462 (Gough, 1987), namely Mp (Managerial Potential; Gough, 1984), Wo (Work Orientation; Gough, 1985), CT (Creative Temperament; Gough, 1992), B–MS and B–FM (Baucom's unipolar scales for masculinity and feminity; Baucom, 1976, 1980; Baucom & Danker-Brown, 1984; Baucom & Weiss, 1986), Anx (Anxiety; Leventhal, 1966, 1968), D–SD (Dicken's scale for social desirability; Dicken, 1963), and D–AC (Dicken's scale for acquiescence; Dicken, 1963).

The five new special purpose scales include Lp (Leadership), Ami (Amicability), Leo (Law Enforcement Orientation), Tm (Tough-mindedness), and Nar (Narcissism; Wink & Gough, 1990).

The Open System

The first research version of the CPI contained 548 items. It was scored for 15 of the 20 folk scales now reported on the profile sheet. When the 480-item

Table 1.1 Relationships Between Form 462 and Form 434 Scales of the CPI

| Scales | Length | New Items | Correlations Between Old and New Scales | | Mean Scores on Form 462 (Old) and Form 434 (New) Scales | | | |
| | | | Males (N = 3,000) | Females (N = 3,000) | Males (N = 3,000) | | Females (N = 3,000) | |
					Old	New	Old	New
Do (Dominance)	36	2	.99	.99	19.50	19.41	19.19	18.95
Cs (Capacity for Status)	28	2	.98	.98	14.92	15.11	15.27	15.56
Sy (Sociability)	32	1	.99	.99	19.78	19.76	20.17	19.93
Sp (Social Presence)	38	2	.98	.98	24.29	24.45	23.20	23.50
Sa (Self-acceptance)	28	3	.96	.96	16.65	16.01	16.72	15.85
In (Independence)	30	1	.99	.99	15.73	15.34	14.59	14.15
Em (Empathy)	38	1	.99	.99	19.28	19.07	19.58	19.44
Re (Responsibility)	36	1	.99	.99	23.98	23.98	25.92	25.98
So (Socialization)	46	2	.99	.99	29.89	29.70	31.71	31.42
Sc (Self-control)	38	0	1.00	1.00	19.19	19.19	20.72	20.72
Gl (Good Impression)	40	0	1.00	1.00	17.20	17.20	17.30	17.30
Cm (Communality)	38	2	.99	.99	34.58	34.58	34.84	34.87
Wb (Well-being)	38	7	.96	.96	30.58	29.47	29.80	28.30
To (Tolerance)	32	3	.98	.98	18.41	18.57	19.71	20.09
Ac (Achievement via Conformance)	38	1	.99	.99	25.14	24.84	26.68	26.33
Ai (Achievement via Independence)	36	0	1.00	1.00	19.27	19.27	19.15	19.15
Ie (Intellectual Efficiency)	42	5	.97	.97	27.93	27.47	27.93	27.55
Py (Psychological-mindedness)	28	2	.97	.97	14.15	14.55	13.81	14.24
Fx (Flexibility)	28	0	1.00	1.00	13.11	13.11	12.92	12.92
F/M (Femininity/Masculinity)	32	0	1.00	1.00	13.46	13.46	20.59	20.59
v.1 (Externality/Internality)	34	0	1.00	1.00	18.38	18.38	19.44	19.44
v.2 (Norm-doubting/Norm-favoring)	36	2	.98	.99	22.32	21.84	23.72	23.28
v.3 (Ego integration)	58	4	.99	.99	31.95	31.13	32.36	31.17

Note: All of the scales have the same length in Forms 462 and 434. "New Items" does not refer to newly written items, but rather to items already included in the CPI that were substituted in each scale for the items dropped from Form 462.

form of the CPI was published in 1956, three new scales were added: Sp (Social Presence), Sa (Self-acceptance), and Sc Self-control). Also, several scales that had been scored on Form 548 were dropped. An example is a scale for neurodermatitis (Gough, Allerhand, & Grais, 1950), whose intentions were hard to reconcile with the theoretical model of folk concepts. In 1986, the 480-item CPI was replaced by Form 462, and two new scales were added to the profile sheet: Em (Empathy; Hogan, 1969; Johnson, Cheek, & Smither, 1981), and In (Independence; Gough, 1989). The three vector scales used to define the cuboid model of personality structure were also introduced in the 1986 edition. As stated above, 28 items were dropped from Form 462 to develop Form 434 (CPI, Third Edition), and five new special purpose scales have been added.

The CPI is by no means the only inventory that has undergone changes over time in accordance with the concept of an open system. Perhaps the prototypical example of an open system in psychological assessment is the *Strong Interest Inventory®*, whose items have dropped from over 400 in 1927 (Strong, 1943), to 399 (Campbell, 1967, 1974), to 325 (Campbell, 1977; Hansen, 1984), to 317 in the current version (Harmon, Hansen, Borgen, & Hammer, 1994). Over the years, scales have been dropped from the *Strong*, and many new scales have been added, including measures for Holland's (1973) six general occupational themes.

Instrumental Versus Definitional Goals

In psychological measurement, two points of view may be noted concerning the purposes of scales. One of these is the *definitional*, which sees scales as specifying or defining a psychological variable. Much of the early writing about the appraisal of intelligence either explicitly or implicitly espoused this viewpoint. A famous early dictum (Boring, 1923) embodying this perspective alleged that "intelligence is what the tests test." The *trait* conception of personality testing also stems from the definitional perspective.

Opposed to the definitional view is the *instrumental*. From the instrumental standpoint, the goals of a scale are utilitarian or pragmatic, and evaluations of the validity of a measure should be based on criteria of this kind. For instance, does a scale for dominance in fact identify people who are described by others as dominant, strong, self-assured, and resourceful, and who, in addition, do things that can consensually be classified as dominant (Buss & Craik, 1980, 1981, 1983a)? In its underlying logic, the CPI is clearly affiliated with this instrumental or pragmatic perspective.

The most consequential of the differences between the definitional and instrumental views about measurement is found in the criteria stipulated for evaluating the worth of the test. From the definitional side, the criteria of choice include the degree to which the items in the scale systematically sample the apparent content of the domain, the degree to which the items are interrelated (so as to establish a homogeneous and unifactorial scale if possible), and the correspondence of the text of the items to an articulated formulation of the meaning of the measure. In regard to dominance, promising items from the definitional standpoint would be: "I am dominant," "Others see me as dominant," "Being dominant is a good thing," "I like to be in charge of and direct others," "I have a natural talent for leadership," and "In conversations, I tend to take the initiative and talk the most." One of the problems with scales based on definitional guidelines, apparent in these illustrations, is that their intentions are easy to discern, and faking, if attempted, is relatively easy.

From the instrumental side, the above criteria are merely means to an end, and if the true goals or purposes of appraisal can be achieved without recourse to them, they are nonbinding. The criteria for the instrumentalist include the degree to which the test classifies people in the way that others classify them and the accuracy with which scores on the test predict or confirm behavior that is significantly relevant to the purposes put forward for the measure. For instance, if a scale for responsibility accurately classifies people who are consensually described as responsible, reliable, dependable, and conscientious (high scorers), or as irresponsible, undependable, erratic, and slipshod (low scorers), and also accurately predicts the behavior of individuals in situations where reliability and diligence are important, then it is of little moment to observe that the scale has low interitem concordance, or that it is factorially multifaceted.

Scales developed by instrumental criteria often contain a mix of both obvious and subtle items. A *subtle* item is one whose scale membership and direction of scoring are hard to identify simply from a reading of the item. The Form 434 Ie (Intellectual Efficiency) scale includes obvious items, such as "I seem to be about as capable and smart as most people around me" ("true"); "I was a slow learner in school" ("false"); and "I am quite a fast reader" ("true"). It also includes more subtle and less obvious items, such as "Most people make friends because friends are likely to be useful to them" ("false"); "People are much too easy on their children nowadays" ("false"); "Success is a matter of will power" ("false"); and "I gossip a little at times" ("true").

Instrumental scales are usually, but not always, developed by so-called empirical item analysis. Empirical technique bases the selection and scoring of items on their demonstrated relationships to external or nontest criteria. The method permits the discovery of items whose content is seemingly unrelated to the objectives of measurement, and also permits the rejection of seemingly relevant items that in fact fail to demonstrate these relationships.

Topographical Intentions

The topographical axiom specifies that correlations among the CPI folk scales should reflect the correlations among the same concepts when used for interpersonal description. Also, each scale, taken individually, is intended to assess the cluster or composite of qualities subsumed under the name for the same concept as used by the folk. Independence, for example, signifies both self-sufficiency and distance or detachment from others. The scale for independence on the inventory must therefore contain both of these components. From the adjectival descriptions by observers (reported in Appendix D), it appears that both elements are discernible in high scorers on the In scale. For example, the adjective *individualistic* had correlations ranging from .16 to .25 in six different samples comprising 1,828 people, with a median of .20. Correlations for the adjective *independent* ranged from .16 to .32, with a median of .22; and for *confident* the range was from .21 to .32, with a median of .28. All of the 18 coefficients just summarized were statistically significant at or beyond the .05 level of probability.

The topographical principle also requires that correlations between scales should converge on the correlations among the same concepts when used by raters or observers. In a sample of 198 college sophomores assessed by means of interviews, group discussions, and a wide variety of informal interactions, staff ratings of independence and social acuity or empathy correlated .63. This finding suggests that the correlation between the In and Em (Empathy) scales should be in the region of .60. In the current norm samples of 3,000 persons of each set, the coefficients for In versus Em were .53 for men and .58 for women.

A more comprehensive topographical analysis was carried out using small clusters of six adjectives

each to mark the 20 folk concepts, with no adjective appearing on more than one cluster. For example, Sc (Self-control) was indexed by moderate, patient, and self-controlled (indicative), and by daring, impulsive, and mischievous (contraindicative). For In, the six adjectives were confident, independent, and individualistic (indicative), and dependent, meek, and mild (contraindicative). For Ie (Intellectual Efficiency), the words were alert, intelligent, and rational (indicative), and dull, nervous, and unintelligent (contraindicative). The 20 ACL clusters were then intercorrelated in six observational samples: 236 men described by their wives or partners, 194 college men, each described by three peers; 612 men assessed at the Institute of Personality Assessment and Research, and each described by a panel of 10 staff observers; 236 women described by their husbands or partners; 192 college women, each described by three peers; and 358 assessed women, each described by a panel of 10 observers. The six 20 × 20 matrices were then correlated with the 20 × 20 CPI matrices for each sample, with these results: male spouses, $r = .76$; male students, $r = .78$; male assessees, $r = .80$; female spouses, $r = .73$; female students, $r = .80$; and female assessees, $r = .95$. Quite clearly, the correlations among the folk scales of the CPI do converge on the correlations among the same concepts as used by observers.

A common criticism of the CPI, based on the tacit (and mistaken) assumption that its goals dictate the development of uncorrelated or orthogonal scales, is that the mean level of correlation among scales is too high. For the 20 × 20 matrix of folk scales on the norm sample of males, the coefficients ranged from a low of –.25 (Sp vs. F/M) to a high of .82 (Sc vs. Gi), with a median of .42. For the matrix in the norm sample of females, the range was from –.40 (In vs. F/M) to .84 (Sc vs. Gi), with a median of .42. How do these values compare with what may be found for other tests? For the *Wechsler Adult Intelligence Test* (Wechsler, 1939), the 10 subscales in the sample of persons ages 20 to 34 ranged in correlations from .16 to .72, with a median of .44. For the MMPI, the 13 × 13 matrix reported by Kassebaum, Couch, and Slater (1959) had correlations ranging from –.28 to .83, with a median of .33.

From a study of the *Millon Clinical Multiaxial Inventory* (MCMI; Millon, 1983) by Holliman and Guthrie (1989), a matrix of the 20 scales was computed for a sample of 236 persons (118 of each sex). One of the MCMI scales (Compulsive Personality) had negative correlations with all of the other 19 measures. When these correlations were reflected to positive values, the range of the coefficients was from −.64 to .95, with a median of .42. The coefficient of .95 was for the Schizotypal and Avoidant Personality scales, and that of −.64 was for the Antisocial and Dependent Personality scales. As stated in the previous paragraph, the largest correlations for any two CPI scales were those of .82 (males) and .84 (females) for the Self-control and Good Impression measures. In the MCMI 20 × 20 matrix, there were 13 coefficients greater than .84.

A reasonable inference from these quick scans of intercorrelation matrices is that in most multivariate tests addressed to a recognizable domain (for example, psychopathology, cognitive functioning, personality disorders, and concepts expressed in the natural language), median values between, say, .35 and .45 may be expected. Rather than being "too high," the median level for the CPI matrix is about at the norm for comparable tests.

Item overlap (items appearing on more than one scale) is another psychometric issue about which experts have different opinions. One viewpoint contends that overlap should be avoided at all costs, opposed to the view that it makes little difference as long as the amount of overlap is small. A major allegation of those who eschew overlap is that it alters, modifies, or obscures the factorial dimensions underlying the intercorrelational matrix of multivariate inventory. Obviously, this is an assertion that should be evaluated empirically to see if, in fact, overlap has a detectable and confounding influence on factorial structure. The amount of overlap should also be explicitly determined, in order to permit comparison among tests on this phenomenon. Let us first look at the specifics of overlap among the scales of the CPI in comparison with several other tests and, after that, at published studies of the influence or lack of influence of overlap on the factor structure of the CPI.

On the CPI, there is only one instance of 10 or more items in common between two scales. This occurs between the 38-item Sc and 40-item Gi scales, which share 12 items. Several scales share eight items, for example, Do and In, Sy and Sp, and Ai and Ie. Shared items are not always scored in the same direction. Sa has four items in common with Sc, but all are scored in opposite directions. The overlap among scales is higher on the MMPI than it is on the CPI. The F and Sc (Schizophrenia) scales have 15 items in common, all scored alike, D (Depression) and Pt (Psychasthenia) share 13 similarly scored items, and Hs (Hypochondriasis) and Hy (Hysteria) have 20 overlapping and similarly scored items. The extent of overlap is even higher for the *Millon Clinical Multiaxial Inventory* and for the *Strong Interest Inventory.*

There is a formula for estimating the correlation between any two scales based on the number of common items scored the same way on both scales and on the length of the two scales. When this formula is applied to the 153 pairs of CPI scales that share items, the range of coefficients goes from a low of −.17 to a high of .29, with a median of .00. For the MMPI, the same formula, when applied to the 78 instances of overlap among the three validity and 10 clinical scales, generated a range of correlations from −.15 to .46, with a median of .04. With the exception of the overlap coefficient for Hs and Hy on the MMPI, the correlations are low in magnitude and converge on .00.

What is the effect of item overlap on the correlation matrix and factor structure of the CPI? There are four published studies dealing with this topic (Cohen & Farley, 1977; Farley & Cohen, 1974, 1980; Rogers & Shure, 1965). Three methods were employed to remove or reduce the effects of item overlap. One was to drop all overlapping items and then score the scales for their unique items only. A second was to assign overlapping items randomly to the two scales in a pair so as to eliminate duplication. A third was to lower the computed correlations between scales according to the magnitude of the correlations that would be produced by overlap alone. For example, the Re and So scales have three items in common, all scored in the same direction. Applying the overlap formula yields a correlation of .07. The observed correlations of .65 for men and .60 for women are then lowered by .07 prior to factoring.

The findings in all of the studies were that the factors extracted and their loadings were close to identical under all four conditions (the scales as scored, and with the three different adjustments). In reflecting on this finding, Rogers and Shure (1965) commented that the interpersonal and intrapersonal themes embedded in the CPI scales are too powerful to be modified by anything as trivial as a few items of overlap between scales. Farley and Cohen (1980) suggested that there might even be an advantage to using overlapping items, in that more extensive and intensive assessment could be conducted with a smaller list of items than would be possible without such overlap.

Intentions of the Scales

As stated above, the intentions stipulated for the scales of the inventory are (a) to predict what people will say and do in specified contexts, and (b) to identify individuals who will be evaluated and described in differentiating and interpersonally significant ways. These purposes should be clearly distinguished from the common psychometric aims of defining psychological traits and generating a factorial matrix of uncorrelated variables. That is, no claims are advanced in regard to defining or assessing psychological traits, even though the names selected for some of the scales are the same as those used in trait nomenclature. Also, as discussed in regard to the topographical principle, intercorrelations among the scales should correspond to the intercorrelations among the same concepts in folk usage rather than to an arbitrary model of orthogonal relationships.

The conceptualization of scales as having classificatory and predictive import, free of any linkage to trait notions, can be illustrated by reference to the *Strong Interest Inventory* (Harmon, Hansen, Borgen, & Hammer, 1994). Consider, for example, the *Strong* scale for Physicist. Including this scale in the *Strong* does not imply that a trait called *physicist* or *physicalism* is being proposed, nor even that there is some single, unidimensional, monofactorial theme being assessed. Rather, the appeal is to instrumental, pragmatic concerns, and the claims of the scale are that people who score high will resemble physicists in ways that are valuable to know, will tend to be described as physicists are described, and will tend to do and say things that physicists say and do. To the extent that these expectations are confirmed, the scale will be of interest and value.

Going further with this example, no claim is made (or needed) that the scale for physicist is

uncorrelated with other scales, for instance, that for mathematician. In fact, these two scales are usually very highly correlated, beyond anything found in the 20 × 20 matrix for the folk scales of the CPI. Does this mean that the two *Strong* scales are redundant, that they overlap too much, that they are psychometrically unworthy, or that one should be dropped? Not at all, because their substantial correlation actually reflects what is known to occur in the scientific and academic domains. Most physicists have mathematical interests and talents, and it would be strange indeed if a scale for the former failed to correlate strongly with a scale for the latter. In the other direction, many mathematicians, but certainly not all, also have an interest in and a talent for the field of physics. Because of these relatively few but important exceptions (mathematicians with little interest in physics) it is good to have both scales instead of only one, so that the infrequent person with discrepant scores on the two scales can be identified.

Turning to the CPI, consider the Do and Sp scales. In the norm samples, their correlation is .59 for men and .60 for women, and both are found in the first sector on the profile sheet dealing with interpersonal style, poise, and self-assurance. Are there differences worth noting in the implications of higher and lower scores on these two scales? In Appendix E, correlations of the 100 items in the *California Q-Set* (Block, 1961) with scales of the CPI are given for 547 men and 393 women described by panels of observers. On certain Q-sort items, there are appreciable differences between Do and Sp. For item 26 ("Is productive; gets things done"), correlations with Do were .21 for men and .29 for women (both coefficients significant beyond the .01 level); but correlations with Sp were .00 for men and .09 for women (neither coefficient significant at the .05 level). For item 58 ("Enjoys sensuous experiences."), values for Do were .06 for men and .03 for women; whereas correlations with Sp were .18 for men and .24 for women. For item 46 ("Engages in personal fantasy and daydreams, fictional speculations"), high scorers on Do are not much given to daydreaming, as indicated by correlations of –.24 and –.20 for men and women; whereas the Sp scale conveys little information in this regard, with correlations of –.04 for men and .04 for women.

In the realm of associated acts (Buss & Craik, 1983a), data are available for a sample of 88 couples studied by David M. Buss. Each partner was described by the other in regard to acts occurring within a recent period. The acts, using dummy weights of 1 and 0, were correlated with CPI scales for the full sample of 176 persons. The five acts with largest positive correlations with Do were the following: "Had more to say than anyone else" ($r = .34$), "Took charge of the group" ($r = .32$), "Talked a great deal at the meeting" ($r = .32$), "Learned everyone's name at the meeting" ($r = .30$), and "Spoke first at the meeting" ($r = .28$). The prosocial, problem-solving, ascendant implications stressed in interpreting the Do scale are clearly visible in these acts.

For the Sp scale, the five acts with largest positive correlations were the following: "Talked to many people at the party" ($r = .44$), "Talked to almost everyone at the party" ($r = .38$), "Danced at the party" ($r = .36$), "Took the lead in livening up a dull party" ($r = .34$), and "Danced in front of the crowd" ($r = .33$). The pleasure-seeking, spontaneous, and quasi-exhibitionistic implications skilled interpreters extract from high scores on Sp are apparent in these behaviors. The loci in which the two scales are of major relevance might also be noted. The implications of the Do scale are important in settings where people gather to conduct serious business and to make decisions, such as at work and in political life. The implications of the Sp scale are more important in informal situations, at parties, and in general where pleasurable experience is a goal.

The Ac (Achievement via Conformance) and Ai (Achievement via Independence) scales are both in the third sector on the profile sheet, and both have similar goals, including the prediction of academic and other forms of intellectual achievement. In the norm samples, their correlations are .55 for men and .50 for women. In the samples of 547 men and 393 women described by five or more observers on Block's 100 Q-sort items, there are some interesting differences between Ac and Ai. For item 7 ("Favors conservative values in a variety of areas."), the correlations with Ac were .14 for men and .20 for women, whereas the correlations with Ai were $-.13$ and $-.22$. All four coefficients are statistically significant beyond the .01 level. Item 50 ("Is unpredictable and changeable in behavior and attitudes") does not relate to the Ai scale (coefficients of $-.06$ for men and $-.04$ for women), but is associated with low scores on the Ac scale, as indicated by correlations of $-.18$ and $-.32$. Item 51 ("Genuinely values intellectual and cognitive matters") has a modest positive association with Ac, with coefficients of .16 for both sexes, but much stronger association with Ai, with coefficients of .31 for men and .45 for women. These and other descriptive relationships bring out the rule-following, self-disciplined dispositions presaged by elevations on Ac, and the more creative, intellectual dispositions associated with Ai.

A final brief example makes use of the So and Sc scales. Both are in the second sector of the profile sheet, both pertain to societal norms and values, and both are associated with rule-following behavior. Two of Block's items may be cited to bring out the differences between So and Sc. Item 15 ("Is skilled in social techniques of imaginative play, pretending, and humor") has no relevance to scores on So, as shown by correlations of .04 and .06 for men and women, respectively. However, the negative correlations with Sc of $-.12$ for men and $-.21$ for women, even though modest in size, suggest that behavior of this kind will seldom, if ever, be found among high scorers on the scale. Item 84 ("Is cheerful") correlates .20 for men and .19 for women with the So scale, but only .05 with Sc for both sexes. These findings, and many others, support the notion that compliance with norms for high scorers on So is easy, automatized, and friction-free in regard to ego functioning. For high scorers on Sc, however, compliance is invested with affect, is a self-aware behavior, and demands expenditure of psychic energy. The element of overcontrol in high scores on Sc is associated with the potential for sudden and explosive outbursts of temper, and even violence.

Itemmetric Considerations

Of the 434 items in the current form of the CPI, 171 were taken from the *Minnesota Multiphasic Personality Inventory* (MMPI; Hathaway & McKinley, 1943); 158 of these items also appear in MMPI-2 (Butcher, Dahlstrom, Graham, Tellegen, & Kaemmer, 1989).* Some of the CPI scales were

---

* Use of the MMPI items (copyright 1943 by the University of Minnesota Press) is made possible by the kind permission of the late Dr. Starke R. Hathaway, and under an agreement with the University of Minnesota Press.

originally developed by contrasting item endorsement percentages for persons classified as high or low on a designated criterion. For example, the Sy (Sociability) scale was first constructed by contrasting item endorsement rates on the MMPI for persons reporting a large number of social activities versus persons reporting none or a small number (Gough, 1952b). Some scales, such as Ie (Intellectual Efficiency; Gough, 1953b) were based on analyses of both MMPI and original items, and other scales, such as Gi (Good Impression; Gough, 1952a) were constructed largely or entirely from original items.

In writing and assembling items for the MMPI, Hathaway and McKinley made a conscious effort to include those that were easy to read, contained only frequently used and readily understood words, and were expressed in everyday idioms and phraseology. The more that these objectives were realized, the greater the possibility that respondents would answer with well-rehearsed and well-established personal reactions. In writing new items for the CPI, these same guidelines were adopted. The relatively simple language of the inventory, in other words, is a matter of policy and not just a happenstance occurrence. A readability analysis of Form 462 of the inventory (Schinka & Borum, 1994) suggests that these goals were reasonably well achieved. The mean number of words per item in this analysis was 11.92, and the mean number of syllables per word was 1.37. Overall, the CPI was readable at the fifth-grade level, as indicated by a computed value of 5.22. The NEO-PI-R (Costa & McCrae, 1992) had a grade level of 5.71, the *Personality Research Form* (Jackson, 1967) had a grade level of 5.22, and the 16PF (Cattell, 1949) had a grade level of 6.51. The most difficult individual scale to read, among the 66 examined in the study of the four inventories, was Factor N (private, observant, shrewd) on the 16PF, with a grade level of 8.97. The easiest scale to read on the CPI was Ie, with a grade level of 4.11, and the most difficult was Ai (Achievement via Independence), with a grade level of 6.53.

Another guideline for writing items was to make them as *ego-syntonic* as possible. An *ego-syntonic* item is one which a respondent finds congenial, and on which giving an opinion is a rewarding act. An example of such an item is, "I regard the right to speak my mind as very important." Most people experience a certain sense of satisfaction in responding "true" to this statement. The item, it should be noted, is scored on the Cm (Communality) scale, because most people, everywhere, give a "true" response. But even after one knows that the item is for the most part nondifferentiating, a small surge of positive affect is still associated with answering "true." A second example from the Cm scale that appears to have ego-syntonic qualities is, "I would fight if someone tried to take my rights away."

A third consideration was to make the items as subtle as possible, so as to reduce the influence of manipulative response sets. A *subtle* item is one whose scale membership is hard to guess, and whose scoring is difficult to determine merely by reading the item. To illustrate this point, examine the following four items and try to deduce, first, from which scale they are taken, and, then, how they are scored:

1. Every citizen should take the time to find out about national affairs, even if it means giving up some personal pleasures.
2. When the community makes a decision, it is up to a person to help carry it out even if he or she had been against it.
3. People should not have to pay taxes for the schools if they do not have children.
4. I have not lived the right kind of life.

Informal checking suggests that most people see these four items as having something to do with social responsibility, civic obligations, and the like. Dominance is never mentioned as the disposition being assessed, even though all four items are from the Do scale (scored as "true," "true," "false," and "false"). Only one of the items (the first) is scored on the Re (Responsibility) scale.

Here is another set of four items that are at least moderately subtle components of the scale on which they appear:

1. I am fascinated by fire.
2. I enjoy a race or game better when I bet on it.
3. I do not dread seeing a doctor about an illness.
4. I would be ashamed not to use my privilege of voting.

These four items come from the Re scale, and are scored for "false," "false," "true," and "true." Only one of the items (item 2) appears on any other of the folk scales presented on the profile sheet. This item is also scored for a "false" response on the Ie (Intellectual Efficiency) scale.

Of course, many obvious items are also included in the inventory, and for most of the folk scales they outnumber the subtle items. However, the obvious items as well as the subtle items were selected not because of their content, but because of their demonstrated relationships to the nontest criteria specified for each scale, or because of their alignment with the psychometric theme inherently defined by the items in the scale.

Methodology of Scale Development

The CPI is sometimes referred to as a prototypical example of empirical methodology. In scale development, empirical methods call for the analysis of items against nontest criteria, and then selection and keying of items in such a way as to maximize the relationships between responses to the test and the outcome or target to be forecast.

A contrasting method, often referred to as internal consistency analysis, is to begin with a set of items that are judged to be relevant to the aim of measurement, and then, by study of intercorrelations among these items, to prune out those that are least consistent with whatever psychometric theme is being assessed by the totality. Although both methods (empirical and internal consistency) have ardent adherents, research has shown that useful scales can be developed by both methods (Gough & Bradley, 1992a).

Of the 20 CPI scales now presented on the profile sheet, 13 were clearly developed by empirical methods, that is, by item analyses against nominations, ratings, life outcomes, or other non-CPI criteria. These 13 scales are for Dominance (Do), Capacity for Status (Cs), Sociability (Sy), Independence (In), Empathy (Em), Responsibility (Re), Socialization (So), Tolerance (To), Achievement via Conformance (Ac), Achievement via Independence (Ai), Intellectual Efficiency (Ie), Psychological-mindedness (Py), and Femininity/Masculinity (F/M).

Four of the 20 scales were clearly developed by the internal consistency method: Social Presence (Sp), Self-acceptance (Sa), Self-control (Sc), and Flexibility (Fx). The three remaining scales, for Good Impression (Gi), Communality (Cm), and Well-being (Wb), were developed by mixtures of strategy cutting across the empirical and internal consistency categories.

Profile and Interpretive Conventions

The 20 folk scales on the CPI profile are presented in a sequence going from the more interactional, socially observable qualities such as dominance and independence, through a second group of scales assessing internal values and controls, to a third group pertaining to achievement-seeking needs, and ending with a fourth cluster of scales dealing with stylistic modes such as flexibility and femininity/masculinity. As will be seen in the section on the factorial structure of the inventory, this sequence is compatible with but not identical to the factorial characteristics of the scales. The three vector or structural scales are separately graphed. The 13 special purpose scales are not included on the profile sheet, although in the computer-generated reports, two sets of standard scores (gender based and combined) are given, as well as raw scores for seven of them.

With the exception of the last scale on the profile sheet (F/M) for femininity/masculinity, all are scored so that higher values are associated with the conventionally favored standing on the variable, and lower scores with a less-favored status. This common directionality of the scales helps to simplify interpretation of a profile, with higher scores indicating areas of strength and lower scores indicating areas of weakness. Table 1.2 lists the 20 folk measures in the order in which they appear on the profile sheet, and also presents synoptic formulations of the meanings of higher and lower scores.

Three profile sheets are available—based on new norm samples of 3,000 males and 3,000 females—for males, for females, and for the total. In the first edition of the CPI (Gough, 1957), profiles were based on samples of 6,200 males and 7,150 females, essentially all of the protocols on file. In spite of the heterogeneity and happenstance nature of these norms, the profiles proved to be very helpful in the analysis of individual records. When the 462-item version of the CPI was introduced in 1987, specified norm samples were introduced that were comprised of 1,000 persons of each sex. Prior to publication,

Table 1.2 The 20 Folk Concept Scales and Their Intended Meanings

Measures of Poise, Self-Assurance, and Interpersonal Proclivities

Scale Name	Implications of Higher and Lower Scores
Do (Dominance)	Higher: confident, assertive, dominant, task-oriented Lower: cautious, quiet, hesitant to take the initiative
Cs (Capacity for Status)	Higher: ambitious, wants to be a success, has many interests Lower: unsure of self, dislikes direct competition, uncomfortable with uncertainty or complexity
Sy (Sociability)	Higher: sociable, likes to be with people, outgoing Lower: shy, often inhibited, prefers to stay in the background in social situations
Sp (Social Presence)	Higher: self-assured, spontaneous; versatile; verbally fluent; pleasure-seeking Lower: reserved, hesitant to express own views or opinions; self-denying
Sa (Self-acceptance)	Higher: has good opinion of self; sees self as talented and personally attractive; talkative. Lower: self-doubting; readily assumes blame when things go wrong; often thinks others are better; gives in easily
In (Independence)	Higher: self-sufficient, resourceful, detached; persistent in seeking goals, whether others agree or not Lower: lacks self-confidence, seeks support from others; tries to avoid conflict; has difficulty in making decisions
Em (Empathy)	Higher: comfortable about self and well-accepted by others; perceptive of social nuances, understands how others feel; optimistic Lower: unempathic, skeptical about the intentions of others; defensive about own feelings and desires; has limited range of interests

Measures of Normative Orientation and Values

Scale Name	Implications of Higher and Lower Scores
Re (Responsibility)	Higher: responsible, reliable, ethically perceptive; serious about duties and obligations Lower: self-indulgent, undisciplined, careless; indifferent to personal obligations
So (Socialization)	Higher: conscientious, well-organized; finds it easy to accept and conform to normative rules; seldom gets in trouble Lower: resists rules, does not like to conform; often rebellious, gets into trouble easily; has unconventional views and attitudes
Sc (Self-control)	Higher: tries to control emotions and temper; suppresses hostile and erotic feelings; takes pride in being self-disciplined Lower: has strong feelings and emotions, and makes little effort to hide them; has problems of undercontrol and impulsivity; likes adventure and new experience
Gi (Good Impression)	Higher: wants to make a good impression; tries to do what will please others, sometimes to the point of being obsequious and sycophantic; short of this level, tends to be conventional, formal, and conservative Lower: insists on being himself or herself, even if this causes friction or problems; dissatisfied in many situations, often complains; easily annoyed and irritated
Cm (Communality)	Higher: fits in easily, reasonable, sees self as a quite average person; makes little effort to change things Lower: sees self as different from others; not conventional or conforming; often changeable and moody; extremely low scores suggest careless or random answering
Wb (Well-being)	Higher: feels self to be in good physical and mental health; optimistic about the future; cheerful Lower: concerned about health and/or personal problems; tends to complain about being treated unfairly or inconsiderately; pessimistic
To (Tolerance)	Higher: is tolerant of others' beliefs and values, even when different from or counter to own beliefs; fair-minded, reasonable, and tactful Lower: distrustful, fault-finding, and extrapunitive; often has hostile and vindictive feelings

Table 1.2 The 20 Folk Concept Scales and Their Intended Meanings continued

Measures of Cognitive and Intellectual Functioning

Scale Name	Implications of Higher and Lower Scores
Ac (Achievement via Conformance)	Higher: has strong drive to do well; likes to work in settings where tasks and expectations are clearly defined; efficient and well-organized
	Lower: has difficulty in doing best work in settings that have strict rules and regulations; easily distracted; tends to stop working when things do not go well
Ai (Achievement via Independence)	Higher: has strong drive to do well; likes to work in settings that encourage freedom and individual initiative; clearthinking and intelligent
	Lower: has difficulty in doing best work in settings that are vague, poorly defined, and lacking in precise specifications; has limited interests in intellectual or cognitive endeavors
le (Intellectual Efficiency)	Higher: efficient in use of intellectual abilities; can keep on at a task where others might give up or get discouraged; insightful and resourceful
	Lower: has a hard time getting started on cognitive tasks, and seeing them through to completion; has difficulty in expressing ideas

Measures of Role and Personal Style

Scale Name	Implications of Higher and Lower Scores
Py (Psychological-mindedness)	Higher: insightful and perceptive; understands the feelings of others, but is not necessarily supportive or nurturant
	Lower: more interested in the practical and concrete than the abstract; looks more at what people do than how they feel or think; often apathetic and seemingly unmotivated
Fx (Flexibility)	Higher: flexible; likes change and variety; easily bored by routine and everyday experience; may be impatient and even erratic; clever and imaginative, but also careless and loosely organized
	Lower: not changeable; likes a steady pace and well-organized and predictable situations; conventional and conservative
F/M (Femininity/Masculinity)	Higher: among males, high-scorers tend to be seen as high-strung, sensitive, and esthetically reactive; females with high scores tend to be seen as sympathetic, warm, and modest, but also dependent
	Lower: decisive, action-oriented; shows initiative; not easily subdued; rather unsentimental; tough-minded

experimentation with the tentative profile sheets revealed some problems in depicting scores on the Do, Cs, Sp, and Sa scales that required minor adjustments in the standard score tables. After these adjustments, the second set of profiles turned out to be fully compatible with the first set and to have the same utility for work with individual cases. The guidelines and profile configurations established by these two prior profile forms were kept clearly in view in developing the new forms to accompany the 434-item edition of the CPI so as to minimize any problems users might have in adapting to the new edition.

The large samples on which the 1956 profile sheets were based consisted of approximately 50% high school students, plus a mixture of adults from various occupations, college students, and about 12% delinquents and prison inmates. Although arbitrary and nonrandom, these norms proved to be quite satisfactory for Form 480. In 1986, for Form 462, two new norm samples were assembled, with 1,000 men and 1,000 women drawn from high school populations (25%), undergraduate and graduate college students (30%), delinquents and prison inmates (13%), and the remainder adults from primarily executive and professional occupations. These norms were somewhat less successful than those for Form 480, in that mean scores were a bit higher on scales associated with status and interpersonal competence. For the new report form, norms of 3,000 persons of each gender are used. For each sample, 50% comes from high school testing, 13.3% from delinquents and prison inmates, 16.7% from college undergraduates (no graduate students are included), and 20% from adults in primarily nonprofessional or nonexecutive occupation. Approximately half of the protocols are from testing done after the publication of Form 462. Tryout experience with the new report form suggests that profile patterns and configurations established for the two prior versions carry over fully to the current format.

It is important to note that norms for the CPI are much more diversified and extensive than the samples used for the new profile sheets. Specifically, in Appendix B, raw score means and standard deviations on the 20 folk, 3 vector, and 13 special purpose scales are given for 52 samples of males, and for 42 samples of females. The same statistics are also presented in Appendix B for simulated protocols (fake good, fake bad, and randomly answered), and of course for the composited samples used to develop the profile forms. Nearly all of the published research on the CPI reports data in raw score terms, making it easy to compare any new samples with comparable samples from prior work. In certain settings, such as that of police and law enforcement populations, special profile report forms have been developed (Roberts, 1995b) to show how a new protocol relates to directly pertinent norms. Another way to take advantage of the specific norm groups reported in Appendix B is to draw the most relevant mean profile, along with the profile for the individual or group under scrutiny. For example, if work is being done with entry-level business executives, the mean profile for the 185 male executives reported in Appendix B should be of interest.

A question often asked about the CPI is whether it is valid when used with minority groups. A minibibliography of studies relevant to this query was prepared several years ago. It listed nine reports on American Indians, 18 on Blacks, 13 on Chinese, 12 on Hispanics, 6 on Japanese, and then 35 on other groups and on cross-cultural testing. It might be noted that there are at present 29 versions of the CPI in foreign languages, and published editions in eight countries. The total bibliography for work published outside of the United States and in non-English languages numbers well over 100 titles. For the most part, these studies support the validity of the inventory in translation and when used with minority groups within the United States. For exam-

ple, on the F/M scale, Baldwin (1987) found no differences between Black male and female students and their white counterparts. Pfeifer and Sedlacek (1974) found that college grades of Black students were predictable from the same CPI scales that predicted grades of white students, and to the same degree. Casey (1986) found that the CPI scales associated with high school dropout among white students functioned in precisely the same way for Hispanic students. On the other hand, Davis, Hoffman, and Nelson (1990) found Native Americans to score lower than whites on several scales, including Re, Ac, and the Managerial Potential index. These authors caution that Native Americans, particularly women, may be at a disadvantage when the CPI is used for selection. More research is clearly needed on the validity and utility of the CPI when used with minority populations. A comprehensive bibliography of publications pertaining to the CPI is in preparation, in which all known studies of minority groups will be reported.

Steps in Profile Interpretation

Step 1. The protocol should first be reviewed for its general reliability by examining scores on the Gi, Cm, and Wb scales. On Gi, raw scores of 30 and above are suggestive of a possible attempt to present self in an overly favorable way, and scores of 8 and below suggest an undue emphasis on the negative. On Cm, scores of 24 or lower suggest atypicality of responding, possibly due to random or careless answering. On Wb, scores of 20 or below suggest the possibility of serious personal problems, or the adoption of a fake bad mode of responding. In the computerized interpretive narrative, a screening is conducted for fake good, fake bad, and random responding, using empirically evolved psychometric algorithms drawing on the three scales just named and on configurations of these and other scales. In work with individuals, invalid or falsified protocols rarely occur, but in research testing of large samples, or in testing of groups under pressure to create favorable impressions, invalid or partially invalid protocols will occasionally be encountered.

Step 2. The protocol should be classified within the three-vector or cuboid model (see chapter 2 of this manual). Classification in regard to lifestyle and ego integration, as provided by the model, will furnish useful guidelines about characteristic goals, interpersonal strategies, and expectable problems, as well as about the individual's general competence or effectiveness.

Step 3. Consider elevations of the scales and profile. Higher scores furnish a crude index of superior functioning. However, on nearly all of the scales, there comes a point where scores can be too high, as it were, indicating problems in the expression of the attribute. For example, higher scores on the Do scale are indicative of leadership, prosocial manifestations of dominance, and self-assurance, but at raw score levels of about 32 and above, there is a risk of domineering behavior, overassertion of self, and an objectionable tendency always to seek power. On the Sc scale, problems of overcontrol and suppression of feelings can be anticipated when the raw score is 32 or above, along with explosive outburst of affect if and when the control over impulse breaks down. On the Fx scale, adaptiveness, receptiveness to change, and a talent for creative thinking are associated with elevations, up to raw scores of around 20 to 21. Above this, however, elements of impatience, easy irritability, and difficulty in holding to a wise course of action may be anticipated. Skilled use of the inventory requires awareness of these curvilinear implicative meanings of the scales and sensitivity to their nuances.

Step 4. Look for configurations and patterns among the scales that have been shown to convey significant meaning. For example, in academic settings, the balance between the Ac and Ai scales can be consequential (Domino, 1968, 1971). Students high on Ac, but average or below on Ai, perform best in structured courses and majors where goals are consensual and where methods for attaining these goals are clearly specified. Students high on Ai, but average or below on Ac, do not respond well in settings like this, but like and are at their best in situations requiring individually established goals and personal initiative in choosing methods for achieving these goals. Managers who are high on Do but average or below on Em will tend to be maladroit and abrasive in directing subordinates. McAllister's (1996) book on interpreting the CPI is an excellent source of information for two-scale configurations, and also for more complex patterns involving three, four, or

more scales at a time. Another valuable source of interpretive information is the book by Meyer and Davis (1992), which offers case illustrations and also examines the functioning of managerial teams. In the hands of a well-trained and perceptive user, the CPI can furnish accurate and insightful information, but in the hands of someone untutored in the test, lacking in intuitive talent, and resistant to inductive thinking, the inventory will yield only trivial, and on occasion even incorrect, information. Supervised experience in the analysis of individual cases is a sine qua non for proper professional use of the CPI.

Administration

The CPI is largely self-administering. The CPI 434 test items are accessible online through CPP's online assessment administration platform or through CPP Web Services. Contact the publisher to confirm the most current test administration options available for the CPI 434 assessment.

When taking the assessment, respondents read the instructions online and then proceed to the test items. Alternatively, the instructions can be read aloud by the examiner while the respondents read them silently.

Usually, testing time is from 45 to 60 minutes. For slow readers, or in special circumstances, testing may be divided into two or more sessions. A sensible statement to the respondents about the aims of testing and the use which will be made of the results will be helpful in winning their attention and cooperation.

If questions arise about the meaning of a word, phrase, or item, the examiner should answer them. Questions concerning the explanation of a concept or the purpose of an item are best dealt with by encouraging the respondents to use their own judgment. Although items can be left blank, it is better for scoring and for any subsequent research analyses if all of the items are answered. If more than 30 items are unanswered, the scoring program will trigger a cautionary remark about the possible invalidity of the protocol.

The inventory may be given under normal conditions to students as low as the seventh grade, or at ages 13 to 14.

No rigorous controls need to be established to achieve dependable and useful results. The CPI has been tried under nearly every conceivable condition, including formal testing sessions, informal sessions, individual administrations, take-home plans, mail-out and mail-back testing, and others. Insofar as can be determined from the accuracy of profiles obtained and from internal indicators of reliability and validity, satisfactory results were the rule in every condition. The implication is that although the inventory may ideally be given under standard supervised testing conditions, it can also be used by a counselee awaiting an interview, as a take-home test in the study of research samples, or on any other reasonable basis.

Scoring

All CPI reports are computer-generated after online administration of the assessment. The following CPI 434 reports are available: the CPI 434 Profile, the CPI 434 Narrative Report, and the CPI 434 Configural Analysis Report. Visit www.cpp.com for the latest information on CPI reports, to view report samples, and for information on online test administration setup.

The Profile Report has four parts. In part 1, the protocol is reviewed for dependability, using empirically developed algorithms to detect any showing significant evidence of fake good, fake bad, or random answering response sets. Part 2 gives the type classification based on the first two vector scales and the level of ego integration as indicated by the score on the third vector scale. Part 3 gives raw and standard scores on each of the 20 folk scales. Part 4 presents information for the special purpose scales for Managerial Potential, Work Orientation, Creative Temperament, Leadership Potential, Amicability, Law Enforcement Orientation, and Tough-mindedness. The Profile Report is a basic "snapshot" report, and as such, is provided without any elaboration. The psychologist must consider the data and develop an interpretation.

The Narrative Report has five parts. The first four are similar to those presented in the Profile Report, but with detailed interpretive comments provided for each scale. Part 5 of the Narrative Report arrays the 100 items in the *California Q-Set* (Block, 1961) so as to estimate or simulate what a knowledgeable, perceptive, and benevolent observer would say about the person being tested.

The Configural Analysis Report: An Interpretation of Scale Combinations, contains six parts. The first five are identical to the Narrative Report. Part 6 contains detailed interpretive remarks based on the folk scale configurations discussed by Loring McAllister (1996) in his book on interpreting the CPI.

The Three Vector Scales

A Background to the Scales

For years it has been known that the folk concept scales of the CPI can be reduced to four or five major factors (see, for instance, Bouchard, 1969; Crites, Bechtold, Goodstein, & Helibrun, 1961; Gowan, 1958; Johnston, 1957; Mitchell & Pierce-Jones, 1960; Springob & Streuning, 1964; Veldman & Pierce-Jones, 1964). Studies in the 1970s and 1980s also identified four or five first-order factors of similar composition (see, for example, Lorr & Burger, 1981; Burger, Pickett & Goldman, 1977). The factor structure found in American work has held up well in applications of the CPI in other countries, for example: mainland China (Yang & Gong, 1993), Israel (Levin, 1971; Levin & Karni, 1981), Malaysia (Awang & Loekmono), Spain (Seisdedos, 1992), and French-speaking Switzerland (Gendre, 1966). In addition, the factor structure has been confirmed in various kinds of subsamples within the U.S. population, for example, young scientists (Parloff, Datta, Kleman, & Handlon, 1968), and for persons within each of three strata of intelligence (Shure & Rogers, 1963).

The two best-established of the CPI factors at the time of Megargee's *CPI Handbook* (Megargee, 1972) were (a) one designated by names such as extraversion, self-confidence, assertive self-assurance, and social poise and (b) one referred to as disciplined effectiveness, personal integrity, and adjustment by social conformity. A subsequent confirmatory factor analysis of the CPI (Bernstein, Garbin, & McClellan, 1983) did identify these two themes as primary. A factor analysis of five CPI factors (Burger, Pickett, & Goldman, 1977) found two second-level dimensions, one with appreciable loadings on all of the folk scales except Fx and F/M, and the other with major loadings on Re, So, Sc, and F/M. The first second-order dimension appears to be associated with self-realization and personal adjustment; the second appears to be associated with rule-respecting and compliant dispositions.

The strong evidence for two major themes—interpersonal poise and assurance, and intrapersonal espousal of traditional values—led Nichols and Schnell (1963) to develop two new scales that they called the Person Orientation or Po scale and the Value Orientation or Vo scale. The Po scale had its largest correlations with the folk scales in the first sector of profile sheet, in particular Do, Sy, and Sa. For men and women separately, the coefficients were .86 and .84 with Sy and .78 and .79 with Sa; the coefficient was .86 with Do for both sexes. Correlations of Po with folk scales from the second sector of the profile were relatively modest, for example, .17 (men) and .16 (women) with So, and .00 (men) and −.05 (women) with Sc. However, with Wb the correlations were .41 and .37.

Correlations for the Vo scale were largest for folk scales in the second sector, in particular for Sc, Gi, Wb, and Ac. For men and women separately, the coefficients were .85 and .84 for Sc, .84 and .82 for Gi, .77 and .81 for Wb, and .78 and .82 for Ac. However, Vo also had appreciable correlations with scales in the first sector, for instance, .54 (men) and .49 (women) with Cs, and .47 (men) and .44 (women) with In. In the norm samples reported for the 1986 edition of the CPI (Gough, 1987), correlations between Po and Vo were .29 for men and .25 for women.

Because of the statistically significant (p < .01) albeit modest correlations between Po and Vo, and because of the rather large crossover correlations of Vo with Sector 1 folk scales, it seemed that purer and more focused measures of the interpersonal and intrapersonal themes should be possible. Guidance for this effort was available from the many factor analyses that had been done on the CPI (see Megargee, 1972, for a summary of work through the 1960s) from the Po and Vo scales themselves, and from the then-new smallest space analyses of the CPI by Karni and Levin (1972). The smallest space technique (Guttman, 1968; 1982) positions any set of correlated variables in a geometric (flat) grid in such a way as to minimize the sum of the distances among them. The distance between any two variables is an inverse of the magnitude of their correlations. Thus, variables with high intercorrelations tend to cluster together in the smallest-space grid, whereas variables with low or negative correlations tend to be far apart.

The analyses by Karni and Levin (Karni & Levin, 1972; Levin & Karni, 1970) were based on testing in Israel with the Hebrew translation of the CPI and on American norm data from the first published manual (Gough, 1957). Figure 2.1 presents the data in visual form. Inspection of the location of the scales in both of the smallest-space displays

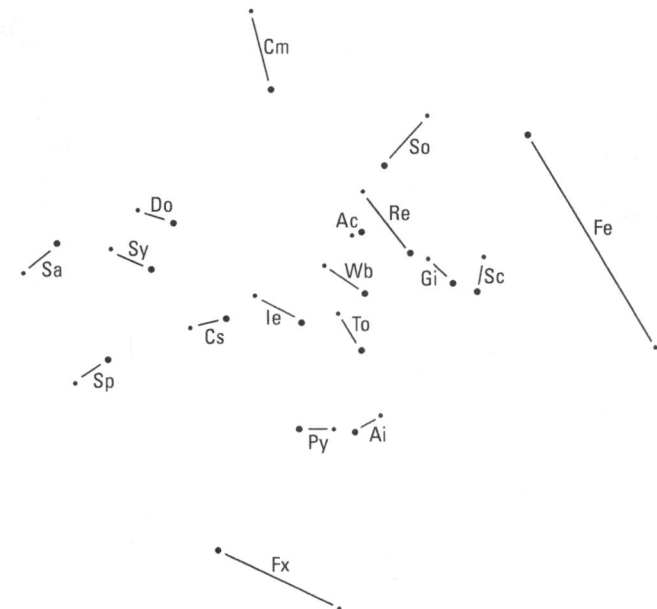

Figure 2.1 Smallest Space Analysis of the CPI for American and Israeli Samples.

From Levin and Karni, 1970.

Note: Small dots correspond to American samples; large dots correspond to Israeli samples.

clearly suggested two implicit axes. The horizontal axis was defined by scales such as Do, Sy, Sa, and Sp at one end, and by the Gi, Sc, and F/M scales at the other. The vertical axis was best defined by Cm, So, Re, and Ac at the high end, and by Py, Ai, and Fx at the low. In the center of the displays was a small cluster of three scales: Wb, To, and Ie.

To develop what eventually turned out to be the three vector scales, experimental indexes were used for each of the three implicit dimensions. For the first, a score was defined by the sum of Sc, Gi, and F/M minus the sum of scores on Do, Sy, Sp, and Sa. For the second, scores were computed by adding So and Cm and subtracting Fx. For the third, the index was provided by the sum of Wb, To, and Ie. In separate samples of 1,000 men and 1,000 women, drawn as a cross section of all cases in the CPI archives, the three experimental markers were correlated with each item in the inventory. These correlational arrays were then searched for items having appreciable correlations with any one of the three markers, but zero or near-zero correlations with the other two. Because only a small number of items met these stringent conditions, items were noted that had a correlation with one of the three themes distinctly larger than its correlation with the other two. In this way, three initial vector (or structural) scales were extracted from the inventory. As might be expected, when scores on the three scales were intercorrelated, the coefficients were too far from zero for the scales to be accepted as independent measures of the three themes.

By this time, a psychological formulation of the meaning of the three themes was also being evolved. The first was conceptualized as an externality to internality dimension, similar but not identical to extraversion-introversion. Persons scoring at the *external* end were hypothesized to be interactive, aware of and responsive to the manifest rewards and punishments of interpersonal life, and expressive in temperament. Persons scoring at the *internal* end were hypothesized to be less inclined towards involvement with others, protective of their own privacy, and reserved in manner. The second vector was conceptualized as one going from norm-questioning (but not norm-breaking) inclinations at one pole to norm-favoring dispositions at the other. High scorers on this second theme were hypothesized to be conscientious, rule-respecting, and pragmatic, whereas low scorers were hypothesized to be adventurous, changeable, and unconventional.

The third vector was originally seen as an index of self-realization, the degree to which the respondents evaluated themselves positively and as having achieved the potentials associated with their own specific temperament. As work on the development of the scale went ahead, and as both formal and informal information accumulated about persons with higher and lower scores, a threefold perspective took shape. That is, from the standpoint of the person taking the inventory, the score on the third vector could serve as an index of self-realization or fulfillment, going from a self-concept filled with doubt, low esteem, and frustrations all the way to a self-view of inner harmony and a reasonably good level of self-actualization. The second perspective was that of others, and stressed the notion of psychological competence. Low scorers were those dealing poorly with life's demands, ill-equipped to cope with trauma and stress. High scorers were those who could make effective use of their talents, and who would persevere even under adverse conditions. The third perspective was that of the professional, the

key concept being ego-integration. Persons with low scores on this third scale were poorly integrated in their ego functioning, at odds with themselves and others, and uninsightful about the impact of their behavior on self and others. High scorers, on the other hand, were well-integrated, more insightful about self and others, and more resilient in coping with ego-threatening forces.

In regard to the development of the three vector scales (called v.1, v.2, and v.3), something like 15 versions of each were created in the search for minimal intercorrelations, absence of any item overlap, and consonance with the three defining folk scale markers. Approximately five years was spent in these efforts, but finally, in about 1980, three scales having the requisite qualities were deemed ready for use. The first presentation of these scales was made in the manual for the 462-item version of the CPI (Gough, 1987). In their first introduction, v.1 had 34 items, v.2 had 36 items, and v.3 had 58 items. The reason for the large number of items on v.3 was to allow for categorization of respondents into seven levels of self-realization, or competence, or ego integration. For Form 434 of the CPI, the three scales have the same number of items, but two items have been changed on the v.2 scale and four on the v.3 scale. These changes were made necessary by the dropping of 28 items from Form 462. Alpha coefficients of reliability for the three scales in the current norm samples of 3,000 men and 3,000 women were .81 and .82 for v.1, .76 and .78 for v.2, and .89 and .88 for v.3. Correlations among the three scales for men in the same sample were −.05 for v.1 and v.2, −.20 for v.1 and v.3, and .10 for v.2 and v.3. The same three correlations for women were .03, −.21, and .06.

Vernon's Circumplex

Aside from the facts that vectors 1 and 2 correlate well with the first two factors from all prior factor analyses of the CPI, and that they are inferrable from and in fact derived from the two implicit dimensions in the Karni-Levin smallest space analyses of the inventory, are there any other reasons for viewing these two vectors as truly basic or fundamental? Other attempts to identify basic dimensions have tended to come up with different dimensions. For example, in his book *Dimensions of Personality*, Eysenck (1947) discussed a factor analysis he had conducted of 39 items on 700 male patients from a military service roster. He identified four factors, but concluded that two were of major importance. The first he identified as general neuroticism and the second as a bipolar dimension of hysteria-dysthymia, or extraversion-introversion. An impressive program of research ensued in which these two basic themes were examined in reference to a wide variety of criteria. Psychoticism as a third key dimension in Eysenck's work came later (see, for example, Eysenck, 1992). Vector 1 in the CPI model can be aligned with Eysenck's introversion-extraversion dimension, but v.2 is conceptually different from Eysenck's neuroticism axis.

Several important analyses have been conducted to identify key dimensions in the MMPI. One of these, by Welsh (1956), found two basic themes called *anxiety* and *repression.* As can be seen in Appendix C, v.l has moderate correlations (.38 for men and .44 for women) with Welsh R, and v.2 has low negative correlations (–.31 for men and –.20 for women) with Welsh A. Nonetheless, the intentions of v.l and R, and v.2 and A, are very different, and their extended implications when one turns to descriptive and biographical data are more or less unrelated. Block (1965) proposed the themes of *ego resilience* and *ego control* as basic to the MMPI. Ego resilience in Block's model has little to do with the v. 1 and v. 2 themes in the CPI, although there are interesting similarities to vector 3. Block's ego control has some conceptual resemblance to vector 2, but important differences remain in that Block's dimension stresses overcontrol at one pole versus undercontrol at the other. Scores on v.2 are intended to reveal nonneurotic rule-favoring dispositions at one pole, and nonneurotic, rule-questioning dispositions at the other.

In another approach to the topic of personality structure and its basic themes, Welsh (1975) introduced the concepts of origence and intellectence. *Origence* refers to a driving force for creative and original thinking and expression, whereas *intellectence* refers to a principle of rationality and reality testing. Welsh's book on the creation of measures for origence and intellectence and their relationships to behavior in many settings amounted to a tour de force. However, any connections between his two dimensions and the v.l and v. 2 themes are tenuous at best.

One of the most widely known and used two-dimensional schema in personality psychology was developed by Leary (1957). In its original form, the

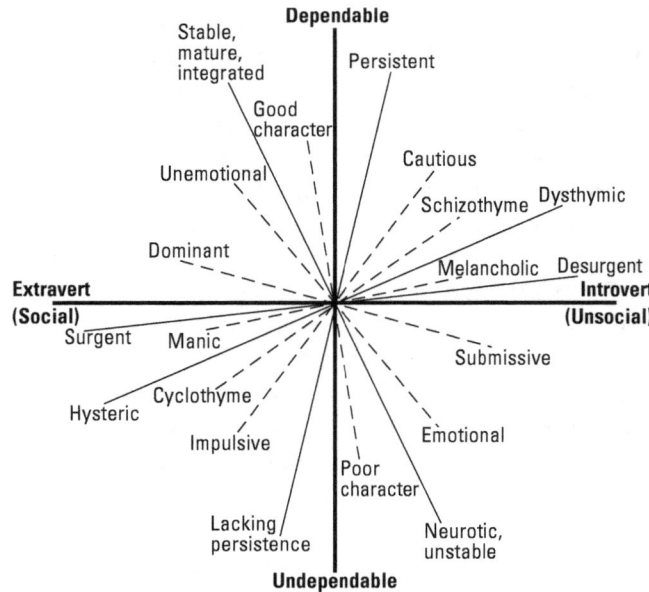

Figure 2.2   The Two Basic Dimensions of Personality as Proposed by Philip E. Vernon

Reproduced from *Personality Tests and Assessments* (1953) by permission of Methuen & Company, publisher, London.

dimensions were described as love versus hate and dominance versus submission. Wiggins (1979) proposed major axes of power (or dominance) and warmth (or love) for his taxonomy of interpersonal traits, and later (Wiggins, 1995) based his *Interpersonal Adjective Scales* on primary dimensions of dominance and nurturance.

Closest to the CPI three-vector model is the circumplex described by Philip Vernon (1953) in his book *Personality Tests and Assessments.* From his survey of factor analytic work, he concluded that "the most pervasive or far-reaching dimension might be termed dependability—a blend of persistence, purposiveness, stability and good character" (p. 12). Vernon identified extraversion-introversion as the other basic theme in personality structure. A graphic display of Vernon's model is shown in Figure 2.2.

Vernon's extraversion-introversion axis is obviously similar to the dimension established by the v.l scale of the CPI, even though Vernon drew more on psychopathological than normal terminology to specify its meaning. Vernon's undependability-dependability axis is similar to the dimension defined by the v.2 scale, with one important proviso: Vernon's axis is heavily loaded with evaluative and even pejorative terms, whereas v.2 is relatively free of any negative or invidious implications at either pole. On the v.2 scale, persons scoring low are characterized by norm-questioning dispositions, which may be expressed in creative and socially useful ways as well as in negative or wayward behavior. Likewise at the high or norm-favoring pole of v.2, behavior may vary from admirable compliance with social values and expectations to undue conventionality, overconformity, and rigid ego control. It might be noted that in Vernon's diagram, Eysenck's major axis of hysteria-dysthymia appears as a subordinate theme, as does Leary's major axis of dominance-submission.

The v.1 Scale

The purpose of the v.1 scale is to assess a continuum going from involvement, participative inclinations, and extraversion at one pole to detachment, a need for privacy, and introversion at the other. By means of item analyses against a criterion of Sc, Gi, and F/M added, and Do, Sy, Sp, and Sa subtracted, 34 items were identified that had good interitem coherence and were relatively uncorrelated with scales v.2 and v.3.

In the total norm sample of 6,000 persons, a principal axis factor analysis of the interitem matrix yielded nine factors with eigen values of 1.00 or greater. Four with values (rounded) of 2.00 or more were retained and rotated by means of Kaiser's normal varimax method. Eighteen items had largest loadings on Factor 1, nine had largest loadings on Factor 2, four were assigned to Factor 3, and three were assigned to Factor 4. Examples of defining items for each factor were the following: (1) "If given the chance I would make a good leader of people" ("false"), "I think I am usually a leader in my group" ("false"), "I like to talk before groups of people" ("false"), and "I usually don't like to talk much unless I am with people I know very well" ("true"); (2) "I am apt to show off in some way if I get the chance" ("false"), "I like to be the center of attention" ("false"), and "I like to boast about my achievements every now and then" ("false"); (3) "I would like the job of a foreign correspondent for a newspaper" ("false") and "I would like to be an actor on the stage or in the movies" ("false"); and (4) "I like large, noisy parties" ("false") and "I like to go to parties and other affairs where there is lots of loud fun" ("false").

Correlations of v.1 with other scales and measures, as reported in Appendix C, were reviewed for

coefficients that would help to illuminate the meaning of v.1. In each example to follow, the first correlation is for males and the second for females: MMPI Si (Social Introversion), .57 and .57; MBTI E–I (Introversion), .51 and .54; *Maudsley Personality Inventory* (Extraversion), –.64 and –.44; *Guilford-Zimmerman Temperament Survey* (Sociability), –.57 and –.60; *Comrey Personality Scales* (Extraversion), –.62 and –.51; *Personality Research Form* (Dominance), –.68 and –.83; *Personality Research Form* (Exhibition), –.67 and –.77; *Millon Clinical Multiaxial Inventory* (Histrionic Personality), –.47 and –.71; *Goldberg's Five-Factor Markers* (adjectival scale for Extraversion), –.55 and–.58; 16PF Factor H (Venturesome, Bold), –.51 and –.53; *Omnibus Personality Inventory* (Social Extraversion), –.53 and –.77; and *Bem Sex-Role Inventory M* (Masculinity), –.69 and –.67. As expected, v.1 is positively correlated with measures of introversion and negatively with measures of extraversion. Measures indicative of self-assertion, self-dramatization, and forcefulness are negatively related to v.1, and measures associated with restraint and inhibition are positively related.

Another source of information concerning the implications of scores on v.1 comes from the ranking of archival samples according to means on the scale. Table 2.1 presents such information for 49 male and 39 female samples. For males, highest scores are found for psychiatric patients, mathematicians, young adults (ages 19–21) in prison, and high school students. In one way or another, each of these groups is concerned with inner or private issues, struggles for wholeness by the patients, solitary intellectual conceptualizations for the mathematicians, the consequences of asocial behavior for the inmates, and the achievement of an adult identity for the students. Lowest scores on v.1, associated with vigorous entry into the interpersonal world, are found for military officers, sales managers, West Point cadets, parole and probation officers, initiators of business activity in Ireland, graduate students in counseling psychology, and candidates for the MBA degree.

Highest scores on v.1 for females are for mathematicians, prison inmates, high school students, pharmacy students, and psychiatric patients. Lowest scores among the female samples are for MBA candidates, law school students, premedical students, critics of books for children, and police officer applicants. There are some interesting contrasts within

Table 2.1 Normative Data for the v.I (Internality) Scale

Male Samples	N	M	SD	Male Samples	N	M	SD
Psychiatric patients	41	19.83	6.34	Members of a club for inventors	14	16.43	5.33
Mathematicians	57	19.56	5.78	Nursing students	149	16.36	6.41
Youth authority inmates	2,899	19.34	5.89	Architecture students	125	16.06	6.14
High school students	4,611	19.18	15.74	Catholic priests	41	16.05	6.29
Correctional officers	221	19.06	5.84	College students	3,235	16.00	5.97
Basic normative sample	3,000	18.38	6.07	Optometry students	100	15.94	5.90
Prison inmates	196	18.02	4.81	High school students nominated as leaders	90	15.89	6.53
Engineers	47	17.98	6.38	High school science fair delegates	363	15.80	6.20
Writers of books for children	29	17.90	4.48	Police officer applicants	883	15.64	4.95
Pharmacy students	439	17.88	5.82	San Francisco area residents	261	15.56	6.10
Art institute students	44	17.77	5.72	Anesthesiologists	98	15.43	5.60
High school students nominated as most attractive	88	17.47	5.87	Research scientists	45	15.42	5.52
Engineering students	66	17.29	6.21	Medical students	551	15.35	5.81
High school students nominated as disciplinary problems	90	17.28	5.13	Creative writers	19	15.32	6.27
Bank managers	49	17.08	5.00	Social welfare graduate students	254	15.26	5.48
High school students nominated as most popular	90	17.06	6.37	Education students	167	15.16	5.40
Business executives	185	16.90	5.60	Critics of books for children	25	15.00	6.16
High school students nominated as best citizens	90	16.88	6.43	Psychology graduate students	623	14.78	5.76
Architects	124	16.69	5.26	Medical school applicants	70	14.63	5.09
Police officers	366	16.58	5.63	Military officers	343	14.43	5.74
Rajneeshpuram residents	33	16.48	6.00	Sales managers	85	14.14	5.52
Juvenile delinquents	76	16.43	6.02	West Point cadets	1,413	13.91	5.24
Commercial writers	14	16.43	8.02	Parole and probation officers	65	13.91	4.91
				Irish entrepreneus	37	13.49	5.83
				Counseling psychology graduate students	67	12.91	5.58
				MBA candidates	71	12.17	5.73

both arrays. For example, male and female writers of books for children had means of 17.90 and 19.41, respectively, whereas critics of books for children had means of 15.00 for both men and women. The writers appear to be more inwardly oriented, and the critics more attuned to the manifest interpersonal world.

More direct information concerning the meaning of the v.l scale can be obtained from descriptions and evaluations of observers. Intensive life-history

interviews were conducted with 504 men and 379 women for whom v.l scores were available. At the end of the interview, the interviewer completed a 99-item checklist, recording observations made during the interview. Dummy weights of 1 were assigned to each item checked, and of 0 to each item left blank. Then these 99 items were correlated with scores on the v.l scale, separately for men and women. The complete set of correlations for all of the CPI scales is given in Appendix G. For the v.l scale, the four items

Table 2.1 Normative Data for the v.l (Internality) Scale continued

Female Samples	N	M	SD	Female Samples	N	M	SD
Mathematicians	41	22.78	5.78	High school students nominated as most attractive	90	17.59	5.34
Prison inmates	345	20.28	5.80	College counselors	42	17.57	6.59
High school students	4,825	20.28	5.80	Architecture students	55	17.36	5.33
Pharmacy students	277	19.61	5.72	High school students nominated as most popular	90	17.17	5.87
Psychiatric patients	34	19.53	5.62	High school science fair delegates	148	17.01	6.23
Basic normative sample	3,000	19.44	6.09	Juvenile delinquents	55	16.98	6.52
Writers of books for children	32	19.41	4.74	Medical students	90	16.98	5.43
Creative writers	10	19.10	6.66	Secondary school teachers	21	16.86	5.05
University clerical personnel	56	19.04	4.40	Psychology graduate students	405	16.76	5.93
High school students nominated as disciplinary problems	90	18.98	5.45	Education students	310	16.64	5.77
Registered nurses	100	18.87	6.68	Optometry students	50	16.56	6.60
Home economic students	176	18.87	5.66	Counseling psychology graduate students	275	15.90	5.60
Art institute students	27	18.74	6.06	Commercial writers	12	15.83	6.32
San Francisco area residents	261	18.48	6.52	Anesthesiologists	17	15.76	6.97
High school students nominated as best citizens	90	18.39	6.06	High school students nominated as leaders	90	15.53	5.37
Social welfare graduate students	446	18.07	5.36	Police officer applicants	200	15.17	5.32
College students	4,126	17.91	6.01	Critics of books for children	36	15.00	6.27
Nursing students	250	17.72	6.74	Premedical students	48	14.77	5.22
Rajneeshpuram residents	34	17.68	4.55	Law students	40	14.05	6.10
				MBA candidates	44	12.89	6.28

with largest positive and four with largest negative correlations are cited below, along with the coefficients for men and for women:f

Reticent and taciturn (.23, .20)
Has difficulty in expressing ideas (.16, .24)
Slow rate of movement (.16, .23)
Unsure of self, doubts own ability (.17, .18)

Unusually self-confident; feels able to meet nearly any situation (−.27, −.25)
Creates a good impression; has effective interpersonal techniques (−.20, −.21)
Witty and animated, an interesting conversationalist (−.16, −.31)
Seemed to enjoy being interviewed (−.15, −.18)

These observations by the interviewers suggest that high scorers on the v.l scale are more diffident than low scorers, less willing or able to disclose their feelings and ideas, and more self-doubting. Low scorers on v.l appeared to enjoy being interviewed, were expressive and animated, and manifested a high degree of self-confidence. Of course, the point-biserial correlations for each item were very low (although all were statistically significant at the .01 level of probability or beyond).

Samples of 547 men and 393 women who had been intensively studied in one-day to three-day assessments were available for analyses of the 100 items in Block's (1961) *California Q-Set*. Each assessee was described on the *Q-Set* by a panel of five or more observers. Their individual Q-sort formulations were composited, and then the consensual Q-sort was rearrayed in the distributions for salience specified in Block's method. The categories numbered nine, and were ranked from very characteristic and salient down to very uncharacteristic. Dummy weights of 9 to 1 were assigned to the items in each category, and then the 100 items were correlated with scores on v.l, separately for women and women. The complete list of correlations for the 100 Q-Set items and the scales of the CPI is given in Appendix E. The five items with largest positive and five items with largest negative correlations with v.l are reported below, along with the coefficients for men and for women:

> Reluctant to commit self to any definite course of action; tends to delay or avoid action (.39, .37)
>
> Is vulnerable to real or fancied threat; generally fearful (.32, .35)
>
> Gives up and withdraws where possible in the face of frustration and adversity (.30, .38)
>
> Tends toward overcontrol of needs and impulses; binds tensions excessively, delays gratification unnecessarily (.31, .31)
>
> Genuinely submissive; accepts domination comfortably (.34, .37)
>
> Behaves in an assertive fashion (−.40, −.38)
>
> Is a talkative individual (−.37, .36)
>
> Has social poise and presence; appears socially at ease (−.34, −33)
>
> Is verbally fluent; can express ideas well (−.30, −.40)
>
> Is power oriented; values power in self or others (−.27, −.36)

The patterns of description for high scorers and low scorers are clearly different in these Q-sort items. High scorers are reluctant to make decisions or to take action, are psychologically vulnerable, use repressive ego defenses, and yield to the dominance of others. Low scorers are assertive, talkative, socially poised, verbally fluent, and confident. They also value power in themselves and others, and may be assumed to seek positions in which they have power over and control of others.

Final evidence for scale v.l based on observational data comes from descriptions on the *Adjective Check List* (Gough & Heilbrun, 1983). In one pair of samples consisting of 236 husbands or partners and 236 wives or partners, each member of the couple described the

other on this 300-item instrument. Dummy weights of 1 were assigned to adjectives checked, and of 0 to adjectives left blank. In a sample of 194 members of a number of fraternities, each man was described on the ACL by three peers. The descriptions were weighted, with values of +2 given to very descriptive adjectives, +1 to moderately descriptive adjectives, 0 to neutral or ambiguous terms, −1 to moderately undescriptive and −2 to very undescriptive adjectives. The protocols from the three observers were combined, and then the composites were standardized for each fraternity separately. The same procedure was carried out for a sample of 192 women in the sororities to which they belonged. The next two samples came from intensive assessments at the Institute of Personality Assessment and Research in Berkeley. Each assessee was described on the ACL by 10 staff members, and then these individual protocols were pooled so as to produce a staff consensus. Using tally weights of 1 for any adjective checked on a protocol and 0 for adjectives left blank, sums on the consensual description could vary from 0 (no observer checked the adjective) to 10 (all 10 observers checked the term). These ACL sums were available for 612 men and 358 women.

Table 2.2 presents the 12 adjectives having largest positive correlations and the 12 adjectives having largest negative correlations with v.l for all six samples. A complete listing of the ACL observers descriptions with the scales of the CPI is given in Appendix D.

One cluster of adjectives associated with high scores on v.l betokens taciturnity, quietness, shyness, and a reserved and retiring demeanor. Caution, inhibition, and even timidity are also indicated. Low scorers on v.l, on the other hand, are described as aggressive, assertive, sharp-witted, spontaneous, and talkative. Low scorers are seen as outgoing and sociable, but also as egotistical. These descriptions are compatible with the concept of the scale as depicting a continuum going from involvement and expressiveness at one pole to detachment and internality at the other.

The v.2 Scale

The purpose of the v.2 scale is to assess a continuum going from a rule-questioning perspective at one pole to a rule-favoring perspective at the other. A first criterion for item analyses was established as the sum of So and Cm minus the score on Fx. Items were sought that had appreciable correlations with the initial marker and low correlations with the

Table 2.2 Adjectival Descriptions by Observers: 12 Most Salient Positive and 12 Most Salient Negative Correlates of the 34-Item v.1 Scale						
	Men, Described By			Women, Described By		
Adjectives	Spouse (N = 386)	3 Peers (N = 194)	10 Staff Members (N = 612)	Spouse (N = 236)	3 Peers (N = 192)	10 Staff Members (N = 358)
Cautious	.20**	.20**	.39**	.19**	.38**	.27**
Gentle	.13*	.12	.24**	.18*	.35**	.20**
Inhibited	.22**	.16*	.39**	.16*	.33**	.30**
Mild	.12	.19**	.32**	.27**	.37**	.34**
Quiet	.29**	.24**	.44**	.34**	.47**	.37**
Reserved	.20**	.21**	.42**	.24**	.48**	.31**
Retiring	.10	.16*	.35**	.15*	.44**	.35**
Shy	.29**	.33**	.39**	.31**	.43**	.33**
Silent	.30**	.30**	.33**	.17*	.34**	.26**
Simple	.16*	.14*	.25**	.17**	.24**	.21**
Timid	.14*	.24**	.29**	.10	.42**	.28**
Withdrawn	.16*	.27**	.33**	.13*	.47**	.23**
Aggressive	−.19**	−.21**	−.31**	−.28**	−.43**	−.36**
Ambitious	−.25**	−.19**	−.33**	−.25**	−.22**	−.32**
Assertive	−.20**	−.15*	−.37**	−.35**	−.39**	−.36**
Egotistical	−.18**	−.22**	−.28**	−.17**	−.36**	−.25**
Enterprising	−.17**	−.16*	−.37**	−.18**	−.22**	−.35**
Outgoing	−.31**	−.36**	−.37**	−.33**	−.38**	−.35**
Pleasure-seeking	−.15*	−.14*	−.28**	−.24**	−.25**	−.22**
Self-confident	−.21**	−.22**	−.37**	−.22**	−.33**	−.40**
Sharp-witted	−.23**	−.17*	−.30**	−.24**	−.18*	−.19**
Sociable	−.17**	−.26**	−.32**	−.25**	−.23**	−.26**
Spontaneous	−.14*	−.15*	−.30**	−.20**	−.34**	−.22**
Talkative	−.29**	−.24**	−.38**	−.27**	−.37**	−.33**

* $p \leq .05$, ** $p \leq .01$

markers for v.1 and v.3. Eventually, 36 items were identified that had the requisite properties.

In the current norm sample of 6,000 persons, a factor analysis was carried out of the interim matrix. To simplify presentation, only the first four (of 10) factors with eigen values of 1.00 or more were retained and rotated by the normal varimax method. Items in Factor 1 dealt almost entirely with recollections of a pleasant home life and childhood, for example: "My

home life was always very pleasant" ("true"), "My home life was always happy" ("true"), and "My parents never really understood me" ("false").

Items in Factor 2 dealt with notions of personal responsibility—in general, in civic activity, and towards individuals. Representative items are: "I take a rather serious attitude toward ethical and moral issues" ("true"), "I would be ashamed not to use my privilege of voting" ("true"), and "We ought

Table 2.3 Normative Data for the v.2 (Norm-Favoring) Scale

Male Samples	N	M	SD	Male Samples	N	M	SD
Sales managers	85	27.29	4.58	College students	3,235	22.44	5.80
Irish entrepreneurs	37	26.22	3.89	Medical students	551	22.39	5.20
West Point cadets	1,413	26.35	4.67	Engineering students	66	22.17	5.77
Bank managers	49	25.78	5.16	Pharmacy students	439	22.12	5.29
High school students nominated as best citizens	90	25.62	4.91	Counseling psychology graduate students	67	21.94	4.76
Military officers	343	25.58	4.45	MBA candidates	71	21.85	4.72
High school students nominated as leaders	90	25.53	4.97	Basic norm sample	3,000	21.84	5.48
Engineers	47	25.34	4.66	Commercial writers	14	21.79	6.12
Catholic priests	41	25.34	3.85	Mathematicians	57	21.75	4.42
Correctional officers	221	25.14	4.83	Research scientists	45	21.62	4.74
Medical school applicants	70	24.84	5.43	Architecture students	125	21.50	6.12
Business executives	185	24.83	5.06	Critics of books for children	25	21.28	4.73
Parole and probation officers	65	24.71	5.37	Psychiatric patients	41	21.12	5.94
Optometry students	100	24.37	5.35	Social welfare graduate students	254	20.97	5.92
Members of a club for inventors	14	24.36	4.75	Nursing students	149	20.81	5.92
Police officer applicants	883	24.32	4.37	San Francisco area residents	261	20.56	5.40
Anesthesiologists	98	23.85	4.27	Creative writers	19	19.74	5.58
Police officers	366	23.73	4.69	Prison inmates	196	19.44	5.88
Architects	124	23.50	5.08	Writers of books for children	29	19.03	4.61
High school students nominated as most popular	90	23.49	5.77	Youth authority inmates	2,899	18.97	5.40
High school science fair delegates	363	23.20	5.56	High school students nominated as disciplinary problems	90	18.88	4.43
Education students	167	23.13	5.04	Juvenile delinquents	76	18.78	5.46
High school students nominated as most attractive	88	22.81	5.11	Psychology graduate students	623	18.28	5.04
				Rajneeshpuram residents	33	14.64	4.19
High school students	4,611	22.53	5.30	Art institute students	44	13.98	4.81

to pay our elected officials better than we do" ("true"). Items in Factor 3 focused on work habits, personal organization, and a liking for routine. Representative items are: "I find that a well-ordered mode of life with regular hours is congenial to my temperament" ("true"), "I always see to it that my work is carefully planned and organized" ("true"), and "I'm known as a hard and steady worker" ("true"). Items in factor 4 pertained to matters such as denial of petty wrong-doing and wayward impulses,

illustrated by items such as: "Sometimes I rather enjoy going against the rules and doing things I'm not supposed to do" ("false") and "I used to steal sometimes when I was a youngster" ("false").

From the correlations of v.2 with other tests and measures presented in full in Appendix C, some examples may be cited here that help to indicate the meaning of the scale. In each instance, the first coefficient is for a male sample and the second for a female. Examples are the following: *Hogan Personality*

Table 2.3 Normative Data for the v.2 (Norm-Favoring) Scale continued

Female Samples	N	M	SD	Female Samples	N	M	SD
High school students nominated as best citizens	90	25.80	5.42	MBA candidates	44	22.80	4.67
Education students	310	25.33	4.79	Medical students	90	22.72	5.35
High school science fair delegates	148	25.32	5.66	Pharmacy students	277	22.69	4.94
High school students nominated as leaders	90	25.29	5.37	Counseling psychology graduate students	275	22.52	4.83
High school students nominated as most attractive	90	25.09	4.85	Psychiatric patients	34	22.44	4.80
Home economics students	176	25.02	4.70	Mathematicians	41	22.10	5.21
High school students nominated as most popular	90	24.81	5.08	Prison inmates	345	21.90	5.75
College counselors	42	24.62	5.67	Critics of books for children	36	21.61	4.73
Police officer applicants	200	24.46	4.21	Social welfare graduate students	446	21.42	5.04
Optometry students	50	24.46	6.31	Architecture students	55	20.91	6.12
Anesthesiologists	17	24.24	4.34	High school students nominated as disciplinary problems	90	20.76	5.39
High school students	4,825	24.14	5.29	San Francisco area residents	261	20.40	5.07
Secondary school teachers	21	23.81	4.51	Writers of books for children	32	20.09	3.92
Basic norm sample	3,000	23.28	5.52	Premedical students	48	19.94	5.13
College students	4,126	23.27	5.34	Psychology graduate students	405	18.97	5.08
University clerical personnel	56	23.27	5.13	Law students	40	18.57	4.83
Nursing students	250	22.99	5.51	Rajneeshpuram residents	34	15.71	3.58
Registered nurses	100	23.02	4.51	Creative writers	10	15.20	4.83
Commercial writers	12	22.92	3.45	Art institute students	27	15.15	5.19
				Juvenile delinquents	55	14.00	5.61

Inventory (Prudence), .63 and .51; *Personality Research Form* (Order), .44 and .51; *Personality Research Form* (Cognitive Structure), .38 and .53; *Omnibus Personality Inventory* (Practical Outlook), .47 and .41; *Goldberg Five Factor Markers* (adjectival scale for Dependability), .33 and .40; Barron's scale for Personal Complexity, −.57 and −.53; Barron's scale for Independence of Judgment, −.51 and −.44; *Omnibus Personality Inventory* (Impulse Expression), −.44 and −.45; and MBTI J–P scale (Perceiving), −.54 and −.45. Positive correlates in this list stress orderliness, clearly structured values, and practicality. Negative correlates stress individuality, personal complexity, and an inquiring versus judging frame of mind.

Ranking of the 49 male and 39 female archival samples according to mean scores on v.2 are offered in Table 2.3. At the norm-favoring and rule-respecting end of the continuum, for men, are sales managers, entrepreneurial executives in Ireland, West Point cadets, bank managers, students nominated as best citizens, and military officers; and, for women, are high school students nominated as as best citizens, majors in education in college, attendees at a national high school science fair, and high school students nominated as leaders. Male samples at the rule-questioning end of the continuum included youth authority inmates, high school disciplinary problems, juvenile delinquents, psychology graduate students, residents in a utopian religious commune, and students at an art institute. Female samples with lowest scores included psychology graduate students, students of law, members of a utopian religious commune, creative writers, art institute students, and juvenile delinquents. It seems clear that rule-doubting dispositions are being expressed in different ways in these samples, from creative reconstruction of reality, to withdrawal from an unacceptable bourgeois world, to frankly recalcitrant and rule-violating behavior.

Let us turn next to the 99-item *Interviewer's Check List* to note the observations most strongly associated with scores on the v.2 scale. A complete listing is found in Appendix G. Cited below are the four items with largest positive and four with largest negative correlations, giving first the coefficient for 504 males and second the coefficient for 379 females.

Family life on the whole was quite happy (.16, .29)
Standards of courteous and polite behavior were emphasized in the home (.22, .13)
Has strong religious beliefs (.23, .17)
Well-groomed and well-dressed (.16, .13)

Unhappy at school and at home (−.20, −.17)
Interviewee had a great deal of friction with parents (−.12, −.27)
Interviewee was ashamed of one or both parents (−.14, −.18)
Considers self to have been an underachiever in high school (−.21, −.11)

Although the correlations are small, all are statistically significant at or beyond the .05 level. The items checked more often for persons scoring high on v.2 mention a happy albeit conventional childhood, attention to personal appearance, and having strong religious beliefs. Items checked more often for those at the rule-questioning pole of v.2 include discord and discomfort at home and underachievement in high school.

California Q-Set formulations of personality by panels of five or more observers were related to scores on v.2 for 547 men and 393 women who had been studied in intensive personality assessment projects. The five items with largest positive and five with largest negative correlations with v.2 are listed below; a complete presentation can be found in Appendix E. The first coefficient in each example is for men, the second for women.

Favors conservative values in a variety of areas (.28, .35)
Is fastidious (.29, .32)

Judges self and others in conventional terms such as "popularity," "the correct thing to do," social pressures, etc. (.26, .27)
Is a genuinely responsible and dependable person (.21, .30)
Is moralistic (.18, .32)

Tends to be rebellious and nonconforming (−.30, −.39)
Engages in personal fantasy and daydreams, fictional speculations (−.22, −.29)
Is unpredictable and changeable in behavior and attitudes (−.20, −.34)
Characteristically pushes and tries to stretch limits; sees what he or she can get away with (−.20, −.28)
Is self-indulgent (−.17, −.30)

The Q-sort descriptions by observers show high scorers on v.2 to be conventional, conservative, and rule-respecting individuals. In fact, their support of normative prescriptions was even characterized as moralistic. They are also seen as genuinely dependable and as fastidious. Low scorers on v.2 were seen as rule-testing and nonconforming, but also as self-indulgent. The imaginative aspect of rule-questioning is discernible in the item about fantasies and fictional speculations.

Adjectival correlates from descriptions by observers are given in Table 2.4. For the spouses, each person was described by the other member of the couple on the *Adjective Check List* (ACL). For peer descriptions, each person was evaluated by three classmates, using a five-step weighted format for the adjectives. For the 612 male and 358 female assessees, each person was described on the ACL by a panel of 10 observers whose individual checklists were summed into a composite. In each of the six subsamples, the 300 adjectives were then correlated with scores on the v.2 scale. A complete listing of these correlations is presented in Appendix D. Table 2.4 contains the 12 items with largest positive and 12 with largest negative correlations.

The 12 adjectives linked to higher scores on v. 2 include expected terms such as conscientious, conservative, and conventional. There is also a cluster pertaining to work habits such as efficient, industrious, and thorough. Emphasis on structure is indicated by the terms organized and practical, with overattention to procedure recognized in the adjective methodical. Adjectival descriptions associated

Table 2.4 Adjectival Descriptions by Observers: 12 Most Salient Positive and 12 Most Salient Negative Correlates of the 36-Item v.2 Scale

Adjectives	Men, Described By			Women, Described By		
	Spouse (N = 236)	3 Peers (N = 194)	10 Staff Members (N = 612)	Spouse (N = 236)	3 Peers (N = 192)	10 Staff Members (N = 358)
Conscientious	.18**	.22**	.10**	.04	.28**	.29**
Conservative	.26**	.12	.19**	.19**	.24**	.35**
Conventional	.20**	.08	.18**	.23**	.24**	.28**
Dignified	.22**	.08	.05	.12	.21**	.17**
Efficient	.22**	.24**	.03	.10	.24**	.18**
Industrious	.03	.22**	.10**	.04	.27**	.23**
Methodical	.15*	.15*	.10**	.14*	.06	.24**
Moderate	.14*	.12	.07	.16*	.07	.15**
Organized	.23**	.35**	.12**	.25**	.33**	.30**
Practical	.19**	.16*	.03	.12	.21**	.14**
Reliable	.13*	.18*	.02	.04	.24**	.19**
Thorough	.03	.23**	.06	.18**	.19**	.22**
Adventurous	−.12	−.13	−.21**	−.14*	−.14*	−.23**
Changeable	−.17**	−.13	−.18**	−.21**	−.28**	−.34**
Cynical	−.13*	−.14*	−.27**	−.12	−.19**	−.25**
Disorderly	−.20**	−.18*	−.16**	−.13*	−.35**	−.35**
Forgetful	−.12	−.12	−.15**	−.20**	−.25**	−.13*
Impulsive	−.23**	−.17	−.16**	−.19**	−.23**	−.29**
Mischievous	−.11	−.23**	−.15**	−.13*	−.21**	−.19**
Pleasure-seeking	−.20**	−.19**	−.15**	−.15*	−.23**	−.21**
Rebellious	−.27**	−.15*	−.26**	−.16*	−.24**	−.32**
Reckless	−.27**	−.18*	−.11**	−.14*	−.27**	−.31**
Restless	−.23	−.13	−.21**	−.13*	−.18*	−.30**
Unconventional	−.21**	−.11	−.27**	−.25**	−.25**	−.31**

* $p \leq .05$, ** $p \leq .01$

with lower scores on v.2 cover anticipated attributes such as unconventionality, adventurousness, impulsivity, and mischievousness—perhaps at times carried to excess, suggested by the terms rebellious, reckless, and disorderly. The adjective cynical offers a hint that the rule-doubting orientation of low scorers on v.2 may be part of a generalized dubiety or disbelief.

The v.3 Scale

The purpose of the v.3 scale is to assess a continuum of self-realization, or psychological competence, or ego integration. Scores on v.3 are related to the respondent's own view of fulfillment, the degree to which the person has realized his or her own potentialities. Those at Levels 1 or 2 see themselves as frustrated, at odds internally and with the culture, and as far from having attained a satisfactory status in living. Those at Levels 6 and 7 see themselves as being in harmony with the circumstances of their lives, as making good use of their own capabilities and talents, and as reasonably self-actualized. It is important to caution, however, that even at Level 7, the inferred psychological status is not one of full satisfaction or of some ideal, quasi-perfect degree of self-realization. From the standpoint of the ordinary observer, scores on v.3 offer a crude index of psychological competence—the degree to which the individual can cope with and adapt to the demands and stresses of life. From the standpoint of the professional observer, the v.3 scale indexes ego integration, that is, the extent to which drives, wishes, controls, and ego defenses are functioning in a relatively friction-free manner.

To develop the v.3 scale, scores on Wb, To, and Ie were summed, and then this sum was correlated with the items of the inventory. The three marker scales were chosen because of their location at the center of the smallest-space analyses reported by Karni and Levin (1972). Wb may be interpreted as an indicator of general psychological and physical well-being. To may be interpreted as a measure of interpersonal maturity and respect for others, and Ie may be interpreted as an indicator of efficacy in the cognitive realm.

Because scores on v.3 were to be used for establishing seven categories of ego integration, more items were needed for v.3 than had been necessary for v.1 and v.2. Of course, as before, the items selected for v.3 had to be aligned with that theme, while being unaligned or minimally associated with v.1 and v.2. The goal, as stated several times above, was to come up with three relatively uncorrelated vector scales, free of any item overlap, and each attuned to the theoretical dimension specified in the model. The limited number of items in the inventory meant that trade-offs were often necessary in the construction of v.3. That is, a good item for v.3 sometimes had an appreciable positive correlation with, say, v.1. In that case, a compensating v.3 item with an appreciable negative correlation with v.1 had to be found. The search for a full set of v.3 items so as to produce a scale having the desired properties was arduous and time-consuming. Eventually, however, 58 items were assembled that in toto fulfilled our objectives.

A principal axis factor analysis of the interitem matrix was conducted in a sample of 6,000 persons (3,000 men and 3,000 women) so as to identify internal themes in the scale. Eleven factors having eigen values of 1.00 or more were found. To simplify discussion of the scale, only the first four were retained, and rotated by means of the normal varimax procedure.

Factor 1 contained 22 items, mostly dealing with positive emotionality, freedom from debilitating worries, and resilient self-control. Illustrative items include: "I am sometimes cross and grouchy without good reason" ("false"), "Every now and then I get into a bad mood, and no one can do anything to please me" ("false"), "Sometimes I just can't seem to get going" ("false"), and "I often lose my temper" ("false"). Factor 2 contained 16 items expressing trust and confidence in others, for instance: "Most people inwardly dislike putting themselves out to help other people" ("false"), "Most people would tell a lie if they could gain by it" ("false"), and "People pretend to care more about one another than they really do" ("false"). Factor 3 also contained 16 items, most indicative of a willingness to accept responsibility for one's own behavior and to take actions needed to protect and enhance the welfare of others. Representative examples are: "Maybe some minority groups do get rough treatment, but it is no business of mine" ("false"), "People don't need to worry about others if only they look after themselves" ("false"), and "There's no use in doing things for other people; you only find that you get it in the neck in the long run" ("false"). Factor 4 had four items with primary loadings, three of which expressed interest in science and in doing research.

Perusal of the correlations between v.3 and other scales and measures in Appendix C led to the identification of a number worth citing here. For each example, the first coefficient is for a male sample and the second for a female. Positive correlations were noted for the *Guilford-Zimmerman* Emotional Stability scale (.54 and .52) and the GZTS scales for Objectivity (.65 and .62) and Friendliness (.53 and .44); the *Omnibus Personality Inventory* scales for Personal Integration (.56 and .50), Low Anxiety Level (.55 and .58), Altruism (.47 and .46), and Nonintellectual Disposition (−.43 and −.53); MMPI K, .68 and .64; Barron's scale for Ego Strength (.44 and .51), and Barron's scale for Personal Soundness (.46 and .53); Loevinger's Ego Development level on her own sentence completion test (.48; for women only, men not tested); NEO-AC-PI N (Neuroticism), –.45 and –.38; *Maudsley Personality Inventory* Neuroticism, (–.48 and –.60); and the *Millon Clinical Multiaxial Inventory* scales for Aggressive Personality (–.59 and –.50), Borderline Personality (–.52 and –.46), Paranoid Personality (–.57 and –.50), and Thought Disorder (–.59 and –.45). In general, v.3 had positive correlations with measures indicative of good adjustment, ego strength, stability, objectivity, and altruism; and negative correlations with measures of complaint, cognitive malfunctioning, and feelings of insufficiency.

Rankings of male and female samples on the v.3 scale are presented in Table 2.8, later in this chapter (in the section on the three-vector or cuboid model). For males, the highest-ranking 9 samples are all from professional groups or from persons in training for professional status. In fact, among the top 12 samples, only the small sample of critics of books for children lies outside of a known professional domain. The research scientists were mostly at the Ph.D. level, in fields such as physics, mathematics, and electrical engineering. The next 3 samples were all students in doctoral programs. In the lowest-ranking 11 samples, 6 were composed of high school students; and the lowest 4 were juvenile delinquents, youth authority wards, prison inmates, and disciplinary problems.

Among women, the top 5 samples all consisted of persons pursuing educational programs leading to professional qualification of one sort or another; and in the bottom 5 were psychiatric patients, high school students in general, juvenile delinquents, high school students nominated as disciplinary problems, and prison inmates. The two arrays were thus similar in placing persons with higher actual or potential attainments near the top, and those with demonstrable ego coping problems near the bottom. There is also an age-developmental theme in the two arrays, with younger persons ranking lower than older.

In the samples of 504 men and 379 women who were seen in intensive life-history interviews, the four items from the *Interviewer's Check List* having largest positive correlations with v.3 and the four having largest negative correlations appear below, along with the coefficient for men and for women:

Was an honor student in high school (.14, .29)

Uses a wide and varied vocabulary (.14, .15)

Seems to be relatively free of neurotic trends and other forms of instability (.14, .14)

Father was a successful man from his own standpoint (as well as from others) (.10, .18)

Had first sexual experience while in high school or before (–.27, –.21)

Makes mistakes in grammar and/or word usage (–.24, –.20)

Seems to be preoccupied with sexual matters (–.14, –.14)

Enjoys children (–.21, –.09)

The eight descriptions by life-history interviews appear to be consonant with the conceptualization of the v.3 scale as pertaining to self-realization, or competence, or ego integration. The correlations for individual items are low (although 14 of the 16 coefficients are significant at or beyond the .01 level), which means that interpretation must be cautious and tentative. Nonetheless, those with higher scores report doing well in school, use language in an interesting and correct way, and come across as relatively free of self-defeating or destabilizing behavior. Two of the items center on sexuality, with low scorers impressing interviewers as preoccupied with such matters; low scorers also reported earlier manifest sexual behavior than did high scorers. The final item about enjoying children was only marginally related to the scale for women, but had a –.21 correlation with v.3 among men. That is, low-scoring men on v.3, when asked about parenting, replied in such a way as to suggest that they did not very much like or want to take care of children. This lead offers promise for some interesting research on parenting and on treatment of children by low scorers on the v.3 scale.

Correlations of v.3 with the 100 items in Block's (1961) *California Q-Set* are reported in full in Appendix E for 547 men and 393 women, each described by a panel of five or more observers. The five items with largest positive and five with largest negative correlations are offered below, along with the coefficient for men and for women:

Genuinely values intellectual and cognitive matters (.24, .35)

Has a wide range of interests (.17, .26)

Has high aspiration level for self (.21, .18)

Is concerned with philosophical problems; e.g., religions, values, the meaning of life, etc. (.17, .21)

Appears to have a high degree of intellectual capacity (.13, .29)

Is self-defeating (−.16, −.15)

Overreactive to minor frustrations; irritable (−.13, −.17)

Feels cheated and victimized by life; self-pitying (−.13, −.14)

Is uncomfortable with uncertainty and complexities (−.11, −.20)

Handles anxiety and conflicts by, in effect, refusing to recognize their presence; repressive or dissociative tendencies (−.14, −.11)

Although these 20 correlations are low, 19 are significant at or beyond the .01 level. High scorers on v.3 are described as intelligent and as valuing things of the mind, as having a wide range of interests, and as having high aspirations for self. Low scorers on v.3 are described as self-defeating, overreactive to minor perturbations, and uncomfortable with complexity. In addition, they feel victimized by life, and they make use of denial and repression in coping with anxiety and conflicts.

From Appendix D, key adjectival descriptions by observers have been selected for presentation in Table 2.5. Among the terms related to higher scores on v.3, there is a strong cluster pertaining to intellectual competence and clarity of thinking—specifically, capable, clear-thinking, foresighted, insightful, intelligent, logical, and rational. Two of the terms (fair-minded and tolerant) suggest prosocial attitudes, and the term imaginative, taken together with the description of low scorers as narrow in interests, betokens a potential for creative attainment.

Low scorers on v.3 are seen as apathetic, confused, and bitter, and as cold, intolerant, nagging, prejudiced, resentful, and suspicious in their interpersonal life. A low level of ego integration is suggested by the further descriptions infantile and shallow.

A recent validational study of the v.3 scale (Weiser & Meyers, 1993) tends to confirm some of the inferences stated above concerning inner-direction, self-esteem, and low levels of anxiety among high scorers on v.3. In samples of from 125 to 140 for males and from 352 to 388 for females, correlations were obtained of .41 and .48 with the inner-directedness scale of the *Personal Orientation*

Inventory (Shostrom, 1963), correlations of −.37 and −.54 with the trait anxiety scale of the *State-Trait Anxiety Index* (Spielberger, Gorsuch, Lushene, Vagg, & Jacobs, 1983), and correlations of .43 and .52 with Coopersmith's (1981) self-esteem inventory.

Summary of the Scales

The three vector scales for the CPI are emergents from the inventory itself, developed so as to sharpen the foci of measurement discernible in the smallest-space analyses of Karni and Levin (1972). Although the vectors are to some extent compatible with factor analytic studies of the CPI, they were not developed by factorial methods and, in fact, do not fully correspond to the factor structure of the inventory (see chapter 3 for factor analytic data on Form 434 of the CPI). Vector 1, it will be recalled, was initially defined by the sum of Do, Sy, Sp, and Sa minus the sum of Gi, Sc, and F/M. The first four scales appear with largest loadings on Factor 1 of the CPI, but Gi and Sc have their largest loadings on Factor 2, and F/M is a major definer of Factor 5. Vector 2 was initially developed against a criterion of So plus Cm minus Fx. In chapter 3, it can be seen that So is most strongly loaded on Factor 2, Cm is found on Factor 3 for men and Factor 4 for women, and Fx is one of two major contributors to Factor 4 for men and Factor 3 for women. Vector 3 began with a marker composed of Wb plus To plus Ie. Factor analysis places these three scales on different dimensions, with Ie found on Factor 1 and the other two scales on Factor 2.

The composites of folk scales used as initial criteria for developing the three vector measures could not be used for the model itself because of their high intercorrelations. However, by selecting items for each vector that had minimal relationships to the other two, it was possible to generate scales having low or near-zero intercorrelations. The observed values for the norm samples of 3,000 men and 3,000 women were as follows: v.1 versus v.2, −.05 for men and .04 for women; v.1 versus v.3, −.20 for men and −.21 for women; and v.2 versus v.3, .10 for men and .06 for women. When correlated with the folk scales as they appear on the profile sheet, v.1 had high negative coefficients with scales in Sector 1 and appreciably lower coefficients with scales in the other three sectors. Vector 2 had high positive correlations with scales in Sector 2, but appreciably lower correlations with scales in the other three sectors. Vector

	Men, Described By			**Women, Described By**		
Adjectives	Spouse (N = 236)	3 Peers (N = 194)	10 Staff Members (N = 612)	Spouse (N = 236)	3 Peers (N = 192)	10 Staff Members (N = 358)

Table 2.5 Adjectival Descriptions by Observers: 12 Most Salient Positive and 12 Most Salient Negative Correlates of the 58-Item v.3 Scale

Adjectives	Spouse (N = 236)	3 Peers (N = 194)	10 Staff Members (N = 612)	Spouse (N = 236)	3 Peers (N = 192)	10 Staff Members (N = 358)
Alert	.13*	.15*	.16**	.07	.09	.08
Capable	.06	.19**	.08*	.16*	.16*	.14**
Clear-thinking	.15*	.16*	.13**	.15*	.18*	.18**
Fair-minded	.14*	.11	.10**	.08	.14*	.08
Foresighted	.13*	.14	.13**	.07	.10	.11*
Imaginative	.08	.03	.15**	.15*	.09	.14**
Insightful	.19**	.12	.16**	.25**	.18*	.16**
Intelligent	.14*	.11	.19**	.12	.17*	.23**
Interests wide	.13*	.06	.16**	.21**	.05	.17**
Logical	.00	.16*	.14**	.12	.16*	.17**
Rational	.07	.18*	.09*	.20**	.18*	.12*
Tolerant	.17**	.15*	.14**	.07	.19**	.06
Apathetic	−.19**	−.06	−.17**	−.06	−.16*	−.08
Bitter	−.19**	−.03	−.20**	−.11	−.26**	−.18**
Cold	−.08	−.20**	−.11**	−.06	−.17*	−.11*
Confused	−.20**	−.15*	−.08*	−.15*	−.15*	−.16**
Infantile	−.06	−.11	−.09*	−.21**	−.16*	−.22**
Interests narrow	−.13*	−.08	−.19**	−.31**	−.14*	−.29**
Intolerant	−.14*	−.12	−.29**	−.20**	−.05	−.17**
Nagging	−.26**	−.16*	−.07	−.07	−.13	−.23**
Prejudiced	−.34**	−.12	−.15**	−.26**	−.19**	−.20**
Resentful	−.11	−.07	−.10**	−.07	−.25**	−.16**
Shallow	−.06	−.17*	−.10**	−.17**	.00	−.23**
Suspicious	−.17**	−.16*	−.15**	−.14*	−.16*	−.14**

* $p \leq .05$, ** $p \leq .01$

3 had high positive correlations with scales in all four sectors of the profile sheet, except for coefficients with F/M of −.02 for men and −.23 for women. These findings lead to a formulation of the three vectors as depicting major orientations toward people (v.1, the interpersonal vector), toward societal values and social norms (v.2, the intrapersonal vector), and toward self (v.3, the self-realization vector).

The first two vectors are also compatible with but not derived from Vernon's (1953) survey of basic themes in personality structure, from which he concluded that the root dimensions are extraversion-introversion and undependability-dependability. Vector 1 more or less corresponds to Vernon's extraversion-introversion dimension, and Vector 2 has partial similarity to Vernon's dependability

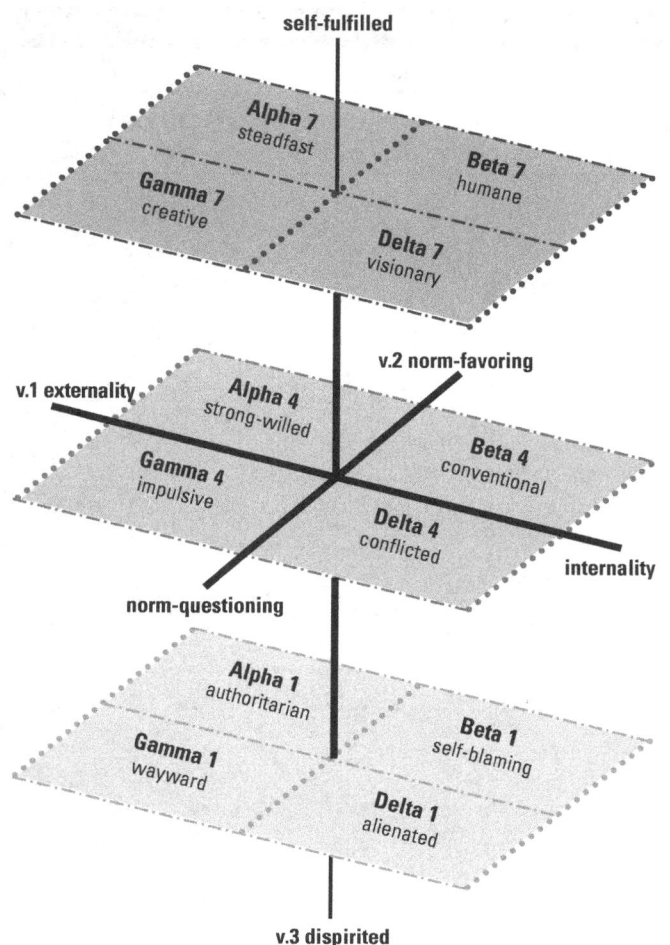

Figure 2.3 Schematic Representation of the Three-Vector or Cuboid Model of Personality Structure Showing Cross-Sections at Levels 1, 4, and 7 of Ego Integration

Table 2.6 Cutting Scores on v.1 and v.2 for Type				
	Males		**Females**	
Type	v.1	v.2	v.1	v.2
Alpha	≤ 17	≥ 22	≤ 19	≥ 23
Beta	≥ 18	≥ 22	≥ 20	≥ 23
Gamma	≤ 17	≤ 21	≤ 19	≤ 22
Delta	≥ 18	≤ 21	≥ 20	≤ 22

Table 2.7 Cutting Scores on v.3 for Level	
v.3	**Level**
49–58	7
45–48	6
40–44	5
33–39	4
26–32	3
20–25	2
0–19	1

continuum. A crucial difference in regard to Vector 2, however, is that insofar as possible, the evaluative and even invidious implications attached to low scores in Vernon's presentation are absent from v.2. The third vector in the three-vector model arrays respondents along a dimension of dissatisfaction, feelings of ineffectiveness, and poor coping abilities at the low end, to self-realization, competence, and ego integration at the other pole.

The Three-Vector Model

The geometric form that best represents the implied and projected psychology of the three-vector model is the cuboid. Figure 2.3 shows the model in this form. Midscale cuts on v.1 and v.2 define four quadrants. The Alpha quadrant is defined by v.1 scores in the participative, extraverted mode, and by v.2

scores presaging norm-favoring or norm-approving dispositions. The Beta cell is composed of persons who are norm-favoring on v.2, and introverted or inwardly oriented on v.1. Gammas are norm-questioning and participative, and Deltas are privacy-seeking and norm- doubting. Because v.1 and v.2 are relatively uncorrelated, approximately 25% of the norm respondents can be expected in each of the quadrants. From the psychological standpoint, each quadrant represents a way of living or a lifestyle, some of whose implications will be elaborated in the text to follow.

On the third vector, cutting scores are set so as to produce seven levels of realization, or competence, or ego integration. Thus, for each of the four life-styles, individuals may range from the despair and frustrations associated with Level 1 on through the midlevels of ordinary stress and feelings of efficacy, on up to the self-actualization associated with Level 7.

Table 2.6 gives the cutting scores for men and women on the v.1 and v.2 scales used to classify respondents in regard to lifestyle. Table 2.7 gives the cutting scores (same for both men end women) on v.3 for the seven levels. Raw scores are used in Tables 2.6 and 2.7 rather than standard scores to

Table 2.8 Type and Level Frequencies for Current Cutting Scores as Applied to the 1987 and 1996 Profile Norm Samples Types

| | Classifications on Level | | | | | | | | |
Types	1	2	3	4	5	6	7	Sum	%
Alphas									
Males 1987	11	15	36	70	55	33	35	255	25.5
Females 1987	9	23	35	50	57	47	29	250	25.0
Males 1996	48	106	157	188	101	53	32	685	22.8
Females 1996	72	124	196	189	111	65	48	805	26.8
Betas									
Males 1987	24	21	45	48	43	22	17	220	22.0
Females 1987	20	34	63	60	39	29	28	263	26.3
Males 1996	92	181	238	220	99	44	25	899	30.0
Females 1996	123	193	244	227	92	41	23	943	31.4
Gammas									
Males 1987	18	35	49	45	43	29	30	249	24.9
Females 1987	24	33	24	70	60	37	23	271	27.1
Males 1996	61	98	139	138	90	41	28	595	19.8
Females 1996	71	77	110	160	111	47	35	611	20.4
Deltas									
Males 1987	25	49	63	57	37	25	20	276	27.6
Females 1987	36	29	51	47	29	13	11	216	21.6
Males 1996	135	192	224	152	60	35	19	821	27.4
Females 1996	130	135	157	121	54	30	14	641	21.4
Sums									
1987 total	167	239	366	447	363	235	183	2000	
1987 %	8.3	12.0	18.3	22.3	18.1	11.8	9.1		
1996 total	732	1106	1465	1399	718	356	224	6000	
1996 %	12.2	18.4	24.4	23.3	12.0	5.9	3.7		

avoid any future ambiguity or uncertainty should a new normative basis be developed for the inventory.

Because the norm sample of women scored higher than the norm sample of men on the v.1 and v.2 scales (see Appendix B), cutting scores are slightly higher for women. On v.3, there are essentially no differences between males and females.

The Type/Level frequencies established for the norm samples in the 1986 edition of the CPI (Gough, 1987) have proved to be valuable in interpreting individual protocols and also in describing groups. So as to minimize changes, and to permit experienced users of the CPI to apply their skills to Form 434 protocols with minimal disruption, the new cutting scores on the vector scales have been set to approximate the outcomes furnished by the prior rules. Table 2.8 presents data for both the 1986 norm samples of 1,000 persons of each sex and the new profile norm groups.

For the 1987 samples, the desired numbers for each of the four lifestyles were 500 in each instance. Using the current cutting scores, the totals come to 505 Alphas, 483 Betas, 520 Gammas, and 492 Deltas. For men and women alone, the desired sums for each Type were 250. Moderate deviations from this figure can be observed for Beta males, Gamma females, Delta males, and Delta females. These deviations, it should be emphasized, have no influence on the interpretations of Type membership, the reason being that the interpretive information to be presented below derives solely from the individuals who were in fact classified under each of the four headings. The desired percentages for each of the seven levels on v. 3 were 8, 12, 19, 22, 19, 12, and 8. The percentages of actual occurrence for the 1987 total sample of 2,000 persons correspond closely to these figures. It therefore appears that the new cutting scores produce results congruent with those used in Form 462 of the inventory.

Table 2.8 also furnished data for the new profile norm samples. In regard to Type frequencies, these sample are somewhat different from the previous ones. There are now 1,490 Alphas, 1,842 Betas, 1,206 Gammas, and 1,462 Deltas—in percentage terms, 24.8, 30.7, 20.1, and 24.4, respectively. Betas are somewhat overrepresented, and Gammas are somewhat underrepresented. The current norm samples are also somewhat lower on the ego integration or self-realization continuum than the prior groups, with percentages of 12.2, 18.4, and 24.4 at Levels 1, 2, and 3, and reduced percentages at Levels 5, 6, and 7. It should be stated again that these differences in frequencies have no bearing on the interpretive meanings for either Type or Level classifications. The observational and other data presented below are based on persons as in fact classified by the current algorithms for the three-vector model.

Table 2.9 furnishes data on the Type classifications for male archival samples, and Table 2.10 provides the same information for female archival samples. There were 27 male samples in the Alpha category, that is, samples having a higher incidence of Alphas than of any of the other three Types. Among those with half or more in the Alpha category, five of eight were persons in leadership posts or in training for such positions. For women, 17 samples were in the Alpha category. Four of these had percentages of 50 or more: commercial writers, police

officer candidates, nominated leaders, and nominated best citizens. For both sexes, students of education, medicine, and optometry were Alphas, as were physicians in the specialty of anesthesiology, police officer applicants, and college students in general. Four subgroups of high school students were also Alphas for both males and females: those nominated as leaders, best citizens, and most attractive, and those who attended a national science fair conference.

Only five male and four female archival samples were in the Beta category, two of which were common: mathematicians and high school students in general. The strongest Beta sample for either sex was composed of correctional officers, but even for them the percentage was less than 50. Betas, it will be recalled, tend toward detachment from others, value and protect their privacy, and tend to approve of or at least accept societal norms.

There were 12 Gamma samples for each sex, including four with percentages great than 50: women law school students, members of a Rajneeshi colony (males and females), and women in a premedical curriculum. Paired samples, beyond the Rajneeshipuram members, included art institute students, psychology graduate students, critics of books for children, social welfare graduate students, juvenile delinquents, San Francisco area residents, and students of architecture. Gammas, it will be recalled, enter into the ongoing flow of interpersonal activity, value the financial and other rewards that the culture provides, but are skeptical of the conventions and practices by which society apportions its approval or disapproval.

Finally, there were four male and five female samples in the Delta category, with only one sample (female creative writers) having more than 50 percent incidence. Common to both lists were high school disciplinary problems and prison inmates. The relative dearth of what could be called "successful" groups in the modal Delta category is not due to any inherent weakness of this lifestyle, but rather to a shortage of samples from settings in which Deltas excel, for example, practicing artists, musicians, and highly theoretical scientists. It might also be noted that women writers and also women students of pharmacy were in the modal Delta category.

Some interesting contrasts in Type membership may be noted for men and women. Male MBA

Table 2.9 California Psychological Inventory Type Frequencies for Male Samples

Samples	N	Percentage of Each Type			
		Alphas	Betas	Gammas	Deltas
Modal Alphas					
Irish managers	37	73.0	10.8	13.5	2.7
West Point cadets	1,413	63.7	21.9	10.4	4.0
Sales managers	85	62.4	25.9	9.4	2.4
Medical school applicants	70	58.6	17.1	15.7	8.6
Air force officers	343	56.0	24.8	13.4	5.8
Parole and probation officers	65	50.8	20.0	21.5	7.7
Nominated high school leaders	90	50.0	30.0	8.9	11.1
Police officer applicants	883	49.6	23.0	14.6	12.8
Bank managers	49	49.0	28.6	4.1	18.4
Nominated high school best citizens	90	48.9	32.2	8.9	10.0
Optometry students	100	48.0	27.0	9.0	16.0
Anesthesiologists	98	45.9	25.5	15.3	13.3
Research scientists	45	44.4	6.7	26.7	22.2
Catholic priests	41	43.9	41.5	9.8	4.9
MBA candidates	71	43.7	7.0	39.4	9.9
Members club for inventors	14	42.9	28.6	21.4	7.1
Education students	167	40.7	24.0	24.6	10.8
Police officers	366	40.7	29.0	13.9	16.4
Engineers	47	40.4	36.2	12.8	10.6
Counseling graduate students	67	40.3	16.4	35.8	7.5
Business executives	185	38.9	33.5	13.0	14.6
Nominated high school most popular	90	38.9	27.8	18.9	14.4
Medical students	551	38.5	20.5	26.3	14.7
High school science fair delegates	363	38.3	24.2	24.0	13.5
College students	3,235	36.7	21.4	23.1	18.8
Architects	124	36.3	25.8	18.5	19.4
Commercial writers	14	35.7	28.6	14.3	21.4
Engineering students	66	33.3	21.2	18.2	27.3

Samples	N	Percentage of Each Type			
		Alphas	Betas	Gammas	Deltas
Modal Betas					
Correctional officers	221	30.3	48.4	7.2	14.0
Nominated high school most attractive	88	25.0	36.4	26.1	12.5
High school students	4,611	22.8	35.3	13.9	27.9
Mathematicians	57	19.3	35.1	22.8	22.8
Pharmacy students	439	26.7	28.2	19.6	25.5
Modal Gammas					
Rajneeshi colony residents	33	3.0	0.0	51.5	45.5
Art institute students	44	4.5	2.3	47.7	45.5
Psychology graduate students	623	19.6	7.2	46.5	26.6
Critics of books for children	25	24.0	20.0	40.0	16.0
Writers of books for children	29	13.8	13.8	37.9	34.5
Social work graduate students	254	28.0	17.3	37.4	17.3
Creative writers	19	21.1	15.8	36.8	26.3
Juvenile delinquents	76	19.7	10.5	36.8	32.9
San Francisco area residents	261	23.4	19.5	36.8	20.3
Architecture students	125	27.2	22.4	32.0	18.4
Nursing students	149	26.8	20.8	28.9	23.5
Modal Deltas					
Young prison inmates	2,899	12.9	19.5	22.2	45.4
High school disciplinary problems	90	15.6	10.0	36.7	37.8
Psychiatric patients	41	17.1	29.3	17.1	36.6
Adult prison inmates	196	16.8	18.4	29.6	35.2

Table 2.10 California Psychological Inventory Type Frequencies for Female Samples

Samples	N	Alphas	Betas	Gammas	Deltas
		Percentage of Each Type			
Modal Alphas					
Commercial writers	12	58.3	0.0	25.0	16.7
Police officer applicants	200	56.0	13.5	20.5	10.0
Nominated high school leaders	90	51.1	17.8	23.3	7.8
Nominated high school best citizens	90	50.0	26.7	8.9	14.4
Education students	310	49.4	24.2	18.4	8.1
Optometry students	50	48.0	14.0	16.0	22.0
Secondary school teachers	21	47.6	14.3	28.6	9.5
Anesthesiologists	17	47.1	23.5	23.5	5.9
Nominated high school most attrractive	90	43.3	26.7	21.1	8.9
College counselors	42	42.9	23.8	21.4	11.9
High school science fair delegates	148	42.6	28.4	18.2	10.8
Nominated high school most popular	90	41.1	27.8	23.3	7.8
Counseling graduate students	275	38.9	10.5	35.3	15.3
Nursing students	250	37.6	17.2	21.6	23.6
Medical students	90	36.7	17.8	31.1	14.4
Home economics students	176	36.4	32.4	15.3	15.9
College students	4,126	34.0	23.0	24.7	18.3
Modal Betas					
Mathematicians	41	14.6	39.0	17.1	29.3
Registered nurses	100	21.0	37.0	25.0	17.0
Modal Betas continued					
High school students	4,825	26.8	36.9	14.7	21.5
University clerical personnel	56	26.8	28.6	25.0	19.6
Modal Gammas					
Law students	40	15.0	2.5	65.0	17.5
Rajneeshi colony residents	34	0.0	2.9	61.8	35.3
Premedical students	48	27.1	6.3	58.3	8.3
Juvenile delinquents	55	7.3	1.8	49.1	41.8
Art institute students	27	0.0	11.1	48.1	40.7
Psychology graduate students	405	15.1	8.4	48.1	28.4
MBA candidates	44	40.9	6.8	45.5	6.8
Critics of books for children	36	33.3	19.4	44.4	2.8
San Francisco area residents	261	17.2	16.1	38.7	28.0
Psychiatric patients	34	14.7	32.4	38.2	14.7
Social work graduate students	446	24.7	17.9	34.5	22.9
Architecture students	55	30.9	9.1	32.7	27.3
Modal Deltas					
Creative writers	10	0.0	0.0	40.0	60.0
Writers of books for children	32	15.6	15.6	25.0	43.8
High school disciplinary problems	90	17.8	18.9	31.1	32.2
Prison inmates	345	22.0	27.8	20.3	29.9
Pharmacy students	277	25.3	24.9	24.2	25.6

candidates were predominantly Alphas, whereas female MBA candidates tended to be Gammas. In a corporate culture, Alphas will be rule-respecting, accepting of the company's traditions, and eager to do well and get ahead. In the same setting, Gammas will be rule-questioning, often at odds with the seemingly petty and arbitrary expectations of the company, but also eager to move up the corporate ladder. Male medical school applicants (hence, premedical students too) were Alphas, whereas female premedical students tended to be Gammas. Medical school itself seems to be an Alpha environment, as suggested by the prevalence of Alphas among male medical students. The Alpha male applicants, if accepted, will tend to fit in and conform to the expectations and folkways of the system; the female applicants, on the other hand, if accepted, will be less conforming, less accepting of the traditions, and more disposed to make changes. Among women, writers of books for children tended to be Deltas, whereas critics of those books tended to be Gammas. Self-expression by way of art, music, and writing is something often found among Deltas, whereas the capacity for criticism and for detecting and explicating the flaws in other peoples' thinking is well-developed among Gammas.

Table 2.11 gives the percentage of persons in each sample (male and female) classified at each of the seven Levels on the v.3 scale, arrayed in rank order for means on the scale. The highest-ranking male sample is comprised of the 45 research scientists. These men held advanced degrees in fields such as physics, mathematics, computer sciences, and electrical engineering and were working in laboratories studying rocketry and the space sciences. None of the men had classifications at Levels 1, 2, or 3, and 71.1% were at Levels 6 and 7. Students of optometry came next, with 64% at Levels 6 and 7; followed by psychology graduate students, with 60.3% at the two highest levels. Male samples with large percentages of persons at Levels 1 and 2 included juvenile delinquents, youth authority wards, prison inmates, and high school disciplinary problems. For females, the four highest-ranking samples were optometry students, psychology graduate students, medical students, and social welfare graduate students, with percentages at Levels 6 and 7 of 68, 64.2, 63.4, and 57.1, respectively. As for males, juvenile delinquents, high school disciplinary problems, and prison inmates anchored the low end, with percentages at Levels 1 and 2 of 40, 51.2, and 54.8, respectively.

The information in Table 2.11 can be useful in interpreting individual protocols. Consider a high school male classified as an Alpha-5. Level 5 is not very high in respect to total norms, but among high school males only 9.7% are at Level 5 or above. Accordingly, for this high school student, good interpersonal skills and excellent leadership potential are indicated. Another example is a female graduate student in psychology classified as a Gamma-4. Level 4

is at the midpoint for people in general, but in the designated subsample, only 12.5% have scores at Level 4 or below. Thus, at least moderate problems of adaptation to the program's rules and expectations would be expected. What about a college student whose v.3 score is at Level 2 and who is thinking of enrolling in a premedical curriculum? The chances of winning eventual admission to a medical school seem remote, the reason being that among both male and female medical students, no one had a v.3 scores as low as this.

Type Characteristics

Psychological implications associated with membership in each of the four quadrants established by the conjoint treatment of the v.1 and v.2 scales can to a certain degree be inferred from what has been said above about the two scales separately. Alphas should be ambitious, energetic, and outgoing. Betas should be reserved, moderate, and patient. Gammas should be spontaneous, restless, and pleasure-seeking. Deltas should be withdrawn, private, and, to some extent, disaffected. These inferences are only starting points, to be modified and sharpened by the information added from a classification on Level. A Delta-7, for example, should be recognizable as having broadly the same perspectives as a Delta-1, but the contrast in self-realization will reflect an enormous difference in the totality of personal expression. Each Type has its own specific mode of self-actualization and attainment, and each Type also has its own specific mode of malfunctioning and ego disintegration.

Data from observational sources are crucial for the development of a psychological portrait for each of the four lifestyles. Four sources of such data are available in the CPI archives. The first is based on adjectival descriptions on the 300-item *Adjective Check List* (ACL; Gough & Heilbrun, 1983). Six samples have adjectival data: 236 men, each described on the ACL by a wife or partner; 236 women, each described by a husband or partner; 194 college males, each described by three peers on the ACL, using a five-step weighted format for rating; 192 college females, each described by three peers on the ACL, using a five-step weighted format; 612 men each described on the ACL by a panel

Table 2.11 Rankings of Male and Female Samples on the v.3 (Ego Integration) Scale and the Percentage of Subjects at Each Level										
		v.3 Scale		**Percentages at Each of the Seven Levels**						
Male Samples	*N*	*M*	*SD*	1	2	3	4	5	6	7
Research scientists	45	46.00	5.32	0.0	0.0	0.0	15.6	13.3	42.2	28.9
Optometry students	100	45.81	8.13	0.0	5.0	1.0	12.0	18.0	23.0	41.0
Psychology graduate students	623	45.49	6.13	0.2	0.3	2.2	12.2	24.7	28.7	31.6
Medical school applicants	70	45.01	5.38	0.0	0.0	1.4	8.6	38.6	27.1	24.3
Education students	167	44.62	6.24	0.0	0.0	3.6	17.4	22.8	26.3	29.9
Social welfare graduate students	254	44.18	6.40	0.4	0.8	2.4	18.9	24.8	23.6	29.1
Medical students	551	43.39	6.89	0.2	1.6	5.1	17.8	28.5	22.7	24.1
Mathematicians	57	43.32	6.92	0.0	1.8	5.3	15.8	31.6	19.3	26.3
Engineering students	66	42.77	6.39	0.0	1.5	6.1	19.7	34.8	18.2	19.7
Critics of books for children	25	42.08	8.10	0.0	4.0	8.0	20.0	20.0	28.0	20.0
Anesthesiologists	98	41.95	5.82	0.0	0.0	6.1	29.6	27.6	21.4	15.3
Engineers	47	41.79	6.60	0.0	0.0	8.5	29.8	27.7	14.9	19.1
Rajneeshpuram residents	33	41.58	5.53	0.0	0.0	3.0	36.4	30.3	18.2	12.1
Catholic priests	41	41.54	7.55	0.0	0.0	12.2	24.4	24.4	22.0	17.1
Parole and probation officers	65	41.43	7.96	0.0	4.6	10.8	23.1	16.9	26.2	18.5
Police officer applicants	883	41.28	8.28	0.9	3.5	11.3	23.9	20.7	17.3	22.3
Business executives	185	41.01	8.71	1.1	2.7	14.1	20.5	24.3	16.2	21.1
MBA candidates	71	40.80	7.98	2.8	2.8	8.5	22.5	25.4	23.9	14.1
Bank managers	49	40.57	7.41	0.0	6.1	8.2	28.6	28.6	10.2	18.4
Counseling graduate students	67	40.19	9.45	0.0	7.5	16.4	22.4	13.4	13.4	26.9
Architects	124	39.99	6.12	0.8	0.8	11.3	30.6	32.3	17.7	6.5
Nursing students	149	39.54	8.03	2.0	2.7	14.1	28.9	23.5	15.4	13.4
Pharmacy students	439	39.38	8.94	1.4	5.2	18.5	21.0	21.6	14.8	17.5
Writers of books for children	29	39.31	7.57	0.0	3.4	17.2	24.1	20.7	27.6	6.9
Police officers	366	38.35	8.10	1.6	4.4	17.5	30.1	23.8	11.5	11.2
Creative writers	19	38.26	6.31	0.0	5.3	10.5	47.4	21.1	10.5	5.3
Members, club for inventors	14	38.14	5.16	0.0	0.0	14.3	42.9	42.9	0.0	0.0
College students	3,235	38.02	7.84	1.3	5.1	17.2	31.7	22.7	13.7	8.4
Military officers	343	37.88	7.16	0.6	6.7	14.0	32.4	29.4	13.4	3.5
Irish managers	37	37.51	6.79	0.0	5.4	18.9	35.1	21.6	16.2	2.7
San Francisco area residents	261	37.33	8.39	3.4	4.6	18.4	30.3	21.8	13.0	8.4
Sales managers	85	37.27	7.70	2.4	4.7	17.6	36.5	22.4	9.4	7.1
Commercial writers	14	36.86	8.32	7.1	0.0	14.3	42.9	21.4	7.1	7.1

| Table 2.11 | Rankings of Male and Female Samples on the v.3 (Ego Integration) Scale and the Percentage of Subjects at Each Level | | continued | | | | | | | |

Male Samples continued	N	v.3 Scale		Percentages at Each of the Seven Levels						
		M	SD	1	2	3	4	5	6	7
Architecture students	125	36.80	7.32	0.8	7.2	18.4	32.8	27.2	8.8	4.8
West Point cadets	1,413	36.57	7.53	1.5	5.4	22.4	35.7	19.7	10.0	5.3
Correctional officers	221	34.47	7.90	2.7	10.9	25.8	32.1	17.6	7.2	3.6
High school science fair delegates	363	34.29	8.30	2.8	12.1	25.1	30.6	17.1	6.9	5.5
High school nominated best citizens	90	33.42	8.42	3.3	17.8	24.4	31.1	12.2	7.8	3.3
Art institute students	44	33.32	7.86	2.3	13.6	31.8	27.3	18.2	4.5	2.3
High school nominated leaders	90	33.03	8.42	3.3	16.7	28.9	27.8	14.4	5.6	3.3
High school nominated most popular	90	30.49	8.01	6.7	25.6	27.8	27.8	8.9	2.2	1.1
High school nominated most attractive	88	28.70	8.34	17.0	23.9	18.2	34.1	4.5	2.3	0.0
High school students	4,611	28.26	8.35	15.5	23.7	30.4	20.7	6.5	2.2	1.0
Juvenile delinquents	76	28.08	8.88	15.8	25.0	28.9	21.1	5.3	2.6	1.3
Youth authority inmates	2,899	26.81	8.99	22.7	24.5	27.3	16.0	6.0	2.5	1.1
Prison inmates	196	26.51	8.90	21.4	30.1	27.0	12.8	2.0	5.1	1.5
High school nominated disciplinary problems	90	25.20	6.68	17.8	38.9	26.7	15.6	1.1	0.0	0.0

Female Samples	N	v.3 Scale		Percentages at Each of the Seven Levels						
		M	SD	1	2	3	4	5	6	7
Optometry students	50	46.20	6.40	0.0	0.0	4.0	8.0	20.0	34.0	34.0
Psychology graduate students	405	46.13	5.83	0.0	0.2	2.2	10.1	23.2	25.2	39.0
Medical students	90	45.60	6.24	0.0	0.0	4.4	12.2	20.0	26.7	36.7
Social welfare graduate students	446	44.68	5.97	0.0	0.2	3.4	15.2	24.0	29.1	28.0
Education students	310	44.13	6.56	0.0	0.3	5.8	18.1	22.3	23.9	29.7
Police officer applicants	200	43.45	8.70	1.0	4.5	7.0	15.5	18.5	21.0	32.5
Secondary school teachers	21	43.24	6.04	0.0	4.8	0.0	19.0	23.8	33.3	19.0
College counselors	42	43.21	3.87	0.0	0.0	0.0	19.0	35.7	38.1	7.1
Law school students	40	43.07	6.98	0.0	0.0	7.5	22.5	25.0	17.5	27.5
Mathematicians	41	42.93	5.85	0.0	0.0	2.4	24.4	29.3	19.5	24.4
Premedical students	48	42.25	6.41	0.0	0.0	6.3	31.3	27.1	16.7	18.8
Anesthesiologists	17	42.18	7.30	0.0	0.0	17.6	5.9	29.4	29.4	17.6
Rajneeshpuram residents	34	41.91	5.91	0.0	2.9	0.0	35.3	26.5	23.5	11.8
Critics of books for children	36	41.75	6.30	0.0	0.0	5.6	33.3	25.0	22.2	13.9
MBA candidates	44	41.59	7.22	0.0	0.0	13.6	25.0	20.5	27.3	13.6

Table 2.11 Rankings of Male and Female Samples on the v.3 (Ego Integration) Scale and the Percentage of Subjects at Each Level continued										
		v.3 Scale		Percentages at Each of the Seven Levels						
Female Samples continued	N	M	SD	1	2	3	4	5	6	7
University clerical personnel	56	41.55	7.19	0.0	1.8	8.9	23.2	32.1	14.3	19.6
Counseling graduate students	275	41.52	7.02	0.4	1.8	8.7	23.3	28.7	20.4	16.7
Home economics students	176	41.16	7.17	0.6	2.3	9.1	22.7	30.1	19.9	15.3
Writers of books for children	32	40.72	5.35	0.0	0.0	6.3	34.4	31.3	21.9	6.3
Commercial writers	12	40.17	5.72	0.0	0.0	8.3	25.0	50.0	8.3	8.3
Nursing students	250	39.87	6.33	0.4	1.2	14.0	28.0	31.6	17.2	7.6
College students	4,126	39.73	7.13	0.6	2.8	12.2	31.4	26.2	16.5	10.3
Creative writers	10	39.70	6.73	0.0	0.0	10.0	40.0	20.0	30.0	0.0
Pharmacy students	277	39.09	8.45	1.4	6.5	13.7	24.2	24.9	18.4	10.8
Registered nurses	100	38.52	6.95	1.0	4.0	15.0	34.0	28.0	11.0	7.0
Architecture students	55	37.91	7.86	0.0	7.3	20.0	27.3	25.5	14.5	5.5
San Francisco area residents	261	37.52	7.88	2.7	5.7	16.1	30.3	26.4	12.6	6.1
High school science fair delegates	148	36.08	7.89	2.7	7.4	16.9	37.8	23.0	8.8	3.4
Art institute students	27	34.78	7.69	0.0	11.1	22.2	37.0	14.8	11.1	3.7
High school nominated most popular	90	33.41	6.80	0.0	12.2	36.7	33.3	12.2	2.2	3.3
High school nominated best citizens	90	32.91	8.66	7.8	13.3	31.1	22.2	16.7	5.6	3.3
High school nominated leaders	90	32.70	7.52	5.6	13.3	26.7	35.6	14.4	3.3	1.1
High school nominated most attractive	90	29.63	7.38	10.0	16.7	44.4	18.9	7.8	1.1	1.1
Psychiatric patients	34	28.85	10.04	11.8	32.4	23.5	14.7	5.9	8.8	2.9
High school students	4,825	28.77	8.49	14.7	21.4	30.7	22.1	7.8	2.6	0.9
Juvenile delinquents	55	27.15	8.02	18.2	21.8	36.4	18.2	3.6	1.8	0.0
High school nominated disciplinary problems	90	25.44	7.55	25.6	25.6	30.0	12.2	6.7	0.0	0.0
Prison inmates	345	25.32	9.95	29.6	25.2	21.7	13.9	5.8	2.6	1.2

of 10 assessment staff observers; and 358 women, each described on the ACL by a panel of 10 assessment staff observers. For the couples, dummy weights of 1 were assigned to adjectives that had been checked, and of 0 for adjectives left blank. For the college students, standard scores on each of the 300 adjectives were computed from the composites, separately for each of the living groups from which students were obtained. For the assessees, the number of

times each adjective was checked by the panel served as the score; these sums could range from a low of 0 (no panel member checked the word) to a high of 10 (all panel members checked the adjective).

The second source of observational data came from Block's 100-item *California Q-Set* (Block, 1961). For each assessee, five or more staff observers contributed Q-sort formulations, which were then composited and rearrayed in the standard *Q-Set*

Table 2.12 Alpha Respondents Versus All Others: 8 Adjectival Descriptions with Largest Positive and 8 with Largest Negative Correlations

Adjectives	Men, Described By			Women, Described By		
	Spouse (N = 236)	3 Peers (N = 194)	10 Staff Members (N = 612)	Spouse (N = 236)	3 Peers (N = 192)	10 Staff Members (N = 358)
Ambitious	.14**	.25**	.14**	.08	.20**	.16**
Confident	.05	.08	.06	.16*	.17*	.18**
Energetic	.16*	.15*	.11**	.10	.22**	.05
Optimistic	.14*	.07	.04	.07	.10	.14**
Outgoing	.11	.11	.14**	.18*	.14*	.07
Resourceful	.15*	.26**	.09*	.12	.07	.03
Self-confident	.11	.11	.04	.20**	.08	.21**
Sociable	.10	.15*	.09*	.16*	.20**	.05
Apathetic	−.02	−.31**	−.17**	−.05	−.15*	−.14**
Forgetful	−.03	−.09	−.14**	−.18*	−.18*	−.06
Meek	−.13*	−.12	−.13**	−.12	−.19**	−.08
Quiet	−.12	−.04	−.22**	−.10	−.22**	−.10*
Quitting	−.11	−.13*	−.09*	−.07	−.13*	−.15**
Shy	−.09	−.06	−.28**	−.15*	−.17*	−.13*
Unambitious	−.13*	−.19**	−.15**	−.06	−.22**	−.15**
Withdrawn	−.08	−.14*	−.21**	−.12	−.24**	−.13*
Number of Alphas	47	59	250	37	66	89
Others	189	135	362	199	126	269

* $p \le .05$, ** $p \le .01$

frequencies. These composites were available for 547 men and 393 women.

The third source of information came from the 99-item *Interviewer's Check List* completed by the life history interview for each assessee. Items checked were given a dummy weight of 1, and items not checked were given a dummy weight of 0. Interviewers' descriptions were available for 504 men and 379 women.

The fourth source of information came from an unpublished 50-item *Interpersonal Q-Sort*. These Q-sort descriptions were furnished by 200 men, each describing his wife or partner, and by 200 women who described their husbands or partners.

For each of the four Types in the three-vector model, analyses were carried out pitting all persons

classified within a Type against the complement, that is, all of the other persons in the sample. For example, in the analyses of the *California Q-Set* items on the Alpha category, 97 of the 393 women and 207 of the 547 men were classified as Alphas. In each contrast, persons in the category were assigned dummy weights of 1, and all of those in the complement were assigned dummy weights of 0.

Alphas

Table 2.12 presents adjectival descriptions by observers having salient relationships to membership in the Alpha category. In each of the six subsamples, the number of Alphas and the number of persons in the complement or non-Alpha categories are found at the bottom of the table. A 1-0 scoring of type membership was correlated with each of the 300 adjectives in each of the six samples, and the eight items with largest overall correlations, both positive and negative, are listed.

Observers tend to see Alphas as ambitious, confident, energetic, and sociable. Optimism and resourcefulness are also qualities viewed as characteristic of Alphas. On the other hand, they are seldom seen as apathetic, meek, quiet, shy, or withdrawn.

California Q-Set items were also correlated with membership in the Alpha category. For men, 207 were classified as Alphas and 340 as non-Alphas. Of the 393 women for whom Q-sort criteria were available, 87 were Alphas and 296 were in the complement. The four Q-sort items with largest positive and four with largest negative correlations with the Alpha classification are listed below, along with the coefficients for men first, and then for women:

Is productive; gets things done (.15, .28)
Behaves in an assertive fashion (.21, .14)
Has high aspiration level for self (.23, .21)
Has social poise and presence; appears socially at ease (.22, .17)

Feels a lack of personal meaning in life (–.20, –.18)
Gives up and withdraws where possible in the face of frustration and adversity (–.21, –.16)
Reluctant to commit self to any definite course of action; tends to delay or avoid action (–.19, –.15)
Is self-defeating (–.22, –.19)

As can be inferred from these descriptions, Alphas are doers, ready to take action, and assertive in dealing with others. They set high goals for themselves and persevere even in the face of frustration or adversity. They are at ease in interpersonal situations and feel that their lives are meaningful.

Interviewer's Check List descriptions were available for 504 men, of whom 128 were Alphas and 376 non-Alphas. Of the 379 women described by interviewers, 70 were Alphas and 309 non-Alphas. The four items having largest positive and four having largest negative correlations with membership in the Alpha category are listed below (the first coefficient is for men, the second for women):

Mother affectionate and loving in disposition (.10, .15)

Family life on the whole was quite happy (.12, .18)
Was an honor student in high school (.17, .16)
Unusually self-confident; feels able to meet nearly any situation (.20, .10)

Interviewee was ashamed of one or both parents (–.11, –.09)
Interviewee had a great deal of friction with parents (–.08, –.16)
Considers self to have been an underachiever in high school (–.13, –.10)
Has many worries and problems (–.09, –.13)

The correlations with *Interviewer's Check List* descriptions are low in magnitude, and therefore of heuristic interest only. They do point toward a new theme in the Alpha lifestyle, however, namely having had a happy childhood and harmonious relationships with parents. The two items about academic performance in high school suggest early evidence of the Alpha's espousal of conventionally endorsed goals. Alphas, that is, tend to do what is seen as good and proper, and work hard to attain sanctioned objectives.

The fourth source of observational information comes from a 50-item Q-sort available for 200 couples. Each man was described by his wife or partner, and each woman was described by her husband or partner. Thirty-five of these men were Alphas, and 165 were in the complement; 29 women were Alphas, and 171 were non-Alphas. The three items with largest positive and three with largest negative correlations are listed below (first coefficient is for men, second for women):

Ambitious; likely to succeed in most things undertaken (.18, .11)
Enterprising and outgoing; enjoys social participation (.15, .17)
Is an effective leader; able to elicit the responses and cooperation of others (.15, .16)

Poorly organized; unable to concentrate attention and effort on intellectual problems (–.11, –.12)
Awkward and ill-at-ease socially; shy and inhibited with others (–.07, –.18)
Worried and preoccupied; tense, nervous, and generally upset (–.16, –.08)

Again, although the correlations are very low, the cumulative picture is congruent with impressions from other samples and other methods of recording observers' impressions. Alphas tend to be seen as ambitious, goal-directed, strong in leadership potential, and well-organized. The item on being an effective leader merits further comment. In a prior study (Gough, 1990), 11 samples ranging in size from 164 to 2,216 were studied in regard to six different criteria of leadership. These included nominations, the Q-sort item just mentioned above, ratings by observers of performance in leaderless group discussions, an adjectival descriptive composite of words directly linked to leadership, and classmates' ratings of leadership for cadets at West Point. In six ANOVAs for persons classified according to CPI type, Alphas ranked well above the average for all subjects.

Consider the samples of 1,857 male and 2,216 female high school students from 15 different schools across the nation. In each school, principals nominated a small number of students who showed visible and outstanding leadership. A total of 180 nominations was submitted, a percentage rate of 4.42. Because leadership is associated with the v.3 level in the model, as well as with lifestyle, both classifications need to be noted. For students at Levels 1 and 2, the nomination rates were 6.0 for Alphas, 2.0 for Betas, 2.0 for Gammas, and 1.0 for Deltas. Thus, even at low levels of ego integration, Alphas are nominated more often than the overall base rate would suggest. For students at Levels 5, 6, and 7, the nomination percentages were 17.6 for Alphas, 4.8 for Betas, 9.8 for Gammas, and 3.7 for Deltas. The F ratios for these contingency tabulations were all significant well beyond the .01 level of probability. High-level Alphas, in other words, constitute a pool from which leaders tend to emerge.

In another study (Kegel-Flom, 1992), 269 students of optometry were studied in regard to leadership and other criteria. Twenty-two of these students were in leadership positions, such as officers of the student association, class representatives to the dean's council, or trustee of the American Optometry Students' Association. Seventy-three percent of these leaders were Alphas, and their mean Level on v.3 was 5.62. At graduation, 31 of the 269 students tested at admission received awards for clinical excellence, leadership, and scholarship; of these, 87% ($N = 27$) were Alphas, and their mean

Level on v.3 was 5.60. In the total groups, the percentage of Alphas was 71, and the overall mean Level on v.3 was 5.54. A third criterion was dropout. Alphas, who comprised 71% of all students, constituted only 57% of the dropout; Gammas, just 10.6% of all students, comprised 29% of the dropouts. Thus, even in an Alpha-dominated academic environment, high-level Alphas tended to occupy slightly more positions of leadership than their classmates, were clearly more numerous among award-winners at graduation, and were underrepresented among dropouts.

What about problems among Alphas? In unpublished studies of over 10,000 applicants for employment as a police officer, Michael D. Roberts (1995a) found that Alphas constituted 62% of the total. For problems at work such as alcohol and drug abuse, unethical behavior, dishonesty, and difficulties in personal relations, Alphas were at or below the rates for these negatives among all officers. In one category, however, Alphas had higher rates than the baseline: excessive or unnecessary use of force. Alphas step forward, take part, and are not hesitant to act. Also, they believe that societal rules are good and proper, and that they should be obeyed. Disciplining of those who violate these rules, up to and including the use of force, is seen by Alphas as justified. Gamma officers, it might be pointed out here, rank far below the overall average when it comes to the excessive or unnecessary use of force, but distinctly above the overall average for dishonesty.

In summary, Alphas can be described as follows:

Alphas invest their values in the shared, interpersonal world and in adherence to norms. Alphas are doers, people who carry out the sanctioned mandates of the culture. At their best, they can be charismatic leaders and instigators of constructive social action. At their worst, they can be opportunistic, manipulative, and hostile towards those whose conformity to conventional values they doubt. Alphas tend to be joiners. At high levels of ego integration, they affiliate with organizations pursuing worthy social aims and with high-status groups. At low levels of ego integration, they affiliate with peripheral or fringe groups, such as survivalist cults and organizations advocating extreme nationalism and primitive patriotism.

Table 2.13 Beta Respondents Versus All Others: 8 Adjectival Descriptions with Largest Positive and 8 with Largest Negative Correlations

	Men, Described By			Women, Described By		
Adjectives	Spouse (N = 236)	3 Peers (N = 194)	10 Staff Members (N = 612)	Spouse (N = 236)	3 Peers (N = 192)	10 Staff Members (N = 358)
Cautious	.06	.03	.24**	.13*	.33**	.22**
Conservative	.18**	.04	.23**	.21**	.23**	.25**
Conventional	.19**	.03	.23**	.20**	.21**	.25**
Mild	.10	.01	.16**	.20**	.21**	.26**
Moderate	.08	.12	.23**	.14*	.22**	.26**
Patient	.08	.16*	.18**	.18**	.22**	.22**
Quiet	.20**	.05	.21**	.24**	.28**	.25**
Reserved	.15*	.07	.19**	.15*	.34**	.19**
Clever	−.17**	−.17*	−.18**	−.06	−.20**	−.19**
Impulsive	−.20**	−.18*	−.14**	−.11	−.21**	−.18**
Outgoing	−.30**	−.20**	−.17**	−.20**	−.14*	−.19**
Pleasure-seeking	−.26**	−.10	−.16**	−.18**	−.25**	−.23**
Spontaneous	−.15*	−.19**	−.15**	−.26**	−.19**	−.17**
Talkative	−.21**	−.11	−.18**	−.23**	−.23**	−.19**
Unconventional	−.16*	−.09	−.14**	−.18**	−.20**	−.19**
Versatile	−.12	−.19**	−.19**	−.06	−.26**	−.22**
Number of Betas	48	23	80	37	30	43
Others	188	171	532	199	162	315

* $p \leq .05$, ** $p \leq .01$

Betas

Table 2.13 presents adjectival descriptions by observers having salient relationships to membership in the Beta category. For each of the six subsamples, the number of Betas and the number in the complement are found at the bottom of the table. Using 1-0 dummy weights, these subgroups were correlated with the 300 adjectives in the ACL, and the eight with largest positive and eight with largest negative correlations selected for inclusion in Table 2.13.

Observers tend to see Betas as cautious, conservative, conventional, moderate, and reserved. Betas tend not to be seen as clever, impulsive, pleasure-seeking, spontaneous, or talkative. The classificatory themes for Betas include an internal orientation

and a need for privacy, along with attitudes of approval of societal norms. In interpersonal life, it is not surprising, they are quiet, forbearing, rule-respecting, prudent, and self-restrained.

In samples of 547 men and 393 women, *California Q-Set* items were correlated with membership in the Beta category. For men, there were 65 Betas and 482 in the complement, and for women there were 49 Betas and 344 in the complement. The four items with largest positive and four with largest negative correlations are given below (first coefficient is for men, second for women):

Tends toward overcontrol of needs and impulses; binds tensions excessively; delays gratification unnecessarily (.21, .29)

Genuinely submissive; accepts domination comfortably (.23, .20)

Favors conservative values in a variety of areas (.18, .29)

Has a readiness to feel guilty (.18, .29)

Characteristically pushes and tries to stretch limits; sees what he or she can get away with (−.20, −.25)

Is an interesting, arresting person (−.16, −.28)

Tends to be rebellious and nonconforming (−.18, −.28)

Is verbally fluent; can express ideas well (−.16, −.25)

The Q-sort descriptions restate the control of impulse, reticence, and conservative values visible in the adjectival data, but also pick up some important new themes. One of these is the item about guilt. Betas tend to be self-punishing, see themselves as at fault, and at low scores on the v.3 scale, are prone to extreme self-doubt and loss of self-esteem. Another new theme involves the item about allure and fascination. Betas in fact avoid the limelight, prefer never to be the center of attention, and seek anonymity. At high levels of ego-integration they will accept positions of leadership, but always in an unselfish and nonegoistic way.

Interviewer's descriptions on the 99-item *Life History Interviewers Check List* were analyzed for 78 Beta males versus 426 in the complement, and for 43 Beta females versus 336 non-Betas. The four items having largest positive and four having largest negative correlations with the Beta classification are given below (first coefficient is for men, second for women):

Has difficulty in expressing ideas (.16, .14)

Speech is difficult to understand; does not enunciate clearly (.10, .18)

Has strong religious beliefs (.18, .23)

Enjoys children (.10, .20)

Attractive, good-looking (−.10, −.11)

Has an alert, "open" face (−.16, −.06)

Uses a wide and varied vocabulary (−.14, −.14)

Witty and animated, an interesting conversationalist (−.11, −.14)

The Betas did not do very well in these interviews, speaking indistinctly, having trouble expressing their views, and making use of a mundane and limited vocabulary. Nonetheless, two substantive items appear in the list, one indicating strong religious beliefs and the other an enjoyment of children, particularly by Beta women.

The 50 items in the *Interpersonal Q-Sort* were correlated with Beta classifications in a sample of 200 couples. There were 43 Beta men, with 157 in the complement, and 31 Beta women, with 169 in the complement. Each person was described on the Q-sort by his or her spouse or partner. The three items with largest positive and three with largest negative correlations are given below (first coefficient is for men, second for women):

A conscientious and serious-minded person (.21, .14)

Unassuming; inhibited, and inattentive; bland and colorless in behavior (.15, .11)

Well-organized, capable, patient, and industrious; values achievement (.16, .14)

Is forceful and self-assured in manner (−.20, −.12)

Enterprising and outgoing; enjoys social participation (−.24, −.11)

Verbally fluent; expresses self easily and with clarity. (−.20, −. 20)

Spouses and partners tend to see Betas much as the other panels of observers did, as conscientious, patient, and well-organized, but not as forceful, enterprising, or participative.

Among the other sources of information about Betas is a study of 858 persons who were classified for prejudice on the basis of descriptions of them by others (Gough & Bradley, 1993). The descriptions scored positively for prejudice included intolerant, prejudiced, and suspicious, among others, and words such as fair-minded and tolerant were scored as contraindicative. Scores for each person on the cluster of adjectives were standardized to a grand mean of 50 and standard deviation of 10. There were 137 Betas in the sample, and for them the mean for prejudice was 48.20. Alphas had a mean of 49.10, Deltas a mean of 50.34, and Gammas a mean of 51.12. The *F* ratio for these means was significant at the .02 level of probability. The greater tolerance of the Betas, in comparison with the other four lifestyles, was most visible for those at above average levels of ego integration. Betas at Level 5 had a mean of

46.63 on the intolerance index, and at Levels 6 and 7 they had a mean of 46.04.

In a talk on leadership styles, Sandra Davis (see Kegel-Flom & Fort, 1995) described Betas in this way:

> Betas are steady, supportive persons who take their responsibilities seriously, preferring order and predictability. They keep organizations running smoothly, often working behind the scene. Introverted Betas are steady workers who can be counted on to get the job done, but who may sometimes adhere too strongly to the status quo, and resist change. And Betas may be so soft-spoken that their ideas are not heard and they fail to receive credit for what they do.

Betas in police work, as found in the unpublished studies of Michael D. Roberts mentioned earlier, had lower rates of unethical behavior, sick-leave abuse, and dishonesty than the other three lifestyles. They also had the best ratings of the four Types for reliability and for good relations with citizens. These findings are consonant with a conception of Betas as conscientious, rule-respecting, and relatively free of narcissistic or egoistic dispositions.

In summary, Betas can be described as follows:

Betas value and protect their internal, private feelings, avoiding public display or disclosure. They are also accepting of societal norms and precepts. Their role is often to preserve values, nurture and support others, and humanize the ways in which societal rules are enforced. At their best, they can be inspirational models of goodness and virtue. At low levels of ego integration, they are overly repressive and self-denying and often have problems of excessively low self-esteem and lack of self-confidence.

Gammas

Table 2.14 presents adjectival descriptions by observers having salient relationships to membership in the Gamma category. For each of the six subsamples, the numbers of Gammas and non-Gammas are shown in the bottom two lines. Using dummy weights of 1 for Gammas and 0 for those in the complements, the subgroups were correlated with the 300 items in the ACL. The eight items with largest positive and eight with largest negative correlations have been selected for inclusion in the table.

Gammas are clearly seen as expressive, unrestrained, restless, and pleasure-seeking, and not as shy, forbearing, or self-effacing. They like and seek attention from others, pursue their own goals with verve and self-confidence, and enjoy change and variety in their daily lives.

Analyses of the *California Q-Set* were conducted in samples of 167 male Gammas versus 380 controls, and 170 female Gammas versus 223 in the complement. The *Q-Set* formulations for each person were based on the composite of five or more independent appraisals by observers, with the 100 items then assigned scores from 9 to 1, going from most salient to least salient. For the type classification, dummy weights of 1 were assigned to Gammas and of 0 to those in the complements. The four items with largest positive and four with largest negative correlations are reported below (first coefficient is for men, second for women):

> Characteristically pushes and tries to stretch limits; sees what he or she can get away with (.22, .55)
> Is self-indulgent (.17, .26)
> Is skilled in social techniques of imaginative play, pretending and humor (.20, .16)
> Is self-dramatizing; histrionic (.15, .29)

> Tends toward overcontrol of needs and impulses; binds tensions excessively; delays gratification unnecessarily (−.15, −.36)
> Is fastidious (−.19, −.29)
> Genuinely submissive; accepts domination comfortably (−.15, −.29)
> Has a readiness to feel guilty (−.17, −.22)

The Q-sort descriptions are more strongly registered for women than for men, particularly the item about pushing against and trying to stretch limits. Objection to restraints, imposed controls, and arbitrary rules can just about be taken for granted among Gamma women. Self-dramatizing and imaginative, witty, and self-assured behavior are also characteristic off the Gamma lifestyle.

Reactions of life history interviewers as recorded on a 99-item checklist were analyzed for 172 Gamma men versus 332 in the complement, and for 169 Gamma women versus 210 in the complement. The four items with largest positive and four with largest negative correlations with the Gamma classification are given below (first coefficient is for men, second is for women):

	Men, Described By			Women, Described By		
Adjectives	Spouse (N = 236)	3 Peers (N = 194)	10 Staff Members (N = 612)	Spouse (N = 236)	3 Peers (N = 192)	10 Staff Members (N = 358)
Assertive	.13*	.13	.18**	.22**	.25**	.26**
Impulsive	.12	.22**	.17**	.27**	.18*	.29**
Outspoken	.16*	.12	.18**	.19**	.31**	.22**
Pleasure-seeking	.13*	.20**	.16**	.28**	.30**	.26**
Restless	.23**	.16*	.20**	.20**	.24**	.27**
Show-off	.27**	.21**	.19**	.11	.14*	.19**
Spontaneous	.13*	.08	.21**	.29**	.21**	.22**
Talkative	.28**	.13	.21**	.11	.25**	.26**
Conscientious	−.11	−.19**	−.08*	−.23**	−.17*	−.24**
Conservative	−.22**	−.02	−.15**	−.23**	−.29**	−.22**
Modest	−.22**	−.18*	−.10**	−.15*	−.16*	−.24**
Patient	−.18**	−.16*	−.09*	−.17**	−.16*−	−.21**
Quiet	−.23**	−.12	−.16**	−.21**	−.20**	−.30**
Reserved	−.21**	−.11	−.15**	−.20**	−.21**	−.22**
Shy	−.19**	−.18*	−.09*	−.23**	−.24**	−.25**
Silent	−.23**	−.11	−.06	−.20**	−.22**	−.24**
Number of Gammas	90	68	169	93	61	156
Others	146	126	443	143	131	287

Table 2.14 Gamma Respondents Versus All Others: 8 Adjectival Descriptions with Largest Positive and 8 with Largest Negative Correlations

* $p \le .05$, ** $p \le .01$

Excited, restless (.13 for men, .11 for women)

Witty and animated, an interesting conversationalist (.20, .17)

Maintained an unusual tempo of social life in adolescence, constant series of dates, parties, etc. (.13, .08)

Unusually self-confident, feels able to meet nearly any situation (.10, .11)

Slow rate of movement (−.10, −.15)

Has difficulty expressing ideas (−.07, −.14)
Reticent and taciturn (−.19, −.09)
Has strong religious beliefs (−.16, −.14)

The correlations for these interviewers' descriptions are very low, even though with samples of 504 men and 379 women they are moderately reliable. The ready wit, animation, and self-confidence noted in the prior adjectival and Q-sort descriptions are detectable in the interviews. An interesting new item is the reporting of a very active social life during adolescence, and another is the relative absence of strong religious beliefs.

Q-sort descriptions by spouses or partners were available for 200 couples. For the men, there were 74 Gammas and 126 in the complement, and for the women there were 79 Gammas and 121 in the complement. The three items with largest positive and three with largest negative correlations with a Gamma classification are reported below (first coefficient is for men, second is for women):

Enterprising and outgoing; enjoys social participation (.26, .11)

Clever and imaginative; a spontaneous and entertaining person (.23, .11)

Verbally fluent; expresses self easily and with clarity (.16, .24).

A conscientious and serious-minded person (−.22, −.20)

Ambitious; commonplace and conventional in thinking and behavior (−.13, −.29)

Gentle, considerate, and tactful in dealing with others; appreciative and helpful (−.13, −.26)

Spouses, like other observers, tend to see their Gamma partners as lively, expressive, clever, and imaginative, and not as conventional, conscientious, serious-minded, or tactful.

Given their penchant for rule-testing and their imaginative fluency, it is not surprising that Gammas at high levels of v.3 tend to be creative in their work. In a study (Gough, 1992) of 1,028 graduate students in psychology tested at entry and then rated by faculty members two or three years later, Gammas ranked above the other three types on the creativity criterion. In standard score terms for the ratings of creativity in research, at Levels 6 and 7, Gammas had a mean of 53.46, Deltas a mean of 50.75, Alphas a mean of 50.43, and Betas a mean of 49.73; the average for all 1,028 students was 50.41. Gammas also get high ratings from observers in leaderless group discussions (Gough, 1990), where their wit, exuberance, and verbal fluency propel them into high visibility. In managerial positions (Meyer & Davis, 1992), Gammas at above-average levels on v.3 tend to be adroit advocates of change, innovative, and resourceful. However, they will sometimes overwhelm others in making a point, and they tend to become bored in routinized, relatively unchanging environments.

A look at Tables 2.9 and 2.10, presented earlier, shows that Gammas tend to favor certain occupations and professions. For men, samples with 40% more in the Gamma category were members of the Rajneeshi mystic religious colony in Oregon, art institute students, psychology graduate students, and critics of books for children. Female samples with 40% or more in the Gamma category were students of law, Rajneeshi colony members, premedical students, juvenile delinquents, art institute students, psychology graduate students, MBA candidates, and critics of books for children.

Mention of the female juvenile delinquents is a reminder that the Gamma way of living carries the danger of rule-testing and noncompliance beyond the point that the society will allow. Realization/ competence/ego integration, as assessed by the v.3 scale, is a crucial differentiator here. Negative manifestations of the Gamma temperament begin to appear at below-average v.3 levels, whereas at above-average levels, Gamma behavior is more norm-changing and norm-correcting than norm-violating.

Michael D. Roberts' studies of police officers, cited several times above, should be mentioned again here. Approximately 10% of the officers (both male and female) in his large sample were Gammas. Alphas, as already stated, comprised about 61% of the sample, Betas 22%, and Deltas the remainder. The problems displayed by Gamma officers were quite predictable from what has been said here about the Gamma way of living. They tended to receive low ratings on performance factors such as reliability, taking proper safety precautions, problem-solving decisions, and written communications, in relation to officers in the other three categories. Their mean rating for dishonesty was higher than for the other three types, even though all four means were low in an absolute sense.

In summary, Gammas can be described as follows:

Gammas attend to and seek the monetary, prestige, and other rewards offered by society, but are often at odds with the culture concerning the criteria by which these rewards are apportioned. Their values are personal and individual, not traditional or conventional. Gammas are the doubters, the skeptics, those who see and resist the arbitrary and unjustified features of the status quo. At their best, they are innovative and insightful creators of new ideas, new products, and new social forms. At their worst, they are rebellious, intolerant, self-indulgent, and disruptive; and at low levels on the v.3 scale, they often behave in wayward, rule-violating, and narcissistic ways.

Table 2.15 Delta Respondents Versus All Others: 8 Adjectival Descriptions with Largest Positive and 8 with Largest Negative Correlations

Adjectives	Men, Described By			Women, Described By		
	Spouse (N = 236)	3 Peers (N = 194)	10 Staff Members (N = 612)	Spouse (N = 236)	3 Peers (N = 192)	10 Staff Members (N = 358)
Awkward	.19**	.12	.20**	.17**	.12	.23**
Inhibited	.18**	.05	.21**	.16*	.21**	.18**
Modest	.13*	.22**	.18**	.10	.16*	.22**
Quiet	.19**	.14*	.28**	.12	.24**	.27**
Retiring	.08	.18*	.18**	.16*	.31**	.23**
Shy	.21**	.14*	.30**	.23**	.31**	.31**
Silent	.21**	.13	.25**	.11	.18*	.29**
Withdrawn	.22**	.04	.27**	.06	.25**	.26**
Ambitious	−.15*	−.05	−.22**	−.14*	−.08	−.22**
Confident	−.09	−.13	−.17**	−.17**	−.17*	−.25**
Demanding	−.15*	−.14*	−.09*	−.04	−.15*	−.22**
Egotistical	−.08	−.17*	−.10**	−.07	−.17*	−.21**
Outgoing	−.12	−.14*	−.22**	−.20**	−.28**	−.23**
Out spoken	−.14*	−.11	−.15**	−.06	−.21**	−.21**
Show-off	−.13*	−.17*	−.15**	−.13*	−.21**	−.15**
Talkative	−.17**	−.16*	−.20**	−.09	−.18*	−.21**
Number of Deltas	51	44	113	69	35	70
Others	185	150	449	167	157	288

* $p \leq .05$, ** $p \leq .01$

Deltas

The defining characteristics of Deltas in the three-vector model are detachment from others and dubiety concerning the conventions and folkways of everyday life. Examination of the adjectival descriptions by observers, as reported in Table 2.15, show that all eight of the most ascriptive terms have something to do with diffidence, withdrawal, and taciturnity. The numbers of Deltas and non-Deltas in each of the six subsamples cited in Table 2.15 were as follows: male spouses, 51 versus 185; male students, 44 versus 150; adult males, 113 versus 499; female spouses, 69 versus 167; female students, 35 versus 157; and adult females, 70 versus 288.

Adjectives checked more often about non-Deltas include at least four (outgoing, outspoken, show-off, and talkative) directly associated with interpersonal activity and participation. Deltas also are described as lacking in ambition and confidence, but as being relatively free of egotism and a desire to control others. All 16 of these most salient adjectives seem to describe the persona, the surface or outer shell that the Delta individual presents to the world. This persona is one that protects and shields the Delta individual from scrutiny of his or her inner life and private feelings.

Analysis of the 100 items in the *California Q-Set* were based on 108 male Deltas versus 439 in the complement, and 77 female Deltas versus 316 in the complement. All 940 persons were described on the Q-items by panels of five or more independent observers, whose Q-formulations were composited into a single array with the 100 items placed in order of saliency. Scores going from 9 (most salient) to 1 (least salient) were assigned according to the frequencies specified by Block (1961). These scores were then correlated with a 1-0 weighting of membership versus nonmembership in the Delta category. The four items with largest positive and four with largest negative correlations are given below (first coefficient is for men, second for women):

Reluctant to commit self to any definite course of action; tends to delay or avoid action (.30, .32)

Is self-defeating (.29, .20)

Gives up and withdraws where possible in the face of frustration and adversity (.21, .34)

Engages in personal fantasy and daydreams; fictional speculations (.24, .20)

Is a talkative individual (−.28, −.31)

Behaves in an assertive fashion (−.30, −.32)

Emphasizes being with others gregarious (−.24, −.15)

Has social poise and presence; appears socially at ease (−.31, −.26)

These Q-sort descriptions show Deltas to be distanced from others, unassertive, ill at ease in social encounters, reluctant to commit to any definite course of action, and in many ways self-defeating. A new theme is the item about private fantasies and daydreams. From case material on highly successful Deltas, this capacity for visualizing things in new and different ways is a primary and powerful resource for persons in the Delta mode.

Life history interviews with 883 persons who had also taken the CPI were available. After the interview, a 99-item check list was completed by the interviewer, and these items were correlated with membership versus nonmembership in the Delta category. For men, there were 126 Deltas and 378 in the complement; the corresponding numbers for women were 97 and 282. The four items with largest positive and four with largest negative correlations for Deltas are given below

(first coefficient in each instance is for men, second for women):

Slow rate of movement (.06, .13)

Unhappy in school and at home (.17, .11)

Has many worries and problems (.11, .16)

Is unsure of self, doubts own ability (.06, .13)

Witty and animated, an interesting conversationalist (−.13, −.18)

Unusually self-confident, feels able to meet nearly any situation (−.23, −.18)

Has a stable, optimistic view of the future (−.13, .13)

Creates a good impression; has effective interpersonal techniques (−.10, −.16)

A dysphoric theme in the Delta personality is apparent in these brief descriptions, although the correlations are of only borderline reliability. Deltas had more worries, less optimism, more doubts about self, and less happiness at home and in school than did the interviewees with other two-vector classifications. When asked directly about their reactions to personal inquiry into feelings, hopes, problems, and the like, a typical Delta reaction is one of resistance and defense. Because their views are so intensely private, Deltas will often feel themselves to be at odds with an interviewer or indeed with anyone in a dyadic relationship.

The next data set comes from a 50-item interpersonal Q-sort done for 200 men by their wives or partners, and for 200 women by their husbands or partners. Forty-eight of the men were Deltas, versus 152 in the complement, and 61 of the women were Deltas, versus 139 in the complement. The three items having largest positive and three having largest negative correlations with these dichotomies are given below (first coefficient is for men, second for women):

Awkward and ill-at-ease socially; shy and inhibited with others (.13, .13)

Easily embarrassed; feels inferior and inadequate (.20, .10)

Gentle, considerate, and tactful in dealing with others; appreciative and helpful (.17, .19)

Enterprising and outgoing; enjoys social participation (−.20, −.16)

Poised and self-confident; not troubled by pressure or criticism (–.10, –.15)

Is an effective leader; able to elicit the responses and cooperation of others (–.15, –.16)

Although the correlations are very low in magnitude, some trends are discernible. Deltas are seen by their spouses or partners as ill at ease in social situations, easily embarrassed, and avoidant of participation. There is also a quality of tact and consideration in their dealings with others. The item about not being an effective leader should also be noted. In a prior study of leadership (Gough, 1990) based on large samples and using more than six different criteria of leadership, Deltas consistently ranked at the bottom in regard to demonstrated leadership and leadership potential.

Tables 2.9 and 2.10, presented earlier, should be reviewed for information about groups having their largest percentage of members in the Delta category. For men, these included young prison inmates, adult prison inmates, high school disciplinary problems, and psychiatric patients. Other samples with a large percentage of Deltas, but more in other classifications, included Rajneeshi colony members, juvenile delinquents, art institute students, and writers of books for children. These samples of men show two Delta themes: marginality and conflict for those ranking low on the ego-integration scale, and imaginative—even visionary—activity for those ranking high.

For women, the Delta samples included creative writers, writers of books for children, high school disciplinary problems, prison inmates, and pharmacy students. The pharmacy students are ambiguously classified, however, having a miniscule prevalence of Deltas over Alphas, and only a slight increase over Betas and Gammas. Other female samples with a high incidence of Deltas, although more persons in other categories, were Rajneeshi colony members, juvenile delinquents, and art institute students. As for men, these samples show two themes for Deltas: marginality and deviation from the norm for those low on v.3, and imaginative and potentially visionary activity for those ranking high.

The nonaffiliative and isolative tendencies of Deltas can be shown in other ways. For example, in a sample of 2,620 high school graduates, college-going rates were 62% for Alphas, 37% for Betas, 37% for Gammas, and only 23% for Deltas (Gough, 1987). Only at the highest levels on v.3 did Deltas'

college-going rates (44%) exceed the overall base rate of 40%. In the Michael D. Roberts sample of over 10,000 applicants for work in law enforcement, only 8% were Deltas. Among 1,413 cadets from two classes at West Point (see Table 2.9), only 4.0% were Deltas. Among sales managers, air force officers, and MBA candidates, Deltas constituted less then 10% of the total. In other words, Deltas tend to be found outside of the ordinary educational and occupational structures of the society.

From unpublished case history material, another problem was detected for persons in the Delta category, namely the control of anger and violence. The case files of persons at Levels 1 and 2 in the Delta mode often contained evidence about child abuse, attacks on spouses or partners, and suicidal behavior. The contradictions, polarities, and dehumanizing aspects of the culture are poorly resolved by Deltas, who struggle inwardly with these problems. High-level Deltas make use of imaginative, creative methods of reformulating these internal conflicts in a new and different way, but low-level Deltas, lacking these talents, reach breaking points at which they lash out against self, others, and the culture in general.

In summary, Deltas may be described as follows:

Deltas center their cathexes on a private, internal world, and on a personal as opposed to traditional or sanctioned system of values. Deltas are reflective, idiosyncratic, and detached. They see things differently from other people, but for the most part keep these perspectives private. At their best, they are imaginatively creative, esthetically perceptive, and visionary. They are most comfortable working alone, as in art, music, literature, or abstract sciences such as mathematics. At their worst, they are fragmented, withdrawn, even decompensated, at risk for chronic criminality, violence against self or others, and disturbances of ego functioning.

Making Use of the Three-Vector Model

How can the three-vector (cuboid) model be used in the study of significant criteria, such as occupational choice and performance, academic attainment, and social attitudes? Of course, the three scales may be examined one at a time, by means of correlational or classificatory statistics, but analyses of this kind do not take full advantage of the postulated

Table 2.16 A Type/Level Analysis for Political Orientation					
		Levels			
Type	**Data**	**1–3**	**4**	**5–7**	**Total**
Alpha	N	31	27	41	99
	M	2.71	2.85	3.02	2.88
	SD	*	*	*	.92
Beta	N	12	10	9	31
	M	3.00	2.80	3.22	3.00
	SD	*	*	*	.86
Gamma	N	44	44	50	138
	M	3.23	3.43	3.46	3.38
	SD	*	*	*	*
Delta	N	23	30	33	86
	M	3.04	3.30	3.27	3.22
	SD	*	*	*	.86
Total	N	110	111	133	354
	M	3.02	3.20	3.26	3.17
	SD	.86	.92	.93	.91

ANOVA for	**df**	**F**	**p**
Type	3	6.50	<.001
Level	2	2.40	.092
T x L	6	0.27	.950

* SD not computed

relationships among the vectors. To illustrate possibilities that do recognize the model's existence, three examples will be given below.

Performance of the U.S. Coast Guard Officers

Multiple regression technique was used in a study of 85 U.S. Coast Guard junior officers (Blake, Potter, & Slimak, 1993). These men took the CPI at entry. Six years later, after graduation and after two years of service as ensigns, comprehensive performance evaluations were obtained from senior officers. These were consolidated into a five-step overall ranking, with men at step 5 characterized as "a rising star," "among the best I have ever seen," and as having

"demonstrated strength from the start"; and men at step 1 characterized as "will never make it" and as being unlikely to win promotion to Lieutenant Junior Grade. In regard to CPI lifestyles, 61 were Alphas, 9 were Betas, 12 were Gammas, and 3 were Deltas.

Correlations of the three vector scales with the overall criterion were –.23 for v.1, .33 for v.2, and .21 for v.3. The regression analysis used these three scales, plus the cross-products for v.1 and v.2, v.1 and v.3, and v.2 and v.3. The strongest set of variables included the three vector scales and the cross-product for v.2 and v.3, with a multiple R of .45 and an R^2 of .20.

The nature of the interaction can be visualized by examining correlations of the three vectors with performance, within two subsamples composed of officers scoring at 36 and above and at 35 and below on v.3. For those low on v.3, the correlations with performance were –.17 for v.1, .10 for v.2, and .22 for v.3. For the officers high on v.3, the three correlations were –.27 for v.1, .50 for v.2, and .08 for v.3. In other words, for officers scoring above average on v.3, scores on v.2 are good predictors of performance.

Political Beliefs

In an unpublished study of the social and political attitudes of 150 male and 204 female college students at the University of California, Berkeley, one of the questions asked for a self-rating along a scale of conservatism to liberalism. Self-ratings of very liberal were given a score of 5, ratings of somewhat liberal a score of 4, ratings of middle-of-the-road a score of 3, ratings of somewhat conservative a rating of 2, and ratings of very conservative a rating of 1. The percentages of the total sample of 354 students at each step, from 5 to 1 respectively, were 6.2, 30.8, 37.9, 23.7, and 1.4. The mean self-rating was 3.17, with a standard deviation of 0.91. Classifications in the CPI typology of lifestyle were 28.0% Alphas, 8.8% Betas, 39.0% Gammas, and 24.3% Deltas.

In Table 2.16, the 354 students are classified into 12 subcells, according to three groups on the v.3 Level and the four lifestyles defined by the v.1 and v.2 scales. An ANOVA for the table produced a significant F ratio for type ($p < .001$), and a borderline F ratio for Level ($p = .09$). There was no observable interaction between Type and Level. Gammas were the most liberal of the four types, with a mean of 3.38; Deltas were next, with a mean of 3.22; and Betas were third, with a mean of 3.00, which was

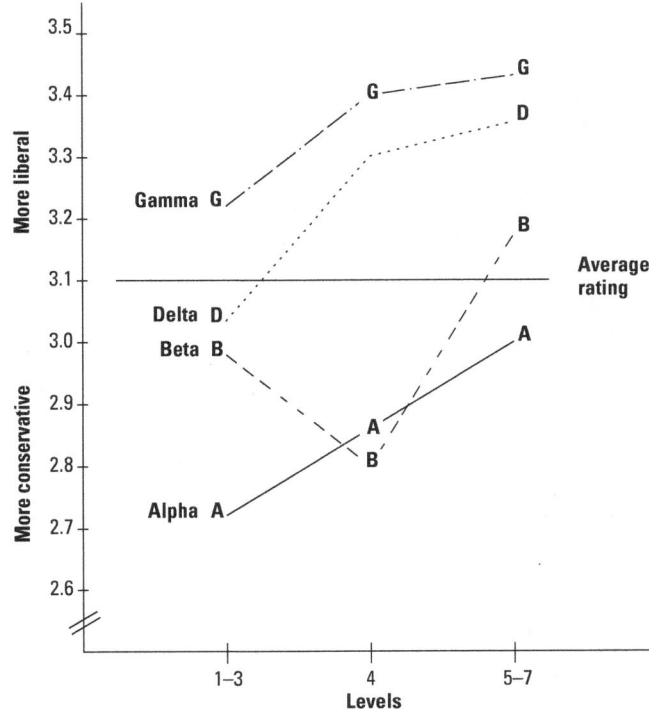

Figure 2.4 Self-Ratings of Political Orientation as Related to the CPI Type/Level Model

College-Going

The third illustrative application focuses on college-going among high school graduates. Data here will be analyzed both by the contingency table method, as in example 2, and by multiple regression technique, as in example 1. As shown in Table 2.17, information on college going was available for 3,487 high school graduates (1,643 males, 1,844 females) from 16 different cities across the nation. Of these, 1,450 went on to college, giving a college-going rate of 41.58 percent. CPI type frequency percentages for the total sample were 24.0 for Alphas, 35.5 for Betas, 14.9 for Gammas, and 25.6 for Deltas.

College-going rates for the four types were significantly different ($p < .001$), as shown in the ANOVA table. College-going percentages were 61 for Alphas, 39 for Betas, 40 for Gammas, and 29 for Deltas. Thus, Alphas go on to college at far above the base rate of 42 percent, Betas and Gammas are just below the base rate, and Deltas are lowest at 29 percent. However, the 44 Deltas classified at Levels 5 through 7 on the v.3 scale had a 61% college-going rate. The highest college-going rate in Table 2.17 is found for Alphas at Levels 5 through 7, among whom 75% went on to college. The lowest rate was found for Deltas at Level 1, with only 15% of the 188 students in this category going on to college. A further observation is that Deltas at Levels 1, 2, 3, and 4 all have college-going rates below the baseline of 42, whereas for Alphas, only those at Level 1 have a college-rate (35%) below the overall average.

Level is monotonically related to college-going among these high school graduates, with rates of 24% for those at Level 1, 35% for those at Level 2, 40% for those at Level 3, 54% for those at Level 4, and 63% for those at Levels 5, 6, and 7. The F ratio of 38.34 for this progression, with 4 degrees of freedom, is significant beyond the .001 level of probability.

Because of the difficulty in visualizing these trends from the data in Table 2.17, the same findings are presented graphically in Figure 2.5. At each of the v.3 levels, Alphas have the highest college-going percentages, and at Levels 1 through 4, Deltas have the lowest. The trend lines are all monotonic, except for the unexpected increase for Gammas at Level 2. Very likely, with even larger samples, the departure from monotonicity for Gammas would disappear.

There are educational implications associated with these differentials. Alphas tend to major in subjects like business administration, engineering

at center on the five-step scale but slightly below the observed average of 3.17 for the total sample. Alphas, with a mean of 2.88, were on the conservative side of the continuum. For all students, there was a slight movement toward more liberal views as Level increased, although this trend was of only borderline significance.

For readers unfamiliar with ANOVA contingency tables, the findings in Table 2.16 may be hard to visualize. For this reason, the trends are graphically illustrated in Figure 2.4. The average self-rating for all 354 students is indicated by the horizontal line at 3.17. Then there are four trend lines, one for each CPI type. Alphas are most conservative, especially at low levels on v.3. They move a little away from this low point at Levels 5 through 7, but even here rank below the total mean. Betas at Levels 1 through 3 are below the total average, and at Level 4 are even farther down. At Levels 5 through 7 Betas score slightly above the overall mean. Deltas at Levels 1 through 3 are on the conservative side of the continuum, but at the two higher groupings are in the liberal category. Gammas at all three groupings on Level rate themselves as liberal.

Table 2.17 Type/Level Analysis for College-Going Rates

Type	Data	Levels 1	2	3	4	5–7	Total
Alpha	N	71	155	273	192	145	836
	rate	35%	52%	57%	71%	75%	61%
Beta	N	175	282	356	270	155	1,238
	rate	27%	30%	36%	50%	53%	39%
Gamma	N	87	109	195	106	24	521
	rate	25%	46%	35%	52%	54%	40%
Delta	N	188	246	267	147	44	892
	rate	15%	25%	30%	41%	61%	29%
Total	N	521	792	1,091	715	368	3,487
	rate	24%	35%	40%	54%	63%	42%

ANOVA For	df	F	p
Type	3	49.14	< .001
Level	4	38.34	< .001
T x L	12	1.26	.235

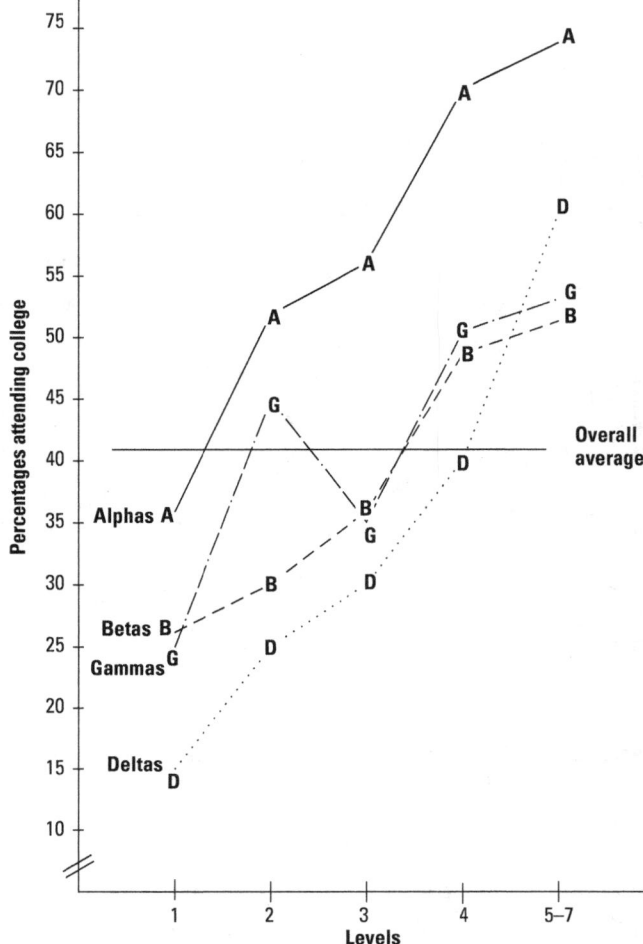

Figure 2.5 Percentages of 3,487 High School Graduates Going on to College as Related to Type and Level

and the applied sciences, and preprofessional programs. Deltas are more often found in subjects such as music, fine arts, and the other humanities. Gammas gravitate to the social sciences, and Betas to the helping disciplines such as nursing and primary education. Colleges themselves differ in their Type atmospherics. As shown previously in Table 2.9, West Point is largely an Alpha environment, with an appreciable number of Betas. Graduate students in psychology are primarily Gammas. Deltas are few and far between at West Point, and Betas are relatively scarce in psychology programs. Students in these minority classifications may well feel isolated and out of place.

A regression analysis was also made of college-going in this same sample, using a dummy weight of 1 for those attending, and of 0 for those who did not continue. Seven variables were processed: v.l, with a correlation of –.24 with college-going; v.2, for which the correlation was .15; v.3, with a correlation of .25; v.l times v.2, with a correlation of –.11; v.l times v.3, with a correlation of .00; v.2 times v.3, with a correlation of .26; and v.l times v.2 times v.3, with a correlation of .06.

The first variable selected in the analysis was v.2 times v.3, and the second was v.l. The third variable was v.l times v.2. However, at later steps, v.l was removed, as was the product of v.2 and v.3. The best combination turned out to be v.2, v.3, and the product of v.l and v.2, with a multiple correlation of .35. Beta weights were .28 for v.2, .20 for v.3, and –.28 for v.l times v.2. The final equation shows that the interaction of v.l and v.2 is significant. The algebra of the equation assigns higher predicted scores to Alphas, particularly at high levels on v.3, and to Betas, Gammas, and Deltas who score high on v.3.

3

Reliability and Factor Analysis

Reliability

This chapter presents statistical data concerning reliability of the CPI scales, as measured in several ways, and the alignment of the scales on the factorial dimensions of the inventory. In interpreting these findings, a number of things should be kept in mind. In regard to reliability as assessed by the intercorrelation of items within a scale, whereas many tests posit this as a high priority, interitem homogeneity is not a goal on the CPI. The reason for this statement is that 13 of the 20 folk scales are developed by empirical methodology, which bases the selection of items solely on their demonstrated relationships to nontest criteria. Empirical technique often turns up items having good predictive and classificatory power, but little or no correlation with each other. In fact, from the standpoint of prediction alone, the lower the intercorrelations among items individually related to the criterion, the stronger will be the scale. Internal consistency technique, which is the contrasting method of scale development, typically begins with a collection of items whose content is judged to be relevant to the aim of measurement. By examining the intercorrelations among these items, and/or the correlations of each items with a total score based on the total, those with low affiliation with the totality are eliminated. This technique produces scales having high interitem homogeneity, but in and of itself does nothing to enhance validity, if validity is conceptualized as predictive or classificatory relationships to nontest criteria. To a certain degree, the magnitudes of single-trial interitem homogeneity measures, such as coefficient alpha, are merely indicators of whether internal consistency or empirical methods of scale construction have been employed.

Both single-trial interitem coefficients of reliability and test-retest correlations for all 36 scales of Form 434 of the CPI are reported in Table 3.1. The alpha coefficients (Cronbach, 1951) were computed on the samples of 3,000 men and 3,000 women, plus the total sample of 6,000 persons, on which the profile report form was based. Test-retest correlations were computed for high school students tested in the 11th grade and then retested as 12th graders, for women tested first as college seniors and then retested five years later (Helson & Moane, 1987; Helson & Wink, 1992), and for adult males tested

Table 3.1 Reliability Data for Form 434 CPI Scales

Scale	No. of Items	Norm Samples: Alpha Coefficients			High School Students: Test-Retest[a]			Adults: Test-Retest[b]	
		Males (N = 3,000)	Females (N = 3,000)	Total (N = 6,000)	Males (N = 108)	Females (N = 129)	Total (N = 237)	Females (N = 91)	Males (N = 44)
Folk Scales									
Do	36	.83	.82	.83	.65	.69	.67	.65	.82
Cs	28	.71	.74	.72	.66	.68	.68	.54	.50
Sy	32	.76	.78	.77	.67	.72	.70	.55	.76
Sp	38	.68	.73	.71	.70	.67	.68	.58	.70
Sa	28	.66	.69	.67	.64	.73	.69	.49	.63
In	30	.73	.75	.74	.61	.65	.64	.50	.78
Em	38	.61	.65	.63	.58	.59	.60	.59	.71
Re	36	.77	.76	.77	.62	.70	.68	.67	.59
So	46	.75	.80	.78	.68	.75	.73	.69	.45
Sc	38	.82	.82	.83	.75	.72	.73	.73	.50
Gi	40	.81	.81	.81	.66	.68	.67	.56	.49
Cm	38	.74	.67	.71	.44	.60	.51	.51	.59
Wb	38	.84	.85	.84	.74	.71	.72	.69	.79
To	32	.77	.80	.79	.77	.69	.74	.54	.47
Ac	38	.78	.78	.78	.65	.78	.74	.36	.50
Ai	36	.79	.81	.80	.69	.58	.62	59	.51
Ie	42	.77	.81	.79	.71	.80	.76	.45	.73
Py	28	.61	.64	.62	.58	.62	.60	.51	.53
Fx	28	.64	.65	.64	.58	.64	.61	.60	.58
F/M	32	.43	.43	.73	.54	.64	.84	.46	.37
Vector Scales									
v.1	34	.81	.82	.82	.68	.76	.72	.70	.74
v.2	36	.76	.78	.77	.62	.75	.70	.65	.71
v.3	58	.84	.89	.88	.77	.72	.74	.68	.59
Special Purpose Scales									
Mp	34	.81	.82	.81	.67	.64	.65	.57	.63
Wo	40	.77	.78	.78	.70	.64	.67	.66	.55
CT	42	.73	.74	.73	.66	.63	.65	.55	.77
Lp	70	.88	.89	.88	.76	.70	.73	.61	.83
Ami	36	.77	.80	.79	.72	.69	.70	.70	.52
Leo	42	.45	.43	.45	.67	.41	.56	.60	.56

		Norm Samples: Alpha Coefficients			High School Students: Test-Retest[a]			Adults: Test-Retest[b]	
Scale	No. of Items	Males (N = 3,000)	Females (N = 3,000)	Total (N = 6,000)	Males (N = 108)	Females (N = 129)	Total (N = 237)	Females (N = 91)	Males (N = 44)
Special Purpose Scales continued									
Tm	36	.79	.79	.79	.71	.61	.65	.46	.52
B–MS	54	.86	.87	.88	.71	.66	.71	.53	.84
B–FM	42	.65	.66	.75	.64	.63	.77	.59	.40
Anx	22	.46	.52	.49	.62	.49	.56	.43	.53
Nar	49	.76	.76	.76	.65	.71	.69	.68	.52
D–SD	32	.69	.70	.69	.64	.67	.66	.56	.70
D–AC	32	.48	.46	.47	.50	.63	.57	.46	.46

Table 3.1 Reliability Data for Form 434 CPI Scales continued

[a]One-year interval between test and retest; [b]Five-year interval between test and retest for females, 25-year interval for males

first at approximately age 40 and then retested 25 years later (Dudek & Hall, 1991). The college women are from Ravenna Helson's studies of life span phenomena among women (Helson & Roberts, 1994; Helson, Roberts, & Agronick, 1995; Helson, Stewart, & Ostrove, 1995), and the adult men are from the MacKinnon and Hall studies of American architects (Hall & MacKinnon, 1969; MacKinnon, 1962).

For the 20 folk concept scales, the alpha coefficients for males ranged from a low of .43 for F/M to a high of .84 for Wb, with a median of .76. For females, the alpha coefficients for the folk scales went from a low of .43 on F/M to a high of .85 on Wb, with a median of .76. For the total sample, the range of the Alphas for the folk scales went from .62 on Py to .84 on Wb, with a median of .77. Alpha coefficient for the three vector scales were at or above .76 in all three samples, with a median of .82. Among the 13 special purpose scales, Alphas in the total sample ranged from lows of .45 on Leo, .47 on Dicken's AC, and .49 on Leventhal's Anx to highs of .81 on Mp, and .88 on both Lp and Baucom's MS.

Looking next at the test-retest correlations, for the high school males, the range was from .44 for Cm to .77 for Sc and v.3. For high school females, the range was from .41 for Leo to .80 for Ie. In the total sample of high school students, the range was

from .51 for Cm to .84 for F/M. For just the 20 folk scales, the median retest correlation was .68.

In Helson's sample of 91 women tested five years apart, the folk concept scales had correlations ranging from a low of .36 on Ac to a high of .73 on Sc. The median was .56. The three vector scales had coefficients of .70, .65, and .68. The 13 special purpose scales ranged from a low of .43 for Anx to a high of .70 for Ami (Amicability).

In the sample of 44 architects tested 25 years apart, correlations for folk scales ranged from .37 on F/M to .82 on Do. The median was .58. The three vector scales had coefficients of .74, .71, and .59. For the 13 special purpose scales, coefficients ranged from a low of .40 on Anx to a high of .84 on B–MS. Because of the small number of men in this sample (N = 44), the test-retest coefficients must be viewed with caution as indicators of stability of the scales over time.

The interitem and retest coefficients reported in Table 3.1 are similar to what is usually found for tests developed by the canons of empirical technique. In empirical methodology, as stated above, the goal is to produce scales capable of forecasting significant nontest behavior, and of classifying people in a way consonant with the evaluations and descriptions of observers, rather than the augmentation of interitem covariance. Given these purposes, moderate heterogeneity among the items in a scale is acceptable and, in fact, to be expected.

Factor Analysis

As indicated in the discussions of Axioms 1 and 3 in chapter 1, the CPI was not developed by factor analytic methods, or according to factor analytic prescriptions. Psychologists and others who wish to use factorial inventories have good possibilities in tests such as the 16PF (Cattell, 1946; Conn & Rieke, 1994), *Comrey's Personality Scales* (Comrey, 1970), and the *Guilford-Zimmerman Temperament Survey* (Guilford, Guilford, & Zimmerman, 1978). The scales of the CPI come from the lexicon of common language, fashioned so as to be as congruent as possible with folk usage of the concepts. That is, in regard to intercorrelations among the scales of the CPI, the designated goal is correspondence with the covariances in folk use of the concepts rather than orthogonality among the measures. The CPI, incidentally, is not alone in its focus on nontest criteria and acceptance of intercorrelation among its scales. Well-known and widely used tests such as the MMPI and the *Strong Interest Inventory* derive from the same logic.

Because of the elegance and power of factor analysis in certain of its uses, many psychologists believe that it must also be the method of choice for defining the variables of personality. Lykken (1971), in a classic paper on the logic and applications of factor analysis in psychology, pointed out three uses: data reduction, whereby a large and unwieldy assembly of measures could be reduced to a smaller and quasi-equivalent set; testing of dimensional hypotheses, such as to examine the presence of some basic concept in a variety of measures; and taxonometrics, in which factorial themes are deemed to be basic or fundamental units of measurements. Lykken's conclusion was that the first two applications are acceptable, but that serious criticisms can be made of the third. Lykkens's two major criticisms of the use of factor analysis for specifying the key variables of personality are, first, that the method is tautological, in that independent or nontest confirmation of the variables is seldom attempted; and, second, that factorially chosen variates have not been shown to be superior in predictive power to variables chosen and constructed in nonfactorial ways.

Paul Meehl (1993) has also proposed four queries or doubts about the claims and animadversions of factor analysis, one of which asked why one should expect factorially constructed measures to predict nontest criteria any better than measures constructed by other methods. Meehl's own answer was that in a purely instrumental task, such as forecasting a specified criterion, there is no reason to employ factor analysis; indeed, better results can be obtained by using a straightforward optimizing procedure such as multiple regression, discriminate function, or an actuarial table. Another point raised by Meehl is that the number of dimensions extracted is dependent on the choice and number of initial variables. Decisions about this matter are arbitrary, there being no clearly agreed upon rules concerning the range and number of variables. Early factoring in the cognitive domain usually specified from five to seven factors, but then Guilford (1967) proposed 120 dimensions. If Guilford had decided to create more tests, and to go outside of his a priori categories, could he have found 240 or even 480 factorial dimensions?

In light of the analyses of Lykken and Meehl, assertions that the true or basic themes in personality are forever three, or five, or seven, or any other number must be viewed with skepticism. For the CPI, the 20 folk measures on the profile sheet appear to be sufficient to forecast or conceptualize most if not all consequential and recurring forms of interpersonal behavior. If not, more can be added, or if any of the 20 proves to be of little use in future work, it can be dropped. This is what is indicated by the *open system* axiom. This is not to deny that organizing or structural themes found within the inventory should be ignored. As was shown in chapter 2 on the cuboid or three-vector model, interpretation of individual protocols can be appreciably improved by beginning with the vector scores. Once this step is taken, interpretation moves on to the individuating nuances and characteristics that can only be found in the configurations of the folk and special purpose scales.

The intercorrelation matrix of the CPI scales may, of course, be examined by means of factor analysis. When this is done, it is recommended that the three higher-order vector scales be excluded, and that Dicken's two response-style scales also be held out of the analysis. Also, the purpose of any such analysis should be the detection of underlying themes, not the discovery of new variables to be used in place of the folk and special purpose scales.

The intercorrelations factored for this manual are given in Table 3.2 for the 3,000 males and the 3,000 females in the profile report samples. For the 20 folk scales (Do through F/M), the ranges are from −.25 to .82 for males, with a median of .40; and from −.40 to .84 for females, with a median of .42. The highest correlations for both sexes were between Sc and Gi. The lowest correlation for men was between Sp and F/M, and the lowest correlation for women was between In and F/M.

Principal axis factor analyses of the 20 folk and 11 special purpose scales were carried out separately for males and females, followed by Kaiser normal varimax rotations of factors having eigen values of 1.00 or greater. Five factors for each analysis met this criterion, as shown in Table 3.3. Sequence of factors and loadings were similar for both sexes, except that Factor 3 for men was best matched with Factor 4 for females, and Factor 4 for males was best matched with Factor 3 for females.

Factor 1 had highest loadings on the seven scales in the first sector of the report form, from Do through Em, and among the special purpose scales, had high loadings on Lp and B–MS. The concept of *ascendance* is compatible with these loadings, and is the name suggested for this factor.

Factor 2 had its largest positive loadings on Sc, Gi, Wo, and Ami, and a large negative loading on Nar. Secondary loadings also occurred on Re and So, Wb, and To. The concept of *dependability* is

relevant to this configuration, and is the name suggested for the factor.

Factor 3 for men and Factor 4 for women are best defined by Cm, followed by So, Wb, and Anx with a negative loading. The name suggested for this factor is *communality*, although *conventionality* is a reasonable alternative.

Factor 4 for men and Factor 3 for women have largest positive loadings on CT and Fx, with secondary loadings on Ai and To. The name suggested for this factor is *originality*.

Factor 5 is largely defined by femininity/masculinity measures, specifically, F/M and B–FM with positive loadings and B–MS with a negative loading. The name suggested for this factor is *femininity/ masculinity*.

These five factors are quite similar to those reported by Megargee (1972) for the 18 folk scales in use at that time. After reviewing 20 different factor analyses of the CPI, Megargee concluded that the consensual dimensions were (1) extraversion, assertive self-assurance, or interpersonal effectiveness; (2) personal integrity, disciplined effectiveness, or conformity; (3) communality, modal response, or conventionality; (4) flexibility, nonauthoritarian attitudes, or adaptive autonomy; and (5) femininity or emotional sensitivity versus masculine toughness.

Table 3.2 Intercorrelations of 36 Form 434 CPI Scales in Samples of 3,000 Males and 3,000 Females

Scales	Do	Cs	Sy	Sp	Sa	In	Em	Re	So	Sc	Gi	Cm	Wb	To	Ac	Ai	Ie	Py	Fx	F/M
Folk Scales																				
Do		.67	.71	.59	.75	.72	.63	.39	.29	.06	.20	.24	.43	.37	.57	.50	.65	.53	.05	−.16
Cs	.67		.70	.61	.65	.63	.69	.44	.29	.17	.29	.19	.48	.55	.58	.66	.69	.62	.22	−.08
Sy	.73	.74		.69	.75	.52	.63	.31	.26	.00	.20	.30	.41	.31	.51	.41	.57	.41	.06	−.20
Sp	.60	.67	.73		.68	.57	.61	.16	.13	−.22	−.08	.32	.40	.32	.30	.46	.58	.41	.34	−.25
Sa	.76	.71	.76	.72		.60	.61	.21	.09	−.15	−.01	.21	.28	.27	.40	.44	.56	.39	.15	−.17
In	.75	.66	.60	.62	.64		.53	.29	.23	.19	.26	.14	.57	.47	.48	.64	.67	.64	.22	−.20
Em	.63	.73	.67	.67	.64	.58		.28	.20	.02	.16	.13	.34	.44	.42	.62	.59	.49	.32	−.10
Re	.35	.42	.31	.17	.21	.26	.33		.65	.49	.41	.42	.53	.66	.72	.45	.58	.50	−.10	.12
So	.21	.22	.24	.11	.03	.12	.22	.60		.51	.41	.38	.57	.53	.64	.30	.42	.41	−.14	.07
Sc	.04	.11	−.01	−.23	−.19	.12	.05	.51	.54		.82	.10	.57	.49	.53	.32	.28	.37	−.17	.15
Gi	.21	.26	.19	−.08	−.03	.23	.19	.47	.44	.84		.06	.57	.40	.51	.31	.28	.34	−.18	.03
Cm	.26	.25	.32	.29	.23	.17	.24	.45	.41	.17	.13		.46	.28	.42	.13	.38	.18	−.19	−.13
Wb	.45	.52	.47	.41	.31	.55	.46	.57	.58	.59	.61	.47		.64	.62	.52	.63	.58	.04	−.22
To	.35	.55	.36	.38	.30	.46	.50	.65	.52	.45	.39	.34	.67		.61	.72	.69	.64	.23	.06
Ac	.51	.54	.48	.27	.33	.44	.44	.72	.62	.57	.58	.47	.67	.59		.55	.68	.58	−.15	.06
Ai	.47	.67	.46	.53	.47	.64	.65	.42	.24	.27	.29	.19	.55	.73	.50		.77	.73	.37	.02
Ie	.64	.75	.61	.61	.58	.71	.66	.56	.34	.26	.32	.38	.66	.71	.64	.80		.69	.20	−.11
Py	.54	.63	.46	.46	.42	.65	.56	.48	.34	.36	.39	.24	.62	.64	.58	.76	.73		.23	−.07
Fx	.12	.28	.18	.45	.24	.27	.37	−.02	−.05	−.19	−.20	−.05	.13	.32	−.11	.45	.29	.28		.00
F/M	−.30	−.27	−.25	−.31	−.30	−.40	−.27	.09	.15	.11	−.03	.06	−.22	−.05	−.01	−.25	−.28	−.24	−.15	
Vector Scales																				
v.1	−.78	−.56	−.68	−.67	−.76	−.56	−.60	−.05	.07	.40	.17	−.10	−.10	−.09	−.18	−.29	−.42	−.27	−.20	.33
v.2	.21	.09	.20	−.11	−.02	−.04	.02	.53	.62	.48	.51	.35	.35	.16	.59	−.06	.11	.12	−.55	.16
v.3	.48	.67	.47	.49	.41	.63	.63	.55	.39	.46	.50	.26	.71	.84	.60	.85	.80	.75	.39	−.23
Special Purpose Scales																				
Mp	.65	.70	.59	.51	.51	.66	.63	.61	.45	.46	.51	.32	.72	.80	.69	.74	.78	.69	.23	−.21
Wo	.36	.50	.40	.33	.23	.46	.43	.63	.62	.66	.65	.44	.85	.70	.71	.58	.64	.63	.09	−.09
CT	.46	.57	.45	.64	.57	.62	.61	.10	−.07	−.20	−.15	.04	.24	.46	.12	.67	.58	.50	.67	−.24
Lp	.79	.73	.72	.57	.61	.73	.66	.59	.52	.44	.54	.41	.79	.63	.77	.64	.77	.70	.07	−.26
Ami	.22	.38	.28	.22	.10	.29	.36	.63	.73	.72	.64	.37	.77	.75	.63	.50	.52	.52	.11	.02
Leo	.38	.18	.27	.03	.16	.26	.13	.47	.44	.51	.55	.33	.51	.30	.55	.18	.30	.29	−.20	−.13
Tm	.64	.59	.51	.41	.43	.76	.49	.42	.31	.50	.55	.23	.69	.55	.63	.66	.69	.70	.08	−.33
B–MS	.78	.74	.74	.66	.70	.81	.65	.34	.20	.24	.41	.25	.67	.47	.52	.60	.72	.64	.24	−.49
B–FM	.08	.20	.12	.00	−.03	.10	.14	.59	.64	.64	.50	.35	.50	.54	.58	.34	.34	.35	−.01	.39
Anx	−.37	−.42	−.41	−.40	−.29	−.40	−.39	−.46	−.51	−.41	−.39	−.48	−.75	−.53	−.55	−.40	−.52	−.47	−.12	.16
Nar	.29	.06	.22	.33	.41	.17	.13	−.40	−.36	−.75	−.63	−.10	−.39	−.40	−.32	−.15	−.08	−.16	.07	−.23
D–SD	.52	.56	.52	.31	.36	.51	.52	.57	.47	.61	.72	.33	.71	.57	.71	.54	.61	.60	−.10	−.13
D–AC	.02	−.13	.03	−.02	.05	−.21	−.09	−.26	−.17	−.43	−.35	−.05	−.40	−.48	−.20	−.39	−.28	−.30	−.30	.03

Note: Males, above diagonal; Females, below diagonal

Table 3.2 Intercorrelations of 36 Form 434 CPI Scales in Samples of 3,000 Males and 3,000 Females

Scales	v.1	v.2	v.3	Mp	Wo	CT	Lp	Ami	Leo	Tm	B–MS	B–FM	Anx	Nar	D–SD	D–AC
Folk Scales																
Do	−.78	.28	−.48	−.66	−.37	−.41	−.81	.19	.39	.64	−.76	−.10	−.38	−.33	−.50	−.01
Cs	−.54	.16	.67	.70	.48	.52	.71	.36	.19	.57	.69	.24	−.38	.06	.51	−.15
Sy	−.67	.27	.43	.56	.36	.33	.71	.23	.31	.47	.71	.08	−.38	.24	.51	.07
Sp	−.64	−.05	.44	.45	.31	.54	.54	.17	.08	.38	.63	−.05	−.39	.35	.26	.00
Sa	−.74	.07	.39	.49	.22	.48	.62	.05	.22	.42	.69	−.04	−.27	.44	.34	.06
In	−.50	.04	.62	.65	.47	.58	.73	.31	.29	.75	.79	.15	−.40	.14	.47	−.24
Em	−.62	.02	.58	.57	.32	.58	.60	.26	.10	.42	.58	.09	−.29	.20	.43	−.08
Re	−.06	.56	.54	.61	.61	.11	.59	.61	.40	.45	.35	.58	−.39	−.32	.57	−.18
So	.02	.61	.41	.49	.63	−.02	.56	.69	.41	.41	.31	.58	−.45	−.29	.51	−.11
Sc	.38	.42	.51	.50	.65	−.11	.43	.73	.43	.52	.28	.64	−.36	−.73	.61	−.46
Gi	.16	.47	.52	.52	.62	−.13	.51	.65	.50	.54	.41	.50	−.35	−.61	.72	−.39
Cm	−.10	.35	.18	.24	.42	−.04	.39	.29	.34	.21	.28	.23	−.45	−.03	.29	.01
Wb	−.06	.34	.68	.67	.84	.21	.75	.74	.50	.70	.70	.45	−.71	−.37	.66	−.39
To	−.09	.20	.82	.79	.67	.46	.61	.71	.27	.55	.47	.52	-.46	-.37	.54	-.45
Ac	−.24	.57	.62	.71	.67	.16	.78	.58	.50	.64	.56	.56	−.49	−.22	.68	−.17
Ai	−.28	.00	.84	.72	.55	.65	.63	.46	.19	.61	.57	.38	−.37	−.14	.47	−.37
Ie	−.40	.18	.75	.75	.62	.52	.76	.49	.32	.66	.70	.34	−.49	−.04	.55	−.24
Py	−.24	.17	.73	.67	.60	.48	.67	.50	.23	.66	.60	.34	−.43	−.13	.51	−.29
Fx	−.14	−.58	.33	.12	−.02	.66	−.03	.02	−.26	.00	.15	−.05	−.02	.03	−.21	−.29
F/M	.19	.04	−.02	−.06	−.10	.02	−.16	.00	−.21	−.20	−.35	.49	.25	−.19	−.05	−.01
Vector Scales																
v.1		−.05	−.20	−.35	.01	−.41	−.48	.17	−.11	−.28	−.50	.25	.12	−.66	−.20	−.25
v.2	.03		.10	.30	.40	−.40	.45	.42	.45	.26	.18	.36	−.28	−.18	.56	.22
v.3	−.21	.06		.83	.70	.55	.70	.66.	.28	.69	.64	.47	−.45	−.32	.61	−.50
Special Purpose Scales																
Mp	−.36	.23	.85		.70	.43	.83	.65	.40	.76	.72	.43	−.49	−.20	.69	−.39
Wo	−.01	.39	.74	.73		.15	.73	.80	.50	.69	.60	.54	−.60	−.45	.67	−.41
CT	−.49	−.43	.57	.48	.19		.32	.11	−.17	.30	.43	.03	−.13	.17	.07	−.25
Lp	−.47	.40	.73	.84	.75	.37		.59	.54	.80	.83	.38	−.61	−.05	.75	−.22
Ami	.13	.42	.69	.68	.82	.14	.63		.39	.54	.42	.61	−.52	−.58	.63	−.43
Leo	−.08	.47	.31	.43	.52	−.15	.54	.44		.50	.46	.25	−.43	−.22	.54	−.16
Tm	−.31	.20	.72	.76	.67	.35	.81	.52	.48		.77	.36	−.50	−.16	.64	−.37
B–MS	−.55	.09	.66	.74	.58	.51	.83	.40	.40	.78		.18	−.55	.02	.60	−.25
B–FM	.25	.40	.46	.44	.59	−.02	.41	.67	.34	.35	.16		−.28	−.54	.42	−.34
Anx	.12	−.29	−.51	−.53	−.64	−.18	−.63	−.59	−.43	−.51	−.52	−.41		.21	−.47	.21
Nar	−.64	−.28	−.34	−.24	−.48	.22	−.12	−.58	−.32	−.18	.03	−.56	.26		−.31	.46
D–SD	−.21	.48	.66	.72	.70	.17	.78	.65	.54	.69	.63	.44	−.52	−.35		−.19
D–AC	−.25	.18	−.50	−.41	−.41	−.23	−.23	−.46	−.19	−.35	−.22	−.37	.26	.47	−.22	

Note: Males, above diagonal; Females, below diagonal

Table 3.3 Rotated Loadings for the Five CPI Factors on Samples of 3,000 Men and 3,000 Women

Scales	M-1	F-1	M-2	F-2	M-3	F-4	M-4	F-3	M-5	F-5
Folk Scales										
Do	.91	.90	.06	.07	.11	.11	−.06	−.07	−.02	−.04
Cs	.76	.78	.21	.19	.13	.12	.24	.27	.07	.03
Sy	.79	.80	.01	.03	.24	.30	−.03	.05	−.08	−.02
Sp	.67	.68	−.15	−.14	.33	.38	.34	.40	−.23	−.13
Sa	.85	.84	−.17	−.17	.12	.18	.06	.12	−.06	−.01
In	.75	.78	.26	.19	−.02	−.02	.24	.22	−.19	−.25
Em	.70	.70	.05	.12	.09	.16	.32	.34	.04	.01
Re	.32	.31	.51	.60	.46	.28	−.03	.02	.33	.34
So	.20	.10	.53	.59	.49	.48	−.09	−.04	.19	.23
Sc	.00	−.04	.93	.93	−.03	−.04	−.12	−.14	.11	−.02
Gi	.17	.16	.83	.83	−.10	−.06	−.21	−.21	−.02	−.12
Cm	.17	.22	.11	.23	.70	.56	−.13	−.04	−.09	.15
Wb	.37	.39	.68	.68	.43	.44	.12	.15	−.30	−.26
To	.36	.36	.58	.61	.32	.20	.41	.48	.18	.17
Ac	.56	.51	.52	.64	.37	.26	−.13	−.12	.25	.23
Ai	.58	.57	.40	.41	.08	−.06	.51	.57	.13	.02
Ie	.68	.70	.34	.39	.33	.16	.29	.35	.03	.02
Py	.55	.58	.44	.47	.14	.02	.34	.33	.03	−.04
Fx	.11	.15	−.09	−.11	−.11	.03	.74	.73	−.04	−.09
F/M	−.17	−.36	.07	.07	−.09	.06	.05	−.07	.69	.62
Special Purpose Scales										
Mp	.66	.66	.56	.57	.17	.11	.18	.25	.07	.02
Wo	.33	.33	.74	.77	.40	.33	.08	.15	−.11	−.08
CT	.50	.55	−.05	−.10	−.06	−.06	.76	.72	.06	−.02
Lp	.80	.78	.47	.51	.28	.26	−.06	−.01	−.06	−.07
Ami	.14	.15	.79	.80	.35	.35	.14	.22	.02	.04
Leo	.29	.27	.45	.53	.22	.21	−.37	−.33	−.20	−.11
Tm	.64	.65	.58	.56	.03	−.04	.02	.05	−.18	−.24
B–MS	.79	.81	.35	.29	.13	.11	.08	.11	−.35	−.36
B–FM	.06	.03	.64	.69	.24	.24	.03	.07	.50	.39
Anx	−.31	−.31	−.42	−.47	−.45	−.52	−.05	−.10	.29	.17
Nar	.38	.34	−.77	−.79	−.02	.03	−.07	−.06	−.09	−.05
Variance Proportion	.29	.30	.23	.26	.09	.09	.08	.07	.05	.04

Note: M signifies male sample; F signifies female sample.

CHAPTER

4

The Detection of Invalid Protocols

An Overview of the Development of Validity Scales

In psychological assessment based on self-reports, the question of the validity or accuracy of what is said is unavoidable. This is particularly true when testing is done in situations, such as applying for a job, in which self-criticism may be seen as a weakness and self-enhancement as a strength. There are also situations in which the strategy of a respondent may be to stress or overstress personal problems, up to and including diagnosable disorders. In research inquiry, where large numbers of persons are tested without any particular attention to them as individuals, those who feel put-upon or exploited by the assessment may decide to answer in a random or meaningless way. The interpreter of any personality inventory needs to have some way of knowing when any of these modes of responding have been carried to the point of rendering the protocols unreliable or invalid.

From the earliest days of self-report inventories, psychologists have been aware of problems such as these. Spencer (1938), for instance, noted that some

individuals react negatively to personal inquiry and tend to give undependable replies. Kelly, Miles, and Terman (1936) observed that faking is easy to elicit, and that scores can thereby be manipulated. Vernon (1934) found that respondents could be strongly influenced by knowledge of the purposes of the testing.

Concerns like these led directly to attempts to control for the validity of the protocol, and to methods for determining whether falsification or dissimulation had occurred. One of the first attempts was that of Hartshorne and May (1928), who developed a *Lie* scale of improbably true assertions for use in their study of children's honesty. The higher the score of any child on their scale, the more likely that false and self-serving answers had been given in the test. Humm and Wadsworth (1934) made use of a *No Count*, a tally of the total number of "no" replies to questions in their inventory for temperament. Beyond a certain frequency, this tally suggested an excessive tendency to deny or disown personal problems. Adams (1941) proposed use of descriptive statements, instead of questions, with respondents then asked to state whether they were similar to or different from each characterization. Ruch (1942) had students respond to an inventory in the normal fashion, and then take the test again under instructions to present a very favorable impression. By contrasting the two sets of protocols, items were identified that yielded significant differences in rates of endorsement, and that could be scored as a scale to distinguish between normal and *fake good* answer sheets.

Although several early personality inventories incorporated one or even two of these methods for detecting invalid protocols, it was not until the appearance of the *Minnesota Multiphasic Personality Inventory* (MMPI; Hathaway & McKinley, 1940, 1943) that separate measures were provided for detecting more than two kinds of invalidity (see Dahlstrom, Welsh, & Dahlstrom, 1972). A first measure was the tally of unanswered items, or the "cannot say" score. Initially, an informal cutoff of 30 unanswered items was suggested, but later, Brown (1950) gave more detailed and explicit instructions for interpreting this indicator. The second MMPI measure was the *Lie* scale, modeled on the work of Hartshorne and May just mentioned. The third was the *F* scale, composed of 64 items very infrequently answered in the scored direction.

A few years after the initial publication of the MMPI, the *K*, or *Correction*, scale was added (McKinley, Hathaway, & Meehl, 1948). The function of the K scale was to identify protocols of psychiatric patients whose scores on the MMPI measures of pathology were too low and nonpatients whose scores on these same scales were too high. In the language of classification, the former group constituted *false negatives* and the latter *false positives*. Adjustments of the scores on MMPI diagnostic scales according to the K score of the respondent permitted the reduction of both kinds of errors. Later, the K scale began to be understood as an indicator of self-presentational style, with higher scores presaging favorable and even defensive views of self, and lower scores betokening self-critical and even self-rejecting attitudes. A useful analysis of the role of self-presentation (as opposed to self-disclosure) in personality testing may be found in a paper by Johnson (1981). Perspicacious interpretation of the scales on any self-report test of personality must take account of the psychology of self-presentation.

As examiners became more adept in persuading clients to answer all or nearly all items in the MMPI, the "cannot say" score diminished in significance, and now often goes unreported, whereas the L, F, and K scores continue to play prominent roles in interpretation. The themes addressed by these three scales—possible self-aggrandizement, erratic or random answering, and an undue emphasis on either positive or negative qualities—cannot now be ignored by any inventory for which operational testing is a possibility.

Patterns or combinations of the three scales have also been studied. In a study of deliberate dissimulation of the MMPI (Gough, 1947), an index derived from the raw score on F minus the raw score on K showed promise as a method for detecting falsified protocols. A more systematic analysis of the F minus K metric (Gough, 1950) found that differences greater than +10 were associated with faking bad, and that differences less than –10 were associated with faking good.

A subsequent investigation of the MMPI at the item level (Gough, 1954) identified 74 items for which the endorsement rates of normal and psychiatric samples were approximately the same, but for which the rates for persons asked to simulate pathology were significantly different. This Ds (Dissimulation) scale has been frequently used in both research and practice with the MMPI.

Fake Bad, Fake Good, and Random Answers

In developing the CPI, it was decided that the Ds scale could furnish a helpful clue for the exaggeration of personal distress, or even of faking bad. However, because of the length of the scale (74 items) and its inclusion of many declarations of rather extreme psychopathology, it was shortened to 44 items when the CPI was first published in 1956. The direction of scoring was also reversed, so as to emphasize positive aspects of mental health and personal well-being. This Wb (Well-being) scale was shortened to 38 items in the 1986 revision of the CPI. In Form 434 of the CPI, Wb also includes 38 items, but seven items from the initial version of the scale have been dropped and replaced by seven other items already present in the inventory.

The second CPI scale to assess response characteristics, this time faking good, was developed by

Ruch's (1942) strategy of testing under normal instructions and then with instructions to fake good. For the Good Impression or Gi scale of the CPI, the instructions for faking asked respondents to imagine themselves as applying for a job they very much wanted, or as being in any other situation in which they wished to be judged as admirable and praiseworthy (Gough, 1952b). The experimental items included modified and updated versions of those used by Ruch, as well as others, based on hunches and intuitions about what people might say when trying to create an extremely favorable impression. Item analysis identified 40 items showing significant differences in endorsement when the two conditions were contrasted. In the 1986 revision of the CPI, five of these items were dropped but replaced by five others already in the inventory. No changes were made in the Gi scale for the current 434-item edition of the CPI.

The third CPI validational measure is called Communality (Cm) and is based on the same strategy used by Hathaway and McKinley for the MMPI F scale. That is, a subset of items answered "true" by a very high percentage of respondents constitutes one portion of the scale, buttressed by another subset of items seldom, if ever, answered "true" and hence scored for "false" on the Cm scale. High scores on the Cm scale suggest that the respondent has reacted to the inventory in a standard or modal fashion, whereas very low scores raise the possibility of erratic, random, or strongly nonnormative responses. In the 1956 edition of the CPI, the Cm scale had 28 items. For the 1986 version, this was increased to 38 items, so as to get more differentiation at the high end. For the present 434-item version of the CPI, the Cm scale also has 38 items, two of which are different from those included in the 1986 edition.

The Wb, Gi, and Cm scales all convey important interpretive meanings for normal protocols, as will be apparent in a number of places in this manual. However, in this chapter, attention is centered on the discovery of invalid protocols; for this purpose the three scales offer a first line of analysis. In raw score terms, scores on Gi of 30 and above are suggestive of faking good. On Wb, scores of 20 and below suggest the presence of serious personal problems and/or the adoption of a fake bad mode of responding. On Cm, raw scores of 24 or below

suggest atypicality of responding and the possibility of merely random answering. For any individual profile, these three indicators of validity should be scanned to see if they are within normal limits.

For more precise classification, these impressionistic scans can be improved upon by combinations of the three validity indicators and by the addition of other scales. For the 1956 edition of the CPI, equations were developed to detect fake good, fake bad, and random protocols (see McAllister, 1986, p. 66). Although the scales were reasonably effective in identifying invalid records, there was a problem in that scores on the fake bad and random equations correlated approximately .95 with each other. As this coefficient indicates, the fake bad equation was just about as effective as the random equation in detecting randomly answered protocols, and the random equation was almost as good as the fake bad equation in detecting fake bad protocols. However, the fake good equation produced scores that were essentially uncorrelated with scores from the other two equations and that functioned well in identifying fake good protocols.

A Decision-Tree Format

For the 1986 edition of the CPI, three new equations were developed by Kevin Lanning (1989) and applied in a new decision-tree format. In the first step, scores on the fake good equation are used to cull out those protocols meeting the prescriptions of this equation for a fake good classification. The remaining protocols are then classified by means of the second or fake bad equation into two groups: fake bad or random, and valid or within normal limits. In the third step, all protocols classified as fake bad or random are examined by means of the random equation and subclassified as either fake bad or random. Cutting scores on the three equations were set so as to maximize the identification of experimentally produced fake good, fake bad, and random protocols and to minimize the misclassification of protocols in the supposedly normal archival files for the CPI. In the 2,000 profile norm sample used in 1986 (1,000 of each sex), 12 protocols were classified as fake good, 9 as fake bad, and 14 as random. These figures show that invalidity, as defined by the three equations and the decision-tree application, is relatively rare in ordinary testing.

Table 4.1 Equations to Detect Fake Good, Fake Bad, and Random Protocols Applied to the Samples Indicated

Samples	N	Fake Good Equation		Called Fake Good		Fake Bad Equation		Called Fake Bad		Random Equation		Called Random	
		M	SD	N	%	M	SD	N	%	M	SD	N	%
Males, faking good	50	60.62	4.90	34	68.0	48.06	2.24	0	0.0	55.42	2.79	0	0.0
Males, faking bad	50	49.18	3.75	0	0.0	65.38	5.75	42	84.0	41.73	2.94	1	2.0
Females, faking good	52	59.24	4.95	30	57.7	47.59	2.01	0	0.0	55.36	2.72	0	0.0
Famales, faking bad	50	48.53	4.22	0	0.0	65.99	7.69	39	78.0	43.10	3.74	2	4.0
Generated by a table of random numbers	100	53.51	1.97	0	0.0	63.59	3.05	24	24.0	48.98	1.35	66	66.0
Generated by the computer	1,000	53.46	2.21	0	0.0	63.27	3.26	225	22.5	48.81	1.26	646	64.6

However, in specific settings, such as among males applying for work as a police officer, higher rates occurred; for 84 men making such application, 10.7% turned in protocols that were classified as fake good.

Protocol Validity Equations

Because of changes in items in the validational scales, as well as in other scales on the profile sheet, new analyses were necessary to develop equations for Form 434. The three equations that best separated experimentally produced invalid records from normative protocols were these:

Fake good = 41.225 + .273Do + .198Em + .538Gi − .255Wb − .168Fx

Fake bad = 86.613 − 1.000Cm − .191Wb + .203Ac − .110Fx

Random = 34.096 + .279Gi + .201Wb + .225Py + .157Fx

Raw scores are used in all three equations. On the fake good algorithm, if the score is equal to or greater than 60.60, the protocol is called *fake good*. On the next two equations, if the score on fake bad is equal to or greater than 59.50, and if the score on random is less than 48.01, the protocol is called *fake bad*. If the score on fake bad is equal to or greater than 59.50, and the score on random is equal to or greater than 48.01, the protocol is called *random*. All other protocols are classified as *normal* or *valid*.

Table 4.1 gives means and standard deviations for the experimental samples on all three scales and the number and percentage of protocols classified as fake good, fake bad, and random.

For both men and women answering experimentally in a fake good mode, no protocols were classified as either fake bad or random. Sixty-four or 62.7% of the 102 protocols were accurately tabbed as fake good. Of the 100 fake bad protocols, none was classified as fake good, 81 were called fake bad, and 3 were misclassified as random. There were 100 answer sheets filled in according to a random-number table. Sixty-six of these were correctly called random, but 24 were called fake bad. A computer-generated set of 1,000 random protocols resulted in 64.6% being correctly classified as random, but 22.5% were classified as fake bad.

Another way to interpret the figures in Table 4.1 is to ask how many protocols were incorrectly classified as valid or normal? Among the protocols produced by students asked to give highly favorable answers, but at the same time to avoid detection for faking, 64 were detected and 38 were not. In the fake bad trials, 84 of the 100 protocols were classified as invalid, but 16 escaped detection. Among the 1,000 computer-generated random records, 871 were classified as invalid, but 129 escaped detection. These figures suggest that fake good protocols will be spotted about 63% of the time, fake bad protocols about 84% of the time, and random protocols about 87% of the time.

Table 4.2 The Equation to Detect Fake Good Protocols Applied to Males

Samples	N	M	SD	Classified as Fake Good N	%	Samples	N	M	SD	Classified as Fake Good N	%
Police officer applicants	883	55.24	3.78	66	7.5	Psychiatric patients	41	51.44	4.08	1	2.4
Juvenile parole and probation officers	65	54.17	3.60	3	4.6	Critics of books for children	25	51.33	3.69	0	0.0
Optometry students	100	54.07	4.16	5	5.0	Pharmacy students	439	51.29	3.83	4	0.9
Irish entrepreneurs	37	54.05	2.67	0	0.0	Architects	124	51.24	3.59	0	0.0
Sales managers	85	53.85	3.43	3	3.5	Engineering students	66	51.06	3.64	1	1.5
Business executives	185	53.49	4.36	7	3.8	College students	3,235	50.91	3.98	36	1.1
Members, club for inventors	14	53.41	4.20	1	7.1	San Francisco area residents	261	50.87	3.64	0	0.0
Education students	167	53.29	3.58	5	3.0	Architecture students	125	50.25	3.31	0	0.0
Police officers	366	53.19	4.08	14	3.8	Psychology graduate students	623	50.22	3.28	1	0.2
Premedical students	70	52.99	3.93	2	2.9	Juvenile delinquents	76	50.02	3.91	0	0.0
Military officers	343	52.98	3.72	8	2.3	Prison inmates	196	50.01	3.79	1	0.5
Bank managers	49	52.94	4.41	2	4.1	High school science fair delegates	363	49.98	3.89	1	0.3
West Point cadets	1,420	52.83	3.97	44	3.1	Nursing students	149	49.95	3.56	0	0.0
Catholic priests	41	52.52	3.38	2	4.9	Profile sheet norm sample	3,000	49.84	3.87	8	0.3
MBA candidates	78	52.40	3.42	1	0.3	Mathematicians	57	49.82	2.98	0	0.0
Correctional officers	221	52.35	3.85	3	1.4	Training school inmates	2,899	49.63	3.84	4	0.4
Engineers	47	52.33	3.54	0	0.0	Commercial writers	16	49.58	4.43	0	0.0
Counseling graduate students	67	52.24	3.17	0	0.0	Creative writers	19	49.52	3.42	0	0.0
Social welfare graduate students	254	52.21	3.36	2	0.8	Writers of books for children	29	49.32	3.32	0	0.0
Anesthesiologists	98	52.15	3.22	0	0.0	High school students	4,611	49.13	3.81	8	0.2
Medical students	551	51.71	3.65	3	0.5	Rajneeshpuram residents	33	49.01	2.99	0	0.0
Research scientists	45	51.63	3.15	0	0.0	Art institute students	44	47.89	2.85	0	0.0

In Table 4.2, the fake good equation has been applied to 44 samples of males; and in Table 4.3, the same equation has been applied to 34 samples of females. The highest incidence of fake good protocols for men was found among the 883 persons applying for work as a police officer in a midsized city on the West coast, for whom the rate was 7.5%. Next came males applying for admission to a doctoral program in optometry, with a rate of 5.0%, and juvenile parole and probation officers tested in a

research project, with a rate of 4.6%. A rate of 7.1% was observed in a very small (N = 14) sample of men who belonged to a club for inventors. Only two other samples had rates greater than 4%, namely 49 banking branch managers and 41 Catholic priests. For all six of these samples, with the possible exception of the aspiring inventors, the circumstances of testing call for self-presentation as honest, ethical, and self-disciplined persons. Seventeen of the male samples had no protocols classified as fake good, and

Table 4.3 The Equation to Detect Fake Good Protocols Applied to Females

Samples	N	M	SD	Classified as Fake Good N	Classified as Fake Good %	Samples	N	M	SD	Classified as Fake Good N	Classified as Fake Good %
Police officer applicants	200	55.30	3.72	17	8.5	Pharmacy students	277	51.21	3.53	2	0.7
Optometry students	50	54.10	4.19	3	6.0	College students	4,126	50.95	3.61	28	0.7
Education students	310	53.37	3.59	4	1.3	Registered nurses	100	50.90	3.34	0	0.0
College counselors	42	52.75	2.94	0	0.0	Nursing students	250	50.88	3.51	1	0.4
Home economics students	176	52.58	3.84	4	2.3	Prison inmates	345	50.75	3.97	1	0.3
Secondary school teachers	21	52.53	4.23	1	4.8	Law students	40	50.38	3.52	0	0.0
Psychiatric patients	34	52.38	3.82	0	0.0	Psychology graduate students	405	50.36	3.13	0	0.0
Critics of books for children	36	52.24	3.58	1	2.8	Writers of books for children	32	50.21	3.43	0	0.0
MBA candidates	64	52.23	2.71	0	0.0	Profile sheet norm sample	3,000	50.17	3.75	11	0.4
University clerical personnel	56	52.22	3.84	0	0.0	High school students	4,823	50.06	3.94	16	0.3
Counseling graduate students	275	52.15	3.34	0	0.0	San Francisco area residents	261	50.05	3.37	0	0.0
Medical students	90	52.06	4.00	1	1.1	Architecture students	55	49.93	3.70	0	0.0
Anesthesiologists	17	51.88	2.82	0	0.0	Mathematicians	41	49.83	3.98	0	0.0
Social welfare graduate students	446	51.69	3.57	2	0.4	Rajneeshpuram residents	34	49.11	3.53	0	0.0
Commercial writers	12	51.58	3.73	0	0.0	Juvenile delinquents	55	47.58	3.35	0	0.0
High school science fair delegates	148	51.55	4.65	2	1.3	Art institute students	27	47.29	2.66	0	0.0
Premedical students	48	51.40	3.15	1	2.1	Creative writers	10	46.69	2.04	0	0.0

others had very low incidence. For example, in the sample of 4,611 high school males tested in 25 schools in various parts of the country, under rather informal conditions, only eight (0.2%) submitted fake good answer sheets.

Three of the 34 samples of females had fake good rates greater than 4.0%, namely women applying for work as a police officer with a rate of 8.5%, women seeking admission to a doctoral program in optometry with a rate of 6.0%, and secondary school teachers tested in a research project with a rate of 4.8%. Seventeen of the samples had no fake good protocols, and five others had rates of less than 0.5%.

Faking good, it may be concluded, is a relatively rare occurrence in both research and operational (as in making application for a job or for admission to an educational program) settings. Even in the police officer setting, applicants with elevated scores on

the equation often turn out to do well in training and on the job (see Roberts, 1995b), as long as the score is not greater than 60.

Table 4.4 presents data for the fake bad and random algorithms, applied to the samples of males. The highest percentages for both kinds of invalidity were observed among the 41 men tested in psychiatric settings (4.9% in each instance). The second highest percentage of fake bad protocols (3.6%) was found in the sample of 196 prison inmates. For 28 of the 44 samples, there were no fake bad occurrences, and for six other samples only one such answer sheet was detected each time. Faking bad among the male samples in the CPI archival database appears to be a relatively infrequent phenomenon.

Randomly answered protocols are somewhat more frequent, with only 23 samples free of any occurrence. In the nationwide sample of 4,611 high

Table 4.4   The Equations to Detect Fake Bad and Random Protocols Applied to Males

Samples	N	Fake Bad Equation		Random Equation		Called Fake Bad		Called Random	
		M	SD	M	SD	N	%	N	%
Psychiatric patients	41	50.33	5.45	50.44	3.95	2	4.9	2	4.9
Art institute students	44	49.15	4.55	49.17	2.90	1	2.3	0	0.0
Prison inmates	196	48.61	4.87	49.15	3.30	7	3.6	3	1.5
Creative writers	19	48.24	2.51	50.72	2.61	0	0.0	0	0.0
Rajneeshpuram residents	33	48.16	3.55	52.64	2.22	0	0.0	0	0.0
Writers of books for children	29	47.92	2.95	51.28	2.71	0	0.0	0	0.0
Critics of books for children	25	47.85	2.94	52.33	3.19	0	0.0	0	0.0
High school students	4,611	47.35	3.94	49.59	2.94	38	0.8	59	1.3
Architecture students	125	47.35	3.88	50.86	2.69	2	1.6	2	1.6
Juvenile delinquents	76	47.26	3.44	49.12	3.10	0	0.0	0	0.0
Training school inmates	2,899	47.22	3.35	49.16	3.29	4	0.1	2	0.1
Mathematicians	57	47.06	2.35	52.89	2.69	0	0.0	0	0.0
Profile sheet norm sample	3,000	47.01	3.47	50.15	3.14	13	0.4	20	0.7
Pharmacy students	439	47.00	3.28	51.95	3.18	3	0.7	3	0.7
High school science fair delegates	363	46.97	3.96	50.28	3.04	2	0.6	3	0.8
Commercial writers	16	46.84	2.27	50.80	3.05	0	0.0	0	0.0
Nursing students	149	46.76	3.54	51.11	3.01	1	0.7	2	1.3
Engineering students	66	46.72	3.51	53.09	2.25	0	0.0	2	3.0
Psychology graduate students	623	46.66	2.52	53.04	2.41	1	0.2	2	0.3
College students	3,235	46.59	2.85	51.37	2.87	13	0.4	8	0.2
San Francisco area residents	261	46.58	3.03	51.25	2.95	1	0.4	2	0.8
Architects	124	46.57	2.01	52.11	2.17	0	0.0	0	0.0
MBA candidates	78	46.56	3.17	52.50	2.31	0	0.0	2	2.6
Social welfare graduate students	254	46.49	2.67	53.49	2.44	0	0.0	2	0.8
Education students	167	46.42	2.24	53.88	2.30	0	0.0	0	0.0
Medical students	551	46.38	2.48	52.98	2.61	0	0.0	1	0.2
Correctional officers	221	46.25	3.29	52.09	2.73	0	0.0	3	1.4
Irish entrepreneurs	37	46.13	2.44	52.41	2.45	0	0.0	0	0.0
West Point cadets	1,420	46.12	2.24	51.56	2.78	1	0.1	3	0.2
Members, club for inventors	14	46.11	1.99	52.87	2.82	0	0.0	0	0.0
Police officer applicants	883	46.09	2.78	53.96	2.64	1	0.1	6	0.7
Optometry students	100	46.07	1.69	54.05	2.89	0	0.0	0	0.0

		Fake Bad Equation		Random Equation		Called Fake Bad		Called Random	
Samples	N	M	SD	M	SD	N	%	N	%
Catholic priests	41	45.87	1.82	52.70	2.56	0	0.0	0	0.0
Business executives	185	45.76	1.68	53.61	2.66	0	0.0	0	0.0
Research scientists	45	45.61	1.81	54.08	2.21	0	0.0	0	0.0
Juvenile parole and probation officers	65	45.60	1.56	53.11	2.72	0	0.0	0	0.0
Premedical students	70	45.53	1.36	53.65	2.07	0	0.0	0	0.0
Engineers	47	45.52	1.58	53.37	1.91	0	0.0	0	0.0
Bank managers	49	45.51	1.51	53.02	2.47	0	0.0	0	0.0
Military officers	343	45.50	2.20	52.33	2.40	0	0.0	1	0.3
Police officers	366	45.42	1.95	52.92	2.70	0	0.0	1	0.3
Anesthesiologists	98	45.39	2.45	52.60	2.07	1	1.0	0	0.0
Counseling graduate students	67	45.39	2.29	52.02	3.11	0	0.0	0	0.0
Sales managers	85	44.98	1.48	52.80	2.07	0	0.0	0	0.0

Table 4.4 The Equations to Detect Fake Bad and Random Protocols Applied to Males continued

school students tested under research conditions, 59 students appear to have answered randomly. In the sample of 3,235 college students tested under similar conditions, eight answered in a random manner. Although the corresponding percentages of 1.3 and 0.2 are low, a reasonable precaution in research inquiry is to screen for such protocols.

Fake bad and random frequencies for the female samples are given in Table 4.5. Three of the 34 female psychiatric patients (8.8%) submitted protocols classified as fake bad. No other sample had an appreciable percentage of fake bad protocols, and 25 of the 34 samples had none at all. The largest number of random records appeared among the 4,823 high school students, among which 182 (3.8%) turned in protocols classified as random. The total number of invalid records among these high school females was 237, with 77% of these protocols classified as random. An inference seems justified that when high school females want to resist taking part in research inquiry of this kind they will do so by submitting random or meaningless responses. Among the 4,611 high school males the total number of invalid records came to 105 (eight fake good, 38 fake bad, and 59 random). Whereas random records were moderately common among high

school females, only six of 4,126 college females contributed protocols of this kind.

A final comment is needed on the classifications derived from the algorithms for fake good, fake bad, and random answering. For instance, when a protocol is classified by these methods as *fake good,* it does not mean that a firm and sure diagnosis has been made of the motivational intentions of the person producing the protocol. Rather, the classification raises a danger signal that the particular protocol deviates markedly from the normative parameters for this phenomenon, and that the dependability or authenticity of the record should be carefully considered before going on to further use or interpretation of the protocol. The same admonition holds for the other two classifications, each of which raises the question as to whether or not the protocol is sufficiently similar to what most people do in taking the inventory to allow interpretation to proceed in the usual manner. A decision as to whether or not any specific protocol is valid, or valid enough to warrant interpretation, is a professional judgment to be made on the basis of the circumstances of testing, knowledge (if available) of the person taking the test, and cues from observational and nontest sources, as well as from the configuration of scores on the profile.

Table 4.5 The Equations to Detect Fake Bad and Random Protocols Applied to Females

Samples	N	Fake Bad Equation		Random Equation		Called Fake Bad		Called Random	
		M	SD	M	SD	N	%	N	%
Psychiatric patients	34	51.98	5.13	48.37	3.91	3	8.8	1	2.9
Prison inmates	345	48.69	3.84	48.68	3.76	3	0.9	3	0.9
Commercial writers	12	48.47	3.69	51.57	2.75	0	0.0	0	0.0
Art institute students	27	48.22	3.75	49.15	2.72	0	0.0	0	0.0
Critics of books for children	36	47.96	1.94	52.07	2.58	0	0.0	0	0.0
Writers of books for children	32	47.94	2.12	51.78	2.40	0	0.0	0	0.0
High school students	4,823	47.79	4.52	49.60	3.04	39	0.8	182	3.8
High school science fair delegates	148	47.63	7.03	50.38	4.96	3	2.0	0	0.0
Mathematicians	41	47.40	2.58	53.01	2.23	0	0.0	0	0.0
Creative writers	10	47.33	3.16	50.62	2.63	0	0.0	0	0.0
College counselors	42	47.31	2.47	53.32	2.07	0	0.0	0	0.0
Juvenile delinquents	55	47.27	3.29	47.89	3.21	0	0.0	0	0.0
Profile sheet norm sample	3,000	47.26	3.07	49.85	3.30	12	0.4	8	0.3
Law students	40	47.18	2.27	52.04	2.82	0	0.0	0	0.0
Premedical students	48	47.09	2.34	51.69	2.86	0	0.0	0	0.0
Architecture students	55	47.06	2.18	50.82	2.95	0	0.0	0	0.0
University clerical personnel	56	47.00	2.62	52.84	2.75	0	0.0	0	0.0
Psychology graduate students	405	46.94	2.40	53.08	2.43	0	0.0	1	0.2
Pharmacy students	277	46.93	2.56	51.90	3.01	1	0.4	1	0.4
Nursing students	250	46.81	2.40	51.42	2.48	0	0.0	1	0.4
College students	4,126	46.71	2.41	51.61	2.74	3	0.1	6	0.1
Social welfare graduate students	446	46.69	2.13	53.42	2.56	0	0.0	0	0.0
San Francisco area residents	261	46.60	2.55	50.85	2.78	1	0.4	0	0.0
Home economics students	176	46.58	2.12	52.77	2.87	0	0.0	0	0.0
Rajneeshpuram residents	34	46.58	2.60	52.39	2.31	0	0.0	0	0.0
Medical students	90	46.56	2.53	53.78	2.51	0	0.0	0	0.0
Education students	310	46.53	1.84	53.49	2.66	0	0.0	0	0.0
Secondary school teachers	21	46.49	2.04	53.44	2.31	0	0.0	0	0.0
Registered nurses	100	46.08	2.47	51.57	2.66	0	0.0	1	1.0
Police officer applicants	200	46.02	2.16	54.13	2.71	1	0.5	1	0.5
Optometry students	50	45.95	1.85	54.14	2.55	0	0.0	0	0.0
MBA candidates	64	45.91	1.57	51.86	2.50	0	0.0	0	0.0
Counseling graduate students	275	45.76	1.86	52.20	2.70	0	0.0	0	0.0
Anesthesiologists	17	45.64	2.52	52.04	2.91	0	0.0	0	0.0

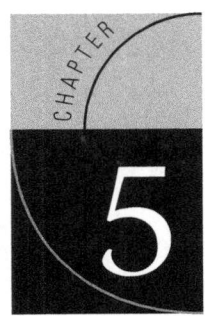

CHAPTER

5

Interpretation
of the Folk Scales

The Sources of Descriptive and Observational Data

The purpose of this chapter is to furnish information about each of the 20 folk scales that an interpreter can use to evolve a valid, perceptive, and coherent picture of individuals scoring high or low on each measure. Much of this information will come from the descriptions and ratings of observers, drawing on the same samples for each scale. For this reason, a single discussion of these samples at the beginning will avoid need to repeat this information as each new scale is considered. The basic intentions of each scale of the CPI, as previously stated, are to forecast what people will say and do in defined situations, and to identify people who will be described in consistent and meaningful terms by those who know them.

Some of the information about what people say and do will come from published reports showing how various criteria can be predicted from CPI measures. Another very useful source of information is found in the *act frequency* studies of Buss and Craik (1980, 1981, 1983a, 1983b, & 1986).

Specifically, for this manual, David Buss has kindly made available unpublished act frequency data for 89 couples. In each couple, the male was rated by his wife or partner, and the female was rated by her husband or partner, on a series of specific acts. The ratings were on an eight-step scale, going from no observations of the act within the last three months, to one occurrence in the same period, to two occurrences, and then on up through several times each week, and culminating in almost daily occurrence. The dummy weights of 0 to 8 were then correlated with each of the 20 CPI scales, in the subsamples of each sex and for the total sample. Because one of the men did not contribute a usable rating form for his wife, the Ns were 88 men, 89 women, and 177 total. For each CPI scale, the five acts with largest positive and the five with largest negative correlations will be reported.

Descriptive correlates for the scales come from items on the *Adjective Check List* (ACL), the *California Q-Set*, an unpublished *Life History Interviewer's Check List*, and an unpublished *Interpersonal Q-Sort*. The adjectival data are drawn from six different samples. The first consists of 236 men who were described on the 300-item ACL by their wives or partners, and the second of 236 women from the same dyads who were described by their husbands or partners. Each checked item was assigned a dummy weight of 1, and each unchecked item a weight of 0. Then the 300 items were correlated with the scales of the CPI. The third sample is composed of 194 college males who were rated on the ACL by three peers, using categories of very descriptive (+2), somewhat descriptive (+1), neutral or irrelevant (0), somewhat undescriptive (–1), and very undescriptive (–2). The ratings were composited for each panel, and then standardized within the fraternities from which the men came. The fourth sample was made up of 192 college females, each rated by three peers in the same way, and then the composites standardized within each sorority from which the subjects were obtained. The fifth sample was composed of 612 men assessed in intensive programs at the Institute of Personality Assessment and Research (IPAR) in Berkeley. A panel of 10 staff observers contributed ACLs for each assessee. Scores on any adjective could therefore range from 0 (unchecked by any member of the panel) to 10 (checked by every member of the panel). The sixth sample was comprised of 358 women studied in intensive assessments at IPAR, and also described on the ACE by panels of 10 observers.

For the *California Q-Set,* assessed samples of 547 men and 393 women were included. Each assessee was rated on the 100-item *Q-Set* by from five to eight judges working independently. Their Q-formulations were then composited and the items rearrayed into the frequencies specified by Jack Block (1961) for each of the nine categories of salience. These values of 9 (most salient) to 1 (least salient or characteristic) were then correlated with each CPI scale.

Data from the life history interviews were available for 504 men and 379 women. After the 90-minute life history interview, the interviewer completed a 99-item check list to describe the assessee's demeanor, speech, family background, adolescent experiences, and current activity. Checked items were given a dummy weight of 1, and items left blank were given a dummy weight of 0. These scores were then correlated with each of the CPI scales.

For the *Interpersonal Q-Sort* of 50 items, 200 men were rated by their wives or partners, and the 200 women were rated by their husbands or partners, on a five-step classification for salience. A third sample of 111 men assessed at IPAR was also included. Each assessee was rated on the Q-sort by three staff observers, drawing on information garnered over the course of the three-day assessment. The three independent Q-sorts were then summed for each assessee, and the items rearrayed into the designated frequencies for each step. The composite scores from 5 (most characteristic) down to 1 (least characteristic) were then correlated with the CPI scales.

A complete listing of ACL, *California Q-Set, Life History Interview* check list items, and *Interpersonal Q-Sort* correlations with scales of the CPI may be found in Appendices D, E, F, and G.

The Do (Dominance) Scale

The Do scale was constructed by analyzing a specially assembled pool of items against peer nominations (Gough, McClosky, & Meehl, 1951) in samples of 100 college and 124 high school students. For the nominators, the dominant person was described as being strong in face-to-face situations and as being able to influence others, to gain their automatic respect, and, if necessary, to control them. Dominant people were further described as having feelings of safety, security, personal rightness, and self-confidence. In addition to nominations of "most dominant" persons in each class or living group, nominations were gathered for those "least dominant." Least dominant persons were described as finding it hard to assert themselves and to stand up for their rights and opinions, and as prone to yield in encounters with more dominant people. Finally, raters were cautioned not to confuse autocratic or domineering dispositions with dominance, to stress actual behavior and not just desires or wishes to dominate, and to distinguish between purely titular or class position (such as personal wealth) and the trait of dominance.

In the initial study, there were 50 persons nominated for the high dominant subsample and also 50 for the low dominant, with 25 males and 25 females in each group. Sixty items were identified that differentiated between the high and low nominees,

32 coming from the specially written pool of items and 28 from the MMPI. Self-ratings were also obtained from all of the students on a graphic item scale. Nominations were scored by counting one point for each "high" nomination and subtracting one point for each "low." Correlations of the peer- and self-ratings were .44 in the high school sample and .42 in the college. In these original samples, the 60-item scale correlated .69 with the high school nominations for dominance, and .60 with the college nominations. Correlations with self-ratings were .56 and .52, respectively.

When the 480-item edition of the CPI was published in 1956, the Do scale was reduced to 46 items by dropping items that did not correlate well with ratings and other criteria of dominance in new samples. For the 462-item form of the CPI published in 1986, the Do scale was further reduced to 36 items, again by dropping items that showed weak or marginal correlations with ratings of dominance in new samples. In Form 434, Do also has 36 items, two of which are different from those in the Form 462 scoring. Correlation of the two 36-item versions of Do was .99 in the profile norm sample of 6,000 respondents.

Factor analysis of the interitem matrix for Do on the norm sample of 6,000 persons identified eight factors with eigen values of 1.00 or greater. For convenience, only the first four were retained and rotated via Kaiser's varimax method. Factor 1 was composed primarily of items describing one's self as a leader, as liking to talk before groups of people, and as having a talent for directing and controlling others. Factor 2 included items such as, "I find it hard to keep my mind on a task or job" ("false"), "I feel like giving up quickly when things to wrong" ("false"), and "I have more trouble concentrating than others seem to have" ("false"), suggestive of a strong sense of self-mastery. Factor 3 contained items such as: "I like to give orders and get things moving," "I think I would enjoy having authority over other people," and "I enjoy planning things and deciding what each person should do." Factor 4 had only two items, both stating that everyone has an obligation to take part in the activities of the group or nation, and to comply with the communal consensus. In toto, the scale has internal clusters indicating self-view as a leader and forceful person, a comfortable sense of

self-mastery, liking for positions of control and authority, and a conviction that everyone should participate in and support legitimate communal activities.

Evidence on what persons with higher and lower scores on Do say and do can be found in the act frequency analyses discussed above. The five acts with largest positive correlations for the 177 subjects were these: took charge of the group ($r = .33$), talked a great deal at the meeting ($r = .33$), had more to say than anyone else ($r = .32$), backed up someone who presented a good idea ($r = .32$), and learned everyone's name in the group ($r = .29$). Note that all of these acts pertain to or assume the existence of a group, and some kind of meeting. High Do people express their dominance via group effort, seek consensual goals, and try to influence others to help achieve those goals.

Not all scales for dominance or ascendancy have these same implications. For instance, in their study of dominance and prototypicality of acts, Buss and Craik (1980) examined the CPI Do scale along with the Dominance scale from the *Personality Research Form* (Jackson, 1967). Among those acts having significantly more association with the PRF than the CPI scale were the following: "I demanded that someone run an errand" (.17 vs. .38), "I chose to sit at the head of the table" (.14 vs. .35), and "I am looked up to by my acquaintances" (.14 vs. .28). Items more strongly associated with the CPI scale than the PRF scale included these: "I solicited funds for a cause in which I was interested" (.27 vs. .12), "I initiated a conversation with a stranger" (.26 vs. .14), and "I advocated an idea that was 'ahead of the times'" (.32 vs. .17). These and other differentiating acts suggest that the self-aggrandizing component of dominance is relatively strong in the PRF scale and relatively weak in the CPI measure.

Another theme in the list of acts associated with high scores on Do is a willingness to support others, and even to take a subordinate role if by so doing the goal-seeking activities of the group will be furthered. An ingenious series of experiments by E. I. Megargee and his colleagues (Fenelon & Megargee, 1971; Megargee, 1969; Megargee, Bogart, & Anderson, 1966) showed that in dyads composed of high-Do and low-Do participants, the high-Do member was perfectly willing to accept a subordinate role if the task for the dyad was to achieve a high productivity score. However, when the experiment was defined as an assessment for *leadership*, the high-Do member took the role of leader in almost every dyad. An exception to this finding occurred in dyads with a high-Do woman paired with a low-Do man. In the *leadership* condition, the high-Do women more or less directed the low-Do men to sit in the leader's chair, while the high-Do woman did the work for the team. There are many parallels to these experiments in everyday life. Vice presidents of many organizations, and of the nation itself, are often high-dominant persons who, for the time being, work diligently and conscientiously in a subordinate status. In fact, in situations where the goals of the endeavor appear to be consensual and worthy, high-dominant people are usually extremely effective followers. In regard to the experiment with men and women, social conventions typically call for the husband to drive the car, pay the check in restaurants, and carve the turkey at Thanksgiving, even if the wife would do a better job in each instance.

Another experiment (Gorecki, Dickson, & Ritzler, 1981) had 53 college women take part in eight role-playing scenes requiring assertive responses, after which they rated each other on a five-step scale for assertiveness. The sum of these 52 ratings for each student produced a criterion measure for assertiveness. Its correlation with the Do scale was .61 ($p < .01$). Another study (Gough, 1990) correlated scores on the Do scale with various criteria of leadership in 11 separate samples ranging in size from 164 to 1,014. The correlations for Do went from a low of .13 to a high of .42, with a median of .33.

The five acts with largest negative correlations with Do were these: "Spoke only when spoken to by someone else" ($r = -.29$), "Entered the conversation only when asked a question" ($r = -.19$), "Gave one-word answers to personal questions" ($r = -.19$), "Waited for the other person to choose a topic to discuss" ($r = -.18$), and "Became quiet when new people walked into the room" ($r = -.17$). All of these items refer to verbal behavior, and taken together show that high scorers on Do are not taciturn, unresponsive, or tongue-tied.

We turn now to descriptions associated with the Do scale, beginning with the ACL. Table 5.1 presents the 12 adjectives with largest positive and 12 with largest negative correlations with Do in the six samples indicated. High scorers on Do are seen by others as ambitious, assertive, energetic, outgoing, and

self-confident, and not as quiet, shy, timid, or withdrawn. The adjective *dominant* was significantly ($p < .01$) correlated with Do in four of the six samples, but only slightly above zero in the other two. The adjective *submissive,* at the other pole, was negatively correlated with Do in five of the six samples, but the coefficient was only −.10 in the sixth.

What would be the best small combination of adjectives from which to estimate scores on the Do scale? To answer this question, 200 of the 300 adjectives were chosen, eliminating all those with a very low frequency of endorsement by observers, and also those seldom if ever checked in self-appraisal. In the two peer samples (194 men, 192 women) the adjectival descriptions were already standardized to means of 50 and sigmas of 10. For the assessed samples of 612 men and 358 women in which descriptions of each person were obtained from 10 judges, the sums were standardized, by sex, to means of 50 and sigmas of 10. Pooling these samples produced a total of 1,356 persons (806 men, 550 women). In this sample of 1,356 persons, the ACL descriptions were then regressed onto the Do scale, terminating the analysis after eight steps so as to keep the number of adjectives small. The eight adjectives most strongly associated with the Do scale and their beta weights in the equation were the following: ambitious (.11), confident (.11), awkward (−.09), informal (−.09), mischievous (−.07), quiet (−.14), reserved (−.11), and shy (−.10). The multiple regression for these eight terms was .47 ($R^2 = .22$).

The four *California Q-Set* items having largest positive and four having largest negative correlations with Do in the samples of 547 assessed men and 393 assessed women were the following:

Behaves in an assertive fashion (.42 for men, .40 for women)

Has social poise and presence; appears socially at ease (.36 and .37)

Is a talkative individual (.32 and .34)

Tends to proffer advice (.34 and .29)

Reluctant to commit self to any definite course of action; tends to delay or avoid action (−.42, −.41)

Genuinely submissive; accepts domination comfortably (−.33, −.34)

Is self-defeating (−.33, −.34)

Is vulnerable to real or fancied threat, generally fearful (−.32, −.29)

Table 5.1 Adjectival Descriptions by Observers: 12 Most Salient Positive and 12 Most Salient Negative Correlates of the 36-Item Do Scale

Adjectives	Men, Described By			Women, Described By		
	Spouse (N = 236)	3 Peers (N = 194)	10 Staff Members (N = 612)	Spouse (N = 236)	3 Peers (N = 192)	10 Staff Members (N = 358)
Aggressive	.14*	.22**	.30**	.23**	.34**	.34**
Alert	.18**	.16*	.20**	.16*	.27**	.27**
Ambitious	.23**	.22**	.35**	.20**	.29**	.35**
Assertive	.22**	.16*	.35**	.36**	.37**	.40**
Confident	.17**	.23**	.28**	.24**	.41**	.41**
Dominant	.10	.25**	.28**	.04	.45**	.39**
Energetic	.19**	.21**	.31**	.15*	.25**	.29**
Enterprising	.11	.26**	.31**	.18**	.23**	.36**
Initiative	.16*	.11	.35**	.18**	.36**	.35**
Outgoing	.17**	.21**	.32**	.28**	.32**	.32**
Resourceful	.13*	.23**	.27**	.19**	.21**	.28**
Self-confident	.18**	.19**	.29**	.29**	.36**	.43**
Awkward	−.16*	−.16*	−.36**	−.17**	−.19**	−.29**
Cautious	−.14*	−.16*	−.38**	−.11	−.23**	−.28**
Mild	−.14*	−.15*	−.35**	−.21**	−.25**	.30**
Quiet	−.19**	−.19**	−.45**	−.21**	−.32**	−.39**
Retiring	−.09	−.14*	−.35**	−.18**	−.35**	−.31**
Shy	−.24**	−.24**	−.44**	−.28**	−.34**	−.39**
Silent	−.28**	−.23**	−.40**	−.14*	−.21**	−.29**
Simple	−.15*	−.13	−.25**	−.25**	−.16*	−.23**
Submissive	−.10	−.22**	−.27**	−.17**	−.31**	−.33**
Timid	−.13*	−.21**	−.34**	−.15*	−.32**	−.33**
Unambitious	−.19**	−.14*	−.29**	−.08	−.21**	−.27**
Wthdrawn	−.21**	−.18*	−.35**	−.15*	−.35**	−.27**

*$p \leq .05$, **$p \leq .01$

Observers of these 940 persons saw them as assertive, not at all submissive, poised, talkative, ready to initiate action and to give advice, and not as either self-defeating or vulnerable to threat.

From the interviewers' descriptions of 504 men and 379 women, the four items with largest positive and four with largest negative correlations with Do were these:

Unusually self-confident; feels able to meet nearly any situation (.27 for men, .24 for women)

Creates a good impression; has effective interpersonal techniques (.24 and .20)

Uses wide and varied vocabulary (.14 and .23)

Witty and animated, an interesting conversationalist (.16 and .26)

Is unsure of self, doubts own ability (−.22 and −.24)

Has many worries and problems (−.18 and −.20)

Reticent and taciturn (−.19 and −.14)

Has difficulty expressing ideas (−.16 and −.20)

High-Do interviewees impressed their interviewers as being self-confident, verbally fluent, and relatively free of worries and problems.

From the *Interpersonal Q-Sort* formulations for 200 couples and 111 assessees, the three items with largest positive and three with largest negative correlations with Do are given below. The first coefficient is for the 200 men as described by their wives or partners, the second is for the 200 women as described by their husbands or partners, and the third is for the 111 male assessees as described by three staff observers.

Is forceful and self-assured in manner (.22, .24, .43)

Enterprising and outgoing; enjoys social participation (.23, .23, .30)

Is an effective leader; able to elicit the responses and cooperation of others (.35, .28, .43)

Awkward and ill at ease socially; shy and inhibited with others (−.20, −.28, −.52)

Submissive; gives in easily; lacking in self-confidence (−.19,−.22, −.46)

Easily embarrassed; feels inferior and inadequate (−.16, −.25, −.40)

A summary of all of the above information may be attempted in these generalizations: Persons scoring high on Do can be expected to be self-confident, ambitious, assertive, talkative, task-centered, outgoing, enterprising, and persuasive. Their dominance is primarily prosocial, in that they exert influence on others in pursuit of worthy and consensual social goals, not merely for self-aggrandizement and ego-fulfillment. Others recognize their leadership abilities and are willing to accept advice and direction from them. Conversely, persons scoring low on Do tend to be reticent, self-doubting, submissive, unambitious, awkward in social situations, easily embarrassed, self-defeating, and worrying. Can high-Do talents for managing and persuading others be abused? From work with individuals, particularly in managerial positions, it does seem

that at very high scores (34–36 raw score totals), domineering and overly controlling behavior is a distinct possibility. This possibility is enhanced if certain other scores are low, for example Re and To. Excellent case illustrations of this point may be found in the books by McAllister (1996) and by Meyer and Davis (1992).

The Cs (Capacity for Status) Scale

The Cs scale was originally developed (Gough, 1948a, 1948b, 1949b) to identify persons who would view themselves as possessing high status, as worthy of high status, and as likely to be judged in the same way by others. The scale began in work with high school students, using various measures of family income, education, and housing as criteria against which to evaluate items. Later, criteria pertaining to upward and downward mobility (Pierce-Jones, 1961) and to aspects of status in adult groups were examined. This led to a reconceptualization of the scale as a measure of qualities of ambition, self-assurance, and optimism that underlie and lead to status, rather than as a measure of achieved or existent status.

In the 1956 Form 480 edition of the CPI, the Cs scale had 32 items. In the 1986 Form 462 edition, this was reduced to 28 items. In the present Form 434 edition, the Cs scale also has 28 items, two of which are different from those in Form 462. The correlations of Cs in Form 462 and Form 434 were .98 for both the male and female norm samples of 3,000 persons.

An interitem matrix was computed in the total norm sample of 6,000 and then factor analyzed. There were seven factors with eigen values greater than 1.00. Four of these were retained for rotation by means of Kaiser's normal varimax method. The first rotated factor contained items indicating poise and self-assurance in interpersonal situations, for example, "It is hard for me to find anything to talk about when I meet a new person" ("false"), and "I usually feel nervous and ill at ease at a formal dance or party" ("false"). The second cluster of items pertained to esthetic and cultural interests, for example, "I would like to hear a great singer in an opera" ("true"), and "I like to listen to symphony orchestra concerts on the radio" ("true"). An interesting additional item in Factor 2 is, "I would like to wear expensive clothes" ("true"). Factor 3 included items indicative of optimism and confidence in one's ability to cope with life's demands, for instance, "The future is too uncertain for a person to make serious plans" ("false"), and "I feel uneasy indoors" ("false"). The fourth factor included items recognizing advantages of status and success, for example, "In most ways a poor person is better off than a rich one" ("false"), and "I would rather be a steady and dependable worker than a brilliant but unstable one" ("false"). In their self-reports, persons with high scores on Cs express feelings of confidence and self-assurance, optimism concerning their present and future prospects, wide ranging interests, and a liking for the good things associated with money and position.

From the act frequency analyses, the five behaviors with largest positive and five with largest negative correlations with the Cs scale are listed below, based on the ratings of 177 persons by their spouses or partners.

Charmed a new acquaintance with clever conversation (.27)

Introduced self to the stranger at a party (.27)

Told a long story to entertain others (.28)

Made witty remarks at the party (.29)

Took the initiative in planning a party (.27)

Entered the conversation only when asked a question (–.19)

Met with someone secretly (–.17)

Let someone take out a loan in his or her name (–.16)

Took a class just because a friend did (–.15)

Waited to be introduced rather than initiating the introduction (–.16)

These acts portray high scorers on Cs as gregarious, talkative, forward, and witty. Low scorers on Cs are more likely to be reserved and diffident and to yield to the opinions or wishes of others.

Some of the data from Appendix A are helpful in interpreting scores on Cs. For example, college-going among high school graduates correlated .30 for 1,514 males and .31 for 1,799 females. In samples of 93 men and 111 women, Cs had correlations of .52 and .54 with the 16PF Factor H scale for venturesomeness and boldness, and of –.36 and –.47 with Factor O (apprehensive and insecure). In samples of 112 males and 122 females, Cs had correlations of .32 and .38 with the O (openness) factor scale of the NEO.

Table 5.2 presents the 12 adjectives with largest positive and the 12 with largest negative correlations with Cs in six samples in which descriptions by observers were analyzed. Persons with high scores on Cs tend to be seen as ambitious, ingenious, outgoing, self-confident, and sophisticated. Those with low scores tend to be seen as cautious, shy, silent, and withdrawn. In a combined sample of persons described by peers (N = 386) and by assessment staff (N = 970), a regression analysis was carried out on the 200 adjectives having more than occasional usage by the assessment staff. Adjectives were standardized to a mean of 50 and sigma of 10 within each subsample. In this total sample of 1,356 persons, the eight adjectives and their beta weights that gave the best approximation of scores on Cs, as either indicative or contraindicative, were these: ambitious (.17), relaxed (.12), and resourceful (.11) as indicative; and contented (–.11), interests narrow (–.12), shy (–.23), strong (–.12), and suspicious (–.07), as contraindicative. The multiple R was .41 (R^2 = .17).

The four *California Q-Set* items with largest positive and four with largest negative correlations with Cs in samples of 547 men and 393 women are reported below. Each assessee was described on the Q-sort by five or more judges, whose independent formulations were then assembled into a composite array, and weights of from 9 to 1 assigned according to the rated salience of each of the 100 items.

Genuinely values intellectual and cognitive matters (.21 for men, .29 for women)

Has a wide range of interests (.23 and .33)

Has high aspiration level for self (.29 and .30)

Has social poise and presence; appears socially at ease (.26 and .29)

Is uncomfortable with uncertainty and complexities (–.22 and –.31)

Gives up and withdraws where possible in the face of frustration and adversity (–.21 and –.31)

Is self-defeating (–.30 and –.28)

Feels cheated and victimized by life; self-pitying (–.21 and –.23)

Assessees with high scores on Cs are seen as socially poised, interested in many things, having high

Table 5.2   Adjectival Descriptions by Observers: 12 Most Salient Positive and 12 Most Salient Negative Correlates of the 28-Item Cs Scale

	Men, Described By			Women, Described By		
Adjectives	Spouse (*N* = 236)	3 Peers (*N* = 194)	10 Staff Members (*N* = 612)	Spouse (*N* = 236)	3 Peers (*N* = 192)	10 Staff Members (*N* = 358)
Ambitious	.15*	.25**	.28**	.22**	.15*	.28**
Enterprising	.08	.16*	.20**	.21**	.11	.27**
Ingenious	.19**	.05	.20**	.16*	.11	.17**
Initiative	.22**	.15*	.20**	.16*	.08	.25**
Insightful	.13*	.10	.16**	.21**	.13	.20**
Intelligent	.15*	.12	.17**	.07	.18*	.22**
Interests wide	.15*	.08	.21**	.25**	.18*	.27**
Outgoing	.12	.15*	.17**	.29**	.16*	.25**
Resourceful	.09	.17*	.21**	.22**	.09	.25**
Self-confident	.10	.16*	.19**	.16*	.15*	.33**
Sophisticated	.13*	.12	.15**	.23**	.08	.23**
Talkative	.08	.13	.18**	.19**	.12	.20**
Awkward	−.18**	−.14*	−.25**	−.05	−.18*	−.23**
Cautious	−.13*	−.18*	−.23**	−.15*	−.19**	−.27**
Interests narrow	−.16*	−.14*	−.28**	−.31**	−.15*	−.33**
Meek	−.14*	−.09	−.26**	−.03	−.29**	−.27**
Quiet	−.13*	−.12	−.25**	−.26**	−.17*	−.29**
Reserved	−.11	−.08	−.22**	−.17**	−.18*	−.22**
Shy	−.26**	−.22**	−.33**	−.24**	−.27**	−.36**
Silent	−.20**	−.20**	−.29**	−.14*	−.13	−.26**
Simple	−.16*	−.10	−.29**	−.14*	−.13	−.26**
Timid	−.08	−.10	−.29**	−.23**	−.18*	−.30**
Unambitious	−.11	−.09	−.24**	−.07	−.13	−.27**
Withdrawn	−.18**	−.14*	−.31**	−.10	−.24**	−.22**

*$p \leq .05$, **$p \leq .01$

aspirations, and valuing intellectual matters. Those with low scores on Cs are seen as self-defeating, self-pitying, uncomfortable in dealing with ambiguity, and as likely to give up when unsuccessful.

From analyses of the descriptions of assessees by interviewers on the 99-item check list, the four items with largest positive and four with largest negative correlations have been selected for presentation below. For each item, the correlations with Cs for the 504 men and 379 women are also cited, in that order.

Witty and animated, an interesting conversationalist (.18 and .26)

Was an honor student in high school (.19 and .29)

Unusually self-confident, feels able to meet near-ly any situation (.20 and .18)

Creates a good impression; has effective interper-sonal techniques (.19 and .28)

Awkward and clumsy in movement (−.19 and −.12)

Slow rate of movement (−.13 and −.23)

Has difficulty in expressing ideas (−.16 and −.22)

Makes mistakes in grammar and/or word usage (−.19 and −.18)

One can visualize persons with higher or lower scores on Cs in the interview situation. Those with high scores are alert, witty, animated, sure that they are making a good impression, and able to report good things about their lives to date. Those with low scores are awkward, bumbling, unprepossessing, and unskilled in their use of language.

Correlations for Cs with the 50 items in the *Interpersonal Q-Sort* were available for 200 men described by their wives or partners, 200 women described by their husbands or partners, and 111 assessees each described by a panel of three assess-ment staff observers. The three items with largest positive and three with largest negative correla-tions have been chosen for citation below, along with the three correlations for the three samples just described.

Enterprising and outgoing; enjoys social participa-tion (.17, .18, .36)

Independent, intelligent, and self-reliant; values achievement (.19, .23, .21)

Verbally fluent; expresses self easily and with clarity (.26, .30, .36)

Dull, lacking in ability and understanding (−.13, −.17, −.27)

Unambitious; commonplace and conventional in thinking and behavior (−.09, −.36, −.31)

Awkward and ill at ease socially; shy and inhib-ited with others (−.20, −.32, −.40)

In summary, high scores on Cs connote attributes such as poise, self-confidence, verbal fluency, wit, ambition, breadth of interests, and feelings of optimism about the pleasures and rewards that life will bring. At very high scores (raw scores of 26–28) elements of self-satisfaction, feelings of entitlement,

and a sort of bemused indifference to bourgeois con-ventions become apparent, occasionally to the point of Kohlbergian (Kohlberg, 1981) morality gone awry ("If I feel justified in doing it, it's ethical"). Low scores connote feelings of inadequacy, difficulty in coping with complex social situations, poor verbal skills, and a tendency to give up in the face of set-backs or adversity.

The Sy (Sociability) Scale

When first developed (Gough, 1952b), this scale was called *social participation* because its criterion was the number of different activities in which individu-als engaged. Its psychological purpose, of course, was to identify people of outgoing, participative temperament, who seek out and enjoy social encounters. In Form 480 of the CPI, the scale had 36 items. In Form 462, it was reduced to 32 items. In Form 434, it also has 32 items, with one item sub-stituted for an item dropped from the prior version. Correlation between Sy in Form 462 and Form 434 is .99 for both norm samples of 3,000 men and 3,000 women.

Factor analysis of the interitem matrix for Sy on the 6,000 norm subjects resulted in eight factors with eigen values of 1.00 or greater. Four were retained and rotated by means of Kaiser's normal varimax method. The first rotated factor had 15 items, most of them indicating comfort and assur-ance in social situations, for example, "It is hard for me to act natural when I am with new people" ("false"), "When in a group I have trouble thinking of the right things to talk about" ("false"), and "I am a good mixer" ("true"). The second factor of four items stressed enjoyment of social functions, for example, "I enjoy social gatherings just to be with people" ("true"), and "I love to go to dances" ("true"). Factor 3 had six items pertaining to self-confidence, for instance, "I seem to be about as capable and smart as most others around me" ("true"), and "If given the chance I would make a good leader of people" ("true"). Factor 4 had seven items suggesting a liking for attention from others, for example, "A person needs to 'show off' a little now and then" ("true"), and "I like to be the center of attention" ("true").

From the act frequency data pool in which 177 persons were rated by their spouses or partners for frequency of specific behaviors during the prior three months, the five acts with largest positive and five with largest negative correlations with Sy are cited below, along with the coefficients for each act.

Talked to almost everyone at the party (.39)

Took the lead in livening up a dull party (.36)

Became the center of attention at the gathering (.32)

Urged the group to go out for the evening (.29)

Took the initiative in planning the party (.29)

Stayed at home to watch TV rather than attend the party (−.24)

Spoke only when spoken to by someone else (−.26)

Said "I don't know" when he or she did not want to answer the question (−.26)

Spent the whole day alone without speaking to anyone (−.21)

Gave one-word answers to personal questions (−.25)

Persons with high scores on Sy plan for, attend, and enjoy parties and get-togethers. If things are not going well, they take the initiative in enlivening the proceedings and readily become the center of attention. Those with low scores prefer to stay home, respond minimally when spoken to, and sometimes spend an entire day alone without speaking to anyone. All of these acts seem to be relevant to the concept of *sociability*.

Table 5.3 presents the 24 adjectives with largest correlations with Sy in six different samples where observers' descriptions were available. One of the obvious themes associated with high scores on Sy is sociability itself, including specifics such as outgoing, enterprising, enthusiastic and talkative. Another cluster suggests confidence and optimism. The start-up inclinations visible in the act frequency data appear again in the adjectives adventurous and initiative.

Adjectives more descriptive of those with low scores on Sy include cautious, inhibited, reserved, shy, silent, and timid. Limited interests and lack of ambition are also mentioned.

Regression analysis of the 200 most frequently checked adjectives in a sample of 1,356 persons described by observers gave rise to an eight-term cluster which had a multiple correlation of .43 with

Sy (R^2 = .18). The adjectives with positive beta weights were ambitious, opportunistic, and sociable. Those with negative beta weights were complicated, frank, interests narrow, painstaking, and shy. The terms ambitious and opportunistic are interesting in regard to work and moving ahead on the job.

In a doctoral thesis at the American Telephone and Telegraph Company, Jacobs (1992) followed the progress of 229 persons hired in the managerial development program. The CPI was among the tests administered at the time of hiring, and the criterion studied was promotion or nonpromotion to middle management seven or more years later. Among the CPI scales, Sy had the largest correlation with the dichotomous criterion, with coefficients of .33 for the 126 men and .31 for the 103 women. In the AT&T corporate culture, the qualities associated with high scores on the Sy scale are conducive to good managerial performance and to promotion.

Findings are next presented from *California Q-Set* descriptions of 547 men and 393 women, each described by panels of five or more observers whose independent evaluations were consolidated into an overall composite. The 100 *Q-Set* items were then correlated with the Sy scale. The four items with largest positive and the four with largest negative correlations are given below, along with the correlations for each item.

Is a talkative individual (.27 for men, .32 for women)

Initiates humor (.26 and .28)

Emphasizes being with others; gregarious (.32 and .35)

Has social poise and presence; appears socially at ease (.30 and .35)

Reluctant to commit self to any definite course of action; tends to delay or avoid action (−.23 and −.29)

Keeps people at a distance; avoids close interpersonal relationships (−.31 and −.29)

Is self-defeating (−.32 and −.31)

Tends to ruminate and have persistent, preoccupying thoughts (−.25 and −.30)

Persons with high scores on Sy are described as gregarious, talkative, and poised, and as initiating humor. Those with low scores tend to be seen as self-defeating, ruminative, reluctant to take

Table 5.3 Adjectival Descriptions by Observers: 12 Most Salient Positive and 12 Most Salient Negative Correlates of the 32-Item Sy Scale

Adjectives	Men, Described By			Women, Described By		
	Spouse (N = 236)	3 Peers (N = 194)	10 Staff Members (N = 612)	Spouse (N = 236)	3 Peers (N = 192)	10 Staff Members (N = 358)
Active	.03	.22**	.21**	.15*	.28**	.28**
Adventurous	.12	.08	.14**	.15*	.21**	.25**
Ambitious	.12	.25**	.24**	.22**	.21**	.23**
Energetic	.11	.12	.23**	.12	.34**	.29**
Enterprising	.08	.16*	.21**	.20**	.21**	.30**
Enthusiastic	.22**	.09	.13**	.17**	.24**	.31**
Initiative	.08	.14*	.22**	.13*	.21**	.27**
Optimistic	.16*	.13	.15**	.13*	.22**	.28**
Outgoing	.27**	.29**	.27**	.30**	.36**	.34**
Self-confident	.15*	.23**	.23**	.19**	.28**	.33**
Sociable	.21**	.33**	.24**	.17**	.28**	.31**
Talkative	.24**	.18*	.21**	.23**	.25**	.31**
Cautious	−.21**	−.17*	−.23**	−.19**	−.26**	−.25**
Inhibited	−.18**	−.11	−.27**	−.20**	−.28**	−.27**
Interests narrow	−.10	−.24**	−.15**	−.25**	−.14*	−.22**
Modest	−.10	−.13	−.21**	−.17**	−.22**	−.27**
Quiet	−.19**	−.22**	−.29**	−.27**	−.33**	−.33**
Reserved	−.24**	−.18*	−.30**	−.27**	−.30**	−.31**
Retiring	−.03	−.13	−.29**	−.13*	−.38**	−.32**
Shy	−.28**	−.23**	−.34**	−.27**	−.37**	−.30**
Silent	−.25**	−.30**	−.30**	−.15*	−.24**	−.29**
Timid	−.10	−.19**	−.22**	−.10	−.34**	−.26**
Unambitious	−.12	−.17*	−.21**	−.16*	−.16*	−.15**
Unexcitable	−.17**	−.18*	−.18**	−.05	−.22**	−.14**

$*p \leq .05, **p \leq .01$

a stand, and as avoidant of close interpersonal relationships.

From the interviewers' descriptions of 504 men and 379 women seen in life history interviews, the four items with largest positive and four with largest negative correlations with Sy from the 99 on the check list are presented below, along with the coefficients for each sex.

Witty and animated, an interesting conversationalist (.15 for men and .29 for women)

Has an alert, "open" face (.11 and .18)

Creates a good impression; has effective interpersonal techniques (.18 and .24)

Seems relatively free of neurotic trends, conflicts, and other forms of instability (.11 and .18)

Reticent and taciturn (–.10 and –.20)

Was nervous and ill at ease during the interview (–.13 and –.11)

Has many worries and problems (–.17 and –.23)

Is unsure of self, doubts own ability (–.14 and –.17)

Those with high scores on Sy are animated and responsive in the interview, make a good impression, and appear to be relatively free of neurotic concerns and worries. Persons with low scores are reticent, unsure of themselves, ill at ease in the interview, and report many worries and problems.

From the 50-item *Interpersonal Q-Sort* used by raters in three different samples, the three items with largest positive and three with largest negative correlations with Sy are reported below. Correlations, in order, are for the 200 men described by their wives or partners, the 200 women described by their husbands or partners, and 111 male assessees each described by three staff observers.

Ambitious, likely to succeed in most things undertaken (.38, .30, .41)

Enterprising and outgoing; enjoys social participation (.14, .15, .29)

Is an effective leader; able to elicit the responses and cooperation of others (.16, .20, .21)

Awkward and ill at ease socially; shy and inhibited with others (–.31, –.27, –.43)

Unassuming, inhibited, and inattentive; bland and colorless in behavior (–.12, –.21, –.39)

Easily embarrassed; feels inferior and inadequate (–.15, –.19, –.36)

Once again, high scorers on Sy appear to others to be outgoing, ambitious, and effective in leadership. Low scorers seem awkward, ill at ease, somewhat bland, and easily embarrassed.

In summary, elevated scores on Sy are indicative of a sort of convivial sociability, a liking for activities involving other people, talkativeness, and enterprise. Those who score high are also likely to be ambitious, to do well at work and elsewhere where interaction with others is important, and to be relatively free of self-doubt, neurotic preoccupations, and self-defeating tendencies. These implications appear to hold even at very high scores on the scale. That is, there does not seem to be any point at which sociability and the need for interaction with others becomes

excessive, or demanding, or neuroticized. Those who score below average on Sy tend to be shy, reticent, ruminative, unsure of themselves, narrow in interests, and ill at ease in most if not all social situations.

The Sp (Social Presence) Scale

The Sp scale is the fourth in the first sector of scales on the profile sheet, containing measures of poise, self-assurance, and interpersonal styles. The seven scales in this sector may, in fact, be viewed as facets or themes within the general domain of interpersonal effectiveness. The special focus of Sp is on spontaneity, sprightliness, versatility, and an engaging social manner. No systematic account of the development of Sp has as yet been published, so important details should be reported here. In the first version of the CPI profile sheet, there were only three scales to assess facets within the interpersonal sector, namely Do, Cs, and Sy. As soon as the inventory began to be used in studies of individuals, it became apparent that additional facets in this realm were needed. When Form 480 was published, Sector 1 of the profile sheet was augmented to five measures by the addition of Sp and Sa (Self-acceptance).

Sp was developed by internal consistency methods. An initial cluster of CPI items suggestive of the attributes just cited, and also of vigorous self-confidence in social settings, was assembled, and then each item was correlated with total score on the cluster for men and women separately. Items with low or marginal correlations for either sex were dropped and the process repeated. When Form 480 was published in 1956, the Sp scale had 56 items. In preparation for Form 462, published in 1986, the 56 items were analyzed for both internal relationships to total score, and to nontest criteria such as assessment staff ratings of social presence and of social poise and assurance. These analyses led to the dropping of 18 items, and the introduction of a 38-item version of Sp. In its current Form 434 scoring, Sp also has 38 items, two of which are different from those in the prior version. Correlations of the two scales were .98 for both men and women in the norm samples.

Factor analysis of the 38 items in Sp in the sample of 6,000 persons constituting most recent norms identified 10 subsets with eigen values of 1.00 or greater. The first four were retained for rotation by Kaiser's normal varimax method. The first rotated factor had 18 items centering primarily on self-confidence and self-assurance, for example, "I seem to be about as capable and smart as most others around me" ("true"), "I am certainly lacking in self-confidence" ("false"), and "I usually feel nervous and ill at ease at a formal dance or party" ("false"). Factor 2 had 10 items, centering on self-assertion and a liking for attention. Examples are "I am apt to show off in some way if I get the chance" ("true"), "I like to be the center of attention" ("true"), and "Sometimes I rather enjoy going against the rules and doing things I'm not supposed to do" ("true"). Factor 3 had eight items pertaining to pleasure-seeking and a zest for new experience, for instance, "I always follow the rule: business before pleasure" ("false"), "I can't really enjoy a rest or vacation unless I have earned it by some hard work" ("false"), and "It bothers me when something unexpected interrupts my daily routine" ("false"). Factor 4 had only two items, "I like to go to parties and other affairs where there is lots of loud fun" ("true"), and "I like large, noisy parties" ("true").

Appendix B presents normative data for 52 male and 42 female samples; the four with highest means on Sp and the four with lowest means for each gender are these:

Female Samples	M
Rajneeshpuram residents	29.00
Education majors	28.06
MBA candidates	28.00
Anesthesiologists	28.00
Faking bad	15.54
Psychiatric patients	19.47
Prison inmates	21.06
High school students nominated as disciplinary problems	22.39

Male Samples	M
Rajneeshpuram residents	29.24
Psychology graduate students	29.05
MBA candidates	29.03
Premedical students	28.91
Faking bad	15.30
Psychiatric patients	20.56
Members of club for inventors	22.79
Training school inmates	23.36

Lowest scores for both men and women were obtained by persons asked to "fake bad" on the inventory. For women, the other three lowest samples were all designated as having some kind of difficulty in adjustment. For men, two of the other three lowest samples also were characterized by problems in adjustment. The remaining male sample was composed of 14 persons who got together on weekends to talk about "inventions." Informal observation suggested that they were somewhat reclusive and felt themselves to be marginal in the general culture. Highest-scoring samples included Rajneeshpuram residents and MBA candidates for both sexes, plus college majors in education and medical anesthesiologists for women, and psychology graduate students and premedical majors for men. Among the high-scoring samples, one discernible theme is the capacity for independent decision–making, along with a willingness to take stands at variance with normative conventions. Another theme is an interest in ideas and in cognitive pursuits.

Several correlations of the Sp scale with other tests, as shown in Appendix C, may be mentioned here. For 55 men and 51 women, the coefficient with Comrey's Emotional Stability scale were .46 and .44, respectively, and .71 and .57 with Comrey's scale for Extraversion. Sp also correlated .56 and .58 with the NEO Extraversion scale, and .68 and .50 with the *Maudsley Personality Inventory* Extraversion scales. Nonintellectual Disposition on the *Omnibus Personality Inventory* correlated –.45 with Sp for men, and –.51 for women. On Jackson's *Personality Research Form*, the scale for Exhibition correlated .49 with Sp for men and .67 for women. On Millon's *Clinical Multiaxial Inventory*, the scale for Histrionic Personality had correlations with Sp of .60 for men and .69 for women. Finally, on Zuckerman's *Sensation Seeking Scale*, total score correlated with Sp at .64 for men and .60 for women. There is a pattern in these correlations of a kind of exuberant, self-indulgent, adventurous seeking of pleasure.

Specific acts associated with the Sp scale are cited below, taken from an analysis of interspousal ratings for frequency in a sample of 177 persons (88 males, 89 females). Correlations of the acts with Sp are also given. The five acts with largest positive correlations come first, followed by the five acts with largest negative correlations.

Talked to many people at the party (.44)

Talked to almost everyone at the party (.38)

Danced at the party (.35)

Took the lead in livening up a dull party (.34)

Told a joke to lighten up a tense situation (.31)

Spoke only when spoken to (–.18)

Followed a religious counselor's instructions without question (–.21)

Walked with face to the ground (–.16)

Stayed at home all day long (–.16)

Walked into the party with head down (–.16)

Four of the five positive acts occurred in party settings, and three other acts took place in interactive situations. Persons with high scores on Sp enjoy entertainments and festivities and take an active part in such affairs. They also use their wit to move things along and to overcome tensions. Those with low scores on Sp avoid doing things that seem self-assertive and comply willingly with instructions from a religious counselor.

Table 5.4 gives the 12 adjectives with largest positive and 12 with largest negative correlations with Sp in six samples in which those taking the CPI were described by observers. One cluster of words pertains to cleverness, humor, and breadth of interest. Another is indicative of self-confidence and poise. A third refers to spontaneity and versatility. High scorers on Sp are expressive, talk easily, seek pleasure, and are interested in many things.

Low scorers on Sp impress others as dull, inhibited, narrow in interests, cautious, and conservative. They do not say very much, tend toward meekness, and are apt to withdraw from social encounters.

In a combined sample of 1,356 persons described by observers on the ACL, a regression analysis was carried out to estimate scores on Sp from the 200 most frequently used adjectives. Adjectival descriptions were standardized within the component samples of 194 college males, 192 college females, 612 assessed males, and 358 assessed females. The multiple correlation between the eight-adjective cluser and Sp was .41 (R^2 = .17). The program was arbitrarily terminated after eight steps. Adjectives with positive beta weights were energetic, self-confident, and versatile; those with negative weights were complicated, forceful, interests narrow, painstaking, and shy.

From the *California Q-Set,* the four items with largest positive and four with largest negative correlations in samples of 547 men and 393 women described by panels of five or more observers are listed below.

Has social poise and presence; appears socially at ease (.29 for men and .29 for women)

Is skilled in social techniques of imaginative play, pretending and humor (.25 and .26)

Initiates humor (.25 and .24)

Tends to perceive many different contexts in sexual terms; eroticizes situations (.25 and .24)

Tends toward overcontrol of needs and impulses; binds tensions excessively; delays gratification unnecessarily (–.26 and –.29)

Is self-defeating (–.24 and –.30)

Genuinely submissive; accepts domination comfortably (–.23 and –.24)

Has a readiness to feel guilty (–.22 and –.26)

A new theme in the Q-Sort items is the tendency of high scorers to perceive sexual implications in many contexts, and apparently to respond to such implications with minimal feelings of guilt. High scores connote social poise, effective use of humor, and a capacity for imaginative play. Low scorers seem to be overcontrolled, self-defeating, and submissive. From case studies of individuals, it appears that the wit and humor of high scorers is often used aggressively, that is to attack and disparage others when the high scorer is annoyed or frustrated by their behavior.

Characteristics associated with Sp in the descriptions of 504 men and 379 women by their life history interviewers are indicated in the list below of four items with largest positive and four with largest negative correlations.

Witty and animated, an interesting conversationalist (.15 for men and .27 for women)

Unusually self-confident; seems able to meet nearly any situation (.23 and .17)

Creates a good impression; has effective interpersonal techniques (.15 and .18)

Seems relatively free of neurotic trends, conflicts, and other forms of instability (.14 and .23)

Has many worries and problems (–.20 and –.26)

Was nervous and ill at ease during the interview (–.15 and –.14)

Table 5.4   Adjectival Descriptions by Observers: 12 Most Salient Positive and 12 Most Salient Negative Correlates of the 38-Item Sp Scale

Adjectives	Men, Described By			Women, Described By		
	Spouse (N = 236)	3 Peers (N = 194)	10 Staff Members (N = 612)	Spouse (N = 236)	3 Peers (N = 192)	10 Staff Members (N = 358)
Adventurous	.17**	.14*	.24**	.20**	.31**	.25**
Clever	.09	.21**	.24**	.19**	.18*	.14**
Humorous	.08	.21**	.19**	.24**	.25**	.19**
Interests wide	.12	.19**	.16**	.22**	.22**	.21**
Optimistic	.16*	.17*	.18**	.13*	.17*	.22**
Outgoing	.24**	.22**	.26**	.32**	.35**	.26**
Pleasure-seeking	.17**	.20**	.26**	.19**	.20**	.22**
Self-confident	.17**	.26**	.28**	.24**	.28**	.30**
Sociable	.15*	.32**	.24**	.20**	.30**	.22**
Spontaneous	.12	.12	.24**	.29**	.36**	.19**
Talkative	.23**	.22**	.26**	.22**	.26**	.24**
Versatile	.12	.22**	.28**	.12	.33**	.24**
Cautious	−.15*	−.18*	−.23**	−.17**	−.36**	−.24**
Conservative	−.14*	−.04	−.16**	−.28**	−.18*	−.23**
Dull	−.08	−.15*	−.20 **	−.13*	−.25**	−.11*
Inhibited	−.22**	−.14*	−.28**	−.15*	−.29**	−.27**
Interests narrow	−.15*	−.24**	−.17**	−.29**	−.16*	−.28**
Meek	−.05	−.19**	−.27**	−.13*	−.26**	−.19**
Quiet	−.18**	−.18*	−.25**	−.25**	−.30**	−.29**
Reserved	−.22**	−.11	−.24**	−.30**	−.35**	−.21**
Shy	−.19**	−.27**	−.27**	−.26**	−.37**	−.25**
Silent	−.24**	−.26**	−.22**	−.19**	−.27**	−.22**
Timid	−.03	−.16*	−.25**	−.14*	−.33**	−.22**
Withdrawn	−.18**	−.19**	−.28**	−.17**	−.39**	−.23**

*$p \leq .05$, **$p \leq .01$

Is unsure of self, doubts own ability (−.17 and −.22)

Has strong religious beliefs (−.17 and −.27)

High scorers on Sp seem to be relatively free of neurotic concerns, whereas low scorers report many worries and problems. High scorers are unusually self-confident, whereas low scorers feel unsure and doubt their own ability. High scorers make a good impression on the interviewers, whereas low scorers were nervous and ill at ease. High scorers were witty and animated and talked in an interesting way. Low scorers spoke of their strong religious beliefs.

From the *Interpersonal Q-Sort*, the three items with largest positive and three with largest negative correlations with Sp in a sample of 200 men described by their wives or partners, of 200 women described by their husbands or partners, and 111 men described by three assessment observers are listed below.

Enterprising and outgoing; enjoys social participation (.31, .28, .40)

Clever and imaginative a spontaneous and entertaining person (.18, .19, .31)

Verbally fluent; expresses self easily and with clarity (.17, .26, .26)

Dull; lacking in ability and understanding (–.19, –.19, –.19)

Awkward and ill at ease socially; shy and inhibited with others (–.20, –.35, –.40)

Wedded to routine; made anxious by change and uncertainty (–.19, –.24, –.19)

In summary, persons with high scores on Sp tend to be talkative, clever, spontaneous, pleasure-seeking, self-indulgent, hedonistic, willful, imaginative, self-assured, and independent. Those with low scores tend to be inhibited, ill at ease in many social situations, worrying, self-defeating, submissive, withdrawn, and prone to feelings of guilt and self-blame.

The Sa (Self-acceptance) Scale

The Sa scale was initially developed to assess feelings of personal worth, accomplishment, and self-esteem. Internal consistency technique was employed, beginning with a list of items that appeared to be relevant to these criteria, and then by examining their intercorrelations and correlations with a total scored based on the full set of items to choose those that were best aligned with the starting concept. In the 1956 Form 480 version of the CPI, the Sa scale had 34 items. In the 1986 Form 462 version the scale was shortened to 28 items by dropping four items that had weak relationships to external or nontest criteria of the concept. In the present Form 434 edition of the CPI, the Sa scale also contains 28 items, of which three are different from those in Form 462. This change was necessary because of the 28 items deleted from Form 462. For the two profile norm samples for Form 434, correlations of the present and prior versions of the Sa scale were .96 for both men and women.

Factor analysis of the 28 items in the norm sample of 6,000 persons identified seven factors with eigen values of 1.00 or greater. The first four were retained for rotation by means of Kaiser's normal varimax method. The first factor of 10 items centered on feelings of comfort and confidence in dealing with others, for example, "It is hard for me to find anything to talk about when I meet a new person" ("false"), "It is hard for me to start a conversation with strangers" ("false"), and "It is hard for me to act natural when I am with new people" ("false"). The second factor of eight items dealt with willingness to admit to self-serving and self-centered behavior, for example, "Sometimes I rather enjoy going against the rules and doing things I'm not supposed to do" ("true"), and "I must admit I often do as little work as I can get by with" ("true"). The third factor contained six items indicating positive self-evaluation, for instance, "I was a slow learner in school" ("false"), and "I have a natural talent for influencing people" ("true"). The fourth factor of four items suggested an interest in adventurous and even unconventional experiences, for example, "I would like to see a bullfight in Spain" ("true"), and "I would disapprove of anyone's drinking to the point of intoxication at a party" ("false").

One of the questions often asked about the Sa scale is whether the self-esteem associated with high scores is reciprocated by positive reactions of others. An early study by Hogan and Mankin (1970) had 34 male college students take part in six 75-minute meetings attended each time by four or five of the men. Each person rated the other 33 on a seven-point scale of general likability; these ratings were accumulated and averaged for each of the 34 men, and then correlated with the scales of the CPI. The coefficient for the Sa scale was .32, but after two men for whom the likability ratings were very discrepant were dropped from the analysis, the coefficient rose to .53. From this study, it does appear that among college men, scores on Sa are positively associated with perceived likability.

Another question is whether self-acceptance as measured by the scale is associated with self-evaluations of physical attractiveness. In a study of 455 college students (Montgomery & Mathis, 1992), including 311 male and 144 female students, self-ratings of own physical attractiveness were obtained, using a 10-point scale. Scores on Sa correlated .22 ($p < .01$) with self-ratings of physical attractiveness.

A third study to be mentioned here is a little farther afield from the primary focus of the Sa scale, but does pertain to an expected implication of the scale to show satisfying adaptations to the demands of daily living. The study (Taub & Hawkins, 1979) compared 18 college males with regular sleep habits versus 18 with irregular sleep records. Those with irregular sleep had no usual time for going to bed, no usual time for waking up, and widely fluctuating amounts of sleep each night. They did not, however, have complaints of disturbed or troubled sleep. The regular sleepers went to bed about the same time each day, awakened at about the same time, and seldom had less than seven hours of sleep. Standard scores were used in the analysis, which when converted to raw score equivalents for the 28-item Sa scale showed a mean of 21.55 for the regular sleepers and of 16.42 for those with irregular sleeping patterns. This difference of 5.13 is highly significant ($p < .01$), and can be represented by a point-biserial correlation of .64. One way to describe these findings is to say that people high on Sa manage their psychological housekeeping in an efficient way, so as to leave time, energy, and affect available for more rewarding and ego-enhancing pursuits.

From Appendix B in which norm data for 52 male and 42 female samples are given, the four samples for each sex with highest Sa means and lowest means are cited below:

Female Samples	M
MBA candidates	20.02
Premedical students	19.67
Commercial writers	19.58
Law school students	19.17
Faking bad	11.14
Psychiatric patients	14.39
High school students	14.95
Prison inmates	15.05

Male Samples	M
Counseling psychology students	20.07
MBA students	19.92
Premedical students	19.89
Parole and probation officers	19.78
Faking bad	12.48
Psychiatric patients	14.39
High school students	15.21
High school disciplinary problems	15.28

For women, three of the four highest-scoring samples were students in preparation for relatively prestigious professions, and the fourth was a small sample of women writing for advertising firms, magazines, and the news media. Three of the lowest-scoring samples were composed of women in difficult situations, or faking a self-defeating and unhappy individual. The other sample was composed of high school students in general, a finding that suggests the kind of ambivalence, self-doubt, and identity problems that beset young people at this stage of their lives.

Three of the four highest-scoring male samples also consisted of students in training for professional careers. Their lives, at this stage, are on-track and aimed for rewarding careers. The fourth sample was a small group of federal parole and probation officers. A common stereotype of persons in this occupation has elements of authoritarian attitudes, personal rigidity, and poor tolerance of frustration. Their high score on the Sa scale, however, suggests contrary themes, such as a therapeutic rather than punitive stance toward their clients, and feelings of personal fulfillment in their work. At the low end of the Sa scale for men were samples asked to fake bad, a cross-section of psychiatric patients, high school students in general, and high school students nominated by their principals as disciplinary problems.

From Appendix C, in which correlations of CPI scales with those from a variety of other inventories are presented, a selection has been made of measures having strong relationships to Sa for both men and women. In the list to follow, the correlation for men is given first, followed by the correlation for women. A first cluster of scales centers on Extraversion and Sociability, for example, Extraversion from the Comrey Personality Scales (.51, .61), Extraversion from the NEO-AC (.45, .62), Extraversion from the *Maudsley Personality Inventory* (.55, .47), and Social Introversion from the MMPI (−.63, −.69). A liking for attention and for being ascendant is visible in Ascendancy on the *Guilford-Zimmerman Temperament Survey* (.54, .63), Ambition on the *Hogan Personality Inventory* (.50, .61), Dominance (.57, .75) and Exhibition (.58, .68) on the *Personality Research Form*, and Histrionic Personality on the *Millon Clinical Multiaxial Inventory* (.55, .68). A masculinity theme is evidenced in correlations with the masculine scale of the *Bem Sex-Role Inventory* (.57, .63) and the M+ (Favorable Masculinity) scale on the *Spence-Helmreich Personal Attributes*

Questionnaire (.57, .57). A possible negative implication of high scores on Sa is indicated by its correlations of .52 and .68 with the narcissistic personality scale of the Millon CMI, and a taste for risk-taking is suggested by correlations of .51 and .61 with the Bold-Venturesomeness Factor H scale of the 16PF.

The next line of evidence for interpreting scores on Sa comes from spouse-reported acts in a sample of 177 persons (88 men, 89 women). The five acts with largest positive correlations with Sa are cited first, followed by the five acts with largest negative correlations.

Took charge of the group (.36)

Talked to almost everyone at the party (.33)

Placed self at the center of activity at the party (.33)

Talked to many people at the party (. 35)

Dressed according to the latest fashion (.32)

Entered the conversation only when asked a question (–.22)

Spoke only when spoken to (–.22)

Waited for the other person to choose a topic to discuss (–.19)

Walked into the room full of people without talking to anyone (–.20)

Waited to be introduced rather than initiating the introduction (–.19)

All of these acts refer in one way or another to taking the initiative in personal interactions, and to seeking a central, visible role. High scorers on Sa are not shrinking violets, and, in fact, do things that bring attention to themselves. They are also talkative and can be counted on to speak up in nearly any situation.

These implications, and also those observed in the correlations with other tests, resemble in many ways those noted for the Sp scale. Are there any differences between the two scales that may help to bring out their nuances of meaning? In the act inventory, certain acts did appear to be associated much more with one scale than the other. For example, the act, "Asked several questions without waiting for answers" correlated .18 with Sa, but only .01 with Sp. "He/she planned his/her career in detail" correlated .18 with Sa, but only .04 with Sp. "He/she boasted about his/her accomplishments" correlated .28 with Sa, but only .10 with Sp. Among the acts more strongly associated with Sp than Sa

were, "Picked up a hitch-hiker" (.18 versus .03), "Openly discussed his/her sex life with friends" (.23 versus .07), and "Willingly bore the cost of an evening on the town" (.18 versus .03). There is more spontaneity and uninhibited expression associated with elevations on Sp, and more egoism and self-concern associated with elevations on Sa.

Adjectival descriptions by observers are presented in Table 5.5 for six different samples. Two consist of men or women each described on the ACL by a spouse or partner. Two are composed of college students, each described on the ACL by three peers using a five-step rating for each adjective. Two are made up of assessees, each described by a panel of 10 observers whose individual protocols were summed into a composite for each assessee. In Table 5.5, the 12 adjectives with largest positive correlations with Sa are given, and also the 12 with largest negative correlations.

One cluster depicts outgoing, sociable, and talkative attributes, along with an absence of shyness, taciturnity, and withdrawal. Another cluster refers to self-confidence and self-assurance. A few adjectives used are suggestive of the overevaluation of self and egoism associated with very high scores on Sa. Still another cluster betokens the initiative, enterprise, and ambition that the scale connotes. Some of the specific terms used to describe high scorers are aggressive, energetic, self-confident, and talkative. Some of the specific terms more associated with low scores on Sa are mild, quiet, shy, and silent.

In a composite sample of 1,356 persons, made up of the peer-described and assessed individuals, standardized scores on the 200 most frequently used adjectives were regressed against the Sa scale, terminating the analsis after eight steps. The multiple regression for the best combination of eight adjectives was .43 (R^2 = .18). Four terms had positive beta weights (ambitious, enterprising, opportunistic, and wary), and four had negative beta weights (interests narrow, painstaking, shy, and tense).

For 547 men and 393 women, formulations on the *California Q-Set* were available from panels of five or more observers for each assessee. These independent Q-sortings were composited into a single array for each assessee, and then the 100 items were correlated with scores on the Sa scale. The four items with largest positive and the four with largest negative correlations are presented

	Men, Described By			Women, Described By		
Adjectives	Spouse (N = 236)	3 Peers (N = 194)	10 Staff Members (N = 612)	Spouse (N = 236)	3 Peers (N = 192)	10 Staff Members (N = 358)
Aggressive	.16*	.19**	.25**	.25**	.31**	.30**
Ambitious	.19**	.16*	.32**	.28**	.17*	.32**
Confident	.15*	.22**	.27**	.25**	.27**	.37**
Egotistical	.10	.20**	.19**	.17**	.20**	.20**
Energetic	.22**	.16*	.30**	.18**	.22**	.29**
Enterprising	.12	.21**	.31**	.24**	.16*	.35**
Initiative	.18**	.12	.29**	.18**	.16*	.34**
Outgoing	.27**	.26**	.29**	.34**	.29**	.29**
Resourceful	.16*	.17*	.25**	.25**	.11	.30**
Self-confident	.22**	.24**	.29**	.32**	.26**	.38**
Sociable	.20**	.21**	.22**	.27**	.16*	.25**
Talkative	.26**	.20**	.24**	.21**	.32**	.30**
Awkward	−.18**	−.12	−.30**	−.08	−.18*	−.30**
Cautious	−.12	−.13	−.28**	−.19**	−.37**	−.30**
Inhibited	−.15*	−.08	−.33**	−.23**	−.28**	−.31**
Interests narrow	−.07	−.28**	−.25**	−.23**	−.12	−.27**
Mild	−.13*	−.15*	−.28**	−.22**	−.31**	−.30**
Quiet	−.23**	−.24**	−.35**	−.27**	−.34**	−.35**
Reserved	−.15*	−.10	−.32**	−.27**	−.37**	−.27**
Retiring	−.14*	−.05	−.34**	−.16*	−.35**	−.36**
Shy	−.25**	−.29**	−.37**	−.31**	−.34**	−.35**
Silent	−.25**	−.24**	−.31**	−.11	−.22**	−.27**
Submissive	−.08	−.18*	−.26**	−.21**	−.23**	−.29**
Withdrawn	−.20**	−.26**	−.33**	−.18**	−.36**	−.28**

Table 5.5 Adjectival Descriptions by Observers: 12 Most Salient Positive and 12 Most Salient Negative Correlates of the 28-Item Sa Scale

*p ≤ .05, **p ≤ .01

below. For each item, the first coefficient is for the sample of 547 men and the second is for the sample of 393 women.

Behaves in an assertive fashion (.31 and .37)

Has high aspiration level for self (.28 and .29)

Has social poise and presence; appears socially at ease (.35 and .38)

Is verbally fluent; can express ideas well (.24 and .40)

Genuinely submissive; accepts domination comfortably (−.30 and −.32)

Gives up and withdraws where possible in the face of frustration and adversity (−.29, −.36)

Reluctant to commit self to any definite course of action; tends to delay or avoid action (–.31 and –.36)

Is self-defeating (–.36 and –.37)

In this sample of 940 assessees, those with higher scores on Sa were seen as assertive, ambitious, socially poised, and verbally fluent. Those with lower scores on Sa were seen as easily dominated, short on perseverance, reluctant to act or take a stand, and self-defeating. The concept of self-acceptance or self-esteem seems to be fully compatible with these specific findings.

In-depth life history interviews were conducted with 504 men and 379 women as part of large assessment programs. After the 90-minute interviews, a 99-item check list was completed by the interviewer, marking each behavior or characteristic observed during the interview. Dummy weights of 1 were assigned to any item checked, and of 0 to any item not checked. Then these weights were correlated with scores on the Sa scale. The four items with largest positive and four with largest negative correlations are reported below. The first coefficient after each item was that for the 504 men, and the second was that for the 379 women.

Witty and animated, an interesting conversationalist (.28, .27)

Unusually self-confident, feels able to meet nearly any situation (.28, .29)

Has a stable, optimistic view of the future (.16, .17)

Creates a good impression; has effective interpersonal techniques (.22, .21)

Reticent and taciturn (–.18, –.18)

Has difficulty in expressing ideas (–.14, –.16)

Has many worries and problems (–.21, –.22)

Is unsure of self, doubts own ability (–.21, –.26)

Interviewees with higher scores on Sa impressed the interviewers as being witty and animated, self-confident, optimistic, and deft in their interpersonal relations. Those with lower scores on Sa were described by their interviewers as taciturn, inept in expressing ideas, worrying, and self-doubting. Although not one of the four items with largest positive correlations, the description "attractive, good-looking" should be mentioned because of its relevance to one of the elements in the self-acceptance syndrome assessed by Sa. This item had correlations of .15 with Sa for both men and women.

The final source of observational data comes from the 50-item *Interpersonal Q-Sort*, completed by 200 women to describe their husbands or partners, by 200 men to describe their wives or partners, and by three assessment staff observers each describing 111 male assessees. The three items with largest positive and three with largest negative correlations are reported below. The first coefficient each time is for the 200 men, then the 200 women, and then the 111 male assessees.

Enterprising and outgoing; enjoys social participation (.31, .29, .25)

Verbally fluent; expresses self easily and with clarity (.19, .31, .35)

Is an effective leader; able to elicit the responses and cooperation of others (.20, .24, .38)

Unassuming, inhibited, and inattentive; bland and colorless in behavior (–.17, –.16, –.45)

Awkward and ill at ease socially; shy and inhibited with others (–.28, –.31, –.48)

Easily embarrassed; feels inferior and inadequate (–.19, –.28, –.43)

In summary, people with high scores on Sa think well of themselves and tend to be liked by others. They are optimistic about the future, and in their careers move toward high status and well-paying occupations. They enjoy social contacts and behave in such a way as to attract attention and favorable responses from others. They are talkative, express ideas easily and with clarity, and take the initiative in meeting and conversing with others. In general, their behavior is ego-enhancing, not at all self-defeating, and in line with their high levels of aspiration. They are not easily embarrassed or subdued. There is, however, a downside to very high scores on Sa (raw scores of 26 to 28), in that narcissistic and egoistic attributes begin to appear. Persons with these very high scores will tend to be opportunistic, exploitative, and demanding.

People with low scores on Sa are usually diffident, hesitant to take firm or decisive actions, and reluctant to get into any situation involving direct competition with others. They doubt their own ability, seek to stay in the background, and have difficulty in expressing their ideas.

The In (Independence) Scale

The In scale was introduced in the 1986 Form 462 of the CPI, and its development was described in a chapter in Newmark's book on psychological assessment methods (Gough, 1989). The method of scale development was empirical, in that a nontest criterion of independence was first established, after which items in the CPI were examined individually for their ability to forecast the ratings of independence. The analyses were conducted in a sample of 236 couples, in which each man was described on the ACL by his wife or partner, and each woman was described on the ACL by her husband or partner. There were 30 items discovered that had correlations significant at or beyond the .05 level for both men and women, and these 30 items were assembled into the In scale. To cross-validate the scale, scores on In were correlated with staff ratings of independence for 198 college students observed in an assessment setting. The number of raters varied from 10 to 18. All ratings on each student were summed and averaged, and then correlated with scores on In. For the total sample of 198 students the validity coefficient was .42. For the 99 men alone the coefficient was .47, and for the 99 women alone the coefficient was .37.

For Form 434, one of the original In items was dropped and a new item substituted. Correlations of the original and Form 434 versions of the scale had correlations of .99 for 3,000 men in the current norm sample, and also of .99 for the 3,000 women in the current norm sample. In the combined sample of 6,000 persons, a factor analysis of the interitem matrix was conducted. Eight factors with eigen values of 1.00 were identified, of which four were retained and rotated by means of Kaiser's normal varimax method. Items in the first rotated factor focused on resoluteness, perseverance, and feelings of competence, for example, "I usually expect to succeed in things I do" ("true"), "I have a tendency to give up easily when I meet difficult problems" ("false"), and "I feel like giving up quickly when things go wrong" ("false"). Factor 2 contained items suggestive of self-confidence and assurance when under scrutiny, for instance, "Even the idea of giving a talk in public makes me afraid" ("false"), and "I dislike having to talk in front of a group of people" ("false").

Factor 3 contains items indicating self-sufficiency, relative unconcern about the wishes or demands of others, and willingness to follow one's own judgment even when others disagree. Representative items are, "I usually try to do what is expected of me, and to avoid criticism" ("false"), "Before I do something I try to consider how my friends will react to it" ("false"), and "It is very important to me to have enough friends and social life" ("false"). The fourth factor contained items indicating a liking for positions of authority and for decision-making prerogatives, for example, "When I work on a committee I like to take charge of things" ("true"), and "I would be willing to describe myself as a pretty 'strong' personality" ("true").

Act frequency data for the In scale come from a sample of 177 persons (88 males and 89 females), each of whom was rated on the list of acts by a spouse or partner. The acts were then correlated with scores on the In scale, and the five with largest positive and five with largest negative correlations are listed below.

Took charge of the group (.31)

Talked to many people at the party (.30)

Set goals for a group (.28)

Interrupted a conversation (.27)

Spoke with a loud, firm voice (.25)

Quarreled with parents about their vacation plans (–.17)

Followed a religious counselor's instructions without question (–.20)

Walked with his/her head down (–.18)

Disliked the mayor because everyone else did (–.17)

Exaggerated his/her personal problems (–.17)

Two important themes are embodied in the In scale, one pertaining to self-assurance, resourcefulness, and competence, and the other to a distancing of self from others and from perfunctory or conventional demands. Both of these dispositions can be discerned in the acts cited above. Talking to many people, taking charge of a group, and setting goals are all manifestations, among other things, of self-confidence and the ability to get things done. Setting self apart from others and behaving independently can be seen in the acts of interrupting a conversation, not complying with a religious counselor's instructions, and not going along with the consensual dislike of the mayor.

The need to go it alone when necessary, plus the strength and resolve to do so, can be at least indirectly illustrated in a recent study by Helson and Picano (1990). They worked with a sample of 104 women who took the CPI as college seniors, and then again 22 years later. The women were placed in one of four research classifications, according to their life experiences. A group of 26 "nonmothers" included those who had never married, or who had married but had not had children. A second group of 26 was made up of mothers who were divorced. A third neotraditional group of 35 were mothers in intact marriages, but who worked more than 20% time. The fourth group, called "traditionals," was composed of mothers in intact marriages who did not engage in paid work. For the first three groups, scores on the In scale increased significantly ($p < .05$) over the 22-year period; whereas for the traditional women, the increase was less than half a point. The stronger life demands for self-sufficiency and financial independence for women in the first three classifications was associated with significant increases in their scores on the In scale.

Table 5.6 lists the 12 adjectives with largest positive and 12 with largest negative correlations with the In scale in six different samples summing to a total of 1,828 persons. In each sample, the respondents were described by one or more observers on the *Adjective Check List,* and then tallies for the 300 adjectives were correlated with scores on the In scale.

Adjectives with positive correlations, hence descriptive of persons with high scores on In, refer to characteristics such as confidence, resourcefulness, determination, and enterprise. The word *independent* appears, along with the adjective *individualistic.* The two key elements postulated for the scale (self-assurance and self-sufficiency) are therefore discernible in the reactions of observers.

Adjectives with negative correlations are associated with lower scores on In. One cluster depicts feelings of inadequacy and self-doubt, for example in the adjectives meek, weak, and worrying. Another

cluster suggests reticence and taciturnity, for example quiet, shy, and silent. The terms awkward and dull suggest a somewhat negative evaluation by observers of those scoring low on the In scale.

In a sample of 1,356, standardized scores on the observers' consensual ACLs were regressed on the In scale to discover the best small combination of descriptions from which to estimate standing on the measure. The analysis included only the 200 most frequently used adjectives, and the iterations were arbitrarily stopped after eight steps. The eight-term ACL cluster for In had a multiple correlation of .40 with scores on In ($R^2 = .16$). Three adjectives had positive beta weights: confident, egotistical, and intelligent. Five had negative beta weights: conventional, dissatisfied, distractible, shy, and unassuming. The "lone wolf" metaphor for the In scale is clearly detectable in this set of eight descriptions.

The next source of observer-based evidence on the meaning of the In scale comes from Block's *California Q-Set.* Assessment staff observers did Q-sorts for 547 men and 393 women, with from five to eight evaluators per person. The independent Q-sorts were composited into consensual arrays, and then items were placed in the nine categories of salience specified by Block, with the designated number of items in each category. The 100 Q-sort items were then correlated with scores on the In scale. The four items with largest positive and the four with largest negative correlations are reported below. The first coefficient each time is for the 547 men, and the second is for the 393 women.

Has a wide range of interests (.21, .31)

Behaves in an assertive fashion (.31, .33)

Has social poise and presence; appears socially at ease (.31, .25)

Is verbally fluent; can express ideas well (.26, .34)

Is uncomfortable with uncertainty and complexities (−.29, −.35)

Genuinely submissive; accepts domination comfortably (−.33, −.33)

Gives up and withdraws where possible in the face of frustration and adversity (−.31, −.38)

Has a readiness to feel guilty (−.30, −.30)

Assessees with high scores on In were seen as assertive, socially poised, verbally fluent, and as

	Men, Described By			Women, Described By		
Adjectives	Spouse (N = 236)	3 Peers (N = 194)	10 Staff Members (N = 612)	Spouse (N = 236)	3 Peers (N = 192)	10 Staff Members (N = 358)
Aggressive	.18**	.10	.26**	.21**	.25**	.33**
Alert	.23**	.14*	.26**	.09	.21**	.20**
Ambitious	.23*	.06	.30**	.20**	.18*	.34**
Assertive	.26**	.12	.32**	.35**	.19**	.35**
Confident	.21**	.22**	.31**	.24**	.32**	.31**
Determined	.14*	.11	.20**	.22**	.21**	.31**
Enterprising	.16*	.11	.30**	.20**	.21**	.30**
Independent	.16*	.22**	.28**	.21**	.18*	.32**
Individualistic	.16*	.16*	.22**	.25**	.17*	.24**
Intelligent	.17**	.23**	.23**	.09	.14*	.25**
Resourceful	.14*	.10	.30**	.22**	.14*	.26**
Self-confident	.23**	.13	.30**	.30**	.27**	.37
Awkward	−.21**	−.16*	−.33**	−.14*	−.12	−.18**
Cautious	−.11	−.22**	−.33**	−.08	−.22**	−.21**
Dull	−.13*	−.17*	−.23**	−.09	−.18*	−.18**
Meek	−.14*	−.20**	−.31**	−.22**	−.22**	−.28**
Mild	−.18**	−.21**	−.28**	−.13*	−.19**	−.24**
Nervous	−.15*	−.17*	−.15**	−.13*	−.18*	−.17**
Quiet	−.07	−.19**	−.35**	−.18**	−.15*	−.26**
Shy	−.18**	−.23**	−.36**	−.32**	−.26**	−.28**
Silent	−.13*	−.20**	−.28**	−.11	−.15*	−.23**
Submissive	−.12	−.18*	−.32**	−.19**	−.20**	−.33**
Weak	−.14*	−.13	−.22**	−.22**	−.19**	−.19**
Worrying	−.17**	−.17*	−.20**	−.13*	−.20**	−.09

Table 5.6 Adjectival Descriptions by Observers: 12 Most Salient Positive and 12 Most Salient Negative Correlates of the 30-Item In Scale

*$p \le .05$, **$p \le .01$

having a wide range of interests. Assessees with low scores were seen as uncomfortable with ambiguity, submissive, easily defeated, and prone to feelings of guilt.

From a 99-item *Interviewer's Check List* completed for 504 men and 379 women by their life history interviewers, the four items with largest positive and four with largest negative correlations are reported below. The first coefficient each time is for the men, and the second for the women.

Uses wide and varied vocabulary (.18, .16)

Witty and animated; an interesting conversationalist (.17, .19)

Unusually self-confident; feels able to meet near-ly any situation (.29, .18)

Was relaxed and at ease during the interview (.14, .14)

Reticent and taciturn (−.15, −.12)

Was nervous and ill at ease during the interview (−.14, −.14)

Has many worries and problems (−.14, −.19)

Is unsure of self, doubts own ability (−.19, −.30)

Although the correlations with check list items are modest in magnitude, all are statistically significant at or beyond the .05 level of probability. Persons with high scores on In tended to be seen by their life history interviewers as animated, self-confident, at ease in the interview, and as possessing a wide and varied vocabulary. Persons with low scores on In tended to be seen as reticent, ill at ease in the interview, worrying, and self-doubting.

A 50-item Q-sort deck for interpersonal behavior was used in three samples. In the first, 200 men were described by their wives or partners. In the second, 200 women were described by their husbands or partners. In the third, 111 men were described by panels of three assessment observers whose independent appraisals were combined into a single composite. The 50 items were then correlated with scores on the In scale. The three with largest positive and the three with largest negative correlations are reported below, along with the three coefficients for each item in this same order.

Is forceful and self-assured in manner (.19, .23, .31)

Verbally fluent; expresses self easily and with clarity (.23, .24, .25)

Is an effective leader; able to elicit the responses and cooperation of others (.27, .19, .24)

Submissive; gives in easily; lacking in self-confidence (−.20, −.27, −.38)

Awkward and ill at ease socially; shy and inhibited with others (−.11, −.21, −.36)

Easily embarrassed; feels inferior and inadequate (−.14, −.27, −.34)

These key descriptions are similar to what has already been noted for persons with higher and lower scores on In. Those with high scores tend to be seen as forceful, verbally fluent, and as possessing leadership skills. Those with low scores tend to be seen as submissive, socially awkward, and easily embarrassed.

The name of the In scale stresses its positive or favorable implications, namely independence and self-sufficiency. Had it been scored in the opposite direction it could well have been called *dependency.* Recent years have witnessed a great interest in the concept and measurement of dependency (Bornstein, 1992, 1993; Mills & Taricone, 1991). A widely used measure of dependency, the *Interpersonal Dependency Inventory* (Bornstein, 1994; Hirschfeld, et al., 1977) was administered to a sample of 145 males and 145 females, who also took the CPI. Correlations of the In scale with the subscales and total score on the IDI were as follows: Emotional Reliance on Others, −.32 and −.43; Lack of Social Self-Confidence, −.66, −.62; Assertion of Autonomy, .09, .12; total score, −.62, −.66. It should be noted that the third subscale (Assertion of Autonomy) is conceptualized as a defensive maneuver, not as an ego-syntonic statement of independence.

In summary, elevated scores on the In scale are indicative of self-confidence, assertiveness, perseverance in pursuit of goals, breadth of interests, good verbal skills, assurance even in complex and demanding situations, and both the strength and inclination to stand apart from others in evaluating situations. A possible problem attending very high scores on In (raw scores of 28 to 30) is too much indifference to the opinions of others, and an unwillingness to compromise or yield.

Persons with low scores on In tend to acquiesce in response to majority views, stay silent, and to submit. They feel inferior and inadequate in many settings, worry, and are cautious about doing anything that will prompt scrutiny from others.

The Em (Empathy) Scale

The Em (Empathy) scale was developed in a doctoral dissertation by Robert Hogan (1967), and first described in a journal report in 1969 (Hogan, 1969). Hogan's conceptualization, much simplified, is that in playing the game of life, the first stage involves assimilating the rules and making them more or less automatic in one's psychology. The CPI So

(Socialization) scale is an acceptable measure of mastery at this stage. The second stage requires learning how to react both overtly and by way of implicit, even intuitionally perceived, cues so as to adapt one's behavior to the needs and wishes of important others. The Em scale is intended to serve as a measure of this set of attitudes and skills. At the highest level of moral development comes the capacity and insight needed to break away from stultifying and dehumanizing constraints, behave in new and liberating ways, and move the social enterprise constructively forward. Among the scales included in the CPI, probably the v.3 scale comes closest to being an acceptable indication of this third level, with important ancillary information furnished by scores on the In (Independence) and Re (Responsibility) scales. Whether or not this theoretical schema is adopted, and whether or not one views the So and v.3 scales as appropriate measures for Levels 1 and 2, the Em scale by itself provides the user of the CPI with very useful and enlightening information.

To develop the Em scale, Hogan posited a cluster of five indicative and five contraindicative items from Block's *California Q-Set*. Two of the indicative items are, "Is socially perceptive of a wide range of interpersonal cues" and "Evaluates the motivation of others in interpreting situations." Two of the contraindicative items are, "Does not vary roles; relates to everyone in the same way" and "Judges self and others in conventional terms like 'popularity,' 'the correct thing to do,' 'social pressures,' etc." Consensual staff Q-sorts were available at that time for 211 men who were studied in intensive assessment programs, and who had also taken the MMPI, the CPI, and an unpublished inventory created by staff members of the Institute of Personality Assessment and Research. Item analyses pitted the highest-scoring 27% versus the lowest-scoring 27% on the Q-sort criterion. Differences were evaluated by chi-square and Fisher's exact test, leading to the selection of 64 items. Of these, 31 came from the CPI, 25 from the MMPI, and eight from the IPAR inventory. In early work with the Em scale, this 64-item version was used, but by the mid-1970s the majority of studies made use of the CPI alone. Because seven of the MMPI items (of the 25) had been used in the CPI, it was possible to score the CPI for a 38-item version of the Em scale. In the

434-item edition of the CPI, one of these items was dropped, and a substitute selected from the next-best items cited in Hogan's initial research. For the two profile norm samples of 3,000 men and 3,000 women, correlations of the Form 462 and Form 434 scoring of Em were .99 for both sexes.

Because the original development of Em was done on samples of men only, it is important to attend to evidence showing its utility and validity for women. For the current profile norm samples, means were 19.44 (SD = 4.85) for women and 19.07 (SD = 4.70) for men. Groups that ought to score high appear to do so, as shown in Appendix B. Women graduate students in psychology had a mean of 24.47, and male graduate students in psychology had a mean of 24.86. Women majoring in education had a mean of 24.03, and men in the same major had a mean of 24.32. Groups that one would expect to score low also appear to do so. For example, women in prison had a mean of 17.10, and men in prison had a mean of 17.33.

Perusal of the correlations of Em with scales from other tests and inventories in Appendix C turned up relatively few strong relationships, supportive of the contention that the Em scale contributes information not easily to be found elsewhere. Among the links to other variables that might be mentioned are those to the Thinking Introversion and Practical Outlook scales of the *Omnibus Personality Inventory*. Correlations of Em with the former were .54 for men and .62 for women, and with the latter the coefficients were −.37 for men and −.60 for women. Zuckerman's *Sensation-Seeking Scale* total score had correlations with Em of .46 for men and .52 for women. Loevinger's Ego Development measure on her sentence completion technique, available for women only, had a correlation of .49 with Em. Barron's scale for Originality had correlations with Em of .55 for men and .56 for women. The MMPI Si (Social Introversion) scale had correlations with Em of −.51 for men and −.65 for women. From this evidence, one can see that high scorers on Em are active, experience-seeking persons, but at the same time, they are capable of complex, creative ideation and are resilient in ego functioning.

Factor analysis of the 38 items in Em on the profile norm total sample of 6,000 persons identified nine factors with eigen values of 1.00 or more. Four of these were arbitrarily retained for rotation by means of Kaiser's normal varimax method. Items in Factor 1 were expressive of progressive ideas and personal flexibility, for example, "People today have forgotten how to feel properly ashamed of themselves" ("false"), "The trouble with many people is that they don't take things seriously enough" ("false"), and "I like to have a place for everything and everything in its place" ("false"). Items in Factor 2 stressed accommodations to others' feelings and wishes, for example, "I must admit I often try to get my own way regardless of what others may want" ("false"), "I like to keep people guessing what I am going to do next" ("false"), and "I am sometimes cross and grouchy without good reason" ("false"). The third factor had items about leadership, a liking for social interaction, and verbal skills, for example, "I think I am usually a leader in my group" ("true"), "I am a good mixer" ("true"), and "I usually don't like to talk much unless I am with people I know well" ("false"). Factor 4 had items indicating interests in imaginative and intellectual endeavors, for example, "I have at one time or another in my life tried my hand at writing poetry" ("true"), and "I liked *Alice in Wonderland* by Lewis Carroll" ("true").

Act frequency analyses were conducted in a sample of 177 persons (88 men and 89 women), in which each person was described by a spouse or partner. The five acts with largest positive and the five with largest negative correlations with Em are reported below.

Talked to almost everyone at the party (.31)

Brought up a topic that was controversial (.30)

Answered questions about self directly and openly (.31)

Entered into the conversation of a group he/she did not know (.32)

Initiated a conversation with a stranger (.30)

Spoke only when spoken to (−.25)

Entered the conversation only when asked a question (−.20)

Waited to be introduced rather than initiate the introduction (−.18)

Stayed at home and watched TV alone on a Saturday night (−.18)

Maintained an expressionless face during the conversation (−.17)

Most of the acts pertain to conversations with others, and to candidness in responding to personal inquiry. The item about bringing up a controversial topic is of interest as a sign of the moderate unconventionality associated with elevated scores on Em.

An early study by Hogan and his colleagues (Hogan, Mankin, Conway, & Fox, 1970) on use of marijuana by college students can be mentioned here in the same regard. Students were classified as frequent users, occasional users, nonusers, and principled or adamant nonusers. The first two groups had means on Em significantly above that for college students in general, whereas the latter two groups had means about the same as for college students overall. Frequent users could be distinguished from occasional users by their lower scores on the So scale, and nonusers could be distinguished from adamant nonusers by the higher So scores of the latter. A later study (Kurtines, Hogan, & Weiss, 1975) of heroin users found the same dynamic interplay for the Em and So scales. Persons high on both Em and So tend to be infrequent users of marijuana and nonusers of heroin or other illegal substances. Persons average on Em and high on So tend to be nonusers of drugs. Persons low on Em and high on So tend to be nonusers with a passion. Finally, persons low on Em and also low on So appear to be at serious risk for addiction to heroin or other drugs.

Adjectival descriptions by observers as they relate to the Em scale are reported in Table 5.7. The 12 adjectives from the ACL with largest positive and the 12 with largest negative correlations with Em in the six samples have been selected for presentation in the table. One cluster of descriptors pertains to sociability, spontaneity, talkativeness, and an outgoing nature, all linked to higher Em scores. Another cluster involves experience-seeking, a wide range of interests, and hedonistic drives. The word *insightful* is worth noting because of its direct pertinence to the goals of measurement for Em.

Persons with low scores on Em are described as relatively unsocial (shy, quiet, reserved, silent, and withdrawn), as experience-avoiding (cautious, inhibited, timid, and interests narrow), and as dispirited (gloomy and nervous).

In the subsamples of 194 male college students, 192 female college students, 612 assessed males, and 358 assessed females, adjectival descriptions by

Table 5.7 Adjectival Descriptions by Observers: 12 Most Salient Positive and 12 Most Salient Negative Correlates of the 38-Item Em Scale

Adjectives	Men, Described By			Women, Described By		
	Spouse (N = 236)	3 Peers (N = 194)	10 Staff Members (N = 612)	Spouse (N = 236)	3 Peers (N = 192)	10 Staff Members (N = 358)
Adventurous	.09	.13	.21**	.15*	.17*	.27**
Insightful	.19**	.11	.26**	.17**	.13	.21**
Interests wide	.13*	.17*	.30**	.22**	.15*	.32**
Optimistic	.15*	.21**	.21**	.16*	.06	.17**
Outgoing	.21**	.24**	.24**	.32**	.23**	.30**
Pleasure-seeking	.10	.12	.20**	.16*	.23**	.14**
Resourceful	.13*	.18*	.30**	.16*	.14*	.27**
Self-confident	.06	.22**	.29**	.11	.17*	.31**
Sharp-witted	.14*	.20**	.21**	.18**	.04	.17**
Sociable	.18**	.28**	.24**	.20**	.24**	.19**
Spontaneous	.14*	.12	.20**	.21**	.24**	.18**
Talkative	.10	.19**	.20**	.17**	.21**	.28**
Cautious	−.15*	−.16*	−.24**	−.14*	−.32**	−.23**
Gloomy	−.17**	−.10	−.17**	−.07	−.17*	−.11*
Inhibited	−.16*	−.08	−.26**	−.14*	−.17*	−.27**
Interests narrow	−.19**	−.20**	−.32**	−.26**	−.10	−.33**
Nervous	−.26**	−.09	−.14**	−.08	−.21**	−.15**
Quiet	−.15*	−.08	−.24**	−.26**	−.22**	−.27**
Reserved	−.17**	−.07	−.21**	−.20**	−.25**	−.26**
Shy	−.16*	−.13	−.25**	−.23**	−.26**	−.26**
Silent	−.18**	−.16*	−.25**	−.18**	−.19**	−.22**
Tense	−.13*	−.21**	−.11**	−.08	−.19**	−.18**
Timid	−.03	−.16*	−.21**	−.12	−.31**	−.25**
Withdrawn	−.21**	−.11	−.27**	−.09	−.29**	−.20**

*$p \leq .05$, **$p \leq .01$

observers were standardized. Then, in the total sample of 1,356 persons, the 200 most frequently used adjectives were regressed onto the Em scores, arbitrarily stopping the iterations at eight steps. The optimum combination of eight descriptions had a multiple correlation with Em of .42 ($R^2 = .18$). The adjectives with positive beta weights were pleasure-seeking, tactful, and versatile. The adjectives with negative beta weights were interests narrow, modest, painstaking, simple, and temperamental.

In samples of 547 men and 393 women described on the *California Q-Set* by panels of five more staff observers, the four items with largest positive and four with largest negative correlations with the Em scale are listed below. The first coefficient for each item is that for men, and the second is that for women.

Initiates humor (.25 and .22)

Is skilled in social techniques of imaginative play, pretending, and humor (.30 and .24)

Has social poise and presence; appears socially at ease (.33 and .27)

Is verbally fluent; can express ideas well (.26, .34)

Is uncomfortable with uncertainty and complexities (−.25 and −.34)

Is vulnerable to real or fancied threat; generally fearful (−.23, −.26)

Is self-defeating (−.30, −.27)

Handles anxiety and conflicts by, in effect, refusing to recognize their presence; repressive or dissociative tendencies (−.25, −.26)

Assessees with high scores on Em were seen as lively, humorous, socially poised, and verbally fluent. Those with low scores on Em were seen as uncomfortable with ambiguity, vulnerable to threat, self-defeating, and repressive in their ego defenses.

The Em scale scores were next correlated with interviewers' check list descriptions of 504 men and 379 women, based on intensive life history interviews. The four items with largest positive and four with largest negative correlations are reported below. The first coefficient for each item is for the 504 men, and the second is for the 379 women.

Uses wide and varied vocabulary (.15, .23)

Witty and animated, an interesting conversationalist (.21, .26)

Unusually self-confident, feels able to meet nearly any situation (.19, .22)

Creates a good impression; has effective interpersonal techniques (.18, .20)

Makes mistakes in grammar and/or word usage (−.17, −.20)

Reticent and taciturn (−.14, −.17)

Father was stern and authoritarian (−.17, −.16)

Slow rate of movement (−.14, −.15)

In the interviews, persons with higher scores on Em made a good impression, expressed self-confidence,

used a wide vocabulary, and talked in a witty and animated way. Persons with lower scores on Em were reticent, made mistakes in grammar or word usage, and had a slow rate of movement. In recalling their families, they described their fathers as stern and authoritarian.

The final source of descriptive evidence comes from the 50-item *Interpersonal Q-Sort,* in which 200 men were described by their wives or partners, 200 women by their husbands or partners, and 111 men by panels of three assessment staff observers. The three items with largest positive and three with largest negative correlations with Em are cited below, along with the three coefficients for the 200 males, the 200 females, and the 111 male assessees.

Enterprising and outgoing; enjoys social participation (.27, .26, .25)

Clever and imaginative; a spontaneous and entertaining person (.17, .22, .34)

Verbally fluent; expresses self easily and with clarity (.26, .27, .43)

Unassuming, inhibited, and inattentive; bland and colorless in behavior (−.12, −.15, −.37)

Awkward and ill at ease socially; shy and inhibited with others (−.22, −.32, −.40)

Wedded to routine; made anxious by change and uncertainty (−.15, −.23, −.13)

Persons with high scores on Em are seen by these observers as enterprising and outgoing, clever, and verbally fluent. Persons with low scores on Em are seen as unassuming and inhibited, ill at ease socially, and as made anxious by change and uncertainty.

In summary, high scores on Em are indicative of versatility, social insight, urbanity, wit, verbal fluency, and initiative. Case work with individuals has not revealed any hidden negatives associated with very high scores, as was the finding, for example, for Dominance and Self-acceptance. Even at the very highest levels of Em the implications are for an effective, insightful, and imaginative way of dealing with social situations and with interpersonal relations. High scorers on Em do seem to be able to put themselves into the psychological frames of others and to sense how they feel and think. Moreover, high scorers on Em facilitate this kind of understanding by an active, outgoing kind of social behavior. Low scorers on Em tend to be unsure of themselves, self-defeating, narrow in interests, reticent in speech, and poor in dealing with uncertainty, change, and complexities.

The Re (Responsibility) Scale

The Re scale was initially developed (Gough, McClosky, & Meehl, 1952) to assess the dimension of social responsibility in a large-scale study of political participation and involvement (Gough, 1991; McClosky, 1969). Hypotheses concerning political participation drew on 83 defined facets of personality and cognition, which in toto constituted a de facto theory of political behavior. However, the three key elements in the formulation were a participative temperament, awareness of ongoing political and social phenomena, and a sense of responsibility regarding the part each citizen should play.

A peer nomination method was used in the initial item analyses for the scale, in samples of 50 male and 50 female university students, 221 ninth grade students, 123 high school students from several classes, and 282 high school seniors. In three of the samples, students nominated the most and least responsible persons in their group or class; and in two of the samples, teachers provided the nominations. Equal numbers of males and females were selected on the basis of these nominations so as to form four pairs of criterion samples: college, first high school, second high school, and the ninth-grade class. Then, items from the MMPI and also from a specially prepared pool of items intended to relate to the concept of social responsibility were evaluated for their ability to differentiate between most and least responsible subsets in each of the four comparisons. Fifty-six items survived this process of selection, of which 31 were obvious in their relations to responsibility and 25 were subtle. The definition of responsibility given to the nominators stressed willingness to accept the consequences of one's own behavior, dependability, trustworthiness, and a sense of obligation to others as indicative of responsibility, and an absence of or deficiency in these attributes as contraindicative. Cross-validation of the 56-item scale on 80 persons studied in an assessment program produced correlations in the vicinity of .35 with staff ratings of such attributes as positive character integration and sense of responsibility.

For the first published version of the CPI in 1956, the Re scale was reduced to 42 items, dropping the

14 items that showed lowest validities against nontest criteria of responsibility. Cross-validated validity coefficients for the 42-item scale approximated .40. In the 1986 462-item version of the CPI, the Re scale was further reduced to 36 items by dropping the six items with lowest nontest validities. In the present 434-item CPI, one of these items was dropped and replaced by another item so as to keep length at 36. Correlations of the Form 434 and Form 462 versions of the Re scale were .99 in both of the profile norm samples of 3,000 males and 3,000 females. A useful review of the validity of the Form 462 version of the Re scale is found in a paper by Weekes (1993), who found the Re scale to be significantly related to good job performance under unobserved conditions of work; nonuse of amphetamines, marijuana, and alcohol; and avoidance of high-risk financial involvement. From these studies, and from work with individuals, it appears that high scores on Re are associated with self-discipline and reliability, but in an informed, enlightened way that permits departures from convention when appropriate.

Factor analysis of the 36 items from Re in the profile norm samples of 6,000 persons (3,000 men, 3,000 women) identified eight factors with eigen values of 1.00 or greater. Four of these were arbitrarily retained for rotation by Kaiser's normal varimax method. The first factor contained items indicative of generalized feelings of responsibility, for instance, "Maybe some minority groups do get rough treatment, but it's no business of mine" ("false"), "We ought to worry about our own country and let the rest of the world take care of itself" ("false"), and "It's no use worrying my head about public affairs; I can't do anything about them anyway" ("false"). Factor 2 has items indicating dependable personal behavior, for example, "As a child I was suspended from school one or more times for disciplinary reasons" ("false"), and "I have never been in trouble with the law" ("true"). Factor 3 contains items pertaining to civic responsibilities for citizens, for example, "Every citizen should take the time to find out about national affairs, even if it means giving up some personal pleasures" ("true"), and "When a person 'pads' an income tax report so as to get out of some taxes, it is just as bad as stealing money from the government" ("true"). Factor 4 had a somewhat miscellaneous group of five items, all at least tangentially indicative of positive attitudes toward education and self-improvement, for example, "I was a slow learner in school" ("false") and "I like to read about science" ("true").

Act frequency implications of the Re scale were examined in a sample of 177 persons (88 men, 89 women), in which each individual was rated for frequency of specific acts by a spouse or partner. The five acts with largest positive and five with largest negative correlations are listed below.

> Listened attentively to the speaker (.26)
>
> Followed a scheduled routine without changing it (.19)
>
> Went to church (.24)
>
> Asked a question out loud in a large class (.20)
>
> Discussed the political issues of the day (.20)
>
> Dressed in "sexy" clothes (−.18)
>
> Went to a night club (−.24)
>
> Did not return an article found on the floor (−.29)
>
> Let others pay for the drinks (−.23)
>
> Brought records to a party, and let others run the stereo (−.26)

These acts are very specific and discrete, but taken together they give something of a picture of what persons with high and low scores on Re do. Acts associated with high scores include attentiveness to others, observance of schedules, church-going, making appropriate inquiry, and taking note of political issues. Acts associated with low scores include going to a night club, dressing provocatively, not trying to return a lost-and-found article, letting others pay the tab for drinks, and letting others make use of one's own possessions.

Adjectival descriptions associated with Re in six different samples are presented in Table 5.8. In the first two samples, men and women were described by their spouses or partners; in the second two samples, college students were described by panels of three peers; and in the third two samples, male and female assessees were described by panels of 10 staff observers. The 12 adjectives with largest positive and 12 with largest negative correlations with Re are reported in the table. Not all of the adjectives in Table 5.8 have statistically significant correlations in all six samples, but in each case, all are in the same direction (positive, or negative), and at least three are at the .05 level of probability.

Persons with high scores on Re are, in fact, described as responsible, reliable, dependable, and conscientious. They are also described as organized, efficient, persevering, logical, and methodical. A third theme is suggested by the descriptors discreet and moderate. Low scorers on Re are seen as impulsive, infantile, pleasure-seeking, rebellious, reckless, and restless. A second theme is suggested by the terms flirtatious and show-off. A third implication is betokened by the adjectives careless and temperamental. The remaining item is suspicious, noted for low scorers on Re.

In a composite sample of 1,356 persons (the 386 college students and 970 assessees), the 200 most frequently used adjectives were regressed onto Re scores, arbitrarily terminating the process after eight steps. The best combination of eight adjectives from which to estimate scores on Re had a multiple correlation of .42 (R^2 = .18). Adjectives with positive beta weights were dependable and organized. Adjectives with negative beta weights were adventurous, cynical, easy-going, pleasure-seeking, silent, and suspicious.

From Appendix E, the four items from the *California Q-Set* with largest positive and the four with largest negative correlations with Re in samples of 547 men and 393 women have been selected for reporting below. Each assessee was described on the Q-sort by a panel of five or more staff observers, after which the 100 items as consensually sorted were correlated with Re scores. The correlations are first for the 504 men and then for the 393 women.

> Is a genuinely responsible and dependable person (.23, .30)
>
> Is productive; gets things done (.16, .30)
>
> Genuinely values intellectual and cognitive matters (.26, .33)
>
> Has high aspiration level for self (.27, .18)
>
> Is unpredictable and changeable in behavior and attitudes (−.15, −.27)
>
> Various needs tend toward relatively direct and uncontrolled expression; unable to delay gratification (−.20, −.31)
>
> Characteristically pushes and tries to stretch limits; sees what he or she can get away with (−.31, −.22)
>
> Is self-indulgent (−.25, −.30)

High scorers on Re were rated as genuinely responsible, productive, attentive to intellectual matters,

Table 5.8 Adjectival Descriptions by Observers: 12 Most Salient Positive and 12 Most Salient Negative Correlates of the 36-Item Re Scale						
	Men, Described By			**Women, Described By**		
Adjectives	Spouse (N = 236)	3 Peers (N = 194)	10 Staff Members (N = 612)	Spouse (N = 236)	3 Peer s (N = 192)	10 Staff Members (N = 358)
Conscientious	.26**	.26**	.14**	.14*	.34**	.19**
Dependable	.16*	.30**	.07	.13*	.28**	.22**
Discreet	.14*	.15*	.06	.07	.23**	.16**
Efficient	.17**	.19**	.14**	.09	.29**	.21**
Logical	.09	.17*	.02	.16*	.19**	.25**
Methodical	.13*	.13	.15**	.08	.14*	.18**
Moderate	.20**	.17*	.09*	.17**	.15*	.06
Organized	.14*	.23**	.16**	.10	.36**	.26**
Persevering	.05	.14*	.12**	.08	.22**	.16**
Reliable	.08	.20**	.05	.07	.31**	.12*
Responsible	.06	.26**	.08*	.03	.32**	.18**
Tactful	.16*	.05	.08*	.07	.25**	.04
Careless	−.08	−.28**	−.15**	−.15*	−.30**	−.23**
Flirtatious	−.29**	−.21**	−.19**	−.23**	−.05	−.26**
Forgetful	−.09	−.25**	−.14**	−.13*	−.23**	−.12*
Impulsive	−.28**	−.23**	−.14**	−.20**	−.18*	−.23**
Infantile	−.17**	−.15*	−.14**	−.12	−.19**	−.24**
Pleasure-seeking	−.18**	−.31**	−.22**	−.17**	−.13	−.31**
Rebellious	−.22**	−.16*	−.16**	−.14*	−.32**	−.17**
Reckless	−.27**	−.22**	−.18**	−.25**	−.27**	−.24**
Restless	−.24**	−.17*	−.11**	−.09	−.27**	−.19**
Show-off	−.18**	−.22**	−.16**	−.17**	−.14*	−.05
Suspicious	−.20**	−.09	−.17**	−.19**	−.15*	−.14**
Temperamental	−.20**	−.06	−.15**	−.16*	−.23**	−.15**

*p ≤ .05, **p ≤ .01

and as having a high level of aspiration. Low scorers on Re were viewed as erratic and unpredictable, uncontrolled, rule-testing, and self-indulgent.

Intensive life history interviews were conducted with 504 men and 379 women, after which the interviewer completed a 99-item check list describing some of the things that occurred. Dummy weights of 1 for items checked and 0 for items left blank were then correlated with scores on the Re scale. The four items with largest positive and four with largest negative correlations with Re are given below, along with the coefficients for men (first) and for women (second).

Standards of courteous and polite behavior were emphasized in the home (.13, .12)

Was an honor student in high school (.24, .15)

Has a stable, optimistic view of the future (.17, .23)

Seems relatively free of neurotic trends, conflicts, and other forms of instability (.14, .19)

Interviewee had a great deal of friction with parents (–.08, –.19)

Had first sexual intercourse while in high school (–.30, –.17)

Led a borderline, delinquent-like existence in high school (–.21, –.16)

Considers self to have been an underachiever in high school (–.22, –.14)

High scorers on Re apparently were brought up with attention to conventional standards of courteous behavior, did well in school, evolved stable, optimistic views of the future, and appear to be relatively free of obvious signs of neuroticism and distress. Low scorers on Re tended to have friction with their parents, began their sexual experiences in high school, had delinquent-like lives then, and were underachievers scholastically. There thus appears to be a strong developmental history related to higher or lower scores on Re, with visible evidence in family life, in school, and in life perspectives.

A final source of observer-based information relevant to scores on Re comes from a 50-item Q-sort completed for 200 men by their wives or partners, for 200 women by their husbands or partners, and for 111 male assessees by panels of three staff observers. The three items from the Q-sort with largest positive and three with largest negative correlations with Re are reported below, along with the coefficients for men, women, and assessees.

A conscientious and serious-minded person (.19, .12, .16)

Honest and direct in behavior; mature and realistic in outlook (.14, .09, .20)

Has a highly developed inner sense of ethics and morality; deeply humanitarian and altruistic (.11, .19, .17)

Distrustful and cynical; dissatisfied with most things; indifferent to the worries and problems of others (–.12, –.16, –.28)

Given to moods; often difficult and recalcitrant (–.22, –.14, –.11)

Coarse and vulgar; inclined to behave in a crude and impolite fashion (–.16, –.18, –.15)

The relationships here are relatively modest, but do point toward ethical behavior and outlook among high scorers on Re, and toward distrust, moodiness, and recalcitrance among low scorers.

In summary, high scores on Re are associated with interpersonal maturity, considerateness toward others, rational enlightened compliance with rules, courtesy, self-discipline, dependability, and perseverance. Low scores on Re are associated with impulsivity, self-indulgence, cynicism, willfulness, and hedonistic immaturity.

The So (Socialization) Scale

The 46-item So scale began life as a 64-item measure for delinquency (Gough & Peterson, 1952), based on a role-taking or perspective-taking theory of psychopathy (Gough, 1948c), and also on clinical lore concerning the interpersonal operations of delinquents. In the initial construction of the scale, five male and four female samples were employed, including high school students, disciplinary problems from the same school, youth authority wards, and reformatory inmates. The goal of the analysis was to develop a measure that would classify individuals and groups along a sociological continuum going from unusual probity and rectitude at one pole, through zones of ordinary rule-compliance, to a region of moderate waywardness and recalcitrance, down to a pole of severe asociality and a strong propensity for norm-violating behavior.

In the 45 years since the scale was first introduced, a great deal of evidence has been published showing that scores are in fact highly diagnostic of positions along this sociological continuum (see Gough, 1994, for an extensive review). For example, when 69 male samples were arrayed in order of their mean scores on So, all of the less-socialized samples had means below 29.50, and all of the more-socialized samples had means above this figure. Anchoring the low end of the distribution were delinquents convicted of violent offenses, multiple offenders, and imprisoned heroin addicts. Just below 29.50 came samples of first offenders, exhibitionists with no other crimes, college students who were moderate users of marijuana, and college shoplifters. At the top of the array were samples of bank managers, medical school applicants, entrepreneurs who had started new companies, and graduate students in engineering. For 40 samples of women, all of the less socialized groups also had means below 29.50, and all of the more socialized had means greater than this.

Within-sample differences were also appreciable, and in the expected direction. One of the studies (DeFrancesco & Taylor, 1993) classified delinquent boys into those with minor offenses only, such as truancy and curfew violations; those with offenses against property, such as stealing and burglary; and those with offenses involving violence, such as armed robbery. A fourth group of boys from the same places of living and of the same age (15 to 16), but with no known record of delinquency, was also tested. Dummy values from 1 to 4 for the four subsamples of 121 boys correlated .71 with scores on the 46-item So scale. For just the 91 boys in the three subsamples of delinquents, the correlation was .48. In another study (Edwards & Nagelberg, 1986), 25 college women with eating disorders were compared with 25 who were free of these problems. The point-biserial correlation for So was .38, with lower So scores for women with eating disorders. A comparison of 601 college students who did not use marijuana with 151 who did (Goldstein, 1974), found higher So scores among the nonusers, with a point-biserial correlation of .38. Schalling (1978), in her review of validity data for the So scale, reported a correlation of .73 for the contrast of delinquents versus nondelinquents in 25 samples involving more than 10,000 persons.

A more recent study (Gough & Bradley, 1992b) compared 272 male delinquents and prison inmates with 1,088 nondelinquents, approximately matched for age and status. The point-biserial correlation for this comparison was .54. The same study compared 400 delinquent and imprisoned women with 2,266 approximately matched controls, giving rise to a point-biserial correlation of .58.

In a monograph on the So scale (Gough, 1994), the arrays of means on So for the 69 male and 40 female samples led to recommendations to treat scores of 32 and over for men and 33 and above for women as indicative of above-average compliance with social norms, scores of 30 to 31 for men and 30 to 32 for women as forecasters of ordinary compliance, scores

of 26 to 29 for men and also for women as predictors of moderate waywardness, and scores of 25 and below for both sexes as diagnostic of severe problems in rule-following and norm-accepting behavior.

One of the intentions for the So scale, and indeed for the entire inventory, is validity in cross-cultural applications. The folk concepts about personality for which the inventory is scaled are conceived of as cultural and historical universals that are natural derivatives of communal living and hence applicable to individuals in any society. An early study of the So scale (Gough, 1965b) examined its cross-cultural validity in eight languages and 10 countries, comparing delinquent and nondelinquent male and female samples in each instance. The total number of persons in the survey came to 21,772 nondelinquents and 5,052 delinquents. Significantly ($p < .001$) higher So scores were found for nondelinquents in every comparison. Point-biserial coefficients for the American comparisons were .59 for males and .46 for females. For all of the other samples treated as a composite, the point-biserials were .43 for males and .56 for females. Using hitmax technique to define a cutting score on So that would maximize the accurate identification of nondelinquents and of delinquents, the best differentiation was given by a raw score of 28. That is, respondents with scores of 28 and over would be called nondelinquents, and those with raw scores below 28 would be called delinquents. This score gave a 78% overall accuracy for males and an 85% overall accuracy for females, based on the theoretical assumptions of a 30% base rate for men and a 20% base rate for women.

As mentioned above, the first version of the So scale had 64 items (but scored in the reverse direction, for delinquency). In the 1956 Form 480 version of the CPI, this was reduced to 54 items. In the 1986 Form 462 version, the So scale was further shortened to 46 items. Two items from the 1986 form had to be dropped because of conflict with the Americans with Disabilities Act, and two other items were substituted. The items dropped were, "I have never done any heavy drinking" and "I have used alcohol excessively." Two other items having approximately equivalent differentiating power for a social behavior were substituted. Correlations between the Form 462 and Form 434 versions of the scale were .99 for both of the profile norm samples of 3,000 men and 3,000 women.

A factor analysis of the interitem matrix was conducted on the total sample of 6,000 persons from the profile norm sample, giving rise to 11 factors with eigen values of 1.00 or more. Four factors were retained for rotation via Kaiser's normal varimax method. Prior factor analyses of the So scale (Butt, 1973; DeFrancesco & Taylor, 1986; Rosen, 1977; Stein, Gough, & Sarbin, 1966) all agreed that from four to six factors will account for the major sources of variation in the interitem matrix.

Factor 1 in the new analysis consisted of items associated with self-discipline and rule-observing behavior. Examples are: "In school I was sometimes sent to the principal because I had misbehaved" ("false"), "I have never been in trouble with the law" ("true"), and "I used to steal sometimes when I was a youngster" ("false"). Factor 2 contained items indicative of optimism, self-confidence, and positive emotionality, for example, "I don't think I'm quite as happy as others seem to be" ("false"), "Life usually hands me a pretty raw deal" ("false"), and "I have had more than my share of things to worry about" ("false"). Factor 3 had items indicative of good upbringing and favorable memories of family, for example, "My home life was always very pleasant" ("true") and "The members of my family were always very close to each other" ("true"). Factor 4 consisted of items indicative of interpersonal awareness and a reflective temperament, for example, "I often think about how I look and what impression I am making upon others" ("true"), and "I often act on the spur of the moment without stopping to think" ("false").

One study (Kubicka et al., 1995) examined findings for the four subscales of the So scale, comparing 190 young adults from unwanted pregnancies in the Czech Republic with pair-matched controls born of accepted pregnancies, at age 30. The 90 men and 100 women from unwanted pregnancies scored significantly lower than the contrast group on the So scale in full, and also on the subscales for self-discipline and favorable memories of childhood. The subscale for optimism and self-confidence differentiated for the female samples, but not for men. The fourth subscale for interpersonal awareness did not differentiate between persons from wanted and unwanted pregnancies, but did show an overall difference of gender, with women scoring higher than men.

Collins and Bagozzi (1999) did a confirmatory factor analysis of the four subscales of the So scale on white collar criminals and white collar controls, finding essential similarity of the four-factor structure in both groups. All four subscales also differentiated between the white collar criminals and their controls, with the largest effect-size of .98 for the interpersonal awareness subscale, next for self-discipline with a d value of .78, followed by optimism and positive emotionality with a d value of .68, and good memories of childhood with a d value of .38. For the total So scale, the difference was highly significant, with a d value of 1.02 (noncriminals had higher scores). A d value of 1.00 indicates a difference in means of the two contrasted groups of one standard deviation on the measure employed.

Relationship of So to recalled childhood experiences of 107 college men and 199 college women (Kosson, Steuerwald, Newman, & Widom, 1994) was appreciable for a number of formative influences. Conflict with mother had correlations of –.26 for men and –.35 for women, and conflict with father had corresponding correlations of –.43 and –.34. Amount criticized by parents had correlations with So of –.30 for men and –.42 for women, but a tally of amount of contact with parents had correlations of .28 and .31, respectively. Scores on So also related significantly ($p < .001$) to no prior use of marijuana, cocaine, and alcohol, and negatively (–.58 and –.39) to extent engaged in stealing. Even in this relatively well-socialized sample of 306 college students, low scores were associated with pathogenic childhood conditions and early appearance of deviant behaviors.

Findings from the Buss-Craik inventory of acts for 88 men and 89 women, rated for frequency of occurrence in a three-month period, are examined next. The five acts with largest positive correlations with So and the five with largest negative correlations are reported below.

Listened attentively to the speaker (.25)

Arrived on time for the meeting (.20)

Listened attentively while a friend talked about a problem (.19)

Went to church (.22)

Returned property that he/she had found (.18)

Told an off-color joke (–.20)

Hitch-hiked a ride (–.22)

Responded slowly and deliberately to a personal question (–.22)

	Men, Described By			Women, Described By		
Adjectives	Spouse (N = 236)	3 Peers (N = 194)	10 Staff Members (N = 612)	Spouse (N = 236)	3 Peers (N = 192)	10 Staff Members (N = 358)
Conscientious	.18**	.20**	.21**	.06	.22**	.26**
Conservative	.15*	.22**	.12**	.06	.27**	.22**
Conventional	.11	.24**	.14**	.13*	.24**	.23**
Cooperative	.12	.19**	.19**	.16*	.18*	.14**
Dependable	.07	.29**	.15**	.08	.20**	.27**
Efficient	.21**	.20**	.10**	.10	.20**	.15**
Honest	.10	.36**	.14**	.13*	.18*	.06
Modest	.08	.27**	.10**	.13*	.13	.12*
Organized	.21**	.32**	.22**	.20**	.26**	.25**
Reliable	.11	.34**	.19**	.03	.27**	.24**
Sincere	.07	.29**	.14**	.13*	.18*	.08
Tactful	.22**	.14*	.17**	.07	.13	.12*
Careless	−.22**	−.31**	−.18**	−.21**	−.23**	−.30**
Changeable	−.23**	−.14*	−.21**	−.24**	−.20**	−.29**
Cynical	−.18**	−.17*	−.31**	−.19**	−.15*	−.24**
Disorderly	−.18**	−.20**	−.13**	−.15*	−.32**	−.35**
Impatient	−.15*	−.14*	−.21**	−.16*	−.14*	−.29**
Impulsive	−.28**	−.30**	−.18**	−.26**	−.24**	−.31**
Pleasure-seeking	−.15*	−.16*	−.16**	−.15*	−.16*	−.20**
Rebellious	−.31**	−.28**	−.28**	−.29**	−.20**	−.33**
Reckless	−.30**	−.30**	−.20**	−.34**	−.24**	−.30**
Restless	−.26**	−.15*	−.25**	−.18**	−.18*	−.31**
Sarcastic	−.14*	−.23**	−.22**	−.22**	−.15*	−.19**
Temperamental	−.27**	−.20**	−.23**	−.18**	−.15*	−.24**

Table 5.9 Adjectival Descriptions by Observers: 12 Most Salient Positive and 12 Most Salient Negative Correlates of the 46-Item So Scale

*$p \leq .05$, **$p \leq .01$

Blamed other people for a mistake, even though it was not their fault (−.21)

Let a casual friend borrow a record album (−.24)

These acts are very specific and narrow in scope, but taken together they show persons with higher scores doing what good citizens are expected to do, and persons with lower scores exhibiting moderately unconventional and self-serving behavior.

Adjective check list descriptions of 1,828 persons in six samples were correlated with scores on the So scale. As shown in Table 5.9, the 12 words with largest positive and 12 with largest negative correlations were selected for presentation.

Persons with high scores on So were described by observers as conscientious, dependable, honest, and reliable, in keeping with the intentions of the measure. They were also seen as cooperative, modest, sincere, and tactful, suggesting sensitivity to the feelings of others. Another theme is suggested by the descriptions efficient and organized. Finally, observers saw them as conservative and conventional.

Persons with low scores on So were seen as careless, changeable, disorderly, impatient, impulsive, rebellious, reckless, and temperamental—terms indicative of willfulness and counter-normative inclinations. The descriptions cynical and sarcastic suggest unempathic reactions to others. Finally, the description pleasure-seeking hints at self-indulgent, self-serving tendencies.

A regression analysis of the 200 most frequently used adjectives in a composite sample of 1,356 persons was carried out to identify the particular subset of observers' descriptions that would best forecast scores on the So scale. The analysis was arbitrarily stopped after eight steps. The multiple correlation for the best set of eight descriptions was .40 (R^2 = .16). Adjectives with positive beta weights were honest and organized. Those with negative beta weights were dissatisfied, easy-going, individualistic, rebellious, tough, and wary.

The 100 items in the *California Q-Set* were correlated with scores on So for 547 men and 393 women, each of whom had been described on the Q-sort by panels of five or more observers. These independent formulations were combined into a single Q-sort for each person, and then the item correlated with scores on So. The four items with largest positive and four with largest negative coefficients are reported below. The first correlation is for the 547 men and the second is for the 393 women.

Is a genuinely dependable and responsible person (.27, .30)

Is fastidious (.22, .28)

Favors conservative values in a variety of areas (.23, .30)

Behaves in an ethically consistent manner; is consistent with own personal standards (.22, .28)

Is unpredictable and changeable in behavior and attitudes (−.23, −.35)

Various needs tend toward relatively direct and uncontrolled expression; unable to delay gratification (−.21, −.35)

Tends to be rebellious and nonconforming (−.30, −.34)

Characteristically pushes and tries to stretch limits; sees what he or she can get away with (−.27, −.28)

The Q-sort formulations for persons with high scores on So stress honesty and ethicality, and also depict the high-scoring individuals as conservative and fastidious. Low-scoring persons are viewed as rebellious, changeable, willful, and refractory.

Life history interviews were conducted with 504 men and 379 women. After each interview, the interviewer completed a 99-item check list recording direct observations and impressions gleaned from the session. These items were given weights of 1 for any checked item and of 0 for those left blank. The four items with largest positive and four with largest negative correlations with So are listed below. The first coefficient each time is for the 504 men and the second is for the 379 women.

Father benevolent and tolerant (.16, .27)

Family life on the whole was quite happy (.24, .40)

Standards of courteous and polite behavior were emphasized in the home (.17, .21)

Has a stable, optimistic view of the future (.17, .28)

Interviewee was ashamed of one or both parents (−.21, −.27)

Interviewee had a great deal of friction with parents (−.27, −.41)

Unhappy in school and at home (−.27, −.26)

Led a borderline, delinquent-like existence in high school (−.24, −.16)

Six of the eight items pertain to family circumstances. Persons with high scores on So reported their fathers to be benevolent and tolerant, had happy recollections of family life, and recalled an emphasis on courteous and polite behavior. Those with low scores on So tended to be ashamed of one parent or both parents, had friction with their parents, and were unhappy at home and also in school. They also reported a delinquent-like existence while in high school. High scorers on So, in other words, were socialized toward compliance and rule-respecting behavior as they grew up, whereas those low on So tended to reject their parents and also parental control, and in their teens began to show rule-testing and rule-violating behavior.

The final source of observational data comes from the 50-item *Interpersonal Q-Sort*, completed by 200 women to describe their husbands or partners, by 200 men to describe their wives or partners, and by three assessment staff judges to describe 111 male assessees. The three items with largest positive and three with largest negative correlations are given below, along with the coefficients for the 200 men, the 200 women, and the 111 male assessees.

A conscientious and serious-minded person (.18, .22, .23)

Honest and direct in behavior; mature and realistic in outlook (.18, .12, .27)

Well-organized, capable, patient, and industrious; values achievement (.18, .12, .27)

Restless and changeable; thinks and behaves differently from others (−.16, −.13, −.21)

Headstrong, rebellious, and resentful of others; lacking in self-discipline; apt to behave in a rash or destructive manner (−.12, −.17, −.26)

Given to moods; often difficult and recalcitrant (−.25, −.16, −.30)

High scorers on So are described as conscientious, honest, and well-organized. Low-scorers are described as restless, headstrong, and moody. These characterizations are similar to what was found for adjectival and other Q-sort descriptions, and are congruent with the stated aims of the So scale.

In summary, high scores on So are indicative of a kind of automatized, friction-free compliance with societal rules and conventions. In growing up, these high-scoring persons were influenced by parental models and prescriptions to accept easily the prevailing norms of the culture. Others see them clearly as reliable, organized, and conscientious. However, there is a downside associated with very high scores on So, beginning with raw scores of about 38, in too much conformity, and in ready acceptance of even those conventions that may be inhibitory and unduly constraining. Persons with very high scores on So can be harsh and punitive judges of deviation or weakness in others.

Low scores on So are indicative of failure or relative failure to internalize societal rules governing interpersonal life, and also presage difficulties in understanding others' inner needs and feelings. As a result, persons with low scores have many conflicts, behave in what seems to others to be rash and self-serving ways, and are poor at establishing long-lasting and mutually rewarding relationships. They also have serious problems with impulse control, and are prone to substance abuse, crime, and violence.

The Sc (Self-control) Scale

The Sc scale is the third of three CPI scales intended to assess internalization of norms and social values, the other two being Re and So. Accumulation of clinical and observational data for the Re scale suggests that persons with high scores are aware of and understand the meaning and nature of normative sanctions, and that their compliance is based on rational and discretionary motives. The purpose of the So scale, as just reviewed above, is to array individuals and groups along a continuum going from nearly automatic adherence to convention at one pole to very strong rule-breaking and norm-violating proclivities at the other. Neither the Re nor the So scale, however, carries any necessary implications for a positive evaluation of societal norms or for feelings that their prescriptions are ethically good and admirable. Also, low scores on Re and So do not presage the kind of joyful, ebullient abandonment of restraint that one might see at certain times, such as during participation in a carnival, or on occasions such as escape from disaster or abrupt release of tensions, or in intensively competitive events. In other words, there seems to be a place for a third measure, one that begins with a cathexis of societal sanctions and ends with a capacity for caprice, high spirits, and exuberant emotionality. This theory and the story of the scale's development were reported in considerable detail in the previous manual (Gough, 1987, pp. 45–52).

In the 1956 Form 480 version of the CPI, the Sc scale had 50 items. In the 1986 Form 462 version, the Sc scale was reduced to 38 items. For the present 434-item version of the inventory, Sc is composed of these same 38 items. A factor analysis of the 38 items in the total profile norm sample of 6,000 persons (3,000 of each sex) identified 10 factors with eigen values of 1.00 or more. Four of these were arbitrarily retained for rotation by means of Kaiser's normal varimax method. The first factor contained 19 items primarily centering on self-control, for example, "I must admit I have a bad temper, once I get angry" ("false"), "I often act on the spur of the moment, without stopping to think" ("false"), "Sometimes I feel like smashing things" ("false"), and "I am often said to be hotheaded" ("false"). Factor 2 had nine items expressing claims to modesty and selflessness, for example, "I like to be the center of attention" ("false") and "I like to boast about my achievements every now and then" ("false"). Factor 3 had seven items denying rule-breaking propensities. Examples are "I keep out of trouble at all cost" ("true") and "Sometimes I rather enjoy going against the rules and doing things I'm not supposed to do" ("false"). The fourth factor had only three items, suggesting suppression of hedonistic or aggressive feelings, for example, "I like large, noisy parties" ("false").

Act frequency data were analyzed in samples of 88 men and 89 women, each person being rated for frequency of occurrence of acts by a spouse or partner. The five acts with largest positive and five with largest negative correlations with Sc are reported below.

Listened attentively to the speaker (.20)

Went to church (.23)

Became deeply involved in a religious movement (.18)

Addressed a public gathering (.17)

Ate lunch alone (.17)

Said something simply to "shock" others (−.25)

Danced at the party (−.28)

Told a sexual joke (−.29)

Wore a sexy outfit to the dance (−.28)

Spent a large sum of money for an outfit for one dance (−.30)

Four of the five acts associated with high scores on Sc involve uplifting or socially commendable behavior. All of the acts associated with low scores involve relatively free and uninhibited expression of impulse, in particular erotic impulse.

Table 5.10 cites the 12 adjectives with largest positive and 12 with largest negative correlations with the Sc scale in six samples in which descriptions by observers were obtained. Several of the adjectives associated with high scores on Sc are compatible with the name of the measure, namely self-controlled, reserved, patient, and organized. One of the internal themes of the scale's 38 items stresses modesty and an absence of any inclinations toward self-aggrandizement. The adjectival descriptions moderate and modest suggest that this persona is to at least some extent acknowledged by observers. High scorers are also seen as conscientious and dependable, conventional and conservative, and mild.

The hedonistic, fun-in-life implications envisaged for low scorers on Sc are visible in the observers' descriptions of adventurous, mischievous, and pleasure-seeking. Problems of impulse control are also noted in the adjectives headstrong, impulsive, reckless, careless, and temperamental. An element of self-seeking is noted in the description boastful.

A regression analysis of the 200 most frequently used adjectives was carried out on a sample of 1,356 persons (806 men, 550 women), for whom the observers' ACL descriptions were first standardized by subsample of origin. The analysis was arbitrarily terminated after eight steps. The best combination of eight adjectives for predicting scores on Sc had a multiple correlation of .37 ($R^2 = .14$). Three adjectives had positive beta weights: alert, obliging, and peaceable. The five adjectives with negative beta weights were adventurous, changeable, easy-going, pleasure-seeking, and sensitive. Even if the maneuver has a superficial basis, high scorers on Sc seem to want to make a good impression and to get along well with others. Low scorers, as anticipated, are experience-seeking, changeable, and easy-going. The item sensitive is of interest in pointing to an element of vulnerability in the otherwise exuberant self-assertion of those with low scores.

The 100 items in the *California Q-Set* were correlated with scores on Sc in samples of 547 men and 393 women, each of whom had been described on the Q-sort by panels of five or more assessment staff observers. The four items with largest positive and the four with largest negative correlations are given below, along with the coefficients for the 547 men and for the 393 women.

	Men, Described By			Women, Described By		
Adjectives	Spouse (N = 236)	3 Peers (N = 194)	10 Staff Members (N = 612)	Spouse (N = 236)	3 Peers (N = 192)	10 Staff Members (N = 358)
Conscientious	.21**	.16*	.14**	.14*	.23**	.23**
Conservative	.21**	.10	.11**	.18**	.34**	.23**
Conventional	.18**	.11	.12**	.17**	.32**	.19**
Dependable	.14*	.19**	.12**	.08	.15*	.19**
Mild	.13*	.16*	.12**	.21**	.28**	.21**
Moderate	.15*	.19**	.17**	.26**	.34**	.24**
Modest	.13*	.20**	.14**	.20**	.29**	.18**
Organized	.26**	.17*	.09*	.20**	.24**	.14**
Patient	.13*	.19**	.16**	.05	.29**	.16**
Quiet	.20**	.14*	.11**	.25**	.31**	.21**
Reserved	.15*	.14*	.14**	.12	.34**	.16**
Self-controlled	.10	.16*	.11**	.12	.26**	.19**
Adventurous	−.27**	−.13	−.26**	−.17**	−.28**	−.34**
Boastful	−.22**	−.15*	−.18**	−.15*	−.22**	−.11*
Careless	−.14*	−.21**	−.11**	−.18**	−.24**	−.19**
Headstrong	−.18**	−.16*	−.18**	−.30**	−.17*	−.22**
Impulsive	−.27**	−.24**	−.20**	−.34**	−.33**	−.26**
Mischievous	−.19**	−.31**	−.25**	−.13*	−.18*	−.20**
Outgoing	−.19**	−.16*	−.16**	−.14*	−.19**	−.19**
Pleasure-seeking	−.24**	−.14*	−.26**	−.24**	−.23**	−.29**
Rebellious	−.21**	−.21**	−.18**	−.22**	−.34**	−.26**
Reckless	−.24**	−.16*	−.19**	−.32**	−.20**	−.24**
Restless	−.25**	−.14*	−.16**	−.20**	−.31**	−.26**
Temperamental	−.21**	−.21**	−.18**	−.28**	−.18*	−.20**

Table 5.10 Adjectival Descriptions by Observers: 12 Most Salient Positive and 12 Most Salient Negative Correlates of the 38-Item Sc Scale

*$p \le .05$, **$p \le .01$

Is a genuinely dependable and responsible person (.25, .31)

Is fastidious (.23, .26)

Tends toward overcontrol of needs and impulses, binds tensions excessively; delays gratification unnecessarily (.24, .33)

Behaves in an ethically consistent manner; is consistent with own personal standards (.21, .35)

Various needs tend toward relatively direct and uncontrolled expression; unable to delay gratification (−.24, −.32)

Tends to be rebellious and nonconforming (−.21, −.29)

Characteristically pushes and tries to stretch limits; sees what he or she can get away with (−.31, −.34)

Is self-indulgent (−.23, −.26)

Overcontrol is associated with higher scores on Sc, and undercontrol with lower. This is an important finding and, among other things, indicates that an optimum score on Sc is somewhere in its middle range. High scorers are also viewed as genuinely dependable, fastidious, and observant of their own personal standards. Low scorers on Sc tend to be rebellious and nonconforming, self-indulgent, and fretful when confronted with constraints or limits.

Check list descriptions by life history interviewers of 547 men and 379 women were correlated with scores on Sc, using dummy weights of 1 for any item checked and of 0 for items left blank. The four items with largest positive and four with largest negative correlations are listed below, along with the coefficients for men and for women. The correlations in this instance are very low, although all of them are statistically significant at or beyond the .05 level of probability.

Reticent and taciturn (.13, .13)

Has strong religious beliefs (.15, .14)

Is happily married (.19, .19)

Has a stable, optimistic view of the future (.10, .18)

Excited, restless during the interview (−.13, −.14)

Made considerable use of hands in talking (−.10, −.12)

Quick tempo of movement (−.10, −.11)

Had first sexual intercourse while in high school or before (−.22, −.10)

Apparently, high scorers on Sc held back in the interviews and were guarded in expression, although they did acknowledge strong religious beliefs and reported their marriages as happy. They also voiced optimism about the future. Most of what impressed the interviewers about the low scorers on Sc was their style and manner of behavior—restlessness, gesturing with their hands, and a quick tempo of movement. One item of content, early manifestation of overt sexuality, is in keeping with suppressive responses to eroticism among high scorers and relatively open manifestation of eroticism among low scorers.

Q-sort descriptions by observers on a 50-item list were available for 200 men described by their wives or partners, 200 women described by their husbands or partners, and 111 men each described by a panel of three assessment staff observers. The three items with largest positive and three with largest negative correlations with Sc are cited below, and the coefficients for the 200 men, 200 women, and 111 men, in that order.

Patient and self-controlled; restrained and self-contained in behavior (.10, .23, .24)

A conscientious and serious-minded person (.23, .19, .16)

Well-organized, capable, patient, and industrious; values achievement (.14, .20, .23)

Impulsive and uninhibited; easily angered and irritated (−.13, −.19, −.18)

Headstrong, rebellious, and resentful of others; lacking in self-discipline; apt to behave in a rash or destructive manner (−.09, −.17, −.20)

Given to moods; often difficult and recalcitrant (−.12, −.12, −.10)

Correlations of the Sc scale with items from the *Interpersonal Q-Sort* are weak at best, with only 10 of the 18 cited above reaching or exceeding the .05 level of confidence. Hence, any interpretive remarks based on these relationships must be considered as highly tentative and as in need of verification from other sources. With those provisos, it is still of interest to note the similarity of the Q-sort items to what the other analyses have shown. That is, those with high scores on Sc are seen as self-controlled, conscientious, and well-organized; whereas those with low scores are seen as impulsive, headstrong, and given to moods.

In summary, scores on Sc do appear to define a continuum going from undercontrol to overcontrol. High scorers bind their tension, seek to please, and want to be accepted as admirable, upstanding people. In particular, they avoid overt or blatant expressions of aggressive and erotic impulses. However, the controls exerted are often excessive, and at raw-score levels of around 32 and above, their repressions exact a cost. One of these costs is that anger, being bottled up and denied, has a tendency toward explosive, destructive breakthroughs. Another is attitudes of judgmentalism toward others who are more candid and open in expressing erotic and aggressive feelings.

Low scorers are indeed less inhibited and more open in regard to their emotions, but they have their own problems with which to contend. One of these is a disposition toward headstrong, undercontrolled behavior that can lead to serious conflict with others. Another is the egoism or narcissism associated with low scores, which interferes with the establishment of long-lasting, deeply experienced relationships.

The configural implications of scores on Re, So, and Sc merit a brief discussion, keeping in mind that Re presages an analytic, rational mode of rule compliance; So involves an automated, friction-free adherence to social norms; and Sc betokens self-restraint, along with feelings that normative sanctions are right and proper. Consider the pattern of moderate elevation on Re, and somewhat below-average scores on So and Sc. This configuration is associated with creativity and guilt-free enjoyment of life, but at the same time with acceptable rule-observing behavior. A second pattern has a somewhat below-average score on Re, a below average score on So, and a quite elevated score on Sc. This configuration suggests undue suppression of impulse, lack of insight concerning aggressive feelings, and a potential for explosive or uncontrolled breakthrough of destructive behavior. McAllister (1996, p.75) has commented on this configuration of low Re and So, along with high Sc, as well as on other configurations involving these three scales.

The Gi (Good Impression) Scale

The development of the Gi scale was described in chapter 4, "The Detection of Invalid Protocols." Gi in fact has two goals: to assist in identifying protocols confounded by too strenuous attempts to claim favorable attributes and virtues, and to define a continuum in which impression management varies from a projected indifference to others' evaluations to a very active desire to be seen as a good and admirable person. Implications of Gi for faking good begin at raw scores of approximately 30 and above. From about 18 to 29, the psychological scale marks an increasing concern about the reactions of others. From about 14 and below, respondents are stating (often rather assertively), a rejection of the idea that their actions and beliefs are guided by any attempt to win favor.

A factor analysis of the 40 items in the Gi scale on a sample of 6,000 persons (3,000 of each sex) found 10 factors with eigen values of 1.00 or more. Four of these were arbitrarily retained for rotation by means of Kaiser's normal varimax method. Factor 1 contained items denying any self-serving or egoistic motives, for example, "I always follow the rule: business before pleasure" ("true"), "I like to boast about my achievements every now and then" ("false"), and "I am apt to show off in some way if I get the chance" ("false"). Factor 2 had items claiming equanimity and absence of any moodiness or irritability, for instance, "Every now and then I get into a bad mood and no one can do anything to please me" ("false") and "If I am not feeling well I am somewhat cross and grouchy" ("false"). Factor 3 included items stating a willingness to accept supervision, work under strictly defined conditions, and avoid any interpersonal friction. Representative items are, "I do not mind taking orders and being told what to do" ("true"), "I have very few quarrels with members of my family" ("true"), and "I always try to consider the other person's feelings before I do something" ("true"). Factor 4 has items expressing faith in the ethicality and goodwill of others, for example, "Most people would tell a lie if they could gain by it" ("false") and "Most people are secretly pleased when someone else gets into trouble" ("false").

Act frequency implications for Gi were examined in a sample of 177 persons (88 men, 89 women) in which each person was rated on the frequency of acts by a spouse or partner. The five acts with largest positive and five with largest negative correlations with Gi are reported below.

Listened attentively to the speaker (.21)

Had the boss over for dinner (.16)

Went to church (.25)

Became deeply involved in a religious movement (.19)

Was active in community or campus affairs (.15)

Withheld affection so as to get his/her way (–.28)

Let others pay for the drinks (–.25)

Refused to acknowledge that he/she was wrong (–.25)

Was unwilling to listen to another person's point of view (–.29)

Refused to change his/her mind (–.26)

Two of the five acts associated with high scores on Gi involve overt religious activity, and one involves

	Men, Described By			Women, Described By		
Adjectives	Spouse (N = 236)	3 Peers (N = 194)	10 Staff Members (N = 612)	Spouse (N = 236)	3 Peers (N = 192)	10 Staff Members (N = 358)
Appreciative	.14*	.10	.01	.10	.26**	.13*
Conscientious	.12	.06	.06	.18*	.20**	.23**
Conservative	.22**	.08	.08*	.05	.29**	.21**
Conventional	.15*	.11	.09*	.11	.30**	.16**
Cooperative	.13*	.05	.02	.21**	.21**	.10*
Dependable	.10	.12	.05	.05	.15*	.18**
Formal	.03	.14*	.05	.11	.11	.13*
Moderate	.14*	.06	.09*	.24**	.29**	.17**
Organized	.19**	.08	.03	.13*	.22**	.20**
Practical	.16*	.06	.03	.10	.19**	.03
Quiet	.10	.05	.01	.14*	.24**	.11*
Thorough	.04	.02	.09*	.08	.14*	.13*
Argumentative	−.13*	−.13	−.07	−.22**	−.23**	−.04
Careless	−.14*	−.13	−.10**	−.11	−.22**	−.18**
Complaining	−.13*	−.15*	−.08*	−.26**	−.22**	−.09
Dissatisfied	−.19**	−.15*	−.15**	−.11	−.14*	−.17**
Emotional	−.12	−.15*	−.12**	−.19**	−.11	−.15**
Headstrong	−.16*	−.14*	−.13**	−.18**	−.18*	−.10*
Impulsive	−.25**	−.10	−.12**	−.24**	−.27**	−.19**
Mischievous	−.12	−.22**	−.18**	−.12	−.18*	−.15**
Pleasure-seeking	−.16*	−.05	−.14**	−.18*	−.20**	−.21**
Rebellious	−.19**	−.08	−.18**	−.16*	−.32**	−.16**
Restless	−.21**	−.18*	−.16**	−.17*	−.28**	−.17**
Temperamental	−.12	−.26**	−.18**	−.16*	−.29**	−.16**

Table 5.11 Adjectival Descriptions by Observers: 12 Most Salient Positive and 12 Most Salient Negative Correlates of the 40-Item Gi Scale

*p ≤ .05, **p ≤ .01

taking part in community affairs. The other two acts pertain to more immediate or personal attention to others. All of the acts associated with low scores on Gi suggest resistance to needs or demands of others and an insistence on having one's own way. Work with individuals having low scores on Gi (raw scores of 12 or below) have revealed a prickly, isolative demeanor that is consonant with these five acts.

Adjectival descriptions by observers for persons in six different samples were correlated with the Gi scale as shown in Table 5.11. The 12 adjectives with largest positive and 12 with largest negative correlations are cited in the table. In examining these relationships it should be remembered that very few if any of the 1,828 respondents on whom these analyses were made had scores on Gi in the fake-good region. Persons with moderately elevated scores on Gi present themselves as agreeable, congenial individuals who try to do what pleases others. Observers do appear to see them as appreciative and cooperative. High scorers are also seen as conscientious and dependable, moderate, thorough, and quiet. Their behavior appears to be somewhat formal, and they are described as conventional and conservative.

Low scorers on Gi are quite differently described, one cluster containing adjectives such as argumentative, dissatisfied, complaining, and temperamental. Another cluster pertains to self-assertion, with adjectives such as headstrong, impulsive, rebellious, and restless. Pleasure-seeking and mischievous constitute a third grouping, and the list is closed out by careless and emotional.

In a sample of 1,356 persons with the adjectival descriptions standardized by subsample, a regression of the 200 most frequently used terms on the Gi scale was carried out, arbitrarily terminating the analysis at eight steps. At that point, the multiple correlation was .31 (R^2 = .10). Only one item had a positive beta weight, submissive. The seven adjectives with negative beta weights were awkward, changeable, cynical, easy-going, sensitive, temperamental, and witty.

Relationship of the Gi scale to the 100 items in the *California Q-Set* were studied in samples of 547 men and 393 women, each of whom had been described on the Q-sort by panels of five or more assessment staff observers. These independent formulations were combined into a consensus for each assessee, and then the Q-sort items were correlated with scores on the Gi scale. The four items with largest positive and four with largest negative correlations are listed below, along with the coefficient for men, and for women.

Is fastidious (.20, .22)

Favors conservative values in a variety of areas (.15, .24)

Is moralistic (.14, .26)

Behaves in a sympathetic or considerate manner (.17, .18)

Is unpredictable and changeable in behavior and attitudes (–.12, –.27)

Tends to be rebellious and nonconforming (–.18, –.26)

Characteristically pushes and tries to stretch limits; sees what he or she can get away with (–.21, –.24)

Is self-indulgent (–.13, –.27)

High scorers on Gi are described as fastidious, conservative, moralistic, and considerate. Low scorers are described as changeable, nonconforming, refractory, and self-indulgent.

Relationships of the Gi scale to interviewers' impressions as recorded in the 99-item check list are almost too small to report. Only one of the items had significant ($p < .05$) negative correlations for both men and women, and only four had significant positive correlations for both subsamples. The item associated with low scores on Gi was, "Had first sexual experience while in high school or before," with coefficients of –.19 for 504 men and –.13 for 379 women. The four items with positive correlations were, "Standards of courteous and polite behavior were emphasized in the home" (.12, .14), "Is happily married" (.11, .10), "Has a stable, optimistic view of the future" (.14, .22), and "Seems relatively free of neurotic trends, conflicts, and other forms of instability" (.11, .13).

For the 50-item *Interpersonal Q-Sort*, relationships with Gi were a bit stronger. This analysis was carried out in three samples: 200 men described by their wives or partners, 200 women described by their husbands or partners, and 111 men described by panels of three assessment staff observers. The three items with largest positive and three with largest negative correlations are reported below, along with the coefficients for men, women, and the 111 male assessees.

A conscientious and serious-minded person (.17, .14, .16)

Well-organized, capable, patient, and industrious; values achievement (.11, .18, .25)

Gentle, considerate, and tactful in dealing with others; appreciative and helpful (.14, .15, .14)

Impulsive and uninhibited; easily angered and irritated (–.19, –.22, –.14)

Distrustful and cynical; dissatisfied with most things; indifferent to the worries and problems of others (–.10, –.18, –.16)

Critical and outspoken; disparages other people and their ideas (–.14, –.09, –.19)

The patience, tact, and concern for others associated with moderate elevations on Gi are apparent in the items with positive correlations, and the indifference to others and tendency to speak critically and disparagingly of others associated with below average scores on Gi are apparent in the items with negative correlations.

In summary, respondents with above average but not extraordinarily high scores on Gi see themselves as cooperative, helpful, and considerate, and in fact are described in these same terms by others. What these high scorers do not see in themselves is their tendency toward moralistic reactions and their opportunistic tendencies. Work with individuals has shown that persons with high scores on Gi often seek to ingratiate themselves with superiors while overlooking or ignoring the feelings of their own subordinates. Low scorers on Gi value their own authenticity, to the point of being aggressively indifferent to what others may think. They are also quick to complain, criticize, and voice skepticism about the alleged purposes and good qualities of their more conventional peers.

The Cm (Communality) Scale

The Cm scale was developed to identify protocols rendered invalid by careless, random, unknowing, or extremely unusual patterns of response to the inventory. The items scored for "true" are answered in this way by a large percentage of respondents from all groups tested to date, and those scored for "false" are answered in this way by most people. This "communality" of response, incidentally, holds for testing with the inventory in non-English versions. Here are some examples, and the percentages answering "true" for the profile norm samples of 3,000 persons of each sex:

My parents wanted me to "make good" in the world. (95% and 91%)

Education is more important than most people think. (90% and 93%)

If I am driving a car, I try to keep others from passing me. (10% and 6%)

Voting is nothing but a nuisance. (3% and 4%)

On the Cm scale, the first two items are scored for "true" and the last two are scored for "false."

Because of the modality effect, scores tend to accumulate at the high end of the scale, with norm means of about 34.5 on the 38-item measure. A long tail of scores extends downward to include respondents who do not understand what they are reading, those answering randomly, and some, of course, whose approach to testing is radically different from that of most people.

In chapter 4, use of the Cm scale as an aid in detecting invalid protocols was spelled out in considerable detail. In the present chapter, attention will be centered on the meaning of the scale for protocols deemed to be valid. A first step in this direction comes from a factor analysis of the 38 items in the total profile norm sample of 6,000 persons. Ten factors were detected with eigen values of 1.00 or more, and four of these were arbitrarily retained for rotation by means of Kaiser's normal varimax method. Factor 1 included items disagreeing with cynical or antagonistic views of human nature, for example, "Most young people get too much education" ("false"), "People should not be expected to do anything for their community unless they are paid for it" ("false"), and "It is impossible for an honest person to get ahead in the world" ("false"). Factor 2 is composed of items expressing optimism about self and the society, for instance, "The future seems hopeless to me" ("false") and "I usually feel that life is worthwhile" ("true"). Factor 3 has items recognizing benefits accruing from life's experiences, for example, "I believe we are made better by the trials and hardships of life" ("true") and "Any person who is willing to work hard has a good chance of succeeding" ("true"). Factor 4 has items admitting to ordinary emotionality and affect, for instance, "There are times when I have been very angry" ("true") and "Some people exaggerate their troubles in order to get sympathy" ("true").

Act frequency data were analyzed in a sample of 177 persons (88 men, 89 women), each of whom had been rated for frequency of specific acts in the last three months by a spouse or partner. The five acts with largest positive and five with largest negative correlations with Cm are reported below.

Arrived on time for the meeting (.20)

Told a joke to lighten a tense situation (.19)

Went to church (.22)

Sent greeting cards on holidays (.20)

Carefully looked at the prices before buying the object (.27)

Hung up the phone on a partner (−.18)

Ate in the corner of the cafeteria alone (–.20)

Mumbled to himself/herself (–.17)

Made no plans for the weekend (–.16)

Avoided eye contact in the conversation (–.16)

The correlations are quite small, but generally compatible with the notion of what most people might do in everyday situations. Those with higher scores on Cm arrived on time for a meeting, used humor to relieve a tense situation, went to church, sent cards on holidays, and checked on the price before buying something. These are all conventional, ordinary bits of behavior. Items associated with lower scores on Cm included hanging up the phone on a partner or spouse, eating alone, mumbling instead of talking clearly, not making weekend plans, and avoiding eye contact. In minor ways, these are all unconventional or at least nonmodal actions.

Adjectival descriptions by observers related to the Cm scale were studied in six samples totaling 1,828 individuals. The 12 adjectives with largest positive and the 12 with largest negative correlations are presented in Table 5.12.

Respondents with higher scores on Cm are, in fact, described as conventional. Then there is a theme of reasonableness, including the terms conscientious, dependable, and reasonable. Another theme is suggested by the terms efficient, organized, and practical. High scorers are also described as ambitious, conservative, contented, mature, and stable. Low scorers on Cm are described as unconventional, and then rather negatively as lazy, moody, quitting, and shiftless. Another theme suggests indifference to ordinary doings, namely absentminded, careless, and forgetful. Additional descriptions include changeable, impulsive, and reckless.

In a sample of 1,356 persons, standardized scores on the 200 most frequently used adjectives were regressed onto the Cm scale, stopping the analysis arbitrarily at eight steps. The multiple correlation for these eight terms was .32 (R^2 = .10). Two of the adjectives had positive beta weights: organized and responsible. Six had negative beta weights: aloof, attractive, awkward, individualistic, logical, and withdrawn.

Observers' descriptions using the *California Q-Set* were related to scores on Cm in samples of 547 men and 393 women, each of whom received a Q-sort by panels of five or more judges. These independent formulations were combined into a single consensu-

al sorting for each assessee, and then the 100 items in the *Q-Set* were correlated with Cm. The four items with largest positive and four with largest negative coefficients are reported below. The first coefficient each time is for the 547 men, and the second is for the 393 women.

Is a genuinely dependable and responsible person (.14, .16)

Is fastidious (.15, .14)

Is turned to for advice and reassurance (.13, .23)

Has social poise and presence; appears socially at ease (.16, .24)

Feels a lack of personal meaning in life (–.12, –.19)

Is self-defeating (–.15, –.27)

Tends to be rebellious and nonconforming (–.15, –.20)

Has fluctuating moods (–.12, –.21)

Persons with high scores on Cm tend to be described as dependable, fastidious, poised, and as worth asking for advice. Those with low scores tend to be seen as self-defeating, nonconforming, fluctuating in mood, and as lacking a sense of meaning in their lives.

Life history interviews were conducted with 504 men and 379 women. After each interview, the interviewer filled in a 99-item check list recording observations and factual information. Items with checks were assigned dummy weights of 1, and items left blank were given weights of 0. These weights were then correlated with scores on Cm. The four items with largest positive and the four with largest negative correlations are cited below, along with the coefficients for men and for women.

Well-groomed and well-dressed (.15, .16)

Is happily married (.14, .13)

Has a stable, optimistic view of the future (.14, .19)

Seems relatively free of neurotic trends, conflicts, and other forms of instability (.12, .24)

Unhappy at school and at home (–.11, –.16)

Dated very little or not at all (–.09, –.10)

Is unsure of self, doubts own ability (–.13, –.12)

Thin, appears weak and frail (–.12, –.10)

Although the correlations reported above are significant at or beyond the .05 level of probability, they

Table 5.12 Adjectival Descriptions by Observers: 12 Most Salient Positive and 12 Most Salient Negative Correlates of the 38-Item Cm Scale

	Men, Described By			Women, Described By		
Adjectives	Spouse (N = 236)	3 Peers (N = 194)	10 Staff Members (N = 612)	Spouse (N = 236)	3 Peers (N = 192)	10 Staff Members (N = 358)
Ambitious	.05	.10	.05	.13*	.18*	.08
Conscientious	.09	.16*	.10**	.11	.18*	.15**
Conservative	.08	.12	.12**	.06	.11	.10*
Contented	.16*	.02	.02	.03	.06	.25**
Conventional	.02	.06	.10**	.02	.08	.17**
Dependable	.04	.20**	.05	.12	.13	.25**
Efficient	.08	.22**	.10**	.11	.20**	.17**
Mature	.12	.18*	.06	.20**	.05	.20**
Organized	.02	.24**	.14**	.12	.17*	.24**
Practical	.04	.21**	.03	.12	.12	.22**
Reasonable	.11	.11	.04	.17*	.19**	.18**
Stable	.11	.15*	.04	.08	.16*	.27**
Absent-minded	−.19*	−.15*	−.11**	−.04	−.11	−.14**
Careless	−.16*	−.22**	−.11**	−.08	−.13	−.11*
Changeable	−.15*	−.05	−.09*	−.12	−.06	−.13*
Cynical	−.10	−.03	−.12**	−.10	−.14*	−.18**
Forgetful	−.09	−.26**	−.11**	−.09	−.13	−.09
Impulsive	−.04	−.10	−.08*	−.15*	−.08	−.11*
Lazy	−.10	−.19*	−.09*	−.20**	−.10	−.10*
Moody	−.28**	−.03	−.11**	−.10	−.11	−.30**
Quitting	−.11	−.17*	−.08*	−.04	−.03	−.14**
Reckless	−.15*	−.24**	−.01	−.18**	−.12	−.16**
Shiftless	−.14*	−.08	−.08*	−.12	−.15*	−.14**
Unconventional	−.17*	−.05	−.13**	−.14*	−.24**	−.19**

*p ≤ .05, **p ≤ .01

are very small. Specific links to higher or lower scores on Cm should therefore be viewed with great caution, although the general tenor of the relationships appears to be meaningful. That is, high scores on Cm seem to be associated with what normal, reasonable people who are in good touch with the culture should do. Low scores on Cm are isolating in one way or another, indicative of dissatisfaction, uncertainty, and peripherality.

Items from the 50-item *Interpersonal Q-Sort* were correlated with Cm in three samples: 200 men described by their wives or partners, 200 women described by their husbands or partners, and 111 male assessees described by panels of three staff observers. The three items with largest positive and three with largest negative correlations with Cm are given below, along with the correlations for the men, the women, and the male assessees.

Alert and energetic in behavior and attitudes; uncomplaining and in good spirits (.10, .15, .11)

Gets along well with others; able to "fit in" easily in most situations (.13, .10, .19)

Independent, intelligent, and self-reliant; values achievement (.05, .06, .28)

Distrustful and cynical; dissatisfied with most things; indifferent to the worries and problems of others (−.03, −.18, −.21)

Undependable; poorly motivated; has difficulty in working toward prescribed goals (−.14, −.05, −.17)

Worried and preoccupied; tense, nervous, and generally upset (−.13, −.17, −.19)

Because of the low magnitude of these correlations, the relationships implied must be seen as tenuous and suggestive only. The three items associated with higher scores on Cm, taken together, depict someone who feels comfortable in the social milieu and who can function effectively. The three items associated with lower scores on Cm, taken together, depict someone who feels marginal, and whose interpersonal functioning is impaired.

In summary, above average scores on Cm can be taken as confirming the validity of the protocol, and also as indicative of someone who fits in, who espouses consensual goals and values, and who gets along well with others. Very high scores (raw scores of 37 to 38) carry an additional meaning of conventionality and undue conformity. Low scores on Cm (below 25 raw score points) are suggestive of random or erratic answering and of possible invalidity of the protocol, but also of poor morale, self-doubt, feelings of alienation, and general instability. Moderately low scores (30 to 34 raw score points), on the other hand, can be indicative of independence of mind, creative differences from the norm, and self-assertion.

The Wb (Well-being) Scale

The Wb scale is a derivative of an early scale (Gough, 1954) developed to distinguish between bona fide psychiatric patients and persons attempting to simulate their reactions. Items showing large differences between the authentic and dissimulated samples were further checked against endorsement rates from normal samples. Those for which patients and normals had essential identical rates of endorsement were retained for the scale. The 74-item scale was called Ds for *Dissimulation*, and has been widely used in work with the MMPI, both in its original 74-item version and in a shortened 40-item version (Friedman, Webb, & Lewak, 1989; Woychyshyn, McElheran, & Romney, 1992).

When the first 480-item edition of the CPI was published in 1956, a 44-item version of the Ds scale was included, but scored in a reverse direction and retitled Wb for *Well-being*. In the 1986 Form 462 of the CPI, Wb was shortened to 38 items. To develop Form 434 of the CPI, items contraindicated by the Americans with Disabilities Act were dropped from Form 462. Seven of the items dropped came from the Wb scale. Two examples are, "I hardly ever feel pain in the back of the neck" ("true"), and "I have a great deal of stomach trouble" ("false"). In order to keep Wb at its same length, seven other items from the CPI were substituted. An example is "Most of the time I feel happy" ("true"). One of the effects of these changes in content was to shift emphasis from physical and psychological well-being to primarily psychological well-being. In spite of the change of items, correlations between the current and prior versions of Wb were .96 for both the 3,000 profile norm men and the 3,000 profile norm women.

As before, the Wb scale serves a validating as well as interpretive function in the inventory. Very low scores (raw scores of 20 and below) raise the possibility of exaggerated or unwarranted emphasis on personal problems, and even of a deliberate attempt to fake bad. Within the range of raw scores from 20 to 38, interpretations are permissible along the lines to be elaborated below.

A factor analysis of the current 38-item form of the Wb scale was carried out on the profile norm sample of 6,000 persons. Eight factors were identified with eigen values of 1.00 or more, of which four were arbitrarily retained for rotation by Kaiser's normal varimax method. Factor 1 contained items indicative of feelings of wholeness and integrity, and the ability to withstand stress. Examples are, "Sometimes I feel that I am about to go to pieces" ("false"), "I feel like giving up quickly when things go wrong" ("false"), and "I get tired more easily than other people seem to" ("false"). Factor 2 included items suggesting trust in others and feelings that life's treatment is fair, for example, "I would have been more successful if people had given me a fair chance" ("false") and "Life usually hands me a pretty raw deal" ("false"). Factor 3 has items suggesting good relations with others and absence of extreme irritations, for instance, "Some of my family have habits that bother and annoy me very much" ("false"), and "At times I have a strong urge to do something harmful or shocking" ("false"). Factor 4 contained items indicative of happiness and good morale. Examples are "Most of the time I feel happy" ("true") and "I don't think I'm quite as happy as others seem to be" ("false").

Act frequency analyses for Wb were conducted in a sample of 187 persons (88 men and 89 women), each of whom had been rated for frequency of a list of acts by a spouse or partner. The five acts with largest positive and five with largest negative correlations with Wb are given below.

> Listened attentively to the speaker (.25)
>
> Arrived on time for the meeting (.25)
>
> Entered a competitive sporting event (.20)
>
> Organized a group to attain its goals (.22)
>
> Willingly tried a new food at the restaurant at the suggestion of a friend (.23)
>
> Turned red when asked a personal question (–.21)
>
> Exaggerated a personal problem (–.20)
>
> Ignored a stranger's "hello" (–.16)
>
> Accused them of talking behind his/her back (–.15)
>
> Wept when he/she couldn't solve a simple problem (–.16)

Acts associated with higher scores on Wb involve paying attention to others, entering a competition, taking the initiative, and trying something new in food. All of these specific acts can be seen as based on a sufficient fund of energy and sense of well-being. Acts associated with low scores on Wb suggest distance from others, feelings of insufficiency, and a dwelling on personal difficulties.

Is there any evidence that Wb scores are related to real-life indices of good health, well-being, and the like? One study (Bayer, Whissell-Buechy, & Honzik, 1980) had two physicians rate the general good health of 51 men and 77 women at age 50, using their combined ratings as a criterion. The correlation of this criterion with the Wb scale of the CPI, from testing at 42, was .27 for men and .43 for women. Another study (Picano, 1989) related CPI data at age

21 to indices of adjustment in various categories at ages 42 to 45 for 75 women. For psychological well-being the correlation with Wb was .27, for physical health the correlation was .21, and for total or overall adjustment the correlation was .33. These two studies agree in showing a moderately positive relationship between scores on the Wb scale and various criteria of good psychological functioning over the life span.

Table 5.13 lists the 12 adjectives with largest positive and 12 with largest negative correlations with the Wb scale in six different samples in which respondents were described on the ACL by observers. It is rather striking in looking at this table how much stronger are the associations with low scores on Wb than with high scores. It is as if the extent to which a high scorer on Wb can be characterized is limited to "This person feels good, has energy, seems stable, and can get things done." One of the adjectival clusters associated with low scores on Wb stresses poor morale and feelings of victimization, for example, bitter, complaining, and self-pitying. Another cluster pertains to nervousness, distractibility, anxiety, and worry. Difficulty in achieving harmonious relations with others is suggested by the descriptors defensive, suspicious, and nagging.

In a composite sample of 1,356 persons for whom the descriptive adjectives were standardized by subsample, the 200 most frequently used words were regressed onto the Wb scale, with the analysis arbitrarily stopped after eight steps. The multiple correlation for this best set of eight adjectives for predicting scores on Wb was .32 (R^2 = .10). Adjectives with positive beta weights were moderate and organized, and those with negative weights were adventurous, confused, dissatisfied, cynical, kind, and silent.

In assessed samples of 547 men and 393 women, panels of five or more staff observers performed a Q-sort from the *California Q-Set* on each person. The staff sortings were then combined into a single consensual formulation for each assessee, and the 100 items correlated with scores on the Wb scale. The four items with largest positive and four with largest negative correlations are reported below, along with the coefficients for men and for women.

> Is productive, gets things done (.15, .27)
>
> Is subjectively unaware of self-concern; feels satisfied with self (.16, .26)

Table 5.13 Adjectival Descriptions by Observers: 12 Most Salient Positive and 12 Most Salient Negative Correlates of the 38-Item Wb Scale

Adjectives	Men, Described By			Women, Described By		
	Spouse (N = 236)	3 Peers (N = 194)	10 Staff Members (N = 612)	Spouse (N = 236)	3 Peers (N = 192)	10 Staff Members (N = 358)
Adaptable	.09	.06	.09*	.07	.27**	.07
Cheerful	.12	.05	.04	.05	.22**	.10*
Confident	.10	.14*	.06	.17**	.17*	.15**
Contented	.22**	.08	.00	.19**	.22**	.11*
Efficient	.10	.05	.17**	.19**	.15*	.15**
Energetic	.04	.04	.10**	.08	.16*	.08
Enterprising	.03	.10	.07	.14*	.13	.14**
Initiative	.03	.13	.08*	.15*	.11	.13*
Organized	.10	.09	.16**	.10	.19**	.21**
Poised	.07	.14*	.09*	.07	.12	.15**
Self-confident	.16*	.08	.05	.19**	.17*	.16**
Stable	.11	.07	.01	.06	.23**	.19**
Anxious	−.14*	−.19**	−.10**	−.19**	−.19**	−.26**
Awkward	−.27**	−.23**	−.23**	−.11	−.12	−.14**
Bitter	−.27**	−.08	−.13**	−.26**	−.24**	−.20**
Complaining	−.32**	−.04	−.11**	−.28**	−.23**	−.19**
Confused	−.31**	−.14*	−.13**	−.21**	−.20**	−.32**
Defensive	−.20**	−.24**	−.10**	−.16*	−.30**	−.09
Distractible	−.16*	−.19**	−.16**	−.13*	−.08	−.22**
Nagging	−.27**	−.16*	−.09*	−.20**	−.16*	−.21**
Nervous	−.27**	−.16*	−.09*	−.17**	−.21**	−.22**
Self-pitying	−.25**	−.07	−.09*	−.22**	−.23**	−.23**
Suspicious	−.23**	−.07	−.14**	−.17*	−.22**	−.16**
Worrying	−.31**	−.13	−.18**	−.23**	−.15*	−.21**

*$p \leq .05$, **$p \leq .01$

Is cheerful (.15, .16)

Has social poise and presence; appears socially at ease (.21, .18)

Has a brittle ego-defense system; has a small reserve of integration; would be disorganized and maladaptive if under stress or trauma (−.17, −.21)

Engages in personal fantasy and daydreams, fictional speculations (−.18, −.21)

Is self-defeating (−.23, −.19)

Feels cheated and victimized by life; self-pitying (−.18, −.21)

Persons with higher scores on Wb are described as productive, satisfied with their lives, cheerful, and socially at ease. Those with lower scores are described as having brittle ego-defense systems, as self-defeating and self-pitying, and as engaging in fantasy and daydreams. Presumably, these fantasies and fictional speculations are to some degree a substitute for life experiences deemed to be unsatisfactory.

Items from a 99-item life history interviewer's check list were correlated with the Wb scale in samples of 504 men and 379 women. The check list was filled out after the 90-minute interview. Items checked were coded as 1 and items not checked were coded as 0. The four items with largest positive and four with largest negative correlations with Wb are cited below, along with the coefficients for men and women.

Family life on the whole was quite happy (.15, .17)

Is happily married (.29, .10)

Has a stable, optimistic view of the future (.21, .26)

Seems relatively free of neurotic trends, conflicts, and other forms of instability (.18, .18)

Unhappy in school and at home (−.16, −.11)

Is generally dissatisfied with life (−.21, −.14)

Has many worries and problems (−.21, −.17)

Is unsure of self, doubts own ability (−.19, −.21)

Interviewees with high scores on Wb were seen by interviewees as generally happy and satisfied with their lives. The notion of psychological well-being seems to be thoroughly consonant with these descriptions. Those with lower scores on Wb were described as generally dissatisfied, unsure of self, and worried.

Items on the 50-item *Interpersonal Q-Sort* were correlated with the Wb scale in three samples: 200 men described by their wives or partners, 200 women described by their husbands or partners, and 111 male assessees described by panels of three staff observers whose independent formulations were combined into a single appraisal for each man. The three items with largest positive and three with largest negative correlations with Wb are cited below, along with the correlations for the three subsamples.

Poised and self-confident; not troubled by pressure or criticism (.16, .15, .25)

Alert and energetic in behavior and attitude; uncomplaining and in good spirits (.15, .13, .18)

Gets along well with others; able to "fit in" easily in most situations (.16, .21, .26)

Awkward and ill at ease socially; shy and inhibited with others (−.08, −.15, −.27)

Worried and preoccupied; tense, nervous, and generally upset (−.17, −.25, −.41)

Headstrong, rebellious, and resentful of others; lacking in self-discipline; apt to behave in a rash or destructive manner (−.14, −.19, −.17)

Persons with high scores on Wb are described as self-confident, good at coping with pressure, alert and energetic, and as able to get along well with others. Those with low scores on Wb are described as ill at ease socially, tense and nervous, and as prone to willful or headstrong behavior.

In summary, very low scores on Wb are suggestive of exaggerated or even feigned worries, but moderately low scores are attained by respondents who in fact are seen as worrying, beset by problems, and unsure about how to deal with them. High scores, on the contrary, betoken general feelings of well-being and competence, favorable life circumstances, and contentment. There does not seem to be any point at which these positive feelings become overdone, leading to narcissistic self-satisfaction or smugness. That is, even for the highest possible scores on Wb, interpretive implications are favorable in regard to psychological well-being.

The To (Tolerance) Scale

When first developed (Gough, 1951), the To scale was called Pr for *Prejudice*. The reason for this was that it was keyed in the direction of intolerance and validated against widely used measures at that time such as the *California F Scale* (Adorno, Frenkel-Brunswik, Levinson, & Sanford, 1950) and the Levinson-Sanford Anti-Semitism scale (Levinson & Sanford, 1944). When the CPI was published in 1956, the scale was reversed in scoring and given its present title.

In the intervening years, the To scale has been validated against demographic and observer-based indices of intolerance. One of the most recent studies (Dunbar, 1995) reported a correlation of −.54 between To and a contemporary measure of anti-Semitism for a sample of 76 Euro-White college students. On the other hand, almost no relationship was found for a sample of 74 Asian-American students.

Another recent study (Gough & Bradley, 1993) related the To scale to an observer-based index of intolerance in samples of 430 men and 428 women. A 12-item intolerance cluster of adjectives was defined for the ACL, with terms such as distrustful, intolerant, and prejudiced scored as indicative and terms such as fair-minded, reasonable, and tolerant scored as contraindicative. Interitem alpha coefficients for the intolerance index ranged from .71 to .88 in the subsamples studied, with a median of .79. In the full composite sample of 430 men and 428 women, correlations of To and the criterion index were −.30 for men and −.28 for women. Although modest in magnitude, the coefficients were the highest for any of the self-report measures considered, including the *California F Scale* (r = .08 for the total sample).

From the correlations of the CPI with other tests and measures, given in full in Appendix C, several may be mentioned here. With Comrey's Trust scale, the coefficients were .51 for men and .58 for women. Coefficients were .58 for men and .50 for women with the *Guilford-Zimmerman Temperament Survey* (GZTS) scale for Objectivity, and .54 for men and .48 for women with the GZTS scale for Friendliness. With the *Omnibus Personality Inventory* scale for Personal Integration, the coefficients were .55 for men and .49 for women, and with the Altruism scale from the OPI, the coefficients were .60 and .54, respectively.

The 32-item To scale in Form 434 has three items that are different from those in the Form 462 version. Correlation between the prior and current versions of the To scale were .98 for both the profile norm samples of 3,000 men and 3,000 women. A factor analysis of the interitem matrix in the total norm sample of 6,000 persons identified seven factors with eigen values of 1.00 or greater. Four of these were arbitrarily retained for rotation by means of Kaiser's normal varimax method. The first factor included items expressing trust in the integrity and goodwill of others, for example, "I think most people would lie to get ahead" ("false"), "Most people are honest chiefly through fear of being caught" ("false"), and "Most people inwardly dislike putting themselves out to help other people" ("false"). Factor 2 had items suggesting feelings of being treated fairly by others and by life's events, for example, "People often talk about me behind my back" ("false"), "Several times a week I feel as if something dreadful is about to happen" ("false"), and "I feel that I have often been punished without cause" ("false"). Factor

3 was composed of items suggesting concern for others, for example, "People do not need to worry about others if only they look after themselves" ("false"). Factor 4 had items expressing belief in ideas of fairness and equity, for example, "It makes me angry when I hear of someone who has been wrongly prevented from voting" ("true"), and "I don't blame people for trying to get all they can get in this world" ("false").

Act frequency analyses were conducted in a sample of 177 persons (88 men, 89 women), each of whom was rated for frequency of a list of acts by a spouse or partner. The five acts with largest positive and the five with largest negative correlations with To are reported below.

Volunteered to make dinner for friends on a weekend (.20)

Dressed drably (.25)

Initiated a conversation with a shy person at a party (.21)

Volunteered an idea to start a conversation in the group (.21)

Took the initiative in planning a party (.24)

Snubbed others at the party (−.19)

Did not return an article he/she found on the floor (−.23)

Accused them of talking behind his/her back (−.23)

Spent a large sum of money on an outfit for one dance (−.19)

Smoked marijuana when everyone else did, even though he/she didn't want to (−.19)

The acts associated with high scores on To promote the well-being of others in a group, or help a group to function for the comfort of all. The item about being dressed drably could be interpreted as minimizing attention to self, in a way compatible with the notion of tolerance as an attitude promoting good feeling among all. Acts associated with low scores on To include snubbing others, not returning a lost article, accusing others of talking behind one's back, spending money on attention-provoking clothing, and giving in to entreaties to smoke marijuana. These acts are diverse, but alike in that they are all divisive or disruptive of interpersonal relations in one manner or another. It seems reasonable to conclude that persons with high scores on To act in such a way as to promote harmony, feelings of involvement

Table 5.14 Adjectival Descriptions by Observers: 12 Most Salient Positive and 12 Most Salient Negative Correlates of the 32-Item To Scale

	Men, Described By			Women, Described By		
Adjectives	Spouse (N = 236)	3 Peers (N = 194)	10 Staff Members (N = 612)	Spouse (N = 236)	3 Peers (N = 192)	10 Staff Members (N = 358)
Appreciative	.16*	.19**	.12**	.05	.14*	.02
Clear-thinking	.20**	.16*	.10**	.21**	.21**	.12*
Cooperative	.15*	.18*	.08*	.19**	.23**	.05
Fair-minded	.22**	.23**	.08*	.16*	.21**	.08
Foresighted	.09	.19**	.15**	.13*	.15*	.10*
Insightful	.17*	.14*	.12**	.21**	.15*	.12*
Intelligent	.17*	.09	.12**	.10	.20**	.15**
Reasonable	.18*	.29**	.05	.18*	.21**	.10*
Sincere	.18*	.16*	.08*	.11	.19**	.04
Tactful	.14*	.12	.11**	.13*	.22**	.07
Thoughtful	.10	.30**	.13**	.12	.17*	.08
Tolerant	.19**	.18*	.11**	.12	.22**	.07
Arrogant	−.14*	−.17*	−.07	−.10	−.21**	−.13*
Bitter	−.24**	−.06	−.19**	−.16*	−.32**	−.20**
Boastful	−.20**	−.24**	−.10**	−.13*	−.11	−.11*
Distrustful	−.07	−.20**	−.11**	−.24**	−.27**	−.20**
Fussy	−.13*	−.16*	−.09*	−.18*	−.19**	−.08
Infantile	−.14*	−.12	−.13**	−.22**	−.21**	−.21**
Intolerant	−.19**	−.21**	−.10**	−.18*	−.17*	−.23**
Prejudiced	−.33**	−.16*	−.15**	−.28**	−.17*	−.24**
Self-centered	−.22**	−.23**	−.10**	−.11	−.27**	−.18**
Suspicious	−.22**	−.22**	−.18**	−.28**	−.19**	−.23**
Temperamental	−.16*	−.23**	−.10**	−.18*	−.22**	−.09
Vindictive	−.13*	−.11	−.12**	−.19**	−.08	−.13*

*p ≤ .05, **p ≤ .01

for everyone, and goodwill. Persons with low scores on To are more self-centered, little concerned about the feelings of others, and ready to criticize others for real or imagined slights.

Adjectival descriptions by observers most strongly associated with scores on To are presented in Table 5.14. One clear cluster related to high scores on To includes the terms cooperative, fair-minded, reasonable, sincere, and tactful. High scorers on To, in other words, are in fact seen as willing to accept and understand others. The most direct evidence for this inference is the adjective tolerant. High scorers on To are also able to make sound judgments and accurate appraisals, as suggested by the descriptions clear-thinking, insightful, and intelligent. Other important attributes among high scorers are indicated by the words appreciative, foresighted, and thoughtful.

Low scorers on To are described as distrustful, intolerant, prejudiced, suspicious, and vindictive, a cluster fully consonant with the stated purposes of the To scale. Overattention to self and underattention to others are implied by the adjectives arrogant, boastful, and self-centered. Dissatisfaction with many things can be inferred from the descriptions bitter, fussy, infantile, and temperamental. Low scores on the To scale certainly are suggestive of intolerance and prejudice, but they go beyond this in indicating a pervasive sense of alienation from others and a desire for retribution.

In a combined sample of 1,356, using adjectival descriptions standardized by subsample, a regression analysis was carried out on the 200 most frequently checked words. The analysis was terminated after eight steps. The best combination of eight adjectives for predicting scores on To has a multiple correlation of .31 (R^2 = .09). Adjectives with positive beta weights were civilized, foresighted, and intelligent. Adjectives with negative beta weights were aloof, humorous, rigid, strong, and suspicious.

California Q-Set items were correlated with To in samples of 547 men and 393 women, each of whom had been described on the Q-sort by panels of five or more assessment observers. The four items with largest positive and the four with largest negative correlations are presented below, along with the coefficients for men and for women.

Has a wide range of interests (.16, .17)

Appears to have a high degree of intellectual capacity (.12, .21)

Genuinely values intellectual and cognitive matters (.22, .29)

Is concerned with philosophical problems; e.g. religions, values, the meaning of life, etc. (.20, .19)

Extrapunitive; tends to transfer or project blame (−.12, −.16)

Is guileful and deceitful, manipulative, opportunistic (−.12, −.18)

Is basically distrustful of people in general; questions their motivations (−.14, −.10)

Characteristically pushes and tries to stretch limits; sees what he or she can get away with (−.17, −.18)

The Q-sort items associated with high scores on To all refer to intellectual or cognitive activity. The tolerance betokened by these high scores seems to rest on a rational, reflective basis more than on an instinctive or spontaneous liking for people. Those with low scores on To are seen as extrapunitive, guileful, distrustful, and oppositional. Such dispositions are associated with intolerance, but go beyond just this one focus. That is, persons scoring low on To are apt to attack others and to exploit them if possible.

Interviewers' check list descriptions were analyzed against To in samples of 504 men and 379 women seen in intensive life history interviews. The four items with largest positive and the four with largest negative correlations are reported below, along with the coefficients for men and for women. The relationships are of borderline level, with two of the coefficients for women and one for men falling short of the .05 level of significance.

Was an honor student in high school (.13, .17)

Is realistic in thinking and social behavior (.07, .19)

Has a stable, optimistic view of the future (.10, .14)

Seems relatively free of neurotic trends, conflicts, and other forms of instability (.10, .15)

Makes mistakes in grammar and/or word usage (−.24, −.15)

Considers self to have been an underachiever in high school (−.15, −.07)

Is generally dissatisfied with life (−.10, −.08)

Had first sexual intercourse while in high school or before (−.26, −.15)

Check list items associated with high scores on To are weakly indicative of generally good adjustment, realistic attitudes, and of superior academic performance in high school. Items associated with low scores on To are weakly indicative of poor verbal skills and underachievement in high school, early expressions of sexuality, and general dissatisfaction. A tantalizing item not cited above is the description "rugged, masculine appearance" with a correlation of −.23 for men. In other words, men scoring low on To in this sample of 504 appeared to be rugged and masculine.

The three *Interpersonal Q-Sort* items with largest positive and the three with largest negative correlations with To are cited below, along with the coefficients for the three subsamples of 200 men, 200 women, and 111 male assessees.

> Honest and direct in behavior; mature and realistic in outlook (.18, .06, .17)
>
> Verbally fluent; expresses self easily and with clarity (.14, .02, .26)
>
> Is an effective leader; able to elicit the response and cooperation of others (.18, .04, .22)
>
> Distrustful and cynical; dissatisfied with most things; indifferent to the worries and problems of others (−.08, −.13, −.22)
>
> Headstrong, rebellious, and resentful of others; lacking in self-discipline; apt to behave in a rash or destructive manner (−.09, −.15, −.19)
>
> Given to moods; often difficult and recalcitrant (−.16, −.10, −.15)

The items associated with high scores on To had moderate relationships for the two male samples, but close to zero links for females. Because of this, only very tentative comments can be justified. For men, high scores on To may carry implications for maturity, verbal fluency, and leadership potential. The three items associated with low scores on To convey slight implications of distrust, resentment against others, and moodiness for both men and women.

In summary, high scores on To do appear to presage tolerance and a willingness to accept others and to accept differences from one's own views. This disposition seems to stem from cognitive, reflective attitudes rather than from warmth and positive feelings. High scorers on To also seem to be intelligent, interested in cognitive matters, realistic in their expectations, stable, and relatively free of serious conflicts or psychological problems. In work with individuals, there does not seem to be any high point at which these attributes veer over into too much intellectuality or detachment. That is, the positive implications of elevations on To hold right on up to the top of the scale.

Low scores on To do point to intolerance, doubt about others, and distrust of their motives, but also go beyond this in suggesting internal conflicts, broad dissatisfactions, and a tendency to seek retribution against others. Very low scores on To, along with low scores on scales such as So and Sc that are associated with impulse control, are diagnostic of a potential for interpersonal violence.

The Ac (Achievement via Conformance) Scale

The Ac scale was initially developed as a predictor of high school academic achievement (Gough, 1949a, 1953c). Items based on hypotheses about motivational and other factors associated with superior scholastic attainment were evaluated for their correlations with high school grades, and those either positively or negatively related were kept for the early versions of the scale. In the 1956 Form 480 edition of the CPI, the Ac scale had 38 items meeting this criterion. In 1964 (Gough, 1964a), a study of 571 male and 813 female students from five high schools found correlations of Ac with cumulative grade point average (GPA) of .35 for both sexes. In cross-validating samples of 649 males and 722 females from nine high schools, the correlations of Ac with GPA were .37 for males and .40 for females. A cross-cultural study of secondary school students in Greece (Repapi, Gough, Lanning, & Stefanis, 1983) reported correlations of Ac and GPA of .21 for over 800 females and of .26 for over 700 males from 19 different schools. In Appendix C, correlations of Ac with high school GPA are given for samples of 2,432 males and 2,852 females from 25 schools in all regions of the country. The coefficients were .40 for males and .40 for females.

In these same schools, information in regard to graduation or dropout was available for 1,760 males and 2,019 females (see also Gough, 1966b). Correlations for Ac with this dichotomy (scored on a 1–0 basis) were .16 for males and .13 for females. Information on attendance or nonattendance in college was available for 1,514 male graduates and for 1,799 female graduates (see also Gough, 1968a). Correlations of Ac with this 1–0 dichotomy were .33 for males and .27 for females. Finally, for 995 males and 441 females from three colleges, correlations of Ac with four-year GPA were .14 for males and .11 for females. From this and other information for Ac, it can be concluded that the measure is predictive of academic performance at the high school level, moderately predictive of graduation and college-going, but only minimally related to academic performance in college. In environments having defined goals, established criteria of evaluation, and more or less fixed routines, Ac assesses dispositions related to superior performance. As the criteria for achievement become more varied, less standard, and more open to individual determination, Ac goes down in predictive power. Findings such as these led to a conceptualization of Ac as an achievement drive related to superior performance in defined settings, in which conformance is rewarded.

Two important studies by Domino (Domino, 1968, 1971) focused explicitly on academic achievement in conforming and independent settings. The Ac scale had positive relations with criteria in the conforming settings, but neutral to even negative relations in those requiring independent goal-setting and effort. In one experiment, he established subgroups according to scores on the Ac scale, and on the Ai (Achievement via Independence) scale, which will be discussed in the following section. One pair of subsamples was made up of students with high scores on Ac and average or low scores on Ai. Another pair of subsamples was composed of students with high scores on Ai and average or low scores on Ac. Classroom instruction was also varied, with one subsample of each pair taught in a way that stressed clarity of the syllabus, assigned readings, and scheduled examinations based directly on those readings. Alternatively, one subsample of each pair was taught in a way allowing great latitude for individual goal-setting, suggested rather than assigned readings, and examinations only tangentially related to the readings. Students high on Ac did best in the structured classrooms, and did poorly in the unstructured. On the contrary, students high on Ai did not achieve well in the structured classes, but did very well in the unstructured. The configurations of the Ac and Ai scales have continued to be among the most powerful for the inventory (McAllister, 1996).

The Ac scale in Form 434 has one item different from those in Forms 462 and 480. Correlation of the current 38-item version with the prior version was .99 for both the 3,000 males and 3,000 females in the profile norm samples. Factor analysis of the 38 items in the total norm sample of 6,000 persons identified nine factors with eigen values of 1.00 or greater. Four of these were arbitrarily retained for rotation by Kaiser's normal varimax method. Factor 1 was composed of items suggesting an ability to concentrate thinking and effort and to persevere. Examples are, "I am often bothered by useless thoughts which keep running through my mind" ("false"), "I cannot keep my mind on one thing" ("false"), and "I must admit I find it very hard to

work under strict rules and regulations" ("false"). Factor 2 has items indicating acceptance of rules and conformity, for instance, "In school I was sometimes sent to the principal because I had misbehaved" ("false") and "In school my marks for conduct were quite regularly bad" ("false"). Factor 3 included items expressing a liking for school, for example, "I liked school" ("true") and "I never cared much for school" ("false"). Factor 4 has items concerning planfulness and an orientation toward the future. Examples are, "In school I always looked far ahead in planning what courses to take" ("true") and "I like to plan out my activities in advance" ("true").

Act frequency data were taken from analyses on a sample of 177 persons (88 males, 89 females), each of whom was rated for frequency of a list of acts by a spouse or partner. The five acts with largest positive correlations with Ac and the five with largest negative correlations are cited below.

Listened attentively to the speaker (.28)

Planned his/her career in detail (.18)

Played tennis (.21)

Went to church (.24)

Was active in community or campus affairs (.22)

Laughed loudly at a joke (−.22)

Said "I don't know" when asked a question he/she didn't want to answer (−.24)

Told a secret about himself/herself (−.21)

Circled around to avoid someone he/she knew (−.21)

Gave one-word answers to personal questions (−.26)

Acts associated with high scores on Ac pertain to planning, church-going, and taking part in community affairs, plus listening to a speaker and playing tennis. These are all things that active and adaptable people might do. Acts associated with low scores on Ac suggest isolative or self-protective tendencies. In the context of the other acts, "Laughing loudly at a joke" may involve an overreaction or a defensive reaction rather than a good sense of humor.

Adjectival descriptions by observers are reported in Table 5.15, which lists the 12 having largest positive and the 12 having largest negative correlations with Ac. One cluster associated with high

Table 5.15 Adjectival Descriptions by Observers: 12 Most Salient Positive and 12 Most Salient Negative Correlates of the 38-Item Ac Scale

Adjectives	Men, Described By			Women, Described By		
	Spouse ($N = 236$)	3 Peers ($N = 194$)	10 Staff Members ($N = 612$)	Spouse ($N = 236$)	3 Peers ($N = 192$)	10 Staff Members ($N = 358$)
Ambitious	.12	.29**	.21**	.19**	.26**	.16**
Clear-thinking	.15*	.20**	.05	.26**	.26**	.11*
Conscientious	.15*	.22**	.14**	.20**	.28**	.23**
Dependable	.05	.28**	.09*	.14*	.23**	.25**
Efficient	.14*	.23**	.18**	.15*	.30**	.19**
Foresighted	.10	.19**	.12**	.12	.23**	.15**
Industrious	.09	.22**	.15**	.12	.22**	.27**
Intelligent	.11	.19**	.04	.18**	.26**	.12*
Mature	.13*	.26**	.04	.17*	.23**	.09
Methodical	.06	.17*	.11**	.23**	.16*	.19**
Moderate	.12	.16*	.03	.18*	.14*	.11*
Organized	.15*	.30**	.23**	.28**	.33**	.29**
Careless	−.25**	−.27**	−.16**	−.10	−.33**	−.28**
Confused	−.23**	−.17*	−.11**	−.19**	−.19**	−.29**
Disorderly	−.18**	−.22**	−.14**	−.12	−.32**	−.32**
Distractible	−.31**	−.22**	−.18**	−.13*	−.20**	−.29**
Impulsive	−.20**	−.22**	−.10**	−.22**	−.30**	−.24**
Mischievous	−.25**	−.32**	−.15**	−.18**	−.21**	−.12*
Pleasure-seeking	−.16*	−.28**	−.15**	−.11	−.19**	−.22**
Quitting	−.16*	−.22**	−.13**	−.09	−.20**	−.22**
Rebellious	−.25**	−.20**	−.21**	−.19**	−.29**	−.25**
Reckless	−.28**	−.26**	−.15**	−.29**	−.22**	−.22**
Restless	−.16*	−.22**	−.15**	−.11	−.28**	−.24**
Shiftless	−.16*	−.29**	−.17**	−.18**	−.18*	−.23**

$*p \le .05, **p \le .01$

scores on Ac depicts good organization and use of personal resources, specifically efficient, industrious, intelligent, methodical, and organized. The adjectives conscientious, dependable, and mature suggest the ability to accept and adapt to social norms. Clear-thinking, foresighted, and intelligent go along with good cognitive ability, and the term ambitious suggests a motive to achieve.

Associated with low scores on Ac are terms suggesting poor self-discipline and the ability to persevere in pursuit of goals, for example careless, distractible, impulsive, rebellious, reckless, restless, disorderly, and shiftless. Emphasis on narcissistic gain is suggested by the descriptions pleasure-seeking and mischievous, and a general lack of will is indicated by the terms confused and quitting.

A regression analysis of the 200 most frequently used adjectives was conducted in a composite sample of 1,356 persons, using standard scores on each adjective based on subsample norms. The best combination of eight adjectives from which to estimate scores on Ac had a multiple correlation of .43 (R^2 = .19). Adjectives with positive beta weights were ambitious, organized, and outgoing. Adjectives with negative beta weights were active, adventurous, awkward, cynical, and easy-going.

The 100 items in Block's *California Q-Set* were correlated with scores on Ac in samples of 547 men and 393 women. Each of these assessees had been described on the Q-sort by panels of five or more judges. The four items with largest positive and the four with largest negative correlations are reported below, along with the coefficients for men and for women.

Is a genuinely responsible and dependable person (.21, .28)

Is fastidious (.24, .25)

Is productive; gets things done (.18, .34)

Has high aspiration level for self (.34, .22)

Feels a lack of personal meaning in life (–.21, –.25)

Is unpredictable and changeable in behavior and attitudes (–.18, –.32)

Is self-defeating (–.24, –.23)

Tends to be rebellious and nonconforming (–.22, –.28)

Persons with high scores on Ac are viewed as responsible, fastidious, productive, and ambitious. Those with low scores are viewed as changeable, self-defeating, rebellious, and as feeling a lack of meaning in their lives. In other words, persons with high scores on Ac have high aspirations and a need to achieve, and tend to do so by way of productivity and conformance to the demands of their world.

Life history interviews were conducted with 504 men and 370 women, after which a 99-item check list was completed by the interviewers. Using a 1–0 scoring of the items, the four with largest positive and four with largest negative correlations with Ac are cited below, along with the coefficients for men and for women.

Well-groomed and well-dressed (.20, .15)

Family life on the whole was quite happy (.15, .26)

Was an honor student in high school (.21, .20)

Has a stable, optimistic view of the future (.15, .31)

Unhappy in school and at home (–.20, –.17)

Led a borderline, delinquent-like existence in high school (–.22, –.15)

Considers self to have been an underachiever in high school (–.23, –.17)

Is unsure of self, doubts own ability (–.15, –.27)

In the interviews, high scorers on Ac showed up well-groomed in proper attire, recalled their family life as happy, stated that they had been honor students in high school, and described their stable and optimistic expectations for the future. Low scorers on Ac recalled unhappy childhoods, nonconformist behavior in high school, and academic underachievement, and voiced doubts about their own coping ability.

Samples of 200 men, 200 women, and 111 male assessees were described by observers on the 50-item *Interpersonal Q-Sort*, and the three items with largest correlations with Ac and the three with largest negative correlations were selected for citation below. The coefficients are for the 200 men, 200 women, and 111 assessees in that order.

Well-organized, capable, patient, and industrious; values achievement (.15, .17, .40)

Independent, intelligent, and self-reliant; values achievement (.18, .21, .19)

Is an effective leader; able to elicit the response and cooperation of others (.23, .13, .25)

Distrustful and cynical; dissatisfied with most things; indifferent to the worries and problems of others (–.14, –.16, –.28)

Poorly organized; unable to concentrate attention and effort on intellectual problems (–.13, –.23, –.22)

Given to moods; often difficult and recalcitrant (–.20, –.14, –.12)

In these samples, persons scoring high on Ac are described as well-organized, independent, and as valuing achievement. Their leadership potential is also noted. Those with low scores on Ac are described as distrustful, cynical, poorly organized, and as given to moods.

In summary, the Ac scale identifies people who have high aspirations, and who are sufficiently self-disciplined and organized to persevere in pursuit of their goals. In settings where both goals and means are clearly specified, they do very well, but in settings where structure is vague or ill-defined, they are uncomfortable and do not achieve to their fullest capacity. Low scorers on Ac give up easily, get confused, and tend to value personal pleasure and short-term gains more than recognized success in school and work. They also tend to be unsure of their own ability, do things that are self-defeating, and are easily distracted. Low scores on Ac, along with low scores on Re and So, are often found among delinquents and others with severe problems in rule-following behavior. However, relatively low scores on Ac, if associated with high scores on Ai and other signs of personal resourcefulness in the full profile, can portend superior creative potential.

The Ai (Achievement via Independence) Scale

Because, as noted above, the Ac scale was ineffective in predicting academic performance in college, a new scale (Gough, 1953a) was constructed. Items embodying hypotheses about academic performance at this level were assembled and then examined for their relationship to grades in several college samples. Items having significant links were retained for the first version of the Ai scale. In the 1956 Form 480 edition of the CPI scale, Ai had 32 items. For the 1986 Form 462 edition of the inventory, Ai was increased in length to 36 items. These same 36 items are included in Form 434.

A validational study of Ai (Gough & Lanning, 1986) on large, composite samples of college students, using concurrent, two-year, and four-year GPAs as criteria, reported correlations for Ai and GPA of .22 for 1,347 males in one composite, and of .31 for 326 males in another; for females, the correlations were .25 for 1,842 in one sample and .31 for 570 in another. In an earlier study (Gough, 1964a), correlations of Ai with high school GPA for samples of 571 and 649 males from 14 high schools were .30 and .33. For samples of 813 and 722 females from these same schools, the correlations were .35 and .42. Thus, although Ac is at best a weak predictor of grades in college, Ai is a reasonably good predictor of grades in high school.

A study by Pfeifer and Sedlacek (1974) attempted to forecast college grades for 79 Black students from the CPI and other measures. A correlation of .35 was obtained for the Ai scale. College-going among the graduates of four high schools had point-biserial correlations of .28 for males and .31 for females (Gough, 1968a).

Besides the differences in forecasting college grades, are there other differences between Ac and Ai? Werner (1988) examined 108 men and 82 women who had distinctly high or low scores on a test of sexual and reproductive knowledge. For both men and women, differences between high scorers and low scorers were small and statistically insignificant (p > 05) on the Ac scale, but large and significant (p < 01) on Ai. Additional information about differences between Ac and Ai can be found in Appendix C; some pertinent contrasts are cited below.

Measures Correlating More Highly with Ac than Ai

16PF Factor G (Dutiful, Persevering): .29 (males) and .36 (females) for Ac, versus .01 (males) and .05 (females) for Ai

Comrey Personality Scales, Orderly: .22 and .43 for Ac, versus −.04 and .08 for Ai

Goldberg's Big-Five marker for Dependability: .22 and .27 for Ac, versus −.14 and −.12 for Ai

Hogan Personality Inventory, Prudence: .57 and .54 for Ac, versus .02 and .15 for Ai

Measures Correlating More Highly with Ai than Ac

16PF Factor Q-1 (Liberal, Free-thinking): −.06 (males) and −.03 (females) for Ac, versus .22 (males) and .32 (females) for Ai

Myers-Briggs Type Indicator, Intuitive: −.10 and −.20 for Ac, versus .31 and .29 for Ai

NEO-AC: Openness to Experience: .05 and .04 for Ac, versus .30 and .30 for Ai

Omnibus Personality Inventory, Autonomy: −.13 and −.10 for Ac, versus .43 and .61 for Ai

The correlates of the Ac scale stress prudence, dependability, self-discipline, and orderly habits. Those of the Ai scale stress openness to experience, autonomuy, independence of mind, and intuitive (as opposd to sense-dominated) perceptual preferences. Thus, in spite of correlations between Ac and Ai of .55 for men (N = 5,000) and .50 for women (N = 5,000), the scales have clearly discernible differences in their implications. High scores on Ac are indicative of an ability to get the most out of a defined set of circumstances, and to maximize achievement where both means and goals are consensually established. High scores on Ai are indicative of an ability to set new and personal goals, and to evolve effective means for their attainment.

The psychological dynamic of Ac, following on this line of reasoning, might be termed *form-enhancement*, whereas the dynamic for Ai might be termed *form-creation*.

Factor analysis of the 36 items in Ai in the total profile norm sample of 6,000 persons identified eight factors with eigen values of 1.00 or more. Four of these were arbitrarily retained for rotation by means of Kaiser's normal varimax method. Factor 1 consisted primarily of items expressing iconoclastic and independent beliefs, for example, "Only a fool would try to change our American way of life" ("false"), "For most questions, there is just one right answer, once a person is able to get all the facts" ("false"), and "Disobedience to any government is never justified" ("false"). Items in Factor 2 suggest confidence in self and in what the future holds, for example, "With things going as they are, it's pretty hard to keep up hope of amounting to something" ("false"), and "I sometimes feel that I am a burden to others" ("false"). Factor 3 had items indicating breadth of interests, for example, "I like poetry" ("true") and "I enjoy hearing lectures on world affairs" ("true"). Factor 4 contained items denying common fears, for example, "I dread the thought of an earthquake" ("false") and "I do not have a great fear of snakes" ("true").

Act frequency implications of Ai are found in spouse or partner reported frequencies of specific acts for 88 men and 89 women. The five acts with largest positive and five with largest negative correlations are given below, along with the correlations with Ai in the total sample of 177 persons.

Did not object to his/her partner spending time with a member of the opposite sex (.27)

Listened attentively to the speaker (.28)

Gave advice, although none was requested (.22)

Volunteered an idea in order to start conversation in the group (.24)

Discussed the political issues of the day (.22)

Made a friendship in order to obtain a favor (−.22)

Befriended someone so that he/she could use that person's car (−.20)

Forgave an acquaintance who had spread a false rumor about him/her (−.20)

Helped a friend get a job where he/she works (−.19)

Accused others of talking behind his/her back (−.21)

Acts associated with high scores on Ai involve taking the initiative, acquiescing in freedom of behavior for a partner, listening to a speaker, and discussing current political issues. There is a sort of "live and let live" flavor to these acts, things that might be done by someone with a secure sense of independence and confidence in one's own abilities. All of the acts associated with low scores on Ai pertain to friends and acquaintances—in two cases, seeking to exploit relationships; in two others, dealing with rumors and gossip; and in one case, helping a friend find a job. The five acts, taken together, suggest dependence on others and concern about their opinions.

Descriptions of persons with high or low scores on Ai are given in Table 5.16, for six samples in which observers recorded their impressions on the ACL. The 12 adjectives with largest positive and the 12 with largest negative correlations appear in the table. The largest cluster of terms associated with high scores on Ai pertain to capabilities, for instance, capable, clear-thinking, insightful, intelligent, logical, and rational. The adjective independent also appears, supported by the terms enterprising and foresighted. In addition, high-scorers are seen as alert and reflective.

Adjectives associated with low scores on Ai depict someone lacking in clarity of thought and intellectual ability, for example, confused, interests narrow, rattlebrained, and simple. Troubled relations with others are suggested by the descriptions distrustful, fussy, prejudiced, and suspicious. More general problems in dealing with life's demands are suggested by the adjectives apathetic, infantile, restless, and weak.

A regression analysis of the 200 most frequently used adjectives was carried out in a combined sample of 1,356 persons, terminating arbitrarily after eight steps. The multiple correlation at that point was .36 (R^2 = .13). Adjectives with positive beta weights were foresighted, intelligent, moderate, and thorough. Adjectives with negative beta weights were affectionate, practical, rigid, and simple.

California Q-Set items were correlated with Ai in samples of 547 males and 393 females. Each assessee had been described on the Q-sort by panels of five or more staff observers. Those independent formulations were combined into a consensual Q-sorting for each person. The four items with largest positive and four with largest negative correlations with Ai are reported below, along with the coefficients for men and for women.

Has a wide range of interests (.21, .34)

Appears to have a high degree of intellectual capacity (.22, .42)

Adjectives	Men, Described By			Women, Described By		
	Spouse (N = 236)	3 Peers (N = 194)	10 Staff Members (N = 612)	Spouse (N = 236)	3 Peers (N = 192)	10 Staff Members (N = 358)
Alert	.19**	.18*	.19**	.10	.15*	.13*
Capable	.11	.21**	.17**	.14*	.20**	.14**
Clear-thinking	.18**	.20**	.24**	.22**	.20**	.26**
Clever	.14*	.17*	.17**	.16*	.10	.19**
Enterprising	.05	.11	.14**	.17**	.14*	.17**
Foresighted	.09	.20**	.23**	.04	.14*	.18**
Independent	.13*	.29**	.09*	.10	.05	.23**
Insightful	.22**	.14*	.23**	.27**	.17*	.21**
Intelligent	.22**	.21**	.30**	.18**	.22**	.30**
Logical	.13*	.19**	.23**	.06	.20**	.25**
Rational	.14*	.17*	.22**	.15*	.20**	.19**
Reflective	.13*	.07	.24**	.27**	.13	.10*
Apathetic	−.23**	−.09	−.19**	−.02	−.11	−.17**
Confused	−.12	−.14*	−.10**	−.13*	−.15*	−.09
Distrustful	−.12	−.14*	−.10**	−.13*	−.15*	−.09
Fussy	−.15*	−.09	−.16**	−.09	−.03	−.13*
Infantile	−.07	−.11	−.08*	−.14*	−.16*	−.24**
Interests narrow	−.18**	−.01	−.25**	−.37**	−.06	−.34**
Prejudiced	−.35**	−.06	−.16**	−.22**	−.03	−.19**
Rattlebrained	−.20**	−.03	−.13**	−.17**	−.10	−.19**
Restless	−.11	−.15*	−.01	−.01	−.16*	−.03
Simple	−.17**	−.01	−.29**	−.17**	−.09	−.31**
Suspicious	−.15*	−.04	−.13**	−.11	−.04	−.12*
Weak	−.18**	−.02	−.11**	−.05	−.04	−.18**

*p ≤ .05, **p ≤ .01

Genuinely values intellectual and cognitive matters (.31, .45)

Has high aspiration level for self (.27, .33)

Favors conservative values in a variety of areas (−.15, −.30)

Is uncomfortable with uncertainty and complexities (−.15, −.30)

Gives up and withdraws where possible in the face of frustration and adversity (−.12, −.25)

Is self-defeating (−.19, −.19)

High scorers on Ai are seen as intelligent, valuing intellectual matters, wide in their interests, and as having high levels of aspiration. Given such characteristics, can achievement be far behind? Low scorers on Ai are viewed as conservative, uncomfortable with ambiguity, self-defeating, and as tending to give up when confronted with obstacles and adversity. Small wonder that low scorers on Ai tend not to do well in situations requiring independent effort and self-direction.

Interviewers' reactions were registered on a 99-item check list for 504 men and 379 women with whom life history interviews had been conducted. The four items with largest positive and the four with largest negative correlations with Ai are given below, along with the coefficients for men and for women.

Uses wide and varied vocabulary (.21, .22)

Witty and animated, an interesting conversationalist (.12, .18)

Was an honor student in high school (.20, .32)

Unusually self-confident, feels able to meet nearly any situation (.12, .11)

Makes mistakes in grammar and/or word usage (−.28, −.23)

Had first sexual intercourse while in high school or before (−.23, −.24)

Is unsure of self, doubts own ability (−.12, −.16)

Enjoys children (−.18, −.18)

Interviewees with high scores on Ai are described as witty, self-confident, superior achievers in high school, and as using a wide and varied vocabulary. Those with low scores are described as unsure of self, as prone to grammatical mistakes, and as having begun overt sexual activity in high school or before.

The item about enjoying children, associated with low scores on Ai, is an interesting finding. In some of the other data sets a certain remoteness from others was noted for high scorers. Perhaps this distancing, or centering of affect on self, extends to a lesser interest in and enjoyment of children.

Fifty *Interpersonal Q-Sort* items were correlated with Ai in samples of 200 men described by wives or partners, 200 women described by husbands or partners, and 111 male assessees each described by three staff observers. The three items with largest positive and three with largest negative correlations are listed below, along with the coefficients for men, women, and the 111 male assessees.

Independent, intelligent, and self-reliant; values achievement (.25, .17, .33)

Observant and perceptive; quick to respond to the subtleties and nuances of others' behavior (.13, .15, .30)

Verbally fluent; expresses self easily and with clarity (.20, .10, .38)

Dull, lacking in ability and understanding (−.15, −.10, −.27)

Unambitious, commonplace and conventional in thinking and behavior (−.05, −.13, −.31)

Warm and unpretentious; a comfortable and uncomplicated person (−.12, −.13, −.22)

High scorers on Ai are perceived as independent and intelligent, perceptive, and verbally fluent. Low scorers are seen as dull, unambitious, but also as warm and uncomplicated.

In summary, Ai is predictive of superior performance in settings requiring independent planning and effort. High scorers appear to be intelligent, clear-thinking individuals with a wide range of interests. They aspire to do well and are capable of self-direction. At the same time, there is a touch of egoism or self-centeredness in the syndrome, in that those high on Ai may be indifferent to the feelings of others and lacking in personal warmth.

Low scorers on Ai are poor risks for academic achievement at all educational levels, have doubts about their own ability, are uncomfortable with ill-defined or ambiguous situations, and have narrow interests. They do not deal well with intellectual demands and are easily distracted or confused. At their best, they are warm, simple, conservative individuals who can get along well in uncomplicated settings where little is required or expected of them. When frustrated or under pressure they tend to be self-defeating and withdrawn.

The Ie (Intellectual Efficiency) Scale

The Ie scale was developed (Gough, 1953b) to assess good access to one's intellectual resources and staying power in the use of these resources over time. To make sure that the scale would also relate to intellectual level, original item analyses also attended to relationships with measures of ability such as the Kuhlman-Anderson test (Kuhlman & Anderson, 1940). Data on group measures of ability such as this were available for large samples of high school students in cities where the CPI had been administered. In early analyses against direct measures of intellectual ability in high school, college, and adult samples, correlations within the range of .40 to .50 were regularly obtained.

In Appendix C, correlations of Ie with several measures of intellectual ability are reported. For 2,625 high school males and 3,096 high school females, using standard scores on whatever measure of ability had been given, the correlations for Ie were

.43 and .44. For 735 college males and 452 college females tested with an unpublished measure of general vocabulary, correlations were .29 for males and .22 for females. From a project on creativity, 158 males and 27 females were given individual administrations of the *Wechsler Adult Intelligence Scale* (WAIS). In these samples of very intelligent persons (the mean WAIS for the 185 persons was approximately 132), Ie had correlations with WAIS total IQ of .28 for the men and .54 for the women. As reported in Appendix C, Ie also is significantly correlated with high school GPA (.43 for 2,432 males and .45 for 2,852 females), with college-going (.35 for males and .32 for females), and with four-year GPA in college for 995 males ($r = .16$) and 441 females ($r = .17$).

Some of the correlations between Ie and scales from other inventories are also of interest: coefficients of .42 for men and .46 for women with Comrey's Emotional Stability scale; .38 for men and .44 for women with Goldberg's Big-5 marker for Intellect; .54 for men and .43 for women with the GZTS Emotional Stability scale; .54 for men and .52 for women with the OPI scale for Theoretical Orientation, and .52 and .53 with Personal Integration; .56 for men and .52 for women with Hogan's scale for Ambition; .48 for men and .57 for women with Barron's Ego Strength scale; and .43 for men and .45 for women with Barron's scale for Originality.

Several studies have related Ie to indices of good health and effective functioning. Overall physical health at age 50, as judged by two physicians, was correlated with CPI scales administered at age 43 (Bayer, Whissell-Buechy, & Honzik, 1980). For 51 men, the correlation for Ie was .28, and for 77 women the correlation was .41. Another study (Cartwright, Wink, & Kmetz, 1995) classified women physicians into those with good health, psychological ill health, and physical ill health. At age 46, the means on Ie for these three subgroups were 35.51, 31.75, and 32.90. The mean for the good health group was significantly ($p < .01$) higher than the combined means for the two subgroups in poor health.

In Form 480 of the CPI, the Ie scale had 52 items. In Form 462, this was reduced to 42 items. In Form 434, the Ie scale also has 42 items, but five different items had to be substituted because of items dropped from Form 462. The reason for such a large number of dropped items was that Ie had an appreciable number of items pertaining to general good health and physical efficiency, and five of these came into conflict with the limitations imposed by the Americans with Disabilities Act. Correlations

between Ie in Forms 462 and 434 are .97 for both the 3,000 profile norm sample of men and the 3,000 profile norm sample of women.

A factor analysis of the 42 items in Ie was carried out on the total profile norm sample of 6,000 persons. Ten factors with eigen values of 1.00 or more were identified, of which four were arbitrarily retained for rotation by means of Kaiser's normal varimax method. The first rotated factor consisted of items expressing good morale and confidence in the future, for example, "I have had more than my share of things to worry about" ("false"), "I often feel as if the world was just passing me by" ("false"), and "The future seems hopeless to me" ("false"). Factor 2 was composed of items denying common fears and worries, for instance, "A windstorm terrifies me" ("false"), and "I am not afraid of picking up a disease or germs from door knobs" ("true"). Factor 3 had items suggesting good intellectual ability and participation in intellectual activity, for example, "I read at least ten books a year" ("true"), "I am quite a fast reader" ("true"), and "I was a slow learner in school" ("false"). Factor 4 was a doublet with items specifically focused on science, that is, "I like to read about science" ("true") and "I like science" ("true").

Act frequency data were analyzed in a sample of 177 persons (88 males, 89 females), each of whom was rated for frequency of acts by a spouse or partner. The five acts with largest positive correlations with Ie and the five with largest negative correlations are listed below:

Listened attentively to the speaker (.34)

Willingly tried a new food at a restaurant, when a friend suggested it (.26)

Followed a scheduled routine, without changing it (.22)

Arrived on time for the meeting (.21)

Voiced opinions in a large class (.18)

Snubbed others at the party (−.20)

Shared hidden feelings about his/her parents with another person (−.19)

Smoked marijuana when everyone else did, even though he/she didn't want to (−.19)

Turned red when someone asked a personal question (−.18)

Forgave an acquaintance for spreading a false rumor about him/her (−.18)

Acts associated with higher scores on Ie suggest ability to focus attention, follow a schedule, and express per-

Table 5.17 Adjectival Descriptions by Observers: 12 Most Salient Positive and 12 Most Salient Negative Correlates of the 42-Item Ie Scale					
	Men, Described By			**Women, Described By**		
Adjectives	Spouse (N = 236)	3 Peers (N = 194)	10 Staff Members (N = 612)	Spouse (N = 236)	3 Peers (N = 192)	10 Staff Members (N = 358)
Alert	.18**	.17*	.22**	.16*	.14*	.20**
Capable	.06	.20**	.15**	.18**	.21**	.17**
Clear-thinking	.15*	.20**	.19**	.22**	.28**	.20**
Clever	.08	.14*	.16**	.19**	.06	.17**
Confident	.05	.14*	.19**	.16*	.21**	.27**
Independent	.08	.29**	.13**	.14*	.12	.24**
Initiative	.14*	.10	.20**	.20**	.15*	.26**
Insightful	.15*	.11	.19**	.27**	.17*	.16**
Intelligent	.18**	.23**	.26**	.16*	.26**	.28**
Rational	.10	.19**	.13**	.13*	.25**	.11*
Resourceful	.08	.09	.24**	.20**	.16*	.27**
Self-confident	.11	.14*	.18**	.17**	.14*	.28**
Apathetic	−.21**	−.18*	−.21**	−.10	−.10	−.22**
Awkward	−.19**	−.16*	−.21**	.00	−.15*	−.18**
Bitter	−.20**	−.03	−.15**	−.10	−.16*	−.11*
Confused	−.22**	−.15*	−.16**	−.12	−.12	−.25**
Dependent	−.11	−.08	−.12**	−.15*	−.09	−.27**
Gloomy	−.14*	−.08	−.12**	−.03	−.15*	−.13*
Interests narrow	−.13*	−.10	−.22**	−.36**	−.11	−.34**
Nervous	−.22**	−.11	−.05	−.08	−.18*	−.24**
Silent	−.11	−.15*	−.20**	−.14*	−.03	−.26**
Simple	−.14*	−.16*	−.26**	−.22**	−.03	−.31**
Slow	−.25**	−.10	−.16**	−.07	−.11	−.20**
Weak	−.22**	−.12	−.10**	−.08	−.09	−.24**

*p ≤ .05, **p ≤ .01

sonal opinions, all compatible with the notion of efficiency in cognition and thinking. At least moderate openess to new experience is indicated by the willingness to try a new food. Acts associated with lower scores are indicative of lack of will, interpersonal ambivalence, and an acquiescent mind-set.

Adjectival descriptions by observers are given in Table 5.17. In each of the six samples, observers recorded their impressions on the 300-item

Adjective Check List. The 12 descriptions with largest positive and 12 with largest negative correlations with Ie are reported in the table. Most of the adjectives associated with high scores on Ie pertain to cognitive ability and cognitive functioning, for example, capable, clear-thinking, clever, insightful, intelligent, and rational. High scorers are also seen as resourceful and self-confident, as independent, alert, and able to take the initiative.

Adjectives associated with low scores on Ie focus less on cognitive activity and more on more general malfunctioning. One cluster is related to low morale and poor adjustment: bitter, gloomy, nervous, and weak. Cognitive shortcomings are suggested by the terms confused and interests narrow. Repressive tendencies may be inferred from the descriptions apathetic, silent, simple, and slow, and interpersonal deficits from the terms awkward and dependent.

A regression analysis of the 200 most frequently used adjectives in a composite sample of 1,356 persons, using adjectival scores standardized by subsample, was conducted, terminating the analysis at eight steps. The best combination of eight descriptions of estimating scores on Ie gave a multiple correlation of .36 ($R^2 = .13$). Adjectives with positive beta weights were civilized, idealistic, and reflective. Adjectives with negative beta weights were complicated, kind, shy, suspicious, and temperamental.

Descriptions by observers using the *California Q-Set* were analyzed in samples of 547 men and 393 women, each of whom had been given the Q-sort by panels of five or more judges. Consensual Q-sorts were derived for each assessee, and then the 100 items were correlated with scores on Ie. The four items with largest positive and four with largest negative correlations are reported below, along with the coefficients for men and for women.

Genuinely values intellectual and cognitive matters (.23, .37)

Has high aspiration level for self (.25, .28)

Has social poise and presence; appears socially at ease (.23, .24)

Is verbally fluent; can express ideas well (.19, .37)

Gives up and withdraws where possible in the face of frustration and adversity (–.17, –.30)

Has a brittle ego-defense system; has a small reserve of integration; would be disorganized and maladaptive if under stress or trauma (–.17, –.29)

Is self-defeating (–.23, –.25)

Feels cheated and victimized by life; self-pitying (–.21, –.25)

High scorers on Ie appear to value intellectual and cognitive matters, have high aspirations, are socially poised, and express themselves well. Low scorers give up and withdraw when stymied, seem to have brittle ego-defenses, and are self-defeating and self-pitying. It might be mentioned that the item "Appears to have a

high degree of intellectual capacity" was also related to scores on Ie, with correlations of .15 for men and .34 for women.

Impressions of life history interviewers to 504 men and 379 women were recorded on a 99-item check list. The four items with largest positive and four with largest negative correlations are cited below, along with the coefficients for men and for women.

Uses wide and varied vocabulary (.24, .23)

Was an honor student in high school (.17, .26)

Unusually self-confident, feels able to meet nearly any situation (.21, .16)

Creates a good impression; has effective interpersonal techniques (.19, .16)

Has difficulty in expressing ideas (–.15, –.13)

Makes mistakes in grammar and/or word usage (–.23, –.18)

Has many worries and problems (–.20, –.14)

Is unsure of self, doubts own ability (–.21, –.18)

High scorers on Ie made use of a wide vocabulary in the interviews, were self-confident, and created a good impression. They also report being honor students in high school. Low scorers have difficulty in expressing ideas, make mistakes in use of language, have many worries, and seem to be self-defeating.

Items from the 50-item *Interpersonal Q-Sort* were correlated with Ie in samples of 200 men described by a wife or partner, 200 women described by a husband or partner, and 111 male assessees described by panels of three staff observers. The three items with largest positive and three with largest negative correlations are cited below, with the coefficients for men, women, and the male assessees.

Independent, intelligent, and self-reliant; values achievement (.16, .21, .33)

Verbally fluent; expresses self easily and with clarity (.13, .22, .43)

Is an effective leader; able to elicit the response and cooperation of others (.18, .17, .35)

Dull; lacking in ability and understanding (–.15, –.15, –.26)

Given to moods; often difficult and recalcitrant (–.21, –.04, –.26)

Wedded to routine; made anxious by change and uncertainty (–.02, –.17, –.25)

On this set of descriptors, high scorers on Ie are seen as independent and intelligent, as verbally fluent, and as having leadership potential. Low scorers on Ie are seen as dull and lacking in ability, as given to moods, and as anxious if required to deal with change or uncertainty.

In summary, high scores on Ie are indicative of good intellectual ability, efficient use of ability, and general good sense in living. Payoffs are visible in better physical and psychological well-being than for low scorers, in superior academic achievement, and in positive reactions from others. Curvilinearity of meaning for scores on Ie does not seem to occur. That is, there is no high point at which respondents become too intellectual, too wrapped up in cognitive endeavor, or too eager to succeed.

Low scores on Ie are suggestive of moderate to below-average intellectual ability, but also of a more far-ranging lack of skills and resources for dealing with the demands of life and work. Persons with low scores on Ie deal poorly with stress and trauma, have feelings of victimization, and are often self-defeating.

The Py (Psychological-mindedness) Scale

In the late 1940s and early 1950s, a pool of some 300 experimental items was given to a sample of 25 outstanding young psychologists, chosen on the basis of personal acquaintance and from nominations gathered informally from senior scholars at several universities. The names of these individuals cannot be revealed, but in following their careers to the present time, it is obvious that they have more than lived up to their potentials. Their many awards and recognitions included presidencies of regional, national, and divisional associations of psychology, gold medals for both research and professional contributions to psychology, elections to the National Academy of Science, and an output of books, papers, reviews, and commentaries sufficient to fill a small library. The item responses for this group of 25 young luminaries were contrasted with those of a large sample of persons in other fields and/or training programs. Some 75 items that showed promise were retained and then administered to both male and female students enrolled in graduate seminars in psychology in several universities. Instructors of these seminars furnished research evaluations of the competence and potential for superior work in psychology for these students. The ratings were correlated with the items, 22 of which had significant relationships to the ratings and agreement in endorsement rates with the first analysis. These 22 items constituted the initial version of the Py scale, as it appeared in Form 480 in 1956.

Table 5.18 Raw Score Means and Standard Deviations on the Py Scale for 22 Different Educational, Occupational, and Clinical Samples				
	Males		**Females**	
Samples	M	SD	M	SD
Psychology graduate students	21.32	2.89	21.17	2.89
Mathematicians	21.05	2.47	21.00	2.69
Medical school students	19.41	2.88	20.27	2.57
Social welfare students	19.45	2.90	19.30	2.93
Premedical students	19.67	2.22	19.06	2.73
Optometry students	19.00	2.98	19.12	2.90
Anesthesiologists	18.44	2.44	18.00	2.85
Majors in education	18.75	2.91	17.88	2.92
Creative writers	19.37	2.81	17.90	3.57
MBA candidates	17.86	2.96	18.61	2.81
Counseling graduate students	17.75	3.66	17.88	2.91
Police officer applicants	17.70	2.73	18.17	2.77
Pharmacy school students	17.31	3.37	17.46	3.24
Nursing school students	16.97	3.75	16.48	2.96
Architecture school students	16.37	2.90	16.98	3.41
College students in general	16.62	3.32	16.46	3.22
Art institute students	15.36	3.22	15.22	3.73
Profile norm samples	14.55	3.78	14.24	3.89
High school students in general	13.89	3.35	13.24	3.35
Psychiatric patients	14.15	4.02	12.38	4.66
Juvenile delinquents	13.13	3.40	12.11	3.64
Prison inmates	12.76	3.48	12.60	3.80

The strategy of scale construction for Py was designed to attain two objectives: first, to produce higher scores for persons interested in the field of psychology and working in the discipline than for other equally talented persons interested and working in other fields; second, to be related to the quality of work in psychology, using criteria normally employed to evaluate such work. Attainment of the first objective is suggested by the data in Table 5.18. For 22 groups for which both male and female samples were available, as reported in full in Appendix B, means on Py are arrayed roughly in order of magnitude.

Highest-scoring samples for both men and women are graduate students in psychology, followed by mathematicians, medical school students, social welfare graduate students, premedical students, optometry students, and physicians specializing in anesthesiology. In the middle of the array are found samples such as police officer applicants, pharmacy and nursing school students, students of architecture, and college students in general. Groups scoring below the baseline established by the profile norm samples are high school students, psychiatric patients, juvenile delinquents, and prison inmates. Presumably, one of the themes concurrent with these arrays is psychological-mindedness, or interest in psychology.

Another bit of evidence pertinent to the stipulated aims of the Py scale is its correlation of .46 with the Psychologist scale on the *Strong Interest Inventory* for a sample of 300 college students (150 of each sex).

In regard to the second goal, to relate to performance in psychological endeavor as ordinarily evaluated, in four samples of undergraduate psychology students ($N = 5,103$), the mean correlation of Py with course grade was .24 (Gough, 1964b). Another study (Sandoval, 1993) related scores on the CPI to those on the *Maslach Burnout Inventory* (MBI; Maslach & Jackson, 1986) in a sample of 50 school psychologists. The first two scales of the MBI focus directly on burnout and its symptoms, whereas the third scale (Personal Accomplishment) assesses attributes that help to counter and resist occupational burnout. The correlation between Py and the Personal Accomplishment scale was .30 ($p < .05$). A third study (Burkhart, Gynther, & Christian, 1978) had 60 college students take the MMPI, first under normal instructions, and then with instructions to either fake good or fake bad. A tally was made of the use of very subtle and somewhat subtle items as opposed to use of obvious and very obvious items. Under standard conditions, Py was significantly ($p < .01$) correlated with endorsement of subtle items and avoidance of obvious, whereas intelligence as measured by the *American College Test* (ACT) was not. The authors concluded that this sensitivity to subtle items "demonstrates that Py also measures the ability to discriminate more sharply the social meaning of an interpersonal communication."

In the 1986 version of the CPI (Form 462), the Py scale was lengthened to 28 items in an attempt to increase its single-trial index of reliability. The six new items were selected on the basis of a reappraisal of the two initial item analyses, with the proviso, of course, that each new item was already included in Form 480 of the inventory. Two of the 28 items in

the scale came into conflict with the prohibitions of the Americans with Disabilities Act and had to be dropped from Form 434. Two other items from Form 434 were substituted so as to keep the length of Py at 28. Correlations of the two 28-item versions of Py were .97 for both male and female profile norm samples. As reported in chapter 3, the interitem alpha coefficient of Py on the profile norm sample of 6,000 persons was .62, indicative of moderate heterogeneity of content.

A factor analysis of the 28 items in Py was carried out on the sample of 6,000 persons in the profile norm sample. Seven factors with eigen values of 1.00 or greater were identified, of which four were arbitrarily retained for rotation by means of Kaiser's normal varimax method. Factor 1 was composed primarily of items indicating the ability to direct and maintain one's intellectual functions, for example, "I find it hard to keep my mind on a task or job" ("false"), "I have a tendency to give up easily when I meet difficult problems" ("false"), and "I cannot keep my mind on one thing" ("false"). Factor 2 has items suggesting indifference to minor conventions, personal neatness, and the like. Representative items are, "I do not like to see people carelessly dressed" ("false") and "I always like to keep my things neat and tidy and in good order" ("false"). Factor 3 has items indicating a liking for intellectual endeavors, for instance, "The idea of doing research appeals to me" ("true") and "I like to read about science" ("true"). Factor 4 was a singleton, its one item being "I never make judgments about people until I am sure of the facts" ("false").

Specific acts associated with higher and lower scores on Py were detected in an analysis of the Buss-Craik act frequency inventory on a sample of 177 persons (88 men, 89 women), each of whom was rated for frequencies of the acts by a spouse or partner. The five acts with largest positive correlations with Py and the five with largest negative correlations are listed below.

Listened carefully to a friend's criticisms of him/her (.24)

Advocated an idea that was "ahead of its time" (.24)

Willingly tried a new food at a restaurant when a friend suggested it (.27)

Picked up the tab for lunch (.25)

Helped a friend with a difficult assignment (.21)

Blushed when speaking to a large group (–.16)

Forgave an acquaintance who had spread a false rumor about him/her (–.16)

Table 5.19 Adjectival Descriptions by Observers: 12 Most Salient Positive and 12 Most Salient Negative Correlates of the 28-Item Py Scale

Adjectives	Men, Described By			Women, Described By		
	Spouse ($N = 236$)	3 Peers ($N = 194$)	10 Staff Members ($N = 612$)	Spouse ($N = 236$)	3 Peers ($N = 192$)	10 Staff Members ($N = 358$)
Alert	.13*	.09	.16**	.12	.16*	.11*
Clear-thinking	.16*	.08	.16**	.20**	.22**	.23**
Confident	.05	.08	.12**	.15*	.23**	.11*
Enterprising	.07	.05	.13**	.16*	.12	.14**
Foresighted	.12	.18*	.18**	.05	.12	.16**
Initiative	.18**	.00	.13**	.22**	.14*	.14**
Insightful	.25**	.14*	.19**	.24**	.11	.13*
Intelligent	.10	.12	.23**	.13*	.13	.29**
Logical	.03	.20**	.20**	.06	.22**	.34**
Rational	.08	.13	.08*	.13*	.19**	.25**
Reflective	.13*	.07	.13**	.25**	.07	.12*
Thorough	.03	.16*	.22**	.10	.20**	.22**
Apathetic	−.16*	−.08	−.18**	−.05	−.11	−.08
Confused	−.18**	−.07	−.14**	−.05	−.10	−.13*
Dependent	−.03	−.03	−.09*	−.09	−.06	−.21**
Infantile	−.02	−.06	−.09*	−.25**	−.06	−.19**
Self-pitying	−.12	−.07	−.03	−.10	−.06	−.10*
Shiftless	−.11	−.06	−.11**	−.08	−.04	−.06
Silent	−.11	−.02	−.11**	−.12	−.03	−.11*
Simple	−.11	−.05	−.19**	−.25**	−.08	−.21**
Superstitious	−.20**	−.01	−.04	−.09	−.04	−.30**
Unambitious	−.10	−.07	−.12**	−.03	−.03	−.23**
Weak	−.19**	−.03	−.13**	−.11	−.08	−.11*
Whiny	−.03	−.05	−.05	−.15*	−.04	−.09

*$p \le .05$, **$p \le .01$

Did not complain when someone used his/her car without permission (−.17)

Accused them of talking behind his/her back (−.20)

Continued to apologize for a minor mistake (−.16)

The acts associated with higher scores on Py suggest an interest in new ideas, openmindedness in regard to criticism and to new experiences, and willingness to help others on intellectual tasks. Acts associated with lower scores on Py involve apologetic behavior,

embarrassment in the limelight, avoidance of conflict with exploitative friends, and sensitivity to behind-the-back remarks.

Adjective Check List correlates with Py in six samples are given in Table 5.19, which lists the 12 adjectives with largest positive and 12 with largest negative correlations. The association of adjectives with higher and lower scores on Py is somewhat weaker than for the other scales, particularly in the subsamples of college men and women. With this caution, let us look first at the descriptions related to higher scores. One theme betokens good intellectual functioning, for example, clear-thinking, insightful, intelligent, logical, rational, and reflective. High scorers are also described as alert and foresighted, as having initiative and confidence, and as being thorough.

Those with lower scores on Py are seen as apathetic, dependent, simple, unambitious, and weak. They also seem given to complaint, as suggested by the adjectives self-pitying and whiny. They tend to be silent, appear to be superstitious, and to some extent are characterized as shiftless. All 12 of the terms associated with lower scores on Py depict some kind of interpersonal or intrapersonal problem.

In a composite sample of 1,356 persons, using standardized scores for the observers' descriptions, the 200 most frequently used adjectives were regressed onto the Py score, stopping the analysis after eight steps. The best combination of eight descriptions for estimating scores on Py had a multiple correlation of .35 (R^2 = .12). Five adjectives had positive beta weights: argumentative, ingenious, logical, thorough, and tolerant. Three had negative beta weights: kind, strong, and suspicious.

The 100 items in the *California Q-Set* were correlated with Py scores in samples of 547 men and 393 women, all of whom had been described on the Q-sort by panels of five or more observers. The four items with largest positive and the four with largest negative correlations are cited below, along with the coefficients for men and for women.

> Has a wide range of interests (.20, .26)
>
> Appears to have a high degree of intellectual capacity (.21, .32)
>
> Genuinely values intellectual and cognitive matters (.30, .40)
>
> Has high aspiration level for self (.25, .27)
>
> Is uncomfortable with uncertainty and complexities (−.11, −.24)
>
> Gives up and withdraws where possible in the face of frustration and adversity (−.18, −.23)
>
> Judges self and others in conventional terms such as "popularity," "the correct thing to do," "social pressures, etc." (−.12, −.23)
>
> Is self-indulgent (−.16, −.12)

A clear cognitive theme is observable in the Q-sort items associated with high scores on Py, namely breadth of interests, superior intellectual ability, and

placing value on intellectual matters. A strong desire to achieve is also presaged by the item on aspirations. Low scores on Py are associated with discomfort in dealing with complexity, lack of perseverance when frustrated or confronted with adversity, conventionality in evaluating self and others, and self-indulgence.

Behaviors and recollections observed during a life history interview were recorded on a 99-item check list by the interviewer for 504 men and 379 women. The four items with largest positive correlations with Py and the four with largest negative correlations are given below, with the coefficients for men and for women.

> Uses wide and varied vocabulary (.14, .22)
>
> Witty and animated, an interesting conversationalist (.11, .18)
>
> Was an honor student in high school (.10, .19)
>
> Unusually self-confident, feels able to meet nearly any situation (.13, .17)
>
> Makes mistakes in grammar and/or word usage (−.20, −.19)
>
> Had first sexual intercourse while in high school or before (−.21, −.16)
>
> Considers self to have been an underachiever in high school (−.13, −.12)
>
> Is unsure of self, doubts own ability (−.10, −.18)

Although the coefficients are low in magnitude, those associated with high scores on Py suggest self-confidence, elan, and effective use of intellectual resources. Those associated with low scores on Py suggest self-doubt, educational lacks, and pursuit of gratifications along nonintellectual, noncognitive lines.

The 50-item *Interpersonal Q-Sort* was used to obtain descriptions by observers of 200 men, 200 women, and 111 men studied in living-in assessments. The three items with largest positive and three with largest negative correlations with Py are cited below, along with the coefficients for the three samples.

> Observant and perceptive; quick to respond to the subtleties and nuances of others' behavior (.14, .14, .27)
>
> Has a talent for creative and original thinking (.13, .11, .35)
>
> Verbally fluent; expresses self easily and with clarity (.17, .11, .27)

Unambitious; commonplace and conventional in thinking and behavior (–.08, –.21, –.27)

Awkward and ill at ease socially; shy and inhibited with others (–.10, –.14, –.25)

Wedded to routine; made anxious by change and uncertainty (–.10, –.16, –.15)

High scorers on Py tend to be described as perceptive, observant of subtleties in the behavior of others, creative, and verbally fluent. Low scorers are described as unambitious, commonplace, ill at ease socially, and as wedded to routine.

In summary, the Py scale assesses an analytic, rational, conceptualizing kind of psychological-mindedness. High scorers tend to be interested in psychological phenomena, including the field itself. In academic pursuits, they do well, drawing on their verbal fluency, superior intelligence, and creative potential. In their relations with others, they tend to be somewhat distant, not usually warm or supportive, and in intimacy, they tend to take more than they give.

Low scorers on Py avoid intellectual and interpersonal complexities when they can, have conventional views, are dubious about their own abilities, and are ill at ease in social situations. They have a tendency to feel put-upon by the vicissitudes of life, rely on devious rather than direct methods of coping, and have a difficult time making good use of whatever talents they might possess.

The Fx (Flexibility) Scale

The Fx scale was constructed in collaboration with Nevitt Sanford in an attempt to get at the rigidity factor found to be of central importance in the authoritarian personality (Adorno, Frenkel-Brunswik, Levinson, & Sanford, 1950). The *California F Scale* has implications for rigidity, along with its more obvious assessment of prejudicial and intolerant attitudes. However, the F scale rigidity is confounded by linkage to a particular politicosocial perspective. The challenge for Fx, as it were, was to provide a purer measure of the rigidity-flexibility axis, unassociated with either progressive or conservative ideology. The methodology of scale development was frankly subjective. That is, items were written to express the psychology of rigidity and flexibility as understood by Gough and Sanford. Some 80 items were assembled and then administered to various samples of

students in classes of the two authors, assessees at the Institute of Personality Assessment and Research, and elsewhere. Psychometric analyses pitted individual items against total score on the initial composite. In this way, the pool of items was reduced to 22, each one aligned with the totality of the others.

This first scale became known as the Gough-Sanford Rigidity scale, and was used in that form by a number of investigators (see, for example, Rokeach, 1960). In 1956, when Form 480 of the CPI was published, the scale was reversed in scoring and retitled Flexibility. In Form 462, published in 1986, Fx was increased in length to 28 items. This version of the scale has been carried over intact to Form 434.

As shown in Appendix C, Fx has zero or near zero correlations with measures of academic performance and progress, and also with measures of intellectual ability. For instance, in samples of 2,625 males and 3,086 females, Fx had correlations of .04 and .06, respectively, with standardized ability test scores as used in the high schools where the students were tested. When examined in relation to personality inventory measures, informative findings appeared. For example, correlations of –.56 for men and –.62 for women were obtained with Comrey's scale for Orderliness, and –.30 and –.47 with his scale for Conformity. Correlations of –.54 for men and –.56 for women were found with the NEO-AC scale for Conscientiousness, of .69 and .54 with the OPI scale for complexity, and of –.65 and –.74 with the OPI scale for practical outlook. With the PRF scale for Cognitive Structure, the correlations were –.49 for men and –.58 for women; with the Lazare-Klerman-Armor scale for Obsessional Personality, the correlations were –.59 for men and –.62 for women; and with Barron's scale for Complexity, the correlations were .60 and .55. An interesting application of the Fx scale was made by Garnham (1974), who found low Fx scores to be a problem in political decision making.

A factor analysis of the 28 Fx items in the profile norm sample of 6,000 persons identified seven factors with eigen values of 1.00 or more. Four of these were arbitrarily retained for rotation by means of Kaiser's normal varimax method. Factor 1 was composed of items indicative of tolerance of ambiguity, for example, "I often wish people would be more definite about things" ("false"), and "For most questions there is just one right answer, once a person is able to get all the facts" ("false"). Factor 2 betokens uncompulsivity, for example, "I like to have a place for everything and everything in its place" ("false") and "I always like to keep my things neat and tidy and in good order" ("false"). Factor 3 has items candidly admitting bias and prejudgment, for instance, "I never make judgments about people until I am sure of the facts" ("false"), and "It is always a good thing to be frank" ("false"). Factor 4 has items suggesting absence of severe or punitive super-ego controls, for example, "I think I am stricter about right and wrong than most people" ("false") and "I set a high standard for myself and feel that others should do the same" ("false").

Act-frequency specifics associated with Fx were examined in a sample of 177 persons (88 men, 89 women), each of whom was rated for frequency of acts by a spouse or partner. The five acts with largest positive and the five with largest negative correlations are reported below.

Willingly bore the cost of the evening out on the town (.30)

Talked to a stranger at a bus stop (.31)

Ignored a stranger's greeting (.29)

Served a fantastic meal for friends at a dinner party (.30)

Entertained the crowd at a party with some jokes (.27)

Planned out a casual conversation (−.16)

Picked a fight with a stranger at a party (−.16)

Drove an expensive car to impress his/her friends (−.17)

Managed to control the outcome of a meeting without the others being aware of it (−.17)

Went to church (−.19)

Acts associated with high scores on Fx have a kind of spontaneity and liveliness, and suggest a readiness to do whatever seems like fun or compatible with one's mood. Acts associated with low scores on Fx involve more deliberation, more planning, and more awareness of consequences.

From correlations of ACL descriptions of persons in six samples, the 12 adjectives with largest positive and 12 with largest negative correlates of Fx are listed in Table 5.20. One cluster associated with high scores on Fx suggests a delight in new experience and impatience with routine: adventurous, changeable, pleasure-seeking, spontaneous,

unconventional, and uninhibited. Another cluster points to wit and humor: clever, humorous, imaginative, and sharp-witted. The description disorderly suggests that spontaneity and the abandonment of restraint may at times go too far, and the adjective individualistic suggests too much attention to self and too little to others in the search for pleasure.

Adjectives associated with low scores on Fx suggest constraint (cautious, conservative, conventional, deliberate, industrious, and painstaking), narrowness of interests, fussiness, prejudice, and prudery. However, there is also an element of practicality that is very much lacking in the implications associated with high scores.

A regression analysis of the 200 most frequently used adjectives in a composite sample of 1,356 persons was carried out to discover the best set of eight descriptions from which to estimate scores on Fx. This optimum set had a multiple correlation of .40 with Fx (R^2 = .16). Adjectives with positive beta weights were curious, imaginative, and rational. Adjectives with negative beta weights were affectionate, conservative, industrious, organized, and rigid.

Analyses of the 100 items in the *California Q-Set* were conducted in samples of 547 men and 393 women, each of whom had been described on the Q-sort by panels of five or more judges. These independent formulations were combined in a consensual composite for each assessee. The four items with largest positive and the four with largest negative correlations with Fx are given below, with the coefficients for men and for women.

Appears to have a high degree of intellectual ability (.18, .21)

Thinks and associates to ideas in unusual ways; has unconventional thought processes (.18, .33)

Enjoys sensuous experiences (including touch, taste, smell, and physical contact) (.16, .22)

Tends to be rebellious and nonconforming (.22, .36)

Is fastidious (−.22, −.34)

Favors conservative values in a variety of areas (−.26, −.40)

Is moralistic (−.20, −.31)

Judges self and others in conventional terms such as "popularity," "the correct thing to do," social pressures, etc. (−.23, −.30)

Table 5.20 Adjectival Descriptions by Observers: 12 Most Salient Positive and 12 Most Salient Negative Correlates of the 28-Item Fx Scale

Adjectives	Men, Described By			Women, Described By		
	Spouse (N = 236)	3 Peers (N = 194)	10 Staff Members (N = 612)	Spouse (N = 236)	3 Peers (N = 192)	10 Staff Members (N = 358)
Adventurous	.18**	.20**	.14**	.15*	.20**	.20**
Changeable	.14*	.17*	.11**	.17**	.21**	.22**
Clever	.22**	.18*	.24**	.11	.18*	.19**
Disorderly	.22**	.19**	.11**	.15*	.26**	.23**
Humorous	.16*	.22**	.09*	.17**	.13	.13*
Imaginative	.23**	.13	.27**	.15*	.24**	.28**
Individualistic	.08	.14*	.16**	.25**	.17*	.24**
Pleasure-seeking	.18**	.25**	.11**	.13*	.30**	.15**
Sharp-witted	.07	.19**	.16**	.18**	.15*	.24**
Spontaneous	.15*	.13	.16**	.34**	.25**	.17**
Unconventional	.23**	.08	.22**	.21**	.19**	.22**
Uninhibited	.17**	.12	.13**	.13*	.16*	.19**
Cautious	−.02	−.14*	−.08*	−.16*	−.38**	−.16**
Conservative	−.26**	−.07	−.26**	−.32**	−.29**	−.42**
Conventional	−.20**	−.07	−.22**	−.14*	−.20**	−.38**
Deliberate	−.12	−.15*	−.10**	−.09	−.10	−.24**
Fussy	−.17**	−.08	−.15**	.00	−.14*	−.12*
Industrious	−.05	−.16*	−.04	−.04	−.19**	−.16**
Interests narrow	−.22**	−.17*	−.17**	−.21**	−.12	−.30**
Painstaking	−.06	−.19**	−.09*	−.09	−.17*	−.12*
Practical	−.10	−.17*	−.08*	−.08	−.23**	−.17**
Prejudiced	−.20**	−.02	−.15**	−.05	−.24**	−.15**
Prudish	−.03	−.19**	−.08*	−.10	−.32**	−.29**
Stern	−.25**	−.24**	−.13**	−.03	−.18*	−.16**

$*p \le .05, **p \le .01$

High scorers on Fx are viewed as superior in intelligence, even though the observed correlation of Fx with measures of ability is not much above zero. They are also seen as having innovative, unconventional thought processes, as rebellious, and as enjoying sensual experiences (remember the act item about serving friends a "fantastic" meal).

Low scorers on Fx are described as fastidious, conservative, moralistic, and given to conventional judgment and standards.

The yield from the 99-item interviewers' check list was relatively scanty for those scoring high on Fx, but somewhat more informative for reactions to those scoring low, as shown below in the listing of the four items with largest positive and four with largest negative correlations with Fx.

Animated facial expressiveness (.17, .05)

Careless, unkempt in grooming and appearance (.11, .12)

Uses wide and varied vocabulary (.15, .13)

Witty and animated, an interesting conversationalist (.16, .17)

Father stern and authoritarian (−.15, −.12)

Has strong religious beliefs (−.19, −.21)

Is happily married (−.11, −.19)

Enjoys children (−.22, −.25)

For the 504 men who were interviewed, correlations of .09 are significant at or beyond the .05 level; and for the 379 women, correlations of .10 are significant at or beyond the .05 level. Thus, even for the very low coefficients in the four items associated with high scores on Fx, only one item is below the .05 level for confidence. From these items, a weak impression is conveyed of high Fx interviewees showing up in rather unkempt attire, speaking in an animated way with a diversified vocabulary, and displaying animated facial expressiveness. These descriptions are quite compatible with the picture of high scorers on Fx that is emerging from the other observational perspectives.

Low scorers on Fx have strong religious beliefs, are happily married, and enjoy children. Their stern fathers seemingly have transmitted strong inclinations to conform, follow conventions, and behave in a controlled manner.

Interpersonal Q-sorts were done for 200 men, 200 women, and 111 male assessees. From the 50 items in the deck, the three with largest positive and three with largest negative correlations with Fx are reported below, along with the coefficients for the three samples.

Clever and imaginative; a spontaneous and entertaining person (.28, .24, .29)

Undependable; poorly motivated; has difficulty in working toward prescribed goals (.17, .09, .33)

Has a talent for creative and original thinking (.17, .20, .28)

A conscientious and serious-minded person (−.17, −.20, −.21)

Deliberate and methodical in behavior; inflexible and stubborn in attitude (−.19, −.15, −.29)

Unimaginative and literal-minded; slow and deliberate; lacking in zest and enthusiasm (−.21, −.17, −.18)

High scorers on Fx are described as clever, entertaining, and original in their thinking, but also as undependable and as inconstant in pursuit of prescribed goals. Low scorers are described as serious and conscientious, but also as stubborn and inflexible, and as literal-minded.

In summary, high scores on Fx are indicative of a number of favorable attributes, including zest, imaginativeness, spontaneity, good ability to adapt to change and the unexpected, and an adventurous spirit. But along with this, especially at very high raw scores of 25 and over, goes undependability, too much volatility, and easy irritability when things move too slowly or are seen as routinized.

Low scores on Fx, likewise, betoken certain favorable qualities such as seriousness of purpose, conscientiousness, practicality, and firm moral beliefs and principles. But at the same time, there are important negative attributes associated with low scores, especially those below six or seven raw score points, including rigidity, moralistic judgment, and a deliberate, slow-moving mode of behavior.

The F/M (Femininity/Masculinity) Scale

The basic purpose of the F/M scale is to array respondents along a dimension that is consonant with folk notions of femininity and masculinity. It is well established (Williams & Best, 1982, 1990) that there are culturally universal perceptions of what is feminine and what is masculine, and even children at age five appear to have acquired this knowledge. In their thirty-nation study, Williams and Best found a common core of adjectival characterizations used and understood by children and adults in every country. Among the terms associated with men and masculinity were aggressive, determined, and robust. Among the terms associated with women and femininity were gentle, sentimental, and warm. For the F/M scale to be compatible with folk psychology, empirically derived descriptive correlates of higher and lower scores must be in agreement with these findings.

A subsidiary requirement for the F/M scale is to differentiate between men and women everywhere, in all cultures. That is, to be compatible with folk notions about femininity and masculinity, women must in general have higher scores on F/M than men. Failure to achieve such differentiation in any culture would cast serious doubt on the validity of the scale. Because folk ideas about homoeroticism tend to assign more femininity to homoerotic than to heteroerotic men, and more masculinity to homo-erotic than to heteroerotic women, a desirable finding would be somewhat elevated scores for homoerotic men and somewhat depressed scores for homoerotic women. These trends, if discernible, would be only moderate for two reasons. First, as is well-known clinically, there are different pathways to homoerotic behavior, only one of which is associated with femi-nization or masculinization of personality. Second, there are strong pancultural taboos against manifest homoerotic behavior, often leading to its suppression or denial.

The first version of the scale (Gough, 1952a) had 58 items, chosen from some 300 for their ability to differentiate between the self-reports of men and women. This scale showed good discriminations between men and women in cross-validating sam-ples, and also showed a significant difference in the expected direction between 38 homoerotic and 38 heteroerotic males, matched for age, education, and intelligence. The scale, however, was too long for inclusion in the CPI and was therefore shortened to 38 items when Form 480 of the inventory was published in 1956. For Form 462 of the CPI, pub-lished in 1986, the scale was further shortened to 32 items. This 32-item scale has been carried over unchanged in the current 434-item edition of the CPI.

A first cross-cultural study (Gough, 1966a) on the ability of the scale to differentiate between men and women reported data for six countries: France, Italy, Norway, Turkey, the United States, and Venezuela. Differences between the means for men and women were significant ($p < .01$) in every case. The point-biserial correlations for the differentiations ranged from .47 to .71, with a median of .54.

An expanded compilation of cross-cultural data is given in Table 5.21, for 17 countries. Information for the 11 new applications was furnished by Prof.

M. A. Torki for Egypt and Kuwait (Torki, 1988); Prof. A. B. Weinert for Germany; Drs. J. Levin and E. S. Karni for Israel (Levin & Karni, 1971); Dr. T. Nishiyama for Japan (Nishiyama, 1975); Drs. K. Chun and Y. Chung for Korea (Gough, Chun, & Chung, 1968); Drs. I. Ahmad for Pakistan (Ahmad, Anis-ul-Haque, & Anila, 1994); Dr. L. Wu for the People's Republic of China; Prof. H. Pitariu for Romania (Pitariu, 1981); Dr. N. Seisdedos for Spain; and Prof. Y. Ying for Taiwan (Ying, 1991).

All 17 of the differences between men and women in Table 5.21 are statistically significant ($p < .01$). The median value for F/M for men is 14.32, and the median value for women is 18.54. The point-biserial correlations ranged from a low of .37 to a high of .71. The correlation of .37 was obtained in a study of 311 grade school children in Korea, and the coefficient of .71 was obtained for two large and heterogeneous samples of adults in the United States. The highest F/M mean for the male samples was that of 15.89 for Japanese college students. The lowest F/M mean for female samples was that of 17.02 for university students in Pakistan. From all of the information so far avail-able, it appears that the scale is succeeding in its objective of differentiating between men and women in any culture.

Itemmetric analyses of the F/M scale have been conducted in nine of the countries named in Table 5.21, and it is hoped that such information will be developed for all 17, and even more. Even though total score on F/M may differentiate in the expected direction between men and women, discrepancies may well be found in regard to individual items. It is also of considerable interest to note items whose differentiations hold constant across all samples. One such item is, "A windstorm terrifies me," which was answered "true" more often by women than men in all nine countries. An example of an item answered "true" more often by men in all nine comparisons (and therefore scored for a "false" response) is, "I think I would like the work of a garage mechanic." An example of an item showing a single reversal is, "I become quite irritated when I see someone spit on the sidewalk." Women answered "true" to this item significantly more often than men in eight of the comparisons; how-ever, in the Japanese samples, the percentages were 56 for men and 53 for women.

| Table 5.21 Cross-Cultural Comparison of Males and Females on the 32-Item F/M Scale | | | | | | | |
| Country of Testing | Males | | | Females | | | $r_{p.bis}$ |
	N	M	SD	N	M	SD	
Egypt	91	15.59	1.50	200	18.71	2.22	.55
France	452	14.83	3.30	382	18.46	3.17	.52
Germany	149	14.01	2.90	123	18.63	3.28	.60
Israel	200	13.78	3.03	200	18.54	2.51	.64
Italy	697	14.69	2.98	171	18.67	2.95	.47
Japan	200	15.89	2.80	300	18.66	1.84	.46
Korea	155	15.20	3.40	156	17.84	3.20	.37
Kuwait	202	15.09	2.46	227	17.63	2.37	.46
Norway	87	13.73	2.91	83	18.09	2.63	.62
Pakistan	90	13.68	3.10	90	17.02	3.15	.47
People's Republic of China	2,671	14.11	2.68	790	17.73	3.40	.43
Romania	570	14.32	3.64	300	18.94	4.11	.58
Spain	455	13.97	2.64	139	18.14	3.13	.54
Taiwan	111	15.11	3.23	104	18.62	3.21	.48
Turkey	88	15.30	2.75	117	18.74	3.54	.47
United States	6,419	13.69	3.06	5,647	19.67	2.85	.71
Venezuela	151	14.32	3.23	175	18.54	2.30	.58

Note: All of the mean differences are significant beyond the .01 level.

Itemmetric data can also give clues about possible mistranslations or poor quality of translation. Consider the item, "I'm pretty sure I know how we can settle the international problems we face today." In eight of the countries, the percentage of "true" responses by men ranged from 5 to 50, with a mean of 26.25. The percentage of "true" responses by women ranged from 4 to 37, with a mean of 14.88. However, in one country, the percentages were 74 for men and 62 for women. Is it probable that in this one country both men and women have vastly superior understanding of international affairs, or is it more likely that something has gone awry in translating the item?

The findings in Table 5.21 pertain to testing in the United States and other countries. What about similarities and differences on F/M for majority and minority populations within the United States? Baldwin (1987) administered the F/M scale to students at a Midwestern college over a 14-year period. The means and standard deviations for both men and women held relatively constant during this period. For Black males (N = 664), the mean on the 32-item F/M scale was 14.80; and for White males (N = 554), the mean was 14.43. For Black females (N = 1,528), the mean was 18.70; and for White females (N = 936), the mean was 18.32. The differences between Black and white subsamples were small and statistically insignificant for both males and females, whereas those for gender were large and significant beyond the .01 level of probability. Also, the means for Baldwin's two male samples were close to the median of 14.32 for males in Table 5.21, and his two female samples had means close to the median of 18.54 for females in Table 5.21.

Certain other lines of research on role and gender implications of the F/M scale can be mentioned. Mazen and Lemkau (1990) classified jobs as traditional feminine or nontraditional, and found that women in the former had significantly higher F/M scores than women in the latter. An earlier study (Block, von der Lippe, & Block, 1973) found that men with low scores on F/M gravitated toward technical fields, accounting, police work, and construction. Men with high scores more often chose careers in teaching, the helping professions, entertainment, and the social sciences. Women with high scores were frequently employed in clerical, receptionist, design, and beautician jobs. Women with low scores often had positions as managers, administrators, and scientists.

A recent study (Gough, 1995) arrayed 36 samples of women according to their mean scores on F/M. At the top were high school students who did not go on to college, writers of books for children, commercial writers, registered nurses, women in traditionally feminine jobs, and critics of books for children, in that order. At the bottom were students of law, architecture, optometry, and medicine, women in traditionally masculine jobs, juvenile delinquents, MBA candidates, and applicants for work as police officers.

From the norms for males in Appendix B, the five samples scoring highest on F/M are critics of books for children, writers of books for children, creative writers, mathematicians, and art institute students. The five samples with lowest means on F/M are West Point cadets, engineers, military officers, high school disciplinary problems, and police officers. Scores on the F/M scale do seem to convey information about occupational preferences and prospects that is not directly available from other measures.

Relationships of F/M to other scales intended to assess masculinity or femininity are reported in Appendix C. With Comrey's scale for Masculinity, the correlations for F/M are –.33 for men and –.31 for women; with the Guilford-Zimmerman scale for Masculinity, the correlations are –.53 for both sexes; with raw scores on the MMPI Mf scale, the correlations are .49 for men and .42 for women. The CPI F/M scale is similar in some ways to these other measures, but not identical.

For the dimensions of the five-factor model, as assessed by self-reports, Appendix C has measures from the NEO-AC and also from Goldberg's adjectival markers. What are the relationships of F/M to

the themes of the FFM? With the five factor scales of the NEO-AC, the correlations for F/M ranged from –.06 to .38 for men, and from –.17 to .30 for women. With Goldberg's five markers, the correlations for F/M ranged from –.24 to .33 for men, and from –.28 to .19 for women. Whatever it is that the F/M scale assesses appears to be absent, or at best weakly present, in these self-report FFM measures.

A number of writers (e.g. Bem, 1974; Constantinople, 1973; Spence & Helmreich, 1979) have pointed out that in the self-report sphere, scales for masculinity and femininity can be constructed so as to produce zero or near-zero correlations with each other. From these findings, some psychologists have concluded that MF is composed of two independent or unipolar themes, and that it is incorrect to conceptualize MF as a bipolar dimension with poles of femininity and masculinity. Among the measures based on these views are the *Bem Sex-Role Inventory* (Bem, 1981) and the *Personal Attributes Questionnaire* of Spence and Helmreich (1979). In regard to the CPI, it should be mentioned that Kanner (1976) found that the two subscales of F/M formed by the indicative items (those scored for "true") and the contraindicative items (those scored for "false"), had essentially zero correlations with each other. In Kanner's method, the 15 "true" items constitute the "F" subscale, and the 17 "false" items, reversed in scoring, constitute the "M" scale. Baucom (1976, 1980) also developed independent or unipolar FEM and MAS scales for the CPI. What this means is that for psychologists who wish to work with unipolar measures, scales of this kind are at hand for the CPI. If this is done, Baucom's two scales are recommended because of the excellent research literature for his two measures (Baucom, 1983; Baucom & Aiken, 1984; Baucom, Besch, & Callahan, 1985; Baucom & Danker-Brown, 1979, 1983, 1984; Baucom & Sanders, 1978; Baucom & Weiss, 1986).

For probes into the realm of self-views, some interesting findings can indeed be turned up by use of CPI unipolar MF measures. One such study, using Kanner's two subscales, is summarized in Table 5.22. In the nationwide high school testing with the CPI, students for whom year in school was indicated were classified as 9th, 10th, 11th, and 12th graders. Then, scores for the F and M subscales were examined for trends. For males, scores on the F subscale stayed relatively constant over

Table 5.22 Developmental Trends on the F/M Subscales for Males and Females

Grade	Males N = 2,502				Females N = 2,880			
	F/M-F		F/M-M		F/M-F		F/M-M	
	M	SD	M	SD	M	SD	M	SD
9	4.36	2.13	7.98	2.20	7.29	2.52	4.68	2.09
10	4.18	2.23	8.58	2.52	7.69	2.47	4.18	2.11
11	4.42	2.28	8.62	2.58	7.89	2.53	4.40	2.27
12	4.43	2.24	9.08	2.53	8.00	2.46	4.37	2.37
F	0 86		9.94		3.18		1.34	
df	3, 2498		3, 2498		3, 2876		3, 2876	
p	.46		.00		.02		.26	

the four samples, and the F ratio for means was insignificant. However, on the M subscale, there was a steady (monotonic) increase by year, and the F ratio was highly significant. In other words, the "masculine" component in the self-psychology of these teenage boys increased in strength over the four years.

For the females, the trend line for the M scale was relatively constant across the four years, and the F ratio for means was statistically insignificant. However, the trend line for the F subscale was monotonic, up, and statistically significant at the .02 level. In other words, the "feminine" component in the self-psychology of these teenage girls increased in strength over the four years. The two developmental trends derive from cross-sectional samples, rather than from longitudinal testing of the same students at each of the four educational levels. Also, even though the samples are reasonably large, cross-validation is a necessity. Nonetheless, and granting these provisos, it is of considerable interest to note the growth of own-sex self-psychology during these years of puberty.

However, for those who contend that only unipolar views and measures are acceptable in the MF domain, there is a serious and invariably overlooked problem. The problem is that in the observational realm, the two dimensions typically have large negative correlations, on the order of –.90 to –.99. As an example, in an assessment project at the Institute of Personality Assessment and Research in Berkeley,

99 male and 99 female college students were studied in two-day programs for each assessee. Each student was rated by from 12 to 18 staff observers on a diverse list of attributes, including femininity and masculinity. The former was defined as "characteristically feminine in style and manner of behavior," and the latter as "characteristically masculine in style and manner of behavior." Interjudge reliabilities were .96 for both ratings. For males alone, the two ratings had a correlation of –.89, and for the women alone the correlation was –.88. For all 198 students, the correlation was –.95. Similar findings have been made for the adjectives feminine and masculine on the *Adjective Check List*. Findings such as these suggest that in the perceptions of observers, MF is a bipolar continuum. Because a major goal of the CPI is to align itself with the way interpersonal concepts are used in the everyday world, it is entirely reasonable to include a bipolar F/M scale.

Very little published research is available in regard to CPI F/M scores of homoerotic men and women. A search of abstracts turned up only one study of women in which the F/M scale had been used (Wilson & Greene, 1971). In this paper, homosexual women had significantly lower F/M scores than heterosexual women. Several studies of male samples were discovered, but only two had large enough samples to warrant generalization (Siegelman, 1972, 1978). In Siegelman's research, both American and British homoerotic men had higher F/M scores than heteroerotic men. These findings are in agreement with the hypothesized functioning of the F/M scale, and also with folk psychology concerning the phenomena. It is important to emphasize, however, that F/M is not offered as nor intended to be a diagnostic measure for homosexuality. For psychologists having such diagnostic aims, other more clinically oriented tests such as the MMPI and *Rorschach* are more appropriate.

The basic purpose of F/M, as stated above, is to define a continuum that corresponds to the folk psychology of femininity and masculinity. Persons at the low pole should be seen as having "masculine" attributes, and those at the high pole should be seen as having "feminine" attributes. Furthermore, differentiations useful to the interpreter should be demonstrable within samples of men and within samples of women. The value of the measure, to put this another way, should be judged by the information it provides and not merely by knowledge of its origins. Let us now turn to data seeking to provide such information.

A factor analysis of the 32 items in F/M was conducted in the profile norm sample of 6,000 persons. Eight factors with eigen values of 1.00 or more were identified, of which four were arbitrarily retained for rotation by means of Kaiser's normal varimax method. Factor 1 was composed primarily of items stating liking for traditionally masculine jobs and activities, for example, "I like mechanics magazines" ("false"), "I think I would like the work of a building contractor" ("false"), and "I would like to be a soldier" ("false"). Factor 2 had items suggesting feelings of vulnerability, for instance, "Sometimes I feel that I am about to go to pieces" ("true") and "I am inclined to take things hard" ("true"). Factor 3 had items expressing liking for traditionally feminine work, for example, "I would like to be a nurse" ("true") and "I think I would like the work of a dress designer" ("true"). Factor 4 had items stating a dislike of horseplay and practical jokes, for example, "I like to be with a crowd who play jokes on one another" ("false") and "I must admit that I enjoy playing practical jokes on people" ("false").

Act frequency analyses were carried out in a sample of 177 persons (88 men, 89 women), each of whom was rated for frequency of the Buss-Craik list of acts by a spouse or partner. The five acts with largest positive correlations with F/M and the five with largest negative are listed below.

Persuaded someone to do something he/she didn't want to do (.26)

Avoided people's glances (.26)

Remembered an acquaintance's birthday, even though no one else did (.24)

Complained about being mistreated by others (.26)

Sent cards to friends on holidays (.29)

Picked up a hitchhiker (−.30)

Took the initiative in a sexual encounter (−.35)

Took charge of things at the committee meeting (−.34)

Rolled down the car window and talked to the person in the next car (−.30)

Thought about how much money he/she would make (−.30)

Acts associated with high scores on F/M all deal with interpersonal relations, that is, persuading someone to do something, avoiding glances, remembering someone's birthday, complaining about mistreatment, and sending cards on holidays. High scorers do things to form and solidify relations to others, and are disappointed when others do not reciprocate. However, they shy away from direct, immediate contact.

Low scores on F/M are associated with taking the initiative, including in sexual matters; with quick and unfearful overtures to others, as in picking up a hitchhiker and talking to someone in the next car; and with thinking about money one might make.

These acts come from analyses of all 177 persons. What would the acts be if analyses were made separately for the 88 men and the 89 women? Because the F/M scale is the only one of the folk measures to stress gender differences, such analyses would be desirable. For the men only, the five acts with largest positive and five with largest negative correlations with F/M are listed below.

Did not complain when he was overcharged at the store (.31)

Asked lots of personal questions (.28)

Circled around to avoid someone he knew (.28)

Complained about how others were mistreating him (.37)

Wrote a confidential letter to someone with whom he was not close (.37)

Loaned his car to an acquaintance he barely knew (–.35)

Rolled down the car window and talked to someone in the next car (–.29)

Took command of the situation after the accident (–.36)

Helped a friend fix his car (–.35)

Spoke first at the meeting (–.34)

Several new items appear in the above list. Men with high scores on F/M did not object when overcharged, let a stranger borrow the key to their apartment, avoided a direct meeting with someone, complained of mistreatment, and wrote a confidential letter to a casual acquaintance. The last item creates an image of intimacy at a distance.

Men with low scores on F/M loaned their cars to persons barely known, talked to someone in the next car, took charge at the scene of an accident, helped a friend work on a car, and spoke first at a meeting. These acts involve task-centered behavior, initiative, and a kind of automatic self-confidence.

The five acts with largest positive correlations with F/M for women are cited next, plus the five acts with largest negative correlations.

Resisted conceding an argument (.18)

Dressed inconspicuously and conservatively (.19)

Walked into a room full of people without talking to anyone (.20)

Avoided someone's glances (.23)

Avoided direct eye contact (.20)

Played a practical joke on someone (–.35)

Borrowed a book from a friend and never returned it (–.34)

Abandoned her work to go out with friends (–.33)

Gossiped about her competitors (–.38)

At the reception, sought out the most important person there (–.33)

Women with high scores on F/M are described by their spouses or partners as avoiding eye contact and as dressing and behaving in such a way as to minimize attention to themselves. They are also described as resisting the loss of an argument. Women with low scores on F/M are described as willing to play a practical joke, not very punctilious about returning things borrowed, ready to stop working in order to go out with friends, inclined to gossip about competitors,

and self-propelling in seeking out important persons at receptions. The acts associated with high scores, for the most part, direct attention away from self and minimize anything pertaining to self-assertion or self-promotion. The acts associated with low scores depict an entirely different social style, one involving vigorous assertion of own interests and a willingness to take the center of the stage.

Before closing discussion on the act indicators, several additional acts whose correlations were only slightly below those cited above might be mentioned, as they help in filling out the picture of men with higher and lower scores on F/M. Associated with high scores on F/M were these additional acts: "Read a book all afternoon" (r = .26), "Threw a big party" (r = .22), "Hugged his friend when they met on the street" (r = .22), and "Walked with his head down" (r = .23). Among the additional acts associated with lower scores on F/M for men were the following: "Played basketball" (r = –.24), "Left his car unlocked while he ran an errand" (r = –.24), "Readily used the authority of his position" (r = –.28), and "Got people together to play a sport" (r = –.24).

Among the additional acts associated with higher F/M scores for women were the following: "Refused to acknowledge that she was wrong" (r = .18) and "Avoided the salesperson's offer of assistance" (r = .17). Illustrative additional acts associated with lower F/M scores for women included these: "Parked illegally for convenience" (r = –.27), "Agreed to go out with someone she didn't like" (r = –.28), "Wore seductive clothes" (r = –.31), and "Went to a nightclub" (r = –.32).

Adjectives associated with higher and lower scores on F/M for both men and women are presented in Table 5.23. The yield is the weakest of that for any of the folk scales, probably because of differences in the way in which observers use terms to characterize role-linked behavior for the two sexes. Nonetheless, the adjectives associated with high scores on F/M do have a general flavor of dependency, submissiveness, and sensitivity, along with an element of emotionality and nervousness. It should be remarked that these are not simply stereotypic comments about men and women, but rather, descriptions in fact associated with high scores on F/M for both sexes. If someone has an elevated score on F/M, then these descriptions can be expected, within broad limits of error and probability. Descriptions associated with low scores on F/M include aggressiveness, determination, masculinity, self-confidence, and independence.

Table 5.23 Adjectival Descriptions by Observers: 12 Most Salient Positive and 12 Most Salient Negative Correlates of the 32-Item F/M Scale

Adjectives	Men, Described By			Women, Described By		
	Spouse (N = 236)	3 Peers (N = 194)	10 Staff Members (N = 612)	Spouse (N = 236)	3 Peers (N = 192)	10 Staff Members (N = 358)
Dependent	.05	.21**	.05	.14*	.02	.29**
Emotional	.13*	.15*	.15**	.00	.10	.19**
Feminine	.07	.33**	.15**	.02	.25**	.16**
Gentle	.04	.12	.21**	.09	.18*	.12*
High-strung	.20**	.14*	.10**	.09	.05	.12*
Mild	.07	.17*	.11**	.07	.15*	.13*
Nervous	.17**	.34**	.12**	.07	.08	.18**
Sensitive	.09	.22**	.30**	.07	.11	.17**
Sentimental	.07	.14*	.11**	.12	.04	.20**
Submissive	.17**	.17*	.04	.07	.16*	.22**
Sympathetic	.07	.10	.17**	.11	.16*	.14**
Worrying	.12	.30**	.18**	.03	.15*	.11*
Aggressive	−.05	−.21**	−.16**	−.10	−.14*	−.14**
Assertive	−.13*	−.06	−.06	−.15*	−.02	−.15**
Boastful	−.03	−.19**	−.06	−.15*	−.21**	.00
Confident	−.20**	−.19**	−.06	−.20**	−.09	−.17**
Determined	−.14*	−.06	−.03	−.14*	.00	−.16**
Forceful	−.05	−.21**	−.03	−.15*	−.08	−.14**
Independent	−.16*	−.17*	−.06	−.22**	−.08	−.19**
Masculine	−.12	−.34**	−.14**	−.01	−.33**	−.08
Robust	−.05	−.18*	−.12**	−.02	−.19**	−.05
Self-confident	−.20**	−.18*	−.08*	−.14*	−.06	−.19**
Strong	−.14*	−.19**	−.08*	−.18**	−.17*	−.21**
Tough	.00	−.15*	−.09*	−.16*	−.22**	−.13*

*p ≤ .05, **p ≤ .01

Of more importance for interpreting scores on F/M are the adjectival correlates analyzed separately for men and women. Table 5.24 gives the 12 terms with largest positive and the 12 with largest negative correlations for men in the three samples cited.

Men who score high on F/M do tend to be described as feminine, but also as complaining, high-strung, nervous, emotional, gloomy, self-pitying, and sensitive. A third theme is suggested by the adjectives shy and timid. A rather uncomplimentary overall impression may be inferred from the adjective peculiar, but more favorable reactions are suggested by the term reflective. The totality, however, is unmistakably that of diffidence, lack of strength and force, and a considerable amount of commiseration for self.

Table 5.24	Adjectival Descriptions by Observers: 12 Most Salient Positive and 12 Most Salient Negative Correlates of the 32-Item F/M Scale for Men		
	Described By		
Adjectives	Spouse (*N* = 236)	3 Peers (*N* = 194)	10 Staff Members (*N* = 612)
Complaining	.20**	.19**	.05
Emotional	.13*	.15*	.15**
Feminine	.07	.33**	.15**
Gloomy	.17**	.18*	.08*
High-strung	.20**	.14*	.10**
Nervous	.17**	.34**	.12**
Peculiar	.13*	.14*	.10**
Reflective	.14*	.24**	.27**
Self-pitying	.25**	.30**	.05
Sensitive	.09	.22**	.30**
Shy	.17**	.13	.14**
Timid	.12	.20**	.10**
Aggressive	−.05	−.21**	−.16**
Ambitious	−.15*	−.08	−.11**
Assertive	−.13*	−.06	−.06
Confident	−.20**	−.19**	−.06
Independent	−.16*	−.17*	−.06
Masculine	−.12	−.34**	−.14**
Opportunistic	−.04	−.11	−.14**
Outgoing	−.01	−.17*	−.09*
Practical	−.06	−.08	−.12**
Robust	−.05	−.18*	−.12**
Self-confident	−.20**	−.18*	−.08*
Strong	−.14*	−.19**	−.08*

*$p \leq .05$, **$p \leq .01$

Table 5.25	Adjectival Descriptions by Observers: 12 Most Salient Positive and 12 Most Salient Negative Correlates of the 32-Item F/M Scale for Women		
	Described By		
Adjectives	Spouse (*N* = 236)	3 Peers (*N* = 192)	10 Staff Members (*N* = 358)
Dependent	.14*	.02	.29**
Feminine	.02	.25**	.16**
Gentle	.09	.18*	.12*
Mild	.07	.15*	.13*
Modest	.08	.19**	.09
Soft-hearted	.11	.13	.18**
Submissive	.07	.16*	.22**
Sympathetic	.11	.16*	.14**
Unassuming	.08	.13	.12*
Unselfish	.05	.15*	.10*
Warm	.18**	.18*	.09
Weak	.10	.17*	.13*
Aggressive	−.10	−.14*	−.14**
Assertive	−.15*	−.02	−.15**
Confident	−.20**	−.09	−.17**
Forceful	−.15*	−.08	−.14**
Hard-headed	−.14*	−.11	−.10*
Headstrong	−.04	−.18*	−.10*
Healthy	−.10	−.15*	−.14**
Independent	−.22**	−.08	−.19**
Self-confident	−.14	−.06	−.19**
Strong	−.18**	−.17*	−.21**
Stubborn	−.11	−.16*	−.13*
Tough	−.16*	−.22**	−.13*

*$p \leq .05$, **$p \leq .01$

The adjectives related to low scores on F/M for men include masculine, along with conventionally masculine attributes such as aggressiveness, assertiveness, ambition, confidence, independence, and robustness. A negative, albeit weak, set of three correlations with the adjective opportunistic may be noted. Other adjectives are outgoing, practical, and strong. The overall picture is of an active, strong, assertive person, interested in the down-to-earth and practical, and not very perceptive about the feelings of others.

Table 5.25 cites the 24 most salient adjectival descriptions for women with higher and lower scores on F/M. The adjective feminine appears as a correlate of high scores, along with stereotypic terms such as gentle, modest, mild, soft-hearted, sympathetic, unselfish, and warm. Another theme is indicated by the adjectives dependent and submissive. It should be noted, again, that these adjectives were in fact used by observers to describe specific individuals, not with any intention of characterizing the concept of "femininity" or to describe something abstract like "feminine" women. The adjectives, in other words, turn out empirically to be correlated with the F/M scale in fairly large samples of women studied one at a time.

The adjectives correlated with low scores on F/M for women include several connoting competence and effectiveness, for instance, confident, healthy, independent, self-confident, and strong. Assertiveness is also a theme, with the terms aggressive, assertive, forceful, and headstrong. Psychological strength is betokened by the descriptions strong and tough. Finally, the adjectives hard-headed and stubborn convey implications of firmness of will.

Three regression analyses were carried out on the 200 most frequently used adjectives, first to estimate F/M score in the total sample of 1,356 persons, then to do the same in the sample of 806 men, and third to do the same in the sample of 550 women. Each analysis was arbitrarily terminated at eight steps. In the total sample, the best combination of eight adjectives generated a multiple correlation of .26 (R^2 = .07). Adjectives with positive beta weights were artistic, feminine, painstaking, reflective, and sensitive. Adjectives with negative beta weights were cool, courageous, and healthy.

For the 806 men alone, the best cluster of eight words had a multiple correlation of .41 (R^2 = .17). Positive weights were assigned to artistic, charming, painstaking, sensitive, unconventional, and worrying. Negative weights were assigned to adventurous and wary.

The multiple correlation for the 550 women alone was .37 (R^2 = .14). Positive indicators were enthusiastic, feminine, retiring, and submissive. Negative indicators were aggressive, courageous, healthy, and relaxed.

Items from the *California Q-Set* were correlated with F/M scores in samples of 547 men and 393 women, each of whom had been described on the Q-sort by panels of five or more observers in assessments. The four items with largest positive and four

with largest negative correlations with F/M in both samples are given below, along with the correlations for men and for women.

Anxiety and tension find outlet in bodily symptoms (.19, .22)

Is basically anxious (.13, .16)

Concerned with own adequacy as a person, either at conscious or unconscious levels (.13, .18)

Has fluctuating moods (.15, .14)

Behaves in an assertive fashion (−.13, −.16)

Is subjectively unaware of self-concern; feels satisfied with self (−.26, −.13)

Is power oriented; values power in self or others (−.17, −.21)

Expresses hostile feelings directly (−.18, −.13)

Both men and women who score above average on F/M impress others as anxious, concerned with their own adequacy, fluctuating in mood, and as manifesting their anxieties in bodily symptoms. Those with below average scores are seen as assertive, unaware of self-concern, power oriented, and as direct and forthright in expressing hostility.

When we turn to the Q-sort items associated with F/M for each sex alone, some new information emerges. The four items most strongly associated with high scores on F/M for men and the four most strongly associated with low scores are listed below.

Thinks and associates to ideas in unusual ways; has unconventional thought processes (.24)

Anxiety and tension find outlet in bodily symptoms (.19)

Enjoys esthetic impressions; is esthetically reactive (.30)

Is concerned with philosophical problems; e.g., religions, values, the meaning of life, etc. (.20)

Tends to judge others in conventional terms such as "popularity," "the correct thing to do," social pressures, etc. (.20)

Is subjectively unaware of self-concern; feels satisfied with self (−.26)

Interested in members of the opposite sex (−.22)

Behaves in a masculine style and manner (−.35)

For men alone, ideational, creative, and esthetic proclivities are associated with high scores, along with a tendency toward somatization attributed to both men and women with elevated scores on F/M. Low-scoring men on F/M judge others in conventional ways, are unaware of any self-concern, show an interest in women, and behave in a masculine way.

Analysis of the Q-sort items for women alone also turned up some new information, as shown below in the citations of the four items with largest positive and four with largest negative correlations.

> Anxiety and tension find outlet in bodily symptoms (.22)
>
> Genuinely submissive; accepts domination comfortably (.24)
>
> Seeks reassurance from others (.19)
>
> Concerned with own adequacy as a person, either at conscious or unconscious levels (.18)
>
> Is critical, skeptical, not easily impressed (−.25)
>
> Extrapunitive; tends to transfer or project blame (−.22)
>
> Has high aspiration level for self (−.28)
>
> Values own independence and autonomy (−.31)

Women with high scores on F/M seem to somaticize their anxieties and tensions, accept dominance from others, seek reassurance from others, and worry about their own adequacy. Women with low scores on F/M seem to be skeptical, extrapunitive, aspiring, and autonomy-seeking.

Interviewers' descriptions of 504 male and 379 female assessees produced only a few items appreciably related to the F/M scale for both sexes. For this reason, only the separate listing of items will be given below. The first set is composed of the four items with largest positive and four with largest negative correlations with F/M for the 504 men.

> Delicate, feminine appearance (.17)
>
> Considerable parental friction and discord (.15)
>
> Dated very little or not at all (.18)
>
> Has many worries and problems (.15)
>
> Rugged, masculine appearance (−.19)
>
> Unusually self-confident, feels able to meet nearly any situation (−.16)
>
> Has a stable, optimistic view of the future (−.21)
>
> Seems relatively free of neurotic trends, conflicts, and other forms of instability (−.17)

Men with high scores on F/M were described as feminine in appearance, as having grown up in families with considerable parental discord, as having many worries, and as having dated little or not at all in high school. Men with low scores on F/M were described as masculine in appearance, unusually self-confident, optimistic about the future, and relatively free of neurotic trends.

The four items with largest positive correlations with F/M among women, and the four with largest negative correlations are reported below.

> Is unsure of self, doubts own ability (.15)
>
> Has strong religious beliefs (.18)
>
> Is happily married (.23)
>
> Enjoys children (.23)
>
> Calm and deliberate (−.12)
>
> Healthy-looking, well-developed and well-nourished (−.11)
>
> Was an honor student in high school (−.22)
>
> Unusually self-confident, feels able to meet nearly any situation (−.13)

The .05 level of significance for correlations in the sample of 379 women is achieved by $r = .10$. Thus, although the correlations reported above are very low in magnitude, they do reach or exceed the .05 level. Women with high scores on F/M are described by their life history interviewers as unsure of their own ability, as having strong religious beliefs, as having a happy marriage, and as enjoying children. These items may appear stereotypic, but it should be remembered that the interviewers had no knowledge whatsoever of scores on the F/M or any other scale, and that the interviewers were doing their best to describe what they observed about each woman.

Check list items associated with low scores on F/M among women included descriptions of being calm and deliberate, healthy-looking, and unusually self-confident. In addition, these low-scoring women reported honors-level performance in high school.

Interpersonal Q-Sort descriptions were examined in samples of 200 men who were given a Q-sort by a wife or partner, 200 women given a Q-sort by a husband or partner, and 111 men given a Q-sort by panels of three assessment staff observers. The three items with largest positive correlations with F/M and the three with largest negative correlations are cited below, along with the coefficients for men, women, and the male assessees.

Awkward, ill at ease socially; shy and inhibited with others (.12, .15, .15)

Easily embarrassed; feels inferior and inadequate (.16, .14, .08)

Worried and preoccupied; tense, nervous, and generally upset (.14, .09, .20)

Ambitious; likely to succeed in most things undertaken (−.08, −.18, −.15)

Enterprising and outgoing; enjoys social participation (−.10, −.09, −.24)

Active and robust in manner; hardheaded and forthright in judgment (−.02, −.10, −.34)

Because of the low magnitudes of these correlations, interpretation must be only tentative. The three items associated with high scores on F/M all report some sort of worry, inhibition, or feelings of inadequacy. The three items associated with low F/M scores all report some sort of initiative, ambition, and enterprise.

The findings were only somewhat different when attention was focused on men alone. Only one new item was found among the three with largest positive correlations: "Given to moods; often difficult and recalcitrant," with coefficients of .10 for the 200 men and .30 for the 111 assessees. Also, only one new item was found among the three associated with low scores on F/M: "Poised and self-confident; not troubled by pressure or criticism," with correlations of .22 for the 200 men and .24 for the 111 assessees.

Somewhat more specificity was found in the items associated with higher and lower F/M scores among women. The three with largest positive and the three with largest negative correlations are reported below.

Tolerant, permissive, and benevolent; considerate and charitable (.22)

Submissive; gives in easily; lacking in self-confidence (.18)

Wedded to routine; made anxious by change and uncertainty (.21)

Ambitious; likely to succeed in most things undertaken (−.18)

Distrustful and cynical; dissatisfied with most things; indifferent to the worries and problems of others (−.21)

Independent, intelligent, and self-reliant; values achievement (−.19)

Husbands or partners describe women with higher F/M scores as tolerant and benevolent, but also as submissive, lacking in confidence, and wedded to routine. They describe women with lower F/M scores as ambitious, intelligent, and competent, but also as distrustful and cynical.

In summary, what should be considered in regard to the F/M scale is the range and utility of the information it provides about persons who have taken the inventory, and the extent to which such information is available from other scales and other dimensions of measurement. Personal objections to bipolar MF scales, even if passionate, should for the moment be set aside so that the value of the information conveyed by the F/M scale can be objectively evaluated. The same caution holds for doctrinaire views concerning the illegitimacy of any form of measurement within the MF sphere. The goal of the F/M scale is not to demean or stigmatize either men or women, but rather to provide information that will be useful in reaching a full and accurate understanding of the individuals who are tested. It is our contention that the F/M scale does in fact furnish important and useful information not generally available from other measures.

Some of the implications of higher or lower scores on F/M apply to anyone who has been tested. Persons who score high dislike and avoid head-on social encounters, and behave and even dress in such a way as to stay out of the limelight and escape intense scrutiny. High scorers are solicitous of their friends, tend to be sensitive, gentle, and worrying, have fluctuations of mood, are easily embarrassed, and have many inhibitions. Low scorers are indifferent to being at the center of things, and, indeed, in some ways invite attention to themselves by dress and manner. They take the initiative, including the initiative in sexual encounters, and appear to be confident, strong, assertive, and enterprising. They value and seek power and express hostility and anger openly.

There are, of course, certain gender specifics in the implications of higher and lower F/M scores. Men who score high were described by interviewers as being feminine and delicate in appearance, and as behaving in feminine ways. Observers in general saw them as nervous, high-strung, easily offended, and emotional. On the positive side, they have a talent for imaginative and even creative thinking, are aware of philosophical and ethical issues, and enjoy esthetic experiences.

Men who score low on F/M seem to look masculine and to behave in masculine ways, are prepared to take decisive action in times of stress or emergency, are seen as confident, independent, robust, strong, and adventurous. However, they also tend to have rather conventional views, are little inclined to introspection, and tend to brush off criticism or complaints from others.

For women with high scores on F/M, some of the specific implications include a strong prohibition against doing anything that is showy or attention-provoking, a willingness to defer or submit to respected others, and dislike of any situations involving uncertainty and unpredictability. Those who know them tend to see them as feminine, gentle, and warm, but also as weak and dependent. They seek and need reassurance from others.

Women with low scores on F/M tend to be openly hedonistic, enjoy center-stage roles, have high aspirations for themselves, and seek and need autonomy. Others see them as assertive, independent, and self-confident, but also as demanding, stubborn, and willful.

In reporting test results, two profile forms are used—one for a same-sex sample, and the other for a combined sample of all 6,000 persons. Visual inspection of the two profiles for any individual will reveal that the only appreciable difference is on the F/M scale. On the form derived from the total sample, women's standard scores fall mainly above 50, and those for men fall mainly below 50. A standard score of 50 on the total sample profile is equivalent to standard scores of 39 for women and 61 for men on the same-sex profile form.

Illustrative Case Analyses

Introduction

The primary goal of the CPI is to furnish information from which a skilled interpreter can formulate an accurate, insightful, and useful characterization of the individual tested. Nomothetic work—such as forecasting academic and job performance criteria, differentiating between samples classified as delinquent or nondelinquent, and identifying attributes related to creativity, drug abuse, leadership, and designated career preferences—is important and can produce findings that will be helpful in applying the inventory to individual cases. There is, in fact, an abundant CPI literature pertaining to the topics just mentioned, as well as many others. However, no amount of information about groups and general trends will substitute for the interpretive skills that can only be developed by the study of case material. In this chapter, eight illustrative cases will be presented in an effort to show something of the relationships to be expected between the scales of the inventory and salient features of the respondent's life.

For readers who want to go beyond the minimal interpretive guidelines that can be offered in this manual, the books by McAllister (1996), on

configurations and patterns among the scales, and by Meyer and Davis (1992), on executives and managerial teams, are strongly recommended. Two computerized interpretive narratives are also available from the publisher. The first is Gough's CPI Narrative Report, which gives a description of the respondent, including lifestyle and level of ego integration, followed by comments on each of the 20 folk scales and on seven special purpose scales, and ends with a CPI-based sorting of the 100 descriptors in Block's (1961) *California Q-Set* that seeks to approximate what a knowledgeable, perceptive, and benevolent observer would say about the person tested. The second is McAllister's CPI Configural Analysis Report, which supplements Gough's narrative and gives extensive attention to the specific profile configurations observable in the protocol.

Case 1: Alpha-5 Male

This record is from an 18-year-old high school graduate who took the CPI in a large-scale research testing program. In the three-vector model of personality structure, he is classified as an Alpha-5 (see Figure 6.1). Alphas are norm-favoring and rule-respecting,

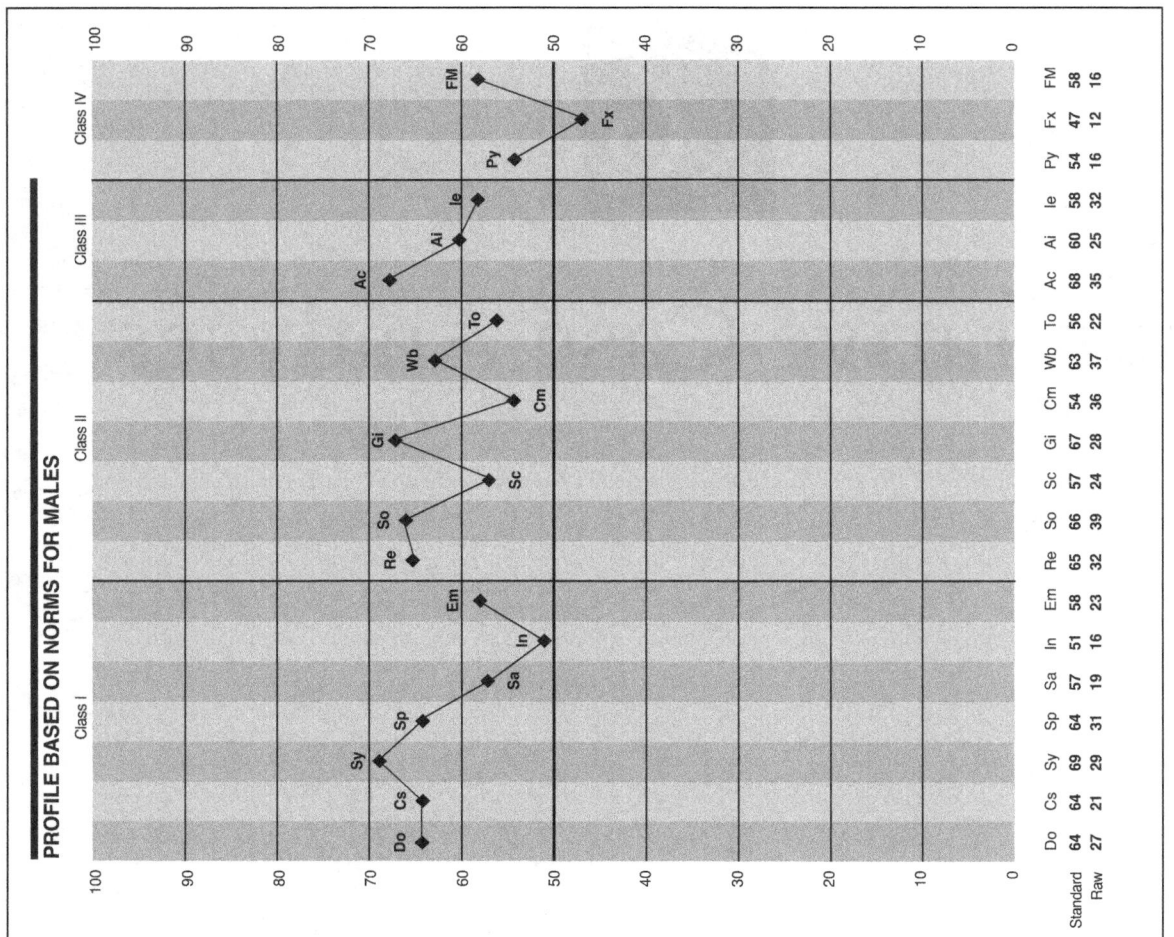

Figure 6.2 CPI Profile for Case 1

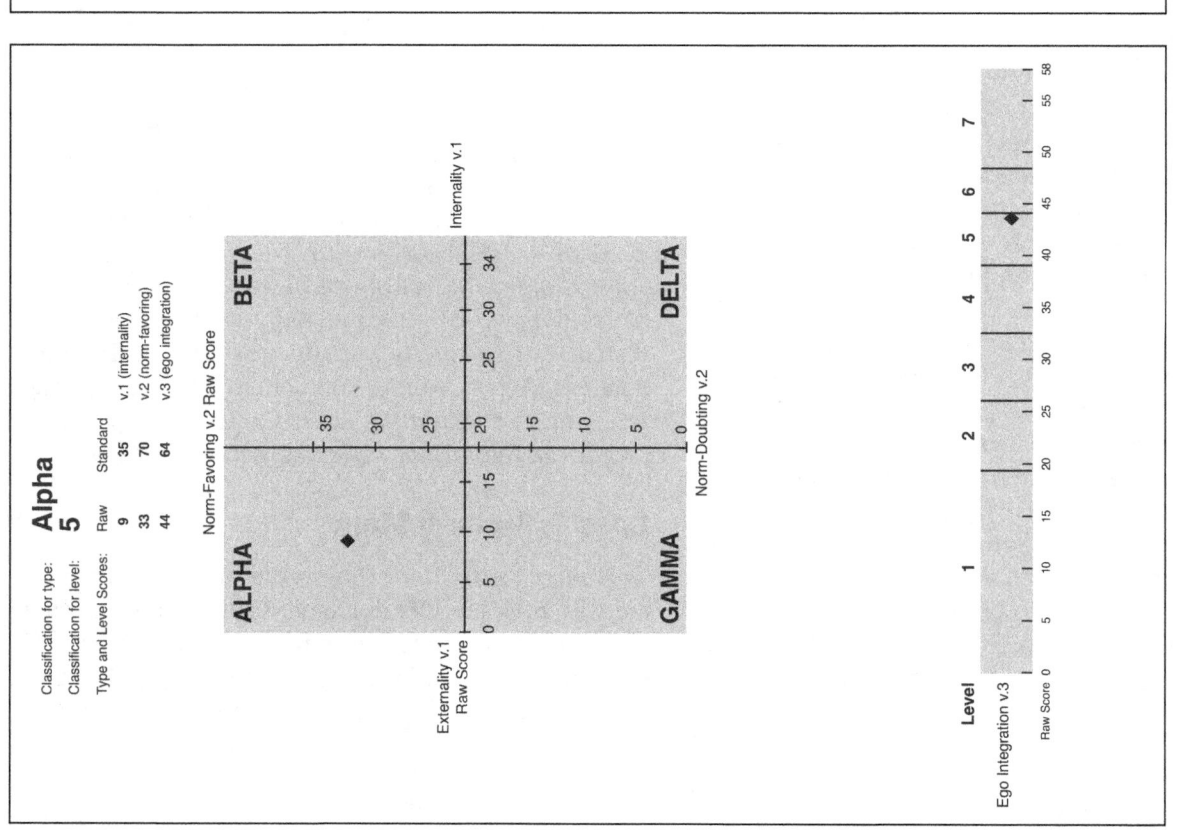

Figure 6.1 Classification in the Three-Vector Model for Case 1

and participative in the social environment. They tend to seek and be accepted in positions of leadership, and are at their best when working with others in pursuit of consensually defined, meritorious goals. His score on v.3 is at Level 5, suggesting good potential for self-realization and attainment in the Alpha mode. It might be noted that only 9.7% of high school males have v.3 scores at Level 5 or above.

On the profile, as shown in Figure 6.2, his highest scores are on the scales for Sociability (Sy), Achievement via Conformance (Ac), Good Impression (Gi), Socialization (So), Responsibility (Re), Dominance (Do), Capacity for Status (Cs), and Social Presence (Sp), all greater than 60 in standard score terms. If we put these scales names into adjectival terms, drawing on their descriptions in chapter 5, Case 1 can be described as outgoing, ambitious, ingratiating, reliable, conscientious, strong, enterprising, and self-confident. His only standard score below 50 is on Flexibility (Fx), at 47. Perhaps from this one low score we can infer that he is a bit stubborn or hard to persuade, but far short of anything like rigidity or dogmatic opinionation.

On the special purpose scales (not shown in the profile), he had standard scores of 65 or above on four: Managerial Potential (69), Leadership Potential (68), Amicability (67), and Tough-mindedness (65). Among the Block Q-sort items ranked high by the CPI algorithms were "Has high aspiration level for self," "Is productive, gets things done," and "Is cheerful." Among the items ranked low, and hence probably not at all descriptive of this young man, were "Genuinely submissive; accepts domination comfortably," "Tends to be rebellious and nonconforming," and "Feels cheated and victimized by life; self-pitying."

One of McAllister's configurations that is relevant to the profile is that for a high score on Ac with significantly lower scores on Ai and Fx. This person's score on Ai is in fact high, although lower than Ac, so McAllister's comments must be somewhat tempered. The configuration, according to McAllister, is found among people who want and need structure, whose approach to problems is pragmatic, and who strongly favor tried-and-true methods as opposed to improvisational or experimental maneuvers. Another configuration is that for high scores on both Cs and Sp, which McAllister found to be associated with a need for personal power. The configuration of high scores on Cs, Sy, and Gi points

toward a manipulative tendency. The combination of high scores on Re, So, and Gi points toward someone who is dutiful, ready to accept obligations, responsive to a leader, and keen to fit in and be successful in the judgment of others.

Due to a number of fortuitous circumstances, it was possible to obtain follow-up information on this individual for an almost 40-year period. He went on to college, studying an engineering curriculum, got married shortly after graduating, and several years after that accepted an appointive position from the governor of his state. Approximately 30 years after taking the CPI, he was appointed to a cabinet position by the president of the United States, where he served with distinction. At last follow-up, he was president of a national association of private businesses.

Case 2: Alpha-2 Female

Case 2 is a 22-year-old married White woman with no children. She was brought up in a very religious family, her father being a Protestant minister and her mother (in her description) "a minister's wife and everything that goes with it." She described her father as "a great human being; very wise; my idol, strong, dependable, honest, loving—in his own way—everything good, he is." She sees herself now as very religious and regularly attends church. She met her husband while in junior high school and dated him off and on in high school. When she was in college, she saw him again when he was on leave from military service, at which time they decided to get married. So far, they have not had any children, although the husband says he would like to start a family. Case 2, however, sees both herself and her husband as too immature for this responsibility. If they have children she would raise them as her parents raised her, with no ambiguity about the parents being in charge, but still with loving respect for the child. Her first goals for her children are that they be honest and trustworthy. In reply to the question, "Do you consider yourself happily married?" she answered, "No, but not unhappy either; many problems just now that we need to straighten out."

Given the above synopsis, it is not surprising to find that Case 2 is an Alpha in the three-vector model (see Figure 6.3). Alphas are rule-supporters and attentive to the interpersonal world. Her Level 2 ranking on the v.3 scale also seems appropriate, considering her expressed concerns about herself

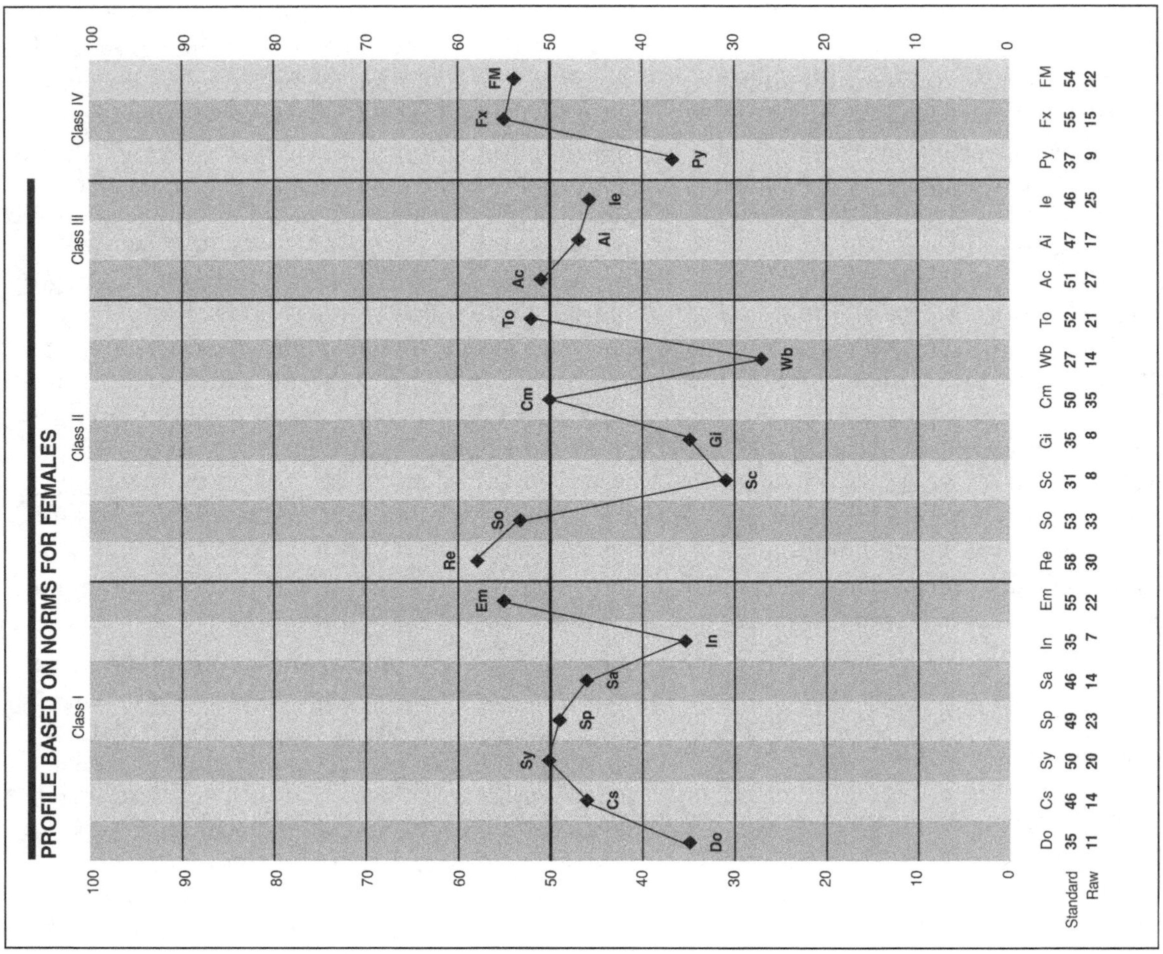

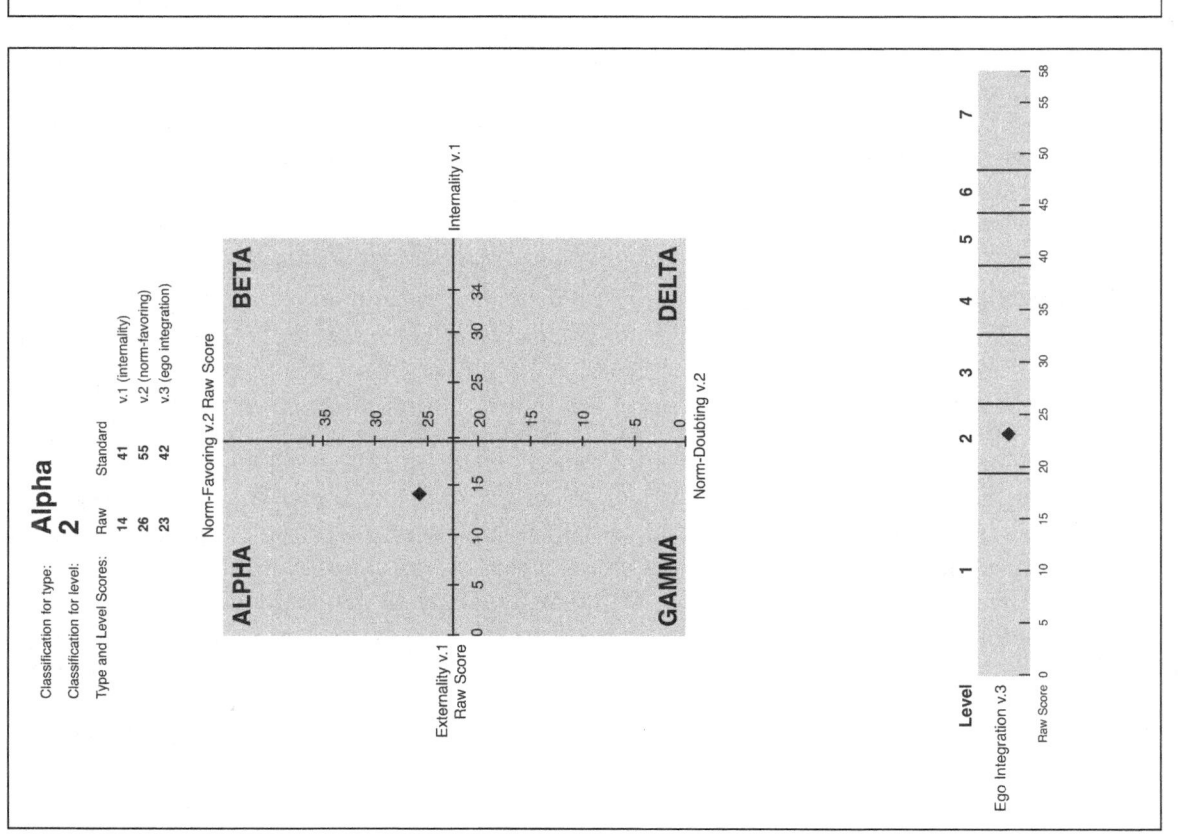

PROFILE BASED ON NORMS FOR FEMALES
Class I
Class II
Class III
Class IV
Do Cs Sy Sp Sa In Em Re So Sc Gi Cm Wb To Ac Ai Ie Py Fx FM
Standard 35 46 50 49 46 35 55 58 53 31 35 50 27 52 51 47 46 37 55 54
Raw 11 14 20 23 14 7 22 30 33 8 8 35 14 21 27 17 25 9 15 22

Figure 6.4 CPI Profile for Case 2

Classification for type: Alpha
Classification for level: 2
Type and Level Scores: Raw Standard
14 41 v.1 (internality)
26 55 v.2 (norm-favoring)
23 42 v.3 (ego integration)
Norm-Favoring v.2 Raw Score
ALPHA
BETA
GAMMA
DELTA
Externality v.1 Raw Score
Internality v.1
Norm-Doubting v.2
Level
Ego Integration v.3
Raw Score

Figure 6.3 Classification in the Three-Vector Model for Case 2

and about her relationship to her husband. As mentioned in the presentation of the v.3 scale, scores may be interpreted from three perspectives. The first is that of self-realization, implicitly stating the question, "How far along are you towards being the person you want to be and feel you are capable of being?" At Level 2 on v.3, the "answer" is something like, "I'm only just starting to realize my full self; I've got a long way to go before I will be the person I want to be." The second perspective is that of the ordinary observer, stressing the notion of psychological competence and the ability to deal with everyday life in a successful and rewarding way. The third perspective is that of the professional observer and embodies the notion of ego integration. That is, how well has this individual integrated her self-knowledge, needs, vulnerabilities, and talents into a resilient whole? At Alpha-2, she has as yet achieved only a minimum level of integration.

As shown in Figure 6.4, her profile has six scales with standard scores less than 40: Do, In, Sc, Gi, Wb, and Py. McAllister suggests that persons low on both Do and Gi are dissatisfied, and that they tend to be moody and touchy. The low scores on Do and In point towards submissive behavior and a tendency to yield to the opinions or demands of others. Wb, her lowest score, suggests problems of self-doubt, poor morale, and a lack of resolve in coping effectively with interpersonal conflict. The most unusual and unexpected of these low scores is that on Sc (Self-control). Her high scores on Re and So, along with the rule-oriented nature of her upbringing and current life, lead to an anticipation of average or above-average scores on Sc. Low scores on Sc are usually indicative of strong aggressive and erotic impulses, and more open expression of these drives than found in most people. In her confidential life history interview, she voiced both worries and complaints about her husband's "lack of desire," and described her own sex drive as much stronger than average.

We will close our discussion of Case 2 with the interviewer's character sketch:

> She is an attractive, friendly, sincere, and conscientious young woman. She was raised with a set of very definite values and expectations for marriage, and knows that her value system has been a source of conflict with her husband. Although she does not expect other people to conform to her values, she does expect conformance from her husband and is very disappointed when he fails to do so. These dissatisfactions with

her marriage, she is quick to acknowledge, come in part from her own behavior. She is far from confident about the future of her marriage and does not want to have any children until things have improved. She sees her husband as fully capable of providing material support, but as less able to provide emotional support for her and any children they may have.

Case 3: Beta-3 Male

This record was obtained from a 20-year-old college senior majoring in engineering. He grew up in a stable, conventional family as an only child. He remembered his childhood as happy but uneventful. In high school he had a part-time job and did well academically. His parents wanted him to go to college, but were not insistent. His preferred subjects were mathematics, chemistry, and physics. In his senior year, he started to date a young woman who later became his wife.

In college, he has maintained approximately a B average, and has decided not to go on to graduate school. He got married a year ago, and now has one child. He and his wife are active in a church group. He feels he is well suited for a career in engineering, given his interest in mechanical things and ability to analyze problems. When asked about the kind of people who go into engineering, he replied, "more masculine men, those with a logical cast of mind." When asked to define "success" he answered, "to enjoy what I am doing, to make enough money to support my family, to have good family relations, and to have peace of mind."

In the three-vector model, he is classified as a Beta-3, with a score on v.1 just one point above the Alpha category (see Figure 6.5). Borderline classifications such as this call for attention to both Beta and Alpha characteristics. Betas tend to be reserved, inwardly oriented, and supportive of societal rules and conventions. They ask little for themselves and give much to others. Problem areas include repression of emotion, self-doubt, and lack of self-confidence. At Level 3 (although almost at Level 4), this man is expressing moderate dissatisfaction with his current degree of self-understanding and ego integration.

As shown in Figure 6.6, his profile of folk concept scales has three scores of 59 or above, and one below 40. His highest score is on Re, presaging dependability, a strong sense of ethicality, and adherence to conventional values. Do is at 59,

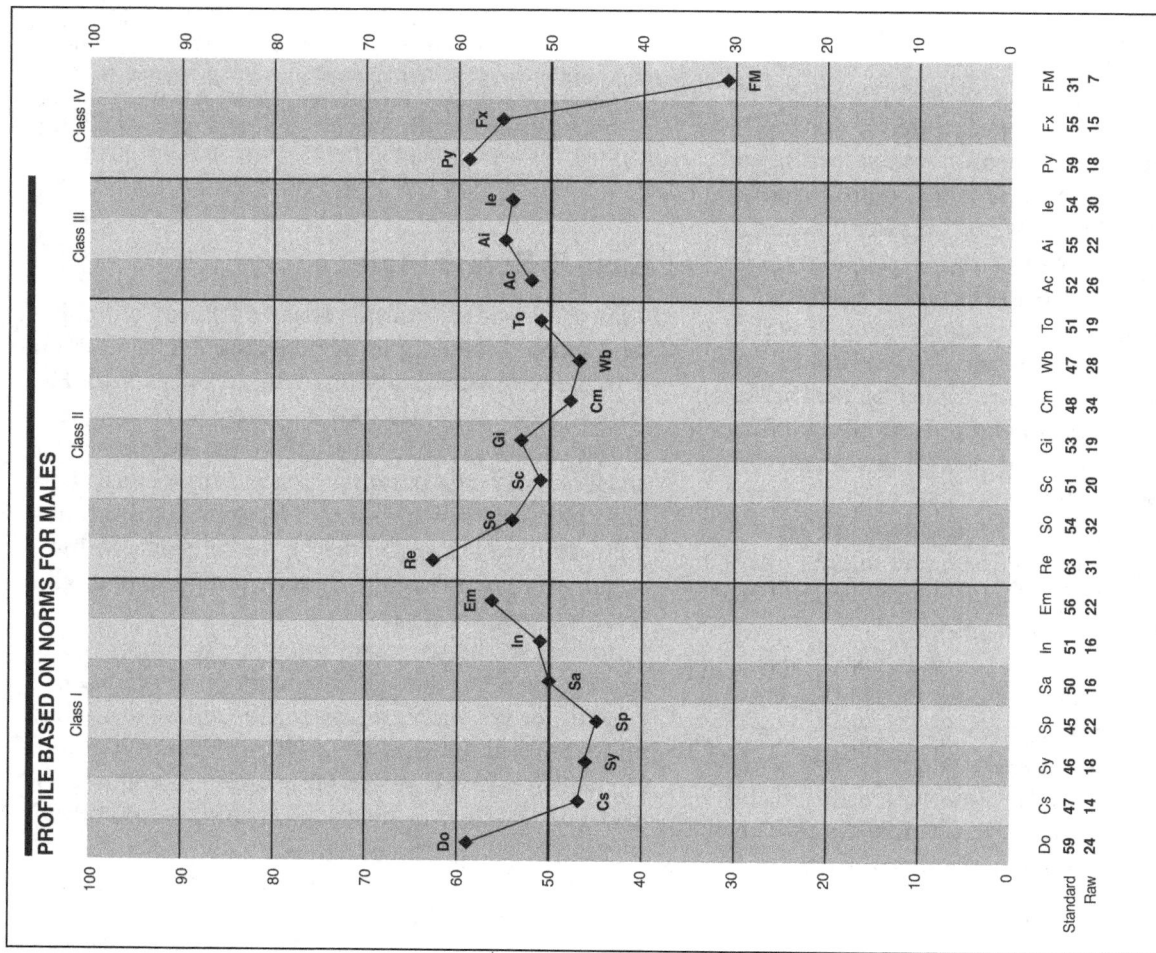

Figure 6.6 CPI Profile for Case 3

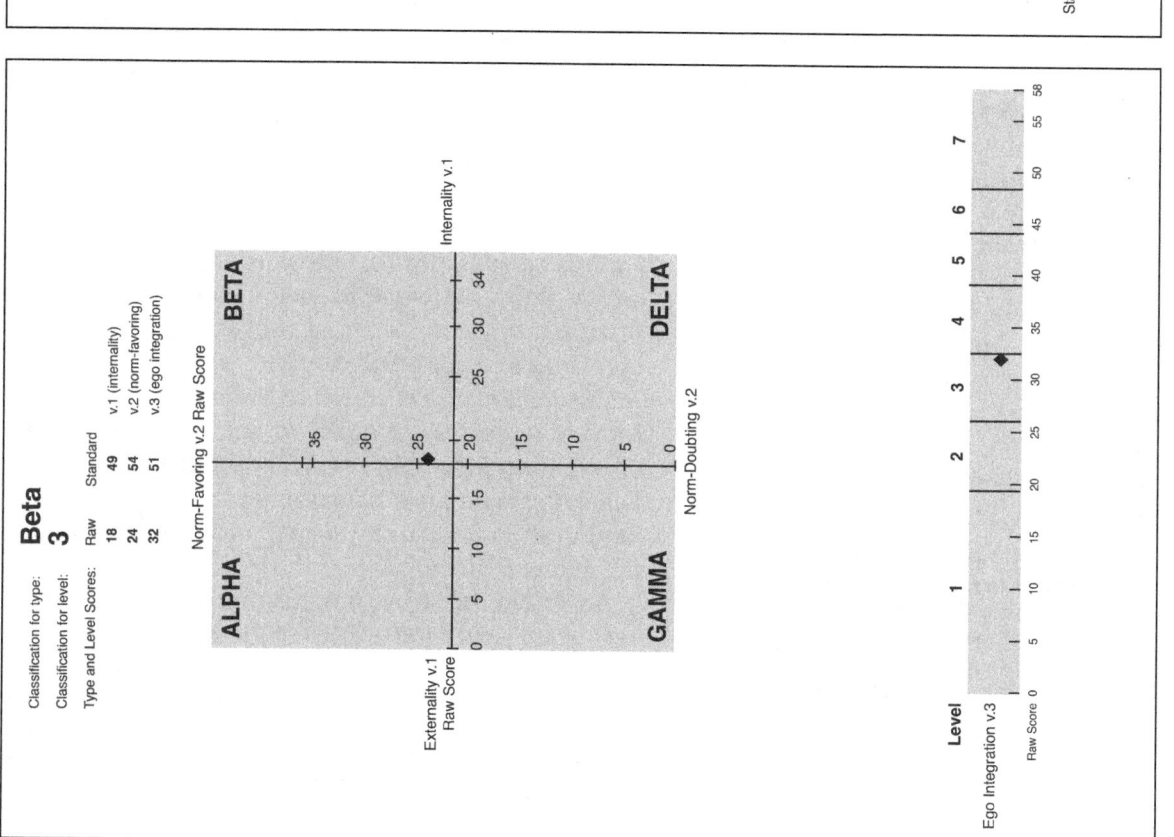

Figure 6.5 Classification in the Three-Vector Model for Case 3

indicating a potential for decisive, assertive behavior and for leadership. This theme is relevant to the Alpha tilt mentioned above. Open expression of his dominance, however, is inhibited by his distancing from others, as revealed in below-50 scores on Cs, Sy, Sp, and Sa. His score of 59 on Py betokens a detached but perceptive understanding of others, independence of mind, and above-average cognitive ability. His very low score of 31 on F/M points toward a problem-centered versus person-centered way of dealing with people, suppression of affect, and a preference for action as opposed to contemplation. In Part 5 of the computerized interpretive narrative, the five Q-sort items ranked as most likely to be descriptive were "Has high aspiration level for self," "Prides self on being 'objective,' rational," "Genuinely values intellectual and cognitive matters," "Judges self and others in conventional terms," and "Is critical, skeptical, not easily impressed."

The psychologist who did the confidential life history interview with this man submitted the following character sketch:

> Subject is a tall, nice-looking man with glasses. He seems mature, but gives the impression of being somewhat slow and stolid. He hides his emotions, even from himself. He is sure of his own ability, has definite opinions of a conservative orientation, and dislikes ambiguity. He values self-reliance and independence, and has achieved considerable independence for himself. However, his ego-coping mechanisms are rigid, and he is lacking in spontaneity and playfulness. He entered into the assessment project with enthusiasm, seemingly eager to be evaluated. He prefers to associate with others who share his social and political views. Although he seems to have a realistic grasp of his abilities, and also his limitations, his "frozen" emotions may prevent him from reaching his full potential as a human being.

Case 4: Beta-7 Female

Case 4 is a 33-year-old married White woman with two children. She describes her most-favorable qualities as honesty, dependability, loyalty to family and friends, and the ability to stay calm. She sees her least-favorable qualities as impatience, lack of ambition, and poor will power in regard to eating. She has one younger sister, who often annoys her with incessant psychological probing into personal feelings and reactions. Her father was hard-working, ambitious, and very church-oriented, but with a drinking problem. She got along well with him as a child, and still has a good relationship. Her mother was devoted to husband and family, did a lot of reading, but never tried to develop her own independence or abilities. When problems surfaced, her mother would "clam up" and not say anything. In high school, Case 4 worked in a church group, sang in the choir, and had excellent grades. She liked to be alone and recalls herself as a sort of solitary person. She first met her husband in a church group, when she was 14 years old. They didn't get along well in high school—both would clam up when angry and couldn't communicate. Later, things went better, and they got married, although they still have trouble confiding in each other. They share strong, conservative political and economic beliefs, but the church now plays almost no role in their life together. When asked what she would do if her husband died or left, she said, "I'd do just fine, although I'd miss him a lot. I would stay where I am, give the kids a stable situation, and continue my job." Swimming and sailing are her two favorite leisure-time activities. She describes her usual mood as "pleasant and easygoing, no big highs or lows."

Her classification in the three-vector model is borderline Beta, just one point away from Delta and two points away from Alpha (see Figure 6.7). Both Betas and Deltas tend to be inwardly oriented, having personal feelings and emotions not easy to express. Betas are rule-accepters, whereas Deltas are rule-questioners. Vacillation between normative compliance and rule-rejecting is probable, possibly illustrated by her on-again off-again relationship to the church. Her Alpha trend is exemplified by her attempts in high school to enter into the social sphere, but then (Beta trend) finding involvement unrewarding. Her Level 7 standing on the v.3 scale indicates an unusually strong sense of self-realization, considering the rather low-key responses she gave in her personal interview.

As shown in Figure 6.8, her profile of folk concept scales has high points above 60 on Ai, To, Py, Wb, and Ac, and only one score (F/M) below 50. For persons high on both Ac and Ai, McAllister states that they are mature, organized, and stable individuals who have broad interests, and are independent yet able to conform. Persons with scores above 70 on Ai usually perform well in academic

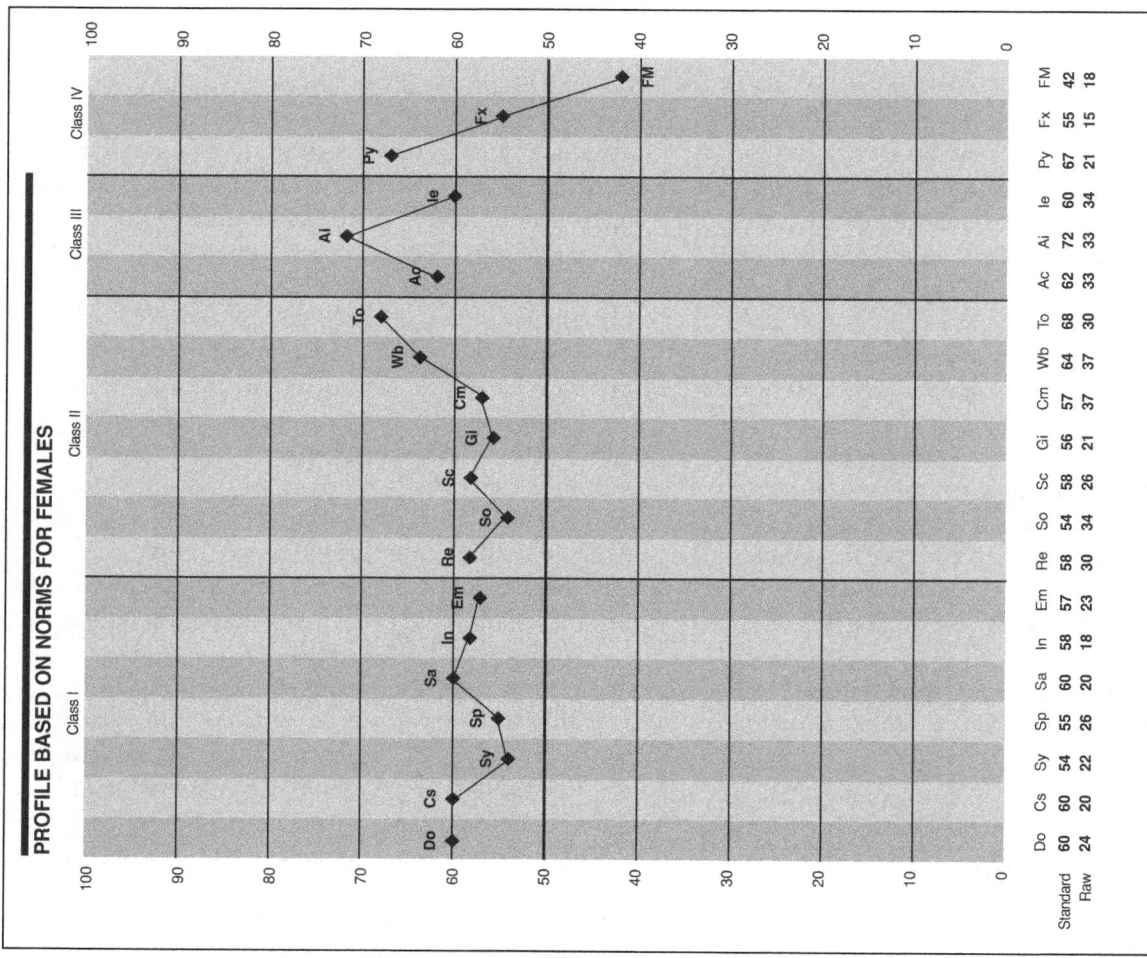

Figure 6.8 CPI Profile for Case 4

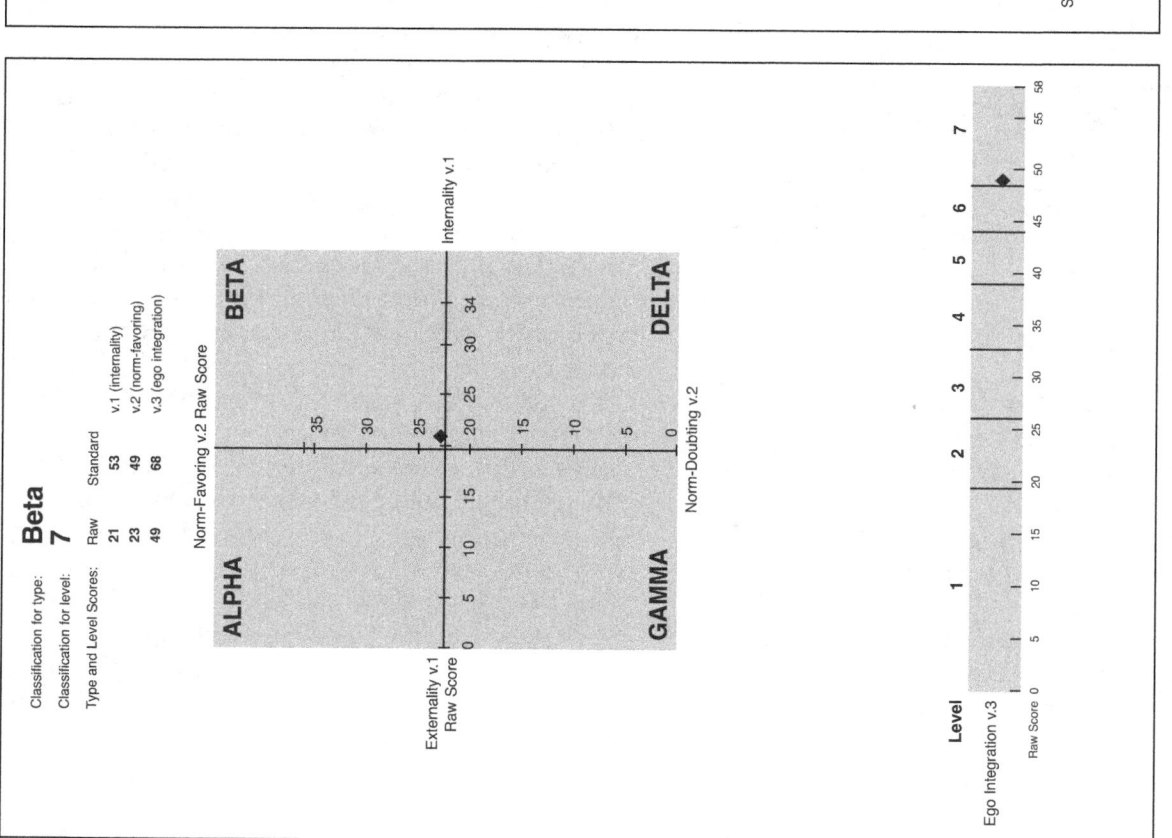

Figure 6.7 Classification in the Three-Vector Model for Case 4

settings, and elsewhere where independent effort is demanded. Her other high scores suggest that she takes ethical issues seriously (To), that she is interpersonally insightful (Py), that she is optimistic about her ability to cope with the demands of everyday life (Wb), and that she is conscientious in carrying out tasks and duties (Ac). From her low score on F/M, we infer that she tries to be objective, rational, and logical in dealing with others, even though she has strong subjective feelings. Her highest score on the special purpose scales was 70 on Mp (Managerial Potential). This seems to be an unrealized talent, inasmuch as she has not as yet held or sought any managerial posts. The five *California Q-Set* items estimated to be most descriptive of her, as seen by observers, are "Values own independence and autonomy," "Is cheerful," "Is protective of those close to her," "Prides self on being 'objective,' rational," and "Behaves in a sympathetic or considerate manner."

We close with the summary statement of her life history interviewer:

> Case 4 was not very expressive in the interview, appearing to be introverted and uninclined to say very much about her personal feelings. She grew up in an upper middle-class family, and had a comfortable, pleasant childhood. At school she was at first shy and self-conscious, but tried hard to gain admission to the most popular group. When she succeeded in this, she realized that she did not quite like it. Although she is not dominant or assertive in behavior, she is not at all submissive and, in fact, is quite independent. She does not appear to be affectionate in nature, perhaps because of a tendency towards overcontrol, but also because of her stress on objectivity and logic in interpersonal dealings. She is uncomfortable when someone else tries to probe into her inner feelings, and finds her sister's efforts along this line to be annoying. Her husband also has a tendency to hold much in reserve, which leads to problems between them because of her own tendency to "clam up" in conflicts. Because of explicit effort to be more open with each other, their communication has improved in recent years.

Case 5: Gamma-1 Male

Case 5 is a 49-year-old Hispanic male being treated for alcoholism in a clinic in southwestern United States. He has a fifth-grade education, and on the *Wechsler Adult Intelligence Test*, he had an overall IQ of 92. On the CPI, his scores on the v.1 and v.2 scales classify him as a Gamma, and on the v.3 scale he ranks at Level 1 (see Figure 6.9). Gammas are responsive to others and more than ready to receive the financial and status rewards associated with interpersonal attainment. They are also rule-doubting, dubious about the conventions and folkways of the law-abiding culture, and frustrated with what they often see as petty restraints. At low levels on the v.3 scale, they tend to behave in impulsive, self-defeating ways and seem to learn little from the lessons of experience. As a Gamma-1, Case 5 can be expected to have many, and serious, problems of adjustment of the "acting out" variety.

His CPI profile, as shown in Figure 6.10, reveals standard scores of 20 or lower on Re, So, Sc, Wb, Ac, and Ie. Surprisingly, for a profile with so many low scores, the Sy and Sp scales are above 50. From the Re and So low points, we can infer that his ethical standards will be opportunistic, that he will often be moody and recalcitrant, that he will overvalue immediate pleasure and rewards, and that he will be almost incapable of objective evaluation of his own behavior. From the low score on Sc, we can add that both aggressive and erotic impulses will be relatively uncontrolled, and that he will be extremely self-indulgent. Wb suggests pessimism about his current status and an almost fatalistic view that nothing much will improve, and from the low Ac and Ie scores, we can anticipate severe underachievement in both school and work, and easy distractibility. His lowest score on the special purpose scales occurred on the Wo (Work Orientation) scale, with a standard score of 16. He would be a poor prospect for any work requiring attention to detail, punctuality, rule-observance, and self-discipline. The five Block *California Q-Set* items forecast to be most descriptive were the following: "Behaves in a masculine style and manner," "Values own independence and autonomy," "Is self-indulgent," "Characteristically pushes and tries to stretch limits; sees what he can get away with," and "Interested in members of the opposite sex." The two Q-sort items expected to be least descriptive of him were these: "Has a high aspiration level for self" and "Genuinely values intellectual and cognitive matters."

From his case file, we learn that he was born and has lived his entire life in the Southwest. Both parents died in an automobile accident when he was three, and he was raised by various relatives and foster parents. His formal schooling stopped after the

Classification for type: Gamma
Classification for level: 1
Type and Level Scores: Raw Standard
11 38 v.1 (internality)
5 19 v.2 (norm-favoring)
4 21 v.3 (ego integration)
Norm-Favoring v.2 Raw Score
ALPHA
BETA
GAMMA
DELTA
Externality v.1 Raw Score
Internality v.1
Norm-Doubting v.2
0 5 10 15 20 25 30 34
0 5 10 15 20 25 30 35
Level
1 2 3 4 5 6 7
Ego Integration v.3
Raw Score 0 5 10 15 20 25 30 35 40 45 50 55 58

Figure 6.9 Classification in the Three-Vector Model for Case 5

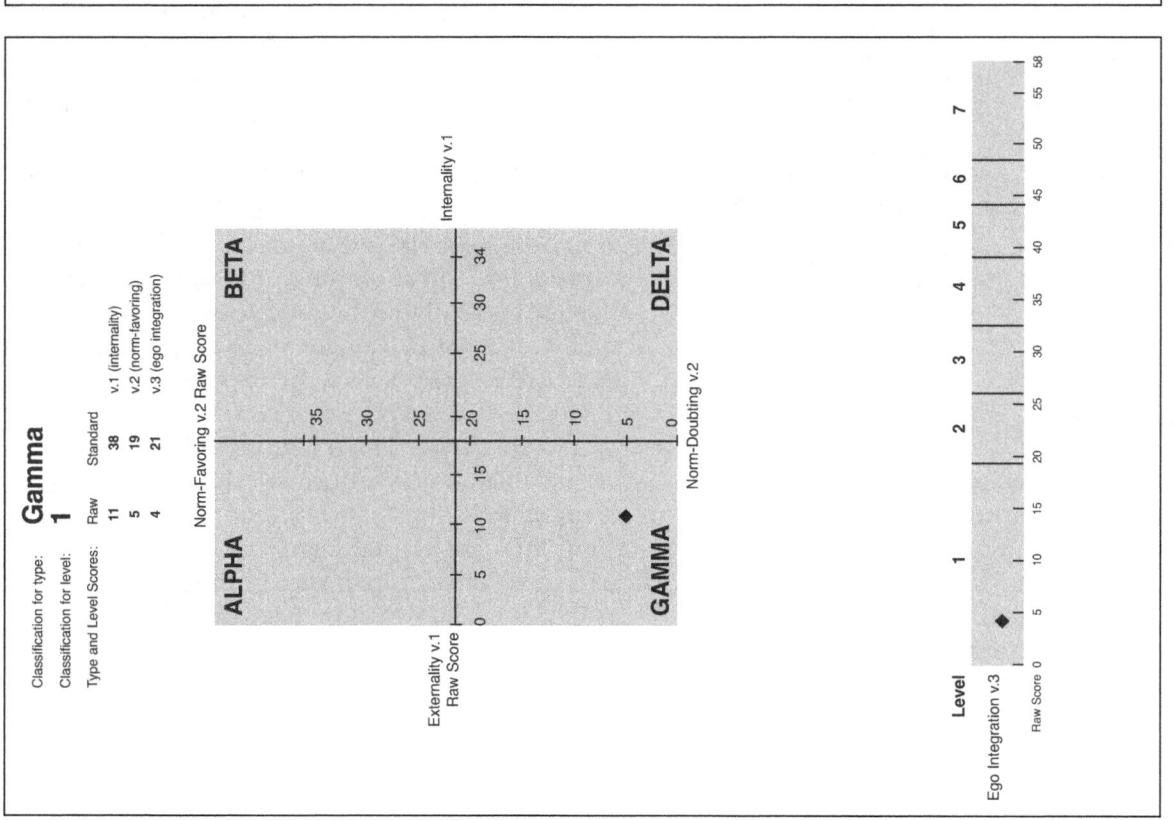

PROFILE BASED ON NORMS FOR MALES
Class I
Class II
Class III
Class IV
0 10 20 30 40 50 60 70 80 90 100
Do Cs Sy Sp Sa In Em Re So Sc Gi Cm Wb To Ac Ai Ie Py Fx FM
Standard 44 36 55 53 50 45 46 9 11 20 26 21 14 21 13 33 20 38 52 37
Raw 16 9 22 26 16 13 17 2 7 0 2 25 9 3 4 9 10 10 14 9

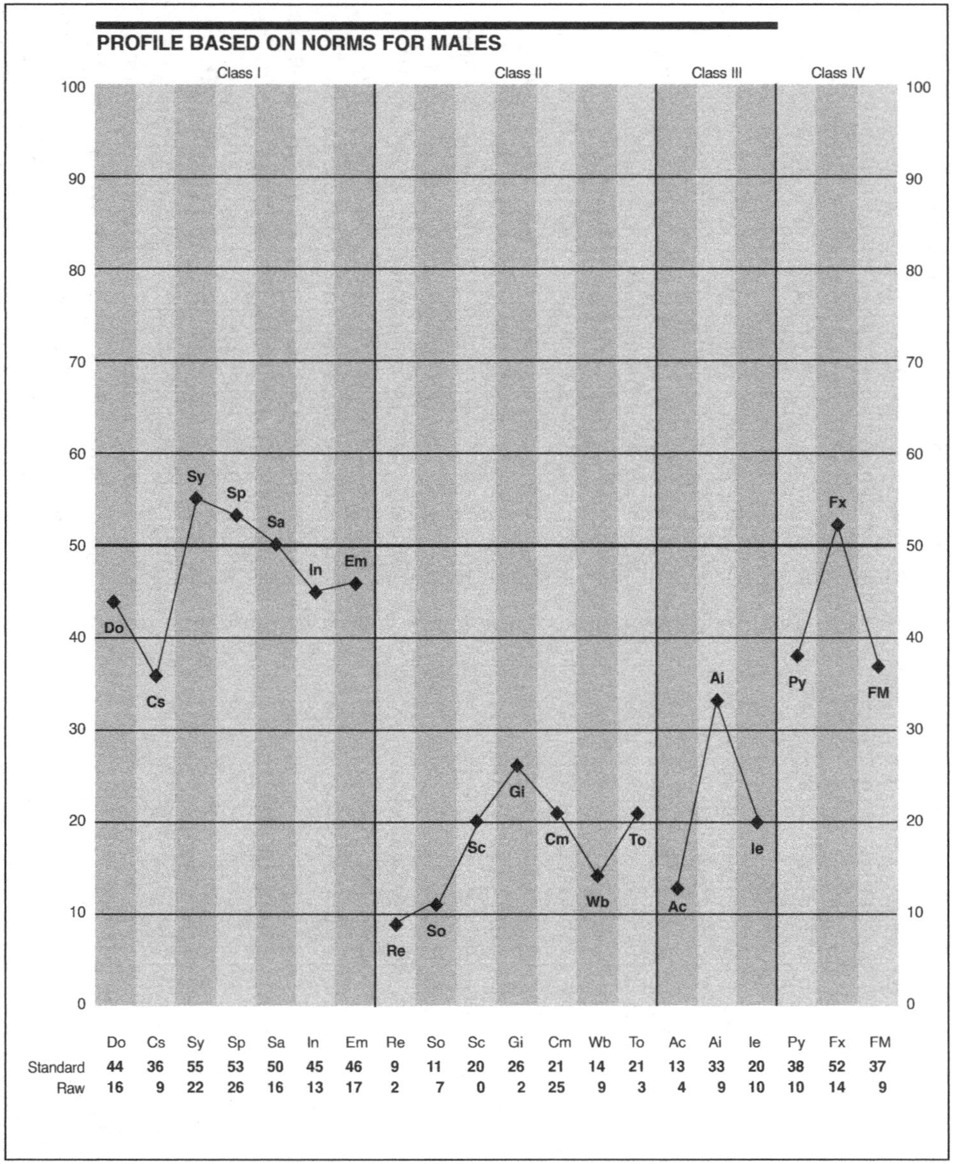

Figure 6.10 CPI Profile for Case 5

fifth grade. Since age nine, he has been in constant trouble with legal authorities, mostly for petty crimes, public intoxication, curfew violations, property damage and vandalism, living from the earnings of prostitutes, and vagrancy. He has been legally married at least four times, but insofar as the records show, has never been divorced. He is currently living with a woman who is "trying to reform him." This liaison has lasted for 14 months, a record for him, and for the last eight months, he has been employed as a maintenance man, his longest period of continuous employment.

His group therapist describes him as a very disruptive man who seems to fluctuate from arrogance and braggadocio on the one hand, to almost total withdrawal on the other. Although the group leader has made several attempts to have him removed from the group, the other members have come to his support for retention. Thus, despite some ups and downs, he seems able to engender at least moderately positive responses from peers, especially as a way to oppose authority. It may be noted that, in his youth, he was apparently the instigator of some criminal gang activity, but it was always the other gang members who were caught and punished. His therapist for individual counseling described him as "very impulsive and self-centered, with almost no understanding of his own psychological functioning and ego defenses, and no awareness of the motives underlying his alcoholic binges."

Case 6: Gamma-7 Female

Case 6 is a 19-year-old college student majoring in psychology. She is the oldest of three children; one of her brothers is in college, and the other is in high school. Her educational goal is to gain admission to a doctoral program in clinical psychology. She sees herself as having academic talent and as being perceptive about people—knowing what they are feeling and what they want. Her mother was "super loving and protective," whereas her father was more of a disciplinarian. The family was secure financially, the father having a good job and the mother working part-time. Both parents spent a lot of time with the children—playing sports like tennis and skiing, traveling together, and just having fun. Although there was a college in her home

town, she wanted to go away to school so as to be more independent. She had excellent grades in high school, but was also very active socially—going to parties, dances, and so forth. Even though she is mostly self-supporting in college, she is getting good grades. She lives off campus with four others, going to parties on Friday and Saturday nights, and often to a bar after work each day. She has had a steady boyfriend for the past few months.

In the three-vector model she is classified as a Gamma-7, as shown in Figure 6.11. Gammas at high levels on v.3 are adept at coping with change, enjoy new experiences and variety, have a talent for creative thinking, and are persuasive in dealing with others. They also tend to be impatient with people who are slow or stodgy (as they often see others), and sometimes behave in ways that impress others as self-serving and self-indulgent.

Her profile, as shown in Figure 6.12, has 11 of 20 scales with standard scores of 60 or greater, suggesting an overvaluation of her productive attributes, at least in her persona. Her score of 62 on Gi (Good Impression) is consonant with this interpretation. Her highest score is on the In (Independence) scale, indicative of both an exceptional degree of resourcefulness in dealing with life's demands and a tendency to stand apart from others. Her high scores on the Em and Py scales agree with her statements about insight into others, and her ability to sense what they feel and think. On the Ac and Ai scales she has an 18-point difference in favor of Ai. This configuration is associated with a striving for independence in any intellectual endeavor, ability to see to the heart of complex issues, and superior achievement in work calling for self-sufficiency and initiative. The elevations on Sy, Sp, and Sa point towards verve, spontaneity, versatility, and self-confidence. Her high score on Fx, along with a moderately low score on Cm, backs up the comments just above concerning creativity and an ability to see beyond and beneath the norm. Her lowest score is F/M, concordant with her expressed needs for independence and autonomy, but also suggesting that she may be suppressing her nurturant and care-giving proclivities.

Her life history interviewer submitted the following remarks in a summary of the interview:

> She is a self-assured young woman who likes to do well in all that she does. She has had consistently high

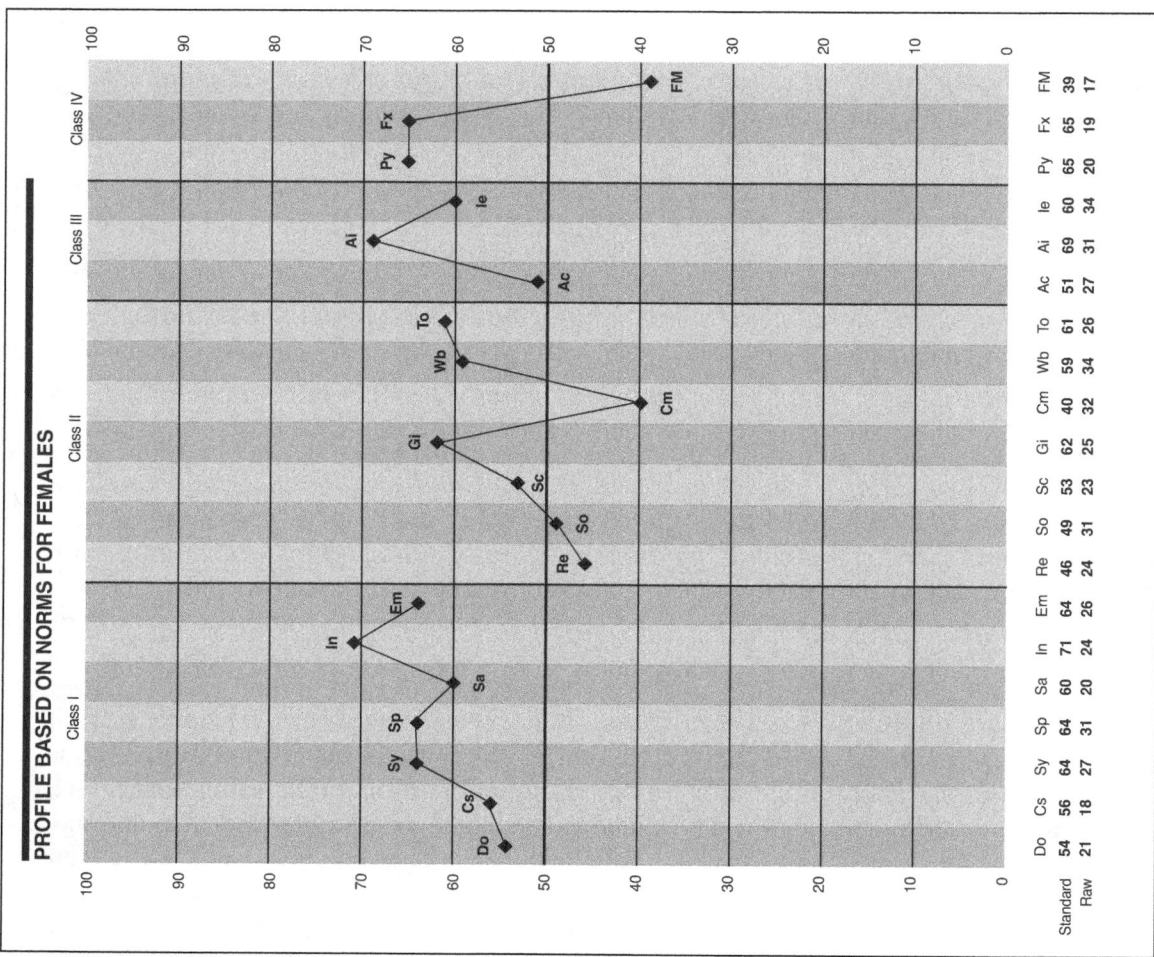

Figure 6.12 CPI Profile for Case 6

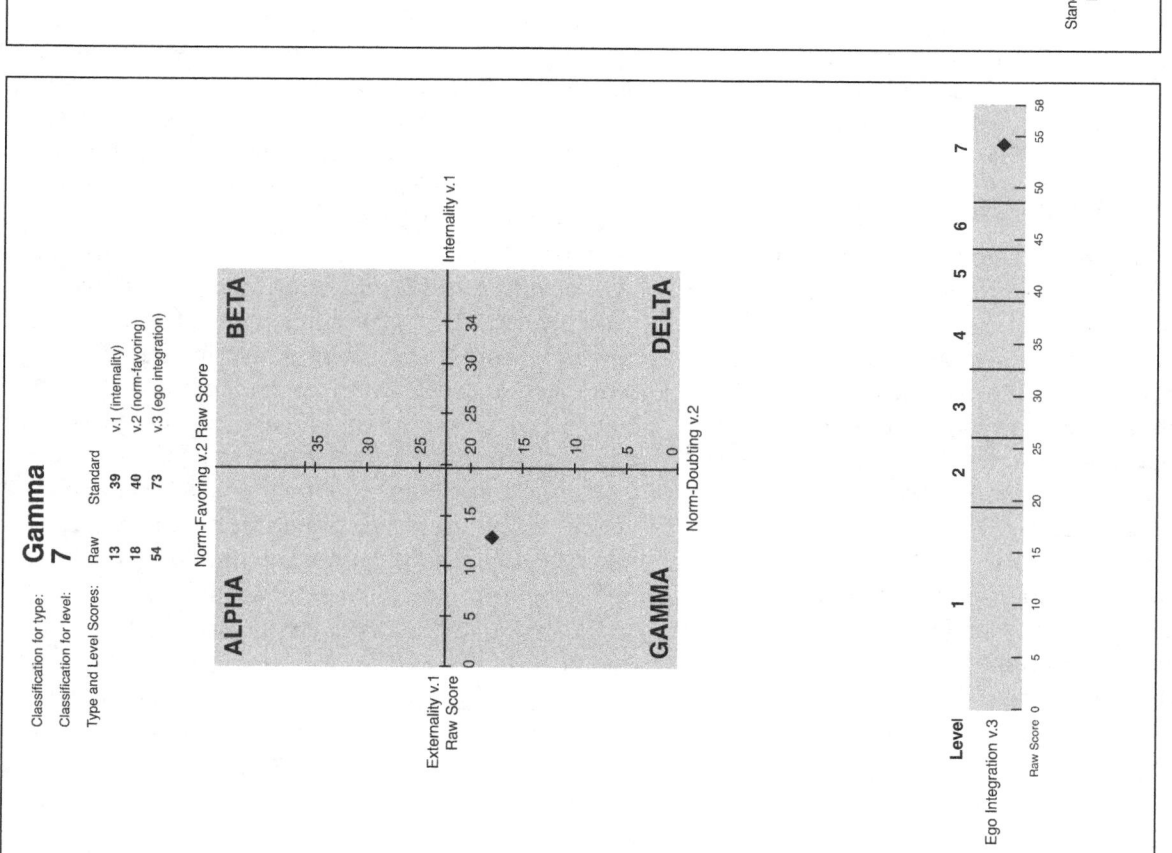

Figure 6.11 Classification in the Three-Vector Model for Case 6

grades in both high school and college, and feels most powerful when she receives tangible evidence of good performance, as in her grade reports or when someone who is important or respected praises her. Her goal is to achieve the financial independence her mother never had, in a profession that exemplifies her mother's values of loving and understanding. Although her behavior is not rule-bound in any conventional sense, she thinks she is too conforming to the wishes of others. She feels good about her life and self-understanding so far, but also feels that she has a lot of learning and a lot of growing to do. She wants to travel widely, to out-of-the-way places to study the cultures and to Europe to appreciate its art, music, and literature. Money looms large in these fantasies, but with her determination, self-sufficiency, and talent she may well succeed in attaining her goals.

Case 7: Delta-7 Male

Case 7 is a 33-year-old Ph.D. in mathematics, working in a research laboratory devoted to rocketry and space exploration. He grew up in the Midwest, the youngest of four children, in an upper middle class family. When subject was eight his father was killed in a robbery, and after that the family moved to the West Coast. Subject remembers himself as a poor student in grade school, and an indifferent student in high school. In college he started in engineering, but was not strongly interested. He left college for several years of military service, during which he did a lot of reading and discovered that he in fact had a desire for further education. He returned to college to major in mathematics, graduated with honors, and went on to a Ph.D. in this field. His achievements have been recognized by several visiting appointments to prominent research institutes. In his present position he works mostly on his own, identifying the topics he believes to be worthy of investigation, and then studying them in his own way. Recently he has been asked to take on some administrative duties, but he prefers the more theoretical mathematics he can do alone. In fact, he finds this work "wonderful, beautiful, exciting." He is married, with one child, and finds considerable satisfaction in his family life. He mentioned, however, that he does not like parties or social gatherings with large numbers of people.

His classification in the three-vector model is Delta-7, as shown in Figure 6.13. Deltas seek privacy and detachment from others, and in their own thinking, question the imperatives of societal conventions. At higher levels of ego integration, they are forward-looking and even visionary, especially in fields such as art, music, literature, and sciences such as mathematics. A basic problem for the Deltas is to achieve an inner reconciliation of the polarities and incongruities they encounter in their lives and in the culture at large.

As shown in Figure 6.14, his CPI profile has four scales with standard scores of 70 or more: Sc, Ai, Ie, and Py. McAllister comments that persons with very high scores on both Sc and Ie are often perfectionists, risk-aversive, and likely to be thinkers rather than doers. High scorers on both Ie and Py, McAllister finds, are intellectually efficient, but are often seen as aloof and detached, resist getting involved in the emotional needs of others, and are strongly task-oriented. This man's very high score on Ai is indicative of independent ways of thinking, superior potential for achievement in intellectual endeavor, and a talent for imaginative, original work. His even higher score on Py betokens good judgment about people, a high level of aspiration, and a cathexis of intellectual activity, but also a somewhat individualistic, impersonal way of dealing with others. His very high score on Sc should also be noted, as it is something of an anomaly in the context of the full profile. That is, for a person of exceptional intellectual and creative talent, this degree of overcontrol will be a barrier against full realization of his outstanding creative potential.

We close this discussion of Case 7 with the final summary from his life history interview:

> He is a tall, dark, impressive-looking man, with a pleasing voice and a self-assured manner. He is enthusiastic about his work in mathematics, but not to the exclusion of other interests or activities. He appears to be unusually free of feelings of anxiety, worry, and guilt, and at the same time, to be unusually mature and self-actualized. His academic history is striking—from near-failure in grade school to indifferent achievement in his first years in college, he seems to have felt completely free to achieve or not. His later intellectual accomplishments seem to stem from a real excitement in learning, not from extrinsic motivations such as good grades, praise, or conformity to rules. Although his interpersonal skills might lead him into administrative work, I suspect that he will resist these blandishments and will remain in more creative and independent activity in mathematics.

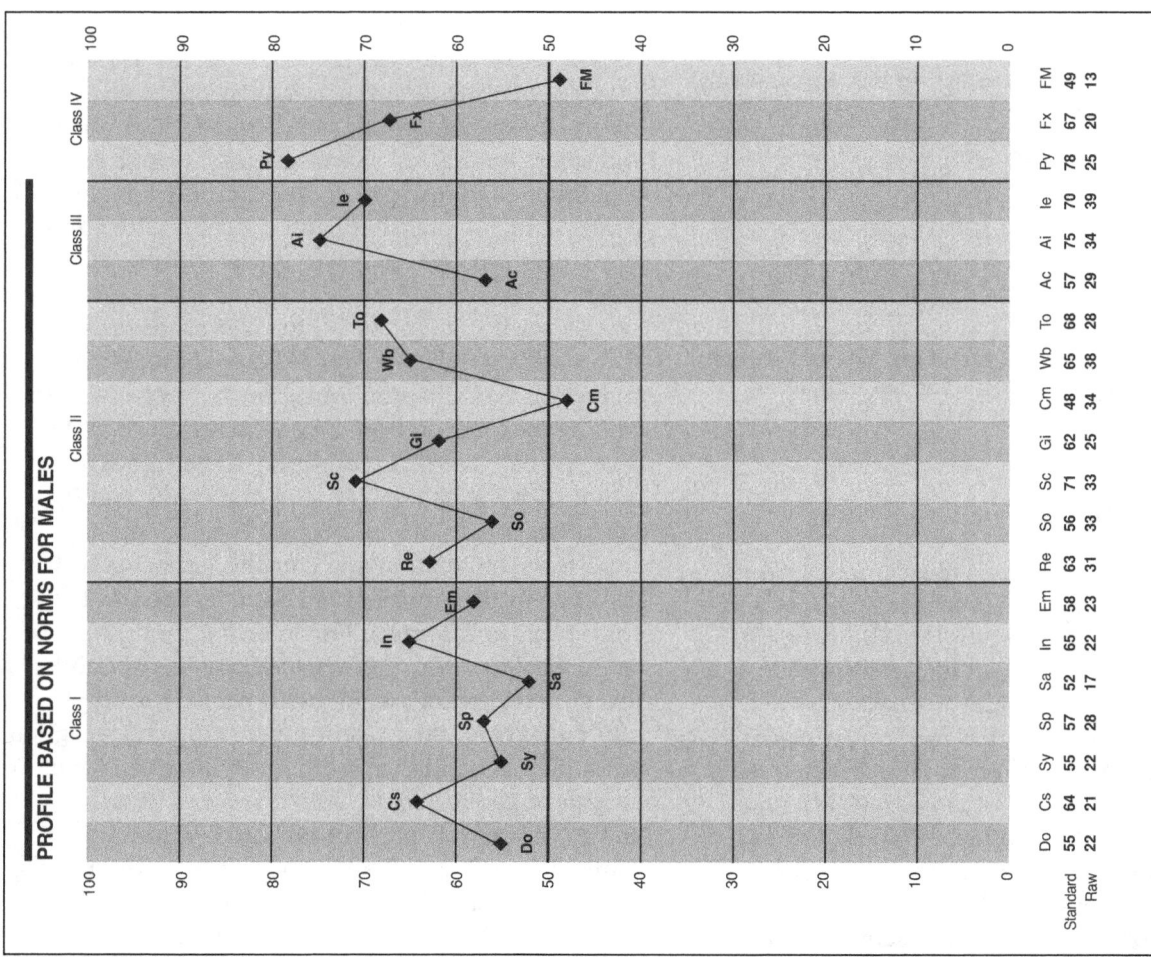

Figure 6.14 CPI Profile for Case 7

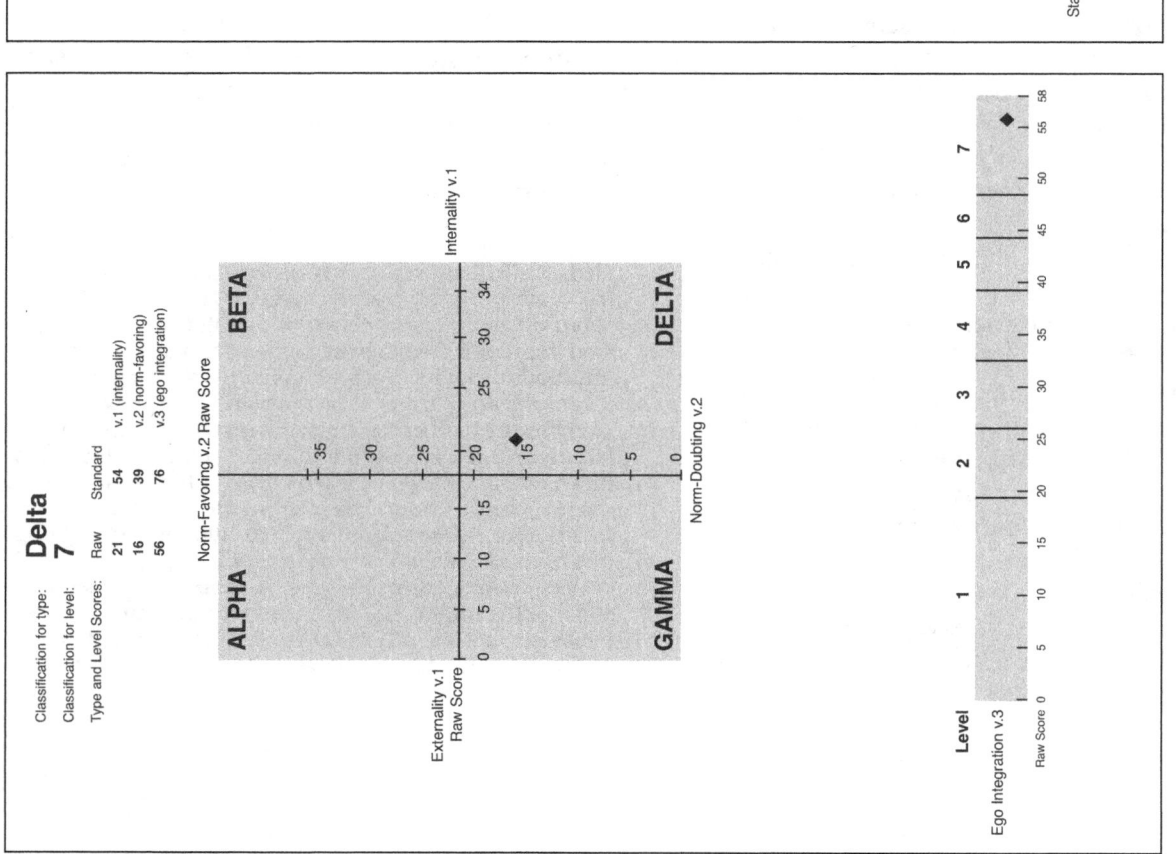

Figure 6.13 Classification in the Three-Vector Model for Case 7

Case 8: Delta-3 Female

Case 8 is an 18-year-old college female who took the CPI in a large class of over 800 students. Her performance in the course was somewhat above average, and she received a grade of B. On later inquiry, the instructor said he had no recollection of her, and that as far as he could remember, she had not come to see him during his office hours. About all his course records showed was that she had done well on the midterm and final examinations.

As shown in Figure 6.15, Case 8 is a Delta-3 in the three-vector model. Deltas tend to distance themselves from others and to protect their privacy. They are also unpersuaded of the merit and wisdom of ordinary conventions and societal norms. At lower levels of ego integration, these contradictions between internal beliefs and the expectations of others can lead to worry, self-doubt, and alienation. At Level 3, this individual seems to be experiencing difficulty in achieving a good sense of identity, and no doubt has many dissatisfactions with her present status.

Turning to her CPI profile in Figure 6.16, we see that she does indeed score low on the Wb scale. She is also low on the Sy scale, indicating a turning away from easy contact with others. Her low score on Do suggests a sort of acquiescence in her present subordinate status, but her moderately elevated score on Ai and high score on Fx rule against anything like true submissiveness in her character. The gestalt is more indicative that she is biding her time, working towards a stronger and more rewarding integration to come later.

The contrast of 26 points between her scores on Ac and Ai make this two-scale configuration crucial in interpreting the profile. McAllister notes that people with this pattern dislike supervision, resist

structure, and rebel against organizational folkways. They are at their best in individual, self-initiated effort. Her highest score is on Fx, indicating a liking for change and variety along with a dislike of routine, a wide range of interests, and progressive sociopolitical views. Her second-highest score is on F/M, superficially associated with dependency on important others and nurturant feelings for those in her sphere of affection, but in this case, more indicative of an inner, private, and complex emotional life.

On the special purpose scales (not shown in the profile) her highest score was on Creative Temperament. This finding, along with her very high score on Fx and configuration of Ai over Ac, does suggest a considerable latent degree of creative potential. The five Block Q-sort items identified by CPI algorithms as most likely to be descriptive of this person were: "Concerned with own adequacy as a person, either at conscious or unconscious levels," "Has fluctuating moods," "Is introspective and concerned with self as as object," "Is basically anxious," and "Compares self to others, is alert to real or fancied differences between self and other people."

After graduating from college, she started a career in journalism, which she pursued for about seven years. During that time, she was a columnist for a widely read magazine and a contributing editor to another. When her first novel appeared, she turned entirely to freelance writing. Her second novel was published eight years after her first. Both novels received critical acclaim and were seen as quasi-autobiographical artistic resolutions of a complex and contradictory inner life. She has continued to publish novels, from two to five years apart, and has also written screenplays for a number of movies. As of now, she is generally recognized as an important, creative writer with a distinctive personal style.

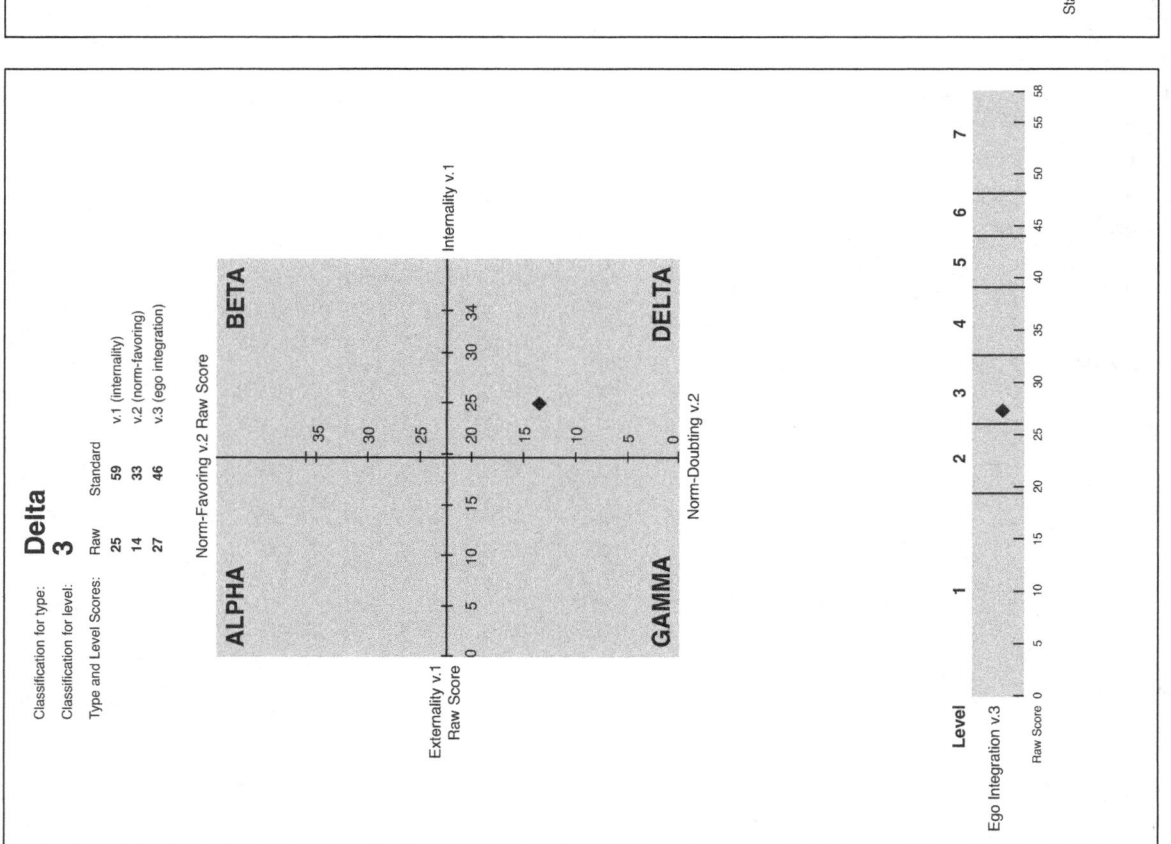

PROFILE BASED ON NORMS FOR FEMALES

	Do	Cs	Sy	Sp	Sa	In	Em	Re	So	Sc	Gi	Cm	Wb	To	Ac	Ai	Ie	Py	Fx	FM
Standard	29	46	28	34	39	35	51	36	48	49	38	33	28	39	29	55	41	44	70	67
Raw	8	14	9	15	11	7	20	19	30	20	10	30	15	14	15	22	22	12	21	26

Figure 6.16 CPI Profile for Case 8

Classification for type: **Delta**
Classification for level: **3**

Type and Level Scores:

	Raw	Standard	
	25	59	v.1 (internality)
	14	33	v.2 (norm-favoring)
	27	46	v.3 (ego integration)

Internality v.1

BETA

DELTA

Norm-Favoring v.2 Raw Score

Norm-Doubting v.2

ALPHA

GAMMA

Externality v.1
Raw Score

Level

Ego Integration v.3

Figure 6.15 Classification in the Three-Vector Model for Case 8

CHAPTER

7

New Research

The basic purpose of the CPI is to furnish information from which a true-to-life and distinctive picture of the person tested may be drawn. Given this fundamental aim, it is not surprising that primary usage of the inventory occurs in work with individuals, such as managerial training and selection (see Meyer & Davis, 1992), selection and evaluation of police officers (see Roberts, 1995b), treatment of alcoholics (Kadden, Cooney, Getter, & Litt, 1989), and the identification of effective telemarketers (Hakstian, Scratchley, MacLeod, Tweed, & Siddarth, 1997). In all of these examples, emphasis is on individuals, one at a time, rather than on nomothetic concerns.

However, there is also a good fund of new information pertaining to the use of the CPI in the study of general trends and relationships. It should be mentioned that a complete bibliography of CPI research is now being prepared for publication, a listing that will include approximately 2,000 titles. As a guide to current users of the CPI, a representative sampling of research appearing after the preparation of the 1996 manual is given below.

Life-Span Trends

One major field of application is life-span psychology, in which trends in personality are charted over significant periods of time. Key contributions of this kind have been made by Ravenna Helson and her colleagues at the University of California, Berkeley, including influences of the women's movement on the life path (Agronick & Duncan, 1998), changes in goals from early to mature adulthood (Harker & Solomon, 1996), personality change in women during adulthood (Helson, 1996), positive and negative affect as related to changes in personality from young adulthood to midlife (Helson & Klohnen, 1998), creative achievement in adulthood as related to personal growth (Helson & Pals, 2000), influence of experiences at work on personality change in women (Roberts, 1997), the psychology of individualism as related to personality change in women (Roberts & Helson, 1997), and changes in personality among self-directed women between ages 40 and 50 (Wink, 1996). Examples from other important programs of research on life-span topics are age

175

trends in responsibility and flexibility (Schaie, 1996) and the evolution of psychological generativity in women (Stewart & Vandewater, 1998). Age differences in adult personality have also been compared between the United States and the People's Republic of China (Labouvie-Vief, Diehl, Tarnowski, & Shen, 2000; Yang, McCrae, & Costa, 1998).

Personal Adjustment

Personal adjustment is another topic of importance. One study (Cook, Young, Taylor, & Bedford, 1996) related scales of the CPI to a criterion of general good health in a sample of 899 persons. A correlation of .51 was found for the Wb (Well-being) scale, and of .40 for the self-realization vector. Leventhal's 1966 scale for anxiety was reanalyzed in a Romanian version (Albu & Pitariu, 1999) and a new 21-item version developed. Good health and adjustment across the adult life span have also been studied (see Adams, Cartwright, Ostrove, Stewart, & Wink, 1998; Harker & Keltner, 2001; Peskin, Jones, & Livson, 1997; Twisk, Snel, Kemper, & van Mechelen, 1998; Vandewater, Ostrove, & Stewart, 1997). Positive CPI profile signs such as elevations on Wb and Ie are consistently associated with better physical and psychological health in adulthood.

Intergenerational Psychology

Intergenerational psychology has been examined in studies of, for instance, the recurrence of addictive vulnerability or "risk" factors across three generations (Brook, Whiteman, & Brook, 1999), links between parental personality and the adjustment of their children (Solomon, 2000), and the relation of adult attachment styles to family context and personality (Diehl, Elnick, Bourbeau, & Labouvie-Vief, 1998). An excellent example of genetic versus environmental influence on CPI scales appeared in 1998, based on the Minnesota twin bank (Bouchard, McGue, Hur, & Horn, 1998), comparing twins reared together and apart.

Managerial Performance

Managerial performance continues to be a focus of research with the CPI. A doctoral thesis (Batista, 1995) in Puerto Rico compared executives at three levels, finding monotonic trends toward higher scores for higher-ranked managers on scales such as Do (Dominance) and In (Independence). For 236 Romanian executives rated on performance, correlations were obtained of .27 for So (Socialization), .26 for Lp (Leadership), and .24 for Tm (Tough-mindedness) (see Pitariu, Pitariu, & Ali Al Mutairi, 1998). In Pakistan, 35 more successful executives were compared with 49 less successful, on selected scales of the CPI (Shujaat, Zehra, & Anila, 1996); for Do, the point-biserial correlation for the split was +.39. British, Czech, Georgian, Lithuanian, and Ukranian managers were compared for their mean CPI profiles (see Cook et al., 1998), with British managers scoring higher in most of the scales, in particular on Do, Cs (Capacity for Status), and Ai (Achievement via Independence).

The So and To Scales

One of the most thoroughly researched scales of the CPI is So (see Gough, 1994). Interest in the So scale has continued in recent years, with studies of the internal structure of the measure (Collins & Bagozzi, 1999; Kadden, Litt, Donovan, & Cooney, 1996) and of its relation to criminal violence (Heilbrun, 1996) and to sexual aggression by men (Kosson, Kelly, & White, 1997). Another study (Taylor, McGue, Iacono, & Lykken, 2000) identified three interpretable factors within the scale, labeled optimism, favorable home background or "family," and behavioral control. Self-reported delinquency was significantly related to total score (correlations of −.49 for 485 boys and −.53 for 382 girls) as well as to all three subscales. Comparison of monozygotic and dizygotic twins suggested primarily a genetic contribution to the covariance of self-reported delinquency and So scores for boys, but a shared genetic and environmental contribution for girls. A review of counterproductive behavior at work (Collins & Griffin, 1998) reported true score validities for the So scale of −.61 with violations of statutory laws, +.28 with prosocial and productive job performance, and −.47 with violation of societal and organizational norms. A seven-month follow-up of patients in methadone treatment maintenance (Alterman, Rutherford, Cacciola, McKay, & Boardman, 1998) produced a biserial correlation of .20 between So and successful (N = 127) versus unsuccessful (N = 62) completion of the program. The To (Tolerance) scale has also been studied as a separate measure (see Dunbar, 1997; Dunbar, Saiz, Stela, & Saez, 2000; Sullaway & Dunbar, 1996).

New Scales

The scales of the CPI are classified into three groups: the 20 folk measures, displayed on the profile sheet, then three vectors intended to chart the underlying structure of personality posited for the full inventory, and a set of special purpose scales, seven of which are reported in the computerized scoring provided by the publisher. In consonance with the "open-system" axiom, which calls for new measures whenever the extant set—either singly or in commonsense combinations—fails to forecast or rationalize a criterion. Given this axiom, it is to be expected that new special purpose scales will be developed. Among those that have been published since the 1996 manual are measures for hostility (Adams & John, 1997), "openness" as conceptual-

ized in the *Five-Factor Model* (Hakstian & Farrell, 2001), the seven social performance themes assessed in the *Hogan Personality Inventory* (Hogan, 1986; Johnson, 1997), ego resilience (Klohnen, 1996a, 1996b), and personal warmth (Peskin, Jones, & Livson, 1997).

A sampling of other studies since 1996 includes those relating the CPI to the *Five-Factor Model* (Fleenor & Eastman, 1997), use of the CPI in counseling (Gough, 2000), career commitments and momentum among women (Roberts & Friend, 1998; Vandewater & Stewart, 1997, 1998), performance of military personnel (Gough & Bradley, 1999), relationship of the CPI to the *Barron-Welsh Art Scale* (Gough, Hall, & Bradley, 1996), selection of telemarketing employees (Hakstian, Scratchley, MacLeod, Tweed, & Siddarth, 1997), religiosity (Park, Meyers, & Czar, 1998), creativity among adolescents (Dincă, 2001), and wisdom in midlife women (Wink & Helson, 1997).

The Special Purpose and Research Scales

As reported in the main text of the manual, there are three classifications for the scales of the inventory: folk concepts, presented on the profile sheet; secondary vector scales, used in defining the cuboid model; and special purpose or research scales that may be added to scoring at the discretion of the examiner. Extensive discussion has already appeared of the folk and vector scales, including items illustrative of major internal themes. Form 434 items included in each of 13 special purpose scales are given in this appendix.

Scale Description

Managerial Potential (Mp) is the first of these scales. It was developed (Gough, 1984) in an attempt to identify persons with a propensity to seek managerial positions and a potentiality for good performance in such roles. A perusal of normative data in Appendix B shows that entrepreneurial innovators (Barron & Egan, 1968), banking and business executives, and sales managers do indeed attain high scores, whereas low scores are found among students in an art institute and prison inmates. A doctoral thesis by Ruth

Jacobs (1992) reported Mp data for 34 men advanced to middle management during a seven-year period after hiring, as compared with 116 who were not advanced; and for 31 women who were advanced to middle management as compared with 98 who were not. For those advanced, means on Mp were 26.35 for men and 25.81 for women; and for those not advanced, Mp means were 23.64 for men and 23.36 for women. The differences are statistically significant beyond the .01 level, and equivalent to point biserial correlations of .26 for men and .23 for women.

Work Orientation (Wo) is the second scale. Its goal (Gough, 1985) is to identify respondents characterized by a strong, selfless, disciplined will to work, compatible with Veblen's (1914) "instinct of workmanship" and Weber's (1930) formulation of the Protestant ethic. Perusal of norms in Appendix B reveals high scores for teachers and students of education, optometry students, and police officers; and low scores for juvenile delinquents and psychiatric patients. Key adjectival correlates (see Appendix D) include conscientious, dependable, moderate, organized, and reasonable associated with higher scores;

and careless, changeable, distractible, reckless, and temperamental with lower scores.

Creative Temperament (CT) is the third scale. It is composed of items found individually to correlate with observers' ratings of creativity (Gough, 1992). Scores on the scale correlated from .25 to .53 with criterion ratings of creativity in nine samples, with a median of .44. Norm samples with high scores on CT include psychologists, creative writers, and members of the Rajneeshi commune; low-scoring samples include high school students, correctional officers, and training school inmates. Adjectival descriptions by observers associated with high scores include adventurous, clever, complicated, unconventional, and spontaneous; and for low scores cautious, conservative, mild, practical, and quiet.

Leadership (Lp) is the fourth scale. Its development has not yet been described in a published report, but an extensive presentation of samples, criteria, and relevant conceptions of leadership may be found in a chapter on testing for leadership (Gough, 1990). High-scoring samples include MBA candidates, sales managers, and military officers; low-scoring samples include high school disciplinary problems, psychiatric patients, and students of art. Adjectival descriptions such as alert, ambitious, energetic, poised, and resourceful are associated with high scores; and descriptions such as awkward, dissatisfied, immature, quitting, and timid with low scores.

Amicability (Ami) is the fifth scale. In a sample of 236 couples, adjectival descriptions of each person by the spouse or partner were scored for a cluster of terms such as cheerful, cooperative, friendly, good-natured, and warm (indicative), and cold, demanding, fault-finding, quarrelsome, and touchy (contraindicative). These criterion scores were then correlated with CPI items as endorsed by the 472 persons. Representative items scored "true" include "I always try to consider the other person's feelings before I do something," and "I have very few quarrels with members of my family." Representative of items scored "false" are "Sometimes I feel like smashing things," and "I think most people would lie to get ahead." Norm samples with high scores include counselors, priests, and home economics majors, and those with low scores include juvenile delinquents and prison inmates. Adjectives in new samples implicated by high scores include appreciative, fair-minded, modest, reasonable, and tactful;

as compared with argumentative, headstrong, intolerant, self-centered, and suspicious for low scores.

Law Enforcement Orientation (Leo) is the sixth scale. The scale is based on item analyses of the inventory, using two criteria: The first was a contrast between persons in police work (using a dummy weight of 1) versus persons in 14 contrasting occupational groups (with a dummy weight of 1); and the second pitted the items against job performance ratings of 141 officers and class standings in a police academy of 137 cadets. Examples of items meeting the requirement of positive correlations with both criteria are "I do not like to see people carelessly dressed," and "I think I am usually a leader in my group" (both true); and "The future is too uncertain for a person to make serious plans," and "There are times when I act like a coward" (both false). In testing of seven male and two female samples of police officers, means on Leo ranged from a low of 29.28 to a high of 33.88, with a median of 31.58. The highest mean for any other occupational group was that of 28.45 for parole and probation officers. Psychology graduate students, social work graduate students, and mathematicians all scored below the basic norm value of 24.99 for men and 23.49 for women. Adjectival descriptions by observers included confident, conventional, healthy, organized, and practical associated with high scores; and absent-minded, artistic, lazy, pessimistic, and worrying associated with low scores.

Tough-mindedness (Tm) is the seventh scale. It has not yet been described in a published report. In his book on pragmatism, William James (1907) distinguished between "toughminded" and "tender-minded" modes of thinking, and commented on the pervasive role these dispositions have played in philosophy, science, and even everyday life. Meehl (1954) made use of these notions in his classic analysis of clinical versus statistical prediction, and Eysenck (1944) concluded that the dimension of tender-to-tough-mindedness is basic in the formation of attitudes. Terms such as idealistic, sensitive, and understanding are indicative of tender-mindedness, and terms such as practical, logical, and unemotional are associated with tough-mindedness. To develop the scale, a cluster of 24 "tough" and 24 "tender" adjectives was defined and then scored on the descriptions 472 spouses (236 men, 236 women) had made of each other. These scores were then correlated with the items of the CPI. Examples of items chosen for the scale are "I hardly ever get excited or thrilled" (true), "I daydream very little" (true), "I often act on the spur of the moment without stopping to think" (false), and "I often start things I never finish" (false). From the correlations in Appendix D, it is clear that descriptions such as assertive, efficient, forceful, and self-confident are associated with high scores; and descriptions such as dreamy, emotional, distractible, and sensitive with low scores. Norm samples with high scores include police officers, parole and probation officers, and research scientists. Norm samples with low scores include students of art, juvenile delinquents, and high school disciplinary problem.

The eighth and ninth scales, the *Baucom scale for masculinity (B–MS)* and the *Baucom scale for feminity (B–FM)*, were developed by Donald Baucom (1976, 1980) to assess masculinity and femininity as unipolar dimensions. Ideally, the scales should be uncorrelated and have equal means for men and women to allow a full range of high and low scores on each scale for both sexes. In the two basic norm samples of 3,000 persons of each sex, the correlations were .18 for men and .16 for women. On the B–MS scale for masculinity, the men had a mean of 34.51 and the women a mean of 28.36. On the B–FM scale for femininity, the men had a mean of 25.06 and the women a mean of 31.07. Although these differences are statistically significant (p ≤.01), the magnitudes are small and not disqualifying for the purposes of the measures. For B–MS, samples of women with high scores include medical students, police officers, and teachers; samples with low scores include psychiatric patients and prison inmates. Male samples with high scores include police officers, military officers, and students of education; low-scoring samples include psychiatric patients and students of art. For B–FM, representative samples with high scores are counselors, clerical personnel, and social work students (women); and creative writers, architects, and critics of books for children (men). Representative samples with low scores are juvenile delinquents and prison inmates (both men and women). Adjectival descriptions associated with the two scales were similar for men and women. For B–MS, the descriptions aggressive, energetic, initiative, and self-confident were linked to high scores, as compared with cautious, mild, reserved, and timid for low scores. For B–FM, high-scorers tended to be

described as appreciative, gentle, patient, and sincere; low-scorers tended to be described as boastful, impulsive, pleasure-seeking, and tough.

Anxiety (Anx) is the 10th scale. It was developed by Leventhal (1966, 1968) as a parallel to anxiety scales on other tests such as the MMPI. Because of the dropping of 28 items referring to disabilities or matters of personal privacy, scoring of Anx in Form 434 is necessarily somewhat modified from its scoring in prior versions of the CPI. Specifically, three items were dropped and three new items were substituted. Correlations between the original and Form 434 versions of Anx were .92 for men and .93 for women, in the basic norm samples of $N = 3,000$, and mean scores increased slightly for both sexes. Samples with high scores on the Form 434 version included, for both sexes, psychiatric patients, prison inmates, and young delinquents. Low-scoring samples included anesthesiologists, police officers, and students of education. Adjectival descriptions such as complaining, evasive, nervous, and tense are associated with high scores, and descriptions such as contented, optimistic, cheerful, and self-confident with low scores. Correlations with anxiety scales in other inventories include .64 (males) and .60 (females) with the Anxiety Disorder scale of the *Millon Clinical Multiaxial Inventory*; .46 (males) and .57 (females) with the Welsh A scale on the MMPI; and .52 (males) and .54 (females) with the Neuroticism scale of *Maudsley Personality Inventory*.

Narcissism (Nar) is the 11th scale. It was developed by Wink and Gough (1990), focusing on the themes of exaggerated self-esteem, devaluation of others, feelings of entitlement, and dissatisfaction with one's own status. Using internal consistency methods, thirteen successive analyses were carried out until a scale compatible with these theoretical goals was evolved. In the empirical sphere, the scale had a correlation of .49 with assessment staff observers' ratings of narcissism in a sample of 57 persons. Its correlation with the Raskin and Hall (1979) scale for narcissism in this same sample was .72. Samples of women with above-average scores included MBA candidates and students of law and of art. High-scoring samples of men included art institute students, MBA candidates, and juvenile delinquents. Low-scoring samples included college counselors, teachers, and priests. Adjectival descriptions by observers associated with higher scores were, for example, argumentative, egotistical, opinionated, and self-centered; descriptions such as moderate, modest, gentle, and quiet were associated with lower scores.

The last two special purpose scales given below are *Dicken Social Desirability (D–SD)* and *Dicken Acquiescence (D–AC)*. These scales were developed by Charles Dicken (1963) in a study of the influence of social desirability and acquiescence on the validity of the other CPI scales. Dicken concluded that neither scale added to or indeed affected the validity of the folk concept measures. However, both scales have appreciable correlations with certain CPI scales. D–SD (Dicken Social Desirability), for example, correlates .72 with the Good Impression (Gi) scale, for both sexes, and .66 (males) and .71 (females) with the Well-being (Wb) scale. Correlations for the D–AC scale were much lower, the largest being with Tolerance (To), –.45 for males and –.48 for females. The D–SD scale consists of 32 items, half scored for a true response and half for a false. The same 32 items define the D–AC scale, but with all items scored for true. This psychometric strategy keeps their intercorrelations as low as possible, with coefficients in the basic norm samples of –.19 for males and –.22 for females. Adjectival description are not cited here, as neither scale is recommended for interpretation of individual protocols. Scoring of the scales is offered for the convenience of researchers interested in these two response styles.

Scoring Keys

Mp (Managerial Potential), 34 items
True: 96, 108, 202, 226, 239, 259, 359, 376
False: 20, 23, 40, 48, 109, 117, 142, 147, 169, 170, 173, 184, 188, 194, 209, 219, 233, 237, 243, 253, 266, 284, 294, 382, 422, 434

Wo (Work Orientation), 40 items
True: 126, 165, 180, 245, 263, 276, 283, 314, 392, 400
False: 26, 47, 48, 74, 77, 92, 93, 132, 137, 178, 190, 192, 194, 232, 237, 252, 257, 267, 274, 290, 299, 309, 351, 353, 366, 390, 398, 402, 405, 422

CT (Creative Temperament), 42 items
True: 47, 120, 122, 161, 172, 191, 213, 239, 244, 259, 267, 275
False: 3, 14, 25, 32, 37, 51, 88, 123, 131, 141, 177, 195, 199, 209, 225, 229, 230, 246, 255, 258, 261, 305, 313, 328, 361, 382, 387, 401, 404, 429

Lp (Leadership), 70 items
True: 21, 61, 86, 96, 123, 135, 160, 162, 179, 202, 226, 239, 245, 246, 260, 276, 304, 310, 317, 319, 320, 359, 403, 412, 413
False: 7, 15, 31, 40, 43, 54, 71, 76, 83, 92, 101, 109, 124, 136, 145, 147, 148, 170, 173, 177, 188, 190, 236, 252, 257, 258, 261, 270, 273, 284, 290, 291, 294, 313, 323, 331, 341, 362, 369, 390, 416, 417, 418, 421, 422

Ami (Amicability), 36 items
True: 45, 127, 135, 151, 168, 230, 245, 259, 276
False: 6, 20, 26, 29, 32, 44, 48, 78, 81, 128, 154, 173, 184, 190, 194, 248, 266, 267, 294, 336, 342, 346, 353, 390, 405, 416, 434

Leo (Law Enforcement Orientation), 42 items
True: 88, 98, 123, 129, 133, 165, 202, 210, 229, 230, 280, 312, 317, 318, 359, 371, 382
False: 4, 7, 31, 99, 103, 105, 139, 160, 164, 181, 215, 237, 244, 250, 255, 275, 287, 300 309, 328, 331,335, 362, 390, 399

Tm (Tough-mindedness), 36 items
True: 53, 126, 156, 320, 359, 380, 392, 412
False: 13, 20, 25, 40, 71, 99, 109, 110, 132, 145, 155, 159, 170, 191, 208, 211, 243, 252, 294, 306, 314, 326, 331, 357, 362, 385, 422, 425

B–MS (Baucom scale for masculinity), 54 items
True: 53, 87, 100, 108, 126, 202, 259, 269, 320, 359, 399
False: 7, 13, 27, 28, 31, 35, 38, 40, 58, 68, 70, 72, 76, 85, 91, 111, 124, 144, 145, 147, 177, 186, 187, 227, 232, 238, 240, 252, 258, 272, 284, 286, 301, 308, 309, 313, 334, 369, 383, 391, 418, 422, 429

B–FM (Baucom scale for femininity), 42 items
True: 110, 122, 146, 150, 151, 212, 230, 328, 348
False: 19, 26, 29, 33, 36, 39, 49, 78, 82, 87, 114, 117, 129, 143, 171, 196, 210, 211, 214, 239, 249, 263, 268, 274, 291, 340, 342, 347, 362, 377, 420, 428, 431

Anx (Leventhal scale for anxiety), 22 items
True: 15, 58, 90, 94, 156, 183, 236, 285, 306, 321, 327, 344, 353, 372, 378, 390, 398
False: 178, 190, 214, 246, 348

Nar (Wink-Gough scale for narcissism), 49 items
True: 4, 32, 39, 53, 60, 78, 80, 81, 102, 112, 128, 129,

130, 142, 146, 171, 175, 179, 206, 209, 225, 231, 250, 262, 267, 275, 293, 296, 307, 320, 327, 329, 375, 376, 397, 399, 403, 407, 412

False: 7, 151, 217, 230, 286, 304, 348, 380, 385, 427

D–SD (Dicken scale for social desirability), 32 items

True: 52, 95, 97, 108, 133, 140, 152, 168, 174, 242, 246, 276, 354, 371, 380, 389

False: 7, 44, 48, 70, 81, 101, 194, 219, 231, 233, 270, 294, 331, 335, 375, 419

D–AC (Dicken scale for aquiescence), 32 items

True: 7, 44, 48, 52, 70, 81, 95, 97, 101, 108, 133, 140, 152, 168, 174, 194, 219, 231, 233, 242, 246, 270, 276, 294, 331, 335, 354, 371, 375, 380, 389, 419

False: no items

Appendix

Normative Data

This appendix presents normative data on the 20 folk, 3 vector, and 13 special purpose or research scales for 52 samples of males and 42 samples of females. It would be difficult if not impossible for one person to test all of these samples. Many psychologists have been kind enough to make data from their own projects available, including in particular these: Frank Baron, William D. Campagna, Kenneth H. Craik, Marvin Dunnette, Mae S. Gowan, Wallace B. Hall, Morag B. Colvin Harris, Ravenna Helson, Robert Hogan, Keith Jacoby, Penelope Kegel-Flom, Donald W. MacKinnon, Mary Adele Monson, Michael D. Roberts, Eric Sanders, Norman D. Sundberg, Rhona Steinberg, and Ernst Wenk. Their generosity is gratefully acknowledged.

Male Samples ($N = 52$)

A. Basic normative sample

B. High school samples
1. General sample
2. National Science Fair delegates
3. Nominated as best citizens
4. Nominated as leaders
5. Nominated as most attractive
6. Nominated as most popular
7. Nominated as disciplinary problems

C. College samples
1. General sample
2. Majors in architecture
3. Majors in education
4. Majors in engineering
5. Premedical majors
6. Art institute students
7. West Point cadets

D. Graduate or professional school
1. Business administration
2. Counseling
3. Medicine
4. Nursing
5. Optometry
6. Pharmacy
7. Psychology
8. Social welfare

E. Occupational samples
1. Anesthesiologists
2. Architects
3. Bankers
4. Business executives
5. Correctional officers
6. Engineers
7. Irish entrepreneurs
8. Mathematicians
9. Military officers
10. Parole and probation officers
11. Police officers
12. Police officer applicants
13. Research scientists
14. Sales managers
15. Commercial writers
16. Creative writers
17. Writers of books for children
18. Critics of books for children

F. Other samples
1. Catholic priests
2. Rajneeshpuram residents
3. Members, club for inventors
4. Juvenile delinquents
5. Youth authority inmates
6. Adult prison inmates
7. Psychiatric patients
8. San Francisco area residents

G. Simulated protocols
1. Fake bad
2. Fake good
3. Randomly answered

Female Samples (*N* = 42)

A. Basic normative sample
B. High school samples
1. General sample
2. National Science Fair delegates

3. Nominated as best citizens
4. Nominated as leaders
5. Nominated as most attractive
6. Nominated as most popular
7. Nominated as disciplinary problems.

C. College samples
1. General sample
2. Majors in architecture
3. Majors in education
4. Majors in home economics
5. Premedical majors
6. Art institute students

D. Graduate or professional school
1. Business administration
2. Counseling
3. Law
4. Medicine
5. Nursing
6. Optometry
7. Pharmacy
8. Psychology
9. Social welfare

E. Occupational samples
1. Anesthesiologists
2. College counselors
3. Mathematicians
4. Police officer applicants
5. Registered nurses
6. Secondary school teachers
7. University clerical personnel
8. Commercial writers
9. Creative writers
10. Writers of books for children
11. Critics of books for children

F. Other samples
1. Rajneeshpuram residents
2. Juvenile delinquents
3. Adult prison inmates
4. Psychiatric patients
5. San Francisco area residents

G. Simulated protocols
1. Fake bad
2. Fake good
3. Randomly answered

CPI Means and Standard Deviations, Part 1: Male Samples

High School Students

Scale	Basic Normative Sample N=3,000		General N=4,611		National Science Fair Delegates N=363		Nominated as Best Citizens N=90		Nominated as Leaders N=90		Nominated as Most Attractive N=88		Nominated as Most Popular N=90		Nominated as Disciplinary Problems N=90		Scale
	M	SD	M	SD	M	SD	M	SD	M	SD	M	SD	M	SD	M	SD	
Do	19.41	5.25	18.31	5.83	22.63	5.85	22.57	6.11	22.86	6.13	20.42	6.26	20.84	6.34	17.80	5.06	Do
Cs	15.11	4.35	14.05	4.16	16.74	3.98	16.87	3.51	16.80	4.09	14.84	4.56	15.67	4.46	13.62	3.67	Cs
Sy	19.76	4.87	19.05	4.87	21.02	4.98	21.89	4.49	22.42	4.35	20.72	4.78	21.21	5.10	19.04	4.31	Sy
Sp	24.45	4.79	23.60	4.58	24.83	4.71	25.51	4.27	25.62	4.59	25.39	4.53	25.44	4.55	24.52	4.39	Sp
Sa	16.01	4.18	15.21	3.99	18.28	3.56	17.16	3.59	17.77	3.81	16.86	3.96	17.32	3.96	15.28	3.73	Sa
In	15.34	4.49	14.37	3.97	17.70	4.23	16.39	3.76	16.44	3.41	15.08	4.19	15.17	4.01	14.20	3.69	In
Em	19.07	4.70	17.92	4.09	20.46	4.53	19.56	3.90	20.20	4.48	18.62	4.09	19.92	4.72	17.51	3.95	Em
Re	23.98	5.35	24.14	5.14	27.16	4.62	28.32	3.22	27.77	4.52	24.20	5.09	26.02	5.03	19.51	4.56	Re
So	29.70	5.89	30.57	5.65	32.47	5.55	33.99	4.71	33.82	5.14	30.70	5.86	31.97	5.84	25.77	4.91	So
Sc	19.19	6.45	18.59	6.34	18.26	6.51	21.27	6.59	20.54	6.50	17.75	7.14	19.11	6.14	15.09	5.53	Sc
Gi	17.20	6.32	16.42	6.14	15.48	6.37	18.51	5.93	18.41	5.51	16.09	6.62	16.81	5.32	13.84	5.93	Gi
Cm	34.58	3.34	34.26	3.80	35.11	3.87	35.74	2.33	35.66	2.23	35.01	3.66	35.57	2.99	32.61	4.52	Cm
Wb	29.47	5.68	28.70	5.61	29.13	5.74	31.90	4.43	31.82	4.03	29.95	6.02	30.63	4.63	26.34	5.51	Wb
To	18.57	5.29	17.51	4.79	20.61	4.81	20.58	4.61	20.20	4.90	17.66	4.73	19.18	4.62	14.80	4.03	To
Ac	24.84	5.67	24.06	5.60	27.53	4.97	29.17	4.07	28.54	4.30	24.55	5.97	26.58	5.43	19.46	4.72	Ac
Ai	19.27	5.87	17.16	4.90	22.50	4.75	20.18	4.43	19.29	4.81	17.05	4.37	18.12	4.46	15.26	4.20	Ai
Ie	27.47	5.81	26.10	5.63	31.02	4.90	30.16	4.39	29.88	4.89	27.31	5.55	28.06	5.36	23.41	5.32	Ie
Py	14.55	3.78	13.89	3.35	16.86	3.18	16.17	3.13	15.47	3.37	14.07	3.43	14.68	3.13	12.79	2.73	Py
Fx	13.11	3.99	12.85	3.64	14.13	4.23	12.89	4.10	12.40	3.79	13.28	3.51	13.08	3.51	13.50	2.89	Fx
F/M	13.46	3.34	12.90	3.26	13.67	3.42	13.14	3.13	12.71	3.22	12.16	3.27	12.97	3.45	11.61	3.15	F/M
v.1	18.38	6.07	19.18	5.74	15.80	6.20	16.88	6.43	15.89	6.53	17.47	5.87	17.06	6.37	17.28	5.13	v.1
v.2	21.84	5.48	22.53	5.30	23.20	5.56	25.62	4.91	25.53	4.97	22.81	5.11	23.49	5.77	18.88	4.43	v.2
v.3	31.13	9.47	28.26	8.35	34.79	8.30	33.42	8.42	33.03	8.42	28.70	8.34	30.49	8.01	25.20	6.68	v.3
Mp	17.54	5.99	16.12	5.26	19.08	5.35	20.13	4.98	20.28	5.11	17.01	5.77	18.44	5.18	14.38	4.41	Mp
Wo	27.94	5.57	26.99	5.31	27.79	5.42	29.90	4.65	29.66	4.51	27.27	5.47	28.86	4.51	23.50	4.74	Wo
CT	19.57	5.49	18.40	4.43	22.50	5.19	19.22	4.52	19.76	4.77	19.24	4.27	19.28	4.01	18.92	3.96	CT
Lp	44.03	10.61	42.02	9.72	46.30	10.26	50.01	8.40	50.62	8.26	44.81	10.69	47.22	9.68	38.21	8.07	Lp
Ami	21.81	5.43	21.49	5.15	21.10	5.55	24.00	4.91	24.13	4.92	21.92	5.41	23.37	4.72	18.60	4.71	Ami
Leo	24.99	4.04	25.23	3.97	26.02	4.26	27.12	3.36	27.02	3.42	25.89	4.06	26.48	3.46	23.89	3.82	Leo
Tm	20.07	5.85	18.94	5.27	20.69	5.34	22.74	4.94	22.13	4.76	19.65	6.24	20.73	5.18	17.62	4.50	Tm
B-MS	34.51	8.56	33.07	7.92	35.50	8.69	38.17	7.03	38.91	7.06	35.89	8.78	36.38	8.14	32.82	7.17	B-MS
B-FM	25.06	5.04	24.09	4.85	25.72	4.52	26.43	4.21	25.87	4.27	23.55	5.33	24.68	4.57	20.00	4.45	B-FM
Anx	6.04	2.52	6.10	2.59	6.39	2.73	5.11	2.04	4.96	2.11	5.49	2.42	5.16	2.24	6.88	2.82	Anx
Nar	24.04	6.35	24.28	6.05	26.57	6.06	23.59	6.07	24.17	6.19	25.60	6.13	24.59	5.91	27.50	5.85	Nar
D-SD	17.71	4.78	16.93	4.75	18.10	4.72	19.39	4.45	19.94	4.43	17.00	5.22	18.39	4.71	14.77	4.11	D-SD
D-AC	15.90	3.78	16.49	3.65	16.89	3.33	15.99	3.24	15.66	3.45	16.64	3.10	15.94	3.14	16.59	3.36	D-AC

CPI Means and Standard Deviations, Part 1: Male Samples continued

College Students: Programs of Study

Scale	General N = 3,235 M	SD	Architecture N = 125 M	SD	Education N = 167 M	SD	Engineering N = 66 M	SD	Premedical N = 70 M	SD	Art Institute N = 44 M	SD	Military Academy N = 1,413 M	SD	Scale
Do	22.45	6.22	21.57	6.18	25.02	4.96	22.32	6.18	25.29	5.52	17.36	6.38	25.21	5.22	Do
Cs	18.26	3.61	17.91	3.46	20.68	2.90	18.80	3.47	21.14	2.89	14.93	3.72	18.63	3.31	Cs
Sy	21.67	4.81	21.70	4.55	23.70	3.86	20.97	4.61	24.33	3.75	17.77	4.53	23.84	3.96	Sy
Sp	26.72	4.54	26.44	5.08	28.49	3.89	26.95	4.26	28.91	4.26	25.16	4.58	26.82	4.14	Sp
Sa	18.17	3.83	18.40	4.05	19.16	3.43	17.55	3.32	19.89	3.06	17.18	3.51	19.14	3.31	Sa
In	17.33	4.05	17.98	4.19	19.12	3.07	18.92	4.10	19.03	3.05	17.32	5.15	17.60	3.59	In
Em	21.99	4.38	21.63	4.38	24.32	3.57	21.70	4.41	25.26	3.65	21.93	3.08	21.75	4.02	Em
Re	27.09	4.35	25.76	4.92	29.10	3.49	28.00	4.06	30.26	3.28	18.16	3.70	29.16	3.58	Re
So	32.00	4.84	32.26	5.69	33.28	4.20	32.48	5.28	34.20	4.52	25.55	4.05	33.78	4.47	So
Sc	20.15	6.05	19.02	6.26	23.44	5.06	23.00	5.70	23.07	5.03	15.34	5.44	20.62	6.23	Sc
Gi	17.85	6.17	16.80	5.95	22.07	5.76	19.62	5.56	20.83	5.74	13.18	5.07	19.66	6.40	Gi
Cm	35.09	2.71	34.37	3.59	35.02	2.30	34.77	3.48	36.29	1.32	31.68	4.49	36.05	2.04	Cm
Wb	31.35	4.93	29.94	5.38	34.74	3.04	33.17	3.95	34.56	2.55	25.73	6.54	32.39	4.40	Wb
To	22.36	4.18	22.25	3.84	25.19	3.32	24.88	3.13	25.80	2.94	18.43	4.44	22.08	4.01	To
Ac	27.74	4.71	27.04	5.02	30.33	3.92	29.32	4.63	31.84	3.36	19.70	4.22	29.45	4.44	Ac
Ai	23.83	4.63	23.82	4.21	26.94	3.82	26.53	3.43	28.24	3.19	22.89	4.72	21.94	4.16	Ai
Ie	31.52	4.54	31.30	4.47	33.93	3.45	33.45	3.61	35.13	2.63	28.23	5.05	32.27	4.20	Ie
Py	16.62	3.32	16.37	2.90	18.75	2.91	19.42	2.90	19.67	2.22	15.36	3.22	16.44	2.91	Py
Fx	14.34	4.41	15.14	4.44	15.43	4.01	15.79	3.05	15.09	3.71	17.68	4.55	11.29	3.71	Fx
F/M	13.48	3.59	14.22	3.75	13.88	3.36	12.42	2.83	13.17	3.18	16.48	4.11	11.89	3.16	F/M
v.1	16.00	5.97	16.06	6.14	15.16	5.40	17.29	6.21	14.63	5.09	17.77	5.72	13.91	5.24	v.1
v.2	22.44	5.80	21.50	6.12	23.13	5.04	22.17	5.77	24.84	5.43	13.98	4.81	26.35	4.67	v.2
v.3	38.02	7.84	36.80	7.32	44.62	6.24	42.77	6.39	45.01	5.38	33.32	7.86	36.57	7.53	v.3
Mp	21.51	5.31	20.26	5.06	25.49	4.38	24.12	4.79	26.03	3.99	14.45	4.49	22.54	5.12	Mp
Wo	30.30	4.76	28.31	4.91	34.03	3.34	32.08	4.49	33.86	3.04	23.45	5.35	31.25	4.53	Wo
CT	22.65	5.46	23.99	5.53	25.09	4.41	24.55	4.98	24.86	4.45	27.45	5.29	19.14	4.12	CT
Lp	49.59	9.73	47.28	9.55	55.31	6.76	51.61	9.26	56.76	6.76	38.11	8.72	53.23	8.99	Lp
Ami	23.91	5.06	22.37	5.43	27.35	4.19	26.33	4.57	27.67	3.83	17.91	4.84	24.40	4.78	Ami
Leo	25.23	4.30	25.14	4.48	25.43	3.62	25.36	4.82	25.99	3.72	19.34	3.82	28.18	3.96	Leo
Tm	22.29	5.42	21.67	4.83	26.13	4.32	24.76	4.65	26.53	3.87	16.48	5.31	23.56	5.31	Tm
B-MS	37.96	8.54	36.92	8.08	43.08	6.47	39.71	7.90	42.93	6.47	31.82	8.70	40.48	7.53	B-MS
B-FM	26.51	4.51	27.28	4.85	28.90	4.37	26.80	4.35	28.24	4.62	24.18	4.77	26.06	4.30	B-FM
Anx	5.32	2.14	5.95	2.44	4.44	1.48	4.98	1.93	4.27	1.50	7.32	2.85	4.88	1.93	Anx
Nar	24.26	6.16	26.14	6.74	20.32	5.87	22.24	5.84	21.97	5.49	28.82	6.62	25.51	5.76	Nar
D-SD	19.34	4.58	18.28	4.81	22.60	4.06	20.36	3.90	22.53	3.98	15.00	3.48	21.05	4.72	D-SD
D-AC	15.21	3.40	15.30	2.96	13.87	2.44	13.30	3.41	14.10	2.97	16.00	4.48	16.45	3.23	D-AC

CPI Means and Standard Deviations, Part 1: Male Samples continued

Graduate or Professional School

Scale	Business Administration N = 71		Counseling N = 67		Medicine N = 551		Nursing N = 149		Optometry N = 100		Pharmacy N = 439		Psychology N = 623		Social Welfare N = 254		Scale
	M	SD	M	SD	M	SD	M	SD	M	SD	M	SD	M	SD	M	SD	
Do	25.56	5.38	25.36	5.45	24.19	5.52	21.49	6.27	24.49	6.04	21.35	5.94	23.63	5.44	24.53	4.96	Do
Cs	19.56	3.59	18.67	3.97	19.98	3.01	18.36	3.34	19.12	3.55	16.62	3.71	20.46	2.92	19.74	2.91	Cs
Sy	22.92	3.98	23.54	4.34	22.67	4.06	21.17	4.75	23.06	4.65	20.61	4.53	22.07	4.19	23.60	3.78	Sy
Sp	29.03	3.91	27.93	4.31	28.08	4.08	26.21	4.48	26.97	4.44	25.72	4.73	29.05	3.94	28.71	3.99	Sp
Sa	19.92	3.83	20.07	3.44	19.25	3.49	18.26	3.97	19.02	3.14	17.42	3.66	19.34	3.36	18.84	3.17	Sa
In	20.70	3.81	19.00	4.11	19.38	3.74	17.74	4.21	19.15	4.03	17.61	4.16	20.66	3.53	18.55	3.27	In
Em	24.23	4.45	24.64	4.32	23.88	4.39	22.01	4.29	24.10	4.48	21.26	4.58	24.86	3.77	24.63	4.01	Em
Re	25.21	4.18	25.01	4.31	28.16	3.82	26.46	4.55	28.94	3.53	25.36	4.19	26.95	4.02	28.37	3.44	Re
So	31.99	4.64	30.97	4.54	33.10	4.20	31.36	5.57	34.50	3.77	32.22	4.47	30.64	4.19	31.56	4.13	So
Sc	21.00	5.61	20.12	5.56	21.90	5.60	19.64	6.21	25.86	4.67	22.19	5.94	20.36	5.29	22.58	5.15	Sc
Gi	19.15	5.85	18.39	5.60	19.13	5.86	16.54	5.93	23.35	6.46	19.38	6.41	16.79	5.41	20.10	5.58	Gi
Cm	34.87	2.42	36.31	2.10	35.18	2.44	34.86	3.21	35.72	1.65	34.79	3.13	34.53	2.46	34.76	2.58	Cm
Wb	32.90	3.96	31.64	4.86	32.97	3.94	30.47	5.54	34.30	3.83	31.36	5.17	32.18	4.06	33.40	4.15	Wb
To	22.70	4.04	23.13	4.30	25.08	3.52	23.11	4.30	26.18	4.05	22.58	4.55	25.58	3.52	25.47	3.42	To
Ac	29.31	3.88	28.78	4.06	29.76	3.95	27.32	4.91	31.10	3.80	28.28	3.97	28.65	3.87	29.06	3.88	Ac
Ai	26.99	4.32	26.45	4.83	27.94	3.80	25.35	4.39	28.03	4.56	25.30	4.86	29.90	3.24	27.54	3.74	Ai
Ie	33.39	3.55	32.34	4.42	33.94	3.63	31.87	4.50	34.05	4.52	30.69	4.82	35.30	3.44	33.58	3.79	Ie
Py	17.86	2.96	17.75	3.66	19.41	2.88	16.97	3.75	19.00	2.98	17.31	3.37	21.32	2.89	19.45	2.90	Py
Fx	15.61	4.05	15.54	4.11	16.26	4.15	15.65	4.00	14.45	4.23	14.30	4.32	19.09	3.94	17.16	4.17	Fx
F/M	13.75	3.40	13.69	3.96	13.46	3.34	14.47	3.53	14.76	2.79	14.96	3.08	14.20	3.14	14.15	3.04	F/M
v.1	12.17	5.73	12.91	5.58	15.35	5.81	16.36	6.41	15.94	5.90	17.88	5.82	14.78	5.76	15.26	5.48	v.1
v.2	21.85	4.72	21.94	4.76	22.39	5.20	20.81	5.92	24.67	5.35	22.12	5.29	18.28	5.04	20.97	5.42	v.2
v.3	40.80	7.98	40.19	9.45	43.39	6.89	39.54	8.03	45.81	8.13	39.38	8.94	45.49	6.13	44.18	6.40	v.3
Mp	23.01	5.08	23.40	4.75	24.18	4.81	21.64	5.37	25.49	5.52	20.97	5.55	24.27	4.33	26.12	4.05	Mp
Wo	30.68	4.33	29.88	4.75	32.24	4.10	29.79	5.50	33.83	3.79	30.58	4.89	31.36	4.01	33.04	3.90	Wo
CT	25.34	5.16	24.93	6.09	25.55	5.37	24.32	5.05	23.98	5.27	23.12	5.21	29.88	4.67	26.32	4.77	CT
Lp	54.07	7.92	53.00	8.21	53.26	8.04	48.32	10.15	55.65	8.68	48.30	9.61	51.84	7.77	54.21	7.38	Lp
Ami	23.97	4.86	23.06	5.18	25.68	4.53	23.50	5.67	27.56	4.54	24.19	5.00	23.73	4.54	26.41	4.46	Ami
Leo	26.01	4.37	26.55	3.76	24.54	4.01	24.83	4.27	27.49	3.50	26.04	3.71	21.94	3.87	24.59	3.59	Leo
Tm	25.83	4.35	23.42	4.51	24.74	4.81	22.11	5.41	26.30	5.18	22.84	5.22	25.14	4.37	25.66	4.24	Tm
B-MS	41.48	7.21	40.82	7.87	41.09	7.03	37.46	8.21	42.35	7.73	37.73	8.40	41.08	7.22	41.52	6.49	B-MS
B-FM	26.66	3.89	26.09	5.04	27.70	4.28	27.23	4.89	30.80	3.58	28.83	4.32	27.60	4.35	29.09	3.91	B-FM
Anx	5.06	1.69	4.96	1.89	4.84	1.73	5.74	2.19	4.77	1.75	5.60	2.15	5.10	1.81	4.61	1.67	Anx
Nar	27.68	6.17	25.88	6.79	23.93	6.10	24.23	6.65	21.06	5.68	22.86	6.21	25.11	6.10	20.54	5.72	Nar
D-SD	21.15	4.39	21.03	4.25	20.60	4.18	18.58	4.45	23.13	4.55	20.01	4.51	19.94	3.59	21.44	4.03	D-SD
D-AC	15.27	3.39	14.73	3.40	14.27	3.28	14.83	3.54	13.83	3.22	14.81	3.68	13.98	3.27	13.47	3.04	D-AC

CPI Means and Standard Deviations, Part 1: Male Samples continued

Occupational Samples

Scale	Anesthesiologists N=98 M	SD	Architects N=124 M	SD	Bankers N=49 M	SD	Business Executives N=185 M	SD	Correctional Officers N=221 M	SD	Engineers N=47 M	SD	Irish Entrepreneurs N=37 M	SD	Mathematicians N=57 M	SD	Military Officers N=343 M	SD	Scale
Do	23.94	5.46	24.76	5.19	25.18	4.38	24.94	5.22	22.46	5.43	23.26	6.28	27.76	5.11	21.00	5.05	26.17	5.09	Do
Cs	18.04	2.70	19.35	2.86	18.63	3.04	19.05	3.70	16.81	3.85	18.79	3.52	18.54	3.19	18.95	2.98	19.03	3.31	Cs
Sy	22.52	4.15	20.80	4.20	22.12	4.17	22.66	4.07	20.95	4.28	21.45	5.55	21.81	3.98	19.44	4.74	23.56	4.04	Sy
Sp	27.78	3.84	26.28	3.78	26.47	3.69	26.35	3.99	24.37	4.08	25.85	5.26	25.30	5.09	25.74	4.53	27.64	4.03	Sp
Sa	19.16	3.46	18.16	3.59	17.20	3.65	17.59	3.94	16.32	3.78	17.96	4.24	19.19	3.65	16.84	3.46	19.03	3.31	Sa
In	18.35	3.30	20.03	3.73	18.94	2.93	18.43	3.26	17.08	3.31	18.77	4.04	20.11	3.13	20.18	3.76	19.05	2.96	In
Em	22.84	4.01	21.73	3.62	20.69	3.96	21.91	5.18	18.84	4.27	21.21	4.50	22.59	4.09	21.72	3.53	21.95	4.64	Em
Re	26.89	3.16	28.79	3.47	29.39	3.05	28.69	4.27	27.03	4.42	29.02	3.54	28.22	3.34	29.54	3.31	28.93	3.57	Re
So	32.53	3.82	32.37	3.99	35.33	4.07	33.17	4.11	31.33	4.55	35.30	4.42	33.05	4.73	32.74	3.76	32.13	4.45	So
Sc	22.71	4.60	22.27	5.31	24.51	6.08	24.62	5.86	23.42	5.96	24.09	5.09	23.08	5.10	23.68	5.90	21.58	5.92	Sc
Gi	19.78	4.64	17.85	5.65	21.65	6.88	22.71	6.58	21.45	6.23	21.32	5.12	21.08	5.13	17.82	5.83	20.36	5.81	Gi
Cm	36.51	2.33	35.29	2.00	36.27	1.44	35.82	1.72	35.58	3.18	36.43	1.36	35.89	2.20	34.40	2.69	36.27	2.07	Cm
Wb	32.79	3.35	32.78	3.49	35.04	2.12	34.91	2.87	33.20	4.26	34.19	2.89	33.11	4.33	32.60	4.33	34.19	3.33	Wb
To	24.17	3.07	23.91	3.48	24.27	3.54	23.68	4.00	20.49	4.51	23.94	3.31	23.30	3.86	25.00	3.60	22.42	3.71	To
Ac	30.16	3.36	29.63	3.69	30.24	3.58	29.92	4.46	28.30	4.71	31.06	3.33	30.16	3.28	28.84	3.86	29.44	4.03	Ac
Ai	27.93	2.96	25.31	3.88	25.14	3.86	24.70	4.90	21.11	4.64	25.98	3.77	23.84	3.84	28.65	3.68	23.04	4.00	Ai
Ie	33.51	3.51	32.55	3.54	32.86	3.96	32.57	4.44	30.04	4.82	33.77	3.43	31.35	4.59	34.12	3.98	32.05	4.05	Ie
Py	18.44	2.44	19.07	2.72	17.80	3.20	18.26	3.02	16.18	2.82	19.55	1.94	16.84	2.96	21.05	2.47	17.07	2.64	Py
Fx	14.33	4.22	13.68	4.67	11.71	4.08	13.07	4.09	10.78	3.81	13.09	3.85	12.65	3.75	16.14	4.21	11.73	3.61	Fx
F/M	12.73	3.44	15.61	3.06	13.59	3.32	13.28	2.93	13.14	2.94	11.43	3.27	15.32	2.93	16.53	3.09	11.46	3.00	F/M
v.1	15.43	5.60	16.69	5.26	17.08	5.00	16.90	5.60	19.06	5.84	17.98	6.38	13.49	5.83	19.56	5.78	14.43	5.74	v.1
v.2	23.85	4.27	23.50	5.08	25.78	5.16	24.83	5.06	25.14	4.83	25.34	4.66	26.22	3.89	21.75	4.42	25.58	4.45	v.2
v.3	41.95	5.82	39.99	6.12	40.57	7.41	41.01	8.71	34.47	7.90	41.79	6.60	37.51	6.79	43.32	6.92	37.88	7.16	v.3
Mp	23.93	3.99	24.79	4.08	26.41	4.49	25.46	4.82	21.57	5.22	24.32	4.16	26.62	4.46	23.91	4.20	24.57	4.78	Mp
Wo	32.22	3.29	31.66	3.69	34.63	3.09	34.14	3.67	32.19	4.83	33.47	2.95	31.89	3.71	32.37	4.39	33.20	3.93	Wo
CT	22.70	4.52	24.15	5.63	21.10	5.24	21.14	5.18	18.05	4.54	20.19	4.51	22.62	4.58	27.39	4.92	19.37	4.44	CT
Lp	53.45	7.02	53.71	7.27	56.41	6.73	55.71	7.51	51.91	8.45	54.19	7.32	57.16	8.50	49.77	7.96	56.05	7.38	Lp
Ami	25.55	3.91	25.35	4.45	27.82	3.87	28.06	4.35	25.03	4.60	26.91	3.01	25.03	4.39	25.63	4.77	25.87	4.59	Ami
Leo	27.44	3.44	22.33	3.93	26.78	3.48	26.30	3.55	26.81	3.68	27.91	3.34	26.73	3.25	21.47	3.22	27.46	3.51	Leo
Tm	25.85	4.02	24.89	4.36	27.71	3.95	26.20	4.81	24.62	4.83	26.23	4.71	26.68	4.44	24.30	4.84	25.95	4.39	Tm
B-MS	41.12	6.86	38.27	7.15	41.00	6.52	41.63	6.90	38.67	7.24	41.15	7.75	39.97	7.27	37.65	8.43	42.15	6.09	B-MS
B-FM	27.73	4.45	29.39	4.01	29.78	3.21	28.45	4.13	27.98	4.38	27.68	3.94	29.59	3.40	30.63	3.65	26.47	4.51	B-FM
Anx	4.66	1.49	5.23	2.00	4.51	1.42	4.19	1.57	4.64	2.07	4.68	1.63	5.27	2.21	5.89	1.84	4.72	1.69	Anx
Nar	24.04	5.02	24.65	5.76	20.43	5.45	20.82	6.29	20.91	5.73	23.36	6.05	25.89	5.56	20.91	6.11	23.82	6.02	Nar
D–SD	21.07	3.48	20.58	3.87	22.04	3.56	22.34	4.55	20.33	4.22	22.00	3.76	22.59	2.98	20.00	3.92	21.72	4.11	D–SD
D–AC	14.13	3.20	14.29	3.02	13.18	2.86	14.14	3.36	14.98	3.46	13.91	3.06	15.78	2.62	13.19	3.93	15.01	3.15	D–AC

CPI Means and Standard Deviations, Part 1: Male Samples continued

Occupational Samples

Scale	Parole and Probation Officers N=65 M	SD	Police Officers N=366 M	SD	Police Officer Applicants N=883 M	SD	Research Scientists N=45 M	SD	Sales Managers N=85 M	SD	Commercial Writers N=14 M	SD	Creative Writers N=19 M	SD	Children's Book Authors N=29 M	SD	Children's Book Critics N=25 M	SD	Scale
Do	28.45	3.65	23.88	5.43	25.52	4.70	24.93	4.87	26.84	4.63	22.79	6.78	23.84	5.63	21.72	5.26	24.80	5.52	Do
Cs	18.98	2.81	16.94	3.43	18.03	3.12	20.91	2.58	19.07	2.92	18.50	4.64	20.26	3.16	18.93	2.62	18.28	3.17	Cs
Sy	23.57	3.48	22.13	4.14	23.14	3.49	22.76	4.28	24.62	3.10	19.71	5.54	22.42	3.99	20.00	4.24	20.60	5.35	Sy
Sp	26.54	3.85	25.92	3.98	25.77	3.63	28.53	3.71	27.21	3.70	25.00	4.59	27.05	4.26	25.97	3.68	24.84	5.47	Sp
Sa	19.78	2.76	18.71	3.33	18.98	2.96	18.96	3.50	19.46	2.39	17.00	4.06	19.26	4.21	17.86	3.95	18.36	3.72	Sa
In	19.85	2.63	18.47	3.43	19.46	2.79	20.69	2.62	18.41	3.13	18.71	3.36	19.79	3.68	20.41	3.51	20.68	3.31	In
Em	23.82	4.63	20.81	4.33	22.46	4.10	23.80	4.03	21.91	4.17	22.21	4.48	23.37	3.39	22.83	3.92	22.72	5.22	Em
Re	29.18	3.84	27.13	3.92	27.93	3.91	30.07	2.78	28.20	3.97	26.93	5.36	27.00	4.86	27.00	3.27	28.08	3.49	Re
So	32.48	4.60	32.56	3.99	32.31	3.69	31.69	4.16	33.58	3.89	28.43	5.33	29.42	4.85	30.14	4.61	31.12	3.15	So
Sc	23.08	5.89	24.51	5.51	26.11	5.44	23.67	4.63	23.21	5.09	20.21	7.15	18.74	6.84	20.86	6.66	21.84	5.76	Sc
Gi	21.11	6.41	22.47	6.40	25.08	6.16	19.51	4.94	21.81	5.17	15.64	6.56	13.68	6.10	15.24	6.04	18.00	6.09	Gi
Cm	36.20	1.62	36.22	1.79	35.77	2.54	35.71	1.75	36.95	1.31	35.00	2.32	33.47	2.37	33.59	3.06	33.88	2.67	Cm
Wb	34.22	3.64	34.17	3.56	34.44	3.74	34.73	2.47	35.13	2.58	31.07	5.90	29.11	5.22	30.34	4.35	31.64	4.17	Wb
To	24.57	4.02	21.84	4.43	22.25	4.66	26.27	3.19	22.45	3.78	23.07	4.98	24.26	3.78	24.41	4.21	25.52	3.40	To
Ac	30.26	3.75	29.08	4.16	30.57	4.00	30.29	3.37	30.64	3.63	28.64	4.31	27.00	4.86	27.28	4.03	29.48	3.75	Ac
Ai	25.03	4.74	23.05	4.68	24.20	4.72	29.16	2.70	21.84	4.01	24.57	3.41	26.89	3.25	27.03	3.40	26.52	4.06	Ai
Ie	32.69	4.18	30.36	4.22	31.81	4.46	35.16	2.98	31.93	3.97	37.64	4.03	33.79	3.87	33.03	3.61	33.60	4.69	Ie
Py	18.78	2.64	16.72	2.91	17.70	2.73	22.16	2.64	17.15	2.32	17.64	3.00	19.37	2.81	18.69	2.98	18.88	3.40	Py
Fx	12.89	4.20	12.24	4.00	12.54	3.74	16.38	4.33	10.80	3.17	13.07	3.85	16.53	5.37	16.76	4.10	16.56	5.40	Fx
F/M	13.06	2.83	12.05	2.73	12.56	2.64	14.29	2.56	12.85	2.93	15.57	2.90	17.63	2.81	18.83	2.84	19.28	3.54	F/M
v.1	13.91	4.91	16.58	5.63	15.64	4.95	15.42	5.52	14.14	5.52	16.43	8.02	15.32	6.27	17.90	4.48	15.00	6.16	v.1
v.2	24.71	5.37	23.73	4.69	24.32	4.37	21.62	4.74	27.29	4.58	21.79	6.12	19.74	5.58	19.03	4.61	21.28	4.73	v.2
v.3	41.43	7.96	38.35	8.10	41.28	8.28	46.00	5.32	37.27	7.70	36.86	8.32	38.26	6.31	39.31	7.57	42.08	8.10	v.3
Mp	26.17	4.94	22.90	5.34	23.70	5.20	27.11	3.62	25.05	4.60	23.21	5.85	23.21	4.55	22.79	5.09	25.28	4.38	Mp
Wo	32.66	4.49	33.07	3.87	33.85	4.03	34.22	3.02	33.60	2.94	30.07	6.03	27.74	4.93	28.69	4.36	30.00	3.75	Wo
CT	22.43	5.25	19.60	4.74	20.90	4.63	27.62	5.06	19.09	3.79	24.36	5.57	29.21	4.37	28.21	3.63	29.20	5.49	CT
Lp	57.68	6.20	54.09	8.15	56.67	7.21	55.96	6.10	58.12	6.35	49.43	11.71	49.47	9.66	48.55	7.56	52.32	8.47	Lp
Ami	25.74	5.30	25.73	4.32	26.33	4.47	26.98	3.56	26.34	3.92	22.50	6.63	22.37	5.18	22.62	5.98	23.72	4.12	Ami
Leo	28.57	3.48	32.03	3.60	31.49	3.49	22.93	4.17	27.92	3.03	22.57	4.05	20.53	4.35	21.45	4.25	23.52	3.16	Leo
Tm	27.08	4.61	26.18	4.83	27.42	4.17	27.29	3.79	26.59	4.40	23.14	5.30	22.74	4.89	23.66	4.34	25.48	4.93	Tm
B-MS	43.98	5.37	42.54	6.86	44.48	5.86	41.96	6.20	43.96	5.25	36.14	8.72	37.05	8.13	35.79	6.67	37.08	8.27	B-MS
B-FM	29.77	5.39	27.59	4.05	28.53	3.90	29.07	3.08	27.62	3.85	28.21	4.34	29.37	4.59	30.86	3.90	31.40	3.32	B-FM
Anx	4.29	1.38	4.19	1.53	4.22	1.77	4.76	1.35	3.76	1.27	5.71	2.49	5.89	2.62	5.90	1.88	5.60	2.00	Anx
Nar	23.11	5.66	22.43	5.72	21.52	5.57	22.98	5.08	23.45	4.59	24.00	6.49	25.37	6.57	24.24	7.36	22.56	6.29	Nar
D-SD	22.37	3.94	22.30	4.05	23.69	3.89	21.69	3.34	23.36	3.13	19.86	4.87	17.79	4.98	19.10	4.17	19.96	4.27	D-SD
D-AC	13.66	3.58	13.96	3.14	14.02	3.11	12.89	3.25	15.34	2.88	14.43	3.65	14.32	2.93	14.62	2.87	13.40	3.11	D-AC

CPI Means and Standard Deviations, Part 1: Male Samples continued

Other Samples

Scale	Catholic Priests N=41 M	SD	Members, Inventors Club N=14 M	SD	Rajneeshpuram Residents N=33 M	SD	Juvenile Delinquents N=76 M	SD	Youth Authority Prison Inmates N=2,899 M	SD	Adult Prison Inmates N=196 M	SD	Psychiatric Patients N=41 M	SD	San Francisco Area Residents N=261 M	SD	Scale
Do	24.66	6.01	24.36	5.08	20.70	4.69	19.93	6.06	16.39	6.13	18.28	5.03	17.88	6.44	23.59	6.01	Do
Cs	18.54	3.56	17.93	3.52	17.27	2.80	14.75	4.12	13.32	4.20	15.05	3.92	14.73	4.58	17.18	3.76	Cs
Sy	22.24	4.05	20.14	3.68	21.91	3.97	20.66	4.36	18.90	4.86	19.84	4.39	17.83	4.68	21.04	4.67	Sy
Sp	24.88	4.83	22.79	3.96	29.24	3.15	25.26	4.99	23.36	4.63	23.67	4.29	20.56	5.63	26.63	4.30	Sp
Sa	18.29	3.50	17.07	3.17	18.55	3.16	17.17	3.83	15.31	4.05	16.48	3.39	14.39	4.52	18.07	3.79	Sa
In	18.39	3.77	19.79	2.81	21.94	2.82	15.62	3.86	13.74	4.17	14.55	3.98	14.63	5.57	19.08	4.00	In
Em	22.73	5.19	20.14	4.24	22.85	3.32	19.09	4.34	17.33	4.20	17.53	4.01	18.02	4.06	21.71	4.59	Em
Re	28.73	2.83	27.64	2.24	21.12	3.98	18.51	4.52	18.68	5.49	19.49	5.85	23.02	5.33	24.40	5.12	Re
So	33.20	3.94	30.29	4.89	26.21	3.94	22.21	5.09	22.53	5.44	22.82	5.30	27.51	6.26	30.07	5.49	So
Sc	24.15	5.05	25.36	6.11	19.24	5.45	16.33	6.56	18.24	6.49	18.31	7.29	21.88	6.99	20.53	6.12	Sc
Gi	20.44	5.18	22.71	7.55	17.21	5.24	16.28	6.05	17.72	6.34	17.28	6.50	20.27	7.44	17.22	6.00	Gi
Cm	36.00	1.53	35.36	1.82	31.48	3.69	34.24	3.11	34.15	3.15	32.92	4.60	31.56	5.44	35.02	2.91	Cm
Wb	33.73	3.40	33.21	4.37	32.76	3.04	28.32	5.89	27.27	6.15	27.12	6.68	27.76	7.40	31.59	5.05	Wb
To	24.78	3.91	21.36	3.65	21.18	4.00	15.51	4.38	14.61	5.10	14.77	5.03	19.02	5.17	21.50	4.87	To
Ac	30.63	3.31	27.79	3.70	21.88	4.16	22.58	6.09	21.33	5.95	21.88	6.04	24.27	6.21	27.23	5.06	Ac
Ai	25.51	4.54	22.64	3.30	26.76	2.66	18.21	5.25	16.56	4.77	17.88	4.45	19.24	5.17	24.28	5.01	Ai
Ie	32.07	4.37	31.50	2.90	32.33	2.94	26.89	5.52	24.93	5.80	26.46	5.67	25.85	5.91	31.05	4.95	Ie
Py	17.56	3.27	16.43	3.34	18.15	2.77	13.13	3.40	11.97	3.55	12.76	3.48	14.15	4.02	17.08	3.59	Py
Fx	13.85	4.69	13.14	4.94	19.61	3.33	11.71	3.76	12.36	3.40	12.21	3.66	12.24	4.16	13.74	4.30	Fx
F/M	15.22	3.47	13.43	3.37	14.55	2.55	12.58	3.63	13.16	3.15	13.62	3.36	15.66	3.69	13.75	3.33	F/M
v.1	16.05	6.29	16.43	5.33	16.48	6.00	16.43	6.02	19.34	5.89	18.02	4.81	19.83	6.34	15.56	6.10	v.1
v.2	25.34	3.85	24.36	4.75	14.64	4.19	18.78	5.46	18.97	5.40	19.44	5.88	21.12	5.94	20.56	5.40	v.2
v.3	41.54	7.55	38.14	5.16	41.58	5.53	28.08	8.88	26.81	8.99	26.51	8.90	32.66	9.85	37.33	8.39	v.3
Mp	25.22	4.47	22.57	3.23	19.18	4.62	16.33	5.05	14.16	5.55	15.51	5.44	17.85	5.26	21.47	5.42	Mp
Wo	33.27	3.71	32.07	4.87	30.24	3.47	26.28	5.37	25.59	5.79	25.97	6.02	26.41	6.28	30.32	5.20	Wo
CT	22.78	4.75	21.21	5.51	30.15	3.60	20.36	4.48	17.24	4.25	18.47	4.41	19.83	5.19	22.88	5.84	CT
Lp	54.05	8.48	52.07	7.42	47.58	6.07	42.83	11.10	38.51	10.64	40.77	10.30	40.88	12.33	50.20	9.83	Lp
Ami	27.34	3.79	24.71	3.73	24.00	3.65	17.16	5.33	18.18	5.58	17.97	5.37	21.12	6.18	23.28	5.65	Ami
Leo	25.02	3.74	25.21	4.34	23.03	3.14	24.63	3.83	24.51	4.00	23.64	3.82	23.59	4.67	25.13	4.34	Leo
Tm	24.71	5.51	25.50	4.13	24.00	4.33	20.28	5.73	18.39	5.70	19.54	5.45	20.37	7.61	24.27	5.48	Tm
B-MS	39.15	8.49	39.07	6.83	40.45	6.56	36.28	8.93	32.11	8.80	34.03	8.07	31.80	11.11	39.45	7.92	B-MS
B-FM	29.44	3.67	27.07	3.81	26.45	3.76	22.16	5.15	22.57	4.63	22.26	5.49	26.34	5.78	26.87	4.95	B-FM
Anx	5.10	1.80	4.93	1.86	5.48	1.15	6.57	2.73	7.35	2.87	7.18	2.99	7.27	3.41	5.26	2.16	Anx
Nar	20.54	6.20	23.07	6.53	24.55	6.31	27.59	6.68	23.63	6.26	25.62	6.52	21.24	7.22	26.10	6.49	Nar
D-SD	21.83	3.42	21.00	4.08	18.09	3.79	17.13	4.46	16.33	4.71	16.65	4.55	18.46	4.82	19.54	4.04	D-SD
D-AC	15.29	2.99	13.86	3.21	12.15	3.56	16.76	3.21	15.34	3.63	16.37	3.58	15.83	4.30	14.82	3.35	D-AC

CPI Means and Standard Deviations, Part 1: Male Samples continued

Simulated Protocols

Scale	Fake Good N=50 M	Fake Good N=50 SD	Fake Bad N=50 M	Fake Bad N=50 SD	Theoretical Values for Total Randomization M	Theoretical Values for Total Randomization SD	Scale
Do	29.84	4.91	12.70	6.73	18.00	3.00	Do
Cs	21.44	3.49	8.72	3.62	14.00	2.65	Cs
Sy	24.72	3.62	11.70	4.61	16.00	2.83	Sy
Sp	25.00	3.60	15.30	5.21	19.00	3.08	Sp
Sa	19.64	2.50	12.48	4.03	14.00	2.65	Sa
In	19.84	2.81	9.40	4.29	15.00	2.74	In
Em	24.94	3.64	14.08	4.18	19.00	3.08	Em
Re	30.92	3.21	10.70	6.33	18.00	3.00	Re
So	35.70	3.29	17.16	5.61	23.00	3.39	So
Sc	29.60	5.17	11.72	6.62	19.00	3.08	Sc
Gi	31.30	7.27	9.78	5.77	20.00	3.16	Gi
Cm	34.70	2.29	18.38	5.42	19.00	3.08	Cm
Wb	34.92	4.01	7.10	5.75	19.00	3.08	Wb
To	22.46	3.05	8.06	4.15	16.00	2.83	To
Ac	33.86	4.41	13.06	5.85	19.00	3.08	Ac
Ai	23.84	3.78	10.98	4.18	18.00	3.00	Ai
Ie	34.10	3.06	14.00	5.56	21.00	3.24	Ie
Py	18.04	2.50	8.18	3.49	14.00	2.65	Py
Fx	9.64	4.23	10.42	3.64	14.00	2.65	Fx
F/M	13.54	3.15	17.78	4.15	16.00	2.83	F/M
v.1	11.58	4.43	19.06	6.95	17.00	2.92	v.1
v.2	30.94	5.29	15.18	6.05	18.00	3.00	v.2
v.3	42.92	6.87	12.06	7.64	29.00	3.81	v.3
Mp	27.74	4.35	8.28	4.07	17.00	2.92	Mp
Wo	34.42	3.94	10.60	5.45	20.00	3.16	Wo
CT	18.70	5.14	16.10	5.11	21.00	3.24	CT
Lp	62.66	9.45	20.00	8.70	35.00	4.18	Lp
Ami	28.20	3.51	8.52	4.92	18.00	3.00	Ami
Leo	30.12	4.08	17.54	3.83	21.00	3.24	Leo
Tm	29.32	4.20	10.52	4.73	18.00	3.00	Tm
B-MS	45.06	6.27	15.82	8.25	27.00	3.67	B-MS
B-FM	28.90	3.47	18.24	5.96	21.00	3.24	B-FM
Anx	4.16	1.74	14.82	2.30	11.00	2.35	Anx
Nar	21.64	4.21	31.34	7.87	24.50	3.50	Nar
D-SD	27.30	4.36	10.14	4.37	16.00	2.83	D-SD
D-AC	16.30	2.50	19.18	3.03	16.00	2.83	D-AC

CPI Means and Standard Deviations, Part 2: Female Samples

Scale	Basic Normative Sample N=3,000		High School Students — General N=4,825		National Science Fair Delegates N=148		Nominated as Best Citizens N=90		Nominated as Leaders N=90		Nominated as Most Attractive N=90		Nominated as Most Popular N=90		Nominated as Disciplinary Problems N=90		Scale
	M	SD	M	SD	M	SD	M	SD	M	SD	M	SD	M	SD	M	SD	
Do	18.95	5.28	17.78	5.81	22.00	6.46	20.30	6.13	22.61	5.53	20.17	5.48	20.72	5.28	17.47	5.13	Do
Cs	15.56	4.25	14.66	4.43	17.64	3.73	16.90	4.43	18.39	3.57	16.88	3.70	17.81	3.92	13.84	4.16	Cs
Sy	19.93	5.02	19.23	4.94	21.66	4.88	20.64	4.89	23.23	4.31	21.38	4.21	22.43	4.01	18.50	4.10	Sy
Sp	23.50	5.19	22.60	4.76	23.99	4.78	23.82	4.84	25.73	4.72	24.23	4.10	25.50	4.52	22.39	4.36	Sp
Sa	15.85	4.25	14.95	4.22	18.20	3.50	16.39	4.10	18.63	3.74	17.48	3.60	17.83	3.31	15.19	3.91	Sa
In	14.15	4.72	12.91	4.01	16.22	4.43	14.78	3.86	15.50	3.77	13.27	3.80	14.84	3.78	13.40	3.70	In
Em	19.44	4.85	18.59	4.23	21.57	4.06	20.30	4.31	22.13	3.60	20.00	4.09	21.32	4.02	18.20	3.73	Em
Re	25.98	4.92	26.04	4.73	28.98	3.85	28.09	4.26	27.91	4.23	26.68	4.22	27.40	4.14	22.36	5.03	Re
So	31.42	6.29	32.54	5.80	34.31	5.50	34.42	5.26	33.57	5.86	33.58	4.75	33.77	5.05	27.44	6.40	So
Sc	20.72	6.63	21.01	6.61	20.45	6.11	22.30	5.81	20.36	5.79	19.93	6.42	21.01	6.12	17.96	6.46	Sc
Gi	17.30	6.24	17.71	6.36	17.74	6.26	18.94	5.90	18.38	6.03	17.09	6.11	19.08	6.24	16.31	6.33	Gi
Cm	34.87	2.85	34.35	4.41	35.32	3.46	34.47	5.47	34.36	5.61	34.38	4.90	33.87	5.88	32.60	5.58	Cm
Wb	28.30	6.12	27.90	5.94	29.15	5.95	29.43	5.73	29.32	5.54	27.82	5.34	29.84	5.56	25.00	6.03	Wb
To	20.09	5.48	19.10	4.93	22.26	4.56	21.47	4.82	21.18	4.64	20.03	4.58	21.36	4.32	16.06	4.72	To
Ac	26.33	5.48	25.82	5.49	29.07	4.57	28.59	5.15	28.87	5.30	27.07	4.80	27.84	5.17	21.61	5.48	Ac
Ai	19.15	6.22	16.86	4.84	22.46	4.31	19.40	4.58	18.43	4.39	17.66	4.33	18.86	4.56	15.40	4.63	Ai
Ie	27.55	6.24	25.91	5.79	31.39	4.63	29.34	5.67	29.39	5.42	24.80	5.25	28.72	5.48	24.07	5.00	Ie
Py	14.24	3.89	13.24	3.35	16.33	3.25	14.32	3.68	14.47	3.18	13.50	2.87	15.08	2.70	12.02	3.09	Py
Fx	12.92	4.01	12.58	3.39	13.55	3.93	12.51	3.08	13.01	3.55	12.57	2.96	13.48	3.33	13.12	3.40	Fx
F/M	20.59	3.27	20.61	3.23	19.43	2.98	14.48	3.04	20.08	3.26	20.81	2.88	19.59	3.21	19.86	3.23	F/M
v.1	19.44	6.09	20.28	5.80	17.01	6.23	18.39	6.06	15.53	5.37	17.59	5.34	17.17	5.87	18.98	5.45	v.1
v.2	23.28	5.52	24.14	5.29	25.32	5.66	25.80	5.42	25.29	5.37	25.09	4.85	24.81	5.08	20.76	5.39	v.2
v.3	31.17	10.02	28.77	8.49	36.08	7.89	32.91	8.66	32.70	7.52	29.63	7.38	33.41	6.80	25.44	7.55	v.3
Mp	17.76	6.06	16.77	5.37	20.09	4.96	19.97	5.12	20.56	5.17	18.47	5.30	19.86	4.88	15.16	4.45	Mp
Wo	27.41	5.69	26.79	5.46	27.84	5.29	28.52	4.76	27.92	5.00	26.64	4.81	28.37	4.41	23.59	5.57	Wo
CT	19.73	5.48	18.17	4.33	21.34	4.78	19.49	4.42	20.89	4.12	19.04	3.79	20.37	3.98	18.90	4.31	CT
Lp	43.62	10.83	42.16	10.88	47.30	10.72	47.49	9.92	49.84	9.56	45.53	9.08	48.03	8.32	38.12	8.44	Lp
Ami	22.58	5.84	22.66	5.28	23.02	5.63	24.80	4.66	24.09	4.47	22.97	4.63	24.57	4.68	19.29	5.26	Ami
Leo	23.49	3.88	24.13	3.78	25.80	4.36	24.91	3.65	24.77	3.29	24.51	3.35	24.72	3.21	23.00	3.60	Leo
Tm	18.56	5.94	17.40	5.41	19.77	5.32	19.76	5.06	19.73	5.05	17.98	5.09	19.81	4.44	16.34	4.19	Tm
B-MS	28.36	9.33	26.85	8.49	30.66	8.64	29.93	8.61	32.47	8.16	27.82	7.73	31.86	7.22	26.83	6.88	B-MS
B-FM	31.07	4.53	30.50	4.45	31.01	4.66	31.32	4.36	30.80	4.86	30.79	4.53	30.81	4.77	27.13	4.79	B-FM
Anx	6.48	2.59	6.46	2.68	6.31	2.72	6.13	2.93	6.32	2.99	6.30	2.42	6.04	2.78	7.57	3.12	Anx
Nar	22.32	6.32	21.67	5.99	23.62	6.01	21.22	5.83	23.28	5.03	23.39	5.86	22.43	6.24	24.48	6.13	Nar
D-SD	17.80	4.87	17.34	4.84	19.43	4.72	19.06	4.76	19.58	4.53	17.87	4.22	19.03	4.54	15.84	4.68	D-SD
D-AC	15.71	3.71	15.79	3.59	16.03	3.12	15.50	3.65	15.60	3.52	16.16	3.47	15.50	3.60	15.73	3.49	D-AC

CPI Means and Standard Deviations, Part 2: Female Samples continued

College Students: Programs of Study

Scale	General N=4,126 M	SD	Architecture N=55 M	SD	Education N=310 M	SD	Home Economics N=176 M	SD	Premedical N=48 M	SD	Art Institute N=27 M	SD	Scale
Do	21.14	5.99	21.24	5.95	24.14	5.11	22.28	5.68	23.85	5.25	17.41	6.12	Do
Cs	19.02	3.43	18.58	3.59	20.71	3.06	18.95	3.40	19.69	3.48	15.81	3.62	Cs
Sy	22.30	4.49	19.93	4.61	24.46	3.80	23.01	4.23	22.62	3.96	17.44	4.18	Sy
Sp	26.64	4.50	24.98	4.74	28.06	4.01	26.28	4.23	27.54	4.13	25.19	5.89	Sp
Sa	18.10	3.76	18.22	3.59	19.09	3.32	18.03	3.53	19.67	3.07	18.00	4.17	Sa
In	16.48	4.17	18.38	4.57	18.00	3.63	16.77	3.90	18.54	4.13	17.78	5.04	In
Em	22.65	4.21	21.64	3.46	24.03	3.76	22.64	3.82	24.85	3.92	21.44	3.70	Em
Re	28.29	3.83	27.35	4.01	30.31	3.08	29.56	3.56	25.65	4.16	19.89	4.13	Re
So	33.70	4.69	31.71	5.10	34.73	4.25	34.62	3.80	30.96	4.87	26.89	5.06	So
Sc	22.06	5.86	20.13	6.24	24.76	5.85	24.76	5.51	19.83	5.97	16.85	5.38	Sc
Gi	18.53	5.87	16.27	6.08	22.25	6.44	21.55	6.49	16.92	5.99	12.63	5.09	Gi
Cm	35.14	2.34	34.67	2.14	35.37	1.88	35.36	2.04	34.75	2.09	32.52	3.41	Cm
Wb	31.17	4.69	29.51	5.58	33.97	3.69	33.07	4.39	29.50	5.21	26.26	6.09	Wb
To	24.23	3.79	22.96	4.27	25.51	3.26	24.24	3.35	23.73	3.55	20.70	3.98	To
Ac	28.88	4.25	26.93	4.25	31.63	3.55	30.53	3.94	28.19	4.24	20.33	4.67	Ac
Ai	24.51	4.51	24.38	4.21	26.51	3.91	24.46	4.19	27.42	4.17	23.00	5.22	Ai
Ie	31.91	4.44	31.24	4.01	33.97	3.65	31.55	4.32	33.85	4.09	28.52	6.05	Ie
Py	16.46	3.22	16.98	3.41	17.88	2.92	16.87	3.13	19.06	2.73	15.22	3.73	Py
Fx	15.15	4.05	15.51	4.32	14.91	3.51	14.10	3.58	16.90	3.12	18.04	4.80	Fx
F/M	19.93	3.09	18.20	2.96	18.88	2.95	19.28	2.76	18.81	3.32	20.52	2.98	F/M
v.1	17.91	6.01	17.36	5.33	16.64	5.77	18.87	5.66	14.77	5.22	18.74	6.06	v.1
v.2	23.27	5.34	20.91	6.12	25.33	4.79	25.02	4.70	19.94	5.13	15.15	5.19	v.2
v.3	39.73	7.13	37.91	7.86	44.13	6.56	41.16	7.17	42.25	6.41	34.78	7.69	v.3
Mp	22.11	4.85	20.09	5.04	25.66	4.46	24.04	4.79	22.31	5.47	15.63	5.11	Mp
Wo	30.27	4.50	27.80	5.09	33.08	3.99	32.14	4.48	29.02	4.49	24.78	4.82	Wo
CT	23.67	5.12	23.29	5.38	24.25	4.55	22.43	4.13	27.21	5.15	27.85	6.32	CT
Lp	49.43	8.88	46.09	10.01	55.37	7.07	52.70	8.52	50.81	8.25	39.41	8.97	Lp
Ami	26.01	4.89	22.29	5.43	28.15	4.76	27.97	4.31	23.27	5.36	19.93	5.24	Ami
Leo	23.54	3.80	23.58	4.36	24.52	3.60	24.89	3.54	22.67	4.23	19.59	3.42	Leo
Tm	21.19	5.21	21.31	5.27	25.05	4.47	23.87	5.05	21.79	4.96	16.11	5.73	Tm
B-MS	32.94	8.31	31.75	8.52	38.36	6.97	35.25	7.94	35.15	8.48	29.52	9.33	B-MS
B-FM	32.65	3.70	30.62	4.23	33.60	3.49	33.39	3.36	30.90	4.10	27.93	3.89	B-FM
Anx	5.55	1.91	6.42	2.39	4.54	1.36	4.86	1.69	5.94	1.99	7.07	2.30	Anx
Nar	21.12	6.13	24.98	6.94	18.88	6.29	19.06	5.45	26.04	6.13	26.67	5.81	Nar
D-SD	19.66	4.24	18.38	5.05	22.70	4.16	20.95	4.20	20.17	3.81	15.78	4.43	D-SD
D-AC	14.28	3.27	14.13	3.39	13.94	3.02	13.38	2.88	14.67	3.42	14.52	3.09	D-AC

CPI Means and Standard Deviations, Part 2: Female Samples continued

Graduate or Professional School

Scale	Business Administration N=44 M	SD	Counseling N=275 M	SD	Law N=40 M	SD	Medicine N=90 M	SD	Nursing N=250 M	SD	Optometry N=50 M	SD	Pharmacy N=277 M	SD	Psychology N=405 M	SD	Social Welfare N=446 M	SD	Scale
Do	25.89	5.73	23.63	5.44	24.10	5.90	23.13	5.37	21.15	6.40	23.80	5.20	20.23	5.71	22.36	5.48	22.62	5.10	Do
Cs	19.52	2.96	18.69	3.63	19.72	3.67	20.87	3.42	19.00	3.39	19.96	3.43	17.23	3.78	20.53	3.22	20.13	2.77	Cs
Sy	23.95	3.96	23.11	4.68	21.65	4.19	22.92	4.23	22.24	4.60	23.70	4.32	20.80	5.05	21.78	4.35	23.08	3.97	Sy
Sp	28.00	3.86	26.62	4.75	27.92	4.46	27.80	4.02	26.25	4.81	27.62	4.08	25.04	4.72	27.77	4.18	27.79	3.80	Sp
Sa	20.02	3.59	19.16	3.50	19.17	3.90	19.08	3.37	18.55	3.72	18.56	3.19	17.13	3.73	18.69	3.58	18.12	3.10	Sa
In	19.45	3.94	17.80	3.93	20.12	3.57	19.81	3.04	16.82	4.22	19.16	3.08	16.68	3.97	19.97	3.95	17.87	3.52	In
Em	24.05	4.02	23.77	4.35	25.62	4.08	24.67	3.87	22.45	4.16	24.98	4.22	21.13	4.40	24.47	3.87	24.32	3.86	Em
Re	26.34	4.27	26.47	3.66	27.22	3.46	29.80	3.28	28.50	3.28	29.30	3.56	26.13	3.78	27.98	3.57	29.23	3.04	Re
So	33.34	4.14	32.42	4.48	31.25	3.86	34.02	3.90	33.83	4.86	35.22	3.68	33.61	4.35	31.72	4.27	32.67	4.09	So
Sc	21.09	6.48	22.82	5.25	19.35	5.89	23.46	5.43	21.78	5.51	26.38	5.76	23.33	5.70	22.35	5.26	23.80	5.60	Sc
Gi	18.07	6.10	19.22	5.59	15.67	5.74	20.49	6.54	18.21	5.27	23.48	6.51	19.53	6.08	17.54	5.37	20.12	6.06	Gi
Cm	35.16	1.98	36.18	1.69	34.02	2.24	34.94	2.38	35.16	2.20	35.82	2.02	35.09	2.37	34.39	2.29	34.60	2.04	Cm
Wb	31.25	4.31	31.17	4.36	30.07	4.53	33.32	3.82	30.66	4.58	34.08	3.36	30.61	5.02	31.71	4.15	32.93	4.08	Wb
To	24.45	3.83	24.94	3.52	25.25	3.68	26.58	3.42	24.48	3.51	26.62	3.34	23.24	4.33	26.56	3.53	26.62	3.06	To
Ac	29.48	3.87	29.55	3.77	26.92	3.67	30.32	3.90	28.94	4.19	31.06	3.96	28.81	3.78	28.78	3.36	29.06	3.48	Ac
Ai	27.55	3.43	26.96	3.88	28.85	3.29	29.22	3.54	25.06	4.21	27.96	3.46	25.06	4.56	29.89	3.27	27.96	3.43	Ai
Ie	33.36	3.78	31.82	4.30	34.07	3.45	34.97	3.89	32.03	4.18	34.62	3.22	30.84	4.83	35.25	3.38	33.79	3.45	Ie
Py	18.61	2.81	17.88	2.91	19.90	3.18	20.27	2.57	16.48	2.96	19.12	2.90	17.46	3.24	21.17	2.89	19.30	2.93	Py
Fx	15.86	3.57	15.64	3.84	19.40	3.73	17.23	3.74	15.12	3.99	14.92	4.19	14.46	4.00	18.81	3.79	17.55	3.82	Fx
F/M	17.75	3.55	19.30	2.92	18.40	2.62	17.98	2.64	20.39	3.07	18.08	2.52	19.42	3.06	19.06	2.88	18.93	2.97	F/M
v.1	12.89	6.28	15.90	5.60	14.05	6.10	16.98	5.43	17.72	6.74	16.56	6.60	19.61	5.72	16.76	5.93	18.07	5.36	v.1
v.2	22.80	4.67	22.52	4.83	18.57	4.83	22.72	5.35	22.99	5.51	24.46	6.31	22.69	4.94	18.97	5.08	21.42	5.04	v.2
v.3	41.59	7.22	41.52	7.02	43.07	6.98	45.60	6.24	39.87	6.33	46.20	6.40	39.09	8.45	46.13	5.83	44.68	5.97	v.3
Mp	24.61	4.91	23.73	4.77	22.85	5.00	24.73	4.77	22.08	4.69	25.40	4.66	20.67	5.11	24.39	4.52	25.79	3.94	Mp
Wo	29.86	3.83	30.20	4.04	29.27	4.22	32.77	3.98	30.07	4.06	34.00	3.34	30.18	4.51	31.26	3.89	32.48	3.89	Wo
CT	25.68	4.56	24.99	5.36	29.87	5.15	26.32	5.00	23.87	4.84	24.16	4.56	22.49	5.18	29.53	5.11	26.57	4.54	CT
Lp	54.34	7.31	52.09	7.95	49.67	8.40	54.22	7.90	49.01	9.25	55.88	8.28	47.77	9.32	51.18	7.73	52.95	7.49	Lp
Ami	24.02	4.96	25.09	4.33	22.77	5.50	27.11	4.34	25.72	4.59	28.42	4.25	25.10	4.88	25.10	4.54	27.65	4.34	Ami
Leo	24.16	2.98	25.72	3.60	21.00	4.08	23.58	4.27	23.76	3.74	25.64	3.43	25.02	3.71	21.07	3.66	23.00	3.70	Leo
Tm	24.82	4.60	23.51	4.63	23.57	5.03	24.97	4.53	21.09	5.18	25.70	4.74	22.00	5.24	24.65	4.31	24.35	4.53	Tm
B-MS	37.64	7.99	35.38	8.32	35.65	8.14	38.49	7.23	32.17	8.29	39.30	6.77	33.22	8.78	36.40	7.68	36.95	7.26	B-MS
B-FM	30.84	4.25	32.45	3.80	31.05	3.63	32.60	3.47	32.89	3.43	33.86	3.29	33.30	3.38	32.25	3.50	33.80	3.23	B-FM
Anx	5.43	1.65	5.40	1.72	6.02	1.94	5.20	1.54	5.76	1.91	4.60	1.51	5.66	2.03	5.72	1.77	5.01	1.70	Anx
Nar	26.98	6.97	22.11	5.78	27.32	6.35	21.32	5.95	21.29	5.84	20.36	5.90	21.55	5.93	22.68	5.95	18.18	5.45	Nar
D-SD	20.95	4.19	20.99	3.55	18.45	4.23	21.58	3.84	20.04	4.13	23.68	4.37	19.80	4.25	20.42	3.64	21.13	3.95	D-SD
D-AC	14.95	3.14	13.51	3.05	13.35	3.29	13.56	3.01	14.54	3.24	13.92	3.13	14.43	3.56	13.37	3.12	12.47	2.88	D-AC

CPI Means and Standard Deviations, Part 2: Female Samples continued

Occupational Samples

Scale	Anesthesiologists N=17 M	SD	College Counselors N=42 M	SD	Mathematicians N=41 M	SD	Police Officer Applicants N=200 M	SD	Registered Nurses N=100 M	SD	Secondary School Teachers N=21 M	SD	University Clerical Personnel N=56 M	SD	Commercial Writers N=12 M	SD	Creative Writers N=10 M	SD	Children's Book Authors N=32 M	SD	Children's Book Critics N=36 M	SD	Scale
Do	23.29	7.07	24.26	5.30	18.83	6.05	25.34	5.17	21.25	6.31	23.81	5.61	21.73	4.22	24.17	6.03	17.40	6.77	21.06	5.29	25.25	6.45	Do
Cs	19.76	3.80	19.40	3.11	18.46	3.03	18.43	3.33	16.78	3.54	20.52	3.12	19.16	3.55	19.58	2.81	19.60	3.84	18.78	2.84	19.36	3.20	Cs
Sy	24.53	4.27	22.98	4.20	18.44	4.40	23.95	3.61	20.55	4.66	23.24	3.05	21.52	3.93	21.25	5.28	20.10	5.53	19.69	4.42	21.31	4.81	Sy
Sp	28.00	6.51	26.48	3.84	23.63	4.54	27.15	3.86	24.28	4.81	27.24	3.02	25.84	3.77	26.58	5.71	26.70	5.33	24.31	3.75	25.72	4.31	Sp
Sa	18.71	4.28	17.55	3.51	15.51	3.54	18.42	2.73	16.76	4.16	18.81	3.34	17.89	3.24	19.58	5.58	18.30	3.59	17.56	3.13	18.89	3.21	Sa
In	17.71	4.25	18.10	3.36	17.83	4.31	19.92	3.15	16.19	4.33	18.81	2.60	18.57	3.29	18.58	3.65	17.70	5.10	20.12	2.94	19.53	4.74	In
Em	22.76	5.19	22.29	4.05	20.39	3.85	22.84	4.15	20.87	4.66	24.14	4.03	21.89	4.25	22.67	4.48	22.60	3.47	22.31	4.00	24.19	3.61	Em
Re	27.88	4.00	30.69	2.80	29.85	2.66	28.30	3.67	27.25	3.60	30.38	2.65	29.09	3.38	29.58	3.60	23.10	3.38	27.72	3.72	27.89	4.86	Re
So	33.71	5.01	33.26	4.12	32.88	3.64	33.21	3.67	33.50	3.95	33.76	4.68	32.89	4.39	32.25	4.59	28.30	4.83	31.50	4.98	31.89	4.04	So
Sc	22.41	5.20	24.21	4.71	25.29	4.89	26.17	5.28	22.43	5.45	24.62	4.58	23.77	6.30	22.75	5.08	17.00	5.93	22.62	5.80	22.33	6.34	Sc
Gi	19.00	5.71	21.33	5.75	19.00	5.62	25.17	6.19	18.61	5.50	20.86	5.53	21.34	6.96	17.58	5.26	12.80	3.55	17.41	5.49	18.25	5.82	Gi
Cm	36.53	2.03	34.83	2.90	34.22	2.38	35.99	1.95	36.06	2.23	35.19	1.81	34.80	2.61	33.83	3.79	33.60	2.55	33.62	2.03	34.08	1.90	Cm
Wb	31.12	5.74	33.55	3.42	32.10	3.72	34.32	3.55	31.34	4.56	33.71	2.83	32.84	4.06	30.42	5.00	27.60	6.42	30.72	4.52	30.92	5.16	Wb
To	24.88	3.52	25.81	2.27	25.83	3.58	24.31	4.51	24.38	4.02	25.81	3.04	24.37	4.28	26.00	3.02	24.00	4.85	26.37	3.49	25.78	2.93	To
Ac	30.24	3.77	32.17	3.81	28.80	3.68	31.34	3.70	29.57	3.90	30.57	4.38	29.66	3.79	30.00	3.79	24.40	4.45	27.56	4.17	29.72	4.19	Ac
Ai	27.82	3.91	26.95	3.18	27.56	3.63	25.52	4.49	24.46	4.58	26.43	3.98	25.34	4.71	27.08	3.94	27.80	3.36	27.62	3.50	27.67	3.22	Ai
Ie	33.18	4.79	33.48	3.50	32.49	3.78	32.19	4.53	31.60	5.03	34.57	3.23	32.71	3.70	32.08	3.03	32.60	4.79	33.34	3.53	33.42	3.80	Ie
Py	18.00	2.85	18.93	2.03	21.00	2.69	18.17	2.77	17.12	3.03	19.19	2.94	17.61	2.97	18.58	3.23	17.90	3.57	18.31	3.02	18.92	2.73	Py
Fx	14.88	3.44	14.48	3.26	15.54	4.83	12.86	3.99	13.57	4.12	15.48	4.33	14.18	3.72	14.50	3.83	21.50	1.96	16.16	4.73	15.47	4.10	Fx
F/M	18.41	2.94	19.98	2.40	19.78	2.47	15.67	2.95	20.80	2.96	19.05	3.20	19.84	2.90	21.50	2.84	20.00	3.62	21.16	2.49	20.61	2.85	F/M
v.1	15.76	6.97	17.57	6.59	22.78	5.78	15.17	5.32	18.87	6.68	16.86	5.05	19.04	4.40	15.83	6.32	19.10	6.66	19.41	4.74	15.00	6.27	v.1
v.2	24.24	4.34	24.62	5.67	22.10	5.21	24.46	4.21	23.02	4.51	23.81	4.51	23.27	5.13	22.92	3.45	15.20	4.83	20.09	3.92	21.61	4.73	v.2
v.3	42.18	7.30	43.21	3.87	42.93	5.85	43.45	8.70	38.52	6.95	43.24	6.04	41.55	7.19	40.17	5.72	39.70	6.73	40.72	5.35	41.75	6.30	v.3
Mp	24.00	4.43	26.40	3.13	23.54	4.07	24.70	5.28	22.00	5.06	25.43	3.71	23.43	4.39	24.92	3.45	19.40	6.06	23.72	3.62	25.47	4.32	Mp
Wo	31.41	4.68	33.50	3.25	31.63	4.15	33.68	3.66	30.92	3.74	33.38	2.91	32.12	3.99	29.58	4.38	25.90	4.63	29.22	4.36	28.97	5.05	Wo
CT	22.76	4.31	23.67	4.18	24.66	6.32	21.65	5.09	21.70	5.65	25.19	4.14	23.20	5.14	26.17	3.74	29.70	4.11	27.53	4.52	26.56	4.33	CT
Lp	52.24	8.68	55.33	5.86	48.78	7.75	56.19	7.58	48.84	9.33	55.38	6.91	51.95	6.53	51.75	8.86	41.90	11.01	48.47	7.80	52.47	9.96	Lp
Ami	25.76	5.36	27.62	3.28	25.88	4.01	27.25	4.72	26.00	4.18	27.86	3.64	27.12	4.10	24.92	4.78	21.90	6.49	25.56	5.81	25.11	5.30	Ami
Leo	25.00	2.52	23.90	3.63	21.46	3.81	30.32	3.35	25.26	3.42	23.62	3.79	23.62	3.67	20.58	3.45	17.60	3.69	20.16	3.19	22.06	4.27	Leo
Tm	24.82	4.53	25.60	3.66	23.85	4.75	28.25	3.96	22.51	4.84	24.95	4.61	24.36	4.64	23.83	4.84	18.10	4.70	22.72	4.13	24.61	4.97	Tm
B-MS	36.59	8.83	36.88	6.04	32.63	8.27	42.21	6.32	31.08	8.56	38.90	5.92	35.48	7.24	34.58	7.72	29.20	8.72	32.50	5.94	35.11	9.44	B-MS
B-FM	32.65	3.50	33.64	2.71	33.20	3.30	31.52	3.71	33.58	3.83	34.43	3.14	33.98	3.50	33.67	2.50	30.00	5.94	32.94	4.26	33.14	3.93	B-FM
Anx	4.88	1.87	4.79	1.24	5.95	1.93	4.64	1.81	5.67	1.89	4.62	1.16	4.98	1.88	6.25	2.34	6.70	3.02	5.91	2.32	5.78	2.31	Anx
Nar	22.29	6.72	17.67	5.51	18.34	5.72	21.69	5.71	21.10	6.01	12.81	5.45	19.68	6.46	20.83	5.78	23.60	5.40	21.31	6.64	22.97	7.12	Nar
D-SD	21.76	3.67	21.57	3.31	19.56	3.59	23.43	3.87	19.85	3.95	22.86	3.60	22.09	4.10	21.00	4.67	16.60	4.62	18.97	3.57	21.00	4.34	D-SD
D-AC	14.47	2.74	13.81	3.52	12.93	2.96	13.41	2.99	14.05	3.17	13.43	3.09	13.95	3.15	14.33	3.60	13.00	2.94	12.84	2.95	13.56	3.05	D-AC

CPI Means and Standard Deviations, Part 2: Female Samples continued

Other Samples / Simulated Protocols

Scale	Rajneeshpuram Residents N=34 M	SD	Juvenile Delinquents N=55 M	SD	Adult Prison Inmates N=345 M	SD	Psychiatric Patients N=34 M	SD	San Francisco Area Residents N=261 M	SD	Fake Good N=52 M	SD	Fake Bad N=50 M	SD	Randomly Answered N=100 M	SD
Do	20.76	4.87	17.73	7.19	17.55	5.99	17.88	6.46	20.36	6.44	28.10	5.10	11.66	6.64	17.91	2.91
Cs	17.91	3.02	14.16	4.32	14.47	4.78	14.50	3.88	16.95	4.05	21.50	3.03	9.68	4.38	13.59	2.80
Sy	23.03	3.00	18.85	5.01	18.70	4.86	18.32	5.51	20.28	4.76	25.25	3.23	10.92	5.35	16.03	2.89
Sp	29.00	3.07	24.73	5.31	21.06	4.94	19.47	5.16	25.27	4.99	25.02	3.20	15.54	5.85	18.42	2.73
Sa	19.09	2.19	16.64	4.21	15.05	4.23	14.91	4.20	16.79	4.23	19.83	2.78	11.14	4.65	13.71	2.43
In	21.15	3.42	13.91	5.04	13.61	4.27	12.56	4.75	16.87	4.74	19.15	3.44	10.66	5.27	15.19	2.67
Em	22.97	3.27	18.22	4.60	17.10	4.75	18.09	4.29	21.44	4.54	24.94	3.60	13.50	4.79	19.19	2.96
Re	22.12	4.27	19.44	5.30	22.29	5.37	22.94	4.89	25.46	4.63	30.52	4.10	11.46	7.45	18.40	3.41
So	27.12	4.73	21.04	4.69	23.07	6.01	27.38	5.75	31.32	4.99	36.06	3.06	17.50	6.49	23.15	3.39
Sc	20.06	5.52	13.80	6.28	19.45	7.29	21.71	6.82	21.52	5.71	29.21	5.36	12.48	6.34	18.98	2.77
Gi	17.12	5.93	12.85	5.59	17.86	7.00	19.00	6.90	16.81	5.25	30.15	7.31	10.84	6.92	20.02	2.88
Cm	33.18	2.81	33.62	3.05	33.69	3.57	31.03	4.73	35.24	2.25	34.94	1.81	17.34	7.49	18.73	2.70
Wb	32.71	3.08	24.98	6.14	25.56	7.42	22.62	7.81	29.71	5.23	35.25	3.27	9.12	8.41	19.10	3.26
To	22.35	3.26	15.27	4.41	15.59	5.48	17.44	5.82	23.22	4.40	22.96	3.86	9.26	5.25	16.09	2.84
Ac	22.09	3.70	18.58	6.15	23.60	6.45	23.97	5.34	27.15	4.52	33.71	4.17	13.80	7.33	19.01	3.27
Ai	26.21	3.10	17.22	4.98	16.58	4.83	18.50	6.03	24.04	4.95	24.65	4.17	12.46	5.44	17.93	3.01
Ie	32.00	3.52	25.51	5.64	25.46	6.57	24.59	6.62	30.55	5.21	33.79	3.44	14.24	7.12	20.45	3.56
Py	17.56	1.97	12.11	3.64	12.60	3.80	12.38	4.66	16.92	3.39	18.04	2.64	9.90	3.55	14.71	2.65
Fx	19.06	2.98	15.71	2.90	10.37	3.61	10.47	3.55	14.57	4.25	10.87	3.94	12.24	4.58	13.70	2.21
F/M	18.85	2.36	17.95	3.22	19.59	3.33	19.91	3.39	20.60	3.01	17.62	3.46	18.62	4.66	15.95	2.89
v.1	17.68	4.55	16.98	6.52	20.36	5.97	19.53	5.62	18.48	6.52	13.25	4.57	20.96	6.50	17.15	2.49
v.2	15.71	3.58	14.00	5.61	21.90	5.75	22.44	4.80	20.40	5.07	30.08	4.72	13.44	6.47	18.29	3.26
v.3	41.91	5.91	27.15	8.02	25.32	9.95	28.85	10.04	37.52	7.88	44.17	6.79	14.76	9.84	29.56	4.05
Mp	20.26	4.81	13.73	5.45	14.48	6.14	17.35	5.69	20.67	5.50	26.75	4.94	8.16	5.83	16.99	3.15
Wo	30.24	4.12	22.44	5.36	24.54	6.57	23.35	6.95	29.15	4.66	34.40	3.66	11.78	6.12	20.10	3.37
CT	28.32	3.36	21.60	3.63	17.49	4.39	17.88	4.97	23.05	5.40	19.23	4.57	18.40	5.85	21.32	3.19
Lp	46.68	5.91	36.18	10.98	38.94	12.01	38.18	11.15	46.81	9.68	61.23	7.87	20.06	12.36	35.25	3.86
Ami	24.68	4.86	15.96	5.14	17.93	5.92	19.03	7.05	24.34	5.00	28.33	3.88	9.64	5.33	18.44	2.80
Leo	21.76	3.54	22.09	4.53	22.06	4.03	21.94	3.91	23.42	3.64	28.92	3.77	17.34	3.89	21.19	3.45
Tm	23.59	4.09	16.29	5.58	18.28	6.07	18.03	5.53	21.64	5.43	28.33	4.56	11.26	6.16	17.80	3.10
B-MS	38.38	5.66	29.53	9.75	27.63	9.44	25.88	10.39	31.24	8.97	41.40	6.51	16.80	10.00	26.59	3.33
B-FM	30.44	3.70	24.29	4.91	27.44	5.25	30.21	5.20	32.89	3.78	32.00	3.92	19.84	7.47	20.79	3.51
Anx	5.76	1.67	7.69	2.91	8.37	3.29	9.00	3.26	5.82	2.01	4.02	1.36	14.20	3.45	11.34	2.30
Nar	24.12	4.71	25.95	6.65	22.88	6.62	22.38	7.54	22.46	6.65	20.02	5.92	29.08	7.75	24.07	3.50
D-SD	19.21	4.40	13.64	4.53	16.95	5.11	17.82	4.07	19.14	3.91	26.46	4.31	10.34	5.27	16.04	2.65
D-AC	12.44	3.33	15.42	3.93	16.99	3.88	16.71	4.27	14.41	3.57	15.58	2.69	17.86	3.12	15.82	2.76

Correlations of CPI™ Scales with Other Tests and Measures

In this appendix, correlations are given for the 20 folk, 3 vector, and 13 special purpose scales with the measures listed below. Many of these analyses were generously furnished by other investigators from their own projects. These contributions are gratefully acknowledged and will be specifically cited as the various tests and variables are listed.

Category 1: Academic and Performance Measures

1. High school grade point averages for students from 25 schools

2. Graduation versus dropout from high school

3. College attendance versus nonattendance by high school graduates

4. Self-reported college two-year grade point averages

5. Registrar's recorded four-year college grade point averages

6. Graduation versus dropout from college

7. Graduate students, take versus not take the Ph.D. degree

Category 2: Cognitive and Intellectual Measures

1. *College Vocabulary Test.* An unpublished 75-item multiple-choice test developed at the Institute of Personality Assessment and Research, Berkeley, California, by Harrison Gough and Harold Sampson.

2. Crutchfield's *Gottschaldt Figures Test.* Crutchfield's (Crutchfield, Woodworth, & Albrecht, 1958) version of the embedded figures method first introduced by Kurt Gottschaldt in 1926.

3. *Miller Analogies Test.* A high-level measure of deductive or analogical thinking used for many years by graduate schools as a test for applicants (Miller, 1970).

4. *Perceptual Acuity Test.* A test of perceptual judgment based on geometric illusions (Gough & McGurk, 1967; Gough & Olton, 1972; Gough & Weiss, 1981).

5. *Scholastic Aptitude Test* (SAT). Verbal score.

6. *Scholastic Aptitude Test* (SAT). Mathematical score.

7. *Standardized high school ability tests.* Scores from tests used in American high schools, standardized by school. Representative tests include the *Henmon-Nelson Tests of Mental Ability* (French, 1973), the *Kuhlmann-Anderson* (Kuhlmann & Anderson, 1985), and the *Otis-Lennon School Ability Test* (Otis & Lennon, 1979).

8. *Wechsler Adult Intelligence Scale* (WAIS; Wechsler, 1955). Verbal scales.

9. *Wechsler Adult Intelligence Scale.* Performance scales.

10. *Wechsler Adult Intelligence Scale.* Full scale total.

Category 3: Personality and Interest Inventories

1. *Cattell 16PF Questionnaire* (16PF; Cattell, 1949; Cattell & Eber, 1964).

2. *Comrey Personality Scales* (CPS; Comrey, 1970).

3. *Costa and McCrae NEO-AC* (Costa & McCrae, 1992). Data furnished by Kevin Lanning.

4. *Eysenck Maudsley Personality Inventory* (MPI; Eysenck, 1959).

5. *Goldberg Adjectival Big-Five Factor Markers* (Big-5; Goldberg, 1992). Data furnished by Lewis R. Goldberg.

6. *Guilford-Zimmerman Temperament Survey* (GZTS; Guilford & Zimmerman, 1949; Guilford, Zimmerman, & Guilford, 1976).

7. *Heist and Yonge Omnibus Personality Inventory* (OPI; Heist & Yonge, 1968).

8. *Hogan Personality Inventory* (HPI; Hogan, 1986). Data furnished by John A. Johnson.

9. *Interpersonal Dependency Inventory* (IDI; Hirschfeld, Klerman, Gough, Barrett, Korchin, & Chodoff, 1977; Bornstein, 1994).

10. *Jackson Personality Research Form* (PRF; Jackson, 1967).

11. *Lazare-Klerman-Armor Inventory* (LKAI; Lazare, Klerman, & Armor, 1966, 1970).

12. *Millon Clinical Multiaxial Inventory* (MCMI; Millon, 1983; Holliman & Guthrie, 1989). Data furnished by Neil B. Holliman

13. *Minnesota Multiphasic Personality Inventory* (MMPI; Hathaway & McKinley, 1943).

14. *Myers-Briggs Type Indicator®* (MBTI; Myers & McCaulley, 1985).

15. *Strong Interest Inventory®* (SII; Harmon, Hansen, Borgen, & Hammer, 1994). Scored for Holland's occupational theme scales (Holland, 1985).

16. *Tellegen's three higher-order traits.* Scored on *Adjective Check List* self-report protocols (Gough, Bradley, & Bedeian, 1996; Tellegen, 1985).

17. *Zuckerman Sensation-Seeking Scale* (SSS; Zuckerman, 1971; Zuckerman, Kolin, Price, & Zoob, 1964).

Category 4: Other Measures

1. *Barron personality scales*
   a. Complexity (Barron, 1953a)
   b. Independence (Barron, 1953b)
   c. Originality (Barron, 1965)
   d. Personal Soundness (Barron, 1954)

2. *Barron-Welsh Art Scale and Welsh Revised Art Scale* (BWAS, RAS; Barron & Welsh, 1952; Welsh, 1975).

3. *Beck Depression Inventory* (BDI; Beck, Steer, & Garbin, 1988; Beck, Ward, Mendelson, Mock, & Erbaugh, 1961).

4. *Bem Sex-Role Inventory* (BSRI; Bem, 1981).

5. *Chapin Social Insight Test* (CSIT; Gough, 1968c).

6. *Hogan Survey of Ethical Attitudes* (SEA; Hogan, 1970; Hogan, & Dickstein, 1972).

7. *Loevinger Sentence Completion Test for Ego Development* (SCT; Helson & Wink, 1989; Loevinger, 1979). Data furnished by Ravenna Helson.

8. *Rotter Locus of Control Scale* (LOC; Rotter, 1966).

9. *Spence-Helmreich Personal Attributes Questionnaire* (PAQ; Spence & Helmreich, 1979).

A. Academic and Performance Measures

Measures	Do	Cs	Sy	Sp	Sa	In	Em	Re	So	Sc	Gi	Cm	Wb	To	Ac	Ai	Ie	Py
1. High school GPA (Ns = 2,432 males, 2,852 females)																		
M	.25	.28	.20	.18	.19	.18	.17	.43	.33	.11	.04	.25	.25	.30	.44	.30	.43	.29
F	.26	.32	.22	.19	.23	.23	.25	.39	.30	.14	.13	.10	.25	.38	.40	.36	.45	.30
2. Graduation versus dropout from high school (Ns = 1,760 males, 2,019 females)																		
M	.05	.12	.10	.12	.08	.06	.07	.21	.19	.06	.05	.12	.17	.16	.19	.09	.17	.08
F	.09	.16	.14	.11	.10	.08	.13	.15	.16	.03	.04	.06	.12	.13	.19	.10	.17	.10
3. College attendance by high school graduates (Ns = 1,514 males, 1,799 females)																		
M	.26	.30	.26	.23	.26	.14	.22	.30	.24	.01	.01	.16	.17	.24	.33	.20	.35	.17
F	.28	.31	.25	.24	.29	.17	.24	.25	.16	−.04	.00	.09	.13	.22	.27	.20	.32	.17
4. Self-reported two-year college GPA (Ns = 99 males, 99 females)																		
M	.23	.20	.15	.05	.17	.23	.14	.24	.14	.18	.13	−.06	.19	.20	.32	.36	.32	.21
F	.13	.20	.14	.17	.17	.20	.21	.19	−.04	−.09	−.10	.04	−.05	.20	.12	.28	.20	.24
5. Registered four-year college GPA (Ns = 995 males, 441 females)																		
M	.10	.13	.08	.07	.06	.10	.08	.16	.12	.01	.01	.05	.08	.11	.14	.13	.16	.10
F	.09	.02	−.06	−.08	.02	.07	.05	.12	.03	.00	−.03	.03	.00	.09	.11	.15	.17	.11
6. Graduation versus dropout from college (Ns = 1,420 males, 727 females)																		
M	.04	.02	.04	.03	.00	.03	.03	.12	.16	.07	.05	.10	.10	.12	.13	.10	.12	.09
F	−.03	.02	.00	.00	−.05	.00	.03	.10	.11	.05	.01	.11	.03	.10	.11	.09	.09	.06
7. Graduate school, take versus not take the Ph.D. degree (Ns = 623 males, 405 females)																		
M	.07	.02	.02	.06	.04	.02	.07	.02	.05	−.07	−.05	.06	.00	.11	.03	.08	.09	.10
F	.10	.03	.00	.00	.04	.11	−.02	−.01	.08	−.02	−.04	.13	.06	−.02	.13	.12	.15	.10

A. Academic and Performance Measures continued

Measures	Fx	F/M	v.1	v.2	v.3	Mp	Wo	CT	Lp	Ami	Leo	Tm	B–MS	B–FM	Anx	Nar	D–SD	D–AC
1. High school GPA (Ns = 2,432 males, 2,852 females)																		
M	−.03	.06	−.12	.23	.27	.28	.27	.12	.31	.21	.16	.21	.19	.27	−.18	−.04	.20	−.03
F	.01	−.03	−.14	.17	.35	.35	.27	.18	.33	.28	.16	.25	.20	.23	−.18	−.10	.26	−.09
2. Graduation versus dropout from high school (Ns = 1,760 males, 2,019 females)																		
M	.00	.02	−.01	.09	.13	.13	.15	.06	.15	.16	.09	.07	.11	.16	−.11	−.06	.12	−.07
F	.02	−.06	−.08	.07	.12	.12	.12	.03	.16	.12	.08	.09	.09	.08	−.11	.00	.11	−.03
3. College attendance by high school graduates (Ns = 1,514 males, 1,799 females)																		
M	.00	.06	−.21	.17	.21	.26	.15	.14	.28	.17	.10	.12	.18	.17	−.13	.05	.17	.01
F	−.01	−.05	−.26	.11	.19	.22	.11	.14	.26	.12	.05	.12	.17	.08	−.09	.08	.16	.02
4. Self-reported two-year college GPA (Ns = 99 males, 99 females)																		
M	.09	−.01	−.17	.14	.22	.19	.09	.21	.27	.13	.00	.23	.15	.16	−.09	.03	.14	.00
F	.10	.06	−.14	.01	.28	.21	.06	.36	.11	−.02	−.32	.08	.12	.02	.02	.03	.05	−.13
5. Registered four-year college GPA (Ns = 995 males, 441 females)																		
M	−.04	−.06	−.06	.09	.11	.13	.10	.04	.16	.07	.03	.08	.07	.01	−.05	.02	.09	.01
F	−.04	.03	−.07	.08	.02	.07	.01	.06	.05	−.02	−.03	.03	.00	.02	.02	.02	.07	.02
6. Graduation versus dropout from college (Ns = 1,420 males, 727 females)																		
M	.00	.00	.02	.07	.11	.11	.15	−.03	.08	.14	.06	.05	.03	.07	−.05	−.08	.04	−.09
F	−.03	.06	.03	.05	.08	.08	.10	.00	.04	.08	.03	.06	−.04	.11	−.05	−.02	.06	−.04
7. Graduate school, take versus not take the Ph.D. degree (Ns = 623 males, 405 females)																		
M	.03	−.01	−.10	.00	.02	.06	.01	.11	.03	.01	−.08	.03	−.01	.01	.03	.08	−.02	.00
F	−.01	−.09	−.05	−.01	.02	.01	.03	.06	.07	−.02	.06	.10	.06	−.02	−.05	.09	−.05	−.02

B. Cognitive and Intellectual Measures

Measures	Do	Cs	Sy	Sp	Sa	In	Em	Re	So	Sc	Gi	Cm	Wb	To	Ac	Ai	Ie	Py
1. College Vocabulary Test (Ns = 735 males, 452 females)																		
M	.01	.14	−.02	.08	.00	.15	.18	.08	.03	.00	−.08	−.05	−.04	.21	.08	.36	.29	.25
F	−.02	.14	−.07	−.03	−.02	.09	.06	.09	−.06	−.02	−.10	−.12	−.04	.12	.04	.26	.22	.25
2. Crutchfield's Gottschaldt Figures Test (Ns = 508 males, 289 females)																		
M	−.02	.16	.02	.06	.00	.12	.08	.09	.09	.03	−.02	.04	.07	.21	.08	.21	.20	.23
F	−.08	.07	−.04	.01	−.03	.03	−.01	.15	.08	.09	−.01	−.03	.15	.18	.02	.21	.19	.17
3. Miller Analogies Test (Ns = 608 males, 379 females)																		
M	−.14	.03	−.08	.03	−.03	−.03	.11	−.05	−.06	−.12	−.20	−.07	−.13	.13	−.15	.20	.11	.09
F	−.01	.13	.04	.10	−.01	.08	.10	.05	−.04	−.04	−.04	.00	.01	.20	−.05	.25	.25	.23
4. Perceptual Acuity Test (Ns = 240 males, 219 females)																		
M	.09	.17	.04	.03	.07	.11	.13	.07	.00	−.04	−.07	.02	.02	.12	.04	.14	.17	.20
F	−.03	.07	−.03	−.02	.05	.15	.05	−.10	−.13	−.04	.00	−.06	.00	−.09	−.01	.10	.03	.08
5. Scholastic Aptitude Test: Verbal (Ns = 99 males, 99 females)																		
M	−.01	.02	−.09	−.02	−.01	.21	.06	.15	.17	.04	−.09	.10	.06	.20	.02	.24	.25	.17
F	−.02	.17	−.02	.04	.08	.12	.16	.15	−.06	−.13	−.19	−.12	−.12	.12	.02	.24	.19	.16
6. Scholastic Aptitude Test: Mathematical (Ns = 99 males, 99 females)																		
M	.00	.03	.06	.08	.05	.09	.08	.25	.29	.02	−.04	.17	.05	.20	.14	.28	.25	.15
F	−.08	.08	−.10	−.02	−.03	.07	−.06	.14	.01	.02	−.18	−.06	.03	.12	−.06	.15	.18	.23
7. Standardized high school ability tests (Ns = 2,625 males, 3,086 females)																		
M	.25	.27	.20	.25	.26	.22	.19	.32	.17	−.03	−.08	.19	.17	.26	.27	.25	.43	.22
F	.28	.33	.26	.28	.32	.26	.29	.34	.18	.01	.02	.09	.19	.34	.31	.31	.44	.27
8. Wechsler Adult Intelligence Scale: Verbal (Ns =158 males, 27 females)																		
M	−.11	.09	.04	.06	.01	.03	.22	.14	.03	.02	−.08	−.18	−.02	.26	.06	.42	.36	.34
F	.21	.22	.13	.17	.14	.15	.18	.50	.31	.09	.10	.14	.31	.01	.47	.12	.34	.25
9. Wechsler Adult Intelligence Scale: Performance (Ns =158 males, 27 females)																		
M	.00	.07	.00	.10	−.02	.04	.05	.00	.05	−.09	−.15	−.16	.06	.06	−.01	.02	.03	.02
F	.25	.27	.10	.36	.19	.09	.07	.50	.26	.03	−.10	−.16	.40	.15	.23	.29	.54	.24
10. Wechsler Adult Intelligence Scale: Full scale total (Ns =158 males, 27 females)																		
M	−.08	.12	.03	.10	.00	.05	.19	.11	.05	−.03	−.14	−.22	.02	.22	.04	.32	.28	.27
F	.28	.28	.13	.33	.20	.13	.15	.57	.33	.06	−.02	−.05	.42	.11	.38	.25	.54	.28

B. Cognitive and Intellectual Measures continued

Measures	Fx	F/M	v.1	v.2	v.3	Mp	Wo	CT	Lp	Ami	Leo	Tm	B–MS	B–FM	Anx	Nar	D–SD	D–AC
1. College Vocabulary Test (Ns = 735 males, 452 females)																		
M	.25	.17	−.07	−.14	.24	.07	−.02	.35	−.01	−.04	−.25	.04	−.05	.13	.04	.02	−.03	−.05
F	.10	−.01	.03	−.11	.15	.09	.04	.22	−.03	−.09	−.22	.05	−.01	.00	.07	−.02	−.05	−.09
2. Crutchfield's Gottschaldt Figures Test (Ns = 508 males, 289 females)																		
M	.15	−.04	.01	−.02	.23	.12	.08	.21	.07	.14	−.09	.04	.04	.01	−.05	.00	.00	−.03
F	.14	−.09	.12	−.03	.21	.11	.13	.13	.00	.13	−.06	−.01	.04	.06	−.08	−.09	−.07	−.07
3. Miller Analogies Test (Ns = 608 males, 379 females)																		
M	.22	−.03	.01	−.25	.07	−.03	−.09	.26	−.16	−.04	−.27	−.11	−.11	−.09	.12	.06	−.20	−.08
F	.16	−.06	−.04	−.16	.19	.12	.10	.15	.03	.07	−.17	.08	.05	.06	.02	.00	−.13	−.06
4. Perceptual Acuity Test (Ns = 240 males, 219 females)																		
M	.07	−.13	−.07	−.01	.15	.12	.02	.15	.08	.02	.03	.09	.09	−.06	.06	.07	.01	−.07
F	.08	−.13	−.01	−.15	.07	.00	.01	.10	−.03	−.05	.01	.08	.07	−.08	.00	.05	−.04	−.14
5. Scholastic Aptitude Test: Verbal (Ns = 99 males, 99 females)																		
M	.15	.08	−.03	−.09	.21	.06	.07	.16	.02	.03	−.03	.02	−.06	.15	−.04	.01	−.18	−.09
F	.25	.14	−.02	−.18	.22	.09	−.02	.40	−.06	−.06	−.32	−.12	−.07	.01	.04	.02	−.14	−.09
6. Scholastic Aptitude Test: Mathematical (Ns = 99 males, 99 females)																		
M	−.01	−.04	−.08	.23	.22	.10	.11	.06	.09	.13	.06	.01	.00	.11	−.02	.01	.05	.08
F	.17	−.02	.15	−.13	.20	.13	.11	.20	−.08	.07	−.18	−.01	−.01	.08	−.02	−.13	−.21	−.17
7. Standardized high school ability tests (Ns = 2,625 males, 3,086 females)																		
M	.04	−.04	−.20	.07	.24	.24	.15	.22	.23	.10	.08	.16	.20	.10	−.13	.07	.10	−.03
F	.06	−.08	−.23	.08	.30	.31	.19	.24	.30	.18	.13	.20	.22	.12	−.14	.02	.19	−.05
8. Wechsler Adult Intelligence Scale: Verbal (Ns =158 males, 27 females)																		
M	.24	.13	.00	−.11	.26	−.01	.04	.33	−.11	.10	−.20	−.05	−.04	.09	.20	−.18	−.01	−.13
F	−.11	−.02	−.11	.27	.18	.15	.27	−.04	.37	.26	.37	.22	.28	.29	−.15	.01	.34	−.12
9. Wechsler Adult Intelligence Scale: Performance (Ns =158 males, 27 females)																		
M	.04	−.03	−.08	−.06	−.02	−.05	−.01	.09	−.01	.02	−.13	−.06	−.03	−.07	.01	.07	−.12	−.03
F	−.15	−.11	−.18	.16	.25	.22	.26	.08	.33	.13	.00	.12	.25	.06	−.48	.04	.01	−.05
10. Wechsler Adult Intelligence Scale: Full scale total (Ns =158 males, 27 females)																		
M	.19	.08	−.04	−.11	.18	−.03	.03	.30	−.08	.09	−.22	−.07	−.04	.03	.15	−.10	−.07	−.11
F	−.15	−.09	−.19	.23	.25	.22	.30	.03	.39	.20	.18	.18	.30	.18	−.39	.04	.16	−.08

C. Personality and Interest Inventories

Measures	Do	Cs	Sy	Sp	Sa	In	Em	Re	So	Sc	Gi	Cm	Wb	To	Ac	Ai	Ie	Py
1. Cattell 16 PF Questionnaire (Ns = 93 males, 111 females)																		
Factor A (outgoing, sociable)																		
M	.25	.15	.32	.22	.25	.00	.22	.09	.04	−.02	.07	−.10	.15	.06	.12	.01	.09	.08
F	.21	.12	.29	.23	.15	.01	.11	.04	.06	.04	.19	.17	.15	−.08	.25	−.11	−.04	−.08
Factor B (intelligent, astute)																		
M	.23	.32	.20	.25	.32	.15	.16	.13	−.10	−.14	−.18	.13	−.05	.17	.14	.34	.34	.34.
F	.03	.12	.03	.05	−.05	.05	.14	.04	.05	−.02	.00	.11	.06	.16	.06	.15	.14	.07
Factor C (emotionally stable, mature)																		
M	.17	.11	.17	.13	.14	.09	.10	.21	.30	.24	.35	.18	.32	.34	.19	.13	.07	.22
F	.35	.43	.39	.33	.20	.40	.34	.40	.47	.49	.56	.27	.66	.44	.54	.44	.51	.44
Factor E (assertive, aggressive)																		
M	.32	.23	.30	.33	.34	.32	.19	.05	.01	−.07	−.03	.09	.22	.07	.29	.17	.32	.11
F	.29	.26	.23	.31	.38	.42	.23	−.24	−.37	−.34	−.17	−.22	−.02	−.02	−.23	.22	.16	.26
Factor F (pleasure-seeking, hedonistic)																		
M	.22	.19	.29	.26	.23	−.03	.28	−.22	−.06	−.36	−.14	−.06	−.21	−.26	−.12	−.13	−.08	−.02
F	.32	.24	.42	.49	.34	.20	.38	−.18	−.08	−.29	−.09	.04	.08	−.06	−.02	.02	.10	−.02
Factor G (dutiful, persevering)																		
M	.20	−.06	.15	−.13	.08	.00	−.04	.29	.32	.25	.32	.05	.22	.12	.29	.01	.00	.01
F	.03	.13	.17	−.04	−.03	−.03	.04	.52	.33	.33	.32	.29	.17	.11	.36	.05	.12	.07
Factor H (venturesome, bold)																		
M	.54	.52	.53	.32	.51	.44	.53	.15	.07	.12	.32	−.05	.29	.14	.29	.17	.27	.26
F	.60	.54	.68	.55	.61	.49	.58	.22	−.03	.06	.33	.16	.45	.16	.32	.26	.34	.35
Factor I (tender-minded, sensitive)																		
M	−.20	.11	−.03	−.05	.05	.01	.12	−.07	−.23	.01	−.09	−.19	−.25	.02	−.07	.18	.08	.05
F	−.27	−.17	−.20	−.25	−.24	−.23	−.21	.03	.05	.07	−.06	.09	−.20	.01	−.16	−.03	−.09	−.08
Factor L (suspicious, wary)																		
M	−.10	−.13	.00	−.04	−.07	−.12	−.12	−.09	−.08	−.16	−.23	−.16	−.24	−.25	−.22	−.28	−.19	−.17
F	−.22	−.34	−.24	−.28	−.09	−.32	−.37	−.33	−.35	−.43	−.41	−.13	−.50	−.53	−.30	−.38	−.40	−.36
Factor M (imaginative, Bohemian)																		
M	−.20	−.08	−.24	−.07	−.07	.08	.06	−.32	−.33	−.09	−.14	−.15	−.19	−.03	−.29	.14	.01	−.05
F	−.14	−.08	−.21	−.14	.03	−.03	−.06	−.19	−.36	−.26	−.28	−.27	−.30	−.01	−.41	.03	−.12	−.05
Factor N (observant, shrewd)																		
M	.24	.26	.17	.14	.31	.26	.22	.05	.01	−.01	−.01	.03	.11	.06	.16	.22	.24	.24
F	.26	.10	.23	.15	.22	−.03	.15	−.03	−.15	−.07	.12	.08	−.05	−.24	.09	−.17	−.15	−.04
Factor O (apprehensive, insecure)																		
M	−.32	−.36	−.30	−.33	−.32	−.29	−.25	−.24	−.22	−.15	−.25	−.18	−.55	−.29	−.36	−.16	−.37	−.32
F	−.52	−.47	−.44	−.37	−.35	−.51	−.40	−.24	−.28	−.45	−.56	−.15	−.61	−.31	−.49	−.37	−.43	−.42
Factor Q-1 (liberal, free-thinking)																		
M	−.03	.07	−.16	.04	.04	.26	.01	−.10	−.16	.10	−.02	−.05	−.02	.11	−.06	.22	.12	.24
F	.22	.24	.09	.27	.14	.39	.15	−.11	.01	−.02	.03	−.12	.10	.24	−.03	.32	.14	.31
Factor Q-2 (self-sufficient, reclusive)																		
M	−.20	−.06	−.28	−.12	−.08	−.02	−.20	−.06	−.04	−.02	−.16	.03	−.17	−.01	−.12	.03	.02	.05
F	−.05	−.02	−.21	−.06	−.07	.11	−.14	−.06	.02	.06	.02	.02	.06	.19	.06	.24	.18	.24
Factor Q-3 (controlled, self-disciplined)																		
M	.06	.06	.06	.00	.13	.18	.08	.06	.03	.24	.31	.04	.17	.12	.25	.25	.18	.14
F	.25	.16	.16	.08	.08	.24	.08	.35	.34	.38	.42	.12	.32	.25	.36	.12	.20	.23
Factor Q-4 (tense, frustrated)																		
M	−.18	−.16	−.08	−.15	−.15	−.31	−.20	−.05	−.22	−.24	−.41	−.18	−.46	−.16	−.24	−.15	−.24	−.15
F	−.47	−.50	−.44	−.35	−.32	−.50	−.37	−.31	−.36	−.51	−.64	−.19	−.69	−.45	−.49	−.44	−.46	−.50

C. Personality and Interest Inventories continued

Measures	Fx	F/M	v.1	v.2	v.3	Mp	Wo	CT	Lp	Ami	Leo	Tm	B–MS	B–FM	Anx	Nar	D–SD	D–AC
1. Cattell 16 PF Questionnaire (Ns = 93 males, 111 females)																		
Factor A (outgoing, sociable)																		
M	−.11	.09	−.27	.15	.13	.18	−.02	.01	.16	.08	.04	.02	.22	.03	−.14	.08	.13	−.03
F	−.15	−.01	−.25	.14	−.04	.16	.15	−.04	.25	.05	.31	.20	.21	.19	−.13	−.02	.17	.10
Factor B (intelligent, astute)																		
M	.31	−.25	−.23	−.07	.23	.24	.04	.31	.16	−.12	−.14	.12	.18	−.19	−.09	.14	−.04	.07
F	.18	−.07	.02	−.01	.20	.12	.06	.18	.08	.06	−.18	−.02	.02	−.11	.01	−.03	.03	.01
Factor C (emotionally stable, mature)																		
M	−.01	−.26	−.08	.21	.36	.27	.35	−.06	.27	.35	.26	.29	.27	.07	−.33	−.19	.23	−.12
F	.03	−.18	−.13	.34	.54	.50	.60	.15	.59	.57	.36	.53	.50	.32	−.47	−.39	.55	−.14
Factor E (assertive, aggressive)																		
M	.08	−.10	−.33	.02	.11	.24	.19	.21	.32	.02	.29	.25	.33	−.06	−.09	.18	.04	.01
F	.35	−.32	−.36	−.26	.21	.10	−.07	.54	.06	−.23	−.12	.09	.34	−.56	.02	.39	.00	.12
Factor F (pleasure-seeking, hedonistic)																		
M	.13	−.08	−.46	−.04	−.09	.04	−.27	.12	.07	−.19	−.09	−.11	.11	−.17	.26	.45	−.06	.14
F	.14	−.22	−.49	−.09	.00	.12	−.04	.25	.19	−.02	.08	.09	.29	−.25	−.14	.34	.08	.32
Factor G (dutiful, persevering)																		
M	−.19	.00	−.02	.38	.12	.19	.20	−.32	.23	.24	.37	.17	.15	.16	−.07	−.21	.28	.01
F	−.19	.11	.08	.45	.11	.18	.18	−.12	.17	.29	.28	.12	.02	.31	−.09	−.30	.35	.10
Factor H (venturesome, bold)																		
M	.03	−.01	−.51	.17	.35	.41	.22	.20	.50	.16	.23	.40	.58	.06	−.13	.04	.45	.01
F	.04	−.21	−.53	.12	.38	.52	.39	.31	.60	.20	.28	.43	.67	−.02	−.39	.10	.49	.00
Factor I (tender-minded, sensitive)																		
M	.33	.32	.20	−.29	.10	−.16	−.17	.28	−.19	−.14	−.23	−.20	−.13	.08	.04	−.09	−.12	.13
F	.00	.18	.29	−.02	−.01	−.12	−.11	−.02	−.20	.01	−.05	−.20	−.30	.09	.25	−.21	−.21	−.07
Factor L (suspicious, wary)																		
M	−.09	−.06	−.06	−.03	−.32	−.26	−.28	−.13	−.23	−.30	−.24	−.16	−.22	−.23	.13	.24	−.15	.14
F	−.22	.26	.04	−.12	−.57	−.52	−.52	−.28	−.39	−.50	−.09	−.40	−.34	−.14	.32	.29	−.40	.24
Factor M (imaginative, Bohemian)																		
M	.21	.32	.19	−.41	.00	−.20	−.08	.33	−.23	−.18	−.17	−.17	−.08	.01	.15	−.06	−.14	−.03
F	.33	.11	.07	−.43	−.02	−.19	−.24	.30	−.31	−.29	−.42	−.25	−.17	−.31	.33	.18	−.25	−.01
Factor N (observant, shrewd)																		
M	.05	−.02	−.16	.04	.14	.18	.06	.17	.20	−.09	.02	.23	.20	−.03	−.03	.13	.16	.04
F	−.15	.10	−.29	.09	−.12	.00	−.04	−.08	.11	−.11	.17	.08	.15	−.04	−.08	.16	.14	.22
Factor O (apprehensive, insecure)																		
M	.12	.23	.21	−.17	−.38	−.51	−.40	−.01	−.51	−.37	−.14	−.40	−.50	−.04	.28	.08	−.24	.17
F	−.09	.34	.28	−.21	−.54	−.58	−.54	−.16	−.66	−.45	−.44	−.67	−.63	−.16	.46	.24	−.52	.13
Factor Q-1 (liberal, free-thinking)																		
M	.19	−.15	.05	−.25	.14	.03	−.01	.30	.00	−.13	.01	.21	.07	−.21	−.03	.03	−.07	−.05
F	.16	−.10	−.22	−.12	.27	.27	.16	.23	.22	.05	−.09	.31	.18	−.14	.06	.09	.17	−.10
Factor Q-2 (self-sufficient, reclusive)																		
M	.24	−.04	.25	−.15	−.10	−.18	−.08	.05	−.22	−.13	−.08	−.12	−.14	−.13	.06	−.05	−.24	.14
F	.02	−.09	.14	.00	.15	.01	.16	.06	.01	.02	−.04	.14	.01	−.09	−.02	−.07	.01	−.04
Factor Q-3 (controlled, self-disciplined)																		
M	−.01	.11	.14	.08	.37	.21	.25	.01	.22	.25	.12	.19	.18	.20	−.15	−.27	.15	−.14
F	−.24	−.12	−.06	.31	.19	.25	.40	−.12	.38	.33	.35	.40	.24	.27	−.27	−.17	.41	.05
Factor Q-4 (tense, frustrated)																		
M	.19	−.05	.06	−.07	−.37	−.32	−.42	−.06	−.37	−.40	−.14	−.39	−.39	−.22	.21	.13	−.32	.26
F	−.03	.30	.18	−.26	−.56	−.52	−.65	−.18	−.67	−.56	−.39	−.60	−.60	−.25	.59	.30	−.63	.16

C. Personality and Interest Inventories continued

Measures	Do	Cs	Sy	Sp	Sa	In	Em	Re	So	Sc	Gi	Cm	Wb	To	Ac	Ai	Ie	Py
2. Comrey Personality Scales (Ns = 55 males, 51 females)																		
Validity																		
M	−.06	−.05	.02	−.10	.04	−.08	−.23	.04	−.15	.10	.17	−.31	−.09	−.06	−.16	−.10	−.07	.01
F	.00	−.11	−.06	−.12	.02	−.03	−.12	−.01	.04	.09	.01	−.17	.03	−.15	.01	−.02	−.05	−.10
Response Bias																		
M	.15	.16	.18	.04	.12	.14	−.05	.13	−.06	.37	.46	−.10	.12	.05	.18	.03	.05	.17
F	.16	−.01	.08	−.14	.00	.06	.04	.51	.52	.60	.58	.09	.40	.13	.47	.12	.25	.15
Trust																		
M	−.07	.24	.16	.27	.09	.00	.32	.43	.19	.18	.17	.27	.33	.51	.30	.33	.22	.23
F	−.07	.29	.12	−.04	.02	−.01	.07	.57	.29	.43	.46	.15	.27	.58	.31	.35	.14	.19
Orderly																		
M	.02	−.12	−.14	−.20	−.05	−.07	−.28	.02	.23	.15	.04	.04	.06	−.05	.22	−.04	−.01	−.19
F	.05	−.12	.02	−.15	−.09	−.05	−.04	.25	.29	.39	.43	.23	.33	.11	.43	.08	.13	.06
Conforming																		
M	−.06	.03	.10	.09	−.03	−.29	−.17	.20	.30	.09	.09	.27	.19	−.06	.15	−.28	−.20	−.17
F	−.30	−.27	−.21	−.35	−.37	−.49	−.34	.29	.29	.25	.21	.22	.04	.04	.17	−.16	−.22	−.17
Activity																		
M	.48	.13	.34	.32	.37	.26	.07	.15	.10	−.08	.18	.37	.40	−.11	.27	−.06	.13	.11
F	.27	.33	.39	.29	.31	.33	.23	.29	.10	.11	.27	.09	.36	−.05	.40	.15	.34	.22
Emotional Stability																		
M	.44	.27	.40	.46	.41	.44	.30	.13	.45	.37	.44	.44	.72	.22	.33	.16	.42	.39
F	.37	.39	.43	.44	.34	.23	.27	.40	.59	.57	.54	.41	.70	.31	.59	.34	.46	.51
Extraversion																		
M	.64	.63	.79	.71	.78	.54	.54	.12	.04	−.05	.22	.42	.40	.07	.41	.28	.47	.35
F	.58	.53	.61	.57	.50	.49	.33	.11	.10	.00	.18	−.08	.31	−.05	.31	.11	.37	.27
Masculinity																		
M	.07	.04	−.03	.00	−.02	.13	−.01	−.03	−.19	.07	.18	−.07	.23	.09	.01	.18	.17	.45
F	−.13	.13	−.05	−.02	−.10	−.02	.02	.11	.02	.14	.09	−.30	.09	.02	−.05	.24	.11	.15
Empathy																		
M	.35	.07	.25	.14	.19	.24	.25	.08	.13	.26	.40	.02	.16	.10	.20	.11	.11	.19
F	.22	.21	.21	.13	.12	.13	.08	.25	.05	.15	.44	−.03	.24	−.02	.22	.02	.09	.10
3. Costa and McCrae NEO-AC (Ns = 112 males, 122 females)																		
Neuroticism																		
M	−.24	−.31	−.22	−.37	−.21	−.46	−.16	−.11	−.22	−.35	−.36	−.13	−.64	−.42	−.32	−.31	−.42	−.42
F	−.38	−.36	−.36	−.43	−.36	−.46	−.29	−.19	−.29	−.31	−.39	−.22	−.62	−.30	−.40	−.27	−.43	−.43
Extraversion																		
M	.44	.38	.53	.56	.45	.22	.47	.10	.28	−.26	−.11	.36	.25	.22	.28	.22	.32	.06
F	.53	.43	.65	.58	.62	.37	.50	−.09	−.01	−.29	−.04	.11	.25	−.02	.15	.10	.24	.21
Openness																		
M	.08	.32	.09	.17	.14	.15	.36	.09	−.06	.02	−.09	.12	.09	.10	.05	.30	.29	.16
F	.15	.38	.26	.25	.23	.09	.31	.16	−.04	−.02	.05	.20	.09	.19	.04	.30	.30	.21
Agreeableness																		
M	−.17	.06	−.12	−.01	−.21	−.11	.25	.29	.37	.38	.32	.23	.32	.36	.19	.34	.23	.10
F	−.19	.00	−.09	−.12	−.19	−.15	.14	.30	.24	.45	.42	.16	.29	.37	.15	.26	.11	.05
Conscientiousness																		
M	.34	.16	.21	.00	.23	.26	−.05	.34	.26	.15	.21	.23	.23	−.01	.45	.09	.22	.13
F	.35	.10	.11	.03	.15	.26	−.07	.29	.43	.31	.31	.19	.35	.02	.52	.01	.23	.20

C. Personality and Interest Inventories continued

Measures	Fx	F/M	v.1	v.2	v.3	Mp	Wo	CT	Lp	Ami	Leo	Tm	B–MS	B–FM	Anx	Nar	D–SD	D–AC
2. Comrey Personality Scales (Ns = 55 males, 51 females)																		
Validity																		
M	−.01	−.06	.04	−.02	−.12	−.03	−.10	−.04	−.06	−.06	.01	.00	−.05	−.04	.19	−.01	−.05	−.01
F	−.01	−.38	.10	.12	.06	−.11	−.11	−.09	.01	−.12	.08	.06	.14	−.03	−.06	−.02	.03	.05
Response Bias																		
M	−.14	.09	−.05	.32	.08	.17	.04	−.01	.24	.07	.26	.20	.10	.20	−.07	−.13	.40	−.18
F	−.37	−.08	.10	.65	.22	.34	.40	−.38	.40	.38	.52	.40	.18	.43	−.24	−.33	.45	.00
Trust																		
M	.23	.03	.14	.06	.49	.27	.39	.20	.19	.47	.01	.08	.13	.15	−.35	−.44	.18	−.31
F	.08	.21	.27	.29	.53	.35	.40	−.05	.14	.52	.04	.05	.09	.47	−.19	−.51	.40	−.25
Orderly																		
M	−.56	.00	.05	.36	−.13	.14	.16	−.43	.11	.09	.12	.19	−.12	.09	−.10	−.02	.11	−.03
F	−.62	−.02	.14	.46	.16	.31	.38	−.36	.32	.22	.43	.33	.07	.35	−.36	−.29	.33	−.19
Conforming																		
M	−.30	−.20	.04	.33	−.12	−.01	.25	−.46	.06	.22	.33	.02	−.03	−.14	−.31	−.19	.13	.06
F	−.47	.15	.37	.55	−.15	−.03	.12	−.66	−.08	.20	.37	−.11	−.39	.30	−.17	−.39	.08	.26
Activity																		
M	−.20	−.50	−.41	.25	−.02	.12	.28	−.13	.44	.06	.60	.36	.36	−.31	−.32	.31	.26	−.04
F	−.04	−.08	−.21	.17	.14	.18	.19	.06	.40	.08	.20	.30	.38	−.05	−.29	.03	.42	.16
Emotional Stability																		
M	−.04	−.49	−.24	.21	.30	.36	.65	.04	.65	.57	.52	.53	.59	.00	−.69	−.05	.54	−.19
F	−.01	−.12	−.09	.41	.43	.58	.66	−.19	.65	.58	.51	.57	.53	.42	−.47	−.19	.59	.11
Extraversion																		
M	.14	−.24	−.62	.01	.30	.32	.24	.34	.60	.08	.40	.39	.71	−.25	−.33	.26	.35	.07
F	.25	−.14	−.51	.02	.20	.27	.11	.25	.43	.07	.07	.26	.57	−.16	−.12	.12	.26	.22
Masculinity																		
M	−.01	−.33	.04	−.15	.19	.10	.11	.06	.09	.05	−.06	.31	.27	−.07	−.04	−.10	.07	−.19
F	.00	−.31	.15	.07	.09	−.10	.04	−.06	.04	.10	−.02	.07	.11	−.08	−.06	−.20	.10	.11
Empathy																		
M	.04	.07	−.20	.29	.16	.16	.09	.14	.32	.14	.32	.21	.18	.11	−.08	.04	.46	−.17
F	.06	.10	−.04	.16	.23	.18	.12	−.01	.18	.19	.12	.16	.25	.12	−.17	−.22	.20	−.14
3. Costa and McCrae NEO-AC (Ns = 112 males, 122 females)																		
Neuroticism																		
M	−.02	.38	.04	−.10	−.45	−.43	−.45	−.14	−.48	−.41	−.32	−.53	−.59	−.12	.47	.16	−.36	.11
F	.06	.30	.16	−.24	−.38	−.43	−.44	−.12	−.58	−.41	−.39	−.54	−.58	−.08	.44	.05	−.48	.09
Extraversion																		
M	.03	−.06	−.45	.22	.21	.29	.14	.21	.44	.06	.19	.18	.42	.05	−.32	.25	.15	.06
F	.16	−.17	−.57	.04	.10	.27	−.03	.29	.42	.00	.20	.19	.56	−.16	−.22	.40	.25	.19
Openness																		
M	.39	.22	.03	−.27	.21	−.02	−.02	.45	.04	−.02	−.30	−.06	.03	.07	−.05	.03	.02	.01
F	.22	.05	−.10	−.10	.28	.14	.11	.31	.14	.04	−.09	.04	.16	−.03	.02	−.03	.15	.09
Agreeableness																		
M	.21	.21	.32	.01	.40	.14	.40	.07	.09	.48	.09	.12	.00	.51	−.19	−.52	.20	−.25
F	.09	.27	.36	.09	.39	.17	.25	.04	.03	.45	.06	−.03	−.10	.42	−.12	−.48	.22	−.18
Conscientiousness																		
M	−.54	.03	−.17	.55	.05	.31	.26	−.26	.46	.11	.44	.41	.24	.16	−.17	.19	.41	.06
F	−.56	−.16	−.16	.66	−.05	.15	.33	−.38	.46	.20	.47	.46	.26	.18	−.36	.07	.38	.04

C. Personality and Interest Inventories continued

Measures	Do	Cs	Sy	Sp	Sa	In	Em	Re	So	Sc	Gi	Cm	Wb	To	Ac	Ai	Ie	Py
4. Eysenck Maudsley Personality Inventory (Ns = 89 males, 86 females)																		
Extraversion																		
M	.52	.43	.76	.68	.55	.42	.44	.08	−.04	−.22	.05	.45	.42	.12	.23	.08	.33	.28
F	.42	.38	.56	.50	.47	.21	.32	.00	.13	−.15	.04	.31	.24	−.04	.10	−.05	.15	.14
Neuroticism																		
M	−.53	−.45	−.47	−.36	−.45	−.62	−.34	−.36	−.31	−.47	−.60	−.40	−.67	−.35	−.54	−.34	−.48	−.62
F	−.46	−.48	−.43	−.36	−.38	−.51	−.44	−.44	−.43	−.49	−.56	−.36	−.71	−.32	−.61	−.44	−.53	−.52
? Score																		
M	−.09	−.07	−.08	−.19	−.01	−.14	−.15	−.19	−.08	−.06	−.04	−.27	−.23	−.10	−.15	−.13	−.13	−.03
F	−.04	.06	−.08	.09	.00	−.02	.08	−.11	−.17	−.19	−.13	−.02	−.12	−.05	−.04	.04	.01	.02
5. Goldberg's Adjectival Big-Five Markers (Ns = 289 males, 411 females)																		
Extraversion/Surgency																		
M	.55	.35	.54	.37	.51	.37	.30	.01	.03	−.17	.08	.15	.21	−.09	.20	−.10	.09	.02
F	.53	.38	.57	.51	.52	.35	.39	−.03	−.02	−.20	−.02	.15	.14	.01	.12	.09	.17	.11
Agreeableness																		
M	−.07	.09	.13	.05	−.09	−.24	.18	.26	.27	.25	.24	.24	.22	.32	.18	.05	.04	.03
F	−.13	−.08	.04	−.03	−.10	−.25	.06	.06	.21	.17	.25	.08	.09	.12	.05	−.06	−.08	−.05
Dependability/Conscientiousness																		
M	.14	−.11	−.01	−.15	.03	.06	−.23	.01	.22	.16	.16	.14	.10	−.13	.22	−.14	−.08	−.05
F	.13	−.13	−.02	−.13	−.01	−.03	−.20	.13	.24	.19	.18	.11	.07	−.07	.27	−.12	−.07	−.07
Emotional Stability																		
M	.12	.15	.10	.07	.03	.27	.19	.27	.35	.46	.44	.06	.50	.27	.30	.22	.28	.35
F	.13	.17	.13	.13	.10	.34	.16	.31	.33	.46	.50	.04	.54	.31	.33	.24	.35	.30
Intellect																		
M	.31	.31	.24	.29	.37	.43	.31	−.05	−.18	−.20	−.11	.13	.04	.02	.10	.37	.38	.32
F	.34	.36	.23	.28	.34	.38	.29	.14	−.13	−.11	−.11	.09	.09	.13	.15	.42	.44	.38
6. Guilford-Zimmerman Temperament Survey (GZTS) (Ns = 112 males, 98 females)																		
General Activity																		
M	.40	.12	.23	.24	.36	.24	−.01	.05	.00	−.10	.01	.14	.19	−.07	.16	−.06	.05	.10
F	.49	.33	.48	.39	.45	.28	.33	.05	−.06	−.21	.10	.30	.14	−.10	.22	.08	.17	.20
Restraint																		
M	.06	.11	−.25	−.34	−.12	.09	−.05	.26	.26	.45	.33	−.13	.10	.11	.28	.21	.17	.17
F	.04	.04	−.16	−.37	−.26	.06	−.19	.38	.23	.37	.31	.13	.07	.25	.36	.22	.16	.24
Ascendance																		
M	.62	.50	.45	.46	.54	.44	.45	.17	.01	−.06	.13	.26	.35	.13	.27	.24	.32	.33
F	.71	.63	.61	.53	.63	.65	.57	.12	−.11	−.06	.25	.15	.34	.10	.33	.25	.33	.39
Sociability																		
M	.62	.46	.76	.54	.50	.30	.48	.34	.25	.10	.32	.38	.47	.31	.38	.17	.30	.21
F	.62	.44	.70	.55	.54	.34	.56	.21	.03	.00	.33	.29	.32	−.01	.40	.07	.20	.24
Emotional Stability																		
M	.53	.41	.43	.44	.27	.58	.31	.40	.53	.51	.60	.40	.76	.40	.61	.39	.50	.45
F	.42	.45	.43	.39	.22	.41	.37	.32	.44	.51	.60	.37	.77	.39	.53	.39	.43	.41
Objectivity																		
M	.31	.37	.29	.29	.11	.47	.35	.47	.51	.58	.62	.26	.72	.58	.48	.49	.54	.47
F	.30	.43	.33	.33	.08	.45	.33	.34	.39	.50	.64	.10	.63	.50	.44	.43	.38	.41
Friendliness																		
M	−.01	.21	.00	.02	−.24	.20	.12	.46	.43	.57	.48	.12	.51	.54	.34	.36	.33	.33
F	−.06	.15	.10	.00	−.22	.00	.14	.36	.45	.47	.52	.10	.42	.48	.29	.34	.26	.16

C. Personality and Interest Inventories continued

Measures	Fx	F/M	v.1	v.2	v.3	Mp	Wo	CT	Lp	Ami	Leo	Tm	B–MS	B–FM	Anx	Nar	D–SD	D–AC
4. Eysenck Maudsley Personality Inventory (Ns = 89 males, 86 females)
Extraversion
M	.06	−.39	−.64	.01	.14	.28	.22	.20	.48	.12	.45	.34	.57	−.31	−.31	.32	.23	.11
F	−.04	−.22	−.44	.10	.00	.18	.09	.07	.36	.08	.21	.10	.41	−.08	−.22	.28	.15	.28
Neuroticism
M	.20	.45	.27	−.32	−.48	−.64	−.66	−.06	−.73	−.52	−.48	−.78	−.71	−.18	.52	.09	−.56	.35
F	.10	.25	.24	−.38	−.60	−.71	−.68	.10	−.73	−.52	−.50	−.76	−.63	−.34	.54	.21	−.67	.17
? Score
M	.09	.06	.07	−.08	−.09	−.08	−.20	.02	−.17	−.21	−.20	−.18	−.13	−.04	.21	−.01	−.10	−.01
F	.19	−.17	−.14	−.08	.06	−.19	−.13	.22	−.13	−.19	−.07	−.13	−.02	−.10	.07	.17	−.12	.03
5. Goldberg's Adjectival Big-Five Markers (Ns = 289 males, 411 females)
Extraversion/Surgency
M	−.08	−.24	−.55	.15	−.01	.23	−.02	.05	.45	−.10	.23	.30	.55	−.21	−.31	.36	.23	.20
F	.11	−.23	−.58	.00	.10	.27	−.01	.26	.41	−.06	.23	.31	.52	−.26	−.19	.39	.23	.06
Agreeableness
M	.07	.33	.10	.07	.23	.13	.25	.05	.12	.36	.03	−.06	−.07	.34	−.19	−.33	.17	−.12
F	.01	.19	.15	.14	.06	.03	.15	−.09	.00	.30	.11	−.11	−.11	.28	−.04	−.31	.10	−.09
Dependability/Conscientiousness
M	−.42	−.14	.01	.33	−.12	.11	.09	−.36	.18	.05	.39	.31	.12	.06	−.13	.04	.14	−.02
F	−.50	−.03	.00	.40	−.13	.09	.11	−.37	.19	.11	.43	.27	.06	.16	−.06	.00	.19	−.06
Emotional Stability
M	.04	−.17	.08	.21	.37	.32	.51	.05	.38	.45	.23	.42	.35	.21	−.31	−.30	.38	−.19
F	.00	−.28	.04	.22	.39	.38	.48	.00	.41	.47	.18	.43	.39	.20	−.38	−.26	.42	−.17
Intellect
M	.23	−.10	−.35	−.16	.19	.14	−.07	.39	.20	−.16	−.10	.15	.24	−.18	−.05	.27	.09	.10
F	.32	−.11	−.30	−.18	.30	.20	.06	.42	.25	−.12	−.16	.18	.29	−.18	−.07	.23	.12	−.03
6. Guilford-Zimmerman Temperament Survey (GZTS) (Ns = 112 males, 98 females)
General Activity
M	−.14	−.18	−.38	.18	−.03	.15	.07	−.08	.30	−.07	.34	.26	.33	−.13	−.08	.26	.12	.11
F	−.10	.02	−.51	.19	.01	.32	.07	.07	.35	−.02	.29	.22	.36	−.04	−.12	.30	.25	.28
Restraint
M	−.20	.10	.19	.24	.19	.18	.21	−.14	.14	.16	.12	.17	−.02	.25	−.04	−.27	.24	−.12
F	−.22	.16	.20	.30	.20	.25	.20	−.18	.16	.11	.18	.28	−.08	.29	.12	−.27	.30	−.12
Ascendance
M	.11	−.28	−.57	.14	.24	.37	.22	.24	.54	.08	.29	.36	.60	−.08	−.28	.30	.31	.02
F	.10	−.28	−.63	.12	.36	.46	.27	.35	.58	.06	.19	.48	.74	−.22	−.34	.29	.42	.12
Sociability
M	.05	−.20	−.57	.29	.31	.57	.41	.13	.63	.37	.40	.42	.64	.15	−.40	.05	.47	.02
F	−.09	−.11	−.60	.25	.14	.40	.23	.07	.56	.13	.36	.36	.62	.02	−.20	.14	.49	.23
Emotional Stability
M	−.09	−.37	−.25	.34	.54	.63	.78	.05	.73	.65	.55	.76	.71	.41	−.56	−.18	.59	−.26
F	−.05	−.12	−.20	.33	.52	.67	.75	−.08	.71	.63	.48	.70	.54	.34	−.56	−.34	.66	−.10
Objectivity
M	.13	−.18	−.03	.25	.65	.56	.77	.19	.56	.69	.39	.61	.56	.49	−.52	−.43	.54	−.33
F	.03	−.09	−.08	.21	.62	.62	.64	.03	.60	.60	.29	.64	.50	.36	−.38	−.40	.63	−.24
Friendliness
M	.18	.00	.24	.13	.53	.34	.57	.14	.25	.62	.18	.32	.21	.47	−.35	−.62	.31	−.41
F	.12	.23	.19	.18	.44	.38	.40	−.03	.23	.62	.15	.20	.04	.45	−.18	−.57	.38	−.35

C. Personality and Interest Inventories continued

Measures	Do	Cs	Sy	Sp	Sa	In	Em	Re	So	Sc	Gi	Cm	Wb	To	Ac	Ai	Ie	Py
6. Guilford-Zimmerman Temperament Survey (GZTS) (*N*s = 112 males, 98 females) continued																		
Thoughtfulness																		
M	.11	.15	−.02	.00	.16	.05	.13	.05	−.01	−.06	−.03	−.09	−.12	−.12	.11	.09	.10	−.05
F	.23	.12	.12	.03	.26	.15	.17	.06	−.11	−.12	−.08	.20	−.06	.00	.09	.08	.11	.13
Personal Relations																		
M	.30	.31	.32	.20	.03	.26	.30	.46	.43	.43	.51	.26	.57	.53	.45	.26	.33	.30
F	.07	.21	.22	.08	−.13	.12	.09	.46	.45	.49	.50	.31	.53	.47	.34	.26	.26	.20
Masculinity																		
M	.23	.18	.01	.22	.18	.39	.09	.15	.10	.25	.21	.17	.41	.25	.16	.27	.32	.45
F	.31	.23	.17	.29	.21	.34	.27	.00	−.15	−.02	.09	−.15	.17	.21	.05	.34	.25	.39
7. Heist and Yonge Omnibus Personality Inventory (OPI) (*N*s = 57 males, 51 females)																		
Thinking Introversion																		
M	.40	.42	.26	.39	.44	.42	.54	.07	−.20	−.11	.04	.04	.00	.31	.05	.49	.40	.44
F	.46	.47	.28	.47	.38	.41	.62	.24	−.01	−.04	.11	.29	.28	.45	.15	.61	.52	.39
Theoretical Orientation																		
M	.42	.45	.24	.39	.48	.66	.29	.18	.05	.03	.12	.13	.28	.28	.31	.49	.54	.57
F	.35	.32	.02	.22	.12	.46	.39	.15	.02	−.21	−.08	.36	.26	.26	.28	.48	.52	.60
Estheticism																		
M	.17	.32	.16	.18	.33	.10	.42	−.01	−.23	−.32	−.21	.04	−.22	.09	−.09	.25	.11	.12
F	.48	.54	.34	.52	.52	.35	.57	.19	.05	−.16	.02	.16	.13	.37	.22	.50	.43	.30
Complexity																		
M	.04	.10	.03	.22	.31	.20	.18	−.20	−.46	−.37	−.23	−.18	−.27	−.01	−.34	.10	.09	.15
F	.29	.52	.29	.52	.37	.44	.52	−.07	−.23	−.28	−.11	−.07	.17	.30	−.18	.43	.42	.32
Autonomy																		
M	−.02	.24	.09	.30	.13	.16	.41	.03	−.05	−.15	−.22	.06	.00	.37	−.13	.43	.36	.28
F	.45	.45	.28	.47	.33	.56	.48	−.06	−.15	−.32	−.17	.17	.13	.29	−.10	.61	.53	.49
Non-Religious Orientation																		
M	−.20	−.06	−.05	.04	−.03	−.01	.15	−.05	−.21	−.19	−.17	−.16	−.11	.04	−.36	.20	.08	.04
F	.16	.03	.05	.13	.14	.09	.15	−.10	−.17	−.14	−.07	−.09	−.18	−.12	−.14	.23	.11	.11
Social Extraversion																		
M	.53	.44	.74	.49	.48	.33	.37	.33	.20	.03	.25	.22	.36	.30	.30	.15	.28	.22
F	.74	.60	.76	.65	.63	.43	.56	.11	.09	−.25	.07	.11	.34	.18	.13	.21	.49	.22
Impulse Expression																		
M	.10	.04	.07	.17	.27	−.02	.27	−.33	−.65	−.76	−.58	−.15	−.50	−.27	−.43	−.09	−.16	−.11
F	.43	.51	.53	.74	.60	.39	.51	−.31	−.46	−.74	−.48	−.10	−.13	−.10	−.39	.15	.31	.11
Personal Integration																		
M	.52	.50	.48	.49	.29	.51	.33	.46	.69	.60	.62	.36	.79	.55	.65	.41	.52	.52
F	.42	.29	.34	.23	.26	.37	.24	.31	.47	.51	.56	.36	.76	.49	.55	.47	.53	.36
Low Anxiety Level																		
M	.56	.46	.48	.59	.38	.62	.36	.31	.58	.54	.65	.30	.81	.47	.65	.44	.53	.47
F	.40	.42	.30	.33	.36	.57	.32	.14	.44	.44	.41	.48	.76	.55	.56	.52	.69	.48
Altruism																		
M	.43	.44	.51	.33	.28	.26	.45	.58	.27	.18	.30	.23	.31	.60	.39	.36	.35	.39
F	.46	.40	.35	.24	.23	.20	.37	.40	.33	.28	.55	.22	.45	.54	.34	.35	.43	.13
Practical Outlook																		
M	−.08	−.32	−.13	−.30	−.19	−.27	−.37	−.09	.12	.00	.05	.06	.03	−.40	−.01	−.46	−.37	−.48
F	−.25	−.50	−.21	−.40	−.23	−.45	−.60	−.19	−.05	.02	.06	−.20	−.31	−.51	.00	−.65	−.43	−.47

C. Personality and Interest Inventories continued

Measures	Fx	F/M	v.1	v.2	v.3	Mp	Wo	CT	Lp	Ami	Leo	Tm	B–MS	B–FM	Anx	Nar	D–SD	D–AC
6. Guilford-Zimmerman Temperament Survey (GZTS) (Ns = 112 males, 98 females) continued																		
Thoughtfulness																		
M	.04	.13	−.13	.07	−.01	−.05	−.18	.06	.06	−.16	−.01	−.09	−.08	−.17	.15	.15	.02	.07
F	−.03	.03	−.25	.05	.04	.05	−.03	.10	.16	−.17	.00	.03	.17	−.11	.03	.27	.09	.11
Personal Relations																		
M	−.01	−.15	−.12	.32	.47	.52	.62	.05	.48	.61	.40	.49	.41	.39	−.35	−.36	.43	−.29
F	−.09	.14	.11	.24	.40	.52	.55	−.18	.37	.56	.32	.38	.13	.45	−.27	−.53	.49	−.22
Masculinity																		
M	.06	−.53	−.03	−.04	.32	.22	.43	.19	.29	.24	.31	.46	.45	−.04	−.27	−.14	.22	−.31
F	.26	−.53	−.26	−.12	.33	.15	.17	.27	.23	.02	.04	.35	.42	−.30	−.22	.11	.08	−.15
7. Heist and Yonge Omnibus Personality Inventory (OPI) (Ns = 57 males, 51 females)																		
Thinking Introversion																		
M	.53	−.02	−.39	−.32	.36	.32	−.02	.63	.23	−.08	−.09	.15	.31	−.28	−.09	.15	.17	−.10
F	.38	−.05	−.38	−.08	.45	.42	.31	.51	.47	.16	−.13	.14	.39	−.21	−.18	.20	.42	−.18
Theoretical Orientation																		
M	.28	−.33	−.28	−.14	.39	.39	.29	.38	.36	.06	.27	.46	.49	−.14	−.27	.15	.28	.02
F	.17	−.25	−.24	−.05	.44	.33	.21	.32	.35	−.05	−.24	.25	.37	−.29	−.29	.22	.04	−.20
Estheticism																		
M	.29	.25	−.35	−.23	.12	.02	−.21	.52	−.02	−.19	−.36	−.19	−.02	−.13	.13	.27	−.08	.05
F	.23	.05	−.46	.02	.31	.34	.17	.47	.41	.07	−.10	.15	.35	−.08	−.04	.33	.28	−.01
Complexity																		
M	.51	.07	−.18	−.48	.13	−.12	−.29	.55	−.19	−.33	−.25	−.19	.04	−.41	.21	.29	−.23	.02
F	.68	−.23	−.30	−.53	.39	.31	.02	.77	.22	−.04	−.23	.00	.48	−.36	.05	.21	.13	−.27
Autonomy																		
M	.69	−.12	−.03	−.51	.47	.24	.06	.67	−.07	.06	−.26	−.03	.10	.01	.01	−.12	−.10	−.36
F	.54	−.28	−.38	−.43	.44	.41	.06	.72	.34	−.15	−.30	.26	.56	−.34	.04	.38	.05	−.23
Non-Religious Orientation																		
M	.47	.06	.08	−.41	.15	.01	−.07	.33	−.23	−.10	−.24	−.17	−.07	−.11	.19	−.02	−.13	−.19
F	.12	.00	−.13	−.17	.10	.05	−.13	.20	.05	−.22	−.27	.18	.20	−.13	.22	.19	.04	.19
Social Extraversion																		
M	.08	−.08	−.53	.31	.22	.32	.27	.08	.51	.24	.36	.26	.51	.07	−.40	.03	.45	.19
F	.19	−.18	−.77	.02	.16	.48	.16	.36	.59	−.03	.39	.36	.57	−.30	−.25	.43	.45	−.01
Impulse Expression																		
M	.22	−.08	−.43	−.44	−.17	−.29	−.50	.45	−.28	−.64	−.40	−.36	−.14	−.61	.38	.70	−.41	.41
F	.34	−.43	−.64	−.45	.02	.15	−.28	.58	.19	−.41	−.27	−.11	.44	−.63	.02	.67	−.11	.24
Personal Integration																		
M	.06	−.21	−.16	.38	.56	.68	.77	−.02	.74	.74	.56	.67	.68	.49	−.76	−.38	.69	−.16
F	−.06	−.01	−.14	.32	.50	.60	.75	.04	.69	.58	.40	.70	.50	.20	−.59	−.07	.62	−.47
Low Anxiety Level																		
M	.01	−.37	−.18	.31	.55	.66	.78	.01	.78	.70	.60	.75	.76	.29	−.73	−.29	.71	−.16
F	.02	−.16	−.15	.15	.58	.65	.77	.19	.75	.55	.19	.64	.57	.12	−.57	−.04	.58	−.32
Altruism																		
M	.19	−.02	−.39	.25	.47	.49	.32	.19	.45	.39	.26	.25	.30	.18	−.36	−.21	.44	−.10
F	.15	.11	−.31	.24	.46	.52	.48	.27	.50	.39	.30	.32	.32	.00	−.18	−.09	.67	−.42
Practical Outlook																		
M	−.65	−.02	.10	.47	−.50	−.32	−.06	−.59	−.01	−.13	.16	−.10	−.17	.06	.01	.11	−.03	.36
F	−.74	.03	.14	.41	−.54	−.42	−.27	−.74	−.33	−.23	.25	−.08	−.41	.05	.12	−.05	−.21	.44

C. Personality and Interest Inventories continued

Measures	Do	Cs	Sy	Sp	Sa	In	Em	Re	So	Sc	Gi	Cm	Wb	To	Ac	Ai	Ie	Py
7. Heist and Yonge Omnibus Personality Inventory (OPI) (*N*s = 57 males, 51 females) continued																		
Masculinity–Femininity																		
M	.20	.01	−.04	.14	.03	.32	−.03	.10	.35	.42	.43	.14	.54	.12	.31	.09	.22	.15
F	−.20	−.31	−.35	−.29	−.27	.04	−.32	−.10	−.05	.25	.14	.13	.19	−.09	.15	.06	.05	.23
Response Bias																		
M	.54	.52	.34	.33	.30	.57	.22	.39	.52	.51	.60	.24	.63	.41	.64	.43	.49	.54
F	.43	.37	.15	.18	.26	.38	.30	.26	.23	.30	.46	.29	.50	.42	.50	.57	.56	.53
Non-Intellectual Disposition																		
M	−.40	−.47	−.22	−.45	−.51	−.54	−.47	−.13	.18	.08	−.05	−.04	−.09	−.32	−.09	−.54	−.48	−.48
F	−.53	−.59	−.25	−.51	−.40	−.67	−.22	−.22	−.01	.22	.04	−.26	−.26	−.45	−.19	−.65	−.62	−.59
8. Hogan Personality Inventory (HPI) (*N*s = 40 males, 92 females)																		
Adjustment																		
M	.41	.19	.53	.30	.15	.43	.01	.27	.61	.50	.38	.18	.70	.26	.55	.07	.51	.18
F	.28	.43	.26	.22	.14	.49	.29	.35	.48	.65	.76	.15	.73	.43	.57	.49	.48	.50
Ambition																		
M	.63	.33	.64	.49	.50	.56	.10	.36	.62	.31	.16	.37	.62	.29	.55	.08	.56	.30
F	.74	.53	.64	.51	.61	.67	.41	.23	.16	.16	.38	.20	.47	.16	.54	.33	.52	.42
Sociability																		
M	.51	.09	.59	.47	.54	.35	.36	−.28	.00	−.47	−.28	.01	.02	−.30	−.15	−.27	.03	−.11
F	.24	.17	.47	.53	.41	.02	.20	−.24	−.32	−.59	−.37	−.01	−.13	−.24	−.19	−.20	−.01	−.03
Likability																		
M	.27	.28	.49	.30	.22	.12	.13	.23	.44	.19	.07	.36	.45	.18	.36	−.10	.23	−.01
F	.13	.12	.27	.24	.18	.08	.16	.37	.27	.21	.27	.29	.35	.28	.32	.19	.18	.10
Prudence																		
M	.11	.10	.27	.02	.05	.05	−.10	.36	.59	.49	.34	.15	.42	.29	.57	.02	.10	.19
F	.04	.08	−.02	−.24	−.14	.03	−.10	.52	.47	.62	.53	.18	.29	.25	.54	.15	−.04	.09
Intellectence																		
M	.33	.22	.42	.34	.42	.19	.33	−.06	−.04	−.29	−.17	−.06	−.05	−.13	−.10	−.09	.09	−.03
F	.29	.50	.37	.46	.41	.35	.44	−.04	−.25	−.15	.08	.12	.12	.14	.05	.28	.39	.45
School Success																		
M	.46	.34	.30	.09	.34	.38	.27	.18	.11	.07	.40	−.17	.24	.17	.17	.30	.38	.25
F	.24	.22	.20	.17	.24	.32	.15	.05	−.09	.02	.11	.02	.12	.10	.20	.21	.37	.25
9. Interpersonal Dependency Inventory (IDI) (*N*s = 145 males, 145 females)																		
Emotional Reliance on Others (A)																		
M	−.09	−.17	−.04	−.12	−.04	−.32	−.11	−.23	−.13	−.39	−.42	−.02	−.43	−.35	−.17	−.25	−.24	−.36
F	−.16	−.28	−.13	−.28	−.24	−.43	−.22	−.23	−.04	−.25	−.29	−.08	−.47	−.29	−.20	−.40	−.35	−.45
Lack of Social Self-Confidence (B)																		
M	−.69	−.44	−.50	−.51	−.55	−.66	−.40	−.03	−.05	.02	−.20	−.14	−.50	−.17	−.29	−.27	−.47	−.31
F	−.65	−.45	−.53	−.50	−.54	−.62	−.46	−.24	−.15	−.07	−.23	−.33	−.57	−.24	−.32	−.37	−.46	−.37
Assertion of Autonomy (C)																		
M	.06	−.05	−.12	−.02	.12	.09	−.13	−.12	−.22	−.02	−.05	−.17	.03	−.29	−.11	−.14	.03	.05
F	.07	−.08	−.21	−.16	.00	.12	−.10	−.16	−.26	−.05	−.04	−.18	−.13	−.11	−.02	−.02	.00	.01
Unweighted Total Score (A + B − C)																		
M	−.40	−.28	−.19	−.30	−.34	−.54	−.19	−.10	.00	−.22	−.32	.01	−.50	−.15	−.18	−.20	−.37	−.39
F	−.48	−.36	−.26	−.35	−.43	−.64	−.32	−.18	.02	−.15	−.27	−.14	−.51	−.24	−.27	−.41	−.45	−.46
Weighted Total Score (40.84 + .20A + .18B − .66C + .55 BC/30)																		
M	−.56	−.40	−.42	−.46	−.47	−.62	−.30	−.03	−.05	−.11	−.27	−.16	−.55	−.19	−.28	−.27	−.49	−.43
F	−.60	−.42	−.41	−.44	−.52	−.66	−.46	−.21	.00	−.09	−.25	−.23	−.52	−.25	−.29	−.40	−.45	−.41

C. Personality and Interest Inventories continued																	
Measures	Fx	F/M	v.1	v.2	v.3	Mp	Wo	CT	Lp	Ami	Leo	Tm	B–MS	B–FM	Anx	Nar	D–SD	D–AC

7. Heist and Yonge Omnibus Personality Inventory (OPI) (Ns = 57 males, 51 females) continued

Masculinity–Femininity

M	−.19	−.45	.17	.19	.21	.29	.54	−.18	.38	.34	.54	.51	.39	.11	−.45	−.24	.34	−.14
F	−.27	−.20	.38	.01	.07	−.06	.19	−.32	−.07	.09	.02	.21	.01	.02	−.25	−.19	−.14	−.19

Response Bias

M	−.10	−.18	−.21	.39	.43	.59	.60	−.06	.67	.52	.58	.69	.63	.26	−.57	−.17	.64	−.05
F	−.10	−.21	−.21	.23	.52	.48	.55	.12	.54	.34	.12	.51	.38	−.13	−.38	.03	.54	−.31

Non-Intellectual Disposition

M	−.50	.09	.33	.29	−.43	−.31	−.07	−.64	−.24	.05	.04	−.24	−.37	.22	.12	−.17	−.19	.06
F	−.45	.26	.46	.16	−.53	−.51	−.24	−.65	−.49	−.04	.19	−.22	−.50	.38	.14	−.36	−.24	.21

8. Hogan Personality Inventory (HPI) (Ns = 40 males, 92 females)

Adjustment

M	−.07	−.09	−.11	.46	.33	.46	.57	−.11	.66	.65	.37	.55	.45	.41	−.40	−.18	.64	−.11
F	.08	−.20	.10	.27	.68	.62	.68	.05	.64	.71	.44	.56	.55	.35	−.51	−.50	.64	−.41

Ambition

M	−.14	−.14	−.33	.45	.18	.58	.53	.01	.76	.49	.44	.64	.62	.31	−.55	.09	.50	−.14
F	−.08	−.27	−.53	.23	.37	.58	.37	.30	.75	.24	.51	.64	.71	.00	−.40	.16	.55	−.12

Sociability

M	.03	−.32	−.73	.00	−.14	.07	−.14	.06	.24	−.22	.09	.06	.36	−.30	.09	.69	.14	.40
F	.08	−.29	−.56	−.15	−.18	−.11	−.28	.16	.01	−.30	−.05	−.17	.17	−.39	.01	.50	−.17	.40

Likability

M	−.16	−.02	−.18	.33	.10	.15	.39	−.06	.47	.27	.15	.15	.29	.29	−.36	−.05	.32	.03
F	.04	−.03	−.05	.26	.29	.30	.35	.07	.29	.32	.32	.04	.25	.35	−.35	−.24	.37	−.13

Prudence

M	−.42	.00	.06	.63	.15	.30	.38	−.23	.50	.52	.26	.31	.27	.23	−.24	−.23	.48	−.07
F	−.45	.19	.25	.51	.23	.27	.39	−.37	.30	.41	.39	.25	.11	.57	−.26	−.43	.44	−.19

Intellectence

M	.12	.03	−.45	−.06	.09	.03	.03	.28	.17	−.13	−.20	−.10	.26	−.27	.20	.45	.09	.54
F	.15	−.35	−.35	−.23	.30	.17	.03	.40	.29	.02	−.03	.17	.34	−.33	−.10	.18	.23	.16

School Success

M	.05	.04	−.36	.19	.34	.42	.11	.18	.42	.22	.19	.28	.44	.02	−.09	.06	.46	.11
F	.05	−.01	−.16	−.08	.19	.23	.13	.20	.19	−.04	.02	.24	.24	−.09	−.09	.05	.19	−.08

9. Interpersonal Dependency Inventory (IDI) (Ns = 145 males, 145 females)

Emotional Reliance on Others (A)

M	−.19	.08	−.09	.03	−.41	−.35	−.39	−.20	−.26	−.41	−.04	−.29	−.27	−.22	.28	.25	−.31	.32
F	−.18	.15	.01	.06	−.44	−.36	−.50	−.33	−.35	−.34	−.08	−.47	−.39	−.06	.31	.15	−.31	.26

Lack of Social Self-Confidence (B)

M	−.04	.38	.55	−.10	−.27	−.54	−.36	−.29	−.68	−.19	−.31	−.58	−.67	.14	.38	−.30	−.37	.12
F	.00	.17	.47	−.17	−.36	−.54	−.42	−.22	−.71	−.24	−.30	−.57	−.68	−.01	.43	−.21	−.45	.05

Assertion of Autonomy (C)

M	−.17	−.20	−.05	−.02	−.20	−.13	−.10	−.07	.03	−.13	.05	.07	.11	−.25	−.05	.15	.04	.13
F	−.20	−.21	−.13	−.09	−.11	−.09	−.23	−.05	−.06	−.24	.08	.07	.01	−.24	−.01	.19	−.04	.12

Unweighted Total Score (A + B − C)

M	−.05	.32	.22	−.02	−.27	−.40	−.36	−.22	−.48	−.27	−.19	−.48	−.53	.05	.37	−.06	−.37	.19
F	.00	.28	.33	−.01	−.39	−.45	−.40	−.27	−.56	−.20	−.25	−.60	−.59	.08	.41	−.13	−.40	.11

Weighted Total Score (40.84 + .20A + .18B − .66C + .55 BC/30)

M	−.05	.39	.41	−.07	−.28	−.48	−.42	−.24	−.62	−.24	−.32	−.58	−.65	.14	.43	−.21	−.44	.14
F	−.04	.22	.46	−.06	−.39	−.49	−.40	−.30	−.64	−.20	−.27	−.58	−.64	.05	.48	−.18	−.41	.14

C. Personality and Interest Inventories continued

Measures	Do	Cs	Sy	Sp	Sa	In	Em	Re	So	Sc	Gi	Cm	Wb	To	Ac	Ai	Ie	Py
10. Jackson Personality Research Form (PRF) (*N*s = 133 males, 84 females)																	
Abasement																		
M	−.21	−.10	−.09	−.16	−.13	−.17	.08	−.04	−.05	.04	.08	−.14	−.07	.04	−.22	−.08	−.14	−.10
F	−.29	−.13	−.09	−.12	−.20	−.32	−.03	−.06	−.07	−.08	−.01	.01	−.12	−.07	−.06	−.13	−.24	−.31
Achievement																		
M	.28	.13	.22	.05	.21	.12	.15	.37	.18	.22	.30	.31	.21	.13	.39	.14	.16	.22
F	.40	.25	.30	.23	.27	.32	.30	.31	.10	−.01	.22	.25	.22	.30	.35	.29	.33	.29
Affiliation																		
M	.11	.10	.35	.12	.15	−.05	.13	.02	.22	.05	.22	.11	.15	−.03	.04	−.12	−.11	−.09
F	.34	.31	.60	.27	.28	−.03	.36	.31	.48	.28	.35	.32	.34	.18	.38	.07	.17	.04
Aggression																		
M	.08	−.15	.04	.11	.12	−.03	−.16	−.24	−.09	−.40	−.43	−.19	−.25	−.35	−.16	−.17	−.19	−.19
F	−.09	−.15	−.20	−.06	.00	−.06	−.12	−.47	−.40	−.61	−.55	−.44	−.31	−.44	−.45	−.27	−.20	−.19
Autonomy																		
M	.11	.23	.06	.19	.18	.33	.16	−.05	−.18	−.01	.03	−.05	.12	.02	−.03	.26	.30	.21
F	.07	.15	−.11	.16	.14	.36	.14	−.16	−.29	−.30	−.24	−.13	.02	.10	−.23	.20	.18	.27
Change																		
M	.02	.19	.07	.09	.09	.15	.29	−.02	−.19	−.04	.02	−.01	.05	.07	−.15	.26	.18	.13
F	.15	.21	.14	.28	.21	.28	.20	−.24	−.03	−.28	−.11	−.03	.10	−.09	−.19	.03	.01	.13
Cognitive Structure																		
M	.03	−.10	.00	−.16	−.09	−.21	−.23	.05	.17	.13	.14	.13	.01	−.06	.17	−.27	−.20	−.17
F	.10	−.16	.11	−.18	.01	−.16	−.14	.27	.20	.08	.13	.24	−.08	−.16	.33	−.27	−.15	−.26
Defendence																		
M	−.04	−.14	−.13	−.08	−.01	−.13	−.27	−.15	.00	−.22	−.22	−.06	−.18	−.38	−.08	−.37	−.26	−.30
F	.09	−.21	−.02	−.21	.03	−.05	−.23	.03	−.04	−.03	−.11	−.24	−.25	−.34	.08	−.21	−.13	−.17
Dominance																		
M	.71	.43	.61	.39	.57	.41	.37	.20	.14	−.04	.15	.12	.15	.05	.45	.14	.25	.12
F	.78	.52	.61	.67	.75	.61	.52	.06	.03	−.23	.13	.07	.42	.11	.21	.34	.48	.42
Endurance																		
M	.39	.21	.30	.14	.28	.24	.19	.29	.03	.19	.32	.19	.20	.06	.37	.12	.15	.23
F	.41	.28	.47	.34	.32	.37	.26	.30	.28	.28	.42	.30	.48	.29	.39	.28	.31	.33
Exhibition																		
M	.55	.39	.61	.49	.58	.42	.40	−.01	.06	−.23	−.04	−.05	.11	−.04	.15	.12	.18	.05
F	.64	.51	.58	.67	.68	.47	.53	.03	−.07	−.36	−.01	.00	.38	.14	.08	.28	.43	.29
Harm Avoidance																		
M	−.03	−.21	−.08	−.19	−.14	−.22	−.22	.23	.28	.13	−.06	.08	−.07	.08	.22	−.19	−.09	−.12
F	−.28	−.44	−.32	−.50	−.38	−.45	−.42	.12	.12	.26	.03	.04	−.36	−.28	.05	−.31	−.43	−.44
Impulsivity																		
M	−.11	−.07	−.06	.07	.02	.00	.04	−.28	−.20	−.36	−.29	−.33	−.23	−.15	−.36	−.03	−.09	−.04
F	−.01	.12	.04	.26	.09	.16	.08	−.41	−.42	−.52	−.44	−.32	−.04	−.06	−.42	.00	.03	.08
Nurturance																		
M	.11	.02	.19	−.05	.05	−.15	.24	.25	.17	.12	.28	.15	.04	.16	.19	−.09	−.08	−.09
F	.19	.09	.14	.16	.08	.06	.30	.16	.09	.17	.16	.13	.20	.06	.20	.04	.11	.10
Order																		
M	.17	.04	.16	−.10	.14	−.10	−.13	.24	.20	.15	.13	.14	.01	.00	.35	−.16	−.13	−.08
F	.12	−.05	.11	−.07	.06	−.04	−.04	.26	.34	.18	.20	.21	.10	.04	.33	−.02	−.05	−.13

C. Personality and Interest Inventories continued

Measures	Fx	F/M	v.1	v.2	v.3	Mp	Wo	CT	Lp	Ami	Leo	Tm	B–MS	B–FM	Anx	Nar	D–SD	D–AC
10. Jackson Personality Research Form (PRF) (Ns = 133 males, 84 females)																		
Abasement																		
M	.09	.20	.15	−.07	−.01	−.14	−.02	.01	−.15	.09	−.06	−.25	−.18	.08	.12	−.17	−.14	−.04
F	.02	.20	.22	.08	−.18	−.26	−.04	−.17	−.22	.06	−.15	−.35	−.27	.07	−.02	−.24	−.07	.10
Achievement																		
M	−.16	−.13	−.16	.39	.13	.24	.20	−.06	.35	.13	.30	.22	.25	−.04	−.21	−.01	.40	.06
F	−.27	−.08	−.35	.35	.21	.31	.25	.00	.40	.05	.28	.34	.29	−.06	−.20	.17	.41	.15
Affiliation																		
M	−.10	−.02	−.13	.26	−.06	.03	.04	−.18	.19	.19	.20	.01	.19	.01	−.23	.01	.22	.11
F	−.28	−.02	−.26	.49	.17	.31	.29	−.11	.45	.41	.29	.20	.32	.33	−.48	−.02	.49	.06
Aggression																		
M	.03	−.06	−.22	.03	−.35	−.19	−.34	−.10	−.12	−.32	−.08	−.13	−.08	−.27	.15	.42	−.32	.29
F	.10	−.07	−.12	−.30	−.36	−.38	−.43	.02	−.35	−.55	−.37	−.30	−.13	−.38	.33	.50	−.50	.28
Autonomy																		
M	.22	−.10	−.13	−.25	.19	.10	.00	.41	.15	−.07	−.08	.17	.25	−.05	−.04	.08	.08	−.01
F	.20	−.16	−.25	−.27	.12	.05	−.06	.42	−.03	−.24	−.12	.11	.15	−.41	.18	.32	−.05	.13
Change																		
M	.29	.02	−.08	−.16	.16	.00	.02	.34	.06	−.03	−.16	.01	.11	−.05	−.06	.09	.02	−.01
F	.14	−.04	−.33	−.09	.03	−.05	.03	.32	.11	−.07	−.06	.03	.20	−.17	−.07	.33	.03	.11
Cognitive Structure																		
M	−.49	−.06	.05	.38	−.19	−.02	.04	−.44	.01	.02	.34	−.06	−.06	−.01	−.06	−.02	.15	.26
F	−.58	.03	−.03	.53	−.27	−.03	−.07	−.52	.12	.01	.28	.00	−.11	.14	.01	.02	.26	.25
Defendence																		
M	−.36	−.05	−.09	.18	−.41	−.26	−.28	−.32	−.15	−.28	.04	−.12	−.16	−.06	.15	.33	−.17	.26
F	−.31	.01	−.05	.05	−.23	−.12	−.21	−.30	−.03	−.34	.11	.06	−.12	−.01	.32	.27	−.05	.08
Dominance																		
M	−.67	−.27	−.68	.30	.08	.39	.08	.13	.57	−.02	.38	.44	.50	−.22	−.24	.38	.34	.06
F	.17	−.37	−.83	−.02	.32	.47	.33	.39	.61	.00	.34	.57	.69	−.39	−.33	.60	.40	.07
Endurance																		
M	−.09	−.16	−.27	.28	.10	.27	.19	.04	.43	.06	.34	.33	.35	−.11	−.16	.01	.38	−.02
F	−.35	−.01	−.28	.36	.29	.39	.45	−.04	.56	.32	.41	.45	.42	.15	−.43	−.02	.56	.09
Exhibition																		
M	.16	−.13	−.67	.06	.03	.22	−.05	.25	.41	−.08	.15	.23	.40	−.20	−.14	.44	.10	.17
F	.27	−.27	−.77	−.05	.30	.43	.28	.40	.47	.03	.15	.37	.58	−.30	−.33	.54	.21	.08
Harm Avoidance																		
M	−.18	.30	.12	.20	−.13	.04	.05	−.26	−.06	.08	.12	−.02	−.23	.27	.01	−.16	−.07	−.01
F	−.28	.43	.44	.16	−.36	−.18	−.18	−.52	−.24	−.05	−.07	−.13	−.44	.37	.24	−.30	−.18	−.06
Impulsivity																		
M	.30	.03	−.09	−.24	−.09	−.24	−.32	.20	−.23	−.23	−.35	−.19	−.09	−.17	.24	.21	−.31	.16
F	.47	−.06	−.13	−.44	−.05	−.14	−.14	.40	−.19	−.24	−.35	−.23	.11	−.28	−.06	.29	−.38	−.02
Nurturance																		
M	.00	.13	−.10	.31	.05	.08	.05	−.09	.10	.20	.11	−.07	.00	.06	−.18	−.06	.16	−.10
F	−.09	.06	−.06	.26	.16	.08	.14	.08	.20	.20	.06	.04	.12	.06	−.19	−.10	.28	.14
Order																		
M	−.47	.00	−.08	.44	−.16	.15	.08	−.38	.19	.02	.36	.06	.03	.11	−.17	.00	.20	.02
F	−.49	−.01	−.05	.51	−.02	.11	.14	−.44	.23	.17	.36	.14	.01	.17	−.11	−.05	.28	.19

C. Personality and Interest Inventories continued

Measures	Do	Cs	Sy	Sp	Sa	In	Em	Re	So	Sc	Gi	Cm	Wb	To	Ac	Ai	Ie	Py
10. Jackson Personality Research Form (PRF) (Ns = 133 males, 84 females) continued																		
Play																		
M	−.21	−.10	.02	.20	−.02	−.21	.04	−.31	.00	−.36	−.23	−.01	−.11	−.22	−.29	−.15	−.13	−.23
F	.06	.15	.28	.38	.16	−.03	.25	−.21	.12	−.23	−.23	−.02	.11	−.03	−.11	−.03	.18	.02
Sentience																		
M	.12	.20	.12	.21	.18	.23	.35	.02	−.07	−.15	−.09	.12	.06	.17	−.05	.24	.25	.14
F	.10	.18	.13	.30	.20	.22	.30	−.03	−.09	−.06	.04	.05	.19	.17	−.11	.22	.13	.24
Social Recognition																		
M	.05	−.15	.11	−.06	.00	−.25	−.14	.03	.16	−.20	−.12	.13	−.17	−.17	.11	−.34	−.29	−.29
F	.03	−.10	.18	−.11	−.03	−.34	.07	.29	.37	.12	.04	.25	.00	.01	.32	−.20	−.08	−.28
Succorance																		
M	.04	−.06	.12	−.04	−.06	−.21	.02	.08	.17	−.08	.05	.16	−.05	.08	.08	−.17	−.16	−.11
F	−.17	−.14	.01	−.16	−.15	−.42	−.07	−.01	.24	.10	−.07	−.02	−.16	−.16	.00	−.28	−.22	−.35
Understanding																		
M	.26	.37	.18	.20	.23	.31	.34	.22	−.10	.05	.09	.09	.08	.25	.22	.52	.39	.50
F	.26	.41	.33	.41	.34	.46	.41	.15	−.03	.05	.12	−.02	.33	−.31	.16	.49	.43	.52
Infrequency																		
M	−.06	−.08	.01	−.02	−.12	.02	.10	−.02	−.01	−.02	.01	−.04	−.10	−.07	−.02	.03	.00	−.02
F	−.12	−.15	.08	.01	.01	−.19	−.06	−.16	−.16	−.22	−.15	−.16	−.16	−.32	−.20	−.26	−.22	−.18
Desirability																		
M	.39	.34	.43	.22	.31	.30	.34	.31	.34	.40	.44	.30	.46	.29	.40	.24	.35	.23
F	.43	.51	.44	.47	.34	.39	.54	.38	.46	.26	.38	.50	.58	.51	.53	.43	.53	.45
11. Lazare-Klerman-Armor Inventory (LKAI) (Ns = 84 males, 84 females)																		
Obsessional Personality																		
M	.05	−.29	−.19	−.34	−.13	−.06	−.32	.23	.24	.50	.37	.20	.24	−.11	.32	−.18	−.01	.06
F	.28	.00	.09	−.18	.11	.21	−.16	.19	.22	.21	.19	.09	.12	−.19	.43	−.19	−.04	−.01
Hysterical Personality																		
M	.10	.12	.19	.33	.31	.10	.19	−.42	−.31	−.66	−.54	−.15	−.25	−.30	−.25	−.04	−.02	−.15
F	.20	.28	.36	.39	.38	.22	.24	−.21	−.17	−.62	−.49	−.13	−.18	−.13	−.18	.08	.08	.13
Oral Personality																		
M	−.37	−.19	−.21	−.21	−.25	−.45	−.07	−.13	−.08	−.36	−.39	−.14	−.52	−.28	−.33	−.17	−.34	−.38
F	−.57	−.46	−.55	−.55	−.46	−.63	−.41	−.27	−.36	−.12	−.23	−.46	−.64	−.30	−.36	−.46	−.57	−.50
12. Millon Clinical Multiaxial Inventory (MCMI) (Ns = 118 males, 118 females)																		
Schizoid Personality																		
M	−.56	−.42	−.65	−.57	−.57	−.55	−.38	−.39	−.23	−.19	−.26	−.38	−.54	−.36	−.41	−.42	−.50	−.41
F	−.53	−.45	−.61	−.51	−.51	−.36	−.46	−.08	−.21	.07	−.16	−.25	−.38	−.17	−.26	−.09	−.25	−.19
Avoidant Personality																		
M	−.49	−.36	−.56	−.54	−.50	−.60	−.26	−.38	−.30	−.30	−.33	−.36	−.65	−.43	−.45	−.49	−.57	−.48
F	−.54	−.42	−.61	−.51	−.48	−.46	−.42	−.14	−.26	−.05	−.24	−.30	−.50	−.33	−.31	−.19	−.33	−.26
Dependent Personality																		
M	−.34	−.14	−.22	−.33	−.28	−.59	−.12	−.13	−.06	−.16	−.15	−.21	−.46	−.22	−.24	−.34	−.38	−.48
F	−.62	−.45	−.40	−.38	−.42	−.65	−.27	−.13	−.05	−.05	−.24	−.15	−.39	−.23	−.22	−.34	−.49	−.40
Histrionic Personality																		
M	.40	.28	.61	.60	.55	.38	.32	.01	−.12	−.29	−.18	.04	.14	−.07	−.07	.08	.16	.12
F	.57	.45	.71	.69	.68	.43	.50	−.18	−.15	−.45	−.21	.07	.10	−.05	−.13	.02	.15	.06
Narcissistic Personality																		
M	.53	.23	.51	.38	.52	.45	.12	.08	−.04	−.06	.03	.03	.19	−.12	.08	.03	.17	.19
F	.72	.48	.67	.56	.68	.58	.41	−.09	−.08	−.25	−.02	.11	.22	−.02	.03	.05	.26	.21

C. Personality and Interest Inventories continued

Measures	Fx	F/M	v.1	v.2	v.3	Mp	Wo	CT	Lp	Ami	Leo	Tm	B–MS	B–FM	Anx	Nar	D–SD	D–AC
10. Jackson Personality Research Form (PRF) (Ns = 133 males, 84 females) continued																		
Play																		
M	.15	.01	−.03	−.03	−.17	−.32	−.21	−.05	−.22	−.06	−.16	−.33	−.14	−.11	−.05	.16	−.23	.29
F	.20	.02	−.17	−.06	.07	−.02	.01	.11	.00	.06	−.08	−.12	.10	−.04	−.09	.19	−.03	.08
Sentience																		
M	.30	.02	−.18	−.15	.22	.09	.05	.34	.08	−.05	−.18	−.02	.10	−.10	−.10	.20	−.07	.01
F	.17	−.04	−.22	−.02	.25	.12	.13	.27	.11	.11	−.03	.11	.16	−.12	−.06	.10	.19	.04
Social Recognition																		
M	−.30	.08	−.14	.31	−.33	−.18	−.15	−.38	−.06	−.10	.13	−.15	−.19	−.01	.01	.17	−.06	.26
F	−.20	.21	−.03	.32	−.11	.13	.11	−.43	.10	.24	.23	−.06	−.16	.36	−.11	−.01	.14	−.02
Succorance																		
M	−.10	.15	−.07	.28	−.09	−.02	.08	−.20	−.01	.12	.11	−.14	−.11	.08	−.03	.03	−.01	.07
F	−.08	.24	.23	.22	−.18	−.16	−.12	−.29	−.13	.14	−.10	−.27	−.23	.28	.02	−.19	−.12	−.07
Understanding																		
M	.25	−.03	−.15	−.04	.33	.25	.21	.42	.27	−.01	−.09	.21	.27	.01	.02	−.01	.20	−.02
F	.23	−.16	−.30	−.08	.42	.31	.29	.52	.30	.15	−.14	.26	.40	−.16	−.13	.11	.33	−.04
Infrequency																		
M	.07	.03	.04	−.02	.07	−.06	−.04	.04	−.06	.04	−.11	−.02	−.03	−.04	.09	−.01	−.04	−.04
F	.03	.10	.03	−.15	−.24	−.22	−.16	−.11	−.19	−.18	−.06	−.23	−.15	−.06	.02	.14	−.16	.04
Desirability																		
M	−.04	−.22	−.15	.26	.26	.44	.47	.02	.56	.44	.41	.37	.50	.09	−.41	−.14	.50	−.17
F	.07	−.06	−.33	.31	.52	.56	.49	.23	.60	.55	.35	.42	.41	.10	−.48	−.10	.60	.04
11. Lazare-Klerman-Armor Inventory (LKAI) (Ns = 84 males, 84 females)																		
Obsessional Personality																		
M	−.59	−.12	.24	.39	−.12	.19	.36	−.60	.20	.19	.42	.29	.10	.31	−.22	−.19	.30	−.16
F	−.62	.03	−.13	.55	−.16	.16	.13	−.42	.27	.02	.41	.33	.12	.18	−.18	−.03	.23	.12
Hysterical Personality																		
M	.20	−.02	−.41	−.22	−.28	−.21	−.46	.24	−.10	−.50	−.09	−.22	−.04	−.58	.22	.59	−.29	.34
F	.26	−.06	−.47	−.16	−.06	−.07	−.24	.38	.01	−.34	−.28	−.07	.15	−.35	.16	.57	−.26	.25
Oral Personality																		
M	.08	.38	.17	−.13	−.26	−.47	−.50	.01	−.49	−.33	−.26	−.57	−.55	−.06	.35	.04	−.39	.37
F	−.06	.17	.39	−.21	−.41	−.65	−.56	−.21	−.72	−.38	−.35	−.66	−.67	−.11	.41	−.13	−.48	.27
12. Millon Clinical Multiaxial Inventory (MCMI) (Ns = 118 males, 118 females)																		
Schizoid Personality																		
M	−.22	.31	.29	−.13	−.42	−.45	−.40	−.34	−.64	−.36	−.45	−.47	−.70	−.05	.60	−.02	−.43	.24
F	.03	.06	.54	−.24	−.12	−.38	−.26	−.12	−.50	−.13	−.38	−.28	−.43	−.17	.48	−.29	−.31	−.08
Avoidant Personality																		
M	−.16	.32	.20	−.10	−.49	−.53	−.52	−.32	−.67	−.44	−.47	−.58	−.73	−.13	.71	.10	−.47	.28
F	.05	.13	.47	−.28	−.25	−.52	−.41	−.14	−.59	−.28	−.42	−.37	−.50	−.20	.53	−.19	−.41	−.03
Dependent Personality																		
M	−.05	.33	.17	−.02	−.33	−.27	−.30	−.20	−.41	−.17	−.26	−.43	−.46	.10	.39	−.09	−.28	.14
F	.09	.37	.44	−.18	−.28	−.46	−.28	−.28	−.52	−.11	−.32	−.57	−.58	.11	.28	−.24	−.32	.01
Histrionic Personality																		
M	.38	−.15	−.50	−.20	.06	.06	−.02	.47	.26	−.06	−.01	.11	.41	−.30	−.21	.37	.04	.05
F	.17	−.25	−.74	−.09	−.10	.19	−.09	.40	.34	−.20	.09	.08	.44	−.28	−.15	.58	.05	.25
Narcissistic Personality																		
M	.01	−.18	−.47	.15	.01	.10	.01	.14	.39	−.05	.19	.24	.46	−.24	−.26	.34	.23	.18
F	−.10	−.31	−.71	.16	−.02	.27	.05	.30	.50	−.14	.24	.33	.56	−.23	−.31	.53	.23	.29

C. Personality and Interest Inventories continued

Measures	Do	Cs	Sy	Sp	Sa	In	Em	Re	So	Sc	Gi	Cm	Wb	To	Ac	Ai	Ie	Py
12. Millon Clinical Multiaxial Inventory (MCMI) (Ns = 118 males, 118 females) continued																		
Antisocial Personality																		
M	.29	−.11	.06	.06	.20	.27	−.16	−.12	−.19	−.21	−.15	−.04	−.03	−.28	−.12	−.14	−.05	.09
F	.57	.26	.40	.35	.48	.48	.17	−.14	−.14	−.23	−.10	.02	.06	−.14	−.05	−.01	.16	.15
Compulsive Personality																		
M	.16	.28	.17	.01	.07	.22	.12	.51	.58	.71	.64	.27	.62	.59	.67	.51	.45	.38
F	.06	.15	−.04	−.14	−.17	.17	.03	.45	.51	.62	.64	.21	.51	.39	.59	.21	.25	.26
Passive-Aggressive Personality																		
M	−.29	−.34	−.33	−.24	−.22	−.39	−.25	−.48	−.50	−.61	−.54	−.38	−.71	−.59	−.61	−.57	−.56	−.48
F	−.20	−.24	−.19	−.12	−.03	−.28	−.24	−.45	−.51	−.51	−.60	−.31	−.67	−.43	−.57	−.27	−.38	−.32
Schizotypal Personality																		
M	−.53	−.37	−.57	−.54	−.53	−.63	−.27	−.39	−.26	−.28	−.32	−.41	−.62	−.40	−.46	−.49	−.56	−.51
F	−.59	−.45	−.59	−.50	−.50	−.53	−.42	−.14	−.24	−.08	−.29	−.28	−.51	−.32	−.33	−.24	−.37	−.31
Borderline Personality																		
M	−.30	−.24	−.33	−.34	−.30	−.52	−.18	−.37	−.34	−.46	−.38	−.33	−.68	−.49	−.46	−.51	−.54	−.50
F	−.28	−.27	−.28	−.25	−.13	−.37	−.27	−.36	−.50	−.41	−.50	−.32	−.70	−.46	−.50	−.29	−.42	−.33
Paranoid Personality																		
M	.08	−.19	−.12	−.27	−.05	−.20	−.25	−.31	−.30	−.30	−.24	−.26	−.46	−.61	−.34	−.55	−.43	−.39
F	.28	.03	.12	.05	.26	.08	−.10	−.30	−.26	−.37	−.33	−.08	−.33	−.46	−.24	−.36	−.20	−.15
Anxiety Disorder																		
M	−.29	−.26	−.35	−.34	−.32	−.54	−.16	−.35	−.30	−.40	−.34	−.32	−.65	−.45	−.44	−.48	−.51	−.53
F	−.34	−.30	−.31	−.30	−.21	−.40	−.28	−.33	−.41	−.32	−.42	−.31	−.65	−.42	−.46	−.29	−.42	−.36
Somatoform Disorder																		
M	−.29	−.19	−.25	−.30	−.27	−.56	−.16	−.25	−.22	−.33	−.31	−.30	−.62	−.42	−.37	−.49	−.52	−.50
F	−.25	−.28	−.18	−.19	−.09	−.41	−.20	−.36	−.38	−.42	−.49	−.33	−.64	−.44	−.49	−.36	−.44	−.34
Hypomanic Disorder																		
M	.25	.02	.30	.19	.30	.01	.08	−.22	−.32	−.47	−.36	−.17	−.34	−.48	−.33	−.38	−.29	−.21
F	.56	.33	.56	.46	.66	.30	.29	−.20	−.18	−.56	−.37	.01	−.17	−.22	−.19	−.17	.00	−.01
Dysthymic Disorder																		
M	−.35	−.25	−.40	−.38	−.37	−.54	−.19	−.34	−.31	−.38	−.33	−.31	−.65	−.39	−.43	−.47	−.53	−.48
F	−.39	−.29	−.42	−.37	−.28	−.40	−.31	−.25	−.40	−.23	−.35	−.31	−.64	−.35	−.41	−.20	−.37	−.29
Alcohol Dependence																		
M	.07	−.12	−.01	−.08	.00	−.32	−.04	−.33	−.35	−.41	−.31	−.34	−.48	−.55	−.42	−.47	−.39	−.44
F	.22	.10	.28	.21	.38	.01	.08	−.34	−.42	−.56	−.46	−.12	−.44	−.39	−.36	−.28	−.16	−.18
Drug Dependence																		
M	.20	−.05	.18	.10	.23	−.03	.00	−.37	−.46	−.49	−.39	−.32	−.41	−.58	−.44	−.45	−.32	−.24
F	.52	.28	.57	.51	.62	.35	.26	−.34	−.33	−.53	−.38	−.07	−.19	−.34	−.29	−.19	−.01	−.02
Thought Disorder																		
M	−.41	−.39	−.50	−.51	−.42	−.54	−.32	−.45	−.37	−.34	−.37	−.46	−.66	−.58	−.53	−.60	−.63	−.48
F	−.24	−.27	−.31	−.27	−.17	−.29	−.32	−.26	−.40	−.31	−.42	−.24	−.56	−.48	−.38	−.30	−.30	−.28
Depressive Disorder																		
M	−.35	−.31	−.40	−.39	−.36	−.53	−.25	−.39	−.37	−.45	−.37	−.38	−.69	−.52	−.50	−.55	−.59	−.49
F	−.25	−.22	−.27	−.24	−.15	−.28	−.26	−.31	−.36	−.35	−.46	−.25	−.61	−.43	−.38	−.24	−.38	−.30
Delusional Disorder																		
M	.01	−.18	−.20	−.37	−.16	−.26	−.27	−.18	−.19	−.11	−.09	−.27	−.36	−.43	−.22	−.45	−.36	−.32
F	.09	−.07	−.02	−.18	−.05	−.03	−.21	−.15	−.04	−.10	−.12	.00	−.24	−.33	−.07	−.37	−.21	−.19

C. Personality and Interest Inventories continued

Measures	Fx	F/M	v.1	v.2	v.3	Mp	Wo	CT	Lp	Ami	Leo	Tm	B–MS	B–FM	Anx	Nar	D–SD	D–AC
12. Millon Clinical Multiaxial Inventory (MCMI) (Ns = 118 males, 118 females) continued
Antisocial Personality
M	−.21	−.12	−.32	.11	−.22	−.16	−.18	−.07	.06	−.30	.03	.05	.10	−.35	.02	.43	.00	.32
F	−.20	−.39	−.52	.11	−.16	.11	−.04	.11	.30	−.22	.20	.26	.39	−.36	−.11	.53	.09	.30
Compulsive Personality
M	−.09	−.14	.27	.35	.55	.59	.67	−.04	.57	.67	.56	.58	.44	.53	−.59	−.54	.54	−.43
F	−.25	.15	.22	.46	.47	.40	.58	−.18	.42	.53	.48	.41	.21	.57	−.42	−.46	.56	−.27
Passive-Aggressive Personality
M	−.10	.27	−.11	−.21	−.59	−.59	−.67	−.12	−.65	−.64	−.57	−.62	−.61	−.39	.69	.42	−.56	.46
F	.13	−.01	−.08	−.47	−.50	−.49	−.67	.06	−.55	−.63	−.48	−.45	−.38	−.55	.61	.36	−.56	.23
Schizotypal Personality
M	−.15	.34	.22	−.13	−.48	−.51	−.49	−.30	−.67	−.39	−.50	−.56	−.73	−.10	.68	.06	−.46	.26
F	.04	.16	.48	−.28	−.29	−.53	−.40	−.15	−.62	−.25	−.46	−.46	−.57	−.21	.52	−.18	−.41	.01
Borderline Personality
M	−.14	.33	−.03	−.08	−.52	−.48	−.57	−.25	−.59	−.53	−.46	−.59	−.62	−.20	.68	.26	−.43	.37
F	.13	.12	.05	−.42	−.46	−.53	−.66	−.02	−.58	−.59	−.46	−.47	−.43	−.43	.64	.19	−.53	.20
Paranoid Personality
M	−.37	.12	−.25	.17	−.57	−.42	−.47	−.39	−.29	−.54	−.18	−.30	−.28	−.31	.36	.46	−.22	.58
F	−.27	−.15	−.36	.05	−.50	−.31	−.39	−.07	−.05	−.48	−.13	−.11	−.02	−.43	.20	.56	−.22	.55
Anxiety Disorder
M	−.15	.32	.00	−.08	−.49	−.45	−.53	−.24	−.57	−.50	−.45	−.56	−.62	−.16	.64	.20	−.43	.37
F	.10	.14	.13	−.39	−.39	−.52	−.60	−.06	−.58	−.47	−.40	−.44	−.45	−.30	.60	.09	−.43	.15
Somatoform Disorder
M	−.16	.37	.03	.00	−.47	−.40	−.49	−.26	−.51	−.39	−.38	−.55	−.58	−.08	.57	.16	−.36	.32
F	.07	.12	.01	−.32	−.45	−.50	−.63	−.06	−.50	−.51	−.45	−.49	−.40	−.36	.53	.22	−.48	.25
Hypomanic Disorder
M	.02	.07	−.49	−.01	−.42	−.33	−.42	.07	−.11	−.45	−.18	−.28	−.05	−.38	.22	.57	−.18	.46
F	−.06	−.18	−.72	.00	−.32	−.05	−.33	.26	.20	−.40	.05	−.05	.25	−.39	.06	.71	−.11	.44
Dysthymic Disorder
M	−.14	.33	.06	−.09	−.45	−.44	−.51	−.23	−.60	−.48	−.45	−.56	−.64	−.15	.66	.16	−.42	.30
F	.10	.18	.23	−.40	−.33	−.47	−.55	−.07	−.59	−.45	−.41	−.41	−.47	−.27	.62	−.01	−.42	.05
Alcohol Dependence
M	−.18	.12	−.32	.01	−.48	−.37	−.49	−.22	−.30	−.47	−.29	−.38	−.29	−.39	.34	.40	−.23	.54
F	.00	−.07	−.40	−.20	−.44	−.30	−.50	.14	−.15	−.56	−.15	−.21	.01	−.45	.33	.50	−.27	.39
Drug Dependence
M	−.04	.05	−.47	−.08	−.44	−.35	−.49	−.01	−.19	−.51	−.34	−.31	−.09	−.52	.29	.57	−.24	.50
F	.01	−.29	−.69	−.10	−.37	−.10	−.31	.26	.16	−.45	−.04	−.01	.32	−.51	.06	.74	−.15	.46
Thought Disorder
M	−.21	.26	.09	−.08	−.59	−.58	−.58	−.36	−.65	−.52	−.48	−.54	−.67	−.27	.67	.25	−.47	.41
F	−.07	−.02	.11	−.26	−.45	−.53	−.53	−.06	−.46	−.50	−.45	−.35	−.35	−.43	.51	.20	−.46	.28
Depressive Disorder
M	−.15	.32	.01	−.09	−.55	−.53	−.58	−.30	−.63	−.52	−.45	−.60	−.64	−.22	.68	.24	−.45	.39
F	.04	.11	.09	−.32	−.43	−.48	−.56	−.05	−.51	−.50	−.39	−.39	−.38	−.35	.57	.17	−.48	.17
Delusional Disorder
M	−.43	.13	−.08	.24	−.44	−.30	−.32	−.43	−.22	−.37	−.15	−.24	−.31	−.19	.26	.24	−.13	.42
F	−.41	.01	−.09	.19	−.36	−.26	−.20	−.21	−.04	−.27	−.02	−.06	−.09	−.18	.17	.26	−.10	.40

C. Personality and Interest Inventories continued

Measures	Do	Cs	Sy	Sp	Sa	In	Em	Re	So	Sc	Gi	Cm	Wb	To	Ac	Ai	Ie	Py
12. Millon Clinical Multiaxial Inventory (MCMI) (Ns = 118 males, 118 females) continued																		
Factor 1 (anxiety and dysphoria)																		
M	−.43	−.37	−.47	−.38	−.39	−.52	−.25	−.47	−.42	−.51	−.48	−.38	−.72	−.52	−.57	−.53	−.58	−.50
F	−.39	−.35	−.40	−.29	−.24	−.39	−.33	−.35	−.48	−.36	−.51	−.34	−.67	−.41	−.52	−.22	−.39	−.32
Factor 2 (impulse under control; errant impulse)																		
M	.40	.19	.53	.45	.50	.19	.22	−.13	−.28	−.45	−.30	−.08	−.16	−.33	−.23	−.20	−.07	−.08
F	.54	.35	.65	.59	.68	.32	.38	−.30	−.28	−.57	−.37	−.02	−.13	−.22	−.26	−.13	.01	−.02
Factor 3 (paranoid thinking; cognitive rigidity)																		
M	.07	−.12	−.15	−.40	−.14	−.22	−.25	−.10	−.05	.08	.08	−.22	−.23	−.36	−.07	−.38	−.29	−.26
F	.21	.04	.04	−.11	.08	.10	−.12	−.02	.06	.04	.06	.04	−.04	−.23	.10	−.26	−.06	−.02
Factor 4 (constriction and dependency)																		
M	−.06	.19	.13	−.02	−.05	−.31	.19	.16	.20	.14	.15	.02	−.05	.14	.14	.01	−.02	−.18
F	−.34	−.14	−.11	−.19	−.21	−.43	−.03	.04	.10	.02	.00	−.03	−.17	−.04	−.01	−.20	−.26	−.22
13. Minnesota Multiphasic Personality Inventory (MMPI) (Ns = 657 males, 461 females)																		
L Scale																		
M	.01	−.02	−.10	−.21	−.11	.08	−.03	.14	.08	.42	.51	−.20	.18	.09	.16	.08	.00	.06
F	.06	−.03	−.04	−.16	−.07	.16	−.03	.16	.08	.46	.56	−.08	.29	.08	.16	.03	.01	.02
F Scale																		
M	−.30	−.30	−.28	−.16	−.19	−.26	−.17	−.36	−.28	−.28	−.27	−.41	−.43	−.31	−.41	−.17	−.28	−.27
F	−.18	−.21	−.27	−.22	−.15	−.09	−.17	−.36	−.40	−.29	−.30	−.46	−.45	−.33	−.37	−.18	−.26	−.16
K Scale																		
M	.29	.42	.34	.26	.20	.36	.31	.37	.30	.52	.61	.09	.60	.54	.43	.43	.44	.42
F	.26	.45	.34	.29	.27	.39	.38	.40	.30	.45	.50	.03	.57	.55	.35	.47	.49	.37
HsK Scale																		
M	−.21	−.18	−.14	−.10	−.17	−.22	−.07	−.17	−.10	−.04	−.01	−.30	−.22	−.06	−.22	−.04	−.16	−.17
F	−.04	−.07	−.08	−.14	−.05	−.08	.01	−.07	−.07	−.01	.03	−.20	−.20	−.12	−.06	−.11	−.16	−.09
D Scale																		
M	−.44	−.33	−.44	−.44	−.42	−.42	−.27	−.20	−.12	.00	−.11	−.37	−.49	−.15	−.30	−.13	−.39	−.27
F	−.40	−.36	−.44	−.50	−.41	−.41	−.33	−.18	−.17	.03	−.10	−.38	−.44	−.18	−.31	−.25	−.44	−.32
Hy Scale																		
M	−.08	.04	.00	−.01	−.03	−.04	.09	−.06	−.10	.04	.04	−.24	−.12	.15	−.10	.12	−.01	.01
F	.06	.10	.08	.01	.11	.03	.19	.08	−.02	.02	.06	−.17	−.04	.13	−.04	.11	.07	.03
PdK Scale																		
M	−.06	−.04	.01	.04	.05	−.06	.02	−.29	−.42	−.21	−.12	−.26	−.28	−.14	−.27	−.02	−.11	−.11
F	.01	.04	.00	−.01	.15	.05	.06	−.30	−.46	−.27	−.21	−.32	−.33	−.19	−.35	.00	−.07	−.08
Mf Scale (raw scores)																		
M	−.09	.09	−.15	−.05	−.01	.01	.21	−.05	−.15	−.14	−.20	−.18	−.30	.14	−.08	.24	.08	.03
F	−.09	.09	−.05	−.05	.01	−.12	.16	.06	−.08	−.01	−.11	.03	−.14	.19	.01	.15	.11	.00
Pa Scale																		
M	−.17	−.11	−.15	−.11	−.10	−.17	−.02	−.14	−.19	−.15	−.11	−.24	−.28	.04	−.21	.01	−.12	−.08
F	−.13	−.04	−.07	−.07	−.06	−.13	−.02	−.12	−.25	−.19	−.13	−.20	−.29	.05	−.23	−.02	−.13	−.13
PtK Scale																		
M	−.39	−.21	−.29	−.27	−.30	−.41	−.10	−.25	−.16	−.13	−.17	−.31	−.52	−.05	−.36	−.08	−.31	−.24
F	−.35	−.23	−.27	−.32	−.22	−.42	−.15	−.19	−.25	−.21	−.25	−.31	−.54	−.16	−.37	−.22	−.37	−.37
ScK Scale																		
M	−.30	−.19	−.20	−.12	−.17	−.26	−.04	−.31	−.28	−.23	−.21	−.38	−.46	−.14	−.38	−.07	−.21	−.23
F	−.21	−.14	−.20	−.16	−.08	−.20	−.06	−.35	−.41	−.38	−.32	−.41	−.55	−.30	−.41	−.20	−.30	−.29

C. Personality and Interest Inventories continued

Measures	Fx	F/M	v.1	v.2	v.3	Mp	Wo	CT	Lp	Ami	Leo	Tm	B–MS	B–FM	Anx	Nar	D–SD	D–AC
12. Millon Clinical Multiaxial Inventory (MCMI) (Ns = 118 males, 118 females) continued																		
Factor 1 (anxiety and dysphoria)																		
M	−.09	.32	.04	−.22	−.55	−.58	−.62	−.20	−.71	−.57	−.57	−.64	−.71	−.27	.75	.27	−.55	.36
F	.17	.05	.17	−.48	−.42	−.54	−.62	.00	−.64	−.52	−.51	−.48	−.47	−.45	.66	.12	−.56	.10
Factor 2 (impulse under control; errant impulse)																		
M	.18	−.03	−.59	−.09	−.21	−.12	−.29	.25	.08	−.31	−.12	−.12	.20	−.39	.03	.53	−.07	.32
F	.11	−.20	−.76	−.12	−.28	.01	−.29	.32	.19	−.40	.00	−.04	.31	−.40	.00	.70	−.10	.38
Factor 3 (paranoid thinking; cognitive rigidity)																		
M	−.48	.09	−.04	.37	−.36	−.19	−.19	−.52	−.09	−.23	.02	−.09	−.18	−.06	.14	.14	.02	.39
F	−.44	−.04	−.10	.33	−.21	−.12	−.02	−.20	.15	−.12	.11	.11	.06	−.06	−.05	.19	.09	.36
Factor 4 (constriction and dependency)																		
M	.06	.16	.10	.09	.08	.15	.09	−.04	.03	.19	.04	−.07	−.05	.29	−.03	−.25	.09	−.13
F	.09	.41	.22	−.02	−.04	−.16	−.10	−.15	−.20	.05	−.11	−.32	−.30	.28	.10	−.24	−.07	−.03
13. Minnesota Multiphasic Personality Inventory (MMPI) (Ns = 657 males, 461 females)																		
L Scale																		
M	−.10	.05	.13	.14	.22	.15	.15	−.08	.12	.20	.17	.24	.11	.16	−.07	−.28	.24	−.23
F	−.23	−.02	.14	.25	.18	.18	.21	−.21	.20	.25	.32	.28	.17	.21	−.16	−.27	.34	−.16
F Scale																		
M	.15	.07	.11	−.34	−.29	−.45	−.44	−.01	−.43	−.37	−.18	−.34	−.33	−.22	.32	.14	−.41	.11
F	.08	−.07	.02	−.25	−.30	−.35	−.44	.05	−.37	−.42	−.32	−.26	−.26	−.33	.40	.22	−.36	.11
K Scale																		
M	.11	−.15	−.10	.22	.68	.63	.58	.20	.53	.60	.25	.54	.53	.28	−.33	−.39	.54	−.36
F	.19	−.17	−.08	.11	.64	.63	.57	.21	.51	.56	.24	.51	.50	.24	−.39	−.33	.47	−.38
HsK Scale																		
M	.19	.11	.12	−.19	−.04	−.17	−.23	.01	−.25	−.05	−.09	−.19	−.19	−.02	.19	−.10	−.21	−.05
F	.04	.09	.00	−.07	−.10	−.03	−.19	.00	−.11	−.06	−.05	−.11	−.10	−.12	.11	−.02	−.05	−.07
D Scale																		
M	.14	.35	.33	−.25	−.20	−.40	−.38	−.06	−.53	−.19	−.25	−.40	−.53	.15	.37	−.16	−.37	−.08
F	−.01	.27	.30	−.15	−.24	−.33	−.35	−.15	−.53	−.15	−.21	−.35	−.52	.02	.38	−.13	−.27	−.09
Hy Scale																		
M	.30	.17	.03	−.20	.18	.04	−.16	.23	−.12	.05	−.14	−.07	−.04	.07	.11	−.13	−.09	−.18
F	.24	.08	−.05	−.13	.15	.19	−.07	.23	.01	.09	−.09	−.05	.03	−.02	.03	−.06	.03	−.19
PdK Scale																		
M	.22	−.02	−.06	−.34	−.05	−.17	−.30	.14	−.20	−.30	−.08	−.13	−.02	−.24	.19	.06	−.18	−.07
F	.23	.02	−.12	−.39	−.30	−.36	−.54	.13	−.40	−.55	−.26	−.30	−.21	−.36	.39	.32	−.41	.05
Mf Scale (raw scores)																		
M	.30	.49	−.03	−.29	.10	−.08	−.32	.40	−.19	−.20	−.40	−.24	−.27	.12	.26	.10	−.18	.00
F	.18	.42	.03	−.16	.12	.01	−.09	.23	−.10	.02	−.22	−.16	−.22	.21	.08	−.07	−.03	−.10
Pa Scale																		
M	.18	.12	.05	−.20	−.01	−.14	−.27	.11	−.23	−.16	−.10	−.20	−.21	−.11	.21	.01	−.19	−.05
F	.17	.09	.00	−.12	−.01	−.10	−.27	.13	−.25	−.15	−.21	−.29	−.19	−.18	.29	.02	−.11	.01
PtK Scale																		
M	.27	.30	.20	−.28	−.12	−.35	−.42	.05	−.49	−.19	−.28	−.47	−.48	−.02	.37	−.08	−.34	.02
F	.17	.26	.11	−.23	−.26	−.35	−.45	.00	−.52	−.23	−.32	−.50	−.50	−.15	.42	.02	−.36	.00
ScK Scale																		
M	.26	.15	.10	−.37	−.13	−.36	−.42	.12	−.42	−.29	−.25	−.38	−.32	−.17	.35	.04	−.34	.07
F	.20	.05	−.05	−.34	−.27	−.36	−.47	.12	−.44	−.39	−.36	−.42	−.32	−.38	.42	.18	−.40	.08

C. Personality and Interest Inventories continued

Measures	Do	Cs	Sy	Sp	Sa	In	Em	Re	So	Sc	Gi	Cm	Wb	To	Ac	Ai	Ie	Py
13. Minnesota Multiphasic Personality Inventory (MMPI) (Ns = 657 males, 461 females) continued																		
MaK Scale																		
M	.12	.05	.22	.25	.28	.05	.15	−.38	−.40	−.47	−.31	−.10	−.30	−.33	−.28	−.19	−.09	−.22
F	.24	.14	.27	.33	.37	.10	.24	−.33	−.39	−.54	−.34	−.01	−.26	−.28	−.24	−.07	.02	−.06
Si Scale																		
M	−.64	−.61	−.79	−.66	−.63	−.46	−.51	−.24	−.14	−.01	−.28	−.32	−.53	−.23	−.38	−.18	−.41	−.27
F	−.65	−.64	−.81	−.74	−.69	−.52	−.65	−.22	−.19	.04	−.21	−.32	−.49	−.31	−.31	−.36	−.54	−.34
Welsh A Scale																		
M	−.48	−.42	−.42	−.39	−.34	−.55	−.29	−.38	−.30	−.41	−.51	−.25	−.74	−.40	−.51	−.36	−.51	−.49
F	−.41	−.44	−.44	−.46	−.35	−.55	−.37	−.36	−.34	−.36	−.43	−.27	−.72	−.44	−.44	−.47	−.57	−.51
Welsh R Scale																		
M	−.27	−.16	−.33	−.24	−.29	−.02	−.14	.06	.13	.41	.25	−.23	.09	.20	.00	.20	.01	.07
F	−.27	−.15	−.30	−.31	−.28	−.03	−.18	.21	.18	.49	.30	−.25	.13	.23	.08	.15	−.03	.09
Barron ES Scale																		
M	.35	.38	.33	.35	.28	.44	.24	.34	.23	.26	.29	.28	.58	.39	.38	.34	.48	.43
F	.31	.44	.32	.43	.29	.45	.31	.30	.20	.20	.24	.14	.59	.41	.29	.49	.57	.48
14. Myers-Briggs Type Indicator (MBTI) (Ns = 401 males, 292 females)																		
E–I (continuous score)																		
M	−.50	−.42	−.63	−.46	−.51	−.27	−.36	−.05	−.06	.12	−.15	−.11	−.21	.04	−.17	.01	−.17	−.03
F	−.53	−.43	−.70	−.57	−.58	−.30	−.56	−.05	−.08	.18	−.07	−.22	−.20	−.07	−.14	−.13	−.29	.01
S–N (continuous score)																		
M	.02	.23	.02	.18	.13	.25	.24	.01	−.20	−.07	−.16	−.11	−.01	.22	−.10	.31	.20	.30
F	.04	.24	.07	.15	.13	.26	.23	.11	−.20	−.12	−.14	−.16	.02	.18	−.20	.29	.25	.31
T–F (continuous score)																		
M	−.20	−.04	−.12	−.14	−.15	−.23	.09	.00	−.05	−.03	−.09	−.08	−.18	.09	−.13	−.10	−.19	−.15
F	−.17	−.02	−.02	.01	−.08	−.17	.05	−.04	.01	.00	.06	−.01	−.09	.04	−.08	−.13	−.09	−.15
J–P (continuous score)																		
M	−.15	.04	−.02	.19	.03	.07	.15	−.32	−.33	−.31	−.34	−.23	−.19	−.01	−.44	.04	−.03	.08
F	−.10	.03	.00	.13	.03	.09	.23	−.14	−.29	−.24	−.25	−.21	−.11	.02	−.44	.03	.04	.05
15. Strong Interest Inventory (SII): Occupational Theme Scales (Ns = 554 males, 223 females)																		
Realistic																		
M	.14	.11	.14	.00	.01	−.02	−.05	.25	.23	.13	.22	.28	.27	.06	.17	−.09	.07	.02
F	.06	.10	.04	.06	.11	.01	.06	.10	−.02	.00	.04	.08	.08	.00	.05	.02	.10	.07
Investigative																		
M	.10	.27	.05	.03	.07	.12	.19	.27	.12	.12	.09	.05	.09	.24	.23	.36	.34	.39
F	.10	.18	.02	.05	.08	.13	.04	.26	.07	.13	.10	.07	.21	.22	.14	.24	.24	.41
Artistic																		
M	.00	.24	.00	.18	.20	.16	.41	−.16	−.21	−.23	−.22	−.15	−.25	.07	−.11	.29	.15	.13
F	.21	.32	.26	.23	.41	.21	.36	−.06	−.20	−.30	−.22	.03	−.16	.00	−.01	.12	.16	.01
Social																		
M	.36	.29	.40	.19	.27	.04	.30	.19	.12	.04	.22	.18	.17	.07	.27	−.01	.13	−.09
F	.31	.17	.23	.05	.25	.04	.15	.12	.15	.05	.13	.25	.00	.03	.25	−.04	.03	−.12
Enterprising																		
M	.34	.19	.41	.19	.24	.01	.12	.15	.12	.02	.22	.24	.21	−.13	.22	−.23	−.01	−.23
F	.27	.20	.38	.24	.30	−.02	.25	−.10	.11	−.13	.02	.29	.01	−.10	.18	−.07	.05	−.17
Conventional																		
M	.23	.11	.26	.00	.03	−.12	−.03	.32	.29	.23	.32	.27	.26	−.03	.37	−.16	.02	−.13
F	.05	−.02	.07	−.04	−.04	−.09	−.08	.06	.26	.13	.17	.23	.11	−.07	.27	−.09	−.06	−.04

C. Personality and Interest Inventories continued

Measures	Fx	F/M	v.1	v.2	v.3	Mp	Wo	CT	Lp	Ami	Leo	Tm	B–MS	B–FM	Anx	Nar	D–SD	D–AC
13. Minnesota Multiphasic Personality Inventory (MMPI) (Ns = 657 males, 461 females) continued																		
MaK Scale																		
M	.08	−.13	−.33	−.23	−.25	−.23	−.40	.11	−.10	−.42	−.13	−.19	.09	−.44	.14	.47	−.16	.31
F	.20	−.14	−.43	−.25	−.20	−.20	−.37	.23	−.03	−.42	−.16	−.23	.16	−.46	.07	.50	−.18	.25
Si Scale																		
M	.01	.33	.57	−.29	−.36	−.56	−.41	−.17	−.69	−.27	−.30	−.47	−.73	.10	.41	−.15	−.53	−.02
F	−.18	.26	.57	−.14	−.43	−.57	−.35	−.36	−.70	−.26	−.29	−.41	−.73	.04	.46	−.16	−.49	−.05
Welsh A Scale																		
M	.07	.29	.23	−.31	−.55	−.67	−.66	−.14	−.69	−.50	−.34	−.71	−.70	−.19	.46	.17	−.57	.27
F	−.04	.29	.18	−.20	−.56	−.61	−.63	−.16	−.67	−.48	−.36	−.65	−.67	−.22	.57	.15	−.53	.21
Welsh R Scale																		
M	.18	.28	.38	−.14	.21	.04	.15	.13	−.11	.24	−.04	.07	−.11	.40	.03	−.44	−.04	−.34
F	.03	.15	.44	.05	.20	.09	.25	−.05	−.07	.32	.00	.15	−.09	.34	.00	−.49	.08	−.36
Barron ES Scale																		
M	−.03	−.30	−.19	.22	.44	.55	.52	.17	.52	.40	.20	.52	.52	.09	−.40	−.08	.41	−.19
F	.15	−.33	−.16	.07	.51	.51	.52	.24	.50	.33	.16	.52	.52	.08	−.42	−.04	.33	−.18
14. Myers-Briggs Type Indicator (MBTI) (Ns = 401 males, 292 females)																		
E–I (continuous score)																		
M	.03	.20	.51	−.24	−.09	−.32	−.05	−.06	−.43	−.04	−.24	−.23	−.50	.14	.26	−.25	−.39	−.12
F	−.15	.14	.54	−.12	−.18	−.33	−.08	−.28	−.47	−.05	−.20	−.19	−.51	.09	.24	−.23	−.31	−.15
S–N (continuous score)																		
M	.39	.09	−.06	−.30	.27	.08	−.08	.53	−.01	−.04	−.33	−.03	.03	−.14	.06	.08	−.07	−.15
F	.43	.01	−.06	−.29	.24	.08	.00	.53	.01	−.07	−.36	−.05	.11	−.20	.02	.09	−.07	−.19
T–F (continuous score)																		
M	.11	.33	.16	−.12	.00	−.13	−.15	.09	−.23	−.01	−.25	−.31	−.28	.20	.14	−.14	−.12	−.07
F	.07	.18	.13	−.07	.04	−.10	−.04	.00	−.15	.11	−.12	−.16	−.14	.14	.01	−.21	.01	−.09
J–P (continuous score)																		
M	.55	.02	−.02	−.54	.02	−.21	−.27	.52	−.28	−.22	−.44	−.26	−.06	−.32	.24	.14	−.38	−.11
F	.51	−.06	−.04	−.45	.04	−.15	−.14	.43	−.21	−.14	−.35	−.19	−.03	−.26	.19	.12	−.27	−.09
15. Strong Interest Inventory (SII): Occupational Theme Scales (Ns = 554 males, 223 females)																		
Realistic																		
M	−.29	−.50	−.03	.37	.00	.17	.29	−.37	.25	.27	.33	.22	.22	−.16	−.26	−.15	.23	.04
F	−.06	−.26	−.05	.04	.03	.04	.07	−.03	.12	.06	.08	.00	.10	−.24	−.12	.08	.05	.08
Investigative																		
M	.10	.03	−.05	.07	.33	.19	.15	.19	.13	.12	−.08	.14	.08	.06	−.10	−.05	.18	−.05
F	.01	−.13	.03	.09	.25	.24	.25	.06	.22	.12	.00	.19	.18	−.04	−.18	−.05	.17	−.04
Artistic																		
M	.35	.37	−.16	−.33	.15	−.10	−.25	.50	−.13	−.23	−.45	−.21	−.12	−.01	.16	.25	−.09	.09
F	.19	.13	−.35	−.15	.02	−.03	−.17	.37	.11	−.18	−.17	−.11	.10	−.21	.01	.28	.03	.13
Social																		
M	−.18	−.18	−.32	.28	.09	.24	.18	−.16	.32	.14	.25	.15	.27	−.02	−.19	.00	.32	.09
F	−.12	.03	−.26	.21	.05	.13	.01	−.03	.26	.06	.22	.07	.10	.01	−.05	.08	.24	.07
Enterprising																		
M	−.34	−.36	−.31	.39	−.11	.18	.19	−.40	.33	.11	.37	.20	.30	−.10	−.19	.03	.29	.18
F	−.10	−.09	−.37	.22	−.11	.04	−.05	−.06	.22	−.05	.22	−.03	.12	−.12	−.15	.19	.16	.24
Conventional																		
M	−.44	−.28	−.09	.49	−.03	.22	.32	−.51	.31	.26	.42	.25	.21	.11	−.20	−.19	.31	.10
F	−.29	−.08	−.01	.36	−.06	.06	.16	−.30	.15	.10	.22	.07	−.01	.09	−.11	−.03	.13	.13

C. Personality and Interest Inventories continued

Measures	Do	Cs	Sy	Sp	Sa	In	Em	Re	So	Sc	Gi	Cm	Wb	To	Ac	Ai	Ie	Py
16. Tellegen's three higher-order traits, as scored on the ACL (Ns = 570 males, 353 females)																		
Positive Emotionality (PEM)																		
M	.50	.38	.45	.35	.48	.35	.33	.05	.06	−.15	.03	.13	.15	.01	.21	.07	.24	.13
F	.43	.35	.44	.39	.44	.33	.42	.09	.07	−.10	.05	.21	.18	.03	.20	.08	.31	.12
Negative Emotionality (NEM)																		
M	−.28	−.25	−.29	−.22	−.20	−.25	−.22	−.33	−.33	−.30	−.38	−.22	−.53	−.25	−.35	−.15	−.31	−.19
F	−.25	−.18	−.22	−.19	−.14	−.30	−.14	−.14	−.24	−.21	−.26	−.16	−.41	−.18	−.20	−.17	−.22	−.23
Constraint (CNS)																		
M	−.02	−.01	−.03	−.24	−.10	−.16	−.07	.26	.24	.32	.30	.16	.14	.04	.34	.00	−.01	−.01
F	−.18	−.14	−.26	−.31	−.26	−.17	−.29	.19	.23	.36	.32	.10	.08	.07	.30	−.07	−.13	−.01
17. Zuckerman Sensation-Seeking Scale (SSS) (Ns = 69 males, 69 females)																		
Thrill and Adventure Seeking (TAS)																		
M	.12	.40	.28	.35	.31	.33	.23	−.14	−.22	−.06	.07	.21	.24	.14	.00	.11	.13	.08
F	.24	.28	.40	.40	.31	.05	.34	.08	.11	−.17	−.04	.35	.11	.16	.07	.26	.25	−.04
Experience Seeking (ES)																		
M	.18	.40	.26	.45	.35	.31	.41	−.13	−.23	−.15	.07	−.16	.21	.22	−.11	.33	.30	.21
F	.23	.21	.19	.40	.39	.26	.47	−.29	−.26	−.29	−.09	.01	.11	.04	−.21	.31	.32	.12
Disinhibition (DIS)																		
M	.14	.34	.43	.55	.40	.19	.28	−.51	−.28	−.32	.01	−.20	.15	−.07	−.28	.12	.02	.03
F	.11	.27	.36	.58	.23	.10	.37	−.18	−.18	−.40	−.18	−.06	.09	.08	−.28	.21	.24	−.04
Boredom Susceptibility (BS)																		
M	.16	.13	.16	.26	.21	.24	.26	−.15	−.09	−.13	−.18	−.11	.19	−.06	−.16	.03	.15	.09
F	.16	.00	.19	.13	.14	.04	.18	−.27	−.14	−.53	−.40	−.23	−.23	−.44	−.25	−.20	−.14	−.17
Total Score																		
M	.24	.50	.45	.64	.51	.42	.48	−.37	−.33	−.27	−.01	−.12	.31	.10	−.22	.25	.24	.17
F	.29	.31	.45	.60	.41	.17	.52	−.24	−.17	−.52	−.26	.05	.04	−.03	−.25	.24	.27	−.05

C. Personality and Interest Inventories continued

Measures	Fx	F/M	v.1	v.2	v.3	Mp	Wo	CT	Lp	Ami	Leo	Tm	B–MS	B–FM	Anx	Nar	D–SD	D–AC
16. Tellegen's three higher-order traits, as scored on the ACL (Ns = 570 males, 353 females)																		
Positive Emotionality (PEM)																		
M	−.05	−.14	−.49	.17	.10	.26	.01	.14	.39	−.04	.10	.24	.41	−.19	−.17	.35	.28	.15
F	.08	−.12	−.40	.11	.13	.25	.12	.21	.39	.04	.14	.21	.43	−.15	−.22	.26	.27	.07
Negative Emotionality (NEM)																		
M	.12	.19	.11	−.33	−.30	−.40	−.49	.04	−.48	−.42	−.33	−.41	−.44	−.17	.35	.17	−.43	.11
F	−.02	.22	.10	−.17	−.26	−.32	−.27	−.06	−.36	−.27	−.26	−.33	−.35	−.10	.25	.05	−.32	.06
Constraint (CNS)																		
M	−.36	−.01	.17	.35	.07	.12	.26	−.34	.14	.25	.22	.16	−.02	.28	−.12	−.28	.23	−.04
F	−.34	.09	.31	.30	.05	.04	.19	−.41	.02	.21	.18	.12	−.14	.30	.04	−.37	.14	−.09
17. Zuckerman Sensation-Seeking Scale (SSS) (Ns = 69 males, 69 females)																		
Thrill and Adventure Seeking (TAS)																		
M	.13	−.12	−.12	−.12	.19	.17	.09	.30	.26	.10	−.13	.22	.39	−.18	−.12	.06	.19	−.27
F	.21	−.05	−.29	.02	.22	.20	.09	.25	.24	.12	−.05	−.01	.23	.00	−.21	.12	.17	.11
Experience Seeking (ES)																		
M	.39	−.07	−.20	−.34	.38	.15	.08	.61	.23	.08	−.27	.15	.31	−.09	−.01	.06	.16	−.17
F	.31	−.16	−.36	−.32	.15	.01	−.09	.49	.16	−.22	−.26	.06	.27	−.31	−.13	.32	.08	.09
Disinhibition (DIS)																		
M	.30	−.22	−.26	−.37	.08	.02	.04	.41	.17	−.05	−.26	.07	.36	−.31	.03	.23	.14	−.24
F	.40	−.10	−.31	−.19	.18	.11	.04	.40	.09	−.03	−.40	.03	.30	−.24	−.07	.31	−.01	.09
Boredom Susceptibility (BS)																		
M	.29	−.11	−.26	−.12	.00	.06	−.02	.24	.14	−.01	−.14	.05	.16	−.22	.06	.31	−.01	.09
F	.14	−.24	−.37	−.11	−.39	−.15	−.33	.13	−.06	−.39	−.19	−.10	.05	−.40	.21	.48	−.35	.26
Total Score																		
M	.45	−.21	−.34	−.39	.27	.15	.07	.63	.32	.04	−.32	.19	.48	−.31	−.01	.26	.19	−.23
F	.41	−.20	−.51	−.22	.09	.08	−.09	.49	.18	−.18	−.35	.00	.33	−.34	−.09	.46	−.03	.21

D. Other Measures

Measures	Do	Cs	Sy	Sp	Sa	In	Em	Re	So	Sc	Gi	Cm	Wb	To	Ac	Ai	Ie	Py
1. Barron personality scales (Ns = 1,358 males, 911 females)																		
Complexity																		
M	−.08	.20	−.08	.20	.09	.26	.26	−.19	−.35	−.24	−.33	−.22	−.18	.23	−.23	.47	.28	.39
F	.07	.25	.00	.23	.20	.35	.28	−.11	−.38	−.22	−.25	−.24	−.07	.22	−.23	.45	.33	.45
Independence																		
M	−.06	.19	−.06	.19	.09	.28	.22	−.12	−.24	−.17	−.27	−.14	−.10	.27	−.15	.48	.34	.42
F	.07	.23	.03	.21	.20	.33	.25	−.04	−.25	−.13	−.21	−.17	.01	.27	−.13	.42	.35	.39
Originality																		
M	.35	.46	.29	.46	.45	.39	.55	−.01	−.30	−.43	−.36	−.03	−.13	.21	.01	.46	.43	.38
F	.51	.50	.38	.52	.56	.46	.56	.00	−.31	−.45	−.34	−.01	−.05	.18	.02	.44	.45	.40
Personal Soundness																		
M	.22	.27	.15	.12	.07	.34	.15	.36	.31	.44	.41	.10	.54	.38	.41	.34	.39	.42
F	.24	.34	.16	.19	.14	.43	.19	.36	.28	.41	.42	.00	.55	.42	.38	.44	.44	.47
2. Barron-Welsh Art Scale (BWAS) and Revised Art Scale (RAS) (Ns = 1,533 males, 549 females)																		
BWAS																		
M	−.09	.11	−.09	.11	.06	.16	.17	−.15	−.18	−.11	−.18	−.20	−.12	.13	−.18	.26	.14	.21
F	.03	.13	.02	.10	.11	.13	.07	.06	−.05	−.06	−.09	−.11	.03	.08	−.12	.12	.10	.12
RAS																		
M	−.09	.13	−.06	.15	.09	.17	.23	−.17	−.18	−.14	−.19	−.21	−.13	.14	−.17	.31	.18	.24
F	.07	.15	.05	.13	.14	.16	.11	.04	−.05	−.06	−.07	−.07	.06	.12	−.09	.14	.14	.14
3. Beck Depression Inventory (BDI) (Ns = 118 males, 118 females)																		
M	−.19	−.16	−.23	−.22	−.17	−.38	−.08	−.32	−.35	−.42	−.30	−.28	−.54	−.42	−.43	−.40	−.47	−.40
F	−.12	−.10	−.18	−.17	−.05	−.18	−.19	−.28	−.44	−.32	−.39	−.32	−.53	−.36	−.38	−.17	−.23	−.24
4. Bem Sex-Role Inventory (BSRI) (Ns = 99 males, 99 females)																		
Masculinity																		
M	.67	.38	.45	.54	.57	.52	.36	−.22	−.08	−.26	.00	.04	.34	−.15	.19	.06	.40	.27
F	.76	.39	.46	.35	.63	.70	.42	.22	.10	−.09	.13	.28	.40	−.05	.36	.26	.32	.31
Femininity																		
M	.10	.12	.15	−.02	.04	−.03	.12	.07	.23	.15	.29	.05	.06	.09	.25	.11	.04	.03
F	.12	.22	.26	.10	.13	−.09	.17	.44	.21	.16	.33	.43	.14	.27	.33	.06	.06	−.03
5. Chapin Social Insight Test (CSIT) (Ns = 766 males, 218 females)																		
M	−.06	.16	−.07	.12	.04	.18	.24	.04	−.06	−.07	−.20	−.06	−.05	.29	.02	.42	.33	.35
F	−.09	.12	−.09	.02	−.03	.15	.04	.10	−.14	.04	−.08	−.02	.11	.18	−.04	.24	.25	.32
6. Hogan Survey of Ethical Attitudes, Form A (SEA-A) (Ns = 49 males, 49 females)																		
M	−.04	−.45	−.20	−.28	−.27	−.15	−.33	.29	.35	.09	−.02	.30	.04	−.12	.24	−.06	.01	−.18
F	−.03	−.10	.04	−.19	−.15	−.26	−.17	.13	.38	.17	−.03	.08	−.09	−.11	.15	−.31	−.27	−.28
7. Loevinger Sentence Completion Test for Ego Development (LSCT) (N = 87 females)																		
F	.33	.36	.25	.35	.30	.32	.49	.36	.06	.07	.19	.13	.20	.16	.24	.45	.39	.35
8. Rotter Locus of Control Scale (LOC) (Ns = 89 males, 89 females)																		
M	−.14	−.10	−.14	−.07	−.03	−.12	−.04	−.31	−.11	−.14	−.24	−.16	−.25	−.31	−.34	−.20	−.20	−.25
F	−.28	−.22	−.13	−.04	−.27	−.14	−.32	−.34	−.24	−.26	−.29	−.24	−.16	−.09	−.42	−.27	−.21	−.24
9. Spence-Helmreich Personal Attributes Questionnaire (PAQ) (Ns = 87 males, 86 females)																		
Masculinity +																		
M	.65	.44	.50	.55	.57	.53	.39	−.09	.04	−.20	.10	.18	.46	−.04	.31	.12	.41	.25
F	.67	.31	.43	.40	.57	.60	.37	.21	.24	−.03	.23	.39	.48	−.16	.41	.20	.26	.37
Masculinity −																		
M	.28	.14	.10	.29	.34	.24	.08	−.26	−.16	−.41	−.43	−.04	−.01	−.32	−.11	−.07	.18	.06
F	.07	.09	.01	.10	.04	.18	.02	−.22	−.21	−.34	−.33	−.29	−.14	−.11	−.23	.03	.08	.03

D. Other Measures continued

Measures	Fx	F/M	v.1	v.2	v.3	Mp	Wo	CT	Lp	Ami	Leo	Tm	B–MS	B–FM	Anx	Nar	D–SD	D–AC
1. Barron personality scales (Ns = 1,358 males, 911 females)																		
Complexity																		
M	.60	.13	−.08	−.57	.29	−.02	−.20	.68	−.18	−.28	−.53	−.07	−.01	−.10	.15	.19	−.25	−.11
F	.55	−.17	−.16	−.53	.31	.12	−.05	.64	−.02	−.24	−.48	.09	.18	−.27	.14	.24	−.11	−.12
Independence																		
M	.52	.10	−.03	−.51	.33	.03	−.08	.62	−.11	−.19	−.42	.00	.05	−.06	.10	.13	−.18	−.19
F	.45	−.14	−.11	−.44	.32	.17	.02	.55	.03	−.12	−.34	.13	.19	−.16	.05	.16	−.06	−.16
Originality																		
M	.48	.01	−.56	−.38	.26	.17	−.18	.64	.12	−.35	−.35	.04	.20	−.26	.02	.46	−.07	.11
F	.43	−.21	−.65	−.35	.25	.28	−.07	.65	.28	−.33	−.27	.18	.39	−.35	.02	.53	.00	.09
Personal Soundness																		
M	.05	−.16	.01	.19	.46	.48	.56	.11	.44	.45	.18	.51	.40	.24	−.34	−.29	.41	−.23
F	.09	−.30	−.04	.13	.53	.51	.58	.16	.49	.40	.13	.56	.45	.16	−.33	−.21	.39	−.26
2. Barron-Welsh Art Scale (BWAS) and Revised Art Scale (RAS) (Ns = 1,533 males, 549 females)																		
BWAS																		
M	.37	.13	−.02	−.37	.15	−.06	−.18	.45	−.14	−.13	−.35	−.10	−.03	−.05	.10	.12	−.14	−.08
F	.20	.06	−.04	−.16	.09	.06	.03	.20	.03	.01	−.17	.04	.07	.03	.03	.06	−.09	−.09
RAS																		
M	.42	.12	−.05	−.39	.18	−.07	−.18	.49	−.14	−.14	−.36	−.11	−.01	−.07	.10	.15	−.13	−.06
F	.20	.02	−.08	−.16	.13	.10	.06	.22	.06	.02	−.13	.08	.11	.00	.01	.08	−.04	−.10
3. Beck Depression Inventory (BDI) (Ns = 118 males, 118 females)																		
M	−.10	.26	−.08	−.13	−.40	−.34	−.46	−.13	−.46	−.47	−.40	−.45	−.45	−.24	.58	.18	−.28	.30
F	.12	−.02	−.03	−.37	−.33	−.40	−.54	.10	−.43	−.46	−.39	−.26	−.27	−.44	.49	.18	−.40	.12
4. Bem Sex-Role Inventory (BSRI) (Ns = 99 males, 99 females)																		
Masculinity																		
M	−.12	−.42	−.69	.12	.02	.30	.07	.10	.59	−.09	.34	.52	.61	−.43	−.35	.55	.32	.15
F	−.20	−.33	−.67	.29	.15	.40	.21	.13	.68	−.06	.35	.58	.62	−.22	−.34	.54	.33	−.06
Femininity																		
M	−.20	.22	−.06	.22	.17	.18	.13	−.15	.11	.19	.14	.10	−.03	.31	−.11	−.07	.21	.00
F	−.07	.19	−.09	.32	.30	.23	.15	−.08	.24	.32	.16	.01	.04	.28	−.13	−.19	.32	.01
5. Chapin Social Insight Test (CSIT) (Ns = 766 males, 218 females)																		
M	.35	.11	−.04	−.28	.28	.06	.01	.41	−.06	−.06	−.23	.02	−.02	.02	.01	.08	−.12	−.08
F	.23	.06	.05	−.28	.25	.06	.14	.28	−.03	.03	−.22	.10	.05	.05	−.01	−.13	−.08	−.19
6. Hogan Survey of Ethical Attitudes, Form A (SEA-A) (Ns = 49 males, 49 females)																		
M	−.29	.03	.17	.28	−.19	−.02	.08	−.51	−.07	.02	.40	−.02	−.12	−.18	−.20	−.02	−.09	.08
F	−.31	.23	.02	.37	−.18	.08	.04	−.43	.04	.19	.24	.04	−.14	.41	−.06	−.20	−.07	−.05
7. Loevinger Sentence Completion Test for Ego Development (LSCT) (N = 87 females)																		
F	.32	−.16	−.22	.02	.48	.28	.22	.40	.32	−.01	.04	.18	.34	−.12	−.01	.09	.24	−.13
8. Rotter Locus of Control Scale (LOC) (Ns = 89 males, 89 females)																		
M	−.02	.03	.04	−.16	−.28	−.25	−.17	−.03	−.17	−.12	−.19	−.17	−.21	−.12	.24	.15	−.16	.09
F	.04	.15	.16	−.26	−.18	−.33	−.11	.01	−.34	−.16	−.29	−.29	−.26	−.02	.14	.00	−.31	.25
9. Spence-Helmreich Personal Attributes Questionnaire (PAQ) (Ns = 87 males, 86 females)																		
Masculinity +																		
M	−.07	−.37	−.62	.19	.07	.32	.23	.18	.63	.14	.36	.54	.64	−.35	−.43	.44	.42	.15
F	−.26	−.41	−.59	.43	.02	.25	.32	−.01	.65	−.07	.45	.55	.64	−.12	−.33	.35	.37	.02
Masculinity −																		
M	.05	−.23	−.40	−.10	−.21	−.03	−.20	.10	.08	−.34	−.01	.01	.19	−.37	−.13	.51	−.19	.32
F	.10	−.12	−.26	−.19	−.15	−.06	−.19	.16	−.05	−.29	−.30	−.07	.03	−.32	.04	.45	−.22	.08

Measures	Do	Cs	Sy	Sp	Sa	In	Em	Re	So	Sc	Gi	Cm	Wb	To	Ac	Ai	Ie	Py

D. Other Measures continued

9. Spence-Helmreich Personal Attributes Questionnaire (PAQ) (Ns = 87 males, 86 females) continued

Femininity +

Measures	Do	Cs	Sy	Sp	Sa	In	Em	Re	So	Sc	Gi	Cm	Wb	To	Ac	Ai	Ie	Py
M	.20	.22	.24	.07	.11	.01	.25	.06	.12	.06	.29	.09	.07	.07	.26	.03	.00	−.08
F	.18	.08	.36	.14	.21	−.09	.20	.29	.23	.07	.29	.38	.15	−.02	.34	−.10	−.07	−.09

Femininity − (compliant)

	Do	Cs	Sy	Sp	Sa	In	Em	Re	So	Sc	Gi	Cm	Wb	To	Ac	Ai	Ie	Py
M	−.53	−.33	−.30	−.40	−.46	−.59	−.29	.13	.00	.03	−.06	−.14	−.37	−.14	−.21	−.20	−.44	−.34
F	−.46	−.31	−.31	−.29	−.40	−.50	−.31	−.09	−.19	.04	−.05	−.12	−.33	−.02	−.31	−.28	−.33	−.30

Femininity − (verbal-aggressive)

	Do	Cs	Sy	Sp	Sa	In	Em	Re	So	Sc	Gi	Cm	Wb	To	Ac	Ai	Ie	Py
M	−.14	−.15	−.14	−.16	−.16	−.15	−.11	.10	−.01	.00	−.21	.00	−.17	.08	.00	.02	−.07	−.06
F	−.21	−.17	−.18	−.21	−.25	−.23	−.29	−.16	−.12	−.19	−.35	−.26	−.31	−.09	−.32	−.23	−.24	−.25

Masculinity-Femininity (bipolar scale)

	Do	Cs	Sy	Sp	Sa	In	Em	Re	So	Sc	Gi	Cm	Wb	To	Ac	Ai	Ie	Py
M	.40	.23	.23	.30	.41	.47	.19	−.01	−.14	−.04	.13	.02	.37	−.10	.13	.05	.35	.18
F	.46	.35	.27	.33	.37	.60	.35	.02	.06	.10	.21	.10	.40	.01	.18	.24	.31	.33

D. Other Measures continued																		
Measures	Fx	F/M	v.1	v.2	v.3	Mp	Wo	CT	Lp	Ami	Leo	Tm	B–MS	B–FM	Anx	Nar	D–SD	D–AC
9. Spence-Helmreich Personal Attributes Questionnaire (PAQ) (Ns = 87 males, 86 females) continued																		
Femininity +																		
M	−.24	.12	−.16	.28	.13	.19	.15	−.07	.21	.19	.19	.10	.07	.18	−.05	.03	.32	−.02
F	−.13	.09	−.18	.38	.03	.07	.10	−.19	.24	.15	.24	.05	.11	.19	−.16	−.14	.26	.04
Femininity – (compliant)																		
M	−.02	.39	.48	−.06	−.19	−.40	−.16	−.24	−.51	−.06	−.24	−.53	−.54	.31	.28	−.37	−.26	−.01
F	.09	.18	.43	−.24	−.13	−.32	−.18	−.11	−.46	−.06	−.23	−.46	−.46	−.08	.26	−.36	−.21	.03
Femininity – (verbal-aggressive)																		
M	.08	.24	.16	−.06	.00	.02	−.13	−.01	−.24	−.16	−.12	−.21	−.31	.20	.14	−.05	−.29	−.08
F	.07	.22	.10	−.22	−.22	−.21	−.24	−.01	−.36	−.14	−.19	−.20	−.37	−.01	.20	.07	−.34	.08
Masculinity-Femininity (bipolar scale)																		
M	−.06	−.42	−.34	.04	−.03	.19	.13	.14	.46	−.01	.25	.42	.48	−.39	−.28	.32	.27	.03
F	−.02	−.52	−.34	.12	.14	.26	.27	.09	.46	.02	.30	.54	.59	−.23	−.25	.21	.23	−.04

Correlations of CPI™ Scales with Adjectival Descriptions by Observers

The correlations presented in this appendix come from three kinds of samples. In the first, college students were described by three of their friends or peers on the 300-item *Adjective Check List* (Gough & Heilbrum, 1983). For these descriptions, each adjective was rated as very descriptive, somewhat descriptive, neutral or irrelevant, somewhat undescriptive, or very undescriptive. Dummy weights of +2, +1, 0, –1, and –2 were used to score the descriptions. Then the three adjectival protocols for each person were pooled into a composite, and scores on each of the 300 adjectives were standardized for the group in which the survey was conducted. The sample of 194 males was drawn from a number of fraternities at the University of California, Berkeley, and the sample of 192 females was drawn from a number of sororities at Berkeley. The standard scores for each of the 300 adjectives were then correlated, by sex, with the 36 CPI scales.

In the next pair of samples, 236 couples described their spouses or partners on the ACL. Adjectives checked or endorsed were coded with a dummy weight of 1, and those left blank were coded with a dummy weight of 0. The descriptions of husbands by their wives or partners were then correlated with scores on each of the 36 CPI scales, and the same was done for descriptions of the wives by their husbands or partners.

The third pair of samples consisted of persons assessed at the Institute of Personality Assessment and Research at the University of California, Berkeley. There were 612 men and 358 in these two groups. Each assessee was described on the ACL by a panel of 10 observers, typically composed of five or six males and four or five females. Dummy weights of 1 were assigned to adjectives checked, and 0 to adjectives left blank. Scores on each adjective for each assessee could therefore range from a low of 0 (adjectives that no judge had checked) to a high of 10 (every judge checked the adjective). These descriptive scores on the 300 adjectives were then correlated with the 36 CPI scales.

To summarize the above, each of the 300 adjectives as checked by observers was correlated with the CPI scales for persons described by opposite-sex spouses or partners, by small panels of same-sex peers, and by 10-person panels of professional observers. The total number of correlations presented below comes to 64,800 (36 CPI scales times 300 adjectives times 6 subsamples). Perusal of the correlations should attend to those adjectives with statistically significant correlations in the same direction for all six subsamples. For example, the adjective "self-confident" had correlations with the Do scale ranging from .18 to .43, with a median of .29, with all six coefficients being significant at or beyond the .01 level. The adjective "rebellious" had negative correlations with the So scale ranging from −.20 to −.33, with a median of −.28; all six coefficients were significant at or beyond the .01 level. The adjective "egotistical" was correlated with the Nar (Narcism) scale with values from .17 to .31, median of .27, with all coefficients significant at or beyond the .01 level. In the main text for the manual, 12 adjectives with largest positive and 12 with largest negative correlations in the six subsamples are reported for the 20 folk and three vector scales.

Correlations of Observers' Adjectival Description with Scales of the CPI

		Scale: Do						Scale: Cs				
		By Peers		By Spouses		By Staff		By Peers		By Spouses		By Staff
Adjectives		M	F	M	F	M	F	M	F	M	F	M	F
001.	absent-minded	−.03	−.26	−.18	.03	−.21	−.10	−.03	−.19	−.11	.00	−.06	−.02
002.	active	.21	.30	.05	.16	.25	.31	.10	.12	.04	.12	.14	.23
003.	adaptable	.05	.09	.07	.06	.15	.16	.08	.12	.05	.06	.14	.12
004.	adventurous	.05	.14	.03	.12	.19	.22	.04	.10	.05	.10	.11	.20
005.	affected	.09	.11	.06	.00	.14	.12	.06	.15	.07	−.05	.08	.07
006.	affectionate	−.05	−.01	.04	.01	−.03	−.03	−.04	−.04	−.01	.05	−.05	−.03
007.	aggressive	.22	.34	.14	.23	.30	.34	.13	.20	−.02	.16	.10	.21
008.	alert	.16	.27	.18	.16	.20	.27	.13	.13	.16	.12	.19	.19
009.	aloof	.04	−.04	−.09	−.02	−.25	−.08	−.03	−.05	.00	−.09	−.20	−.05
010.	ambitious	.22	.29	.23	.20	.35	.35	.25	.15	.15	.22	.28	.28
011.	anxious	.00	.00	.00	−.06	−.24	−.30	.02	−.15	−.10	.00	−.09	−.27
012.	apathetic	−.22	−.16	−.14	−.04	−.29	−.21	−.22	−.11	−.17	−.06	−.24	−.20
013.	appreciative	−.04	.03	.04	.01	−.10	−.11	−.05	−.01	.05	.01	.03	−.08
014.	argumentative	.17	.18	.12	.21	.28	.23	.00	.04	−.04	.06	.18	.14
015.	arrogant	.16	.16	.05	.13	.18	.20	−.02	.08	−.05	.09	.08	.09
016.	artistic	−.17	−.08	−.07	.04	.02	−.09	−.07	.03	.03	.03	.13	.13
017.	assertive	.16	.37	.22	.36	.35	.40	.03	.20	.06	.34	.15	.24
018.	attractive	.03	.10	−.03	.00	.04	.10	.02	.06	−.03	−.05	.01	.10
019.	autocratic	.06	.13	.08	.08	.12	.20	−.01	.06	.05	.02	.01	.14
020.	awkward	−.16	−.19	−.16	−.17	−.36	−.29	−.14	−.18	−.18	−.05	−.25	−.23
021.	bitter	−.06	−.02	−.15	−.05	−.04	.00	−.08	−.12	−.25	−.06	−.11	−.08
022.	blustery	.08	.01	.03	−.06	.15	.06	.07	.00	−.01	−.01	.01	.01
023.	boastful	.13	.26	.03	.06	.24	.17	.08	.14	−.05	−.01	.02	.12
024.	bossy	.10	.25	−.04	.11	.20	.22	−.01	.13	−.15	−.05	.02	.05
025.	calm	−.14	−.08	−.14	−.14	−.16	.01	−.04	.07	−.03	−.10	−.13	.01
026.	capable	.13	.14	.01	.18	.10	.27	.16	.07	−.02	.15	.06	.18
027.	careless	−.04	−.13	−.21	−.02	−.04	−.06	−.03	.04	−.12	−.06	−.00	.02
028.	cautious	−.16	−.23	−.14	−.11	−.38	−.28	−.18	−.19	−.13	−.15	−.23	−.27
029.	changeable	.01	−.01	−.14	.08	.02	−.07	.06	.05	−.10	.08	.00	.01
030.	charming	−.03	.10	−.03	.06	.11	.11	.01	.05	−.05	.00	.10	.14
031.	cheerful	−.03	.03	.09	−.01	.09	.14	−.03	.04	.07	−.06	.10	.07
032.	civilized	.11	−.01	.03	−.01	.00	.09	.05	.01	.08	.00	.09	.05
033.	clear-thinking	.12	.18	.05	.09	.08	.24	.11	.16	.10	.10	.08	.24
034.	clever	.06	.12	.09	.16	.20	.20	.12	.05	.07	.20	.16	.22
035.	coarse	−.06	.01	−.17	.04	.05	.07	−.03	.04	−.15	.06	−.06	.01
036.	cold	−.08	−.02	−.12	.01	−.08	.00	−.09	−.10	−.08	−.03	−.18	−.06
037.	commonplace	−.22	−.13	−.01	−.14	−.19	−.16	−.02	−.07	.00	−.13	−.25	−.26
038.	complaining	−.07	−.05	−.14	.01	−.05	.05	−.11	−.09	−.22	−.07	−.02	−.06
039.	complicated	.02	−.06	.11	.07	−.05	−.02	.01	.07	.14	.09	−.02	.03
040.	conceited	.16	.26	.00	.10	.25	.17	.10	.14	−.06	.06	.15	.13
041.	confident	.23	.41	.17	.24	.28	.41	.15	.21	.04	.19	.17	.30
042.	confused	−.12	−.19	−.18	−.04	−.18	−.20	−.10	−.10	−.22	−.07	−.12	−.16
043.	conscientious	−.01	.09	.10	.07	−.15	−.02	.02	−.05	.05	.12	−.07	−.05
044.	conservative	.07	−.12	−.06	−.21	−.13	−.09	.01	−.07	−.05	−.18	−.20	−.20

Correlations of Observers' Adjectival Description with Scales of the CPI continued

| | Scale: Do | | | | | | Scale: Cs | | | | | |
| | By Peers | | By Spouses | | By Staff | | By Peers | | By Spouses | | By Staff | |
Adjectives	M	F	M	F	M	F	M	F	M	F	M	F
045. considerate	−.01	−.07	.01	−.17	−.18	−.09	.00	−.08	−.03	−.06	−.08	−.12
046. contented	−.05	.00	.03	−.13	−.10	.03	−.08	.02	.02	−.07	−.14	−.13
047. conventional	.00	−.09	.04	−.12	−.17	−.11	.05	−.06	.01	−.07	−.22	−.22
048. cool	.01	.05	−.05	−.01	−.05	.03	.02	−.07	.00	−.01	−.07	.04
049. cooperative	−.08	−.04	.08	−.04	−.10	−.07	−.00	−.02	.08	.01	−.03	−.04
050. courageous	.01	.11	.11	.08	.08	.14	.04	.01	.07	.06	.00	.03
051. cowardly	−.12	−.22	−.04	−.05	−.11	−.07	−.03	−.07	−.06	−.03	−.08	−.07
052. cruel	−.11	−.03	−.13	.06	.00	−.02	−.08	.03	−.16	.01	−.07	−.03
053. curious	.01	−.02	.02	.04	.01	.15	.01	−.01	.03	.13	.13	.15
054. cynical	.03	−.02	−.07	.12	.02	.10	.02	−.06	−.08	.08	−.06	.07
055. daring	.02	.14	−.04	−.03	.21	.15	−.05	.11	−.05	.00	.08	.15
056. deceitful	.09	.04	−.13	.07	.11	.03	.09	.04	−.15	−.02	.12	.03
057. defensive	−.10	−.13	.05	−.01	−.07	−.11	−.12	−.14	−.09	.07	−.13	−.14
058. deliberate	.08	.15	.00	−.02	−.21	−.05	−.08	.02	−.02	.00	−.26	−.10
059. demanding	.15	.24	.10	.10	.21	.21	−.03	.11	.04	.00	.08	.09
060. dependable	.06	.08	.02	−.07	−.10	.02	.04	.03	.02	−.07	−.07	−.01
061. dependent	−.08	−.19	−.04	−.13	−.26	−.24	.12	−.16	−.05	−.14	−.17	−.25
062. despondent	−.02	−.18	.02	.03	−.15	−.27	.02	−.16	.00	.07	−.13	−.23
063. determined	.20	.34	.10	.18	.18	.32	.08	.17	−.02	.13	.06	.20
064. dignified	.10	.10	.01	.04	−.02	−.02	.02	.07	−.04	.07	−.01	−.08
065. discreet	−.04	−.01	.02	.05	−.16	−.13	.11	.01	.09	.07	−.08	−.12
066. disorderly	−.04	−.09	.08	.05	−.02	−.07	−.01	.00	.02	.00	.00	−.06
067. dissatisfied	−.08	−.08	−.03	−.07	−.05	−.11	.00	−.04	−.10	.00	−.05	−.03
068. distractible	−.10	−.03	−.14	−.03	−.14	−.11	−.08	−.05	−.20	−.05	−.08	−.11
069. distrustful	−.10	−.06	−.08	−.07	−.02	−.03	−.03	−.04	−.17	−.09	−.05	−.10
070. dominant	.25	.45	.10	.04	.28	.39	.15	.17	.02	−.02	.09	.23
071. dreamy	−.11	−.13	−.06	−.03	−.22	−.22	.01	−.05	−.05	.04	−.11	−.15
072. dull	−.19	−.21	−.07	−.10	−.21	−.12	−.04	−.09	−.03	−.05	−.23	−.16
073. easygoing	−.12	−.04	−.23	−.11	−.15	−.02	−.08	.04	−.11	−.12	−.10	−.05
074. effeminate	.00	−.04	.04	.07	−.06	.08	.02	.01	.03	.07	.05	.00
075. efficient	.14	.22	.02	.01	.18	.22	.01	.12	−.03	.06	.12	.14
076. egotistical	.23	.25	.08	.15	.23	.22	.11	.15	.05	.11	.08	.14
077. emotional	−.01	.03	.04	−.01	.02	−.03	−.05	−.05	−.07	.00	.05	−.09
078. energetic	.21	.25	.19	.15	.31	.29	.02	.14	.09	.09	.19	.21
079. enterprising	.26	.23	.11	.18	.31	.36	.16	.11	.08	.21	.20	.27
080. enthusiastic	.10	.16	.21	.15	.17	.24	.02	.07	.14	.16	.11	.18
081. evasive	−.03	−.07	−.03	−.06	−.17	−.04	−.02	.06	−.06	−.10	−.17	−.04
082. excitable	.01	.24	−.04	.03	.12	.06	.00	.03	−.15	.01	.10	−.02
083. fair-minded	.02	−.03	−.02	−.02	−.12	−.01	.00	−.02	.04	.03	.00	.04
084. fault-finding	.04	.08	.02	−.07	.08	.11	−.10	−.04	.00	−.09	−.03	.05
085. fearful	−.06	−.13	−.14	−.09	−.27	−.26	−.09	−.10	−.16	−.05	−.16	−.30
086. feminine	−.17	−.05	−.05	−.11	−.13	−.08	−.06	−.02	−.06	−.01	−.01	−.05
087. fickle	−.12	.11	−.06	−.05	−.05	.06	−.03	.11	−.13	−.05	−.05	.02
088. flirtatious	.01	.20	−.12	.02	.06	.08	−.05	.13	−.27	.00	.03	.08

			Scale: Do						Scale: Cs			
		By Peers		By Spouses		By Staff		By Peers		By Spouses		By Staff
Adjectives		M	F	M	F	M	F	M	F	M	F	M	F
089.	foolish	.00	−.11	−.06	.01	.00	−.06	−.01	−.04	−.04	−.02	−.07	−.11
090.	forceful	.25	.30	.10	.12	.26	.33	.03	.14	−.04	.05	.03	.23
091.	foresighted	.11	.20	.08	−.07	.10	.23	.07	.07	.08	−.07	.05	.18
092.	forgetful	−.04	−.27	−.08	.01	−.15	−.08	−.10	−.12	−.08	.07	−.09	−.06
093.	forgiving	.12	−.06	−.08	−.10	−.14	−.09	.12	.00	.02	−.13	−.10	−.15
094.	formal	.17	.03	.01	.04	−.08	−.05	.13	.01	.12	.02	−.07	−.10
095.	frank	−.04	.14	.04	−.03	.03	.23	−.03	.02	.01	.11	−.04	.14
096.	friendly	−.04	.11	.10	−.02	.05	.08	.00	.14	.11	−.03	.04	.04
097.	frivolous	−.04	.09	−.03	−.01	.02	.02	.02	.04	−.03	.01	−.02	−.04
098.	fussy	−.09	.03	−.11	−.03	−.05	−.07	−.17	−.02	−.07	−.06	−.06	−.07
099.	generous	−.10	−.07	−.01	−.07	−.05	.01	.04	−.03	.00	−.06	−.08	−.02
100.	gentle	−.09	−.23	−.04	−.17	−.31	−.24	−.07	−.14	−.03	−.07	−.15	−.22
101.	gloomy	−.09	−.17	−.16	.03	−.19	−.05	−.06	−.18	−.23	−.02	−.15	−.13
102.	good-looking	.09	.17	−.02	−.06	−.02	.08	.05	.09	.00	−.01	−.04	.10
103.	good-natured	−.10	.02	.04	−.01	−.07	.01	.00	.06	.01	.03	−.04	.02
104.	greedy	.00	−.01	−.01	−.06	.02	−.01	−.12	−.07	−.07	−.08	−.02	−.01
105.	handsome	.09	−.06	.02	.07	.02	.06	−.04	−.04	.04	.05	−.02	.06
106.	hard-headed	.09	.15	.03	.04	.15	.13	−.02	.03	−.06	−.05	−.02	.08
107.	hard-hearted	−.07	.11	−.10	−.05	.05	.10	.01	−.03	−.10	−.03	−.06	.09
108.	hasty	−.03	−.05	−.10	.02	.09	.06	−.03	−.06	−.23	.03	.07	−.04
109.	headstrong	.06	.15	.07	.07	.17	.21	−.05	.00	−.10	.04	.04	.14
110.	healthy	−.09	.03	.01	.04	−.01	.17	−.04	.03	−.08	.04	−.12	.13
111.	helpful	.04	.08	−.02	.11	−.11	−.03	.05	.04	−.03	.01	−.06	−.09
112.	high-strung	−.04	.04	−.09	.08	.00	−.06	−.03	−.04	−.16	.02	.04	−.08
113.	honest	−.06	−.08	−.04	−.04	−.16	.01	−.01	−.08	.02	.03	−.06	−.02
114.	hostile	.00	.01	−.10	.10	.03	.05	−.05	−.09	−.13	.06	−.02	.01
115.	humorous	.00	.08	.01	.14	.13	.19	.02	.02	−.01	.25	.04	.14
116.	hurried	−.08	.10	.10	.04	.06	.04	−.01	−.02	.01	.10	.06	.02
117.	idealistic	.18	.11	.11	.18	−.05	.01	−.02	.09	.13	.10	.05	.07
118.	imaginative	.01	.13	.01	.18	.13	.07	.10	.09	.08	.22	.19	.21
119.	immature	−.05	−.18	−.06	−.07	−.14	−.18	−.03	−.14	−.14	−.08	−.02	−.12
120.	impatient	.07	−.02	.01	.08	.17	.15	−.05	−.08	.00	.03	.08	.07
121.	impulsive	.03	.04	−.01	.09	.16	.03	−.01	.05	−.09	.08	.09	.02
122.	independent	.06	.23	.06	.16	.17	.28	.15	.15	.02	.14	.10	.22
123.	indifferent	−.17	−.17	−.07	.05	−.19	−.10	−.05	−.02	−.06	.03	−.14	−.10
124.	individualistic	.04	.18	.09	.25	.08	.15	.01	.17	.04	.28	.02	.17
125.	industrious	.09	.16	.12	.04	.06	.25	.06	−.03	.03	.08	.02	.11
126.	infantile	−.10	−.02	−.04	−.16	−.06	−.12	−.06	−.03	−.10	−.20	−.08	−.19
127.	informal	−.14	−.05	.00	.02	−.04	.04	−.09	.00	−.07	.03	−.03	.06
128.	ingenious	.13	.18	.03	.13	.17	.09	.05	.11	.19	.16	.20	.17
129.	inhibited	−.06	−.19	−.11	−.15	−.38	−.32	.00	−.11	−.12	−.12	−.26	−.25
130.	initiative	.11	.36	.16	.18	.35	.35	.15	.08	.22	.16	.20	.25
131.	insightful	.03	.20	.08	.15	.09	.11	.10	.13	.13	.21	.16	.20
132.	intelligent	.13	.17	.15	.06	.12	.21	.12	.18	.15	.07	.17	.22

		Scale: Do						Scale: Cs				
		By Peers		By Spouses		By Staff		By Peers		By Spouses		By Staff	
Adjectives		M	F	M	F	M	F	M	F	M	F	M	F
133.	interests—narrow	−.24	−.18	−.04	−.21	−.25	−.20	−.14	−.15	−.16	−.31	−.28	−.33
134.	interests—wide	.13	.28	.09	.17	.18	.18	.08	.18	.15	.25	.21	.27
135.	intolerant	.01	.15	−.11	−.11	.03	.04	−.15	.10	−.09	−.09	−.03	−.05
136.	inventive	.00	.13	.07	.17	.13	.08	.05	.01	.08	.12	.16	.11
137.	irresponsible	−.07	−.17	.00	.03	−.01	−.05	−.07	−.01	−.03	.01	.02	.01
138.	irritable	.05	−.06	−.07	−.03	.02	.08	−.08	−.11	−.07	−.08	.01	−.01
139.	jolly	−.02	.19	−.10	−.04	.16	.10	−.02	.14	−.06	.06	.05	.00
140.	kind	−.03	−.05	−.06	.01	−.21	−.05	−.01	−.10	−.02	−.02	−.16	−.11
141.	lazy	−.02	−.15	.09	−.08	−.10	−.11	−.02	.00	.08	−.09	−.10	−.03
142.	leisurely	−.07	−.01	.06	.06	−.14	−.06	−.09	.05	−.03	.02	−.08	−.08
143.	logical	.14	.19	.04	−.13	−.02	.16	.14	.11	.01	−.05	.02	.12
144.	loud	.04	.14	.07	.09	.18	.18	−.02	.07	−.06	.03	.03	.07
145.	loyal	.04	.01	−.09	−.16	−.12	−.01	.03	−.11	−.07	−.12	−.17	−.17
146.	mannerly	.06	.04	.03	.12	−.20	−.06	.08	.02	.04	.05	−.09	−.08
147.	masculine	.06	.09	.02	.07	.07	.06	−.05	.06	−.05	.00	−.12	.04
148.	mature	.14	.18	.02	.02	.07	.22	.12	.11	.01	.02	.04	.07
149.	meek	−.18	−.32	−.06	−.16	−.32	−.30	−.09	−.29	−.14	−.03	−.26	−.27
150.	methodical	.00	−.03	−.01	.12	−.12	.02	−.05	−.02	.01	.09	−.13	−.05
151.	mild	−.15	−.25	−.14	−.21	−.35	−.30	−.14	−.14	−.02	−.16	−.17	−.24
152.	mischievous	−.06	.00	−.12	−.03	.15	.05	.00	.06	−.12	−.01	.06	.08
153.	moderate	.01	−.18	.04	−.02	−.26	−.12	.06	−.05	.08	.07	−.16	−.11
154.	modest	−.08	−.21	−.06	−.15	−.35	−.32	−.05	−.18	−.02	−.09	−.20	−.31
155.	moody	−.03	−.11	−.09	−.04	−.15	−.12	−.04	−.18	−.14	−.07	−.14	−.10
156.	nagging	−.05	.03	−.11	−.04	−.07	.08	−.16	.02	−.18	−.04	−.09	−.07
157.	natural	−.01	−.09	−.10	−.06	.08	.09	.03	−.02	.02	.06	.05	.09
158.	nervous	−.14	−.11	−.11	−.02	−.21	−.25	.00	−.18	−.23	−.04	−.07	−.23
159.	noisy	.03	.16	.04	−.02	.17	.10	.01	.11	−.08	−.08	.04	.05
160.	obliging	−.05	−.01	−.06	−.04	−.19	−.19	.04	−.01	−.01	−.01	−.05	−.14
161.	obnoxious	.04	.06	.05	.11	.13	.04	−.03	.08	.00	.07	.08	−.04
162.	opinionated	.19	.20	.03	.12	.18	.21	−.01	.09	.02	.08	.03	.11
163.	opportunistic	.23	.13	.04	.09	.26	.23	.19	.07	−.02	.05	.11	.19
164.	optimistic	.16	.16	.18	.13	.13	.23	.00	.10	.11	.15	.09	.13
165.	organized	.17	.17	−.01	−.02	.15	.23	.05	.03	−.01	−.03	.11	.15
166.	original	.05	.13	.02	.11	.12	.05	.00	.10	.01	.11	.17	.17
167.	outgoing	.21	.32	.17	.28	.32	.32	.15	.16	.12	.29	.17	.25
168.	outspoken	.15	.31	.09	.23	.28	.28	.00	.21	−.02	.18	.12	.17
169.	painstaking	−.06	.02	.00	−.04	−.22	−.17	−.10	−.01	.04	.01	−.18	−.16
170.	patient	−.06	−.10	−.03	−.20	−.31	−.13	−.05	−.05	.04	−.11	−.18	−.18
171.	peaceable	−.16	−.12	−.07	−.15	−.33	−.22	−.05	−.10	−.03	−.03	−.18	−.23
172.	peculiar	−.07	−.14	−.12	.03	−.21	−.08	−.04	−.03	−.24	−.03	−.15	−.10
173.	persevering	.13	.12	−.11	.05	.05	.08	.13	.06	.02	.08	−.01	−.01
174.	persistent	.10	.29	.03	.20	.11	.23	.05	.16	−.01	.15	−.07	.11
175.	pessimistic	−.13	−.17	−.04	−.02	−.15	−.13	−.07	−.14	−.02	−.06	−.05	−.16
176.	planful	.14	.17	−.04	.00	.08	.18	.04	.06	−.08	.03	.01	.15

Correlations of Observers' Adjectival Description with Scales of the CPI continued											
	Scale: Do						**Scale: Cs**				
	By Peers		By Spouses		By Staff		By Peers		By Spouses		By Staff	
Adjectives	M	F	M	F	M	F	M	F	M	F	M	F
177. pleasant	.05	.01	.00	−.01	−.07	−.03	.07	.00	−.05	.05	−.02	.01
178. pleasure-seeking	.04	.10	.06	.13	.16	.08	.02	.01	−.06	.11	.10	.06
179. poised	.15	.14	.11	.19	.19	.26	.06	.07	.13	.21	.14	.21
180. polished	.16	.19	.14	.22	.16	.18	.10	.09	.07	.25	.11	.18
181. practical	.09	.01	.06	−.05	.02	.19	.08	−.08	.00	.04	−.13	.00
182. praising	−.01	.08	.02	.03	−.01	.00	.16	−.08	−.05	.00	.02	−.03
183. precise	.13	.06	.10	.04	−.09	.06	.01	−.04	.04	.11	−.06	.06
184. prejudiced	.04	.05	−.10	−.07	.01	−.03	−.04	−.02	−.27	−.11	−.09	−.12
185. preoccupied	−.02	−.03	.05	.05	−.28	−.19	.09	−.12	−.01	.04	−.16	−.17
186. progressive	.09	.15	−.01	.05	.15	.16	.14	.03	.08	.16	.09	.19
187. prudish	.04	−.01	−.03	−.12	−.12	−.18	−.03	−.02	−.05	−.17	−.17	−.25
188. quarrelsome	.16	.01	−.14	−.08	.15	.09	−.05	.00	−.17	−.10	.08	.03
189. queer	−.14	−.08	−.02	.00	−.14	−.01	−.06	−.10	−.07	.00	−.09	−.05
190. quick	.01	.31	.01	.13	.23	.22	−.02	.11	.00	.13	.18	.16
191. quiet	−.19	−.32	−.19	−.21	−.45	−.39	−.12	−.17	−.13	−.26	−.25	−.29
192. quitting	−.18	−.21	−.14	−.09	−.19	−.13	−.09	−.12	−.12	−.07	−.11	−.19
193. rational	.13	.19	.14	−.01	−.09	.20	.19	.15	.13	.14	−.04	.10
194. rattle-brained	−.03	−.07	−.13	−.13	−.02	−.08	.00	−.04	−.17	−.15	.02	−.10
195. realistic	.08	.21	.05	−.04	.03	.24	.13	.10	−.01	.02	−.01	.11
196. reasonable	.10	.06	.11	.05	−.11	.02	.19	.02	.04	.11	−.06	.03
197. rebellious	−.01	.01	−.07	.10	.04	.04	−.05	.00	−.19	.01	−.01	.07
198. reckless	−.05	.01	−.13	.03	.08	−.02	.00	.00	−.14	−.06	.02	−.01
199. reflective	−.05	.01	−.04	.09	−.15	−.05	−.04	.05	.05	.21	.00	−.01
200. relaxed	−.04	.02	−.02	−.12	−.02	.20	.03	.14	−.06	−.11	.01	.13
201. reliable	.08	.08	.00	−.09	−.09	.01	.02	−.01	−.01	−.03	−.05	−.07
202. resentful	.11	−.08	−.11	−.03	−.02	.03	−.01	−.06	−.16	.03	−.07	−.05
203. reserved	−.11	−.31	−.11	−.17	−.42	−.30	−.08	−.18	−.11	−.17	−.22	−.22
204. resourceful	.23	.21	.13	.19	.27	.28	.17	.09	.09	.22	.21	.25
205. responsible	.14	.15	.01	.00	−.04	.06	.10	.01	.02	.09	−.04	−.03
206. restless	−.02	.04	.07	.09	.08	.04	−.06	−.03	−.09	.09	.02	.04
207. retiring	−.14	−.35	−.09	−.18	−.35	−.31	−.05	−.25	.01	−.11	−.25	−.27
208. rigid	−.06	.04	.01	−.16	−.11	−.09	.01	.00	.01	−.13	−.17	−.13
209. robust	.05	.19	.12	.04	.11	.19	−.10	.10	.04	.04	−.06	.13
210. rude	−.13	.04	−.02	.09	.11	.08	−.06	.05	−.10	.03	.03	.01
211. sarcastic	.01	.08	.03	.09	.10	.14	−.01	−.01	−.03	.04	.05	.12
212. self-centered	.10	.16	−.08	.06	.16	.10	.09	.08	−.14	.02	.06	.06
213. self-confident	.19	.36	.18	.29	.29	.43	.16	.15	.10	.16	.19	.33
214. self-controlled	.09	.07	.03	.06	−.19	−.09	.07	−.01	.07	.06	−.14	−.13
215. self-denying	−.04	−.04	−.06	−.09	−.26	−.21	−.07	−.05	−.05	−.14	−.25	−.21
216. self-pitying	−.09	−.06	−.05	−.13	−.11	−.06	−.03	−.09	−.13	−.04	−.06	−.10
217. self-punishing	.07	−.08	−.05	.00	−.14	−.07	−.03	−.08	−.07	.06	−.13	−.09
218. self-seeking	.11	.11	.05	.03	.24	.16	.05	−.02	.03	.07	.13	.10
219. selfish	.13	.09	.00	.01	.13	.05	.06	.10	.04	.02	.04	−.03
220. sensitive	−.04	−.17	−.12	.04	−.25	−.19	−.03	−.20	−.06	.01	−.05	−.12

Correlations of Observers' Adjectival Description with Scales of the CPI *continued*											
	Scale: Do						**Scale: Cs**				
	By Peers		By Spouses		By Staff		By Peers		By Spouses		By Staff	
Adjectives	M	F	M	F	M	F	M	F	M	F	M	F
221. sentimental	−.01	.06	−.08	−.09	−.07	−.13	−.03	−.03	−.11	−.06	−.10	−.14
222. serious	.11	−.02	.03	−.04	−.22	−.02	−.03	−.15	.03	−.02	−.17	.02
223. severe	.05	.07	.00	−.04	−.02	−.03	−.02	.05	−.01	.01	−.17	−.07
224. sexy	.09	.11	−.01	.05	.09	.11	.02	.12	−.13	.06	.01	.11
225. shallow	−.18	.03	−.05	−.10	−.08	−.14	−.09	.06	−.05	−.15	−.10	−.19
226. sharp-witted	.11	.07	.17	.18	.23	.16	.11	−.05	.09	.22	.13	.14
227. shiftless	−.11	−.03	−.10	−.02	−.16	−.04	−.04	−.05	−.10	−.09	−.12	−.08
228. show-off	.04	.13	.09	.04	.23	.17	.06	.14	−.03	−.04	.08	.13
229. shrewd	.13	.05	−.02	.15	.31	.22	.16	.03	−.07	.09	.15	.15
230. shy	−.24	−.34	−.24	−.28	−.44	−.39	−.22	−.27	−.26	−.24	−.33	−.36
231. silent	−.23	−.21	−.28	−.14	−.40	−.29	−.20	−.13	−.20	−.14	−.29	−.26
232. simple	−.13	−.16	−.15	−.25	−.25	−.23	−.10	−.18	−.16	−.23	−.29	−.30
233. sincere	.04	−.05	−.06	−.11	−.21	−.05	−.03	−.01	.00	.02	−.09	−.07
234. slipshod	.03	−.04	−.04	.01	.00	.01	.06	−.01	−.07	−.02	.01	−.05
235. slow	−.17	−.22	−.22	−.07	−.27	−.24	−.06	−.09	−.15	−.12	−.22	−.26
236. sly	−.04	−.01	−.15	.11	.04	.03	.06	.00	−.21	.03	.01	.00
237. smug	.08	.12	.00	.00	.14	.11	.06	.13	.00	−.03	.07	.09
238. snobbish	.12	.18	.01	.07	.11	.07	.11	.07	−.01	.05	.10	.06
239. sociable	.16	.20	.06	.18	.22	.22	.13	.16	.10	.20	.15	.15
240. soft-hearted	−.09	−.04	−.11	−.14	−.15	−.14	−.04	−.03	−.13	−.13	−.08	−.16
241. sophisticated	.13	.09	.13	.18	.19	.22	.12	.08	.13	.23	.15	.23
242. spendthrift	.04	−.11	.00	−.02	.01	.05	.01	.01	.08	−.14	.01	.02
243. spineless	−.11	−.24	.08	−.10	−.19	−.13	−.03	−.24	.12	−.08	−.16	−.11
244. spontaneous	.03	.22	.08	.15	.20	.16	.00	.11	.03	.21	.16	.13
245. spunky	−.12	.14	−.02	.14	.17	.14	−.15	.02	−.15	.11	.09	.07
246. stable	.10	.14	−.06	−.02	−.05	.16	.15	.10	−.05	.06	−.08	.05
247. steady	.06	.06	−.06	−.04	−.10	.05	.08	.02	−.05	−.02	−.19	−.03
248. stern	.16	.10	−.07	−.09	−.03	.10	.01	.03	−.16	−.09	−.18	−.01
249. stingy	.01	.05	−.03	.02	−.12	.04	−.05	−.03	−.14	−.08	−.14	−.02
250. stolid	.09	−.03	.00	−.03	−.17	−.08	−.01	.00	.03	−.01	−.28	−.17
251. strong	.10	.24	.05	.11	.08	.35	.00	.06	.00	.00	−.10	.20
252. stubborn	.11	.22	−.05	.05	.11	.13	−.04	.00	−.07	.04	−.04	.06
253. submissive	−.22	−.31	−.10	−.17	−.27	−.33	−.03	−.19	−.03	−.08	−.17	−.26
254. suggestible	−.08	−.02	−.09	.01	−.13	−.23	.06	−.08	−.04	.01	−.04	−.18
255. sulky	−.07	−.11	−.02	−.06	−.12	−.01	−.07	−.11	−.01	−.05	−.17	−.12
256. superstitious	−.03	−.14	−.15	−.01	−.04	−.03	.02	.01	−.24	−.09	−.06	−.21
257. suspicious	−.04	−.12	−.11	.00	−.11	.01	−.01	−.17	−.21	−.07	−.14	−.09
258. sympathetic	.01	−.06	−.04	−.07	−.09	−.10	.05	−.08	.00	−.05	−.04	−.09
259. tactful	.09	.05	.14	.11	−.02	.01	.08	.05	.09	.16	.05	.01
260. tactless	−.04	−.03	−.07	−.02	.07	.08	−.02	.01	−.15	.02	.00	.04
261. talkative	.11	.28	.22	.13	.31	.30	.13	.12	.08	.19	.18	.20
262. temperamental	.08	−.03	−.02	.12	.01	.10	−.04	−.10	−.05	.00	−.03	.05
263. tense	−.05	−.20	−.04	.02	−.14	−.20	−.03	−.17	−.09	−.01	−.10	−.17
264. thankless	−.01	−.13	−.03	.00	.02	.02	.04	−.14	−.05	−.03	−.04	.02

Correlations of Observers' Adjectival Description with Scales of the CPI continued											
	Scale: Do						**Scale: Cs**				
	By Peers		By Spouses		By Staff		By Peers		By Spouses		By Staff	
Adjectives	M	F	M	F	M	F	M	F	M	F	M	F
265. thorough	.12	.17	−.02	.00	−.03	.14	.09	.02	.04	.03	.01	.06
266. thoughtful	.06	.03	−.07	−.09	−.11	.04	.04	.02	−.02	−.05	−.01	.00
267. thrifty	.06	.06	−.02	−.08	−.18	−.02	.01	−.02	−.06	−.06	−.22	−.09
268. timid	−.21	−.32	−.13	−.15	−.34	−.33	−.10	−.26	−.08	−.10	−.25	−.29
269. tolerant	.02	.02	.05	−.09	−.14	−.01	.14	.02	.08	.07	.03	.03
270. touchy	.03	.06	−.16	.00	−.06	−.04	−.15	.01	−.15	−.09	−.04	−.10
271. tough	.06	.14	−.07	.04	.13	.30	.00	.07	−.13	.02	−.10	.16
272. trusting	.02	−.09	.09	−.02	−.21	−.10	.12	−.04	.09	.01	−.05	−.07
273. unaffected	−.14	−.08	−.02	.10	−.19	−.21	−.05	−.05	.01	.00	−.05	−.10
274. unambitious	−.14	−.21	−.19	−.08	−.29	−.27	−.09	−.13	−.11	−.07	−.24	−.27
275. unassuming	−.25	−.20	−.02	−.02	−.36	−.32	.01	−.15	−.02	−.04	−.14	−.28
276. unconventional	.01	−.04	−.06	.07	−.04	.02	.05	.06	.02	.07	−.02	.07
277. undependable	−.02	−.03	.02	.00	.02	−.04	.02	.04	.04	−.02	.03	.02
278. understanding	.02	.05	−.02	.06	−.11	.04	.11	.03	.08	.02	−.05	.00
279. unemotional	−.04	−.18	−.04	−.04	−.23	−.09	−.15	−.04	.04	−.06	−.25	−.02
280. unexcitable	−.17	−.19	−.16	−.05	−.19	−.11	−.11	.00	−.13	.00	−.19	−.11
281. unfriendly	−.03	.00	−.08	.07	−.08	−.01	.00	−.06	−.18	.00	−.09	−.07
282. uninhibited	.05	.03	−.06	.14	.23	.13	.04	.02	−.03	.16	.14	.14
283. unintelligent	−.03	−.05	.00	−.04	−.10	−.14	−.02	.01	.00	.00	−.11	−.13
284. unkind	−.14	−.02	−.05	.03	.00	.09	−.07	−.03	−.05	−.02	−.03	.02
285. unrealistic	−.04	−.01	.04	.01	−.11	−.08	.01	−.05	.03	−.02	−.09	−.11
286. unscrupulous	−.01	−.10	−.20	.10	−.02	.01	.01	.01	−.24	.07	.00	.01
287. unselfish	.03	−.08	−.11	−.06	−.06	−.14	.07	−.04	−.10	−.10	−.01	−.18
288. unstable	−.04	−.17	−.18	.03	−.10	−.18	.03	−.10	−.24	−.03	.00	−.08
289. vindictive	.06	.12	.01	−.01	.04	.08	.03	.11	.01	−.02	−.02	−.02
290. versatile	.09	.26	.03	.07	.22	.25	.10	.19	.03	.13	.22	.22
291. warm	−.02	−.04	−.01	−.11	.08	.05	−.02	.06	−.03	−.01	.08	.01
292. wary	.12	−.06	−.02	.02	−.13	−.09	.13	−.07	−.06	−.01	−.16	−.18
293. weak	−.14	−.31	−.12	−.11	−.19	−.21	−.02	−.24	−.15	−.11	−.10	−.22
294. whiny	−.12	−.06	−.06	−.01	.03	−.04	−.04	−.07	−.02	−.02	.02	−.08
295. wholesome	−.07	.04	.02	.02	−.04	.13	−.08	.04	−.02	.05	−.09	.06
296. wise	.18	.18	.05	.02	.00	.15	.12	.11	.03	.09	.03	.08
297. withdrawn	−.18	−.35	−.21	−.15	−.38	−.27	−.14	−.24	−.18	−.10	−.31	−.22
298. witty	.04	.17	.00	.08	.16	.19	.09	.04	.03	.11	.11	.16
299. worrying	−.11	−.10	−.22	−.02	−.23	−.16	−.09	−.11	−.23	−.01	−.15	−.19
300. zany	−.04	.09	−.04	.12	.05	.00	−.05	.11	−.04	.10	.02	.06

Correlations of Observers' Adjectival Description with Scales of the CPI continued

		Scale: Sy						Scale: Sp				
		By Peers		By Spouses		By Staff		By Peers		By Spouses		By Staff	
Adjectives		M	F	M	F	M	F	M	F	M	F	M	F
001.	absent-minded	−.09	−.16	−.06	.03	−.17	−.03	−.15	−.16	−.10	.06	−.12	.02
002.	active	.22	.28	.03	.15	.21	.28	.12	.26	.07	.12	.27	.23
003.	adaptable	.05	.15	.02	.06	.15	.20	.07	.23	.04	.09	.22	.19
004.	adventurous	.08	.21	.12	.15	.14	.25	.14	.31	.17	.20	.24	.25
005.	affected	.05	.18	.04	−.04	.06	.09	.02	.15	.01	.03	.08	.07
006.	affectionate	−.01	.03	.02	.00	−.02	.07	.01	.07	.00	.08	−.01	.05
007.	aggressive	.18	.27	.09	.16	.17	.20	.10	.24	.09	.16	.18	.21
008.	alert	.12	.20	−.02	.06	.16	.17	.16	.23	.11	.06	.24	.11
009.	aloof	−.04	−.10	−.10	−.16	−.23	−.18	.03	−.13	−.05	−.08	−.12	−.12
010.	ambitious	.25	.21	.12	.22	.24	.23	.16	.14	.09	.15	.23	.19
011.	anxious	−.11	−.04	−.10	−.02	−.18	−.26	−.10	−.17	−.10	−.05	−.17	−.24
012.	apathetic	−.22	−.20	−.08	−.05	−.21	−.19	−.15	−.13	−.12	−.04	−.18	−.14
013.	appreciative	−.05	.04	−.05	−.03	−.05	−.03	−.07	.03	.00	−.01	−.01	−.05
014.	argumentative	.04	.06	.04	.16	.19	.09	.03	.07	.02	.19	.23	.10
015.	arrogant	.04	.06	−.04	.09	.09	.10	.05	.00	.04	.08	.15	.10
016.	artistic	−.17	−.07	−.07	.09	−.08	−.01	−.08	.05	−.06	.05	.06	.01
017.	assertive	.05	.21	.09	.25	.22	.27	−.01	.15	.11	.32	.24	.23
018.	attractive	−.03	.13	−.05	.03	.02	.12	−.04	.13	−.03	−.02	.10	.10
019.	autocratic	−.11	.01	.02	.00	.04	.11	−.14	−.03	.06	.07	.07	.13
020.	awkward	−.25	−.19	−.13	−.05	−.27	−.23	−.24	−.17	−.11	.00	−.27	−.18
021.	bitter	−.08	−.12	−.16	−.04	−.12	−.09	−.05	−.13	−.11	−.02	−.07	−.06
022.	blustery	.07	.01	.02	.01	.07	.04	.04	−.05	.12	.00	.10	.02
023.	boastful	.13	.20	.11	.09	.09	.14	.09	.14	.09	.08	.10	.15
024.	bossy	−.01	.12	−.09	.05	.10	.11	−.06	.05	−.05	.03	.09	.08
025.	calm	−.07	−.06	−.08	−.21	−.09	−.01	−.03	−.03	−.07	−.13	−.01	−.01
026.	capable	.12	.12	−.08	.08	.06	.16	.12	.08	.01	.12	.17	.13
027.	careless	−.01	.00	−.10	−.09	−.01	.01	−.03	.09	−.09	−.09	.06	.07
028.	cautious	−.17	−.26	−.21	−.19	−.23	−.25	−.18	−.36	−.15	−.17	−.23	−.24
029.	changeable	.05	.02	−.08	.04	.03	.03	.01	.04	−.05	.11	.10	.07
030.	charming	.11	.14	−.01	.00	.05	.14	.08	.13	.01	.00	.15	.14
031.	cheerful	.08	.15	.08	.04	.12	.20	.09	.20	.03	.02	.15	.13
032.	civilized	.02	.03	.02	−.05	−.04	.03	.04	.13	−.03	−.04	.04	.00
033.	clear-thinking	.13	.12	−.04	−.03	.03	.14	.13	.13	.00	.02	.14	.16
034.	clever	.14	.11	.00	.17	.12	.17	.21	.18	.09	.19	.24	.14
035.	coarse	−.04	−.05	−.11	−.01	.04	.04	−.04	.01	−.13	.07	.08	.07
036.	cold	−.19	−.17	−.07	−.04	−.11	−.10	−.29	−.22	−.03	−.07	−.10	−.05
037.	commonplace	−.15	−.15	.00	−.14	−.10	−.09	−.17	−.14	−.03	−.10	−.12	−.14
038.	complaining	−.08	−.13	−.09	.01	−.05	−.01	−.03	−.17	−.12	−.01	.01	−.02
039.	complicated	−.09	−.08	.04	.02	−.14	−.14	−.06	−.06	.00	.10	−.04	−.06
040.	conceited	.10	.17	.00	.10	.16	.11	.04	.06	.01	.10	.15	.11
041.	confident	.19	.34	.07	.19	.20	.32	.20	.32	.01	.20	.27	.28
042.	confused	−.17	−.07	−.09	−.03	−.13	−.18	−.18	−.09	−.12	−.01	−.17	−.20
043.	conscientious	−.04	.06	−.04	.04	−.09	−.06	−.08	−.03	−.05	.07	−.11	−.14
044.	conservative	−.01	−.14	−.06	−.22	−.05	−.09	−.04	−.18	−.14	−.28	−.16	−.23

Correlations of Observers' Adjectival Description with Scales of the CPI continued

	Scale: Sy						Scale: Sp					
	By Peers		By Spouses		By Staff		By Peers		By Spouses		By Staff	
Adjectives	M	F	M	F	M	F	M	F	M	F	M	F
045. considerate	.00	−.02	.01	−.09	−.13	−.01	−.01	−.04	−.05	−.03	−.08	−.03
046. contented	−.06	.06	−.01	−.11	.01	.04	−.03	.14	.04	−.04	.02	.03
047. conventional	−.04	−.09	.01	−.16	−.05	−.03	−.02	−.19	−.11	−.16	−.16	−.17
048. cool	.01	−.08	−.04	−.06	−.01	−.09	.05	−.05	.00	.05	.04	.01
049. cooperative	−.09	.04	.03	−.07	−.03	.05	−.08	.04	−.01	−.05	.00	−.02
050. courageous	−.02	.08	.09	.04	.04	.04	−.04	.06	.09	.04	.08	.05
051. cowardly	−.05	−.17	−.10	−.01	−.10	−.02	−.10	−.10	−.09	−.01	−.11	−.06
052. cruel	−.14	−.11	−.10	.02	−.07	.03	−.13	−.17	−.06	.02	.01	−.01
053. curious	.04	−.01	−.03	−.01	−.02	.12	.09	.14	.01	.06	.12	.18
054. cynical	−.03	−.11	−.13	.00	−.05	.02	.01	−.10	−.09	.07	.09	.08
055. daring	.02	.19	.05	−.02	.14	.18	−.02	.27	.08	.02	.19	.20
056. deceitful	.08	.01	−.15	.05	.13	.01	.04	−.04	−.03	.04	.11	−.02
057. defensive	−.12	−.21	.01	.01	−.10	−.18	−.13	−.27	.02	.03	−.09	−.15
058. deliberate	−.07	.02	−.03	.02	−.23	−.14	−.09	.00	−.07	.05	−.19	−.14
059. demanding	.07	.12	.07	.08	.11	.08	.02	.03	.06	.04	.15	.09
060. dependable	.03	.07	−.06	−.19	−.08	.00	.02	.05	.06	−.12	−.04	−.08
061. dependent	−.05	−.11	−.01	−.16	−.16	−.12	−.04	−.15	−.05	−.15	−.22	−.15
062. despondent	−.02	−.20	.01	.08	−.14	−.30	.04	−.21	.04	.07	−.14	−.29
063. determined	.09	.27	.04	.13	.10	.17	.02	.14	−.04	.16	.16	.15
064. dignified	−.01	.03	−.08	.04	−.09	−.19	.03	−.02	−.07	.04	−.09	−.20
065. discreet	−.03	.00	−.02	.01	−.14	−.17	−.01	−.08	.04	.10	−.11	−.19
066. disorderly	−.05	−.07	.07	.02	−.02	.00	−.02	.00	.10	.05	.07	.05
067. dissatisfied	−.09	−.14	−.03	−.03	−.08	−.16	−.03	−.14	−.07	−.10	.00	−.08
068. distractible	−.13	−.07	−.08	.01	−.07	−.03	−.16	−.07	−.01	.04	−.01	−.04
069. distrustful	−.08	−.14	−.08	−.11	−.03	−.10	−.09	−.17	−.07	−.11	.00	−.03
070. dominant	.15	.28	.01	.01	.14	.24	.07	.17	.01	−.01	.22	.22
071. dreamy	−.08	−.09	.03	.05	−.19	−.15	−.01	−.04	.02	.08	−.18	−.14
072. dull	−.15	−.24	.01	−.10	−.18	−.08	−.15	−.25	−.08	−.13	−.20	−.11
073. easygoing	.05	.02	−.08	−.15	−.01	.11	.11	.21	−.01	−.03	.04	.10
074. effeminate	.00	.01	.06	.02	−.05	.07	−.05	.00	.01	.11	−.07	.01
075. efficient	.04	.13	−.12	.00	.11	.13	.00	.11	−.11	.02	.15	.09
076. egotistical	.16	.16	.07	.12	.11	.11	.13	.08	.07	.10	.18	.14
077. emotional	−.05	.00	.02	.04	.02	.02	−.06	−.01	.00	.02	.07	.04
078. energetic	.12	.34	.11	.12	.23	.29	.10	.31	.11	.06	.29	.23
079. enterprising	.16	.21	.08	.20	.21	.30	.11	.20	.06	.19	.25	.24
080. enthusiastic	.09	.24	.22	.17	.13	.31	.06	.21	.24	.15	.18	.24
081. evasive	−.10	−.13	.01	−.05	−.15	−.06	−.04	−.11	.01	−.08	−.12	.00
082. excitable	−.03	.23	−.02	.07	.11	.12	.02	.21	−.04	.07	.16	.09
083. fair-minded	.03	.05	−.03	−.03	−.06	.02	.01	.06	.09	−.01	.03	.00
084. fault-finding	−.04	−.07	.01	−.08	−.02	.01	.02	−.14	−.04	−.03	.03	.02
085. fearful	−.04	−.13	−.06	−.02	−.19	−.27	−.03	−.22	−.09	−.02	−.20	−.24
086. feminine	−.09	.03	−.11	−.04	−.09	.02	−.14	−.01	−.06	−.01	−.06	−.01
087. fickle	−.08	.12	−.04	.01	−.05	.03	.00	.15	−.10	.07	.04	.06
088. flirtatious	.03	.26	.00	−.01	.02	.16	.05	.31	−.02	.05	.13	.17

Correlations of Observers' Adjectival Description with Scales of the CPI continued

	Scale: Sy						Scale: Sp					
	By Peers		By Spouses		By Staff		By Peers		By Spouses		By Staff	
Adjectives	M	F	M	F	M	F	M	F	M	F	M	F
089. foolish	−.04	.00	−.01	.00	.00	−.01	.04	.03	−.02	.02	.01	−.04
090. forceful	.12	.16	−.06	.12	.08	.18	.03	.09	−.06	.09	.13	.15
091. foresighted	.01	.07	−.01	−.05	.01	.13	.03	.06	.00	−.05	.09	.10
092. forgetful	−.03	−.10	−.01	.00	−.13	−.04	−.07	−.10	−.06	.07	−.04	−.04
093. forgiving	.10	.02	.04	−.06	−.08	−.02	.12	.04	.07	−.06	−.05	−.05
094. formal	.02	−.02	−.04	.01	−.11	−.14	−.11	−.21	.09	−.02	−.10	−.16
095. frank	−.07	.00	−.01	.00	.05	.16	.01	.10	.09	.09	.14	.17
096. friendly	.08	.22	.11	−.01	.09	.17	.10	.27	.13	.05	.10	.11
097. frivolous	−.12	.20	.01	−.03	.00	.07	−.14	.17	.01	−.03	.06	.10
098. fussy	−.16	−.04	−.11	−.01	−.04	−.09	−.13	−.16	−.17	−.03	−.10	−.10
099. generous	.04	.04	.05	−.08	−.05	.09	.05	.08	.14	−.07	−.01	.04
100. gentle	−.09	−.13	−.04	−.14	−.21	−.13	−.10	−.15	−.06	−.09	−.15	−.14
101. gloomy	−.06	−.19	−.19	−.08	−.19	−.17	−.04	−.27	−.15	−.08	−.13	−.10
102. good-looking	.11	.20	−.07	−.06	−.02	.12	.05	.16	−.03	.00	.08	.09
103. good-natured	.02	.13	.04	.01	.02	.16	.09	.15	.09	.02	.08	.13
104. greedy	−.09	−.10	.02	−.07	−.01	.00	−.13	−.13	.06	−.08	.05	.06
105. handsome	−.01	−.10	.00	.03	.02	.01	−.03	−.02	.04	.02	.06	−.01
106. hard-headed	.00	.04	−.01	.09	.04	−.04	−.01	.01	−.06	.11	.09	−.01
107. hard-hearted	−.10	−.08	−.04	−.04	.01	.06	−.15	−.12	−.07	−.03	.03	.05
108. hasty	−.06	.06	−.14	.06	.08	.11	−.05	.04	−.08	.04	.15	.09
109. headstrong	.00	.02	.04	.10	.07	.11	−.05	.00	.04	.11	.14	.14
110. healthy	.02	.06	−.12	.01	.01	.27	.11	.06	−.17	.07	.09	.25
111. helpful	.05	.08	−.04	.03	−.01	.06	.07	.13	−.10	.08	.01	−.01
112. high-strung	−.11	.02	−.09	.11	−.03	−.09	−.10	−.03	−.14	.05	.02	−.08
113. honest	−.07	−.09	−.12	−.05	−.05	−.02	−.02	−.09	−.03	−.01	−.01	−.06
114. hostile	.01	−.11	−.13	.05	.00	−.06	.00	−.14	−.12	.01	.02	−.01
115. humorous	.12	.11	−.03	.14	.12	.21	.21	.25	.08	.24	.19	.19
116. hurried	−.05	.14	.05	.10	.02	.05	−.03	.09	.03	.10	.09	.01
117. idealistic	−.03	.12	.09	.08	−.06	−.01	−.05	.00	.08	.07	−.04	.01
118. imaginative	.04	.13	−.06	.18	.03	.11	.07	.18	.11	.19	.16	.17
119. immature	−.10	−.08	−.01	−.02	−.02	−.10	−.02	.00	−.04	−.02	−.06	−.13
120. impatient	.00	−.06	.04	.10	.10	.05	−.01	−.07	−.01	.11	.19	.09
121. impulsive	.03	.09	.00	.08	.10	.07	.03	.15	−.02	.13	.17	.10
122. independent	.08	.11	.01	.11	.08	.16	.20	.12	.04	.16	.23	.21
123. indifferent	−.17	−.19	−.03	−.01	−.12	−.14	−.13	−.10	−.10	−.02	−.04	−.02
124. individualistic	.01	.09	.00	.26	.01	.05	.08	.16	.03	.32	.16	.12
125. industrious	.09	.05	.06	.00	.01	.11	.05	−.01	−.02	.06	.02	.04
126. infantile	−.09	.06	−.04	−.15	−.05	−.13	−.06	.06	−.08	−.15	−.04	−.18
127. informal	−.02	.03	−.05	−.00	.03	.15	.03	.15	.06	.09	.13	.18
128. ingenious	.08	.16	.03	.12	.12	.13	.11	.18	.04	.15	.21	.11
129. inhibited	−.11	−.28	−.18	−.20	−.27	−.27	−.14	−.29	−.22	−.15	−.28	−.27
130. initiative	.14	.21	.08	.13	.22	.27	.13	.23	.11	.15	.24	.24
131. insightful	−.02	.16	.04	.08	.02	.09	.09	.12	.09	.12	.12	.12
132. intelligent	.06	.22	−.02	.04	.05	.08	.10	.19	.02	.09	.19	.10

Correlations of Observers' Adjectival Description with Scales of the CPI continued

		Scale: Sy						Scale: Sp				
		By Peers		By Spouses		By Staff		By Peers		By Spouses		By Staff	
Adjectives		M	F	M	F	M	F	M	F	M	F	M	F
133.	interests—narrow	−.24	−.14	−.10	−.25	−.15	−.22	−.24	−.16	−.15	−.29	−.17	−.28
134.	interests—wide	.15	.21	.07	.16	.08	.17	.19	.22	.12	.22	.16	.21
135.	intolerant	−.18	−.04	−.06	−.09	.02	−.08	−.17	.00	−.13	−.10	.01	−.11
136.	inventive	.08	.09	.08	.10	.03	.10	.06	.19	.09	.14	.15	.16
137.	irresponsible	−.06	−.08	.01	.05	.02	−.03	−.08	.00	−.03	.01	.06	.02
138.	irritable	−.05	−.16	−.09	−.04	−.01	−.03	−.07	−.17	−.07	−.04	.06	−.01
139.	jolly	.12	.21	−.04	.03	.14	.14	.13	.30	.02	.07	.12	.12
140.	kind	.01	.02	−.02	−.06	−.13	.05	−.01	.01	−.02	−.03	−.07	−.02
141.	lazy	−.01	−.12	.16	−.07	−.01	−.04	.06	.03	.17	−.01	.04	.04
142.	leisurely	−.02	.02	.09	−.01	.00	−.01	.04	.19	.14	.07	.05	.02
143.	logical	.12	.08	−.10	−.18	−.02	−.03	.15	.07	−.04	−.10	.06	−.04
144.	loud	.02	.19	.07	.09	.11	.14	.01	.18	.07	.09	.17	.12
145.	loyal	.11	−.03	−.07	−.15	−.06	−.04	.03	−.04	−.10	−.08	−.12	−.07
146.	mannerly	.04	.03	.06	.02	−.12	−.05	.00	−.01	.00	.01	−.13	−.09
147.	masculine	.11	−.01	.08	.00	.01	−.02	.09	.05	.06	.00	.08	.02
148.	mature	.16	.07	−.05	.00	.04	.10	.14	.00	−.06	.06	.09	.07
149.	meek	−.20	−.31	−.02	−.10	−.24	−.22	−.19	−.26	−.05	−.13	−.27	−.19
150.	methodical	−.09	−.14	−.10	.05	−.13	−.12	−.09	−.16	−.11	.04	−.14	−.17
151.	mild	−.15	−.26	−.02	−.19	−.20	−.24	−.13	−.23	−.06	−.19	−.22	−.24
152.	mischievous	.00	.11	−.06	.04	.11	.15	.08	.18	−.02	.07	.19	.15
153.	moderate	.00	−.20	.05	−.01	−.12	−.08	−.01	−.13	−.04	−.08	−.16	−.10
154.	modest	−.13	−.22	−.10	−.17	−.21	−.27	−.09	−.20	−.09	−.16	−.21	−.27
155.	moody	−.04	−.21	−.13	.01	−.16	−.19	−.08	−.20	−.17	.06	−.08	−.10
156.	nagging	−.15	−.02	−.03	−.03	−.04	.01	−.15	−.06	−.09	.02	−.01	−.04
157.	natural	.03	−.03	.01	−.01	.16	.14	.11	.08	.04	.06	.17	.12
158.	nervous	−.16	−.13	−.12	.03	−.15	−.22	−.16	−.21	−.25	−.02	−.15	−.17
159.	noisy	.02	.20	.03	.02	.13	.15	.05	.22	.04	.05	.14	.11
160.	obliging	.00	.05	−.06	.00	−.10	−.07	−.05	−.01	−.02	.06	−.11	−.11
161.	obnoxious	−.03	.04	.01	.07	.10	.02	−.06	.03	.03	.10	.14	−.02
162.	opinionated	.01	.07	.05	.08	.09	.11	.01	.03	.07	.13	.12	.07
163.	opportunistic	.26	.14	−.02	.03	.19	.18	.15	.07	−.02	.11	.20	.19
164.	optimistic	.13	.22	.16	.13	.15	.28	.17	.17	.16	.13	.18	.22
165.	organized	.07	.03	−.12	−.09	.11	.10	.03	.02	−.14	−.10	.12	.05
166.	original	.09	.11	.00	.08	.02	.03	.18	.20	.03	.15	.17	.10
167.	outgoing	.29	.36	.27	.30	.27	.34	.22	.35	.24	.32	.26	.26
168.	outspoken	.09	.21	.06	.16	.14	.18	.09	.21	.06	.17	.22	.13
169.	painstaking	−.14	−.05	−.01	−.01	−.25	−.22	−.22	−.12	.02	−.06	−.24	−.24
170.	patient	−.08	−.08	−.03	−.19	−.24	−.13	−.14	−.07	−.02	−.15	−.18	−.13
171.	peaceable	−.07	−.07	−.05	−.14	−.20	−.17	−.06	−.10	−.01	−.08	−.21	−.19
172.	peculiar	−.14	−.12	−.12	.01	−.17	−.16	−.19	−.09	−.18	.01	−.17	−.12
173.	persevering	−.03	.05	−.08	.03	−.03	−.02	−.01	.01	−.10	−.01	−.01	−.12
174.	persistent	−.01	.19	.07	.20	−.02	.13	.03	.13	−.07	.11	.01	.11
175.	pessimistic	−.11	−.25	−.02	−.02	−.11	−.20	−.11	−.20	−.02	.01	−.07	−.15
176.	planful	.03	.10	−.09	.01	.01	.13	−.03	−.04	−.09	−.03	.07	.08

Correlations of Observers' Adjectival Description with Scales of the CPI continued

	Scale: Sy						Scale: Sp					
	By Peers		By Spouses		By Staff		By Peers		By Spouses		By Staff	
Adjectives	M	F	M	F	M	F	M	F	M	F	M	F
177. pleasant	.12	.10	.04	−.01	−.02	.07	.13	.14	.04	.01	.06	.02
178. pleasure-seeking	.13	.12	.12	.13	.19	.17	.20	.20	.17	.19	.26	.22
179. poised	.14	.15	.07	.09	.10	.15	.10	.06	.12	.10	.14	.08
180. polished	.17	.14	.10	.13	.05	.11	.16	.03	.10	.12	.07	.06
181. practical	.06	−.10	.01	−.08	.01	.15	.03	−.11	−.04	.01	.03	.09
182. praising	.10	−.01	.06	−.02	−.02	.06	.07	−.07	.00	−.06	.03	.02
183. precise	−.07	−.02	−.01	−.01	−.11	−.07	−.14	−.10	−.02	.01	−.08	−.06
184. prejudiced	−.05	−.04	−.06	−.11	−.01	−.08	−.11	−.11	−.12	−.16	−.05	−.12
185. preoccupied	−.06	−.05	.02	.01	−.24	−.24	−.08	−.06	−.01	.02	−.21	−.21
186. progressive	.14	.07	.01	.04	.03	.14	.12	.10	.08	.09	.15	.17
187. prudish	−.08	−.10	−.03	−.14	−.15	−.17	−.15	−.17	.00	−.21	−.19	−.29
188. quarrelsome	.07	−.07	−.09	−.01	.10	.02	.09	−.06	−.08	.00	.12	.04
189. queer	−.11	−.10	.03	.00	−.10	−.10	−.13	−.17	.04	.00	−.13	−.05
190. quick	.06	.22	−.13	.13	.20	.19	.10	.17	−.03	.14	.29	.17
191. quiet	−.22	−.33	−.19	−.27	−.29	−.33	−.18	−.30	−.18	−.25	−.25	−.29
192. quitting	−.24	−.24	−.04	−.07	−.15	−.18	−.20	−.19	−.04	−.05	−.06	−.09
193. rational	.16	.12	.04	−.07	−.04	.06	.16	.14	.08	.00	.06	.04
194. rattle-brained	−.07	.08	.02	−.07	−.01	.00	−.08	.06	−.04	−.07	−.01	.02
195. realistic	.06	.08	−.01	−.08	.05	.15	.11	.06	−.01	.00	.15	.14
196. reasonable	.11	.04	.05	−.05	−.05	.03	.07	.03	−.01	.03	.04	.00
197. rebellious	−.06	.02	−.15	.03	−.04	.00	.01	.06	−.06	.09	.08	.09
198. reckless	−.06	.02	−.12	−.01	.08	−.02	−.07	.08	.01	.01	.14	.03
199. reflective	−.14	.01	−.06	.06	−.14	−.14	−.14	−.07	−.01	.14	−.05	−.09
200. relaxed	.08	.05	.07	−.22	.05	.19	.14	.22	.11	−.10	.10	.18
201. reliable	.03	.05	.03	−.15	−.03	−.03	−.01	.01	.04	−.07	−.02	−.10
202. resentful	.04	−.15	−.12	−.02	−.05	−.07	.00	−.12	−.17	.01	.01	−.04
203. reserved	−.18	−.30	−.24	−.27	−.30	−.31	−.11	−.35	−.22	−.30	−.24	−.21
204. resourceful	.18	.17	.03	.21	.19	.20	.10	.11	.05	.22	.26	.20
205. responsible	.07	.08	.08	−.06	−.06	−.02	.03	.01	.12	−.04	−.02	−.09
206. restless	.00	.06	.05	.14	.00	.05	−.05	.06	.06	.17	.10	.08
207. retiring	−.13	−.38	−.03	−.13	−.29	−.32	−.17	−.35	.00	−.11	−.24	−.27
208. rigid	−.05	−.08	−.03	−.18	−.08	−.19	−.04	−.15	−.08	−.15	−.14	−.24
209. robust	.03	.15	.11	.02	.03	.20	.01	.21	.17	.07	.09	.19
210. rude	−.07	−.04	.00	.06	.07	.05	.04	.01	−.01	.05	.11	.03
211. sarcastic	−.03	−.01	−.03	.06	.05	.12	.02	.03	.02	.08	.15	.15
212. self-centered	−.02	.06	−.06	.06	.12	.05	−.06	.01	−.06	.02	.16	.05
213. self-confident	.23	.28	.15	.19	.23	.33	.26	.28	.17	.24	.28	.30
214. self-controlled	.08	−.02	−.07	−.03	−.15	−.18	.10	−.05	−.06	.03	−.10	−.17
215. self-denying	−.11	−.09	−.08	−.11	−.24	−.25	−.09	−.10	−.11	−.13	−.27	−.32
216. self-pitying	−.04	−.14	.01	−.04	−.09	−.10	−.09	−.18	−.04	−.12	−.07	−.12
217. self-punishing	.08	−.14	.01	.02	−.17	−.12	−.01	−.23	.03	−.02	−.17	−.19
218. self-seeking	.06	.00	.07	.08	.19	.15	.09	−.01	.08	.12	.22	.13
219. selfish	.03	−.01	.02	.05	.12	.02	−.03	−.02	−.02	.06	.11	.01
220. sensitive	−.01	−.16	−.08	.01	−.18	−.13	−.07	−.16	−.03	.03	−.05	−.09

Correlations of Observers' Adjectival Description with Scales of the CPI continued

| | | Scale: Sy | | | | | | Scale: Sp | | | | |
| | | By Peers | | By Spouses | | By Staff | | By Peers | | By Spouses | | By Staff | |
Adjectives		M	F	M	F	M	F	M	F	M	F	M	F
221.	sentimental	−.02	.02	−.05	.00	−.06	.00	−.01	−.02	−.07	−.01	−.05	−.03
222.	serious	−.02	−.15	−.04	−.11	−.23	−.15	−.07	−.23	−.06	−.03	−.17	−.13
223.	severe	−.08	−.05	−.01	−.03	−.14	−.16	−.11	−.07	.04	−.04	−.10	−.11
224.	sexy	.11	.12	−.02	.07	.04	.15	.09	.17	.04	.13	.15	.14
225.	shallow	−.15	.10	−.01	−.06	.02	−.05	−.11	.04	−.02	−.13	−.03	−.08
226.	sharp-witted	.15	.05	−.01	.15	.14	.09	.19	.07	.11	.23	.23	.11
227.	shiftless	−.04	−.08	−.06	.01	−.08	−.13	−.02	−.07	−.09	.01	−.03	−.05
228.	show-off	.02	.21	.18	.10	.15	.20	.00	.17	.16	.10	.20	.15
229.	shrewd	.10	−.04	−.05	.08	.19	.11	.08	−.06	−.03	.14	.20	.10
230.	shy	−.23	−.37	−.28	−.27	−.34	−.30	−.27	−.37	−.19	−.26	−.27	−.25
231.	silent	−.30	−.24	−.25	−.15	−.30	−.29	−.26	−.27	−.24	−.19	−.22	−.22
232.	simple	−.11	−.18	−.11	−.19	−.17	−.15	−.09	−.16	−.04	−.17	−.19	−.16
233.	sincere	.07	−.04	−.03	−.14	−.11	−.07	.06	−.05	−.03	−.08	−.08	−.11
234.	slipshod	.03	−.06	−.04	−.08	.03	−.02	.01	−.05	−.01	.00	.04	.01
235.	slow	−.16	−.19	−.04	−.05	−.24	−.23	−.10	−.12	−.06	−.07	−.22	−.22
236.	sly	.05	−.01	−.12	.13	.01	.04	.04	−.01	−.12	.11	.06	.05
237.	smug	.04	.08	.03	−.04	.12	.04	.07	.08	−.04	−.06	.13	.05
238.	snobbish	.05	.02	−.03	.05	.07	.09	.00	−.07	.04	.05	.04	.05
239.	sociable	.33	.28	.21	.17	.24	.31	.32	.30	.15	.20	.24	.22
240.	soft-hearted	−.05	.03	−.03	−.10	−.05	−.02	−.05	.06	.00	−.09	−.05	−.06
241.	sophisticated	.14	.08	.19	.15	.06	.17	.08	−.03	.08	.11	.15	.17
242.	spendthrift	.09	−.03	.09	−.07	−.01	.09	.09	−.03	.00	−.06	.07	.10
243.	spineless	−.09	−.20	.10	−.15	−.17	−.10	−.11	−.24	.08	−.05	−.16	−.07
244.	spontaneous	.07	.26	.12	.18	.19	.21	.12	.36	.12	.29	.24	.19
245.	spunky	−.08	.17	.03	.14	.15	.13	−.03	.21	−.04	.17	.17	.14
246.	stable	.12	.08	−.12	−.12	−.02	.13	.10	.05	−.03	−.03	.03	.05
247.	steady	.08	−.01	−.07	−.08	−.10	−.01	.05	−.02	−.06	−.07	−.09	−.05
248.	stern	.03	−.08	−.12	−.04	−.10	−.07	−.06	−.19	−.18	−.02	−.08	−.07
249.	stingy	−.08	−.08	−.03	−.03	−.12	.01	−.11	−.07	−.05	.02	−.10	−.02
250.	stolid	.03	−.10	−.09	.00	−.17	−.12	−.04	−.06	−.01	.00	−.18	−.16
251.	strong	.03	.10	.05	.03	.00	.24	.00	.09	.05	.00	.08	.22
252.	stubborn	.03	.06	.01	.11	.03	−.01	−.01	.03	−.07	.12	.08	.02
253.	submissive	−.09	−.19	−.10	−.18	−.18	−.20	−.04	−.20	−.06	−.14	−.24	−.22
254.	suggestible	.04	.01	−.07	.07	−.02	−.09	.06	.16	−.01	.03	−.10	−.14
255.	sulky	−.08	−.15	−.06	−.06	−.12	−.05	−.10	−.20	.05	−.03	−.04	−.02
256.	superstitious	.03	−.07	−.15	.02	−.04	−.12	−.03	−.03	−.08	.00	−.07	−.17
257.	suspicious	−.05	−.14	−.15	−.02	−.09	−.09	−.07	−.17	−.14	−.02	−.04	−.11
258.	sympathetic	.06	.01	.02	−.05	−.03	.01	.08	.03	.10	−.02	−.01	−.02
259.	tactful	.14	.06	.08	.03	.05	.04	.11	.02	.03	.11	.04	.03
260.	tactless	−.10	−.05	−.10	.05	.02	.02	−.06	.00	−.09	.03	.06	.02
261.	talkative	.18	.25	.24	.23	.21	.31	.22	.26	.23	.22	.26	.24
262.	temperamental	.02	−.09	−.01	.12	−.05	.04	−.02	−.14	−.04	.10	.08	.08
263.	tense	−.15	−.20	−.08	−.01	−.14	−.25	−.13	−.25	−.13	−.01	−.10	−.19
264.	thankless	−.05	−.14	−.01	.00	−.06	.01	−.11	−.13	−.06	−.05	−.04	−.03

Correlations of Observers' Adjectival Description with Scales of the CPI continued

	Scale: Sy						Scale: Sp					
	By Peers		By Spouses		By Staff		By Peers		By Spouses		By Staff	
Adjectives	M	F	M	F	M	F	M	F	M	F	M	F
265. thorough	.03	.02	−.11	−.01	−.06	.03	.03	−.07	−.06	.02	−.04	−.01
266. thoughtful	.02	.05	−.06	−.10	−.10	.00	.07	.02	.02	.00	−.01	−.03
267. thrifty	−.02	−.04	.01	−.03	−.14	−.01	−.04	−.01	−.10	−.10	−.17	−.10
268. timid	−.19	−.34	−.10	−.10	−.22	−.26	−.16	−.33	−.03	−.14	−.25	−.22
269. tolerant	.09	.06	.07	−.05	−.03	.07	.09	.10	.14	.02	.07	.07
270. touchy	−.03	−.05	−.13	.05	−.05	−.11	−.02	−.06	−.11	.08	.02	−.12
271. tough	.05	.04	−.06	−.02	.01	.14	−.04	.05	−.11	.02	.09	.15
272. trusting	.11	−.02	.11	.03	−.09	.04	.12	.02	.09	.04	−.06	.00
273. unaffected	.02	−.08	.01	.02	−.09	−.12	.03	.02	.05	.10	−.05	−.04
274. unambitious	−.17	−.16	−.12	−.16	−.21	−.15	−.13	−.04	−.06	−.05	−.11	−.13
275. unassuming	−.12	−.20	.00	−.07	−.18	−.22	−.09	−.09	−.04	.02	−.19	−.19
276. unconventional	.02	−.05	−.11	.01	−.06	−.03	.06	.05	−.01	.19	.06	.05
277. undependable	−.05	−.03	.05	−.01	.04	−.06	−.04	.05	.10	.02	.04	.00
278. understanding	.12	.09	.06	.03	−.07	.13	.14	.11	.12	.10	.04	.10
279. unemotional	−.09	−.24	.01	−.05	−.20	−.08	−.18	−.17	.04	−.02	−.14	−.03
280. unexcitable	−.18	−.22	−.17	−.05	−.18	−.14	−.15	−.16	−.15	−.05	−.12	−.10
281. unfriendly	−.14	−.18	−.19	.08	−.09	−.07	−.08	−.18	−.19	.06	−.06	−.02
282. uninhibited	.12	.08	−.04	.15	.17	.21	.15	.17	.01	.22	.25	.20
283. unintelligent	−.08	.03	.00	−.04	−.09	−.07	−.10	.03	.00	−.05	−.13	−.05
284. unkind	−.17	−.16	.00	.03	−.02	.08	−.13	−.18	−.02	−.04	.01	.09
285. unrealistic	−.05	.07	−.01	−.02	−.10	−.10	.02	−.01	.04	−.02	−.08	−.12
286. unscrupulous	.01	−.10	.07	.02	−.01	.03	−.03	−.06	−.13	.05	.06	.05
287. unselfish	.08	−.06	−.18	.02	−.03	−.07	.13	−.05	−.19	.01	.00	−.09
288. unstable	−.01	−.12	−.16	.04	−.10	−.14	.01	−.17	−.12	.05	−.06	−.09
289. vindictive	.00	−.01	−.14	−.07	.00	−.01	.03	−.04	.00	−.03	.03	−.01
290. versatile	.16	.25	.03	.06	.17	.22	.22	.33	.12	.12	.28	.24
291. warm	.02	.07	.06	−.06	.09	.14	.01	.13	−.04	−.01	.09	.07
292. wary	.09	−.14	.00	−.08	−.13	−.20	.06	−.25	.00	−.04	−.08	−.11
293. weak	−.11	−.25	−.03	−.07	−.09	−.21	−.09	−.21	−.08	−.10	−.17	−.20
294. whiny	−.13	−.08	−.08	−.03	.04	−.01	−.08	−.09	.03	−.01	.01	−.09
295. wholesome	−.01	.07	.08	.00	−.03	.20	−.04	.11	−.02	.03	.00	.12
296. wise	.14	.07	.06	−.04	−.06	.09	.13	.04	.06	.02	.00	.08
297. withdrawn	−.24	−.37	.06	−.15	−.34	−.30	−.19	−.39	−.18	−.17	−.28	−.23
298. witty	.15	.12	−.20	.05	.14	.22	.26	.21	.08	.09	.23	.18
299. worrying	−.11	−.12	.04	−.03	−.21	−.22	−.06	−.26	−.11	−.05	−.18	−.21
300. zany	−.01	.19	−.10	.13	.04	.12	.07	.28	.00	.17	.12	.12

Correlations of Observers' Adjectival Description with Scales of the CPI continued

		Scale: Sa						Scale: In				
		By Peers		By Spouses		By Staff		By Peers		By Spouses		By Staff	
Adjectives		M	F	M	F	M	F	M	F	M	F	M	F
001.	absent-minded	−.05	−.09	−.17	.10	−.16	−.06	−.07	−.18	−.10	.04	−.14	−.08
002.	active	.10	.19	.13	.17	.26	.31	.04	.23	.04	.18	.28	.22
003.	adaptable	.00	.11	.12	.11	.17	.20	.02	.09	.09	.09	.16	.10
004.	adventurous	.05	.24	.10	.19	.25	.29	.07	.14	.05	.23	.23	.20
005.	affected	.13	.13	.03	.01	.10	.11	−.08	.12	.09	.00	.14	.13
006.	affectionate	−.01	−.11	.05	.03	.01	.01	−.11	−.06	−.07	.03	−.03	−.10
007.	aggressive	.19	.31	.16	.25	.25	.30	.10	.25	.18	.21	.26	.33
008.	alert	.07	.20	.15	.16	.19	.22	.14	.20	.23	.09	.26	.20
009.	aloof	.07	.01	−.03	−.06	−.18	−.12	.09	.00	.05	−.01	−.08	.05
010.	ambitious	.16	.17	.19	.28	.32	.32	.06	.18	.23	.20	.30	.34
011.	anxious	−.01	−.07	−.07	−.03	−.20	−.28	−.12	−.08	−.03	−.10	−.17	−.20
012.	apathetic	−.14	−.16	−.08	−.08	−.26	−.26	−.04	−.08	−.13	.01	−.27	−.21
013.	appreciative	−.09	−.04	.01	−.02	−.06	−.08	−.12	−.01	.03	−.04	−.03	−.15
014.	argumentative	.17	.15	.04	.19	.22	.19	.15	.20	.10	.11	.25	.25
015.	arrogant	.11	.15	.07	.13	.19	.19	.14	.10	.09	.12	.23	.20
016.	artistic	−.02	−.05	.01	.14	.06	.02	−.13	.04	.06	.07	.16	.05
017.	assertive	.13	.27	.11	.36	.29	.34	.12	.19	.26	.35	.32	.35
018.	attractive	−.05	.09	.03	.03	.10	.10	.04	.04	.10	.01	.09	.07
019.	autocratic	−.03	.12	.05	.11	.10	.19	.03	.00	.13	.13	.13	.20
020.	awkward	−.12	−.18	−.18	−.08	−.30	−.30	−.16	−.12	−.21	−.14	−.33	−.18
021.	bitter	−.06	.00	−.14	.02	−.04	−.02	−.03	−.05	−.11	−.10	−.07	.04
022.	blustery	.08	.02	.04	.01	.10	.06	.05	−.01	.01	−.10	.10	.05
023.	boastful	.15	.20	.09	.14	.18	.21	.07	.19	−.02	−.01	.21	.15
024.	bossy	.04	.19	−.02	.11	.13	.15	.03	.18	−.06	−.01	.14	.18
025.	calm	−.09	−.16	−.10	−.14	−.11	−.01	−.03	.06	−.10	−.04	−.11	.01
026.	capable	.06	.02	−.08	.13	.11	.23	.09	.13	.11	.14	.14	.26
027.	careless	.05	.06	−.14	.00	.01	.01	.02	−.02	−.14	−.06	.01	−.02
028.	cautious	−.13	−.37	−.12	−.19	−.28	−.30	−.22	−.22	−.11	−.08	−.33	−.21
029.	changeable	.07	.09	−.10	.15	.06	.04	−.03	−.03	−.06	.02	.04	−.02
030.	charming	.05	.06	.04	.06	.14	.16	−.08	.04	−.03	.06	.23	.09
031.	cheerful	.03	.02	.06	.04	.10	.11	−.10	.01	.02	−.04	.12	.00
032.	civilized	.12	−.02	−.01	−.01	.01	.05	.09	.05	−.01	−.05	.09	.04
033.	clear-thinking	.06	.08	.04	.02	.07	.19	.09	.10	.08	.11	.14	.23
034.	clever	.17	.17	.11	.17	.21	.24	.16	.10	.11	.16	.27	.19
035.	coarse	.02	.01	−.13	.03	.04	.08	.03	.03	−.10	.13	.05	.07
036.	cold	−.10	−.06	−.07	−.01	−.07	−.02	−.02	.01	.02	−.01	−.04	.08
037.	commonplace	−.18	−.14	−.02	−.14	−.19	−.19	−.26	−.08	−.03	−.09	−.20	−.20
038.	complaining	−.03	−.05	−.12	.06	−.03	−.01	−.07	−.08	−.19	−.12	−.01	.04
039.	complicated	−.02	.05	.06	.08	−.03	.04	.06	−.02	.11	.11	.08	.14
040.	conceited	.15	.22	−.02	.16	.20	.19	.13	.18	.01	.06	.24	.15
041.	confident	.22	.27	.15	.25	.27	.37	.22	.32	.21	.24	.31	.31
042.	confused	−.03	−.04	−.16	.03	−.15	−.16	−.09	−.20	−.16	−.10	−.20	−.13
043.	conscientious	−.12	−.04	.02	.05	−.15	−.07	−.13	−.02	.14	.06	−.15	−.06
044.	conservative	−.02	−.24	−.06	−.21	−.14	−.17	.01	−.12	−.02	−.14	−.24	−.17

Correlations of Observers' Adjectival Description with Scales of the CPI continued

	Scale: Sa						Scale: In					
	By Peers		By Spouses		By Staff		By Peers		By Spouses		By Staff	
Adjectives	M	F	M	F	M	F	M	F	M	F	M	F
045. considerate	−.04	−.10	.01	−.10	−.14	−.08	−.10	−.10	.00	−.12	−.12	−.16
046. contented	−.07	−.04	.04	−.12	−.07	−.02	−.01	.07	.09	−.03	−.07	−.07
047. conventional	−.03	−.21	−.03	−.18	−.18	−.18	−.08	−.10	.04	−.14	−.28	−.22
048. cool	.15	.04	−.01	−.02	.00	.00	.08	.04	.03	.07	−.02	.10
049. cooperative	−.14	−.07	.06	−.08	−.08	−.03	−.11	−.05	.08	−.02	−.05	−.18
050. courageous	−.01	.10	.09	.07	.09	.11	.02	.10	.17	.11	.10	.15
051. cowardly	−.09	−.18	−.04	.00	−.06	−.01	−.15	−.19	−.11	−.06	−.08	−.02
052. cruel	−.06	−.05	−.05	.08	−.03	.02	−.06	−.02	.01	.07	.02	.02
053. curious	.06	.01	−.02	.04	.05	.21	.09	−.03	.07	.09	.21	.17
054. cynical	.06	.05	−.06	.11	.03	.11	.17	.03	.08	.09	.11	.17
055. daring	−.04	.19	.04	.00	.22	.23	.08	.19	.02	.00	.21	.15
056. deceitful	.13	.03	−.12	.10	.12	.03	.09	.02	−.05	.00	.08	−.02
057. defensive	−.02	−.09	−.01	.02	−.06	−.16	−.04	−.16	.00	−.09	−.08	.02
058. deliberate	.02	.05	−.01	.04	−.25	−.09	.02	.11	.11	.04	−.16	.00
059. demanding	.13	.17	.13	.14	.20	.17	.09	.17	.10	−.04	.20	.19
060. dependable	−.01	−.01	−.05	−.08	−.11	−.01	−.07	−.02	.05	−.02	−.06	−.03
061. dependent	−.04	−.17	−.02	−.08	−.24	−.22	−.13	−.09	−.09	−.20	−.28	−.29
062. despondent	.09	−.12	.03	.06	−.14	−.29	.01	−.17	.00	.01	−.15	−.25
063. determined	.15	.21	.08	.25	.17	.29	.11	.21	.14	.22	.20	.31
064. dignified	.00	−.01	.04	.06	−.07	−.09	−.02	−.02	−.04	.10	.01	.00
065. discreet	−.03	−.09	.03	.09	−.13	−.13	−.02	−.04	.07	.05	−.09	−.10
066. disorderly	.03	.05	.01	.06	.02	.01	.10	−.05	−.02	.02	.09	−.05
067. dissatisfied	.00	−.01	.02	−.02	−.02	−.05	−.01	−.03	−.08	−.16	−.01	−.04
068. distractible	−.05	−.01	−.09	.05	−.08	−.10	−.11	−.02	−.16	−.12	−.11	−.14
069. distrustful	−.07	−.04	−.11	−.05	.01	−.04	−.06	−.09	−.04	−.13	.02	.09
070. dominant	.18	.28	.13	.01	.23	.34	.09	.26	.16	.06	.27	.34
071. dreamy	−.02	−.12	−.01	.03	−.17	−.18	−.18	−.12	−.07	−.01	−.16	−.12
072. dull	−.14	−.27	−.02	−.06	−.20	−.14	−.17	−.18	−.13	−.09	−.23	−.18
073. easygoing	.02	.05	−.13	−.10	−.08	.02	−.05	−.03	−.17	.00	−.10	−.12
074. effeminate	.00	−.01	−.02	.13	−.01	.02	−.09	.00	.05	.09	−.04	−.04
075. efficient	−.02	.08	−.05	.02	.14	.15	−.01	.15	.06	.02	.21	.18
076. egotistical	.20	.20	.10	.17	.19	.20	.20	.17	.09	.08	.25	.22
077. emotional	.06	.06	.03	−.02	.08	.01	−.14	−.03	−.07	−.09	.05	−.04
078. energetic	.16	.22	.22	.18	.30	.29	−.01	.19	.19	.15	.31	.24
079. enterprising	.21	.16	.12	.24	.31	.35	.11	.21	.16	.20	.30	.30
080. enthusiastic	.08	.13	.29	.21	.17	.27	−.03	.07	.16	.13	.22	.11
081. evasive	−.03	−.03	−.07	.02	−.14	−.07	.01	−.06	.01	−.14	−.11	.04
082. excitable	.04	.24	−.06	.09	.15	.08	−.10	.13	−.12	−.04	.14	.04
083. fair-minded	−.02	−.01	−.03	−.01	−.06	.02	−.05	−.03	.09	.02	−.04	.00
084. fault-finding	.09	.01	.00	−.01	.04	.08	.03	.04	.01	−.10	.09	.14
085. fearful	−.05	−.13	−.07	−.04	−.21	−.30	.02	−.16	−.11	−.08	−.19	−.20
086. feminine	−.16	−.08	−.08	−.02	−.07	−.05	−.14	−.09	−.02	−.09	−.07	−.11
087. fickle	−.05	.16	−.10	.06	−.03	.09	−.09	.13	.03	−.09	.09	−.01
088. flirtatious	−.02	.22	−.05	.05	.10	.12	.02	.13	−.14	.02	.16	−.01

Correlations of Observers' Adjectival Description with Scales of the CPI continued

		Scale: Sa						Scale: In				
		By Peers		By Spouses		By Staff		By Peers		By Spouses		By Staff	
Adjectives		M	F	M	F	M	F	M	F	M	F	M	F
089.	foolish	.09	.00	−.06	.09	−.02	−.07	.02	−.09	−.04	−.08	.01	−.11
090.	forceful	.17	.18	.04	.09	.18	.26	.04	.18	.15	.08	.22	.32
091.	foresighted	−.03	.06	.00	−.06	.09	.20	.08	.15	.16	.00	.13	.17
092.	forgetful	.01	−.13	−.11	.07	−.10	−.02	−.04	−.19	−.03	.08	−.04	−.10
093.	forgiving	.08	−.07	−.08	−.06	−.09	−.06	.02	−.07	−.08	−.13	−.09	−.17
094.	formal	.04	−.10	.06	.03	−.10	−.08	−.01	.03	.04	.11	−.06	−.03
095.	frank	−.03	.10	.12	.10	.07	.24	.02	.05	.10	.06	.06	.20
096.	friendly	.02	.16	.07	−.01	.06	.12	−.06	.04	.08	.00	.05	−.01
097.	frivolous	.00	.13	−.06	.06	.02	.02	−.08	.04	−.07	−.06	.08	−.06
098.	fussy	−.07	−.03	−.10	.02	−.05	−.09	−.09	.00	−.12	−.10	−.03	−.03
099.	generous	−.06	−.05	.00	−.07	−.04	.07	−.10	−.06	−.02	−.07	.00	−.06
100.	gentle	−.09	−.23	−.02	−.13	−.23	−.20	−.08	−.19	−.01	−.15	−.19	−.24
101.	gloomy	−.03	−.13	−.19	−.02	−.17	−.09	−.08	−.20	−.12	−.01	−.12	−.03
102.	good-looking	.06	.16	.02	.02	.06	.08	.03	.09	.05	−.01	.08	.05
103.	good-natured	−.06	.03	.06	.04	−.02	.08	−.04	−.07	.09	.02	−.05	−.07
104.	greedy	−.04	−.02	.02	.00	.05	.05	−.03	−.06	.03	−.04	.08	.02
105.	handsome	−.02	−.02	.06	.01	.07	.03	.04	−.01	.04	.06	.03	.11
106.	hard-headed	.06	.13	−.01	.12	.14	.07	.11	.08	.06	−.04	.18	.23
107.	hard-hearted	−.03	.06	−.05	.01	.04	.12	−.01	.06	.03	−.06	.04	.07
108.	hasty	.02	.05	−.09	.11	.13	.13	−.20	.03	−.11	−.09	.14	.01
109.	headstrong	.07	.07	.04	.16	.16	.21	.02	.11	.08	.00	.20	.24
110.	healthy	−.04	−.02	−.08	.03	.06	.22	.04	.03	.03	.12	.04	.11
111.	helpful	.03	.04	−.07	.06	−.06	−.03	−.01	.00	.01	.04	−.06	−.11
112.	high-strung	−.02	.02	−.10	.15	.06	−.06	−.09	.00	−.12	−.02	.07	−.01
113.	honest	−.06	−.11	−.06	−.05	−.10	.02	−.07	−.10	−.01	−.01	−.08	−.02
114.	hostile	.05	−.01	−.10	.08	.03	.02	.03	.00	−.02	.02	.05	.12
115.	humorous	.16	.16	.04	.17	.14	.20	.02	−.03	−.02	.15	.16	.09
116.	hurried	−.04	.12	.07	.05	.06	.05	−.18	.01	.05	−.01	.14	.00
117.	idealistic	.12	.00	.12	.13	−.01	.07	.04	.02	.10	.08	.02	.08
118.	imaginative	.09	.13	.07	.23	.15	.17	−.02	.16	.18	.16	.25	.16
119.	immature	−.02	−.10	.00	−.02	−.06	−.15	−.01	−.12	−.08	−.16	−.10	−.15
120.	impatient	.09	.02	.06	.12	.19	.18	.01	.02	.05	.05	.22	.18
121.	impulsive	.04	.18	.08	.17	.17	.08	.05	.04	−.03	−.01	.19	.02
122.	independent	.08	.16	.08	.22	.20	.27	.22	.18	.16	.21	.28	.32
123.	indifferent	−.07	−.09	−.01	.05	−.14	−.11	−.03	−.01	.05	.08	−.11	−.05
124.	individualistic	.05	.17	.05	.37	.13	.18	.16	.17	.16	.25	.22	.24
125.	industrious	.09	−.06	.12	.04	.01	.17	−.05	.07	.08	.09	.09	.23
126.	infantile	−.06	.00	.01	−.09	−.03	−.17	−.15	−.01	.04	−.24	−.03	−.19
127.	informal	−.02	.07	−.07	.07	.04	.14	−.05	.02	.04	.03	.04	.03
128.	ingenious	.18	.15	.08	.16	.16	.16	.10	.19	.12	.12	.26	.13
129.	inhibited	−.08	−.28	−.15	−.23	−.33	−.31	−.17	−.12	.00	−.12	−.35	−.20
130.	initiative	.12	.16	.18	.18	.29	.34	.04	.26	.24	.11	.32	.33
131.	insightful	.05	.16	.11	.13	.07	.17	.02	.10	.14	.09	.16	.19
132.	intelligent	.05	.14	.08	.07	.13	.14	.23	.14	.17	.09	.23	.25

Correlations of Observers' Adjectival Description with Scales of the CPI continued

		Scale: Sa						Scale: In					
		By Peers		By Spouses		By Staff		By Peers		By Spouses		By Staff	
Adjectives		M	F	M	F	M	F	M	F	M	F	M	F
133.	interests—narrow	−.28	−.12	−.07	−.23	−.25	−.27	−.18	−.07	−.03	−.25	−.27	−.29
134.	interests—wide	.17	.21	.10	.23	.17	.23	.16	.14	.11	.17	.25	.24
135.	intolerant	.00	.06	−.09	−.03	.02	.01	−.01	.13	−.01	−.14	.03	.03
136.	inventive	.07	.13	.08	.13	.15	.14	.00	.17	.12	.10	.26	.13
137.	irresponsible	−.01	−.06	−.01	.08	.02	.01	.07	−.03	.01	−.04	.04	−.07
138.	irritable	.00	−.05	−.10	.01	.07	.05	−.06	−.03	−.02	−.12	.06	.13
139.	jolly	.13	.20	−.05	−.02	.12	.09	−.05	.11	−.15	−.05	.09	.01
140.	kind	−.07	−.08	−.16	.01	−.17	−.01	−.17	−.11	−.05	.02	−.13	−.18
141.	lazy	.06	.03	.14	.00	−.04	−.01	.12	−.05	.06	−.02	−.08	−.11
142.	leisurely	.04	.12	.06	.07	−.06	−.04	.03	.07	.06	.06	−.11	−.01
143.	logical	−.00	.06	.05	−.13	.00	.08	.12	.17	.10	.00	.10	.22
144.	loud	.02	.21	.02	.12	.15	.20	−.01	.10	−.01	.05	.16	.12
145.	loyal	.07	−.11	−.06	−.10	−.12	−.06	−.08	−.05	−.16	−.11	−.18	−.06
146.	mannerly	.03	−.06	.08	.07	−.15	−.04	−.09	−.02	.02	.18	−.18	−.08
147.	masculine	.08	.12	.06	.06	.07	.07	.10	.13	.04	.05	.07	.14
148.	mature	.11	.05	−.09	.04	.06	.18	.09	.14	.05	.11	.08	.15
149.	meek	−.14	−.35	−.02	−.20	−.28	−.32	−.20	−.22	−.14	−.22	−.31	−.28
150.	methodical	−.08	−.16	−.04	.07	−.16	−.11	−.06	−.01	.04	.13	−.10	.02
151.	mild	−.15	−.31	−.13	−.22	−.28	−.30	−.21	−.19	−.18	−.13	−.28	−.24
152.	mischievous	.11	.06	−.08	.04	.15	.10	.00	.07	−.10	−.03	.16	.03
153.	moderate	.00	−.27	−.02	−.05	−.21	−.14	−.04	−.06	.02	−.04	−.27	−.07
154.	modest	−.18	−.27	−.01	−.23	−.30	−.32	−.06	−.17	−.06	−.16	−.29	−.28
155.	moody	−.01	−.11	−.13	.01	−.12	−.10	−.01	−.13	−.07	−.11	−.08	.00
156.	nagging	−.11	.02	−.06	.01	−.05	.06	−.10	.03	−.16	−.11	−.04	−.02
157.	natural	.01	−.03	−.04	.01	.12	.12	.02	−.08	−.03	.04	.06	.09
158.	nervous	−.11	−.14	−.13	.03	−.17	−.19	−.17	−.18	−.15	−.13	−.15	−.17
159.	noisy	.02	.21	−.01	.03	.14	.13	−.03	.11	−.01	−.05	.13	.03
160.	obliging	−.06	−.03	−.05	.01	−.17	−.15	−.07	−.05	−.04	.01	−.11	−.21
161.	obnoxious	.04	.10	.09	.11	.13	.09	.03	.08	.05	.00	.10	.02
162.	opinionated	.17	.15	.08	.15	.15	.19	.07	.16	.09	.03	.17	.20
163.	opportunistic	.20	.07	.05	.13	.26	.26	.09	.06	.08	.14	.23	.17
164.	optimistic	.09	.08	.21	.16	.16	.22	.17	.07	.15	.13	.12	.09
165.	organized	.06	−.07	−.04	−.01	.13	.12	−.02	.09	.04	.01	.16	.14
166.	original	.14	.16	.06	.17	.15	.11	.07	.15	.10	.08	.27	.18
167.	outgoing	.26	.29	.27	.34	.29	.29	.06	.21	.07	.16	.24	.17
168.	outspoken	.15	.28	.10	.22	.22	.23	.10	.20	.05	.11	.27	.25
169.	painstaking	−.14	−.10	.03	−.03	−.23	−.19	−.08	−.07	.03	−.00	−.15	−.11
170.	patient	−.11	−.20	−.05	−.15	−.26	−.14	−.11	−.08	.01	−.08	−.19	−.17
171.	peaceable	−.12	−.21	−.08	−.14	−.28	−.23	−.12	−.08	−.02	−.09	−.26	−.22
172.	peculiar	−.06	−.06	−.14	.08	−.16	−.14	−.03	−.04	−.08	.01	−.13	.03
173.	persevering	−.01	.04	−.06	.05	−.01	.03	.06	.06	.02	.10	.05	.06
174.	persistent	.03	.17	.03	.21	.07	.21	.08	.19	.09	.19	.12	.23
175.	pessimistic	−.07	−.13	−.02	.04	−.07	−.09	−.07	−.20	.05	−.13	−.07	−.09
176.	planful	.05	−.02	−.05	.04	.08	.16	−.06	.10	.06	.02	.11	.15

Correlations of Observers' Adjectival Description with Scales of the CPI continued

	Scale: Sa						Scale: In					
	By Peers		By Spouses		By Staff		By Peers		By Spouses		By Staff	
Adjectives	M	F	M	F	M	F	M	F	M	F	M	F
177. pleasant	.05	.06	.02	−.01	−.04	−.01	−.01	−.06	.01	−.02	−.01	−.07
178. pleasure-seeking	.09	.17	.07	.19	.21	.14	.08	.18	−.02	.07	.18	.03
179. poised	.11	.08	.17	.21	.17	.20	.12	.09	.13	.15	.19	.21
180. polished	.19	.09	.19	.14	.09	.20	.07	.06	.06	.17	.14	.14
181. practical	−.01	−.14	.05	−.01	.01	.12	.05	−.03	.07	−.03	.00	.06
182. praising	.08	−.10	.03	.01	.00	.03	−.03	−.03	−.03	−.05	.07	−.09
183. precise	−.02	−.10	.13	.01	−.07	.01	.04	.02	.16	.07	.02	.13
184. prejudiced	.00	−.02	−.02	.01	−.01	−.04	.02	.02	−.07	−.14	−.03	−.07
185. preoccupied	−.03	−.01	.00	.07	−.25	−.22	−.05	.03	.09	.05	−.22	−.11
186. progressive	.12	.15	.07	.04	.14	.21	.07	.09	−.02	.11	.21	.15
187. prudish	.02	−.11	−.01	−.11	−.16	−.27	−.06	−.05	−.02	−.17	−.12	−.17
188. quarrelsome	.19	.03	−.16	.02	.13	.13	.13	.01	−.11	−.10	.10	.14
189. queer	−.05	−.03	−.06	.00	−.12	−.07	−.14	−.04	.03	.00	−.08	.03
190. quick	.03	.24	.04	.18	.25	.23	.07	.19	.12	.13	.27	.17
191. quiet	−.24	−.34	−.23	−.27	−.35	−.35	−.19	−.15	−.07	−.18	−.35	−.26
192. quitting	−.10	−.17	−.06	−.06	−.12	−.09	−.15	−.16	−.10	−.18	−.07	−.11
193. rational	.07	.12	.10	−.04	−.04	.16	.13	.17	.15	.07	.01	.22
194. rattle-brained	−.02	.01	−.09	.01	.02	−.06	−.09	−.07	−.17	−.17	−.02	−.14
195. realistic	−.03	.09	.05	−.02	.07	.20	.06	.18	.09	.06	.04	.18
196. reasonable	−.02	.01	.06	.00	−.07	.01	.06	.03	.12	.04	−.06	.02
197. rebellious	.06	.11	−.08	.19	.05	.11	.08	.02	−.07	.08	.12	.13
198. reckless	−.02	.11	−.08	.10	.12	.01	.06	.08	−.04	−.02	.12	.02
199. reflective	−.05	−.05	−.04	.04	−.11	−.04	−.07	.00	.03	.13	−.02	.04
200. relaxed	.08	.00	.03	−.18	.02	.19	−.01	.05	.03	−.06	.04	.14
201. reliable	−.02	−.07	.00	−.11	−.05	−.05	−.05	.04	.02	−.03	−.05	−.01
202. resentful	.06	−.04	−.12	.04	.01	−.02	.13	−.05	−.05	−.13	.00	.06
203. reserved	−.10	−.37	−.15	−.27	−.32	−.27	−.09	−.17	−.01	−.16	−.30	−.16
204. resourceful	.17	.11	.16	.25	.25	.30	.10	.14	.14	.22	.30	.26
205. responsible	.03	−.01	.09	−.01	−.05	.01	−.01	.08	.06	.04	.02	.03
206. restless	−.02	.12	.09	.21	.10	.10	−.10	.02	.05	.03	.17	.06
207. retiring	−.05	−.35	−.14	−.16	−.34	−.36	−.14	−.34	−.01	−.13	−.29	−.23
208. rigid	−.03	−.08	−.03	−.13	−.13	−.17	−.05	.02	.08	−.11	−.16	−.03
209. robust	.01	.17	.23	.04	.12	.22	−.03	.09	.09	.01	.09	.14
210. rude	.01	.07	.04	.05	.11	.10	.01	.06	.05	.06	.08	.07
211. sarcastic	.05	.07	.04	.11	.12	.20	.12	.06	.05	.03	.15	.16
212. self-centered	.06	.11	−.03	.10	.18	.09	.17	.13	−.04	−.03	.15	.08
213. self-confident	.24	.26	.22	.32	.29	.38	.13	.27	.23	.30	.30	.37
214. self-controlled	.06	−.09	−.01	.04	−.16	−.15	.07	.04	.06	.12	−.15	−.01
215. self-denying	−.08	−.13	−.07	−.14	−.32	−.26	−.09	−.03	−.12	−.11	−.22	−.17
216. self-pitying	−.07	−.04	−.07	−.04	−.07	−.09	−.11	−.05	−.14	−.24	−.11	−.11
217. self-punishing	.08	−.10	−.06	.01	−.13	−.10	.07	−.05	−.02	−.12	−.08	−.08
218. self-seeking	.16	.07	.07	.11	.24	.20	−.02	.05	.05	.07	.20	.10
219. selfish	.06	.09	.00	.06	.12	.06	.09	.06	.08	.00	.07	.03
220. sensitive	.02	−.11	−.02	.03	−.15	−.11	−.14	−.19	−.10	−.04	−.09	−.14

	Scale: Sa						**Scale: In**					
	By Peers		By Spouses		By Staff		By Peers		By Spouses		By Staff	
Adjectives	M	F	M	F	M	F	M	F	M	F	M	F
221. sentimental	.04	.00	−.07	−.11	−.04	−.04	−.17	.05	−.16	−.12	−.05	−.12
222. serious	.00	−.17	−.02	−.06	−.20	−.03	−.03	−.02	.04	.04	−.17	.11
223. severe	−.04	−.02	.08	.02	−.05	−.05	−.05	.11	.03	−.05	.00	.04
224. sexy	.03	.11	.05	.10	.12	.13	.04	.11	−.03	.08	.11	.04
225. shallow	−.07	.07	−.03	−.03	−.04	−.16	−.18	.04	.02	−.17	−.11	−.24
226. sharp-witted	.14	.11	.15	.18	.21	.17	.13	.04	.15	.10	.24	.19
227. shiftless	.00	−.03	−.13	.02	−.11	−.01	−.12	−.01	−.12	−.07	−.04	−.02
228. show-off	.09	.22	.11	.11	.21	.20	.05	.11	.00	.02	.22	.12
229. shrewd	.06	.06	.01	.13	.26	.17	.11	.02	.00	.07	.29	.23
230. shy	−.29	−.34	−.25	−.31	−.37	−.35	−.23	−.26	−.18	−.32	−.36	−.28
231. silent	−.24	−.22	−.25	−.11	−.31	−.27	−.20	−.15	−.13	−.11	−.28	−.23
232. simple	−.08	−.23	−.07	−.19	−.24	−.23	−.14	−.13	−.06	−.26	−.26	−.26
233. sincere	.01	−.06	−.06	−.11	−.15	−.08	−.10	−.14	.00	−.08	−.14	−.06
234. slipshod	.10	.04	−.01	.02	.01	.00	.11	−.01	.01	−.03	.02	−.05
235. slow	−.08	−.16	−.18	−.03	−.27	−.24	−.12	−.11	−.26	−.08	−.23	−.20
236. sly	.02	−.03	−.10	.16	.05	.02	.07	−.04	−.14	.08	.08	.04
237. smug	.13	.11	.02	.00	.14	.07	.15	.06	.06	−.04	.08	.15
238. snobbish	.10	.05	.04	.10	.10	.11	.11	.10	.09	.02	.07	.09
239. sociable	.21	.16	.20	.27	.22	.25	.02	.07	−.03	.09	.18	.06
240. soft-hearted	−.05	−.04	−.07	−.09	−.09	−.10	−.13	−.05	−.17	−.17	−.12	−.21
241. sophisticated	.09	.09	.17	.20	.14	.25	.14	.01	.04	.19	.22	.21
242. spendthrift	.07	.02	−.02	−.03	.01	.08	.15	−.08	−.01	−.05	.07	−.01
243. spineless	−.04	−.23	.07	−.11	−.17	−.06	−.09	−.21	.11	−.09	−.13	−.11
244. spontaneous	.04	.30	.16	.21	.21	.19	−.03	.18	.08	.19	.21	.12
245. spunky	−.01	.13	.05	.20	.17	.16	−.13	.05	−.08	.16	.13	.13
246. stable	.04	−.04	−.06	−.05	−.03	.09	.02	.13	−.01	.05	−.02	.07
247. steady	.02	−.06	−.09	−.04	−.11	−.03	.03	.05	−.01	−.03	−.12	.00
248. stern	.05	−.01	−.06	−.04	−.04	−.01	.03	.02	.01	−.06	−.06	.11
249. stingy	.01	.02	−.02	.07	−.09	.06	.01	.03	−.07	−.03	−.09	.06
250. stolid	.09	−.05	−.01	−.04	−.16	−.13	−.04	−.03	.01	.03	−.18	−.09
251. strong	.10	.11	.12	.10	.09	.32	.07	.20	.12	.13	.07	.34
252. stubborn	.06	.05	−.01	.16	.08	.07	.02	.11	−.06	.00	.13	.22
253. submissive	−.18	−.23	−.08	−.21	−.26	−.29	−.18	−.20	−.12	−.19	−.32	−.33
254. suggestible	.02	−.02	−.01	.11	−.13	−.19	−.16	.08	−.10	.01	−.16	−.27
255. sulky	−.03	−.11	.01	−.06	−.11	−.04	−.06	−.16	.01	−.12	−.11	.02
256. superstitious	−.06	−.05	−.08	.02	−.03	−.10	−.12	−.13	−.07	−.06	−.02	−.12
257. suspicious	−.06	−.10	−.05	.03	−.05	−.07	−.02	−.14	−.06	.00	−.06	.07
258. sympathetic	.06	−.02	.02	−.04	−.03	−.03	−.06	−.11	−.04	−.03	−.04	−.14
259. tactful	.09	.01	.09	.11	.03	.02	.10	.03	.06	.15	−.01	−.01
260. tactless	−.02	.00	−.04	.03	.06	.09	.00	.01	−.06	−.13	.09	.12
261. talkative	.20	.32	.26	.21	.24	.30	.03	.13	.10	.06	.28	.16
262. temperamental	.04	−.01	.02	.14	.03	.14	.04	−.06	−.03	−.02	.08	.13
263. tense	−.08	−.15	−.03	.06	−.12	−.21	.01	−.21	−.04	−.07	−.11	−.09
264. thankless	.01	−.10	.05	−.01	−.03	−.01	.02	−.12	.02	.01	.03	.04

Correlations of Observers' Adjectival Description with Scales of the CPI continued

		Scale: Sa						Scale: In				
		By Peers		By Spouses		By Staff		By Peers		By Spouses		By Staff
Adjectives		M	F	M	F	M	F	M	F	M	F	M	F
265.	thorough	.03	−.03	.01	.01	−.07	.06	.00	.10	.11	.03	.05	.15
266.	thoughtful	.02	−.02	.00	−.11	−.07	.01	.04	−.05	−.01	−.06	−.01	.01
267.	thrifty	−.03	−.07	−.07	−.09	−.14	−.04	−.10	−.01	−.07	−.08	−.20	−.05
268.	timid	−.12	−.33	−.11	−.17	−.31	−.33	−.22	−.28	−.04	−.20	−.31	−.30
269.	tolerant	.05	.01	.08	−.03	−.07	.02	.05	.00	.10	−.01	−.02	−.04
270.	touchy	.02	.07	−.15	.11	.01	−.07	−.03	.01	−.12	−.04	−.02	.02
271.	tough	.07	.11	−.03	.01	.14	.26	−.03	.15	−.02	.12	.11	.30
272.	trusting	.07	−.18	.08	.00	−.12	−.04	−.04	−.09	.00	−.03	−.11	−.13
273.	unaffected	−.08	−.05	.05	.07	−.13	−.11	.00	−.09	.01	.09	−.14	−.11
274.	unambitious	−.09	−.15	−.05	−.13	−.25	−.20	.02	−.08	−.15	−.11	−.21	−.32
275.	unassuming	−.13	−.25	.02	−.02	−.30	−.29	−.20	−.17	−.07	−.05	−.30	−.32
276.	unconventional	.09	.06	−.01	.19	.02	.08	.08	.03	.07	.12	.11	.12
277.	undependable	.05	.06	.01	.06	.03	.01	.12	.03	.02	−.08	.01	−.04
278.	understanding	.09	.06	.08	.07	−.03	.10	.00	−.03	.04	.06	.02	−.03
279.	unemotional	−.09	−.16	.00	.01	−.19	−.06	−.02	−.12	.16	−.06	−.14	−.05
280.	unexcitable	−.16	−.21	−.14	−.03	−.17	−.15	−.03	−.10	−.02	−.05	−.08	−.07
281.	unfriendly	−.08	−.07	−.12	.13	−.05	−.03	.09	.02	−.03	.03	−.02	.06
282.	uninhibited	.10	.13	−.01	.22	.23	.21	.09	.06	.03	.18	.24	.12
283.	unintelligent	−.05	−.05	.00	−.03	−.08	−.09	−.06	−.03	.00	−.01	−.10	−.11
284.	unkind	−.13	−.04	−.03	.03	.02	.13	−.09	−.02	.02	.02	.02	.13
285.	unrealistic	.03	.04	.07	.04	−.11	−.12	.02	−.04	.02	−.11	−.08	−.10
286.	unscrupulous	.03	−.04	−.16	.07	.02	.09	−.01	−.01	−.17	.10	.09	.02
287.	unselfish	.07	−.12	−.14	−.04	−.07	−.13	−.02	−.06	−.20	−.11	−.01	−.19
288.	unstable	.04	−.05	−.12	.05	−.07	−.10	.02	−.21	−.16	−.03	.00	−.11
289.	vindictive	.01	.08	.02	.02	.04	.05	.05	.12	.04	−.03	.02	.08
290.	versatile	.11	.30	.14	.13	.26	.28	.11	.16	.01	.15	.30	.22
291.	warm	.02	−.02	−.01	−.04	.08	.07	−.14	−.06	−.09	−.05	.08	−.06
292.	wary	.10	−.03	.03	−.01	−.08	−.14	.16	−.03	.07	.03	−.09	.02
293.	weak	−.14	−.30	−.12	−.08	−.16	−.23	−.13	−.19	−.14	−.22	−.22	−.19
294.	whiny	−.07	−.05	.01	.05	.07	−.08	−.12	−.14	−.18	−.13	−.02	−.06
295.	wholesome	−.11	−.01	−.02	.05	−.03	.13	−.14	.03	−.06	.03	−.01	.03
296.	wise	.19	.02	−.01	.01	−.02	.18	.10	.14	.09	.01	.13	.10
297.	withdrawn	−.26	−.36	−.20	−.18	−.33	−.28	−.09	−.27	−.12	−.16	−.30	−.17
298.	witty	.16	.23	.07	.05	.15	.23	.08	.07	.02	.02	.21	.11
299.	worrying	−.06	−.13	−.15	.01	−.21	−.21	−.17	−.20	−.17	−.13	−.20	−.09
300.	zany	.02	.22	.02	.17	.08	.08	−.01	.08	−.09	.11	.11	.00

Correlations of Observers' Adjectival Description with Scales of the CPI continued

		Scale: Em						Scale: Re					
		By Peers		By Spouses		By Staff		By Peers		By Spouses		By Staff	
Adjectives		M	F	M	F	M	F	M	F	M	F	M	F
001.	absent-minded	.08	−.02	−.08	.08	−.08	−.01	−.13	−.26	−.11	−.07	−.04	−.17
002.	active	.09	.17	.05	.12	.26	.22	.16	.21	−.06	−.06	−.11	.03
003.	adaptable	.12	.18	.15	.08	.28	.19	.14	.27	.06	−.03	−.02	−.02
004.	adventurous	.13	.17	.09	.15	.21	.27	−.17	−.03	−.13	−.18	−.24	−.19
005.	affected	.01	.19	.05	.02	.06	.09	.04	−.02	.10	−.03	−.02	−.04
006.	affectionate	.05	.05	.07	.00	.06	.00	−.02	.00	−.11	−.04	−.07	−.15
007.	aggressive	.02	.23	−.01	.19	.07	.27	−.01	−.03	−.15	−.14	−.06	.03
008.	alert	.09	.13	.07	.12	.27	.18	.16	.20	.15	.04	−.01	.10
009.	aloof	−.04	.00	−.10	−.07	−.16	−.11	−.02	−.20	−.06	−.13	−.11	.01
010.	ambitious	.18	.06	.09	.11	.22	.28	.22	.27	.05	−.08	.11	.13
011.	anxious	−.05	−.17	−.10	−.03	−.14	−.21	.05	−.03	.00	−.08	.05	−.12
012.	apathetic	−.11	−.10	−.14	−.04	−.26	−.14	−.29	−.24	−.16	.01	−.10	−.06
013.	appreciative	.10	−.06	.15	−.06	.11	−.09	.17	.13	.12	.06	.04	.01
014.	argumentative	−.12	.02	−.02	.12	.13	.16	−.12	−.12	−.01	−.18	−.01	.05
015.	arrogant	−.04	.02	.00	.05	.04	.09	−.11	−.16	−.16	−.02	−.13	−.04
016.	artistic	−.06	.05	−.01	.03	.11	.08	−.12	−.09	.01	−.12	.00	−.06
017.	assertive	−.05	.09	.06	.28	.19	.26	−.02	.12	.01	.02	−.05	.05
018.	attractive	.14	.08	−.03	.01	.15	.10	−.05	.01	−.04	−.08	−.21	−.13
019.	autocratic	−.01	.00	.01	.01	−.05	.08	.04	−.08	−.05	−.05	−.10	.06
020.	awkward	−.21	−.20	−.07	−.05	−.29	−.16	−.11	−.18	−.18	.00	−.09	−.10
021.	bitter	−.18	−.12	−.14	.00	−.16	−.04	.02	−.21	−.30	−.20	−.09	−.14
022.	blustery	.01	.03	.00	−.01	−.04	.01	−.08	−.11	−.03	−.01	−.08	−.09
023.	boastful	−.02	.10	.04	.03	.01	.13	−.11	−.07	−.16	−.09	−.08	−.04
024.	bossy	−.13	.07	−.10	−.04	−.01	.13	−.01	−.05	−.17	−.01	−.03	.02
025.	calm	.07	−.01	.01	−.08	.01	−.02	.10	.19	.08	.07	−.12	.02
026.	capable	.16	.00	−.02	.10	.23	.15	.24	.25	.10	.14	−.08	.12
027.	careless	.06	.13	−.06	−.06	.00	.03	−.28	−.30	−.15	−.08	−.15	−.23
028.	cautious	−.16	−.32	−.15	−.14	−.24	−.23	.17	.21	.03	.01	.01	−.01
029.	changeable	.13	.05	−.03	.04	.05	.06	−.05	−.16	−.12	−.11	−.10	−.28
030.	charming	.20	.10	.01	.08	.19	.11	−.16	.15	−.15	.03	−.18	−.02
031.	cheerful	.18	.15	.15	.03	.16	.11	.00	.14	.11	.07	−.06	.00
032.	civilized	.12	.04	−.04	−.07	.17	.02	.00	.16	.12	.01	−.05	.13
033.	clear-thinking	.08	.06	.05	.07	.25	.18	.23	.24	.23	.26	−.06	.16
034.	clever	.10	.13	.15	.14	.27	.25	−.05	.03	−.01	.03	−.12	.00
035.	coarse	−.01	−.03	−.07	.09	−.13	.05	−.08	−.20	−.18	−.04	−.18	−.15
036.	cold	−.24	−.18	−.17	−.03	−.16	−.07	−.14	−.10	.01	−.08	−.11	−.04
037.	commonplace	−.09	−.12	−.04	−.14	−.29	−.22	−.01	−.02	.04	−.06	−.10	−.12
038.	complaining	−.15	−.15	−.16	−.02	−.08	−.03	−.09	−.14	−.15	−.11	−.08	−.05
039.	complicated	.03	−.01	.07	.07	.07	.03	.04	−.08	.13	−.12	−.09	−.08
040.	conceited	−.03	.10	−.02	.05	.08	.13	−.13	−.09	−.16	−.01	.01	.01
041.	confident	.13	.17	−.02	.15	.27	.30	−.01	.19	.03	−.01	−.12	.05
042.	confused	−.04	−.01	−.15	−.02	−.12	−.15	−.09	−.14	−.23	−.13	−.01	−.24
043.	conscientious	.07	−.17	.01	.06	−.04	−.08	.26	.34	.26	.14	.14	.19
044.	conservative	−.01	−.10	−.16	−.23	−.23	−.27	.05	.18	.16	.03	.05	.09

Correlations of Observers' Adjectival Description with Scales of the CPI continued

		Scale: Em						Scale: Re				
		By Peers		By Spouses		By Staff		By Peers		By Spouses		By Staff
Adjectives		M	F	M	F	M	F	M	F	M	F	M	F
045.	considerate	.10	−.09	.07	−.01	.04	−.05	.16	.21	.10	.07	−.06	−.06
046.	contented	.07	.12	−.02	−.12	−.02	−.13	−.06	.13	.25	.00	−.18	−.02
047.	conventional	−.01	−.08	−.08	−.11	−.23	−.26	.07	.23	.11	.09	.05	.02
048.	cool	.16	−.01	−.02	−.01	.02	.00	−.16	−.11	.00	−.09	−.09	−.01
049.	cooperative	.05	−.03	.10	−.07	.10	.02	.06	.27	.11	.18	−.01	.01
050.	courageous	.08	.02	.06	−.04	.06	.13	−.03	.00	−.03	.01	−.08	−.09
051.	cowardly	−.05	.00	−.04	−.08	−.11	−.08	−.08	−.02	−.04	.04	−.06	−.08
052.	cruel	−.20	−.09	−.14	.05	−.07	.00	−.10	−.07	−.21	−.08	−.17	−.09
053.	curious	.05	.02	.02	.09	.19	.25	−.02	−.06	−.04	−.04	−.08	−.08
054.	cynical	−.06	−.05	−.04	.02	−.02	.13	−.05	−.19	−.09	−.19	−.26	−.09
055.	daring	.03	.17	.05	.02	.15	.20	−.19	−.07	−.13	−.08	−.19	−.24
056.	deceitful	.02	.00	−.14	.00	.04	.05	−.02	−.08	−.19	−.08	.00	−.11
057.	defensive	−.16	−.19	−.02	−.03	−.17	−.11	−.08	−.14	−.03	−.04	−.05	−.02
058.	deliberate	−.08	−.11	−.03	−.10	−.18	−.11	.22	.09	.05	−.09	−.03	.12
059.	demanding	−.04	.02	.01	−.02	.08	.13	.04	−.02	−.05	−.10	−.09	−.06
060.	dependable	.01	−.07	.00	−.10	−.01	−.08	.30	.28	.16	.13	.07	.22
061.	dependent	.07	−.07	−.04	−.15	−.18	−.20	.02	−.07	.00	.08	.05	−.17
062.	despondent	−.03	−.15	.06	.05	−.12	−.23	.00	−.18	−.13	.05	−.02	−.07
063.	determined	−.02	.06	−.08	.05	.12	.21	.20	.21	.01	.00	−.06	.06
064.	dignified	.10	.00	−.06	−.04	.03	−.19	.08	.17	.11	.05	.10	.11
065.	discreet	.16	.02	−.01	−.03	−.03	−.15	.15	.23	.14	.07	.06	.16
066.	disorderly	.04	.06	.15	.04	.03	.03	−.23	−.24	−.17	.00	−.17	−.25
067.	dissatisfied	−.07	−.10	−.07	−.02	−.05	−.01	−.08	−.17	−.18	.01	−.11	−.19
068.	distractible	−.06	.02	−.09	−.03	.00	−.02	−.21	−.13	−.28	−.02	−.15	−.30
069.	distrustful	−.13	−.14	−.13	−.09	−.11	−.07	−.14	−.15	−.04	−.15	−.10	−.16
070.	dominant	.07	.17	−.01	−.02	.15	.26	.10	.01	.09	−.15	−.15	.11
071.	dreamy	.14	.05	−.03	.10	−.05	−.09	−.09	−.06	−.21	−.14	−.06	−.21
072.	dull	−.12	−.18	.00	−.08	−.24	−.13	.02	−.01	−.06	−.01	−.08	−.09
073.	easygoing	.16	.11	−.02	−.12	.02	.05	−.14	−.01	−.10	.04	−.26	−.20
074.	effeminate	.01	−.03	.11	−.04	.00	−.05	.01	.00	−.03	−.03	.04	−.08
075.	efficient	−.05	−.05	−.11	−.04	.19	.10	.19	.29	.17	.09	.14	.21
076.	egotistical	−.09	.12	.01	.10	.11	.17	−.08	−.07	−.11	−.05	−.10	.02
077.	emotional	−.05	−.02	.03	−.05	.05	.02	−.09	−.10	−.10	−.15	−.08	−.28
078.	energetic	.09	.07	.11	.07	.23	.25	−.04	.21	−.06	−.01	−.01	.03
079.	enterprising	.14	.06	.07	.10	.26	.29	.15	.22	−.05	.07	−.03	.08
080.	enthusiastic	.09	.10	.23	.13	.19	.24	.05	.13	−.02	.04	−.09	−.05
081.	evasive	−.07	.03	−.13	−.09	−.18	−.05	−.06	−.09	−.05	−.12	−.16	−.11
082.	excitable	−.04	.10	−.01	.02	.07	.09	−.06	−.08	−.13	−.23	−.08	−.18
083.	fair-minded	.10	−.02	.09	−.02	.14	.06	.10	.19	.09	.13	−.04	.05
084.	fault-finding	−.16	−.14	−.08	−.09	−.05	.05	−.08	−.07	−.05	−.08	−.12	−.06
085.	fearful	−.08	−.14	−.11	.00	−.15	−.20	−.05	−.12	−.20	−.05	−.06	−.16
086.	feminine	−.06	.00	−.05	−.04	.03	−.01	.20	.12	.01	−.12	−.03	−.12
087.	fickle	.03	.14	−.07	.01	.01	.07	−.14	−.19	.02	−.15	−.14	−.21
088.	flirtatious	.02	.32	−.14	−.01	.10	.19	−.21	−.05	−.29	−.23	−.19	−.26

Correlations of Observers' Adjectival Description with Scales of the CPI continued

		Scale: Em						Scale: Re				
		By Peers		By Spouses		By Staff		By Peers		By Spouses		By Staff
Adjectives		M	F	M	F	M	F	M	F	M	F	M	F
089.	foolish	.00	.02	.04	.01	−.13	−.03	−.17	−.23	−.01	−.15	−.12	−.23
090.	forceful	.01	.05	−.01	.05	.09	.21	.06	.01	−.08	−.06	−.06	.07
091.	foresighted	.07	.07	.02	−.08	.19	.19	.19	.26	.16	.10	.01	.18
092.	forgetful	.02	−.02	−.01	.07	−.03	−.07	−.25	−.23	−.09	−.13	−.14	−.12
093.	forgiving	.21	.07	.07	−.05	−.01	−.09	.21	.06	.00	−.02	−.11	−.15
094.	formal	−.02	−.10	.01	−.06	−.07	−.17	.21	.13	.09	.03	.07	.11
095.	frank	−.05	.02	.06	.01	.11	.22	.05	.00	−.02	.01	−.19	−.08
096.	friendly	.21	.14	.20	.04	.12	.11	−.02	.09	.07	.01	−.09	−.06
097.	frivolous	−.04	.15	.03	.03	.02	.03	−.04	−.05	−.03	−.03	−.19	−.25
098.	fussy	−.19	−.06	−.08	−.06	−.17	−.12	−.12	.00	−.01	−.07	−.01	.05
099.	generous	.05	.00	.13	−.02	.06	−.01	.08	.10	.02	.07	−.10	−.07
100.	gentle	.08	−.12	.01	−.10	−.04	−.14	.10	.13	.07	.02	−.13	−.15
101.	gloomy	−.10	−.17	−.17	−.07	−.17	−.11	−.02	−.15	−.13	−.03	.00	−.04
102.	good-looking	.17	.19	−.02	−.03	.07	.08	.04	−.01	−.02	−.08	−.24	−.13
103.	good-natured	.10	.07	.04	.01	.11	.06	.02	.18	.06	.10	−.15	−.11
104.	greedy	−.15	−.06	−.07	.01	−.01	.04	−.15	−.12	−.17	−.10	−.11	−.05
105.	handsome	.12	.02	.10	.08	.07	−.03	−.07	.03	.03	.03	−.22	.02
106.	hard-headed	−.19	−.09	−.06	−.02	−.03	.03	.00	−.07	−.07	−.14	−.04	.07
107.	hard-hearted	−.15	−.12	−.17	−.02	−.10	.04	−.09	−.09	−.05	−.11	−.13	.00
108.	hasty	−.10	.07	−.15	.02	.05	.09	−.09	−.17	−.20	−.04	−.02	−.16
109.	headstrong	−.07	.02	−.08	.14	.05	.18	−.04	−.08	−.12	−.12	−.13	−.10
110.	healthy	.06	−.02	−.09	.03	.07	.19	−.10	.04	.10	−.02	−.25	−.13
111.	helpful	.09	−.03	.01	.05	.06	−.02	.10	.22	.06	−.01	−.06	−.06
112.	high-strung	−.13	−.04	−.09	.02	.03	−.03	−.11	−.10	−.12	−.07	−.02	−.10
113.	honest	−.02	−.09	.04	−.02	.05	.01	.13	.19	.15	.15	−.01	.01
114.	hostile	−.18	−.11	−.19	.07	−.09	−.02	−.13	−.16	−.10	−.01	−.06	−.04
115.	humorous	.16	.11	.09	.23	.14	.18	−.17	−.03	−.11	.01	−.25	−.03
116.	hurried	−.05	.04	−.03	.11	.03	.07	−.08	−.10	−.01	.05	−.07	−.04
117.	idealistic	.04	.05	.13	.10	.13	.10	.03	.12	.02	.08	.03	−.05
118.	imaginative	.16	.15	.10	.18	.23	.21	−.08	−.03	−.05	−.01	−.06	−.06
119.	immature	−.07	−.06	−.07	−.03	−.05	−.11	−.19	−.26	−.19	−.08	−.03	−.15
120.	impatient	−.11	−.10	−.08	.02	.09	.13	−.11	−.22	−.06	−.18	−.08	−.09
121.	impulsive	.06	.12	.01	.12	.09	.07	−.23	−.18	−.28	−.20	−.14	−.23
122.	independent	.18	.08	−.05	.02	.18	.25	.12	.08	.10	−.07	−.19	.02
123.	indifferent	−.14	−.06	−.12	−.06	−.15	−.09	−.16	−.13	−.04	−.09	−.19	−.16
124.	individualistic	.09	.13	.08	.26	.11	.18	−.03	−.07	−.03	−.10	−.21	−.06
125.	industrious	.10	−.15	−.02	−.04	.00	.07	.21	.30	.04	−.01	.08	.20
126.	infantile	−.10	.00	−.09	−.14	−.08	−.13	−.15	−.19	−.17	−.12	−.14	−.24
127.	informal	.05	.07	.00	.02	.09	.16	−.12	−.01	−.11	.02	−.29	−.21
128.	ingenious	.08	.10	.16	.08	.22	.16	−.03	−.03	.07	−.02	.04	.01
129.	inhibited	−.08	−.17	−.16	−.14	−.26	−.27	.21	.02	.00	.01	.03	−.01
130.	initiative	.07	.10	.13	.12	.25	.28	.05	.14	.07	.21	−.01	.07
131.	insightful	.11	.13	.19	.17	.26	.21	.06	.20	.12	.18	.00	.05
132.	intelligent	.04	.09	.13	.08	.28	.19	.11	.18	.16	.02	−.02	.19

		Scale: Em						Scale: Re				
		By Peers		By Spouses		By Staff		By Peers		By Spouses		By Staff
Adjectives		M	F	M	F	M	F	M	F	M	F	M	F
133.	interests—narrow	−.20	−.10	−.19	−.26	−.32	−.33	.04	−.09	−.11	−.12	−.07	−.13
134.	interests—wide	.17	.15	.13	.22	.30	.32	−.12	.12	.14	.09	.01	.06
135.	intolerant	−.18	.06	−.12	−.14	−.08	−.12	−.10	−.15	−.14	−.06	−.10	−.04
136.	inventive	−.01	.08	.10	.10	.18	.18	.02	−.02	.02	.01	−.06	−.01
137.	irresponsible	−.01	.06	.00	.01	.08	.06	−.24	−.28	−.07	−.08	−.12	−.22
138.	irritable	−.17	−.15	−.06	−.08	−.07	−.01	−.06	−.18	−.04	−.12	−.05	.03
139.	jolly	.17	.27	−.02	.09	.05	.08	−.13	.09	−.08	−.06	−.10	−.08
140.	kind	.08	−.03	.04	−.02	−.01	−.02	.08	.13	.08	.00	−.21	−.10
141.	lazy	.07	.08	.15	−.01	−.01	.01	−.28	−.32	−.08	−.12	−.19	−.18
142.	leisurely	.11	.22	.07	.03	.00	−.01	−.21	−.05	−.07	−.07	−.20	−.20
143.	logical	.10	−.01	−.01	−.14	.11	.04	.17	.19	.09	.16	.02	.25
144.	loud	−.04	.10	−.05	.02	.04	.15	−.11	−.14	−.01	−.18	−.13	−.07
145.	loyal	.14	−.12	−.03	−.14	−.06	−.15	.13	.06	−.02	−.05	−.07	−.09
146.	mannerly	.09	−.05	−.01	.05	−.05	−.11	.12	.25	.16	.08	.01	.02
147.	masculine	.02	.10	−.06	.02	.01	.01	.02	−.18	−.12	−.05	−.27	.03
148.	mature	.18	.05	.02	−.04	.16	.04	.24	.23	.25	.10	−.05	.14
149.	meek	−.12	−.19	.00	−.13	−.22	−.18	−.03	−.09	−.14	.08	−.09	−.13
150.	methodical	−.11	−.21	−.12	.04	−.14	−.15	.13	.14	.13	.08	.15	.18
151.	mild	−.07	−.07	.03	−.19	−.13	−.26	.06	.08	.04	.07	−.03	−.05
152.	mischievous	−.05	.21	−.11	−.02	.14	.16	−.34	−.06	−.23	−.12	−.21	−.15
153.	moderate	.11	−.01	−.06	−.06	−.14	−.12	.17	.15	.20	.17	.09	.06
154.	modest	−.04	−.17	.00	−.12	−.16	−.27	.13	.11	.07	.13	.04	−.04
155.	moody	−.11	−.14	−.11	−.01	−.15	−.08	−.04	−.25	−.14	−.18	−.08	−.22
156.	nagging	−.16	−.07	−.17	−.04	−.08	−.04	.03	−.02	−.23	−.08	−.09	−.09
157.	natural	.16	−.03	.02	.03	.17	.11	−.05	.03	−.03	.03	−.07	−.01
158.	nervous	−.09	−.21	−.26	−.08	−.14	−.15	−.02	−.10	−.14	−.09	.06	−.11
159.	noisy	.00	.16	−.04	−.05	.01	.11	−.18	−.03	.03	−.18	−.08	−.09
160.	obliging	.12	−.01	−.04	−.01	−.04	−.11	−.02	.18	.05	.06	.07	−.03
161.	obnoxious	−.16	−.04	.03	.12	.03	.01	−.08	−.19	−.10	−.08	−.12	−.09
162.	opinionated	−.09	−.01	.03	.05	.00	.13	−.02	−.06	−.10	−.18	−.07	.00
163.	opportunistic	.10	.08	.01	.05	.12	.23	.07	.04	−.09	−.12	−.10	−.10
164.	optimistic	.21	.06	.15	.16	.21	.17	−.04	.17	.06	.05	−.07	−.01
165.	organized	.00	−.11	−.11	−.11	.15	.06	.23	.36	.14	.10	.16	.26
166.	original	.08	.16	.11	.15	.24	.16	−.03	−.04	−.04	−.07	−.05	−.06
167.	outgoing	.24	.23	.21	.32	.24	.30	−.12	.11	−.06	−.03	−.09	.01
168.	outspoken	.00	.20	.03	.16	.13	.20	−.07	−.01	−.10	−.03	−.06	.01
169.	painstaking	−.10	−.13	−.02	−.04	−.24	−.23	.15	.23	.05	−.07	.12	.06
170.	patient	.12	−.13	.11	−.15	−.13	−.16	.11	.27	.10	.04	.00	.00
171.	peaceable	−.02	−.03	.02	−.08	−.13	−.23	.07	.23	−.04	.02	−.01	.00
172.	peculiar	−.16	−.09	−.19	−.03	−.18	−.06	.01	−.14	−.15	−.16	−.09	−.06
173.	persevering	.04	−.10	−.03	.05	.01	−.05	.14	.22	.05	.08	.12	.16
174.	persistent	−.01	.01	.01	.09	−.03	.19	.09	.19	.01	.02	−.05	.05
175.	pessimistic	−.14	−.16	−.07	−.06	−.08	−.14	−.01	−.24	−.10	−.12	−.07	−.05
176.	planful	.00	−.05	−.13	−.05	.11	.09	.22	.25	.07	.02	.03	.19

Correlations of Observers' Adjectival Description with Scales of the CPI continued

		Scale: Em						Scale: Re					
		By Peers		By Spouses		By Staff		By Peers		By Spouses		By Staff	
Adjectives		M	F	M	F	M	F	M	F	M	F	M	F
177.	pleasant	.25	.07	.00	.06	.11	.02	.08	.12	.03	.15	−.12	.04
178.	pleasure-seeking	.12	.23	.10	.16	.20	.14	−.31	−.13	−.18	−.17	−.22	−.31
179.	poised	.11	.08	.04	.08	.22	.14	.06	.17	.08	−.03	.01	.19
180.	polished	.21	.03	.11	.13	.16	.12	.09	.15	.08	.10	.03	.07
181.	practical	.07	−.12	−.02	−.06	−.02	.01	.21	.21	.12	.09	−.11	.01
182.	praising	.16	.04	.11	−.04	.07	−.04	.12	.17	−.03	.03	.00	−.03
183.	precise	−.04	−.18	−.02	.05	−.05	−.03	.19	.12	.19	.11	−.01	.15
184.	prejudiced	−.06	−.09	−.21	−.14	−.15	−.15	−.13	−.05	−.28	−.20	−.08	−.08
185.	preoccupied	.04	−.03	.01	.06	−.17	−.11	−.03	−.20	−.06	−.10	−.03	−.15
186.	progressive	.19	.11	.05	.08	.21	.27	.10	−.02	.04	.10	−.11	.00
187.	prudish	−.15	−.18	−.02	−.10	−.18	−.30	.04	.17	−.09	−.09	−.02	.08
188.	quarrelsome	−.14	−.10	−.14	−.04	.02	.08	−.10	−.10	−.18	−.15	−.06	−.08
189.	queer	−.13	−.17	.05	.00	−.13	−.01	.00	−.17	−.04	.00	−.01	.02
190.	quick	.05	.11	.01	.07	.25	.20	−.14	.03	−.03	−.06	−.11	−.01
191.	quiet	−.08	−.22	−.15	−.26	−.24	−.27	.13	.05	.12	.12	−.02	−.05
192.	quitting	−.11	−.08	−.02	−.12	−.05	−.15	−.04	−.16	−.17	.04	−.11	−.15
193.	rational	.12	.04	.13	.05	.12	.12	.17	.31	.14	.12	−.10	.13
194.	rattle-brained	−.04	.08	−.03	−.05	−.07	.00	−.11	−.18	−.19	−.04	−.07	−.25
195.	realistic	.12	.08	.05	−.04	.12	.13	.19	.20	.01	.11	−.10	.00
196.	reasonable	.16	.07	.09	.04	.07	−.02	.27	.25	.11	.13	−.03	.09
197.	rebellious	−.07	.09	−.02	.03	.04	.15	−.16	−.32	−.22	−.14	−.16	−.17
198.	reckless	.03	.18	−.13	−.03	.07	.05	−.22	−.27	−.27	−.25	−.18	−.24
199.	reflective	.04	.03	.10	.14	.10	.04	.12	.08	.01	.17	−.01	−.02
200.	relaxed	.19	.12	.11	−.11	.13	.16	−.08	.20	−.01	.00	−.19	−.01
201.	reliable	.04	−.03	.01	−.03	.03	−.08	.20	.31	.08	.07	.05	.12
202.	resentful	−.05	−.09	−.14	.02	−.11	−.03	.01	−.27	−.16	−.08	−.08	−.12
203.	reserved	−.07	−.25	−.17	−.20	−.21	−.26	.20	.08	.09	.11	.00	−.03
204.	resourceful	.18	.14	.13	.16	.30	.27	.19	.24	.01	−.05	.02	.10
205.	responsible	.04	−.04	.03	.00	.04	−.06	.26	.32	.06	.03	.08	.18
206.	restless	−.07	.01	.05	.12	.03	.11	−.17	−.27	−.24	−.09	−.11	−.19
207.	retiring	−.05	−.28	.02	−.16	−.27	−.27	.02	−.06	−.02	.04	−.01	.01
208.	rigid	−.13	−.15	−.07	−.12	−.24	−.25	−.02	.02	−.06	−.08	−.04	.06
209.	robust	.14	.12	.08	.08	.01	.16	−.06	−.07	−.04	.06	−.23	−.07
210.	rude	−.11	.02	−.08	.02	−.05	.05	−.15	−.21	−.15	.00	−.15	−.03
211.	sarcastic	.00	.04	.03	.01	.06	.20	−.12	−.21	−.08	−.13	−.19	−.09
212.	self-centered	−.04	.01	−.15	.03	.07	.10	−.12	−.12	−.20	−.11	−.10	−.11
213.	self-confident	.22	.17	.06	.11	.29	.31	.01	.10	.00	−.03	−.11	.08
214.	self-controlled	.05	−.01	.06	−.02	−.02	−.14	.12	.27	.11	.06	.02	.15
215.	self-denying	−.04	−.09	−.08	−.16	−.24	−.27	.17	.06	−.03	.00	.05	.05
216.	self-pitying	−.07	−.13	−.05	−.05	−.07	−.09	.05	−.12	−.12	−.06	−.01	−.07
217.	self-punishing	.02	−.16	.00	−.02	−.12	−.11	.09	−.02	−.15	−.06	.01	−.10
218.	self-seeking	.01	.05	.02	.10	.12	.17	−.05	−.10	−.14	−.10	−.09	−.13
219.	selfish	−.02	.01	.03	.02	.03	.02	−.13	−.13	.01	.00	−.07	−.13
220.	sensitive	−.10	−.18	.06	.02	.04	−.04	.15	−.05	−.02	.05	−.10	−.19

Correlations of Observers' Adjectival Description with Scales of the CPI continued

| | | Scale: Em | | | | | | | Scale: Re | | | | |
| | | By Peers | | By Spouses | | By Staff | | By Peers | | By Spouses | | By Staff | |
Adjectives		M	F	M	F	M	F	M	F	M	F	M	F
221.	sentimental	.13	.00	.01	−.04	.00	−.06	−.05	−.03	−.03	.04	−.08	−.20
222.	serious	−.03	−.25	.03	−.04	−.10	−.03	.27	.11	.09	.02	.03	.12
223.	severe	−.04	−.05	−.02	−.02	−.14	−.13	−.05	.02	−.12	−.01	−.12	.04
224.	sexy	.03	.21	.03	.07	.10	.13	−.07	−.12	−.22	−.15	−.27	−.20
225.	shallow	−.15	.12	−.12	−.17	−.12	−.16	−.15	−.10	.00	−.03	−.09	−.24
226.	sharp-witted	.20	.04	.14	.18	.21	.17	−.07	−.05	−.01	−.08	−.10	−.04
227.	shiftless	−.03	−.03	−.03	−.04	−.05	−.05	−.08	−.20	−.12	−.21	−.19	−.18
228.	show-off	−.06	.19	.11	.04	.10	.20	−.22	−.14	−.18	−.17	−.16	−.05
229.	shrewd	.05	−.09	−.04	.13	.16	.13	.02	−.05	−.17	−.05	.02	.02
230.	shy	−.13	−.26	−.16	−.23	−.25	−.26	.12	.03	−.01	.03	−.11	−.20
231.	silent	−.16	−.19	−.18	−.18	−.25	−.22	.00	.06	.00	−.04	−.17	−.11
232.	simple	−.04	−.17	−.08	−.14	−.31	−.28	−.07	.05	−.10	−.10	−.09	−.16
233.	sincere	.13	−.10	.09	−.09	.01	−.04	.18	.18	.08	.13	.04	.01
234.	slipshod	−.02	.07	−.11	.05	.01	.02	−.15	−.21	−.07	−.09	−.05	−.12
235.	slow	−.04	−.12	−.02	−.04	−.29	−.24	−.05	−.13	−.13	−.09	.03	−.09
236.	sly	−.01	−.01	−.18	.12	.04	.06	−.02	−.09	−.32	−.16	−.10	−.16
237.	smug	.00	.11	−.04	−.06	.07	.05	−.08	−.04	−.09	−.11	−.08	−.06
238.	snobbish	−.04	.01	−.02	.11	.05	.04	−.06	−.04	−.10	.01	−.01	−.04
239.	sociable	.28	.24	.18	.20	.24	.19	−.10	.15	−.04	−.07	−.11	−.07
240.	soft-hearted	.11	.03	.01	−.13	.01	−.09	.03	.05	−.09	.00	−.04	−.18
241.	sophisticated	.10	.04	.09	.11	.20	.22	−.06	.03	.07	−.01	−.06	.07
242.	spendthrift	.05	.07	.02	−.04	.02	.07	−.18	−.11	.00	−.12	−.07	−.12
243.	spineless	−.10	−.16	.15	−.08	−.17	−.10	−.11	−.17	.06	−.03	−.09	−.04
244.	spontaneous	.12	.24	.14	.21	.20	.18	−.15	.02	−.07	−.08	−.11	−.12
245.	spunky	−.02	.16	−.06	.14	.10	.17	−.17	.06	−.19	−.13	−.08	−.09
246.	stable	.16	−.04	−.04	−.02	.06	.01	.23	.21	.10	.08	−.06	.17
247.	steady	.07	−.10	−.05	−.06	−.09	−.06	.19	.22	.06	.08	−.09	.07
248.	stern	.02	−.13	−.23	.01	−.18	−.06	.05	.06	−.08	−.13	−.06	.05
249.	stingy	−.12	−.13	−.12	.05	−.17	−.02	−.03	−.17	−.18	−.15	−.06	−.03
250.	stolid	−.01	−.18	.05	−.03	−.30	−.18	−.04	−.03	.02	−.08	−.11	.04
251.	strong	.08	.03	.00	−.01	.05	.26	.05	.12	−.07	−.13	−.23	.03
252.	stubborn	−.05	−.07	−.05	.04	−.09	.07	−.04	−.08	−.08	−.14	−.09	.04
253.	submissive	.04	−.08	−.07	−.11	−.21	−.21	−.06	.03	−.02	.03	.09	−.05
254.	suggestible	.18	.11	−.08	.05	−.11	−.16	−.07	−.01	−.11	−.04	.05	−.08
255.	sulky	−.14	−.19	−.01	−.02	−.12	−.07	−.04	−.19	−.11	−.11	−.10	−.24
256.	superstitious	−.04	−.05	−.15	.01	−.10	−.15	.02	.00	−.30	−.19	.01	−.22
257.	suspicious	−.07	−.18	−.17	−.04	−.18	−.06	−.09	−.15	−.20	−.19	−.17	−.14
258.	sympathetic	.16	.00	.14	−.08	.11	−.05	.07	.06	−.02	.06	−.08	−.10
259.	tactful	.21	.09	.14	.10	.18	.02	.05	.25	.16	.07	.08	.04
260.	tactless	−.14	−.05	−.14	.02	−.06	.05	−.09	−.13	−.06	.02	−.11	−.05
261.	talkative	.19	.21	.10	.17	.20	.28	−.11	−.02	−.11	−.14	−.07	−.01
262.	temperamental	−.13	−.08	−.04	.01	−.03	.07	−.06	−.23	−.20	−.16	−.15	−.15
263.	tense	−.21	−.19	−.13	−.08	−.11	−.18	.04	−.09	−.08	−.03	.03	−.09
264.	thankless	−.14	−.15	−.08	−.01	−.09	−.01	−.13	−.16	−.01	.04	−.10	−.03

Correlations of Observers' Adjectival Description with Scales of the CPI continued

	Scale: Em						Scale: Re					
	By Peers		By Spouses		By Staff		By Peers		By Spouses		By Staff	
Adjectives	M	F	M	F	M	F	M	F	M	F	M	F
265. thorough	.03	−.05	−.05	−.02	.03	.02	.27	.23	−.02	.09	.17	.22
266. thoughtful	.10	.04	.05	.01	.13	.06	.23	.14	.05	.13	−.02	.07
267. thrifty	.04	−.11	−.04	−.15	−.18	−.11	.17	.21	.09	.05	−.09	−.04
268. timid	−.16	−.31	−.03	−.12	−.21	−.25	−.01	−.02	−.03	−.01	−.06	−.14
269. tolerant	.19	.06	.22	−.03	.13	.08	.08	.18	.04	.06	−.08	−.02
270. touchy	−.12	−.04	−.13	−.04	−.06	−.14	−.04	−.18	−.05	−.17	−.06	−.12
271. tough	−.09	.04	−.13	.02	−.03	.18	.09	−.09	−.13	−.08	−.21	−.06
272. trusting	.18	.00	.22	.02	.00	−.07	.15	.17	.05	.06	−.07	−.11
273. unaffected	.08	−.03	.10	.01	−.02	−.13	.04	.08	−.07	−.03	.03	−.03
274. unambitious	−.07	.04	−.09	−.10	−.17	−.23	−.07	−.21	−.16	.08	−.14	−.16
275. unassuming	−.01	−.18	.00	−.07	−.12	−.22	−.04	.11	−.03	.13	.03	−.05
276. unconventional	.09	.01	.06	.07	.09	.09	−.08	−.30	−.10	−.13	−.18	−.14
277. undependable	−.01	.11	.05	−.02	.00	.00	−.21	−.28	−.03	−.16	−.07	−.16
278. understanding	.17	.06	.10	.08	.15	.08	.08	.13	−.04	.09	−.15	−.08
279. unemotional	−.10	−.13	.02	−.03	−.18	−.08	.01	−.03	.06	.04	−.22	−.03
280. unexcitable	−.10	−.14	−.09	−.10	−.13	−.17	.03	−.04	−.01	.03	−.08	.05
281. unfriendly	−.12	−.11	−.18	−.03	−.14	−.07	−.11	−.13	−.06	−.07	−.08	−.05
282. uninhibited	.16	.05	.08	.13	.19	.22	−.14	−.14	−.06	−.03	−.12	−.20
283. unintelligent	.01	.09	.00	−.03	−.12	−.15	.01	−.17	.00	−.07	−.04	−.05
284. unkind	−.13	−.10	−.12	−.02	−.03	.03	.03	−.17	.00	.02	−.14	−.11
285. unrealistic	.00	.01	.05	−.02	−.08	−.08	−.11	−.11	−.03	−.12	−.06	−.20
286. unscrupulous	−.02	.05	−.14	.11	.03	−.01	−.16	−.17	−.25	.00	−.09	−.11
287. unselfish	.10	−.10	−.07	−.06	.06	−.17	.15	.18	.01	−.01	−.09	−.05
288. unstable	.00	−.04	−.25	.08	−.02	−.07	−.13	−.18	−.23	−.13	−.04	−.16
289. vindictive	−.08	.04	−.05	−.04	−.07	.03	−.15	−.06	−.14	−.22	−.10	−.05
290. versatile	.21	.22	.05	.02	.32	.28	−.05	−.01	−.10	−.10	−.05	−.02
291. warm	.20	.14	.08	−.03	.15	.06	−.02	.20	.01	.01	−.08	−.05
292. wary	.07	−.13	−.07	−.01	−.17	−.11	.04	−.05	−.13	−.05	−.12	−.09
293. weak	.03	−.11	−.08	−.08	−.15	−.19	−.01	−.03	−.14	.05	−.01	−.13
294. whiny	−.07	−.14	.02	.01	−.03	−.05	−.07	.00	−.12	−.13	.03	−.06
295. wholesome	.09	−.01	.05	.07	.04	.08	.11	.18	.07	.08	−.09	.02
296. wise	.17	.06	.14	.03	.09	.13	.11	.19	.14	.05	−.05	.12
297. withdrawn	−.11	−.29	−.21	−.09	−.27	−.20	.10	−.08	−.16	.07	−.11	−.14
298. witty	.14	.13	.12	.09	.23	.22	−.14	−.02	−.08	−.06	−.17	−.01
299. worrying	−.06	−.20	−.23	−.01	−.15	−.14	.03	.01	−.26	−.01	.00	−.06
300. zany	−.07	.15	.04	.13	.05	.10	−.11	−.08	−.20	−.18	−.15	−.22

Correlations of Observers' Adjectival Description with Scales of the CPI continued

		Scale: So						Scale: Sc				
		By Peers		By Spouses		By Staff		By Peers		By Spouses		By Staff
Adjectives		M	F	M	F	M	F	M	F	M	F	M	F
001.	absent-minded	−.08	−.13	−.12	−.22	−.04	−.20	.00	−.10	.02	−.13	.03	−.10
002.	active	.18	.13	−.08	−.03	−.05	−.07	−.06	−.07	−.13	−.06	−.18	−.18
003.	adaptable	.23	.19	.00	−.05	.11	.04	.08	.14	.01	−.03	−.05	−.09
004.	adventurous	−.15	−.14	−.17	−.15	−.15	−.22	−.13	−.28	−.27	−.17	−.26	−.34
005.	affected	−.06	.02	−.07	−.04	−.14	−.12	−.07	−.08	−.01	−.02	−.06	−.13
006.	affectionate	.14	.02	−.10	.04	−.01	−.02	.00	.05	−.11	.01	−.03	−.09
007.	aggressive	−.09	−.03	−.13	−.22	−.14	−.18	−.13	−.21	−.17	−.23	−.15	−.17
008.	alert	.15	.11	.07	.02	.00	.02	−.01	−.05	−.02	.02	−.08	−.06
009.	aloof	−.04	−.15	−.06	−.19	−.15	−.04	−.01	−.05	−.03	−.08	.00	.11
010.	ambitious	.13	.22	−.02	−.05	.06	.03	.05	.07	−.05	−.08	−.01	−.09
011.	anxious	−.00	.01	−.09	−.13	−.12	−.26	−.10	−.01	−.02	−.10	.03	−.05
012.	apathetic	−.19	−.05	−.21	−.08	−.11	−.05	−.09	−.09	−.08	−.03	−.01	.06
013.	appreciative	.21	.08	.11	.09	.07	.07	.14	.18	.10	.05	.06	.13
014.	argumentative	−.22	−.11	−.07	−.21	−.15	−.14	−.14	−.18	−.08	−.25	−.13	−.08
015.	arrogant	−.23	−.08	−.16	−.10	−.22	−.14	−.13	−.22	−.21	−.07	−.19	−.13
016.	artistic	−.02	−.09	−.06	−.14	−.03	−.13	−.12	−.17	−.01	−.06	−.06	−.01
017.	assertive	−.08	−.05	−.06	−.15	−.04	−.06	.00	−.20	−.09	−.14	−.13	−.17
018.	attractive	.12	−.01	−.05	−.08	.00	.02	.04	−.03	.00	−.04	−.11	−.09
019.	autocratic	−.09	−.06	−.08	−.07	−.13	−.08	.00	−.16	−.09	−.13	−.11	−.09
020.	awkward	−.05	−.08	−.23	−.06	−.10	−.16	−.05	−.04	−.17	−.09	.02	.03
021.	bitter	−.08	−.12	−.28	−.27	−.20	−.27	−.03	−.21	−.17	−.23	−.12	−.20
022.	blustery	−.16	−.09	−.07	−.14	−.16	−.17	−.18	−.20	−.10	−.13	−.11	−.10
023.	boastful	−.21	−.08	−.13	−.17	−.16	−.15	−.15	−.22	−.23	−.15	−.18	−.11
024.	bossy	−.17	−.03	−.23	−.10	−.14	−.11	−.08	−.15	−.22	−.21	−.12	−.09
025.	calm	.18	.10	.13	.06	.02	.16	.13	.32	.20	.22	.00	.14
026.	capable	.24	.18	.09	.09	.00	.12	.13	.14	.07	.12	−.08	.02
027.	careless	−.31	−.23	−.22	−.21	−.18	−.30	−.21	−.24	−.14	−.18	−.11	−.19
028.	cautious	.21	.24	−.03	.08	.01	.10	.05	.34	.07	.17	.12	.18
029.	changeable	−.14	−.20	−.23	−.24	−.21	−.29	−.13	−.28	−.14	−.24	−.19	−.26
030.	charming	.06	.12	−.08	−.02	−.02	−.02	.03	.04	−.10	−.02	−.14	−.10
031.	cheerful	.13	.12	.10	.05	.09	.14	−.06	.09	.08	.06	−.05	−.03
032.	civilized	.12	.11	.16	−.07	.04	.13	.12	.05	.08	.03	−.04	.07
033.	clear-thinking	.18	.19	.19	.09	.07	.10	.08	.13	.18	.20	−.03	−.02
034.	clever	−.03	−.08	−.08	−.04	−.06	−.10	−.08	−.19	−.09	−.05	−.19	−.13
035.	coarse	−.23	−.19	−.22	−.06	−.19	−.23	−.08	−.22	−.11	−.04	−.17	−.15
036.	cold	−.25	−.06	−.05	−.10	−.15	−.09	−.04	−.03	−.01	−.10	.04	−.06
037.	commonplace	−.05	.00	.05	.06	−.08	.03	.02	.10	.14	−.02	−.01	.07
038.	complaining	−.10	−.08	−.12	−.27	−.18	−.22	−.05	−.13	−.16	−.29	−.07	−.13
039.	complicated	.00	−.14	.00	−.20	−.16	−.31	.02	−.16	.10	−.13	−.10	−.13
040.	conceited	−.21	−.08	−.03	−.05	−.12	−.10	−.15	−.13	−.20	−.10	−.08	−.09
041.	confident	−.01	.03	.05	−.03	−.01	.07	−.04	−.09	.05	−.01	−.15	−.13
042.	confused	−.08	−.11	−.19	−.21	−.12	−.33	−.03	−.15	−.16	−.22	−.01	−.12
043.	conscientious	.20	.22	.18	.06	.21	.26	.16	.23	.21	.14	.14	.23
044.	conservative	.22	.27	.15	.06	.12	.22	.10	.34	.21	.18	.11	.23

		Scale: So						Scale: Sc				
		By Peers		By Spouses		By Staff		By Peers		By Spouses		By Staff
Adjectives		M	F	M	F	M	F	M	F	M	F	M	F
045.	considerate	.25	.12	.13	.11	.12	.06	.18	.21	.12	.04	.08	.07
046.	contented	.15	.16	.18	.09	.04	.14	.10	.16	.20	.14	−.02	.09
047.	conventional	.24	.24	.11	.13	.14	.23	.11	.32	.18	.17	.12	.19
048.	cool	−.12	−.20	.03	−.14	−.10	−.03	−.14	−.14	.06	.02	−.02	.03
049.	cooperative	.19	.18	.12	.16	.19	.14	.09	.24	.14	.24	.07	.08
050.	courageous	−.02	−.05	−.09	.00	−.09	−.14	−.09	−.07	−.06	.04	−.13	−.12
051.	cowardly	−.13	.08	−.11	.06	−.06	−.09	−.08	.05	.00	.04	.01	.01
052.	cruel	−.33	−.14	−.16	−.08	−.13	−.15	−.04	−.07	−.16	−.06	−.12	−.14
053.	curious	−.05	−.06	−.11	.03	−.03	−.21	−.10	−.18	−.04	.08	−.03	−.22
054.	cynical	−.17	−.15	−.18	−.19	−.31	−.24	−.04	−.21	−.05	−.16	−.20	−.19
055.	daring	−.11	−.17	−.18	.00	−.13	−.17	−.09	−.25	−.21	−.09	−.22	−.26
056.	deceitful	−.30	−.10	−.22	−.10	−.12	−.21	−.12	−.11	−.15	−.12	−.10	−.15
057.	defensive	−.28	−.18	−.12	−.17	−.21	−.14	−.13	−.11	−.16	−.20	−.05	.03
058.	deliberate	.09	.03	−.02	−.07	.00	.12	.15	−.08	.03	−.14	.07	.20
059.	demanding	−.09	−.06	−.10	−.21	−.18	−.18	.08	−.22	−.16	−.27	−.16	−.18
060.	dependable	.29	.20	.07	.08	.15	.27	.19	.15	.14	.08	.12	.19
061.	dependent	.11	.07	−.04	−.01	−.01	−.01	−.02	.16	.00	−.02	.05	.01
062.	despondent	−.08	−.19	−.13	.03	−.07	−.18	.00	−.10	−.13	.05	−.06	.02
063.	determined	.08	.15	−.05	−.07	−.03	−.05	.04	−.01	−.02	−.04	−.11	−.08
064.	dignified	.11	.08	.05	.04	.07	.09	.06	.11	.09	.08	.07	.17
065.	discreet	.14	.12	.10	.01	.07	.17	.04	.22	.05	−.01	.13	.23
066.	disorderly	−.20	−.32	−.18	−.15	−.13	−.35	−.12	−.28	−.23	−.17	−.10	−.24
067.	dissatisfied	−.18	−.19	−.24	−.12	−.28	−.38	−.06	−.11	−.25	−.13	−.13	−.18
068.	distractible	−.16	−.10	−.23	−.13	−.16	−.28	−.07	−.08	−.26	−.19	−.12	−.21
069.	distrustful	−.23	−.18	−.13	−.14	−.22	−.26	−.09	−.09	−.06	−.14	−.08	−.12
070.	dominant	−.10	−.01	−.05	−.15	−.10	−.09	.00	−.18	−.05	−.14	−.18	−.10
071.	dreamy	−.02	−.01	−.17	−.09	−.04	−.14	−.01	−.01	−.16	−.10	.04	−.01
072.	dull	−.01	.06	−.11	.02	−.03	.05	.11	.13	−.08	.05	.03	.09
073.	easygoing	.03	−.08	−.03	.07	−.03	.05	.00	−.07	.01	.14	−.12	−.08
074.	effeminate	.06	.03	−.04	.02	−.03	.10	.01	.05	.04	−.11	.08	−.03
075.	efficient	.26	.20	.21	.10	.10	.15	.11	.16	.19	.01	.07	.03
076.	egotistical	−.19	−.01	−.09	−.09	−.15	−.09	−.07	−.18	−.21	−.08	−.17	−.12
077.	emotional	−.03	−.08	−.13	−.06	−.10	−.23	−.08	−.12	−.19	−.17	−.13	−.23
078.	energetic	.03	.13	−.07	−.05	.01	−.03	−.12	−.11	−.10	−.02	−.12	−.13
079.	enterprising	.17	.14	−.07	.02	.02	.02	.04	.00	−.13	−.02	−.11	−.11
080.	enthusiastic	.13	.12	−.03	.02	.03	−.01	−.07	−.04	−.17	.01	−.10	−.17
081.	evasive	−.07	−.10	−.12	−.10	−.19	−.11	.06	−.05	−.04	−.17	−.07	−.07
082.	excitable	−.10	−.02	−.14	−.15	−.09	−.15	−.16	−.23	−.12	−.23	−.11	−.16
083.	fair-minded	.18	.17	.12	.09	.11	.12	.08	.12	.08	.12	.02	.08
084.	fault-finding	−.11	−.08	−.08	−.18	−.18	−.20	−.14	−.09	−.02	−.19	−.08	−.09
085.	fearful	−.08	−.02	−.15	.00	−.12	−.17	−.02	.03	−.09	−.01	.03	−.04
086.	feminine	.06	.00	.09	−.02	−.03	.07	.24	.13	.07	−.01	.04	.04
087.	fickle	−.12	−.24	−.06	−.18	−.13	−.20	−.02	−.24	.02	−.21	−.07	−.14
088.	flirtatious	−.08	−.07	−.20	−.18	−.09	−.16	−.09	−.21	−.25	−.16	−.12	−.24

Correlations of Observers' Adjectival Description with Scales of the CPI continued

	Scale: So						Scale: Sc					
	By Peers		By Spouses		By Staff		By Peers		By Spouses		By Staff	
Adjectives	M	F	M	F	M	F	M	F	M	F	M	F
089. foolish	−.12	−.20	−.04	−.22	−.11	−.14	−.15	−.20	−.01	−.25	−.08	−.10
090. forceful	−.07	−.04	−.11	−.16	−.08	−.08	−.11	−.18	−.09	−.24	−.13	−.05
091. foresighted	.24	.16	.06	.11	.11	.07	.07	.12	.09	.22	.05	.02
092. forgetful	−.13	−.14	−.05	−.17	−.08	−.11	−.09	−.09	−.02	−.07	−.02	−.02
093. forgiving	.19	.08	.05	.03	−.02	−.07	.03	.12	.03	.00	−.04	−.05
094. formal	.21	.06	.04	−.06	.06	.10	.18	.15	.04	.04	.13	.17
095. frank	.02	−.06	−.05	−.11	−.04	−.15	−.05	−.19	−.10	−.08	−.14	−.17
096. friendly	.09	.03	−.01	.08	.07	.06	.03	.00	−.05	.07	−.04	−.02
097. frivolous	−.01	−.02	−.06	−.05	−.13	−.12	−.03	−.12	−.01	−.01	−.11	−.13
098. fussy	−.04	−.05	−.06	−.08	−.09	−.08	−.01	.07	−.06	−.14	.03	.04
099. generous	.17	.06	−.06	.00	−.01	−.03	.07	.06	−.12	.12	−.01	−.07
100. gentle	.24	.14	.04	.01	.01	.05	.17	.25	.14	.10	.05	.06
101. gloomy	−.06	−.15	−.18	−.11	−.08	−.16	.01	−.05	−.10	.06	.00	−.05
102. good-looking	.05	−.05	−.04	−.07	−.02	.03	.00	−.07	−.01	−.01	−.11	−.08
103. good-natured	.17	.09	.02	.07	.08	.04	.07	.05	.06	.15	−.06	−.06
104. greedy	−.17	−.06	−.09	−.07	−.12	−.13	.03	−.10	−.12	−.04	−.06	−.14
105. handsome	.00	.00	−.01	−.05	−.03	.06	−.02	.02	−.04	.01	−.13	.06
106. hard-headed	−.09	−.11	−.11	−.21	−.13	−.08	.05	−.21	−.08	−.27	−.07	−.04
107. hard-hearted	−.27	−.08	−.08	−.08	−.13	−.05	−.07	−.10	−.02	−.08	−.09	−.09
108. hasty	−.17	−.16	−.23	−.24	−.11	−.16	−.21	−.20	−.18	−.22	−.10	−.21
109. headstrong	−.26	−.13	−.11	−.29	−.22	−.27	−.16	−.17	−.18	−.30	−.18	−.22
110. healthy	.06	−.02	.09	.03	−.05	.10	−.14	−.02	.09	.02	−.11	−.05
111. helpful	.17	.12	.06	.07	.12	.11	.03	.09	.11	.05	.06	.02
112. high-strung	−.06	−.03	−.17	−.16	−.13	−.28	−.05	−.09	−.08	−.16	−.07	−.16
113. honest	.36	.18	.10	.13	.14	.06	.11	.16	.10	.15	.08	.09
114. hostile	−.15	−.11	−.15	−.04	−.20	−.22	−.04	−.12	−.08	−.07	−.05	−.10
115. humorous	−.08	−.08	−.09	.10	−.11	−.05	−.15	−.28	−.13	−.02	−.22	−.17
116. hurried	−.18	−.08	−.09	−.03	−.06	−.13	−.15	−.20	−.13	−.01	−.10	−.07
117. idealistic	.09	.14	−.05	.02	.03	−.10	.03	.14	.00	−.04	.06	−.06
118. imaginative	.03	.04	−.08	−.12	−.05	−.19	−.09	−.12	−.13	−.06	−.11	−.15
119. immature	−.15	−.10	−.26	−.11	−.05	−.12	−.05	−.18	−.19	−.11	−.02	−.07
120. impatient	−.14	−.14	−.15	−.16	−.21	−.29	−.05	−.18	−.14	−.27	−.16	−.19
121. impulsive	−.30	−.24	−.28	−.26	−.18	−.31	−.24	−.33	−.27	−.34	−.20	−.26
122. independent	−.02	−.11	.10	−.15	−.17	−.13	.04	−.09	.10	−.03	−.18	−.15
123. indifferent	−.14	−.18	−.17	−.12	−.15	−.13	−.01	−.12	−.06	−.07	−.11	−.02
124. individualistic	−.17	−.17	−.02	−.21	−.23	−.25	−.12	−.19	−.03	−.17	−.19	−.15
125. industrious	.19	.19	.01	−.02	.16	.16	.01	.10	.02	.03	.10	.09
126. infantile	−.09	−.05	−.17	−.14	−.14	−.20	−.06	−.17	−.10	−.17	−.10	−.13
127. informal	.01	−.08	−.08	−.12	−.14	−.16	−.03	−.17	−.03	.00	−.20	−.20
128. ingenious	−.01	−.09	.00	.00	−.03	−.11	−.02	−.18	−.02	−.06	−.06	−.09
129. inhibited	.19	.09	−.06	.04	.00	.05	.14	.30	.06	.08	.12	.18
130. initiative	.05	.07	−.13	−.01	.03	−.02	−.08	−.01	−.07	.00	−.11	−.10
131. insightful	.12	.07	−.02	−.02	.04	−.12	.04	.07	−.07	.06	−.04	−.09
132. intelligent	.13	.19	.11	−.01	.01	.02	.07	.08	.08	.04	−.05	.00

Correlations of Observers' Adjectival Description with Scales of the CPI continued

		Scale: So						Scale: Sc					
		By Peers		By Spouses		By Staff		By Peers		By Spouses		By Staff	
Adjectives		M	F	M	F	M	F	M	F	M	F	M	F
133.	interests—narrow	.02	−.01	−.08	.02	−.02	.02	.09	−.02	.04	−.03	.03	.09
134.	interests—wide	−.01	−.04	.08	−.13	−.04	−.15	−.08	−.09	−.02	−.08	−.08	−.10
135.	intolerant	−.11	−.04	−.12	−.07	−.14	−.17	−.01	−.05	−.11	−.12	−.10	−.05
136.	inventive	.08	−.01	.01	−.09	−.07	−.12	.03	−.16	−.03	−.05	−.09	−.08
137.	irresponsible	−.34	−.15	−.11	−.22	−.14	−.28	−.08	−.17	−.10	−.21	−.09	−.19
138.	irritable	−.15	−.17	−.17	−.12	−.19	−.23	−.09	−.15	−.05	−.14	−.11	−.07
139.	jolly	−.04	.08	−.08	.03	−.04	−.04	−.07	−.12	−.08	−.01	−.17	−.12
140.	kind	.34	.17	.05	.01	−.01	.04	.16	.12	.07	.06	−.03	.02
141.	lazy	−.22	−.18	−.07	−.08	−.14	−.21	−.07	−.21	−.12	−.05	−.14	−.13
142.	leisurely	−.10	−.06	−.08	−.18	−.08	−.09	−.08	−.09	−.09	−.08	−.11	−.03
143.	logical	.20	.06	.07	.07	.02	.10	.12	.11	.03	.23	.02	.13
144.	loud	−.13	−.05	−.04	−.21	−.14	−.12	−.12	−.25	−.19	−.24	−.17	−.11
145.	loyal	.23	.11	−.02	−.04	.06	.03	.04	.11	−.04	.00	.03	.01
146.	mannerly	.25	.17	.13	.02	.10	.16	.17	.23	.06	.12	.07	.12
147.	masculine	−.06	−.12	−.12	−.08	−.09	−.09	−.12	−.10	−.12	−.12	−.15	.07
148.	mature	.19	.10	.22	.09	.09	.06	.09	.17	.21	.11	−.02	−.01
149.	meek	.18	−.01	.00	−.06	−.07	.04	.10	.15	−.01	.06	.04	.12
150.	methodical	.21	.08	.09	.08	.13	.24	.06	.15	.11	.10	.12	.26
151.	mild	.25	.04	.05	.14	.09	.14	.16	.28	.13	.21	.12	.21
152.	mischievous	−.28	−.04	−.18	−.15	−.11	−.12	−.31	−.18	−.19	−.13	−.25	−.20
153.	moderate	.31	.12	.10	.08	.16	.20	.19	.34	.15	.26	.17	.24
154.	modest	.27	.13	.08	.13	.10	.12	.20	.29	.13	.10	.14	.18
155.	moody	−.16	−.23	−.23	−.11	−.21	−.37	−.08	−.21	−.08	−.17	−.06	−.15
156.	nagging	−.09	−.04	−.16	−.13	−.12	−.18	−.03	−.08	−.14	−.11	−.07	−.12
157.	natural	.07	−.02	−.05	−.01	.07	.05	−.02	−.02	.00	.00	−.07	−.01
158.	nervous	−.01	−.03	−.12	−.06	−.11	−.24	.05	−.05	−.08	−.10	.04	−.10
159.	noisy	−.17	−.03	−.04	−.17	−.12	−.09	−.12	−.22	−.12	−.22	−.16	−.12
160.	obliging	.17	.20	−.04	−.02	.11	.07	.14	.28	−.01	−.01	.13	.12
161.	obnoxious	−.17	−.09	−.12	−.08	−.18	−.21	−.08	−.25	−.15	−.15	−.20	−.12
162.	opinionated	−.07	−.02	−.07	−.28	−.15	−.15	−.09	−.16	−.13	−.26	−.13	−.12
163.	opportunistic	−.09	.02	−.08	−.16	−.11	−.14	−.04	−.09	−.04	−.16	−.17	−.17
164.	optimistic	.18	.19	.03	−.06	.14	.10	.06	.06	−.08	.05	−.07	−.12
165.	organized	.32	.26	.21	.20	.22	.25	.17	.24	.26	.20	.09	.14
166.	original	−.02	−.07	.01	−.19	−.06	−.21	−.15	−.17	−.06	−.10	−.11	−.13
167.	outgoing	−.05	.03	−.07	−.07	.04	−.01	−.16	−.19	−.19	−.14	−.16	−.19
168.	outspoken	−.10	−.08	−.18	−.20	−.11	−.09	−.09	−.22	−.24	−.15	−.14	−.11
169.	painstaking	.20	.12	−.04	−.01	.13	.08	.19	.18	.03	−.02	.17	.19
170.	patient	.24	.20	.06	.08	.12	.12	.19	.29	.13	.05	.16	.16
171.	peaceable	.19	.18	−.01	−.03	.10	.13	.14	.31	.02	.03	.13	.23
172.	peculiar	−.11	−.21	−.15	−.22	−.15	−.16	.04	−.12	−.02	−.14	.01	.02
173.	persevering	.18	.20	−.04	.09	.12	.10	.13	.05	−.01	.14	.10	.07
174.	persistent	.12	.04	−.08	.00	−.04	−.06	.09	−.10	.01	−.04	−.08	−.06
175.	pessimistic	−.07	−.23	−.08	−.13	−.18	−.24	.00	−.21	−.01	−.14	−.08	−.07
176.	planful	.28	.20	.05	.03	.09	.19	.06	.22	.05	.04	.03	.10

Correlations of Observers' Adjectival Description with Scales of the CPI continued

		Scale: So							Scale: Sc			
		By Peers		By Spouses		By Staff		By Peers		By Spouses		By Staff	
Adjectives		M	F	M	F	M	F	M	F	M	F	M	F
177.	pleasant	.20	.08	.08	.06	.09	.14	.05	.06	.06	.12	−.02	.09
178.	pleasure-seeking	−.16	−.16	−.15	−.15	−.16	−.20	−.14	−.23	−.24	−.24	−.26	−.29
179.	poised	.10	.04	.01	−.05	.08	.12	.11	.14	−.03	−.02	.01	.02
180.	polished	.09	.05	.03	−.02	.04	.10	.00	.07	−.05	.01	−.01	.01
181.	practical	.23	.20	.19	.07	.03	.13	.10	.22	.20	.12	.00	.01
182.	praising	.16	.10	−.05	−.04	.09	.00	.06	.13	−.01	−.01	.06	.01
183.	precise	.26	.00	.07	.06	.03	.08	.21	.03	.11	.10	.05	.12
184.	prejudiced	−.05	.00	−.17	−.18	−.12	−.14	−.04	.00	−.16	−.11	−.07	−.06
185.	preoccupied	−.08	−.06	−.04	−.23	−.12	−.24	.03	−.12	−.05	−.10	.00	−.03
186.	progressive	.03	−.12	−.05	−.09	−.10	−.19	.01	−.16	−.07	−.02	−.15	−.15
187.	prudish	.04	.11	−.13	−.03	.02	.13	.03	.18	−.13	−.04	.10	.22
188.	quarrelsome	−.25	−.08	−.19	−.14	−.19	−.22	−.18	−.18	−.13	−.20	−.13	−.14
189.	queer	−.08	−.16	−.06	.00	−.06	−.09	−.01	−.09	.02	.00	.06	−.01
190.	quick	−.09	−.02	−.08	−.16	−.05	−.13	−.16	−.13	−.04	−.08	−.19	−.20
191.	quiet	.18	.03	.10	.11	.01	.07	.14	.31	.20	.25	.11	.21
192.	quitting	−.17	−.15	−.18	−.05	−.08	−.21	.01	−.05	−.11	.05	−.03	−.05
193.	rational	.27	.19	.04	.07	.05	.08	.08	.18	−.03	.15	−.03	.02
194.	rattle-brained	−.04	−.05	−.14	−.15	−.08	−.13	−.05	−.19	−.15	−.12	−.07	−.16
195.	realistic	.22	.10	.07	.07	.01	.11	.08	.09	.05	.16	−.09	−.01
196.	reasonable	.34	.16	.15	.00	.10	.15	.20	.21	.15	.10	.04	.13
197.	rebellious	−.28	−.20	−.31	−.29	−.28	−.33	−.21	−.34	−.21	−.22	−.18	−.26
198.	reckless	−.30	−.24	−.30	−.34	−.20	−.30	−.16	−.20	−.24	−.32	−.19	−.24
199.	reflective	.08	.02	−.09	−.09	−.02	−.10	.12	.16	.03	.00	.03	.03
200.	relaxed	.11	.11	.03	−.01	.03	.08	.04	.05	.04	.12	−.08	−.04
201.	reliable	.34	.27	.11	.03	.19	.24	.18	.29	.06	.14	.08	.20
202.	resentful	−.09	−.10	−.16	−.12	−.22	−.24	−.01	−.19	−.06	−.17	−.13	−.18
203.	reserved	.22	.04	.03	.08	.02	.04	.14	.34	.15	.12	.14	.16
204.	resourceful	.20	.14	−.07	−.11	.04	−.08	.15	.07	−.06	−.13	−.09	−.12
205.	responsible	.31	.28	.10	−.06	.17	.20	.19	.26	.03	.08	.09	.19
206.	restless	−.15	−.18	−.26	−.18	−.25	−.31	−.14	−.31	−.25	−.20	−.16	−.26
207.	retiring	.01	.02	−.02	.04	−.05	.04	.02	.13	.07	.07	.08	.19
208.	rigid	−.12	.03	−.07	−.16	−.08	.00	−.04	.07	−.01	−.01	−.02	.12
209.	robust	−.01	.05	−.07	−.04	−.14	−.13	−.13	−.16	−.16	−.03	−.17	−.11
210.	rude	−.23	−.12	−.09	−.10	−.23	−.14	−.18	−.26	−.11	−.07	−.20	−.11
211.	sarcastic	−.23	−.15	−.14	−.22	−.22	−.19	−.13	−.34	−.07	−.21	−.22	−.18
212.	self-centered	−.24	−.05	−.16	−.13	−.19	−.22	−.03	−.11	−.17	−.16	−.19	−.17
213.	self-confident	−.08	.01	.04	−.04	.01	.05	−.11	−.09	−.04	.00	−.15	−.11
214.	self-controlled	.24	.22	.10	−.06	.08	.14	.16	.26	.10	.12	.11	.19
215.	self-denying	.15	−.04	−.16	.05	.02	.00	.15	.13	−.05	.05	.12	.18
216.	self-pitying	−.05	−.17	−.13	−.10	−.12	−.22	.11	−.12	−.15	−.08	−.04	−.10
217.	self-punishing	.01	−.08	−.18	−.09	−.07	−.23	.02	.05	−.16	−.10	.00	−.07
218.	self-seeking	−.11	−.06	−.14	.02	−.14	−.18	−.14	−.13	−.17	−.08	−.19	−.19
219.	selfish	−.20	−.17	.01	.03	−.12	−.23	−.07	−.11	−.03	−.09	−.15	−.17
220.	sensitive	.09	−.04	−.04	.01	−.07	−.20	−.08	−.02	−.08	−.05	−.04	−.08

Correlations of Observers' Adjectival Description with Scales of the CPI continued

		Scale: So						Scale: Sc				
		By Peers		By Spouses		By Staff		By Peers		By Spouses		By Staff	
Adjectives		M	F	M	F	M	F	M	F	M	F	M	F
221.	sentimental	.15	−.01	−.01	.12	−.05	−.09	−.01	.08	−.02	.01	−.04	−.07
222.	serious	.21	.12	−.01	.12	.04	.02	.11	.16	.00	.04	.09	.14
223.	severe	−.11	−.07	−.12	−.10	−.10	−.08	−.04	.01	−.19	−.05	−.04	.01
224.	sexy	.02	−.15	−.16	−.16	−.16	−.16	−.08	−.16	−.17	−.09	−.22	−.20
225.	shallow	−.23	.02	.00	−.01	−.08	−.06	−.13	.00	−.04	−.04	−.01	−.05
226.	sharp-witted	−.01	−.15	−.08	−.21	−.07	−.16	−.04	−.26	−.16	−.19	−.20	−.13
227.	shiftless	−.14	−.23	−.15	−.12	−.08	−.24	−.11	−.15	−.08	−.12	−.06	−.11
228.	show-off	−.25	−.09	−.12	−.12	−.19	−.10	−.16	−.26	−.23	−.13	−.24	−.12
229.	shrewd	.03	−.10	−.18	−.19	−.10	−.16	.11	−.12	−.11	−.18	−.14	−.09
230.	shy	.20	.08	−.03	.16	−.06	.01	.19	.26	.06	.17	.04	.09
231.	silent	.12	.04	−.08	−.03	−.11	.00	.09	.18	.10	.09	−.01	.10
232.	simple	.04	.11	.03	−.05	−.04	.01	.10	.13	.06	−.07	.03	.07
233.	sincere	.29	.18	.07	.13	.14	.08	.06	.17	.06	.20	.08	.15
234.	slipshod	−.21	−.16	−.13	−.10	−.12	−.19	−.06	−.17	−.14	−.12	−.05	−.10
235.	slow	−.03	.03	−.09	−.15	−.01	−.03	−.01	.02	−.10	−.09	.10	.14
236.	sly	−.15	−.09	−.22	−.23	−.11	−.18	−.04	−.14	−.16	−.17	−.15	−.16
237.	smug	−.27	−.05	−.04	−.06	−.10	−.07	−.08	−.13	−.06	−.04	−.16	−.12
238.	snobbish	−.20	.05	−.01	−.11	−.04	−.05	−.04	−.05	−.09	−.13	−.05	−.09
239.	sociable	.10	.08	.01	−.15	.04	.05	−.07	−.14	−.08	−.15	−.15	−.15
240.	soft-hearted	.11	.12	−.06	−.02	.01	.00	.15	.11	−.11	−.04	.02	−.02
241.	sophisticated	−.02	−.08	.07	−.07	−.04	−.04	.15	−.01	−.03	−.02	−.15	−.09
242.	spendthrift	−.13	−.06	.01	−.19	−.08	−.14	−.01	−.12	−.04	−.07	−.13	−.14
243.	spineless	−.05	−.03	−.05	−.15	−.06	−.10	.02	−.01	−.04	−.06	.02	.06
244.	spontaneous	−.10	−.04	−.13	−.23	−.05	−.10	−.13	−.27	−.16	−.19	−.17	−.20
245.	spunky	−.06	.05	−.12	−.11	−.10	−.15	−.27	−.11	−.22	−.18	−.17	−.20
246.	stable	.26	.24	.11	−.03	.13	.25	.12	.15	.13	.10	.04	.16
247.	steady	.33	.22	.02	−.03	.11	.21	.13	.22	.07	.06	.05	.12
248.	stern	−.02	.05	.00	−.10	−.07	−.02	.01	.11	−.05	.06	−.03	.06
249.	stingy	−.11	−.01	−.13	−.02	−.11	−.04	−.06	−.09	−.17	−.16	.03	.03
250.	stolid	−.02	.02	−.14	−.04	−.10	.05	−.07	−.11	−.02	.03	.00	.12
251.	strong	−.06	.05	−.04	−.09	−.09	−.07	−.07	−.03	−.09	.01	−.16	−.11
252.	stubborn	−.19	.03	−.09	−.14	−.22	−.18	−.10	−.16	−.12	−.22	−.12	−.07
253.	submissive	.03	.10	−.06	−.02	.03	.07	.13	.25	−.04	.03	.14	.16
254.	suggestible	.08	.06	−.17	−.05	.05	−.02	.01	.00	−.10	.00	.04	.01
255.	sulky	−.10	−.18	−.23	−.06	−.17	−.23	−.07	−.13	−.16	−.11	−.07	−.18
256.	superstitious	.12	.07	−.28	−.21	−.08	−.18	.09	.02	−.21	−.25	−.01	−.20
257.	suspicious	−.21	−.08	−.22	−.22	−.26	−.19	−.11	−.10	−.08	−.17	−.12	−.11
258.	sympathetic	.16	−.01	.05	.04	.05	−.02	.02	.04	−.02	.06	.01	.01
259.	tactful	.14	.13	.22	.07	.17	.12	.11	.23	.09	.05	.12	.08
260.	tactless	−.14	−.03	−.09	−.04	−.21	−.22	.00	−.10	−.08	−.04	−.15	−.12
261.	talkative	.00	−.01	−.04	−.21	−.06	−.07	−.13	−.27	−.12	−.25	−.17	−.22
262.	temperamental	−.20	−.15	−.27	−.18	−.23	−.24	−.21	−.18	−.21	−.28	−.18	−.20
263.	tense	−.04	−.05	−.19	−.10	−.14	−.26	.10	−.03	−.11	−.13	−.01	−.10
264.	thankless	−.24	−.16	−.12	.10	−.18	−.10	−.07	−.16	−.13	.02	−.11	.02

Correlations of Observers' Adjectival Description with Scales of the CPI continued

		Scale: So						Scale: Sc				
		By Peers		By Spouses		By Staff		By Peers		By Spouses		By Staff
Adjectives		M	F	M	F	M	F	M	F	M	F	M	F
265.	thorough	.33	.09	−.02	.13	.18	.18	.12	.18	.03	.08	.16	.15
266.	thoughtful	.24	.16	.04	.15	.08	.07	.20	.14	.05	.12	.06	.09
267.	thrifty	.19	.10	.13	.20	−.05	.07	.03	.10	.12	.15	.00	.08
268.	timid	.04	.01	−.05	−.08	−.03	.00	.09	.19	.01	.02	.07	.08
269.	tolerant	.14	.08	.06	.03	.07	.04	.04	.10	−.03	.08	.04	−.02
270.	touchy	−.17	−.12	−.18	−.14	−.22	−.24	−.11	−.14	−.05	−.27	−.09	−.11
271.	tough	−.08	−.11	−.16	−.13	−.18	−.19	−.11	−.16	−.12	−.11	−.19	−.13
272.	trusting	.23	.22	.06	.06	.07	.06	.00	.23	−.05	.09	.05	.02
273.	unaffected	.06	.01	−.05	−.19	.13	.02	−.02	.09	−.05	−.14	.08	.10
274.	unambitious	−.08	−.13	−.21	.03	−.11	−.13	−.05	−.06	−.09	.03	−.03	−.02
275.	unassuming	.08	.16	−.03	.05	.10	.07	.06	.17	−.05	.10	.13	.11
276.	unconventional	−.13	−.32	−.24	−.26	−.17	−.31	.00	−.32	−.10	−.18	−.12	−.14
277.	undependable	−.33	−.25	−.01	−.18	−.12	−.23	−.12	−.26	−.07	−.15	−.05	−.17
278.	understanding	.17	.13	−.02	.05	.00	.01	.09	.10	−.03	.08	−.05	−.05
279.	unemotional	.03	−.07	.03	−.10	−.13	.04	.04	.06	.18	−.06	−.05	.11
280.	unexcitable	−.04	.00	−.07	−.06	−.04	.08	.09	.15	.08	.07	.03	.17
281.	unfriendly	−.24	−.09	−.20	−.06	−.14	−.03	−.03	−.04	−.08	−.08	−.01	−.04
282.	uninhibited	−.18	−.09	−.05	−.12	−.08	−.18	−.09	−.32	−.02	−.12	−.19	−.23
283.	unintelligent	−.06	−.17	.00	.05	.00	−.06	.08	−.04	.00	.05	.04	.07
284.	unkind	−.03	−.18	.00	.00	−.13	−.18	.03	−.04	−.04	−.01	−.12	−.13
285.	unrealistic	−.18	−.08	−.12	−.20	−.10	−.20	−.16	−.12	−.05	−.16	−.06	−.14
286.	unscrupulous	−.24	−.11	−.24	−.12	−.09	−.18	−.11	−.09	−.11	.00	−.06	−.14
287.	unselfish	.19	.06	.02	.07	.05	.05	.18	.16	−.02	−.04	.03	.07
288.	unstable	−.23	−.12	−.19	−.21	−.09	−.34	−.09	−.17	−.13	−.14	−.01	−.14
289.	vindictive	−.11	−.12	−.13	−.24	−.14	−.13	.04	−.08	−.12	−.18	−.11	−.14
290.	versatile	.02	−.06	−.07	−.02	−.03	−.12	−.08	−.26	−.20	.00	−.12	−.22
291.	warm	.15	.13	.03	.00	.03	.05	.01	.10	.02	.06	−.04	−.05
292.	wary	−.20	−.04	−.17	−.11	−.25	−.14	−.11	.07	−.07	−.00	−.08	.00
293.	weak	−.01	.11	−.16	−.04	−.05	−.13	.02	.12	−.13	−.03	.01	.03
294.	whiny	−.02	.00	−.06	−.21	−.03	−.12	−.03	−.08	−.14	−.24	−.04	−.03
295.	wholesome	.27	.18	.06	−.00	.17	.23	.05	.11	.01	−.00	.04	.04
296.	wise	.17	.17	.15	−.04	.05	−.04	.03	.14	.12	.04	−.01	.01
297.	withdrawn	.11	−.01	−.31	−.01	−.13	−.10	.15	.17	−.14	.02	.01	.04
298.	witty	−.13	−.11	−.03	−.06	−.06	−.08	−.19	−.33	−.11	−.04	−.18	−.19
299.	worrying	.00	.00	−.16	−.14	−.15	−.22	−.05	.10	−.13	−.09	.01	−.02
300.	zany	−.08	−.07	−.19	−.10	−.10	−.12	−.15	−.27	−.16	−.19	−.16	−.14

Correlations of Observers' Adjectival Description with Scales of the CPI continued											
	Scale: Gi						**Scale: Cm**				
	By Peers		By Spouses		By Staff		By Peers		By Spouses		By Staff	
Adjectives	M	F	M	F	M	F	M	F	M	F	M	F
001. absent-minded	−.01	−.15	.05	−.09	−.03	−.11	−.15	−.11	−.19	−.04	−.11	−.14
002. active	.05	.01	−.10	−.02	−.13	−.03	.16	.15	−.06	.11	−.03	.13
003. adaptable	.16	.14	.05	−.02	−.03	−.02	.01	.17	−.07	−.02	.07	.20
004. adventurous	.03	−.17	−.19	−.15	−.18	−.22	−.02	.04	−.05	−.02	−.05	.04
005. affected	.00	.02	.09	−.01	−.04	−.11	.05	−.01	.03	−.04	−.06	−.11
006. affectionate	.01	.12	−.02	.01	−.04	−.04	−.12	.14	−.05	.03	−.06	.18
007. aggressive	−.04	−.16	−.14	−.17	−.07	−.06	.08	−.01	.02	−.03	.04	−.03
008. alert	.08	−.05	−.05	.07	−.06	.03	.17	.13	−.03	.09	.01	.15
009. aloof	.00	−.12	−.07	−.06	−.09	.03	−.05	−.15	−.02	−.09	−.12	−.16
010. ambitious	.11	.00	−.01	−.02	.04	−.01	.10	.18	.05	.13	.05	.08
011. anxious	−.15	−.04	.04	−.05	−.05	−.09	−.07	−.05	−.10	−.19	−.09	−.28
012. apathetic	−.11	−.11	−.07	−.09	−.05	−.01	−.19	−.09	−.05	.00	−.06	−.12
013. appreciative	.10	.26	.14	.10	.01	.13	−.07	.03	.08	.10	−.01	.15
014. argumentative	−.13	−.23	−.13	−.22	−.07	−.04	.01	−.04	.05	.02	.02	−.10
015. arrogant	−.05	−.21	−.22	.03	−.16	−.08	−.01	−.05	−.03	−.04	−.04	−.06
016. artistic	−.16	−.11	−.04	−.05	−.12	−.01	−.04	−.09	.00	−.09	−.09	−.08
017. assertive	.03	−.20	−.07	−.07	−.09	−.08	.03	.14	−.05	.09	.06	.04
018. attractive	.09	.00	.03	−.06	−.10	−.01	−.21	.05	−.03	−.08	−.06	.17
019. autocratic	.00	−.19	−.07	−.10	−.09	−.06	−.08	.03	.01	.03	.01	−.01
020. awkward	−.14	−.04	−.17	−.10	−.03	−.07	−.03	−.14	−.18	.06	−.16	−.26
021. bitter	−.06	−.21	−.13	−.18	−.16	−.15	.03	−.13	−.19	−.20	−.06	−.14
022. blustery	−.11	−.20	−.12	−.11	−.05	−.09	−.02	−.09	.07	−.04	−.02	−.12
023. boastful	−.05	−.11	−.22	−.10	−.08	.01	.04	.01	.03	−.16	−.01	−.05
024. bossy	−.09	−.14	−.18	−.16	−.06	.01	.07	.03	−.12	−.02	.04	−.05
025. calm	.12	.31	.16	.16	−.03	.12	−.04	.05	−.01	.02	.00	.13
026. capable	.07	.12	.01	.08	−.08	.09	.22	.20	.04	.14	−.01	.19
027. careless	−.13	−.22	−.14	−.11	−.10	−.18	−.22	−.13	−.16	−.08	−.11	−.11
028. cautious	−.03	.24	.05	.09	.02	.11	.11	.11	−.02	.04	−.01	−.05
029. changeable	−.09	−.31	−.07	−.23	−.15	−.24	−.05	−.06	−.15	−.12	−.09	−.13
030. charming	.07	.11	−.05	−.04	−.13	−.03	−.17	.15	.08	.01	−.04	.17
031. cheerful	−.04	.17	.13	.03	−.01	.04	.07	.15	.11	.17	−.03	.26
032. civilized	.08	.08	.11	.06	−.11	.10	−.05	.08	.03	.08	−.04	.15
033. clear-thinking	.08	.08	.09	.14	−.06	.05	.19	.20	.08	.15	−.01	.13
034. clever	−.03	−.19	−.04	−.07	−.15	−.05	.06	.00	.01	.07	−.04	.03
035. coarse	−.02	−.18	−.08	−.07	−.12	−.11	−.04	−.10	−.11	−.08	−.05	−.18
036. cold	−.05	−.11	−.04	−.15	.00	−.07	−.13	−.20	.00	−.03	−.12	−.15
037. commonplace	−.02	.06	.16	−.04	.00	.04	.00	−.05	.00	.02	.01	−.04
038. complaining	−.15	−.22	−.13	−.26	−.08	−.09	.01	−.07	−.07	−.11	−.03	−.15
039. complicated	−.05	−.23	.04	−.10	−.18	−.13	.05	−.12	−.04	−.08	−.12	−.27
040. conceited	−.08	−.06	−.24	−.08	−.06	−.04	−.03	−.01	−.04	.01	.00	−.04
041. confident	.05	−.03	.01	.04	−.11	.00	.05	.24	−.02	.08	.03	.20
042. confused	−.07	−.11	−.14	−.21	−.03	−.14	−.13	−.02	−.22	−.06	−.07	−.35
043. conscientious	.06	.20	.12	.18	.06	.23	.16	.18	.09	.11	.10	.15
044. conservative	.08	.29	.22	.05	.08	.21	.12	.11	.08	.06	.12	.10

Correlations of Observers' Adjectival Description with Scales of the CPI continued											
	Scale: Gi						**Scale: Cm**					
	By Peers		By Spouses		By Staff		By Peers		By Spouses		By Staff	
Adjectives	M	F	M	F	M	F	M	F	M	F	M	F
045. considerate	.08	.21	.17	−.02	.01	.05	.05	.04	.12	.02	−.09	.16
046. contented	.07	.20	.22	.12	.00	.07	.02	.06	.16	.03	.02	.25
047. conventional	.11	.30	.15	.11	.09	.16	.06	.08	.02	.02	.10	.17
048. cool	−.04	−.21	.00	−.02	−.03	.01	−.17	−.10	.05	−.05	.00	−.02
049. cooperative	.05	.21	.13	.21	.02	.10	−.06	.10	.03	.10	.00	.24
050. courageous	−.03	−.07	.06	.05	−.09	−.01	−.16	.04	−.02	.02	−.05	.01
051. cowardly	−.05	.03	.05	.02	−.02	−.04	−.04	.04	−.09	.01	−.05	−.05
052. cruel	−.01	−.09	−.16	−.09	−.13	−.11	−.07	−.06	−.10	−.04	−.07	−.13
053. curious	−.08	−.13	−.01	.07	−.11	−.16	−.05	.04	−.05	−.13	−.14	−.04
054. cynical	−.11	−.30	−.07	−.13	−.19	−.19	−.03	−.14	−.10	−.10	−.12	−.18
055. daring	.05	−.16	−.15	−.12	−.12	−.13	−.13	−.04	.03	.10	−.04	−.02
056. deceitful	−.02	−.08	−.15	−.11	−.03	−.11	.00	−.12	−.03	−.12	−.06	−.10
057. defensive	−.18	−.16	−.13	−.15	−.06	.03	−.04	−.13	−.03	−.03	−.09	−.22
058. deliberate	.09	−.11	−.04	−.08	−.02	.16	.13	.02	−.13	.00	.00	.02
059. demanding	.02	−.23	−.11	−.20	−.11	−.08	.03	.01	−.01	−.11	−.02	−.07
060. dependable	.12	.15	.10	.05	.05	.18	.20	.13	.04	.12	.05	.25
061. dependent	−.09	.13	.05	−.03	−.01	−.04	.01	−.02	−.15	−.11	−.01	−.01
062. despondent	−.02	−.17	−.07	.04	−.08	−.05	.00	−.12	−.06	−.01	−.04	−.23
063. determined	.02	−.02	.01	−.04	−.09	.03	.16	.09	.00	.09	.04	.07
064. dignified	.04	.07	.11	.13	.01	.13	−.01	.23	.05	.10	.03	.03
065. discreet	−.03	.18	.00	.02	.04	.17	−.05	.17	.02	.06	.00	.05
066. disorderly	−.08	−.20	−.20	−.20	−.09	−.23	−.16	−.19	.01	.04	−.13	−.25
067. dissatisfied	−.15	−.14	−.19	−.11	−.15	−.17	.02	−.16	−.20	−.04	−.11	−.26
068. distractible	−.10	−.08	−.15	−.16	−.12	−.19	−.24	−.11	−.03	−.03	−.11	−.22
069. distrustful	−.06	−.11	−.06	−.12	−.09	−.10	−.07	−.08	−.04	−.10	−.05	−.24
070. dominant	.08	−.14	−.01	−.15	−.14	.00	.05	.12	.02	−.04	.02	.07
071. dreamy	.01	.04	−.09	−.04	.00	−.05	−.20	.06	−.06	−.12	−.16	−.19
072. dull	.00	.05	.01	.01	.00	.08	−.04	.01	−.21	−.06	−.03	−.04
073. easygoing	.02	−.01	.01	.10	−.09	−.07	−.09	.04	−.05	.01	−.09	.14
074. effeminate	.01	−.01	.09	−.12	.01	.02	.02	−.01	−.01	.02	−.10	.05
075. efficient	.01	.12	.18	.02	.03	.10	.22	.20	.08	.11	.10	.17
076. egotistical	−.03	−.13	−.24	−.04	−.15	−.04	.04	.01	−.03	−.02	−.03	−.04
077. emotional	−.15	−.11	−.12	−.19	−.12	−.15	.02	−.02	−.06	−.10	−.05	−.03
078. energetic	−.02	−.01	−.04	.02	−.07	.01	.10	.19	−.08	.05	.05	.16
079. enterprising	.05	−.01	−.04	.01	−.04	.00	.12	.13	−.04	.16	.01	.16
080. enthusiastic	−.08	.03	−.05	.06	−.06	−.04	.12	.18	.02	.17	−.04	.19
081. evasive	.00	−.10	−.04	−.18	−.09	−.08	−.02	−.09	−.02	−.03	−.11	−.09
082. excitable	−.16	−.14	.00	−.16	−.07	−.06	.07	.03	−.09	−.12	−.08	−.02
083. fair-minded	.11	.14	.07	.08	−.01	.06	.05	.07	.07	.11	−.03	.11
084. fault-finding	−.14	−.16	.04	−.20	−.10	−.04	.06	−.08	−.07	.01	−.06	−.12
085. fearful	−.11	.05	−.11	−.03	−.05	−.08	−.03	.00	−.08	−.13	−.12	−.19
086. feminine	.12	.14	.00	−.02	−.01	.06	.09	.11	.03	−.03	−.14	.19
087. fickle	−.07	−.18	.03	−.19	−.09	−.08	−.08	−.03	−.03	−.03	−.07	−.06
088. flirtatious	.07	−.10	−.20	−.12	−.11	−.13	−.17	.10	−.12	−.14	−.04	.00

		Scale: Gi						Scale: Cm				
		By Peers		By Spouses		By Staff		By Peers		By Spouses		By Staff
Adjectives		M	F	M	F	M	F	M	F	M	F	M	F
089.	foolish	−.13	−.18	.03	−.23	−.02	−.08	−.04	−.02	−.03	−.06	−.01	−.06
090.	forceful	.03	−.10	−.16	−.17	−.10	.05	.11	.01	.03	−.03	.04	.04
091.	foresighted	.05	.10	.12	.13	−.01	.05	.14	.14	−.05	.12	.02	.14
092.	forgetful	−.06	−.12	.03	−.04	−.06	−.04	−.26	−.13	−.09	−.09	−.11	−.09
093.	forgiving	.01	.19	.12	.07	−.07	−.07	.10	.05	.00	.00	−.09	.13
094.	formal	.14	.11	.03	.11	.05	.13	.08	.01	.02	.08	.04	−.01
095.	frank	−.11	−.24	−.02	−.03	−.13	−.10	.14	.11	−.04	.05	.00	.02
096.	friendly	.01	.11	.08	.09	−.03	.04	−.02	.12	.01	.06	−.04	.22
097.	frivolous	−.03	−.05	.06	.02	−.09	−.07	−.09	.07	−.06	−.15	−.03	−.03
098.	fussy	−.15	.02	−.04	−.11	.00	.01	−.10	−.03	.00	−.13	−.05	−.06
099.	generous	.02	.14	−.05	.14	−.03	−.05	.07	.10	.13	−.07	−.07	.10
100.	gentle	.04	.23	.15	.09	−.05	.01	−.01	.12	.12	−.02	−.13	.11
101.	gloomy	−.02	−.15	−.11	.03	−.05	−.06	.00	−.11	−.07	−.04	−.06	−.23
102.	good-looking	.04	−.02	−.01	.01	−.09	−.01	−.11	.08	−.06	−.05	−.07	.14
103.	good-natured	.07	.08	.09	.12	−.06	−.03	−.01	.13	.04	.10	−.04	.16
104.	greedy	−.02	−.13	−.07	−.06	−.06	−.16	−.10	−.08	−.06	−.10	−.05	−.02
105.	handsome	.03	−.09	.04	.03	−.11	.03	−.18	.01	−.01	−.01	−.06	.09
106.	hard-headed	.01	−.24	−.06	−.22	−.05	.01	.08	.05	.05	−.02	.04	−.14
107.	hard-hearted	−.07	−.10	−.05	−.14	−.07	−.02	−.02	−.04	−.05	−.12	−.01	.01
108.	hasty	−.20	−.22	−.16	−.15	−.05	−.14	.00	−.09	−.05	−.14	.01	.00
109.	headstrong	−.14	−.18	−.16	−.18	−.13	−.10	.03	−.11	.04	−.07	−.05	−.10
110.	healthy	−.11	.04	.05	−.01	−.10	.05	.01	.01	.06	.09	−.04	.26
111.	helpful	−.02	.15	.09	.09	.02	.05	.07	.17	.07	.06	.01	.26
112.	high-strung	−.10	−.13	−.02	−.11	−.09	−.15	−.01	−.01	−.13	−.05	−.07	−.19
113.	honest	.02	.07	.07	.08	.03	.09	.07	.10	.08	.09	.01	.12
114.	hostile	−.02	−.17	−.08	−.07	−.04	−.06	−.05	−.09	−.12	−.05	−.05	−.15
115.	humorous	−.03	−.23	−.11	−.01	−.15	−.12	−.02	.12	−.05	.11	−.05	.08
116.	hurried	−.19	−.20	−.03	.02	−.09	−.02	.01	.01	.02	−.04	−.07	−.05
117.	idealistic	−.06	.20	.06	−.01	.00	−.01	.00	.11	−.02	.13	−.06	−.05
118.	imaginative	−.11	−.07	−.14	.00	−.12	−.10	.05	.03	.05	−.03	−.08	−.04
119.	immature	−.06	−.08	−.12	−.08	−.02	−.06	−.03	−.08	−.09	−.06	−.07	−.11
120.	impatient	−.10	−.26	−.13	−.24	−.12	−.13	.05	−.12	−.07	−.12	−.04	−.14
121.	impulsive	−.10	−.27	−.25	−.24	−.12	−.19	−.10	−.08	−.04	−.15	−.08	−.11
122.	independent	.05	−.11	.04	−.01	−.15	−.10	.14	.06	.00	.02	−.06	−.02
123.	indifferent	−.07	−.21	−.07	−.10	−.08	−.07	−.10	−.19	−.08	.04	−.10	−.13
124.	individualistic	−.10	−.12	−.06	−.06	−.16	−.10	−.06	−.04	−.03	.07	−.15	−.13
125.	industrious	.03	.12	.06	.04	.05	.17	.20	.13	.00	.11	.06	.12
126.	infantile	−.11	−.06	−.01	−.18	−.10	−.15	−.01	.06	−.09	−.11	−.11	−.14
127.	informal	.00	−.16	−.01	.03	−.15	−.20	−.01	−.05	−.07	−.04	−.16	.01
128.	ingenious	.02	−.13	.01	−.03	−.04	−.07	.08	.00	−.10	.03	−.04	−.03
129.	inhibited	.07	.24	.01	−.01	.02	.07	.07	.01	−.14	−.07	−.04	−.11
130.	initiative	−.06	.01	.02	−.01	−.05	.01	.18	.17	−.08	.12	.04	.13
131.	insightful	−.02	.10	−.03	.09	−.06	−.03	.12	.12	−.04	.16	−.05	−.02
132.	intelligent	−.01	.10	.01	.01	−.10	.03	.10	.11	.08	−.01	−.04	.04

		Scale: Gi						Scale: Cm				
		By Peers		By Spouses		By Staff		By Peers		By Spouses		By Staff
Adjectives		M	F	M	F	M	F	M	F	M	F	M	F
133.	interests—narrow	.01	−.07	.04	−.07	.00	.02	−.01	.02	−.09	−.11	−.01	−.02
134.	interests—wide	.01	−.04	.00	−.04	−.09	−.03	−.01	.05	.09	.07	−.04	.02
135.	intolerant	−.08	−.09	−.13	−.19	−.10	−.04	−.07	−.03	−.10	−.08	−.02	−.11
136.	inventive	.04	−.11	−.03	−.03	−.13	−.05	.08	.03	.03	.06	−.07	−.04
137.	irresponsible	−.01	−.19	−.05	−.13	−.07	−.17	−.29	−.18	−.01	−.01	−.07	−.09
138.	irritable	−.12	−.23	−.09	−.20	−.11	−.06	.12	−.14	−.06	−.09	−.02	−.17
139.	jolly	.05	.01	−.06	.05	−.05	−.06	−.01	.13	.00	.04	.02	.00
140.	kind	.14	.17	.14	.05	−.08	.01	.01	.12	.07	−.02	−.13	.17
141.	lazy	−.03	−.21	−.09	−.09	−.11	−.17	−.19	−.10	−.10	−.20	−.09	−.10
142.	leisurely	−.02	−.05	−.03	−.04	−.05	−.08	−.19	.03	−.03	−.04	−.06	−.03
143.	logical	.02	.07	−.05	.08	−.05	.11	.13	.03	−.02	.12	.00	−.04
144.	loud	−.07	−.18	−.14	−.17	−.09	−.02	.04	−.04	.01	−.16	.00	−.05
145.	loyal	.06	.13	.03	−.02	.03	.06	.04	.16	−.04	−.05	.06	.17
146.	mannerly	.12	.20	.11	.10	.01	.12	.03	.13	.10	.08	−.05	.15
147.	masculine	−.03	−.10	−.01	−.10	−.11	.04	.07	−.10	−.04	.03	−.02	−.09
148.	mature	.13	.13	.17	.09	−.04	.03	.18	.05	.12	.20	.06	.20
149.	meek	−.06	.11	.01	.05	−.02	.06	.00	−.11	−.08	.04	−.13	−.06
150.	methodical	−.04	.07	.06	.07	.03	.25	.14	.07	−.04	.00	.09	.02
151.	mild	.05	.23	.11	.10	.03	.11	−.01	−.06	−.02	.05	−.08	.05
152.	mischievous	−.22	−.18	−.12	−.12	−.18	−.15	−.16	−.07	−.14	−.15	−.04	−.04
153.	moderate	.06	.29	.14	.24	.09	.17	.07	.06	−.01	.09	.04	.13
154.	modest	.05	.22	.07	−.02	.05	.09	.02	.01	−.04	.10	−.02	.07
155.	moody	−.10	−.31	−.05	−.19	−.12	−.17	−.03	−.11	−.28	−.10	−.11	−.30
156.	nagging	−.11	−.09	−.09	−.07	−.07	−.05	−.01	.00	−.15	−.11	−.02	−.09
157.	natural	−.02	.00	.01	−.01	.01	−.02	.01	.04	.04	.06	.02	.14
158.	nervous	−.08	−.13	−.07	−.07	−.04	−.11	−.06	−.11	−.16	−.12	−.12	−.15
159.	noisy	−.04	−.18	−.05	−.19	−.05	−.04	.00	−.01	.03	−.13	.01	−.03
160.	obliging	.01	.28	.01	−.01	.07	.05	−.12	.18	−.04	.04	−.04	.02
161.	obnoxious	−.11	−.22	−.16	−.08	−.12	−.09	.02	.00	.02	−.07	.00	−.21
162.	opinionated	−.08	−.19	−.07	−.20	−.11	−.03	.03	−.01	.02	−.10	−.02	−.08
163.	opportunistic	.07	−.08	−.06	−.13	−.09	−.05	.04	.04	−.13	−.06	.00	.03
164.	optimistic	.05	.13	.01	.11	−.02	−.02	.00	.21	.11	.13	−.01	.29
165.	organized	.08	.22	.19	.13	.03	.20	.24	.17	.02	.12	.14	.24
166.	original	−.08	−.12	−.02	−.10	−.16	−.10	.01	.02	−.03	.10	−.06	−.12
167.	outgoing	.00	−.10	−.08	−.04	−.04	−.05	.00	.17	.04	.05	.03	.19
168.	outspoken	−.05	−.19	−.19	−.05	−.10	−.01	.06	.06	−.05	−.01	.00	−.01
169.	painstaking	.05	.13	.06	−.05	.06	.15	.06	.08	−.02	−.07	.03	−.12
170.	patient	.14	.31	.14	−.07	.04	.13	−.06	.13	.07	.15	−.06	.15
171.	peaceable	.05	.29	.06	.05	.03	.15	−.05	.15	−.03	.03	−.06	.12
172.	peculiar	.01	−.11	.04	−.13	−.05	.02	.00	−.20	−.08	−.06	−.10	−.26
173.	persevering	−.01	−.01	−.02	.12	.05	.11	.17	.13	−.06	.07	.08	.00
174.	persistent	.00	−.06	.02	.05	−.06	.08	.13	.12	.03	.14	−.05	.02
175.	pessimistic	−.14	−.29	−.02	−.14	−.13	−.11	.00	−.08	−.11	−.04	−.11	−.30
176.	planful	−.02	.18	.04	−.01	−.03	.17	.20	.18	−.07	.18	.07	.19

APPENDIX D

Correlations of Observers' Adjectival Description with Scales of the CPI continued

	Scale: Gi						Scale: Cm					
	By Peers		By Spouses		By Staff		By Peers		By Spouses		By Staff	
Adjectives	M	F	M	F	M	F	M	F	M	F	M	F
177. pleasant	.03	.09	.14	.11	−.03	.11	.02	.14	.07	.06	−.06	.26
178. pleasure-seeking	−.05	−.20	−.16	−.18	−.14	−.21	−.11	−.11	−.10	−.03	−.04	.04
179. poised	.11	.14	.01	.04	−.01	.11	.00	.11	.07	.07	.05	.20
180. polished	.04	.08	.04	.00	−.02	.06	.08	.18	.11	.15	.01	.13
181. practical	.06	.19	.16	.10	.03	.03	.21	.12	.04	.12	.03	.22
182. praising	.05	.21	.07	−.02	.04	.04	.00	.08	.03	.07	−.01	.16
183. precise	.13	.00	.10	.05	−.05	.12	.09	.01	−.02	.11	.00	−.03
184. prejudiced	−.06	−.08	−.13	−.14	−.08	−.04	−.04	−.07	−.07	−.18	.00	−.09
185. preoccupied	.00	−.19	.01	−.07	−.08	−.05	−.07	−.07	−.09	−.10	−.10	−.31
186. progressive	.04	−.14	−.03	.05	−.13	−.07	.08	.02	−.02	.02	−.07	.01
187. prudish	−.07	.13	−.13	−.04	.04	.18	−.05	.10	−.08	.00	−.04	−.04
188. quarrelsome	−.13	−.25	−.16	−.20	−.08	−.08	−.00	−.02	−.11	−.13	−.02	−.12
189. queer	−.06	−.14	.06	.00	.00	.00	−.05	−.09	−.06	.00	−.05	−.22
190. quick	−.07	−.09	−.12	−.01	−.12	−.06	.04	.01	.00	−.01	−.01	.07
191. quiet	.05	.24	.10	.14	.01	.11	.00	−.06	.04	.01	−.08	−.03
192. quitting	.01	−.14	−.11	.05	−.07	−.12	−.17	−.03	−.11	−.04	−.08	−.14
193. rational	−.04	.08	−.02	.08	−.11	.05	.23	.15	.04	.09	−.03	.06
194. rattle-brained	−.02	−.14	−.10	−.06	−.02	−.11	−.06	.02	−.08	−.12	−.02	−.19
195. realistic	.00	.05	.01	.06	−.08	.05	.18	.16	−.03	.18	.05	.19
196. reasonable	.13	.17	.09	.10	.00	.10	.11	.19	.11	.17	.04	.18
197. rebellious	−.08	−.32	−.19	−.16	−.18	−.16	−.07	−.10	−.11	−.04	−.12	−.17
198. reckless	−.03	−.19	−.20	−.26	−.12	−.17	−.24	−.12	−.15	−.18	−.01	−.16
199. reflective	−.02	.14	.05	.06	−.07	−.03	−.07	.07	−.19	.03	−.06	−.07
200. relaxed	.06	.14	.01	.08	−.08	−.03	−.02	.18	.12	−.01	−.02	.19
201. reliable	.07	.26	.08	.08	.00	.18	.19	.14	.11	.00	.08	.17
202. resentful	−.03	−.25	−.06	−.15	−.14	−.13	−.01	−.03	−.13	−.12	−.07	−.13
203. reserved	.03	.25	.14	.03	−.01	.06	.03	−.01	−.11	−.02	−.06	−.07
204. resourceful	.10	.11	−.02	−.07	−.05	−.02	.15	.14	−.05	.08	.02	.08
205. responsible	.06	.18	.03	.07	−.03	.18	.26	.25	.08	−.03	.10	.20
206. restless	−.18	−.28	−.21	−.17	−.16	−.17	−.05	−.12	−.13	−.09	−.11	−.10
207. retiring	−.03	.05	.01	.03	−.02	.09	−.05	.00	−.01	−.04	−.09	−.04
208. rigid	−.07	.04	.00	−.13	−.03	.09	−.01	−.03	−.11	−.09	.02	−.11
209. robust	.00	−.11	−.08	.02	−.13	−.06	−.04	.01	.02	.11	−.03	.06
210. rude	−.16	−.25	−.06	−.08	−.14	−.06	.09	−.06	−.12	.01	−.03	−.09
211. sarcastic	−.11	−.39	−.10	−.18	−.18	−.12	.01	−.10	−.01	−.04	−.06	−.09
212. self-centered	−.04	−.08	−.17	−.19	−.14	−.11	−.04	.00	−.11	−.11	−.03	−.16
213. self-confident	.02	−.03	−.05	.04	−.08	.03	.15	.18	.13	.09	−.01	.20
214. self-controlled	−.01	.19	.07	.08	.01	.15	.08	.16	.04	.11	.06	.05
215. self-denying	.09	.09	−.02	.04	.05	.07	.06	−.01	−.12	.02	−.04	−.11
216. self-pitying	−.05	−.11	−.11	−.09	−.09	−.09	.00	−.06	−.15	−.05	−.04	−.21
217. self-punishing	−.07	.04	−.09	−.07	−.07	−.08	.06	−.10	−.07	−.11	−.01	−.22
218. self-seeking	−.09	−.18	−.10	−.17	−.08	−.09	−.03	.03	.00	.06	.00	−.02
219. selfish	−.01	−.13	−.02	−.11	−.10	−.10	−.06	.06	.01	.03	.01	−.14
220. sensitive	−.20	.01	−.05	−.07	−.14	−.08	.10	.00	.07	.07	−.16	−.02

Correlations of Observers' Adjectival Description with Scales of the CPI continued

	Scale: Gi						Scale: Cm					
	By Peers		By Spouses		By Staff		By Peers		By Spouses		By Staff	
Adjectives	M	F	M	F	M	F	M	F	M	F	M	F
221. sentimental	.00	.09	.01	−.01	−.05	−.09	.02	.11	.01	−.03	−.05	.02
222. serious	.07	.03	.01	.01	−.03	.15	.11	.01	.00	−.06	.00	−.07
223. severe	−.06	−.06	−.16	−.01	−.10	.01	−.10	−.07	−.09	−.02	−.04	−.11
224. sexy	−.07	−.11	−.18	.00	−.12	−.10	−.05	−.02	−.03	−.02	−.06	.03
225. shallow	−.11	.03	.03	−.09	.05	−.07	−.04	−.04	−.02	−.09	−.04	−.01
226. sharp-witted	.02	−.29	−.17	−.14	−.15	−.09	.07	−.04	.06	.04	−.02	−.06
227. shiftless	−.03	−.16	−.04	−.10	−.06	−.13	−.08	−.15	−.14	−.12	−.08	−.14
228. show-off	−.08	−.22	−.13	−.09	−.16	.00	−.06	−.01	.04	−.07	−.01	−.01
229. shrewd	.11	−.24	−.13	−.08	−.07	−.02	.00	−.16	−.20	−.02	.02	−.08
230. shy	.10	.13	−.03	.01	−.04	.00	−.02	.00	−.09	−.04	−.18	−.07
231. silent	−.01	.13	.06	.09	−.08	.04	−.10	−.05	−.05	−.06	−.14	−.02
232. simple	.04	.14	.09	−.07	.04	.02	−.04	.04	.00	−.10	−.03	.01
233. sincere	.02	.17	.07	.22	.01	.13	.09	.11	.08	.06	−.01	.08
234. slipshod	−.02	−.21	−.11	−.12	−.01	−.06	−.12	−.16	−.05	−.10	−.05	−.02
235. slow	−.02	.00	−.04	−.02	.06	.06	−.13	.01	−.15	−.05	.00	−.09
236. sly	.06	−.22	−.14	−.12	−.15	−.12	−.08	−.13	−.22	−.09	−.05	−.11
237. smug	.01	−.12	−.07	−.09	−.12	−.11	.00	.01	−.08	−.01	−.01	−.09
238. snobbish	−.05	−.06	−.11	−.11	−.03	−.10	.00	−.05	−.05	−.08	−.03	−.04
239. sociable	.03	−.04	−.01	−.02	−.07	−.05	.09	.18	.04	−.08	.02	.24
240. soft-hearted	.12	.16	−.07	−.11	.01	−.01	.01	.15	.03	.06	−.08	.07
241. sophisticated	.10	−.03	.03	.02	−.14	−.03	−.06	.05	.02	.11	−.03	.06
242. spendthrift	.04	−.10	−.06	−.08	−.10	−.12	−.13	−.09	.04	−.13	−.05	.03
243. spineless	−.06	−.04	.03	−.08	−.03	.01	−.01	−.09	.02	−.07	−.09	−.04
244. spontaneous	−.07	−.17	−.09	−.11	−.10	−.12	.00	.07	.02	−.02	−.01	.07
245. spunky	−.22	−.06	−.12	−.11	−.07	−.10	−.01	.07	−.06	−.04	.00	.01
246. stable	.06	.11	.03	.04	.00	.16	.15	.16	.11	.08	.04	.27
247. steady	.01	.15	.04	.00	.01	.09	.19	.14	−.02	.07	.06	.21
248. stern	.05	−.03	−.09	.06	−.08	.07	.07	.04	−.04	.01	.03	−.08
249. stingy	−.05	−.18	−.15	−.17	−.04	.02	−.04	−.02	−.07	−.09	.01	−.03
250. stolid	−.08	−.15	.01	.05	−.04	.08	.04	.03	−.03	−.10	−.07	−.03
251. strong	.03	−.02	−.02	.02	−.15	.00	.02	.14	.06	.09	−.02	.10
252. stubborn	−.07	−.18	−.13	−.15	−.10	−.03	.07	.07	−.07	−.01	−.03	−.13
253. submissive	−.02	.18	−.08	.01	.11	.06	.05	−.02	−.03	.00	−.06	.01
254. suggestible	−.02	.00	−.11	−.02	.03	−.01	.02	−.07	−.04	−.08	−.06	−.05
255. sulky	−.08	−.20	−.07	−.14	−.07	−.17	.02	−.04	−.08	−.01	−.06	−.16
256. superstitious	.01	−.02	−.20	−.17	−.02	−.15	.01	−.03	−.19	−.09	−.01	−.17
257. suspicious	−.15	−.16	−.08	−.16	−.15	−.08	.01	−.13	−.13	−.16	−.06	−.19
258. sympathetic	−.04	.08	.04	.04	−.02	.03	−.03	.14	.05	.06	−.08	.18
259. tactful	.16	.16	.10	−.03	.09	.09	−.08	.16	.24	.09	.08	.26
260. tactless	−.01	−.12	−.08	.05	−.11	−.05	.09	−.07	−.05	.00	−.05	−.07
261. talkative	−.06	−.18	−.05	−.14	−.09	−.11	.06	.08	.06	−.06	−.01	.12
262. temperamental	−.26	−.29	−.12	−.16	−.18	−.16	.03	−.09	−.15	−.02	−.10	−.12
263. tense	−.07	−.13	−.10	−.08	−.06	−.15	.01	−.08	−.13	−.07	−.07	−.26
264. thankless	−.09	−.24	−.04	−.06	−.10	.02	−.10	−.10	−.16	−.01	−.02	−.09

Correlations of Observers' Adjectival Description with Scales of the CPI continued

		Scale: Gi						Scale: Cm				
		By Peers		By Spouses		By Staff		By Peers		By Spouses		By Staff	
Adjectives		M	F	M	F	M	F	M	F	M	F	M	F
265.	thorough	.02	.14	.04	.08	.09	.18	.24	.13	−.11	.16	.08	.07
266.	thoughtful	.15	.20	.08	.03	−.02	.09	.13	.14	.11	.16	−.03	.14
267.	thrifty	−.01	.05	.08	.04	−.06	.10	.19	.10	.06	.04	−.02	.04
268.	timid	−.05	.10	.01	.03	.00	.03	−.04	−.05	−.01	−.11	−.10	−.06
269.	tolerant	.04	.16	−.02	.05	−.01	−.02	−.07	.17	.07	.04	−.08	.14
270.	touchy	−.09	−.20	−.03	−.24	−.13	−.11	.06	−.07	−.07	−.11	−.05	−.16
271.	tough	−.04	−.18	−.04	−.06	−.16	−.03	.01	−.04	−.05	−.04	.00	−.02
272.	trusting	−.02	.27	.08	.14	.00	.02	.15	.14	.04	.10	−.11	.11
273.	unaffected	−.09	.05	−.07	−.10	.04	.00	.08	.09	−.10	−.16	.00	.01
274.	unambitious	−.05	−.12	−.13	−.01	−.09	−.07	−.12	−.03	−.19	−.12	−.08	−.01
275.	unassuming	.00	.10	−.03	.17	.06	.03	−.04	.11	.03	.03	−.07	.02
276.	unconventional	.00	−.31	−.07	−.15	−.14	−.14	−.05	−.24	−.17	−.14	−.13	−.19
277.	undependable	−.06	−.18	−.07	−.13	.00	−.11	−.23	−.10	.01	−.13	−.08	−.09
278.	understanding	.04	.17	.05	.13	−.07	−.03	.08	.17	.03	.09	−.09	.18
279.	unemotional	−.01	.01	.09	.00	−.11	.07	−.03	−.04	−.08	.06	−.15	.01
280.	unexcitable	.07	.10	.02	.07	−.03	.10	−.09	−.13	−.10	−.04	−.01	.01
281.	unfriendly	−.04	−.10	−.15	−.08	−.05	−.08	−.07	−.12	−.01	.02	−.06	−.07
282.	uninhibited	.08	−.26	−.02	−.02	−.10	−.10	−.05	−.04	.05	.05	−.03	−.01
283.	unintelligent	.08	.00	.00	.04	.00	.00	−.03	−.04	.00	−.09	.01	−.10
284.	unkind	−.01	−.12	.03	−.09	−.14	−.08	.00	−.18	−.02	.00	−.04	−.06
285.	unrealistic	−.15	−.08	−.01	−.09	−.09	−.10	−.04	−.03	−.10	−.16	−.01	−.24
286.	unscrupulous	−.08	−.10	−.10	.01	−.07	−.13	−.02	−.15	−.09	−.09	−.06	−.11
287.	unselfish	.12	.17	.06	−.01	.01	.08	.12	.01	−.02	.16	−.06	.08
288.	unstable	−.11	−.22	−.16	−.03	−.05	−.16	.01	−.01	−.20	−.07	−.10	−.35
289.	vindictive	.03	−.07	−.07	−.21	−.11	−.06	.00	−.03	−.04	−.08	−.04	−.11
290.	versatile	.01	−.17	−.12	.04	−.10	−.14	.11	.09	.03	.13	−.01	.14
291.	warm	.03	.17	.06	.09	.00	−.01	−.07	.19	−.04	.03	−.05	.23
292.	wary	−.06	.01	−.03	.02	−.10	−.02	.01	−.10	−.05	−.03	−.07	−.18
293.	weak	−.03	.07	−.15	.01	−.02	−.01	.03	.08	−.21	−.03	−.03	−.13
294.	whiny	−.12	−.16	−.07	−.18	−.03	−.01	−.04	.04	−.14	−.15	.02	−.19
295.	wholesome	.07	.09	.07	−.01	.02	.05	.04	.12	.14	.07	.01	.25
296.	wise	.08	.12	.18	.05	−.09	.02	.09	.09	.08	.11	−.03	.04
297.	withdrawn	.09	.09	−.09	−.06	−.07	−.06	−.03	−.05	−.19	.01	−.23	−.16
298.	witty	−.13	−.37	−.06	−.02	−.13	−.12	.06	.01	.01	.02	−.05	.01
299.	worrying	−.15	.07	−.10	−.04	−.08	−.04	.05	−.03	−.18	−.14	−.08	−.22
300.	zany	−.13	−.19	−.10	−.16	−.12	−.08	.04	.00	−.05	.02	.01	−.10

Correlations of Observers' Adjectival Description with Scales of the CPI continued

		Scale: Wb						Scale: To				
		By Peers		By Spouses		By Staff		By Peers		By Spouses		By Staff	
Adjectives		M	F	M	F	M	F	M	F	M	F	M	F
001.	absent-minded	−.10	−.18	−.07	−.10	−.10	−.11	.02	−.05	−.02	−.03	−.01	−.06
002.	active	.10	.11	−.07	.07	.02	.03	.08	.10	−.03	−.05	.00	−.01
003.	adaptable	.06	.27	.09	.07	.09	.07	.15	.30	.08	−.09	.10	.04
004.	adventurous	.08	.06	−.05	.01	−.04	−.06	.03	−.01	−.01	−.05	−.08	−.11
005.	affected	−.02	.03	.05	−.05	−.02	−.04	−.13	−.03	−.02	−.16	−.01	−.04
006.	affectionate	−.01	.11	−.07	.09	−.07	−.01	.13	.05	.01	−.07	−.04	−.03
007.	aggressive	.06	.00	−.09	−.07	.05	.04	−.17	−.01	−.16	−.13	−.08	−.02
008.	alert	.20	.15	.09	.07	.04	.07	.10	.12	.10	.04	.06	.05
009.	aloof	.05	−.19	.01	−.09	−.11	.03	−.02	−.22	−.05	−.02	−.09	−.04
010.	ambitious	.10	.09	.04	.08	.15	.11	.03	.16	.04	−.07	.08	.07
011.	anxious	−.19	−.19	−.14	−.19	−.10	−.26	−.06	−.16	−.04	−.12	.04	−.19
012.	apathetic	−.12	−.12	−.13	−.03	−.13	−.07	−.05	−.17	−.20	−.02	−.11	−.08
013.	appreciative	−.06	.17	.12	.10	.03	.07	.19	.14	.16	.05	.12	.02
014.	argumentative	−.10	−.16	−.05	−.04	.05	.02	−.21	−.02	−.09	−.09	.00	.00
015.	arrogant	.01	−.21	−.16	.00	−.07	−.04	−.17	−.21	−.14	−.10	−.07	−.13
016.	artistic	−.04	−.06	.03	−.06	−.06	.01	−.03	−.01	.08	−.07	.05	.03
017.	assertive	.03	−.10	.04	.17	.06	.06	−.16	.03	.03	.09	−.03	.00
018.	attractive	.05	.07	.07	−.07	−.06	.03	.07	.02	−.03	−.14	.00	−.02
019.	autocratic	−.11	−.18	−.05	.04	.00	.04	−.07	−.15	−.06	.05	−.09	−.09
020.	awkward	−.23	−.12	−.27	−.11	−.23	−.14	−.10	−.13	−.16	.07	−.12	−.05
021.	bitter	−.08	−.24	−.27	−.26	−.13	−.20	−.06	−.32	−.24	−.16	−.19	−.20
022.	blustery	−.17	−.16	.01	−.12	−.01	−.11	−.21	−.10	.00	−.14	−.12	−.11
023.	boastful	.02	−.06	−.14	−.13	−.04	.01	−.24	−.11	−.20	−.13	−.10	−.11
024.	bossy	−.05	−.07	−.25	−.09	.02	−.01	−.19	−.07	−.26	−.07	−.09	−.03
025.	calm	.04	.22	.09	.08	−.05	.11	.21	.24	.11	.09	−.06	.08
026.	capable	.14	.16	.13	.21	−.03	.17	.17	.22	.07	.15	.01	.09
027.	careless	−.17	−.15	−.11	−.20	−.07	−.10	−.14	−.07	−.11	−.09	−.01	−.04
028.	cautious	−.13	.03	−.10	−.01	−.09	−.05	.03	.06	−.11	−.06	−.02	−.03
029.	changeable	−.07	−.15	−.08	−.08	−.12	−.20	.03	−.06	−.05	−.12	−.08	−.15
030.	charming	−.03	.12	−.01	−.02	−.02	.04	−.03	.13	−.11	−.06	.02	.02
031.	cheerful	.05	.22	.12	.05	.04	.10	.10	.20	.12	.05	.04	.06
032.	civilized	.05	.10	.06	.04	−.11	.05	.11	.14	.05	−.04	.04	.05
033.	clear-thinking	.18	.21	.10	.18	−.02	.13	.16	.21	.20	.21	.10	.12
034.	clever	.14	.01	.05	.09	−.04	.00	−.02	.11	−.03	.09	.02	.02
035.	coarse	−.01	−.15	−.23	.02	−.07	−.14	−.07	−.18	−.14	.01	−.19	−.12
036.	cold	−.18	−.18	−.04	−.11	−.06	−.04	−.24	−.23	−.09	−.05	−.09	−.16
037.	commonplace	−.13	−.04	.04	−.04	−.03	−.05	−.01	.02	−.03	−.04	−.13	−.09
038.	complaining	−.04	−.23	−.32	−.28	−.11	−.19	−.16	−.13	−.23	−.09	−.06	−.15
039.	complicated	−.02	−.27	.10	−.07	−.17	−.15	.00	−.12	.17	−.05	−.01	−.08
040.	conceited	−.07	−.05	−.16	.00	.04	.04	−.22	−.18	−.18	−.03	−.01	−.03
041.	confident	.14	.17	.10	.17	.06	.15	−.04	.10	.04	.02	.00	.04
042.	confused	−.14	−.20	−.31	−.21	−.13	−.32	−.09	−.17	−.20	−.19	−.07	−.20
043.	conscientious	−.01	.13	.13	.20	.03	.08	.12	.20	.11	.16	.10	.04
044.	conservative	.06	.12	.09	−.01	.01	.03	.11	.11	.05	−.05	−.10	−.10

Correlations of Observers' Adjectival Description with Scales of the CPI continued

| | Scale: Wb | | | | | | Scale: To | | | | | |
| | By Peers | | By Spouses | | By Staff | | By Peers | | By Spouses | | By Staff | |
Adjectives	M	F	M	F	M	F	M	F	M	F	M	F
045. considerate	.01	.12	.13	.06	−.11	−.02	.19	.20	.08	.09	.05	.00
046. contented	.08	.22	.22	.19	.00	.11	.18	.23	.15	.00	−.07	−.02
047. conventional	−.03	.11	.05	.06	.01	.02	.11	.13	.00	−.01	−.07	−.12
048. cool	.03	−.16	.02	.00	.01	.08	−.08	−.18	.04	−.04	−.04	−.03
049. cooperative	−.09	.20	.11	.15	−.01	−.02	.18	.23	.15	.19	.08	.05
050. courageous	−.01	.05	.09	.06	.04	.00	.04	.01	−.02	−.03	.00	−.12
051. cowardly	−.15	−.05	−.12	−.02	−.07	−.04	−.09	−.02	−.06	.00	−.06	.02
052. cruel	−.11	−.16	−.18	−.03	−.06	−.11	−.18	−.14	−.20	−.01	−.06	−.11
053. curious	−.02	.02	−.02	.08	−.08	−.06	.08	−.02	−.02	.05	.12	−.05
054. cynical	−.03	−.23	−.14	−.04	−.15	−.09	−.06	−.14	−.08	−.12	−.16	−.05
055. daring	.01	.09	−.02	.03	−.02	−.02	−.08	.01	−.05	−.05	−.09	−.15
056. deceitful	−.04	−.10	−.15	−.12	.03	−.14	−.19	−.09	−.08	−.13	.01	−.12
057. defensive	−.24	−.30	−.20	−.16	−.10	−.09	−.13	−.24	−.08	−.04	−.10	−.12
058. deliberate	.12	−.10	−.06	−.01	−.09	.11	.03	−.07	.04	−.09	−.09	−.02
059. demanding	.04	−.16	−.08	−.19	−.02	−.06	−.09	−.14	−.08	−.17	−.06	−.11
060. dependable	.09	.13	.13	.04	.04	.13	.20	.15	.12	.09	.06	.10
061. dependent	−.06	.00	−.09	−.18	−.06	−.15	.09	−.09	−.10	−.08	.00	−.11
062. despondent	.00	−.23	−.10	.09	−.17	−.22	−.06	−.19	−.05	.14	−.10	−.12
063. determined	.04	.04	.02	.10	.02	.09	.00	.06	−.05	.00	.00	−.04
064. dignified	−.01	.06	.00	.05	.00	.05	.07	.04	−.01	−.05	.02	−.03
065. discreet	.00	.11	.05	.04	−.04	.05	.13	.13	.14	.00	.05	.06
066. disorderly	−.05	−.17	−.09	−.09	−.05	−.24	.00	−.09	−.05	.01	.01	−.17
067. dissatisfied	−.03	−.27	−.24	−.21	−.17	−.26	−.13	−.17	−.13	−.07	−.08	−.13
068. distractible	−.19	−.08	−.16	−.13	−.16	−.22	−.10	−.04	−.21	−.16	−.02	−.18
069. distrustful	−.13	−.19	−.11	−.25	−.09	−.17	−.20	−.27	−.07	−.24	−.11	−.20
070. dominant	.03	−.03	.03	−.03	.00	.11	−.12	−.05	−.01	−.05	−.05	.01
071. dreamy	−.08	.03	−.06	−.04	−.19	−.08	.06	−.08	−.09	−.05	.00	−.04
072. dull	−.13	−.11	−.14	−.12	−.10	−.08	.06	−.09	−.14	−.05	−.09	−.13
073. easygoing	.05	.07	−.01	.10	−.13	−.02	.15	.08	−.03	.02	−.09	−.03
074. effeminate	−.06	.00	.06	−.03	−.05	−.03	−.03	.03	−.02	−.04	.05	−.07
075. efficient	.05	.15	.10	.03	.17	.15	−.02	.18	.05	.03	.15	.10
076. egotistical	.07	−.15	−.15	.01	−.03	.03	−.23	−.17	−.14	−.07	−.05	−.05
077. emotional	−.07	−.14	−.17	−.12	−.07	−.18	−.11	−.06	−.10	−.10	−.01	−.17
078. energetic	.04	.16	.04	.08	.10	.08	−.01	.08	.00	−.05	.05	.01
079. enterprising	.10	.13	.03	.14	.07	.14	.00	.16	−.03	.13	.02	.05
080. enthusiastic	.04	.12	.08	.17	.00	.00	.07	.11	.08	.10	.04	−.07
081. evasive	−.01	−.12	−.03	−.16	−.15	−.07	.04	−.16	−.10	−.23	−.17	−.11
082. excitable	−.07	−.08	−.11	−.16	−.03	−.06	−.07	−.12	−.11	−.20	−.03	−.12
083. fair-minded	.03	.17	.21	.13	−.03	.08	.23	.21	.22	.16	.08	.08
084. fault-finding	−.03	−.24	−.12	−.11	−.09	−.07	−.24	−.16	−.06	−.10	−.06	−.11
085. fearful	−.04	−.11	−.21	−.03	−.15	−.25	−.06	−.16	−.18	−.01	−.04	−.14
086. feminine	.02	.10	.00	−.06	−.10	−.01	.15	.09	.06	−.05	.05	−.02
087. fickle	−.07	−.04	−.01	−.13	−.05	−.13	−.03	−.12	−.02	−.10	.01	−.14
088. flirtatious	−.01	.08	−.15	−.07	−.04	−.10	−.07	−.04	−.31	−.20	.00	−.14

Correlations of Observers' Adjectival Description with Scales of the CPI continued

		Scale: Wb						Scale: To				
		By Peers		By Spouses		By Staff		By Peers		By Spouses		By Staff	
Adjectives		M	F	M	F	M	F	M	F	M	F	M	F
089.	foolish	−.05	−.13	.04	−.24	−.04	−.10	−.04	−.13	.00	−.16	−.09	−.16
090.	forceful	.00	−.03	−.08	−.05	.01	.13	−.13	−.05	−.09	−.01	−.05	.03
091.	foresighted	.10	.10	.07	.16	.05	.11	.19	.15	.09	.13	.15	.10
092.	forgetful	−.23	−.09	−.03	.01	−.11	−.03	−.06	−.02	−.05	−.04	.02	−.10
093.	forgiving	.06	.14	.04	−.05	−.10	−.07	.26	.15	.07	.01	−.03	−.09
094.	formal	.07	.03	.07	.08	.02	.03	.06	.04	.07	.07	.04	−.03
095.	frank	.02	−.06	.02	−.03	−.03	−.01	.10	.05	−.02	.11	−.02	−.07
096.	friendly	.04	.18	.10	.09	−.03	.04	.17	.16	.14	.08	−.02	.08
097.	frivolous	−.03	.04	.02	−.11	−.05	−.07	−.02	−.04	−.06	−.03	−.02	−.16
098.	fussy	−.17	−.10	−.19	−.17	−.04	−.08	−.16	−.19	−.13	−.18	−.09	−.08
099.	generous	.05	.11	.10	.01	−.08	−.01	.19	.10	.08	.08	.01	−.03
100.	gentle	.02	.14	.13	.02	−.17	−.08	.23	.17	.13	.04	.02	−.09
101.	gloomy	−.06	−.26	−.22	−.05	−.10	−.19	−.09	−.23	−.11	−.05	.00	−.12
102.	good-looking	.01	.06	.04	−.04	−.05	.02	.04	−.02	.04	−.04	−.01	−.06
103.	good-natured	.15	.13	.18	.16	−.09	.00	.21	.23	.11	.10	−.01	.00
104.	greedy	−.14	−.19	−.10	−.07	−.04	−.09	−.15	−.15	−.18	−.07	.02	−.08
105.	handsome	−.06	−.06	.04	.04	−.09	.04	−.02	.08	.08	.06	−.07	.08
106.	hard-headed	.02	−.18	−.03	−.12	.05	.04	−.16	−.23	−.09	−.16	−.07	−.02
107.	hard-hearted	−.04	−.11	−.07	−.16	−.04	.00	−.21	−.24	−.14	−.12	−.16	−.05
108.	hasty	−.13	−.14	−.15	−.18	.03	−.11	−.17	−.08	−.13	−.09	.03	−.11
109.	headstrong	−.08	−.10	−.04	−.16	−.04	−.05	−.17	−.06	−.08	−.11	−.08	−.11
110.	healthy	−.03	.08	.10	.09	−.08	.11	.08	.03	.03	.03	−.07	−.02
111.	helpful	−.02	.15	−.02	.06	−.03	.01	.20	.15	.04	−.01	.05	.02
112.	high-strung	−.06	−.13	−.23	−.17	−.08	−.20	−.11	−.09	−.13	−.12	.03	−.13
113.	honest	.06	.09	.13	.07	.01	.04	.26	.15	.21	.13	.06	.01
114.	hostile	.01	−.19	−.13	−.06	−.03	−.06	−.11	−.20	−.12	−.02	−.07	−.12
115.	humorous	.07	−.05	−.02	.21	−.09	−.02	−.03	.02	.00	.16	−.14	.01
116.	hurried	−.14	−.15	−.07	.03	−.04	−.06	−.12	−.11	−.09	.09	.04	−.03
117.	idealistic	−.08	.11	−.03	.07	−.05	−.04	.00	.02	.04	.11	.14	−.07
118.	imaginative	.03	.08	.04	.06	−.03	−.02	.03	.10	.11	.05	.11	.02
119.	immature	.01	−.13	−.23	−.16	−.07	−.14	−.11	−.24	−.21	.01	.03	−.09
120.	impatient	−.07	−.23	−.07	−.15	.01	−.10	−.13	−.20	−.06	−.16	−.01	−.10
121.	impulsive	−.08	−.14	−.17	−.13	−.04	−.14	−.09	−.13	−.15	−.11	−.05	−.13
122.	independent	.18	.09	.18	.05	.00	.06	.22	.10	.13	−.02	−.05	.01
123.	indifferent	−.04	−.18	−.04	−.01	−.12	−.11	−.05	−.12	−.14	−.01	−.12	−.14
124.	individualistic	−.06	.00	.03	.10	−.09	−.01	.07	−.02	.06	.09	−.09	−.06
125.	industrious	.04	.08	.08	.05	.07	.19	.07	.13	.02	.05	.05	.04
126.	infantile	−.06	−.12	−.11	−.30	−.15	−.24	−.12	−.21	−.14	−.22	−.13	−.21
127.	informal	.05	.10	.02	.01	−.08	−.09	.11	.11	.03	.01	−.10	−.04
128.	ingenious	.11	.03	.06	.06	.07	.02	−.06	.01	.12	.01	.13	.05
129.	inhibited	−.02	.04	−.08	−.06	−.11	−.10	.09	−.03	−.05	.01	−.02	−.05
130.	initiative	.13	.11	.03	.15	.08	.13	−.04	.05	.11	.13	.03	.04
131.	insightful	.12	.17	.04	.14	−.01	−.01	.14	.15	.17	.21	.12	.12
132.	intelligent	.10	.22	.09	.05	−.03	.14	.09	.20	.17	.10	.12	.15

Correlations of Observers' Adjectival Description with Scales of the CPI continued

		Scale: Wb						Scale: To					
		By Peers		By Spouses		By Staff		By Peers		By Spouses		By Staff	
Adjectives		M	F	M	F	M	F	M	F	M	F	M	F
133.	interests—narrow	−.05	−.10	−.05	−.26	−.04	−.14	.00	−.12	−.15	−.23	−.13	−.25
134.	interests—wide	.02	.07	.12	.12	−.04	.05	.02	.05	.14	.18	.11	.08
135.	intolerant	−.11	−.13	−.13	−.21	−.06	−.13	−.21	−.17	−.19	−.18	−.10	−.23
136.	inventive	.15	.04	.03	.13	−.02	.05	.01	.00	.05	.05	.06	.05
137.	irresponsible	−.07	−.13	−.05	−.19	−.03	−.18	−.10	−.08	−.03	−.14	.06	−.13
138.	irritable	−.08	−.23	−.10	−.18	−.04	−.11	−.21	−.21	−.05	−.08	−.05	−.06
139.	jolly	.05	.14	−.06	.06	−.01	−.01	.01	.14	−.12	.06	−.13	−.08
140.	kind	−.02	.13	.12	.05	−.17	−.04	.15	.12	.13	.11	−.07	−.02
141.	lazy	.01	−.10	−.04	−.09	−.09	−.16	−.04	−.16	.00	−.02	−.04	−.14
142.	leisurely	−.02	.12	.04	−.02	−.05	−.01	.06	.09	.03	.02	−.08	−.05
143.	logical	.12	.15	.02	.11	−.01	.13	.12	.17	.09	.16	.09	.07
144.	loud	−.01	−.12	−.14	−.12	−.04	−.02	−.16	−.09	−.11	−.16	−.10	−.06
145.	loyal	.01	.12	−.08	−.12	−.03	.01	.16	.05	.05	−.09	−.05	−.10
146.	mannerly	.01	.14	.10	.17	−.10	.00	.15	.21	.08	.10	.03	−.10
147.	masculine	.09	−.06	.00	−.02	−.05	.05	.05	−.10	−.07	−.06	−.16	.00
148.	mature	.17	.13	.19	.17	.02	.07	.14	.19	.21	.06	.02	.05
149.	meek	−.11	−.08	−.08	−.14	−.19	−.10	.11	−.07	−.06	.04	−.07	−.06
150.	methodical	−.01	.02	.05	.14	.05	.13	.02	.01	.02	.09	.07	.01
151.	mild	−.07	.05	−.04	.04	−.09	−.02	.15	.09	.08	.05	.01	−.02
152.	mischievous	−.07	.03	−.10	−.12	−.05	−.05	−.16	.08	−.16	−.14	−.06	−.05
153.	moderate	.11	.21	.08	.15	−.01	.10	.21	.17	.20	.13	.03	.04
154.	modest	.01	.02	.04	.01	−.06	−.07	.22	.05	.09	.03	.05	−.03
155.	moody	−.05	−.29	−.17	−.17	−.13	−.23	−.05	−.28	−.08	−.15	−.06	−.16
156.	nagging	−.16	−.16	−.27	−.20	−.09	−.21	−.17	−.09	−.26	−.11	−.05	−.20
157.	natural	.01	.05	.08	.05	.06	.08	.18	.14	.05	.11	−.01	.08
158.	nervous	−.16	−.21	−.27	−.17	−.12	−.22	−.02	−.19	−.20	−.11	.02	−.11
159.	noisy	−.03	−.05	−.05	−.13	−.02	−.04	−.19	.04	−.03	−.14	−.09	−.07
160.	obliging	−.02	.22	.01	.05	.00	−.03	.17	.14	.05	.05	.14	−.01
161.	obnoxious	−.01	−.22	−.07	−.08	−.06	−.16	−.20	−.24	−.14	.04	−.06	−.19
162.	opinionated	−.09	−.11	−.03	−.13	−.03	−.01	−.23	−.06	.01	−.11	−.09	−.11
163.	opportunistic	.07	−.04	−.08	.02	.02	.00	−.12	−.04	−.03	−.04	−.07	−.11
164.	optimistic	.11	.18	.12	.16	.01	.08	.09	.14	.05	.15	.03	−.02
165.	organized	.09	.19	.10	.10	.16	.21	−.01	.14	.02	.01	.14	.10
166.	original	.03	.06	.02	.02	.00	−.03	.01	.08	.08	.02	.13	−.04
167.	outgoing	.03	.09	.03	.13	.08	.06	−.03	.07	−.03	.13	−.02	.02
168.	outspoken	.07	−.07	−.16	−.01	.02	.05	−.10	.04	−.15	.05	−.03	−.04
169.	painstaking	.04	.01	.05	−.03	−.03	−.04	.05	.04	.04	−.06	.04	−.11
170.	patient	−.02	.19	.09	.00	−.05	.03	.12	.22	.17	.00	.06	−.02
171.	peaceable	−.07	.21	.05	.03	−.08	.04	.22	.19	.01	.09	.07	−.01
172.	peculiar	−.12	−.15	−.09	−.07	−.14	−.07	−.06	−.08	−.23	−.14	−.08	−.07
173.	persevering	.10	.06	−.04	.13	.08	.04	.17	.08	.05	.10	.08	−.07
174.	persistent	.08	−.01	.03	.11	−.02	.06	.07	.03	.01	.00	−.08	−.05
175.	pessimistic	−.11	−.30	−.09	−.12	−.16	−.24	−.03	−.19	−.07	−.11	−.02	−.15
176.	planful	.04	.11	.03	.08	.03	.16	−.02	.06	.00	−.01	.08	.05

Correlations of Observers' Adjectival Description with Scales of the CPI continued

	Scale: Wb						Scale: To					
	By Peers		By Spouses		By Staff		By Peers		By Spouses		By Staff	
Adjectives	M	F	M	F	M	F	M	F	M	F	M	F
177. pleasant	.09	.19	.16	.09	−.05	.08	.28	.19	.06	.14	.01	.13
178. pleasure-seeking	.10	.02	−.10	−.09	−.01	−.07	−.09	.06	−.08	−.14	−.07	−.15
179. poised	.14	.12	.07	.07	.09	.15	.09	.12	.04	.00	.03	.09
180. polished	.12	.05	.04	.17	.05	.07	.06	.06	.01	.07	.01	.02
181. practical	.09	.14	.13	.09	.02	.07	.16	.14	.11	.03	−.09	−.03
182. praising	.02	.14	.01	−.02	.09	.00	.16	−.03	.04	−.07	.10	−.07
183. precise	.00	−.01	.06	.14	−.03	.09	.09	.00	.07	.13	.05	.05
184. prejudiced	−.03	−.19	−.15	−.21	−.06	−.17	−.16	−.17	−.33	−.28	−.15	−.24
185. preoccupied	−.07	−.14	−.04	−.14	−.19	−.18	−.09	−.18	.01	−.15	−.05	−.14
186. progressive	.03	−.07	−.04	.04	−.07	.02	.12	.01	.03	.16	−.01	.04
187. prudish	−.17	.00	−.15	−.14	−.07	−.05	−.10	−.02	−.16	−.11	−.04	−.09
188. quarrelsome	−.01	−.22	−.22	−.15	−.05	−.12	−.21	−.11	−.17	−.15	−.04	−.12
189. queer	−.21	−.18	.05	.00	−.08	−.07	−.14	−.22	.05	.00	−.03	−.02
190. quick	.08	.04	−.03	.06	.02	−.03	−.02	.06	−.01	−.01	.06	−.04
191. quiet	−.08	.02	.12	.02	−.13	−.04	.13	.01	.12	.07	.01	.01
192. quitting	−.15	−.19	−.14	−.07	−.09	−.14	−.02	−.18	−.09	.00	.01	−.11
193. rational	.14	.26	.06	.18	−.11	.10	.20	.23	.09	.14	.06	.02
194. rattle-brained	−.07	−.11	−.21	−.13	−.06	−.15	.02	−.12	−.14	−.14	−.06	−.18
195. realistic	.17	.16	.01	.10	−.03	.10	.22	.17	.06	.07	−.04	.02
196. reasonable	.13	.21	.10	.14	.00	.11	.29	.21	.18	.18	.05	.10
197. rebellious	−.03	−.22	−.20	−.14	−.11	−.08	−.17	−.22	−.10	−.16	−.07	−.07
198. reckless	−.08	−.08	−.16	−.27	−.05	−.15	−.19	−.09	−.15	−.29	−.07	−.15
199. reflective	−.12	.04	−.09	.08	−.12	−.11	.14	.04	.04	.22	.13	.01
200. relaxed	.09	.25	.12	.04	.00	.07	.14	.21	.07	.02	−.06	.07
201. reliable	.09	.24	.12	.09	.04	.12	.19	.27	.01	.12	.06	.07
202. resentful	.02	−.30	−.20	−.20	−.09	−.15	−.13	−.34	−.10	−.04	−.14	−.21
203. reserved	−.02	.05	.00	−.06	−.12	−.02	.16	.02	.03	−.02	.01	−.03
204. resourceful	.14	.19	.00	.07	.09	.10	.15	.13	.08	.00	.07	.09
205. responsible	.13	.24	.08	.08	.02	.13	.18	.26	.12	.09	.06	.06
206. restless	−.09	−.16	−.15	−.11	−.08	−.16	−.18	−.20	−.10	−.12	−.06	−.11
207. retiring	−.10	−.11	.00	−.04	−.13	.00	−.01	−.08	.03	−.06	−.05	−.02
208. rigid	−.06	−.10	−.03	−.12	−.07	−.04	−.15	−.07	−.07	−.07	−.15	−.18
209. robust	−.01	−.01	.00	.06	−.04	.02	.05	−.03	−.06	.01	−.13	−.07
210. rude	−.03	−.22	−.07	−.02	−.09	−.16	−.14	−.16	−.14	−.02	−.11	−.12
211. sarcastic	.00	−.26	−.07	−.08	−.11	−.09	.02	−.16	−.12	−.10	−.10	−.06
212. self-centered	−.02	−.11	−.19	−.16	−.06	−.13	−.23	−.27	−.22	−.11	−.10	−.18
213. self-confident	.08	.17	.16	.19	.05	.16	−.03	.08	.06	.00	.00	.04
214. self-controlled	.07	.21	.10	.14	−.02	.07	.17	.22	.12	.03	.02	.01
215. self-denying	.00	.04	−.14	−.07	−.05	−.08	.09	−.03	−.07	−.04	.01	−.04
216. self-pitying	−.07	−.23	−.25	−.22	−.09	−.23	−.07	−.22	−.09	−.07	−.03	−.21
217. self-punishing	−.05	−.08	−.17	−.12	−.08	−.21	−.01	−.10	−.13	−.01	−.01	−.16
218. self-seeking	−.03	−.12	−.08	.05	.01	−.02	−.14	−.14	−.07	.02	−.07	−.13
219. selfish	.03	−.14	.00	.01	−.02	−.12	−.14	−.22	−.02	.00	−.08	−.17
220. sensitive	−.10	−.10	−.07	−.08	−.19	−.18	−.03	.00	.00	.03	.07	−.08

Correlations of Observers' Adjectival Description with Scales of the CPI *continued*											
	Scale: Wb						**Scale: To**				
	By Peers		By Spouses		By Staff		By Peers		By Spouses		By Staff	
Adjectives	M	F	M	F	M	F	M	F	M	F	M	F
221. sentimental	−.03	.09	−.03	.01	−.08	−.11	.07	.00	−.05	−.01	−.05	−.12
222. serious	.00	−.02	−.05	.04	−.11	.05	.13	.02	.08	.04	.04	.01
223. severe	−.17	.02	−.12	−.03	−.10	−.05	−.10	.00	−.14	.00	−.10	−.10
224. sexy	.03	−.03	−.08	−.03	−.10	−.02	−.03	−.04	−.07	−.05	−.13	−.12
225. shallow	−.20	.00	.01	−.19	−.01	−.09	−.21	−.07	−.05	−.19	−.11	−.22
226. sharp-witted	.14	−.13	−.08	−.01	−.01	−.05	.03	−.05	.04	.04	−.01	−.04
227. shiftless	−.07	−.15	−.13	−.15	−.05	−.14	−.04	−.18	−.17	−.14	−.06	−.02
228. show-off	−.02	−.14	−.10	−.03	−.07	.02	−.24	−.05	−.11	−.15	−.07	−.09
229. shrewd	.11	−.14	−.09	−.05	.09	−.02	.03	−.02	−.11	−.03	.00	−.04
230. shy	−.02	−.07	−.01	−.05	−.24	−.14	.13	−.03	.05	−.04	−.05	−.09
231. silent	−.16	−.06	−.05	−.04	−.21	−.11	.01	−.02	−.02	−.07	−.05	−.07
232. simple	−.03	.00	.03	−.22	−.05	−.07	.08	−.01	−.04	−.20	−.14	−.13
233. sincere	.01	.12	.13	.10	−.06	.05	.16	.19	.18	.11	.08	.04
234. slipshod	.02	−.17	−.11	−.11	.00	−.09	−.08	−.15	−.10	−.06	.00	−.05
235. slow	−.16	−.02	−.13	−.12	−.05	−.04	.07	−.05	−.13	−.05	−.03	−.08
236. sly	.03	−.17	−.24	−.02	−.01	−.12	−.04	−.06	−.21	−.18	−.01	−.18
237. smug	.05	−.09	−.10	−.02	−.02	−.05	−.13	−.08	−.12	−.11	−.11	−.15
238. snobbish	−.03	−.07	−.05	−.13	−.04	.00	−.17	−.04	.00	−.09	−.04	−.07
239. sociable	.13	.16	.03	−.04	.03	.03	.05	.10	.01	−.06	−.01	−.02
240. soft-hearted	.06	.19	−.08	−.14	−.06	−.06	.26	.14	−.07	−.08	−.01	−.09
241. sophisticated	.14	−.06	.01	.14	−.05	.04	−.04	−.01	.01	.01	.01	.06
242. spendthrift	.05	−.09	.04	−.11	−.02	−.12	−.08	−.05	.04	−.14	−.03	−.14
243. spineless	−.02	−.14	.02	−.09	−.10	−.03	−.03	−.13	.06	−.05	−.10	−.02
244. spontaneous	−.02	.07	.02	.05	.01	−.01	−.03	.04	.00	.06	.00	−.04
245. spunky	−.05	.08	−.16	.03	.01	−.05	.01	.08	−.17	−.04	−.04	−.12
246. stable	.07	.23	.11	.06	.01	.19	.18	.22	.18	.06	.01	.11
247. steady	.05	.17	.06	.01	−.03	.09	.23	.19	.05	.00	−.09	.00
248. stern	−.05	−.07	−.14	.03	−.06	.03	−.11	−.04	−.21	.01	−.10	−.12
249. stingy	−.19	−.16	−.16	−.11	−.02	.00	−.12	−.21	−.24	−.13	−.05	−.05
250. stolid	−.06	−.12	.03	−.03	−.11	.03	−.08	−.13	.02	−.02	−.17	−.12
251. strong	.01	.16	.05	.04	−.07	.11	−.04	.03	−.03	−.09	−.14	−.01
252. stubborn	−.03	−.08	−.10	−.06	.00	.03	−.23	−.18	−.09	−.16	−.13	−.08
253. submissive	.01	.07	−.17	−.13	−.07	−.05	.16	.09	−.05	−.05	−.01	.02
254. suggestible	.00	.10	−.12	.02	−.03	−.11	.12	.10	−.06	−.07	.00	−.08
255. sulky	−.02	−.27	−.07	−.11	−.12	−.20	−.14	−.23	−.08	−.05	−.10	−.20
256. superstitious	.00	−.09	−.27	−.26	−.04	−.29	.01	.03	−.23	−.21	−.07	−.27
257. suspicious	−.07	−.22	−.23	−.17	−.14	−.16	−.22	−.19	−.22	−.28	−.18	−.23
258. sympathetic	−.04	.14	.08	.07	−.07	−.07	.16	.12	.13	.04	.05	−.02
259. tactful	.11	.16	.16	.14	.06	.03	.12	.22	.14	.13	.11	.07
260. tactless	.00	−.17	−.15	−.08	−.07	−.09	−.09	−.09	−.12	.02	−.09	−.16
261. talkative	.07	.00	−.01	−.05	.01	−.02	.02	−.01	−.08	−.05	−.01	−.07
262. temperamental	−.12	−.25	−.14	−.16	−.12	−.10	−.23	−.22	−.16	−.18	−.10	−.09
263. tense	−.07	−.24	−.20	−.15	−.09	−.23	−.04	−.17	−.13	−.09	−.04	−.10
264. thankless	−.09	−.24	−.14	−.01	−.12	−.02	−.19	−.19	−.13	.00	−.09	−.09

Correlations of Observers' Adjectival Description with Scales of the CPI continued

| | Scale: Wb | | | | | | Scale: To | | | | | |
| | By Peers | | By Spouses | | By Staff | | By Peers | | By Spouses | | By Staff | |
Adjectives	M	F	M	F	M	F	M	F	M	F	M	F
265. thorough	.10	.08	.00	.12	.10	.15	.12	.04	−.02	.07	.19	.02
266. thoughtful	.14	.15	.06	.17	−.07	.05	.30	.17	.10	.12	.13	.08
267. thrifty	−.02	.08	−.02	.05	−.10	.02	.04	.10	.03	.00	−.10	−.10
268. timid	−.14	−.10	−.02	−.18	−.19	−.15	.07	−.07	.01	−.07	−.05	−.09
269. tolerant	−.01	.22	.12	.06	−.03	.04	.18	.22	.19	.12	.11	.07
270. touchy	−.02	−.20	−.15	−.22	−.08	−.22	−.11	−.17	−.05	−.18	−.03	−.20
271. tough	−.02	−.11	−.11	.01	−.03	.02	−.13	−.08	−.17	−.01	−.17	−.07
272. trusting	.02	.26	.07	.14	−.06	.00	.25	.21	.08	.10	.11	−.06
273. unaffected	.05	.09	.07	−.04	.02	.04	.13	.24	.04	−.06	.10	.09
274. unambitious	.03	−.03	−.16	−.06	−.09	−.15	.11	−.02	−.13	.06	−.03	−.14
275. unassuming	−.02	.04	.03	.06	−.07	−.06	.14	.15	.01	.06	.07	.04
276. unconventional	.06	−.25	−.02	−.05	−.10	−.05	.01	−.10	−.03	−.02	−.01	−.06
277. undependable	−.06	−.11	.00	−.16	−.01	−.12	−.19	−.17	.06	−.17	.04	−.08
278. understanding	.09	.20	.06	.16	−.09	.01	.14	.23	.11	.15	.06	.02
279. unemotional	−.04	−.07	.11	−.05	−.17	.02	−.03	−.12	.13	−.02	−.17	−.09
280. unexcitable	−.03	−.02	.00	−.08	−.03	.08	.03	−.02	−.02	.00	−.05	.02
281. unfriendly	−.10	−.16	−.18	.02	−.02	−.03	−.12	−.21	−.11	−.07	−.04	−.13
282. uninhibited	.10	−.13	.05	.03	.00	−.07	−.01	−.01	.02	.02	−.03	−.12
283. unintelligent	.06	−.06	.00	−.05	.02	.01	.05	−.08	.00	−.12	−.06	−.02
284. unkind	.00	−.23	.01	−.04	−.10	−.09	−.07	−.18	−.05	−.10	−.02	−.20
285. unrealistic	−.08	−.11	−.10	−.22	−.12	−.19	−.08	−.14	−.02	−.27	−.02	−.20
286. unscrupulous	−.04	−.15	−.27	−.01	−.01	−.10	−.18	−.15	−.16	−.06	.04	−.14
287. unselfish	.13	.07	−.07	.03	−.04	−.02	.18	.21	−.07	.04	.07	.00
288. unstable	.00	−.28	−.23	−.11	−.05	−.24	−.12	−.21	−.16	−.13	.04	−.14
289. vindictive	.01	−.05	−.08	−.16	−.05	−.14	−.11	−.08	−.13	−.19	−.12	−.13
290. versatile	.15	.03	−.01	.09	.06	.02	.10	.02	−.03	.02	.08	.03
291. warm	−.03	.20	−.04	.01	−.03	.02	.10	.23	.05	.06	−.01	.06
292. wary	.01	−.09	−.04	−.02	−.15	−.09	−.11	−.12	−.11	−.10	−.16	−.12
293. weak	−.04	−.04	−.33	−.23	−.09	−.18	.11	−.04	−.11	−.08	−.06	−.07
294. whiny	−.12	−.14	−.25	−.29	−.03	−.15	−.10	−.07	−.13	−.18	−.03	−.11
295. wholesome	.04	.17	.02	.11	−.01	.11	.14	.17	.02	.09	.04	.05
296. wise	.11	.15	.11	.05	.00	.02	.07	.14	.06	.05	.09	.01
297. withdrawn	−.03	−.10	−.19	−.04	−.24	−.16	.12	−.08	−.21	.01	−.10	−.08
298. witty	.05	−.12	.00	−.04	−.03	−.05	−.04	.02	.02	.00	−.02	−.03
299. worrying	−.13	−.15	−.31	−.23	−.18	−.21	−.12	−.05	−.28	−.10	.01	−.13
300. zany	−.05	.00	−.08	−.03	−.06	−.07	−.10	.01	−.09	−.07	.00	−.15

Correlations of Observers' Adjectival Description with Scales of the CPI continued											
	Scale: Ac						Scale: Ai					
	By Peers		By Spouses		By Staff		By Peers		By Spouses		By Staff	
Adjectives	M	F	M	F	M	F	M	F	M	F	M	F
001. absent-minded	−.10	−.26	−.12	−.13	−.08	−.22	−.05	−.17	−.03	.03	−.08	−.05
002. active	.19	.07	−.06	.10	.00	.06	.08	.11	.02	.05	.08	.07
003. adaptable	.16	.18	−.02	.06	.04	.05	.11	.16	.05	.03	.15	.02
004. adventurous	−.09	−.19	−.14	−.06	−.17	−.15	.08	−.03	.03	.03	.02	.05
005. affected	.02	.11	.02	−.05	−.02	−.04	−.09	.10	.04	−.05	.01	.02
006. affectionate	−.05	.03	−.11	.04	−.08	−.04	.01	−.04	−.08	−.08	−.03	−.19
007. aggressive	.06	.02	−.07	−.01	.02	−.03	−.05	.04	−.10	.03	−.01	.14
008. alert	.13	.13	.09	.15	.05	.14	.18	.15	.19	.10	.19	.13
009. aloof	−.01	−.08	−.02	−.23	−.19	−.05	.04	−.05	−.01	.01	−.06	.01
010. ambitious	.29	.26	.12	.19	.21	.16	.16	.15	.14	.03	.17	.28
011. anxious	−.02	.00	−.06	−.09	−.07	−.27	−.10	−.09	−.02	−.04	.02	−.14
012. apathetic	−.34	−.08	−.17	−.03	−.16	−.17	−.09	−.11	−.23	−.02	−.19	−.17
013. appreciative	.13	.07	.08	.11	.01	.10	.06	.02	.12	.00	.12	−.12
014. argumentative	−.08	−.04	.01	−.07	.03	−.05	−.12	.08	−.03	.05	.11	.15
015. arrogant	−.05	−.01	−.12	−.04	−.11	−.06	−.04	−.06	−.03	.00	.02	.00
016. artistic	−.17	−.08	−.03	−.17	−.06	−.05	−.09	.05	.08	−.03	.09	.07
017. assertive	.02	.10	.00	.14	.07	.05	−.06	.05	.09	.25	.09	.18
018. attractive	−.07	.04	−.03	−.08	−.07	.04	.04	−.02	.06	−.11	.11	.00
019. autocratic	−.02	−.04	−.03	−.03	−.08	.01	.04	−.03	.01	.11	−.09	.04
020. awkward	−.08	−.17	−.25	−.14	−.15	−.24	−.12	−.15	−.19	.06	−.13	−.03
021. bitter	−.04	−.24	−.27	−.24	−.17	−.17	.01	−.14	−.22	−.06	−.20	−.13
022. blustery	−.09	−.11	−.07	−.15	−.10	−.16	−.12	−.05	.00	.00	−.11	−.04
023. boastful	−.08	.04	−.08	−.09	−.06	.02	−.11	.01	−.18	−.08	−.06	−.01
024. bossy	.02	.07	−.20	−.05	−.04	−.04	−.09	.06	−.18	−.08	−.05	.02
025. calm	.10	.22	.06	.03	−.10	.07	.09	.21	.05	.05	−.03	.02
026. capable	.29	.26	−.01	.17	.00	.19	.21	.20	.11	.14	.17	.14
027. careless	−.27	−.33	−.25	−.10	−.16	−.28	−.08	−.05	−.17	−.08	−.05	−.07
028. cautious	.03	.24	−.11	.06	−.05	−.01	.01	.00	−.08	−.02	−.04	−.15
029. changeable	−.09	−.27	−.19	−.16	−.16	−.23	.11	.00	−.01	−.03	−.06	−.06
030. charming	−.06	.10	−.12	.04	−.08	.03	−.02	.01	−.06	−.09	.12	.03
031. cheerful	.01	.07	.06	.09	.04	.13	.03	.07	.05	−.04	.08	−.04
032. civilized	.07	.12	.07	.02	−.01	.11	.11	.10	−.02	−.03	.16	.05
033. clear-thinking	.20	.26	.15	.26	.05	.11	.20	.20	.18	.22	.24	.26
034. clever	.02	−.10	−.02	.10	−.07	−.02	.17	.10	.14	.16	.17	.19
035. coarse	−.14	−.22	−.13	−.07	−.18	−.22	−.05	−.11	−.14	.16	−.18	−.05
036. cold	−.12	−.04	−.02	−.04	−.13	−.11	−.13	−.05	−.06	−.05	−.12	−.07
037. commonplace	−.06	.02	−.02	−.08	−.15	−.10	−.06	.00	−.04	−.06	−.25	−.23
038. complaining	−.13	−.17	−.21	−.19	−.11	−.13	−.12	−.05	−.26	−.06	−.07	−.09
039. complicated	−.04	−.16	.15	−.15	−.16	−.19	.03	.05	.21	.13	.11	.15
040. conceited	−.07	.10	−.11	.00	.02	.01	−.07	−.02	−.13	.03	.03	.05
041. confident	.09	.25	.07	.18	.06	.14	.10	.11	.06	.05	.15	.16
042. confused	−.17	−.19	−.23	−.19	−.11	−.29	−.13	−.14	−.22	−.11	−.13	−.12
043. conscientious	.22	.28	.15	.20	.14	.23	.12	.14	.13	.18	.10	.02
044. conservative	.11	.26	.17	.05	.06	.21	.10	.07	.00	−.15	−.18	−.25

Correlations of Observers' Adjectival Description with Scales of the CPI continued

		Scale: Ac						Scale: Ai				
		By Peers		By Spouses		By Staff		By Peers		By Spouses		By Staff	
Adjectives		M	F	M	F	M	F	M	F	M	F	M	F
045.	considerate	.15	.13	.12	−.02	−.02	.03	.06	.05	.04	.00	.08	−.12
046.	contented	−.03	.11	.17	.04	−.08	.06	.17	.06	.07	−.01	−.07	−.18
047.	conventional	.11	.23	.10	.06	.06	.17	.06	.07	−.01	−.01	−.16	−.30
048.	cool	−.10	−.14	.03	−.04	−.10	.01	.01	−.07	.03	.04	−.02	.07
049.	cooperative	.01	.18	.11	.15	.05	.11	.00	.10	.08	.14	.12	−.07
050.	courageous	−.04	−.05	.00	.07	−.11	−.08	.03	.03	.00	−.01	.02	.01
051.	cowardly	−.02	.00	−.10	.01	−.07	−.05	−.02	.01	−.07	−.08	−.06	−.04
052.	cruel	−.14	−.09	−.12	−.06	−.16	−.16	−.09	−.02	−.12	.04	−.08	−.06
053.	curious	−.06	−.23	−.03	.05	−.09	−.13	.02	−.05	.07	.13	.24	.11
054.	cynical	−.04	−.15	−.07	−.18	−.28	−.20	.09	−.06	−.01	.05	−.08	.08
055.	daring	−.12	−.16	−.11	−.09	−.11	−.15	−.11	.08	.02	−.07	.03	.03
056.	deceitful	−.05	−.09	−.16	−.04	−.05	−.15	−.02	.05	−.11	−.06	−.01	−.02
057.	defensive	−.11	−.11	−.07	−.14	−.12	−.09	−.06	−.14	−.16	.07	−.11	−.06
058.	deliberate	.07	.06	.01	−.04	−.05	.09	.04	.02	.07	−.05	−.09	.00
059.	demanding	.04	.06	−.03	−.10	−.05	−.06	−.02	.01	−.05	−.06	.02	.03
060.	dependable	.28	.23	.05	.14	.09	.25	.14	.13	.04	.02	.08	.02
061.	dependent	−.01	−.05	−.05	−.10	−.05	−.11	−.01	−.09	−.12	−.12	−.08	−.24
062.	despondent	−.06	−.21	−.08	.07	−.15	−.15	.04	−.12	.01	.15	−.15	−.17
063.	determined	.23	.28	.02	.03	.05	.13	.09	.10	−.08	.05	.12	.14
064.	dignified	.09	.16	.04	.11	.05	.08	.05	.07	−.06	.01	.04	−.06
065.	discreet	.08	.14	.08	.07	.04	.08	.16	.13	.07	.18	.08	−.03
066.	disorderly	−.22	−.32	−.18	−.12	−.14	−.32	−.03	−.17	.00	.04	.04	−.09
067.	dissatisfied	−.10	−.12	−.18	−.10	−.18	−.29	−.15	−.03	−.09	−.05	−.05	−.05
068.	distractible	−.22	−.20	−.31	−.13	−.18	−.29	−.04	−.03	−.21	−.15	−.04	−.14
069.	distrustful	−.15	−.11	−.13	−.13	−.14	−.22	−.14	−.15	−.12	−.13	−.10	−.09
070.	dominant	.15	.08	.03	−.06	−.02	.04	.03	.05	.01	−.06	.05	.16
071.	dreamy	−.09	−.06	−.12	−.14	−.11	−.20	.04	−.05	−.03	−.05	−.02	−.07
072.	dull	−.01	.07	−.10	−.03	−.08	−.06	−.02	−.02	−.10	−.09	−.21	−.15
073.	easygoing	−.12	−.13	−.13	.05	−.17	−.07	.01	.01	−.10	.01	−.06	−.13
074.	effeminate	.07	.07	.04	.00	.01	.08	.04	−.01	−.04	.02	.01	−.06
075.	efficient	.23	.30	.14	.15	.18	.19	.03	.17	.08	.11	.19	.15
076.	egotistical	.06	.07	−.03	−.01	−.05	−.01	−.12	−.01	−.05	.08	.04	.08
077.	emotional	−.04	−.11	−.15	−.16	−.06	−.23	−.09	.00	−.13	−.10	.04	−.16
078.	energetic	−.03	.10	.02	.10	.10	.07	.04	.06	.07	.00	.12	.07
079.	enterprising	.15	.14	−.01	.15	.10	.14	.11	.14	.05	.17	.14	.17
080.	enthusiastic	.03	.06	.03	.17	.02	.09	.06	−.02	.10	.07	.14	−.04
081.	evasive	−.06	−.10	−.04	−.11	−.19	−.10	.11	−.01	−.10	−.16	−.19	−.03
082.	excitable	−.01	−.08	−.18	−.17	−.04	−.10	−.05	−.08	−.15	−.17	.04	−.09
083.	fair-minded	.17	.04	.05	.13	.00	.07	.07	.12	.15	.07	.13	.06
084.	fault-finding	−.04	.01	.00	−.15	−.10	−.10	−.09	−.03	−.08	−.04	−.01	−.04
085.	fearful	.00	.01	−.15	−.09	−.10	−.21	−.14	−.10	−.10	−.01	−.06	−.14
086.	feminine	.04	.10	.04	−.06	−.01	.05	.07	.01	.10	−.04	.06	−.13
087.	fickle	−.20	−.08	.03	−.21	−.15	−.13	.00	.04	−.04	−.01	.03	−.09
088.	flirtatious	−.16	.03	−.27	−.18	−.11	−.13	−.07	.01	−.30	−.13	.03	−.08

Correlations of Observers' Adjectival Description with Scales of the CPI continued

	Scale: Ac						Scale: Ai					
	By Peers		By Spouses		By Staff		By Peers		By Spouses		By Staff	
Adjectives	M	F	M	F	M	F	M	F	M	F	M	F
089. foolish	−.13	−.19	−.03	−.20	−.10	−.15	−.05	−.16	−.09	−.07	−.15	−.17
090. forceful	.11	.06	−.04	−.06	.02	.05	−.03	−.01	−.06	.03	.02	.14
091. foresighted	.19	.23	.10	.12	.12	.15	.20	.14	.09	.04	.23	.18
092. forgetful	−.16	−.24	−.08	−.14	−.10	−.13	−.11	−.13	−.06	.09	.00	−.09
093. forgiving	.18	.04	−.05	.04	−.07	−.06	.22	.05	−.05	−.11	.03	−.21
094. formal	.29	.19	.09	−.01	.07	.10	.08	.11	.06	.05	.04	−.08
095. frank	−.03	−.09	.01	−.04	−.10	−.08	.02	.01	−.01	.15	.06	.04
096. friendly	−.02	.10	.03	.02	.00	.03	.10	.05	.03	.00	.05	−.02
097. frivolous	−.10	.05	−.12	.01	−.15	−.13	−.10	.02	−.07	−.03	.00	−.18
098. fussy	−.15	.05	−.07	−.09	−.04	−.01	−.09	−.03	−.15	−.09	−.16	−.13
099. generous	.07	.02	−.07	.01	−.06	−.06	.05	−.05	−.04	.04	.02	−.12
100. gentle	.12	.05	.06	−.04	−.13	−.03	.09	−.05	.04	.00	.04	−.22
101. gloomy	−.10	−.14	−.16	−.04	−.13	−.11	−.05	−.13	−.14	.03	−.08	−.08
102. good-looking	.00	.06	.00	−.11	−.11	.03	.03	−.02	.04	−.05	.06	.00
103. good-natured	.03	.07	.05	.11	−.06	−.04	.13	.07	.05	.01	.05	−.08
104. greedy	−.16	−.06	−.04	−.07	−.09	−.12	−.09	−.03	−.16	−.02	.00	−.05
105. handsome	−.03	−.05	.02	.02	−.10	.00	.04	.12	.03	.07	.01	.05
106. hard-headed	.09	.05	−.06	−.13	−.01	−.04	−.08	−.04	−.14	−.09	−.03	.09
107. hard-hearted	−.21	.01	−.07	−.02	−.10	−.03	−.07	−.04	−.06	−.04	−.12	.03
108. hasty	−.20	−.15	−.23	−.10	−.02	−.18	−.13	−.06	−.20	−.03	.06	−.11
109. headstrong	−.05	−.11	−.13	−.14	−.09	−.13	−.07	−.03	−.11	−.04	.03	.08
110. healthy	−.07	−.01	.00	.05	−.10	.08	.08	−.02	−.06	.07	.04	.02
111. helpful	.13	.12	.04	.15	.01	.07	.09	.04	.03	.02	.12	−.15
112. high-strung	−.02	−.06	−.15	−.07	−.06	−.19	−.05	.00	−.08	−.05	.06	.01
113. honest	.08	.05	.03	.17	.05	.06	.12	.03	.14	.04	.12	−.03
114. hostile	−.12	−.16	−.14	.03	−.11	−.09	−.16	−.02	−.12	.02	−.08	−.01
115. humorous	−.13	−.13	−.13	.11	−.13	−.04	.03	−.07	−.02	.16	−.03	.03
116. hurried	−.14	−.08	−.07	.06	−.03	−.07	−.07	−.08	−.06	.10	.09	−.02
117. idealistic	.08	.20	.05	.11	.08	.04	.09	.02	.06	.21	.20	.02
118. imaginative	−.05	−.10	−.04	.07	−.05	−.08	.05	.05	.15	.13	.18	.18
119. immature	−.27	−.20	−.14	−.13	−.05	−.10	−.09	−.23	−.14	.00	.01	−.15
120. impatient	−.07	−.20	−.03	−.13	−.08	−.19	−.07	−.06	−.06	−.04	.06	.04
121. impulsive	−.22	−.30	−.20	−.22	−.10	−.24	−.12	−.14	−.12	−.04	.00	−.07
122. independent	.13	.00	.06	.04	−.10	−.05	.29	.05	.13	.10	.09	.23
123. indifferent	−.18	−.14	−.03	−.09	−.21	−.16	−.06	−.03	−.11	.03	−.18	−.09
124. individualistic	−.05	−.13	.01	.05	−.19	−.16	.10	.04	.09	.21	.04	.14
125. industrious	.22	.22	.09	.12	.15	.27	.13	.09	.05	.06	.11	.12
126. infantile	−.17	−.09	−.07	−.23	−.14	−.16	−.11	−.16	−.07	−.14	−.08	−.24
127. informal	−.11	−.20	−.10	.03	−.20	−.20	.05	.02	.04	.11	−.04	−.01
128. ingenious	.05	−.05	.05	.00	.01	.00	.03	.07	.26	.07	.14	.13
129. inhibited	.12	.14	−.06	−.10	−.03	−.03	.04	.08	.02	.06	−.04	−.13
130. initiative	.06	.11	.06	.11	.11	.10	−.02	.10	.24	.22	.12	.18
131. insightful	.10	.09	.02	.11	.03	−.04	.14	.17	.22	.27	.23	.21
132. intelligent	.19	.26	.11	.18	.04	.12	.21	.22	.22	.18	.30	.30

Correlations of Observers' Adjectival Description with Scales of the CPI continued

		Scale: Ac						Scale: Ai					
		By Peers		By Spouses		By Staff		By Peers		By Spouses		By Staff	
Adjectives		M	F	M	F	M	F	M	F	M	F	M	F
133.	interests—narrow	−.06	.06	−.02	−.12	−.10	−.06	−.01	−.06	−.18	−.37	−.25	−.34
134.	interests—wide	.02	.00	.05	.05	.03	−.02	.09	.00	.20	.24	.23	.24
135.	intolerant	−.03	.02	−.13	−.11	−.08	−.04	−.06	.07	−.05	−.14	−.10	−.13
136.	inventive	.08	−.10	.04	.04	−.06	−.06	.04	.05	.12	.08	.15	.13
137.	irresponsible	−.25	−.31	.00	−.11	−.12	−.23	−.08	−.09	−.03	−.07	.04	−.09
138.	irritable	−.01	−.15	−.13	−.12	−.09	−.11	−.13	−.07	−.03	−.01	−.04	−.01
139.	jolly	−.03	−.01	−.13	−.06	−.04	−.06	−.03	.05	−.18	−.03	−.08	−.13
140.	kind	.13	.04	.00	.04	−.14	.00	−.01	−.08	.01	.03	−.01	−.17
141.	lazy	−.29	−.27	.00	−.19	−.24	−.21	.01	−.12	.04	.04	−.10	−.12
142.	leisurely	−.21	−.03	−.05	−.07	−.19	−.20	.02	.05	−.05	.04	−.11	−.12
143.	logical	.22	.21	.08	.11	.07	.10	.19	.20	.13	.06	.23	.25
144.	loud	−.12	−.09	−.09	−.14	−.07	−.07	−.10	−.08	−.13	−.08	−.04	−.02
145.	loyal	.17	.06	−.09	−.07	−.04	.06	.03	−.03	.01	−.10	−.08	−.21
146.	mannerly	.13	.20	.11	.14	.01	.12	.01	.11	.01	.09	.02	−.05
147.	masculine	−.02	−.16	−.12	−.03	−.14	−.05	.03	.01	−.11	−.03	−.11	.05
148.	mature	.26	.23	.13	.17	.04	.09	.15	.19	.11	.01	.07	.02
149.	meek	−.08	−.09	−.08	−.07	−.09	−.08	.00	−.04	−.13	.06	−.13	−.13
150.	methodical	.17	.16	.06	.23	.11	.19	.06	.07	.04	.20	.02	.00
151.	mild	.01	.02	−.02	.08	−.09	−.01	.00	.03	−.04	.00	−.01	−.14
152.	mischievous	−.32	−.21	−.25	−.18	−.15	−.12	−.09	.05	−.18	−.10	.00	.03
153.	moderate	.16	.14	.12	.18	.03	.11	.15	.13	.04	.10	.00	−.03
154.	modest	.08	.01	.01	.08	−.02	−.03	.16	−.02	.01	−.06	.01	−.17
155.	moody	−.11	−.23	−.16	−.19	−.19	−.29	−.06	−.09	−.10	−.04	−.07	−.07
156.	nagging	−.03	.05	−.17	−.10	−.15	−.09	−.13	.00	−.28	−.03	−.08	−.20
157.	natural	−.05	−.13	−.10	−.04	.01	.02	.06	−.04	.05	.09	.04	.02
158.	nervous	−.05	−.12	−.13	−.12	−.08	−.26	−.02	−.10	−.15	−.08	.02	−.09
159.	noisy	−.16	−.07	−.06	−.21	−.03	−.12	−.09	−.01	−.12	−.12	−.05	−.07
160.	obliging	−.01	.17	−.04	−.05	.02	−.01	.07	.03	−.05	−.06	.09	−.14
161.	obnoxious	−.17	−.08	−.06	−.08	−.11	−.16	−.10	−.10	−.05	.06	−.04	−.11
162.	opinionated	.03	.06	−.01	−.19	−.03	.01	−.05	.00	−.01	−.07	.03	.03
163.	opportunistic	.03	.10	−.05	−.03	−.03	−.04	−.01	−.01	−.03	.05	.00	.05
164.	optimistic	.05	.15	.11	.15	.04	.13	.10	−.02	.12	.17	.12	−.06
165.	organized	.30	.33	.15	.28	.23	.29	.10	.11	.05	.06	.20	.11
166.	original	−.03	−.09	−.01	−.04	−.05	−.12	.00	.08	.10	.15	.19	.12
167.	outgoing	.02	.05	−.04	.08	.05	.08	.00	.05	−.05	.15	.06	.04
168.	outspoken	−.03	.04	−.13	.00	.03	.02	−.05	.07	−.08	.11	.07	.12
169.	painstaking	.11	.15	−.01	.03	.02	.05	.07	.11	.06	−.03	.01	−.13
170.	patient	.13	.20	.03	.03	−.03	.05	.04	.08	.12	−.07	.03	−.09
171.	peaceable	.06	.18	−.05	−.03	−.05	.04	.05	.07	−.06	−.02	.03	−.14
172.	peculiar	−.05	−.17	−.11	−.15	−.13	−.12	−.05	.00	−.21	−.07	−.09	.00
173.	persevering	.25	.29	−.03	.15	.17	.19	.15	.11	.06	.14	.15	.03
174.	persistent	.06	.20	.05	.12	.04	.06	.05	.08	.03	.07	−.02	.10
175.	pessimistic	−.05	−.20	−.04	−.15	−.14	−.21	−.08	−.14	.01	−.04	−.04	−.12
176.	planful	.23	.34	−.02	.09	.12	.22	.09	.07	−.03	.00	.16	.10

Correlations of Observers' Adjectival Description with Scales of the CPI continued											
	Scale: Ac						Scale: Ai				
	By Peers		By Spouses		By Staff		By Peers		By Spouses		By Staff	
Adjectives	M	F	M	F	M	F	M	F	M	F	M	F
177. pleasant	.10	.03	.06	.07	−.03	.12	.11	.08	.04	.10	.09	−.03
178. pleasure-seeking	−.28	−.19	−.16	−.11	−.15	−.22	−.06	.09	−.08	−.01	.02	−.14
179. poised	.08	.22	.09	.11	.10	.20	.12	.12	.13	−.01	.10	.14
180. polished	.09	.21	.04	.14	.05	.13	.09	.08	−.01	.07	.03	.14
181. practical	.20	.20	.14	.14	−.01	.08	.18	.05	.02	.07	−.07	−.08
182. praising	.09	.03	−.03	.00	.04	.05	.07	−.05	−.06	−.11	.08	−.18
183. precise	.21	.11	.13	.16	.02	.11	.14	.05	.08	.16	.05	.18
184. prejudiced	−.10	.10	−.23	−.15	−.08	−.08	−.06	−.03	−.35	−.22	−.16	−.19
185. preoccupied	.02	−.11	−.04	−.11	−.14	−.21	.02	−.03	.00	−.01	−.06	−.06
186. progressive	.09	−.06	−.01	.05	−.09	−.08	.06	−.02	.07	.21	.10	.14
187. prudish	.02	.19	−.18	−.06	−.02	.11	−.04	.03	−.05	−.12	−.10	−.21
188. quarrelsome	−.09	−.06	−.15	−.17	−.07	−.17	−.14	−.04	−.20	−.10	−.01	.01
189. queer	−.02	−.09	−.05	.00	−.05	−.07	−.06	−.04	.02	.00	−.04	.06
190. quick	−.13	.03	−.05	.03	−.03	.00	.04	.06	.09	.08	.14	.08
191. quiet	.00	.06	.06	.02	−.12	−.06	.02	.07	.04	−.04	−.03	−.10
192. quitting	−.22	−.20	−.16	−.09	−.13	−.22	−.06	−.14	−.06	.02	−.08	−.12
193. rational	.24	.24	.08	.13	−.01	.07	.17	.20	.14	.15	.22	.19
194. rattle-brained	−.08	−.13	−.12	−.14	−.07	−.21	−.03	−.10	−.20	−.17	−.13	−.19
195. realistic	.18	.21	.04	.16	−.02	.11	.12	.16	.09	.05	.07	.08
196. reasonable	.24	.17	.16	.12	.02	.12	.16	.16	.10	.17	.10	.03
197. rebellious	−.20	−.29	−.25	−.19	−.21	−.25	−.14	−.06	−.07	.06	.01	.07
198. reckless	−.26	−.22	−.28	−.29	−.15	−.22	−.11	−.04	−.08	−.13	.00	−.09
199. reflective	.00	.10	−.06	.09	.00	−.05	.07	.13	.13	.27	.24	.10
200. relaxed	−.02	.10	.00	−.01	−.11	.05	.11	.15	.01	−.05	.00	.05
201. reliable	.23	.31	.07	.07	.09	.20	.15	.18	−.04	.10	.09	−.01
202. resentful	−.03	−.19	−.12	−.10	−.17	−.14	−.09	−.09	−.14	−.01	−.11	−.13
203. reserved	.08	.13	−.05	−.02	−.09	−.06	.15	.04	.01	−.07	−.01	−.06
204. resourceful	.21	.19	−.02	.12	.09	.06	.08	.13	.12	.13	.19	.19
205. responsible	.29	.34	.08	.07	.12	.21	.17	.18	.01	.02	.12	.02
206. restless	−.22	−.28	−.16	−.11	−.15	−.24	−.15	−.16	−.11	−.01	−.01	−.03
207. retiring	−.11	−.08	−.04	−.11	−.09	−.06	.06	−.08	.04	−.02	−.08	−.10
208. rigid	.05	.14	−.06	−.16	−.05	.07	−.01	.02	−.01	−.08	−.20	−.12
209. robust	−.02	−.06	.01	.06	−.11	−.06	.01	−.04	−.04	.08	−.08	−.05
210. rude	−.24	−.12	−.09	.01	−.13	−.12	−.08	−.03	−.10	.01	−.06	−.07
211. sarcastic	−.11	−.19	−.04	−.11	−.17	−.12	.07	−.07	−.06	.03	.00	.05
212. self-centered	−.07	.03	−.13	−.15	−.08	−.15	−.08	−.03	−.17	−.02	−.01	−.06
213. self-confident	.11	.16	.12	.17	.07	.16	.17	.06	.11	.02	.16	.20
214. self-controlled	.12	.23	.08	.12	.03	.08	.19	.11	.06	.07	.07	−.05
215. self-denying	.07	.01	−.10	−.03	−.07	−.01	−.02	.07	−.10	−.14	−.06	−.14
216. self-pitying	−.03	−.12	−.15	−.08	−.08	−.10	−.10	−.10	−.12	−.06	−.04	−.16
217. self-punishing	.05	−.03	−.13	−.10	−.10	−.13	−.05	−.03	−.14	.02	−.03	−.06
218. self-seeking	−.08	−.06	−.04	−.05	−.01	−.08	.04	.03	−.05	.00	.02	−.02
219. selfish	−.05	.01	.09	−.04	−.09	−.18	.04	−.05	.01	.02	−.04	−.12
220. sensitive	.02	−.10	−.11	−.02	−.15	−.17	−.09	−.09	.03	−.01	.15	−.06

Correlations of Observers' Adjectival Description with Scales of the CPI continued

		Scale: Ac						Scale: Ai				
		By Peers		By Spouses		By Staff		By Peers		By Spouses		By Staff	
Adjectives		M	F	M	F	M	F	M	F	M	F	M	F
221.	sentimental	.04	.03	−.12	−.05	−.08	−.14	.13	.02	−.09	−.07	−.03	−.24
222.	serious	.26	.12	.05	.07	.00	.08	.15	.08	.03	.07	.07	.14
223.	severe	.02	−.03	−.07	−.02	−.11	−.01	−.02	.10	−.03	.00	−.12	−.03
224.	sexy	−.06	−.01	−.17	−.16	−.18	−.13	.01	.08	−.09	−.01	−.01	−.02
225.	shallow	−.21	.05	−.05	−.02	−.06	−.16	−.20	.03	−.08	−.11	−.19	−.31
226.	sharp-witted	.03	−.17	.04	−.05	−.06	−.06	.14	−.03	.11	.17	.11	.12
227.	shiftless	−.29	−.18	−.16	−.18	−.17	−.23	−.13	−.03	−.22	−.08	−.08	−.06
228.	show-off	−.17	−.01	−.07	−.10	−.09	.01	−.14	.00	−.11	−.10	.01	−.02
229.	shrewd	.15	−.10	−.17	−.06	.00	−.05	.14	.03	−.03	−.02	.02	.09
230.	shy	.00	.02	−.12	−.05	−.16	−.16	.00	−.04	.01	−.08	−.07	−.16
231.	silent	−.09	.08	−.12	−.03	−.19	−.11	−.03	.02	−.11	−.05	−.08	−.13
232.	simple	−.09	.00	−.08	−.16	−.12	−.10	−.01	−.09	−.17	−.17	−.29	−.31
233.	sincere	.17	.10	.05	.05	.05	.11	.01	−.03	.12	.02	.10	−.01
234.	slipshod	−.13	−.26	−.11	−.13	−.06	−.20	−.02	−.05	−.07	.05	.00	−.04
235.	slow	−.13	.00	−.23	−.10	−.05	−.14	.00	−.08	−.20	−.09	−.16	−.17
236.	sly	−.06	−.10	−.28	−.11	−.13	−.16	.07	.03	−.20	−.04	−.01	−.05
237.	smug	−.05	.07	.00	−.07	−.06	.04	−.03	.04	−.06	−.08	−.03	−.02
238.	snobbish	−.07	.09	−.01	−.01	.01	−.02	−.04	.04	.04	.02	.00	.01
239.	sociable	.01	.06	−.03	.00	.00	.06	.03	−.02	−.07	.06	.06	−.04
240.	soft-hearted	.05	.02	−.15	−.13	−.06	−.08	.04	−.01	−.11	−.10	−.01	−.25
241.	sophisticated	−.03	.06	.06	.06	−.05	.03	.02	.02	.02	.12	.09	.18
242.	spendthrift	−.18	−.11	.04	−.10	−.12	−.05	−.07	−.06	−.03	−.03	−.01	−.16
243.	spineless	−.12	−.14	.11	−.19	−.12	−.07	−.02	−.11	.10	.04	−.16	−.04
244.	spontaneous	−.16	−.08	−.05	−.06	.00	−.05	−.12	.02	.01	.21	.10	.01
245.	spunky	−.22	−.05	−.12	−.10	−.04	−.10	−.10	.01	−.22	.06	−.01	.02
246.	stable	.23	.27	.06	.08	.03	.22	.18	.16	.07	.04	.06	.03
247.	steady	.23	.23	.00	.09	.01	.16	.15	.06	−.01	−.05	−.04	−.05
248.	stern	.10	.13	−.08	−.13	−.08	.05	−.06	.07	−.23	−.01	−.12	−.04
249.	stingy	−.08	−.06	−.21	−.14	−.08	−.05	−.05	−.04	−.15	−.03	−.11	−.03
250.	stolid	.06	.00	−.10	−.01	−.14	−.01	−.10	−.06	−.03	−.01	−.24	−.15
251.	strong	.07	.12	.00	.06	−.12	.06	.03	.04	−.02	−.04	−.04	.10
252.	stubborn	−.02	.06	−.10	−.10	−.10	−.08	−.08	−.06	−.12	−.02	−.07	.07
253.	submissive	−.06	.04	−.09	−.08	.02	−.06	.08	.00	−.05	−.04	−.09	−.14
254.	suggestible	−.12	−.04	−.12	−.03	−.02	−.04	−.03	−.03	−.09	.01	−.08	−.22
255.	sulky	−.08	−.18	−.17	−.19	−.17	−.20	−.12	−.11	−.01	−.05	−.12	−.19
256.	superstitious	.00	.00	−.27	−.18	−.01	−.19	−.08	.03	−.13	−.10	−.06	−.29
257.	suspicious	−.07	−.11	−.19	−.13	−.20	−.09	−.04	−.04	−.15	−.11	−.13	−.12
258.	sympathetic	.06	.00	.00	.02	−.05	−.01	.11	−.03	.05	.02	.09	−.16
259.	tactful	.04	.13	.15	.14	.11	.10	.11	.13	.07	.14	.17	−.03
260.	tactless	.00	−.02	−.08	−.01	−.12	−.06	−.07	−.01	−.17	.06	−.04	−.06
261.	talkative	−.01	−.06	−.02	−.07	.01	.03	−.04	−.03	−.09	.00	.10	.02
262.	temperamental	−.07	−.20	−.15	−.13	−.19	−.19	−.13	−.08	−.13	−.01	−.03	−.03
263.	tense	−.04	−.12	−.14	−.11	−.06	−.23	−.03	−.07	−.10	−.02	−.02	−.02
264.	thankless	−.15	−.10	−.08	.03	−.11	−.03	−.09	−.06	−.13	−.06	−.07	−.05

Correlations of Observers' Adjectival Description with Scales of the CPI continued												
	Scale: Ac						**Scale: Ai**					
	By Peers		By Spouses		By Staff		By Peers		By Spouses		By Staff	
Adjectives	M	F	M	F	M	F	M	F	M	F	M	F
265. thorough	.26	.22	−.02	.21	.20	.19	.13	.17	.05	.13	.21	.13
266. thoughtful	.20	.13	.04	.08	.01	.07	.21	.02	.05	.05	.24	.03
267. thrifty	.12	.14	.05	.16	−.09	.03	.09	.04	.06	−.01	−.13	−.15
268. timid	−.05	−.03	−.04	−.08	−.09	−.11	.00	−.07	−.04	−.01	−.07	−.15
269. tolerant	.07	.05	.07	.09	−.06	.01	.22	.04	.14	.06	.18	.04
270. touchy	−.04	−.15	−.18	−.19	−.13	−.17	−.03	−.02	−.10	−.11	.00	−.12
271. tough	.07	−.03	−.16	−.07	−.16	−.07	−.07	.02	−.19	.05	−.08	.08
272. trusting	.09	.08	.04	.07	−.04	.03	.12	.02	−.04	.02	.10	−.16
273. unaffected	.02	−.04	−.09	−.06	−.03	−.03	.11	.01	.07	.10	.06	−.07
274. unambitious	−.16	−.11	−.20	−.07	−.23	−.22	.03	−.05	−.08	.02	−.14	−.32
275. unassuming	−.09	.00	−.06	.11	−.03	−.13	.07	−.03	−.04	.05	−.01	−.14
276. unconventional	.01	−.34	−.18	−.19	−.20	−.21	.02	−.08	.07	.15	.07	.04
277. undependable	−.26	−.23	.07	−.12	−.07	−.21	−.07	−.10	−.01	−.08	−.03	−.02
278. understanding	.09	.05	.04	.11	−.08	−.02	.10	.02	.09	.02	.13	−.04
279. unemotional	.00	−.02	.11	−.12	−.22	−.01	.06	−.10	.18	−.01	−.16	−.06
280. unexcitable	−.06	.01	−.02	.03	−.11	.01	−.02	.03	−.04	.00	−.09	−.04
281. unfriendly	−.07	−.03	−.12	−.03	−.11	−.05	.03	−.02	−.11	−.06	−.04	−.10
282. uninhibited	−.11	−.18	−.11	−.02	−.03	−.09	−.01	−.11	.05	.14	.11	.03
283. unintelligent	−.03	−.14	.00	.03	−.04	−.12	.01	−.03	.00	−.05	−.14	−.13
284. unkind	−.07	−.10	−.05	.04	−.12	−.09	−.07	−.01	−.08	−.08	−.06	−.09
285. unrealistic	−.14	−.09	−.05	−.15	−.11	−.14	−.03	−.10	−.02	−.13	−.07	−.14
286. unscrupulous	−.22	−.12	−.18	.00	−.09	−.12	−.01	.01	−.16	.04	.02	−.06
287. unselfish	.08	.03	−.11	.01	−.02	−.01	.05	.03	−.20	−.06	.07	−.12
288. unstable	−.15	−.21	−.17	−.15	−.09	−.29	−.10	−.16	−.20	.00	−.01	−.01
289. vindictive	−.01	.04	−.06	−.23	−.14	−.10	−.01	.02	−.05	−.09	−.12	−.04
290. versatile	.06	−.06	−.11	−.02	.02	−.01	.10	−.02	.03	.03	.21	.15
291. warm	−.04	.11	−.02	−.03	.00	.02	−.04	.02	.00	.01	.04	−.07
292. wary	.00	.02	−.14	−.05	−.16	−.17	.06	.00	−.07	.02	−.09	−.06
293. weak	−.07	−.05	−.18	−.04	−.04	−.11	−.02	−.04	−.18	−.05	−.11	−.18
294. whiny	−.12	−.04	−.13	−.16	−.01	−.14	−.09	−.06	−.10	−.04	−.06	−.14
295. wholesome	.11	.16	.03	.04	.05	.19	.08	.09	−.04	.06	.06	.00
296. wise	.18	.19	.14	.13	−.02	.00	.12	.13	.10	.03	.11	.07
297. withdrawn	.04	−.10	−.22	−.04	−.18	−.18	.09	−.08	−.11	.02	−.12	−.06
298. witty	−.04	−.17	−.02	.07	−.10	−.03	.07	−.03	.07	.00	.10	.06
299. worrying	.00	.01	−.17	−.04	−.12	−.16	−.10	−.08	−.26	.04	−.01	−.11
300. zany	−.11	−.22	−.22	−.13	−.09	−.12	−.06	−.02	−.15	.02	.01	−.10

Correlations of Observers' Adjectival Description with Scales of the CPI continued

	Adjectives	Scale: Ie						Scale: Py					
		By Peers		By Spouses		By Staff		By Peers		By Spouses		By Staff	
		M	F	M	F	M	F	M	F	M	F	M	F
001.	absent-minded	−.15	−.26	−.11	.03	−.11	−.06	.04	−.14	.00	.07	−.06	−.06
002.	active	.07	.15	−.03	.08	.13	.19	−.11	.10	.01	.10	.08	.05
003.	adaptable	.06	.17	.03	.00	.19	.11	.00	.10	.13	.08	.07	.02
004.	adventurous	.05	.05	−.01	.09	.05	.16	−.05	−.01	.06	.12	.00	−.02
005.	affected	−.01	.06	.02	−.08	.04	.09	−.08	.12	.05	−.04	.03	.03
006.	affectionate	−.04	.00	−.03	.01	−.03	−.09	−.02	−.04	.00	.03	−.07	−.20
007.	aggressive	.04	.11	−.07	.04	.08	.20	−.06	.11	−.08	.12	.01	.15
008.	alert	.17	.14	.18	.16	.22	.20	.09	.16	.13	.12	.16	.11
009.	aloof	.07	−.14	.03	−.06	−.15	−.03	.14	.03	.03	.04	−.07	.07
010.	ambitious	.11	.19	.06	.10	.23	.25	.13	.18	.11	.05	.18	.24
011.	anxious	−.03	−.09	−.04	−.09	−.05	−.31	.07	−.09	.01	−.03	.03	−.09
012.	apathetic	−.18	−.10	−.21	−.10	−.21	−.22	−.08	−.11	−.16	−.05	−.18	−.08
013.	appreciative	.01	.05	.06	.02	.07	−.09	−.01	−.01	.08	.04	.12	−.10
014.	argumentative	−.04	.05	.04	.07	.14	.19	.14	.11	−.05	.08	.11	.21
015.	arrogant	.04	−.04	.04	.02	−.01	.05	.09	−.04	−.01	.04	−.01	.03
016.	artistic	−.09	−.07	.05	.04	.06	.06	−.06	−.02	.10	−.05	.15	−.01
017.	assertive	.00	.12	.07	.31	.15	.25	.05	.13	.06	.31	.09	.15
018.	attractive	.01	.01	−.01	−.08	.05	.00	−.04	.06	.00	−.08	.01	−.06
019.	autocratic	−.04	−.02	.08	.12	−.04	.15	.12	.00	−.01	.11	−.01	.11
020.	awkward	−.16	−.15	−.19	.00	−.21	−.18	−.01	−.13	−.16	.05	−.12	−.04
021.	bitter	−.03	−.16	−.20	−.10	−.15	−.11	.13	−.14	−.19	−.12	−.18	−.03
022.	blustery	−.11	−.06	.04	−.04	−.09	.04	.04	.00	−.04	−.09	−.02	−.01
023.	boastful	−.01	.07	−.10	−.09	−.04	.10	−.12	.07	−.16	−.06	−.03	.01
024.	bossy	−.05	.10	−.17	−.03	.00	.05	.04	.13	−.19	−.03	−.03	.08
025.	calm	.08	.13	.03	.03	−.05	−.01	.01	.13	.01	.03	−.10	.06
026.	capable	.20	.21	.06	.18	.15	.17	.11	.24	−.01	.12	.10	.20
027.	careless	−.16	−.09	−.17	−.05	−.08	.01	−.16	−.07	−.10	.00	−.02	−.03
028.	cautious	−.04	−.02	−.08	−.12	−.12	−.27	.02	−.03	−.05	−.01	−.07	−.09
029.	changeable	.02	−.04	−.10	.04	−.09	−.07	.05	.00	−.02	.10	−.03	−.10
030.	charming	−.13	−.01	−.03	−.01	.08	.09	−.13	.01	−.02	.03	.10	−.01
031.	cheerful	−.03	.08	.10	−.05	.11	.07	−.18	.01	.09	.02	.10	−.08
032.	civilized	.08	.10	.00	−.01	.10	.03	.01	.10	.03	.03	.10	.07
033.	clear-thinking	.20	.28	.15	.22	.19	.20	.08	.22	.16	.20	.16	.23
034.	clever	.14	.06	.08	.19	.16	.19	.01	.08	.04	.09	.13	.09
035.	coarse	−.11	.00	−.17	.09	−.16	−.01	.02	−.02	−.10	.09	−.12	−.01
036.	cold	−.15	−.07	−.02	−.07	−.15	−.08	−.03	.03	−.04	−.11	−.08	.03
037.	commonplace	−.14	−.03	−.04	−.13	−.21	−.22	.03	−.03	−.01	.00	−.19	−.15
038.	complaining	−.10	−.14	−.21	−.09	−.06	−.07	−.04	−.03	−.22	−.07	−.04	−.03
039.	complicated	−.02	−.02	.22	.10	.01	.00	.18	.00	.29	.14	.06	.09
040.	conceited	.01	.05	−.13	.05	.08	.13	−.04	.12	−.17	.05	.09	.10
041.	confident	.14	.21	.05	.16	.19	.27	.08	.23	.05	.15	.12	.11
042.	confused	−.15	−.12	−.22	−.12	−.16	−.25	−.07	−.10	−.18	−.05	−.14	−.13
043.	conscientious	.05	.13	.14	.15	.08	−.07	.18	.09	.06	.15	.07	.05
044.	conservative	.01	.09	−.03	−.17	−.12	−.23	.05	.05	−.02	−.10	−.12	−.14

Correlations of Observers' Adjectival Description with Scales of the CPI continued											
	Scale: Ie						**Scale: Py**					
	By Peers		By Spouses		By Staff		By Peers		By Spouses		By Staff	
Adjectives	M	F	M	F	M	F	M	F	M	F	M	F
045. considerate	.00	.00	.03	−.01	.01	−.11	.01	−.02	.07	−.01	−.01	−.07
046. contented	−.03	.08	.08	−.02	−.06	−.07	.01	.06	.06	.02	−.10	−.07
047. conventional	.00	.07	.00	−.04	−.13	−.21	.05	−.01	−.02	−.03	−.13	−.19
048. cool	.08	−.09	.08	.06	−.04	.03	.01	.04	.03	.06	−.06	.11
049. cooperative	−.04	.08	.10	.07	.09	−.08	−.03	.05	.11	.14	.06	−.06
050. courageous	−.04	.07	.02	.06	.04	.02	.06	.04	.06	.08	−.01	.03
051. cowardly	−.17	−.04	−.02	−.06	−.10	−.02	−.10	−.05	.00	−.08	−.08	.00
052. cruel	−.12	−.13	−.15	.00	−.10	−.03	−.01	.02	−.14	.00	−.05	.01
053. curious	.08	.00	.05	.15	.15	.16	.06	−.11	.04	.16	.21	.11
054. cynical	.11	−.09	−.01	.04	−.10	.07	.23	−.01	−.01	.11	−.08	.10
055. daring	−.10	.14	−.03	−.03	.03	.07	−.07	.09	−.06	−.05	−.02	−.03
056. deceitful	−.04	−.03	−.13	−.08	.02	−.06	.04	.06	−.05	−.06	−.01	−.02
057. defensive	−.08	−.15	−.09	−.03	−.11	−.14	−.07	−.08	−.03	.03	−.06	.04
058. deliberate	.08	.03	.02	−.07	−.10	−.08	.12	−.02	.06	−.04	−.06	.13
059. demanding	.03	.09	−.04	−.07	.04	.05	.04	.10	−.09	−.02	−.01	.05
060. dependable	.12	.14	.05	.02	.08	.01	.11	.06	.02	.08	.05	.09
061. dependent	−.08	−.09	−.11	−.15	−.12	−.27	−.03	−.06	−.03	−.09	−.09	−.21
062. despondent	.00	−.16	.01	.12	−.16	−.26	.09	−.07	.09	.06	−.14	−.16
063. determined	.10	.15	−.05	.13	.14	.17	.16	.09	−.01	.17	.08	.15
064. dignified	.10	.01	−.04	−.01	.02	−.05	.14	.07	−.01	−.02	.05	.08
065. discreet	.10	.11	.07	.12	−.02	−.08	.11	.10	.09	.06	.01	.04
066. disorderly	−.08	−.10	−.05	.05	−.03	−.04	−.08	−.05	.00	.08	.03	−.10
067. dissatisfied	−.01	−.10	−.11	−.10	−.07	−.12	−.00	−.01	−.08	−.06	−.07	.00
068. distractible	−.11	−.05	−.20	−.11	−.08	−.16	−.09	−.06	−.14	−.03	−.04	−.17
069. distrustful	−.17	−.12	−.05	−.14	−.07	−.12	−.09	−.01	−.06	−.10	−.05	−.04
070. dominant	.01	.17	−.01	−.05	.08	.26	.04	.14	−.05	−.03	.04	.18
071. dreamy	−.02	−.04	−.05	.05	−.12	−.18	.02	−.03	−.01	−.05	−.06	−.07
072. dull	−.13	−.07	−.09	−.11	−.21	−.22	.06	−.04	−.05	−.10	−.16	−.12
073. easygoing	−.01	.00	−.10	.00	−.09	−.07	−.16	−.04	−.07	.00	−.10	−.17
074. effeminate	−.05	−.03	.01	.09	.01	−.10	−.05	.02	.00	.02	−.01	−.13
075. efficient	.03	.23	.06	.06	.25	.15	.06	.24	.08	.01	.22	.18
076. egotistical	.08	.04	.00	.09	.05	.15	.00	.04	−.08	.09	.08	.12
077. emotional	−.02	−.05	−.12	−.02	.03	−.13	−.01	−.06	−.07	−.06	.04	−.19
078. energetic	.01	.16	−.01	.06	.18	.17	−.02	.08	.09	.10	.16	.07
079. enterprising	.10	.16	.03	.19	.16	.23	.05	.12	.07	.16	.13	.14
080. enthusiastic	.03	.07	.08	.08	.11	.12	−.01	−.02	.11	.15	.09	−.09
081. evasive	.06	.02	−.01	−.17	−.21	−.08	.09	.05	.00	−.07	−.14	.00
082. excitable	−.02	.02	−.18	−.15	.04	−.05	−.05	−.04	−.11	−.09	.07	−.10
083. fair-minded	.01	.14	.09	.08	.06	.02	−.09	.01	.11	.09	.08	.11
084. fault-finding	.00	−.06	−.04	−.10	−.02	−.01	.02	.08	−.02	−.01	−.01	.04
085. fearful	.01	−.10	−.12	−.03	−.13	−.29	.04	−.09	−.11	.05	−.09	−.12
086. feminine	.00	−.03	.05	−.02	.01	−.16	.12	−.01	.08	−.06	.02	−.20
087. fickle	−.08	.05	.00	−.06	−.02	−.08	−.05	.10	.04	−.08	−.02	−.06
088. flirtatious	−.09	.04	−.27	−.11	.00	−.04	−.06	.11	−.22	−.07	.03	−.12

Correlations of Observers' Adjectival Description with Scales of the CPI continued											
	Scale: Ie						Scale: Py					
	By Peers		By Spouses		By Staff		By Peers		By Spouses		By Staff	
Adjectives	M	F	M	F	M	F	M	F	M	F	M	F
089. foolish	−.06	−.10	.00	−.07	−.11	−.12	.01	−.04	.01	−.01	−.11	−.15
090. forceful	−.04	.10	−.11	.05	.06	.21	−.04	.09	−.10	.00	.02	.20
091. foresighted	.13	.09	.13	.04	.19	.20	.18	.12	.12	.05	.18	.16
092. forgetful	−.15	−.25	−.12	.08	−.06	−.08	−.04	−.13	−.02	.10	−.02	−.06
093. forgiving	.14	.03	−.09	−.09	−.02	−.19	.17	−.09	−.02	−.12	−.07	−.17
094. formal	.08	.04	.13	.03	.02	−.08	.10	.08	.07	.06	.05	.00
095. frank	.07	.01	−.02	.10	.03	.13	.14	.01	.01	.15	.02	.07
096. friendly	.03	.10	.02	.01	.05	.02	−.03	−.03	.07	.06	.04	−.07
097. frivolous	−.13	.03	−.04	−.06	−.05	−.03	−.07	.11	.07	.02	.02	−.16
098. fussy	−.09	−.01	−.13	−.12	−.09	−.09	.00	.06	−.10	−.08	−.10	−.03
099. generous	.04	−.02	.04	.03	.00	−.06	.07	−.14	−.03	.01	−.03	−.09
100. gentle	.09	−.08	.02	−.05	−.08	−.26	.09	−.10	.06	.00	−.03	−.17
101. gloomy	−.08	−.15	−.14	−.03	−.12	−.13	.02	−.11	−.10	.00	−.07	.03
102. good-looking	.04	.00	.00	−.02	−.01	−.01	−.12	.05	.00	−.06	−.04	−.05
103. good-natured	.06	.04	.06	.03	.02	−.01	.04	.02	.10	.03	−.03	−.08
104. greedy	−.07	−.09	−.04	−.08	−.05	.04	−.06	.00	−.06	−.05	−.02	−.01
105. handsome	.03	.00	.01	.00	−.01	−.01	−.07	.02	.03	.07	−.06	.09
106. hard-headed	.05	.01	−.07	−.10	.02	.07	.14	.02	−.09	−.08	.04	.14
107. hard-hearted	−.10	−.01	−.03	−.03	−.11	.01	.02	.05	−.08	−.09	−.11	.00
108. hasty	−.09	−.05	−.13	.00	.05	.01	−.07	.01	−.06	.04	.11	−.08
109. headstrong	.00	−.02	−.09	−.05	.02	.11	.07	.01	−.10	−.06	.02	.07
110. healthy	.00	.04	−.08	.07	.01	.11	−.02	−.07	−.02	.16	−.09	−.02
111. helpful	.08	.12	.02	.02	.06	−.11	.09	.06	.12	.13	.02	−.14
112. high-strung	−.04	.00	−.11	−.04	.03	−.10	.01	.03	−.07	−.03	.09	.00
113. honest	.03	.08	.06	.14	.08	−.03	.10	−.08	.07	.03	.05	.05
114. hostile	−.05	−.08	−.03	.02	−.05	−.02	−.11	−.03	−.08	.04	−.04	.06
115. humorous	−.02	−.09	−.03	.15	−.01	.13	−.10	−.10	−.04	.25	−.03	.00
116. hurried	−.01	−.08	−.04	.08	.05	.01	−.05	−.01	.01	.08	.14	−.02
117. idealistic	.08	.01	.07	.26	.12	.05	.13	−.03	.15	.20	.11	.02
118. imaginative	−.03	.01	.10	.21	.17	.16	−.02	.03	.11	.19	.21	.08
119. immature	−.09	−.16	−.13	−.02	−.05	−.13	−.01	−.15	−.11	−.01	−.01	−.13
120. impatient	−.04	−.09	.01	.01	.08	.06	.05	.04	.00	−.03	.08	.05
121. impulsive	−.05	−.06	−.12	.03	.02	−.01	−.03	−.06	.01	.02	.04	−.07
122. independent	.29	.12	.08	.14	.13	.24	.24	.11	.02	.09	.06	.23
123. indifferent	−.03	−.07	−.02	.00	−.20	−.11	−.04	−.02	.01	.05	−.14	−.03
124. individualistic	.13	.04	.06	.24	.01	.15	.08	.04	.08	.26	.03	.14
125. industrious	.05	.06	.05	.08	.12	.12	.05	.10	.03	.10	.13	.20
126. infantile	−.16	−.09	−.03	−.18	−.11	−.19	−.06	−.06	−.02	−.25	−.09	−.19
127. informal	−.03	.10	.03	.11	−.05	.06	−.03	.03	.07	.11	−.03	.02
128. ingenious	.04	.10	.14	.11	.14	.17	.06	.09	.17	.12	.24	.07
129. inhibited	.01	.05	−.04	−.05	−.13	−.25	.01	.02	.03	.02	−.05	−.09
130. initiative	.10	.15	.14	.20	.20	.26	.00	.14	.18	.22	.13	.14
131. insightful	.11	.17	.15	.27	.19	.16	.14	.11	.25	.24	.19	.13
132. intelligent	.23	.26	.18	.16	.26	.28	.12	.13	.10	.13	.23	.29

Correlations of Observers' Adjectival Description with Scales of the CPI continued

		Scale: le							Scale: Py				
		By Peers		By Spouses		By Staff		By Peers		By Spouses		By Staff	
Adjectives		M	F	M	F	M	F	M	F	M	F	M	F
133.	interests—narrow	−.10	−.11	−.13	−.36	−.22	−.34	.06	.05	−.08	−.32	−.15	−.22
134.	interests—wide	.02	.10	.15	.28	.22	.22	−.11	.02	.12	.26	.20	.18
135.	intolerant	−.05	.08	−.09	−.16	−.08	−.08	.02	.10	−.11	−.19	−.09	−.03
136.	inventive	.01	.03	.12	.12	.16	.16	−.02	.08	.14	.13	.22	.06
137.	irresponsible	−.15	−.14	−.02	−.04	−.02	−.04	−.02	−.04	.03	−.04	.01	−.09
138.	irritable	−.09	−.12	−.08	−.06	−.02	−.01	−.05	.03	−.02	−.08	.03	.08
139.	jolly	−.11	.09	−.16	.02	−.03	.05	−.15	.00	−.16	.00	−.02	−.11
140.	kind	−.05	−.06	−.02	.05	−.10	−.15	−.03	−.12	.02	.05	−.09	−.14
141.	lazy	−.04	−.09	.06	.06	−.15	−.04	−.03	−.09	.07	.02	−.08	−.10
142.	leisurely	−.03	.06	−.03	.06	−.11	−.08	−.04	.01	−.01	.02	−.11	−.06
143.	logical	.19	.22	.03	.03	.18	.14	.20	.22	.03	.06	.20	.34
144.	loud	−.10	.01	−.07	−.06	−.01	.09	−.03	−.04	−.05	−.05	−.01	.00
145.	loyal	−.04	.00	−.08	−.11	−.08	−.21	−.04	−.01	−.03	−.07	−.11	−.13
146.	mannerly	.01	.10	.03	.16	−.04	−.13	.01	.06	.08	.11	−.03	−.03
147.	masculine	.11	.05	−.14	−.05	−.07	.09	−.07	.05	−.08	.00	−.14	.13
148.	mature	.16	.12	.09	.05	.09	.05	.05	.17	.13	.05	.00	.06
149.	meek	−.09	−.13	−.12	−.02	−.20	−.28	.05	−.11	−.11	.05	−.15	−.12
150.	methodical	.08	.10	.02	.18	.01	−.03	.17	.13	.09	.20	.04	.16
151.	mild	−.03	−.01	−.03	−.05	−.12	−.27	−.03	−.06	−.06	−.04	−.08	−.10
152.	mischievous	−.07	.05	−.20	−.06	.00	.10	−.08	.01	−.11	−.06	.01	−.03
153.	moderate	.04	.06	.04	.11	−.05	−.13	.07	.03	.06	.11	−.04	.03
154.	modest	.05	−.08	−.03	−.05	−.06	−.28	.14	−.15	−.02	−.08	−.07	−.11
155.	moody	.02	−.16	−.13	−.09	−.12	−.17	.11	−.06	−.05	−.10	−.05	−.06
156.	nagging	−.11	−.01	−.21	−.07	−.09	−.12	−.02	.05	−.24	−.09	−.07	−.15
157.	natural	.01	−.01	.04	.11	.08	.11	−.05	−.08	.04	.09	.03	.08
158.	nervous	−.11	−.18	−.22	−.08	−.05	−.24	−.06	−.06	−.15	−.08	.06	−.07
159.	noisy	−.11	.06	−.03	−.13	−.01	.07	−.09	−.01	−.08	−.13	.01	−.06
160.	obliging	−.01	.08	−.03	.05	.03	−.17	.05	−.06	.12	.03	.12	−.07
161.	obnoxious	−.05	−.02	−.01	.09	−.02	−.03	.01	−.05	.01	.07	−.05	−.08
162.	opinionated	.04	.08	.00	−.02	.05	.09	.14	.07	.02	.04	.02	.07
163.	opportunistic	.04	.07	−.02	.07	.04	.08	−.05	.01	−.03	.08	−.03	.03
164.	optimistic	.08	.03	.10	.19	.12	.12	.06	−.03	.08	.20	.06	−.09
165.	organized	.11	.17	.00	−.01	.23	.14	.10	.18	.03	.02	.19	.14
166.	original	.05	.05	.06	.18	.14	.15	−.04	.06	.12	.14	.22	.12
167.	outgoing	.01	.07	−.07	.24	.13	.21	−.16	.06	−.01	.18	.05	.00
168.	outspoken	.05	.11	−.12	.10	.11	.17	−.03	.08	−.12	.12	.09	.12
169.	painstaking	−.04	.08	.04	−.01	−.06	−.19	.13	.01	.09	−.03	.03	.06
170.	patient	−.08	.07	.04	−.06	−.05	−.17	−.02	.02	.10	−.09	−.01	−.03
171.	peaceable	.03	.03	.00	−.01	−.08	−.21	−.01	−.02	−.01	−.02	−.03	−.05
172.	peculiar	−.12	−.03	−.20	−.05	−.12	−.07	.05	−.01	−.12	−.06	−.07	.04
173.	persevering	.15	.12	−.01	.15	.14	−.01	.23	.01	.05	.16	.11	.13
174.	persistent	.05	.18	.01	.16	.01	.08	.19	.08	.05	.20	−.06	.15
175.	pessimistic	−.01	−.17	−.01	−.08	−.08	−.18	.04	−.09	.03	−.07	−.02	−.04
176.	planful	.05	.12	−.06	−.03	.16	.11	.14	.11	−.04	.06	.13	.15

	Scale: Ie						Scale: Py					
	By Peers		By Spouses		By Staff		By Peers		By Spouses		By Staff	
Adjectives	M	F	M	F	M	F	M	F	M	F	M	F
177. pleasant	.13	.03	.02	.10	.04	.02	.00	.03	.04	.05	.04	−.05
178. pleasure-seeking	−.03	.05	−.07	.06	.02	−.01	−.11	.03	−.09	.02	−.03	−.15
179. poised	.10	.07	.09	.12	.14	.18	.01	.08	.12	.05	.07	.16
180. polished	.18	.06	−.01	.14	.06	.12	−.06	.13	.01	.15	.07	.04
181. practical	.11	.07	.05	−.02	−.04	−.03	.23	−.02	.01	.04	−.09	−.02
182. praising	.05	−.06	−.06	−.06	.08	−.13	−.02	−.09	−.01	.01	.05	−.12
183. precise	.05	.03	.10	.11	−.01	.10	.19	.05	.14	.17	.05	.23
184. prejudiced	−.08	−.05	−.28	−.16	−.10	−.10	.07	.00	−.27	−.19	−.13	−.11
185. preoccupied	−.02	−.05	.00	−.01	−.16	−.22	.07	.04	.08	.03	−.05	−.05
186. progressive	.02	.05	−.01	.21	.11	.17	.03	−.04	.04	.19	.04	.17
187. prudish	−.05	.03	−.06	−.15	−.12	−.24	.02	.00	−.06	−.10	−.10	−.08
188. quarrelsome	−.03	.02	−.21	−.14	.00	−.01	.02	.01	−.21	−.13	−.01	.05
189. queer	−.20	−.03	−.01	.00	−.06	−.01	−.04	−.05	.01	.00	−.02	.06
190. quick	.04	.08	.02	.14	.16	.13	−.06	.05	.01	.09	.09	.01
191. quiet	−.04	−.04	.03	−.13	−.15	−.28	.06	.00	.02	−.10	−.07	−.07
192. quitting	−.12	−.12	−.07	−.05	−.13	−.15	−.03	−.12	−.01	−.00	−.06	−.05
193. rational	.19	.25	.10	.13	.13	.11	.13	.19	.08	.13	.08	.25
194. rattle-brained	−.11	−.07	−.22	−.19	−.09	−.09	.06	−.07	−.13	−.07	−.10	−.16
195. realistic	.21	.20	.02	.01	.08	.11	.13	.17	.03	.09	.02	.07
196. reasonable	.11	.15	.05	.17	.08	.02	.07	.09	.14	.10	.04	.10
197. rebellious	−.07	−.09	−.09	.06	−.04	.07	−.07	−.03	.00	.06	.01	.05
198. reckless	−.13	−.03	−.08	−.13	−.05	−.03	−.01	−.01	−.01	−.09	−.02	−.11
199. reflective	.07	.10	.02	.27	.12	−.01	.07	.07	.13	.25	.13	.12
200. relaxed	.02	.16	.06	−.03	−.03	.13	−.04	.08	.07	−.07	−.05	.02
201. reliable	.10	.16	.00	.06	.09	−.02	.04	.16	−.02	.02	.04	.08
202. resentful	−.02	−.13	−.14	.00	−.07	−.13	.03	−.12	−.07	−.01	−.09	−.02
203. reserved	.06	−.05	−.05	−.13	−.11	−.20	.14	.02	−.05	−.08	−.06	.02
204. resourceful	.09	.16	.08	.20	.24	.27	.07	.09	.11	.19	.20	.17
205. responsible	.17	.20	.03	.00	.11	.02	.07	.19	.02	.07	.10	.14
206. restless	−.09	−.08	−.08	−.02	−.02	.00	−.06	−.12	−.05	.04	.06	−.05
207. retiring	.00	−.15	.04	−.08	−.15	−.26	.06	−.14	.04	−.11	−.06	−.01
208. rigid	−.04	.03	−.01	−.13	−.13	−.17	−.03	.05	−.03	−.09	−.12	.03
209. robust	−.07	.04	.04	.06	−.05	.09	−.03	−.04	.02	.14	−.08	.00
210. rude	−.07	.01	−.03	.04	−.06	−.05	.00	−.05	−.06	.02	−.06	−.03
211. sarcastic	.04	−.08	.00	.01	−.04	.08	.06	−.02	−.03	.07	−.03	.06
212. self-centered	−.03	.03	−.13	−.02	.01	−.01	−.02	.04	−.15	.00	−.01	−.01
213. self-confident	.14	.14	.11	.17	.18	.28	.00	.22	.11	.11	.11	.16
214. self-controlled	.19	.10	.07	.11	.03	−.08	.19	.15	.13	.12	−.01	.06
215. self-denying	.02	.06	−.07	−.08	−.12	−.24	.04	.01	−.10	−.12	−.09	−.05
216. self-pitying	−.08	−.08	−.07	−.09	−.05	−.11	−.07	−.06	−.12	−.10	−.03	−.10
217. self-punishing	.02	−.08	−.06	−.01	−.06	−.09	−.03	−.06	−.11	.05	−.02	−.08
218. self-seeking	.07	.00	.02	.05	.05	.02	−.08	.00	.01	.08	−.01	−.05
219. selfish	.05	.03	.01	.04	.01	−.06	.02	−.02	.09	.04	−.05	−.10
220. sensitive	.02	−.16	−.07	.03	.02	−.18	−.06	−.15	−.02	.01	.08	−.13

		Scale: Ie						Scale: Py					
		By Peers		By Spouses		By Staff		By Peers		By Spouses		By Staff	
Adjectives		M	F	M	F	M	F	M	F	M	F	M	F
221.	sentimental	−.02	.03	−.06	−.08	−.07	−.15	−.02	.00	−.08	−.03	−.06	−.19
222.	serious	.09	.02	−.02	.06	−.01	.01	.07	.04	.07	.04	−.02	.22
223.	severe	−.02	.12	.00	.00	−.14	−.09	.07	.17	−.06	.08	−.10	.07
224.	sexy	.10	−.01	−.11	.01	−.04	−.01	−.05	.12	−.09	.01	−.07	−.07
225.	shallow	−.27	.07	−.03	−.16	−.14	−.24	−.15	.06	−.05	−.23	−.11	−.25
226.	sharp-witted	.14	−.09	.06	.23	.12	.14	.02	−.03	.07	.13	.07	.12
227.	shiftless	−.15	−.04	−.15	−.10	−.13	−.03	−.06	−.04	−.11	−.08	−.11	−.06
228.	show-off	−.06	.04	−.02	−.06	.02	.10	−.17	.04	−.07	−.05	.02	.01
229.	shrewd	.08	−.01	−.10	−.02	.09	.09	.17	.03	−.08	.06	.09	.09
230.	shy	−.11	−.09	.00	−.17	−.19	−.32	.02	−.11	−.04	−.12	−.13	−.15
231.	silent	−.15	−.03	−.11	−.14	−.20	−.26	−.02	−.03	−.11	−.12	−.11	−.11
232.	simple	−.16	−.03	−.14	−.22	−.26	−.31	.05	−.08	−.11	−.25	−.19	−.21
233.	sincere	.00	.01	.01	.03	.07	−.06	−.05	−.03	.08	.01	.03	.03
234.	slipshod	−.01	−.05	.00	.03	−.04	.00	.07	−.06	−.09	.08	.01	−.02
235.	slow	−.10	−.11	−.25	−.07	−.16	−.20	.06	−.08	−.14	−.10	−.08	−.14
236.	sly	−.07	−.06	−.25	−.01	−.06	−.01	.04	−.07	−.27	−.01	.00	−.05
237.	smug	.03	.00	.01	−.04	−.02	.03	.09	.06	−.03	−.05	−.04	.01
238.	snobbish	−.01	.00	.06	.06	.01	.06	.04	.07	.03	−.02	.01	.00
239.	sociable	.00	.05	−.06	.12	.09	.07	−.13	.02	−.01	.09	.05	−.09
240.	soft-hearted	.00	.06	−.08	−.09	−.03	−.24	.06	−.05	−.10	−.07	−.08	−.20
241.	sophisticated	.06	−.06	−.01	.21	.10	.18	.00	.04	.09	.14	.06	.13
242.	spendthrift	−.12	−.04	.00	−.06	−.02	.00	−.07	−.07	.04	−.03	.02	−.10
243.	spineless	−.10	−.15	.08	−.02	−.20	−.06	−.04	−.11	.12	−.01	−.12	−.04
244.	spontaneous	−.07	.06	.01	.19	.13	.12	−.04	−.02	.11	.19	.12	−.03
245.	spunky	−.11	.05	−.23	.16	.02	.05	−.13	−.04	−.20	.10	−.01	.03
246.	stable	.08	.18	−.02	.04	.05	.09	.10	.15	.06	.09	.00	.09
247.	steady	.14	.08	−.06	−.05	−.05	−.06	.06	.09	−.02	−.04	−.10	.06
248.	stern	−.01	.05	−.18	−.09	−.09	−.05	.10	.08	−.11	.00	−.14	.05
249.	stingy	−.12	−.01	−.12	−.07	−.08	.00	.02	.03	−.14	−.03	−.04	−.02
250.	stolid	−.10	.01	−.10	−.02	−.20	−.15	−.03	.02	.02	.07	−.17	−.05
251.	strong	.05	.09	−.03	.02	−.04	.19	−.07	.03	.07	.04	−.11	.14
252.	stubborn	−.04	−.04	−.10	−.09	−.01	.09	.06	−.03	−.11	−.10	.00	.16
253.	submissive	.04	−.03	−.06	−.13	−.14	−.26	.00	−.03	−.02	−.05	−.09	−.12
254.	suggestible	−.04	.05	−.03	−.04	−.08	−.23	−.05	.02	−.04	.06	−.03	−.17
255.	sulky	−.05	−.10	−.01	−.02	−.15	−.15	−.03	−.03	.01	−.06	−.14	−.10
256.	superstitious	−.12	.00	−.20	−.09	−.07	−.26	−.01	−.04	−.20	−.09	−.04	−.30
257.	suspicious	−.02	−.11	−.14	−.15	−.13	−.12	.02	−.10	−.08	−.07	−.12	−.06
258.	sympathetic	.07	−.03	.02	.07	.03	−.15	.03	−.06	.07	.04	.01	−.15
259.	tactful	.05	.07	.12	.16	.12	−.02	.03	.06	.12	.11	.06	−.04
260.	tactless	−.02	−.01	−.09	.01	−.06	.00	.04	−.03	−.14	.02	−.05	.02
261.	talkative	.06	.03	.04	.09	.13	.18	−.07	.07	−.05	.05	.11	−.03
262.	temperamental	−.04	−.11	−.12	−.02	−.06	.00	.04	−.06	−.06	−.04	.01	−.02
263.	tense	.02	−.19	−.10	.00	−.06	−.18	.11	−.11	−.06	−.01	.00	.01
264.	thankless	−.07	−.13	−.08	−.01	−.07	−.05	.00	−.08	−.04	−.08	−.07	.00

	Scale: Ie						Scale: Py					
	By Peers		By Spouses		By Staff		By Peers		By Spouses		By Staff	
Adjectives	M	F	M	F	M	F	M	F	M	F	M	F
265. thorough	.13	.16	.01	.11	.17	.09	.16	.20	.03	.10	.22	.22
266. thoughtful	.21	.05	.07	.04	.12	.00	.10	−.02	.07	.06	.10	.10
267. thrifty	−.02	.11	.01	−.03	−.15	−.18	.09	.01	−.08	.03	−.14	−.07
268. timid	−.08	−.12	−.05	−.10	−.18	−.31	.08	−.15	.00	−.03	−.13	−.15
269. tolerant	.05	.08	.12	.08	.11	.01	.06	−.02	.18	.06	.08	.07
270. touchy	.00	−.04	−.12	−.10	−.03	−.16	−.01	.01	−.06	−.13	.02	−.09
271. tough	−.03	.04	−.15	.03	−.06	.10	.00	.04	−.13	.05	−.11	.13
272. trusting	.09	.05	−.05	.02	.02	−.14	.07	−.06	−.03	.05	.03	−.10
273. unaffected	.03	−.01	.01	.14	.01	−.05	.05	−.05	.02	.12	.04	.01
274. unambitious	.01	−.06	−.08	.04	−.16	−.26	−.07	−.03	−.10	−.03	−.12	−.23
275. unassuming	−.12	−.02	−.02	.04	−.08	−.21	−.03	−.15	.04	.09	−.02	−.07
276. unconventional	.00	−.11	−.03	.10	−.02	.06	.04	−.09	.04	.10	.03	.09
277. undependable	−.13	−.09	.02	−.11	−.02	−.04	−.06	−.01	.02	−.02	−.02	−.02
278. understanding	.10	.04	.04	.09	.04	−.02	.00	−.01	.14	.09	.01	−.08
279. unemotional	−.04	−.06	.10	−.03	−.22	−.09	.05	−.03	.16	−.02	−.14	−.04
280. unexcitable	−.04	.01	−.02	−.03	−.09	−.10	.01	.02	−.03	.07	−.08	.02
281. unfriendly	.01	−.04	−.11	−.05	−.07	−.03	.08	.01	−.14	−.02	−.04	−.01
282. uninhibited	−.06	−.04	.06	.19	.12	.08	−.02	−.03	.05	.13	.08	−.04
283. unintelligent	−.08	−.08	.00	−.02	−.15	−.12	.03	.00	.00	−.05	−.06	−.09
284. unkind	−.12	−.05	−.03	−.08	−.06	.00	−.02	.08	−.05	−.16	−.06	−.03
285. unrealistic	.03	−.09	.00	−.07	−.05	−.13	−.01	−.06	.08	−.09	−.04	−.15
286. unscrupulous	−.10	.00	−.24	.00	.00	.00	−.01	.01	−.17	.04	−.01	−.03
287. unselfish	.06	−.01	−.18	−.04	.01	−.19	.08	−.06	−.13	−.07	.02	−.11
288. unstable	−.04	−.17	−.19	.00	−.06	−.09	−.06	−.10	−.17	.00	−.01	−.05
289. vindictive	.02	.09	.01	−.09	−.05	−.02	−.03	.06	.01	−.04	−.09	−.04
290. versatile	.04	.02	.00	.08	.22	.23	−.06	.02	.07	.14	.18	.07
291. warm	−.01	.05	−.03	−.06	.07	−.05	−.08	−.07	.03	−.03	.06	−.09
292. wary	.10	−.04	.02	−.04	−.12	−.15	.11	.03	−.01	.04	−.08	.00
293. weak	−.12	−.09	−.22	−.08	−.10	−.24	−.03	−.08	−.19	−.11	−.13	−.11
294. whiny	−.09	−.02	−.05	−.09	−.03	−.14	−.05	−.04	−.03	−.15	−.05	−.09
295. wholesome	.02	.11	−.08	.07	.05	.06	−.04	−.01	.01	.11	.00	−.03
296. wise	.09	.07	.05	.02	.05	.10	.01	.10	.12	.02	.09	.10
297. withdrawn	.05	−.13	−.12	−.03	−.21	−.26	.15	−.10	−.08	.06	−.12	−.08
298. witty	.06	−.07	.03	.08	.09	.15	−.05	−.04	.05	.02	.05	.02
299. worrying	−.07	−.12	−.24	−.03	−.07	−.23	−.02	−.07	−.20	.05	.01	−.03
300. zany	−.05	.05	−.11	.10	−.03	.03	.02	.02	−.10	.05	.03	−.12

Correlations of Observers' Adjectival Description with Scales of the CPI continued

Correlations of Observers' Adjectival Description with Scales of the CPI continued												
		Scale: Fx						Scale: F/M					
		By Peers		By Spouses		By Staff		By Peers		By Spouses		By Staff	
Adjectives		M	F	M	F	M	F	M	F	M	F	M	F
001.	absent-minded	.08	.16	.08	.11	.01	.11	.15	−.02	.03	−.10	.10	.04
002.	active	−.03	.18	.09	−.03	.12	.05	−.17	−.02	.08	−.09	−.08	−.04
003.	adaptable	.01	.13	.12	.01	.14	.07	.09	.09	−.09	−.07	−.03	−.03
004.	adventurous	.20	.20	.18	.15	.14	.20	−.27	−.09	−.02	−.12	−.07	−.07
005.	affected	−.11	−.02	.01	.05	.02	.06	.05	−.20	−.04	.04	.04	.03
006.	affectionate	.01	.04	.03	−.05	.04	−.03	.20	.15	−.03	−.03	.10	.15
007.	aggressive	−.10	.12	−.01	.07	−.04	.16	−.21	−.14	−.05	−.10	−.16	−.14
008.	alert	.01	.04	.09	.02	.19	.02	−.20	−.06	.05	.08	.00	−.06
009.	aloof	−.03	.00	−.04	.12	−.01	−.03	.00	−.03	−.01	−.02	.09	−.08
010.	ambitious	−.13	−.09	−.02	−.08	.03	.07	−.08	.06	−.15	−.09	−.11	−.22
011.	anxious	−.05	−.06	−.04	.03	.03	.03	.19	−.05	.10	.09	.11	.17
012.	apathetic	.11	−.08	−.08	.03	−.10	−.01	.05	−.07	.02	.03	−.05	.03
013.	appreciative	−.08	−.10	.10	−.01	.15	−.10	.17	.06	.01	.05	.13	.16
014.	argumentative	−.10	.09	−.06	.19	.10	.17	−.04	−.21	.03	−.09	−.09	−.13
015.	arrogant	−.04	−.03	.05	−.02	.04	.04	−.01	−.11	−.01	−.11	−.08	−.04
016.	artistic	.03	.05	.10	.06	.20	.13	.09	.06	−.01	−.02	.29	.13
017.	assertive	−.09	−.02	.01	.11	.05	.09	−.06	−.02	−.13	−.15	−.06	−.15
018.	attractive	.05	.05	.13	−.01	.15	.05	−.08	.11	.03	.01	.10	−.06
019.	autocratic	−.08	−.12	−.07	.04	−.08	.00	.11	−.06	.01	−.16	−.09	−.01
020.	awkward	−.08	−.04	.01	.14	−.01	.11	.21	.00	.04	.02	.07	.12
021.	bitter	−.03	−.09	.02	.05	−.12	−.05	.07	−.06	.05	−.10	−.02	.01
022.	blustery	−.04	.06	.03	.10	−.01	.07	.01	.01	−.06	.02	−.09	.05
023.	boastful	−.01	−.06	−.03	−.02	−.06	.00	−.19	−.21	−.03	−.15	−.06	.00
024.	bossy	−.14	.02	−.04	−.01	−.06	.03	.01	−.11	.08	.00	−.13	.02
025.	calm	.00	−.13	.05	−.03	.02	−.13	.02	.07	−.02	−.11	−.03	−.15
026.	capable	−.04	−.09	−.03	.00	.16	−.04	−.10	.11	.01	−.02	.04	−.14
027.	careless	.23	.34	.08	−.11	.09	.19	.06	−.11	.06	.10	−.08	.03
028.	cautious	−.14	−.38	−.02	−.16	−.08	−.16	.18	.10	.01	.11	.08	.06
029.	changeable	.17	.21	.14	.17	.11	.22	.05	−.11	.06	−.09	.04	.11
030.	charming	.05	.00	.11	.00	.21	.08	.03	.13	.04	.07	.17	.03
031.	cheerful	.08	.04	.03	−.01	.12	.00	.02	−.03	−.07	.14	−.02	.04
032.	civilized	.04	−.05	−.02	−.08	.17	−.07	.00	.06	−.03	.03	.25	.00
033.	clear-thinking	−.09	−.06	.04	.01	.19	.06	−.19	.08	.04	−.07	.10	−.16
034.	clever	.18	.18	.22	.11	.24	.19	−.18	−.01	.06	−.18	.10	−.08
035.	coarse	−.04	.02	.00	.18	−.03	.19	−.05	−.16	.13	−.11	−.16	−.02
036.	cold	−.16	−.07	−.01	.02	−.12	−.06	.04	−.08	.12	.06	−.02	−.09
037.	commonplace	−.09	−.11	−.07	.05	−.17	−.14	.16	−.06	.10	.05	−.16	.07
038.	complaining	.03	−.01	−.04	.10	.03	−.03	.19	.00	.20	.08	.05	.01
039.	complicated	.05	.08	.14	.18	.22	.21	.04	.07	.04	−.11	.24	−.05
040.	conceited	.01	−.01	−.03	−.01	.00	.07	−.07	−.16	.05	−.08	−.05	−.04
041.	confident	.07	.00	−.03	.00	.13	.06	−.19	−.09	−.20	−.20	−.06	−.17
042.	confused	−.03	.09	.01	.08	−.02	.06	.10	.07	.13	.11	.03	.08
043.	conscientious	−.22	−.27	−.12	.01	−.01	−.25	.06	.14	.05	.02	.07	.00
044.	conservative	−.07	−.29	−.26	−.32	−.26	−.42	−.02	.03	−.03	.08	−.14	.06

Correlations of Observers' Adjectival Description with Scales of the CPI continued

	Scale: Fx						Scale: F/M					
	By Peers		By Spouses		By Staff		By Peers		By Spouses		By Staff	
Adjectives	M	F	M	F	M	F	M	F	M	F	M	F
045. considerate	−.01	−.14	−.03	.08	.14	−.11	.09	.11	.06	.01	.19	.07
046. contented	.09	−.03	−.01	−.14	.00	−.16	−.03	−.01	−.04	.02	−.10	.05
047. conventional	−.07	−.20	−.20	−.14	−.22	−.38	.09	.08	−.07	.03	−.15	.09
048. cool	.01	.08	.02	−.02	.01	−.02	−.08	−.07	−.02	−.08	−.11	−.14
049. cooperative	.06	−.03	.06	.01	.09	−.10	.00	.08	−.04	.02	.07	.11
050. courageous	.12	.09	.12	−.12	.04	.02	−.17	−.13	−.04	−.03	−.05	−.15
051. cowardly	−.01	−.04	.06	−.07	−.07	.02	.09	.13	.08	−.01	−.01	.04
052. cruel	−.05	−.12	−.09	−.02	−.01	.09	.03	−.03	−.05	−.11	.00	.02
053. curious	.12	.17	.04	.11	.35	.23	−.02	−.08	−.04	−.06	.20	−.06
054. cynical	.08	.02	−.02	.10	.07	.23	−.03	−.07	−.01	−.11	−.05	−.12
055. daring	.09	.28	.11	−.03	.08	.16	−.31	−.18	−.03	−.02	−.02	−.08
056. deceitful	.04	.10	.03	−.07	.00	.13	−.05	−.03	−.03	.00	−.11	−.03
057. defensive	.01	−.11	.04	.10	−.05	−.07	.14	.04	.11	−.03	−.02	−.02
058. deliberate	−.15	−.10	−.12	−.09	−.10	−.24	−.09	.03	.03	−.06	.07	−.10
059. demanding	−.12	.02	−.07	.05	.01	.03	−.01	−.09	.07	−.03	−.05	−.03
060. dependable	−.15	−.16	−.04	−.07	.01	−.21	−.08	.12	−.03	.06	.07	−.02
061. dependent	.14	−.08	.08	−.06	−.07	−.05	.21	.02	.05	.14	.05	.29
062. despondent	.05	.02	.05	.07	−.07	−.06	.09	.13	.09	.00	.08	.12
063. determined	−.18	−.11	−.10	.02	.06	−.01	−.06	.00	−.14	−.14	−.03	−.16
064. dignified	.00	−.19	−.09	−.15	−.03	−.26	.08	.15	.07	.02	.11	−.02
065. discreet	.05	−.14	.04	.01	.01	−.15	.09	.19	.09	−.03	.15	−.01
066. disorderly	.19	.26	.22	.15	.11	.23	.02	−.03	.02	−.03	−.03	.04
067. dissatisfied	.00	.00	.01	.04	.08	.09	.18	−.08	.11	.08	.06	−.01
068. distractible	.05	.18	.06	.05	.11	.18	.14	−.09	−.02	.04	.07	.12
069. distrustful	−.03	−.01	.01	−.03	−.02	.04	.04	.02	.01	.02	−.05	−.07
070. dominant	−.14	.02	−.06	.07	.05	.09	−.09	−.14	−.03	−.07	−.07	−.13
071. dreamy	.08	.05	.05	.06	.07	.12	.16	.07	−.08	−.12	.18	.11
072. dull	−.03	−.19	.00	−.09	−.16	−.16	.26	.02	.11	−.01	−.04	.00
073. easygoing	.23	.10	.16	−.08	.11	.05	−.01	−.03	.00	−.06	−.06	.02
074. effeminate	.01	−.02	.04	−.04	.04	−.10	.17	.01	.07	.05	.16	.08
075. efficient	−.25	−.19	−.11	−.11	.08	−.06	−.02	.05	−.03	.06	−.06	−.17
076. egotistical	−.05	−.03	−.02	.03	.05	.08	−.12	−.12	−.01	−.16	−.05	−.08
077. emotional	−.03	.11	.08	.07	.14	.10	.15	.10	.13	.00	.15	.19
078. energetic	−.01	.06	.07	−.07	.09	.08	−.15	−.02	−.10	−.03	−.04	−.06
079. enterprising	−.05	.04	.05	.06	.09	.09	−.13	−.08	−.08	−.05	−.02	−.11
080. enthusiastic	−.09	.09	.18	.00	.15	.05	−.08	−.01	−.02	.01	.06	.06
081. evasive	.09	.12	−.02	.00	−.06	−.01	.05	.07	−.04	−.02	−.04	.02
082. excitable	.00	.11	.04	.07	.10	.10	−.06	−.07	.02	.09	.06	.14
083. fair-minded	−.04	−.01	.07	−.05	.12	−.03	−.02	.06	−.04	−.01	.06	−.04
084. fault-finding	−.10	−.14	−.12	.04	.04	.00	.01	−.04	.06	−.05	.03	−.04
085. fearful	.00	−.18	−.03	.15	.01	.00	.13	.08	−.05	−.04	.08	.11
086. feminine	.00	.00	.03	.00	.10	−.10	.33	.25	.07	.02	.15	.16
087. fickle	.23	.18	−.03	.14	.04	.05	.24	−.23	.07	.03	.01	.07
088. flirtatious	.05	.21	−.04	.05	.08	.09	−.06	−.07	−.06	−.01	.03	.05

Correlations of Observers' Adjectival Description with Scales of the CPI continued											
	Scale: Fx						Scale: F/M					
	By Peers		By Spouses		By Staff		By Peers		By Spouses		By Staff	
Adjectives	M	F	M	F	M	F	M	F	M	F	M	F
089. foolish	.08	.09	.09	.01	−.10	.01	.05	−.05	.12	−.05	−.09	.12
090. forceful	−.17	−.07	−.08	.06	−.01	.09	−.21	−.08	−.05	−.15	−.03	−.14
091. foresighted	−.03	−.10	−.01	−.01	.12	.04	−.07	.07	−.15	−.01	.12	−.12
092. forgetful	.08	.18	.03	.14	.07	.03	.10	.00	−.02	−.13	.09	.08
093. forgiving	.03	−.02	.15	−.11	.08	−.07	.12	.09	−.06	.07	.09	.16
094. formal	−.20	−.21	.01	−.08	−.08	−.24	.15	.01	.04	−.10	.08	.00
095. frank	.00	.06	−.02	.11	.14	.13	−.04	−.02	−.03	.00	.00	−.10
096. friendly	.12	−.01	.15	.05	.09	.00	−.06	.01	−.13	−.01	.05	.03
097. frivolous	−.01	.13	.05	−.06	.05	.05	.08	−.04	.02	.10	−.01	.08
098. fussy	−.08	−.14	−.17	.00	−.15	−.12	.20	−.01	.12	−.03	.07	.14
099. generous	.06	−.03	.20	.06	.11	.01	.01	.17	.00	.02	.09	.12
100. gentle	−.02	−.14	.03	.04	.14	−.12	.12	.18	.04	.09	.21	.12
101. gloomy	.06	.03	−.01	−.02	−.04	.02	.18	.08	.17	−.06	.08	.04
102. good-looking	.07	.06	.06	.00	.09	.03	−.13	.03	−.02	−.06	.02	−.08
103. good-natured	.10	.02	.11	−.07	.13	.06	−.08	.12	−.08	.03	.05	.07
104. greedy	.00	−.04	−.04	−.09	−.01	.07	.07	−.04	.03	.00	.00	.03
105. handsome	.02	−.03	.08	.02	.09	−.02	−.14	.00	.06	−.06	.02	−.06
106. hard-headed	−.18	−.11	−.12	.00	−.06	.02	−.11	−.11	.05	−.14	−.10	−.10
107. hard-hearted	−.03	−.07	−.08	−.03	−.09	−.02	−.09	−.07	−.03	−.01	−.07	−.07
108. hasty	−.01	.20	.05	.05	.09	.16	−.01	−.12	.04	.05	−.06	.05
109. headstrong	−.12	.05	−.07	.06	.08	.13	−.07	−.18	.02	−.04	−.05	−.10
110. healthy	.13	−.05	−.06	.03	.08	.01	−.20	−.15	−.01	−.10	−.04	−.14
111. helpful	.04	−.06	−.02	−.06	.09	−.14	−.03	.16	.04	.01	.09	.06
112. high-strung	−.04	.09	−.03	.06	.11	.16	.14	.05	.20	.09	.10	.12
113. honest	−.02	−.14	.03	.03	.08	−.08	.06	.15	.11	.05	.09	.03
114. hostile	−.06	−.03	−.04	.01	−.04	.02	−.13	−.07	.02	−.03	−.10	−.03
115. humorous	.22	.13	.16	.17	.09	.13	−.10	−.01	−.04	−.13	.02	−.02
116. hurried	.01	.13	−.04	.11	.11	.12	.05	.08	−.03	.02	.05	.14
117. idealistic	−.13	−.08	.10	.07	.18	.10	.09	.01	.00	−.03	.21	.10
118. imaginative	.13	.24	.23	.15	.27	.28	.12	.02	−.04	−.18	.20	.03
119. immature	.09	.09	−.01	.09	.06	.02	.03	−.08	.11	.05	−.10	.08
120. impatient	−.02	.11	−.05	.15	.10	.18	.06	−.12	−.12	−.04	−.07	.02
121. impulsive	.12	.28	.10	.21	.10	.24	−.16	−.09	.09	.06	−.06	.07
122. independent	.15	.07	−.03	.04	.14	.17	−.17	−.08	−.16	−.22	−.06	−.19
123. indifferent	.03	.06	−.07	.07	−.02	.02	.13	.01	.01	−.13	−.10	.03
124. individualistic	.14	.17	.08	.25	.16	.24	−.07	−.08	−.03	−.18	.06	−.07
125. industrious	−.16	−.19	−.05	−.04	−.04	−.16	−.09	.12	−.08	−.06	.03	−.16
126. infantile	−.07	.00	−.04	−.06	.02	−.04	.10	−.13	.00	.09	−.02	.09
127. informal	.13	.37	.11	.09	.16	.25	−.05	−.04	−.01	−.15	−.06	.01
128. ingenious	.04	.13	.12	.05	.20	.18	−.08	−.02	.04	.08	.06	−.04
129. inhibited	−.17	−.25	.03	.06	−.09	−.13	.09	.03	.05	−.08	.06	.08
130. initiative	−.02	.00	.07	.11	.06	.10	−.13	−.08	−.12	.06	−.04	−.08
131. insightful	.09	.07	.20	.18	.23	.18	.08	.04	.01	.00	.17	−.06
132. intelligent	.10	−.05	−.01	.09	.26	.12	−.01	.01	−.04	−.10	.13	−.14

Correlations of Observers' Adjectival Description with Scales of the CPI continued

		Scale: Fx						Scale: F/M				
		By Peers		By Spouses		By Staff		By Peers		By Spouses		By Staff	
Adjectives		M	F	M	F	M	F	M	F	M	F	M	F
133.	interests—narrow	−.17	−.12	−.22	−.21	−.17	−.30	.14	.01	.00	.14	−.16	.06
134.	interests—wide	.07	.06	.15	.23	.25	.23	−.06	.01	.00	−.10	.20	−.02
135.	intolerant	−.16	−.02	−.02	−.02	−.05	−.14	.01	−.15	−.02	.02	−.06	.00
136.	inventive	−.08	.08	.12	.04	.20	.20	−.03	−.07	−.05	.02	.13	−.04
137.	irresponsible	.17	.24	.00	.06	.08	.14	.05	−.06	.02	−.04	−.04	.07
138.	irritable	−.09	−.07	.05	.09	.02	.06	.10	−.12	.08	−.01	.00	.01
139.	jolly	.07	.12	.07	.03	−.02	.06	−.07	−.04	.01	−.05	−.10	.07
140.	kind	−.16	−.15	.04	.07	.14	−.08	.08	.11	.05	−.01	.20	.13
141.	lazy	.31	.18	.16	.17	.02	.16	.01	−.20	.00	−.12	−.14	.06
142.	leisurely	.24	.20	.14	.02	.04	.06	.03	−.10	−.01	.00	−.10	.03
143.	logical	.05	−.10	−.09	−.04	.15	.00	−.04	.00	.00	.02	.04	−.18
144.	loud	−.04	.05	.06	.01	−.01	.09	−.04	−.15	.11	−.09	−.11	.02
145.	loyal	−.06	−.14	.00	−.02	−.07	−.20	.03	.05	.09	.01	−.04	.08
146.	mannerly	−.14	−.15	−.08	−.05	.03	−.22	.07	.11	−.01	−.13	.11	.06
147.	masculine	.03	.06	−.07	.03	−.03	.07	−.34	−.33	−.12	.01	−.14	−.08
148.	mature	−.04	−.11	−.04	−.04	.04	−.12	−.16	.05	−.01	−.07	.06	−.08
149.	meek	.03	−.17	−.05	−.06	−.07	−.04	.26	.08	.08	.04	.08	.11
150.	methodical	−.12	−.18	−.16	.04	−.11	−.26	.07	.18	.09	−.03	.06	−.11
151.	mild	−.06	−.16	.00	−.11	.00	−.15	.17	.15	.07	.07	.11	.13
152.	mischievous	.17	.34	.02	.07	.15	.23	−.13	−.12	−.06	−.02	−.01	.07
153.	moderate	−.06	−.13	−.01	−.05	−.06	−.17	.09	.08	−.07	−.05	−.03	.00
154.	modest	−.04	−.17	−.07	−.10	.01	−.17	.10	.19	.08	.08	.08	.09
155.	moody	.02	−.01	.02	.12	.03	.16	.05	−.03	.10	−.06	.10	.05
156.	nagging	−.09	−.14	−.08	.10	.01	−.10	.22	−.07	.08	.02	.03	.15
157.	natural	.15	.04	.14	.09	.11	.08	−.10	.08	.03	−.08	−.12	−.04
158.	nervous	−.01	.02	−.15	.00	.03	.09	.34	.08	.17	.07	.12	.18
159.	noisy	.05	.16	−.02	.01	−.01	.12	−.04	−.18	.00	.05	−.08	.07
160.	obliging	.06	−.08	.06	.01	.11	−.02	.05	.15	.02	−.08	.10	.16
161.	obnoxious	−.04	−.02	−.01	.10	.01	.06	−.03	−.18	−.12	−.02	−.12	.04
162.	opinionated	−.10	−.07	.02	.08	.01	−.03	.01	−.18	.01	−.06	−.04	−.08
163.	opportunistic	.02	.02	.04	.03	−.02	.12	−.11	.00	−.04	−.11	−.14	.00
164.	optimistic	.16	−.14	.15	.07	.10	−.01	−.10	−.03	−.03	−.03	.02	.00
165.	organized	−.28	−.24	−.18	−.22	.01	−.21	.11	.12	.10	.09	.00	−.13
166.	original	.08	.17	.19	.11	.29	.25	−.16	−.05	.04	−.07	.21	−.02
167.	outgoing	.06	.14	.17	.19	.07	.11	−.17	−.05	−.01	−.05	−.09	−.01
168.	outspoken	−.05	.06	.01	.12	.08	.08	−.16	−.12	.02	.03	−.03	−.07
169.	painstaking	−.19	−.17	−.01	−.06	−.09	−.17	.12	.13	.03	.05	.18	.01
170.	patient	−.09	−.17	.08	−.19	.02	−.19	.09	.09	−.05	.05	.11	.02
171.	peaceable	.01	−.17	.04	−.04	.05	−.18	.14	.18	−.03	−.05	.07	.12
172.	peculiar	−.01	.03	−.12	.02	.00	.03	.14	−.05	.13	−.10	.10	.03
173.	persevering	−.11	−.18	−.03	−.02	.01	−.16	.01	.05	.05	−.08	.04	−.06
174.	persistent	.00	−.08	−.01	−.03	−.03	.04	−.03	.00	−.10	−.06	.00	−.13
175.	pessimistic	−.04	.05	−.07	.13	.03	.03	.14	.05	.06	.04	.08	.13
176.	planful	−.25	−.20	−.11	−.06	.05	−.14	.02	.13	.04	.04	.07	−.08

Correlations of Observers' Adjectival Description with Scales of the CPI continued												
	Scale: Fx						Scale: F/M					
	By Peers		By Spouses		By Staff		By Peers		By Spouses		By Staff	
Adjectives	M	F	M	F	M	F	M	F	M	F	M	F
177. pleasant	.15	.05	.00	.03	.15	−.02	−.08	.05	−.11	.08	.09	.09
178. pleasure-seeking	.25	.30	.18	.13	.11	.15	−.13	−.19	.03	−.11	−.09	.04
179. poised	.10	−.07	−.01	−.01	.03	−.11	.02	.10	−.02	.00	.05	−.11
180. polished	.01	−.10	.01	.01	.00	−.07	−.06	.12	.08	−.03	.07	−.11
181. practical	−.17	−.23	−.10	−.08	−.08	−.17	−.08	.11	−.06	−.01	−.12	−.07
182. praising	.03	−.13	.05	−.12	.07	−.09	.07	.07	.02	.05	.09	.19
183. precise	−.23	−.19	−.08	.03	.02	−.09	.05	.06	.02	−.04	.16	−.16
184. prejudiced	−.02	−.24	−.20	−.05	−.15	−.15	.03	.00	−.10	−.06	−.11	.06
185. preoccupied	−.02	.06	.04	.07	−.01	.07	.04	−.03	−.03	−.05	.15	.04
186. progressive	.11	.07	.11	.14	.19	.25	−.05	−.03	.02	−.07	.16	−.08
187. prudish	−.19	−.32	−.03	−.10	−.08	−.29	.23	−.04	.07	.08	.07	.10
188. quarrelsome	−.08	−.06	−.04	.09	.02	.11	−.09	−.09	.18	.00	−.08	−.05
189. queer	−.04	−.10	.08	.00	.02	.04	.20	−.08	.02	.00	.08	−.04
190. quick	.16	.07	.05	.07	.18	.14	−.16	−.13	.04	−.10	.01	.03
191. quiet	−.09	−.17	−.10	−.12	−.03	−.14	.14	.16	.05	.10	.09	.04
192. quitting	.06	.05	.12	.06	.00	.03	.25	.05	.03	.03	.06	.04
193. rational	.02	−.09	.02	.08	.18	.02	−.06	−.03	.07	−.12	.07	−.17
194. rattle-brained	.06	.15	.03	−.05	−.07	.10	.08	−.02	.05	.05	−.03	.15
195. realistic	−.05	−.06	.03	.01	.06	−.04	−.08	−.03	.05	.01	−.06	−.11
196. reasonable	−.07	−.15	.01	.07	.10	−.11	−.01	−.01	−.07	−.04	.02	−.02
197. rebellious	.08	.21	.18	.11	.17	.25	−.11	−.11	.09	−.19	.03	−.07
198. reckless	.14	.24	.14	.04	.05	.18	−.06	−.12	−.04	−.09	−.06	.06
199. reflective	.09	−.05	.23	.20	.21	.09	.24	.13	.14	−.11	.27	.04
200. relaxed	.18	−.03	.15	−.11	.10	.03	.01	−.06	−.15	−.08	−.05	−.16
201. reliable	−.10	−.18	−.09	−.06	.04	−.19	−.01	.09	−.11	−.05	.04	−.02
202. resentful	−.04	−.02	−.06	.06	−.05	−.02	−.01	−.06	.02	−.06	−.08	−.01
203. reserved	−.07	−.20	−.09	−.14	.01	−.11	.14	.13	.04	.09	.10	−.01
204. resourceful	−.04	−.08	.08	.09	.18	.13	−.08	.04	−.07	−.19	.02	−.09
205. responsible	−.18	−.18	.02	.01	.04	−.22	−.10	.10	−.02	−.04	.12	−.02
206. restless	.08	.17	.07	.09	.12	.23	.04	−.19	−.11	−.09	.04	.07
207. retiring	−.07	−.20	.09	−.08	−.07	−.12	.08	.15	.09	−.05	.06	.16
208. rigid	−.18	−.28	−.03	.03	−.22	−.27	.03	−.11	.10	.04	−.08	−.04
209. robust	.03	.04	.03	.09	−.02	.06	−.18	−.19	−.05	−.02	−.12	−.05
210. rude	−.01	.02	.01	.00	.01	.04	−.08	−.14	.00	.02	−.12	−.02
211. sarcastic	.17	.09	−.05	.12	.08	.17	−.02	−.17	−.04	−.03	−.07	−.09
212. self-centered	−.07	−.10	−.05	.06	.03	.11	−.05	−.15	.06	−.07	−.05	.05
213. self-confident	.05	.05	.01	−.01	.13	.03	−.18	−.06	−.20	−.14	−.08	−.19
214. self-controlled	.01	−.17	.02	−.09	.00	−.18	.03	.11	.00	−.13	.05	−.08
215. self-denying	−.05	−.10	−.06	−.13	−.09	−.14	.10	.12	.08	.01	.08	.16
216. self-pitying	.02	−.08	.04	.00	−.02	−.03	.30	−.04	.25	.04	.05	.14
217. self-punishing	.00	−.13	.05	.08	−.04	.03	.02	.01	.13	.01	.04	.10
218. self-seeking	−.01	.01	.12	.05	−.01	.11	−.04	−.04	.05	−.07	−.13	−.01
219. selfish	.00	−.07	.04	.01	−.04	.06	−.01	−.11	.05	−.08	−.12	−.01
220. sensitive	−.04	−.08	.13	.04	.27	.09	.22	.11	.09	.07	.30	.17

		Scale: Fx						Scale: F/M					
		By Peers		By Spouses		By Staff		By Peers		By Spouses		By Staff	
Adjectives		M	F	M	F	M	F	M	F	M	F	M	F
221.	sentimental	−.03	−.03	−.06	.06	.02	−.01	.14	.04	.07	.12	.11	.20
222.	serious	−.17	−.20	−.02	−.02	.04	−.03	.04	.14	.06	−.04	.17	−.10
223.	severe	−.04	.04	−.02	.03	−.07	−.11	.01	−.09	−.02	−.03	.09	.03
224.	sexy	.11	.14	.11	.14	.11	.11	−.15	.05	−.04	−.09	.02	−.02
225.	shallow	−.09	.00	−.03	−.17	−.15	−.11	.12	−.06	.09	.15	−.17	.07
226.	sharp-witted	.19	.15	.07	.18	.16	.24	−.07	−.08	.05	−.16	.04	−.06
227.	shiftless	.06	.07	.00	.09	.05	.06	.01	−.02	.08	−.04	−.03	.02
228.	show-off	.05	.11	.17	−.04	.06	.09	−.14	−.12	−.01	−.03	−.04	.05
229.	shrewd	.02	−.02	.01	.14	.02	.13	−.07	−.02	.06	−.07	−.08	−.05
230.	shy	−.14	−.19	.01	−.09	.02	−.04	.13	.15	.17	.08	.14	.06
231.	silent	−.10	−.19	−.10	−.16	−.01	−.07	.17	.13	.05	−.01	.05	.02
232.	simple	−.05	−.17	−.02	−.01	−.17	−.14	.11	−.03	−.02	.07	−.13	.10
233.	sincere	−.08	−.17	.00	−.06	.08	−.10	.11	.15	−.07	.11	.12	.02
234.	slipshod	−.01	.14	.00	.07	.03	.13	−.14	−.11	.10	−.04	−.06	.05
235.	slow	.02	−.08	.08	.07	−.10	−.10	.15	.01	.03	−.04	.01	.06
236.	sly	.14	.04	.00	.06	.07	.07	−.02	−.06	−.07	−.18	−.02	.03
237.	smug	−.06	−.04	−.09	−.01	−.01	−.03	−.12	−.07	−.08	−.02	−.05	−.07
238.	snobbish	−.06	−.07	.05	−.06	−.02	−.01	.01	−.01	.00	−.05	.02	.00
239.	sociable	.14	.15	.16	.16	.11	.03	−.11	.03	−.12	−.16	−.01	.03
240.	soft-hearted	.07	.02	.13	.02	.04	−.07	.13	.13	−.01	.11	.09	.18
241.	sophisticated	.06	−.04	.05	.08	.15	.15	.01	.15	.02	−.13	.19	−.02
242.	spendthrift	.23	.04	.01	.04	.01	.01	−.06	−.09	.13	−.03	−.04	.06
243.	spineless	−.01	−.09	.08	.12	−.07	−.01	.16	−.01	.09	.00	.00	.09
244.	spontaneous	.13	.25	.15	.34	.16	.17	−.08	−.08	−.08	−.02	.00	.07
245.	spunky	.07	.18	−.02	.16	.02	.14	−.11	−.09	.04	−.17	−.02	−.02
246.	stable	−.08	−.14	−.03	−.09	.01	−.19	−.05	−.05	.05	−.03	−.04	−.12
247.	steady	−.09	−.20	.00	−.08	−.07	−.25	−.03	−.02	.01	−.06	−.02	−.12
248.	stern	−.24	−.18	−.25	−.03	−.13	−.16	−.03	−.04	.11	−.01	.01	−.07
249.	stingy	−.02	−.06	−.08	.04	−.08	−.03	.17	−.09	.00	−.04	.00	−.01
250.	stolid	−.15	−.11	.03	−.08	−.14	−.25	−.06	−.05	.03	−.23	−.05	−.02
251.	strong	−.08	−.13	.07	−.13	.00	.03	−.19	−.17	−.14	−.18	−.08	−.21
252.	stubborn	−.17	−.11	−.12	.00	−.05	.04	−.05	−.16	.09	−.11	−.08	−.13
253.	submissive	.02	−.13	.02	−.07	−.09	−.02	.17	.16	.17	.07	.04	.22
254.	suggestible	.15	.16	.07	.03	−.04	−.05	.10	−.08	−.01	.09	.00	.28
255.	sulky	−.01	.00	.08	.11	−.07	−.01	.00	.00	.12	.03	.01	.02
256.	superstitious	−.04	−.02	−.01	−.04	−.01	−.13	.22	.02	−.08	−.01	.07	.10
257.	suspicious	−.02	−.03	.01	.03	−.03	−.04	.01	.01	.03	−.07	−.02	−.03
258.	sympathetic	.03	−.03	.14	.00	.17	−.05	.10	.16	.07	.11	.17	.14
259.	tactful	.09	−.03	.06	.06	.08	−.07	.00	.17	.01	−.04	.13	.03
260.	tactless	−.13	−.06	−.18	.08	.03	.05	.04	−.09	.02	.06	−.09	−.02
261.	talkative	.13	.19	.11	.11	.12	.11	−.01	−.09	−.06	−.07	.02	.04
262.	temperamental	−.04	.03	−.04	.03	.09	.17	.07	−.05	.05	−.04	.09	.01
263.	tense	−.03	−.02	−.05	.02	−.05	.11	.07	.08	.11	.07	.04	.08
264.	thankless	−.06	.01	−.02	−.02	−.01	−.01	.05	−.02	.04	.07	−.03	−.01

Correlations of Observers' Adjectival Description with Scales of the CPI continued

		Scale: Fx						Scale: F/M					
		By Peers		By Spouses		By Staff		By Peers		By Spouses		By Staff	
Adjectives		M	F	M	F	M	F	M	F	M	F	M	F
265.	thorough	−.19	−.23	−.02	−.07	.06	−.10	−.02	.07	.00	−.07	.12	−.14
266.	thoughtful	.01	−.12	.05	.05	.23	−.04	−.01	.14	.05	−.01	.24	.00
267.	thrifty	−.12	−.09	−.07	−.09	−.06	−.16	.04	.11	.11	.09	.01	.03
268.	timid	−.04	−.20	−.01	−.07	−.04	−.04	.20	.16	.12	.00	.10	.11
269.	tolerant	.18	.04	.15	.00	.21	.08	.01	.08	−.03	−.01	.11	.02
270.	touchy	.00	.03	−.01	.02	.09	−.05	.02	−.10	.16	−.04	.04	.03
271.	tough	−.16	−.05	−.17	.03	−.02	.10	−.15	−.22	.00	−.16	−.09	−.13
272.	trusting	.03	−.05	.07	−.05	.14	−.04	−.05	.05	.00	.06	.07	.12
273.	unaffected	.12	.02	.07	.04	.08	.06	−.02	.05	−.06	−.09	−.06	.05
274.	unambitious	.05	.14	.09	.10	.02	−.06	.04	.03	.07	−.02	.00	.14
275.	unassuming	.02	−.05	−.04	−.04	.03	−.02	.12	.13	−.07	.08	.01	.12
276.	unconventional	.08	.19	.23	.21	.22	.22	.12	−.05	.03	−.08	.16	−.05
277.	undependable	.09	.13	.05	−.05	.02	.13	.02	−.12	.05	.04	−.10	−.01
278.	understanding	.03	.00	.17	.07	.18	.02	.01	.10	−.01	−.07	.15	.06
279.	unemotional	−.08	−.15	.00	.02	−.04	−.14	.01	−.03	−.03	.07	−.10	−.07
280.	unexcitable	.02	−.09	−.06	−.01	−.07	−.19	.10	.04	.08	−.02	−.06	−.03
281.	unfriendly	−.06	−.01	−.12	−.04	−.04	−.07	.02	−.04	.02	−.16	−.02	−.10
282.	uninhibited	.12	.16	.17	.13	.13	.19	−.08	−.01	−.04	−.02	−.04	−.04
283.	unintelligent	.01	.07	.00	−.05	−.10	.01	.02	−.04	.00	.05	−.03	.07
284.	unkind	−.03	−.03	−.03	−.08	−.02	−.01	.08	−.05	.09	.08	−.03	−.02
285.	unrealistic	.12	.00	.10	−.04	.03	.02	−.01	−.08	.14	.04	.01	.08
286.	unscrupulous	.05	.10	.00	−.01	.01	.11	−.08	.02	.05	.03	−.03	.05
287.	unselfish	−.06	−.02	−.02	.02	.08	−.06	.04	.15	.13	.05	.05	.10
288.	unstable	.09	.14	−.04	.13	.08	.18	.02	.10	−.01	−.17	.06	.11
289.	vindictive	.04	−.03	−.05	.04	−.07	−.01	−.03	−.09	−.01	−.08	−.07	.03
290.	versatile	.16	.14	.12	.06	.20	.23	−.11	−.12	−.03	−.05	.05	−.05
291.	warm	.04	.05	.06	.01	.12	−.02	.02	.18	.00	.18	.10	.09
292.	wary	.08	−.05	.05	−.02	−.03	−.01	−.08	.06	−.03	−.15	−.06	−.03
293.	weak	.05	−.08	.02	−.07	−.10	−.06	.32	.17	.15	.10	.02	.13
294.	whiny	.05	−.04	.06	.01	−.04	.01	.28	.13	.14	.05	.04	.06
295.	wholesome	−.08	−.07	−.03	.03	.10	−.07	−.01	.02	−.02	−.08	.01	−.04
296.	wise	−.04	−.07	.02	−.04	.11	.04	−.10	.02	.02	−.08	.18	−.01
297.	withdrawn	−.03	−.16	.00	−.01	−.02	.00	.10	.17	.10	.02	.11	.04
298.	witty	.23	.17	.16	−.06	.15	.18	−.04	−.03	−.03	−.09	.07	.04
299.	worrying	−.04	−.04	−.08	.10	.00	−.01	.30	.15	.12	.03	.18	.11
300.	zany	.10	.22	.04	.19	.06	.12	.04	−.11	−.07	.01	−.02	.03

Correlations of Observers' Adjectival Description with Scales of the CPI continued

		Scale: v.1						Scale: v.2					
		By Peers		By Spouses		By Staff		By Peers		By Spouses		By Staff	
Adjectives		M	F	M	F	M	F	M	F	M	F	M	F
001.	absent-minded	−.05	.14	.17	−.08	.19	.04	−.02	−.29	−.13	−.19	−.06	−.21
002.	active	−.19	−.31	−.13	−.14	−.36	−.31	.21	.08	−.10	.08	−.11	−.02
003.	adaptable	−.04	−.08	−.09	−.07	−.19	−.19	.16	.12	−.04	.00	−.07	−.04
004.	adventurous	−.12	−.24	−.18	−.17	−.30	−.34	−.13	−.14	−.12	−.14	−.21	−.23
005.	affected	−.14	−.19	−.07	−.07	−.16	−.18	.08	.06	.02	.01	−.07	−.04
006.	affectionate	.01	.07	−.07	−.03	.00	−.02	.06	.06	−.12	.05	−.09	−.03
007.	aggressive	−.21	−.43	−.19	−.28	−.31	−.36	.05	−.03	−.05	−.13	−.06	−.11
008.	alert	−.09	−.26	−.15	−.12	−.27	−.23	.08	.10	.05	.07	−.11	.08
009.	aloof	.05	.05	.09	.04	.23	.10	−.07	−.16	−.04	−.12	−.14	−.03
010.	ambitious	−.19	−.22	−.25	−.25	−.33	−.32	.22	.21	.12	.02	.07	.07
011.	anxious	−.02	−.01	.04	−.02	.21	.22	−.01	.02	.01	−.05	−.11	−.17
012.	apathetic	.14	.13	.12	.06	.27	.19	−.24	−.08	−.15	−.07	−.05	−.04
013.	appreciative	.06	.10	−.02	.03	.07	.15	.16	.13	.07	.18	−.09	.06
014.	argumentative	−.18	−.24	−.07	−.23	−.29	−.21	−.01	−.17	−.01	−.11	−.09	−.14
015.	arrogant	−.18	−.26	−.10	−.12	−.23	−.24	−.10	−.03	−.16	−.03	−.15	−.04
016.	artistic	.11	.00	.09	−.07	−.03	.07	−.12	−.08	−.13	−.17	−.14	−.19
017.	assertive	−.15	−.39	−.20	−.35	−.37	−.36	.05	.01	−.03	−.06	−.05	−.03
018.	attractive	.01	−.08	.04	.01	−.13	−.14	−.01	.01	−.04	−.06	−.14	−.03
019.	autocratic	−.02	−.16	−.08	−.09	−.15	−.19	−.01	−.03	−.02	−.08	−.07	.03
020.	awkward	.15	.16	.12	.09	.33	.26	.00	−.18	−.16	−.11	−.09	−.17
021.	bitter	.10	−.04	.09	−.09	.02	−.12	−.02	−.05	−.25	−.14	−.10	−.10
022.	blustery	−.17	−.12	−.04	−.02	−.15	−.11	−.06	−.11	.00	−.06	−.07	−.12
023.	boastful	−.16	−.35	−.17	−.16	−.27	−.22	−.02	.03	−.09	.00	−.03	−.06
024.	bossy	−.08	−.29	−.02	−.15	−.20	−.23	.00	−.04	−.10	.02	−.03	.00
025.	calm	.13	.23	.18	.21	.14	.04	.01	.13	.02	.04	−.06	.10
026.	capable	−.09	−.04	.04	−.12	−.16	−.20	.10	.19	.04	.10	−.12	.12
027.	careless	−.11	−.02	.12	−.03	−.05	−.05	−.24	−.37	−.21	−.04	−.18	−.33
028.	cautious	.20	.38	.20	.19	.39	.27	.09	.27	.02	.08	.00	.11
029.	changeable	−.10	−.06	.05	−.16	−.12	−.08	−.13	−.28	−.17	−.21	−.18	−.34
030.	charming	−.05	−.06	.02	−.03	−.18	−.13	−.02	.12	−.04	.07	−.16	−.03
031.	cheerful	−.04	.00	−.01	.02	−.16	−.11	.05	.03	.11	.08	−.03	.09
032.	civilized	−.06	.06	.02	.07	−.07	−.03	.05	.08	.15	.00	−.12	.14
033.	clear-thinking	−.04	−.09	.03	.07	−.14	−.19	.12	.17	.12	.15	−.10	.07
034.	clever	−.10	−.22	−.11	−.17	−.30	−.22	−.15	−.12	−.10	−.02	−.17	−.14
035.	coarse	.05	−.12	.11	−.02	−.11	−.15	−.08	−.17	−.17	−.12	−.11	−.22
036.	cold	.11	.06	.15	−.02	.08	−.06	−.09	−.02	−.04	−.08	−.06	−.01
037.	commonplace	.19	.17	.09	.13	.20	.15	−.04	−.04	.07	.04	.00	.00
038.	complaining	.10	.03	.10	−.13	.01	−.10	−.05	−.12	−.11	−.18	−.14	−.11
039.	complicated	−.02	−.02	.00	−.10	−.01	−.05	−.07	−.13	.02	−.16	−.25	−.29
040.	conceited	−.21	−.30	−.10	−.14	−.26	−.20	−.14	.07	−.06	.02	−.03	−.02
041.	confident	−.23	−.36	−.10	−.24	−.35	−.40	.00	.11	.07	.09	−.08	.05
042.	confused	.08	.02	.11	−.05	.14	.13	−.05	−.14	−.15	−.16	−.06	−.25
043.	conscientious	.11	.08	.01	.00	.21	.14	.22	.28	.18	.04	.10	.29
044.	conservative	.03	.24	.15	.25	.19	.14	.12	.24	.26	.19	.19	.35

Correlations of Observers' Adjectival Description with Scales of the CPI continued

		Scale: v.1						Scale: v.2				
		By Peers		By Spouses		By Staff		By Peers		By Spouses		By Staff
Adjectives		M	F	M	F	M	F	M	F	M	F	M	F
045.	considerate	.07	.17	.07	.12	.14	.08	.15	.20	.11	−.02	−.09	.07
046.	contented	.11	.08	.05	.17	.05	.01	−.06	.11	.17	.11	−.03	.12
047.	conventional	.01	.25	.04	.16	.21	.15	.08	.24	.20	.23	.18	.28
048.	cool	−.12	−.08	.11	.01	.04	−.02	−.10	−.17	−.03	−.04	−.10	.00
049.	cooperative	.08	.15	−.01	.15	.06	.08	−.01	.19	.08	.13	.00	.10
050.	courageous	−.01	−.14	−.11	−.03	−.10	−.16	−.10	−.08	−.02	.08	−.12	−.08
051.	cowardly	.01	.20	.05	.04	.09	.05	−.04	.02	−.10	.10	−.03	−.10
052.	cruel	.11	.02	.06	−.10	−.03	−.05	−.07	−.01	−.10	−.02	−.12	−.15
053.	curious	−.06	−.07	−.05	−.01	−.10	−.21	−.05	−.19	−.04	−.01	−.27	−.22
054.	cynical	.01	−.11	.08	−.16	−.11	−.19	−.14	−.19	−.13	−.12	−.27	−.25
055.	daring	−.05	−.24	−.06	.01	−.29	−.27	−.06	−.21	−.12	.01	−.12	−.21
056.	deceitful	−.08	−.09	.08	−.13	−.14	−.13	−.09	−.11	−.16	−.01	−.05	−.18
057.	defensive	.00	.03	−.05	−.07	.05	.09	−.18	−.07	−.11	−.09	−.08	−.03
058.	deliberate	.08	−.12	.03	−.05	.24	.14	.15	.00	.04	.02	−.02	.18
059.	demanding	−.08	−.34	−.15	−.15	−.25	−.26	.00	−.02	.01	−.08	−.10	−.09
060.	dependable	.05	.00	.04	.12	.14	.09	.20	.23	.06	.08	.03	.28
061.	dependent	.03	.21	.01	.06	.25	.18	−.07	−.02	−.05	.05	−.01	−.05
062.	despondent	.02	.13	−.07	.01	.13	.24	−.06	−.21	−.14	−.03	−.05	−.08
063.	determined	−.12	−.30	−.06	−.17	−.22	−.28	.15	.21	.07	.00	−.07	.05
064.	dignified	−.09	.00	.04	−.02	.09	.13	.08	.21	.22	.12	.05	.17
065.	discreet	.02	.17	−.01	−.02	.19	.19	−.01	.12	.13	.02	.02	.16
066.	disorderly	−.08	−.07	−.14	−.05	−.06	−.04	−.18	−.35	−.20	−.13	−.16	−.35
067.	dissatisfied	.07	−.05	−.05	.00	−.02	−.02	−.07	−.20	−.18	−.02	−.22	−.30
068.	distractible	.02	.00	.03	−.08	.02	−.03	−.13	−.16	−.20	−.05	−.19	−.30
069.	distrustful	.05	.05	.10	−.04	−.01	−.05	−.14	−.11	−.04	−.05	−.13	−.18
070.	dominant	−.18	−.45	−.07	−.06	−.33	−.35	.10	.01	.10	−.07	−.10	.00
071.	dreamy	.05	.15	.03	−.09	.20	.18	−.11	.00	−.17	−.12	−.11	−.21
072.	dull	.20	.24	−.01	.08	.23	.12	−.04	.04	−.10	−.03	.03	.09
073.	easygoing	.06	.00	.15	.15	.03	−.05	−.10	−.11	−.12	.07	−.15	−.09
074.	effeminate	−.01	.07	−.04	−.08	.07	−.07	.05	−.01	−.07	.00	−.04	.13
075.	efficient	−.01	−.09	.08	−.01	−.14	−.16	.24	.24	.22	.10	.03	.18
076.	egotistical	−.22	−.36	−.18	−.17	−.28	−.25	−.05	.06	−.07	.02	−.10	−.05
077.	emotional	−.04	−.09	−.10	−.06	−.09	−.09	.04	−.13	−.10	−.06	−.18	−.21
078.	energetic	−.19	−.27	−.23	−.11	−.36	−.30	.05	.15	.02	.06	−.03	.00
079.	enterprising	−.16	−.22	−.17	−.18	−.37	−.35	.14	.07	−.02	.04	−.02	.03
080.	enthusiastic	−.09	−.17	−.31	−.14	−.25	−.30	.13	.09	−.02	.12	−.08	.02
081.	evasive	.05	.06	.01	−.04	.12	−.04	−.10	−.14	−.02	.00	−.11	−.05
082.	excitable	−.10	−.30	.01	−.17	−.19	−.13	.01	−.03	−.09	−.03	−.10	−.12
083.	fair-minded	−.01	.10	.03	.06	.05	.06	.12	.09	.04	.09	−.09	.04
084.	fault-finding	.00	−.10	.00	−.01	−.09	−.16	−.02	−.02	.02	−.08	−.14	−.10
085.	fearful	.02	.15	.09	.05	.22	.19	−.05	.04	−.12	−.07	−.11	−.11
086.	feminine	.23	.14	.11	.07	.11	.02	.07	.05	.02	−.06	−.11	.05
087.	fickle	.06	−.22	.08	−.02	−.01	−.13	−.18	−.17	−.02	−.14	−.16	−.17
088.	flirtatious	−.05	−.31	.00	−.10	−.13	−.22	−.01	−.04	−.15	−.12	−.14	−.15

	Scale: v.1						Scale: v.2					
	By Peers		By Spouses		By Staff		By Peers		By Spouses		By Staff	
Adjectives	M	F	M	F	M	F	M	F	M	F	M	F
089. foolish	−.08	−.04	.05	−.12	−.03	−.01	−.13	−.20	−.04	−.11	−.03	−.09
090. forceful	−.19	−.31	−.09	−.17	−.24	−.27	.15	.05	−.01	−.09	−.04	−.02
091. foresighted	−.02	−.08	−.02	.15	−.10	−.15	.14	.16	.12	.11	−.03	.05
092. forgetful	−.07	.17	.06	−.05	.10	.07	−.12	−.25	−.12	−.20	−.15	−.13
093. forgiving	−.10	.12	.04	.06	.07	.05	.13	.07	.00	.08	−.14	−.08
094. formal	−.04	.07	.02	.01	.13	.06	.26	.16	.11	.06	.04	.22
095. frank	.05	−.23	−.09	−.01	−.12	−.24	−.05	−.14	.03	−.09	−.19	−.15
096. friendly	.01	−.10	−.13	.01	−.10	−.08	.01	.04	.00	.00	−.06	.01
097. frivolous	.01	−.19	.05	−.04	−.08	−.11	.03	−.02	−.10	.05	−.11	−.11
098. fussy	.13	.03	.09	−.06	.09	.06	−.04	.04	−.01	.08	.02	.04
099. generous	.08	.07	−.04	.12	.02	−.05	.09	.11	−.10	.11	−.12	−.05
100. gentle	.12	.35	.13	.18	.24	.20	.07	.14	.04	.02	−.17	.01
101. gloomy	.14	.12	.17	.04	.17	.03	−.09	−.11	−.12	.02	−.05	−.09
102. good-looking	−.11	−.16	.01	.00	−.07	−.13	−.02	.02	−.02	−.05	−.14	−.01
103. good-natured	.12	.02	−.07	.05	−.03	−.05	.04	.11	.02	.11	−.09	−.06
104. greedy	.03	−.05	−.06	.02	−.05	−.08	−.11	−.02	−.06	−.03	−.08	−.11
105. handsome	−.07	.09	−.05	−.04	−.11	.02	−.05	−.09	.03	.04	−.10	.02
106. hard-headed	−.04	−.21	.01	−.13	−.13	−.12	.04	−.06	.02	−.03	−.05	−.02
107. hard-hearted	.09	−.08	.11	−.06	−.05	−.11	−.09	−.04	.00	−.01	−.06	−.01
108. hasty	−.03	−.06	.05	−.12	−.15	−.15	−.04	−.17	−.16	−.09	−.05	−.19
109. headstrong	−.05	−.21	−.12	−.18	−.22	−.28	−.07	−.14	−.04	−.11	−.17	−.20
110. healthy	.01	−.01	.10	.00	−.10	−.19	−.10	.00	.13	.00	−.15	.00
111. helpful	−.03	.02	.09	−.06	.05	.01	.11	.17	.07	.17	−.04	.11
112. high-strung	.06	−.07	.05	−.13	−.05	−.03	−.06	−.05	−.04	−.03	−.15	−.22
113. honest	.11	.18	.11	.11	.13	.04	.11	.09	.07	−.02	−.05	.03
114. hostile	.00	−.06	.12	−.11	−.03	−.10	−.05	−.12	−.13	.02	−.09	−.12
115. humorous	−.14	−.23	−.08	−.17	−.25	−.24	−.13	−.09	−.09	.01	−.16	−.11
116. hurried	.01	−.21	−.14	−.06	−.12	−.06	−.04	−.10	.04	.06	−.09	−.10
117. idealistic	−.11	−.03	−.11	−.17	.04	−.02	.10	.18	.00	.03	−.10	−.08
118. imaginative	−.09	−.14	−.09	−.18	−.19	−.13	−.10	−.07	−.17	−.05	−.20	−.21
119. immature	.05	.02	−.02	.02	.04	.13	−.17	−.11	−.16	−.07	−.05	−.08
120. impatient	−.07	−.05	−.08	−.18	−.23	−.20	−.04	−.20	−.09	−.10	−.15	−.21
121. impulsive	−.17	−.20	−.08	−.24	−.24	−.16	−.17	−.23	−.23	−.19	−.16	−.29
122. independent	−.06	−.20	−.01	−.12	−.23	−.27	−.06	−.08	.13	−.09	−.24	−.13
123. indifferent	.12	.10	.06	−.05	.11	.06	−.16	−.20	−.07	−.01	−.11	−.11
124. individualistic	−.11	−.20	−.06	−.26	−.18	−.16	−.18	−.14	.00	−.20	−.27	−.25
125. industrious	−.05	−.03	−.09	−.03	−.02	−.14	.22	.27	.03	.04	.10	.23
126. infantile	.12	−.07	.01	.04	−.02	.05	−.08	−.04	−.11	−.07	−.12	−.15
127. informal	.09	−.02	.03	−.01	−.12	−.15	−.12	−.27	−.12	−.09	−.22	−.29
128. ingenious	−.13	−.23	−.04	−.13	−.22	−.11	.00	−.06	−.07	−.01	−.08	−.12
129. inhibited	.16	.33	.22	.16	.39	.30	.12	.04	−.09	−.03	.00	.06
130. initiative	−.14	−.33	−.19	−.12	−.37	−.32	.08	.10	−.03	−.01	−.01	.02
131. insightful	−.05	−.09	−.09	−.05	−.14	−.11	−.04	.06	−.05	−.06	−.11	−.17
132. intelligent	−.13	−.11	−.10	−.05	−.18	−.13	.01	.13	.11	−.04	−.17	.03

		Scale: v.1						Scale: v.2				
		By Peers		By Spouses		By Staff		By Peers		By Spouses		By Staff
Adjectives		M	F	M	F	M	F	M	F	M	F	M	F
133.	interests—narrow	.27	.19	.11	.15	.25	.19	.04	.01	.05	.12	.04	.12
134.	interests—wide	−.20	−.30	−.14	−.15	−.24	−.17	−.02	.03	.01	−.12	−.17	−.15
135.	intolerant	.02	−.15	.07	.00	−.08	−.06	−.04	−.12	−.13	.03	−.07	−.01
136.	inventive	.04	−.16	−.10	−.14	−.18	−.13	.07	−.07	−.08	−.02	−.19	−.16
137.	irresponsible	.00	.07	−.02	−.08	−.06	−.04	−.21	−.27	−.09	−.07	−.14	−.29
138.	irritable	−.02	.00	.09	−.01	−.05	−.09	−.06	−.12	−.09	−.14	−.11	−.14
139.	jolly	−.10	−.26	.05	−.02	−.21	−.14	−.02	−.04	−.03	.03	.00	.01
140.	kind	.03	.11	.10	.02	.12	.03	.25	.16	.04	−.01	−.17	.04
141.	lazy	−.02	.03	−.14	.06	.01	.00	−.29	−.30	−.07	−.16	−.13	−.23
142.	leisurely	−.01	−.03	−.10	−.06	.04	.02	−.18	−.13	−.11	−.06	−.12	−.17
143.	logical	−.08	−.09	.02	.23	−.03	−.01	.03	.12	.08	.02	−.10	.09
144.	loud	−.04	−.30	−.13	−.18	−.24	−.21	−.04	−.05	−.03	−.09	−.07	−.09
145.	loyal	−.07	.11	.08	.12	.11	.03	.13	.11	.01	−.03	.00	.09
146.	mannerly	−.03	.14	−.03	−.04	.16	.08	.17	.17	.17	.09	−.02	.17
147.	masculine	−.04	−.17	−.08	−.10	−.13	.01	−.02	−.19	.02	−.04	−.10	−.09
148.	mature	−.09	−.03	.10	.07	−.09	−.14	.14	.14	.21	.07	−.02	.10
149.	meek	.23	.38	.05	.14	.28	.28	−.06	−.02	−.02	.02	−.08	.02
150.	methodical	.08	.19	.10	−.07	.18	.12	.15	.06	.15	.14	.10	.24
151.	mild	.19	.37	.12	.27	.32	.34	.08	.07	.01	.10	−.04	.08
152.	mischievous	−.07	−.11	.03	−.07	−.25	−.15	−.23	−.21	−.11	−.13	−.15	−.19
153.	moderate	.07	.32	.06	.11	.32	.19	.12	.07	.14	.16	.07	.15
154.	modest	.19	.32	.09	.16	.37	.33	.01	.10	.08	.12	−.04	.07
155.	moody	.05	.02	.09	−.03	.12	.03	−.14	−.21	−.15	−.06	−.18	−.32
156.	nagging	.08	−.08	.08	−.04	.01	−.12	−.01	.04	−.09	−.07	−.07	−.02
157.	natural	−.03	.10	.06	.04	−.12	−.04	−.10	−.09	−.07	−.10	−.02	−.06
158.	nervous	.13	.06	.08	−.02	.17	.16	−.05	−.05	.00	.01	−.09	−.16
159.	noisy	−.06	−.31	−.07	−.08	−.21	−.17	−.08	−.06	.03	−.15	−.02	−.07
160.	obliging	.05	.18	.07	.02	.18	.20	.03	.09	.01	−.03	−.02	−.02
161.	obnoxious	.00	−.22	−.15	−.16	−.21	−.08	−.10	−.06	−.08	−.08	−.09	−.13
162.	opinionated	−.16	−.26	−.08	−.23	−.20	−.24	.07	−.03	−.10	−.08	−.08	−.04
163.	opportunistic	−.25	−.18	−.04	−.13	−.32	−.31	.02	.01	−.07	−.11	−.06	−.09
164.	optimistic	−.17	−.11	−.23	−.09	−.22	−.23	.03	.16	.06	.02	−.01	.07
165.	organized	−.03	−.01	.10	.11	−.11	−.11	.35	.33	.23	.25	.12	.30
166.	original	−.12	−.16	−.09	−.12	−.17	−.06	−.04	−.14	−.05	−.12	−.21	−.25
167.	outgoing	−.36	−.38	−.31	−.33	−.37	−.35	−.02	.00	−.05	.00	.00	.00
168.	outspoken	−.13	−.41	−.18	−.26	−.31	−.25	−.03	−.08	−.08	−.04	−.09	−.03
169.	painstaking	.20	.10	.03	.03	.29	.23	.12	.12	.06	−.01	.08	.14
170.	patient	.08	.25	.09	.19	.32	.18	.16	.19	.03	.11	−.03	.12
171.	peaceable	.15	.27	.04	.14	.32	.27	.07	.18	−.05	.02	−.04	.11
172.	peculiar	.06	.07	.13	−.07	.20	.09	.01	−.19	−.03	−.09	−.11	−.11
173.	persevering	−.04	−.03	.07	.03	.01	−.02	.03	.18	.03	.10	.07	.20
174.	persistent	−.06	−.26	.00	−.17	−.13	−.21	.05	.11	.02	.08	−.03	.01
175.	pessimistic	.16	.07	.02	−.06	.09	.09	−.09	−.20	−.08	−.13	−.16	−.17
176.	planful	−.03	.01	.09	.03	−.07	−.08	.29	.26	.06	.04	.01	.20

Correlations of Observers' Adjectival Description with Scales of the CPI continued

| | Scale: v.1 | | | | | | Scale: v.2 | | | | | |
| | By Peers | | By Spouses | | By Staff | | By Peers | | By Spouses | | By Staff | |
Adjectives	M	F	M	F	M	F	M	F	M	F	M	F
177. pleasant	−.04	.08	.03	.03	.00	.06	.04	.01	.12	−.02	−.09	.06
178. pleasure-seeking	−.14	−.25	−.15	−.24	−.28	−.22	−.19	−.23	−.20	−.15	−.15	−.21
179. poised	−.13	−.06	−.13	−.14	−.18	−.20	.03	.14	.10	.03	.02	.19
180. polished	−.16	−.10	−.14	−.14	−.16	−.16	.03	.19	.14	.07	.06	.11
181. practical	.03	.15	.01	.12	−.02	−.17	.16	.21	.19	.12	.03	.14
182. praising	−.06	.05	.00	−.04	.02	−.05	.09	.14	−.02	.08	−.02	.08
183. precise	.04	.04	−.02	.00	.08	.03	.26	.12	.16	.07	−.06	.13
184. prejudiced	−.03	−.05	.05	−.02	−.04	.02	−.01	.05	−.06	−.04	−.03	.00
185. preoccupied	−.02	.05	−.05	−.07	.25	.14	−.09	−.12	−.09	−.15	−.13	−.21
186. progressive	−.14	−.23	−.07	−.04	−.24	−.19	.03	−.13	.02	−.11	−.17	−.18
187. prudish	.01	.11	−.03	.06	.17	.23	.09	.21	−.12	.09	.02	.24
188. quarrelsome	−.16	−.12	.10	−.03	−.18	−.14	−.03	−.09	−.12	−.08	−.08	−.17
189. queer	.07	.05	.05	.00	.18	.03	−.01	−.05	−.11	.00	−.06	−.06
190. quick	−.05	−.32	.00	−.15	−.34	−.27	−.10	.03	−.14	−.07	−.14	−.07
191. quiet	.24	.47	.29	.34	.44	.37	.03	.05	.04	.12	−.07	.04
192. quitting	.17	.15	.06	.11	.11	.10	−.11	−.12	−.24	.03	−.10	−.18
193. rational	−.13	−.05	−.13	.08	−.01	−.13	.06	.15	.07	−.01	−.15	.05
194. rattle-brained	−.04	−.05	.04	.02	−.04	.00	.00	−.12	−.04	−.01	−.02	−.17
195. realistic	−.02	−.07	−.04	.13	−.10	−.18	.06	.09	.09	.04	−.09	.05
196. reasonable	−.04	.06	−.04	.02	.09	.05	.19	.15	.12	.01	−.07	.09
197. rebellious	−.06	−.17	.02	−.15	−.09	−.15	−.15	−.24	−.27	−.16	−.26	−.32
198. reckless	−.03	−.14	.04	−.13	−.17	−.10	−.18	−.27	−.27	−.14	−.11	−.31
199. reflective	.08	.08	.06	−.07	.11	.08	−.07	.05	−.15	−.04	−.17	−.13
200. relaxed	−.01	.02	−.01	.17	−.05	−.17	−.11	.07	−.08	.01	−.11	.00
201. reliable	.01	.09	.00	.13	.11	.10	.18	.24	.13	.04	.02	.19
202. resentful	−.07	−.05	.13	−.10	−.02	−.11	.01	−.15	−.11	−.04	−.09	−.13
203. reserved	.21	.48	.20	.24	.42	.31	.06	.07	.07	.11	−.07	.02
204. resourceful	−.14	−.15	−.20	−.21	−.31	−.27	.16	.15	.01	−.01	−.05	−.05
205. responsible	−.01	.05	−.07	.01	.07	.06	.21	.24	.07	−.07	.02	.22
206. restless	−.07	−.17	−.15	−.19	−.15	−.15	−.13	−.18	−.23	−.13	−.21	−.30
207. retiring	.16	.44	.10	.15	.35	.35	−.06	−.02	−.08	.06	−.04	.05
208. rigid	.07	.04	.04	.10	.11	.11	−.04	.08	−.12	−.09	.05	.16
209. robust	−.07	−.27	−.18	−.06	−.15	−.22	.00	−.03	.00	.01	−.11	−.06
210. rude	.05	−.19	−.01	−.05	−.16	−.12	−.12	−.12	−.14	−.02	−.15	−.09
211. sarcastic	−.01	−.23	−.03	−.15	−.19	−.24	−.22	−.19	−.06	−.07	−.19	−.18
212. self-centered	−.07	−.22	−.02	−.10	−.24	−.19	−.12	.00	−.11	−.08	−.10	−.16
213. self-confident	−.22	−.33	−.21	−.22	−.37	−.40	.03	.04	.04	.06	−.07	.06
214. self-controlled	−.02	.13	.00	.02	.20	.15	.05	.20	.10	.05	−.01	.18
215. self-denying	.12	.10	.03	.08	.29	.25	.07	.08	−.07	.11	.00	.06
216. self-pitying	.10	−.01	−.02	.03	.09	−.01	−.05	−.08	−.11	−.03	−.08	−.08
217. self-punishing	−.07	.10	−.08	−.08	.14	.04	−.01	.03	−.14	−.06	−.07	−.16
218. self-seeking	−.10	−.19	−.11	−.10	−.29	−.25	−.11	−.03	−.13	−.04	−.04	−.13
219. selfish	−.11	−.17	.04	−.05	−.18	−.12	−.19	−.10	−.01	.02	−.04	−.15
220. sensitive	.00	.17	.06	−.03	.15	.12	.07	−.09	−.06	−.05	−.26	−.21

		Scale: v.1						Scale: v.2					
		By Peers		By Spouses		By Staff		By Peers		By Spouses		By Staff	
Adjectives		M	F	M	F	M	F	M	F	M	F	M	F
221.	sentimental	−.02	.01	.07	.09	.03	.06	.03	.00	−.05	.05	−.09	−.10
222.	serious	.04	.19	.00	.05	.23	.10	.20	.11	.09	.09	−.07	.04
223.	severe	−.01	−.03	−.09	.00	.04	.00	−.09	−.11	−.09	.05	−.09	.05
224.	sexy	−.07	−.18	−.09	−.08	−.18	−.23	−.09	−.06	−.13	−.15	−.16	−.14
225.	shallow	.10	−.06	.04	.07	.03	.04	−.11	−.03	.00	.02	.03	−.04
226.	sharp-witted	−.17	−.18	−.23	−.24	−.30	−.19	−.10	−.12	−.02	−.09	−.13	−.19
227.	shiftless	.03	−.04	.02	−.02	.10	−.02	−.09	−.15	−.16	−.15	−.12	−.17
228.	show-off	−.11	−.35	−.22	−.13	−.33	−.22	−.13	−.07	−.19	−.04	−.12	−.03
229.	shrewd	−.12	−.09	−.04	−.22	−.32	−.23	.05	−.07	−.12	−.08	−.02	−.06
230.	shy	.33	.43	.29	.31	.39	.33	.07	.03	−.09	.07	−.15	−.05
231.	silent	.30	.34	.30	.17	.33	.26	.01	.07	−.02	.12	−.15	.00
232.	simple	.14	.24	.16	.17	.25	.21	−.01	.09	.04	−.01	.02	.00
233.	sincere	−.02	.18	.09	.13	.18	.13	.17	.17	.04	.07	−.04	.08
234.	slipshod	−.07	−.02	.01	−.03	−.02	−.03	−.12	−.26	−.12	−.05	−.05	−.16
235.	slow	.09	.25	.10	.04	.32	.27	−.05	−.11	−.13	−.13	.03	−.02
236.	sly	−.03	−.08	.08	−.20	−.10	−.12	−.08	−.08	−.17	−.13	−.08	−.14
237.	smug	−.12	−.21	−.02	.00	−.18	−.14	−.11	.02	−.02	−.02	−.03	−.01
238.	snobbish	−.10	−.13	.01	−.17	−.13	−.15	−.09	.09	−.11	.04	.01	−.00
239.	sociable	−.26	−.23	−.17	−.25	−.32	−.26	.03	.07	−.07	−.04	−.04	.03
240.	soft-hearted	.10	.11	.04	.12	.11	.08	.04	.04	−.13	−.04	−.08	.00
241.	sophisticated	−.05	−.05	−.14	−.14	−.22	−.23	−.02	.01	.16	.00	−.11	−.03
242.	spendthrift	−.11	.01	.00	.03	−.08	−.11	−.15	−.09	.01	−.12	−.08	−.08
243.	spineless	.13	.18	−.14	.09	.16	.14	−.11	−.05	−.03	−.11	−.04	−.05
244.	spontaneous	−.15	−.34	−.14	−.20	−.30	−.22	−.06	−.12	−.08	−.21	−.12	−.14
245.	spunky	.02	−.20	−.07	−.22	−.24	−.23	−.11	−.04	−.04	−.14	−.04	−.13
246.	stable	−.05	.02	.11	.09	.04	−.04	.21	.15	.08	.04	.00	.22
247.	steady	−.02	.11	.11	.05	.12	.02	.17	.17	.04	.11	.05	.22
248.	stern	−.12	.01	.07	.09	.06	−.08	.10	.01	.08	−.06	−.01	.09
249.	stingy	−.01	−.03	−.02	−.12	.13	−.03	−.01	−.06	−.06	−.03	−.02	−.04
250.	stolid	−.11	.03	.03	−.01	.19	.13	.05	−.03	−.07	.10	−.01	.12
251.	strong	−.09	−.18	−.07	−.07	−.14	−.36	.06	.09	.03	.02	−.12	−.01
252.	stubborn	−.08	−.22	.01	−.12	−.10	−.15	.03	.03	−.06	−.06	−.08	−.08
253.	submissive	.21	.41	.06	.11	.28	.32	−.10	.08	−.07	.10	.05	.01
254.	suggestible	.01	.02	.02	−.07	.11	.17	−.09	−.09	−.16	.02	.03	−.02
255.	sulky	.10	.07	−.02	.01	.07	−.09	−.05	−.13	−.21	−.02	−.07	−.15
256.	superstitious	.07	.07	.04	−.12	.04	−.06	.09	−.04	−.16	−.08	−.05	−.05
257.	suspicious	.03	.05	.09	−.08	.04	−.09	−.09	−.08	−.11	−.12	−.15	−.09
258.	sympathetic	−.05	.08	.01	.10	.05	.07	.05	.01	−.05	−.03	−.13	.00
259.	tactful	−.10	.08	−.09	−.05	.02	.00	.02	.17	.17	.04	.02	.09
260.	tactless	.03	−.06	.07	.00	−.12	−.11	−.03	−.08	−.01	−.03	−.14	−.11
261.	talkative	−.24	−.37	−.29	−.27	−.38	−.33	.01	−.07	−.05	−.07	−.07	−.06
262.	temperamental	−.09	−.04	−.04	−.20	−.08	−.19	−.10	−.21	−.12	−.01	−.20	−.24
263.	tense	.11	.13	.03	−.05	.10	.12	−.07	−.08	−.08	.03	−.06	−.21
264.	thankless	−.01	.03	−.05	−.01	−.03	−.04	−.11	−.11	−.05	.02	−.11	−.03

Correlations of Observers' Adjectival Description with Scales of the CPI continued

		Scale: v.1						Scale: v.2				
		By Peers		By Spouses		By Staff		By Peers		By Spouses		By Staff
Adjectives		M	F	M	F	M	F	M	F	M	F	M	F
265.	thorough	.00	−.07	.04	.00	.08	.01	.23	.19	.03	.18	.06	.22
266.	thoughtful	.03	.05	.04	.10	.07	.04	.14	.16	.06	.10	−.14	.04
267.	thrifty	.02	.02	.03	.13	.18	.05	.16	.09	.10	.20	−.04	.11
268.	timid	.24	.42	.14	.10	.29	.28	−.06	.00	−.05	.06	−.05	−.01
269.	tolerant	−.07	.07	−.10	.08	.06	.04	.03	.06	−.04	.06	−.15	−.07
270.	touchy	−.02	−.11	.14	−.12	.02	−.02	−.07	−.16	−.05	−.05	−.17	−.10
271.	tough	−.07	−.22	.03	−.10	−.15	−.33	.10	−.10	.00	−.03	−.13	−.10
272.	trusting	−.06	.20	−.12	.05	.14	.09	.14	.18	.02	.10	−.12	−.01
273.	unaffected	.11	.10	.01	−.12	.18	.25	−.13	.00	−.10	−.10	−.02	−.11
274.	unambitious	.11	.13	.13	.08	.24	.20	−.18	−.20	−.24	−.11	−.17	−.10
275.	unassuming	.19	.27	.00	.06	.34	.32	−.03	.06	−.03	.12	−.03	−.03
276.	unconventional	−.07	−.12	.01	−.11	−.07	−.07	−.11	−.25	−.21	−.25	−.27	−.31
277.	undependable	−.02	−.11	−.05	−.05	−.07	−.01	−.13	−.24	−.05	−.06	−.05	−.23
278.	understanding	−.05	.04	.00	−.02	.01	−.07	.08	.12	−.03	.07	−.18	−.07
279.	unemotional	.11	.16	.08	.01	.16	.08	.00	−.06	.03	.00	−.12	.08
280.	unexcitable	.23	.21	.17	.11	.19	.13	−.03	−.01	−.03	−.04	−.04	.12
281.	unfriendly	.05	.00	.10	−.11	.08	−.01	−.12	−.04	−.07	.05	−.09	.02
282.	uninhibited	−.15	−.18	.01	−.15	−.33	−.25	−.10	−.12	−.14	−.12	−.11	−.19
283.	unintelligent	.10	−.06	.00	.00	.11	.12	.07	−.16	.00	.00	.03	−.08
284.	unkind	.16	.01	.04	.01	−.05	−.12	.01	−.09	.00	−.04	−.12	−.09
285.	unrealistic	−.07	−.06	−.10	−.10	.07	.00	−.15	−.03	−.13	−.04	−.09	−.16
286.	unscrupulous	−.01	.00	.18	−.08	−.03	−.07	−.15	−.14	−.16	−.02	−.10	−.16
287.	unselfish	.01	.16	.10	.03	.01	.13	.11	.07	.02	.06	−.06	.02
288.	unstable	−.01	.03	.14	−.09	.07	.09	−.15	−.10	−.14	−.06	−.12	−.32
289.	vindictive	−.04	−.17	−.02	−.04	−.08	−.14	−.11	−.03	−.06	−.13	−.08	−.05
290.	versatile	−.16	−.34	−.14	−.09	−.31	−.28	−.07	−.04	−.04	−.04	−.14	−.15
291.	warm	−.01	.05	.04	.09	−.11	−.08	.08	.13	.00	−.01	−.07	.03
292.	wary	−.16	.14	.00	−.05	.08	.03	−.15	−.08	−.13	−.01	−.14	−.08
293.	weak	.11	.32	.01	.04	.17	.19	−.01	.02	−.16	.07	.01	−.06
294.	whiny	.09	.05	−.05	−.11	−.05	−.01	−.11	.00	−.10	−.09	.02	−.06
295.	wholesome	.08	.00	−.04	−.03	.03	−.07	.13	.10	.13	.02	−.02	.12
296.	wise	−.16	−.05	−.04	.00	−.02	−.11	.13	.13	.11	.08	−.10	−.01
297.	withdrawn	.27	.47	.16	.13	.33	.23	.00	−.04	−.17	−.01	−.14	−.09
298.	witty	−.18	−.30	−.09	−.15	−.25	−.25	−.16	−.16	−.10	.05	−.15	−.10
299.	worrying	.10	.12	.10	−.04	.20	.11	.01	.01	−.07	−.02	−.11	−.10
300.	zany	−.08	−.22	−.06	−.22	−.13	−.11	−.01	−.16	−.15	−.14	−.09	−.15

Correlations of Observers' Adjectival Description with Scales of the CPI continued

		Scale: v.3						Scale: Mp					
		By Peers		By Spouses		By Staff		By Peers		By Spouses		By Staff	
Adjectives		M	F	M	F	M	F	M	F	M	F	M	F
001.	absent-minded	−.04	−.12	.00	−.04	.00	−.08	−.01	−.21	−.06	−.05	−.11	−.14
002.	active	.05	.10	−.06	.01	.06	.02	.15	.21	−.05	.08	.09	.10
003.	adaptable	.16	.21	.08	.03	.13	.03	.16	.24	.08	.04	.10	.06
004.	adventurous	.10	−.01	−.07	.04	−.01	−.04	.05	−.05	−.07	.03	−.04	−.06
005.	affected	−.13	.02	.01	−.06	.04	−.03	−.03	.13	.00	−.04	.06	−.01
006.	affectionate	.03	.09	−.06	−.04	−.03	−.12	.02	−.01	−.05	.01	−.09	−.12
007.	aggressive	−.09	−.01	−.13	−.02	−.03	.04	.02	.12	−.06	.01	.10	.11
008.	alert	.15	.09	.13	.07	.16	.08	.13	.15	.13	.13	.12	.12
009.	aloof	.03	−.11	−.03	.01	−.11	.02	.03	−.12	−.08	−.08	−.18	−.03
010.	ambitious	.09	.08	.03	.03	.13	.14	.19	.28	.14	.09	.23	.20
011.	anxious	−.13	−.14	−.04	−.10	.02	−.18	−.08	−.09	−.05	−.11	−.14	−.27
012.	apathetic	−.06	−.16	−.19	−.06	−.17	−.08	−.21	−.21	−.15	−.05	−.20	−.15
013.	appreciative	.04	.15	.10	.03	.12	−.01	.08	.15	.07	.03	.00	−.03
014.	argumentative	−.14	−.06	−.07	−.06	.06	.08	−.09	.02	−.03	−.03	.12	.08
015.	arrogant	−.11	−.22	−.09	.01	−.05	−.07	−.08	−.07	−.07	.00	.01	.03
016.	artistic	−.13	.01	.04	−.05	.08	.08	−.18	−.06	−.02	−.02	−.01	.00
017.	assertive	−.07	−.03	.04	.22	.04	.07	−.01	.12	.16	.24	.13	.15
018.	attractive	.08	.00	.01	−.09	.01	.00	.10	.02	−.04	−.10	−.04	−.03
019.	autocratic	−.04	−.15	−.04	.06	−.10	−.03	−.04	−.03	.00	.03	−.01	.07
020.	awkward	−.18	−.13	−.18	.03	−.12	−.05	−.23	−.14	−.20	−.12	−.27	−.15
021.	bitter	−.03	−.26	−.19	−.11	−.20	−.18	−.07	−.24	−.21	−.17	−.15	−.20
022.	blustery	−.13	−.12	−.05	−.04	−.09	−.06	−.11	−.12	−.05	−.10	−.01	−.04
023.	boastful	−.13	−.10	−.17	−.10	−.08	.01	−.07	.07	−.11	−.06	−.01	.02
024.	bossy	−.14	−.04	−.22	−.13	−.08	.00	−.06	.11	−.21	−.08	.03	.08
025.	calm	.14	.25	.09	.08	−.07	.08	.08	.17	.02	.02	−.16	.03
026.	capable	.19	.16	.06	.16	.08	.14	.22	.19	.10	.20	.02	.16
027.	careless	−.11	−.03	−.14	−.10	.00	−.05	−.10	−.16	−.18	−.14	−.08	−.13
028.	cautious	−.08	−.04	−.05	−.07	−.08	−.09	−.10	−.02	−.12	−.08	−.21	−.14
029.	changeable	.02	−.07	−.03	−.05	−.03	−.13	.00	−.12	−.14	−.05	−.10	−.20
030.	charming	.02	.09	−.09	−.03	.06	.02	−.03	.10	−.12	.01	.01	.03
031.	cheerful	.03	.14	.10	−.02	.10	.00	.04	.17	.07	.03	.05	.06
032.	civilized	.13	.11	.01	−.05	.04	.06	.13	.07	.01	−.02	−.03	.08
033.	clear-thinking	.16	.18	.15	.19	.13	.18	.18	.22	.13	.19	.05	.18
034.	clever	.13	.05	.01	.12	.08	.10	.06	.05	−.04	.16	.05	.09
035.	coarse	−.03	−.18	−.14	.09	−.17	−.06	−.06	−.13	−.15	.03	−.09	−.04
036.	cold	−.20	−.17	−.08	−.06	−.11	−.11	−.22	−.09	−.12	−.05	−.09	−.12
037.	commonplace	−.02	−.06	.03	−.09	−.21	−.16	−.09	.01	.04	−.18	−.19	−.12
038.	complaining	−.17	−.19	−.23	−.14	−.02	−.12	−.14	−.14	−.21	−.13	−.07	−.10
039.	complicated	.02	−.11	.20	.07	.03	.02	−.14	−.10	.14	.01	−.10	−.09
040.	conceited	−.17	−.10	−.18	−.03	.03	.04	−.10	.09	−.12	.02	.10	.07
041.	confident	.10	.07	−.01	.11	.08	.10	.13	.27	.08	.19	.10	.17
042.	confused	−.15	−.15	−.20	−.15	−.08	−.16	−.21	−.22	−.16	−.19	−.17	−.24
043.	conscientious	.07	.09	.10	.20	.06	.03	.08	.18	.19	.21	−.01	.05
044.	conservative	.09	.10	−.01	−.13	−.16	−.14	.08	.09	.07	−.11	−.10	−.03

		Scale: v.3						Scale: Mp				
		By Peers		By Spouses		By Staff		By Peers		By Spouses		By Staff
Adjectives		M	F	M	F	M	F	M	F	M	F	M	F
045.	considerate	.14	.10	.02	.01	.06	−.04	.12	.08	.03	−.06	−.12	−.06
046.	contented	.15	.19	.12	.03	−.05	−.08	.09	.17	.10	−.03	−.13	−.03
047.	conventional	.08	.09	.02	.00	−.12	−.19	.07	.10	.13	−.01	−.11	−.08
048.	cool	−.01	−.12	.03	.01	−.02	.01	−.05	−.08	−.04	−.06	−.05	−.03
049.	cooperative	.06	.17	.09	.16	.11	−.01	.03	.20	.10	.10	−.04	.01
050.	courageous	.01	.05	.02	−.01	−.01	−.04	.04	.01	.02	.01	−.01	−.07
051.	cowardly	−.10	−.03	−.01	−.05	−.06	−.04	−.12	−.04	−.07	−.04	−.12	−.01
052.	cruel	−.15	−.16	−.17	−.03	−.11	−.08	−.15	−.08	−.14	−.01	−.10	−.07
053.	curious	.03	−.11	.03	.13	.19	.03	−.02	−.14	−.01	.06	.01	−.01
054.	cynical	.01	−.20	−.02	−.01	−.11	−.01	−.08	−.17	−.06	.00	−.13	−.05
055.	daring	−.09	.05	−.09	−.09	−.05	−.02	−.06	−.02	−.12	−.09	.00	−.09
056.	deceitful	−.10	−.02	−.10	−.10	.02	−.08	−.04	−.03	−.16	−.07	.07	−.05
057.	defensive	−.14	−.24	−.07	−.04	−.09	−.08	−.18	−.24	−.08	−.10	−.10	−.14
058.	deliberate	.02	−.12	.03	−.12	−.13	.01	.07	.00	.05	−.09	−.18	.01
059.	demanding	−.02	−.15	−.09	−.16	−.03	−.04	.04	.02	.00	−.11	.05	−.01
060.	dependable	.13	.10	.07	.02	.06	.06	.17	.19	.09	.02	.00	.10
061.	dependent	.04	−.06	−.04	−.14	−.05	−.20	−.04	−.08	−.03	−.13	−.14	−.21
062.	despondent	.02	−.14	−.02	.08	−.10	−.12	−.12	−.21	−.01	.10	−.14	−.18
063.	determined	.00	.01	−.05	.07	.03	.03	.07	.22	.01	.14	.04	.08
064.	dignified	.02	.02	−.05	.03	−.01	−.05	.11	.08	−.01	.06	.00	−.02
065.	discreet	.10	.16	.06	.10	.03	.04	.03	.13	.09	.09	−.03	.03
066.	disorderly	.00	−.05	−.03	.00	.05	−.13	−.05	−.21	−.05	−.01	−.05	−.18
067.	dissatisfied	−.16	−.13	−.15	−.12	−.06	−.07	−.20	−.14	−.15	−.12	−.10	−.19
068.	distractible	−.10	.00	−.22	−.16	.00	−.18	−.14	−.06	−.23	−.17	−.14	−.22
069.	distrustful	−.09	−.16	−.10	−.19	−.05	−.11	−.15	−.18	−.10	−.22	−.08	−.17
070.	dominant	−.01	−.03	−.05	−.12	−.03	.10	.07	.12	.03	−.04	.08	.17
071.	dreamy	.03	−.03	−.08	−.03	.01	−.04	−.07	−.11	−.08	−.09	−.17	−.16
072.	dull	.01	−.11	−.06	−.09	−.16	−.11	−.05	−.07	−.10	−.08	−.17	−.10
073.	easygoing	.11	.05	−.01	.05	−.06	−.08	.04	.00	−.15	.00	−.22	−.09
074.	effeminate	−.09	.03	.09	.00	.07	−.08	−.03	.03	.07	−.01	.03	−.02
075.	efficient	−.02	.13	.08	.07	.16	.10	.04	.25	.03	.08	.23	.16
076.	egotistical	−.13	−.15	−.12	.01	.02	.03	−.02	.02	−.06	.04	.05	.03
077.	emotional	−.14	−.05	−.13	−.11	.04	−.16	−.14	−.06	−.13	−.17	−.05	−.21
078.	energetic	.02	.06	−.02	.00	.11	.05	.03	.17	.09	.08	.17	.10
079.	enterprising	.05	.13	−.01	.12	.11	.10	.09	.24	.05	.20	.14	.16
080.	enthusiastic	−.02	.06	.03	.09	.12	−.04	.05	.13	.11	.10	.06	.04
081.	evasive	.06	−.05	−.07	−.19	−.16	−.10	.08	−.10	−.03	−.19	−.19	−.10
082.	excitable	−.09	−.09	−.13	−.15	.04	−.10	−.05	.01	−.12	−.16	.00	−.08
083.	fair-minded	.11	.14	.14	.08	.10	.08	.14	.12	.14	.12	−.05	.03
084.	fault-finding	−.17	−.17	−.01	−.14	−.04	−.07	−.13	−.07	.00	−.17	−.03	−.03
085.	fearful	−.12	−.15	−.15	−.03	−.04	−.15	−.14	−.13	−.15	−.08	−.18	−.23
086.	feminine	.06	.05	.00	−.03	.06	−.06	.05	.01	.01	−.11	−.06	−.09
087.	fickle	.02	−.06	−.01	−.05	.00	−.09	−.09	−.05	−.10	−.13	−.05	−.09
088.	flirtatious	−.06	.01	−.31	−.13	.01	−.09	−.03	.03	−.22	−.17	−.03	−.11

Correlations of Observers' Adjectival Description with Scales of the CPI continued

| | Scale: v.3 | | | | | | Scale: Mp | | | | | |
| | By Peers | | By Spouses | | By Staff | | By Peers | | By Spouses | | By Staff | |
Adjectives	M	F	M	F	M	F	M	F	M	F	M	F
089. foolish	−.04	−.15	.04	−.12	−.10	−.17	−.05	−.16	−.01	−.17	−.10	−.18
090. forceful	−.09	−.11	−.12	−.04	−.06	.14	.02	.06	−.03	.05	.08	.18
091. foresighted	.14	.10	.13	.07	.13	.11	.12	.23	.19	.05	.11	.17
092. forgetful	−.09	−.03	−.03	.06	.01	−.09	−.06	−.20	−.06	−.02	−.10	−.10
093. forgiving	.17	.10	.07	−.10	.00	−.18	.20	.09	.01	−.12	−.15	−.17
094. formal	.00	.01	.05	.04	−.01	−.08	.11	.07	.04	.05	.00	.00
095. frank	.08	−.07	−.02	.14	.02	.00	−.03	−.02	.01	.05	−.07	.01
096. friendly	.17	.10	.10	.04	.03	.02	.12	.17	.12	.04	−.03	.04
097. frivolous	−.10	.00	.05	−.03	−.01	−.15	−.08	−.01	.02	−.05	−.04	−.14
098. fussy	−.13	−.09	−.11	−.14	−.11	−.09	−.14	.00	−.13	−.14	−.04	−.05
099. generous	.15	.02	.04	.06	.02	−.06	.06	−.01	.00	.03	−.06	−.04
100. gentle	.09	.09	.05	.01	.01	−.15	.11	−.02	.00	−.07	−.23	−.18
101. gloomy	−.04	−.15	−.18	.01	−.05	−.07	−.08	−.22	−.21	.01	−.13	−.09
102. good-looking	.03	−.01	−.01	−.02	.00	.00	.15	.07	−.06	−.09	−.05	−.04
103. good-natured	.16	.11	.10	.08	.01	−.03	.13	.10	.06	.06	−.12	−.05
104. greedy	−.11	−.15	−.12	−.04	−.01	−.09	−.09	−.07	−.08	−.05	−.02	−.05
105. handsome	.00	.00	.06	.07	−.04	.06	.06	.02	.03	.07	−.08	.07
106. hard-headed	−.07	−.21	−.09	−.16	−.05	.00	−.04	−.06	−.08	−.15	.06	.05
107. hard-hearted	−.13	−.15	−.08	−.09	−.14	−.03	−.18	.00	−.08	−.08	−.07	−.01
108. hasty	−.21	−.06	−.18	−.07	.08	−.14	−.17	−.10	−.18	−.10	.03	−.12
109. headstrong	−.16	−.09	−.11	−.10	−.02	.00	−.11	−.01	−.04	−.14	.01	−.03
110. healthy	.07	.00	−.01	.04	−.02	.05	.02	.05	−.01	.03	−.10	.02
111. helpful	.10	.10	.03	.02	.09	−.06	.09	.15	.02	.03	−.06	−.03
112. high-strung	−.11	−.09	−.07	−.11	.07	−.09	−.16	−.05	−.04	−.07	−.01	−.12
113. honest	.15	.03	.15	.11	.08	.02	.09	.03	.08	.05	−.06	−.01
114. hostile	−.08	−.16	−.11	.03	−.04	−.05	−.06	−.15	−.11	.00	−.02	−.09
115. humorous	.05	−.09	−.02	.21	−.08	.02	.00	−.04	−.08	.19	−.07	.04
116. hurried	−.16	−.12	−.08	.10	.08	−.06	−.12	−.08	.01	.07	.01	−.01
117. idealistic	−.05	.05	.12	.11	.16	.00	.01	.13	.11	.11	.00	−.09
118. imaginative	.03	.09	.08	.15	.15	.14	.02	.08	.01	.12	.08	.03
119. immature	−.07	−.16	−.14	−.07	.05	−.13	−.12	−.23	−.12	−.13	−.08	−.19
120. impatient	−.07	−.13	−.09	−.13	.05	−.02	−.06	−.14	−.02	−.09	.05	−.05
121. impulsive	−.10	−.13	−.15	−.11	.03	−.12	−.12	−.16	−.18	−.12	.00	−.15
122. independent	.27	.06	.08	.12	.03	.12	.18	.09	.12	.11	.01	.08
123. indifferent	.00	−.08	−.11	.01	−.14	−.10	−.10	−.12	−.09	.00	−.18	−.14
124. individualistic	.05	.05	.03	.20	.02	.07	.04	.00	.03	.18	−.07	.02
125. industrious	.06	.04	.02	.08	.06	.09	.10	.13	.14	.08	.09	.18
126. infantile	−.11	−.16	−.06	−.21	−.09	−.22	−.14	−.13	−.02	−.24	−.14	−.23
127. informal	.10	.10	.04	.09	−.01	−.02	−.02	−.05	.00	.04	−.14	−.08
128. ingenious	.00	.02	.15	.04	.16	.08	.04	.08	.10	.04	.14	.06
129. inhibited	.02	.02	.01	−.01	−.08	−.08	.02	−.01	−.07	−.10	−.20	−.15
130. initiative	−.01	.07	.18	.19	.09	.12	.00	.19	.19	.19	.18	.16
131. insightful	.12	.18	.19	.25	.16	.16	.10	.20	.15	.18	.09	.10
132. intelligent	.11	.17	.14	.12	.19	.23	.14	.21	.17	.10	.10	.21

		Scale: v.3						Scale: Mp					
		By Peers		By Spouses		By Staff		By Peers		By Spouses		By Staff	
Adjectives		M	F	M	F	M	F	M	F	M	F	M	F
133.	interests—narrow	−.08	−.14	−.13	−.31	−.19	−.29	−.15	−.11	−.06	−.32	−.19	−.25
134.	interests—wide	.06	.05	.13	.21	.16	.17	.08	.12	.10	.20	.08	.11
135.	intolerant	−.12	−.05	−.14	−.20	−.09	−.17	−.10	.04	−.14	−.17	−.07	−.11
136.	inventive	.01	.02	.09	.08	.11	.09	.00	.02	.06	.08	.05	.09
137.	irresponsible	−.04	−.02	−.03	−.07	.07	−.09	−.05	−.21	−.04	−.10	−.01	−.17
138.	irritable	−.18	−.17	−.05	−.11	−.04	−.03	−.15	−.19	−.07	−.08	−.05	−.02
139.	jolly	.03	.07	−.13	.01	−.08	−.06	.03	.15	−.17	−.01	−.04	−.02
140.	kind	.03	.05	.07	.04	−.04	−.09	.07	.00	.02	.08	−.22	−.07
141.	lazy	.06	−.12	.06	.05	−.07	−.10	−.03	−.20	.05	−.05	−.14	−.15
142.	leisurely	.05	.09	.01	−.01	−.07	−.06	.01	.05	.03	−.04	−.17	−.12
143.	logical	.16	.16	.00	.12	.14	.17	.18	.20	.02	.07	.03	.16
144.	loud	−.11	−.14	−.13	−.14	−.08	−.01	−.08	−.06	−.05	−.12	−.01	.04
145.	loyal	.05	.04	.00	−.11	−.06	−.15	.06	.06	−.04	−.20	−.13	−.14
146.	mannerly	.05	.14	.03	.11	−.01	−.05	.12	.16	.06	.12	−.13	−.04
147.	masculine	.05	−.05	−.09	−.06	−.13	.07	.11	.00	−.02	.02	−.09	.06
148.	mature	.17	.17	.14	.07	.02	.01	.22	.23	.12	.09	.02	.11
149.	meek	−.01	−.06	−.09	−.02	−.11	−.07	−.06	−.12	−.07	−.11	−.22	−.16
150.	methodical	−.06	.00	.01	.15	−.01	.06	−.01	.03	.06	.18	.02	.09
151.	mild	.03	.07	.03	−.02	−.03	−.08	.03	−.06	−.05	−.07	−.19	−.12
152.	mischievous	−.07	.06	−.18	−.11	−.03	−.03	−.16	−.02	−.17	−.18	−.02	−.07
153.	moderate	.18	.18	.13	.14	−.01	.02	.17	.11	.12	.15	−.09	.02
154.	modest	.13	.02	.01	−.06	.00	−.09	.12	−.02	.06	−.04	−.16	−.17
155.	moody	−.09	−.24	−.08	−.12	−.06	−.11	−.13	−.27	−.14	−.14	−.16	−.20
156.	nagging	−.16	−.13	−.26	−.07	−.07	−.23	−.17	−.04	−.18	−.13	−.08	−.10
157.	natural	.12	.05	.07	.10	.05	.05	.08	−.05	−.05	.08	.00	.03
158.	nervous	−.08	−.15	−.23	−.13	.01	−.15	−.11	−.17	−.16	−.16	−.10	−.20
159.	noisy	−.11	−.05	−.09	−.19	−.06	−.06	−.09	.04	−.04	−.17	.00	−.02
160.	obliging	.16	.10	.02	.00	.13	−.04	.10	.10	.00	−.01	−.02	−.09
161.	obnoxious	−.15	−.23	−.10	.06	−.04	−.12	−.15	−.13	−.04	.06	−.01	−.07
162.	opinionated	−.16	−.13	−.02	−.07	−.04	−.03	−.10	.01	.02	−.08	.02	.02
163.	opportunistic	−.03	−.07	.02	.00	−.03	.02	.06	.10	.07	−.06	.08	.02
164.	optimistic	.15	.04	.07	.16	.09	−.04	.12	.18	.09	.20	.05	.04
165.	organized	.00	.14	.05	.05	.14	.11	.11	.21	.06	.04	.21	.22
166.	original	.01	.06	.10	.09	.15	.09	−.01	.07	.05	.08	.08	.01
167.	outgoing	.05	.02	−.06	.19	.04	.04	.09	.15	−.01	.20	.10	.11
168.	outspoken	−.08	−.03	−.16	.12	.03	.04	−.02	.12	−.08	.12	.09	.05
169.	painstaking	.00	.02	.01	−.07	−.04	−.08	.00	.12	.08	−.04	−.07	−.07
170.	patient	.05	.17	.12	−.09	.03	−.04	.04	.15	.06	−.06	−.14	−.05
171.	peaceable	.10	.17	−.01	.02	.02	−.05	.02	.11	−.06	−.05	−.15	−.08
172.	peculiar	−.08	−.07	−.12	−.08	−.04	.02	−.16	−.15	−.13	−.10	−.16	−.04
173.	persevering	.09	−.02	−.01	.17	.08	.00	.08	.13	.01	.15	.09	.06
174.	persistent	.05	−.04	.03	.06	−.08	.06	.03	.13	.10	.14	−.01	.07
175.	pessimistic	−.13	−.20	−.02	−.05	−.03	−.11	−.16	−.27	−.01	−.14	−.14	−.12
176.	planful	.00	.08	−.01	−.02	.08	.09	.01	.21	.01	.01	.08	.11

Correlations of Observers' Adjectival Description with Scales of the CPI continued

		Scale: v.3						Scale: Mp				
		By Peers		By Spouses		By Staff		By Peers		By Spouses		By Staff	
Adjectives		M	F	M	F	M	F	M	F	M	F	M	F
177.	pleasant	.20	.13	.05	.12	.06	.08	.17	.14	.06	.10	−.06	.05
178.	pleasure-seeking	.03	.04	−.08	−.05	−.02	−.13	−.01	.00	−.08	−.08	−.02	−.15
179.	poised	.14	.11	.04	.05	.05	.13	.17	.16	.08	.09	.11	.18
180.	polished	.03	.08	.01	.07	.00	.07	.12	.17	.08	.17	.10	.12
181.	practical	.18	.06	.06	.08	−.09	−.09	.18	.08	.11	.03	−.04	.04
182.	praising	.09	.03	.00	−.09	.11	−.11	.07	.04	.02	−.01	.06	−.06
183.	precise	.08	−.02	.08	.13	.01	.12	.14	.05	.10	.14	−.01	.12
184.	prejudiced	−.12	−.19	−.34	−.26	−.15	−.20	−.08	−.05	−.24	−.21	−.11	−.14
185.	preoccupied	−.03	−.11	.02	−.02	−.06	−.10	−.12	−.13	.07	−.05	−.19	−.19
186.	progressive	.09	−.04	.02	.20	.04	.11	.11	.02	.01	.11	.02	.03
187.	prudish	−.15	−.05	−.09	−.19	−.06	−.10	−.11	.02	−.08	−.12	−.08	−.10
188.	quarrelsome	−.14	−.13	−.21	−.17	−.02	−.05	−.06	−.10	−.18	−.20	.00	−.08
189.	queer	−.14	−.18	.10	.00	−.01	.02	−.16	−.16	.07	.00	−.07	.01
190.	quick	.00	.05	−.03	.05	.10	.02	−.03	.12	−.02	.07	.08	.05
191.	quiet	.03	.09	.07	−.01	−.04	−.03	−.03	−.09	−.02	−.03	−.24	−.17
192.	quitting	−.09	−.15	−.08	.04	−.03	−.13	−.15	−.26	−.12	−.08	−.13	−.15
193.	rational	.18	.18	.07	.20	.09	.12	.18	.25	.10	.15	−.08	.08
194.	rattle-brained	−.05	−.09	−.19	−.14	−.08	−.21	.00	−.14	−.18	−.23	−.10	−.22
195.	realistic	.18	.14	.02	.07	.02	.05	.19	.19	.00	.07	−.04	.09
196.	reasonable	.23	.17	.11	.17	.07	.06	.25	.18	.10	.13	−.04	.07
197.	rebellious	−.16	−.14	−.12	−.05	−.01	.02	−.20	−.21	−.20	−.09	−.07	−.12
198.	reckless	−.13	−.06	−.13	−.16	−.04	−.12	−.16	−.09	−.18	−.18	−.08	−.17
199.	reflective	.04	.13	.09	.27	.14	.08	−.01	.13	.01	.19	−.05	−.03
200.	relaxed	.19	.17	.06	.04	−.02	.07	.08	.13	−.01	−.05	−.09	.07
201.	reliable	.08	.20	−.02	.10	.04	.05	.13	.27	.02	.08	.00	.06
202.	resentful	−.07	−.25	−.11	−.07	−.10	−.16	−.01	−.23	−.12	−.06	−.09	−.17
203.	reserved	.13	.08	.02	−.12	−.03	−.02	.08	−.04	.01	−.07	−.20	−.12
204.	resourceful	.11	.12	.07	.08	.13	.15	.17	.14	.09	.14	.17	.14
205.	responsible	.11	.19	.05	.08	.06	.04	.16	.27	.07	.09	.02	.07
206.	restless	−.19	−.17	−.12	−.04	−.02	−.08	−.16	−.19	−.09	−.06	−.03	−.14
207.	retiring	−.01	−.09	.04	−.07	−.11	−.06	−.10	−.18	.00	−.07	−.22	−.15
208.	rigid	−.13	−.08	−.03	−.08	−.17	−.13	−.13	.02	.03	−.08	−.11	−.11
209.	robust	.01	−.09	−.03	.07	−.13	−.01	.04	.05	.01	.04	−.07	.00
210.	rude	−.12	−.20	−.11	.00	−.09	−.07	−.20	−.14	−.05	.04	−.04	−.02
211.	sarcastic	.05	−.24	−.08	−.05	−.06	.02	.00	−.13	−.05	−.06	−.08	−.01
212.	self-centered	−.09	−.16	−.18	−.04	−.04	−.08	−.10	−.02	−.13	−.05	−.02	−.09
213.	self-confident	.07	.08	.04	.09	.09	.12	.12	.20	.08	.18	.11	.20
214.	self-controlled	.15	.17	.08	.08	.00	−.01	.17	.17	.05	.14	−.08	−.03
215.	self-denying	.00	.04	−.13	−.11	−.04	−.07	.00	.02	−.09	−.05	−.14	−.14
216.	self-pitying	−.10	−.18	−.13	−.11	−.03	−.17	−.09	−.15	−.14	−.13	−.09	−.13
217.	self-punishing	−.07	−.08	−.07	−.06	−.02	−.09	−.04	−.07	−.06	−.08	−.12	−.11
218.	self-seeking	−.05	−.15	−.04	−.01	−.01	−.04	−.04	−.05	−.03	.01	.07	−.06
219.	selfish	−.05	−.21	.03	.00	−.05	−.12	.02	−.07	.00	−.03	−.02	−.10
220.	sensitive	−.16	−.07	−.06	−.01	.09	−.08	−.13	−.11	−.16	−.01	−.18	−.22

Correlations of Observers' Adjectival Description with Scales of the CPI continued

		Scale: v.3							Scale: Mp			
		By Peers		By Spouses		By Staff		By Peers		By Spouses		By Staff	
Adjectives		M	F	M	F	M	F	M	F	M	F	M	F
221.	sentimental	.02	.02	−.08	−.06	−.04	−.18	.01	.03	−.11	−.07	−.10	−.20
222.	serious	.07	−.01	.01	.00	.00	.09	.10	.00	.01	.00	−.12	.02
223.	severe	−.10	.02	−.13	−.02	−.16	−.07	−.09	.05	−.04	−.08	−.08	−.09
224.	sexy	−.04	.04	−.11	−.01	−.08	−.05	−.05	.01	−.12	−.06	−.12	−.08
225.	shallow	−.17	.00	−.06	−.17	−.10	−.23	−.21	.09	.00	−.17	−.08	−.23
226.	sharp-witted	.16	−.08	−.01	.07	.05	.04	.09	−.11	.05	.08	.05	.05
227.	shiftless	−.05	−.08	−.11	−.05	−.05	−.02	−.08	−.15	−.17	−.16	−.15	−.08
228.	show-off	−.16	−.07	−.06	−.13	−.04	.03	−.14	.01	−.08	−.08	.01	.02
229.	shrewd	.15	−.08	−.12	−.02	.00	.02	.14	−.03	−.06	−.02	.17	.11
230.	shy	.00	−.02	.00	−.11	−.09	−.13	.02	−.15	−.14	−.23	−.30	−.26
231.	silent	−.06	.01	−.05	−.08	−.12	−.09	−.07	−.07	−.15	−.11	−.27	−.19
232.	simple	.01	−.03	−.04	−.20	−.20	−.20	−.06	−.06	−.06	−.29	−.22	−.21
233.	sincere	.02	.07	.10	.11	.08	.02	.12	.02	.10	.06	−.10	−.04
234.	slipshod	.03	−.11	−.15	.01	.05	−.02	.01	−.10	−.07	−.05	−.02	−.09
235.	slow	−.04	−.09	−.11	−.07	−.10	−.10	−.10	−.06	−.15	−.14	−.15	−.12
236.	sly	.08	−.10	−.23	−.13	−.04	−.10	−.01	−.07	−.21	−.07	−.04	−.06
237.	smug	.00	−.12	−.08	−.07	−.08	−.08	−.05	.03	−.07	−.05	.00	−.03
238.	snobbish	−.09	−.07	.01	−.06	−.02	−.06	−.05	.05	.01	−.01	.03	−.02
239.	sociable	.08	.05	−.02	.10	.06	−.04	.15	.11	.03	.09	.04	.03
240.	soft-hearted	.14	.08	−.13	−.13	.00	−.17	.10	.08	−.18	−.15	−.13	−.17
241.	sophisticated	.02	−.01	−.02	.09	.02	.14	.06	.03	.04	.13	.04	.13
242.	spendthrift	.02	−.04	−.04	−.09	−.03	−.11	.00	−.07	−.05	−.13	−.07	−.06
243.	spineless	−.04	−.16	.10	.00	−.12	−.03	−.11	−.19	.12	−.06	−.17	−.04
244.	spontaneous	.01	−.01	−.03	.16	.09	−.02	−.09	.03	−.06	.06	.05	−.01
245.	spunky	−.10	.04	−.25	.02	−.01	−.05	−.18	.06	−.17	.02	.02	−.05
246.	stable	.16	.17	.05	.06	.01	.07	.20	.21	.04	.02	−.04	.13
247.	steady	.13	.14	.00	−.04	−.11	−.02	.16	.16	−.01	.01	−.12	.04
248.	stern	−.07	−.06	−.22	−.04	−.17	−.07	−.04	.01	−.15	−.06	−.07	.01
249.	stingy	−.11	−.14	−.20	−.10	−.09	−.01	−.12	−.07	−.17	−.09	−.05	−.02
250.	stolid	−.09	−.17	.03	−.06	−.22	−.10	−.04	−.08	.01	−.03	−.22	−.07
251.	strong	−.01	.02	−.01	−.06	−.14	.06	.03	.08	−.02	.02	−.10	.09
252.	stubborn	−.15	−.18	−.13	−.04	−.08	.00	−.05	−.04	−.13	−.06	.00	−.01
253.	submissive	.06	.05	−.08	−.05	−.06	−.08	.00	−.03	−.14	−.11	−.13	−.12
254.	suggestible	.04	.03	−.09	−.01	−.02	−.16	.02	.00	−.13	.01	−.08	−.18
255.	sulky	−.09	−.19	−.04	−.04	−.08	−.19	−.13	−.22	−.07	−.08	−.13	−.20
256.	superstitious	−.04	−.02	−.24	−.14	−.06	−.32	.01	−.08	−.22	−.19	−.07	−.26
257.	suspicious	−.16	−.16	−.17	−.14	−.15	−.14	−.18	−.19	−.18	−.18	−.17	−.14
258.	sympathetic	.08	.01	.05	.06	.08	−.05	.07	.00	−.01	.00	−.08	−.11
259.	tactful	.16	.16	.08	.14	.14	.02	.13	.17	.10	.19	.07	.02
260.	tactless	−.07	−.12	−.13	−.02	−.05	−.07	−.11	−.09	−.09	−.06	−.07	−.07
261.	talkative	.04	−.05	−.04	−.02	.05	−.05	.05	.02	.06	−.01	.09	.05
262.	temperamental	−.23	−.19	−.14	−.13	−.05	−.07	−.21	−.17	−.14	−.08	−.11	−.05
263.	tense	−.06	−.15	−.11	−.08	−.05	−.11	−.05	−.17	−.10	−.09	−.09	−.19
264.	thankless	−.16	−.23	−.12	−.05	−.09	−.01	−.16	−.22	−.07	.01	−.09	.03

Correlations of Observers' Adjectival Description with Scales of the CPI continued												
		Scale: v.3						Scale: Mp				
		By Peers		By Spouses		By Staff		By Peers		By Spouses		By Staff	
Adjectives		M	F	M	F	M	F	M	F	M	F	M	F
265.	thorough	.07	.08	.01	.08	.18	.13	.10	.18	.04	.09	.16	.14
266.	thoughtful	.20	.11	.06	.09	.14	.08	.21	.08	−.01	.04	−.03	.04
267.	thrifty	.01	.05	−.02	−.03	−.15	−.11	.02	.07	−.03	.02	−.16	−.04
268.	timid	.00	−.07	−.01	−.07	−.08	−.14	−.11	−.16	−.05	−.10	−.23	−.22
269.	tolerant	.15	.19	.17	.07	.14	.06	.10	.14	.12	.07	−.07	−.02
270.	touchy	−.09	−.15	−.05	−.15	.01	−.16	−.04	−.08	−.10	−.17	−.08	−.17
271.	tough	−.11	−.13	−.16	.01	−.18	.03	−.03	.02	−.16	−.02	−.06	.07
272.	trusting	.13	.16	.07	.04	.11	−.06	.09	.10	.08	.05	−.10	−.10
273.	unaffected	.15	.09	.00	−.02	.09	.04	−.01	.02	−.01	.00	−.06	−.06
274.	unambitious	.04	−.02	−.14	.04	−.10	−.21	−.04	−.12	−.17	−.03	−.23	−.22
275.	unassuming	.11	.02	−.07	.06	.01	−.05	−.08	−.10	−.04	.04	−.17	−.11
276.	unconventional	.04	−.12	.03	.08	.07	.03	−.02	−.20	−.07	−.03	−.10	−.08
277.	undependable	−.05	−.09	.01	−.06	.03	−.01	−.09	−.17	.01	−.13	.01	−.12
278.	understanding	.13	.16	.10	.12	.07	.00	.14	.12	−.01	.08	−.10	−.02
279.	unemotional	−.01	−.13	.16	.01	−.17	−.06	−.05	−.10	.12	−.03	−.24	−.07
280.	unexcitable	−.02	.03	−.03	.03	−.08	−.02	−.09	−.07	−.09	−.05	−.13	−.02
281.	unfriendly	−.06	−.13	−.13	−.10	−.03	−.11	−.09	−.08	−.10	−.04	−.04	−.08
282.	uninhibited	.05	−.10	.01	.13	.06	−.02	.01	−.11	−.01	.08	.05	−.06
283.	unintelligent	.04	−.07	.00	−.07	−.11	−.04	.02	−.03	.00	−.06	−.10	−.05
284.	unkind	−.03	−.09	−.06	−.11	−.09	−.10	−.09	−.09	.00	−.02	−.08	−.04
285.	unrealistic	−.07	−.11	.05	−.17	−.05	−.17	−.10	−.09	.06	−.16	−.15	−.18
286.	unscrupulous	−.08	−.03	−.18	.03	.01	−.06	−.06	−.14	−.19	.08	−.01	−.03
287.	unselfish	.13	.13	−.10	−.07	.09	−.05	.12	.09	−.10	.01	−.05	−.11
288.	unstable	−.08	−.18	−.22	−.02	.04	−.08	−.13	−.26	−.20	−.09	−.04	−.15
289.	vindictive	−.04	−.08	−.04	−.12	−.15	−.08	−.03	.00	−.01	−.12	−.09	−.02
290.	versatile	.11	−.02	−.07	.07	.14	.08	.13	.09	−.09	.04	.11	.09
291.	warm	.03	.15	.00	−.01	.05	.00	.09	.08	−.06	−.04	−.01	.01
292.	wary	−.04	−.10	−.02	−.01	−.12	−.09	−.05	−.09	−.08	−.05	−.17	−.14
293.	weak	−.02	−.07	−.12	−.06	−.09	−.15	−.02	−.14	−.13	−.13	−.13	−.17
294.	whiny	−.10	−.14	−.06	−.13	−.03	−.10	−.14	−.10	−.10	−.14	.00	−.07
295.	wholesome	.05	.09	−.02	.03	.06	.03	.05	.13	−.02	.07	−.02	.06
296.	wise	.03	.13	.13	.03	.07	.01	.12	.16	.11	.02	.03	.08
297.	withdrawn	.04	−.04	−.14	−.05	−.12	−.07	−.04	−.22	−.20	−.05	−.28	−.18
298.	witty	.05	−.10	.04	−.01	.04	−.00	.00	−.03	−.04	−.02	.03	.06
299.	worrying	−.16	−.04	−.27	−.05	−.04	−.12	−.13	−.04	−.27	−.13	−.18	−.16
300.	zany	−.08	−.03	−.09	−.02	−.01	−.07	−.18	−.06	−.13	−.05	−.05	−.09

Correlations of Observers' Adjectival Description with Scales of the CPI continued

		Scale: Wo						Scale: CT					
		By Peers		By Spouses		By Staff		By Peers		By Spouses		By Staff	
Adjectives		M	F	M	F	M	F	M	F	M	F	M	F
001.	absent-minded	−.14	−.22	−.12	−.12	−.07	−.10	.08	.03	.03	.13	−.01	.06
002.	active	.09	.06	−.14	.01	−.11	−.05	−.10	.12	.15	.05	.21	.21
003.	adaptable	.07	.31	.07	.06	.02	−.03	.06	.10	.09	.10	.17	.11
004.	adventurous	.04	−.10	−.14	−.06	−.21	−.16	.14	.20	.18	.23	.22	.34
005.	affected	−.02	−.01	−.01	−.03	−.04	−.11	−.08	.07	.02	−.02	.09	.09
006.	affectionate	.00	.10	−.10	.01	−.11	−.07	.04	.00	.00	−.01	.03	−.05
007.	aggressive	.02	−.11	−.14	−.16	−.03	−.02	−.12	.24	.05	.18	.04	.31
008.	alert	.19	.10	.09	.09	−.03	−.01	.04	.15	.17	.07	.25	.16
009.	aloof	−.03	−.18	.04	−.15	−.05	.05	.07	.06	.01	.10	.02	−.03
010.	ambitious	.09	.14	.00	.08	.07	.03	−.03	.07	.04	.08	.15	.30
011.	anxious	−.20	−.18	−.13	−.17	−.05	−.17	−.02	−.10	−.04	−.01	.00	−.05
012.	apathetic	−.12	−.15	−.15	.00	−.06	−.01	.07	−.06	−.07	.00	−.18	−.15
013.	appreciative	−.03	.24	.09	.04	.01	.06	−.02	−.16	.02	−.04	.12	−.17
014.	argumentative	−.11	−.22	−.13	−.15	−.03	.00	−.04	.23	.05	.17	.17	.29
015.	arrogant	−.07	−.25	−.19	−.04	−.14	−.09	.02	.05	.11	.06	.12	.14
016.	artistic	−.11	−.05	−.02	−.08	−.08	−.03	.03	.09	.11	.08	.32	.22
017.	assertive	.03	−.11	.04	.12	−.05	−.04	−.13	.19	.10	.25	.15	.31
018.	attractive	.04	.05	.00	−.07	−.13	−.09	.06	.06	.05	−.05	.20	.09
019.	autocratic	−.07	−.13	−.10	−.03	−.05	−.02	−.03	.03	.04	−.02	−.02	.09
020.	awkward	−.21	−.16	−.26	−.05	−.12	−.04	−.05	−.11	−.04	.03	−.14	.00
021.	bitter	−.07	−.29	−.33	−.30	−.10	−.22	−.05	−.06	.00	.12	−.12	.03
022.	blustery	−.09	−.21	.02	−.12	−.08	−.10	−.02	.16	−.01	.05	−.03	.14
023.	boastful	−.04	−.15	−.17	−.19	−.13	−.03	−.06	.06	−.02	.03	.04	.14
024.	bossy	−.06	−.11	−.23	−.17	−.04	−.04	−.11	.15	−.07	.04	−.04	.14
025.	calm	.10	.36	.13	.11	.00	.10	.07	−.04	−.03	−.07	−.05	−.14
026.	capable	.12	.26	.11	.24	−.08	.10	.07	.04	−.01	.03	.17	.11
027.	careless	−.25	−.23	−.20	−.20	−.11	−.16	.16	.24	.03	−.02	.13	.18
028.	cautious	−.03	.19	−.04	.10	.04	.04	−.15	−.36	−.12	−.18	−.19	−.29
029.	changeable	−.07	−.23	−.19	−.13	−.15	−.25	.13	.20	.10	.17	.12	.20
030.	charming	−.02	.20	−.07	−.05	−.13	−.03	.07	.03	.00	.00	.30	.13
031.	cheerful	−.02	.25	.13	.08	−.04	.05	.07	.00	.04	−.02	.13	.00
032.	civilized	.03	.16	.09	.04	−.11	.10	.16	.03	−.10	−.09	.24	−.07
033.	clear-thinking	.17	.26	.19	.25	−.05	.09	.01	.06	.04	.01	.25	.15
034.	clever	.05	−.05	−.06	.11	−.16	−.03	.17	.21	.14	.15	.32	.31
035.	coarse	−.04	−.22	−.26	.06	−.11	−.14	.00	.04	.01	.17	−.07	.18
036.	cold	−.15	−.16	−.07	−.12	−.03	−.09	−.12	−.01	−.05	.03	−.12	−.03
037.	commonplace	−.07	.03	.05	−.01	.00	−.01	−.09	−.12	−.08	−.06	−.28	−.22
038.	complaining	−.06	−.26	−.28	−.34	−.06	−.16	.02	−.01	−.10	.12	.02	.01
039.	complicated	−.09	−.27	.08	−.10	−.19	−.16	.13	.14	.14	.18	.27	.27
040.	conceited	−.14	−.11	−.15	−.03	−.01	−.03	.01	.05	−.02	.01	.10	.16
041.	confident	.08	.14	.08	.15	−.06	.01	.06	.18	.01	.06	.22	.22
042.	confused	−.21	−.28	−.30	−.25	−.08	−.25	.03	.02	.02	.07	−.11	.02
043.	conscientious	.08	.28	.21	.23	.11	.12	−.07	−.16	−.10	.07	−.09	−.24
044.	conservative	.13	.26	.15	.04	.10	.09	−.04	−.27	−.25	−.31	−.40	−.47

Correlations of Observers' Adjectival Description with Scales of the CPI continued

	Scale: Wo						Scale: CT					
	By Peers		By Spouses		By Staff		By Peers		By Spouses		By Staff	
Adjectives	M	F	M	F	M	F	M	F	M	F	M	F
045. considerate	.10	.27	.08	.07	−.06	.00	.01	−.20	−.06	.00	.06	−.18
046. contented	.09	.28	.24	.14	.00	.08	.06	.03	−.05	−.13	−.12	−.25
047. conventional	.05	.24	.12	.11	.09	.07	−.06	−.21	−.18	−.20	−.37	−.45
048. cool	−.07	−.22	.03	.03	.04	.02	.13	.12	.06	.02	.00	.01
049. cooperative	.01	.29	.12	.20	.01	.03	.05	−.14	.04	−.13	.05	−.14
050. courageous	−.02	.00	.00	.04	−.07	−.11	.00	.06	.10	−.06	.07	.13
051. cowardly	−.17	−.04	−.10	.00	−.05	.03	−.06	−.10	.00	−.08	−.05	.01
052. cruel	−.13	−.11	−.19	−.01	−.11	−.15	−.07	−.10	−.01	.04	.03	.08
053. curious	−.04	−.08	−.05	.09	−.11	−.11	.20	.07	.11	.09	.39	.31
054. cynical	−.05	−.30	−.14	−.15	−.19	−.15	.14	.13	.05	.16	.11	.28
055. daring	.00	−.10	−.06	−.06	−.15	−.11	−.07	.24	.11	−.03	.14	.27
056. deceitful	−.11	−.14	−.18	−.14	.01	−.21	.01	.06	.04	.01	.04	.09
057. defensive	−.26	−.34	−.18	−.15	−.06	−.05	.04	−.07	.07	.10	−.09	−.05
058. deliberate	.16	−.05	−.03	−.05	−.01	.14	−.20	.01	−.01	−.09	−.17	−.25
059. demanding	.04	−.21	−.15	−.27	−.11	−.12	−.07	.13	.03	.10	.09	.15
060. dependable	.18	.27	.14	.06	.08	.14	−.12	−.13	.00	−.07	−.04	−.20
061. dependent	−.11	.02	−.07	−.14	.00	−.09	.05	−.09	.01	−.14	−.17	−.20
062. despondent	−.06	−.28	−.14	.10	−.12	−.14	.03	−.01	.09	.05	−.07	−.13
063. determined	.05	.05	−.03	.01	−.04	−.01	−.05	.01	−.08	.05	.13	.17
064. dignified	−.02	.17	.04	.09	.07	.08	.01	−.08	−.13	−.04	−.01	−.25
065. discreet	−.02	.25	.16	.09	.06	.11	.07	−.10	.03	.02	−.01	−.22
066. disorderly	−.13	−.31	−.19	−.05	−.10	−.25	.17	.18	.18	.11	.17	.19
067. dissatisfied	−.05	−.26	−.31	−.15	−.17	−.22	.03	.06	.08	−.01	.09	.10
068. distractible	−.22	−.17	−.29	−.11	−.17	−.23	.04	.00	−.01	−.02	.09	.09
069. distrustful	−.14	−.23	−.15	−.25	−.05	−.15	−.07	−.01	−.02	−.08	−.01	.03
070. dominant	.03	−.12	−.01	−.10	−.10	.04	−.15	.18	−.03	.01	.15	.25
071. dreamy	−.08	.01	−.12	−.11	−.13	−.07	.06	−.04	.04	.06	.07	.02
072. dull	−.02	.02	−.12	−.08	−.02	.02	−.07	−.21	−.02	−.06	−.21	−.25
073. easygoing	.05	.07	.01	.13	−.15	−.05	.17	.04	−.03	−.10	.03	−.02
074. effeminate	−.08	.06	.03	−.04	−.03	−.05	−.07	.06	.04	.03	.05	−.09
075. efficient	.14	.26	.13	.06	.15	.09	−.16	−.03	−.08	−.06	.12	.02
076. egotistical	−.02	−.17	−.14	−.01	−.10	−.05	−.05	.08	.03	.05	.16	.18
077. emotional	−.12	−.18	−.26	−.19	−.13	−.26	.00	.09	.04	.05	.18	.13
078. energetic	.05	.10	.00	.00	−.04	.00	−.02	.06	.10	.00	.20	.23
079. enterprising	.11	.17	−.06	.09	−.06	.05	−.05	.10	.11	.10	.20	.25
080. enthusiastic	.04	.08	−.02	.10	−.12	−.07	−.03	.05	.15	.10	.22	.15
081. evasive	−.03	−.12	−.07	−.16	−.10	−.04	.11	.04	−.03	−.05	−.08	−.02
082. excitable	−.11	−.18	−.20	−.20	−.12	−.12	−.07	.13	.00	.04	.15	.14
083. fair-minded	.10	.26	.19	.15	−.01	.07	−.03	−.08	.06	−.01	.11	−.03
084. fault-finding	−.04	−.25	−.10	−.16	−.11	−.08	−.02	.00	−.07	−.02	.07	.09
085. fearful	−.07	−.10	−.20	−.09	−.10	−.15	.06	−.14	−.05	.05	−.07	−.08
086. feminine	−.02	.15	.06	−.12	−.07	−.06	.01	−.03	.03	.00	.12	−.12
087. fickle	−.08	−.17	−.06	−.17	−.07	−.16	.11	.19	.00	.13	.12	.04
088. flirtatious	.00	−.01	−.23	−.16	−.12	−.16	.04	.24	−.06	.02	.17	.12

Correlations of Observers' Adjectival Description with Scales of the CPI continued

	Scale: Wo						Scale: CT					
	By Peers		By Spouses		By Staff		By Peers		By Spouses		By Staff	
Adjectives	M	F	M	F	M	F	M	F	M	F	M	F
089. foolish	−.11	−.23	.01	−.19	−.07	−.12	.11	.03	.05	.05	−.10	−.05
090. forceful	−.01	−.11	−.10	−.10	−.08	.06	−.21	.05	.02	.12	.09	.24
091. foresighted	.13	.23	.12	.21	.02	.08	.02	.03	.03	−.05	.21	.13
092. forgetful	−.14	−.17	−.11	−.06	−.11	−.02	.05	.03	.00	.15	.11	−.06
093. forgiving	.04	.15	.05	−.01	−.13	−.10	.12	−.07	.03	−.08	.05	−.10
094. formal	.11	.07	.10	.04	.09	.06	−.17	−.10	.03	−.03	−.08	−.28
095. frank	.04	−.10	−.02	.00	−.11	−.05	.05	.08	.04	.11	.11	.23
096. friendly	.02	.17	.07	.08	−.09	−.01	.14	.02	.15	.06	.07	.02
097. frivolous	−.06	−.06	−.01	−.10	−.14	−.12	−.05	.07	.03	.03	.09	−.01
098. fussy	−.15	−.09	−.13	−.22	−.01	−.04	−.06	−.10	−.12	−.01	−.14	−.09
099. generous	.06	.16	.03	.05	−.11	−.05	.05	−.08	.11	−.05	.09	−.01
100. gentle	.05	.24	.12	.02	−.11	−.05	.06	−.18	−.02	−.06	.07	−.23
101. gloomy	−.03	−.26	−.24	−.03	−.03	−.13	.02	−.07	−.09	.00	−.05	.00
102. good-looking	.03	.01	−.02	−.06	−.12	−.08	.06	.09	.03	.04	.14	.06
103. good-natured	.14	.21	.15	.19	−.12	.01	.03	−.04	.05	−.03	.08	.01
104. greedy	−.09	−.19	−.14	−.10	−.05	−.08	−.01	−.06	.00	−.05	.08	.08
105. handsome	−.04	.00	.03	.06	−.15	.06	.06	.00	.07	.03	.10	−.01
106. hard-headed	.03	−.22	−.10	−.23	.00	−.04	−.14	.02	−.08	.04	.00	.11
107. hard-hearted	−.10	−.11	−.08	−.13	−.07	−.06	−.11	−.03	−.06	−.05	−.12	.06
108. hasty	−.14	−.24	−.23	−.15	−.04	−.17	−.09	.15	−.01	.07	.14	.15
109. headstrong	−.12	−.21	−.11	−.22	−.14	−.13	−.08	.09	.00	.12	.12	.26
110. healthy	.00	.11	.09	.09	−.13	.04	.08	−.08	−.11	.08	.07	.07
111. helpful	.05	.21	.05	.06	−.01	−.01	.04	−.07	−.03	−.04	.04	−.17
112. high-strung	−.13	−.18	−.21	−.26	−.10	−.24	.04	.00	−.02	.07	.16	.16
113. honest	.12	.14	.14	.18	.02	.05	.03	−.08	.03	−.05	.03	−.05
114. hostile	−.02	−.22	−.17	−.06	−.02	−.08	−.11	−.03	−.03	.04	−.03	.10
115. humorous	−.03	−.11	−.06	.19	−.21	−.07	.13	.11	.09	.22	.11	.20
116. hurried	−.17	−.22	−.14	−.02	−.10	−.07	−.01	.08	−.02	.08	.16	.14
117. idealistic	−.07	.13	−.01	.02	−.05	−.09	.06	−.07	.12	.15	.20	.16
118. imaginative	−.06	.03	−.03	.03	−.10	−.07	.15	.23	.21	.25	.39	.35
119. immature	−.05	−.22	−.25	−.12	−.06	−.14	.05	−.07	.06	.01	.01	−.06
120. impatient	−.06	−.27	−.15	−.26	−.06	−.15	−.03	.05	.00	.10	.17	.27
121. impulsive	−.16	−.28	−.27	−.25	−.16	−.20	.10	.21	.06	.21	.16	.24
122. independent	.17	.00	.18	−.01	−.12	−.04	.19	.21	−.02	.18	.24	.35
123. indifferent	−.09	−.21	−.07	−.04	−.08	−.05	.04	.08	−.04	.06	−.07	−.06
124. individualistic	−.08	−.14	−.06	.01	−.17	−.10	.20	.25	.16	.30	.24	.34
125. industrious	.09	.13	.05	.09	.08	.13	−.06	−.13	.00	.00	−.01	−.03
126. infantile	−.08	−.16	−.16	−.29	−.17	−.27	−.05	−.03	.00	−.08	.00	−.09
127. informal	.03	−.01	−.03	.01	−.21	−.09	.13	.24	.07	.08	.13	.24
128. ingenious	.03	−.04	.03	.02	−.01	−.05	.09	.22	.13	.08	.29	.23
129. inhibited	.01	.13	−.09	−.02	.02	.01	−.13	−.25	.01	.00	−.20	−.26
130. initiative	.11	.09	.01	.13	−.03	.00	−.10	.06	.15	.13	.18	.26
131. insightful	.12	.20	.07	.14	−.07	.01	.12	.10	.21	.21	.30	.26
132. intelligent	.06	.20	.10	.10	−.06	.10	.19	.13	.04	.12	.36	.23

		Scale: Wo						Scale: CT				
		By Peers		By Spouses		By Staff		By Peers		By Spouses		By Staff
Adjectives		M	F	M	F	M	F	M	F	M	F	M	F
133.	interests—narrow	−.07	−.09	−.07	−.27	.00	−.10	−.19	−.10	−.13	−.28	−.33	−.40
134.	interests—wide	−.02	.01	.09	.14	−.09	.05	.19	.16	.09	.26	.38	.35
135.	intolerant	−.13	−.11	−.20	−.24	−.08	−.14	−.16	.05	−.05	−.03	−.06	−.09
136.	inventive	.13	.01	.05	.06	−.11	.00	−.03	.12	.14	.10	.32	.23
137.	irresponsible	−.16	−.23	−.12	−.22	−.09	−.20	.10	.15	.08	.07	.15	.09
138.	irritable	−.10	−.28	−.12	−.20	−.06	−.09	−.11	.01	.03	.04	.05	.11
139.	jolly	.02	.03	−.05	.06	−.12	−.02	.01	.16	−.06	.03	−.04	.04
140.	kind	.02	.17	.09	.03	−.17	−.03	−.09	−.17	−.05	.08	.04	−.14
141.	lazy	−.07	−.21	−.06	−.08	−.10	−.13	.26	.12	.19	.15	−.01	.04
142.	leisurely	−.08	.04	−.01	−.06	−.06	.00	.20	.14	.08	.08	−.04	−.01
143.	logical	.13	.20	.05	.21	.01	.16	.09	.08	.03	−.02	.15	.05
144.	loud	−.07	−.21	−.14	−.19	−.14	−.05	−.04	.12	.01	.03	.05	.19
145.	loyal	.07	.18	−.05	−.10	.00	−.04	−.07	−.13	−.07	−.13	−.17	−.21
146.	mannerly	.05	.25	.13	.13	−.04	.04	−.07	−.12	−.09	.03	−.04	−.24
147.	masculine	.07	−.08	−.07	−.04	−.11	.09	.01	.07	−.10	.03	−.03	.10
148.	mature	.21	.18	.25	.18	.01	.05	.00	.05	−.03	−.08	.07	−.04
149.	meek	−.07	.02	−.11	−.08	−.11	.01	.00	−.23	−.07	−.03	−.12	−.21
150.	methodical	.01	.07	.15	.11	.13	.18	−.06	−.08	−.09	.10	−.15	−.28
151.	mild	.05	.15	−.01	.08	.00	.07	−.03	−.19	−.06	−.17	−.09	−.28
152.	mischievous	−.16	−.09	−.20	−.15	−.17	−.13	.09	.23	.02	.11	.17	.24
153.	moderate	.19	.28	.13	.21	.13	.17	−.03	−.15	−.06	−.11	−.19	−.27
154.	modest	.07	.16	.07	.06	.04	.04	.03	−.24	−.04	−.20	−.13	−.32
155.	moody	−.10	−.37	−.21	−.26	−.10	−.21	.05	.00	.03	.06	.02	.12
156.	nagging	−.17	−.15	−.28	−.18	−.08	−.23	−.08	−.01	−.11	.02	−.03	−.01
157.	natural	.02	.08	.04	.13	−.01	.05	.11	.03	.09	.10	.06	.10
158.	nervous	−.18	−.23	−.28	−.22	−.07	−.15	.01	−.15	−.15	.00	−.01	−.01
159.	noisy	−.12	−.13	−.08	−.21	−.10	−.09	.01	.15	−.05	−.02	.01	.15
160.	obliging	.04	.25	.04	.10	.04	.04	.10	−.11	−.01	.00	.03	−.15
161.	obnoxious	−.06	−.25	−.12	−.07	−.10	−.13	−.06	−.02	−.01	.11	.05	.07
162.	opinionated	−.05	−.17	−.08	−.21	−.09	−.08	−.04	.13	.04	.12	.05	.15
163.	opportunistic	.02	−.06	−.07	−.03	−.07	−.10	−.02	.10	.08	.05	.06	.21
164.	optimistic	.13	.25	.07	.15	−.06	.01	.14	−.07	.14	.16	.13	.04
165.	organized	.12	.27	.14	.12	.17	.18	−.17	−.12	−.14	−.14	.07	−.12
166.	original	−.01	.00	−.01	.03	−.10	−.08	.13	.24	.18	.21	.42	.33
167.	outgoing	.00	−.03	−.04	.05	−.07	−.02	.06	.17	.12	.25	.12	.20
168.	outspoken	.06	−.11	−.20	−.11	−.09	−.04	−.05	.24	.05	.24	.16	.22
169.	painstaking	.08	.15	.08	−.03	.10	.04	−.10	−.13	−.03	−.07	−.14	−.26
170.	patient	.03	.36	.10	.10	.05	.06	−.02	−.19	.03	−.14	−.06	−.26
171.	peaceable	.01	.34	.03	.02	.02	.10	.04	−.17	.00	−.04	−.06	−.31
172.	peculiar	−.13	−.20	−.17	−.10	−.10	−.08	−.03	.02	−.09	.06	−.06	.01
173.	persevering	.11	.11	−.01	.11	.12	−.01	.00	−.05	.01	.02	−.01	−.09
174.	persistent	.06	.01	.00	.05	−.10	.00	−.01	.04	.00	.03	−.02	.16
175.	pessimistic	−.06	−.37	−.07	−.15	−.12	−.17	.04	.08	.00	.03	.07	.01
176.	planful	.08	.19	.06	.10	.02	.12	−.16	−.07	−.08	−.04	.11	−.03

Correlations of Observers' Adjectival Description with Scales of the CPI continued

	Scale: Wo						Scale: CT					
	By Peers		By Spouses		By Staff		By Peers		By Spouses		By Staff	
Adjectives	M	F	M	F	M	F	M	F	M	F	M	F
177. pleasant	.14	.24	.12	.21	−.06	.08	.16	−.03	−.03	−.02	.10	−.07
178. pleasure-seeking	−.02	−.11	−.18	−.18	−.15	−.17	.14	.25	.15	.18	.16	.15
179. poised	.06	.18	.09	.01	.03	.06	.10	.03	.05	.08	.12	.02
180. polished	.13	.12	.08	.11	.01	.02	.10	.01	.00	.04	.10	.03
181. practical	.17	.20	.17	.14	.01	.03	−.02	−.16	−.12	−.05	−.13	−.12
182. praising	.04	.11	−.03	−.01	.04	.00	.03	−.16	.02	−.09	.07	−.16
183. precise	.07	.04	.13	.12	.00	.12	−.06	−.05	−.03	.06	.02	−.02
184. prejudiced	−.02	−.14	−.18	−.24	−.06	−.16	−.05	−.11	−.27	−.13	−.17	−.15
185. preoccupied	−.10	−.20	−.07	−.16	−.09	−.16	−.01	.05	−.01	.12	−.03	−.01
186. progressive	.11	−.08	−.03	.11	−.17	−.04	.07	.18	.10	.16	.26	.31
187. prudish	−.14	.03	−.11	−.16	−.02	.03	−.10	−.19	−.01	−.07	−.16	−.39
188. quarrelsome	−.10	−.21	−.23	−.19	−.08	−.13	−.07	.05	−.05	.00	.07	.18
189. queer	−.23	−.18	.03	.00	−.04	−.05	−.04	−.07	.05	.00	−.02	.04
190. quick	.00	−.03	−.08	−.04	−.12	−.08	.11	.12	.11	.15	.27	.23
191. quiet	.03	.15	.15	.04	.02	.06	−.06	−.19	−.10	−.21	−.12	−.28
192. quitting	−.16	−.22	−.17	−.03	−.06	−.08	.00	−.11	.13	−.05	.01	−.02
193. rational	.12	.31	.07	.24	−.08	.05	.09	.01	.09	.05	.19	.10
194. rattle-brained	−.07	−.18	−.19	−.18	−.08	−.14	.02	.03	−.03	−.08	−.04	.02
195. realistic	.19	.22	.02	.21	−.03	.07	.05	.07	.03	−.02	.05	.05
196. reasonable	.17	.30	.16	.18	.05	.12	−.01	−.06	.05	.03	.05	−.08
197. rebellious	−.17	−.32	−.31	−.20	−.18	−.15	.01	.19	.13	.16	.20	.32
198. reckless	−.11	−.22	−.26	−.34	−.13	−.20	.05	.18	.07	.10	.10	.15
199. reflective	−.06	.16	−.05	.12	−.05	−.05	.12	.00	.18	.25	.25	.13
200. relaxed	.08	.24	.11	.12	−.06	.06	.15	.00	.05	−.08	.07	.09
201. reliable	.15	.38	.13	.13	.07	.13	−.08	−.12	−.12	−.08	−.02	−.16
202. resentful	−.01	−.26	−.21	−.17	−.07	−.16	−.03	−.03	−.02	.00	−.07	.03
203. reserved	.04	.15	.05	.02	.03	.06	.05	−.22	−.13	−.23	−.08	−.23
204. resourceful	.16	.19	−.01	.05	−.02	.01	.00	.00	.11	.20	.27	.29
205. responsible	.20	.35	.12	.10	.05	.14	−.11	−.09	.05	.04	.02	−.15
206. restless	−.15	−.29	−.25	−.16	−.18	−.22	.01	.06	.13	.14	.17	.25
207. retiring	−.11	−.01	−.03	.00	−.02	.06	.01	−.25	.04	−.09	−.14	−.24
208. rigid	−.07	−.02	−.10	−.10	−.03	.01	−.16	−.10	.00	−.03	−.28	−.27
209. robust	−.02	−.07	−.03	.05	−.13	−.01	−.02	.03	.08	.06	.00	.13
210. rude	−.08	−.25	−.14	.04	−.12	−.11	.00	.10	.03	.05	.02	.07
211. sarcastic	−.07	−.31	−.08	−.14	−.17	−.11	.22	.16	−.02	.13	.12	.24
212. self-centered	−.13	−.18	−.19	−.18	−.12	−.17	.01	.00	−.06	.10	.09	.16
213. self-confident	.02	.09	.13	.13	−.06	.04	.10	.24	.08	.08	.22	.22
214. self-controlled	.09	.29	.13	.15	.08	.06	.08	−.10	.00	.02	−.06	−.22
215. self-denying	.04	.11	−.11	−.03	−.01	−.03	−.04	−.08	−.06	−.12	−.16	−.21
216. self-pitying	−.06	−.28	−.26	−.18	−.07	−.24	−.04	−.05	.08	.04	.00	−.05
217. self-punishing	.00	−.09	−.24	−.14	−.05	−.21	−.01	−.13	.10	.04	−.04	.02
218. self-seeking	−.02	−.18	−.13	−.02	−.06	−.14	.01	.06	.12	.08	.09	.15
219. selfish	−.02	−.18	−.02	−.01	−.05	−.18	.01	−.01	.04	.03	−.01	.07
220. sensitive	−.13	−.05	−.11	−.03	−.15	−.18	.01	−.10	.04	.08	.25	.04

		Scale: Wo						Scale: CT				
		By Peers		By Spouses		By Staff		By Peers		By Spouses		By Staff
Adjectives		M	F	M	F	M	F	M	F	M	F	M	F
221.	sentimental	−.02	.08	−.06	.01	−.10	−.09	.05	.00	−.04	−.06	.01	−.06
222.	serious	.10	.07	−.04	.07	−.02	.07	−.04	−.14	−.02	−.05	−.01	−.01
223.	severe	−.14	−.03	−.11	−.05	−.11	−.01	−.02	.07	.05	−.03	−.06	−.10
224.	sexy	.00	−.06	−.12	−.12	−.21	−.14	.06	.21	.00	.13	.15	.14
225.	shallow	−.17	−.05	−.09	−.12	−.01	−.14	−.11	−.01	−.03	−.05	−.18	−.21
226.	sharp-witted	.07	−.20	−.10	.00	−.13	−.05	.20	.13	.15	.20	.23	.27
227.	shiftless	−.07	−.21	−.15	−.21	−.08	−.13	−.05	.08	.00	.08	.03	.05
228.	show-off	−.12	−.15	−.17	−.13	−.16	−.05	.00	.19	.10	−.04	.14	.19
229.	shrewd	.07	−.18	−.13	−.12	−.01	−.05	.07	.09	.07	.15	.12	.20
230.	shy	.06	.06	−.02	−.04	−.13	−.04	−.09	−.24	−.06	−.22	−.08	−.20
231.	silent	−.04	.08	−.10	−.06	−.12	−.02	−.10	−.16	−.15	−.16	−.08	−.20
232.	simple	.03	.06	.01	−.20	.01	−.03	−.06	−.24	−.09	−.11	−.31	−.30
233.	sincere	.10	.19	.12	.20	−.01	.06	−.02	−.13	−.03	−.07	.02	−.14
234.	slipshod	−.03	−.24	−.18	−.11	−.02	−.11	.08	.10	.02	.10	.04	.07
235.	slow	−.13	.03	−.17	−.16	.07	.03	.04	−.08	−.05	−.03	−.17	−.26
236.	sly	−.04	−.22	−.30	−.16	−.09	−.12	.05	.05	−.09	.12	.07	.10
237.	smug	−.02	−.08	−.08	−.08	−.05	−.07	.08	.10	−.01	−.05	−.01	.04
238.	snobbish	−.07	−.09	−.04	−.14	−.06	−.07	.02	.02	.08	.08	.04	.05
239.	sociable	.05	.09	.02	−.10	−.09	−.05	.06	.11	.04	.18	.13	.08
240.	soft-hearted	.07	.19	−.10	−.09	−.08	−.07	.11	.03	−.02	−.02	−.02	−.16
241.	sophisticated	.03	−.01	.00	.04	−.13	−.01	.07	.12	.07	.12	.25	.23
242.	spendthrift	.05	−.09	.00	−.12	−.06	−.14	.11	.08	.09	.05	.06	.01
243.	spineless	−.06	−.15	.01	−.08	−.08	.02	.04	−.14	.12	.04	−.09	−.05
244.	spontaneous	−.03	−.07	−.09	−.04	−.12	−.08	.05	.25	.13	.33	.22	.24
245.	spunky	−.07	.00	−.22	−.10	−.10	−.10	.02	.11	−.09	.21	.07	.21
246.	stable	.15	.27	.20	.17	.04	.15	.01	−.02	−.03	−.03	−.01	−.16
247.	steady	.11	.26	.05	.11	.02	.10	.00	−.09	−.01	−.15	−.18	−.22
248.	stern	−.02	−.01	−.12	.02	−.03	.04	−.13	−.07	−.18	−.07	−.16	−.14
249.	stingy	−.18	−.13	−.23	−.15	.02	−.01	−.03	−.02	−.07	.05	−.14	−.01
250.	stolid	−.06	−.08	.04	.01	−.05	.08	−.13	−.01	.00	.02	−.25	−.27
251.	strong	.00	.13	−.02	.03	−.14	.04	−.06	−.01	−.01	−.04	.01	.19
252.	stubborn	−.06	−.16	−.16	−.12	−.03	−.03	−.13	−.03	−.03	.04	−.02	.14
253.	submissive	.02	.17	−.14	−.09	.03	.06	.09	−.18	.00	−.08	−.21	−.22
254.	suggestible	−.02	.06	−.11	−.01	−.02	−.07	.05	.07	.02	.03	−.09	−.16
255.	sulky	−.06	−.28	−.13	−.14	−.06	−.24	−.08	−.03	.10	.07	−.10	.03
256.	superstitious	.02	−.03	−.30	−.27	−.02	−.36	−.07	−.05	−.04	.01	−.06	−.08
257.	suspicious	−.12	−.23	−.22	−.20	−.11	−.16	−.04	−.07	−.05	−.01	−.07	−.02
258.	sympathetic	.02	.13	.07	.07	−.08	−.06	.07	−.07	.04	−.01	.13	−.12
259.	tactful	.07	.25	.17	.11	.11	.09	.15	.01	−.09	.12	.07	−.12
260.	tactless	−.03	−.17	−.16	.01	−.11	−.11	−.04	.00	−.07	.00	.05	.13
261.	talkative	.00	−.14	−.05	−.16	−.12	−.10	.13	.21	.06	.17	.19	.25
262.	temperamental	−.16	−.30	−.21	−.28	−.17	−.20	−.04	.04	.01	.07	.13	.23
263.	tense	−.07	−.17	−.21	−.18	−.03	−.20	−.01	−.15	.02	.02	−.04	.05
264.	thankless	−.15	−.25	−.14	−.04	−.11	−.03	.00	.00	−.01	.06	−.01	−.02

Correlations of Observers' Adjectival Description with Scales of the CPI continued

	Scale: Wo						Scale: CT					
	By Peers		By Spouses		By Staff		By Peers		By Spouses		By Staff	
Adjectives	M	F	M	F	M	F	M	F	M	F	M	F
265. thorough	.19	.17	.02	.15	.17	.16	−.08	−.06	.01	.00	.06	−.07
266. thoughtful	.18	.21	.09	.19	−.02	.04	.08	−.10	.02	−.01	.21	−.05
267. thrifty	.05	.14	−.04	.11	−.06	.04	−.03	.00	−.09	−.14	−.16	−.21
268. timid	−.07	.01	−.01	−.12	−.09	−.05	−.01	−.28	−.02	−.05	−.11	−.23
269. tolerant	.03	.23	.12	.14	−.04	.04	.15	.06	.17	.03	.20	.05
270. touchy	−.07	−.22	−.14	−.28	−.08	−.20	−.04	.04	−.05	.06	.07	−.04
271. tough	−.01	−.15	−.19	−.06	−.13	−.01	−.27	.05	−.14	.09	−.01	.22
272. trusting	.03	.27	.03	.11	−.04	−.01	.09	−.13	.06	−.01	.09	−.11
273. unaffected	.05	.15	.04	−.06	.07	.11	.14	−.07	.06	.11	−.01	−.01
274. unambitious	−.01	−.12	−.16	−.02	−.07	−.08	.09	.08	.09	.07	−.04	−.23
275. unassuming	.00	.13	−.02	.08	.00	.04	.03	−.15	−.04	−.03	−.08	−.22
276. unconventional	−.02	−.33	−.13	−.14	−.18	−.12	.14	.24	.20	.30	.28	.26
277. undependable	−.18	−.23	−.04	−.17	−.03	−.15	.10	.13	.12	.01	.03	.07
278. understanding	.07	.23	.03	.14	−.12	.00	.06	−.01	.17	.07	.21	.00
279. unemotional	.03	−.03	.15	−.04	−.11	.06	−.01	−.11	.09	−.03	−.10	−.17
280. unexcitable	.03	.09	−.02	.00	.04	.09	.01	−.08	.01	−.01	−.07	−.23
281. unfriendly	−.13	−.14	−.13	−.05	.00	−.01	.04	−.02	−.08	−.06	−.02	−.06
282. uninhibited	.02	−.20	.01	.02	−.12	−.14	.10	.21	.11	.22	.20	.25
283. unintelligent	.07	−.11	.00	−.03	.01	.02	−.09	−.01	.00	−.07	−.12	−.08
284. unkind	−.04	−.21	−.09	−.04	−.10	−.11	−.12	−.03	−.03	−.04	.05	.04
285. unrealistic	−.08	−.21	−.11	−.25	−.09	−.27	.06	.01	.13	−.01	.01	−.05
286. unscrupulous	−.12	−.20	−.26	.00	−.04	−.09	.01	.12	−.07	.02	.09	.07
287. unselfish	.12	.16	−.05	.04	−.04	.03	−.03	−.03	−.11	−.03	.09	−.18
288. unstable	−.09	−.32	−.24	−.19	−.05	−.21	.12	.01	−.02	.12	.08	.11
289. vindictive	.01	−.11	−.16	−.20	−.09	−.15	−.03	.04	.02	.03	−.07	.04
290. versatile	.12	−.04	−.06	.08	−.07	−.07	.13	.22	.09	.12	.33	.33
291. warm	.04	.23	−.02	.04	−.10	−.04	.03	.02	.04	.00	.12	−.01
292. wary	−.03	−.06	−.08	−.06	−.10	−.05	.09	−.04	.04	.01	−.08	−.05
293. weak	−.12	.02	−.28	−.18	−.06	−.10	.10	−.19	.05	−.08	−.13	−.13
294. whiny	−.11	−.16	−.22	−.26	−.01	−.12	.07	−.09	.02	.08	−.04	−.05
295. wholesome	.05	.23	.03	.06	.01	.07	−.03	−.04	−.12	.05	.01	−.06
296. wise	.11	.20	.13	.07	−.04	.05	−.01	.04	−.01	−.07	.19	.04
297. withdrawn	.03	−.02	−.26	−.07	−.14	−.05	−.01	−.24	−.06	−.03	−.09	−.09
298. witty	−.07	−.20	−.05	−.02	−.17	−.07	.22	.24	.03	.05	.24	.26
299. worrying	−.16	−.12	−.34	−.23	−.11	−.12	−.05	−.11	−.11	.09	−.02	−.06
300. zany	−.15	−.10	−.18	−.12	−.13	−.09	.08	.19	.05	.24	.10	.11

Correlations of Observers' Adjectival Description with Scales of the CPI continued

		Scale: Lp						Scale: Ami				
		By Peers		By Spouses		By Staff		By Peers		By Spouses		By Staff	
Adjectives		M	F	M	F	M	F	M	F	M	F	M	F
001.	absent-minded	−.10	−.28	−.16	−.07	−.17	−.14	−.06	−.08	−.06	−.16	−.01	−.10
002.	active	.21	.23	−.04	.14	.15	.19	.13	.07	−.16	.00	−.10	−.10
003.	adaptable	.10	.22	.11	.07	.14	.12	.27	.31	.13	−.02	.08	.01
004.	adventurous	.03	.02	−.04	.07	.03	.06	.03	−.09	−.11	−.09	−.22	−.25
005.	affected	.02	.16	.04	−.08	.05	.02	−.11	−.10	−.08	−.06	−.08	−.15
006.	affectionate	−.03	.03	−.04	.05	−.05	−.07	.20	.15	−.03	.05	−.02	.03
007.	aggressive	.16	.15	.02	.09	.17	.18	−.20	−.20	−.20	−.24	−.17	−.16
008.	alert	.20	.20	.15	.15	.14	.18	.16	−.01	.06	.08	−.01	−.04
009.	aloof	.02	−.12	−.06	−.11	−.24	−.06	−.06	−.28	−.05	−.13	−.07	.01
010.	ambitious	.29	.24	.17	.22	.28	.28	.06	.02	−.04	.00	.03	−.08
011.	anxious	−.10	−.04	−.11	−.17	−.21	−.35	−.14	−.18	−.14	−.18	−.05	−.14
012.	apathetic	−.26	−.18	−.19	−.06	−.26	−.18	−.11	−.19	−.16	−.05	−.04	.03
013.	appreciative	.00	.11	.10	.02	−.02	−.02	.26	.29	.19	.15	.11	.17
014.	argumentative	.03	−.01	−.02	.03	.15	.11	−.34	−.31	−.17	−.27	−.13	−.14
015.	arrogant	.00	−.02	−.08	.05	.03	.09	−.27	−.37	−.27	−.13	−.23	−.19
016.	artistic	−.15	−.11	−.03	−.02	−.03	−.04	−.01	−.11	.03	−.13	−.04	.03
017.	assertive	.13	.16	.12	.30	.21	.25	−.17	−.22	−.04	−.02	−.11	−.14
018.	attractive	.05	.07	−.01	−.05	−.01	.06	.20	−.01	−.01	−.10	−.08	−.04
019.	autocratic	−.02	−.01	.00	.02	.02	.16	−.15	−.24	−.11	−.06	−.15	−.09
020.	awkward	−.21	−.16	−.28	−.20	−.35	−.27	−.13	−.07	−.21	−.03	−.08	−.04
021.	bitter	−.09	−.17	−.28	−.18	−.14	−.15	−.17	−.32	−.27	−.33	−.21	−.26
022.	blustery	−.02	−.08	.00	−.14	.03	−.06	−.26	−.20	−.03	−.22	−.16	−.17
023.	boastful	.06	.14	−.07	−.07	.07	.10	−.20	−.28	−.23	−.21	−.24	−.13
024.	bossy	.02	.14	−.19	.00	.07	.11	−.26	−.25	−.25	−.20	−.15	−.11
025.	calm	−.04	.13	.02	.01	−.10	.07	.28	.28	.25	.19	.05	.12
026.	capable	.20	.22	.06	.24	.04	.23	.22	.17	.09	.15	−.04	.05
027.	careless	−.15	−.21	−.23	−.14	−.10	−.14	−.27	−.21	−.19	−.18	−.11	−.16
028.	cautious	−.12	−.02	−.09	−.06	−.23	−.19	.07	.23	.00	.09	.07	.08
029.	changeable	−.03	−.14	−.18	−.04	−.08	−.19	−.02	−.26	−.14	−.21	−.20	−.26
030.	charming	−.01	.14	−.06	.01	.05	.09	.13	.14	−.04	.00	−.08	−.03
031.	cheerful	.01	.15	.11	.02	.09	.12	.19	.30	.21	.17	.04	.07
032.	civilized	.11	.09	.06	−.05	−.03	.09	.20	.16	.13	.06	−.04	.08
033.	clear-thinking	.19	.22	.11	.20	.03	.20	.18	.18	.22	.19	.01	.03
034.	clever	.09	.02	.03	.15	.05	.10	.02	−.18	−.06	.05	−.14	−.12
035.	coarse	−.07	−.13	−.26	.01	−.07	−.06	−.19	−.28	−.25	−.02	−.18	−.16
036.	cold	−.18	−.07	−.13	−.08	−.11	−.07	−.37	−.28	−.04	−.15	−.10	−.13
037.	commonplace	−.19	−.04	.00	−.13	−.15	−.14	−.03	.05	.07	−.01	.00	.03
038.	complaining	−.15	−.14	−.25	−.18	−.11	−.08	−.19	−.25	−.24	−.32	−.13	−.22
039.	complicated	−.07	−.18	.11	−.05	−.15	−.15	−.13	−.28	.07	−.17	−.20	−.22
040.	conceited	.02	.17	−.04	.04	.15	.10	−.29	−.28	−.22	−.06	−.11	−.10
041.	confident	.22	.32	.17	.25	.18	.31	.01	−.05	.03	.04	−.08	−.06
042.	confused	−.17	−.20	−.30	−.21	−.19	−.31	−.12	−.14	−.26	−.25	−.10	−.23
043.	conscientious	.07	.18	.17	.15	−.02	.07	.18	.26	.19	.17	.17	.15
044.	conservative	.06	.08	.03	−.13	−.04	−.01	.14	.30	.14	.11	.11	.15

Correlations of Observers' Adjectival Description with Scales of the CPI continued

| | | Scale: Lp | | | | | | Scale: Ami | | | | |
| | | By Peers | | By Spouses | | By Staff | | By Peers | | By Spouses | | By Staff | |
Adjectives		M	F	M	F	M	F	M	F	M	F	M	F
045.	considerate	.06	.03	.11	−.09	−.13	−.03	.34	.33	.17	.12	.05	.09
046.	contented	.01	.12	.14	−.01	−.05	.02	.26	.30	.26	.18	.06	.11
047.	conventional	.01	.10	.11	−.06	−.06	−.03	.17	.33	.09	.14	.14	.15
048.	cool	.00	−.07	.01	−.01	−.04	.02	−.10	−.29	.06	−.04	−.01	−.02
049.	cooperative	−.05	.14	.14	.08	−.02	.00	.24	.36	.17	.27	.12	.14
050.	courageous	.00	.06	.08	.08	.02	.05	−.01	−.08	−.01	.04	−.11	−.16
051.	cowardly	−.18	−.10	−.09	−.01	−.14	−.04	−.15	.06	−.09	.03	−.05	−.03
052.	cruel	−.15	−.07	−.20	.00	−.10	−.05	−.27	−.21	−.20	−.05	−.15	−.12
053.	curious	−.05	−.09	−.03	.03	−.04	.03	−.02	−.06	−.04	.05	−.05	−.20
054.	cynical	−.08	−.17	−.10	−.03	−.13	−.06	−.20	−.39	−.18	−.20	−.28	−.20
055.	daring	−.01	.03	−.07	−.02	.09	.02	−.05	−.16	−.12	−.05	−.20	−.24
056.	deceitful	.00	−.03	−.25	−.05	.06	−.10	−.24	−.21	−.16	−.16	−.06	−.17
057.	defensive	−.19	−.22	−.08	−.15	−.14	−.15	−.30	−.29	−.20	−.20	−.13	−.11
058.	deliberate	.13	.06	.01	−.01	−.17	.03	.06	−.15	−.03	−.05	−.01	.10
059.	demanding	.11	.09	−.01	−.07	.08	.06	−.14	−.34	−.19	−.31	−.18	−.23
060.	dependable	.17	.18	.06	.02	.00	.11	.24	.25	.16	.09	.13	.18
061.	dependent	−.11	−.08	−.07	−.21	−.19	−.25	.05	.11	−.04	−.06	.02	.03
062.	despondent	−.05	−.25	−.06	.07	−.19	−.29	−.10	−.23	−.17	.07	−.09	−.05
063.	determined	.19	.28	.07	.18	.10	.22	−.03	−.05	−.03	.00	−.11	−.14
064.	dignified	.09	.12	.03	.11	.01	.03	.12	.04	.08	.07	.06	.04
065.	discreet	.02	.08	.06	.06	−.08	−.04	.16	.21	.10	.02	.13	.17
066.	disorderly	−.13	−.26	−.09	−.08	−.07	−.21	−.12	−.26	−.18	−.15	−.11	−.23
067.	dissatisfied	−.14	−.14	−.21	−.16	−.17	−.25	−.19	−.30	−.35	−.18	−.24	−.28
068.	distractible	−.19	−.12	−.24	−.13	−.18	−.24	−.22	−.08	−.23	−.16	−.14	−.20
069.	distrustful	−.17	−.14	−.16	−.18	−.09	−.17	−.28	−.27	−.13	−.29	−.17	−.23
070.	dominant	.21	.21	.07	−.03	.12	.26	−.15	−.25	−.03	−.14	−.16	−.11
071.	dreamy	−.14	−.08	−.07	−.09	−.23	−.24	.04	.04	−.16	−.09	−.06	−.03
072.	dull	−.15	−.09	−.08	−.12	−.17	−.09	−.03	.03	−.15	−.09	.00	.04
073.	easygoing	−.09	−.04	−.13	.01	−.16	−.03	.27	.11	.11	.15	−.05	.03
074.	effeminate	−.01	−.01	.04	.05	−.06	.04	.01	−.05	.01	−.03	.02	−.03
075.	efficient	.16	.27	.06	.09	.20	.21	.09	.17	.19	.08	.13	.07
076.	egotistical	.12	.11	−.01	.08	.08	.12	−.28	−.33	−.28	−.10	−.19	−.15
077.	emotional	−.12	−.05	−.12	−.15	−.04	−.18	−.14	−.12	−.24	−.13	−.16	−.19
078.	energetic	.17	.21	.13	.14	.22	.20	−.02	.07	−.10	−.02	−.05	−.08
079.	enterprising	.27	.21	.05	.20	.22	.27	.04	.06	−.09	.15	−.06	−.06
080.	enthusiastic	.10	.11	.17	.17	.09	.15	.08	.13	−.02	.12	−.06	−.08
081.	evasive	−.06	−.14	−.08	−.17	−.21	−.09	−.06	−.15	−.11	−.22	−.13	−.12
082.	excitable	−.04	.09	−.14	−.11	.03	−.04	−.10	−.14	−.14	−.22	−.14	−.14
083.	fair-minded	.08	.09	.11	.08	−.05	.04	.28	.29	.24	.15	.08	.12
084.	fault-finding	−.03	−.02	−.08	−.13	−.05	.00	−.26	−.30	−.12	−.19	−.17	−.18
085.	fearful	−.11	−.10	−.19	−.11	−.25	−.32	−.16	−.08	−.21	−.01	−.08	−.12
086.	feminine	−.09	.04	−.03	−.10	−.12	−.05	.12	.13	.00	.00	.00	.07
087.	fickle	−.15	.01	−.06	−.15	−.09	−.04	−.10	−.29	−.05	−.21	−.09	−.13
088.	flirtatious	.02	.14	−.17	−.08	−.01	−.03	.01	−.11	−.24	−.20	−.12	−.17

	Correlations of Observers' Adjectival Description with Scales of the CPI continued											

		Scale: Lp						Scale: Ami					
		By Peers		By Spouses		By Staff		By Peers		By Spouses		By Staff	
Adjectives		M	F	M	F	M	F	M	F	M	F	M	F
089.	foolish	−.05	−.15	−.04	−.13	−.07	−.13	−.11	−.18	−.02	−.21	−.11	−.10
090.	forceful	.18	.12	−.01	.02	.12	.22	−.18	−.20	−.17	−.18	−.15	−.07
091.	foresighted	.15	.24	.09	.05	.09	.19	.17	.17	.13	.23	.06	.04
092.	forgetful	−.12	−.25	−.09	−.01	−.16	−.07	−.12	−.07	−.06	−.08	−.07	−.04
093.	forgiving	.14	.03	−.04	−.07	−.13	−.13	.27	.29	.16	.05	−.04	−.03
094.	formal	.23	.09	.06	.09	−.05	.00	.10	.00	.06	.02	.06	.05
095.	frank	−.04	−.02	.01	−.01	−.04	.09	−.07	−.14	−.04	−.04	−.10	−.18
096.	friendly	.03	.16	.09	.03	.03	.08	.24	.21	.14	.16	−.01	.05
097.	frivolous	−.07	.09	−.05	−.04	−.04	−.07	−.01	−.06	−.03	−.05	−.11	−.10
098.	fussy	−.14	.02	−.13	−.12	−.04	−.07	−.15	−.12	−.16	−.19	−.04	−.03
099.	generous	−.02	.00	.02	−.05	−.07	−.03	.26	.24	.04	.11	−.02	.00
100.	gentle	.01	−.06	.06	−.13	−.25	−.18	.28	.33	.18	.10	.01	.06
101.	gloomy	−.10	−.27	−.27	−.05	−.21	−.13	−.07	−.23	−.23	−.03	−.08	−.10
102.	good-looking	.10	.11	−.02	−.06	−.05	.05	.12	−.04	−.02	−.06	−.07	−.06
103.	good-natured	.02	.12	.10	.08	−.07	.00	.34	.26	.14	.19	.00	.04
104.	greedy	−.13	−.09	−.11	−.09	−.05	−.06	−.21	−.24	−.19	−.10	−.09	−.12
105.	handsome	.07	−.05	.04	.05	−.04	.06	.05	−.06	.05	.04	−.10	.06
106.	hard-headed	.07	.00	−.04	−.08	.08	.05	−.21	−.40	−.10	−.26	−.14	−.10
107.	hard-hearted	−.11	.00	−.11	−.08	−.02	.05	−.27	−.27	−.05	−.10	−.14	−.11
108.	hasty	−.15	−.13	−.22	−.14	.04	−.06	−.18	−.22	−.19	−.20	−.09	−.19
109.	headstrong	−.05	−.04	−.04	−.06	.03	.05	−.30	−.31	−.17	−.25	−.24	−.26
110.	healthy	−.06	.05	.04	.07	−.03	.16	.08	.11	.08	.06	−.09	.01
111.	helpful	.08	.13	.01	.10	−.04	.00	.21	.25	.09	.08	.07	.09
112.	high-strung	−.09	−.05	−.16	−.07	−.06	−.18	−.16	−.18	−.18	−.22	−.13	−.25
113.	honest	.04	.02	.02	.07	−.05	.02	.29	.25	.21	.15	.10	.05
114.	hostile	−.03	−.11	−.15	.03	−.04	−.04	−.13	−.31	−.17	−.10	−.11	−.18
115.	humorous	−.01	−.03	−.03	.18	.00	.07	.04	−.15	−.04	.17	−.21	−.10
116.	hurried	−.15	−.03	.00	.01	.01	−.03	−.22	−.19	−.17	.00	−.11	−.10
117.	idealistic	.08	.20	.10	.13	−.01	−.03	−.03	.12	−.01	.01	.02	−.08
118.	imaginative	.02	.07	.01	.11	.04	.02	.03	.00	−.04	−.07	−.08	−.08
119.	immature	−.14	−.19	−.20	−.16	−.12	−.21	−.12	−.16	−.30	−.12	−.05	−.06
120.	impatient	−.06	−.14	−.03	−.05	.06	−.03	−.22	−.29	−.19	−.21	−.17	−.25
121.	impulsive	−.12	−.16	−.16	−.11	.03	−.14	−.21	−.25	−.28	−.21	−.19	−.24
122.	independent	.09	.08	.11	.17	.05	.16	.07	−.11	.19	−.08	−.16	−.15
123.	indifferent	−.19	−.20	−.10	−.01	−.18	−.14	−.13	−.25	−.16	−.07	−.09	−.09
124.	individualistic	−.02	−.01	.04	.19	−.06	.04	−.13	−.20	−.03	−.09	−.24	−.18
125.	industrious	.17	.16	.09	.10	.10	.25	.09	.09	−.01	.05	.09	.08
126.	infantile	−.15	−.05	−.11	−.26	−.13	−.23	−.11	−.14	−.19	−.27	−.16	−.21
127.	informal	−.13	−.12	−.05	.01	−.10	−.05	.09	.04	−.02	−.04	−.16	−.09
128.	ingenious	.11	.07	.05	.08	.11	.05	.00	−.17	.02	−.06	.01	−.09
129.	inhibited	.01	−.03	−.16	−.14	−.27	−.24	.09	.15	−.07	−.03	.03	.08
130.	initiative	.14	.26	.12	.14	.24	.25	−.03	−.01	−.07	.10	−.06	−.07
131.	insightful	.08	.20	.07	.13	.04	.07	.13	.14	.02	.10	.00	−.03
132.	intelligent	.15	.21	.18	.08	.06	.18	.09	.13	.09	.00	−.04	.01

Correlations of Observers' Adjectival Description with Scales of the CPI continued

		Scale: Lp						Scale: Ami				
		By Peers		By Spouses		By Staff		By Peers		By Spouses		By Staff
Adjectives		M	F	M	F	M	F	M	F	M	F	M	F
133.	interests—narrow	−.23	−.10	−.11	−.29	−.19	−.21	−.01	−.09	−.08	−.14	.01	−.05
134.	interests—wide	.12	.16	.13	.13	.09	.12	.03	−.04	.07	.04	−.07	−.05
135.	intolerant	−.07	.05	−.19	−.19	−.05	−.06	−.26	−.25	−.21	−.23	−.16	−.19
136.	inventive	.09	.05	.05	.08	.03	.05	.12	−.08	.03	.00	−.11	−.03
137.	irresponsible	−.15	−.23	−.04	−.07	−.04	−.14	−.15	−.20	−.16	−.23	−.07	−.17
138.	irritable	−.07	−.18	−.15	−.13	−.07	−.03	−.30	−.37	−.14	−.25	−.14	−.17
139.	jolly	.02	.14	−.11	.01	.07	.01	.13	.08	−.03	.09	−.10	−.05
140.	kind	.03	.05	.02	.02	−.19	−.06	.35	.27	.19	.12	−.06	.07
141.	lazy	−.12	−.22	.03	−.14	−.14	−.17	−.08	−.20	−.08	−.11	−.07	−.12
142.	leisurely	−.13	−.01	.02	−.01	−.10	−.10	.06	.03	−.02	−.05	−.02	−.01
143.	logical	.20	.19	.03	.00	−.01	.17	.18	.06	.04	.20	.00	.03
144.	loud	−.03	.00	−.05	−.06	.04	.07	−.14	−.22	−.16	−.24	−.19	−.12
145.	loyal	.11	.06	−.07	−.17	−.07	−.04	.17	.18	.01	−.04	.04	.00
146.	mannerly	.12	.15	.09	.18	−.15	.02	.24	.25	.14	.06	.04	.06
147.	masculine	.07	.00	−.01	.00	.00	.04	.07	−.16	−.08	−.13	−.14	.00
148.	mature	.21	.19	.16	.13	.05	.17	.22	.11	.31	.19	.04	.01
149.	meek	−.16	−.18	−.06	−.17	−.29	−.23	.08	.10	−.03	−.03	−.07	.08
150.	methodical	.03	.03	.04	.15	−.02	.10	.06	.07	.07	.06	.13	.14
151.	mild	−.08	−.11	−.06	−.10	−.22	−.19	.22	.25	.10	.18	.10	.14
152.	mischievous	−.17	−.06	−.19	−.13	.02	−.04	−.18	−.10	−.16	−.18	−.19	−.14
153.	moderate	.11	.05	.10	.09	−.10	.02	.30	.30	.16	.20	.22	.19
154.	modest	.01	−.08	.01	−.10	−.21	−.22	.23	.25	.15	.15	.15	.11
155.	moody	−.12	−.25	−.18	−.16	−.21	−.25	−.19	−.39	−.18	−.24	−.16	−.23
156.	nagging	−.17	−.01	−.24	−.13	−.13	−.06	−.20	−.20	−.28	−.17	−.09	−.21
157.	natural	.02	−.11	−.04	.04	.08	.09	.16	.14	.07	.11	.05	.07
158.	nervous	−.18	−.15	−.22	−.15	−.18	−.31	−.11	−.15	−.26	−.18	−.06	−.14
159.	noisy	−.04	.04	−.01	−.12	.06	.01	−.10	−.19	−.09	−.25	−.16	−.12
160.	obliging	.02	.13	−.05	.01	−.08	−.12	.24	.33	.02	.10	.13	.11
161.	obnoxious	−.05	−.07	−.01	.02	.00	−.07	−.26	−.34	−.16	−.10	−.18	−.19
162.	opinionated	.04	.05	.00	−.06	.05	.09	−.26	−.30	−.12	−.27	−.20	−.18
163.	opportunistic	.17	.08	−.02	.03	.13	.12	−.03	−.14	−.07	−.16	−.16	−.17
164.	optimistic	.15	.22	.17	.17	.11	.18	.22	.21	.01	.08	.02	−.01
165.	organized	.23	.25	.10	.13	.21	.28	.16	.19	.15	.18	.17	.14
166.	original	.05	.03	.03	.04	.03	.01	.04	−.08	.02	−.06	−.09	−.14
167.	outgoing	.17	.22	.10	.23	.21	.21	.01	−.04	−.06	.01	−.06	−.09
168.	outspoken	.09	.13	−.05	.12	.13	.15	−.16	−.25	−.26	−.15	−.16	−.14
169.	painstaking	−.01	.09	.04	−.04	−.11	−.10	.13	.09	.04	−.03	.09	.06
170.	patient	.03	.09	.06	−.08	−.17	−.05	.29	.33	.19	.12	.15	.12
171.	peaceable	−.09	.08	−.02	−.08	−.20	−.10	.30	.37	.06	.09	.15	.17
172.	peculiar	−.15	−.22	−.18	−.11	−.21	−.10	−.19	−.20	−.16	−.19	−.10	−.06
173.	persevering	.15	.12	−.05	.12	.10	.07	.07	.03	−.04	.11	.09	−.03
174.	persistent	.10	.18	.03	.19	.03	.15	.03	−.12	−.02	.01	−.12	−.10
175.	pessimistic	−.17	−.31	−.07	−.15	−.20	−.22	−.18	−.36	−.12	−.13	−.15	−.15
176.	planful	.17	.25	.00	.04	.08	.22	.09	.14	.04	.08	.04	.11

| | **Correlations of Observers' Adjectival Description with Scales of the CPI** continued | | | | | | | | | | | |

		Scale: Lp						**Scale: Ami**					
		By Peers		By Spouses		By Staff		By Peers		By Spouses		By Staff	
Adjectives		M	F	M	F	M	F	M	F	M	F	M	F
177.	pleasant	.10	.10	.08	.07	−.05	.04	.30	.23	.17	.18	.03	.18
178.	pleasure-seeking	−.01	−.03	−.09	.00	.07	−.04	−.01	−.15	−.13	−.24	−.16	−.17
179.	poised	.14	.18	.13	.15	.16	.26	.18	.08	.03	−.01	.07	.03
180.	polished	.18	.19	.16	.21	.12	.18	.12	−.01	.07	.08	.01	.01
181.	practical	.18	.09	.13	.05	.03	.12	.23	.21	.23	.10	.00	.02
182.	praising	.04	.11	.03	−.02	.06	−.02	.20	.21	.01	.01	.11	.05
183.	precise	.15	.06	.15	.12	−.06	.10	.14	−.04	.10	.08	.00	.06
184.	prejudiced	−.08	.03	−.16	−.20	−.05	−.09	−.21	−.16	−.21	−.27	−.15	−.19
185.	preoccupied	−.08	−.11	.02	−.08	−.27	−.25	−.13	−.23	−.08	−.20	−.11	−.11
186.	progressive	.12	.00	.00	.08	.04	.06	.09	−.17	−.01	.07	−.14	−.13
187.	prudish	−.08	.06	−.10	−.14	−.11	−.12	−.09	.06	−.18	−.09	.01	.08
188.	quarrelsome	.03	−.12	−.27	−.16	.01	−.04	−.29	−.31	−.26	−.21	−.17	−.21
189.	queer	−.21	−.13	−.01	.00	−.13	−.07	−.17	−.25	.05	.00	−.03	−.04
190.	quick	.00	.15	−.04	.09	.09	.09	−.04	−.13	−.10	−.05	−.11	−.17
191.	quiet	−.09	−.14	−.05	−.14	−.30	−.25	.17	.18	.22	.15	.07	.14
192.	quitting	−.27	−.22	−.21	−.13	−.17	−.18	−.11	−.15	−.15	.04	−.07	−.15
193.	rational	.18	.26	.12	.10	−.10	.14	.23	.19	.02	.17	−.02	−.04
194.	rattle-brained	−.07	−.10	−.18	−.22	−.06	−.17	−.04	−.11	−.18	−.15	−.09	−.14
195.	realistic	.14	.22	.04	.09	.01	.18	.21	.14	.07	.16	−.04	.02
196.	reasonable	.20	.16	.17	.11	−.04	.10	.36	.30	.20	.13	.12	.16
197.	rebellious	−.12	−.20	−.22	−.05	−.09	−.09	−.28	−.40	−.26	−.29	−.24	−.24
198.	reckless	−.12	−.10	−.21	−.20	−.01	−.17	−.19	−.25	−.28	−.41	−.19	−.21
199.	reflective	−.09	.08	−.07	.09	−.12	−.07	.09	.08	−.03	.08	−.01	−.05
200.	relaxed	.01	.07	.06	−.06	−.02	.17	.21	.21	.13	.14	.01	.02
201.	reliable	.17	.22	.05	.00	.01	.07	.27	.35	.14	.11	.14	.17
202.	resentful	.03	−.19	−.18	−.12	−.10	−.11	−.16	−.38	−.18	−.19	−.17	−.26
203.	reserved	−.02	−.11	−.05	−.12	−.29	−.18	.16	.18	.12	.07	.08	.09
204.	resourceful	.28	.21	.07	.19	.21	.19	.12	.14	.01	−.06	−.02	−.07
205.	responsible	.21	.27	.05	.03	.02	.11	.24	.28	.08	.05	.10	.14
206.	restless	−.12	−.15	−.09	−.05	−.04	−.13	−.24	−.31	−.25	−.20	−.24	−.23
207.	retiring	−.11	−.25	−.08	−.14	−.28	−.20	−.02	.07	.00	−.01	.01	.07
208.	rigid	−.07	.05	−.06	−.22	−.12	−.08	−.19	−.09	−.10	−.12	−.10	−.07
209.	robust	.05	.07	.06	.06	.03	.09	.01	−.10	−.08	−.02	−.18	−.11
210.	rude	−.16	−.09	−.09	.01	−.04	−.01	−.24	−.36	−.13	−.02	−.23	−.15
211.	sarcastic	−.07	−.14	−.03	−.03	−.04	.02	−.15	−.42	−.15	−.20	−.24	−.16
212.	self-centered	.00	.09	−.18	−.08	.02	−.04	−.26	−.30	−.26	−.21	−.22	−.23
213.	self-confident	.18	.26	.19	.28	.20	.35	−.02	−.07	.01	.05	−.08	−.07
214.	self-controlled	.16	.16	.10	.11	−.09	−.02	.19	.25	.11	.09	.10	.10
215.	self-denying	−.01	.03	−.13	−.08	−.19	−.19	.10	.11	−.15	.05	.03	.04
216.	self-pitying	−.13	−.11	−.17	−.17	−.12	−.16	−.11	−.25	−.23	−.14	−.09	−.18
217.	self-punishing	.05	−.04	−.16	−.08	−.15	−.18	−.04	−.08	−.19	−.12	−.06	−.17
218.	self-seeking	.04	.00	−.02	.03	.12	.03	−.19	−.21	−.19	−.03	−.16	−.20
219.	selfish	.06	.04	.03	.00	.02	−.08	−.23	−.27	−.06	−.06	−.11	−.21
220.	sensitive	−.11	−.13	−.10	−.03	−.24	−.24	−.04	.02	−.03	.01	−.08	−.09

Correlations of Observers' Adjectival Description with Scales of the CPI continued

		Scale: Lp						Scale: Ami				
		By Peers		By Spouses		By Staff		By Peers		By Spouses		By Staff
Adjectives		M	F	M	F	M	F	M	F	M	F	M	F
221.	sentimental	−.02	.10	−.09	−.09	−.07	−.15	.13	.08	−.01	.09	−.07	−.03
222.	serious	.12	.00	.00	.00	−.18	.02	.11	.05	.02	.08	.00	.02
223.	severe	−.07	.03	−.07	−.04	−.10	−.07	−.24	−.11	−.18	−.05	−.17	−.12
224.	sexy	.05	.03	−.06	−.02	−.03	.01	.01	−.17	−.12	−.07	−.22	−.17
225.	shallow	−.22	.07	−.07	−.13	−.05	−.17	−.24	−.01	−.03	−.12	−.02	−.07
226.	sharp-witted	.10	−.12	.03	.07	.08	.04	.00	−.28	−.13	−.10	−.15	−.14
227.	shiftless	−.13	−.15	−.15	−.11	−.14	−.14	−.01	−.27	−.17	−.22	−.07	−.15
228.	show-off	−.02	.03	−.01	−.02	.06	.09	−.20	−.28	−.18	−.13	−.23	−.11
229.	shrewd	.11	−.09	−.10	.02	.17	.08	−.02	−.24	−.21	−.17	−.10	−.15
230.	shy	−.13	−.18	−.19	−.23	−.39	−.32	.17	.14	.03	.05	−.07	.02
231.	silent	−.15	−.10	−.19	−.11	−.34	−.24	.06	.12	.04	.01	−.08	.00
232.	simple	−.10	−.05	−.05	−.28	−.17	−.21	.06	.19	.09	−.14	.02	.03
233.	sincere	.08	.02	.07	.00	−.10	.00	.23	.28	.16	.18	.08	.09
234.	slipshod	−.03	−.17	−.14	−.08	−.02	−.08	−.11	−.23	−.15	−.13	−.08	−.11
235.	slow	−.18	−.11	−.20	−.16	−.17	−.18	−.05	.01	−.10	−.11	.04	.05
236.	sly	−.06	−.12	−.28	−.02	−.04	−.07	−.05	−.31	−.26	−.17	−.12	−.18
237.	smug	.00	.02	−.04	−.05	.05	.03	−.22	−.26	−.10	−.09	−.14	−.18
238.	snobbish	.00	.11	−.02	−.02	.03	.03	−.26	−.17	−.10	−.22	−.09	−.11
239.	sociable	.19	.17	.05	.08	.14	.14	.19	.08	.00	−.11	−.05	−.04
240.	soft-hearted	−.02	.07	−.10	−.21	−.11	−.15	.27	.30	−.04	−.03	.02	.02
241.	sophisticated	.11	.03	.11	.16	.05	.17	.03	−.11	.02	.01	−.11	−.07
242.	spendthrift	−.03	−.10	−.02	−.10	−.04	−.02	−.04	−.17	−.04	−.20	−.12	−.13
243.	spineless	−.14	−.19	.09	−.16	−.19	−.07	−.07	−.07	−.05	−.12	−.06	.01
244.	spontaneous	−.07	.11	.03	.03	.10	.05	−.02	−.09	−.09	−.10	−.11	−.15
245.	spunky	−.15	.07	−.12	.06	.08	.03	−.06	.01	−.17	−.11	−.16	−.19
246.	stable	.18	.23	.01	.02	.01	.23	.28	.20	.19	.05	.10	.16
247.	steady	.14	.14	−.02	−.01	−.05	.10	.29	.20	.11	.04	.05	.09
248.	stern	.08	.05	−.11	−.05	−.07	.05	−.16	−.12	−.16	.03	−.10	−.07
249.	stingy	−.09	−.03	−.15	−.06	−.08	.02	−.23	−.27	−.24	−.16	−.02	−.04
250.	stolid	.01	−.08	.00	.03	−.18	−.04	−.06	−.18	.00	.04	−.07	.03
251.	strong	.10	.17	.04	.10	−.01	.24	−.04	−.01	−.02	−.03	−.18	−.09
252.	stubborn	.02	.09	−.11	−.02	.02	.03	−.24	−.29	−.17	−.24	−.17	−.15
253.	submissive	−.13	−.10	−.15	−.17	−.18	−.24	.15	.23	−.16	−.02	.07	.15
254.	suggestible	−.06	.01	−.15	−.01	−.07	−.21	.25	.05	−.11	−.02	.03	.04
255.	sulky	−.13	−.24	−.10	−.14	−.16	−.16	−.17	−.33	−.17	−.13	−.11	−.25
256.	superstitious	−.02	−.10	−.25	−.15	−.04	−.22	.02	.00	−.28	−.26	−.09	−.28
257.	suspicious	−.12	−.16	−.22	−.13	−.18	−.13	−.29	−.23	−.22	−.28	−.23	−.24
258.	sympathetic	.05	.01	.02	−.04	−.08	−.10	.20	.21	.14	.12	.02	.05
259.	tactful	.12	.14	.21	.18	.06	.06	.22	.30	.16	.14	.16	.11
260.	tactless	−.06	−.08	−.12	−.08	−.05	−.02	−.17	−.17	−.15	.00	−.21	−.19
261.	talkative	.08	.10	.11	.02	.16	.15	.00	−.13	−.09	−.20	−.16	−.14
262.	temperamental	−.09	−.18	−.13	−.05	−.10	−.06	−.34	−.32	−.28	−.29	−.24	−.20
263.	tense	−.07	−.17	−.17	−.11	−.14	−.29	−.12	−.15	−.25	−.16	−.10	−.19
264.	thankless	−.12	−.20	−.11	.01	−.08	.01	−.25	−.33	−.18	−.04	−.21	−.07

Correlations of Observers' Adjectival Description with Scales of the CPI continued

		Scale: Lp						Scale: Ami					
		By Peers		By Spouses		By Staff		By Peers		By Spouses		By Staff	
Adjectives		M	F	M	F	M	F	M	F	M	F	M	F
265.	thorough	.23	.20	.01	.12	.08	.18	.16	.07	−.02	.14	.18	.08
266.	thoughtful	.14	.12	.02	−.02	−.07	.06	.37	.24	.12	.21	.06	.10
267.	thrifty	.08	.06	−.04	.03	−.16	−.02	.04	.06	.05	.11	−.01	.06
268.	timid	−.16	−.22	−.10	−.18	−.30	−.30	.05	.07	−.02	−.08	−.04	.00
269.	tolerant	.03	.08	.11	.00	−.09	.02	.23	.25	.13	.13	.08	.05
270.	touchy	−.07	−.09	−.19	−.13	−.12	−.17	−.19	−.29	−.10	−.31	−.15	−.23
271.	tough	.03	.00	−.11	−.02	.00	.15	−.16	−.30	−.12	−.09	−.24	−.16
272.	trusting	.09	.09	.10	.03	−.13	−.05	.28	.34	.08	.16	.07	.09
273.	unaffected	−.08	−.06	.00	.00	−.08	−.09	.11	.21	.02	−.15	.16	.13
274.	unambitious	−.12	−.16	−.23	−.15	−.25	−.27	−.06	−.08	−.15	−.03	−.02	.00
275.	unassuming	−.17	−.07	−.02	.00	−.22	−.22	.13	.23	.01	.07	.16	.13
276.	unconventional	−.04	−.23	−.12	−.06	−.12	−.07	−.07	−.35	−.11	−.22	−.17	−.18
277.	undependable	−.12	−.14	−.01	−.10	.00	−.10	−.24	−.30	−.06	−.17	−.05	−.15
278.	understanding	.11	.11	.03	.11	−.10	.02	.26	.30	.11	.22	−.03	.04
279.	unemotional	−.03	−.14	.07	−.07	−.25	−.05	−.03	−.07	.13	−.02	−.12	.03
280.	unexcitable	−.13	−.12	−.10	−.06	−.12	−.04	.07	.02	−.03	−.01	.02	.08
281.	unfriendly	−.08	−.05	−.18	.03	−.09	−.01	−.25	−.25	−.18	−.08	−.06	−.06
282.	uninhibited	.04	−.12	−.02	.11	.11	.02	−.03	−.22	.03	−.07	−.15	−.20
283.	unintelligent	.00	−.06	.00	−.02	−.08	−.09	.05	−.05	.00	.00	.01	.05
284.	unkind	−.15	−.12	−.07	.01	−.08	.05	.00	−.27	−.03	−.09	−.14	−.19
285.	unrealistic	−.11	−.05	−.03	−.14	−.14	−.19	−.18	−.22	−.14	−.27	−.11	−.18
286.	unscrupulous	−.08	−.14	−.31	.00	−.04	−.04	−.20	−.21	−.21	−.07	−.05	−.14
287.	unselfish	.13	−.01	−.08	−.04	−.06	−.11	.31	.26	.02	.06	.01	.07
288.	unstable	−.08	−.27	−.29	−.09	−.11	−.26	−.18	−.23	−.21	−.20	−.06	−.15
289.	vindictive	.03	.04	−.09	−.13	−.06	−.02	−.13	−.21	−.18	−.23	−.16	−.18
290.	versatile	.14	.09	.01	.09	.14	.13	.11	−.13	−.06	.08	−.06	−.15
291.	warm	.01	.08	−.02	−.05	.05	.03	.27	.32	.07	.17	−.01	.05
292.	wary	−.01	−.04	−.08	−.05	−.19	−.15	−.27	−.09	−.09	−.10	−.18	−.13
293.	weak	−.13	−.13	−.24	−.16	−.17	−.24	.02	.10	−.25	−.15	−.07	−.04
294.	whiny	−.21	−.10	−.14	−.16	.00	−.12	−.14	−.13	−.20	−.33	−.03	−.07
295.	wholesome	.01	.14	.02	.07	.02	.15	.21	.22	.01	.11	.09	.09
296.	wise	.21	.20	.13	.02	−.03	.12	.15	.10	.18	.05	.00	−.02
297.	withdrawn	−.12	−.26	−.27	−.16	−.36	−.27	.07	.05	−.29	−.08	−.12	−.06
298.	witty	.00	−.04	.01	.02	.03	.08	−.06	−.26	−.06	−.01	−.14	−.13
299.	worrying	−.15	−.08	−.32	−.14	−.25	−.22	−.13	.00	−.25	−.20	−.13	−.10
300.	zany	−.10	−.03	−.12	.01	−.03	−.05	−.09	−.09	−.15	−.14	−.15	−.14

CPI MANUAL

Correlations of Observers' Adjectival Description with Scales of the CPI continued

| | | Scale: Leo | | | | | | Scale: Tm | | | | | |
| | | By Peers | | By Spouses | | By Staff | | By Peers | | By Spouses | | By Staff | |
Adjectives		M	F	M	F	M	F	M	F	M	F	M	F
001.	absent-minded	−.16	−.15	−.21	−.10	−.12	−.17	−.20	−.27	−.09	−.03	−.19	−.10
002.	active	.29	.14	−.07	.03	.01	.06	.13	.12	−.05	.12	.08	.11
003.	adaptable	.06	.11	.07	−.01	.02	.05	.10	.05	.03	.05	.06	.04
004.	adventurous	.07	−.07	−.08	−.12	−.06	−.10	.04	−.09	−.06	.02	−.01	−.05
005.	affected	.12	.08	.04	.00	−.03	−.06	−.05	.12	.10	.03	.04	.04
006.	affectionate	−.09	−.02	−.05	.00	−.04	.05	−.10	−.14	−.13	.01	−.12	−.12
007.	aggressive	.18	.04	.05	−.07	.10	.02	.17	.11	.08	.05	.17	.16
008.	alert	.27	.02	.02	.04	−.04	.09	.26	.16	.16	.11	.09	.10
009.	aloof	−.02	−.18	−.12	−.16	−.16	−.04	.08	−.02	.02	−.10	−.09	.06
010.	ambitious	.22	.10	.10	.13	.13	.07	.22	.22	.22	.14	.23	.21
011.	anxious	−.04	.02	−.02	−.14	−.11	−.21	−.16	−.04	−.01	−.09	−.16	−.23
012.	apathetic	−.22	−.12	−.09	.06	−.05	−.05	−.13	−.12	−.11	−.02	−.18	−.12
013.	appreciative	−.01	.08	−.01	−.05	−.13	.07	−.07	.03	−.03	−.02	−.07	−.02
014.	argumentative	.01	−.07	.03	−.09	−.01	−.06	.07	.10	.06	.02	.16	.15
015.	arrogant	.04	.01	−.05	.03	−.06	−.03	.08	.04	−.02	.02	.08	.08
016.	artistic	−.21	−.22	−.11	−.09	−.28	−.18	−.16	−.10	−.04	−.01	−.07	−.07
017.	assertive	.13	.04	−.03	−.01	.04	.04	.17	.12	.15	.29	.18	.18
018.	attractive	.05	.03	.03	−.04	−.02	.15	.03	.03	.02	.00	−.06	.04
019.	autocratic	.02	−.07	−.10	−.05	.01	−.05	.04	.00	.09	.01	.09	.11
020.	awkward	−.16	−.09	−.16	−.09	−.09	−.20	−.25	−.10	−.21	−.12	−.28	−.16
021.	bitter	−.10	−.13	−.18	−.21	−.07	−.10	−.05	−.12	−.14	−.19	−.07	−.07
022.	blustery	−.09	−.17	.00	−.12	.03	−.08	−.03	−.10	−.04	−.14	.04	−.01
023.	boastful	.12	.10	−.02	−.09	.03	−.01	−.01	.13	−.08	−.07	.09	.06
024.	bossy	.05	.06	−.07	.00	.06	.02	.01	.13	−.09	−.04	.10	.13
025.	calm	−.01	.06	−.02	.06	−.01	.14	−.02	.18	−.08	.00	−.09	.13
026.	capable	.19	.09	.00	.21	−.06	.14	.24	.21	.12	.22	.03	.22
027.	careless	−.24	−.22	−.18	−.07	−.10	−.20	−.19	−.21	−.13	−.11	−.09	−.09
028.	cautious	.02	.14	−.01	.00	.00	.03	−.16	.06	−.09	.01	−.16	−.07
029.	changeable	−.14	−.15	−.07	−.11	−.08	−.22	−.12	−.15	−.13	−.08	−.10	−.22
030.	charming	−.06	.05	−.02	.00	−.19	.06	−.05	.01	−.07	.01	−.03	.04
031.	cheerful	−.02	.11	.06	.06	.01	.16	−.08	.04	.04	−.05	.01	.03
032.	civilized	.02	.01	.08	.07	−.21	.12	.10	.09	.02	−.06	−.07	.15
033.	clear-thinking	.22	.08	.10	.12	−.11	.06	.30	.20	.09	.22	.03	.19
034.	clever	.04	−.10	−.07	.04	−.16	−.07	.20	−.04	−.01	.10	.03	.05
035.	coarse	−.07	−.10	−.16	−.13	.01	−.11	−.03	−.05	−.10	.02	−.01	−.01
036.	cold	−.08	−.02	−.01	−.03	.00	−.08	−.05	.04	.01	−.08	.00	.04
037.	commonplace	−.11	.11	.02	.03	.09	.07	−.19	.04	.03	−.09	−.10	−.06
038.	complaining	−.17	−.15	−.12	−.16	−.09	−.05	−.17	−.11	−.20	−.16	−.04	−.01
039.	complicated	−.07	−.23	−.08	−.17	−.27	−.24	−.09	−.14	.13	.01	−.12	−.06
040.	conceited	−.01	.14	.00	.01	−.01	−.05	.04	.16	−.06	.02	.15	.06
041.	confident	.20	.18	.13	.11	.01	.17	.29	.28	.16	.26	.15	.23
042.	confused	−.07	−.14	−.27	−.13	−.04	−.20	−.24	−.29	−.20	−.18	−.18	−.23
043.	conscientious	.13	.17	.11	.05	.04	.19	.04	.21	.18	.15	−.04	.09
044.	conservative	.06	.23	.26	.06	.26	.31	.07	.19	.12	−.08	−.01	.06

Correlations of Observers' Adjectival Description with Scales of the CPI continued

		Scale: Leo						Scale: Tm				
		By Peers		By Spouses		By Staff		By Peers		By Spouses		By Staff
Adjectives		M	F	M	F	M	F	M	F	M	F	M	F
045.	considerate	.07	.08	.09	−.09	−.08	.04	−.01	.01	−.03	−.10	−.15	−.03
046.	contented	.02	.01	.13	.01	.10	.22	.04	.09	.10	.00	−.05	.07
047.	conventional	.07	.23	.13	.06	.21	.29	−.01	.13	.16	−.02	−.03	.01
048.	cool	−.06	−.07	−.02	−.05	.00	−.02	.02	−.03	.00	.03	.03	.09
049.	cooperative	.03	.13	.09	.11	−.03	.10	−.07	.06	.04	.07	−.07	−.04
050.	courageous	.07	.04	.09	.06	−.01	−.01	.07	.02	.11	.04	.03	.05
051.	cowardly	−.11	−.05	−.06	.10	−.04	.00	−.19	−.10	−.04	.00	−.05	.03
052.	cruel	−.10	.10	−.04	−.07	−.08	−.11	−.07	.03	−.04	.01	.00	−.06
053.	curious	−.12	−.14	−.15	−.10	−.25	−.16	−.04	−.15	.02	.07	−.04	.01
054.	cynical	−.01	−.10	−.13	−.14	−.14	−.16	.05	−.08	.03	−.01	−.04	.01
055.	daring	.06	−.08	.01	.02	.01	−.08	.07	−.02	−.08	−.07	.00	−.05
056.	deceitful	.02	.01	−.09	−.07	.01	−.09	.00	.03	−.06	−.08	.06	−.10
057.	defensive	−.15	−.09	−.05	−.10	.00	−.04	−.19	−.14	−.07	−.13	−.06	−.02
058.	deliberate	.21	.12	−.09	.04	−.01	.09	.13	.08	.09	−.04	−.11	.15
059.	demanding	.08	.08	.01	−.11	.00	−.02	.13	.08	.04	−.08	.09	.07
060.	dependable	.24	.15	.03	.10	.01	.20	.17	.17	.11	.06	−.01	.12
061.	dependent	−.18	.00	.03	.01	.00	−.01	−.15	−.01	−.02	−.15	−.19	−.23
062.	despondent	−.10	−.14	−.13	−.06	−.10	−.15	−.06	−.21	−.04	.04	−.16	−.21
063.	determined	.24	.14	.13	.17	.01	.10	.25	.21	.09	.15	.10	.16
064.	dignified	.05	.07	.11	.10	−.07	.09	.04	.10	.00	.06	.04	.15
065.	discreet	−.05	.10	−.08	.07	−.08	.08	.02	.10	.04	.03	−.04	.09
066.	disorderly	−.26	−.21	−.17	−.08	−.10	−.31	−.17	−.26	−.14	−.07	−.06	−.21
067.	dissatisfied	−.16	−.13	−.22	−.11	−.12	−.22	−.18	−.06	−.16	−.16	−.10	−.13
068.	distractible	−.21	−.01	−.16	−.04	−.11	−.19	−.23	−.11	−.19	−.20	−.21	−.21
069.	distrustful	−.14	−.03	−.01	.01	−.03	−.11	−.06	−.12	−.03	−.14	.00	−.05
070.	dominant	.17	.11	.08	−.05	−.02	.08	.22	.20	.14	−.03	.12	.20
071.	dreamy	−.15	−.07	−.06	−.08	−.11	−.18	−.22	−.21	−.15	−.10	−.20	−.14
072.	dull	−.18	.07	−.02	−.03	.02	.03	−.13	−.01	−.08	−.01	−.12	−.06
073.	easygoing	−.13	−.07	−.03	.03	−.05	.03	−.11	−.08	−.19	.03	−.20	−.07
074.	effeminate	−.13	−.01	−.03	−.09	−.06	.12	−.06	.05	.01	.05	−.04	.03
075.	efficient	.18	.18	.14	.04	.05	.19	.22	.30	.13	.08	.21	.21
076.	egotistical	.15	.06	.00	−.01	−.04	−.03	.16	.09	.01	.09	.11	.14
077.	emotional	−.04	−.11	−.08	−.09	−.13	−.13	−.18	−.15	−.20	−.17	−.09	−.16
078.	energetic	.20	.17	.09	.12	.04	.11	.09	.08	.14	.16	.16	.12
079.	enterprising	.15	.07	.00	.10	.04	.11	.26	.18	.06	.19	.14	.16
080.	enthusiastic	.13	.15	.07	.11	−.02	.06	.05	−.03	.03	.12	.03	.03
081.	evasive	−.06	−.09	−.04	−.01	−.05	−.08	.00	−.11	.03	−.16	−.13	−.04
082.	excitable	.00	.01	−.06	−.06	−.04	−.04	−.07	−.03	−.10	−.12	−.02	−.07
083.	fair-minded	.12	.07	−.04	.04	−.09	.00	.05	.01	.01	.09	−.09	.05
084.	fault-finding	−.02	−.04	.00	−.05	−.06	−.06	.01	.05	.08	−.13	.04	.09
085.	fearful	−.08	.00	−.02	−.15	−.13	−.18	−.13	−.12	−.11	−.10	−.18	−.19
086.	feminine	−.16	.00	.05	−.05	−.15	.13	−.14	−.03	−.04	−.09	−.12	−.03
087.	fickle	−.29	.05	.03	−.07	−.14	−.06	−.24	.03	−.02	−.17	−.01	−.08
088.	flirtatious	−.07	.02	−.06	.02	−.12	−.06	−.04	.03	−.17	−.10	−.01	−.09

Correlations of Observers' Adjectival Description with Scales of the CPI continued

		Scale: Leo						Scale: Tm				
		By Peers		By Spouses		By Staff		By Peers		By Spouses		By Staff	
Adjectives		M	F	M	F	M	F	M	F	M	F	M	F
089.	foolish	−.09	−.01	−.01	−.13	.03	−.03	−.11	−.23	−.09	−.21	−.01	−.13
090.	forceful	.25	.12	−.04	−.02	.02	.07	.18	.15	.10	.07	.11	.24
091.	foresighted	.11	.09	.05	.05	−.05	.10	.20	.25	.15	.08	.10	.19
092.	forgetful	−.18	−.21	−.07	−.06	−.18	−.10	−.15	−.27	−.02	.01	−.12	−.07
093.	forgiving	.03	.02	.00	.05	−.02	.03	.04	−.09	−.07	−.09	−.17	−.14
094.	formal	.15	.11	.00	.07	.01	.14	.16	.18	.04	.04	.05	.10
095.	frank	.01	−.01	−.05	−.06	−.06	−.02	.06	.01	.02	.02	−.03	.09
096.	friendly	−.02	.14	.00	.05	−.01	.10	−.05	.02	−.01	−.03	−.03	.04
097.	frivolous	−.04	.06	−.02	−.03	−.02	.02	−.14	−.01	−.02	−.09	−.05	−.08
098.	fussy	−.19	.00	−.04	−.09	−.03	−.01	−.13	.05	−.09	−.16	−.02	.02
099.	generous	−.09	.02	−.00	−.01	−.03	.02	−.07	−.13	−.10	−.07	−.10	−.05
100.	gentle	−.07	.01	.09	.01	−.15	.03	−.01	−.13	−.01	−.11	−.25	−.13
101.	gloomy	−.13	−.07	−.11	−.05	−.11	−.12	−.16	−.19	−.19	.00	−.09	−.06
102.	good-looking	.09	.07	.03	.03	−.01	.14	.09	.06	.02	−.04	−.04	.04
103.	good-natured	.01	.08	.11	.15	−.03	.06	.01	−.03	.01	.03	−.15	−.03
104.	greedy	−.07	.00	−.02	−.07	−.09	−.13	−.02	−.01	.01	−.06	.01	−.04
105.	handsome	.11	−.08	.02	−.02	.00	.08	.09	.01	.01	.04	−.07	.14
106.	hard-headed	.14	.02	.00	−.05	.01	−.03	.20	.06	.06	−.14	.17	.14
107.	hard-hearted	−.01	.11	−.01	−.08	.02	.00	−.04	.12	.04	−.09	.06	.05
108.	hasty	−.05	−.14	−.10	−.09	−.01	−.08	−.22	−.14	−.11	−.14	.04	−.10
109.	headstrong	.05	.02	.11	−.09	−.05	−.05	.00	.04	.06	−.08	.06	.07
110.	healthy	.05	.12	.13	.08	.08	.17	.01	.08	.06	.10	−.04	.12
111.	helpful	.07	.13	−.02	.06	.00	.16	.03	.03	.04	.08	−.09	−.03
112.	high-strung	−.05	−.01	−.09	−.06	−.14	−.17	−.11	−.05	−.09	−.06	−.05	−.13
113.	honest	.08	−.02	−.04	.07	−.04	.10	.03	−.04	−.02	.05	−.07	.08
114.	hostile	.01	−.03	.03	−.03	−.02	−.09	.00	−.02	−.05	−.02	.04	.01
115.	humorous	−.09	−.09	−.03	.01	−.06	−.02	−.04	−.15	−.07	.09	−.07	.01
116.	hurried	−.03	−.05	.04	−.06	−.14	−.05	−.16	−.13	.09	.00	.01	−.04
117.	idealistic	.03	.13	−.03	−.05	−.12	−.09	.07	.06	.07	.06	−.06	−.09
118.	imaginative	−.10	−.19	−.08	−.05	−.24	−.20	−.04	−.05	−.05	.15	.01	−.04
119.	immature	−.11	−.04	−.13	−.07	.06	−.08	−.14	−.22	−.09	−.12	−.07	−.22
120.	impatient	−.02	−.15	−.02	−.14	−.02	−.15	−.02	−.03	.07	−.07	.07	.00
121.	impulsive	−.07	−.16	−.10	−.17	−.05	−.16	−.11	−.19	−.12	−.15	.01	−.16
122.	independent	.09	.02	.16	.07	−.11	−.08	.26	.12	.16	.16	.07	.15
123.	indifferent	−.17	−.15	.03	−.03	−.06	−.08	−.10	−.08	.06	.00	−.11	−.04
124.	individualistic	−.06	−.19	−.10	−.07	−.19	−.19	.06	.00	.04	.17	.00	.03
125.	industrious	.16	.20	.07	.04	.08	.23	.13	.18	.15	.12	.10	.27
126.	infantile	−.10	−.03	−.01	−.07	−.02	−.09	−.19	−.10	.02	−.20	−.08	−.19
127.	informal	.02	−.12	−.11	.01	−.10	−.14	−.05	−.16	−.03	.04	−.15	−.11
128.	ingenious	.11	−.13	−.10	−.02	−.15	−.12	.10	−.01	.04	.06	.11	.00
129.	inhibited	.05	.15	−.08	−.11	−.01	−.02	−.03	.10	−.02	−.04	−.17	−.11
130.	initiative	.13	.15	.00	.02	.04	.08	.12	.18	.19	.11	.19	.17
131.	insightful	.07	.02	−.07	−.04	−.19	−.12	.08	.08	.02	.08	.03	.07
132.	intelligent	.06	.00	−.06	−.03	−.17	−.06	.19	.18	.09	.12	.04	.19

Correlations of Observers' Adjectival Description with Scales of the CPI continued

		Scale: Leo						Scale: Tm				
		By Peers		By Spouses		By Staff		By Peers		By Spouses		By Staff
Adjectives		M	F	M	F	M	F	M	F	M	F	M	F
133.	interests—narrow	−.10	.08	.07	−.01	.13	.14	−.12	−.01	.11	−.21	−.10	−.11
134.	interests—wide	.01	−.05	.01	−.06	−.22	−.15	.05	.02	−.01	.11	.02	.07
135.	intolerant	.02	.01	−.10	−.04	−.03	.03	.04	.18	−.04	−.18	.03	.01
136.	inventive	.06	−.13	−.04	−.01	−.22	−.09	.12	−.01	.06	.08	.02	.01
137.	irresponsible	−.20	−.27	−.04	−.07	−.07	−.24	−.13	−.23	.00	−.15	−.04	−.19
138.	irritable	.04	−.11	−.12	−.15	−.08	−.05	−.08	−.03	−.02	−.10	.02	.08
139.	jolly	−.03	.09	−.01	.02	.06	−.01	−.02	−.01	−.16	−.05	−.02	−.04
140.	kind	.07	.06	.04	.08	−.09	.09	−.07	−.08	−.07	.04	−.23	−.08
141.	lazy	−.23	−.17	−.05	−.16	−.03	−.19	−.05	−.18	−.05	−.08	−.11	−.16
142.	leisurely	−.18	−.11	−.01	−.07	−.01	−.06	−.09	−.02	−.08	−.08	−.13	−.04
143.	logical	.08	.10	−.03	.02	−.06	.03	.29	.26	.03	.04	.06	.25
144.	loud	.03	−.03	.05	−.04	.03	−.01	.00	−.06	−.05	−.08	.03	.08
145.	loyal	.06	.08	−.12	−.05	.12	.14	.01	.01	−.14	−.13	−.09	−.02
146.	mannerly	.08	.10	.11	.10	−.03	.13	.05	.12	.06	.19	−.14	.08
147.	masculine	.22	−.04	.05	−.03	.08	−.06	.14	.06	.00	.03	.00	.10
148.	mature	.20	.06	.07	.15	−.03	.16	.21	.21	.07	.13	.03	.21
149.	meek	−.16	−.04	.04	−.06	−.07	−.06	−.21	−.12	−.12	−.11	−.23	−.17
150.	methodical	.09	.03	.01	−.05	.01	.19	.05	.08	.08	.22	.01	.21
151.	mild	−.05	.03	−.03	−.03	−.06	.01	−.14	−.05	−.10	−.04	−.20	−.10
152.	mischievous	−.15	−.14	−.15	−.13	−.08	−.15	−.13	−.10	−.13	−.14	−.05	−.12
153.	moderate	.04	.09	.07	.13	.09	.18	.10	.11	.09	.12	−.11	.12
154.	modest	−.01	−.01	.01	.02	−.02	.03	.04	−.01	.07	−.09	−.19	−.08
155.	moody	−.02	−.16	−.11	−.16	−.11	−.26	−.11	−.18	−.09	−.17	−.12	−.13
156.	nagging	−.06	.01	−.06	−.10	−.10	−.01	−.10	.06	−.13	−.10	−.06	−.04
157.	natural	−.03	−.06	−.10	−.03	.06	.04	.02	−.16	−.07	.00	.00	.05
158.	nervous	−.20	−.07	.00	−.09	−.10	−.15	−.22	−.13	−.10	−.13	−.12	−.21
159.	noisy	−.02	−.05	.10	−.10	.06	−.02	−.06	−.05	−.01	−.15	.02	−.02
160.	obliging	−.13	.22	−.05	.07	−.09	.02	−.02	.04	−.04	−.05	−.10	−.10
161.	obnoxious	.05	.03	.05	−.14	−.02	−.08	.02	−.04	.02	−.05	.00	−.06
162.	opinionated	.11	.02	−.04	−.17	.00	.02	.07	.08	.03	−.12	.10	.09
163.	opportunistic	.13	.04	−.04	−.05	.06	−.03	.09	.03	.04	.01	.12	.04
164.	optimistic	.09	.19	.14	.06	.04	.20	.19	.07	.07	.17	.03	.04
165.	organized	.21	.20	.13	.11	.07	.26	.21	.25	.12	.14	.21	.26
166.	original	.01	−.20	−.08	−.10	−.30	−.25	.11	−.01	−.01	.00	.00	−.05
167.	outgoing	.11	.10	.06	−.01	.09	.08	.08	.06	.00	.11	.10	.08
168.	outspoken	.12	−.03	−.04	.00	.00	.03	.08	.10	−.02	.06	.12	.13
169.	painstaking	.07	.12	.02	−.07	−.04	.05	.08	.09	.02	.04	−.05	.04
170.	patient	.09	.15	−.01	.06	−.06	.09	−.03	.07	.01	−.07	−.14	.03
171.	peaceable	−.08	.10	−.03	−.03	−.03	.10	−.12	.04	−.07	−.10	−.18	−.01
172.	peculiar	−.05	−.11	.02	−.12	−.10	−.17	−.16	−.12	−.04	−.11	−.13	−.03
173.	persevering	.14	.13	−.11	.02	.07	.06	.19	.15	−.03	.13	.10	.07
174.	persistent	.08	.15	.04	.06	.04	.03	.11	.17	.05	.17	.05	.16
175.	pessimistic	−.14	−.23	−.09	−.15	−.19	−.23	−.09	−.22	.06	−.15	−.15	−.13
176.	planful	.15	.18	.06	.11	.00	.20	.09	.24	.02	.02	.10	.18

Correlations of Observers' Adjectival Description with Scales of the CPI continued

	Scale: Leo						Scale: Tm					
	By Peers		By Spouses		By Staff		By Peers		By Spouses		By Staff	
Adjectives	M	F	M	F	M	F	M	F	M	F	M	F
177. pleasant	−.01	.12	.11	.02	−.08	.14	.03	−.01	−.01	.04	−.08	.02
178. pleasure-seeking	−.07	−.08	−.11	−.08	−.03	−.10	.01	−.01	−.12	−.08	−.02	−.12
179. poised	.09	.09	.08	.03	−.01	.20	.14	.14	.12	.10	.13	.24
180. polished	.13	.10	.08	.04	−.07	.15	.05	.15	.04	.13	.10	.18
181. practical	.17	.08	.09	.12	.17	.23	.27	.11	.10	.04	.05	.13
182. praising	.02	.16	−.03	.09	−.05	.14	−.03	.00	−.06	−.01	.03	−.02
183. precise	.11	.09	.09	−.01	−.08	.06	.26	.12	.13	.14	−.01	.18
184. prejudiced	−.10	.08	.06	−.01	.06	−.01	−.02	.12	−.07	−.15	.02	−.07
185. preoccupied	−.04	−.11	.03	−.13	−.16	−.16	−.07	−.11	.04	−.05	−.18	−.13
186. progressive	.05	−.05	−.04	−.02	−.15	−.11	.10	−.02	−.03	.08	−.04	.02
187. prudish	−.04	.19	−.12	−.06	.06	.16	−.04	.18	−.08	−.13	−.05	.00
188. quarrelsome	.03	−.04	−.08	−.11	−.02	−.07	.04	−.03	−.11	−.15	.06	.04
189. queer	−.13	−.08	−.08	.00	−.07	−.11	−.21	−.08	−.03	.00	−.07	.01
190. quick	−.02	.11	−.08	.06	−.08	−.03	.07	.12	.06	.11	.08	.04
191. quiet	−.03	−.02	.06	.02	−.10	−.01	−.11	.01	−.01	−.05	−.21	−.11
192. quitting	−.10	−.10	−.19	−.03	−.09	−.07	−.29	−.17	−.14	−.10	−.08	−.10
193. rational	.09	.15	−.05	−.02	−.09	.06	.21	.28	.07	.12	−.07	.20
194. rattle-brained	−.07	−.05	−.12	−.06	−.01	−.13	−.20	−.19	−.18	−.24	−.09	−.18
195. realistic	.19	.11	−.01	.04	.00	.18	.24	.26	.00	.13	.02	.21
196. reasonable	.17	.15	.12	.06	−.04	.09	.21	.17	.10	.13	−.07	.12
197. rebellious	−.03	−.20	−.17	−.14	−.16	−.20	−.13	−.19	−.16	−.05	−.04	−.12
198. reckless	−.12	−.15	−.15	−.21	−.05	−.16	−.11	−.11	−.11	−.16	−.02	−.12
199. reflective	−.11	−.04	−.15	−.16	−.22	−.09	−.07	.03	−.07	.06	−.10	.00
200. relaxed	−.06	.04	.06	.00	−.03	.10	.03	.08	−.04	−.02	−.05	.15
201. reliable	.21	.20	.05	.04	.01	.15	.15	.24	.06	.06	−.02	.14
202. resentful	.02	−.15	−.09	−.18	−.07	−.07	.07	−.09	−.04	−.12	−.04	−.03
203. reserved	−.04	.01	.04	.06	−.10	−.01	−.03	.04	−.01	−.09	−.19	−.03
204. resourceful	.20	.14	−.01	−.01	−.05	−.03	.22	.17	.05	.18	.15	.13
205. responsible	.27	.23	.08	.01	−.01	.17	.18	.30	.05	.08	.01	.17
206. restless	−.09	−.12	.01	−.04	−.13	−.19	−.14	−.20	−.05	−.10	−.03	−.12
207. retiring	−.06	−.03	−.06	−.06	−.08	−.06	−.11	−.15	−.03	−.03	−.19	−.09
208. rigid	.01	.09	−.01	−.10	.06	.07	.01	.17	.08	−.13	−.03	.07
209. robust	.10	.06	−.01	.00	.04	.02	.05	.04	.02	−.04	−.01	.04
210. rude	−.10	−.10	−.04	−.02	−.02	−.06	−.12	−.03	.03	.04	.01	.00
211. sarcastic	−.09	−.17	−.02	−.10	−.09	−.11	.04	−.07	.01	−.03	−.03	.03
212. self-centered	−.02	.08	−.01	−.15	−.01	−.11	.06	.11	−.07	−.05	.03	−.04
213. self-confident	.11	.14	.17	.18	.01	.17	.20	.21	.19	.24	.13	.26
214. self-controlled	.04	.12	.06	.04	−.01	.10	.21	.16	.07	.15	−.04	.08
215. self-denying	.13	−.04	−.02	−.03	−.01	.06	−.01	.00	−.05	−.11	−.11	−.10
216. self-pitying	−.08	−.11	−.13	−.09	−.12	−.10	−.20	−.12	−.19	−.19	−.10	−.13
217. self-punishing	.03	−.04	−.19	−.13	−.05	−.11	−.06	−.06	−.10	−.11	−.10	−.10
218. self-seeking	.01	−.02	−.01	−.12	.04	.00	.04	−.02	−.03	.01	.10	−.02
219. selfish	.02	.09	.03	−.01	.02	−.08	.07	.06	.04	−.01	.02	−.04
220. sensitive	−.01	−.10	−.06	−.03	−.27	−.12	−.24	−.20	−.22	−.02	−.22	−.19

		Scale: Leo						Scale: Tm				
		By Peers		By Spouses		By Staff		By Peers		By Spouses		By Staff	
Adjectives		M	F	M	F	M	F	M	F	M	F	M	F
221.	sentimental	−.04	.09	−.02	−.02	−.04	−.02	−.14	−.01	−.12	−.05	−.14	−.14
222.	serious	.22	.02	−.03	−.07	−.07	.03	.08	.09	−.04	.01	−.13	.12
223.	severe	.04	.06	−.07	.00	−.01	.00	.02	.10	.02	−.09	−.01	.04
224.	sexy	−.03	−.17	−.02	.01	−.09	.01	.03	−.01	−.13	−.05	−.07	−.04
225.	shallow	−.18	.02	.00	−.01	.14	.07	−.23	.07	.03	−.16	−.01	−.11
226.	sharp-witted	.00	−.14	−.09	−.14	−.11	−.08	.15	−.07	.03	.06	.04	.01
227.	shiftless	−.01	−.08	−.09	−.09	−.10	−.09	−.19	−.08	−.11	−.15	−.09	−.02
228.	show-off	−.04	−.08	−.04	−.07	−.02	−.02	−.01	−.03	−.13	−.12	.03	.02
229.	shrewd	.07	−.08	−.11	−.02	.00	−.03	.22	−.05	−.07	−.06	.18	.09
230.	shy	.01	.03	−.12	−.03	−.11	−.05	−.07	−.07	−.18	−.23	−.29	−.20
231.	silent	−.09	.03	−.01	.07	−.12	.00	−.11	.00	−.15	−.10	−.23	−.13
232.	simple	−.04	.13	−.01	−.06	.09	.05	−.10	−.01	−.08	−.26	−.12	−.16
233.	sincere	.11	.03	−.01	.07	−.06	.12	−.04	−.06	.00	.05	−.12	.09
234.	slipshod	−.09	−.11	−.10	−.15	.00	−.08	.02	−.13	−.02	−.06	−.01	−.06
235.	slow	−.15	−.03	−.12	−.03	−.02	−.02	−.22	−.06	−.24	−.10	−.14	−.09
236.	sly	−.05	−.08	−.07	.00	−.10	−.14	.06	−.07	−.14	.02	−.04	−.09
237.	smug	.04	.04	−.06	.00	−.02	−.05	.12	.10	.05	−.05	.06	.07
238.	snobbish	−.04	.12	−.07	−.09	−.02	−.05	.10	.13	.01	−.02	.05	.04
239.	sociable	.07	.10	.07	−.07	.01	.12	.05	.02	−.04	−.01	.03	.04
240.	soft-hearted	−.04	.03	.02	−.10	−.04	.03	−.13	−.09	−.22	−.22	−.16	−.15
241.	sophisticated	−.07	−.03	.01	.01	−.19	.00	.17	.04	.02	.16	.02	.14
242.	spendthrift	−.05	−.15	−.13	−.01	−.07	−.09	.04	−.12	−.06	−.09	−.02	−.05
243.	spineless	−.13	−.07	.00	−.11	−.07	−.02	−.19	−.16	.03	−.07	−.13	−.05
244.	spontaneous	−.03	−.02	.00	−.12	−.06	−.04	−.09	−.04	−.02	.09	.02	−.03
245.	spunky	−.04	.06	−.05	−.09	−.01	−.05	−.12	−.02	−.12	.03	.03	−.01
246.	stable	.11	.07	.02	.04	.07	.27	.14	.25	.04	.07	.03	.23
247.	steady	.11	.17	−.03	.05	.14	.18	.16	.18	−.01	.06	−.01	.12
248.	stern	.15	.12	−.04	.02	.06	.09	.09	.15	.00	−.04	.01	.16
249.	stingy	−.08	−.03	−.08	−.11	−.02	.04	−.08	.05	−.10	−.10	−.01	.06
250.	stolid	.07	.06	−.04	−.07	.05	.10	.04	.00	.04	.01	−.11	.05
251.	strong	.17	.18	.06	.09	.05	.12	.10	.21	.07	.13	−.02	.25
252.	stubborn	.09	.09	−.03	−.06	−.01	−.04	.08	.10	−.07	−.06	.10	.10
253.	submissive	−.19	.00	−.10	−.10	.05	.00	−.16	−.08	−.16	−.13	−.16	−.18
254.	suggestible	−.09	−.02	−.08	.00	.00	−.04	−.16	.05	−.10	−.04	−.10	−.23
255.	sulky	−.01	−.08	−.16	−.13	−.02	−.09	−.14	−.16	−.11	−.17	−.07	−.11
256.	superstitious	−.06	−.06	−.10	−.15	.02	−.03	−.12	−.08	−.11	−.15	−.03	−.19
257.	suspicious	−.04	−.12	−.08	.04	−.07	−.05	−.09	−.13	−.07	−.09	−.07	−.04
258.	sympathetic	−.04	.04	−.03	−.02	−.08	.07	−.07	−.08	−.10	−.02	−.14	−.06
259.	tactful	.03	.02	.14	−.07	.02	.15	.05	.08	.05	.15	.01	.10
260.	tactless	−.05	−.09	−.06	.05	−.06	−.08	−.02	−.04	−.03	−.05	.01	.00
261.	talkative	−.06	.02	.07	−.05	−.05	.03	−.01	−.05	.01	−.03	.08	.00
262.	temperamental	.02	−.13	−.10	−.02	−.18	−.14	−.07	−.09	−.07	−.08	−.05	−.05
263.	tense	−.02	−.07	−.11	−.10	−.04	−.21	.00	−.15	−.04	−.13	−.06	−.15
264.	thankless	−.03	−.13	.02	.00	−.07	−.01	−.04	−.13	.02	−.01	−.02	.05

Correlations of Observers' Adjectival Description with Scales of the CPI continued

		Scale: Leo						Scale: Tm				
		By Peers		By Spouses		By Staff		By Peers		By Spouses		By Staff	
Adjectives		M	F	M	F	M	F	M	F	M	F	M	F
265.	thorough	.15	.18	−.05	.05	−.01	.15	.21	.27	.08	.11	.11	.20
266.	thoughtful	.14	.08	.11	.01	−.12	.09	.13	.01	−.03	.03	−.10	.07
267.	thrifty	.07	.05	.04	.09	.04	.13	.07	.03	−.01	.06	−.13	.04
268.	timid	−.18	.01	−.05	−.08	−.08	−.04	−.17	−.09	−.07	−.11	−.25	−.21
269.	tolerant	−.06	.03	−.01	−.07	−.13	−.05	.01	−.03	.03	.01	−.13	.02
270.	touchy	.06	−.05	−.11	−.15	−.09	−.04	−.03	−.03	−.11	−.16	−.05	−.08
271.	tough	.20	.03	−.01	−.07	.01	.03	.11	.09	−.02	.02	.06	.18
272.	trusting	.01	.01	.05	.06	−.09	.08	−.05	−.05	−.06	−.01	−.13	−.07
273.	unaffected	−.11	−.02	−.09	−.08	.00	−.07	−.04	−.08	−.02	.06	−.06	−.06
274.	unambitious	−.09	−.12	−.23	−.16	−.12	−.07	−.07	−.16	−.18	−.08	−.18	−.24
275.	unassuming	−.21	−.06	−.03	−.07	−.08	−.04	−.16	−.14	−.08	−.01	−.20	−.17
276.	unconventional	−.12	−.26	−.16	−.24	−.22	−.23	−.02	−.22	−.11	−.03	−.09	−.06
277.	undependable	−.19	−.17	−.03	−.13	.01	−.16	−.10	−.15	.01	−.13	.02	−.12
278.	understanding	.00	.02	−.05	.10	−.15	.04	.03	−.04	.00	.10	−.12	.00
279.	unemotional	−.01	.04	.00	.00	−.09	.06	.05	.02	.15	−.03	−.13	.05
280.	unexcitable	−.13	−.03	−.01	−.02	−.05	.06	−.06	.02	−.04	.02	−.07	.06
281.	unfriendly	−.17	−.12	−.09	.05	−.05	−.02	.02	.04	−.01	.01	.01	.05
282.	uninhibited	−.03	−.16	−.04	−.08	−.03	−.08	.01	−.17	−.07	.07	.05	−.08
283.	unintelligent	.02	.07	.00	.05	.00	−.04	−.04	−.04	.00	−.04	−.03	−.06
284.	unkind	−.09	−.05	.00	.02	−.10	−.01	−.04	.03	.03	.02	−.04	.04
285.	unrealistic	−.10	−.04	−.06	−.05	−.08	−.08	−.16	−.13	.00	−.13	−.13	−.20
286.	unscrupulous	−.02	−.15	−.11	−.07	−.11	−.15	−.02	−.13	−.12	.08	.02	−.11
287.	unselfish	.09	−.05	−.03	−.03	−.05	.04	.05	−.05	−.12	−.07	−.06	−.06
288.	unstable	−.07	−.11	−.11	−.10	−.11	−.31	−.15	−.31	−.09	−.11	−.06	−.22
289.	vindictive	.01	.06	−.10	−.14	−.02	−.03	.02	.13	.04	−.12	.01	.03
290.	versatile	.09	−.08	−.04	.03	−.12	−.02	.16	−.01	−.09	.06	.08	.05
291.	warm	.00	.05	−.06	.01	−.06	.09	−.12	−.11	−.15	−.09	−.03	.00
292.	wary	.07	.07	−.01	.00	−.06	−.03	.06	.01	.03	−.01	−.04	−.01
293.	weak	−.27	−.04	−.15	.00	−.06	−.03	−.23	−.15	−.18	−.15	−.15	−.15
294.	whiny	−.16	.01	−.11	−.19	.00	−.03	−.21	−.12	−.17	−.19	−.03	−.05
295.	wholesome	.16	.12	.06	.06	.08	.25	.01	.07	−.03	−.02	−.03	.08
296.	wise	.22	.04	.08	.07	−.22	.00	.18	.19	.06	.00	.00	.12
297.	withdrawn	−.02	−.13	−.16	−.05	−.11	−.10	−.08	−.14	−.13	−.05	−.23	−.14
298.	witty	−.13	−.14	−.04	−.01	−.13	−.04	.03	−.11	−.03	−.03	−.01	−.04
299.	worrying	−.20	−.04	−.15	−.14	−.16	−.14	−.22	−.13	−.21	−.12	−.18	−.11
300.	zany	−.12	−.12	−.11	−.17	−.07	−.13	−.14	−.07	−.18	−.01	−.05	−.10

Correlations of Observers' Adjectival Description with Scales of the CPI continued												

	Scale: B–MS						Scale: B–FM					
	By Peers		By Spouses		By Staff		By Peers		By Spouses		By Staff	
Adjectives	M	F	M	F	M	F	M	F	M	F	M	F
001. absent-minded	−.09	−.24	−.09	.06	−.18	−.06	.00	−.21	−.07	−.20	.00	−.13
002. active	.15	.27	.02	.13	.21	.27	.03	.02	−.14	−.04	−.17	−.02
003. adaptable	.02	.17	.12	.09	.15	.14	.18	.19	.01	−.02	.02	.06
004. adventurous	.17	.16	.04	.15	.15	.20	−.21	−.21	−.22	−.17	−.25	−.21
005. affected	−.01	.17	.06	.02	.09	.07	.00	−.09	−.01	−.05	−.04	−.03
006. affectionate	−.08	.01	−.03	.07	−.06	−.06	.14	.02	−.07	.02	.01	.10
007. aggressive	.18	.26	.13	.17	.25	.31	−.17	−.18	−.16	−.25	−.20	−.19
008. alert	.14	.23	.11	.11	.16	.19	−.05	.07	.01	.10	−.02	.02
009. aloof	.01	−.09	−.02	−.04	−.20	−.04	.03	−.20	−.03	−.10	.02	−.06
010. ambitious	.15	.17	.17	.22	.28	.31	.03	.13	−.11	−.09	−.03	−.10
011. anxious	−.14	−.09	−.08	−.07	−.20	−.31	.10	−.06	.01	−.09	.04	−.04
012. apathetic	−.13	−.18	−.10	−.02	−.21	−.18	−.15	−.15	−.07	.01	−.03	.00
013. appreciative	−.12	.07	.01	−.01	−.06	−.07	.21	.14	.14	.08	.08	.20
014. argumentative	.06	.09	.03	.14	.23	.24	−.18	−.22	−.07	−.17	−.15	−.14
015. arrogant	.08	.05	−.03	.12	.13	.15	−.11	−.23	−.17	−.19	−.22	−.12
016. artistic	−.16	−.07	.00	.07	−.06	−.02	−.07	−.13	−.02	−.09	.06	.00
017. assertive	.09	.18	.14	.34	.25	.34	−.08	−.09	−.10	−.11	−.10	−.13
018. attractive	.04	.05	.07	.01	.01	.08	.03	.00	−.05	−.04	−.02	.03
019. autocratic	−.08	.03	.06	.07	.08	.19	.06	−.17	−.04	−.07	−.17	−.08
020. awkward	−.23	−.16	−.21	−.13	−.31	−.23	.05	−.10	−.10	−.03	.03	−.02
021. bitter	−.12	−.10	−.15	−.07	−.10	−.07	−.03	−.21	−.20	−.35	−.10	−.16
022. blustery	.02	.00	.01	−.06	.10	.04	−.10	−.10	−.06	−.17	−.16	−.12
023. boastful	.16	.21	−.04	.05	.13	.16	−.18	−.18	−.22	−.25	−.20	−.07
024. bossy	−.06	.16	−.10	.01	.13	.16	−.10	−.13	−.16	−.16	−.13	−.02
025. calm	−.05	−.01	−.06	−.04	−.09	.04	.11	.23	.09	.08	.03	.04
026. capable	.08	.10	.03	.17	.06	.26	.11	.23	.05	.17	.01	.07
027. careless	.02	−.07	−.13	−.09	.00	.01	−.15	−.25	−.13	−.09	−.19	−.21
028. cautious	−.25	−.20	−.14	−.10	−.25	−.26	.17	.28	.03	.12	.13	.14
029. changeable	−.02	−.06	−.06	.07	.01	−.08	−.05	−.18	−.14	−.25	−.13	−.19
030. charming	.00	.06	.00	.02	.05	.10	.01	.08	−.07	.02	−.04	.06
031. cheerful	.01	.16	.09	−.03	.10	.11	.05	.10	.00	.09	−.02	.13
032. civilized	.07	.05	−.03	−.01	−.09	.07	.03	.13	.08	−.01	.11	.16
033. clear-thinking	.10	.16	.02	.10	.02	.21	.02	.25	.14	.12	.10	.06
034. clever	.19	.08	.05	.19	.10	.20	−.08	−.08	−.12	−.14	−.07	−.06
035. coarse	−.01	−.02	−.18	.07	.05	.04	−.17	−.30	−.08	−.12	−.24	−.22
036. cold	−.16	−.07	−.07	−.06	−.07	.00	−.17	−.15	.07	−.09	−.04	−.09
037. commonplace	−.19	−.09	.06	−.11	−.10	−.14	.05	.00	.11	−.03	−.08	.09
038. complaining	−.10	−.11	−.23	−.09	−.05	.00	−.03	−.08	−.14	−.17	−.07	−.12
039. complicated	−.08	−.10	.07	.07	−.12	−.01	−.10	−.13	.09	−.17	.02	−.19
040. conceited	.11	.19	−.10	.06	.19	.16	−.17	−.14	−.15	−.07	−.12	−.07
041. confident	.24	.32	.14	.30	.24	.35	−.11	.01	−.16	−.05	−.08	−.04
042. confused	−.15	−.16	−.24	−.12	−.15	−.19	−.10	−.17	−.13	−.19	−.01	−.21
043. conscientious	−.12	.04	.04	.10	−.12	−.06	.14	.31	.19	.16	.20	.23
044. conservative	.00	−.06	.02	−.17	−.09	−.13	.09	.28	.15	.08	.05	.18

Correlations of Observers' Adjectival Description with Scales of the CPI continued

	Scale: B–MS						Scale: B–FM					
	By Peers		By Spouses		By Staff		By Peers		By Spouses		By Staff	
Adjectives	M	F	M	F	M	F	M	F	M	F	M	F
045. considerate	−.05	−.04	−.01	−.09	−.18	−.12	.15	.21	.12	.03	.12	.15
046. contented	−.01	.11	.08	−.01	.01	.02	.08	.18	.17	.08	−.02	.18
047. conventional	−.07	−.04	.04	−.11	−.08	−.14	.15	.25	.06	.14	.07	.24
048. cool	.00	−.04	−.01	.03	.04	.05	−.24	−.22	.01	−.08	−.06	−.07
049. cooperative	−.09	.03	.08	.03	−.08	−.07	.12	.24	.03	.16	.10	.18
050. courageous	.02	.11	.17	.05	.08	.14	−.13	−.06	−.04	−.03	−.10	−.19
051. cowardly	−.17	−.17	−.14	−.01	−.09	−.01	−.05	.03	.01	−.04	−.01	.02
052. cruel	−.07	−.06	−.12	.02	−.03	.00	−.12	−.04	−.21	−.17	−.15	−.10
053. curious	.05	.00	−.02	.06	.00	.16	−.08	−.09	−.11	−.09	.03	−.16
054. cynical	.01	−.09	−.09	.07	−.01	.10	−.15	−.15	−.09	−.22	−.20	−.22
055. daring	.09	.19	.01	−.02	.13	.17	−.23	−.19	−.16	−.12	−.16	−.21
056. deceitful	.10	−.01	−.13	−.01	.12	−.02	−.11	−.12	−.15	−.19	−.18	−.20
057. defensive	−.14	−.16	−.07	−.04	−.06	−.10	−.04	−.12	−.07	−.07	−.08	−.05
058. deliberate	.04	.04	−.05	.00	−.20	−.02	.02	.01	.02	−.11	.11	.10
059. demanding	.08	.11	.01	.03	.15	.15	−.05	−.18	−.12	−.22	−.14	−.15
060. dependable	.02	.08	.04	−.03	−.06	.03	.17	.26	.09	.15	.16	.21
061. dependent	−.11	−.09	−.02	−.17	−.22	−.27	.10	.05	.07	−.05	.11	.11
062. despondent	.00	−.25	−.04	.04	−.20	−.30	.04	−.10	−.06	.02	.00	−.02
063. determined	.09	.19	.10	.21	.14	.28	−.06	.09	−.07	−.10	−.08	−.10
064. dignified	−.05	−.01	−.03	.09	−.08	−.07	.03	.12	.08	.03	.12	.09
065. discreet	−.07	−.03	−.05	.05	−.15	−.11	.16	.28	.07	.01	.19	.18
066. disorderly	.04	−.12	.03	.00	.01	−.06	−.13	−.31	−.16	−.22	−.16	−.26
067. dissatisfied	−.07	−.10	−.16	−.14	−.07	−.10	−.07	−.20	−.20	−.11	−.11	−.21
068. distractible	−.13	−.06	−.10	−.07	−.15	−.14	−.07	−.17	−.22	−.17	−.09	−.16
069. distrustful	−.06	−.10	−.13	−.12	.01	−.04	−.08	−.21	−.09	−.11	−.11	−.20
070. dominant	.12	.27	.09	.00	.18	.34	−.12	−.14	−.04	−.13	−.14	−.12
071. dreamy	−.10	−.11	−.05	.02	−.23	−.16	.03	−.03	−.21	−.20	.10	−.02
072. dull	−.19	−.19	−.08	−.09	−.18	−.12	.17	.00	.03	−.01	−.02	.05
073. easygoing	.02	.03	−.10	.02	−.08	−.01	−.01	−.04	−.02	.06	−.11	.05
074. effeminate	−.09	−.02	.05	.04	−.06	.00	.12	−.03	.05	−.06	.13	.05
075. efficient	−.01	.18	.00	.00	.17	.21	.14	.25	.15	.11	.06	.06
076. egotistical	.21	.13	−.04	.14	.16	.20	−.16	−.17	−.17	−.09	−.15	−.09
077. emotional	−.15	−.02	−.10	−.10	−.01	−.07	−.04	−.13	−.13	−.16	−.04	−.04
078. energetic	.16	.27	.18	.14	.26	.29	−.07	.01	−.18	−.02	−.09	−.03
079. enterprising	.21	.20	.08	.18	.23	.32	.00	.08	−.13	.00	−.08	−.02
080. enthusiastic	.07	.16	.19	.15	.11	.20	−.03	.02	−.11	.09	−.05	.02
081. evasive	−.03	−.11	.00	−.11	−.11	−.07	.01	−.13	−.08	−.13	−.10	−.04
082. excitable	−.02	.15	−.06	−.04	.09	.06	−.07	−.21	−.13	−.14	−.11	−.03
083. fair-minded	−.01	.04	.04	.02	−.08	.01	.12	.20	.10	.15	.07	.09
084. fault-finding	−.02	−.05	−.02	−.08	.03	.10	−.15	−.09	−.03	−.14	−.07	−.13
085. fearful	−.13	−.13	−.14	−.05	−.21	−.30	−.10	−.06	−.14	−.14	.01	−.01
086. feminine	−.21	−.05	−.05	−.08	−.14	−.09	.26	.19	.09	−.02	.09	.19
087. fickle	−.11	.10	−.06	−.06	−.03	−.02	.03	−.22	−.01	−.20	−.08	−.04
088. flirtatious	.02	.16	−.04	.00	.05	.03	−.15	−.12	−.24	−.17	−.15	−.06

		Scale: B–MS						Scale: B–FM					
		By Peers		By Spouses		By Staff		By Peers		By Spouses		By Staff	
Adjectives		M	F	M	F	M	F	M	F	M	F	M	F
089.	foolish	.02	−.08	−.03	−.06	−.02	−.08	−.03	−.28	.05	−.26	−.13	−.05
090.	forceful	.12	.18	.03	.11	.16	.31	−.15	−.05	−.11	−.17	−.10	−.13
091.	foresighted	.03	.10	.06	.00	.04	.19	.15	.25	−.02	.12	.15	.02
092.	forgetful	−.09	−.21	−.02	.09	−.12	−.07	−.06	−.13	.00	−.17	−.04	−.02
093.	forgiving	.03	.01	.00	−.11	−.11	−.15	.18	.12	.01	.03	.03	.09
094.	formal	−.01	−.02	.04	.06	−.10	−.07	.27	.13	.08	−.04	.12	.10
095.	frank	−.05	.01	.02	.02	.04	.21	−.12	−.08	−.08	−.09	−.07	−.10
096.	friendly	.03	.18	.15	−.01	.03	.09	.01	.09	−.07	.05	.00	.11
097.	frivolous	−.07	.06	.02	−.08	.01	.00	−.07	−.14	.04	−.08	−.15	−.01
098.	fussy	−.15	.00	−.15	−.07	−.06	−.08	.06	−.02	−.04	−.16	.00	.10
099.	generous	−.04	−.01	.05	−.04	−.07	.02	.02	.10	−.02	.05	.00	.05
100.	gentle	−.06	−.15	−.01	−.11	−.28	−.24	.25	.23	.09	.09	.10	.12
101.	gloomy	−.10	−.24	−.22	−.01	−.18	−.13	.07	−.06	−.08	−.03	.02	−.06
102.	good-looking	.09	.11	.02	−.01	.01	.07	−.01	.01	−.11	−.04	−.08	.04
103.	good-natured	.03	.07	.09	.04	−.06	.03	.10	.16	−.02	.10	.00	.09
104.	greedy	−.03	−.11	−.03	−.05	.01	−.01	−.05	−.10	−.09	−.05	−.11	−.08
105.	handsome	.05	−.05	.04	.06	.02	.07	−.05	−.05	.01	.02	−.07	.02
106.	hard-headed	.07	.06	.03	.01	.14	.14	−.11	−.14	−.04	−.26	−.10	−.13
107.	hard-hearted	−.04	.01	−.04	−.07	.04	.12	−.22	−.16	−.07	−.08	−.10	−.07
108.	hasty	−.10	.00	−.13	−.04	.13	.05	−.12	−.17	−.22	−.14	−.13	−.16
109.	headstrong	.00	.07	.01	.01	.13	.20	−.21	−.18	−.15	−.33	−.17	−.25
110.	healthy	.04	.10	−.02	.08	.02	.22	−.02	−.01	.08	−.01	−.09	.02
111.	helpful	.01	.10	−.03	.05	−.09	−.07	.08	.17	.06	.06	.09	.16
112.	high-strung	−.11	−.05	−.14	.01	−.01	−.11	.01	−.08	−.06	−.16	.00	−.10
113.	honest	−.07	−.04	−.06	−.02	−.09	.03	.22	.27	.10	.23	.10	.13
114.	hostile	.05	−.05	−.08	.04	.07	.05	−.09	−.16	−.09	−.05	−.14	−.15
115.	humorous	.10	.00	.02	.19	.06	.15	−.13	−.15	−.11	.00	−.12	−.04
116.	hurried	−.10	.00	.05	.07	.03	.00	−.04	−.16	−.08	−.01	−.10	−.02
117.	idealistic	−.02	.07	.09	.07	−.08	.00	.02	.08	−.06	−.04	.12	−.05
118.	imaginative	.00	.10	.02	.22	.04	.11	−.02	−.03	−.16	−.14	.00	−.11
119.	immature	.02	−.10	−.09	−.09	−.03	−.18	−.08	−.28	−.11	−.04	−.06	−.12
120.	impatient	−.01	−.03	.06	.03	.17	.14	−.07	−.15	−.21	−.13	−.17	−.21
121.	impulsive	.05	.04	−.02	.01	.13	.04	−.29	−.32	−.20	−.26	−.20	−.17
122.	independent	.17	.15	.08	.18	.16	.26	−.02	−.02	−.04	−.19	−.16	−.20
123.	indifferent	−.08	−.17	−.03	.02	−.10	−.10	−.04	−.12	−.05	−.15	−.15	−.08
124.	individualistic	.04	.10	.05	.27	.05	.16	−.14	−.14	−.08	−.16	−.14	−.21
125.	industrious	.04	.07	.12	.09	.06	.25	.06	.26	.01	−.05	.09	.06
126.	infantile	−.09	.02	−.03	−.21	−.07	−.18	.00	−.24	−.11	−.11	−.07	−.12
127.	informal	.01	.04	−.05	.04	.03	.08	−.01	−.10	−.13	−.17	−.19	−.13
128.	ingenious	.11	.12	.02	.10	.13	.15	−.15	−.09	.03	−.09	−.02	−.10
129.	inhibited	−.10	−.14	−.12	−.13	−.29	−.29	.22	.21	.03	.01	.14	.09
130.	initiative	.12	.24	.17	.14	.25	.32	−.08	−.03	−.10	.07	−.05	−.06
131.	insightful	.06	.18	.03	.09	.01	.13	.15	.13	−.03	.03	.09	−.06
132.	intelligent	.09	.20	.02	.05	.06	.21	.09	.25	.03	.06	.04	.01

Correlations of Observers' Adjectival Description with Scales of the CPI continued

| | | Scale: B–MS | | | | | | Scale: B–FM | | | | |
| | | By Peers | | By Spouses | | By Staff | | By Peers | | By Spouses | | By Staff | |
Adjectives		M	F	M	F	M	F	M	F	M	F	M	F
133.	interests—narrow	−.25	−.12	.00	−.27	−.14	−.23	.14	−.02	.01	−.07	−.05	.03
134.	interests—wide	.13	.18	.07	.17	.06	.22	−.04	−.02	.02	−.07	.04	−.04
135.	intolerant	−.09	.08	−.12	−.14	.03	.00	−.07	−.14	−.13	−.11	−.16	−.11
136.	inventive	.09	.13	.09	.14	.06	.12	.01	−.11	−.01	−.04	−.06	−.06
137.	irresponsible	.00	−.10	−.02	−.01	.00	−.03	−.19	−.22	−.07	−.17	−.16	−.19
138.	irritable	−.10	−.08	−.06	−.09	.03	.06	−.07	−.13	−.03	−.11	−.12	−.04
139.	jolly	.08	.20	−.03	.04	.12	.08	−.09	−.05	−.03	−.04	−.14	.00
140.	kind	−.10	−.02	.00	.00	−.21	−.10	.18	.19	.07	.08	.03	.14
141.	lazy	.10	−.09	.07	−.02	−.04	−.08	−.13	−.33	−.07	−.14	−.19	−.14
142.	leisurely	.00	.04	.04	.04	−.01	−.04	−.06	−.05	−.06	−.16	−.11	.03
143.	logical	.10	.14	−.04	−.08	−.01	.18	.12	.20	.02	.14	.07	.03
144.	loud	.03	.14	.00	.06	.13	.18	−.15	−.28	.01	−.24	−.19	−.08
145.	loyal	−.03	.01	−.13	−.15	−.10	−.06	.16	.15	.04	−.07	.03	.10
146.	mannerly	−.03	.01	.06	.14	−.19	−.09	.20	.25	.09	−.01	.11	.16
147.	masculine	.15	.10	.01	.02	.08	.13	−.16	−.34	−.24	−.04	−.20	−.12
148.	mature	.13	.12	−.01	.10	.04	.14	.05	.21	.13	.06	.08	.06
149.	meek	−.23	−.25	−.08	−.14	−.30	−.29	.19	.02	.01	−.02	.05	.10
150.	methodical	−.10	−.09	−.06	.14	−.12	.02	.14	.17	.13	.09	.16	.16
151.	mild	−.15	−.19	−.13	−.16	−.28	−.26	.26	.17	.10	.15	.13	.19
152.	mischievous	.03	.07	−.08	−.01	.09	.03	−.28	−.13	−.17	−.24	−.15	−.06
153.	moderate	.00	−.05	.03	.04	−.15	−.05	.23	.25	.08	.08	.14	.21
154.	modest	−.09	−.18	−.02	−.17	−.24	−.28	.26	.20	.10	.11	.16	.17
155.	moody	−.08	−.21	−.17	−.04	−.15	−.14	−.09	−.15	−.11	−.19	−.03	−.15
156.	nagging	−.16	.01	−.14	−.04	−.08	−.04	.09	−.05	−.17	−.04	−.04	−.04
157.	natural	.07	−.04	.00	.03	.14	.13	−.07	.05	.04	−.04	−.07	.02
158.	nervous	−.20	−.18	−.19	−.04	−.19	−.25	.19	−.02	−.04	−.11	.07	.01
159.	noisy	.04	.14	−.02	−.02	.12	.09	−.12	−.22	−.08	−.13	−.14	−.06
160.	obliging	−.04	.05	−.08	.04	−.13	−.14	.11	.25	−.02	−.03	.10	.17
161.	obnoxious	.05	.04	.04	.04	.08	.01	−.13	−.29	−.19	−.15	−.23	−.13
162.	opinionated	−.01	.10	.05	.02	.13	.19	−.16	−.15	−.04	−.32	−.13	−.10
163.	opportunistic	.22	.05	.01	.10	.22	.18	−.07	−.07	−.08	−.16	−.20	−.09
164.	optimistic	.19	.17	.15	.16	.10	.18	.04	.10	−.01	−.01	.02	.05
165.	organized	.01	.14	−.01	−.01	.15	.18	.23	.27	.17	.15	.15	.14
166.	original	.10	.12	.04	.09	.04	.11	−.17	−.07	−.04	−.19	−.01	−.16
167.	outgoing	.21	.26	.19	.25	.24	.25	−.16	−.01	−.08	−.05	−.13	−.01
168.	outspoken	.12	.21	−.01	.14	.18	.25	−.18	−.17	−.18	−.13	−.10	−.09
169.	painstaking	−.13	.00	.00	−.02	−.23	−.13	.14	.12	.03	.04	.20	.08
170.	patient	−.09	−.01	.00	−.13	−.23	−.13	.14	.25	.09	.11	.14	.15
171.	peaceable	−.16	−.07	−.02	−.11	−.25	−.18	.22	.26	.01	−.03	.13	.24
172.	peculiar	−.13	−.10	−.09	−.01	−.18	−.07	−.05	−.11	−.01	−.28	.03	−.14
173.	persevering	.03	.06	−.15	.09	.03	.04	.12	.16	−.05	.01	.09	.04
174.	persistent	.06	.18	.07	.21	.03	.23	.04	.04	−.11	−.11	−.07	−.03
175.	pessimistic	−.17	−.23	−.04	−.06	−.15	−.18	−.04	−.13	−.05	−.09	−.11	−.05
176.	planful	−.05	.11	−.05	.03	.04	.16	.09	.29	.04	.06	.10	.11

	Scale: B–MS						Scale: B–FM					
	By Peers		By Spouses		By Staff		By Peers		By Spouses		By Staff	
Adjectives	M	F	M	F	M	F	M	F	M	F	M	F
177. pleasant	.10	.08	.10	.02	−.06	−.01	.12	.12	.02	.13	.06	.19
178. pleasure-seeking	.15	.07	−.01	.08	.17	.08	−.19	−.26	−.18	−.25	−.23	−.11
179. poised	.09	.08	.10	.15	.12	.21	.15	.10	.01	−.03	.07	.12
180. polished	.11	.06	.10	.20	.05	.15	.03	.12	.01	.04	.02	.07
181. practical	.06	−.01	.07	.00	.06	.12	.07	.29	.14	.11	−.02	.09
182. praising	.03	.05	.03	.00	.02	−.04	.12	.13	−.01	.00	.05	.14
183. precise	.00	−.02	.07	.08	−.10	.08	.17	.11	.06	.07	.11	.05
184. prejudiced	−.05	−.06	−.08	−.15	.02	−.07	−.12	−.03	−.20	−.21	−.16	−.08
185. preoccupied	−.04	−.11	.04	.06	−.26	−.19	−.10	−.11	−.02	−.16	.06	−.11
186. progressive	.10	.05	.00	.11	.03	.16	−.07	−.14	−.02	−.04	.00	−.10
187. prudish	−.13	−.01	−.06	−.16	−.14	−.17	.15	.11	−.07	−.02	.08	.16
188. quarrelsome	.13	−.03	−.17	−.08	.10	.10	−.21	−.14	−.07	−.12	−.19	−.14
189. queer	−.24	−.07	.03	.00	−.12	−.01	−.07	−.19	.03	.00	.06	−.15
190. quick	.12	.21	.01	.17	.16	.17	−.09	−.11	−.01	−.14	−.10	−.06
191. quiet	−.20	−.23	−.12	−.18	−.32	−.29	.21	.21	.17	.13	.14	.11
192. quitting	−.22	−.21	−.11	−.08	−.14	−.12	−.02	−.12	−.16	.05	−.06	−.06
193. rational	.11	.19	.03	.04	−.08	.19	.15	.24	.01	.04	.06	.03
194. rattle-brained	−.08	−.06	−.14	−.12	−.03	−.08	−.06	−.16	−.14	−.22	−.08	−.09
195. realistic	.06	.18	−.01	.01	.04	.20	.07	.24	.05	.07	−.02	.06
196. reasonable	.07	.10	.07	.08	−.05	.04	.23	.31	.06	.10	.11	.20
197. rebellious	.03	−.03	−.15	.08	.03	.08	−.27	−.30	−.22	−.30	−.16	−.28
198. reckless	−.02	.03	−.07	−.06	.08	−.01	−.23	−.27	−.22	−.34	−.21	−.21
199. reflective	−.12	.02	−.08	.12	−.18	−.08	.19	.15	.07	−.02	.15	.02
200. relaxed	.07	.09	.07	−.06	.02	.20	.05	.09	−.06	−.01	−.06	.01
201. reliable	.01	.07	.06	−.05	−.06	.02	.20	.36	.02	.12	.15	.20
202. resentful	.11	−.13	−.13	−.05	−.02	−.01	.00	−.24	−.11	−.13	−.16	−.17
203. reserved	−.15	−.23	−.13	−.19	−.31	−.23	.19	.20	.08	.07	.15	.08
204. resourceful	.20	.14	.09	.21	.21	.27	.05	.16	−.11	−.12	−.01	−.08
205. responsible	.04	.10	.05	.03	−.05	.05	.16	.35	.00	.04	.15	.21
206. restless	−.04	.00	.04	.06	.06	.03	−.12	−.30	−.29	−.25	−.15	−.18
207. retiring	−.14	−.34	−.06	−.10	−.30	−.30	.05	.12	.06	−.04	.09	.12
208. rigid	−.10	.02	.03	−.16	−.10	−.10	.04	.01	.04	−.13	−.07	−.01
209. robust	.01	.20	.10	.01	.10	.16	−.13	−.21	−.04	−.10	−.20	−.16
210. rude	−.01	−.02	.02	.03	.06	.04	−.14	−.21	−.06	−.09	−.22	−.13
211. sarcastic	.03	−.05	−.02	.03	.04	.14	−.13	−.26	−.13	−.19	−.19	−.15
212. self-centered	.10	.11	−.12	.00	.12	.05	−.16	−.17	−.17	−.14	−.15	−.14
213. self-confident	.19	.29	.20	.30	.25	.38	−.09	−.04	−.13	−.08	−.12	−.06
214. self-controlled	.07	.02	−.02	.13	−.14	−.08	.20	.27	.08	−.01	.14	.11
215. self-denying	−.11	−.03	−.14	−.12	−.24	−.23	.12	.04	−.05	−.10	.13	.08
216. self-pitying	−.14	−.09	−.20	−.14	−.10	−.16	.11	−.20	−.06	−.10	−.01	−.07
217. self-punishing	.02	−.10	−.06	−.07	−.13	−.14	−.05	−.08	−.11	−.05	−.04	−.11
218. self-seeking	.09	.00	.00	.07	.19	.13	−.05	−.11	−.10	−.10	−.19	−.13
219. selfish	.08	.03	.01	.06	.10	.05	−.06	−.15	.03	−.06	−.16	−.14
220. sensitive	−.17	−.14	−.15	−.03	−.24	−.22	.09	−.02	−.04	−.02	.11	−.04

Correlations of Observers' Adjectival Description with Scales of the CPI continued

		Scale: B–MS						Scale: B–FM					
		By Peers		By Spouses		By Staff		By Peers		By Spouses		By Staff	
Adjectives		M	F	M	F	M	F	M	F	M	F	M	F
221.	sentimental	−.13	.07	−.06	−.09	−.11	−.12	.10	.05	.07	.07	.01	.07
222.	serious	−.03	−.14	−.09	−.04	−.23	.04	.21	.25	−.01	−.02	.16	.02
223.	severe	−.10	.03	−.01	−.04	−.07	−.04	−.07	.00	−.13	−.12	.00	−.03
224.	sexy	.08	.03	.00	.06	.07	.08	−.06	−.12	−.20	−.14	−.17	−.08
225.	shallow	−.16	.05	.00	−.16	.03	−.13	−.09	−.06	.02	−.04	−.10	.01
226.	sharp-witted	.15	−.02	.00	.14	.12	.15	−.07	−.15	−.07	−.22	−.06	−.13
227.	shiftless	−.04	−.06	−.10	−.05	−.06	−.05	−.10	−.18	−.05	−.20	−.10	−.11
228.	show-off	.10	.09	.06	.03	.14	.16	−.19	−.24	−.17	−.13	−.19	−.02
229.	shrewd	.10	−.06	−.07	.08	.21	.17	.02	−.10	−.14	−.17	−.11	−.10
230.	shy	−.18	−.29	−.26	−.28	−.39	−.32	.22	.15	.04	.05	.09	.04
231.	silent	−.25	−.21	−.19	−.09	−.32	−.26	.18	.13	.06	.00	−.03	.04
232.	simple	−.07	−.13	−.04	−.25	−.13	−.19	.08	.03	.01	−.14	−.03	.13
233.	sincere	−.08	−.05	−.04	−.07	−.16	−.04	.17	.23	.02	.22	.13	.16
234.	slipshod	.08	−.04	−.05	−.03	.02	.01	−.23	−.21	−.02	−.13	−.09	−.14
235.	slow	−.18	−.12	−.13	−.09	−.19	−.18	−.01	.04	−.07	−.10	.07	.10
236.	sly	.03	−.05	−.15	.14	−.01	.00	−.05	−.12	−.20	−.23	−.16	−.14
237.	smug	.10	.07	−.01	−.02	.09	.09	−.19	−.09	−.12	−.08	−.09	−.10
238.	snobbish	.09	.01	−.01	.05	.03	.08	−.09	−.02	−.04	−.11	−.08	.03
239.	sociable	.18	.16	.17	.17	.17	.16	−.06	.03	−.03	−.17	−.09	.08
240.	soft-hearted	−.04	.05	−.11	−.18	−.11	−.15	.13	.17	−.09	−.05	.03	.09
241.	sophisticated	.12	−.05	.05	.23	.03	.20	.00	.04	.01	−.07	.01	.01
242.	spendthrift	.13	−.09	−.02	−.04	.00	.02	−.09	−.10	.01	−.17	−.15	−.04
243.	spineless	−.11	−.18	.05	−.08	−.14	−.09	.05	−.08	.00	−.04	−.03	.07
244.	spontaneous	.03	.21	.08	.17	.16	.16	−.15	−.15	−.19	−.15	−.09	−.07
245.	spunky	−.10	.17	−.09	.14	.11	.14	−.18	−.07	−.18	−.21	−.15	−.13
246.	stable	.05	.15	−.03	−.03	−.01	.16	.14	.27	.12	−.04	.04	.14
247.	steady	.02	.07	−.04	−.05	−.06	.01	.18	.21	.07	−.02	.07	.08
248.	stern	.00	−.01	−.10	−.03	−.05	.05	−.05	.09	−.03	−.14	.00	−.01
249.	stingy	−.06	−.03	−.08	−.04	−.04	.08	.06	−.18	−.18	−.15	.01	−.06
250.	stolid	−.03	−.05	.02	.03	−.15	−.07	−.07	−.04	.01	−.13	−.06	.02
251.	strong	.11	.19	.11	.10	.05	.33	−.17	.00	−.13	−.11	−.13	−.14
252.	stubborn	.02	.12	−.07	.05	.12	.16	−.13	−.10	−.13	−.19	−.17	−.18
253.	submissive	−.15	−.19	−.19	−.19	−.22	−.30	.19	.19	−.03	.03	.13	.15
254.	suggestible	−.04	.03	−.09	.02	−.07	−.26	.09	−.06	−.14	−.04	.01	.05
255.	sulky	−.06	−.18	−.05	−.07	−.09	−.07	−.07	−.09	−.10	−.13	−.05	−.18
256.	superstitious	−.11	−.10	−.16	−.05	−.04	−.17	.04	−.07	−.26	−.22	.01	−.19
257.	suspicious	−.11	−.13	−.11	−.02	−.06	−.05	−.16	−.11	−.11	−.25	−.14	−.15
258.	sympathetic	−.03	−.04	.00	−.02	−.09	−.11	.09	.16	.06	.13	.08	.14
259.	tactful	.08	.04	.09	.10	.01	−.01	.01	.25	.11	.07	.19	.17
260.	tactless	−.01	.00	−.08	−.04	.03	.11	.02	−.12	−.07	−.03	−.20	−.17
261.	talkative	.14	.18	.20	.12	.19	.23	−.09	−.19	−.08	−.22	−.10	−.05
262.	temperamental	−.04	−.09	−.05	.05	−.02	.08	−.11	−.13	−.17	−.18	−.13	−.19
263.	tense	−.07	−.23	−.09	−.05	−.12	−.23	.04	−.04	−.11	−.12	.02	−.07
264.	thankless	−.05	−.16	−.05	−.02	−.05	.03	−.12	−.17	−.05	−.02	−.12	−.06

		Scale: B–MS						Scale: B–FM				
		By Peers		By Spouses		By Staff		By Peers		By Spouses		By Staff	
Adjectives		M	F	M	F	M	F	M	F	M	F	M	F
265.	thorough	.03	.07	.02	.05	−.02	.13	.13	.21	−.01	.09	.22	.05
266.	thoughtful	.04	.03	−.02	−.03	−.14	−.01	.21	.21	.05	.12	.16	.11
267.	thrifty	−.05	.00	−.11	−.04	−.13	−.02	.19	.13	.07	.19	.00	.10
268.	timid	−.21	−.29	−.12	−.12	−.31	−.33	.17	.13	.04	−.09	.08	.08
269.	tolerant	.02	.06	.09	−.06	−.08	.04	.08	.18	−.03	−.01	.08	.12
270.	touchy	−.02	.00	−.14	−.03	−.02	−.10	−.02	−.17	−.03	−.23	−.10	−.11
271.	tough	.04	.08	−.08	.05	.09	.26	−.13	−.22	−.13	−.20	−.19	−.20
272.	trusting	.00	−.01	.08	−.01	−.14	−.06	.02	.18	.04	.07	.03	.13
273.	unaffected	−.02	−.06	.01	.07	−.07	−.07	.05	.08	−.07	−.09	.01	.08
274.	unambitious	−.02	−.16	−.14	−.09	−.17	−.23	.07	−.14	−.10	−.07	−.02	.01
275.	unassuming	−.14	−.15	.00	−.02	−.24	−.25	.13	.12	−.06	.04	.08	.09
276.	unconventional	.09	−.08	−.04	.12	−.04	.08	−.05	−.27	−.14	−.25	−.05	−.24
277.	undependable	.04	−.03	−.02	−.05	.04	.01	−.18	−.34	−.01	−.10	−.14	−.20
278.	understanding	.06	.07	.07	.09	−.11	.03	.12	.16	−.01	.02	−.01	.11
279.	unemotional	−.09	−.16	.04	−.02	−.18	−.03	.04	−.02	.05	−.01	−.11	−.01
280.	unexcitable	−.13	−.14	−.14	−.01	−.11	−.09	.01	.07	.05	.02	−.04	.05
281.	unfriendly	−.08	−.10	−.14	.07	−.03	.01	−.11	−.09	−.13	−.17	−.09	−.10
282.	uninhibited	.11	.00	.03	.17	.17	.12	−.18	−.21	−.01	−.07	−.16	−.18
283.	unintelligent	−.01	.00	.00	−.01	−.06	−.06	−.01	−.23	.00	.04	−.05	.07
284.	unkind	−.13	−.12	.00	−.03	−.04	.12	.07	−.13	.02	−.01	−.18	−.15
285.	unrealistic	−.03	.01	.01	−.04	−.12	−.13	−.10	−.22	−.04	−.17	−.07	−.16
286.	unscrupulous	.00	−.09	−.21	.05	.01	.01	−.20	−.18	−.10	−.12	−.13	−.13
287.	unselfish	.06	−.05	−.17	−.04	−.06	−.11	.09	.14	.02	−.01	−.02	.11
288.	unstable	.00	−.25	−.17	.06	−.05	−.16	−.12	−.21	−.18	−.23	−.05	−.17
289.	vindictive	.06	.06	.02	−.03	.00	.02	−.07	−.06	−.12	−.21	−.13	−.08
290.	versatile	.17	.19	.03	.12	.17	.21	−.04	−.18	−.12	−.05	−.06	−.04
291.	warm	−.02	.05	−.03	−.09	.04	.01	.04	.13	−.01	.07	.00	.12
292.	wary	.07	−.07	.00	.04	−.09	−.10	−.09	−.01	−.11	−.15	−.12	−.10
293.	weak	−.16	−.23	−.23	−.13	−.15	−.23	.17	.09	−.12	.00	.04	.05
294.	whiny	−.17	−.13	−.15	−.13	.00	−.09	.07	.01	−.06	−.23	.01	−.02
295.	wholesome	−.03	.11	.01	.04	−.01	.09	.16	.14	.01	.00	.06	.14
296.	wise	.14	.10	.08	.01	−.06	.09	.01	.18	.11	.00	.05	.03
297.	withdrawn	−.18	−.33	−.18	−.12	−.33	−.27	.15	.11	−.16	−.03	.03	−.02
298.	witty	.11	.01	.03	.02	.08	.12	−.07	−.21	−.09	−.13	−.08	−.05
299.	worrying	−.21	−.15	−.24	−.06	−.26	−.23	.11	.08	−.12	−.10	.04	.00
300.	zany	−.02	.12	−.02	.09	.02	.02	−.03	−.24	−.20	−.16	−.15	−.08

Correlations of Observers' Adjectival Description with Scales of the CPI continued

		Scale: Anx						Scale: Nar				
		By Peers		By Spouses		By Staff		By Peers		By Spouses		By Staff	
Adjectives		M	F	M	F	M	F	M	F	M	F	M	F
001.	absent-minded	.07	.19	.14	.10	.05	.09	.06	.04	−.09	.16	−.08	.04
002.	active	−.21	−.08	.05	−.08	−.04	−.10	.03	.12	.14	.11	.27	.19
003.	adaptable	−.02	−.22	−.10	.00	−.10	−.15	−.14	−.15	−.01	.08	.07	.09
004.	adventurous	−.11	−.02	.01	−.02	.03	.00	.11	.25	.19	.24	.32	.32
005.	affected	−.02	−.10	.06	.00	.02	.05	.10	.10	.02	.02	.10	.18
006.	affectionate	.02	−.12	−.01	.00	.03	−.15	−.08	−.12	.03	.06	.04	−.02
007.	aggressive	−.16	.00	−.01	.01	−.04	−.05	.24	.31	.27	.27	.23	.29
008.	alert	−.19	−.05	.01	−.07	−.05	−.08	−.02	.12	.11	.00	.14	.12
009.	aloof	−.01	.20	.03	.19	.10	.08	.01	.11	.06	.06	−.04	−.04
010.	ambitious	−.14	−.11	−.04	−.08	−.12	−.06	.03	.02	.25	.18	.15	.24
011.	anxious	.09	.11	.10	.11	.08	.21	.06	.06	.00	.04	−.13	−.07
012.	apathetic	.10	.12	.02	.01	.11	.11	.00	.10	.00	−.04	−.12	−.12
013.	appreciative	.06	−.07	−.05	−.04	−.03	−.16	−.17	−.20	−.07	−.06	−.09	−.22
014.	argumentative	.00	.14	.02	.07	−.03	−.03	.28	.24	.14	.22	.18	.18
015.	arrogant	.00	.12	.14	−.08	.07	.04	.24	.31	.27	.11	.26	.21
016.	artistic	.06	.15	−.01	.11	.03	.04	.06	.08	−.01	.14	.11	−.03
017.	assertive	.03	.01	.02	−.03	−.06	−.09	.18	.27	.19	.26	.26	.29
018.	attractive	−.01	−.04	−.01	.04	.01	−.05	−.07	.04	.02	.04	.16	.08
019.	autocratic	.09	.11	.02	−.04	.02	−.07	.04	.22	.19	.14	.16	.18
020.	awkward	.07	.14	.21	.14	.18	.14	−.07	−.02	.07	−.05	−.19	−.12
021.	bitter	−.01	.29	.24	.18	.11	.13	.03	.23	.07	.14	.08	.21
022.	blustery	.06	.22	.02	.05	.01	.04	.17	.14	.07	.06	.11	.11
023.	boastful	−.13	.07	.10	.00	.06	−.02	.16	.31	.20	.15	.27	.14
024.	bossy	.01	−.05	.19	.04	.00	.01	.19	.23	.17	.18	.14	.17
025.	calm	.00	−.14	−.04	−.09	−.02	−.13	−.21	−.36	−.19	−.19	−.05	−.04
026.	capable	−.07	−.11	−.01	−.15	.00	−.16	−.02	−.10	−.04	.00	.14	.07
027.	careless	.11	.25	.17	.24	.08	.01	.22	.17	.01	.13	.08	.08
028.	cautious	.08	−.15	.01	.03	.05	.09	−.15	−.39	−.05	−.19	−.25	−.19
029.	changeable	.05	.19	.10	.13	.08	.06	.10	.19	.05	.24	.15	.14
030.	charming	.08	−.04	.01	−.01	−.02	−.07	−.05	−.06	.05	.06	.22	.08
031.	cheerful	−.10	−.18	−.11	−.13	−.06	−.13	−.03	−.12	−.08	−.03	.10	.01
032.	civilized	−.04	−.08	−.01	.03	.05	−.05	−.05	−.04	−.03	−.07	.09	−.02
033.	clear-thinking	−.12	−.10	−.02	−.17	.01	−.11	−.02	−.07	−.15	−.20	.08	.12
034.	clever	−.07	.09	.02	−.07	.00	.03	.15	.20	.15	.06	.29	.18
035.	coarse	−.06	.15	.15	.05	.07	.05	.01	.24	.01	.09	.14	.18
036.	cold	.15	.14	.13	.16	.11	.08	.11	.08	.00	.07	−.02	.12
037.	commonplace	.08	−.05	−.01	.03	.07	−.03	−.12	−.12	−.14	−.08	−.11	−.17
038.	complaining	.08	.17	.20	.18	.09	.08	.04	.14	.06	.18	.05	.14
039.	complicated	.02	.21	−.02	.15	.10	.19	.05	.11	−.05	.15	.11	.12
040.	conceited	.02	.04	.14	−.04	−.02	−.01	.30	.28	.23	.18	.19	.13
041.	confident	−.09	−.15	−.03	−.10	−.05	−.15	.15	.17	.12	.14	.26	.27
042.	confused	.11	.12	.20	.20	.11	.24	.01	.13	.10	.14	−.08	−.01
043.	conscientious	.02	−.10	−.02	−.04	−.06	−.01	−.20	−.23	−.04	−.15	−.20	−.17
044.	conservative	−.03	−.19	−.06	−.02	−.03	−.05	−.14	−.29	−.11	−.21	−.17	−.21

Correlations of Observers' Adjectival Description with Scales of the CPI continued

| | Scale: Anx | | | | | | Scale: Nar | | | | | |
| | By Peers | | By Spouses | | By Staff | | By Peers | | By Spouses | | By Staff | |
Adjectives	M	F	M	F	M	F	M	F	M	F	M	F
045. considerate	−.09	−.11	−.06	.01	.06	−.08	−.22	−.25	−.07	−.12	−.10	−.08
046. contented	−.08	−.20	−.15	−.15	−.01	−.18	−.12	−.22	−.18	−.14	−.04	−.09
047. conventional	−.02	−.21	−.10	.00	−.06	−.07	−.17	−.34	−.03	−.21	−.19	−.21
048. cool	.09	.21	−.06	−.06	.00	−.05	.18	.22	−.04	.03	−.03	.05
049. cooperative	.03	−.20	−.07	−.15	−.03	−.09	−.16	−.26	−.05	−.20	−.08	−.14
050. courageous	.05	−.02	−.02	−.08	−.01	.07	.04	.10	.03	.01	.10	.19
051. cowardly	.19	.01	.10	−.03	.08	.03	.02	−.10	−.01	−.05	−.02	−.02
052. cruel	.04	.19	.17	−.02	.11	.07	.04	.10	.13	.14	.11	.11
053. curious	−.05	.01	.04	.06	.08	.03	.07	.13	.04	.02	.08	.24
054. cynical	.02	.24	.14	.16	.16	.05	.16	.26	.09	.25	.22	.25
055. daring	−.02	.03	.08	−.05	.01	.05	.09	.20	.14	.11	.28	.26
056. deceitful	.02	.15	.15	.01	.01	.10	.22	.10	.01	.20	.10	.13
057. defensive	.17	.18	.11	.09	.08	.09	.09	.16	.11	.09	.01	−.01
058. deliberate	−.06	−.01	.11	.03	.03	.00	−.11	.09	.04	.13	−.12	−.08
059. demanding	−.08	.02	.07	.08	.01	−.02	.11	.31	.22	.25	.21	.22
060. dependable	−.06	−.17	−.09	−.07	−.04	−.12	−.16	−.18	−.09	−.15	−.16	−.17
061. dependent	.08	−.03	.13	.18	.01	.00	−.04	−.16	−.06	−.06	−.16	−.16
062. despondent	.04	.18	.10	.00	.11	.21	.02	.06	.14	.01	−.03	−.16
063. determined	−.11	−.09	−.06	−.04	−.04	−.08	.06	.14	.10	.14	.18	.21
064. dignified	.07	−.06	−.01	.06	−.04	.02	−.06	−.12	.00	−.03	−.07	−.07
065. discreet	.06	−.07	−.03	−.03	.03	.01	−.05	−.26	−.01	−.02	−.15	−.16
066. disorderly	.04	.31	.09	.07	.07	.10	.19	.25	.13	.09	.09	.14
067. dissatisfied	.00	.22	.22	.23	.15	.15	.09	.15	.19	.03	.11	.12
068. distractible	.14	.05	.14	.07	.08	.12	.12	.12	.10	.12	.05	.08
069. distrustful	.13	.18	.09	.23	.10	.14	.08	.16	.03	.12	.05	.16
070. dominant	−.11	−.02	.03	.08	−.03	−.09	.18	.34	.16	.11	.28	.25
071. dreamy	.11	.05	.07	.02	.12	.07	−.06	−.02	.07	.16	−.10	−.07
072. dull	.10	−.02	.15	.05	.06	.05	−.16	−.18	.02	−.03	−.11	−.09
073. easygoing	−.05	.00	−.03	−.15	.09	−.04	−.11	.02	−.16	−.15	.06	.04
074. effeminate	.14	.02	−.07	.01	.07	.00	−.08	−.01	−.05	.09	−.05	.02
075. efficient	−.07	−.16	−.10	−.05	−.11	−.15	−.06	−.13	−.09	−.03	.03	.05
076. egotistical	−.11	.09	.07	.03	.02	.00	.27	.31	.31	.17	.27	.21
077. emotional	.04	.12	.09	.12	.06	.03	.09	.17	.14	.13	.10	.09
078. energetic	−.13	−.11	−.10	−.08	−.11	−.10	.11	.11	.20	.08	.24	.18
079. enterprising	−.05	−.04	.01	−.11	−.07	−.12	.05	.05	.21	.08	.25	.20
080. enthusiastic	−.15	−.12	−.12	−.14	.00	−.08	.07	.06	.26	.01	.20	.16
081. evasive	.15	.15	.11	.18	.12	.09	.00	.10	.07	.12	.01	.11
082. excitable	−.11	.02	.01	.10	−.01	−.03	.12	.32	.07	.18	.18	.09
083. fair-minded	−.02	−.11	−.13	−.05	.00	−.05	−.16	−.21	−.08	−.15	−.06	−.04
084. fault-finding	−.01	.15	.13	.11	.11	.04	.16	.19	.08	.10	.12	.15
085. fearful	−.01	.03	.16	−.04	.18	.18	.05	−.06	.08	−.03	−.12	−.07
086. feminine	.04	−.09	−.03	.10	.11	−.06	−.28	−.19	−.06	.01	−.07	−.08
087. fickle	.12	.10	.05	.14	.14	.09	−.07	.26	−.05	.09	.08	.13
088. flirtatious	−.01	−.05	.10	.03	.07	.00	.04	.21	.14	.16	.21	.21

Correlations of Observers' Adjectival Description with Scales of the CPI continued

		Scale: Anx						Scale: Nar				
		By Peers		By Spouses		By Staff		By Peers		By Spouses		By Staff	
Adjectives		M	F	M	F	M	F	M	F	M	F	M	F
089.	foolish	−.01	.12	.01	.21	.11	.06	.17	.19	−.07	.21	.07	.04
090.	forceful	−.13	−.01	.08	.02	−.03	−.08	.14	.25	.23	.23	.22	.19
091.	foresighted	−.03	−.08	.03	−.13	−.04	−.14	−.08	−.08	−.03	−.17	.00	.04
092.	forgetful	.17	.15	.04	.02	.15	.04	.10	−.01	−.04	.10	.00	−.03
093.	forgiving	−.08	−.18	−.03	−.04	.07	−.01	−.10	−.22	−.12	−.07	−.03	−.04
094.	formal	−.03	−.02	−.10	−.07	−.01	.01	−.09	−.16	−.01	.01	−.09	−.05
095.	frank	−.06	.07	−.02	.04	.01	−.04	−.02	.21	.12	.03	.10	.21
096.	friendly	−.04	−.22	−.14	−.12	−.01	−.09	−.05	−.06	−.04	−.07	.08	.00
097.	frivolous	−.05	−.02	.01	.13	.05	−.02	.05	.19	−.08	.05	.14	.09
098.	fussy	.12	.02	.15	.03	.08	.06	.04	.04	.02	.10	.00	−.07
099.	generous	−.14	−.15	−.06	.05	.07	−.08	−.15	−.15	−.02	−.18	.00	−.01
100.	gentle	.06	−.12	−.06	.04	.11	.01	−.18	−.37	−.17	−.15	−.12	−.13
101.	gloomy	.05	.27	.21	.07	.13	.20	−.03	.11	.00	.02	−.08	.05
102.	good-looking	−.03	−.02	−.04	.01	.01	−.04	.03	.12	.07	−.02	.16	.07
103.	good-natured	−.11	−.21	−.09	−.08	.02	−.06	−.19	−.12	−.03	−.12	.04	.00
104.	greedy	.11	.10	.08	.14	.09	−.01	.04	.17	.12	.06	.09	.14
105.	handsome	.07	.02	−.04	−.02	−.01	−.06	.04	−.01	.07	−.03	.17	−.04
106.	hard-headed	−.06	.05	.05	.08	.00	.02	.13	.26	.05	.20	.13	.13
107.	hard-hearted	.03	.05	.15	.14	.03	.01	.09	.16	.04	.12	.11	.12
108.	hasty	.02	.10	.17	.18	−.05	−.06	.15	.16	.07	.14	.12	.14
109.	headstrong	−.01	.11	.02	.11	.04	−.01	.23	.20	.21	.25	.23	.24
110.	healthy	−.05	−.05	−.06	−.10	.03	−.13	.01	.00	−.10	−.02	.14	.10
111.	helpful	−.06	−.14	−.05	−.08	−.02	−.12	−.09	−.14	−.11	.04	−.06	−.06
112.	high-strung	.08	.08	.20	.10	.06	.11	.00	.14	.00	.13	.07	.07
113.	honest	−.03	−.15	−.06	.02	−.02	−.03	−.18	−.21	−.13	−.20	−.12	−.05
114.	hostile	−.06	.27	.09	.09	.04	.08	.06	.19	.07	.11	.06	.13
115.	humorous	−.02	.06	.03	−.12	.03	.00	.10	.27	.09	.05	.28	.20
116.	hurried	.02	.11	.04	.00	.00	.05	.02	.26	.16	.00	.15	.02
117.	idealistic	.02	−.13	.03	.00	.02	.02	.08	−.13	.07	.14	−.05	.04
118.	imaginative	.01	.04	−.05	.00	.00	.01	.11	.09	.17	.17	.19	.11
119.	immature	−.08	.06	.24	.09	.03	.11	.05	.14	.11	−.03	−.03	−.04
120.	impatient	−.01	.21	−.04	.04	.00	.03	.10	.20	.16	.24	.19	.21
121.	impulsive	−.03	.17	.11	.10	.02	.06	.23	.32	.18	.28	.21	.16
122.	independent	−.07	.03	−.14	−.07	.01	.01	−.02	.07	−.01	.10	.25	.26
123.	indifferent	.11	.16	.09	.00	.09	.11	.04	.09	.06	.10	.03	.02
124.	individualistic	.12	.13	−.01	.03	.07	.06	.09	.16	.13	.21	.22	.22
125.	industrious	−.11	−.10	−.07	.02	−.08	−.09	−.05	−.14	.08	−.01	−.03	.04
126.	infantile	−.04	.01	.13	.21	.13	.15	.02	.19	.10	.03	.05	.11
127.	informal	−.10	−.01	.10	−.08	.06	−.02	−.07	.08	.03	.01	.18	.16
128.	ingenious	−.04	.06	.00	.00	−.04	−.02	.03	.15	.07	.06	.13	.10
129.	inhibited	.02	−.09	.18	.11	.06	.13	−.15	−.34	−.07	−.07	−.25	−.20
130.	initiative	−.09	−.02	.03	−.04	−.08	−.15	.10	.12	.10	.03	.24	.21
131.	insightful	−.09	−.09	.02	.00	−.02	−.03	−.08	−.06	.01	.04	.07	.09
132.	intelligent	−.05	−.16	.07	−.03	.00	−.05	.03	−.06	.08	.00	.15	.09

Correlations of Observers' Adjectival Description with Scales of the CPI continued

		Scale: Anx						Scale: Nar					
		By Peers		By Spouses		By Staff		By Peers		By Spouses		By Staff	
Adjectives		M	F	M	F	M	F	M	F	M	F	M	F
133.	interests—narrow	.11	.04	.10	.10	.04	.05	−.13	.01	−.02	−.05	−.17	−.13
134.	interests—wide	−.03	.03	−.07	−.07	.02	−.03	.11	.13	.01	.07	.18	.11
135.	intolerant	.12	.13	.15	.23	.05	.07	.13	.22	.12	.08	.09	.11
136.	inventive	−.15	.10	.00	−.03	.07	.01	−.02	.17	.09	.02	.20	.12
137.	irresponsible	.11	.29	.13	.18	.07	.13	.17	.12	.04	.12	.08	.08
138.	irritable	.06	.31	.08	.25	.08	.07	.10	.18	.02	.10	.07	.11
139.	jolly	−.07	−.12	.00	−.09	−.01	−.04	.00	.11	−.03	−.04	.19	.08
140.	kind	−.04	−.10	−.11	−.04	.09	−.07	−.19	−.17	−.15	−.08	−.03	−.05
141.	lazy	.09	.21	.07	.13	.08	.06	.15	.22	.11	.06	.06	.10
142.	leisurely	.11	−.06	.00	−.04	.01	−.03	.08	.08	.06	.07	.00	.04
143.	logical	−.09	−.06	.05	−.06	.01	−.04	−.02	−.04	.05	−.23	.00	.01
144.	loud	−.12	.03	.12	.05	.00	−.04	.09	.32	.12	.21	.24	.16
145.	loyal	.02	−.09	.08	.06	−.03	−.07	−.07	−.16	.00	−.08	−.14	−.07
146.	mannerly	−.04	−.16	−.09	−.10	.02	.01	−.11	−.24	−.06	−.01	−.11	−.07
147.	masculine	−.13	.05	.07	−.06	.01	.03	.07	.23	.14	.07	.16	.05
148.	mature	−.12	−.02	−.11	−.13	−.06	−.09	−.05	−.13	−.12	−.09	.03	.09
149.	meek	.07	.02	−.05	.12	.17	.10	−.19	−.24	.03	−.14	−.16	−.20
150.	methodical	−.01	−.07	−.01	−.06	−.06	.00	−.12	−.18	−.05	.00	−.14	−.14
151.	mild	.10	−.05	.00	−.03	.07	.01	−.19	−.34	−.17	−.23	−.22	−.27
152.	mischievous	.04	.02	.14	.03	.02	.02	.26	.09	.08	.13	.28	.14
153.	moderate	−.04	−.19	−.08	−.07	−.04	−.07	−.14	−.34	−.16	−.21	−.27	−.20
154.	modest	.10	−.02	−.04	.07	.01	.07	−.22	−.35	−.14	−.14	−.28	−.27
155.	moody	.08	.27	.21	.09	.08	.17	.05	.19	.01	.11	.01	.10
156.	nagging	.10	.11	.16	.20	.11	.05	.03	.12	.05	.06	.06	.11
157.	natural	−.07	−.03	.02	.02	−.06	−.09	−.03	−.07	−.13	−.02	.04	.01
158.	nervous	.16	.13	.19	.08	.07	.16	−.12	.06	.05	.06	−.11	−.06
159.	noisy	−.09	.02	.04	.12	−.01	−.01	.11	.29	.08	.18	.18	.09
160.	obliging	.03	−.19	.03	−.03	.02	.02	−.10	−.28	−.06	−.02	−.18	−.22
161.	obnoxious	−.04	.06	−.01	.16	.05	.07	.13	.30	.16	.15	.21	.10
162.	opinionated	.00	.05	.05	.19	.03	−.01	.21	.23	.17	.27	.17	.20
163.	opportunistic	−.07	−.04	.07	−.05	−.01	−.07	.14	.12	.07	.19	.26	.21
164.	optimistic	−.11	−.19	−.11	−.07	−.05	−.12	.05	−.04	.11	.01	.12	.11
165.	organized	−.11	−.18	−.11	−.09	−.12	−.13	−.09	−.20	−.16	−.13	.01	.02
166.	original	−.02	.07	.04	.07	.00	.11	.17	.15	.07	.12	.19	.13
167.	outgoing	−.15	−.11	−.13	−.13	−.09	−.14	.16	.22	.16	.16	.25	.19
168.	outspoken	−.13	.04	.09	−.02	−.01	−.06	.25	.30	.26	.14	.24	.18
169.	painstaking	.03	.04	.04	.05	.02	.11	−.14	−.18	−.03	−.02	−.17	−.17
170.	patient	.11	−.17	−.05	.03	.05	−.04	−.16	−.36	−.15	−.09	−.24	−.15
171.	peaceable	.07	−.15	−.06	.00	.03	−.01	−.22	−.36	−.09	−.11	−.26	−.24
172.	peculiar	.04	.19	.14	.08	.15	.19	−.05	.04	−.08	.15	−.09	−.01
173.	persevering	−.02	−.08	.11	−.02	−.10	.03	−.02	−.03	.03	−.04	−.07	−.01
174.	persistent	−.11	−.10	.01	−.07	.03	−.03	.03	.15	.03	.14	.12	.16
175.	pessimistic	.08	.27	.13	.16	.14	.17	.01	.15	.04	.08	.03	.01
176.	planful	−.13	−.12	−.04	−.08	−.03	−.13	−.01	−.16	.00	−.05	.03	−.02

Correlations of Observers' Adjectival Description with Scales of the CPI continued

		Scale: Anx						Scale: Nar				
		By Peers		By Spouses		By Staff		By Peers		By Spouses		By Staff	
Adjectives		M	F	M	F	M	F	M	F	M	F	M	F
177.	pleasant	−.14	−.15	−.16	.03	.00	−.11	−.11	−.10	−.09	−.12	.03	−.15
178.	pleasure-seeking	−.06	.10	.06	.07	.00	−.04	.15	.28	.21	.28	.28	.21
179.	poised	−.05	−.06	−.05	.03	−.09	−.11	−.03	−.10	.14	.08	.11	.09
180.	polished	−.05	.00	−.08	−.09	−.06	−.04	.09	−.03	.07	.03	.13	.08
181.	practical	−.13	−.18	−.14	−.06	−.04	−.15	−.13	−.23	−.11	−.15	−.02	.08
182.	praising	−.10	−.16	−.01	.02	−.06	−.07	−.08	−.16	−.04	.04	−.03	−.05
183.	precise	.01	−.01	−.04	−.04	.02	−.03	−.11	−.08	.02	−.06	−.04	−.02
184.	prejudiced	.07	.02	.06	.17	.04	.07	.13	.09	.17	.13	.06	.05
185.	preoccupied	.03	.16	.10	.10	.10	.18	.02	.12	.07	.12	−.09	−.02
186.	progressive	−.08	.01	.05	−.02	.10	−.01	.06	.20	.06	−.03	.21	.17
187.	prudish	.10	−.04	.18	.17	.07	.09	−.02	−.11	.14	−.01	−.13	−.21
188.	quarrelsome	−.04	.11	.14	.19	.05	.06	.28	.22	.06	.10	.14	.16
189.	queer	.13	.21	−.06	.00	.08	.15	.00	.11	−.11	.00	−.10	.03
190.	quick	−.08	−.01	.04	.00	−.03	−.01	.12	.20	.12	.09	.26	.20
191.	quiet	.19	.04	−.02	−.05	.08	.10	−.19	−.35	−.22	−.32	−.26	−.25
192.	quitting	.20	.13	.14	.05	.06	.09	−.17	.04	−.03	−.15	.01	.02
193.	rational	−.09	−.16	.10	−.03	.05	−.04	.01	−.10	.12	−.10	.02	.10
194.	rattle-brained	.01	.13	.04	.12	.07	.10	.00	.19	.07	.03	.03	.04
195.	realistic	−.13	−.11	.04	−.07	−.02	−.14	−.08	−.05	.05	−.13	.07	.08
196.	reasonable	−.11	−.13	−.17	−.06	−.02	−.13	−.16	−.17	−.06	−.10	−.10	−.08
197.	rebellious	.03	.25	.15	.07	.09	.09	.19	.31	.12	.26	.15	.20
198.	reckless	.07	.10	.21	.24	.01	.11	.15	.25	.10	.29	.20	.14
199.	reflective	.14	.05	.11	−.02	.07	.13	−.12	−.16	.01	−.02	−.06	−.02
200.	relaxed	−.05	−.10	−.12	−.03	−.02	−.16	−.10	−.02	−.03	−.16	.06	.13
201.	reliable	−.06	−.22	−.09	.00	−.03	−.10	−.17	−.30	−.04	−.18	−.09	−.17
202.	resentful	−.02	.28	.10	.23	.09	.10	.13	.25	.04	.13	.08	.17
203.	reserved	.14	−.03	.05	.13	.07	.08	−.13	−.38	−.12	−.21	−.24	−.18
204.	resourceful	−.20	−.14	.07	−.01	−.08	−.11	−.02	−.03	.20	.22	.20	.17
205.	responsible	−.16	−.19	−.10	.00	−.06	−.12	−.12	−.26	.02	−.04	−.07	−.12
206.	restless	.05	.21	.03	.05	.08	.11	.16	.31	.21	.20	.20	.18
207.	retiring	.09	.02	.10	.10	.07	.07	−.07	−.22	−.05	−.07	−.20	−.24
208.	rigid	.06	.04	.05	.13	.05	.11	.01	−.03	.03	−.06	−.05	−.03
209.	robust	−.06	−.02	−.04	.03	.03	−.03	.04	.23	.17	.02	.19	.20
210.	rude	−.02	.15	.06	.05	.06	.09	.15	.29	.12	.06	.20	.12
211.	sarcastic	−.01	.24	.05	.15	.10	.02	.16	.34	.18	.16	.26	.24
212.	self-centered	−.03	.09	.20	.12	.02	.11	.19	.24	.19	.16	.23	.19
213.	self-confident	−.09	−.08	−.13	−.16	−.05	−.13	.14	.20	.17	.16	.26	.27
214.	self-controlled	−.03	−.21	−.10	−.06	.00	.01	−.09	−.27	−.01	−.04	−.15	−.11
215.	self-denying	.02	.05	.12	.10	.11	.12	−.22	−.17	−.01	−.06	−.23	−.22
216.	self-pitying	.13	.23	.18	.19	.08	.17	−.14	.17	.06	.01	−.01	.08
217.	self-punishing	.03	.11	.19	.11	.09	.16	−.02	−.03	.12	.08	−.07	.02
218.	self-seeking	.03	.04	.10	−.01	−.01	−.02	.13	.21	.10	.17	.25	.18
219.	selfish	.06	.07	−.02	.06	−.02	.05	.18	.21	.01	.10	.17	.12
220.	sensitive	.01	.14	.05	.07	.12	.08	−.02	−.06	.00	.02	−.03	−.07

Correlations of Observers' Adjectival Description with Scales of the CPI continued

		Scale: Anx						Scale: Nar				
		By Peers		By Spouses		By Staff		By Peers		By Spouses		By Staff	
Adjectives		M	F	M	F	M	F	M	F	M	F	M	F
221.	sentimental	.09	−.05	.01	.03	.04	−.02	.00	−.10	−.06	−.11	.02	−.05
222.	serious	.07	.02	.04	.11	.06	.06	−.14	−.16	.07	.02	−.16	−.06
223.	severe	.09	.00	.07	.07	.09	.09	.10	.01	.19	−.03	.07	.06
224.	sexy	−.12	.07	.02	.00	.01	−.03	.11	.17	.19	.08	.26	.19
225.	shallow	.20	.02	.08	.14	−.03	−.02	.04	.08	.02	.04	−.05	−.02
226.	sharp-witted	−.04	.19	.07	.09	.02	.05	.12	.26	.26	.20	.28	.16
227.	shiftless	−.03	.14	.14	.09	.04	.11	−.01	.13	−.02	.07	.01	.06
228.	show-off	−.10	.09	.13	.05	.00	.00	.17	.32	.24	.16	.30	.12
229.	shrewd	−.02	.19	.10	.07	−.05	.03	.02	.13	.16	.19	.24	.18
230.	shy	.07	.04	.10	.09	.15	.14	−.28	−.30	−.13	−.18	−.19	−.18
231.	silent	.21	.00	.11	.03	.15	.14	−.18	−.22	−.16	−.10	−.13	−.13
232.	simple	−.07	−.06	−.07	.12	.06	−.03	−.20	−.17	−.11	−.05	−.14	−.18
233.	sincere	.02	−.11	−.12	.03	.00	−.04	−.09	−.22	−.02	−.21	−.15	−.11
234.	slipshod	.01	.21	.15	.20	−.01	.05	.12	.18	.10	.11	.02	.01
235.	slow	.18	−.02	.11	.07	.00	.09	−.06	−.11	−.04	.00	−.18	−.15
236.	sly	.08	.16	.22	−.04	.04	.05	.02	.11	.12	.23	.16	.19
237.	smug	−.05	.05	−.02	.09	−.01	.06	.15	.17	.11	.11	.19	.16
238.	snobbish	.01	.01	−.05	.12	.02	−.03	.16	.07	.11	.21	.11	.15
239.	sociable	−.23	−.12	−.13	.02	−.07	−.15	.05	.10	.07	.19	.22	.12
240.	soft-hearted	−.10	−.18	−.04	.13	.05	−.04	−.20	−.21	.01	−.01	−.08	−.10
241.	sophisticated	−.02	.06	−.06	−.02	.01	−.04	.00	−.01	.12	.11	.23	.16
242.	spendthrift	.03	.07	−.05	.16	.01	.00	.10	.08	.02	.08	.11	.11
243.	spineless	.05	.04	.05	.14	.13	.00	−.10	−.06	.06	−.03	−.06	−.08
244.	spontaneous	−.06	−.03	−.03	.00	−.02	−.04	.11	.26	.16	.14	.23	.15
245.	spunky	.03	−.08	.12	.03	−.01	.03	.09	.15	.21	.28	.21	.20
246.	stable	−.06	−.17	−.13	.04	−.01	−.20	−.05	−.14	−.11	−.08	−.03	−.04
247.	steady	−.09	−.17	−.03	.11	−.01	−.12	−.13	−.20	−.10	−.07	−.07	−.03
248.	stern	−.01	.07	.15	.03	.06	.02	.14	−.04	.10	−.05	−.01	.14
249.	stingy	.19	.13	.21	.14	.04	−.08	.03	.17	.19	.22	−.05	.03
250.	stolid	.02	.09	−.05	.01	.11	−.01	.09	.07	.01	.04	−.08	−.06
251.	strong	−.03	−.06	−.03	−.01	.03	−.13	.09	.09	.11	.15	.19	.30
252.	stubborn	.01	.06	.09	.07	.01	.00	.21	.23	.06	.17	.13	.17
253.	submissive	.07	−.13	.13	.08	.04	.03	−.16	−.31	.00	−.11	−.25	−.29
254.	suggestible	−.13	.01	.13	.04	.00	.04	−.09	.06	.05	.05	−.11	−.18
255.	sulky	.01	.25	.14	.17	.09	.07	.02	.10	.09	.05	−.01	.17
256.	superstitious	−.01	.03	.23	.27	.01	.16	−.14	−.02	.17	.21	−.01	.13
257.	suspicious	.06	.19	.17	.11	.12	.15	.12	.11	.10	.16	.08	.18
258.	sympathetic	.01	−.12	−.03	−.02	.04	−.04	−.05	−.13	−.05	−.05	−.06	−.10
259.	tactful	.03	−.13	−.21	−.07	−.10	−.12	−.04	−.22	−.03	.00	−.10	−.06
260.	tactless	−.12	.05	.10	.10	.10	.07	.02	.12	.05	−.02	.16	.14
261.	talkative	−.26	−.06	−.01	.07	−.03	−.09	.15	.35	.16	.23	.27	.20
262.	temperamental	.10	.20	.13	.11	.07	−.02	.22	.19	.12	.27	.17	.22
263.	tense	.11	.16	.16	.13	.06	.21	−.06	−.01	.07	.12	−.02	.01
264.	thankless	.13	.14	.20	.01	.04	.08	.12	.12	.09	.03	.11	.05

Correlations of Observers' Adjectival Description with Scales of the CPI continued

		Scale: Anx						Scale: Nar				
		By Peers		By Spouses		By Staff		By Peers		By Spouses		By Staff	
Adjectives		M	F	M	F	M	F	M	F	M	F	M	F
265.	thorough	−.12	−.05	.06	−.01	−.08	−.04	−.08	−.09	.00	−.05	−.14	−.02
266.	thoughtful	−.14	−.15	−.04	−.13	.03	−.04	−.24	−.16	−.06	−.09	−.07	−.07
267.	thrifty	.01	−.07	.09	.08	.06	.03	−.06	−.10	−.05	−.15	−.08	−.05
268.	timid	.08	.06	.00	.19	.12	.12	−.24	−.25	−.07	−.08	−.19	−.15
269.	tolerant	−.02	−.11	−.13	−.02	.05	−.08	−.07	−.20	−.01	−.09	−.07	−.05
270.	touchy	.03	.20	.20	.10	.06	.16	.08	.21	−.06	.23	.04	.09
271.	tough	−.03	.09	.13	−.03	.01	−.01	.13	.24	.14	.09	.20	.30
272.	trusting	−.12	−.22	−.11	−.03	.08	−.12	−.03	−.31	.03	−.12	−.09	−.10
273.	unaffected	−.02	−.05	−.08	.14	.01	−.06	−.03	−.13	.02	.19	−.18	−.22
274.	unambitious	.06	−.01	.10	.06	.09	.02	−.02	.01	−.03	−.02	−.10	−.14
275.	unassuming	.09	−.08	−.06	−.04	.05	.05	−.22	−.24	.04	−.06	−.27	−.24
276.	unconventional	.03	.34	.08	.05	.12	.12	.02	.22	.04	.19	.14	.16
277.	undependable	.13	.19	.02	.21	.04	.08	.15	.26	.04	.15	.05	.05
278.	understanding	−.10	−.16	−.05	−.17	.09	−.09	−.07	−.15	−.05	−.08	.03	.02
279.	unemotional	.10	.00	−.05	.05	.16	.01	−.06	−.09	−.09	−.05	.00	−.06
280.	unexcitable	.10	.08	.05	.03	.06	−.03	−.15	−.17	−.08	−.10	−.07	−.10
281.	unfriendly	.07	.16	.17	−.06	.05	.04	.07	.11	.06	.17	.01	.10
282.	uninhibited	−.09	.08	.00	−.07	.02	.02	.09	.25	.01	.11	.27	.22
283.	unintelligent	−.03	.00	.00	.00	.05	.01	−.10	.05	.00	−.01	−.07	−.10
284.	unkind	−.01	.16	.08	.12	.07	.04	−.06	.12	.02	.07	.17	.16
285.	unrealistic	.04	.05	.10	.21	.02	.15	.12	.11	.11	.13	.02	.07
286.	unscrupulous	.05	.19	.16	.12	.08	.05	.12	.13	.01	.09	.10	.11
287.	unselfish	−.19	−.09	−.06	.02	.07	−.02	−.18	−.26	−.08	−.05	−.02	−.15
288.	unstable	−.02	.22	.20	.08	.07	.21	.04	.15	.03	.12	−.01	−.01
289.	vindictive	.01	.10	.08	.27	.08	.08	.10	.17	.11	.20	.11	.16
290.	versatile	−.18	.00	−.03	.00	−.06	−.07	.04	.31	.17	.06	.23	.21
291.	warm	−.05	−.21	.00	.04	−.01	−.12	−.11	−.19	−.05	−.14	.08	−.01
292.	wary	.08	.07	.07	.07	.12	.11	.24	−.06	.11	.11	.02	.05
293.	weak	.07	−.07	.30	.24	.08	.10	−.15	−.20	.09	−.05	−.11	−.12
294.	whiny	.15	.02	.15	.26	.03	.05	−.04	.05	.09	.19	.02	.04
295.	wholesome	−.14	−.18	−.05	−.09	−.01	−.13	−.16	−.11	.00	.00	−.03	−.01
296.	wise	−.12	−.09	.04	.02	.02	−.08	.01	−.12	−.08	−.04	.06	.08
297.	withdrawn	.19	.12	.23	.09	.17	.19	−.20	−.28	.05	−.08	−.14	−.08
298.	witty	.02	.12	−.05	−.03	−.01	.04	.18	.32	.07	.08	.27	.20
299.	worrying	.08	.04	.24	.17	.10	.19	−.05	−.12	.11	.03	−.08	−.03
300.	zany	−.06	.07	.05	.06	.01	.10	.12	.28	.13	.24	.20	.12

Correlations of Observers' Adjectival Description with Scales of the CPI continued											
	Scale: D–SD						**Scale: D–AC**					
	By Peers		By Spouses		By Staff		By Peers		By Spouses		By Staff	
Adjectives	M	F	M	F	M	F	M	F	M	F	M	F
001. absent-minded	.00	−.28	−.02	−.04	−.09	−.11	.05	−.08	−.06	−.01	.00	.01
002. active	.13	.21	−.01	.10	.04	.12	.11	.08	.10	.12	.06	.07
003. adaptable	.13	.24	.08	−.02	.07	.12	−.02	−.04	−.05	.11	−.01	.06
004. adventurous	.08	−.03	−.06	.00	−.03	−.03	.05	.09	.14	.10	.07	.14
005. affected	.01	.07	.05	−.07	.06	−.03	.07	.08	−.03	.09	−.03	.02
006. affectionate	−.07	.07	−.01	−.04	−.02	.02	.00	.02	.01	.07	−.02	.07
007. aggressive	.11	.10	−.06	.01	.04	.06	.14	.11	.13	.07	.04	.02
008. alert	.08	.14	.03	.12	.04	.13	−.02	.09	.00	.09	.00	.06
009. aloof	−.03	−.17	−.06	−.06	−.16	−.09	−.02	−.02	.01	−.02	−.02	−.11
010. ambitious	.17	.22	.11	.17	.18	.16	.03	−.02	.09	.01	.01	.01
011. anxious	−.11	−.08	−.02	−.14	−.10	−.26	.05	.02	−.06	.06	−.11	−.05
012. apathetic	−.17	−.23	−.15	−.06	−.16	−.18	−.12	.00	−.02	−.11	.00	.00
013. appreciative	.09	.13	.08	.04	.03	.11	.01	−.04	−.03	.05	−.07	.01
014. argumentative	.01	−.03	−.02	−.04	.04	−.01	.11	.05	.07	.04	.02	−.01
015. arrogant	.02	−.03	−.18	.07	−.05	−.03	.06	.15	.02	.05	.05	.09
016. artistic	−.15	−.09	−.01	−.01	−.05	−.03	−.01	.04	−.02	.09	−.04	−.14
017. assertive	.05	.02	.00	.16	.06	.10	.03	.15	−.10	.02	.06	.08
018. attractive	.04	.08	−.01	−.02	−.02	.08	−.10	.04	.03	.08	.04	.00
019. autocratic	.02	−.03	−.01	−.05	−.01	−.01	.00	.07	.05	.02	.07	.07
020. awkward	−.16	−.21	−.25	−.14	−.23	−.21	.13	−.09	−.05	−.10	−.01	−.04
021. bitter	−.03	−.16	−.18	−.13	−.19	−.15	.07	.15	−.01	.11	.09	.10
022. blustery	.02	−.03	−.08	−.11	−.01	−.08	.19	.10	.04	.08	.03	.08
023. boastful	.05	.01	−.07	−.03	.02	.07	.10	.14	.17	.17	.10	.03
024. bossy	−.06	.05	−.21	−.03	.01	.04	.10	.07	.14	.06	.06	.04
025. calm	.05	.18	.08	.04	−.07	.12	−.13	−.16	−.08	−.03	.02	−.03
026. capable	.13	.21	−.03	.12	.00	.21	−.16	−.05	−.05	−.09	.03	.00
027. careless	−.12	−.24	−.18	−.10	−.14	−.16	.11	−.02	−.06	.10	.02	−.04
028. cautious	−.08	.10	−.04	−.01	−.09	−.07	−.07	−.15	−.10	−.07	−.05	−.06
029. changeable	−.04	−.25	−.11	−.12	−.13	−.23	.02	.00	−.03	.08	.02	.02
030. charming	.01	.12	−.01	−.05	−.01	.05	−.02	.01	.09	.05	.02	.01
031. cheerful	.02	.15	.14	.04	.06	.14	.04	−.05	−.02	.03	.02	.10
032. civilized	.03	.05	.11	.03	−.03	.13	−.18	−.05	−.03	.06	.04	−.03
033. clear-thinking	.08	.18	.07	.18	.01	.16	−.15	−.11	−.11	−.05	.00	−.01
034. clever	−.06	−.04	−.06	.12	−.02	.04	−.11	.04	.12	.07	.05	.03
035. coarse	.05	−.16	−.17	−.02	−.12	−.14	.09	.09	−.01	−.11	.09	.02
036. cold	−.09	−.07	−.03	−.06	−.02	−.12	.03	.01	−.01	.00	−.05	.00
037. commonplace	−.08	−.01	.08	−.08	−.10	−.08	.06	−.10	.01	.03	.03	.09
038. complaining	−.13	−.18	−.19	−.18	−.12	−.11	.04	.08	.08	.01	.00	.06
039. complicated	.08	−.15	.05	−.10	−.14	−.16	.05	.03	−.21	−.01	−.04	−.11
040. conceited	.00	.08	−.12	−.01	.07	.03	.11	.15	.23	.05	.03	.03
041. confident	.13	.22	.07	.19	.04	.18	−.04	.04	.08	.09	.08	.10
042. confused	−.01	−.20	−.19	−.16	−.15	−.22	.06	.08	.05	.04	−.02	.00
043. conscientious	.11	.26	.18	.17	.03	.15	−.05	−.02	−.11	−.13	−.05	.01
044. conservative	.04	.12	.10	−.03	.03	.08	−.10	−.13	−.03	.01	.02	.07

Correlations of Observers' Adjectival Description with Scales of the CPI continued

	Scale: D–SD						Scale: D–AC					
	By Peers		By Spouses		By Staff		By Peers		By Spouses		By Staff	
Adjectives	M	F	M	F	M	F	M	F	M	F	M	F
045. considerate	.06	.14	.16	−.02	−.05	.07	−.13	.04	−.08	.08	−.04	.07
046. contented	−.04	.15	.12	.02	−.02	.07	−.16	.01	−.01	−.01	.05	.10
047. conventional	.02	.15	.11	.01	.01	.09	−.00	−.13	−.07	−.03	.01	.11
048. cool	−.02	−.20	−.03	.04	−.06	−.04	−.01	−.03	−.05	.09	−.02	−.01
049. cooperative	−.08	.17	.11	.07	.02	.14	−.14	−.08	−.05	−.08	−.02	.03
050. courageous	−.05	.03	.04	.09	−.02	.03	−.03	.02	−.05	.08	.02	.07
051. cowardly	−.02	−.12	−.06	.00	−.07	−.05	.15	−.11	−.12	.08	.00	.00
052. cruel	−.07	−.12	−.16	−.03	−.10	−.13	.05	−.02	−.03	.07	.02	.00
053. curious	−.06	−.10	.01	.05	−.07	−.06	.00	.05	−.05	.03	−.09	.02
054. cynical	.03	−.20	−.08	−.09	−.17	−.16	−.04	.06	−.07	.07	.05	−.04
055. daring	.05	.01	−.03	−.05	.00	−.06	.05	.02	.07	.11	.08	.08
056. deceitful	−.03	−.10	−.17	−.03	.00	−.11	.00	−.07	−.01	.11	.00	.00
057. defensive	−.15	−.20	−.15	−.13	−.08	−.10	.01	.06	.01	.00	−.03	−.02
058. deliberate	.05	−.05	−.03	−.06	−.11	.06	−.07	.13	−.06	.09	−.01	−.03
059. demanding	.06	−.04	−.04	−.13	−.01	−.03	.01	.15	.11	.06	.08	.08
060. dependable	.09	.21	.06	−.05	.04	.19	−.11	−.01	−.10	−.08	−.06	.04
061. dependent	−.07	−.07	.00	−.11	−.06	−.14	.03	−.08	−.05	.10	−.09	.07
062. despondent	−.07	−.23	−.13	.05	−.11	−.18	.02	−.09	−.01	−.06	.04	−.06
063. determined	.07	.18	.02	.08	.04	.15	.01	.08	.01	−.01	.06	.07
064. dignified	.05	.16	.06	.12	.03	.02	−.02	−.01	.05	.10	−.02	−.01
065. discreet	.01	.10	.04	.03	.02	.08	−.11	−.14	−.01	.13	−.05	−.12
066. disorderly	−.04	−.22	−.12	−.09	−.07	−.25	.07	.01	.12	.03	−.03	.05
067. dissatisfied	−.01	−.26	−.22	−.11	−.17	−.22	.11	.00	.10	−.03	.00	.00
068. distractible	−.05	−.16	−.22	−.15	−.13	−.20	.11	−.09	.14	.08	.03	.05
069. distrustful	−.09	−.13	−.14	−.12	−.09	−.20	.07	.03	−.06	.11	.01	−.02
070. dominant	.16	.10	.02	−.10	.00	.13	.17	.15	−.02	−.01	.08	.07
071. dreamy	−.04	.00	−.15	−.07	−.11	−.15	−.03	−.04	−.02	.13	−.02	−.10
072. dull	−.03	−.09	−.07	−.12	−.09	−.02	−.01	−.07	−.04	.00	.01	.06
073. easygoing	−.05	−.01	−.04	.02	−.13	.00	−.07	.03	−.04	.04	.08	.11
074. effeminate	−.05	−.04	.03	−.04	.01	.07	.03	−.04	.01	.14	−.10	.08
075. efficient	−.02	.28	.13	.10	.14	.19	−.06	−.02	.02	−.05	−.06	.03
076. egotistical	.03	.04	−.11	.06	.00	.03	.12	.16	.19	.01	.04	.04
077. emotional	−.06	−.07	−.11	−.17	−.08	−.13	.12	.03	.08	.11	−.01	.06
078. energetic	.08	.20	.10	.09	.11	.14	.09	.10	.04	.02	.02	.06
079. enterprising	.08	.13	.02	.16	.13	.17	.01	−.04	.05	.00	.07	.08
080. enthusiastic	.05	.15	.12	.10	.04	.13	.00	.08	.05	.01	.01	.15
081. evasive	.08	−.13	.00	−.16	−.16	−.11	−.07	.04	−.06	.11	.01	.06
082. excitable	−.09	−.06	−.07	−.12	.01	−.04	.09	.17	.05	.13	−.01	.06
083. fair-minded	.10	.12	.08	.01	.00	.11	−.04	−.05	−.09	.00	−.02	−.02
084. fault-finding	−.07	−.11	−.02	−.18	−.09	−.09	.12	.07	.05	.00	.02	.02
085. fearful	−.10	−.06	−.17	−.10	−.12	−.24	.05	.00	.01	.05	−.09	.02
086. feminine	.11	.09	.04	−.07	−.04	.08	−.05	−.06	−.05	.12	−.06	.01
087. fickle	−.05	−.06	−.01	−.09	−.06	−.05	.03	.04	−.14	.08	−.02	.05
088. flirtatious	.02	.06	−.19	−.11	−.02	−.02	.07	.09	.10	.17	.03	.08

Correlations of Observers' Adjectival Description with Scales of the CPI *continued*											
	Scale: D–SD						Scale: D–AC					
	By Peers		By Spouses		By Staff		By Peers		By Spouses		By Staff	
Adjectives	M	F	M	F	M	F	M	F	M	F	M	F
089. foolish	−.09	−.21	−.07	−.11	−.04	−.08	.05	.09	.00	.13	.10	.07
090. forceful	.10	.09	−.06	−.03	.01	.14	.19	.13	.08	.04	.06	.02
091. foresighted	.04	.20	.12	.10	.07	.15	−.11	−.02	−.19	−.04	−.04	−.04
092. forgetful	−.14	−.25	−.04	.01	−.11	−.10	.09	−.13	−.03	.02	.01	.03
093. forgiving	.08	.12	−.04	−.01	−.05	−.06	−.02	−.06	−.07	.08	.01	.10
094. formal	.13	.13	.04	.04	.03	.02	−.07	−.06	.00	.00	−.03	.00
095. frank	.02	−.09	−.04	.03	−.09	.00	−.06	.08	.09	−.05	.02	.07
096. friendly	.04	.13	.09	.05	.02	.15	−.16	.04	−.06	.08	.01	.08
097. frivolous	−.02	−.04	−.06	.05	−.04	−.04	.03	.07	−.12	.04	.02	.07
098. fussy	−.16	−.03	−.06	−.12	−.01	−.04	.01	.00	.06	.12	.03	.03
099. generous	.01	.17	−.04	.07	−.04	−.01	.02	−.02	−.03	.04	−.01	.01
100. gentle	−.01	.05	.01	−.08	−.13	−.03	−.12	−.10	−.10	−.03	−.02	.04
101. gloomy	−.07	−.21	−.21	.00	−.11	−.14	.00	.03	−.05	−.09	−.01	−.02
102. good-looking	.06	.09	−.03	−.08	−.03	.07	−.14	.03	.07	.06	.05	.01
103. good-natured	−.01	.16	.11	.08	−.05	.07	−.10	.05	−.02	−.06	.07	.06
104. greedy	−.08	−.16	−.10	−.04	−.03	−.13	.01	.08	.05	.01	−.02	.07
105. handsome	.03	.02	.04	−.01	−.05	.05	−.14	−.02	.07	−.06	.08	−.01
106. hard-headed	.03	−.09	−.07	−.10	.00	−.02	.05	.11	.09	.13	.06	−.02
107. hard-hearted	−.08	−.07	−.05	−.10	−.06	−.01	−.05	.02	−.03	.16	.07	.03
108. hasty	−.12	−.14	−.22	−.16	.02	−.09	.17	.09	−.05	.07	−.03	.04
109. headstrong	−.04	−.04	−.07	−.07	−.05	−.04	.11	−.01	.10	.09	.04	.04
110. healthy	−.07	.04	.00	.03	−.04	.17	−.03	−.05	.02	.00	.06	.06
111. helpful	.03	.20	.04	.12	.01	.10	.06	.02	−.11	.13	.00	.09
112. high-strung	−.09	−.08	−.12	.00	−.06	−.19	.07	.09	.00	.01	−.07	−.04
113. honest	−.01	.09	−.02	−.03	.00	.10	−.09	−.07	−.05	−.14	−.04	.00
114. hostile	−.01	−.15	−.16	.03	−.03	−.15	.05	.02	−.10	.04	.01	−.03
115. humorous	.01	−.18	−.12	.12	−.08	.00	.00	.18	.08	−.01	.10	.07
116. hurried	−.10	−.08	.02	.07	−.03	−.04	.14	.08	.01	−.05	−.01	.02
117. idealistic	.04	.15	.06	.06	.01	.00	.07	−.05	.03	.08	−.06	−.05
118. imaginative	−.01	.03	−.04	.10	−.03	.00	−.03	.00	.00	.08	−.04	−.06
119. immature	−.04	−.20	−.15	−.12	−.08	−.14	.02	.11	.04	−.01	−.03	−.04
120. impatient	−.02	−.20	−.04	−.15	−.03	−.11	.18	.04	.01	.10	−.02	−.01
121. impulsive	−.04	−.22	−.15	−.14	−.05	−.18	.14	.12	.08	.17	−.01	.02
122. independent	.14	.06	.09	.10	−.05	.01	−.07	.01	−.07	.04	.02	.04
123. indifferent	−.14	−.21	−.08	−.04	−.20	−.15	−.09	−.09	−.07	.01	.02	.04
124. individualistic	.05	−.03	.00	.08	−.07	−.05	−.01	−.01	−.01	.06	.01	−.02
125. industrious	.09	.26	.07	.05	.10	.21	.01	.04	.01	.02	−.01	.02
126. infantile	−.06	−.10	−.07	−.19	−.12	−.19	.06	.11	−.03	.10	.07	.06
127. informal	.04	−.15	−.01	.00	−.11	−.08	.02	−.07	−.07	.05	.02	.07
128. ingenious	.03	.03	.03	.01	.06	−.01	−.04	.04	.03	.11	−.07	−.06
129. inhibited	.02	.07	−.14	−.12	−.10	−.09	−.05	−.23	−.15	−.03	−.06	−.05
130. initiative	.04	.15	.07	.09	.12	.17	.08	.10	−.03	.00	.04	.04
131. insightful	.05	.15	−.01	.13	.01	.07	−.07	−.11	−.07	−.07	−.01	−.10
132. intelligent	.01	.24	.05	.05	.02	.11	−.14	−.09	−.07	−.05	−.03	−.04

354
CPI MANUAL

Correlations of Observers' Adjectival Description with Scales of the CPI continued

		Scale: D–SD						Scale: D–AC					
		By Peers		By Spouses		By Staff		By Peers		By Spouses		By Staff	
Adjectives		M	F	M	F	M	F	M	F	M	F	M	F
133.	interests—narrow	−.07	−.10	−.07	−.21	−.14	−.15	.07	−.01	−.12	.04	−.01	.14
134.	interests—wide	.11	.09	.06	.05	.04	.09	.01	.11	.02	.05	−.04	−.05
135.	intolerant	−.03	−.10	−.14	−.17	−.08	−.12	.00	−.02	.05	.07	.09	.06
136.	inventive	.04	.02	.01	.13	.00	−.01	−.10	.03	.01	.03	−.01	−.11
137.	irresponsible	−.08	−.19	−.08	−.10	−.06	−.13	−.05	.01	.02	.03	−.01	.00
138.	irritable	−.04	−.24	−.11	−.15	−.09	−.10	.10	.01	−.10	.01	.02	−.04
139.	jolly	.03	.13	−.10	.02	−.01	.01	−.02	.05	.10	.08	.10	.11
140.	kind	.09	.15	.04	.02	−.10	.05	.03	.06	−.09	−.02	.02	.10
141.	lazy	−.10	−.29	−.01	−.12	−.15	−.19	−.11	.00	.02	−.01	.01	.06
142.	leisurely	−.09	−.06	−.01	−.05	−.09	−.10	−.08	−.05	.01	.06	.04	.08
143.	logical	.08	.16	−.09	−.02	−.01	.09	−.06	−.13	−.02	−.12	−.06	−.09
144.	loud	.03	−.04	−.09	−.05	.00	.02	.09	.22	.14	.10	.07	.01
145.	loyal	.05	.04	−.04	−.19	−.03	.04	.04	−.01	.01	.10	.03	.07
146.	mannerly	.06	.12	.11	.16	−.03	.07	−.06	−.12	.04	.01	−.02	.02
147.	masculine	.04	−.09	.05	−.07	−.06	−.04	−.07	.05	.11	.00	.10	−.06
148.	mature	.19	.19	.15	.08	.03	.13	−.09	−.03	−.06	.02	.04	.07
149.	meek	−.13	−.10	−.06	−.07	−.16	−.06	−.03	−.05	.10	.02	−.03	.01
150.	methodical	−.03	.06	−.04	.13	.01	.14	.09	−.11	−.08	−.02	−.04	−.06
151.	mild	−.12	.06	−.03	−.04	−.08	−.02	−.10	−.08	.04	−.03	−.03	−.04
152.	mischievous	−.19	−.09	−.16	−.19	−.07	−.07	.08	.04	.07	.14	.08	.02
153.	moderate	.09	.16	.03	.13	−.01	.09	−.13	−.18	−.12	−.05	−.04	−.02
154.	modest	−.01	.04	.02	−.02	−.09	−.05	−.13	−.09	−.01	.12	−.08	−.02
155.	moody	−.04	−.33	−.12	−.12	−.16	−.27	.04	.00	−.07	.14	−.01	−.03
156.	nagging	−.11	−.08	−.15	−.11	−.06	−.09	.08	.11	.09	−.01	.04	.14
157.	natural	.03	−.03	.01	−.07	.02	.07	−.07	−.05	−.07	.01	.01	−.01
158.	nervous	−.04	−.19	−.14	−.05	−.10	−.24	.07	.01	.03	.13	−.08	.00
159.	noisy	.03	−.02	−.02	−.15	.01	−.02	.08	.14	.10	.14	.03	.08
160.	obliging	.02	.18	−.05	−.08	−.01	−.02	−.09	−.11	−.06	.01	−.13	.00
161.	obnoxious	−.06	−.13	−.09	.00	−.04	−.17	.06	.17	.05	.03	.09	.05
162.	opinionated	.01	−.06	−.07	−.11	−.03	.03	.14	.05	.02	.18	.05	.10
163.	opportunistic	.08	.01	−.02	−.02	.03	.02	.00	.00	−.09	.12	.07	.05
164.	optimistic	.07	.16	.08	.14	.08	.12	−.07	.09	.06	−.02	.06	.16
165.	organized	.09	.33	.11	.14	.16	.25	.03	−.02	−.01	−.05	−.04	.02
166.	original	−.07	−.02	−.04	.02	−.05	−.10	.02	.01	.02	.12	−.05	−.07
167.	outgoing	.07	.07	.08	.14	.10	.11	.10	.13	.21	.11	.07	.11
168.	outspoken	.03	.01	−.08	.09	.02	.06	.02	.12	.18	−.01	.04	.06
169.	painstaking	.03	.14	.01	−.03	−.01	−.04	−.15	−.08	−.06	.02	−.04	−.06
170.	patient	.05	.14	.08	−.12	−.05	.05	−.08	−.15	−.11	.09	−.10	−.02
171.	peaceable	−.01	.16	−.07	−.05	−.10	.06	−.04	−.13	−.03	.08	−.06	−.04
172.	peculiar	.05	−.15	−.11	−.09	−.17	−.08	.07	−.09	−.03	.04	−.01	−.04
173.	persevering	.07	.11	−.04	.11	.10	.09	−.01	.01	−.03	−.03	−.04	.01
174.	persistent	.07	.14	.01	.11	−.01	.09	.02	.07	−.03	.10	.06	−.02
175.	pessimistic	−.09	−.29	.02	−.10	−.17	−.21	.05	.03	−.02	.01	−.01	−.03
176.	planful	.04	.22	−.01	−.02	.06	.20	.08	−.12	−.01	−.07	.00	.03

Correlations of Observers' Adjectival Description with Scales of the CPI continued												
		Scale: D–SD						Scale: D–AC				
		By Peers		By Spouses		By Staff		By Peers		By Spouses		By Staff	
Adjectives		M	F	M	F	M	F	M	F	M	F	M	F
177.	pleasant	.04	.10	.10	.04	−.02	.17	−.08	−.04	−.03	−.06	.01	.02
178.	pleasure-seeking	.01	−.13	−.08	−.06	−.03	−.08	.05	.03	.18	.17	.09	.13
179.	poised	.09	.16	.08	.07	.13	.23	−.17	−.05	.10	.13	.02	.01
180.	polished	.08	.18	.11	.09	.07	.11	−.13	.01	.09	.09	.03	.02
181.	practical	.11	.20	.13	.07	.02	.13	−.13	−.08	−.07	.03	.07	.17
182.	praising	.08	.18	.03	−.03	.07	.08	−.03	−.03	.00	.03	−.09	.07
183.	precise	.13	.07	.10	.09	−.03	.05	−.11	−.13	−.04	−.06	−.05	−.07
184.	prejudiced	−.04	−.08	−.11	−.17	−.05	−.11	.04	.03	.10	.11	.07	.07
185.	preoccupied	.02	−.20	.01	−.07	−.17	−.17	.02	−.01	−.07	.05	−.03	−.01
186.	progressive	.09	−.04	.00	.06	−.03	.05	−.04	.07	.09	−.04	.04	.01
187.	prudish	−.06	.10	−.17	−.09	−.06	.03	.08	−.05	−.01	.08	−.01	−.02
188.	quarrelsome	−.11	−.19	−.16	−.15	−.04	−.11	.08	.09	.04	−.01	.05	.00
189.	queer	−.04	−.11	−.01	.00	−.11	−.08	.14	.12	−.02	.00	−.05	.01
190.	quick	−.06	.11	−.03	.10	.03	.01	.01	.10	−.03	.04	.04	.04
191.	quiet	−.06	.01	−.05	−.07	−.14	−.07	−.14	−.17	−.16	−.06	−.09	−.10
192.	quitting	−.03	−.24	−.20	−.01	−.13	−.19	.06	.04	−.02	−.01	.02	−.04
193.	rational	.02	.19	−.02	.05	−.07	.08	−.09	−.06	−.01	−.06	.02	−.02
194.	rattle-brained	.02	−.16	−.13	−.07	−.06	−.14	.08	.04	.14	.04	.08	.06
195.	realistic	.12	.17	.06	.00	−.03	.15	−.13	−.01	.02	−.02	.05	.05
196.	reasonable	.21	.15	.11	.07	−.02	.14	−.09	−.03	.01	−.04	−.07	.00
197.	rebellious	.00	−.18	−.19	−.07	−.16	−.15	.16	.14	.01	.12	−.03	.01
198.	reckless	−.05	−.15	−.26	−.19	−.04	−.16	.07	−.01	−.01	.10	.05	−.04
199.	reflective	−.06	.06	−.05	.06	−.08	−.03	−.14	−.12	−.11	.00	−.05	−.12
200.	relaxed	.04	.08	.02	−.04	−.06	.10	−.10	−.05	.01	.03	.05	.04
201.	reliable	.08	.26	.07	.03	.03	.14	−.04	−.08	.02	−.11	−.02	−.04
202.	resentful	.02	−.22	−.07	−.12	−.13	−.17	−.05	.08	−.03	.09	.04	.07
203.	reserved	−.02	.02	−.03	−.10	−.10	−.09	−.13	−.26	−.15	.03	−.08	−.08
204.	resourceful	.14	.26	.03	.10	.09	.13	−.08	.03	.05	.06	.03	−.01
205.	responsible	.14	.25	.04	.00	.03	.17	−.01	−.08	.04	−.01	−.01	−.01
206.	restless	−.06	−.22	−.11	−.08	−.09	−.18	.15	.10	.06	.11	−.03	.02
207.	retiring	−.02	−.18	−.04	−.05	−.14	−.08	−.06	−.13	−.06	.07	−.06	−.09
208.	rigid	−.05	.03	−.03	−.17	−.07	−.06	.05	−.03	−.09	−.04	.03	.01
209.	robust	.05	.03	.04	.06	−.07	.06	.02	.12	.10	−.02	.10	.11
210.	rude	−.04	−.19	−.06	.05	−.09	−.07	.13	.11	.00	.00	.08	.04
211.	sarcastic	−.11	−.25	−.04	−.11	−.13	−.09	−.12	.18	.02	.03	.10	.04
212.	self-centered	.05	−.07	−.19	−.08	−.05	−.11	.00	.07	.07	.08	.09	.07
213.	self-confident	.11	.19	.07	.18	.06	.22	.00	.03	.15	.05	.08	.10
214.	self-controlled	.04	.16	.07	.09	−.02	.05	−.13	−.10	.00	.04	−.06	−.04
215.	self-denying	.09	.10	−.07	−.11	−.06	−.07	−.04	−.07	.02	.08	−.07	−.04
216.	self-pitying	.05	−.12	−.10	−.15	−.10	−.13	.06	.07	.09	.06	.02	.07
217.	self-punishing	.04	−.04	−.12	−.09	−.12	−.15	−.02	−.04	.03	.01	−.02	−.05
218.	self-seeking	−.02	−.08	−.06	−.06	.05	.00	−.02	.04	.03	.09	.09	.10
219.	selfish	−.02	−.10	−.01	.01	−.02	−.11	−.07	.05	−.02	.10	.10	.05
220.	sensitive	−.15	−.14	−.08	−.08	−.17	−.12	.07	−.02	.10	.08	−.06	−.01

Correlations of Observers' Adjectival Description with Scales of the CPI continued

		Scale: D–SD						Scale: D–AC				
		By Peers		By Spouses		By Staff		By Peers		By Spouses		By Staff	
Adjectives		M	F	M	F	M	F	M	F	M	F	M	F
221.	sentimental	−.03	.05	−.04	−.08	−.05	−.10	−.07	−.01	−.02	.10	.00	.05
222.	serious	.05	.03	−.01	.00	−.08	.05	−.09	−.12	.03	.14	−.05	−.16
223.	severe	−.03	.04	−.11	−.01	−.10	−.07	.10	−.06	.03	.06	.07	−.01
224.	sexy	−.05	.03	−.12	−.03	−.04	−.02	.04	.02	.09	.03	.12	.08
225.	shallow	−.16	−.01	.01	−.05	−.01	−.11	.04	.00	.06	.03	.02	.15
226.	sharp-witted	.08	−.16	−.05	−.03	−.04	−.05	−.01	.12	.16	.15	.06	−.02
227.	shiftless	−.01	−.15	−.14	−.10	−.15	−.12	.05	.01	.00	.00	.06	.00
228.	show-off	−.04	−.07	−.10	−.05	−.02	.06	.04	.19	.15	.15	.08	.04
229.	shrewd	.11	.00	−.09	−.02	.05	.05	.00	.01	.12	.16	.05	.01
230.	shy	.02	−.10	−.15	−.15	−.23	−.17	−.14	−.14	−.10	−.02	−.05	−.03
231.	silent	−.09	−.04	−.02	−.06	−.24	−.13	−.10	−.12	−.12	.07	−.04	−.07
232.	simple	−.01	.01	−.01	−.14	−.09	−.11	.07	−.03	.00	.10	.01	.08
233.	sincere	.04	.12	.05	.05	−.03	.09	−.03	.02	−.06	−.11	−.04	−.03
234.	slipshod	.02	−.13	−.08	−.04	−.03	−.06	−.03	−.02	.04	.13	−.01	−.01
235.	slow	−.02	−.13	−.13	−.09	−.10	−.12	.11	−.11	.04	.04	−.03	.00
236.	sly	−.03	−.11	−.23	−.05	−.10	−.11	−.04	.04	.05	.07	.03	.08
237.	smug	.04	.01	−.04	−.03	−.02	−.08	.01	.04	.01	−.03	.05	.07
238.	snobbish	.05	.04	−.13	.02	.02	−.04	.02	.04	−.03	.13	.07	.08
239.	sociable	.11	.09	.05	.06	.06	.11	.01	.16	.05	.11	.07	.17
240.	soft-hearted	.07	.10	−.11	−.18	−.02	−.03	−.04	−.05	.05	.10	.02	.09
241.	sophisticated	.11	.02	.11	.09	−.01	.08	−.08	.00	.11	.12	.04	.03
242.	spendthrift	−.01	−.16	−.05	−.07	−.05	−.05	−.08	.01	.09	.02	.06	.04
243.	spineless	−.08	−.19	.04	−.13	−.07	−.04	.07	−.01	−.02	−.08	−.01	−.04
244.	spontaneous	.02	.02	.01	.00	.01	−.01	.16	.08	.05	−.01	.04	.09
245.	spunky	−.16	.06	−.05	−.02	.04	−.01	.12	.04	.19	.10	.10	.08
246.	stable	.11	.16	−.05	.01	.02	.24	−.12	−.02	.00	.06	.01	.02
247.	steady	.07	.16	−.02	−.05	−.02	.12	−.06	−.03	−.06	.04	.03	.08
248.	stern	.11	.03	−.11	−.02	−.09	.00	.15	−.04	.15	−.03	.06	.03
249.	stingy	−.05	−.13	−.14	−.11	−.07	.02	.09	.07	.14	.18	−.01	.04
250.	stolid	.02	−.12	−.02	.00	−.12	−.02	.06	.00	−.07	.04	.02	.03
251.	strong	.10	.17	.05	.07	−.09	.13	.03	−.01	.09	.09	.12	.07
252.	stubborn	.07	−.07	−.08	−.07	−.02	−.01	.12	.12	.17	.16	.05	.03
253.	submissive	−.04	.06	−.11	−.12	−.02	−.08	−.06	−.12	.04	.06	−.07	−.04
254.	suggestible	−.04	−.02	−.11	.01	−.01	−.08	−.03	.04	.01	.03	−.01	.03
255.	sulky	−.04	−.24	−.17	−.05	−.11	−.18	.03	−.01	.02	.11	.05	.09
256.	superstitious	.07	−.06	−.29	−.12	−.04	−.16	.06	−.04	.08	.16	−.04	.21
257.	suspicious	−.11	−.20	−.10	−.12	−.16	−.16	.09	.03	−.02	.10	.03	.05
258.	sympathetic	−.01	.05	−.03	.03	−.02	.04	.00	.03	−.03	.02	−.02	.03
259.	tactful	.13	.16	.11	.10	.10	.10	−.14	−.06	.07	.01	−.07	.02
260.	tactless	−.01	−.07	−.12	−.05	−.11	−.11	.05	.02	.05	−.01	.04	.00
261.	talkative	.06	.02	.08	−.07	.03	.06	.15	.19	.15	.14	.04	.14
262.	temperamental	−.12	−.23	−.11	−.04	−.13	−.13	.08	.00	.04	.12	.04	.01
263.	tense	.00	−.22	−.08	−.07	−.09	−.25	−.04	−.11	.02	.10	−.02	−.04
264.	thankless	−.06	−.25	−.11	−.02	−.14	−.02	.04	.07	−.01	.04	.08	.04

		Scale: D–SD						Scale: D–AC				
		By Peers		By Spouses		By Staff		By Peers		By Spouses		By Staff	
Adjectives		M	F	M	F	M	F	M	F	M	F	M	F
265.	thorough	.04	.23	−.02	.12	.08	.17	−.08	−.08	−.02	.03	−.11	−.01
266.	thoughtful	.06	.14	.05	.02	−.01	.12	−.12	−.07	−.06	.00	−.04	−.00
267.	thrifty	−.05	.14	.04	.00	−.10	.04	−.12	−.05	.06	−.03	.01	.02
268.	timid	−.10	−.12	−.08	−.12	−.14	−.12	−.03	−.10	.02	.04	−.03	.03
269.	tolerant	.03	.14	.02	−.04	−.03	.05	−.08	−.11	.02	.05	−.07	.02
270.	touchy	−.09	−.18	−.09	−.14	−.14	−.15	.01	−.05	−.05	.11	.00	.05
271.	tough	.02	.00	.00	−.03	−.11	.03	.09	.06	.06	.03	.13	.05
272.	trusting	.09	.18	.06	.09	−.05	.01	.04	−.07	.12	.05	−.07	.01
273.	unaffected	−.03	.00	−.02	−.07	−.06	−.04	−.10	−.05	−.01	.10	−.06	−.14
274.	unambitious	−.12	−.21	−.18	−.15	−.18	−.20	−.14	−.08	−.01	−.09	−.04	.09
275.	unassuming	.00	−.03	−.01	.05	−.11	−.09	−.01	−.05	.10	.04	−.06	−.02
276.	unconventional	.10	−.20	−.15	−.11	−.14	−.11	.04	.13	.00	−.01	−.05	−.04
277.	undependable	−.06	−.19	−.06	−.06	−.02	−.13	.05	.00	.02	.02	−.01	−.01
278.	understanding	.08	.14	−.01	.09	−.06	.06	−.04	−.07	−.01	−.10	.02	.02
279.	unemotional	.02	−.10	.17	−.05	−.18	.03	−.06	−.17	−.07	−.03	.03	−.01
280.	unexcitable	−.02	−.08	−.06	−.03	−.10	.07	−.16	−.14	−.11	−.08	−.03	.00
281.	unfriendly	.00	−.13	−.21	−.05	−.08	−.13	.07	−.03	−.03	.10	−.06	.08
282.	uninhibited	.12	−.17	.00	.04	.00	−.05	.05	.16	.01	.05	.04	.09
283.	unintelligent	.05	−.18	.00	.02	−.07	−.09	.00	−.03	.00	.13	.01	−.04
284.	unkind	−.05	−.13	.01	−.01	−.12	−.07	.04	−.01	.06	−.02	.07	.09
285.	unrealistic	−.09	−.07	.03	−.05	−.14	−.14	.08	.06	−.03	.18	.04	.07
286.	unscrupulous	.01	−.05	−.20	.06	−.03	−.14	.00	.06	−.04	.02	−.02	−.02
287.	unselfish	.18	.09	−.04	−.09	.02	.02	.00	−.16	.05	.10	−.03	−.01
288.	unstable	−.03	−.19	−.16	−.05	−.09	−.23	.09	.03	.00	.09	−.11	−.08
289.	vindictive	.01	.00	−.10	−.13	−.08	−.07	−.03	−.04	.01	.05	.06	.04
290.	versatile	.08	.01	−.06	.01	.07	.00	−.04	.13	.18	.02	.01	.02
291.	warm	.02	.14	.03	.00	.03	.10	−.09	.03	.03	.00	.00	.07
292.	wary	.01	−.04	−.09	−.06	−.16	−.13	−.04	−.10	−.02	.04	.02	−.03
293.	weak	−.11	−.06	−.17	−.06	−.10	−.11	.07	−.05	.09	.03	.03	.02
294.	whiny	−.12	−.13	−.12	−.08	.01	−.06	.09	.14	.05	.07	.03	.06
295.	wholesome	.02	.14	.01	−.01	−.01	.15	.00	−.02	.18	.09	−.04	.04
296.	wise	.12	.18	.12	.06	−.04	.08	−.03	−.08	.02	.10	−.03	.01
297.	withdrawn	.07	−.12	−.18	−.09	−.22	−.19	−.05	−.13	−.04	−.01	−.02	−.02
298.	witty	−.08	−.18	−.11	.03	−.03	−.01	.02	.17	.07	.15	.05	.05
299.	worrying	−.15	−.06	−.19	−.07	−.13	−.14	.09	−.16	.11	.07	−.03	−.02
300.	zany	−.07	−.10	−.13	−.04	−.04	−.05	.21	.18	.16	.16	.07	.06

Correlations of Observers' Adjectival Description with Scales of the CPI continued

Correlations of CPI™ Scales with *California Q-Set* Descriptions by Observers

This appendix presents correlations of the 36 CPI scales with each of the 100 items on the *California Q-Set* (Block, 1961). There were 547 men and 393 women so described, participants in various assessment programs conducted by the Institute of Personality Assessment and Research. Each assessee was described on the *Q-Set* by from five to nine judges, each judge using the fixed distribution of the 100 items as specified by Block. Then, these independent formulations for each assessee were composited, and the composites were rearrayed in the stipulated nine-step categories, with frequencies of 5, 8, 12, 16, 18, 12, 8, and 5 for items varying from most salient and descriptive to least salient and hence not descriptive. Weights of 9 to 1 were assigned to the items within each category, for purposes of correlating the items with the CPI scales. The 7,200 correlations generated in this analysis follow, along with the text of each *Q-Set* item.

Correlations of CPI Scales with California Q-Set Descriptions by Observers

Q-Sort Items	Do	Cs	Sy	Sp	Sa	In	Em	Re	So	Sc	Gi	Cm	Wb	To	Ac	Ai	Ie	Py
1. Is critical, skeptical, not easily impressed																		
M	.05	.02	−.10	.02	.05	.17	−.04	−.02	−.14	−.05	−.06	−.06	.00	−.02	−.06	.02	.01	.07
F	.13	.14	.00	.06	.08	.21	.07	.19	−.05	.01	−.01	−.08	.07	.08	.03	.23	.17	.23
2. Is a genuinely dependable and responsible person																		
M	−.05	.01	−.06	−.11	−.08	−.09	−.05	.23	.27	.25	.19	.14	.13	.10	.21	.09	.10	.08
F	.06	.06	.05	−.05	−.02	.05	−.01	.30	.30	.31	.28	.16	.22	.20	.28	.13	.10	.13
3. Has a wide range of interests																		
M	.16	.23	.10	.11	.16	.21	.21	.16	.05	.04	.04	.03	.08	.16	.10	.21	.20	.20
F	.26	.33	.21	.23	.31	.31	.29	.18	−.05	−.06	.01	.02	.12	.17	.10	.34	.28	.26
4. Is a talkative individual																		
M	.36	.20	.27	.22	.27	.27	.23	.04	.08	−.08	.00	.09	.11	.02	.14	.08	.15	.05
F	.34	.19	.32	.25	.33	.24	.22	.01	−.05	−.18	−.06	.06	.02	−.03	.09	.05	.19	.03
5. Behaves in a giving way toward others																		
M	−.05	−.02	−.01	−.06	−.08	−.12	.05	.04	.18	.12	.10	.04	.01	.03	.04	−.02	−.02	−.05
F	−.03	−.07	.04	−.01	−.02	−.09	.00	.03	.11	.17	.17	.19	.14	.13	.08	−.05	−.04	.00
6. Is fastidious																		
M	−.02	.02	−.02	−.13	−.05	−.14	−.04	.25	.22	.23	.20	.15	.11	.07	.24	.04	.04	−.04
F	−.07	−.10	−.12	−.19	−.13	−.12	−.21	.15	.28	.26	.22	.14	.10	.02	.25	−.10	−.12	−.09
7. Favors conservative values in a variety of areas																		
M	−.10	−.15	−.02	−.14	−.14	−.24	−.20	.09	.23	.17	.15	.10	.05	−.05	.14	−.13	−.08	−.10
F	−.11	−.19	−.09	−.23	−.21	−.18	−.28	.11	.30	.30	.24	.11	.09	−.03	.20	−.22	−.17	−.17
8. Appears to have a high degree of intellectual capacity																		
M	.09	.17	.00	.03	.09	.18	.14	.10	.02	.01	−.01	−.03	.00	.12	.08	.22	.15	.21
F	.21	.30	.09	.14	.19	.28	.25	.26	.02	−.02	.03	−.04	.10	.21	.14	.42	.34	.32
9. Is uncomfortable with uncertainty and complexities																		
M	−.24	−.22	−.14	−.17	−.23	−.29	−.25	.01	.05	.06	.01	.00	−.05	−.05	−.05	−.15	−.15	−.11
F	−.30	−.31	−.22	−.32	−.35	−.35	−.34	−.04	.11	.17	.09	.00	−.09	−.09	−.02	−.30	−.34	−.24
10. Anxiety and tension find outlet in bodily symptoms																		
M	−.24	−.08	−.21	−.20	−.24	−.19	−.19	.03	−.03	.09	.01	−.08	−.11	.01	−.01	−.07	−.15	−.02
F	−.22	−.21	−.20	−.24	−.22	−.27	−.21	−.01	−.10	.00	−.09	−.14	−.20	−.11	−.11	−.15	−.19	−.14
11. Is protective of those close to him or her																		
M	−.09	−.11	−.01	−.09	−.11	−.18	−.10	−.02	.16	.11	.09	.09	.05	−.07	.04	−.14	−.08	−.11
F	−.06	−.13	−.05	−.11	−.11	−.11	−.11	.10	.20	.28	.24	.16	.18	.07	.12	−.11	−.11	.01
12. Tends to be self-defensive																		
M	−.17	−.20	−.17	−.14	−.15	−.13	−.20	−.09	−.19	−.08	−.11	−.07	−.14	−.09	−.15	−.12	−.16	−.07
F	−.21	−.22	−.22	−.19	−.29	−.15	−.18	−.01	.00	.09	.03	−.13	−.06	−.06	−.09	−.06	−.15	−.06
13. Is thin-skinned; sensitive to anything that can be construed as criticism or an interpersonal slight																		
M	−.20	−.16	−.18	−.17	−.19	−.19	−.21	−.03	−.11	−.01	−.07	−.06	−.13	−.04	−.13	−.06	−.13	−.05
F	−.25	−.22	−.19	−.22	−.25	−.22	−.15	−.10	−.04	−.01	−.07	−.12	−.16	−.11	−.15	−.12	−.17	−.11
14. Genuinely submissive; accepts domination comfortably																		
M	−.33	−.13	−.19	−.23	−.30	−.33	−.15	.12	.16	.18	.12	−.06	−.04	.06	.01	−.06	−.10	−.06
F	−.34	−.26	−.23	−.24	−.32	−.33	−.26	−.03	.12	.20	.11	.03	−.01	.03	−.05	−.20	−.27	−.14
15. Is skilled in social techniques of imaginative play, pretending, and humor																		
M	.22	.20	.24	.25	.26	.20	.30	−.08	.04	−.12	−.03	.04	.06	.03	.02	.12	.11	.03
F	.20	.17	.29	.26	.28	.11	.24	−.11	−.06	−.21	−.11	.15	−.04	.00	.02	.04	.15	−.05
16. Is introspective and concerned with self as an object																		
M	−.21	.03	−.14	−.11	−.12	−.13	−.02	.10	−.01	.07	−.02	−.06	−.08	.13	.00	.15	.04	.08
F	−.10	.09	−.11	−.03	−.01	.02	.11	.02	−.18	−.12	−.12	−.19	−.18	.07	−.09	.21	.10	.06

Correlations of CPI Scales with California Q-Set Descriptions by Observers continued

Q-Sort Items	Fx	F/M	v.1	v.2	v.3	Mp	Wo	CT	Lp	Ami	Leo	Tm	B–MS	B–FM	Anx	Nar	D–SD	D–AC
1. Is critical, skeptical, not easily impressed																		
M	.03	.02	-.02	-.08	-.05	-.02	-.01	.11	-.01	-.11	-.09	.09	.03	-.05	.05	.08	-.04	.00
F	.08	-.25	-.09	.01	.15	.13	.06	.17	.10	-.06	-.05	.16	.14	-.13	.05	.14	-.02	-.06
2. Is a genuinely dependable and responsible person																		
M	-.13	-.03	.15	.21	.04	.09	.21	-.17	.10	.28	.15	.08	-.04	.20	-.10	-.22	.15	-.05
F	-.20	-.06	.09	.30	.18	.23	.27	-.16	.20	.28	.24	.25	.07	.22	-.12	-.18	.26	-.09
3. Has a wide range of interests																		
M	.16	.17	-.11	-.02	.17	.15	.04	.28	.14	.05	-.16	.07	.07	.15	.00	.05	.12	-.02
F	.24	-.11	-.23	-.07	.26	.22	.11	.35	.22	.01	-.09	.20	.27	-.08	-.07	.14	.13	-.12
4. Is a talkative individual																		
M	.01	.01	-.37	.09	.08	.20	-.02	.09	.27	-.02	.07	.16	.26	-.01	-.08	.19	.15	.08
F	.06	-.03	-.36	-.01	.01	.13	-.04	.18	.22	-.11	.09	.12	.29	-.04	-.10	.20	.10	.13
5. Behaves in a giving way toward others																		
M	-.02	.06	.08	.09	.02	.00	.06	-.07	.02	.16	.02	-.06	-.08	.12	-.01	-.14	.06	-.02
F	-.09	.10	.11	.08	.09	.10	.19	-.12	.07	.24	.14	.05	.01	.17	-.13	-.22	.16	-.02
6. Is fastidious																		
M	-.22	.08	.13	.29	.02	.10	.22	-.23	.11	.23	.18	.07	-.03	.25	-.08	-.22	.18	-.02
F	-.34	.10	.17	.32	-.08	.06	.13	-.35	.06	.18	.25	.06	-.11	.26	-.04	-.19	.12	-.01
7. Favors conservative values in a variety of areas																		
M	-.26	-.19	.15	.28	-.10	-.03	.16	-.43	.02	.19	.27	.03	-.05	.07	-.10	-.18	.10	.04
F	-.40	.09	.22	.35	-.11	.04	.11	-.45	.01	.21	.28	.07	-.12	.26	-.09	-.26	.12	-.01
8. Appears to have a high degree of intellectual capacity																		
M	.18	.13	-.09	-.06	.13	.10	-.01	.25	.04	-.01	-.11	.04	-.01	.12	.03	.06	.00	-.03
F	.21	-.15	-.16	.02	.29	.22	.09	.30	.18	-.01	-.09	.18	.18	-.05	.04	.11	.10	-.13
9. Is uncomfortable with uncertainty and complexities																		
M	-.15	-.13	.24	.07	-.11	-.14	.05	-.29	-.14	.06	.09	-.10	-.13	-.01	.00	-.19	-.06	.00
F	-.29	.09	.32	.17	-.20	-.17	-.05	-.38	-.22	.09	.09	-.16	-.29	.14	.07	-.24	-.07	.04
10. Anxiety and tension find outlet in bodily symptoms																		
M	-.03	.19	.27	-.05	.02	-.09	-.04	-.07	-.20	.00	-.17	-.15	-.22	.13	.07	-.21	-.11	-.10
F	-.05	.22	.20	.00	-.18	-.18	-.16	-.16	-.26	-.07	-.10	-.24	-.28	.02	.08	-.10	-.13	.05
11. Is protective of those close to him or her																		
M	-.14	-.05	.13	.13	-.09	-.07	.10	-.25	.01	.13	.16	-.03	-.03	.10	-.09	-.18	.07	.02
F	-.19	.06	.18	.21	.02	.09	.23	-.26	.08	.25	.18	.10	-.01	.19	-.15	-.23	.16	-.01
12. Tends to be self-defensive																		
M	-.04	.04	.13	-.13	-.10	-.15	-.09	-.08	-.20	-.13	-.09	-.13	-.16	-.03	.13	.00	-.16	.02
F	-.09	.01	.19	.00	-.07	-.16	-.02	-.12	-.19	.00	-.03	-.09	-.21	.00	.08	-.10	-.08	-.04
13. Is thin-skinned; sensitive to anything that can be construed as criticism or an interpersonal slight																		
M	.02	.10	.19	-.08	-.08	-.13	-.07	-.04	-.21	-.10	-.05	-.15	-.18	.02	.09	-.09	-.16	-.01
F	-.03	.10	.18	-.06	-.15	-.23	-.14	-.12	-.26	-.06	-.10	-.22	-.27	.00	.11	-.10	-.17	.00
14. Genuinely submissive; accepts domination comfortably																		
M	-.06	.08	.34	.07	.00	-.11	.04	-.16	-.19	.18	-.01	-.19	-.26	.18	.03	-.30	-.03	-.08
F	-.11	.24	.37	.06	-.10	-.12	.06	-.28	-.21	.19	-.02	-.19	-.27	.21	-.03	-.34	-.04	-.05
15. Is skilled in social techniques of imaginative play, pretending, and humor																		
M	.15	.01	-.27	-.06	.09	.09	-.04	.21	.14	-.02	.01	.04	.17	-.05	-.07	.20	.06	.08
F	.13	.05	-.28	-.08	.01	.04	-.06	.20	.09	-.10	-.03	-.04	.12	-.04	-.04	.20	.02	.12
16. Is introspective and concerned with self as an object																		
M	.11	.17	.20	-.07	.10	-.05	.00	.11	-.16	.03	-.19	-.14	-.20	.12	.09	-.15	-.09	-.10
F	.23	.03	.03	-.22	.10	-.04	-.11	.27	-.12	-.09	-.25	-.14	-.14	-.14	.17	.01	-.14	-.14

Correlations of CPI Scales with California Q-Set Descriptions by Observers continued

Q-Sort Items	Do	Cs	Sy	Sp	Sa	In	Em	Re	So	Sc	Gi	Cm	Wb	To	Ac	Ai	Ie	Py
17. Behaves in a sympathetic or considerate manner																		
M	−.13	.00	−.03	−.11	−.13	−.18	.02	.14	.26	.22	.17	.04	.06	.12	.13	.07	.04	−.01
F	−.12	−.08	−.02	−.04	−.11	−.12	−.04	.04	.14	.20	.18	.15	.11	.16	.08	.00	−.05	−.01
18. Initiates humor																		
M	.24	.15	.26	.25	.22	.20	.25	−.10	.07	−.15	−.03	.06	.08	−.04	.00	.03	.08	−.04
F	.23	.14	.28	.24	.25	.14	.22	−.07	−.08	−.17	−.09	.05	.03	−.01	−.03	.04	.13	.04
19. Seeks reassurance from others																		
M	−.16	−.02	−.03	−.15	−.17	−.25	−.10	.11	.11	.11	.08	−.08	−.04	.03	.04	−.06	−.06	−.04
F	−.28	−.20	−.13	−.15	−.25	−.29	−.16	−.18	−.03	.04	.01	−.07	−.11	−.07	−.13	−.18	−.24	−.14
20. Has a rapid personal tempo; behaves and acts quickly																		
M	.26	.16	.20	.17	.27	.21	.16	.02	.01	−.10	−.04	.06	.07	.03	.05	.06	.09	.07
F	.28	.16	.26	.23	.28	.18	.18	.01	−.01	−.17	−.05	.08	.07	−.01	.04	.07	.17	−.01
21. Arouses nurturant feelings in others																		
M	−.26	−.11	−.15	−.20	−.25	−.27	−.11	.02	.15	.14	.12	−.09	−.08	.03	.01	−.01	−.08	−.09
F	−.24	−.18	−.11	−.11	−.19	−.19	−.10	−.16	.05	.10	.07	.07	−.02	.01	−.03	−.10	−.20	−.11
22. Feels a lack of personal meaning in life																		
M	−.27	−.18	−.23	−.17	−.23	−.21	−.18	−.09	−.20	−.05	−.11	−.12	−.22	−.09	−.21	−.08	−.17	−.09
F	−.36	−.20	−.28	−.25	−.32	−.31	−.24	−.12	−.18	−.01	−.10	−.19	−.26	−.09	−.25	−.16	−.25	−.10
23. Extrapunitive; tends to transfer or project blame																		
M	.07	−.07	.04	.05	.06	.07	−.05	−.06	−.14	−.12	−.05	.00	.00	−.12	−.08	−.09	−.06	−.06
F	.04	−.07	−.01	.01	.04	−.01	−.12	−.08	−.09	−.15	−.11	.00	−.03	−.16	−.05	−.20	−.08	−.07
24. Prides self on being "objective," rational																		
M	.02	−.01	−.05	−.03	−.03	.05	−.10	.05	.02	.05	.00	.06	.02	−.01	.09	.03	.04	.09
F	.11	.16	−.01	.00	.02	.12	.02	.29	.17	.17	.15	−.01	.19	.13	.19	.25	.18	.27
25. Tends toward over-control of needs and impulses; binds tensions excessively, delays gratification unnecessarily																		
M	−.24	−.16	−.23	−.26	−.27	−.21	−.23	.14	.16	.24	.14	.02	.01	.04	.10	.01	−.06	.00
F	−.19	−.13	−.22	−.29	−.26	−.18	−.23	.23	.27	.33	.23	.04	.06	.08	.20	−.04	−.13	−.02
26. Is productive; gets things done																		
M	.21	.08	.07	.00	.14	.18	−.01	.16	.18	.10	.10	.11	.15	.06	.18	.04	.12	.16
F	.29	.21	.19	.09	.16	.27	.15	.30	.27	.17	.21	.18	.27	.20	.34	.24	.25	.21
27. Shows condescending behavior in relations with others																		
M	.18	.13	.15	.15	.17	.16	.14	.09	−.01	−.04	−.02	.06	.09	.03	.09	.09	.10	.10
F	.23	.20	.12	.10	.19	.23	.10	.12	.02	−.06	−.05	−.05	.05	−.06	.09	.07	.13	.10
28. Tends to arouse liking and acceptance in people																		
M	−.01	.06	.04	.01	.00	−.01	.10	.03	.22	.12	.09	.06	.09	.07	.07	.06	.07	.03
F	−.01	.00	.09	.12	.06	−.03	.04	.01	.08	.05	.08	.19	.12	.12	.05	.03	.05	.00
29. Is turned to for advice and reassurance																		
M	.16	.09	.12	.08	.11	.12	.14	.06	.15	.07	.06	.13	.13	.06	.15	.09	.14	.05
F	.24	.10	.16	.10	.18	.15	.06	.15	.17	.12	.16	.23	.21	.08	.18	.06	.14	.09
30. Gives up and withdraws where possible in the face of frustration and adversity																		
M	−.36	−.21	−.22	−.19	−.29	−.31	−.18	−.08	−.09	.02	−.01	−.13	−.18	−.03	−.15	−.12	−.17	−.18
F	−.40	−.31	−.26	−.24	−.36	−.38	−.28	−.17	.00	.09	−.06	−.09	−.15	−.13	−.16	−.25	−.30	−.23
31. Regards self as physically attractive																		
M	.10	−.02	.11	.13	.15	.06	.06	−.14	−.03	−.11	−.05	.08	.04	−.04	−.05	−.05	−.02	−.08
F	.13	.11	.20	.18	.17	.14	.07	−.14	.07	−.10	−.01	.13	.06	−.03	.02	−.06	.00	−.07
32. Seems to be aware of the impression he or she makes on others																		
M	.02	.04	.04	.05	.02	.02	.12	.03	.16	.06	.04	.05	.11	.08	.08	.09	.08	.02
F	.06	.08	.10	.18	.14	.03	.13	−.05	−.03	−.10	−.06	.14	.00	.10	−.01	.04	.06	−.02

Correlations of CPI Scales with California Q-Set Descriptions by Observers continued

Q-Sort Items	Fx	F/M	v.1	v.2	v.3	Mp	Wo	CT	Lp	Ami	Leo	Tm	B-MS	B-FM	Anx	Nar	D-SD	D-AC
17. Behaves in a sympathetic or considerate manner																		
M	.01	.07	.19	.15	.09	.04	.13	−.09	.00	.27	.06	−.06	−.10	.20	−.06	−.27	.08	−.07
F	−.09	.11	.18	.11	.11	.10	.20	−.14	.02	.26	.10	.05	−.07	.20	−.10	−.24	.17	−.08
18. Initiates humor																		
M	.08	−.03	−.30	.01	.01	.08	−.08	.11	.16	−.03	.01	.06	.19	−.07	−.07	.22	.03	.14
F	.15	−.03	−.26	−.09	.01	.07	−.04	.17	.11	−.09	.02	.04	.21	−.03	−.10	.18	.04	.08
19. Seeks reassurance from others																		
M	−.04	.07	.16	.12	.02	−.03	.01	−.14	−.09	.09	.03	−.12	−.13	.10	.04	−.18	.02	−.07
F	.01	.19	.21	−.11	−.10	−.15	−.06	−.12	−.24	.04	−.05	−.21	−.24	.10	.05	−.22	−.07	−.01
20. Has a rapid personal tempo; behaves and acts quickly																		
M	.07	−.01	−.28	.03	.06	.15	−.04	.13	.17	−.03	.05	.11	.21	−.04	−.06	.18	.07	.03
F	.10	.03	−.29	−.01	.01	.11	−.01	.21	.17	−.09	.08	.07	.25	.00	−.07	.15	.07	.08
21. Arouses nurturant feelings in others																		
M	.01	.06	.26	.05	.03	−.09	.01	−.08	−.16	.13	−.01	−.15	−.19	.11	.04	−.24	−.03	−.06
F	.00	.11	.24	−.03	−.02	−.12	.02	−.11	−.15	.13	−.01	−.16	−.20	.09	.01	−.20	.00	−.08
22. Feels a lack of personal meaning in life																		
M	.02	.13	.23	−.17	−.10	−.19	−.12	−.04	−.29	−.16	−.18	−.22	−.28	−.05	.15	−.06	−.19	−.05
F	.04	.11	.28	−.17	−.09	−.23	−.13	−.09	−.36	−.08	−.25	−.25	−.33	−.07	.25	−.17	−.24	.00
23. Extrapunitive; tends to transfer or project blame																		
M	−.08	−.14	−.08	−.02	−.08	−.04	−.03	−.07	.02	−.12	.06	.07	.12	−.12	.02	.12	−.04	.05
F	−.12	−.07	−.06	.01	.19	−.15	−.13	−.09	−.04	−.18	.06	−.05	.04	−.10	.05	.11	−.10	.18
24. Prides self on being "objective," rational																		
M	−.09	−.11	−.01	.05	−.03	.03	.08	−.09	.03	.00	.05	.12	.02	.00	.01	.02	.01	.03
F	−.06	−.22	.00	.19	.18	.19	.21	−.01	.19	.09	.09	.25	.15	.01	−.06	−.01	.16	−.04
25. Tends toward over-control of needs and impulses; binds tensions excessively, delays gratification unnecessarily																		
M	−.16	.02	.31	.14	−.02	−.06	.15	−.24	−.11	.17	.08	−.03	−.20	.20	−.02	−.29	.04	−.06
F	−.26	.07	.31	.29	.02	.05	.16	−.33	−.03	.22	.14	.02	−.19	.21	.03	−.31	.11	−.09
26. Is productive; gets things done																		
M	−.09	−.07	−.12	.18	.02	.20	.15	−.04	.23	.14	.16	.24	.13	.08	−.08	.04	.16	.01
F	−.14	−.18	−.16	.29	.20	.33	.25	.00	.35	.16	.25	.37	.27	.11	−.16	.04	.30	−.07
27. Shows condescending behavior in relations with others																		
M	−.02	−.08	−.18	.06	.08	.13	.06	.02	.14	−.01	.06	.15	.16	−.06	−.05	.11	.06	.03
F	−.08	−.16	−.23	.10	.00	.08	−.01	.07	.18	−.11	.05	.17	.20	−.08	−.02	.20	.04	.06
28. Tends to arouse liking and acceptance in people																		
M	.06	−.03	.05	.06	.08	.08	.09	.02	.07	.21	.06	.03	.03	.09	−.09	−.09	.06	−.03
F	.04	.01	.03	.02	.08	.08	.13	−.02	.07	.15	.06	.01	.04	.09	−.15	−.11	.11	−.06
29. Is turned to for advice and reassurance																		
M	−.02	−.04	−.10	.12	.05	.16	.12	.00	.20	.14	.07	.13	.12	.08	−.10	.01	.14	.02
F	−.14	−.06	−.10	.17	.11	.22	.23	−.09	.26	.14	.22	.25	.22	.09	−.17	.00	.27	.02
30. Gives up and withdraws where possible in the face of frustration and adversity																		
M	.02	.05	.30	−.13	−.05	−.21	−.09	−.10	−.30	−.01	−.07	−.27	−.26	.02	.09	−.18	−.18	−.06
F	−.05	.17	.38	−.06	−.19	−.24	−.07	−.26	−.32	.06	−.12	−.27	−.35	.09	.08	−.24	−.20	.03
31. Regards self as physically attractive																		
M	−.05	−.15	−.16	.00	−.04	.02	.01	−.02	.08	−.02	.18	.07	.13	−.14	−.10	.18	.04	.05
F	.00	−.10	−.19	.00	−.03	.02	−.03	.03	.12	−.02	.14	.09	.15	−.04	−.05	.16	.08	.03
32. Seems to be aware of the impression he or she makes on others																		
M	.08	−.02	.00	.06	.07	.06	.09	.03	.07	.16	.06	.04	.05	.09	−.08	−.04	.00	−.03
F	.09	.10	−.14	−.05	.10	.05	.01	.12	.06	.03	−.06	.00	.03	−.01	−.09	.06	.02	.06

Correlations of CPI Scales with California Q-Set Descriptions by Observers continued

Q-Sort Items	Do	Cs	Sy	Sp	Sa	In	Em	Re	So	Sc	Gi	Cm	Wb	To	Ac	Ai	Ie	Py
33. Is calm, relaxed in manner
M	−.04	−.06	.00	.05	−.01	−.01	.04	−.08	.07	.06	.08	−.02	.05	−.03	−.04	−.02	−.01	−.08
F	.08	.12	.05	.04	.05	.10	.04	.10	.21	.19	.17	.13	.24	.13	.19	.08	.10	.14
34. Over-reactive to minor frustrations; irritable
M	−.01	−.12	−.08	−.03	−.03	−.03	−.14	−.10	−.14	−.10	−.12	−.04	−.09	−.12	−.11	−.15	−.12	−.03
F	−.12	−.18	−.15	−.11	−.18	−.08	−.16	−.08	−.16	−.06	−.13	−.22	−.16	−.15	−.20	−.15	−.15	−.08
35. Has warmth; has the capacity for close relationships; compassionate
M	.01	.11	.11	.06	.03	−.05	.17	.06	.20	.09	.11	.10	.07	.10	.09	.09	.09	.02
F	.01	−.03	.07	.08	.03	−.06	.07	−.06	.05	.06	.09	.15	.09	.09	.01	−.04	−.03	−.05
36. Is subtly negativistic; tends to undermine and obstruct or sabotage
M	−.04	−.07	−.05	.03	−.01	.03	−.06	−.12	−.25	−.14	−.12	−.12	−.09	−.06	−.12	−.02	−.07	−.05
F	−.05	−.09	−.13	−.11	−.08	−.03	−.11	−.07	−.16	−.10	−.14	−.15	−.16	−.13	−.14	−.12	−.09	−.06
37. Is guileful and deceitful, manipulative, opportunistic
M	.18	.05	.15	.17	.19	.14	.07	−.13	−.18	−.18	−.07	−.03	.02	−.12	−.05	−.04	−.04	−.07
F	.09	−.05	.05	.04	.07	.03	−.04	−.16	−.16	−.17	−.16	−.02	−.06	−.18	−.10	−.14	−.08	−.10
38. Has hostility toward others
M	−.03	−.03	−.04	.02	.00	−.02	−.08	.03	−.15	−.08	−.08	.04	.00	−.01	−.03	−.06	−.05	.02
F	−.07	−.04	−.18	−.15	−.11	.04	−.12	.03	−.17	−.02	−.07	−.20	−.10	−.09	−.08	−.03	−.04	.07
39. Thinks and associates to ideas in unusual ways; has unconventional thought processes
M	.01	.12	−.09	−.02	.01	.16	.06	.03	−.13	.00	−.03	−.08	−.04	.08	−.06	.07	.04	.16
F	−.01	.11	−.08	.01	.03	.12	.11	.02	−.19	−.10	−.13	−.20	−.04	.08	−.12	.20	.12	.19
40. Is vulnerable to real or fancied threat, generally fearful
M	−.32	−.10	−.20	−.21	−.27	−.29	−.23	.12	−.03	.09	.00	−.04	−.12	.01	−.03	−.05	−.12	−.02
F	−.37	−.31	−.27	−.27	−.36	−.28	−.26	−.07	−.06	.08	−.02	−.17	−.13	−.09	−.17	−.15	−.28	−.10
41. Is moralistic
M	−.06	−.15	−.10	−.18	−.16	−.14	−.23	.13	.15	.16	.14	.06	.04	−.03	.11	−.12	−.10	−.05
F	−.05	−.15	−.14	−.26	−.22	−.06	−.23	.21	.24	.29	.26	.02	.10	−.01	.24	−.12	−.11	−.01
42. Reluctant to commit self to any definite course of action; tends to delay or avoid action
M	−.42	−.14	−.23	−.22	−.31	−.31	−.15	.02	.02	.12	.03	−.08	−.10	.07	−.09	−.02	−.11	−.05
F	−.41	−.25	−.29	−.25	−.36	−.34	−.23	−.06	−.01	.09	−.04	−.11	−.14	−.03	−.17	−.13	−.25	−.11
43. Is facially and/or gesturally expressive
M	.26	.16	.21	.15	.25	.15	.22	.02	.07	−.07	.00	.02	.04	.01	.08	.03	.10	−.02
F	.16	.07	.21	.19	.19	.05	.13	−.15	−.08	−.22	−.14	.03	−.08	−.09	−.06	−.03	.05	−.08
44. Evaluates the motives of others in interpreting situations
M	.05	.14	.02	.03	.07	.03	.10	.08	−.02	.03	.03	−.01	.00	.08	.04	.10	.07	.09
F	.02	.08	.02	.03	.01	.02	.10	.00	−.08	−.07	−.06	−.03	−.06	.04	−.02	.09	.05	.04
45. Has a brittle ego-defense system; has a small reserve of integration; would be disorganized and maladaptive when under stress or trauma
M	−.23	−.15	−.16	−.16	−.21	−.21	−.14	−.03	−.14	.00	−.07	−.10	−.17	−.01	−.13	−.09	−.17	−.07
F	−.33	−.30	−.27	−.34	−.37	−.32	−.33	−.10	−.09	.06	−.04	−.22	−.21	−.15	−.17	−.23	−.29	−.17
46. Engages in personal fantasy and daydreams, fictional speculations
M	−.24	−.02	−.15	−.04	−.15	−.09	−.11	−.09	−.15	−.05	−.11	−.16	−.18	−.02	−.18	.01	−.05	.03
F	−.20	−.02	−.05	.04	−.02	−.11	.05	−.21	−.24	−.24	−.27	−.06	−.21	−.06	−.21	.03	−.03	−.12
47. Has a readiness to feel guilty
M	−.26	−.13	−.21	−.22	−.24	−.30	−.19	.11	.09	.14	.02	−.01	−.08	.04	.02	.00	−.08	−.02
F	−.26	−.23	−.18	−.26	−.27	−.30	−.14	.02	.10	.12	.06	.00	−.11	−.02	.00	−.10	−.19	−.12
48. Keeps people at a distance; avoids close interpersonal relationships
M	−.28	−.26	−.31	−.21	−.27	−.14	−.28	−.10	−.20	.02	−.04	−.13	−.13	−.12	−.16	−.13	−.19	−.05
F	−.24	−.17	−.29	−.23	−.25	−.11	−.21	−.01	.00	.09	.01	−.13	−.10	−.07	−.06	−.03	−.14	−.03

Correlations of CPI Scales with California Q-Set Descriptions by Observers continued

Q-Sort Items	Fx	F/M	v.1	v.2	v.3	Mp	Wo	CT	Lp	Ami	Leo	Tm	B–MS	B–FM	Anx	Nar	D–SD	D–AC
33. Is calm, relaxed in manner																		
M	−.01	−.14	.03	.00	−.03	−.05	.08	−.05	.01	.11	.10	.03	.03	−.02	−.02	−.05	.04	.04
F	−.11	−.15	.03	.15	.13	.17	.21	−.11	.20	.21	.15	.23	.12	.07	−.17	−.04	.17	−.07
34. Over-reactive to minor frustrations; irritable																		
M	−.05	.04	.01	−.03	−.13	−.07	−.08	−.07	−.08	−.15	−.03	−.06	−.05	−.08	.05	.07	−.09	.05
F	−.02	.00	.05	−.10	−.17	−.17	−.15	−.08	−.19	−.15	−.11	−.08	−.10	−.10	.11	.04	−.19	.06
35. Has warmth; has the capacity for close relationships; compassionate																		
M	.07	.00	.00	.08	.12	.08	.09	.04	.09	.20	.05	.00	.05	.09	−.05	−.12	.10	−.03
F	.05	.10	.01	−.02	.07	.05	.11	−.02	.04	.17	.08	.03	.02	.10	−.13	−.09	.10	−.03
36. Is subtly negativistic; tends to undermine and obstruct or sabotage																		
M	.03	.04	−.01	−.14	−.01	−.06	−.10	.08	−.10	−.19	−.11	−.03	−.01	−.12	.10	.09	−.13	.00
F	−.05	−.10	.00	−.08	−.15	−.15	−.13	−.06	−.12	−.21	−.09	−.07	−.06	−.17	.14	.11	−.16	.09
37. Is guileful and deceitful, manipulative, opportunistic																		
M	−.01	−.12	−.24	−.02	−.05	.00	−.07	.03	.07	−.18	.06	.10	.18	−.18	−.02	.21	.00	.10
F	−.04	−.03	−.13	−.07	−.17	−.11	−.13	−.02	−.01	−.22	.00	−.05	.07	−.05	.02	.17	−.08	.08
38. Has hostility toward others																		
M	−.06	−.03	.03	−.01	−.03	−.02	.01	−.05	−.02	−.09	−.03	.04	.02	−.08	−.03	.01	−.05	.00
F	−.02	−.08	.06	−.08	−.08	−.11	−.07	.01	−.10	−.14	−.10	−.02	−.04	−.12	.11	.03	−.15	.00
39. Thinks and associates to ideas in unusual ways; has unconventional thought processes																		
M	.18	.24	.02	−.16	.07	.04	−.08	.29	−.06	−.10	−.29	−.01	−.06	.04	.07	.03	−.06	−.08
F	.33	−.01	.01	−.22	.12	.02	−.08	.33	−.08	−.09	−.32	−.08	.01	−.17	.15	.08	−.18	−.12
40. Is vulnerable to real or fancied threat, generally fearful																		
M	−.04	.12	.32	.00	−.02	−.13	.01	−.15	−.23	.01	−.09	−.20	−.27	.08	.06	−.23	−.12	−.11
F	−.09	.14	.35	−.05	−.13	−.23	−.08	−.18	−.30	.01	−.12	−.22	−.31	.04	.12	−.23	−.18	.00
41. Is moralistic																		
M	−.20	−.05	.14	.18	−.07	−.02	.11	−.29	.02	.12	.17	.04	−.08	.13	−.07	−.16	.06	−.01
F	−.31	−.02	.18	.32	−.04	.03	.11	−.33	.04	.16	.26	.10	−.06	.15	−.05	−.20	.12	−.06
42. Reluctant to commit self to any definite course of action; tends to delay or avoid action																		
M	.05	.05	.39	−.09	.04	−.16	.06	−.08	−.27	.11	−.12	−.22	−.27	.10	.08	−.27	−.14	−.11
F	.02	.14	.37	−.05	−.07	−.22	−.03	−.16	−.32	.06	−.19	−.29	−.36	.04	.10	−.25	−.20	−.03
43. Is facially and/or gesturally expressive																		
M	.05	.09	−.27	.05	.04	.12	−.09	.12	.16	−.04	.06	.06	.15	−.02	−.02	.17	.09	.07
F	.10	.11	−.21	−.08	.09	−.02	−.15	.15	.03	−.17	−.06	−.05	.10	.00	.04	.16	−.03	.13
44. Evaluates the motives of others in interpreting situations																		
M	.09	.13	−.06	−.01	.07	.08	.02	.11	.03	.00	−.05	.02	.02	.12	.01	.00	.02	−.07
F	.15	.00	−.07	−.08	.05	.05	−.03	.09	.00	−.07	−.09	−.03	−.03	−.09	.05	.08	−.05	−.03
45. Has a brittle ego-defense system; has a small reserve of integration; would be disorganized and maladaptive when under stress or trauma																		
M	.02	.07	.18	−.09	−.03	−.13	−.09	−.05	−.24	−.08	−.10	−.19	−.20	−.01	.10	−.10	−.13	−.08
F	−.10	.16	.30	−.03	−.20	−.22	−.18	−.23	−.33	−.04	−.09	−.25	−.32	.03	.21	−.19	−.20	.05
46. Engages in personal fantasy and daydreams, fictional speculations																		
M	.14	.12	.16	−.22	.01	−.19	−.15	.15	−.26	−.13	−.26	−.22	−.19	−.04	.12	−.02	−.19	−.07
F	.25	.11	.03	−.29	.04	−.20	−.22	.21	−.25	−.15	−.30	−.30	−.18	−.21	.13	.10	−.24	−.04
47. Has a readiness to feel guilty																		
M	−.04	.12	.32	.05	−.03	−.11	.02	−.11	−.19	.08	−.04	−.19	−.25	.15	−.01	−.25	−.05	−.09
F	−.11	.16	.25	.09	−.05	−.10	.00	−.19	−.19	.08	−.04	−.17	−.28	.11	.13	−.21	−.01	.01
48. Keeps people at a distance; avoids close interpersonal relationships																		
M	−.04	−.03	.27	−.15	−.12	−.22	−.06	−.11	−.28	−.12	−.08	−.10	−.21	−.03	.09	−.11	−.19	−.03
F	−.11	−.06	.23	.01	−.09	−.17	−.03	−.13	−.20	−.04	−.06	−.08	−.22	−.07	.18	−.05	−.13	−.04

Correlations of CPI Scales with California Q-Set Descriptions by Observers continued

Q-Sort Items	Do	Cs	Sy	Sp	Sa	In	Em	Re	So	Sc	Gi	Cm	Wb	To	Ac	Ai	Ie	Py
49. Is basically distrustful of people in general; questions their motivations																		
M	−.08	−.13	−.11	−.05	−.06	−.02	−.16	−.14	−.26	−.13	−.12	−.05	−.13	−.14	−.17	−.11	−.14	−.05
F	−.07	−.09	−.18	−.13	−.13	.02	−.10	−.04	−.11	−.06	−.07	−.16	−.09	−.10	−.11	−.04	−.08	−.01
50. Is unpredictable and changeable in behavior and attitudes																		
M	−.06	−.02	−.03	.02	.00	.02	.01	−.15	−.23	−.14	−.12	−.13	−.14	−.06	−.18	−.06	−.10	−.02
F	−.07	−.08	−.06	.08	−.02	−.01	.05	−.27	−.35	−.28	−.27	−.14	−.19	−.15	−.32	−.04	−.08	−.08
51. Genuinely values intellectual and cognitive matters																		
M	.04	.21	.00	.00	.01	.12	.11	.26	.09	.13	.05	−.02	.05	.22	.16	.31	.23	.30
F	.13	.29	.03	.07	.14	.25	.18	.33	.07	.11	.09	−.10	.16	.29	.16	.45	.37	.40
52. Behaves in an assertive fashion																		
M	.42	.13	.24	.20	.31	.31	.18	−.07	−.02	−.12	−.05	.13	.10	−.08	.07	.00	.10	.02
F	.40	.27	.31	.28	.37	.33	.25	.05	−.01	−.14	−.03	.07	.09	−.02	.11	.15	.25	.11
53. Various needs tend toward relatively direct and uncontrolled expression; unable to delay gratification																		
M	.15	.09	.17	.19	.18	.15	.11	−.20	−.21	−.24	−.14	−.06	−.04	−.08	−.15	−.06	.00	−.02
F	.04	.00	.09	.18	.12	.03	.10	−.31	−.35	−.32	−.27	−.08	−.17	−.19	−.27	−.12	−.01	−.10
54. Emphasizes being with others; gregarious																		
M	.25	.22	.32	.22	.21	.10	.25	.12	.18	−.05	.03	.12	.17	.13	.15	.11	.17	.04
F	.23	.12	.35	.25	.24	.02	.17	−.01	.09	−.09	.00	.18	.13	.04	.09	−.05	.12	−.06
55. Is self-defeating																		
M	−.33	−.30	−.32	−.24	−.36	−.27	−.30	−.15	−.23	−.04	−.11	−.15	−.23	−.11	−.24	−.19	−.23	−.13
F	−.34	−.28	−.31	−.30	−.37	−.27	−.27	−.11	−.14	.02	−.09	−.27	−.19	−.10	−.23	−.19	−.25	−.14
56. Responds to humor																		
M	.02	.03	.11	.10	.05	−.02	.14	−.14	.07	−.08	.01	−.06	−.01	−.05	−.07	−.03	−.02	−.12
F	.10	.04	.21	.20	.16	.02	.13	−.13	.01	−.10	−.04	.10	.02	.01	−.01	−.01	.07	−.09
57. Is an interesting, arresting person																		
M	.22	.11	.08	.10	.20	.24	.21	−.12	−.06	−.10	−.04	−.01	−.02	−.04	−.08	.01	.02	−.05
F	.22	.25	.19	.23	.30	.23	.27	−.04	−.15	−.19	−.08	−.02	.01	.01	−.06	.17	.19	.12
58. Enjoys sensuous experiences (including touch, taste, smell, physical contact)																		
M	.06	.14	.07	.18	.11	.14	.15	−.07	−.07	−.10	−.06	.00	.06	.04	−.10	.06	.10	.04
F	.03	.12	.12	.24	.18	.06	.20	−.22	−.17	−.20	−.15	.05	−.01	−.03	−.16	.01	.07	−.07
59. Is concerned with own body and the adequacy of its physiological functioning																		
M	−.13	−.09	−.10	−.11	−.09	−.09	−.10	−.08	−.07	.04	.04	−.09	−.06	−.11	−.02	−.10	−.08	−.10
F	−.15	−.16	−.12	−.14	−.18	−.21	−.15	−.09	.02	.01	−.06	.05	−.10	−.07	−.03	−.19	−.17	−.15
60. Has insight into own motives and behavior																		
M	.03	.07	.03	.04	.04	.05	.13	−.08	.07	.01	.03	.04	−.01	.05	.02	.10	.05	−.01
F	.11	.13	.10	.14	.16	.16	.14	.05	−.02	−.04	.00	.06	.10	.13	.00	.19	.12	.16
61. Creates and exploits dependency in people																		
M	.10	−.09	.04	−.01	.04	.12	−.02	−.15	−.09	−.05	−.02	−.07	.01	−.15	−.06	−.14	−.09	−.09
F	.07	−.01	−.01	−.06	.00	−.01	−.11	.08	−.02	.06	.05	.05	.02	−.07	.01	−.19	−.07	−.01
62. Tends to be rebellious and nonconforming																		
M	.05	.04	.00	.13	.10	.20	.09	−.20	−.30	−.21	−.18	−.15	−.06	−.04	−.22	.02	.01	.04
F	.06	.11	.01	.17	.15	.21	.16	−.18	−.34	−.29	−.26	−.20	−.09	−.06	−.28	.12	.11	.11
63. Judges self and others in conventional terms like "popularity," "the correct thing to do," social pressures, etc.																		
M	−.06	−.11	.06	−.05	−.10	−.21	−.13	.09	.21	.09	.11	.10	.05	−.02	.12	−.11	−.06	−.12
F	−.07	−.13	.04	−.09	−.14	−.22	−.17	.00	.28	.16	.13	.20	.04	−.08	.15	−.26	−.18	−.23
64. Is socially perceptive of a wide range of interpersonal cues																		
M	.12	.21	.13	.12	.16	.12	.22	.08	.15	.02	.04	.07	.11	.14	.11	.17	.17	.09
F	.13	.19	.17	.19	.19	.17	.24	−.02	−.03	−.04	.02	.15	.06	.13	.07	.14	.16	.11

Correlations of CPI Scales with California Q-Set Descriptions by Observers continued

Q-Sort Items	Fx	F/M	v.1	v.2	v.3	Mp	Wo	CT	Lp	Ami	Leo	Tm	B–MS	B–FM	Anx	Nar	D–SD	D–AC
49. Is basically distrustful of people in general; questions their motivations																		
M	−.04	.00	.03	−.15	−.14	−.14	−.10	−.03	−.14	−.24	−.07	−.04	−.07	−.11	.07	.07	−.13	.06
F	.00	−.12	.02	−.06	−.08	−.13	−.11	.00	−.13	−.16	−.07	−.05	−.06	−.18	.15	.08	−.13	−.01
50. Is unpredictable and changeable in behavior and attitudes																		
M	.12	.08	.00	−.20	−.01	−.08	−.19	.14	−.14	−.22	−.16	−.08	−.05	−.13	.11	.11	−.16	−.03
F	.23	.08	−.06	−.34	−.10	−.20	−.21	.22	−.21	−.24	−.31	−.21	−.09	−.23	.10	.16	−.26	.05
51. Genuinely values intellectual and cognitive matters																		
M	.17	.13	.03	−.01	.24	.12	.11	.23	.05	.11	−.16	.07	−.03	.16	.04	−.09	.05	−.07
F	.18	−.12	−.03	.05	.35	.27	.20	.27	.18	.09	−.10	.20	.15	.01	−.01	−.02	.11	−.18
52. Behaves in an assertive fashion																		
M	−.04	−.13	−.40	.06	−.03	.17	−.02	.04	.28	−.09	.13	.25	.31	−.12	−.07	.28	.11	.11
F	.01	−.16	−.38	.03	.07	.17	.03	.20	.29	−.11	.14	.22	.37	−.10	−.09	.27	.15	.10
53. Various needs tend toward relatively direct and uncontrolled expression; unable to delay gratification																		
M	.13	−.09	−.23	−.16	−.02	−.01	−.17	.17	.03	−.20	−.05	−.01	.16	−.27	.03	.26	−.06	.07
F	.20	.04	−.15	−.31	−.16	−.18	−.23	.21	−.10	−.26	−.22	−.16	.06	−.23	.05	.22	−.20	.12
54. Emphasizes being with others; gregarious																		
M	.03	−.10	−.26	.16	.14	.20	.08	.04	.25	.15	.12	.10	.23	−.03	−.11	.07	.16	.05
F	.00	.01	−.23	.06	.02	.13	.04	.02	.21	.07	.15	.07	.22	.09	−.24	.03	.14	.11
55. Is self-defeating																		
M	−.01	.10	.29	−.19	−.16	−.24	−.16	−.10	−.35	−.17	−.18	−.26	−.31	−.07	.15	−.09	−.23	−.07
F	−.01	.11	.29	−.11	−.15	−.23	−.12	−.15	−.35	−.04	−.17	−.30	−.33	−.05	.18	−.15	−.24	−.01
56. Responds to humor																		
M	.06	−.07	−.10	−.03	.00	−.07	−.10	.01	−.02	.03	.03	−.11	.03	−.05	.04	.07	−.05	.10
F	.06	.01	−.16	−.05	.01	.02	.02	.09	.06	.01	.06	−.01	.10	.02	−.09	.07	.05	.12
57. Is an interesting, arresting person																		
M	.08	.11	−.23	−.11	−.03	.06	−.14	.19	.09	−.12	−.04	.06	.09	−.03	.02	.20	.02	.03
F	.23	−.08	−.30	−.16	.08	.08	−.08	.30	.11	−.14	−.06	.05	.20	−.16	.01	.25	.03	.01
58. Enjoys sensuous experiences (including touch, taste, smell, physical contact)																		
M	.16	.00	−.07	−.14	.08	.05	.00	.24	.06	−.01	−.12	.02	.12	−.14	−.03	.10	−.01	−.05
F	.22	−.03	−.15	−.22	.00	−.06	−.08	.24	.01	−.06	−.17	−.11	.09	−.17	−.04	.18	−.08	.06
59. Is concerned with own body and the adequacy of its physiological functioning																		
M	−.08	.05	.13	.00	−.02	−.08	−.03	−.11	−.10	−.02	−.03	−.08	−.08	.00	.07	−.11	−.01	−.08
F	−.17	.17	.14	.02	−.15	−.12	−.08	−.19	−.13	.04	.03	−.11	−.20	.07	−.05	−.06	−.07	.06
60. Has insight into own motives and behavior																		
M	.09	.05	−.06	−.06	.06	.04	.00	.13	.03	.03	.00	−.01	−.01	.07	.05	−.01	.01	.00
F	.12	−.09	−.12	−.04	.19	.13	.11	.17	.10	.02	−.02	.13	.11	−.02	−.10	.08	.08	−.04
61. Creates and exploits dependency in people																		
M	−.04	−.02	−.09	−.01	−.10	−.01	−.03	−.04	.03	−.09	.02	.06	.09	−.04	.02	.09	.01	.01
F	−.12	.01	.01	.06	−.08	.03	.00	−.13	.08	.01	.08	.04	.06	.04	−.06	−.04	.03	.00
62. Tends to be rebellious and nonconforming																		
M	.22	.03	−.14	−.30	.01	−.04	−.19	.32	−.08	−.24	−.24	−.03	.05	−.19	.08	.21	−.14	.00
F	.36	−.15	−.15	−.39	.03	−.10	−.15	.39	−.08	−.25	−.25	−.08	.12	−.34	.12	.26	−.21	.00
63. Judges self and others in conventional terms like "popularity," "the correct thing to do," social pressures, etc.																		
M	−.23	−.20	.06	.26	−.06	.03	.15	−.33	.05	.18	.25	.04	.01	.04	−.08	−.12	.10	.00
F	−.30	.12	.11	.27	−.15	−.02	.06	−.38	.03	.16	.25	.00	−.10	.28	−.15	−.18	.10	.08
64. Is socially perceptive of a wide range of interpersonal cues																		
M	.08	.09	−.09	.08	.13	.12	.06	.14	.15	.13	−.02	.04	.07	.12	−.09	.00	.08	−.02
F	.12	.06	−.16	−.05	.19	.17	.12	.18	.15	.05	−.02	.12	.12	.02	−.14	.05	.10	−.03

Correlations of CPI Scales with California Q-Set Descriptions by Observers continued

Q-Sort Items	Do	Cs	Sy	Sp	Sa	In	Em	Re	So	Sc	Gi	Cm	Wb	To	Ac	Ai	Ie	Py
65. Characteristically pushes and tries to stretch limits; sees what he or she can get away with																		
M	.22	.03	.17	.23	.24	.24	.11	−.31	−.27	−.31	−.21	−.10	−.07	−.17	−.17	−.07	−.04	−.06
F	.18	.07	.13	.19	.20	.15	.16	−.22	−.28	−.34	−.24	−.10	−.13	−.18	−.24	−.02	.02	−.01
66. Enjoys esthetic impressions; is esthetically reactive																		
M	.06	.26	−.03	.04	.08	.15	.15	.17	.03	.05	.02	−.03	.04	.16	.06	.15	.14	.16
F	−.08	.11	−.01	.05	.05	.05	.09	−.01	−.09	.01	−.02	−.06	.03	.04	.00	.08	.05	.01
67. Is self-indulgent																		
M	.07	.00	.12	.16	.09	.08	.10	−.25	−.21	−.23	−.13	−.08	−.08	−.13	−.18	−.13	−.05	−.16
F	.00	.00	.04	.16	.06	.00	.10	−.30	−.26	−.26	−.27	−.10	−.16	−.16	−.26	−.13	−.05	−.12
68. Is basically anxious																		
M	−.25	−.09	−.21	−.21	−.24	−.24	−.19	.16	−.04	.13	.02	−.07	−.07	.08	.01	.01	−.05	.04
F	−.35	−.29	−.34	−.30	−.35	−.29	−.25	−.06	−.11	.04	−.05	−.30	−.24	−.09	−.18	−.13	−.25	−.10
69. Is sensitive to anything that can be construed as a demand																		
M	−.09	−.11	−.10	−.05	−.11	−.06	−.15	−.09	−.17	−.08	−.11	−.06	−.08	−.05	−.17	−.10	−.11	−.02
F	−.23	−.16	−.23	−.18	−.25	−.16	−.13	−.04	−.09	.10	.01	−.13	−.10	−.11	−.08	−.10	−.17	−.05
70. Behaves in an ethically consistent manner; is consistent with own personal standards																		
M	−.15	−.16	−.18	−.22	−.22	−.16	−.15	.12	.22	.21	.13	.02	.03	.04	.10	.00	−.01	−.03
F	−.08	−.03	−.12	−.14	−.12	−.01	−.06	.26	.28	.35	.28	.05	.17	.20	.22	.10	.05	.14
71. Has high aspiration level for self																		
M	.25	.29	.18	.10	.28	.18	.13	.27	.16	.09	.13	.07	.15	.19	.34	.27	.25	.25
F	.29	.30	.18	.18	.29	.30	.27	.18	.11	−.06	.02	.05	.13	.11	.22	.33	.28	.27
72. Concerned with own adequacy as a person, either at conscious or unconscious levels																		
M	−.22	−.12	−.19	−.16	−.19	−.21	−.14	.08	−.08	.05	−.04	−.04	−.14	.03	−.09	−.05	−.08	−.01
F	−.33	−.16	−.29	−.26	−.26	−.22	−.17	−.04	−.13	.04	−.09	−.25	−.21	.02	−.17	.00	−.11	−.05
73. Tends to perceive many different contexts in sexual terms; eroticizes situations																		
M	.17	.11	.15	.25	.22	.19	.14	−.15	−.17	−.20	−.12	.00	.05	−.08	−.10	.00	.01	.02
F	.13	.12	.17	.24	.17	.07	.21	−.15	−.10	−.23	−.18	.05	−.02	−.03	−.13	.05	.09	.00
74. Is subjectively unaware of self-concern; feels satisfied with self																		
M	.21	.07	.23	.20	.20	.17	.12	−.08	.05	−.04	.09	.05	.16	−.07	.04	−.05	.07	−.02
F	.25	.07	.20	.17	.16	.19	.07	.07	.27	.11	.15	.28	.26	.03	.22	−.03	.09	.04
75. Has a clear-cut, internally consistent personality																		
M	.00	−.08	.03	.01	.01	−.02	−.04	−.06	.10	.01	.03	.08	.03	−.06	.02	−.07	−.02	−.06
F	.10	.08	.10	.02	.08	.02	.01	.18	.27	.23	.25	.14	.19	.13	.20	.03	.04	.02
76. Tends to project own feelings and motivations onto others																		
M	−.05	−.06	−.01	−.02	−.05	−.04	−.13	.01	−.07	−.03	−.02	−.01	−.01	.00	.01	−.04	.00	.05
F	−.10	−.18	−.10	−.16	−.12	−.12	−.20	−.01	.03	.05	−.01	−.03	−.05	−.14	.01	−.24	−.17	−.07
77. Appears straightforward, forthright, candid in dealing with others																		
M	−.05	−.03	−.01	−.04	−.06	−.09	−.02	−.01	.14	.11	.07	.06	.09	.04	.05	.01	.03	.00
F	.14	.13	.06	.05	.16	.08	.09	.18	.10	.12	.12	.15	.13	.13	.13	.14	.17	.09
78. Feels cheated and victimized by life; self-pitying																		
M	−.22	−.21	−.23	−.20	−.26	−.19	−.24	−.06	−.19	−.02	−.09	−.09	−.18	−.09	−.15	−.15	−.21	−.12
F	−.24	−.23	−.27	−.29	−.31	−.22	−.27	−.01	−.13	.06	−.02	−.21	−.21	−.12	−.13	−.18	−.25	−.09
79. Tends to ruminate and have persistent, pre-occupying thoughts																		
M	−.25	−.13	−.25	−.19	−.28	−.14	−.20	.02	−.08	.03	−.08	−.10	−.12	.01	−.11	−.04	−.09	.04
F	−.27	−.17	−.30	−.25	−.25	−.18	−.21	.00	−.10	.07	−.04	−.20	−.16	−.04	−.13	−.10	−.18	−.05
80. Interested in members of the opposite sex																		
M	.08	.01	.12	.16	.11	.05	.08	−.14	−.06	−.10	−.03	.03	.08	−.04	−.06	−.04	.01	−.04
F	.11	.10	.20	.26	.17	.06	.20	−.25	−.10	−.26	−.18	.02	−.05	−.08	−.13	−.01	−.01	−.09

Correlations of CPI Scales with California Q-Set Descriptions by Observers continued

Q-Sort Items	Fx	F/M	v.1	v.2	v.3	Mp	Wo	CT	Lp	Ami	Leo	Tm	B–MS	B–FM	Anx	Nar	D–SD	D–AC
65. Characteristically pushes and tries to stretch limits; sees what he or she can get away with																		
M	.08	−.10	−.32	−.20	−.09	−.04	−.23	.19	.04	−.30	−.05	.05	.18	−.31	.05	.39	−.12	.13
F	.19	−.11	−.27	−.28	−.10	−.12	−.22	.24	.00	−.33	−.10	−.04	.15	−.27	.10	.34	−.15	.11
66. Enjoys esthetic impressions; is esthetically reactive																		
M	.11	.30	.00	−.02	.14	.11	.02	.27	.06	.05	−.23	.00	−.04	.13	.02	.01	.05	−.06
F	.10	.05	.06	−.08	.10	.01	.04	.11	−.01	.07	−.17	−.06	.00	−.01	−.02	−.03	−.01	−.10
67. Is self-indulgent																		
M	.06	−.06	−.18	−.17	−.07	−.08	−.17	.08	−.03	−.18	−.03	−.05	.08	−.21	.09	.25	−.09	.07
F	.17	.01	−.14	−.30	−.15	−.18	−.20	.16	−.12	−.20	−.18	−.11	.00	−.13	−.01	.21	−.22	.13
68. Is basically anxious																		
M	−.07	.13	.29	.01	.03	−.07	.03	−.11	−.19	.04	−.10	−.12	−.21	.10	.06	−.23	−.07	−.12
F	−.02	.16	.31	−.12	−.12	−.19	−.13	−.12	−.34	−.06	−.18	−.24	−.35	.03	.22	−.19	−.23	−.07
69. Is sensitive to anything that can be construed as a demand																		
M	.05	.08	.09	−.14	−.06	−.13	−.05	.03	−.15	−.13	−.15	−.12	−.11	−.02	.04	.01	−.11	.01
F	.03	.12	.21	−.05	−.05	−.18	−.04	−.08	−.22	−.04	−.10	−.12	−.22	.03	.11	−.13	−.12	−.04
70. *Behaves* in an ethically consistent manner; is consistent with own personal standards																		
M	−.11	.03	.25	.13	−.02	−.04	.11	−.19	−.03	.20	.08	−.03	−.15	.19	−.01	−.24	.04	−.03
F	−.12	.00	.22	.24	.17	.11	.25	−.17	.07	.31	.15	.12	−.06	.20	−.07	−.24	.17	−.15
71. Has high aspiration level for self																		
M	.01	−.03	−.17	.23	.21	.27	.13	.13	.27	.11	.11	.21	.16	.06	−.06	.03	.19	.00
F	.08	−.28	−.27	.12	.18	.21	.07	.27	.27	−.04	.06	.21	.26	−.14	−.04	.22	.15	−.05
72. Concerned with own adequacy as a person, either at conscious or unconscious levels																		
M	−.02	.13	.22	−.04	−.01	−.10	−.03	−.07	−.21	−.03	−.11	−.15	−.20	.09	.09	−.16	−.12	−.09
F	.07	.18	.24	−.14	−.02	−.18	−.08	.01	−.31	−.06	−.21	−.22	−.34	.02	.20	−.16	−.21	−.06
73. Tends to perceive many different contexts in sexual terms; eroticizes situations																		
M	.10	−.05	−.21	−.12	−.02	−.01	−.06	.18	.10	−.15	−.06	.08	.19	−.19	−.09	.23	−.02	.03
F	.25	.04	−.22	−.17	−.02	−.01	−.08	.19	.05	−.08	−.12	−.06	.10	−.07	−.02	.19	−.07	.06
74. Is subjectively unaware of self-concern; feels satisfied with self																		
M	−.06	−.26	−.23	.08	.00	.08	.08	−.06	.22	.07	.19	.21	.27	−.12	−.10	.13	.15	.14
F	−.18	−.13	−.15	.24	.03	.17	.19	−.15	.33	.14	.28	.27	.27	.09	−.20	.07	.22	.06
75. Has a clear-cut, internally consistent personality																		
M	−.11	−.19	−.03	.08	−.09	−.06	.03	−.14	.05	.08	.16	.04	.03	−.05	−.02	.02	.04	.07
F	−.19	−.12	.00	.26	.08	.17	.21	−.18	.19	.22	.26	.22	.12	.16	−.18	−.08	.23	−.02
76. Tends to project own feelings and motivations onto others																		
M	−.06	−.09	.06	−.03	.01	−.01	.01	−.04	−.03	−.05	.01	.02	.05	−.07	.01	−.05	−.06	−.09
F	−.19	.10	.13	.07	−.19	−.13	−.08	−.22	−.09	−.01	.06	−.06	−.11	−.01	.01	−.04	−.09	.03
77. Appears straightforward, forthright, candid in dealing with others																		
M	−.04	−.11	.10	.04	−.01	.02	.10	−.06	.04	.18	.06	.04	.00	.05	−.05	−.14	.03	−.07
F	.01	−.03	−.04	.08	.15	.19	.15	.03	.16	.14	.13	.17	.17	.08	−.08	−.09	.15	−.11
78. Feels cheated and victimized by life; self-pitying																		
M	−.07	.12	.20	−.14	−.13	−.17	−.09	−.11	−.24	−.19	−.10	−.17	−.24	−.01	.13	−.07	−.15	−.04
F	−.13	.14	.24	−.04	−.14	−.20	−.14	−.18	−.26	−.09	−.11	−.16	−.27	.00	.21	−.13	−.17	−.07
79. Tends to ruminate and have persistent, pre-occupying thoughts																		
M	−.01	.12	.27	−.11	−.03	−.15	−.03	−.05	−.23	−.08	−.19	−.19	−.26	.06	.08	−.14	−.14	−.07
F	−.01	.12	.28	−.11	−.08	−.15	−.11	−.09	−.25	−.02	−.17	−.19	−.27	−.04	.18	−.15	−.18	−.11
80. Interested in members of the opposite sex																		
M	−.03	−.22	−.12	.00	−.03	−.01	−.02	.01	.09	.00	.11	.06	.16	−.22	−.11	.12	.06	.10
F	.19	−.05	−.25	−.20	−.06	−.07	−.13	.19	.02	−.11	−.05	−.08	.07	−.14	−.03	.23	−.08	.10

Correlations of CPI Scales with California Q-Set Descriptions by Observers continued

Q-Sort Items	Do	Cs	Sy	Sp	Sa	In	Em	Re	So	Sc	Gi	Cm	Wb	To	Ac	Ai	Ie	Py
81. Is physically attractive; good-looking
M	.05	.04	.08	.09	.10	.02	.09	−.05	.06	−.03	.04	.05	.07	.04	−.02	.04	.01	−.04
F	.08	.09	.14	.12	.12	.07	.07	−.14	.03	−.08	.00	.12	.04	−.04	.05	−.03	.00	−.07
82. Has fluctuating moods
M	−.15	−.06	−.13	−.11	−.11	−.14	−.04	.01	−.15	−.04	−.11	−.12	−.13	.03	−.13	−.03	−.07	.00
F	−.29	−.20	−.20	−.10	−.18	−.19	−.16	−.28	−.29	−.19	−.25	−.21	−.28	−.18	−.34	−.14	−.21	−.19
83. Able to see to the heart of important problems
M	.12	.13	.02	.04	.10	.18	.09	.13	.10	.06	.03	.07	.09	.11	.13	.19	.17	.19
F	.19	.20	.07	.12	.18	.23	.19	.23	.08	.06	.06	.04	.12	.20	.11	.32	.27	.29
84. Is cheerful
M	.12	.11	.21	.13	.13	.05	.15	.03	.20	.05	.10	.05	.15	.06	.11	.07	.11	.03
F	.12	.07	.20	.16	.13	.04	.07	−.01	.19	.05	.08	.22	.16	.09	.15	−.01	.11	−.03
85. Emphasizes communication through action and nonverbal behavior
M	−.06	−.09	−.01	−.03	−.03	−.05	−.04	−.15	−.08	−.07	−.04	.02	−.06	−.13	−.15	−.15	−.14	−.11
F	−.05	−.11	.02	.01	−.07	−.10	−.07	−.10	.03	.02	−.05	.08	.02	.00	−.05	−.07	−.07	−.10
86. Handles anxiety and conflicts by, in effect, refusing to recognize their presence; repressive or dissociative tendencies
M	−.15	−.26	−.16	−.15	−.20	−.13	−.25	−.06	−.09	.03	.01	−.13	−.07	−.15	−.09	−.18	−.15	−.08
F	−.18	−.16	−.18	−.20	−.22	−.16	−.26	.06	.14	.21	.11	−.02	.04	−.05	.06	−.14	−.10	−.04
87. Interprets basically simple and clear-cut situations in complicated and particularizing ways
M	−.09	−.02	−.13	−.11	−.09	.01	−.09	.06	−.11	.06	−.01	−.07	−.09	.04	.00	.04	.03	.06
F	−.04	.03	−.04	−.04	−.01	.02	.00	.00	−.09	−.05	−.04	−.14	−.09	−.02	.00	.07	.02	.01
88. Is personally charming
M	.16	.12	.11	.10	.14	.14	.17	.02	.11	.00	.04	.09	.11	.03	.06	.06	.07	.00
F	.08	.10	.14	.17	.16	.05	.09	−.04	−.01	−.07	−.01	.16	.05	.06	.00	.03	.06	−.05
89. Compares self to others. Is alert to real or fancied differences between self and other people
M	−.15	−.19	−.18	−.15	−.17	−.07	−.20	−.10	−.12	−.04	−.09	−.12	−.14	−.11	−.15	−.10	−.18	−.10
F	−.08	−.08	−.04	−.05	−.09	−.13	.00	−.12	−.07	−.09	−.09	−.05	−.12	−.12	−.09	−.13	−.11	−.14
90. Is concerned with philosophical problems; e.g., religions, values, the meaning of life, etc.
M	.00	.12	−.06	−.08	−.04	.05	.07	.24	.05	.16	.10	−.01	.03	.20	.15	.19	.16	.15
F	.07	.09	−.09	−.11	.02	.15	.09	.17	.01	.12	.09	−.12	.03	.19	.12	.27	.20	.18
91. Is power oriented; values power in self or others
M	.24	−.03	.11	.13	.22	.17	−.02	−.15	−.09	−.20	−.15	.08	.00	−.18	.00	−.08	−.04	−.06
F	.35	.21	.24	.19	.29	.25	.20	.04	.05	−.11	.00	.12	.05	−.03	.13	.12	.16	.08
92. Has social poise and presence; appears socially at ease
M	.36	.26	.30	.29	.35	.31	.33	.07	.14	−.03	.02	.16	.21	.12	.17	.17	.23	.10
F	.37	.29	.35	.29	.38	.25	.27	.11	.12	−.05	.07	.24	.18	.09	.24	.11	.24	.07
93. Behaves in a masculine style and manner (if a male), or behaves in a feminine style and manner (if a female)
M	.10	−.09	.09	.09	.06	.05	−.03	−.17	−.03	−.13	−.07	.12	.04	−.14	−.05	−.14	−.05	−.09
F	−.12	−.15	−.03	−.04	−.11	−.15	−.07	−.12	.09	.05	.07	.13	−.04	−.03	.02	−.16	−.20	−.20
94. Expresses hostile feelings directly
M	.18	.03	.11	.12	.18	.15	.02	−.13	−.12	−.15	−.09	.04	.06	−.09	−.05	−.06	.01	.04
F	.15	.08	.05	.10	.12	.17	.03	.00	−.17	−.12	−.06	−.09	.03	−.07	−.09	−.01	.07	.09
95. Tends to proffer advice
M	.34	.18	.22	.15	.26	.25	.16	.13	.08	.00	.04	.12	.14	.04	.20	.04	.15	.09
F	.29	.14	.15	.05	.19	.19	.11	.20	.07	.03	.08	.04	.13	.07	.15	.10	.19	.12
96. Values own independence and autonomy
M	.07	.00	−.02	.09	.14	.18	−.01	−.16	−.21	−.11	−.11	−.11	−.01	−.08	−.13	.00	−.01	.09
F	.17	.21	.07	.20	.20	.27	.22	.05	−.11	−.15	−.09	−.03	.06	.05	−.01	.28	.26	.19

Correlations of CPI Scales with California Q-Set Descriptions by Observers continued

Q-Sort Items	Fx	F/M	v.1	v.2	v.3	Mp	Wo	CT	Lp	Ami	Leo	Tm	B–MS	B–FM	Anx	Nar	D–SD	D–AC
81. Is physically attractive; good-looking																		
M	-.01	-.13	-.08	.05	.03	.05	.06	.00	.08	.09	.16	.08	.11	-.06	-.12	.06	.09	.03
F	.00	-.09	-.14	-.01	-.01	-.01	-.03	.02	.08	-.02	.13	.05	.10	-.01	-.05	.12	.06	.01
82. Has fluctuating moods																		
M	.10	.15	.14	-.15	-.01	-.07	-.10	.07	-.20	-.11	-.16	-.18	-.14	-.02	.15	-.05	-.15	-.04
F	.16	.14	.13	-.31	-.21	-.33	-.31	.09	-.38	-.19	-.35	-.33	-.28	-.12	.20	.00	-.33	.03
83. Able to see to the heart of important problems																		
M	.09	.04	-.08	.02	.08	.12	.06	.14	.11	.08	.00	.14	.04	.08	-.07	.01	.05	.01
F	.12	-.12	-.12	.03	.24	.22	.17	.19	.18	.05	-.05	.21	.16	.00	-.04	.08	.13	-.09
84. Is cheerful																		
M	.06	-.11	-.13	.11	.11	.10	.08	.00	.16	.17	.14	.07	.16	.03	-.08	.00	.11	.02
F	-.03	.03	-.09	.12	.04	.12	.13	-.04	.17	.14	.17	.09	.14	.12	-.17	-.04	.18	.08
85. Emphasizes communication through action and nonverbal behavior																		
M	-.07	-.11	.01	-.06	-.13	-.11	-.09	-.08	-.08	-.07	.02	-.07	-.02	-.13	.03	.07	-.05	.08
F	-.01	.01	.07	-.02	-.07	-.03	.00	-.04	-.03	.05	.08	-.05	-.02	.02	.00	-.03	-.04	.01
86. Handles anxiety and conflicts by, in effect, refusing to recognize their presence; repressive or dissociative tendencies																		
M	-.14	-.05	.17	-.01	-.14	-.15	-.04	-.17	-.13	-.05	.00	-.05	-.10	-.04	.02	-.08	-.08	-.01
F	-.18	.08	.25	.13	-.11	-.07	.04	-.29	-.08	.12	.09	-.04	-.14	.13	-.03	-.25	.02	.00
87. Interprets basically simple and clear-cut situations in complicated and particularizing ways																		
M	.01	.17	.11	-.09	.06	-.01	-.03	.08	-.10	-.09	-.17	-.08	-.12	.04	.11	-.06	-.05	-.10
F	.03	-.02	.03	-.07	.03	.00	-.08	.06	-.04	-.06	-.12	-.04	-.05	-.11	.14	.02	-.05	-.01
88. Is personally charming																		
M	.03	.04	-.12	.07	.03	.10	.02	-.03	.16	.08	.04	.09	.11	.06	-.11	.09	.10	.03
F	.09	.03	-.11	-.04	.03	.07	.01	.07	.08	.03	.07	.02	.08	.03	-.09	.04	.07	.00
89. Compares self to others. Is alert to real or fancied differences between self and other people																		
M	-.01	.05	.12	-.14	-.10	-.14	-.11	.13	.20	-.15	-.07	-.13	-.16	-.01	.15	.01	-.14	-.03
F	-.05	-.02	-.02	.01	-.12	-.13	-.14	-.05	-.13	-.10	-.03	-.14	-.15	-.05	.07	.06	-.08	.07
90. Is concerned with philosophical problems; e.g., religions, values, the meaning of life, etc.																		
M	.06	.20	.07	.02	.17	.09	.05	-.06	.04	.08	-.10	.01	-.07	.19	.04	-.13	.08	-.10
F	.08	-.01	.05	.00	.21	.14	.06	.16	.07	.04	-.01	.09	.02	-.02	.05	-.04	.05	-.18
91. Is power oriented; values power in self or others																		
M	-.10	-.17	-.27	.05	-.17	.01	-.07	.16	.14	-.20	.15	.13	.17	-.16	-.02	.27	.01	.15
F	-.02	-.21	-.36	.11	.02	.14	-.02	.12	.25	-.12	.17	.22	.27	-.07	-.08	.27	.14	.08
92. Has social poise and presence; appears socially at ease																		
M	.04	-.08	-.34	.11	.12	.28	.11	-.13	.35	.11	.12	.24	.32	.00	-.15	.18	.21	.05
F	-.02	-.05	-.33	.13	.12	.25	.09	.10	.35	.06	.19	.23	.31	.07	-.20	.13	.25	.04
93. Behaves in a masculine style and manner (if a male), or behaves in a feminine style and manner (if a female)																		
M	-.10	-.35	-.13	.02	-.16	-.03	.02	.04	.08	-.06	.18	.10	.15	-.23	-.08	.15	-.01	.11
F	-.10	.18	.08	.09	-.09	-.07	-.04	-.17	-.06	.10	.07	-.09	-.16	.20	-.03	-.10	.04	.01
94. Expresses hostile feelings directly																		
M	.01	-.18	-.18	-.04	-.07	.03	-.05	.04	.11	-.15	.07	.14	.21	-.20	-.06	.18	.00	.05
F	.03	-.13	-.14	-.08	-.03	-.01	-.06	.12	.07	-.16	-.02	.08	.19	-.15	.01	.17	-.05	.07
95. Tends to proffer advice																		
M	-.08	-.03	-.30	.14	.04	.21	.07	.04	.29	.02	.10	.22	.24	-.01	-.08	.14	.18	.01
F	-.04	-.09	-.20	.13	.07	.19	.06	.05	.23	-.01	.16	.23	.23	.05	-.09	.08	.13	.01
96. Values own independence and autonomy																		
M	.08	-.10	-.09	-.17	-.04	-.06	-.11	.14	-.02	-.16	-.07	.06	.08	-.21	.05	.16	-.06	.02
F	.13	-.31	-.18	-.08	.16	.10	.01	.27	.14	-.13	-.11	.13	.20	-.27	.05	.24	.03	.01

Q-Sort Items	Do	Cs	Sy	Sp	Sa	In	Em	Re	So	Sc	Gi	Cm	Wb	To	Ac	Ai	Ie	Py
97. Is emotionally bland; has flattened affect																		
M	−.19	−.07	−.05	−.08	−.15	−.21	−.06	.10	.08	.12	.12	.03	.02	.02	.07	.03	.00	−.02
F	−.22	−.19	−.26	−.23	−.29	−.10	−.22	.04	.12	.21	.09	−.03	.03	.03	.01	−.07	−.16	.01
98. Is verbally fluent; can express ideas well																		
M	.27	.18	.17	.19	.24	.26	.26	.01	.04	−.10	−.08	.05	.02	.06	.06	.20	.19	.09
F	.39	.34	.28	.27	.40	.34	.34	.15	.00	−.14	.00	.11	.09	.15	.18	.30	.37	.19
99. Is self-dramatizing; histrionic																		
M	.30	.11	.16	.15	.24	.25	.14	−.06	−.14	−.18	−.09	−.01	−.02	−.08	−.03	−.06	.04	−.01
F	.16	.10	.15	.12	.18	.08	.10	−.09	−.19	−.24	−.16	−.06	−.10	−.11	−.07	−.05	.07	−.04
100. Does not vary roles; relates to everyone in the same way																		
M	−.22	−.20	−.16	−.20	−.20	−.18	−.24	−.03	−.04	.09	.06	−.03	−.06	−.08	−.04	−.13	−.11	−.07
F	−.15	−.17	−.18	−.17	−.22	−.11	−.24	.02	.15	.20	.13	−.03	.07	−.03	.03	−.12	−.14	−.02

Correlations of CPI Scales with California Q-Set Descriptions by Observers continued

Q-Sort Items	Fx	F/M	v.1	v.2	v.3	Mp	Wo	CT	Lp	Ami	Leo	Tm	B–MS	B–FM	Anx	Nar	D–SD	D–AC
97. Is emotionally bland; has flattened affect																		
M	−.08	−.09	.20	.09	.03	−.07	.15	−.17	−.06	.14	.07	−.02	−.09	.06	−.07	−.23	.05	−.01
F	−.16	−.07	.27	.08	.00	−.06	.11	−.23	−.11	.15	.03	.03	−.17	.02	.04	−.15	−.03	−.09
98. Is verbally fluent; can express ideas well																		
M	.13	.10	−.30	−.03	.09	.15	−.06	.24	.16	−.07	−.03	.11	.13	.05	−.01	.21	.07	.05
F	.17	−.12	−.40	.00	.22	.23	.03	.32	.29	−.06	.04	.22	.30	−.05	−.09	.21	.15	.00
99. Is self-dramatizing; histrionic																		
M	.03	.08	−.33	−.03	−.05	.09	−.16	.14	.13	−.20	−.03	.08	.15	−.13	.03	.28	.05	.10
F	.08	.08	−.23	−.11	−.09	−.04	−.21	.17	.00	−.22	−.10	−.07	.11	−.08	.02	.19	−.06	.10
100. Does not vary roles; relates to everyone in the same way																		
M	−.13	−.08	.22	.01	−.12	−.18	.03	−.21	−.15	.00	.03	−.07	−.14	−.05	.07	−.14	−.03	.00
F	−.20	−.05	.24	.13	−.05	−.01	.11	−.25	−.02	.11	.11	.05	−.08	.08	.00	−.17	.04	.02

Correlations of CPI Scales with California Q-Set Descriptions by Observers continued

Correlations of CPI™ Scales with *Interpersonal Q-Sort* Descriptions by Observers

This appendix reports correlations of the 36 CPI scales with the 50 items of the *Interpersonal Q-Sort*, as formulated by observers. The first sample of men included 200 who were described on the *Q-Sort* by their wives or partners. The sample of women included 200 who were described on the *Q-Sort* by their husbands or partners. The 50 items were sorted into a fixed distribution of five categories according to their descriptive salience, with frequencies of 4, 10, 22, 10, and 4 items per category. For the second sample of 111 men, three assessment staff observers independently furnished *Q-Sort* appraisals of each assessee, and then these independent appraisals were composited into a single formulation. The 5,400 correlations resulting from these analyses follow, along with the text of each of the *Q-Sort* items.

Correlations of CPI Scales with Items of the Interpersonal Q-Sort

Item	Do	Cs	Sy	Sp	Sa	In	Em	Re	So	Sc	Gi	Cm	Wb	To	Ac	Ai	Ie	Py
1. Is forceful and self-assured in manner																		
M[a]	.22	.07	.11	.10	.15	.19	.10	−.03	−.04	−.10	−.12	.02	.02	−.05	.05	.02	−.02	−.01
F[b]	.24	.10	.11	.12	.19	.23	.15	−.02	−.01	−.06	−.05	.05	.08	.05	.11	.04	.14	.05
M[c]	.43	.28	.27	.26	.40	.31	.27	.13	.09	−.11	−.07	.33	.24	.20	.33	.20	.43	.10
2. Impulsive and uninhibited; easily angered and irritated																		
M[a]	−.07	−.09	−.09	−.03	−.03	.02	−.12	−.08	−.14	−.13	−.19	−.04	−.09	−.05	−.15	−.05	−.10	−.06
F[b]	.02	.01	.01	.01	.05	.03	.01	−.10	−.16	−.19	−.22	−.11	−.10	−.06	−.13	.01	.01	.07
M[c]	.20	.17	.29	.22	−.25	.17	.13	.04	−.04	−.18	−.14	.00	−.05	.01	.10	−.02	.18	.00
3. Ambitious; likely to succeed in most things undertaken																		
M[a]	.24	.12	.14	.01	.12	.18	−.02	.12	.08	.05	.08	.00	.10	.03	.19	.05	.04	.08
F[b]	.10	.15	.15	.07	.14	.18	.07	−.09	.00	−.05	−.01	.13	.03	−.04	.10	.01	.03	.06
M[c]	.45	.28	.29	.20	.31	.25	.25	.24	.16	−.03	.04	.20	.25	.16	.32	.15	.22	.15
4. Distrustful and cynical; dissatisfied with most things; indifferent to the worries and problems of others																		
M[a]	−.12	−.16	−.08	−.03	−.13	.05	−.13	−.12	−.07	−.01	−.10	−.03	.00	−.08	−.14	−.05	−.01	−.12
F[b]	−.03	−.06	−.07	−.04	.00	−.03	−.02	−.16	−.17	−.15	−.18	−.18	−.09	−.13	−.16	.01	−.03	−.04
M[c]	−.28	−.11	−.17	−.09	−.22	−.19	−.17	−.28	−.21	−.07	−.16	−.21	−.27	−.22	−.28	−.09	−.16	−.15
5. Enterprising and outgoing; enjoys social participation																		
M[a]	.23	.17	.38	.31	.31	.12	.27	−.05	−.02	−.17	−.04	.09	.10	−.01	.02	−.01	.04	.03
F[b]	.23	.18	.30	.28	.29	.10	.26	.11	−.05	−.15	−.08	−.01	.09	.03	.04	−.01	.09	.05
M[c]	.30	.36	.41	.40	.25	.25	.25	.09	.23	.05	.17	.23	.37	.21	.19	.11	.31	.16
6. Shrewd and self-centered; inclined to be selfish and opportunistic																		
M[a]	.13	.09	.03	.09	.10	.15	−.04	−.01	−.06	−.05	−.04	.01	.01	−.09	.00	.07	.10	.01
F[b]	.17	.15	.09	.15	.19	.19	.15	−.08	−.15	−.07	−.03	.05	.02	.02	−.05	.05	.09	.06
M[c]	.11	.21	.19	.20	.20	.16	.14	−.10	−.07	−.19	−.19	−.05	−.06	.00	−.05	.09	.21	.06
7. Clever and imaginative; a spontaneous and entertaining person																		
M[a]	.05	.14	.07	.18	.18	.08	.17	−.19	−.06	−.22	−.14	−.09	−.08	−.06	−.09	.01	−.02	.07
F[b]	.12	.13	.15	.19	.16	.10	.22	−.08	−.02	−.06	−.07	.01	.08	.15	−.10	.12	.12	.13
M[c]	.20	.27	.16	.31	.21	.23	.34	.03	−.02	−.02	−.02	.17	.11	.24	.03	.29	.32	.28
8. Restless and changeable; thinks and behaves differently from others																		
M[a]	−.11	−.08	−.08	−.10	−.01	−.03	−.07	−.05	−.16	−.08	−.02	−.17	−.09	−.09	−.07	−.01	−.10	−.08
F[b]	.16	.06	.15	.17	.14	.09	.06	−.06	−.13	−.21	−.16	−.11	−.06	−.12	−.01	.04	.09	.11
M[c]	.02	.12	.09	.08	−.07	.00	.01	−.05	−.21	−.04	−.12	.04	−.14	−.05	−.08	.07	−.04	.09
9. Poised and self-confident; not troubled by pressure or criticism																		
M[a]	.16	.11	.08	.10	.15	.17	.03	.04	.12	.03	−.02	.08	.16	.04	.11	.08	.08	.06
F[b]	.14	.13	.10	.14	.13	.23	.11	.02	.03	.06	.08	.01	.15	.08	.13	.04	.11	.00
M[c]	.22	.27	.28	.30	.28	.34	.20	.13	.28	.00	−.02	.20	.25	.14	.24	.25	.42	.15
10. Undependable; poorly motivated; has difficulty in working toward prescribed goals																		
M[a]	−.07	−.10	−.02	−.06	−.04	−.11	.05	−.10	.00	−.02	.00	−.14	−.04	−.07	−.13	−.06	−.06	−.09
F[b]	.01	.02	.03	−.03	.00	−.06	.06	.03	−.03	−.02	−.04	−.05	.04	−.01	−.09	.04	.02	.09
M[c]	−.14	−.05	−.07	−.02	−.04	−.14	.02	.29	−.26	−.09	−.07	−.17	−.23	−.06	−.30	−.10	−.14	−.04
11. Alert and energetic in behavior and attitude; uncomplaining and in good spirits																		
M[a]	.13	.15	.04	.10	.02	.07	.14	.16	.16	.08	.14	.10	.15	.10	.20	.08	.08	.19
F[b]	−.04	−.07	.01	.01	−.02	.00	.01	.05	.11	.07	.04	.15	.13	.02	.02	−.03	−.04	−.03
M[c]	.08	.16	.07	.06	.06	.18	.14	.07	.21	.12	.16	.11	.18	.04	.20	.03	.11	.05

[a] for men described by their wives or partners; $N = 200$
[b] for women described by their husbands or partners; $N = 200$
[c] for men described by three assessment staff observers; $N = 111$

Correlations of CPI Scales with Items of the Interpersonal Q-Sort continued

Measures	Fx	F/M	v.1	v.2	v.3	Mp	Wo	CT	Lp	Ami	Leo	Tm	B-MS	B-FM	Anx	Nar	D-SD	D-AC
1. Is forceful and self-assured in manner																		
M[a]	-.08	-.06	-.21	.02	-.07	.06	.00	.03	.12	-.10	.10	.16	.13	-.11	-.07	.22	.08	.11
F[b]	-.04	-.10	-.21	.00	.04	.12	-.02	.08	.23	-.05	.04	.12	.16	-.05	-.10	.21	.11	-.01
M[c]	-.16	-.12	-.35	.13	.22	.37	.13	.14	.46	.14	.11	.29	.30	-.07	-.19	.21	.23	.05
2. Impulsive and uninhibited; easily angered and irritated																		
M[a]	.03	.01	.03	-.07	-.13	-.09	-.16	-.02	-.15	-.15	-.06	-.04	-.06	-.12	.13	.12	-.12	-.01
F[b]	.17	.03	-.04	-.26	-.04	-.09	-.17	.17	-.08	-.25	-.16	-.03	.02	-.15	.04	.15	-.19	-.05
M[c]	.05	.01	-.24	.02	.02	.03	-.11	.12	.14	-.14	-.04	.04	.18	-.15	-.02	.12	-.04	.19
3. Ambitious; likely to succeed in most things undertaken																		
M[a]	-.07	-.08	-.16	.17	.03	.17	.09	-.07	.20	.01	.24	.20	.15	-.01	-.09	.11	.13	.02
F[b]	.04	-.18	-.09	-.02	-.01	.04	.02	.06	.11	-.02	.08	.10	.15	-.12	.01	.09	.10	.01
M[c]	-.15	-.15	-.40	.25	.20	.29	.11	.12	.43	.08	.11	.28	.32	-.06	-.16	.20	.18	.06
4. Distrustful and cynical; dissatisfied with most things; indifferent to the worries and problems of others																		
M[a]	-.05	-.05	.16	-.10	-.06	-.02	-.03	-.02	-.11	-.05	-.15	.04	-.06	-.07	.07	.01	-.06	-.11
F[b]	.02	-.21	-.05	-.11	-.06	-.10	-.15	-.03	-.12	-.17	-.07	-.05	-.03	-.17	.13	.11	-.10	.06
M[c]	.06	.15	.14	-.24	-.21	-.35	-.25	-.05	-.31	-.14	-.13	-.24	-.31	-.09	.10	.02	-.15	.10
5. Enterprising and outgoing; enjoys social participation																		
M[a]	.16	-.10	-.33	-.09	.01	.07	.08	.14	.16	.00	.08	.05	.27	-.01	-.14	.11	.11	.13
F[b]	.15	-.09	-.29	-.02	.07	.12	-.02	.19	.14	-.09	.06	.07	.20	-.12	-.06	.22	.15	.08
M[c]	-.03	-.24	-.29	.21	.37	.38	.25	.09	.41	-.31	.10	.28	.34	.01	-.28	.06	.30	.08
6. Shrewd and self-centered; inclined to be selfish and opportunistic																		
M[a]	-.06	-.12	-.10	.01	.03	.08	.01	.02	.09	-.11	-.03	.14	.11	-.09	.02	.14	.02	.00
F[b]	.04	-.09	-.15	-.09	.08	.10	-.01	.17	.11	-.10	-.03	.12	.21	-.14	-.02	.16	.08	-.01
M[c]	.16	-.04	-.22	-.11	.05	-.04	-.09	.18	.06	-.15	-.12	.04	.12	-.18	.14	.20	-.04	.13
7. Clever and imaginative; a spontaneous and entertaining person																		
M[a]	.28	.02	-.25	-.19	.00	-.07	-.14	.28	-.01	-.17	-.12	-.09	.07	-.12	-.02	.21	-.04	.14
F[b]	.24	-.09	-.14	-.12	.14	.10	.04	.24	.08	.04	-.07	.09	.15	-.07	-.07	.11	.10	.02
M[c]	.29	-.01	-.19	-.17	.22	.20	.06	.43	.22	.05	-.15	.17	.23	-.09	-.13	.06	.05	-.03
8. Restless and changeable; thinks and behaves differently from others																		
M[a]	-.11	.03	.06	-.05	-.08	-.12	-.15	.00	-.11	-.19	-.03	-.03	-.10	-.04	.20	.08	.01	-.02
F[b]	.13	-.01	-.20	-.05	-.04	.00	-.16	.17	.00	-.17	-.06	.05	.10	-.09	-.06	.15	-.03	.08
M[c]	.10	.17	-.03	-.13	.02	-.06	-.11	.13	-.08	-.21	-.17	-.01	-.04	-.03	-.21	-.03	-.02	.08
9. Poised and self-confident; not troubled by pressure or criticism																		
M[a]	.02	-.12	-.14	.07	.05	.10	.22	.00	.20	.14	.16	.16	.15	.01	-.13	.16	.10	.08
F[b]	-.04	-.08	-.14	.04	.14	.17	.13	.10	.20	.08	.12	.17	.19	.04	-.08	.03	.14	-.02
M[c]	.02	-.24	-.19	.14	.19	.25	.07	.15	.36	.13	-.04	.21	.32	.01	-.14	.04	.14	.14
10. Undependable; poorly motivated; has difficulty in working toward prescribed goals																		
M[a]	.17	.11	.04	-.09	-.05	-.07	-.16	.10	-.09	-.06	-.05	-.20	-.02	.07	.05	-.06	-.06	.02
F[b]	.09	.04	.00	-.10	.00	-.04	.05	.06	-.04	-.04	-.03	-.02	.03	-.03	-.08	.01	.01	-.02
M[c]	.33	.04	.02	-.27	-.06	-.21	-.23	.12	-.27	-.14	-.13	-.23	-.15	-.21	.01	.06	-.16	-.04
11. Alert and energetic in behavior and attitude; uncomplaining and in good spirits																		
M[a]	.02	.07	-.10	.11	.16	.10	.20	.00	.18	.14	.10	.14	.13	.14	-.21	-.04	.08	-.03
F[b]	-.02	-.07	.05	.05	-.02	.05	.13	.00	.05	.14	.09	.00	.02	.03	-.09	-.03	.04	-.02
M[c]	-.11	-.21	.00	.13	.15	.10	.14	-.03	.17	.14	.14	.10	.16	-.04	-.08	-.02	.14	-.04

[a] for men described by their wives or partners; $N = 200$
[b] for women described by their husbands or partners; $N = 200$
[c] for men described by three assessment staff observers; $N = 111$

Correlations of CPI Scales with Items of the Interpersonal Q-Sort continued

Item	Do	Cs	Sy	Sp	Sa	In	Em	Re	So	Sc	Gi	Cm	Wb	To	Ac	Ai	Ie	Py
12. Dull; lacking in ability and understanding																		
M[a]	−.06	−.13	−.05	−.19	−.13	−.10	−.15	.02	.03	.11	.13	−.05	.00	−.10	−.03	−.15	−.15	−.08
F[b]	−.13	−.17	−.15	−.19	−.17	−.05	−.15	−.10	−.09	.09	.03	.03	−.06	−.05	−.07	−.10	−.15	.01
M[c]	−.22	−.27	−.15	−.19	−.20	−.31	−.17	−.14	−.02	−.11	−.04	.28	−.26	−.18	−.28	−.27	−.26	−.28
13. A conscientious and serious-minded person																		
M[a]	−.02	.02	−.03	−.03	−.05	−.03	−.05	.19	.18	.23	.17	.14	.05	.19	.16	.13	.07	.08
F[b]	−.04	−.07	−.12	−.17	−.10	−.06	−.12	.12	.22	.19	.14	.09	.09	.01	.17	−.05	−.04	−.04
M[c]	−.18	−.23	−.20	−.20	−.21	−.19	−.17	.06	.23	.16	.16	−.03	.10	.01	−.02	−.07	−.22	−.17
14. Poorly organized; unable to concentrate attention and effort on intellectual problems																		
M[a]	−.07	−.01	.05	.02	.01	−.16	.05	−.10	−.11	−.10	−.03	−.06	−.02	−.02	−.13	−.09	−.10	−.07
F[b]	−.13	−.03	−.04	.03	−.06	−.07	.06	−.05	−.10	−.16	−.20	−.07	−.09	.06	−.23	.09	.06	.00
M[c]	−.21	−.26	−.29	−.34	−.28	−.27	−.11	−.10	−.07	.20	.12	−.14	−.21	.02	−.22	−.16	−.40	−.09
15. Honest and direct in behavior; mature and realistic in outlook																		
M[a]	.12	.04	.02	.01	.01	.09	.03	.14	.18	.10	.05	.05	.16	.18	.07	.12	.11	.09
F[b]	−.01	−.04	.01	.04	.00	.02	−.11	.09	.12	.11	.12	.02	.08	.06	.09	−.03	−.06	−.01
M[c]	.14	.05	.08	.15	.13	.13	.08	.20	.27	.15	.22	.11	.26	.17	.17	.09	.13	.05
16. Unassuming, inhibited, and inattentive; bland and colorless in behavior																		
M[a]	−.13	−.07	−.12	−.14	−.17	−.09	−.12	.23	.18	.21	.15	.04	.05	.08	.09	−.06	−.03	−.04
F[b]	−.10	−.11	−.21	−.14	−.16	−.06	−.12	.03	.08	.15	.10	.10	−.03	.04	.00	.00	−.05	−.02
M[c]	−.43	−.40	−.39	−.42	−.45	−.41	−.37	−.19	−.16	.09	.08	−.23	−.29	−.26	−.30	−.28	−.52	−.33
17. Patient and self-controlled; restrained and self-contained in behavior																		
M[a]	−.17	−.09	−.11	−.07	−.21	−.12	−.12	.01	.03	.10	.01	.01	.05	.01	.02	−.01	−.03	.02
F[b]	−.11	.01	−.07	−.08	−.16	.03	−.07	.01	.06	.23	.21	.00	.13	.07	.11	−.03	−.03	.03
M[c]	−.22	−.26	−.26	−.31	−.32	−.20	−.16	.04	.16	.24	.22	−.06	.06	.01	−.05	−.04	−.20	−.14
18. Deliberate and methodical in behavior; inflexible and stubborn in attitude																		
M[a]	−.14	−.11	−.07	−.18	−.12	−.05	−.18	.06	−.01	.11	.05	−.04	−.04	−.01	.00	−.01	−.02	−.04
F[b]	−.11	−.06	−.08	−.06	−.05	.03	−.10	−.07	.00	.01	.03	−.07	.00	−.06	−.04	−.02	−.01	−.12
M[c]	−.06	−.20	−.08	−.16	−.10	−.10	−.32	−.02	−.05	−.17	−.17	−.01	−.11	−.28	−.02	−.33	−.22	−.29
19. Tolerant, permissive, and benevolent; considerate and charitable																		
M[a]	−.06	−.03	−.06	.07	−.09	−.20	.10	−.05	−.03	−.08	−.03	.12	−.01	.03	−.08	−.05	.00	.03
F[b]	−.24	−.12	−.14	−.14	−.26	−.26	−.12	.14	.12	.09	.04	.04	−.08	.06	−.04	−.07	−.11	−.06
M[c]	−.07	−.11	−.18	−.16	−.14	.09	−.04	.02	.01	.24	.16	−.08	.10	.08	−.02	.06	−.01	.09
20. Submissive; gives in easily; lacking in self-confidence																		
M[a]	−.19	−.11	−.08	−.12	−.13	−.20	−.09	−.02	.00	.01	.06	−.05	−.11	−.08	−.04	−.09	−.08	−.12
F[b]	−.22	−.08	−.12	−.15	−.24	−.27	−.12	.19	.14	.18	.12	.03	−.03	.14	.07	.06	−.05	.01
M[c]	−.46	−.34	−.30	−.30	−.37	−.38	−.23	−.23	−.16	−.01	.02	−.36	−.34	−.16	−.35	−.33	−.53	−.32
21. Eager to please; attentive to the needs and wants of others																		
M[a]	−.07	−.12	.00	−.02	−.04	−.23	−.03	−.07	−.07	−.11	−.11	.02	−.16	−.09	−.13	−.21	−.10	−.18
F[b]	−.09	−.04	.01	−.01	−.11	−.12	.00	.06	.17	.07	.05	−.06	−.05	−.04	.02	−.04	.01	−.07
M[c]	−.16	−.16	−.09	−.12	−.16	−.02	−.12	.06	.21	.13	.28	−.09	.06	.20	−.06	−.02	−.09	−.05
22. Unambitious; commonplace and conventional in thinking and behavior																		
M[a]	−.12	−.09	−.02	−.08	−.05	−.11	−.05	−.03	.08	.17	.17	.08	.10	.00	.08	−.05	.04	−.08
F[b]	−.33	−.36	−.26	−.19	−.29	−.25	−.24	.03	.08	.10	.03	−.02	−.03	.00	−.15	−.13	−.18	−.21
M[c]	−.19	−.31	−.18	−.14	−.17	−.31	−.17	−.10	−.11	.02	.04	−.11	−.12	−.09	−.17	−.31	−.29	−.27

[a] for men described by their wives or partners; $N = 200$
[b] for women described by their husbands or partners; $N = 200$
[c] for men described by three assessment staff observers; $N = 111$

Correlations of CPI Scales with Items of the Interpersonal Q-Sort continued

Measures	Fx	F/M	v.1	v.2	v.3	Mp	Wo	CT	Lp	Ami	Leo	Tm	B–MS	B–FM	Anx	Nar	D–SD	D–AC
12. Dull; lacking in ability and understanding																		
M[a]	−.17	−.04	.12	.10	−.11	−.03	.01	−.19	−.01	.04	.12	.04	−.02	.01	.07	−.13	.04	.08
F[b]	−.06	.06	.17	−.04	−.11	−.14	−.04	−.07	−.12	.04	−.02	−.07	−.12	.01	.01	−.14	−.08	−.04
M[c]	−.02	−.09	.13	.04	−.29	−.30	−.18	−.25	−.27	−.08	.03	−.27	−.28	−.12	.15	.01	−.10	.16
13. A conscientious and serious-minded person																		
M[a]	−.17	.15	.16	.20	.08	.15	.15	−.12	.07	.22	.07	.05	−.06	.25	−.11	−.21	.06	−.10
F[b]	−.20	.00	.16	.20	−.05	.04	.14	−.30	.08	.19	.15	.02	−.07	.21	.01	−.15	.08	−.02
M[c]	−.21	−.05	.19	.13	−.14	−.03	.15	−.27	−.12	.19	.17	−.11	−.20	.21	.11	−.16	.08	−.07
14. Poorly organized; unable to concentrate attention and effort on intellectual problems																		
M[a]	.09	−.05	−.03	−.06	−.07	−.06	−.12	.08	−.12	−.04	−.09	−.14	.01	−.08	.07	−.06	−.01	.01
F[b]	.19	−.02	.01	−.22	.00	−.05	−.12	.15	−.18	−.12	−.21	−.10	−.07	−.10	.03	.06	−.16	.02
M[c]	.08	.05	.26	.00	−.03	−.21	−.12	−.11	−.29	.04	.10	−.18	−.29	−.05	.07	−.21	−.03	−.08
15. Honest and direct in behavior; mature and realistic in outlook																		
M[a]	−.02	−.05	−.02	.14	.09	.07	.12	−.02	.18	.15	.07	.05	.03	.02	−.10	−.01	.03	−.04
F[b]	−.06	−.01	.04	.10	.03	.03	.07	−.13	.05	.15	.20	.05	.08	.12	−.03	−.15	.12	−.04
M[c]	−.02	−.06	−.10	.15	.20	.26	.19	−.04	.23	.25	.09	.15	.17	.11	−.12	−.02	.21	−.06
16. Unassuming, inhibited, and inattentive; bland and colorless in behavior																		
M[a]	−.23	−.03	.19	.20	.04	.12	.18	−.22	.02	.23	.12	.04	−.04	.18	−.05	−.24	.06	−.21
F[b]	−.03	.03	.16	.08	−.03	−.05	.04	−.14	−.05	.13	.12	.03	−.10	.15	−.06	−.20	−.02	−.03
M[c]	−.05	.07	.39	−.04	−.30	−.39	−.19	−.34	−.46	−.10	−.01	−.36	−.45	.05	.25	−.14	−.21	−.03
17. Patient and self-controlled; restrained and self-contained in behavior																		
M[a]	−.03	−.10	.22	.04	−.01	−.07	.12	−.07	−.05	.14	−.11	−.05	−.12	.01	−.13	−.12	−.08	−.03
F[b]	−.11	−.05	.15	.02	.06	.02	.21	−.11	.03	.18	.12	.06	.01	.06	−.02	−.18	.01	−.07
M[c]	−.08	−.07	.33	.12	−.11	−.07	.11	−.29	−.13	.20	.16	−.07	−.17	.16	.04	−.25	.03	−.11
18. Deliberate and methodical in behavior; inflexible and stubborn in attitude																		
M[a]	−.19	.13	.19	.08	−.04	−.04	.04	−.19	−.08	−.01	.04	.06	−.11	.12	.10	−.12	.03	−.12
F[b]	−.15	−.06	.10	.00	−.04	−.05	−.03	−.13	−.03	.01	.00	−.03	−.02	−.05	.07	.02	−.06	.03
M[c]	−.29	−.03	.05	.11	−.40	−.20	−.10	−.31	−.13	−.21	.12	−.15	−.20	−.05	.14	.17	−.09	.15
19. Tolerant, permissive, and benevolent; considerate and charitable																		
M[a]	.14	.01	.05	−.11	.01	−.13	−.02	.02	−.07	.03	−.11	−.19	−.08	−.04	−.05	−.07	−.09	.00
F[b]	−.09	.22	.22	.06	−.08	−.11	.03	−.20	−.17	.13	.01	−.23	−.21	.18	.04	−.26	−.13	.02
M[c]	.02	−.02	.16	−.06	.03	.07	.06	.03	−.03	.10	.06	.09	−.02	.01	−.03	−.15	.07	−.20
20. Submissive; gives in easily; lacking in self-confidence																		
M[a]	.00	.08	.14	−.02	−.07	−.16	−.12	−.03	−.18	−.06	−.04	−.19	−.16	.04	.13	−.11	−.07	.09
F[b]	−.02	.18	.22	.07	.05	−.03	.09	−.12	−.14	.20	−.04	−.10	−.23	.18	.07	−.33	−.06	−.11
M[c]	.07	−.02	.32	−.13	−.26	−.40	−.27	−.21	−.52	−.11	−.11	−.39	−.36	.01	.25	−.14	−.32	−.10
21. Eager to please; attentive to the needs and wants of others																		
M[a]	.05	.03	.01	−.09	−.16	−.19	−.14	−.09	−.14	−.05	−.02	−.26	−.11	−.05	.05	−.01	−.17	.11
F[b]	.01	.04	.06	.08	−.04	−.06	.03	−.12	−.10	.12	.00	−.09	−.09	.09	.02	−.10	−.11	.05
M[c]	.02	−.14	.16	.12	.14	.01	.10	−.10	−.07	.19	.12	−.04	−.05	.00	.06	−.17	.02	−.14
22. Unambitious; commonplace and conventional in thinking and behavior																		
M[a]	−.18	−.04	.16	.07	.03	.05	.12	−.15	.02	.14	.10	.00	.03	.08	−.08	−.21	.08	−.04
F[b]	−.13	.10	.31	.07	−.13	−.16	.04	−.23	−.23	.15	−.07	−.20	−.22	.11	.00	−.26	−.18	.02
M[c]	−.06	−.02	.14	.03	−.17	−.07	−.12	−.26	−.23	−.02	.11	−.22	−.25	−.02	−.04	−.05	−.04	−.05

[a]for men described by their wives or partners; N = 200
[b]for women described by their husbands or partners; N = 200
[c] for men described by three assessment staff observers; N = 111

Correlations of CPI Scales with Items of the Interpersonal Q-Sort continued

Item	Do	Cs	Sy	Sp	Sa	In	Em	Re	So	Sc	Gi	Cm	Wb	To	Ac	Ai	Ie	Py
23. Gets along well with others; able to "fit in" easily in most situations																		
M[a]	.15	.13	.28	.16	.23	.02	.18	.04	.04	.02	.13	.13	.16	.02	.04	-.09	.03	-.02
F[b]	.14	.10	.18	.20	.12	.13	.13	.09	.17	.08	.12	.10	.21	.09	.08	-.03	.12	.02
M[c]	.13	.04	.06	.10	.13	.13	.11	.01	.15	.04	.06	.19	.26	.07	.15	.14	.13	.15
24. Awkward and ill-at-ease socially; shy and inhibited with others																		
M[a]	-.20	-.20	-.31	-.20	-.28	-.11	-.22	.06	-.01	.09	-.02	-.02	-.08	.02	-.02	.02	.00	-.10
F[b]	-.28	-.32	-.27	-.35	-.31	-.21	-.32	-.07	.04	.04	-.02	-.08	-.15	-.16	-.01	-.11	-.24	-.14
M[c]	-.52	-.40	-.43	-.40	-.48	-.36	-.40	-.19	-.16	.16	.06	-.24	-.27	-.18	-.37	-.22	-.45	-.25
25. Well-organized, capable, patient, and industrious; values achievement																		
M[a]	-.02	-.04	-.05	-.10	-.11	.00	-.14	.05	.14	.14	.11	.01	-.02	-.03	.15	.02	-.02	.06
F[b]	-.02	.05	-.04	-.03	-.02	.03	-.08	.06	.22	.20	.18	.16	.22	.05	.17	.02	-.03	.04
M[c]	.21	.13	.10	.00	.18	.16	.14	.29	.32	.23	.25	.05	.32	.13	.40	.17	.23	.10
26. Unimaginative and literal-minded; slow and deliberate; lacking in zest and enthusiasm																		
M[a]	-.01	-.07	.06	-.03	-.03	-.10	-.04	.04	.05	.07	.11	.04	.02	-.08	.08	-.08	-.01	-.08
F[b]	-.11	-.19	-.22	-.19	-.18	-.05	-.24	.13	.03	.13	.04	.05	-.02	-.01	.06	-.10	-.13	-.05
M[c]	-.13	-.24	-.13	-.10	-.14	-.10	-.31	-.07	-.07	-.01	.03	-.24	-.07	-.12	-.12	-.18	-.22	-.21
27. Independent, intelligent, and self-reliant; values achievement																		
M[a]	.15	.19	.03	.05	.07	.23	.06	.11	.09	.04	-.02	.05	.13	.18	.18	.25	.16	.13
F[b]	.28	.23	.21	.24	.23	.27	.15	.02	.10	.01	.05	.06	.13	-.06	-.21	.17	.21	.14
M[c]	.20	.21	.16	.15	.27	.10	.15	.27	.09	-.01	-.06	.28	.15	.13	.19	.33	.33	.24
28. Easily embarrassed; feels inferior and inadequate																		
M[a]	-.16	-.08	-.15	-.07	-.19	-.14	-.01	.08	-.06	.05	.05	-.01	-.09	.10	-.04	.09	.02	.07
F[b]	-.25	-.20	-.19	-.23	-.28	-.27	-.12	-.01	.12	.06	-.02	-.10	-.17	-.01	-.08	-.05	-.15	-.13
M[c]	-.40	-.35	-.36	-.39	-.43	-.34	-.32	-.22	-.31	.11	.04	-.36	-.38	-.30	-.37	-.30	-.49	-.25
29. Efficient; able to mobilize personal resources quickly and effectively																		
M[a]	.10	.07	-.02	-.03	.06	.15	-.11	.07	.04	.05	.05	.02	.09	.03	.12	.01	.06	.04
F[b]	-.03	.00	-.07	-.04	-.02	.08	-.08	-.03	.07	.03	-.03	.00	.00	-.10	.07	-.01	-.02	-.06
M[c]	.34	.39	.28	.33	.39	.45	.29	.31	.18	.02	-.01	.36	.42	.28	.37	.43	.58	.41
30. Worried and preoccupied; tense, nervous, and generally upset																		
M[a]	-.10	-.11	-.13	-.20	-.11	-.12	-.12	.04	-.09	.05	.06	-.13	-.17	-.04	-.11	-.03	-.13	-.02
F[b]	.01	.01	.03	.03	.06	-.07	.01	-.12	-.24	-.19	-.14	-.17	-.25	-.11	-.10	-.04	-.04	-.05
M[c]	-.23	-.13	-.14	-.09	-.15	-.30	-.06	-.13	-.32	-.25	-.19	-.19	-.41	-.23	-.38	-.14	-.27	-.03
31. Observant and perceptive; quick to respond to the subtleties and nuances of others' behavior																		
M[a]	.03	.09	.00	.13	.06	.09	.08	-.01	.03	.05	.05	-.06	.04	.06	-.02	.13	.10	.14
F[b]	.13	.14	.03	.13	.15	.19	.13	.00	-.02	-.01	-.03	-.03	.10	.05	.02	.15	.22	.14
M[c]	.11	.22	.09	.18	.09	.18	.21	.08	-.03	-.07	-.04	.14	.08	.10	.16	.30	.23	.27
32. Lazy, indifferent about duties and obligations; generally undependable and immature																		
M[a]	.00	-.04	.03	.09	.02	-.05	.05	-.09	-.02	-.08	-.04	.00	-.05	-.05	-.05	-.08	-.03	-.08
F[b]	.02	-.03	-.01	.03	.01	-.01	.07	-.08	-.14	-.12	-.11	-.14	-.09	.01	-.20	.01	.01	.06
M[c]	-.22	-.19	-.13	-.13	-.17	-.30	-.17	-.26	-.31	-.10	-.13	-.29	-.31	-.32	-.24	-.23	-.28	-.20
33. Quick and alert in manner; likes the new and different; impatient with and critical of delay or hesitation																		
M[a]	.03	.02	.01	.01	.09	.18	-.04	-.05	-.10	-.06	-.02	-.10	-.01	-.05	-.04	.03	.01	.04
F[b]	.10	.16	.16	.13	.16	.08	.15	-.04	-.12	-.13	-.06	-.12	.02	-.01	-.01	.04	.06	.03
M[c]	.08	.26	.17	.15	.22	.09	.19	-.05	-.11	.02	.00	.01	.01	.18	.03	.09	.14	.20

[a] for men described by their wives or partners; N = 200
[b] for women described by their husbands or partners; N = 200
[c] for men described by three assessment staff observers; N = 111

Correlations of CPI Scales with Items of the Interpersonal Q-Sort continued

Measures	Fx	F/M	v.1	v.2	v.3	Mp	Wo	CT	Lp	Ami	Leo	Tm	B-MS	B-FM	Anx	Nar	D-SD	D-AC
23. Gets along well with others; able to "fit in" easily in most situations																		
M[a]	.13	-.08	-.18	-.01	.04	.09	.12	.04	.17	.13	.12	.01	.21	.03	-.17	-.04	.15	.04
F[b]	.03	-.11	-.12	.16	.08	.12	.14	.01	.20	.16	.14	.08	.19	.10	-.17	.03	.18	.07
M[c]	-.07	.01	-.04	.06	.22	.27	.30	.03	.22	.20	.09	.19	.25	.17	-.16	-.02	.05	-.10
24. Awkward and ill-at-ease socially; shy and inhibited with others																		
M[a]	-.19	.12	.26	.03	-.02	-.10	-.05	-.11	-.16	.00	-.06	-.02	-.27	.03	.13	-.10	-.12	-.07
F[b]	-.11	.15	.31	.03	-.17	-.19	-.12	-.21	-.25	-.02	-.06	-.16	-.30	.09	.11	-.17	-.20	-.10
M[c]	.03	.15	.49	-.18	-.25	-.40	-.14	-.18	-.55	-.07	-.07	-.37	-.41	.11	.22	-.28	-.23	-.13
25. Well-organized, capable, patient, and industrious; values achievement																		
M[a]	-.19	-.02	.07	.20	.02	.03	.10	-.20	.06	.07	.15	.14	-.02	.06	-.04	-.05	.04	-.02
F[b]	-.14	.03	.12	.19	.06	.07	.21	-.10	.16	.22	.15	.15	.06	.19	-.21	-.16	.15	-.07
M[c]	-.25	.10	-.04	.26	.23	.37	.35	-.09	.36	.33	.14	.34	.21	.31	-.04	-.08	.30	-.15
26. Unimaginative and literal-minded; slow and deliberate; lacking in zest and enthusiasm																		
M[a]	-.21	-.13	.03	.14	-.08	.06	.12	-.23	.03	.08	.12	.09	.03	.00	.00	-.11	.07	-.01
F[b]	-.17	.16	.17	.11	-.05	-.06	.08	-.22	-.10	.07	.02	.03	-.14	.10	-.03	-.14	-.08	-.06
M[c]	-.18	.15	.08	-.01	-.21	-.14	-.01	-.22	-.20	-.10	.02	-.16	-.18	.05	.22	.03	-.05	-.07
27. Independent, intelligent, and self-reliant; values achievement																		
M[a]	-.04	-.10	-.08	.09	.11	.19	.16	.06	.19	.04	.02	.20	.08	.00	-.13	.11	.04	-.05
F[b]	.08	-.19	-.22	.06	.11	.18	.11	.10	.25	.00	.00	.30	.28	-.05	-.03	.19	.16	.10
M[c]	.05	.01	-.16	-.03	.16	.24	.14	.20	.22	.05	.02	.22	.22	.15	-.11	.06	.06	.00
28. Easily embarrassed; feels inferior and inadequate																		
M[a]	.01	.16	.19	-.07	.09	.00	-.06	.02	-.17	.03	-.08	-.04	-.13	.12	.12	-.18	.00	-.05
F[b]	-.02	.14	.24	.03	-.10	-.16	-.15	-.12	-.26	-.01	-.09	-.16	-.29	.08	.08	-.16	-.17	-.01
M[c]	.12	.08	.34	-.19	-.32	-.47	-.27	-.14	-.54	-.20	.00	-.35	-.36	-.02	.20	-.17	-.21	-.07
29. Efficient; able to mobilize personal resources quickly and effectively																		
M[a]	-.18	-.11	-.07	.19	.03	.11	.11	-.06	.13	.05	.13	.23	.11	.01	-.10	.05	.10	.05
F[b]	-.16	-.07	-.02	.14	-.06	.00	.02	-.11	.01	-.05	.06	.07	-.01	.05	.05	.07	.00	.00
M[c]	.02	-.09	-.27	.09	.38	.50	.33	.29	.47	.24	-.10	.40	.39	.16	-.20	.05	.22	-.12
30. Worried and preoccupied; tense, nervous, and generally upset																		
M[a]	-.06	.14	.14	.00	-.02	-.07	-.18	-.07	-.20	-.11	-.10	-.08	-.17	.10	.19	-.11	.02	-.05
F[b]	.16	.09	-.07	-.15	-.07	-.06	-.26	.16	-.13	-.24	-.27	-.06	-.06	-.11	.13	.10	-.13	.07
M[c]	.19	.20	.07	-.18	-.27	-.41	-.31	-.02	-.42	-.31	-.18	-.34	-.36	-.08	.04	.09	-.17	.17
31. Observant and perceptive; quick to respond to the subtleties and nuances of others' behavior																		
M[a]	.19	.10	-.04	-.12	.11	.04	.04	.18	.03	.04	.01	-.02	.02	.10	-.05	-.05	-.03	-.11
F[b]	.10	-.01	-.12	-.06	.18	.15	.05	.18	.10	.00	-.10	.11	.08	.00	.01	.14	.01	.01
M[c]	.10	.17	-.13	-.08	.17	.10	.08	.25	.12	-.01	-.18	.15	.12	.10	-.12	.05	-.11	-.05
32. Lazy, indifferent about duties and obligations; generally undependable and immature																		
M[a]	.11	.09	-.05	-.05	-.01	-.03	-.10	.10	-.03	-.02	-.04	-.10	-.01	.06	.07	.02	-.02	.02
F[b]	.12	-.01	-.09	-.15	-.01	-.06	-.10	.12	-.10	-.12	-.11	-.06	.00	-.14	.02	.06	-.13	.06
M[c]	.05	.11	.16	-.26	-.31	-.36	-.32	-.09	-.33	-.32	-.08	-.27	-.20	-.18	.08	.02	-.25	.00
33. Quick and alert in manner; likes the new and different; impatient with and critical of delay or hesitation																		
M[a]	.00	-.08	-.07	-.09	-.01	-.01	-.02	.09	.00	-.07	.02	.13	.10	-.14	-.02	.14	-.02	-.01
F[b]	.20	-.01	-.16	-.14	.03	.06	-.03	.18	.02	-.08	-.05	.03	.09	-.08	-.01	.15	.06	.00
M[c]	.11	-.06	-.11	-.15	.25	.13	-.01	.22	.09	-.01	-.10	.09	.25	-.04	-.05	-.01	-.04	.02

[a] for men described by their wives or partners; $N = 200$
[b] for women described by their husbands or partners; $N = 200$
[c] for men described by three assessment staff observers; $N = 111$

Correlations of CPI Scales with Items of the Interpersonal Q-Sort continued

Item	Do	Cs	Sy	Sp	Sa	In	Em	Re	So	Sc	Gi	Cm	Wb	To	Ac	Ai	Ie	Py
34. Headstrong, rebellious, and resentful of others; lacking in self-discipline; apt to behave in a rash or destructive manner																		
M[a]	−.03	−.07	−.06	−.03	−.03	−.03	−.03	−.09	−.12	−.09	−.08	−.03	−.14	−.09	−.11	−.08	−.11	−.12
F[b]	.05	.01	.00	−.01	.10	.01	.06	−.21	−.17	−.17	−.18	−.07	−.19	−.15	−.17	−.04	−.07	−.01
M[c]	−.01	−.01	.00	.06	−.03	−.04	−.17	−.16	−.26	−.20	−.19	−.06	−.17	−.19	−.03	−.17	−.04	−.07
35. Gentle, considerate, and tactful in dealing with others; appreciative and helpful																		
M[a]	−.11	−.01	.00	.05	−.13	−.17	.11	.08	.13	.14	.14	.19	.11	.17	.03	.02	.04	.08
F[b]	−.20	−.18	−.12	−.13	−.21	−.18	−.18	.10	.15	.21	.15	.13	.05	.04	.03	−.14	−.14	−.12
M[c]	−.10	−.25	−.26	−.28	−.24	−.06	−.10	.11	.00	.16	.14	.05	.02	.04	.00	−.01	−.16	−.01
36. Active and robust in manner; hard-headed and forthright in judgment																		
M[a]	.11	.02	.08	.06	.16	.14	−.03	−.05	−.04	−.14	−.16	−.02	.01	−.10	−.06	−.05	−.02	.01
F[b]	.14	.11	.18	.19	.14	.11	.11	.03	−.03	−.14	−.02	.06	−.02	.03	.04	.08	.08	.02
M[c]	.21	.19	.15	.22	.29	.34	.08	−.03	.16	−.05	−.06	.23	.25	.15	.07	.04	.31	.13
37. Is a likable person; interesting and pleasant to be with																		
M[a]	.09	.13	.09	.08	.10	−.03	.14	.04	.02	.03	.08	.06	.10	.07	.06	−.01	.08	.03
F[b]	−.05	−.06	−.01	.02	.00	−.11	.01	.09	.13	.07	.08	.13	.02	.05	.05	−.07	−.08	−.04
M[c]	.01	−.07	.02	.02	.03	−.01	.01	−.01	.07	−.01	.01	.02	.09	−.02	.05	−.01	.00	−.03
38. Is vain, self-centered, and egotistical																		
M[a]	.06	.05	−.01	.02	.07	.13	−.03	−.05	−.03	−.12	−.13	.05	−.01	−.09	−.01	.02	.02	.02
F[b]	.16	.21	.10	.06	.13	.14	.16	.04	−.07	.04	.10	−.03	.05	.16	.09	.16	.17	.16
M[c]	.23	.32	.33	.22	.25	.12	.26	−.02	−.13	−.14	−.15	.01	.00	−.03	.10	.05	.22	.10
39. Is a good listener, draws other people out; has a knack for getting others to "be themselves"																		
M[a]	.05	.00	.13	.06	.07	−.05	.12	−.13	−.10	−.09	−.09	.02	−.03	−.05	−.08	−.06	.03	−.02
F[b]	.04	.04	−.02	.05	.06	.09	.03	.09	.03	.13	.14	.01	.11	.16	−.01	.05	.09	.08
M[c]	.16	−.02	.05	.05	−.01	.08	.13	.28	.11	.12	.09	.07	.21	.10	.11	.20	.07	.19
40. Self-pitying and martyr-like; tries to make others feel guilty																		
M[a]	−.05	−.10	.00	−.06	.00	−.10	.01	−.04	−.03	−.03	−.07	−.03	−.14	−.11	−.06	−.10	−.05	−.09
F[b]	−.05	−.03	−.09	−.10	−.11	−.11	−.07	−.04	−.05	−.04	−.03	.02	−.05	−.02	−.04	.00	−.02	−.02
M[c]	−.10	−.05	−.04	−.10	−.08	−.08	−.20	−.05	−.21	−.02	−.13	−.14	−.22	−.07	−.11	−.07	−.21	−.11
41. Has a talent for creative and original thinking																		
M[a]	−.01	.09	−.04	−.03	−.02	.09	.04	.00	.02	.00	.01	−.07	.03	.10	.01	.12	.11	.13
F[b]	.11	.10	.12	.07	.17	.06	.02	−.07	−.03	−.03	−.05	.01	−.01	.03	−.01	.11	.12	.11
M[c]	.05	.20	.11	.12	.11	.13	.24	.01	−.08	.06	.02	.02	.00	−.02	.02	.24	.26	.35
42. Critical and outspoken; disparages other people and their ideas																		
M[a]	−.04	−.08	−.02	.09	.04	.07	.01	−.06	−.05	−.06	.14	.13	−.06	−.07	−.01	−.05	−.02	−.08
F[b]	.04	.04	.00	.05	.06	.06	.03	−.21	−.22	−.17	−.09	−.16	−.11	−.15	−.20	.06	.00	.03
M[c]	.08	.22	.20	.12	.16	.12	.09	.00	−.02	−.15	−.19	.17	−.03	−.10	.06	.11	.22	.18
43. Verbally fluent; expresses self easily and with clarity																		
M[a]	.16	.26	.03	.17	.19	.23	.26	.04	.03	−.08	−.07	−.06	.06	.14	.08	.20	.13	.17
F[b]	.35	.30	.30	.26	.31	.24	.27	.06	−.04	−.14	.02	−.04	.04	.02	.12	.10	.22	.11
M[c]	.32	.36	.25	.26	.35	.25	.43	.18	.12	−.10	−.06	.30	.23	.26	.27	.38	.43	.27
44. Given to moods; often difficult and recalcitrant																		
M[a]	−.21	−.16	−.19	−.13	−.12	−.15	−.16	−.22	−.25	−.12	−.09	−.18	−.22	−.16	−.20	−.11	−.21	−.10
F[b]	.01	−.01	.09	.03	−.01	−.03	.04	−.14	−.16	−.12	−.09	.00	−.02	−.10	−.14	−.04	−.04	−.09
M[c]	−.11	−.09	−.10	−.10	−.10	−.13	−.20	−.11	−.30	−.10	−.23	−.06	−.21	−.15	−.12	−.14	−.26	−.09

[a] for men described by their wives or partners; *N* = 200
[b] for women described by their husbands or partners; *N* = 200
[c] for men described by three assessment staff observers; *N* = 111

Correlations of CPI Scales with Items of the Interpersonal Q-Sort continued

Measures	Fx	F/M	v.1	v.2	v.3	Mp	Wo	CT	Lp	Ami	Leo	Tm	B–MS	B–FM	Anx	Nar	D–SD	D–AC
34. Headstrong, rebellious, and resentful of others; lacking in self-discipline; apt to behave in a rash or destructive manner
M[a]	.01	.02	−.01	−.10	−.04	−.08	−.15	.01	−.13	−.16	−.06	−.01	−.08	−.07	.11	.07	−.06	−.01
F[b]	.04	−.03	−.12	−.18	−.10	−.12	−.21	.12	−.07	−.28	−.15	−.11	−.02	−.24	.15	.18	−.09	.04
M[c]	.01	.16	−.06	−.18	−.18	−.17	−.22	.06	−.10	−.28	−.01	−.07	−.04	−.09	−.06	.08	−.14	.10
35. Gentle, considerate, and tactful in dealing with others; appreciative and helpful
M[a]	.13	.05	.16	−.05	.12	.02	.16	−.02	.03	.22	.00	−.13	−.03	.14	−.17	−.22	−.05	−.12
F[b]	−.12	.04	.25	.10	−.07	−.08	.14	−.25	−.08	.21	.04	−.07	−.14	.20	−.01	−.20	−.06	−.02
M[c]	−.10	.19	.20	.05	−.10	.00	.08	−.15	−.06	.09	.13	−.07	−.14	.17	.09	−.14	−.04	−.08
36. Active and robust in manner; hard-headed and forthright in judgment
M[a]	−.03	−.02	−.14	.03	−.11	−.01	−.05	.01	.01	−.09	−.05	.06	.10	−.11	.01	.14	−.03	.11
F[b]	.13	−.10	−.14	−.01	.07	.04	−.02	.12	.13	−.06	.03	.00	.12	−.13	−.02	.09	.02	.00
M[c]	−.02	−.34	−.16	−.01	.17	.21	.12	.19	.29	.15	.03	.27	.39	−.16	−.12	.13	.11	−.01
37. Is a likable person; interesting and pleasant to be with
M[a]	.15	−.12	−.10	−.06	.04	−.02	.03	.02	.08	.05	.04	−.02	.08	−.02	−.10	−.01	−.02	−.01
F[b]	−.07	.05	.06	.10	−.02	.00	.07	−.08	.02	.11	.12	−.08	−.07	.07	−.09	−.09	−.01	.02
M[c]	−.08	−.07	.04	−.01	−.02	.01	.02	.00	.04	.00	.05	−.01	.04	−.04	−.11	−.08	.01	.06
38. Is vain, self-centered, and egotistical
M[a]	.00	−.05	−.10	−.04	−.03	.01	−.06	.04	.03	−.18	.02	.08	.04	−.07	.04	.21	−.02	.10
F[b]	.08	−.09	−.11	−.01	.18	.17	.07	.13	.17	−.01	−.04	.15	.15	−.04	.00	.06	.18	−.01
M[c]	.09	−.09	−.30	−.06	.04	.09	−.06	.22	.17	−.14	−.15	.10	.23	−.22	.03	.22	.07	.11
39. Is a good listener, draws other people out; has a knack for getting others to "be themselves"
M[a]	.08	−.06	−.08	−.06	−.05	−.08	−.03	.04	.01	−.02	−.04	−.13	.01	−.14	.06	.08	−.06	.04
F[b]	.04	.03	.03	.02	.15	.08	.09	.02	.08	.16	.01	.02	.01	.02	−.05	−.03	.11	−.13
M[c]	−.05	.11	−.04	.06	.12	.16	.13	.04	.18	.03	−.07	.17	.04	.14	.07	−.05	.04	−.06
40. Self-pitying and martyr-like; tries to make others feel guilty
M[a]	.00	.07	.01	−.03	−.06	−.07	−.12	.06	−.09	−.11	−.13	−.11	−.07	−.01	.09	.02	−.04	.10
F[b]	−.07	.17	.06	.01	−.02	−.03	−.03	.00	−.08	−.10	−.04	−.07	−.11	.06	.09	−.03	−.06	.04
M[c]	.04	.06	.02	−.05	−.16	−.19	−.12	−.04	−.17	−.19	−.06	−.11	−.20	−.11	.15	.06	−.10	.14
41. Has a talent for creative and original thinking
M[a]	.17	.02	−.02	−.06	.16	.11	.00	.16	.04	.05	−.03	−.04	.04	−.05	−.01	.01	.06	−.07
F[b]	.20	.04	−.10	−.11	.07	.06	.01	.23	.01	−.03	−.03	.00	.06	−.07	−.01	.12	.02	−.04
M[c]	.28	.07	−.02	−.16	.21	.11	−.04	.29	.07	−.04	−.21	.19	.10	.01	.00	.00	.07	−.07
42. Critical and outspoken; disparages other people and their ideas
M[a]	−.08	.06	−.03	−.04	−.07	−.03	−.03	−.01	−.04	−.08	−.02	.01	−.04	−.01	.09	.10	−.02	.04
F[b]	.07	−.16	−.07	−.16	−.03	−.07	−.23	.09	−.09	−.29	−.13	−.03	.03	−.22	.03	.19	−.03	.07
M[c]	.11	.00	−.13	.01	.04	−.05	−.06	.11	.08	−.10	−.11	.03	.07	−.03	−.07	.13	.02	.24
43. Verbally fluent; expresses self easily and with clarity
M[a]	.29	.03	−.19	−.07	.16	.11	.07	.29	.13	.01	−.05	.05	.08	−.04	−.05	.08	−.04	.01
F[b]	.05	−.10	−.39	−.01	.12	.19	−.03	.20	.25	−.11	.02	.16	.30	−.09	−.08	.24	.18	.05
M[c]	.11	.03	−.30	.04	.33	.36	.18	.27	.41	.11	−.09	.24	.23	.06	−.21	.12	.13	−.01
44. Given to moods; often difficult and recalcitrant
M[a]	.01	.10	.20	−.18	−.17	−.24	−.27	−.02	−.33	−.21	−.18	−.15	−.18	−.07	.23	−.01	−.18	−.03
F[b]	.13	−.02	−.02	−.12	−.06	−.07	−.11	.04	−.08	−.17	−.01	−.08	−.01	−.11	.12	.02	−.03	−.07
M[c]	−.09	.30	.11	−.14	−.18	−.20	−.06	−.08	−.18	−.25	−.15	−.09	−.18	.02	−.01	.04	−.08	.00

[a] for men described by their wives or partners; N = 200
[b] for women described by their husbands or partners; N = 200
[c] for men described by three assessment staff observers; N = 111

Correlations of CPI Scales with Items of the Interpersonal Q-Sort continued

Item	Do	Cs	Sy	Sp	Sa	In	Em	Re	So	Sc	Gi	Cm	Wb	To	Ac	Ai	Ie	Py
45. Has highly developed inner sense of ethics and morality; deeply humanitarian and altruistic																		
M[a]	−.02	.05	−.06	−.10	−.06	.02	.02	.11	.03	.09	.08	−.12	−.02	.11	−.01	.13	.02	.11
F[b]	−.11	−.07	−.08	−.16	−.14	−.20	−.17	.19	.14	.02	−.01	.13	−.05	−.10	.06	−.15	−.08	−.14
M[c]	−.01	−.18	−.12	−.19	−.14	−.07	.02	.17	.13	.18	.19	.06	.03	.10	.12	.00	−.09	−.13
46. Overly concerned with success; too dominated by own ambition and desire to win approval																		
M[a]	.12	−.02	.08	.00	.17	.07	−.02	−.04	−.08	−.12	−.07	.12	−.04	−.09	−.01	−.03	−.07	.01
F[b]	.08	.08	.06	.04	.14	.03	.03	.02	−.10	−.03	.07	−.02	−.02	−.03	.13	.04	.02	.01
M[c]	.12	.21	.21	.05	.16	.08	.11	.14	.20	.07	.10	−.13	.05	.11	.20	.04	.04	.07
47. Warm and unpretentious; a comfortable and uncomplicated person																		
M[a]	−.12	−.04	.10	.07	−.05	−.20	.05	−.10	−.01	−.08	−.04	−.04	−.06	−.04	−.08	−.12	−.08	−.05
F[b]	−.19	−.20	−.12	−.15	−.21	−.20	−.16	.14	.10	.11	.04	.09	.03	.13	−.02	−.13	−.19	−.07
M[c]	−.07	−.10	−.10	−.08	−.10	−.08	−.08	−.06	.12	−.10	−.07	.01	−.05	−.17	−.05	−.22	−.15	−.20
48. Wedded to routine; made anxious by change and uncertainty																		
M[a]	−.18	−.04	−.22	−.19	−.14	−.12	−.15	.08	−.01	.11	.02	−.11	−.14	−.01	−.01	.00	−.02	−.10
F[b]	−.15	−.19	−.15	−.24	−.13	−.20	−.23	.01	.10	.09	.06	.00	−.09	−.09	.05	−.17	−.17	−.16
M[c]	−.05	−.19	−.09	−.19	−.10	−.18	−.13	.04	−.07	−.05	.00	−.18	−.15	−.07	.00	−.22	−.25	−.15
49. Is an effective leader; able to elicit the responses and cooperation of others																		
M[a]	.35	.21	.16	.05	.20	.27	.14	.21	.13	.07	.13	.02	.17	.18	.23	.15	.18	.16
F[b]	.28	.22	.20	.14	.24	.19	.24	.04	.01	−.04	−.01	.13	.10	.04	.13	.06	.17	.08
M[c]	.43	.19	.21	.27	.38	.24	.19	.14	.20	−.07	−.11	.29	.28	.22	.25	.14	.35	.14
50. Coarse and vulgar; inclined to behave in a crude and impolite fashion																		
M[a]	−.01	.05	.06	.11	.00	.03	.06	−.16	−.06	−.07	−.11	−.01	.02	−.02	−.04	−.01	.01	−.02
F[b]	−.04	−.05	−.10	.03	−.05	.04	.02	−.18	−.25	−.14	−.11	−.15	−.14	−.03	−.14	.04	−.08	−.02
M[c]	.00	−.06	.00	.09	.02	.04	−.13	−.13	.04	−.17	−.13	.06	−.05	−.09	.05	.04	.13	−.02

[a] for men described by their wives or partners; $N = 200$
[b] for women described by their husbands or partners; $N = 200$
[c] for men described by three assessment staff observers; $N = 111$

Correlations of CPI Scales with Items of the Interpersonal Q-Sort continued

Measures	Fx	F/M	v.1	v.2	v.3	Mp	Wo	CT	Lp	Ami	Leo	Tm	B–MS	B–FM	Anx	Nar	D–SD	D–AC
45. Has highly developed inner sense of ethics and morality; deeply humanitarian and altruistic																		
M[a]	.08	.11	.08	.03	.08	.03	.01	.06	.01	.10	−.04	−.01	−.03	.11	.07	−.10	−.03	−.04
F[b]	−.24	.13	.09	.19	−.15	−.07	−.03	−.25	−.08	−.01	.11	−.11	−.13	.17	.03	−.07	−.06	.02
M[c]	−.07	−.02	.14	.18	−.04	.02	.06	−.09	.04	.11	.24	.03	−.02	.04	.00	−.16	.09	−.10
46. Overly concerned with success; too dominated by own ambition and desire to win approval																		
M[a]	.00	−.01	−.13	.05	−.07	.02	−.12	.00	.00	−.15	.03	.05	.07	−.05	.08	.19	.07	.08
F[b]	−.03	−.06	−.11	.04	.03	.05	.02	.04	.06	.00	.06	.08	.07	−.05	.01	.05	.09	.06
M[c]	−.04	.16	−.20	.16	.20	.16	.09	.00	.16	.07	.00	.12	.12	.17	.16	−.04	.18	−.04
47. Warm and unpretentious; a comfortable and uncomplicated person																		
M[a]	.02	−.09	.01	−.07	−.09	−.15	−.08	−.04	−.07	.01	−.05	−.23	−.07	−.16	−.09	−.01	−.08	.08
F[b]	−.14	.17	.18	.09	−.07	−.06	.09	−.15	−.08	.18	.10	−.17	−.18	.17	−.02	−.18	−.03	−.06
M[c]	−.18	−.16	.07	.13	−.19	−.09	−.06	−.15	−.08	−.03	.04	−.07	−.05	−.04	.12	.08	−.17	.13
48. Wedded to routine; made anxious by change and uncertainty																		
M[a]	−.10	.14	.20	.01	−.05	−.14	−.02	−.11	−.14	−.01	−.05	−.07	−.23	.13	.12	−.12	−.07	−.01
F[b]	−.23	.21	.20	.17	−.14	−.13	.01	−.26	−.09	.06	.03	−.06	−.19	.08	.13	−.17	−.03	−.03
M[c]	−.21	.03	.06	.12	−.18	−.08	.01	−.27	−.11	−.01	.10	−.10	−.12	.04	.22	.01	.01	−.05
49. Is an effective leader; able to elicit the responses and cooperation of others																		
M[a]	.08	−.08	−.26	.13	.20	.30	.16	.10	.35	.12	.14	.22	.22	.03	−.11	.07	.18	−.07
F[b]	−.05	−.08	−.24	.10	.10	.19	.11	.05	.35	.07	.12	.18	.20	.00	−.06	.12	.23	.07
M[c]	−.06	−.06	−.32	.17	.17	.39	.18	.17	.42	.11	.09	.26	.31	.00	−.23	.10	.17	−.04
50. Coarse and vulgar; inclined to behave in a crude and impolite fashion																		
M[a]	−.06	−.11	−.02	−.08	−.01	.02	−.02	.08	−.01	−.05	−.16	.02	.04	−.13	−.04	.03	.06	−.02
F[b]	−.01	−.04	−.01	−.18	−.05	−.11	−.17	.15	−.11	−.20	−.14	.04	−.06	−.19	.01	.10	−.09	.03
M[c]	.00	−.02	−.01	.00	−.12	−.12	−.05	−.01	.02	−.12	.09	.01	.06	−.15	−.08	.04	−.11	.10

[a] for men described by their wives or partners; N = 200
[b] for women described by their husbands or partners; N = 200
[c] for men described by three assessment staff observers; N = 111

G

Correlations of CPI™ Scales with Items in the *Interviewer's Check List*

This appendix reports correlations of the 36 CPI scales with the 99 items in the *Interviewer's Check List* (ICL), for samples of 504 men and 379 women. The descriptions by interviewers were based on observations made during a 90-minute to two-hour life history interview with each person. After the interview, the observer checked those items in the list of 99 that characterized the behavior, background, or remarks made by the interviewee. Checked items were assigned dummy weights of 1, with weights of 0 assigned to items left blank. The specific categories covered by the ICL include (a) activity during the interview, (b) physical movement, (c) physique and bearing, (d) personal appearance and expression, (e) speech, (f) reaction to the interview, (g) family background, (h) behavior during adolescence, and (i) current behavior and experience. The interviewers were staff psychologists at the Institute of Personality Assessment and Research in Berkeley, or doctoral candidates in fields such as clinical, counseling, and personality psychology. The 7,128 correlations generated by this analysis follow.

Correlations of CPI Scales with Items in the Interviewer's Check List

Item	Do	Cs	Sy	Sp	Sa	In	Em	Re	So	Sc	Gi	Cm	Wb	To	Ac	Ai	Ie	Py
Activity																		
1. Excited, restless																		
M	.08	.05	.09	.00	.11	.06	−.01	−.05	−.08	−.13	−.04	−.09	−.07	−.05	−.03	−.04	−.08	.01
F	.09	.07	.06	.08	.11	.06	.11	−.03	−.06	−.14	−.08	−.06	−.07	−.04	−.02	−.01	.04	−.03
2. Calm and deliberate																		
M	.02	−.06	−.03	.00	−.03	.00	.02	−.01	.02	.05	.00	.03	.05	−.02	.01	−.04	.00	−.05
F	.00	.07	.00	.04	.01	.04	−.05	−.02	.03	.01	.03	.08	.02	.01	.04	.05	.00	.04
3. Nervous and fidgety																		
M	−.10	−.07	−.10	−.10	−.08	−.07	−.06	−.05	−.06	−.02	−.04	−.07	−.06	−.08	−.08	−.05	−.13	−.06
F	−.07	−.12	−.07	−.09	−.08	−.08	−.04	.00	−.07	−.01	−.03	−.05	−.06	−.01	−.09	−.07	−.05	−.06
4. Made considerable use of hands in talking																		
M	.06	.09	.04	.04	.10	.09	.05	−.10	−.10	−.10	−.08	−.10	−.04	−.03	−.09	.01	−.02	.01
F	.14	.09	.16	.12	.15	.09	.16	−.04	−.02	−.12	−.05	−.02	−.03	−.02	−.02	.02	.11	−.02
5. Tended to pull at ears, put hands to face, etc																		
M	−.07	−.08	−.08	−.11	−.08	−.09	−.08	.06	−.01	.05	.02	.00	−.06	−.04	−.01	−.04	−.09	.00
F	−.11	−.06	−.14	−.09	−.09	−.12	−.08	.05	−.04	.05	.01	−.10	−.09	.03	−.09	.02	−.04	.00
Movement																		
6. Graceful and well-coordinated in movement																		
M	.12	.12	.10	.12	.12	.08	.18	.02	.05	.00	.00	.08	.13	.12	.04	.13	.14	.04
F	.02	.08	.08	.06	.06	.01	.05	.02	.08	.02	.08	.04	.01	.01	.05	.03	.00	−.03
7. Awkward and clumsy in movement																		
M	−.11	−.19	−.15	−.16	−.12	−.12	−.18	−.10	−.07	−.06	−.08	−.13	−.21	−.22	−.15	−.22	−.28	−.22
F	−.04	−.12	−.05	−.06	.00	−.03	.01	.00	−.04	−.04	−.10	.00	−.02	.01	−.09	−.02	−.02	−.04
8. Quick tempo of movement																		
M	.09	.10	.07	.08	.12	.08	.07	−.05	−.04	−.10	−.04	−.03	.00	.00	−.01	−.01	.05	.06
F	.11	.15	.15	.11	.11	.04	.15	.04	−.06	−.11	−.04	−.04	−.02	−.05	.09	.04	.08	.02
9. Slow rate of movement																		
M	−.10	−.13	−.10	−.12	−.12	−.12	−.14	.02	.02	.09	.01	.00	−.03	−.09	.03	−.09	−.08	−.06
F	−.17	−.23	−.20	−.18	−.16	−.18	−.15	−.08	.02	.14	.06	.02	−.04	−.04	−.09	−.10	−.17	−.10
Physique and Bearing																		
10. Impressive bearing and posture																		
M	.11	.00	.08	.04	.16	.03	.07	−.07	−.09	−.05	−.03	.00	−.01	−.04	.01	−.03	.03	−.06
F	.09	.08	.07	.05	.05	.05	.02	.11	.12	.12	.13	.10	.11	.08	.18	.06	.07	.06
11. Poor posture, generally unimpressive bearing																		
M	−.11	−.05	−.07	−.04	−.12	−.07	−.05	−.03	−.05	−.02	−.03	−.10	−.10	−.08	−.13	−.08	−.10	−.05
F	−.07	−.07	−.09	−.05	−.07	−.07	.00	.08	−.01	.06	−.02	−.07	.00	.15	−.05	.09	.01	.02
12. Healthy-looking, well-developed and nourished																		
M	.11	.00	.09	.08	.13	.00	.03	−.07	−.02	−.04	.02	.08	.08	.02	.01	−.02	.06	−.03
F	.02	.12	.08	.08	.04	.05	.09	−.07	.08	.00	.05	.03	.04	.00	.09	.05	.01	.02
13. Thin, appears weak and frail																		
M	−.15	−.07	−.14	−.14	−.13	−.03	−.07	.07	.08	.07	.00	−.12	−.06	.05	.02	.06	−.04	.06
F	−.01	.03	−.03	.04	−.02	.04	.00	.00	−.06	−.01	−.03	−.10	.00	.00	.00	.05	.05	.03
14. Obese, overly heavy for height and build																		
M	.08	−.01	.06	.02	.06	.01	−.05	.00	−.07	−.05	−.01	−.02	−.02	−.04	−.01	−.06	−.01	−.05
F	.00	−.14	−.09	−.09	−.02	−.07	−.07	.03	−.04	−.06	−.13	−.03	−.06	−.06	−.15	−.10	−.06	−.02

Correlations of CPI Scales with Items in the Interviewer's Check List continued

Measures	Fx	F/M	v.1	v.2	v.3	Mp	Wo	CT	Lp	Ami	Leo	Tm	B–MS	B–FM	Anx	Nar	D–SD	D–AC
Activity																		
1. Excited, restless																		
M	.00	−.03	−.13	.03	−.06	−.04	−.13	.01	.01	−.14	.01	.02	.02	−.17	.01	.15	.01	.08
F	.09	.03	−.16	−.04	−.07	−.01	−.09	.11	.02	−.15	−.06	.01	.04	−.03	.08	.15	−.05	.08
2. Calm and deliberate																		
M	−.09	−.03	.00	−.01	.00	.03	.07	−.07	.04	.03	.06	.05	.02	.04	−.05	−.03	−.01	.01
F	−.07	−.12	−.01	.06	.02	−.03	.00	−.02	.02	−.01	.06	.03	.02	−.04	.04	.00	.04	.01
3. Nervous and fidgety																		
M	.00	−.03	.09	−.02	−.11	−.12	−.10	−.04	−.10	−.03	−.08	−.10	−.08	−.05	.04	−.01	−.05	.04
F	.03	.09	.06	−.05	−.05	−.03	−.06	.05	−.10	−.02	−.09	−.12	−.11	−.04	−.03	−.01	−.07	−.05
4. Made considerable use of hands in talking																		
M	.11	.02	−.06	−.09	.00	.03	−.11	.11	.00	−.09	−.06	.00	.07	−.11	.07	.08	−.04	−.03
F	.03	.02	−.16	.00	.00	.03	−.05	.12	.07	−.10	−.03	.01	.10	−.09	−.06	.13	.04	.16
5. Tended to pull at ears, put hands to face, etc.																		
M	−.11	.11	.12	.03	−.07	−.06	.02	−.10	−.06	−.02	−.03	.00	−.10	.12	.03	−.04	−.03	−.03
F	.06	.10	.12	−.10	.01	−.05	−.01	−.02	−.10	.01	−.08	−.07	−.11	.09	.07	−.09	−.07	−.05
Movement																		
6. Graceful and well-coordinated in movement																		
M	.07	−.01	−.16	−.03	.12	.13	.10	.10	.15	.08	.11	.10	.12	.05	−.05	.04	.07	−.01
F	.01	−.01	−.01	.02	.04	.01	.01	.03	.05	.03	.05	.02	.05	.06	.02	−.02	.06	.01
7. Awkward and clumsy in movement																		
M	−.12	.07	.08	.02	−.23	−.19	−.20	−.18	−.20	−.16	−.05	−.15	−.18	−.06	.14	.04	−.14	.09
F	.07	.02	.04	−.08	−.04	−.07	−.06	.04	−.06	−.02	−.08	−.04	−.02	−.04	−.05	.00	−.08	−.02
8. Quick tempo of movement																		
M	.11	−.03	−.13	−.05	.04	.02	−.05	.12	.04	−.06	−.03	.04	.06	−.13	−.03	.12	.02	−.03
F	−.03	.01	−.18	.01	.00	.05	−.02	.07	.07	−.09	−.04	.03	.09	−.01	.02	.13	.08	.08
9. Slow rate of movement																		
M	−.17	.00	.16	.08	−.11	−.08	.03	−.17	−.05	.02	.01	−.03	−.08	.04	−.02	−.07	−.02	.06
F	−.09	.08	.23	.03	−.09	−.10	−.02	−.18	−.14	.03	.07	−.11	−.18	.01	.00	−.16	−.03	−.03
Physique and Bearing																		
10. Impressive bearing and posture																		
M	−.05	−.08	−.14	−.01	−.05	.02	−.02	−.02	.07	−.07	.13	.05	.10	−.07	−.06	.10	.04	.04
F	−.04	.03	−.02	.13	.09	.14	.13	−.02	.14	.11	.14	.14	.08	.15	−.10	−.05	.12	−.07
11. Poor posture, generally unimpressive bearing																		
M	.06	.01	.09	−.04	−.06	−.12	−.09	.02	−.12	−.06	−.15	−.12	−.11	−.05	.07	−.03	−.11	−.02
F	.11	.09	.08	−.06	.08	.02	.03	.05	−.07	.07	−.08	−.06	−.11	.01	.00	−.09	−.01	−.07
12. Healthy-looking, well-developed and nourished																		
M	−.03	−.11	−.13	.00	.00	.08	.06	−.06	.10	.02	.20	.08	.12	−.08	−.08	.09	.09	−.01
F	.05	−.11	−.06	.00	.04	.01	.04	.05	.06	.00	.03	.07	.06	.02	−.01	.01	.07	.05
13. Thin, appears weak and frail																		
M	.00	.10	.16	−.01	.03	−.09	−.04	.05	−.11	.01	−.13	−.07	−.15	.13	.08	−.12	−.09	−.02
F	.04	−.04	.04	−.06	.05	.01	−.03	.06	−.04	.02	−.11	.01	.02	.01	.00	−.01	−.06	−.05
14. Obese, overly heavy for height and build																		
M	−.07	−.10	−.08	.06	−.05	.00	−.05	−.07	.02	−.05	.06	.02	.04	−.08	.03	.07	.06	.06
F	−.07	.10	.01	.02	−.13	−.07	−.04	−.08	−.10	−.08	−.02	−.06	−.06	−.07	−.02	.06	−.09	.04

Correlations of CPI Scales with Items in the Interviewer's Check List continued

Item	Do	Cs	Sy	Sp	Sa	In	Em	Re	So	Sc	Gi	Cm	Wb	To	Ac	Ai	Ie	Py
Personal Appearance and Expression																		
15. Attractive, good-looking																		
M	.12	.05	.10	.11	.15	.07	.12	−.08	.00	−.07	−.02	.09	.04	.02	.00	.04	.09	.00
F	.14	.16	.22	.18	.15	.10	.15	.03	.08	−.06	.04	.05	.04	−.04	.14	−.02	.06	−.05
16. Unattractive, below average in personal appearance																		
M	−.09	−.01	−.04	−.03	−.12	−.05	−.06	.03	.00	.02	.00	−.10	−.08	−.07	−.02	−.05	−.07	−.03
F	−.04	−.09	−.09	−.09	−.03	−.05	−.04	.05	−.05	.01	−.05	.00	−.02	−.01	−.10	−.01	−.02	.01
17. Animated facial expressiveness																		
M	.11	.15	.08	.09	.10	.12	.14	−.05	−.06	−.07	−.04	−.09	−.01	.02	−.04	.10	.08	.08
F	.09	.08	.15	.13	.11	.04	.13	−.02	−.02	−.13	−.06	−.03	−.04	−.06	.01	.03	.04	.02
18. Deadpan face; expressionless																		
M	−.06	−.10	−.05	−.05	−.10	−.06	−.09	.03	−.01	.05	.03	−.02	−.05	−.08	−.03	−.12	−.07	−.07
F	−.15	−.15	−.17	−.16	−.15	−.13	−.11	.01	.05	.12	.03	.03	−.01	.06	−.05	−.03	−.12	−.04
19. Diverts gaze; seldom looked directly at the interviewer																		
M	−.07	−.06	−.08	−.07	−.09	−.06	−.06	−.05	−.06	.02	.01	−.05	−.07	−.11	−.04	−.10	−.11	−.12
F	−.07	−.09	−.14	−.11	−.11	−.09	.01	−.02	.03	.06	.02	−.03	−.03	.02	−.05	−.01	−.03	.00
20. Has an alert, "open" face																		
M	.13	.15	.11	.13	.19	.13	.14	.00	.00	−.07	−.02	.05	.04	.05	.04	.11	.14	.10
F	.07	.12	.18	.11	.12	.03	.09	−.07	−.01	−.09	−.02	.03	−.05	−.02	.06	.03	.08	−.03
21. Tough, hard-boiled in appearance																		
M	.00	−.14	−.07	−.10	−.04	−.05	−.10	−.15	−.06	−.03	−.05	.04	−.02	−.18	−.10	−.20	−.15	−.14
F	.01	.02	−.04	−.02	.04	.03	.06	−.04	−.09	−.04	−.03	−.09	−.02	−.01	−.01	.04	.03	.02
22. Looks older than actual age																		
M	.04	−.04	.00	−.01	.04	.02	−.01	−.08	−.05	−.06	−.05	−.07	−.06	−.08	−.09	−.05	−.01	−.03
F	.00	−.10	−.11	−.13	−.04	−.07	−.05	.04	−.01	.02	.00	.03	−.02	−.05	−.08	−.11	−.07	−.07
23. Looks younger than actual age																		
M	−.03	.06	−.04	−.04	−.02	.00	.03	.04	.01	.06	.08	−.03	.05	.06	.02	.03	.02	.05
F	.04	.07	.06	.07	.06	.02	.02	−.03	.01	−.02	.02	−.01	.04	.05	−.02	.06	.06	.01
24. Well-groomed and well-dressed																		
M	.10	.12	.07	.01	.11	.03	.06	.16	.15	.10	.11	.15	.12	.08	.20	.01	.08	.03
F	.06	.04	.04	.01	.01	.07	−.04	.04	.15	.04	.11	.12	.06	−.05	.15	−.03	−.03	−.05
25. Careless, unkempt in grooming and appearance																		
M	−.07	−.13	−.04	.01	−.06	−.07	.06	−.20	−.21	−.17	−.14	−.08	−.13	−.12	−.20	−.06	−.11	−.06
F	−.05	−.03	−.04	.01	.01	−.02	.01	.09	.03	.07	−.02	−.08	.07	.16	−.01	.14	.10	.11
26. Shoes clean and well-shined																		
M	.10	.00	.00	−.10	.04	.03	−.07	.16	.11	.17	.20	.07	.14	.01	.18	−.05	−.01	.00
F	.06	.03	.00	.05	.01	.07	.00	.07	.08	.05	.04	.10	.08	.06	.09	.04	.04	.10
27. Florid face, blotchy complexion of nose and face																		
M	−.10	.03	−.01	.01	−.06	−.06	.02	.00	−.03	−.04	−.04	−.08	−.08	.00	−.07	.00	−.06	.00
F	−.05	.02	−.03	−.07	.01	−.02	.00	.11	−.03	.00	−.07	−.09	−.06	.03	.04	.09	.04	.06
28. Rugged, masculine appearance																		
M	.08	−.10	.03	−.02	.04	−.04	−.08	−.22	−.18	−.15	−.09	−.01	−.06	−.23	−.11	−.21	−.11	−.13
F	−.06	−.02	−.02	−.05	.00	.00	−.03	−.09	−.01	−.03	−.02	−.04	−.05	−.08	−.07	−.01	−.05	−.02
29. Delicate, feminine appearance																		
M	−.10	−.02	−.07	−.09	−.04	−.03	.03	−.07	−.06	.00	−.02	−.05	−.12	.02	−.02	.07	−.03	.01
F	.05	.01	.05	.07	.01	.06	−.05	.01	.06	.07	.14	.10	.07	−.03	.12	−.05	.01	.01

Correlations of CPI Scales with Items in the Interviewer's Check List *continued*																	
Measures	**Fx**	**F/M**	**v.1**	**v.2**	**v.3**	**Mp**	**Wo**	**CT**	**Lp**	**Ami**	**Leo**	**Tm**	**B–MS**	**B–FM**	**Anx**	**Nar**	**D–SD**	**D–AC**

Personal Appearance and Expression

15. Attractive, good-looking

	Fx	F/M	v.1	v.2	v.3	Mp	Wo	CT	Lp	Ami	Leo	Tm	B–MS	B–FM	Anx	Nar	D–SD	D–AC
M	.06	−.04	−.15	−.06	.03	.04	.06	.06	.11	−.02	.18	.06	.12	−.08	−.06	.13	.03	.01
F	.03	−.05	−.14	.04	.02	.05	.00	.04	.13	.00	.15	.07	.16	.06	−.01	.09	.12	.08

16. Unattractive, below average in personal appearance

M	−.02	.00	.06	.00	−.08	−.09	−.07	−.04	−.09	−.05	−.11	−.05	−.09	.00	.05	−.05	−.06	.04
F	−.04	.03	.06	.03	−.03	−.01	.04	−.03	−.04	−.01	−.04	.00	−.02	−.05	.02	−.03	−.05	−.03

17. Animated facial expressiveness

M	.17	.05	−.14	−.09	.08	.07	−.06	.20	.04	−.06	−.08	.02	.07	−.09	.00	.11	.01	.01
F	.05	−.01	−.15	−.05	−.02	.00	−.04	.07	.04	−.10	−.01	.01	.07	−.05	.02	.12	.03	.13

18. Deadpan face; expressionless

M	−.09	.00	.07	.04	−.09	−.09	−.01	−.11	−.06	.01	.01	.00	−.05	.07	.02	−.05	−.05	.04
F	−.02	.05	.17	.01	−.02	−.05	.02	−.07	−.14	.09	−.04	−.10	−.16	.07	.02	−.16	−.03	−.05

19. Diverts gaze; seldom looked directly at the interviewer

M	−.09	.07	.09	−.01	−.08	−.08	−.06	−.07	−.11	−.02	.01	−.03	−.08	.02	−.04	−.09	.01	.01
F	.04	.00	.08	−.04	.00	−.02	−.04	.02	−.08	.00	.00	−.01	−.08	.01	.06	−.06	−.02	−.03

20. Has an alert, "open" face

M	.10	−.05	−.16	−.07	.08	.09	.01	.15	.13	−.02	.04	.08	.12	−.09	.02	.13	.05	.01
F	.06	−.02	−.11	−.03	.01	.00	−.04	.07	.07	−.06	.02	.01	.06	−.06	.00	.10	.04	.11

21. Tough, hard-boiled in appearance

M	−.18	−.03	.02	.02	−.21	−.10	−.07	−.19	−.02	−.06	.00	.01	.01	−.05	−.03	.04	−.04	.05
F	.00	−.08	−.05	−.06	.01	.01	.00	.03	.01	−.08	−.06	.03	.05	−.06	.01	.01	−.02	−.06

22. Looks older than actual age

M	.02	−.06	−.04	−.04	−.06	−.02	−.07	−.03	−.03	−.06	.00	.01	.00	−.11	.02	.07	−.03	−.04
F	−.11	.02	.05	.07	−.08	−.07	−.07	−.10	−.04	−.06	.12	−.07	−.05	−.08	−.05	−.03	.00	.01

23. Looks younger than actual age

M	.03	−.03	.02	.01	.07	.02	.04	.05	.02	.08	.03	.02	.04	.03	−.03	−.06	−.02	−.02
F	.05	.07	.00	−.03	.05	.10	.02	.06	.03	.01	−.08	.03	.07	.04	.03	.00	.04	−.03

24. Well-groomed and well-dressed

M	−.14	.04	−.05	.16	.05	.14	.15	−.10	.18	.14	.14	.11	.10	.11	−.11	−.02	.13	.02
F	−.12	.02	−.03	.13	−.03	.03	.10	−.10	.10	.06	.26	.12	.08	.12	−.10	−.06	.07	.00

25. Careless, unkempt in grooming and appearance

M	.11	−.09	−.03	−.21	−.10	−.17	−.20	.10	−.17	−.18	−.09	−.13	−.05	−.22	.09	.09	−.13	.03
F	.12	.00	.09	−.07	.13	.03	.08	.08	−.01	.08	−.07	.01	.00	.01	−.04	−.05	−.02	−.11

26. Shoes clean and well-shined

M	−.24	−.02	.00	.24	−.01	.13	.16	−.21	.17	.13	.24	.20	.11	.13	−.11	−.08	.11	−.02
F	−.05	.00	−.02	.07	.06	.08	.11	.00	.08	.07	.03	.15	.05	.09	−.06	−.06	.03	−.06

27. Florid face, blotchy complexion of nose and face

M	.08	−.05	.03	−.06	.00	−.04	−.04	.02	−.09	−.03	−.07	−.07	−.05	−.03	.10	−.02	−.12	.03
F	.04	.03	.02	−.02	.05	.02	−.02	.06	−.05	−.03	−.13	.02	−.06	−.01	.11	.00	−.05	−.03

28. Rugged, masculine appearance

M	−.12	−.19	−.07	−.04	−.21	−.14	−.12	−.16	−.01	−.15	.11	.01	.07	−.20	−.04	.14	−.03	.08
F	−.04	−.03	.03	−.02	−.06	−.10	−.04	−.02	−.05	−.06	−.04	−.11	−.03	.00	.09	.03	−.05	.06

29. Delicate, feminine appearance

M	.07	.17	.09	−.12	.06	−.06	−.10	.11	−.14	−.08	−.06	−.11	−.11	.09	.09	−.07	−.09	−.04
F	−.08	.10	.00	.09	.00	.04	.06	−.09	.09	.10	.12	.10	.06	.18	−.10	−.04	.05	.01

Correlations of CPI Scales with Items in the Interviewer's Check List continued																	
Item	Do	Cs	Sy	Sp	Sa	In	Em	Re	So	Sc	Gi	Cm	Wb	To	Ac	Ai	Ie	Py

Speech

30. Pleasing, resonant voice

	Do	Cs	Sy	Sp	Sa	In	Em	Re	So	Sc	Gi	Cm	Wb	To	Ac	Ai	Ie	Py
M	.15	.05	.06	.06	.14	.10	.12	−.06	.01	−.05	.00	.03	.05	.00	−.01	.03	.10	−.01
F	.14	.10	.11	.08	.16	.12	.14	.02	−.04	−.11	−.02	.00	−.06	−.04	.12	.05	.06	−.01

31. Has difficulty in expressing ideas

	Do	Cs	Sy	Sp	Sa	In	Em	Re	So	Sc	Gi	Cm	Wb	To	Ac	Ai	Ie	Py
M	−.16	−.16	−.08	−.07	−.14	−.20	−.13	.00	−.02	.01	.03	.02	−.08	−.06	−.04	−.16	−.15	−.12
F	−.20	−.22	−.17	−.14	−.16	−.11	−.14	−.04	.07	.12	.00	.01	.02	.03	−.12	−.10	−.13	−.04

32. Uses wide and varied vocabulary

	Do	Cs	Sy	Sp	Sa	In	Em	Re	So	Sc	Gi	Cm	Wb	To	Ac	Ai	Ie	Py
M	.14	.20	.08	.10	.14	.18	.15	.09	.03	−.03	−.09	.05	.03	.13	.10	.21	.24	.14
F	.23	.21	.16	.18	.19	.16	.23	.06	−.04	−.06	−.02	−.03	.05	.07	.14	.22	.23	.22

33. Redundant and repetitious in speech

	Do	Cs	Sy	Sp	Sa	In	Em	Re	So	Sc	Gi	Cm	Wb	To	Ac	Ai	Ie	Py
M	−.07	−.16	−.05	−.07	−.09	−.07	−.17	−.15	−.07	.01	.03	.01	−.02	−.15	−.07	−.25	−.17	−.15
F	−.09	−.16	−.09	−.07	−.08	−.08	−.03	.01	.06	−.01	−.02	.02	−.04	−.03	−.11	−.09	−.08	−.07

34. Makes mistakes in grammar and/or word usage

	Do	Cs	Sy	Sp	Sa	In	Em	Re	So	Sc	Gi	Cm	Wb	To	Ac	Ai	Ie	Py
M	−.14	−.19	−.08	−.12	−.10	−.15	−.17	−.20	−.15	−.03	−.03	−.07	−.11	−.24	−.18	−.28	−.23	−.20
F	−.08	−.18	−.05	−.09	−.10	−.10	−.20	−.08	.02	.03	.01	.00	−.03	−.15	−.12	−.23	−.18	−.19

35. Reticent and taciturn

	Do	Cs	Sy	Sp	Sa	In	Em	Re	So	Sc	Gi	Cm	Wb	To	Ac	Ai	Ie	Py
M	−.19	−.12	−.11	−.11	−.18	−.15	−.14	.05	.08	.13	.06	.01	−.02	.03	.04	.03	−.04	−.02
F	−.14	−.17	−.17	−.15	−.18	−.12	−.17	.00	.04	.13	.00	.08	.05	.02	−.06	−.08	−.11	.01

36. Given to clichés and trite expressions

	Do	Cs	Sy	Sp	Sa	In	Em	Re	So	Sc	Gi	Cm	Wb	To	Ac	Ai	Ie	Py
M	−.07	−.09	.01	−.04	−.04	−.12	−.05	−.09	−.07	−.08	−.07	−.04	−.10	−.13	−.09	−.18	−.17	−.15
F	−.06	−.03	.00	.00	−.04	−.03	−.02	−.09	.08	−.02	.00	.08	.03	−.04	−.03	−.09	−.07	−.07

37. Witty and animated, an interesting conversationalist

	Do	Cs	Sy	Sp	Sa	In	Em	Re	So	Sc	Gi	Cm	Wb	To	Ac	Ai	Ie	Py
M	.16	.18	.15	.15	.18	.17	.21	−.01	−.02	−.06	.01	−.04	.01	.07	.04	.12	.12	.11
F	.26	.26	.29	.27	.27	.19	.26	.03	−.03	−.17	−.06	−.02	.04	.04	.10	.18	.23	.18

38. Makes economical but effective use of words

	Do	Cs	Sy	Sp	Sa	In	Em	Re	So	Sc	Gi	Cm	Wb	To	Ac	Ai	Ie	Py
M	.07	.13	.07	.11	.09	.13	.08	.03	.01	−.04	−.02	.00	.10	.04	.00	.08	.14	.14
F	−.06	−.02	−.09	−.07	−.09	−.02	−.02	.01	−.01	.02	.00	−.01	−.02	−.03	−.03	.04	−.03	−.03

39. Speech is difficult to understand; does not enunciate clearly

	Do	Cs	Sy	Sp	Sa	In	Em	Re	So	Sc	Gi	Cm	Wb	To	Ac	Ai	Ie	Py
M	−.08	−.11	−.08	−.05	−.07	−.09	−.14	−.07	−.03	−.02	.00	.01	.02	−.12	−.06	−.12	−.10	−.08
F	.00	−.02	.02	−.02	.00	−.01	−.03	.01	.05	.08	.10	.02	.05	−.01	.05	−.01	−.03	.03

40. Simple and direct in manner of expression

	Do	Cs	Sy	Sp	Sa	In	Em	Re	So	Sc	Gi	Cm	Wb	To	Ac	Ai	Ie	Py
M	−.02	−.07	−.03	−.06	.00	−.07	−.01	−.10	−.08	−.01	−.01	−.05	−.03	−.07	−.13	−.10	−.10	−.08
F	.03	.05	.00	.00	−.01	−.04	.03	.01	.00	−.05	.01	.00	−.03	−.03	.06	.01	.03	−.05

41. Circumstantial and roundabout in speech

	Do	Cs	Sy	Sp	Sa	In	Em	Re	So	Sc	Gi	Cm	Wb	To	Ac	Ai	Ie	Py
M	−.03	−.04	−.05	−.06	−.07	−.04	−.03	.04	−.01	.02	−.01	.00	−.09	−.03	.03	−.04	−.06	.00
F	−.09	−.08	−.07	−.09	−.05	−.04	−.04	−.04	.00	.00	−.05	.00	−.07	−.04	−.07	−.09	−.11	−.08

Reaction to the Interview

42. Defensive and guarded in manner

	Do	Cs	Sy	Sp	Sa	In	Em	Re	So	Sc	Gi	Cm	Wb	To	Ac	Ai	Ie	Py
M	−.12	−.11	−.10	−.14	−.14	−.09	−.15	−.04	.01	.08	.06	−.06	−.04	−.05	−.02	−.08	−.11	−.02
F	−.08	−.10	−.13	−.12	−.09	−.07	−.06	.05	.01	.03	.00	.01	−.02	.07	−.01	.00	−.08	.01

43. Showed hostility toward the interviewer

	Do	Cs	Sy	Sp	Sa	In	Em	Re	So	Sc	Gi	Cm	Wb	To	Ac	Ai	Ie	Py
M	−.04	−.06	−.02	−.01	.03	.02	−.07	−.08	.03	−.10	−.11	−.02	−.06	−.07	−.05	−.07	−.05	−.04
F	−.01	−.04	.00	−.02	−.04	−.03	−.01	.07	.09	.05	.04	.03	.02	.05	.01	.04	.00	.01

44. Was relaxed and at ease during the interview

	Do	Cs	Sy	Sp	Sa	In	Em	Re	So	Sc	Gi	Cm	Wb	To	Ac	Ai	Ie	Py
M	.14	.06	.11	.14	.13	.12	.14	−.06	.04	−.05	−.03	.01	.08	.04	.00	.05	.12	−.03
F	.18	.22	.19	.13	.23	.14	.14	.11	.02	−.06	−.02	.11	.02	.06	.16	.13	.15	.12

Correlations of CPI Scales with Items in the Interviewer's Check List continued

Measures	Fx	F/M	v.1	v.2	v.3	Mp	Wo	CT	Lp	Ami	Leo	Tm	B–MS	B–FM	Anx	Nar	D–SD	D–AC

Speech

30. Pleasing, resonant voice

M	.01	−.04	−.14	−.07	.02	.06	.02	.03	.13	−.02	.08	.09	.12	−.02	−.05	.09	.06	.01
F	.05	−.08	−.16	.00	.05	.02	−.12	.11	.08	−.14	.02	.06	.07	−.11	.06	.13	.03	.09

31. Has difficulty in expressing ideas

M	−.07	.03	.16	.04	−.12	−.11	−.07	−.17	−.14	−.02	.02	−.11	−.12	−.01	.06	−.10	−.06	.02
F	−.03	.06	.24	−.02	−.08	−.08	.02	−.08	−.11	.11	−.02	−.12	−.16	.04	−.02	−.11	−.10	−.05

32. Uses wide and varied vocabulary

M	.15	.01	−.14	−.06	.14	.12	.05	.24	.11	−.01	−.11	.08	.06	.01	−.01	.08	−.04	−.06
F	.13	−.07	−.24	.01	.15	.13	.02	.20	.18	−.05	−.08	.12	.15	−.10	−.02	.18	.10	.03

33. Redundant and repetitious in speech

M	−.11	−.08	.09	−.01	−.14	−.09	−.06	−.18	−.08	−.03	.09	−.02	.00	−.06	−.04	−.03	−.03	−.01
F	.00	.09	.08	.02	−.06	−.05	.03	−.04	−.10	.02	−.03	−.13	−.10	.02	.02	−.02	−.07	.07

34. Makes mistakes in grammar and/or word usage

M	−.15	−.10	.09	−.06	−.24	−.22	−.14	−.20	−.16	−.13	.02	−.08	−.07	−.14	.04	−.01	−.09	.01
F	−.18	.06	.12	.00	−.20	−.15	−.05	−.22	−.08	−.01	.15	−.09	−.09	.02	−.01	−.05	−.07	.04

35. Reticent and taciturn

M	−.10	.04	.23	.11	.00	−.05	.07	−.14	−.08	.10	.01	−.08	−.16	.14	−.01	−.18	.05	−.05
F	−.03	.04	.20	.01	−.06	−.08	.04	−.08	−.10	.07	.03	−.07	−.14	.07	−.07	−.12	−.08	−.08

36. Given to clichés and trite expressions

M	−.10	−.02	.00	−.01	−.17	−.14	−.13	−.11	−.10	−.12	−.01	−.12	−.08	−.11	.02	.04	−.05	.14
F	−.03	.07	.04	.00	−.09	−.09	.02	−.03	−.04	.03	.04	−.05	−.02	.03	−.09	−.03	.01	.05

37. Witty and animated, an interesting conversationalist

M	.16	.04	−.16	−.11	.13	.11	−.02	.24	.10	−.04	−.10	.07	.11	−.03	−.01	.08	.03	−.06
F	.17	−.07	−.31	.00	.13	.15	−.01	.26	.17	−.12	−.04	.10	.22	−.12	−.05	.21	.08	.07

38. Makes economical but effective use of words

M	.07	−.04	−.09	−.04	.08	.07	.09	.13	.10	.04	−.01	.08	.11	−.02	−.05	.04	.02	.02
F	−.02	−.07	.03	.04	.00	−.05	−.05	−.02	−.05	−.06	−.07	.03	−.05	−.03	.02	.00	−.02	.05

39. Speech is difficult to understand; does not enunciate clearl

M	−.08	−.03	.09	.03	−.10	−.12	−.03	−.12	−.08	−.06	−.04	−.05	−.06	−.06	−.01	.01	−.06	.03
F	−.07	−.08	.01	.11	−.03	.04	.04	−.04	.05	.01	.09	.03	.03	−.02	−.01	−.03	.07	.04

40. Simple and direct in manner of expression

M	.01	−.08	.02	−.09	−.08	−.08	−.05	−.03	−.06	.00	.08	−.04	.04	−.07	.02	.00	.00	−.01
F	−.11	−.10	−.06	.04	−.03	−.01	−.04	−.09	.03	−.04	.04	.05	.00	−.08	.02	.05	.05	.06

41. Circumstantial and roundabout in speech

M	−.05	.08	.02	.03	−.05	−.01	−.07	−.03	−.05	−.06	−.06	−.06	−.10	.02	.06	.02	−.07	.06
F	−.04	.07	.07	−.04	−.07	−.08	−.01	−.03	−.10	.01	.00	−.05	−.09	.03	.04	.00	−.02	.00

Reaction to the Interview

42. Defensive and guarded in manner

M	−.09	.03	.15	.05	−.04	−.05	.02	−.11	−.08	.06	−.01	−.04	−.08	.09	−.01	−.12	−.01	−.04
F	−.03	−.02	.08	.01	−.01	−.04	.01	.00	−.08	.02	−.01	−.03	−.10	.00	−.02	−.06	−.05	−.08

43. Showed hostility toward the interviewer

M	−.08	.03	.02	.00	−.09	−.08	−.05	−.04	−.05	−.03	−.04	−.05	−.04	−.02	.00	.09	−.08	.07
F	.06	.10	.07	.00	.02	.04	.10	−.01	−.01	.06	.04	.03	−.02	.09	.00	−.06	.03	−.02

44. Was relaxed and at ease during the interview

M	.07	−.01	−.14	−.08	.07	.08	.03	.13	.10	.01	.06	.06	.12	−.02	−.04	.09	.02	.02
F	.03	−.08	−.16	.01	.09	.10	.02	.10	.16	−.06	.03	.13	.16	.00	.02	.13	.05	.01

Correlations of CPI Scales with Items in the Interviewer's Check List continued

Item	Do	Cs	Sy	Sp	Sa	In	Em	Re	So	Sc	Gi	Cm	Wb	To	Ac	Ai	Ie	Py
Reaction to the Interview continued																		
45. Seemed to enjoy being interviewed																		
M	.16	.08	.07	.06	.12	.09	.12	.00	.05	−.05	−.04	.04	.08	.03	.06	.04	.11	.05
F	.14	.20	.20	.12	.16	.04	.17	.05	.06	−.06	.00	.03	.00	.03	.09	.05	.09	−.04
46. Poised and overtly cooperative, but nevertheless evasive																		
M	−.05	−.08	−.05	−.04	−.04	−.06	−.10	.02	.02	.02	.02	.06	.03	−.06	.04	−.07	−.06	−.02
F	−.14	−.13	−.18	−.11	−.16	−.06	−.12	−.08	−.04	.01	−.01	.02	−.05	−.06	−.12	−.08	−.07	−.05
47. Asked questions of the interviewer																		
M	.06	−.01	.05	.00	.07	.03	.06	−.05	−.05	−.06	.00	−.01	.00	−.07	−.05	−.04	.02	−.02
F	.08	.12	.00	.01	.07	.04	.11	.10	.04	.03	.04	.05	.00	.11	.10	.14	.13	.10
48. Was nervous and ill at ease during the interview																		
M	−.17	−.09	−.13	−.15	−.13	−.14	−.07	.05	.04	.09	.06	−.03	−.05	−.01	−.02	−.01	−.08	−.02
F	−.13	−.17	−.11	−.14	−.11	−.14	−.09	.03	.03	.05	.01	.00	−.03	.06	−.09	−.06	−.09	−.07
Family Background																		
49. Father stern and authoritarian																		
M	−.06	−.11	−.09	−.09	−.09	−.08	−.17	−.01	−.10	.03	.05	.05	−.01	−.11	−.07	−.15	−.12	−.08
F	−.10	−.11	−.15	−.14	−.13	−.08	−.16	.03	−.13	.04	.06	−.06	−.07	.01	−.08	−.05	−.08	−.03
50. Father benevolent and tolerant																		
M	.14	.11	.12	.13	.13	.14	.12	.09	.16	.00	.02	.05	.11	.11	.14	.06	.19	.09
F	.07	.06	.13	.08	.10	−.01	.11	.05	.27	−.05	−.05	.04	.00	−.03	.10	−.02	.06	.04
51. Father weak, dominated by mother																		
M	−.03	.01	−.06	−.06	.00	.00	−.02	−.03	−.01	.06	.04	−.13	−.02	.01	−.02	.02	−.06	.06
F	−.07	−.05	−.16	−.14	−.11	−.01	−.03	−.01	−.07	.04	.01	−.09	−.03	−.02	−.02	.02	−.02	−.03
52. Father absent from home much of the time																		
M	.00	.01	−.08	−.03	.02	−.03	.04	.00	−.08	−.04	−.06	−.02	−.05	−.04	.02	.02	−.02	.00
F	−.01	.08	−.01	.01	.03	.02	.03	.04	−.08	−.03	−.05	.04	.04	.09	−.02	.08	.08	.07
53. Father a successful man from his own viewpoint (as well as from others)																		
M	.04	.18	.13	.08	.11	−.01	.11	.05	.09	−.03	−.01	.03	−.01	.08	.07	.04	.11	.06
F	.08	.19	.16	.12	.08	.06	.17	.18	.22	.09	.08	.00	.08	.14	.15	.14	.14	.12
54. Mother nervous, dissatisfied with her life																		
M	−.01	.03	−.04	.02	−.01	−.01	.04	.00	−.12	−.06	−.07	−.06	−.12	−.02	−.04	.03	−.02	.02
F	−.01	.02	−.08	−.07	−.01	−.01	−.04	−.04	−.24	−.13	−.09	−.09	−.18	−.09	−.11	−.01	−.05	−.04
55. Mother affectionate and loving in disposition																		
M	−.03	.00	−.02	.00	−.04	.00	.01	.04	.13	.06	.03	−.01	.05	.08	.01	.03	.04	.01
F	.12	.13	.17	.12	.14	.09	.10	.10	.24	.10	.13	.10	.16	.13	.24	.05	.11	.05
56. Considerable parental friction and discord																		
M	−.09	−.03	−.10	−.10	−.08	−.08	−.05	−.03	−.15	.02	−.05	−.05	−.11	−.01	−.06	.02	−.10	−.03
F	−.01	.13	−.06	.01	.07	.08	.03	−.09	−.26	−.10	−.05	−.13	−.09	−.04	−.11	.08	.01	.03
57. Parents were churchgoers																		
M	.03	.01	.03	−.04	.00	−.03	−.10	.07	.05	.11	.12	.02	.11	.00	.07	−.06	−.01	−.03
F	−.05	−.07	−.12	−.15	−.11	−.08	−.12	.06	.07	.05	−.01	.08	−.02	−.04	.03	−.07	−.03	−.01
58. Social and economic status of the family was marginal																		
M	−.04	−.13	−.14	−.16	−.10	−.06	−.10	.04	−.05	.08	.08	−.04	−.03	−.03	−.03	−.06	−.10	−.06
F	−.01	−.05	−.06	−.04	.01	−.05	−.09	.04	−.23	−.10	−.06	−.02	−.10	−.06	−.07	−.01	−.04	.00
59. Great emphasis in the family on achievement in school and elsewhere																		
M	.05	.04	.04	−.02	.06	−.02	.00	.11	.04	.00	−.03	.03	−.01	.03	.10	.04	.08	.06
F	.10	.12	.05	.06	.09	.01	.08	.05	.06	−.03	−.03	.06	.02	.01	.09	.10	.11	.09

Correlations of CPI Scales with Items in the Interviewer's Check List continued

Measures	Fx	F/M	v.1	v.2	v.3	Mp	Wo	CT	Lp	Ami	Leo	Tm	B–MS	B–FM	Anx	Nar	D–SD	D–AC
Reaction to the Interview continued																		
45. Seemed to enjoy being interviewed																		
M	.07	−.02	−.15	−.03	.02	.04	.00	.08	.09	−.02	.04	.05	.10	−.04	−.02	.10	.02	.04
F	.00	.06	−.18	.06	.05	.08	.02	.05	.11	.01	.05	.03	.10	−.03	−.01	.06	.07	.07
46. Poised and overtly cooperative, but nevertheless evasive																		
M	−.11	−.05	.06	.13	−.06	−.01	.04	−.17	.01	.08	.05	.00	−.04	.02	−.04	.00	.01	.02
F	−.05	−.01	.13	−.03	−.10	−.12	−.03	−.07	−.14	−.06	−.04	−.10	−.13	−.05	.07	−.03	−.10	−.02
47. Asked questions of the interviewer																		
M	−.06	−.02	−.06	.02	−.03	−.03	−.05	−.01	.04	−.04	.03	.04	.05	−.06	.00	.06	.02	.04
F	.04	.00	−.06	.02	.15	.13	.06	.08	.05	.01	−.01	.08	.02	.04	.07	.05	.07	−.02
48. Was nervous and ill at ease during the interview																		
M	−.01	.07	.18	.04	−.03	−.09	.00	−.09	−.11	.04	−.02	−.08	−.14	.08	.05	−.14	−.03	−.04
F	.01	.07	.13	.03	−.04	−.06	−.05	−.03	−.11	.03	.00	−.13	−.15	.08	−.01	−.08	−.03	.01
Family Background																		
49. Father stern and authoritarian																		
M	−.15	−.03	.11	.03	−.13	−.06	−.02	−.21	−.05	−.06	.10	−.03	−.07	−.04	−.01	−.07	.02	−.01
F	−.12	.06	.10	−.03	−.04	−.08	−.07	−.11	−.13	−.05	.00	−.04	−.10	.04	.04	−.07	−.02	−.04
50. Father benevolent and tolerant																		
M	.06	−.10	−.13	.06	.12	.10	.08	.10	.14	.09	.09	.11	.15	.02	−.11	.07	.04	−.01
F	.03	−.08	−.08	.19	−.02	.01	.00	−.01	.08	.07	−.02	−.03	.05	−.03	.02	.10	.04	.16
51. Father weak, dominated by mother																		
M	.08	.00	.04	−.05	.01	−.01	−.01	.02	−.04	−.01	−.02	.00	−.01	.03	.02	−.03	−.01	−.02
F	.01	.04	.09	−.09	−.01	−.01	−.01	−.02	−.08	−.04	−.03	−.04	−.09	.01	.08	−.08	−.12	−.10
52. Father absent from home much of the time																		
M	−.03	.07	.01	−.06	−.04	−.07	−.09	.02	−.05	−.12	−.04	−.06	−.07	−.03	.02	.03	−.01	.03
F	.10	−.09	.03	−.12	.07	.07	−.02	.10	.01	−.04	−.02	.00	.02	−.06	−.07	−.03	−.06	−.06
53. Father a successful man from his own viewpoint (as well as from others)																		
M	.08	.00	−.07	.09	.10	.07	−.01	.04	.05	.05	−.03	−.05	.01	.00	.05	.05	.01	.01
F	.09	.03	−.05	.10	.18	.12	.12	.12	.11	.14	−.01	.09	.05	.14	.02	.00	.16	−.01
54. Mother nervous, dissatisfied with her life																		
M	.01	.11	−.03	−.08	.00	−.04	−.10	.02	−.06	−.15	−.11	−.07	−.08	−.03	.08	.05	−.03	.01
F	.03	−.02	.00	−.14	−.01	−.01	−.13	.06	−.11	−.20	−.09	−.06	−.06	−.16	.11	.04	−.13	−.01
55. Mother affectionate and loving in disposition																		
M	−.01	−.02	.06	.06	.04	−.01	.08	.00	.03	.13	.07	−.01	−.02	.04	−.08	−.03	.02	−.03
F	−.04	.04	−.10	.18	.09	.13	.10	−.01	.21	.17	.13	.15	.16	.18	−.15	.00	.23	−.05
56. Considerable parental friction and discord																		
M	.00	.15	.07	−.10	−.02	−.07	−.08	.01	−.12	−.14	−.08	−.10	−.16	−.03	.07	−.05	−.07	−.01
F	.06	−.07	−.02	−.23	.04	−.02	−.09	.16	−.06	−.19	−.09	−.03	.03	−.16	.06	.02	−.12	−.08
57. Parents were churchgoers																		
M	−.15	−.11	.01	.17	−.04	.04	.10	−.16	.06	.10	.15	.06	.07	.06	−.10	−.07	.06	−.05
F	−.03	.05	.08	.05	−.07	−.05	−.02	−.12	−.08	−.01	.06	−.02	−.09	.07	.08	−.03	−.04	.07
58. Social and economic status of the family was marginal																		
M	−.11	.04	.06	−.03	−.05	−.05	−.01	−.08	−.05	−.03	.02	.02	−.04	.02	−.01	−.09	.05	−.04
F	.00	.00	.00	−.08	−.04	−.01	−.06	−.02	−.07	−.16	−.03	−.04	−.04	−.17	.05	.00	−.12	.00
59. Great emphasis in the family on achievement in school and elsewhere																		
M	−.04	.04	−.03	.13	.00	.04	.01	−.02	.05	−.01	.02	.04	−.01	.00	.00	.01	.03	.09
F	.01	−.03	−.06	.07	.05	.06	.04	.05	.07	−.04	−.07	.07	.04	−.06	.04	.08	.03	.07

Correlations of CPI Scales with Items in the Interviewer's Check List continued

Item	Do	Cs	Sy	Sp	Sa	In	Em	Re	So	Sc	Gi	Cm	Wb	To	Ac	Ai	Ie	Py
Family Background continued																		
60. Family life on the whole was quite happy																		
M	.13	.06	.09	.07	.09	.11	.07	.10	.26	.06	.08	.10	.15	.12	.15	.06	.15	.05
F	.10	.06	.17	.10	.07	.04	.06	.15	.40	.12	.10	.19	.17	.05	.26	.00	.07	.07
61. Interviewee was ashamed of one or both parents																		
M	−.10	−.09	−.13	−.07	−.08	−.06	−.06	−.03	−.21	−.04	−.02	.00	−.05	−.06	−.10	.03	−.04	−.01
F	−.10	.01	−.09	−.04	−.01	−.07	−.02	−.12	−.27	−.12	−.06	−.09	−.17	.01	−.14	.02	−.02	−.01
62. Father drank to excess, was an alcoholic																		
M	−.02	−.08	−.07	−.04	−.04	.00	−.03	−.12	−.09	.02	.00	−.08	−.01	−.06	−.07	−.05	−.08	−.10
F	−.02	.00	.00	.05	−.02	−.04	.00	−.10	−.20	−.11	−.06	−.04	−.06	−.04	−.10	.00	.00	−.02
63. Mother drank to excess, was an alcoholic																		
M	−.02	−.07	−.03	−.01	−.01	.01	−.01	−.10	−.05	.01	−.06	−.01	−.04	−.05	−.04	−.04	−.05	−.07
F	−.01	−.02	−.02	.01	.05	−.02	−.02	−.07	−.20	−.10	−.02	−.04	−.08	−.07	−.08	−.05	−.04	−.06
64. Family carried out activities together, e.g., picnics, outings, trips, etc.																		
M	.04	−.02	.07	−.02	.05	−.04	−.02	.04	.12	.04	.02	.06	.06	.01	.04	−.06	.03	.01
F	.07	−.08	.03	−.03	.01	.07	−.01	.09	.24	.06	.03	.06	.07	.01	.10	−.02	.02	.01
65. Interviewee was proud of mother's appearance																		
M	−.03	−.02	−.05	−.07	.00	.05	.00	.05	.08	.06	.03	.05	.06	.07	.02	−.02	.03	.02
F	.03	.16	.13	.11	.12	.03	.11	.05	−.06	−.10	−.03	.02	.00	.05	.07	.04	.03	.00
66. Interviewee was proud of father's job																		
M	.06	.14	.13	.08	.15	−.02	.12	.01	.06	−.09	−.06	−.02	−.04	.00	.01	−.03	.04	−.01
F	.11	.16	.18	.14	.12	.06	.15	.11	.21	.02	.05	.02	.06	.04	.11	.03	.08	.03
67. Family maintained definite traditions, e.g., certain foods at holidays, trips at certain times, family sayings, events, etc.																		
M	.02	.04	.05	.03	.00	.01	.00	.06	.11	.02	.04	.09	.04	.02	.07	−.02	.04	.05
F	.03	−.02	.03	−.01	−.03	.02	.01	.11	.19	.09	.02	.03	.07	.05	.08	−.02	.03	−.03
68. Subject can remember learning certain songs, stories, etc., from mother																		
M	.06	−.02	.01	.00	.02	.03	.00	.07	.10	.05	.04	.10	.09	.06	.09	.01	.08	.03
F	.10	.14	.14	.14	.08	.05	.12	.12	.10	−.08	−.01	.01	.05	.02	.09	.08	.10	.03
69. Went on outings (fishing, hunting, camping, etc.) with father																		
M	.08	.02	.07	.02	.07	.00	.01	.04	.08	−.02	.00	.08	.05	−.01	.05	−.07	.04	.00
F	−.03	−.08	.00	−.03	−.01	−.04	−.05	.09	.18	.07	−.01	.04	.03	.06	.02	.01	.03	.01
70. Cooked, sewed, etc. with mother																		
M	.05	−.03	−.02	−.07	−.01	.00	.01	.02	.03	.05	.04	.01	.00	−.02	.05	−.06	.03	−.07
F	.04	−.01	.08	−.03	.03	−.05	−.03	.16	.21	.14	.12	.11	.09	.03	.19	−.01	.02	−.03
71. Liked to have friends come home to play																		
M	−.01	.08	.00	.10	.05	.00	.07	.01	.09	.00	.01	−.01	.07	.07	.02	.03	.07	.05
F	.09	.12	.09	.08	.13	.04	.14	.08	.20	−.05	−.01	.08	.03	.05	.14	.08	.09	.04
72. Had certain home chores or duties to carry out																		
M	−.03	−.09	.01	−.05	−.01	−.11	−.05	−.07	−.04	−.07	−.04	.02	−.07	−.08	−.07	−.13	−.08	−.11
F	.03	.02	.05	.05	.03	.01	.00	.06	.00	.02	.05	.12	−.01	−.01	.08	.01	.02	.00
73. Standards of courteous and polite behavior were emphasized in the home																		
M	−.01	.04	.00	−.03	−.03	−.04	−.04	.13	.17	.09	.12	.06	.06	.01	.13	−.07	−.03	.01
F	.01	.04	.06	.03	.00	.01	.02	.12	.21	.13	.14	.02	.12	.06	.15	.04	.05	.01

Correlations of CPI Scales with Items in the Interviewer's Check List continued

Measures	Fx	F/M	v.1	v.2	v.3	Mp	Wo	CT	Lp	Ami	Leo	Tm	B–MS	B–FM	Anx	Nar	D–SD	D–AC

Family Background continued

60. Family life on the whole was quite happy

M	.05	−.07	−.05	.16	.11	.12	.15	.04	.16	.22	.15	.09	.13	.08	−.12	−.02	.10	.03
F	−.09	.02	−.05	.29	.01	.05	.14	−.13	.20	.25	.16	.09	.09	.19	−.12	.03	.19	.07

61. Interviewee was ashamed of one or both parents

M	.00	.04	.08	−.14	−.04	−.07	−.04	−.01	−.08	−.11	−.02	−.04	−.07	.00	.08	−.06	−.08	−.07
F	.07	.03	.02	−.18	.03	−.04	−.10	.08	−.15	−.15	−.15	−.12	−.12	−.12	.11	−.01	−.18	−.07

62. Father drank to excess, was an alcoholic

M	−.08	−.03	.02	−.07	−.04	−.02	−.01	−.01	−.04	−.07	.05	.02	.01	−.03	−.07	−.03	−.02	−.04
F	.04	.03	−.03	−.16	.00	−.05	−.05	.08	−.06	−.12	−.08	−.07	−.02	−.02	.03	.00	−.08	−.02

63. Mother drank to excess, was an alcoholic

M	−.07	−.07	.01	−.04	−.07	−.02	−.03	.00	−.03	−.05	−.03	.00	−.01	−.06	.01	.06	−.02	.03
F	−.05	−.01	−.03	−.11	−.01	−.04	−.08	.04	−.01	−.16	−.01	−.04	−.03	−.09	−.02	.04	−.07	.01

64. Family carried out activities together, e.g., picnics, outings, trips, etc.

M	−.03	−.07	.02	.11	−.03	.01	.05	−.07	.05	.11	.11	.02	.06	.05	−.08	−.01	.02	.02
F	−.03	.01	−.03	.18	−.03	.02	.07	−.06	.07	.13	.10	.06	.02	.12	−.05	.05	.07	.00

65. Interviewee was proud of mother's appearance

M	.03	.06	.08	.01	.04	.05	.06	.03	.04	.11	.02	.00	.01	.06	−.03	−.09	−.04	−.09
F	.09	−.05	−.07	−.01	.07	.02	−.01	.10	.02	−.01	−.02	−.03	.06	−.04	.03	.07	.03	.03

66. Interviewee was proud of father's job.

M	.06	.01	−.14	.03	.01	.00	−.08	.04	.03	−.02	.00	−.08	.04	−.06	.05	.09	−.01	.08
F	.03	.02	−.12	.15	.07	.09	.06	.08	.11	.09	.05	.04	.07	.04	−.02	.07	.13	.04

67. Family maintained definite traditions, e.g., certain foods at holidays, trips at certain times, family sayings, events, etc.

M	.03	−.04	.01	.10	.02	.02	.04	−.03	.06	.10	.05	.03	.04	.04	−.03	−.05	.02	.05
F	−.05	.00	.03	.13	−.01	.04	.08	−.06	.05	.14	.05	.02	.01	.08	−.03	−.03	.07	.09

68. Subject can remember learning certain songs, stories, etc., from mother

M	−.01	−.05	.00	.10	.01	.04	.08	−.03	.07	.07	.08	.06	.06	.04	−.07	−.03	.03	.00
F	.06	−.01	−.10	.06	.04	.06	.02	.08	.08	.02	.07	−.02	.08	.04	.04	.05	.06	.02

69. Went on outings (fishing, hunting, camping, etc.) with father

M	−.05	−.11	−.05	.11	−.04	.03	.01	−.11	.08	.03	.09	.02	.09	−.05	−.04	.05	.06	.08
F	−.03	−.04	.09	.11	.03	.01	.05	−.09	.01	.10	.04	−.01	−.01	.07	−.03	−.03	.04	.08

70. Cooked, sewed, etc. with mother

M	−.09	−.01	−.04	.06	−.03	.00	−.02	−.10	.02	.00	.09	.01	−.02	.02	.03	.02	.07	.07
F	−.14	.05	.00	.22	−.01	.07	.08	−.16	.10	.14	.22	.06	.03	.18	−.03	−.06	.16	−.01

71. Liked to have friends come home to play

M	.07	−.03	−.02	.00	.06	.03	.07	.09	.04	.09	−.01	−.01	.05	−.03	−.04	−.01	.00	−.01
F	.01	.02	−.11	.11	.05	.08	.00	.03	.12	.04	.09	.04	.04	.05	−.01	−.09	.07	.00

72. Had certain home chores or duties to carry out

M	−.10	−.01	.04	−.01	−.10	−.11	−.10	−.14	−.05	−.08	.09	−.07	−.04	−.03	.05	.01	−.03	.10
F	−.03	−.03	.00	.08	.02	−.03	−.01	.02	.03	.02	.08	.00	.01	−.03	−.06	−.07	.02	−.01

73. Standards of courteous and polite behavior were emphasized in the home

M	−.07	−.02	.06	.22	.02	.01	.06	−.08	.05	.12	.10	.03	.00	.10	.00	−.11	.06	.02
F	−.04	.01	.02	.13	.06	.07	.14	−.06	.10	.18	.11	.07	.05	.11	−.06	−.10	.07	−.01

Item	Do	Cs	Sy	Sp	Sa	In	Em	Re	So	Sc	Gi	Cm	Wb	To	Ac	Ai	Ie	Py

Correlations of CPI Scales with Items in the Interviewer's Check List continued

Adolescence

74. Interviewee had a great deal of friction with parents

	Do	Cs	Sy	Sp	Sa	In	Em	Re	So	Sc	Gi	Cm	Wb	To	Ac	Ai	Ie	Py
M	−.02	−.01	−.05	−.01	.01	.00	−.03	−.08	−.27	−.07	−.05	−.04	−.06	−.07	−.11	−.01	−.08	.02
F	−.03	.00	−.10	.00	.01	.02	−.01	−.19	−.41	−.17	−.13	−.02	−.15	−.10	−.26	−.04	−.03	−.06

75. Unhappy in school and at home

	Do	Cs	Sy	Sp	Sa	In	Em	Re	So	Sc	Gi	Cm	Wb	To	Ac	Ai	Ie	Py
M	−.10	−.13	−.16	−.11	−.14	−.08	−.13	−.13	−.27	−.10	−.14	−.11	−.16	−.07	−.20	−.06	−.11	−.09
F	−.05	.04	−.06	−.03	.00	.00	.07	−.08	−.26	−.10	−.02	−.16	−.11	−.02	−.17	.05	−.01	−.02

76. Dated very little or not at all

	Do	Cs	Sy	Sp	Sa	In	Em	Re	So	Sc	Gi	Cm	Wb	To	Ac	Ai	Ie	Py
M	−.20	−.12	−.23	−.20	−.25	−.14	−.14	.09	.01	.06	.01	−.09	−.17	.01	−.07	.00	−.08	.00
F	.04	.05	−.02	−.01	−.03	.07	.07	.18	.04	.11	.11	−.10	.03	.13	.11	.16	.08	.14

77. Maintained an unusual tempo of social life, constant series of dates, parties, etc.

	Do	Cs	Sy	Sp	Sa	In	Em	Re	So	Sc	Gi	Cm	Wb	To	Ac	Ai	Ie	Py
M	.11	.06	.17	.13	.15	.05	.03	−.11	−.04	−.10	−.09	.05	.03	−.10	.01	−.06	.01	−.03
F	.05	.02	.05	.03	.10	−.03	.02	−.12	−.10	−.11	−.04	.08	−.07	−.08	−.01	−.06	.00	−.06

78. Had first sexual intercourse while in high school or before

	Do	Cs	Sy	Sp	Sa	In	Em	Re	So	Sc	Gi	Cm	Wb	To	Ac	Ai	Ie	Py
M	.02	−.11	−.01	.01	.09	−.04	−.06	−.30	−.28	−.22	−.19	−.02	−.07	−.26	−.20	−.23	−.17	−.21
F	−.15	−.20	−.12	−.08	−.13	−.09	−.16	−.17	−.20	−.10	−.13	.10	−.07	−.15	−.17	−.24	−.21	−.16

79. Had serious conflicts and worries about sexual matters in adolescence

	Do	Cs	Sy	Sp	Sa	In	Em	Re	So	Sc	Gi	Cm	Wb	To	Ac	Ai	Ie	Py
M	−.12	−.02	−.11	−.13	−.11	−.10	−.04	.06	−.06	.04	−.03	−.02	−.09	.05	−.09	.05	−.07	.04
F	−.10	−.12	−.11	−.14	−.12	−.18	−.14	−.05	−.15	−.07	−.08	−.06	−.21	−.12	−.10	−.14	−.17	−.16

80. Was an honor student in high school

	Do	Cs	Sy	Sp	Sa	In	Em	Re	So	Sc	Gi	Cm	Wb	To	Ac	Ai	Ie	Py
M	.06	.19	.07	.07	.09	.05	.13	.24	.12	.03	.06	.00	.01	.13	.21	.20	.17	.10
F	.15	.29	.19	.21	.20	.15	.31	.15	.16	.01	.10	−.02	.09	.17	.20	.32	.26	.19

81. Led a borderline, delinquent-like existence in high school

	Do	Cs	Sy	Sp	Sa	In	Em	Re	So	Sc	Gi	Cm	Wb	To	Ac	Ai	Ie	Py
M	−.03	−.08	−.06	−.02	−.02	−.03	−.05	−.21	−.24	−.18	−.11	−.05	−.05	−.11	−.22	−.07	−.09	−.06
F	−.03	−.04	−.07	−.01	−.01	.04	.01	−.16	−.16	−.05	−.04	−.03	.00	−.05	−.15	−.04	.00	−.04

82. Considers self to have been an underachiever in high school

	Do	Cs	Sy	Sp	Sa	In	Em	Re	So	Sc	Gi	Cm	Wb	To	Ac	Ai	Ie	Py
M	−.15	−.14	−.18	−.09	−.11	−.10	−.09	−.22	−.23	−.12	−.13	−.04	−.12	−.15	−.23	−.18	−.20	−.13
F	−.11	−.07	−.10	−.06	−.06	−.07	−.06	−.14	−.14	−.08	−.08	−.02	−.10	−.07	−.17	−.10	−.10	−.12

Current

83. Is generally dissatisfied with life

	Do	Cs	Sy	Sp	Sa	In	Em	Re	So	Sc	Gi	Cm	Wb	To	Ac	Ai	Ie	Py
M	−.13	−.13	−.08	−.10	−.08	−.10	−.04	−.02	−.15	−.09	−.09	−.16	−.21	−.10	−.14	−.08	−.17	−.10
F	−.12	−.09	−.14	−.12	−.09	−.11	−.09	−.07	−.10	−.04	−.06	−.09	−.14	−.08	−.12	−.02	−.07	−.07

84. Has many worries and problems

	Do	Cs	Sy	Sp	Sa	In	Em	Re	So	Sc	Gi	Cm	Wb	To	Ac	Ai	Ie	Py
M	−.18	−.14	−.17	−.20	−.21	−.14	−.11	.01	−.10	−.01	−.03	−.13	−.21	−.10	−.14	−.08	−.20	−.07
F	−.20	−.17	−.23	−.26	−.22	−.19	−.17	−.01	−.18	.03	−.02	−.10	−.17	−.02	−.15	−.06	−.14	−.10

85. Drinking is a problem

	Do	Cs	Sy	Sp	Sa	In	Em	Re	So	Sc	Gi	Cm	Wb	To	Ac	Ai	Ie	Py
M	−.08	−.15	−.06	−.08	−.05	−.12	−.12	−.15	−.15	−.11	−.07	−.02	−.12	−.17	−.11	−.18	−.14	−.09
F	.03	.01	.06	.04	.06	.03	.07	.04	−.03	.00	.00	−.01	.01	.00	−.01	.08	.04	.04

86. Has been fired from a job or asked to resign

	Do	Cs	Sy	Sp	Sa	In	Em	Re	So	Sc	Gi	Cm	Wb	To	Ac	Ai	Ie	Py
M	.04	.01	.05	.03	.03	.00	.01	−.03	−.05	−.05	−.05	.02	.03	.02	.02	.00	.03	.08
F	−.02	.09	.00	.02	.05	.05	.08	.04	.00	.06	.03	−.08	.05	.10	.00	.12	.08	.12

87. Has been convicted of one or more felonies

	Do	Cs	Sy	Sp	Sa	In	Em	Re	So	Sc	Gi	Cm	Wb	To	Ac	Ai	Ie	Py
M	−.06	−.08	−.06	−.01	−.02	−.05	−.06	−.19	−.22	−.16	−.11	−.03	−.11	−.14	−.18	−.10	−.08	−.13
F*	.....	.....	.....	.....	.....	.....	.....	.....	.....	.....	.....	.....	.....	.....	.....	.....	.....	.....

88. Unusually self-confident, feels able to meet nearly any situation

	Do	Cs	Sy	Sp	Sa	In	Em	Re	So	Sc	Gi	Cm	Wb	To	Ac	Ai	Ie	Py
M	.27	.20	.19	.23	.28	.29	.19	.04	.02	−.06	.03	.11	.15	.11	.15	.12	.21	.13
F	.24	.18	.21	.17	.29	.18	.22	.03	.00	−.09	.01	.07	.08	−.03	.14	.11	.16	.17

*There were no convictions for felonies among these 379 women.

Correlations of CPI Scales with Items in the Interviewer's Check List continued

Measures	Fx	F/M	v.1	v.2	v.3	Mp	Wo	CT	Lp	Ami	Leo	Tm	B–MS	B–FM	Anx	Nar	D–SD	D–AC
Adolescence																		
74. Interviewee had a great deal of friction with parents																		
M	−.06	−.02	.01	−.12	−.03	−.01	−.05	−.01	−.04	−.15	−.06	.01	.00	−.13	.02	.03	−.03	−.11
F	.08	−.06	−.01	−.27	−.06	−.11	−.15	.11	−.13	−.27	−.14	−.11	−.03	−.27	.10	.07	−.14	.04
75. Unhappy in school and at home																		
M	−.03	.00	.08	−.20	−.12	−.13	−.12	.00	−.18	−.20	−.08	−.07	−.14	−.13	.14	.03	−.18	−.05
F	.10	−.02	.00	−.17	.06	−.03	−.12	.14	−.14	−.13	−.18	−.10	−.03	−.15	.08	.04	−.10	−.03
76. Dated very little or not at all																		
M	.10	.18	.20	−.02	−.02	−.12	−.08	−.03	−.22	−.04	−.14	−.14	−.27	.11	.20	−.16	−.16	−.04
F	.06	.01	.01	.07	.13	.11	.09	.06	.04	.08	−.05	.09	.03	.08	.02	−.12	.07	−.12
77. Maintained an unusual tempo of social life, constant series of dates, parties, etc.																		
M	−.10	−.12	−.15	.01	−.08	.02	−.02	−.05	.09	−.07	.12	.06	.14	−.11	−.15	.13	.03	.11
F	−.08	.09	−.07	.02	−.08	−.03	−.11	.02	.00	−.12	.04	−.03	−.02	−.04	−.02	.10	.05	.11
78. Had first sexual intercourse while in high school or before																		
M	−.16	−.10	−.08	−.15	−.27	−.16	−.15	−.05	−.07	−.24	.01	−.03	.01	−.27	−.01	.23	−.06	.10
F	−.09	.03	.11	−.12	−.21	−.19	−.13	−.10	−.18	−.11	−.02	.13	−.12	−.04	−.09	.02	−.15	.07
79. Had serious conflicts and worries about sexual matters in adolescence																		
M	.08	.13	.12	−.07	.01	−.06	−.02	−.02	−.12	−.02	−.07	−.08	−.15	.06	.08	−.11	−.08	−.05
F	−.08	.13	.05	−.05	−.15	−.12	−.12	−.10	−.18	−.13	−.02	−.14	−.19	−.01	.14	−.04	−.10	.05
80. Was an honor student in high school																		
M	.06	.06	−.06	.15	.14	.09	.06	.11	.09	.06	−.06	.05	−.01	.12	.04	−.04	.04	.05
F	.18	−.22	−.16	.08	.29	.21	.15	.24	.17	.05	−.09	.15	.18	−.07	.06	.09	.15	−.04
81. Led a borderline, delinquent-like existence in high school																		
M	.03	−.10	−.02	−.16	−.12	−.11	−.09	.00	−.10	−.15	.02	−.04	.00	−.25	−.03	.08	−.13	−.05
F	−.02	−.04	.02	−.08	−.01	−.03	−.03	.04	−.06	−.06	−.01	−.04	−.01	−.14	−.07	.05	−.06	.03
82. Considers self to have been an underachiever in high school																		
M	.04	.00	.08	−.21	−.15	−.16	−.14	−.01	−.18	−.15	−.09	−.16	−.09	−.17	.06	.04	−.16	−.01
F	−.02	−.02	.05	−.11	−.09	−.14	−.13	−.04	−.12	−.05	−.07	−.17	−.11	−.14	.06	.06	−.12	.05
Current																		
83. Is generally dissatisfied with life																		
M	.00	.10	.04	−.04	−.13	−.13	−.20	.00	−.18	−.17	−.11	−.14	−.17	−.05	.18	.01	−.09	.00
F	.07	.05	.10	−.09	−.03	−.11	−.08	.00	−.19	−.06	−.07	−.08	−.12	−.05	.10	−.04	−.10	−.02
84. Has many worries and problems																		
M	−.03	.15	.14	−.07	−.08	−.14	−.14	−.08	−.22	−.15	−.13	−.14	−.21	−.02	.15	−.04	−.13	−.04
F	−.03	.15	.19	−.10	−.05	−.10	−.09	−.05	−.24	−.05	−.09	−.14	−.21	−.01	.12	−.16	−.10	−.16
85. Drinking is a problem																		
M	−.12	.00	.03	−.05	−.19	−.16	−.11	−.09	−.17	−.16	−.03	−.08	−.07	−.12	.09	.03	−.07	.06
F	.02	.04	−.03	−.01	.02	.04	−.08	.06	−.03	.00	−.03	.01	.03	−.05	.04	.05	.02	−.01
86. Has been fired from a job or asked to resign																		
M	.00	−.07	−.06	−.02	.03	.04	.00	.04	.04	.01	.00	.03	.07	−.04	−.03	.01	−.03	−.07
F	.11	−.09	.06	−.12	.14	.07	.12	.08	.04	.05	−.05	.06	.08	.01	−.01	−.05	.00	−.09
87. Has been convicted of one or more felonies																		
M	−.02	−.05	.01	−.14	−.16	−.13	−.17	−.03	−.12	−.16	−.05	−.08	−.04	−.18	−.01	.07	−.07	.01
F*	.....	.....	.....	.....	.....	.....	.....	.....	.....	.....	.....	.....	.....	.....	.....	.....	.....	.....
88. Unusually self-confident, feels able to meet nearly any situation																		
M	.05	−.16	−.27	.07	.11	.21	.08	.16	.25	.02	.10	.19	.26	−.09	−.13	.16	.14	.00
F	−.01	−.13	−.25	.06	.06	.09	.01	.13	.21	−.05	.07	.10	.20	−.11	−.04	.19	.13	.07

*There were no convictions for felonies among these 379 women.

Item	Do	Cs	Sy	Sp	Sa	In	Em	Re	So	Sc	Gi	Cm	Wb	To	Ac	Ai	Ie	Py
Correlations of CPI Scales with Items in the Interviewer's Check List continued																		

Current continued

89. Is unsure of self, doubts own ability

	Do	Cs	Sy	Sp	Sa	In	Em	Re	So	Sc	Gi	Cm	Wb	To	Ac	Ai	Ie	Py
M	−.22	−.16	−.14	−.17	−.21	−.19	−.10	.02	−.10	.00	−.02	−.13	−.19	−.05	−.15	−.12	−.21	−.10
F	−.24	−.19	−.17	−.22	−.26	−.30	−.16	−.10	−.10	−.04	−.08	−.12	−.21	−.01	−.27	−.16	−.18	−.18

90. Holds unrealistic standards for self and others

	Do	Cs	Sy	Sp	Sa	In	Em	Re	So	Sc	Gi	Cm	Wb	To	Ac	Ai	Ie	Py
M	.02	−.06	−.01	−.02	.04	.00	−.03	−.08	−.06	−.09	−.09	−.05	−.08	−.11	−.05	−.09	−.11	−.07
F	.00	−.03	−.10	−.12	.00	−.06	−.04	−.07	−.07	−.03	.02	−.04	−.14	−.10	−.05	−.10	−.11	−.08

91. Arrogant and overbearing, fails to see own deficiencies and limitations

	Do	Cs	Sy	Sp	Sa	In	Em	Re	So	Sc	Gi	Cm	Wb	To	Ac	Ai	Ie	Py
M	.08	−.01	.06	.06	.04	.06	.01	−.05	−.05	−.12	−.12	−.04	−.05	−.11	−.04	−.08	−.03	−.05
F	.07	.02	.02	.08	.10	.09	.04	−.07	.02	−.05	−.04	.05	.03	−.05	.00	.06	.04	.04

92. Seems to be preoccupied with sexual matters

	Do	Cs	Sy	Sp	Sa	In	Em	Re	So	Sc	Gi	Cm	Wb	To	Ac	Ai	Ie	Py
M	−.03	−.05	−.05	−.08	−.03	−.06	−.06	−.03	−.10	−.08	−.09	−.10	−.12	−.09	−.16	−.10	−.10	−.08
F	−.06	−.06	−.05	−.07	−.06	−.07	−.04	−.20	−.07	−.10	−.12	−.01	−.18	−.12	−.14	−.11	−.12	−.12

93. Has strong religious beliefs

	Do	Cs	Sy	Sp	Sa	In	Em	Re	So	Sc	Gi	Cm	Wb	To	Ac	Ai	Ie	Py
M	.03	−.09	.01	−.17	−.07	−.06	−.06	.16	.12	.15	.19	.11	.09	.04	.12	−.08	−.02	−.06
F	−.08	−.15	−.14	−.27	−.12	−.12	−.18	.10	.11	.14	.08	.08	−.02	−.06	.10	−.22	−.13	−.15

94. Is realistic in thinking and social behavior

	Do	Cs	Sy	Sp	Sa	In	Em	Re	So	Sc	Gi	Cm	Wb	To	Ac	Ai	Ie	Py
M	.10	.09	.06	.10	.10	.09	.07	.05	.05	.04	.04	.10	.11	.07	.07	.06	.10	.05
F	.12	.14	.12	.10	.09	.09	.10	.19	.12	.10	.12	.12	.16	.19	.21	.14	.15	.10

95. Is happily married

	Do	Cs	Sy	Sp	Sa	In	Em	Re	So	Sc	Gi	Cm	Wb	To	Ac	Ai	Ie	Py
M	.13	.04	.02	−.01	.08	.15	−.05	.10	.10	.19	.11	.14	.29	.11	.16	.08	.15	.14
F	−.05	−.15	−.11	−.11	−.14	−.10	−.20	.17	.12	.19	.10	.13	.10	.09	.04	−.12	−.07	−.04

96. Has a stable, optimistic view of the future

	Do	Cs	Sy	Sp	Sa	In	Em	Re	So	Sc	Gi	Cm	Wb	To	Ac	Ai	Ie	Py
M	.16	.14	.11	.08	.16	.12	.06	.17	.17	.10	.14	.14	.21	.10	.15	.04	.16	.04
F	.19	.16	.20	.16	.17	.13	.11	.23	.28	.18	.22	.19	.26	.14	.31	.12	.16	.17

97. Creates a good impression; has effective interpersonal techniques

	Do	Cs	Sy	Sp	Sa	In	Em	Re	So	Sc	Gi	Cm	Wb	To	Ac	Ai	Ie	Py
M	.23	.19	.18	.15	.22	.18	.18	.08	.08	−.01	.03	.12	.16	.08	.14	.10	.19	.07
F	.20	.28	.24	.18	.21	.08	.20	.18	.06	−.02	.10	.09	.05	.14	.22	.11	.16	.04

98. Seems relatively free of neurotic trends, conflicts, and other forms of instability

	Do	Cs	Sy	Sp	Sa	In	Em	Re	So	Sc	Gi	Cm	Wb	To	Ac	Ai	Ie	Py
M	.11	.12	.14	.14	.13	.10	.10	.14	.14	.10	.11	.12	.18	.10	.12	.07	.16	.04
F	.21	.19	.22	.23	.16	.13	.16	.19	.20	.04	.13	.24	.18	.15	.25	.13	.19	.10

99. Enjoys children

	Do	Cs	Sy	Sp	Sa	In	Em	Re	So	Sc	Gi	Cm	Wb	To	Ac	Ai	Ie	Py
M	.03	−.12	.04	−.08	.00	−.06	−.06	−.04	−.04	−.02	−.02	.05	.00	−.18	−.10	−.18	−.11	−.20
F	−.11	−.18	−.11	−.19	−.20	−.17	−.23	.13	.05	.19	.10	.12	.03	.07	.06	−.18	−.08	−.06

Correlations of CPI Scales with Items in the Interviewer's Check List continued

Measures	Fx	F/M	v.1	v.2	v.3	Mp	Wo	CT	Lp	Ami	Leo	Tm	B–MS	B–FM	Anx	Nar	D–SD	D–AC
Current continued																		
89. Is unsure of self, doubts own ability																		
M	.04	.12	.17	−.09	−.08	−.14	−.15	−.08	−.24	−.10	−.05	−.19	−.24	.01	.14	−.12	−.11	−.03
F	.07	.15	.18	−.12	−.14	−.19	−.19	−.05	−.32	−.06	−.14	−.26	−.28	−.02	.15	−.14	−.21	.01
90. Holds unrealistic standards for self and others																		
M	−.07	.04	−.07	.00	−.12	−.08	−.12	−.02	−.06	−.12	−.02	−.05	−.03	−.09	.06	.12	−.06	.11
F	−.11	.04	−.02	.01	−.09	−.10	−.10	−.06	−.08	−.12	−.06	−.04	−.08	−.06	.07	.07	−.05	.00
91. Arrogant and overbearing, fails to see own deficiencies and limitations																		
M	−.11	−.04	−.14	.04	−.13	−.06	−.05	−.04	.02	−.11	.01	.03	.04	−.12	.03	.13	−.02	.15
F	.01	.01	−.07	−.01	.01	.01	.05	.03	.05	−.05	−.03	.04	.09	.02	.01	.10	.01	.01
92. Seems to be preoccupied with sexual matters																		
M	−.01	.08	−.02	−.01	−.14	−.12	−.18	−.01	−.13	−.13	−.07	−.11	−.09	−.05	.13	−.09	−.06	.07
F	−.04	.10	.00	−.10	−.14	−.12	−.16	−.02	−.12	−.16	−.06	−.09	−.11	−.04	.10	.06	−.08	.14
93. Has strong religious beliefs																		
M	−.19	−.02	.05	.23	−.03	.04	.08	−.24	.08	.12	.21	.01	.01	.14	−.05	−.15	.11	.00
F	−.21	.18	.16	.17	−.15	−.08	−.04	−.25	−.05	.08	.22	−.10	−.15	.19	−.03	−.15	−.04	−.02
94. Is realistic in thinking and social behavior																		
M	.04	−.14	−.07	.02	.10	.09	.13	.03	.14	.10	.08	.12	.13	−.02	−.09	−.02	.05	−.03
F	.01	−.06	−.04	.10	.17	.20	.17	.01	.17	.16	.16	.19	.14	.10	−.13	−.10	.17	−.11
95. Is happily married																		
M	−.11	−.10	.05	.08	.06	.19	.29	−.05	.22	.22	.17	.23	.21	.09	−.25	−.08	.16	−.18
F	−.19	.23	.15	.14	−.08	.03	.16	−.22	.01	.21	.13	.02	−.08	.24	−.13	−.18	.03	−.05
96. Has a stable, optimistic view of the future																		
M	−.05	−.21	−.10	.11	.11	.17	.18	−.02	.23	.19	.23	.18	.23	.00	−.18	−.03	.14	−.02
F	−.10	.00	−.08	.27	.16	.21	.23	−.04	.28	.21	.19	.21	.18	.17	−.20	−.04	.23	−.03
97. Creates a good impression; has effective interpersonal techniques																		
M	.00	−.08	−.20	.03	.12	.16	.11	.09	.23	.06	.10	.14	.21	−.02	−.11	.09	.10	−.02
F	−.02	−.01	−.21	.13	.14	.17	.06	.08	.19	.05	.14	.11	.13	.02	−.02	.00	.18	.03
98. Seems relatively free of neurotic trends, conflicts, and other forms of instability																		
M	.02	−.17	−.08	.05	.14	.13	.16	.01	.18	.17	.20	.17	.22	.04	−.13	−.03	.12	−.06
F	.01	−.03	−.14	.17	.14	.15	.14	.03	.24	.13	.14	.13	.17	.10	−.14	−.01	.19	.04
99. Enjoys children																		
M	−.22	−.12	.00	.01	−.21	−.11	−.04	−.22	−.02	−.04	.15	.00	.08	−.06	−.06	.03	−.02	.04
F	−.25	.23	.18	.12	−.09	.02	.10	−.25	−.04	.16	.13	−.04	−.15	.22	−.06	−.22	.05	−.04

Itemmetric Data

This appendix provides data pertaining to the 434 items in the inventory. Columns 1 and 2 give item numbers in form 434 and in the previous 462-item form of the inventory. Columns 3 and 4 cite endorsement rates (percentage of "true" responses) for the basic norm samples of 3,000 men and 3,000 women. Columns 5 and 6 give mean social desirability ratings for the items, as gathered from judges in 1994. These ratings were kindly made available by Paul D. Werner. Columns 7 and 8 give mean social desirability ratings in 1964, as taken from an article by Mees, Gocka, and Holloway (1964). The social desirability ratings are made on a 9-step scale, with higher values

indicative of greater social desirability. Columns 9 and 10 list the percentage of 96 males and 108 females giving the same response ("true" or "false") to an item when the CPI was administered to the same person on two different occasions. These data are taken from a report of Goldberg and Rorer (1964). The last two columns indicate the percentage of identical answers to each item for 115 monozygotic (MZ) and 120 dizygotic (DZ) pairs of male twins. These data were kindly developed for this manual by Joseph Horn, based on a research analysis published by Horn, Plomin, and Rosenman (1976).

Itemmetric Data

Items		Percent Saying True		Rating of Social Desirability				Test-Retest % Same Answer		Twins % Same Answer	
				In 1994		In 1964					
Form 434	Form 462	3,000 Males	3,000 Females	For Males	For Females	For Males	For Females	96 Males	108 Females	115 MZ Pairs	120 DZ Pairs
001	001	74	80	7.4	7.4	7.1	7.2	81	83	63	58
002	002	10	09	3.4	3.5	2.6	3.0	97	98	98	96
003	003	56	55	6.6	6.2	6.8	7.4	87	90	62	71
004	004	52	48	5.3	4.6	4.0	4.3	83	82	60	50
005	005	30	33	4.5	4.4	4.5	4.5	89	94	61	68
006	006	87	79	8.0	7.6	8.0	7.9	86	90	64	51
007	007	36	38	3.7	3.2	3.8	4.0	81	79	62	64
008	008	44	65	5.7	5.9	5.1	5.6	87	94	66	50
009	009	25	23	4.6	4.0	3.6	3.8	98	99	99	98
010	010	91	93	4.0	3.6	3.7	3.3	91	88	95	96
011	011	24	26	3.1	2.7	2.9	3.2	84	84	77	77
012	012	25	22	3.5	3.1	3.5	3.3	81	81	74	58
013	013	34	36	3.4	3.6	3.6	3.7	81	85	82	69
014	014	30	29	5.2	5.3	6.0	5.4	87	92	72	60
015	015	19	19	3.2	3.1	2.9	2.8	93	95	94	93
016	016	13	09	2.4	2.3	2.8	1.7	96	95	89	82
017	017	25	35	4.9	5.5	5.3	5.5	88	88	84	82
018	018	58	61	4.5	5.1	5.5	4.9	77	80	56	55
019	019	37	09	4.5	4.3	5.6	5.0	76	90	66	55
020	020	48	41	6.0	5.7	5.8	4.9	81	89	50	50
021	021	74	73	7.4	7.5	7.5	7.7	88	88	81	74
022	022	77	80	5.0	5.2	5.0	4.2	80	80	69	75
023	023	43	45	3.9	4.0	5.0	5.2	86	91	74	74
024	024	78	82	6.5	7.0	7.5	8.2	84	87	74	66
025	025	48	57	4.4	4.2	4.7	4.7	75	71	61	60
026	026	44	31	5.3	5.0	3.6	3.0	75	75	72	70
027	027	26	26	3.1	3.4	3.1	3.2	86	92	84	78
028	028	07	45	4.2	5.4	3.8	6.4	98	81	96	93
029	029	27	30	3.2	3.4	2.8	2.8	87	90	82	72
030	030	77	91	4.4	4.5	3.3	3.7	85	95	76	76
031	031	33	44	3.6	3.3	3.4	3.9	87	81	75	63
032	032	54	52	4.4	4.6	4.7	4.4	84	81	60	53
033	033	25	41	5.4	4.5	4.7	4.4	84	81	90	86
034	034	89	86	5.4	5.5	5.3	4.3	83	87	91	88
035	035	41	72	5.4	5.8	5.3	5.4	83	79	60	58
036	036	19	12	4.0	3.3	3.1	2.4	98	94	88	85
037	037	52	52	6.1	6.0	5.5	6.1	68	70	57	59
038	038	46	40	4.3	4.1	4.0	3.9	87	90	69	51
039	039	50	35	5.1	4.4	4.8	4.0	85	91	67	57
040	040	40	57	4.5	4.7	4.1	4.0	83	79	82	53
041	041	60	53	3.8	3.6	4.4	4.9	76	78	61	58
042	042	71	63	4.0	4.1	4.1	4.2	82	85	55	52
043	043	31	30	3.1	3.0	2.7	2.4	87	92	66	68
044	044	55	58	3.6	3.6	3.1	3.2	71	81	60	63

Itemmetric Data continued

Items		Percent Saying True		Rating of Social Desirability				Test-Retest % Same Answer		Twins % Same Answer	
				In 1994		In 1964					
Form 434	Form 462	3,000 Males	3,000 Females	For Males	For Females	For Males	For Females	96 Males	108 Females	115 MZ Pairs	120 DZ Pairs
045	045	64	66	6.6	6.4	6.9	7.7	87	86	61	67
046	046	31	40	5.4	5.7	6.8	6.8	86	91	67	59
047	435	20	16	4.4	4.5	5.1	5.4	86	92	80	84
048	048	67	62	4.5	4.1	3.1	2.9	73	78	62	57
049	049	34	21	4.1	3.6	2.5	1.7	79	89	72	70
050	050	82	79	6.9	7.0	6.2	5.9	87	80	91	86
051	051	77	82	5.5	6.0	7.0	7.4	88	84	71	74
052	052	52	56	6.8	6.6	6.7	6.7	84	84	58	58
053	053	56	43	5.4	5.8	5.8	5.6	79	79	58	59
054	054	20	22	3.3	3.2	3.3	3.3	77	78	92	88
055	055	67	74	4.3	4.7	3.6	4.2	91	86	65	65
056	056	73	74	5.4	5.5	5.4	5.0	73	79	67	60
057	057	54	59	4.9	4.9	4.6	4.9	73	73	64	57
058	058	52	63	4.5	4.6	4.4	4.4	77	78	63	53
059	059	69	68	4.9	5.1	5.0	5.0	79	61	58	51
060	060	62	52	5.2	4.9	4.6	4.5	66	81	70	69
061	061	73	82	6.6	7.3	7.1	7.7	94	96	70	66
062	062	55	54	5.4	5.6	5.6	5.7	84	87	66	49
063	063	61	55	6.0	6.3	6.4	6.5	74	86	61	57
064	064	11	32	3.8	4.6	3.8	4.1	96	94	95	92
065	065	19	35	3.6	4.0	4.6	5.2	88	83	88	94
066	066	84	87	5.2	4.8	4.2	3.7	93	92	82	87
067	436	23	19	3.2	2.9	3.0	2.8	94	96	74	63
068	068	18	55	3.8	4.7	4.3	5.9	89	90	80	71
069	069	59	72	4.9	5.1	5.4	6.3	78	81	70	53
070	070	37	43	4.0	4.3	3.1	3.2	80	79	65	65
071	071	32	52	4.8	5.4	4.2	4.6	83	82	80	68
072	072	14	59	4.7	5.8	4.5	5.6	97	94	87	90
073	073	27	23	2.6	2.3	2.7	2.8	87	92	86	79
074	074	40	38	3.8	3.9	4.2	3.9	82	78	72	63
075	075	22	19	3.5	3.1	2.7	2.5	89	96	66	63
076	076	24	29	3.9	3.7	3.2	3.3	80	78	80	76
077	077	62	60	6.0	6.3	5.1	5.4	85	87	63	58
078	078	60	53	4.6	4.6	4.4	3.9	80	86	61	50
079	079	21	46	3.6	4.2	4.1	4.3	94	95	84	70
080	080	85	89	5.4	6.0	4.7	4.8	87	88	83	88
081	081	44	42	3.9	4.1	3.4	2.8	75	68	57	55
082	082	38	07	3.0	3.4	4.4	4.6	81	98	75	72
083	083	35	33	3.6	3.6	3.8	3.2	84	85	61	48
084	084	52	64	5.6	6.4	5.7	6.3	87	88	77	72
085	085	59	60	4.5	4.7	4.6	4.6	78	80	59	56
086	086	54	51	5.7	6.1	5.4	5.3	79	78	50	48
087	087	81	32	5.8	5.1	5.6	5.2	85	86	88	89
088	088	71	82	5.0	5.2	6.0	6.5	82	93	72	58

Itemmetric Data continued

Items		Percent Saying True		Rating of Social Desirability In 1994		In 1964		Test-Retest % Same Answer		Twins % Same Answer	
Form 434	Form 462	3,000 Males	3,000 Females	For Males	For Females	For Males	For Females	96 Males	108 Females	115 MZ Pairs	120 DZ Pairs
089	438	20	16	3.5	3.5	3.2	3.1	96	96	88	94
090	090	09	09	3.1	3.2	2.0	2.0	99	100	94	95
091	091	56	48	4.6	4.3	3.8	3.1	78	77	57	53
092	092	40	41	4.6	4.5	3.9	3.9	78	92	66	69
093	093	10	11	3.7	3.9	3.0	2.5	93	96	95	89
094	094	23	22	3.2	3.0	2.7	2.4	89	85	78	80
095	095	60	51	5.8	6.2	6.6	7.1	80	83	62	61
096	096	63	76	6.4	7.2	7.3	7.9	84	88	72	74
097	097	37	42	5.8	6.4	6.5	6.6	77	84	67	58
098	098	44	48	4.7	4.4	5.4	5.5	75	84	70	54
099	099	32	31	3.8	3.4	3.6	3.8	85	84	86	80
100	100	74	45	5.7	5.6	5.6	5.2	92	94	86	79
101	101	47	42	4.0	3.6	3.6	2.6	82	85	72	73
102	102	31	30	5.1	5.0	4.4	3.8	81	82	64	75
103	103	32	50	5.2	5.5	6.1	6.0	88	84	68	65
104	104	70	58	5.7	5.4	6.1	6.3	91	94	59	53
105	105	28	28	4.7	4.5	3.9	4.4	84	90	76	78
106	106	53	48	4.1	4.4	4.6	4.3	82	77	51	51
107	107	69	74	5.1	5.3	5.8	5.9	84	86	65	52
108	108	63	56	6.8	6.8	6.8	6.9	75	70	70	63
109	109	72	79	4.6	4.8	4.4	4.6	73	81	63	50
110	110	59	78	6.1	6.4	5.5	5.7	80	83	64	60
111	111	41	38	3.8	3.8	3.7	3.8	91	82	75	55
112	112	60	70	6.3	6.6	6.5	6.5	75	92	65	56
113	113	32	26	3.4	2.9	3.6	4.0	91	92	68	60
114	114	42	24	3.6	2.8	2.9	2.7	87	87	75	82
115	115	39	53	5.3	5.2	4.6	4.6	79	86	70	74
116	116	87	90	6.4	6.3	5.6	5.1	85	92	90	88
117	117	38	26	4.7	4.6	3.1	3.0	86	88	72	64
118	118	86	85	6.9	6.8	7.1	7.0	93	91	83	86
119	119	32	29	4.8	4.7	4.2	4.2	79	81	65	57
120	120	78	71	4.4	3.9	3.1	2.6	96	86	72	63
121	121	36	26	3.5	3.2	4.1	3.9	86	92	75	56
122	122	43	69	5.7	6.4	5.9	6.4	82	95	67	62
123	123	38	39	5.5	5.8	6.0	5.9	87	83	68	57
124	124	40	38	4.0	3.8	4.1	3.5	78	86	70	55
125	125	78	78	5.2	5.2	5.4	5.3	84	78	66	86
126	126	73	61	6.2	6.4	6.4	6.8	87	82	71	76
127	127	75	81	7.6	7.8	7.8	7.9	80	77	75	78
128	128	56	50	5.3	5.2	5.1	5.0	74	74	65	58
129	129	51	19	5.7	5.1	6.1	4.4	89	86	71	62
130	130	59	68	6.2	6.6	6.0	6.7	83	85	59	54
131	131	80	79	6.9	6.5	6.7	7.4	86	85	63	61
132	132	26	22	3.9	3.2	3.6	3.7	85	85	80	87

Itemmetric Data continued

Items		Percent Saying True		Rating of Social Desirability				Test-Retest % Same Answer		Twins % Same Answer	
				In 1994		In 1964					
Form 434	Form 462	3,000 Males	3,000 Females	For Males	For Females	For Males	For Females	96 Males	108 Females	115 MZ Pairs	120 DZ Pairs
133	133	59	66	6.4	6.7	6.2	6.2	77	68	65	62
134	134	39	45	4.8	5.1	4.1	4.3	83	81	61	59
135	439	67	68	6.8	6.9	7.5	7.8	91	89	70	68
136	136	43	33	4.0	3.7	3.4	2.9	86	88	80	66
137	137	48	46	4.3	4.4	4.3	4.5	93	84	67	58
138	440	93	95	5.2	5.4	5.1	5.0	88	93	89	84
139	139	55	42	4.8	4.4	3.4	2.6	79	82	64	56
140	140	50	46	5.7	6.4	6.5	7.0	80	87	64	63
141	141	55	50	5.1	5.2	5.4	4.9	82	85	77	74
142	142	75	69	4.8	4.5	3.7	3.4	72	69	60	56
143	143	41	29	5.2	4.7	4.7	4.4	76	87	72	66
144	144	15	38	3.7	4.2	3.5	3.9	86	84	77	74
145	145	26	34	2.8	2.6	2.6	2.7	84	77	81	75
146	146	60	73	5.7	6.1	5.9	5.7	86	94	65	60
147	147	57	62	3.3	3.6	3.7	3.9	71	79	66	51
148	441	77	56	4.3	4.3	5.4	3.4	83	86	71	66
149	149	51	52	7.3	7.4	7.1	7.6	75	82	65	61
150	150	67	79	5.0	5.1	4.4	4.7	81	76	61	59
151	443	73	84	4.7	4.8	4.9	5.1	86	89	74	74
152	152	63	73	6.1	7.0	7.0	6.9	92	88	73	64
153	153	65	80	4.3	4.5	4.2	4.1	77	70	57	54
154	444	73	84	3.9	4.1	3.2	3.2	88	87	88	82
155	155	57	52	4.4	3.4	4.5	4.9	73	78	55	52
156	156	16	11	3.1	2.7	3.7	3.2	92	94	70	62
157	157	26	18	4.2	4.2	4.3	4.0	91	93	80	75
158	445	91	89	7.0	7.3	7.9	7.3	97	95	89	94
159	159	45	49	4.1	3.6	3.8	3.7	81	78	65	59
160	160	35	59	5.6	5.8	5.9	6.5	83	87	62	61
161	161	48	60	3.4	3.6	3.2	3.5	69	78	59	49
162	162	77	80	5.7	6.1	7.3	7.1	80	91	70	74
163	163	79	85	7.0	7.1	6.8	7.0	93	91	63	62
164	164	35	32	4.3	3.7	3.7	3.7	87	93	81	83
165	165	64	60	4.4	4.4	6.3	6.7	81	78	74	74
166	166	47	60	6.2	6.8	6.9	6.8	83	77	66	70
167	167	47	52	5.9	6.4	6.5	6.3	82	88	75	68
168	168	53	52	6.8	6.8	7.6	8.1	80	83	64	56
169	169	49	50	4.7	4.6	4.5	4.6	76	70	69	60
170	170	57	60	4.5	4.7	4.1	3.8	81	81	62	57
171	171	21	12	5.1	4.8	4.3	3.8	84	96	66	67
172	172	64	36	5.5	5.2	5.3	5.6	77	72	69	53
173	173	60	56	4.6	4.3	4.3	4.5	78	82	74	52
174	174	55	45	6.8	6.8	7.3	7.4	80	81	71	51
175	446	88	90	5.6	5.8	5.6	5.5	93	94	87	86
176	176	53	50	4.1	3.8	4.4	3.7	84	82	73	58

Itemmetric Data continued

Items		Percent Saying True		Rating of Social Desirability				Test-Retest % Same Answer		Twins % Same Answer	
				In 1994		In 1964					
Form 434	Form 462	3,000 Males	3,000 Females	For Males	For Females	For Males	For Females	96 Males	108 Females	115 MZ Pairs	120 DZ Pairs
177	177	28	36	2.6	2.9	3.0	3.0	82	83	83	73
178	178	35	30	3.6	3.5	2.8	2.6	82	94	78	68
179	179	35	37	6.0	6.1	5.6	5.5	79	81	64	64
180	180	76	76	6.7	7.3	6.8	6.5	92	87	74	79
181	181	46	64	7.5	7.7	7.7	8.1	89	92	65	55
182	182	40	42	5.1	4.8	5.4	4.8	76	87	61	61
183	183	18	15	2.7	2.2	2.9	2.2	85	86	94	92
184	184	34	31	4.4	4.3	3.7	3.7	85	86	80	60
185	185	56	50	4.2	4.7	3.7	3.6	78	74	62	57
186	186	61	54	4.6	4.6	4.2	4.1	82	83	58	52
187	187	41	56	4.0	4.4	3.9	3.9	77	78	59	49
188	188	50	45	4.6	5.0	4.5	5.0	79	82	56	56
189	189	20	09	3.0	2.5	2.8	2.4	93	98	87	82
190	190	26	27	4.3	4.2	3.1	2.9	92	96	81	78
191	191	65	60	4.6	4.3	3.5	2.8	77	92	59	64
192	192	31	34	3.6	3.2	4.0	3.9	87	80	80	74
193	193	66	74	5.7	5.8	6.8	7.1	79	90	71	65
194	194	38	32	5.5	5.3	4.5	4.2	74	84	79	70
195	195	57	55	6.4	6.2	6.8	7.2	76	69	66	50
196	196	35	05	4.1	3.3	4.9	3.8	85	97	89	81
197	197	91	87	5.9	5.9	5.3	4.5	99	93	89	87
198	198	65	65	5.7	5.1	6.5	6.8	74	75	56	55
199	199	35	12	3.9	3.8	5.4	5.5	95	93	79	74
200	200	72	69	7.2	7.1	6.9	7.7	78	74	76	69
201	447	89	95	7.1	7.6	7.7	7.7	92	95	97	95
202	202	55	44	6.7	6.6	6.5	6.3	84	84	67	58
203	203	60	60	3.3	3.6	3.2	3.0	63	70	63	59
204	204	37	46	5.9	6.4	6.9	7.2	74	81	69	56
205	205	32	20	4.6	4.4	4.8	3.7	85	87	64	62
206	206	38	34	4.6	3.9	4.1	3.7	85	85	80	64
207	207	39	38	3.8	3.5	3.4	3.1	77	76	75	72
208	208	58	46	6.1	6.1	5.0	4.6	82	82	66	58
209	209	49	44	4.4	4.6	4.2	3.8	66	79	62	56
210	210	61	25	4.1	3.2	6.2	5.6	89	89	81	69
211	211	51	46	5.7	6.1	6.6	6.0	76	83	70	50
212	212	60	80	6.7	7.3	7.8	8.0	86	93	68	63
213	213	75	81	6.5	6.8	4.8	7.8	87	84	70	67
214	214	42	14	3.8	3.2	3.5	3.3	86	96	69	65
215	215	22	09	5.4	4.5	5.9	5.8	85	94	79	82
216	216	62	69	5.2	5.7	5.1	5.0	76	89	66	66
217	217	13	35	4.0	4.1	4.9	5.5	91	97	86	87
218	218	51	70	6.5	6.8	6.1	7.0	89	86	65	61
219	219	52	47	4.0	3.6	3.5	3.0	76	77	58	50
220	220	30	17	3.9	3.8	3.7	3.8	94	89	84	78

Itemmetric Data continued

Items		Percent Saying True		Rating of Social Desirability				Test-Retest % Same Answer		Twins % Same Answer	
				In 1994		In 1964					
Form 434	Form 462	3,000 Males	3,000 Females	For Males	For Females	For Males	For Females	96 Males	108 Females	115 MZ Pairs	120 DZ Pairs
221	221	86	86	7.2	7.0	7.4	7.0	84	93	88	86
222	222	33	40	5.8	6.0	6.3	6.6	78	80	68	59
223	223	39	44	5.1	5.5	6.3	6.5	79	76	60	62
224	224	88	85	7.0	7.0	7.1	6.9	88	88	92	86
225	225	68	59	4.4	4.4	4.0	3.8	72	77	71	55
226	448	33	40	6.5	6.9	6.8	7.0	79	84	66	50
227	227	42	36	3.8	3.8	3.5	3.7	86	91	75	53
228	228	64	56	5.7	5.6	6.1	6.1	85	85	74	65
229	229	57	49	5.2	5.3	5.5	5.2	83	80	67	62
230	230	80	83	5.8	5.8	6.9	7.2	84	86	83	87
231	231	47	37	4.6	4.5	4.0	3.8	81	80	62	60
232	232	27	44	3.7	4.0	3.1	3.4	84	76	82	71
233	233	32	30	3.6	3.4	3.3	2.8	85	92	79	69
234	234	28	25	4.0	4.0	5.3	5.5	82	80	78	68
235	235	72	76	5.6	5.3	7.3	7.3	83	78	60	55
236	236	22	29	3.7	3.9	3.0	3.2	88	89	88	73
237	237	40	36	3.9	3.6	3.1	3.5	95	89	85	80
238	238	74	74	4.1	4.1	3.9	3.7	78	75	68	56
239	239	28	24	6.0	6.2	6.4	6.7	85	90	75	69
240	240	06	44	4.7	5.3	5.6	6.7	98	90	92	91
241	241	61	66	4.0	4.5	4.5	5.1	76	82	67	60
242	242	58	60	6.3	6.4	6.7	7.2	81	81	75	61
243	243	45	49	4.5	4.4	3.8	4.2	69	70	72	70
244	244	25	54	5.0	5.3	5.3	5.7	92	84	79	81
245	245	84	86	7.2	7.5	7.3	7.7	91	93	87	86
246	246	62	66	6.2	6.2	7.1	7.0	81	81	70	59
247	247	75	82	6.4	6.9	6.1	6.2	76	86	80	76
248	248	63	66	4.0	4.2	3.7	3.7	80	84	62	65
249	249	64	10	4.5	3.8	5.4	4.8	82	95	74	70
250	250	45	44	5.0	4.8	4.3	3.6	80	77	64	55
251	251	43	32	5.4	5.5	5.0	4.1	74	84	70	61
252	252	39	44	4.1	4.0	3.7	3.7	82	72	84	83
253	253	49	46	5.0	5.0	3.9	4.0	75	68	62	56
254	254	11	20	5.5	5.6	6.4	7.2	94	94	84	71
255	255	63	60	4.1	4.1	5.1	5.0	78	80	72	55
256	256	62	58	6.7	6.7	6.8	6.6	87	75	64	55
257	257	33	31	3.7	3.5	3.6	3.7	77	79	82	80
258	258	47	52	4.0	4.1	3.8	4.0	81	80	67	61
259	259	90	88	7.4	7.4	7.3	7.8	96	92	96	95
260	260	78	80	7.2	7.7	7.7	8.0	79	70	86	88
261	261	25	21	3.8	3.8	3.1	2.5	92	94	65	64
262	262	77	79	4.3	4.6	3.8	3.5	85	77	58	55
263	263	65	63	4.6	5.0	6.9	7.1	79	81	53	56
264	264	75	80	5.6	6.5	6.1	5.9	80	81	70	67

Itemmetric Data continued

Items		Percent Saying True		Rating of Social Desirability In 1994		In 1964		Test-Retest % Same Answer		Twins % Same Answer	
Form 434	Form 462	3,000 Males	3,000 Females	For Males	For Females	For Males	For Females	96 Males	108 Females	115 MZ Pairs	120 DZ Pairs
265	265	42	65	5.0	5.2	4.4	4.6	87	90	68	60
266	266	50	40	4.4	4.4	3.5	3.0	86	80	66	56
267	267	20	20	4.4	4.0	4.1	3.4	88	88	69	64
268	268	60	66	5.2	5.3	4.6	4.2	83	82	60	62
269	269	69	53	6.2	6.0	6.7	6.5	92	91	74	64
270	270	25	39	3.3	3.5	2.9	2.9	89	90	82	79
271	271	26	28	4.8	4.7	5.0	5.2	88	92	77	65
272	272	37	54	4.8	5.1	4.1	4.9	80	77	73	66
273	273	20	25	3.8	4.1	3.5	3.3	93	84	88	83
274	274	15	10	4.7	5.0	5.1	4.8	92	93	79	86
275	275	50	48	4.8	5.2	4.2	3.0	85	83	69	58
276	276	62	58	6.2	6.6	6.7	7.3	79	76	70	69
277	277	71	52	6.3	6.5	6.1	6.7	86	92	74	63
278	278	54	69	6.6	6.0	7.8	8.0	83	84	64	67
279	279	61	71	4.3	3.4	4.8	4.5	76	80	68	55
280	280	89	89	7.1	7.6	7.3	7.7	95	92	71	67
281	281	24	20	3.3	3.4	3.3	3.5	87	93	76	65
282	449	06	07	3.5	3.1	3.2	3.1	99	98	97	100
283	283	65	46	5.9	5.8	6.4	6.4	81	84	73	70
284	284	42	40	4.5	4.0	3.7	4.0	75	78	72	62
285	285	36	39	3.8	3.6	3.5	3.1	87	86	60	68
286	286	30	47	4.1	4.5	4.7	5.5	88	82	69	67
287	287	35	55	4.6	5.5	5.6	6.4	91	89	79	72
288	288	16	06	3.2	2.8	3.0	2.5	92	99	82	79
289	289	78	87	4.5	4.8	4.1	4.1	82	83	68	53
290	290	22	31	4.2	4.6	4.1	4.0	84	91	72	60
291	291	34	15	3.9	3.8	4.9	4.4	81	94	86	73
292	292	62	69	6.1	6.4	6.4	6.3	82	92	68	52
293	293	48	60	3.7	4.2	3.3	3.7	67	78	68	54
294	294	33	33	4.1	4.2	3.4	3.9	84	88	89	76
295	295	48	56	5.6	5.6	6.3	6.2	78	81	62	54
296	296	38	41	5.5	5.9	5.8	5.6	80	91	75	72
297	297	31	28	3.5	3.3	3.2	2.6	82	78	88	88
298	450	55	49	5.1	4.9	4.5	4.3	77	78	59	55
299	299	10	08	2.6	2.4	2.3	2.3	96	95	96	94
300	300	56	50	5.4	5.5	4.7	4.4	79	81	56	60
301	301	07	27	3.6	3.8	3.1	3.7	93	83	92	91
302	302	58	44	4.3	4.1	3.1	2.5	75	81	73	74
303	303	52	54	6.1	6.3	5.4	4.8	82	75	63	51
304	304	78	82	5.6	5.4	6.8	6.8	81	83	70	80
305	305	86	87	6.1	6.3	6.4	6.4	82	81	74	69
306	306	10	12	3.8	3.6	3.5	3.8	94	94	94	94
307	307	10	06	3.9	3.7	2.4	2.3	93	95	90	90
308	451	14	53	4.7	5.1	3.7	4.7	95	84	89	87

Itemmetric Data continued

Items		Percent Saying True		Rating of Social Desirability In 1994		Rating of Social Desirability In 1964		Test-Retest % Same Answer		Twins % Same Answer	
Form 434	Form 462	3,000 Males	3,000 Females	For Males	For Females	For Males	For Females	96 Males	108 Females	115 MZ Pairs	120 DZ Pairs
309	309	27	38	3.5	3.3	2.9	3.1	73	74	77	84
310	310	68	70	5.0	5.7	4.9	4.8	77	81	60	56
311	311	07	07	2.5	2.2	2.4	2.5	97	97	96	98
312	312	92	94	7.1	7.4	7.5	7.6	96	93	83	82
313	452	52	58	4.2	4.2	3.9	4.2	86	86	72	58
314	314	63	64	5.3	4.8	5.1	5.7	65	75	62	56
315	315	17	15	3.6	3.6	2.9	3.3	91	94	76	79
316	316	95	91	6.4	6.5	7.3	7.3	96	89	88	73
317	317	84	90	5.8	5.5	6.9	6.8	89	90	73	73
318	318	38	31	5.6	5.7	4.9	5.2	71	86	69	54
319	319	32	42	6.3	6.7	6.8	7.5	83	75	73	61
320	320	50	50	6.6	7.1	5.8	6.0	84	80	74	50
321	321	09	08	3.7	3.8	3.6	3.1	98	90	93	95
322	322	93	95	6.2	6.7	6.6	6.9	94	99	96	92
323	453	26	29	4.4	4.9	4.2	4.3	83	79	58	54
324	324	03	04	2.8	2.8	1.8	1.5	97	100	96	96
325	325	25	31	3.6	3.4	3.6	3.5	85	88	84	70
326	326	44	59	5.5	5.7	4.5	5.0	84	91	64	55
327	327	19	14	3.0	2.7	3.1	2.9	86	90	74	74
328	328	63	69	5.3	5.5	6.3	6.7	80	77	81	56
329	329	61	56	5.1	5.0	4.8	4.6	73	74	74	72
330	330	04	02	3.2	2.9	3.4	3.2	98	99	98	98
331	331	48	52	3.2	3.1	2.8	2.4	80	82	76	74
332	332	07	05	2.9	2.7	2.6	2.0	96	98	96	90
333	333	90	93	6.7	7.1	7.8	7.7	87	91	77	72
334	334	54	62	4.8	4.3	4.6	4.5	78	83	65	57
335	335	57	62	3.7	3.9	3.3	3.3	79	80	60	59
336	336	62	65	5.0	5.2	3.9	3.8	85	84	66	62
337	454	12	12	3.8	4.0	3.8	3.3	96	93	90	92
338	338	15	07	4.4	4.2	3.4	3.1	93	97	81	71
339	339	43	44	3.0	2.7	2.7	2.5	86	78	77	82
340	340	38	23	3.9	3.2	4.1	3.7	80	88	70	55
341	341	21	25	3.6	3.2	3.1	3.3	92	92	96	95
342	342	40	34	4.6	4.2	3.9	3.7	75	87	68	58
343	343	92	94	6.4	6.8	7.3	7.7	97	98	96	97
344	344	38	54	4.5	4.9	4.6	4.3	76	81	65	58
345	345	14	12	3.6	3.6	3.8	3.0	85	91	82	77
346	346	49	58	5.9	6.4	5.3	5.5	82	81	70	52
347	347	50	47	4.8	4.3	4.8	4.5	78	70	54	64
348	348	84	85	5.1	5.2	5.9	6.3	78	85	83	92
349	349	08	06	2.6	2.6	1.9	1.7	95	96	95	98
350	350	06	03	2.8	2.4	1.9	2.0	96	96	96	97
351	351	48	56	4.4	4.6	4.0	3.9	76	75	62	63
352	352	08	08	2.4	2.3	2.6	2.7	97	94	83	80

Itemmetric Data continued

Items		Percent Saying True		Rating of Social Desirability				Test-Retest % Same Answer		Twins % Same Answer	
				In 1994		In 1964					
Form 434	Form 462	3,000 Males	3,000 Females	For Males	For Females	For Males	For Females	96 Males	108 Females	115 MZ Pairs	120 DZ Pairs
353	353	16	17	3.7	3.3	2.9	2.9	93	91	90	96
354	354	51	55	5.8	6.1	6.7	6.6	80	76	67	58
355	355	37	35	5.5	5.9	6.3	6.6	88	83	70	49
356	455	08	10	3.5	3.1	3.6	3.3	98	94	96	97
357	357	34	38	4.2	4.2	4.9	5.2	83	77	76	65
358	358	42	39	4.8	4.8	4.3	4.2	81	84	78	80
359	359	35	31	6.2	6.2	5.9	6.1	86	80	59	53
360	360	11	10	3.7	3.4	2.6	2.4	96	95	91	87
361	361	77	81	5.6	5.9	6.7	6.9	81	84	81	73
362	456	38	34	3.5	3.6	3.7	3.4	78	84	81	70
363	363	49	50	4.2	4.1	4.5	4.2	75	73	64	54
364	364	36	36	4.2	4.3	3.9	3.8	79	88	63	53
365	365	08	08	2.7	2.2	2.2	2.0	97	98	94	97
366	366	06	05	4.5	4.5	4.6	4.1	95	94	89	88
367	367	57	58	6.5	7.0	7.3	8.0	72	86	64	52
368	368	70	73	6.6	6.5	7.4	7.3	80	81	60	48
369	369	32	33	4.0	3.8	3.5	3.3	88	88	89	82
370	370	40	47	3.8	4.2	4.4	5.0	88	80	71	64
371	371	37	28	5.0	5.2	6.5	6.6	82	85	74	66
372	372	12	16	3.4	3.4	3.2	3.1	95	94	94	94
373	373	73	66	4.5	4.4	4.7	4.3	88	94	57	69
374	374	08	05	2.9	2.4	2.6	2.0	95	96	97	98
375	375	51	43	4.4	4.3	3.2	2.6	75	81	55	61
376	376	45	52	5.2	5.6	5.8	6.0	71	82	64	53
377	377	44	30	3.8	3.5	3.8	3.7	79	84	74	69
378	378	10	10	3.0	2.8	2.8	2.8	93	93	87	88
379	379	49	51	4.1	4.1	4.0	3.6	77	72	57	59
380	380	61	58	6.9	7.2	7.2	8.0	80	86	83	88
381	457	10	08	3.0	2.9	2.7	2.0	96	96	90	89
382	382	77	75	6.3	6.5	6.4	6.2	74	72	60	60
383	383	44	48	4.5	5.0	4.5	4.8	84	85	74	74
384	384	08	06	2.6	2.3	2.0	1.6	98	98	98	97
385	385	22	26	3.5	2.9	3.2	3.5	91	87	79	75
386	386	53	59	4.6	4.3	4.5	4.9	75	74	56	49
387	387	72	76	5.3	5.3	5.0	5.3	77	81	72	72
388	388	57	55	4.6	4.8	3.3	3.4	69	80	60	50
389	389	57	62	6.6	6.6	5.9	6.0	82	69	66	63
390	390	31	22	3.3	3.3	3.1	2.7	89	94	86	91
391	391	40	54	6.0	6.2	6.4	7.1	79	90	71	63
392	392	45	38	4.9	4.6	5.8	6.0	66	73	61	56
393	458	53	60	4.6	4.6	4.9	4.4	82	70	62	53
394	394	51	62	6.2	6.3	5.7	5.9	82	76	63	71
395	395	71	75	6.6	6.6	6.0	5.8	87	84	61	56
396	396	48	53	4.1	4.2	3.8	3.6	75	84	68	63

Itemmetric Data continued

Items		Percent Saying True		Rating of Social Desirability				Test-Retest % Same Answer		Twins % Same Answer	
				In 1994		In 1964					
Form 434	Form 462	3,000 Males	3,000 Females	For Males	For Females	For Males	For Females	96 Males	108 Females	115 MZ Pairs	120 DZ Pairs
397	397	47	49	4.6	5.0	4.9	5.5	84	79	63	52
398	398	12	11	3.8	3.6	2.9	2.4	99	99	96	97
399	399	48	33	4.3	4.1	3.8	3.0	79	85	60	59
400	400	91	89	6.0	5.9	6.1	6.6	94	94	92	88
401	401	06	04	3.2	2.8	2.5	2.5	98	99	91	86
402	459	11	12	3.3	3.6	3.2	2.8	93	94	88	86
403	403	33	31	5.9	6.3	6.1	6.2	84	91	65	53
404	404	34	36	4.6	4.6	5.5	5.8	86	78	69	52
405	405	28	30	3.3	2.9	3.2	2.7	86	92	85	79
406	406	19	16	3.1	3.0	2.8	2.5	84	95	82	67
407	407	24	30	4.0	4.2	3.7	3.6	84	77	92	81
408	408	47	49	6.3	6.4	6.7	7.5	76	80	66	58
409	409	51	60	4.6	5.0	5.0	5.2	80	81	66	57
410	410	86	86	6.8	7.5	7.0	7.3	97	97	88	89
411	460	29	28	4.1	3.6	5.0	4.1	80	83	69	60
412	412	61	54	5.9	5.8	5.9	5.8	82	83	68	63
413	413	85	83	5.3	4.7	5.8	5.7	92	92	84	82
414	414	90	92	5.4	5.4	5.3	5.0	93	92	88	84
415	415	11	11	3.8	3.4	3.7	3.3	89	93	85	86
416	416	26	26	4.0	3.8	3.6	3.4	88	90	77	70
417	417	18	09	4.0	3.6	3.1	3.0	86	95	83	80
418	418	26	28	3.9	3.7	3.4	3.6	83	81	76	70
419	462	37	36	3.3	3.1	3.4	3.3	91	83	71	63
420	420	50	26	3.4	2.9	2.9	2.3	85	87	65	65
421	421	21	15	4.4	4.2	3.4	2.6	85	95	80	74
422	422	25	35	2.9	2.8	2.6	2.4	91	81	85	83
423	423	10	07	3.1	2.9	2.8	2.3	99	97	93	96
424	424	58	68	5.3	5.5	5.5	5.7	69	81	67	64
425	425	40	41	4.9	4.6	4.4	4.9	72	81	77	77
426	426	17	28	3.9	4.2	3.9	4.0	87	83	81	81
427	427	46	46	4.5	3.9	4.9	5.0	79	77	63	60
428	428	28	28	4.3	4.4	4.2	4.0	82	87	83	73
429	429	48	56	3.8	3.9	3.5	3.9	85	80	72	50
430	430	19	24	4.1	3.6	3.8	3.4	91	92	84	82
431	431	31	14	3.7	3.0	3.0	2.4	86	96	88	85
432	432	75	72	5.7	5.6	5.3	5.2	89	79	83	82
433	433	75	87	6.2	7.0	6.7	6.5	83	86	75	75
434	461	36	35	4.4	4.3	4.2	4.3	89	89	65	57

References

Adams, C. R. (1941). A new measure of personality. *Journal of Applied Psychology, 25,* 141–151.

Adams, S. H., Cartwright, L. K., Ostrove, J. M., Stewart, A. J., & Wink, P. (1998). Psychological predictors of good health in three longitudinal samples of educated midlife women. *Health Psychology, 17,* 412–420.

Adams, S. H., & John, O. P. (1997). A hostility scale for the California Psychological Inventory: MMPI, observer Q-sort, and Big Five correlates. *Journal of Personality Assessment, 69,* 408–424.

Adorno, T. W., Frenkel-Brunswik, E., Levinson, D. J., & Sanford, R. (1950). *The authoritarian personality.* New York: Harper.

Agronick, G. S., & Duncan, L. E. (1998). Personality and social change: Individual differences in life path, and importance attributed to the women's movement. *Journal of Personality and Social Psychology, 74,* 1545–1555.

Ahmad, I., Anis-ul-Haque, M., & Anila. (1994). Validation of Femininity/Masculinity scale of California Psychological Inventory in Pakistan. *Pakistan Journal of Psychological Research, 9,* 27–35.

Albu, M., & Pitariu, H. D. (1999). Evaluarea anxietajii cu ajutorul inventarului Psihologic California (CPI). (Assessment of anxiety with the California Psychological Inventory). *Studii de Psihologie, 4,* 19–32.

Alterman, A. I., Rutherford, M. J., Cacciola, J. S., McKay, J. R., & Boardman, C. R. (1998). Prediction of 7 months methadone treatment responses by four measures of antisociality. *Drug and Alcohol Dependence, 49,* 217–223.

Awang, A., & Loekmono, J. T. L. (1994). *Normative and factorial analyses of a Malaysian translation of the California Psychological Inventory.* Pulau Pinang, Malaysia: Universiti Sains Malaysia.

Baldwin, R. O. (1987). Femininity-masculinity of Blacks and Whites over a fourteen-year period. *Psychological Reports, 60,* 455–458.

Barron, F. (1953a). Complexity-simplicity as a personality dimension. *Journal of Abnormal and Social Psychology, 48,* 163–172.

Barron, F. (1953b). Some personality correlates of independence of judgment. *Journal of Personality, 21,* 287–297.

Barron, F. (1954). Personal soundness in university graduate students: An experimental study of young men in the sciences and the professions. *University of California Publications in Personality Assessment and Research,* No. 1.

Barron, F. (1965). The psychology of creativity. In T. E. Newcomb (Ed.), *New directions in psychology* (Vol. 2, pp. 3–134). New York: Holt, Rinehart & Winston.

Barron, F., & Egan, D. (1968). Leaders and innovators in Irish management. *Journal of Management Studies (Dublin), 5*, 41–60.

Barron, F., & Welsh, G. S. (1952). Artistic perception as a factor in personality style and its measurement by a figure-preference test. *Journal of Psychology, 33*, 193–203.

Batista, M. I. (1995). Profile of first and second level managers in Puerto Rico using the revised California Psychological Inventory. Unpublished doctoral dissertation, Caribbean Center for Advanced Studies, San Juan, PR.

Baucom, D. H. (1976). Independent masculinity and femininity scales on the California Psychological Inventory. *Journal of Consulting and Clinical Psychology, 44*, 876.

Baucom, D. H. (1980). Independent CPI masculinity and femininity scales: Psychological correlates and sex role typology. *Journal of Personality Assessment, 44*, 262–271.

Baucom, D. H. (1983). Sex-role identity and the decision to regain control among women: A learned helplessness investigation. *Journal of Personality and Social Psychology, 44*, 334–343.

Baucom, D. H., & Aiken, P. A. (1984). Sex-role identity, marital satisfaction, and response to marital therapy. *Journal of Consulting and Clinical Psychology, 52*, 438–444.

Baucom, D. H., Besch, P. K., & Callahan, S. (1985). The relation between testosterone and concentration, sex role identity, and personality among females. *Journal of Personality and Social Psychology, 48*, 1218–1226.

Baucom, D. H., & Danker-Brown, P. S. (1979). Influence of sex roles on learned helplessness. *Journal of Consulting and Clinical Psychology, 47*, 928–936.

Baucom, D. H., & Danker-Brown, P. S. (1983). Peer ratings of males and females possessing different sex role identities. *Journal of Personality Assessment, 47*, 494–506.

Baucom, D. H., & Danker-Brown, P. S. (1984). Sex role identity and gender-stereotyped tasks in the development of learned helplessness in women. *Journal of Personality and Social Psychology, 46*, 422–430.

Baucom, D. H., & Sanders, B. S. (1978). Masculinity and femininity as factors in feminism. *Journal of Personality Assessment, 42*, 378–384.

Baucom, D. H., & Weiss, B. (1986). Peers' granting of control to women with different sex role identities: Implications for depression. *Journal of Personality and Social Psychology, 51*, 1075–1080.

Bayer, L. M., Whissell-Buechy, D., & Honzik, M. P. (1980). Adolescent health and personality. *Journal of Adolescent Health Care, 1*, 101–107.

Beck, A. T., Steer, R. A., & Garbin, M. G. (1988). Psychometric properties of the Beck Depression Inventory: Twenty-five years of evaluation. *Clinical Psychology Review, 8*, 77–100.

Beck, A. T., Ward, C. H., Mendelson, M., Mock, J. E., & Erbaugh, J. K. (1961). An inventory for measuring depression. *Archives of General Psychiatry, 4*, 561–571.

Bem, S. L. (1974). The measurement of psychological androgyny. *Journal of Consulting and Clinical Psychology, 42*, 155–162.

Bem, S. L. (1981). *Manual for the Bem Sex-Role Inventory.* Mountain View, CA: CPP, Inc.

Bernstein, I. H., Garbin, C. P., & McClellan, P. G. (1983). A confirmatory factoring of the California Psychological Inventory. *Educational and Psychological Measurement, 43*, 687–691.

Blake, R. J., Potter, E. H., Jr., & Slimak, R. E. (1993). Validation of the structural scales of the CPI for predicting the performance of junior officers in the Coast Guard. *Journal of Business and Psychology, 7*, 431–448.

Block, J. (1961). *The Q-sort method in personality assessment and psychiatric research.* Springfield, IL: Charles C. Thomas. (Reprinted by CPP, Inc., Mountain View, CA).

Block, J. (1965). *The challenge of response sets: Unconfounding meaning, acquiescence, and social desirability in the MMPI.* New York: Appleton-Century-Crofts.

Block, J., von der Lippe, A., & Block, J. H. (1973). Sex-role and socialization patterns: Some personality concomitants and environmental antecedents. *Journal of Consulting and Clinical Psychology, 41*, 321–341.

Boring, E. G. (1923). Intelligence as the tests test it. *New Republic, 35*, 35–37.

Bornstein, R. F. (1992). The dependent personality: Developmental, social, and clinical perspectives. *Psychological Bulletin, 112*, 3–23.

Bornstein, R. F. (1993). *The dependent personality.* New York: Guilford.

Bornstein, R. F. (1994). Construct validity of the Interpersonal Dependency Inventory: 1977–1992. *Journal of Personality Disorders, 8*, 64–76.

Bouchard, T. J., Jr. (1969). Personality, problem-solving procedure, and performance in small groups [Monograph]. *Journal of Applied Psychology, 53* (No. 1, part 2), 1–29.

Bouchard, T. J., Jr., McGue, M., Hur, Y., & Horn, J. M. (1998). A genetic and environmental analysis of the California Psychological Inventory using adult twins reared together and apart. *European Journal of Personality, 12*, 307–320.

Brook, J. S., Whiteman, M., & Brook, D. W. (1999). Transmission of risk factors across three generations. *Psychological Reports, 85*, 227–241.

Brown, M. N. (1950). Evaluating and scoring the Minnesota Multiphasic "Cannot Say" items. *Journal of Clinical Psychology, 6*, 180–184.

Burger, G. K., Pickett, L., & Goldman, M. (1977). Second-order factors in the California Psychological Inventory. *Journal of Personality Assessment, 41,* 58–62.

Burkhart, B. R., Gynther, M. D., & Christian, W. L. (1978). Psychological-mindedness, intelligence, and item subtlety endorsement patterns on the MMPI. *Journal of Clinical Psychology, 34,* 77–79.

Buss, D. M., & Craik, K. H. (1980). The frequency concept of disposition: Dominance and prototypically dominant acts. *Journal of Personality, 48,* 379–392.

Buss, D. M., & Craik, K. H. (1981). The act frequency analysis of personal dispositions: Aloofness, gregariousness, dominance, and submissiveness. *Journal of Personality, 49,* 174–192.

Buss, D. M., & Craik, K. H. (1983a). The act frequency approach to personality. *Psychological Review, 90,* 105–126.

Buss, D. M., & Craik, K. H. (1983b). Act prediction and the conceptual analysis of personality scales: Indices of density, polarity, and extensity. *Journal of Personality and Social Psychology, 45,* 1081–1095.

Buss, D. M., & Craik, K. H. (1986). The act frequency approach and the construction of personality. In A. Angleitner, A. Furnham, & G. Van Heck (Eds.), *Personality psychology in Europe: Vol. 2. Current trends and controversies* (pp. 141–156). Lisse, The Netherlands: Swets & Zeitlinger.

Butcher, J. N., Dahlstrom, W. G., Graham, J. R., Tellegen, A., & Kaemmer, B. (1989). *Manual for the restandardized Minnesota Multiphasic Personality: MMPI-2. An administrative and interpretive guide.* Minneapolis: University of Minnesota Press.

Butt, D. S. (1973). A factorial facet analysis of Gough's socialization scale. *Social Behavior and Personality, 1,* 50–57.

Campbell, D. P. (1967). The Strong Vocational Interest Blank: 1927–1967. In P. McReynolds (Ed.), *Advances in psychological assessment* (Vol. 1, pp. 105–130). Palo Alto, CA: Science and Behavior Books.

Campbell, D. P. (1974). *Manual for the Strong-Campbell Interest Inventory.* Stanford, CA: Stanford University Press.

Campbell, D. P. (1977). *Manual for the Strong-Campbell Interest Inventory* (rev. ed.). Stanford, CA: Stanford University Press.

Cartwright, L. K., Wink, P., & Kmetz, C. (1995). What leads to good health in midlife women physicians? Some clues from a longitudinal study. *Psychosomatic Medicine, 57,* 284–292.

Casey, L. (1986). *Personality characteristics associated with academic achievement of Hispanic high school students.* Unpublished doctoral dissertation, University of California, Berkeley.

Cattell, R. B. (1946). *Description and measurement of personality.* New York: Harcourt, Brace & World.

Cattell, R. B. (1949). *Manual for forms A and B: Sixteen Personality Factor Questionnaire.* Champaign, IL: Institute for Personality and Ability Testing.

Cattell, R. B., & Eber, H. W. (1964). *Handbook for the 16PF questionnaire.* Champaign, IL: Institute for Personality and Ability Testing.

Cohen, A., & Farley, F. H. (1977). The common-item problem in measurement: Effects on cross-cultural invariance of personality inventory structure. *Educational and Psychological Measurement, 37,* 757–760.

Collins, J. M., & Bagozzi, R. P. (1999). Testing the equivalence of the socialization factor structure for criminals and noncriminals. *Journal of Personality Assessment, 72,* 68–73.

Collins, J. M., & Griffin, R. W. (1998). The psychology of counterproductive job performance. In R. W. Griffith, A. O'Leary-Kelly, & J. M. Collins (Eds.), Dysfunctional behavior in organizations: Non-violent dysfunctional behavior. *Monographs in Organizational Behavior and Relations, 23* (Part B), 219–242. Stamford, CT: JAI.

Comrey, A. L. (1970). *Manual for the Comrey Personality Scales.* San Diego, CA: EDITS.

Conn, S. R., & Rieke, M. L. (Eds.) (1994). *The 16PF fifth edition technical manual.* Champaign, IL: Institute for Personality and Ability Testing.

Constantinople, A. (1973). Masculinity-femininity: An exception to a famous dictum? *Psychological Bulletin, 80,* 389–407.

Cook, M., Young, A., Taylor, D., & Bedford, A. P. (1996). Personality correlates of psychological distress. *Personality and Individual Differences, 20,* 313–319.

Cook, M., Young, A., Taylor, D., O'Shea, A., Chitashvili, M., Lepeska, V., Choumentauskas, G., Ventskovsky, C., Hermochova, S., & Uhler, P. (1998). Personality profiles of managers in former Soviet countries. *Journal of Managerial Psychology, 13,* 567–579.

Coopersmith, S. (1981). *SEI: Self-esteem inventories.* Mountain View, CA: CPP, Inc.

Costa, P. T., Jr., & McCrae, R. R. (1992). *The revised NEO Personality Inventory (NEO-PI-R) and NEO Five-Factor Inventory (NEO-FFI) professional manual.* Odessa, FL: Psychological Assessment Resources.

Craig, R. J. (1999). *Interpreting personality tests: A clinical manual for the MMPI-2, MCMI-III, CPI-R, and 16PF.* New York: John Wiley & Sons.

Crites, J. O., Bechtold, H. P., Goodstein, L. D., & Heilbrun, A. B., Jr. (1961). A factor analysis of the California Psychological Inventory. *Journal of Applied Psychology, 45,* 408–414.

Cronbach, L. J. (1951). Coefficient alpha and the internal structure of tests. *Psychometrika, 16,* 297–334.

Crutchfield, R. S., Woodworth, D. G., & Albrecht, R. E. (1958). *Perceptual performance and the effective* person. (Tech. Note WADC-TN-58-60, ASTIA No. 151039). Lackland Air Force Base, TX: Personnel Laboratory, Wright Air Development Center.

Dahlstrom, W. G., Welsh, G. S., & Dahlstrom, L. E. (1972). *An MMPI handbook: Vol. 1. Clinical interpretation* (Rev. ed.). Minneapolis: University of Minnesota Press.

Dahlstrom, W. G., Welsh, G. S., & Dahlstrom, L. E. (1975). *An MMPI handbook: Vol. 2. Research applications* (Rev. ed.). Minneapolis: University of Minnesota Press.

Davis, G. L., Hoffman, R. G., & Nelson, K. S. (1990). Differences between Native Americans and Whites on the California Psychological Inventory. *Psychological Assessment, 2,* 238–242.

DeFrancesco, J. J., & Taylor, J. (1986). Confirmatory factor analysis of Gough's socialization scale. *Psychological Reports, 58,* 759–762.

DeFrancesco, J. J., & Taylor, J. (1993). A validational note on the revised socialization scale of the California Psychological Inventory. *Journal of Psychopathology and Behavioral Assessment, 15,* 53–56.

Dicken, C. F. (1963). Good impression, social desirability, and acquiescence as suppressor variables. *Educational and Psychological Measurement, 23,* 699–720.

Diehl, M., Elnick, A. B., Bourbeau, L. S., & Labouvie-Vief, G. (1998). Adult attachment styles: Their relation to family context and personality. *Journal of Personality and Social Psychology, 74,* 1656–1669.

Dinca, M. (2001). *Teste de creativitate* (tests of creativity). Bucharest: Editura Paideia.

Domino, G. (1968). Differential prediction of academic achievement in conforming and independent settings. *Journal of Educational Psychology, 59,* 256–260.

Domino, G. (1971). Interactive effects of achievement orientation and teaching style on academic achievement. *Journal of Educational Psychology, 62,* 427–431.

Dudek, S. Z., & Hall, W. B. (1991). Personality consistency: Eminent architects 25 years later. *Creativity Research Journal, 4,* 213–231.

Dunbar, E. (1995). The prejudiced personality, racism, and anti-Semitism: The Pr scale forty years later. *Journal of Personality Assessment, 65,* 270–277.

Dunbar, E. (1997). The relationship of DSM diagnostic criteria and Gough's prejudice scale: Exploring the clinical manifestations of the prejudiced personality. *Cultural Diversity and Mental Health, 3,* 247–257.

Dunbar, E., Saiz, J. L., Stela, K., & Saez, R. (2000). Personality and social group determinants of out-group bias: A cross-national comparison of Gough's Pr/To scale. *Journal of Cross-Cultural Psychology, 31,* 267–275.

Edwards, F. E., & Nagelberg, D. B. (1986). Personality characteristics of restrained/binge eaters versus unrestrained/nonbinge eaters. *Addictive Behaviors, 11,* 207–211.

Eysenck, H. J. (1944). General social attitudes. *Journal of Social Psychology, 19,* 207–227.

Eysenck, H. J. (1947). *Dimensions of Personality.* London: Routledge & Kegan Paul, Ltd.

Eysenck, H. J. (1959). *Maudsley Personality Inventory.* London: University of London Press.

Eysenck, H. J. (1992). The definition and measurement of psychoticism. *Personality and Individual Differences, 13,* 757–785.

Farley, F. H., & Cohen, A. (1974). Common-item effects and the smallest space analysis of structure. *Psychological Bulletin, 81,* 766–772.

Farley, F. H., & Cohen, A. (1980). Common items and reliability in personality measurement. *Journal of Research in Personality, 14,* 207–211.

Fenelon, J. R., & Megargee, E. I. (1971). Influence of race on the manifestation of leadership. *Journal of Applied Psychology, 55,* 353–358.

Fleenor, J. W., & Eastman, L. (1997). The relationship between the five-factor model of personality and the California Psychological Inventory. *Educational and Psychological Measurement, 57,* 698–703.

French, J. L. (1973). *Henmon-Nelson tests of mental ability* (rev. ed.). Boston: Houghton-Mifflin.

Friedman, A. F., Webb, J. T., & Lewak, R. (1989). *Psychological assessment with the MMPI.* Hillsdale, NJ: Erlbaum.

Garnham, D. (1974). State Department rigidity: Testing a psychological hypothesis. *International Studies Quarterly, 18,* 31–39.

Gendre, F. (1966). Evaluation de la personnalité et situation de sélection. *Bulletin d'Etudes et Recherches Psychologiques, 15,* 259–261.

Goldberg, L. R. (1992). The development of markers for the Big-Five factor structure. *Psychological Assessment, 4,* 26–42.

Goldberg, L. R., & Rorer, L. G. (1964). Test-retest item statistics for the California Psychological Inventory. *Research Bulletin, 4*(1). Eugene, OR: Oregon Research Institute.

Goldstein, J. W. (1974). Motivations for psychoactive drug use among students. In B. Kleinmuntz (Ed.), *Readings in the essentials of abnormal psychology* (pp. 371–375). New York: Harper & Row.

Gorecki, P. R., Dickson, A. L., & Ritzler, B. A. (1981). Convergent and concurrent validation of four measures of assertion. *Journal of Behavioral Assessment, 3,* 85–91.

Gough, H. G. (1947). Simulated patterns on the Minnesota Multiphasic Personality Inventory. *Journal of Abnormal and Social Psychology, 42,* 215–225.

Gough, H. G. (1948a). A new dimension of status: I. Development of a personality scale. *American Sociological Review, 13,* 401–409.

Gough, H. G. (1948b). A new dimension of status: II. Relationship of the St scale to other variables. *American Sociological Review, 13*, 534–537.

Gough, H. G. (1948c). A sociological theory of psychopathy. *American Journal of Sociology, 53*, 359–366.

Gough, H. G. (1949a). Factors relating to the academic achievement of high school students. *Journal of Educational Psychology, 40*, 65–78.

Gough, H. G. (1949b). A new dimension of status: III. Discrepancies between the St scale and "objective" status. *American Sociological Review, 14*, 275–281.

Gough, H. G. (1950). The F minus K dissimulation index on the Minnesota Multiphasic Personality Inventory. *Journal of Consulting Psychology, 14*, 408–413.

Gough, H. G. (1951). Studies of social intolerance: II. A personality scale for anti-Semitism. *Journal of Social Psychology, 33*, 247–255.

Gough, H. G. (1952a). Identifying psychological femininity. *Educational and Psychological Measurement, 12*, 427–439.

Gough, H. G. (1952b). On making a good impression. *Journal of Educational Research, 46*, 33–42.

Gough, H. G. (1952c). Predicting social participation. *Journal of Social Psychology, 35*, 227–233.

Gough, H. G. (1953a). The construction of a personality scale to predict scholastic performance. *Journal of Applied Psychology, 37*, 361–366.

Gough, H. G. (1953b). A nonintellectual intelligence test. *Journal of Consulting Psychology, 17*, 242–246.

Gough, H. G. (1953c). What determines the academic achievement of high school students? *Journal of Educational Research, 46*, 321–331.

Gough, H. G. (1954). Some common misconceptions about neuroticism. *Journal of Consulting Psychology, 18*, 287–292.

Gough, H. G. (1957). *Manual for the California Psychological Inventory.* Mountain View, CA: CPP, Inc.

Gough, H. G. (1964a). Academic achievement in high school as predicted from the California Psychological Inventory. *Journal of Educational Psychology, 55*, 174–180.

Gough, H. G. (1964b). Achievement in the first course in psychology as predicted from the California Psychological Inventory. *Journal of Psychology, 57*, 419–430.

Gough, H. G. (1965a). Conceptual analysis of psychological test scores and other diagnostic variables. *Journal of Abnormal Psychology, 70*, 294–302.

Gough, H. G. (1965b). A cross-cultural validation of a measure of asocial behavior. *Psychological Reports, 17*, 379–387.

Gough, H. G. (1966a). A cross-cultural analysis of the CPI femininity scale. *Journal of Consulting Psychology, 30*, 136–141.

Gough, H. G. (1966b). Graduation from high school as predicted from the California Psychological Inventory. *Psychology in the Schools, 3*, 208–216.

Gough, H. G. (1968a). College attendance among high-aptitude students as predicted from the California Psychological Inventory. *Journal of Counseling Psychology, 15*, 269–278.

Gough, H. G. (1968b). An interpreter's syllabus for the CPI. In P. McReynolds (Ed.), *Advances in psychological assessment* (Vol. 1, pp. 55–79). Palo Alto, CA: Science and Behavior Books.

Gough, H. G. (1968c). *Manual for the Chapin Social Insight Test.* Mountain View, CA: CPP, Inc.

Gough, H. G. (1984). A managerial potential scale for the California Psychological Inventory. *Journal of Applied Psychology, 69*, 233–240.

Gough, H. G. (1985). A work orientation scale for the California Psychological Inventory. *Journal of Applied Psychology, 70*, 505–513.

Gough, H. G. (1987). *The California Psychological Inventory administrator's guide.* Mountain View, CA: CPP, Inc.

Gough, H. G. (1989). The California Psychological Inventory. In C. S. Newmark (Ed.), *Major psychological assessment instruments* (Vol. 2, pp. 67–98). Boston: Allyn and Bacon.

Gough, H. G. (1990). Testing for leadership with the California Psychological Inventory. In K. E. Clark & M. B. Clark (Eds.), *Measures of leadership* (pp. 355–379). West Orange, NJ: Leadership Library of America.

Gough, H. G. (1991). Some unfinished business. In W. M. Grove & D. Cicchetti (Eds.), *Thinking clearly about psychology: Vol. 2. Personality and psychopathology* (pp. 114–136). Minneapolis, MN: University of Minnesota Press.

Gough, H. G. (1992). Assessment of creative potential in psychology and the development of a creative temperament scale for the CPI. In J. C. Rosen & P. McReynolds (Eds.), *Advances in psychological assessment* (Vol. 8, pp. 227–259). New York: Plenum.

Gough, H. G. (1994). Theory, development, and interpretation of the CPI socialization scale. *Psychological Reports, 75*, 651–700.

Gough, H. G. (1995). Career assessment and the California Psychological Inventory. *Journal of Career Assessment, 3*, 101–122.

Gough, H. G. (2000). The California Psychological Inventory. In C. E. Watkins, Jr., & V. L. Campbell (Eds.), *Testing and assessment in counseling practice—Second edition* (pp. 45–71). Mahwah, NJ: Lawrence Erlbaum Associates.

Gough, H. G., Allerhand, M. E., & Grais, M. L. (1950). Psychological factors in neurodermatitis. *Psychosomatic Medicine, 12*, 386–390.

Gough, H. G., & Bradley, P. (1992a). Comparing two strategies for developing personality scales. In M. Zeidner & R. Most (Eds.), *Psychological testing: An inside view* (pp. 215–246). Mountain View, CA: CPP, Inc.

Gough, H. G., & Bradley, P. (1992b). Delinquent and criminal behavior as assessed by the revised California Psychological Inventory. *Journal of Clinical Psychology, 48,* 298–308.

Gough, H. G., & Bradley, P. (1993). Personal attributes of people described by others as intolerant. In P. M. Sniderman, P. E. Tetlock, & E. G. Carmines (Eds.), *Prejudice, politics, and the American dilemma* (pp. 60–85). Stanford, CA: Stanford University Press.

Gough, H. G., & Bradley, P. (1999). Use of the California Psychological Inventory with military personnel. Paper given at the 41st Annual Meeting of the International Military Testing Association, Monterey, CA, November 8–10, 1999.

Gough, H. G., Bradley, P., & Bedeian, A. W. (1996). *Development of self-report Adjective Check List scales for Tellegen's three higher-order traits.* Manuscript on file. Institute of Personality and Social Research, University of California, Berkeley.

Gough, H. G., Chun, K., & Chung, Y. (1968). Validation of the CPI femininity scale in Korea. *Psychological Reports, 22,* 155–160.

Gough, H. G., Hall, W. B., & Bradley, P. (1996). Forty years of experience with the Barron-Welsh Art Scale. In A. Montuori (Ed.), *Unusual associates: A festschrift for Frank Barron* (pp. 252–301). Cresskill, NJ: Hampton Press.

Gough, H. G., & Heilbrun, A. B., Jr. (1983). *The Adjective Check List Manual – 1983 Edition.* Mountain View, CA: CPP, Inc.

Gough, H. G., & Lanning, K. (1986). Predicting grades in college from the California Psychological Inventory. *Educational and Psychological Measurement, 46,* 205–213.

Gough, H. G., McClosky, H., & Meehl, P. E. (1951). A personality scale for dominance. *Journal of Abnormal and Social Psychology, 46,* 360–366.

Gough, H. G., McClosky, H., & Meehl, P. E. (1952). A personality scale for social responsibility. *Journal of Abnormal and Social Psychology, 47,* 73–80.

Gough, H. G., & McGurk, E. (1967). A group test of perceptual acuity. *Perceptual and Motor Skills, 24,* 1107–1115.

Gough, H. G., & Olton, R. M. (1972). Field independence as related to nonverbal measures of perceptual performance and cognitive ability. *Journal of Consulting and Clinical Psychology, 38,* 338–342.

Gough, H. G., & Peterson, D. R. (1952). The identification and measurement of predispositional factors in crime and delinquency. *Journal of Consulting Psychology, 16,* 207–212.

Gough, H. G., & Weiss, D. S. (1981). A nontransformational test of intellectual competence. *Journal of Applied Psychology, 66,* 102–110.

Gowan, J. C. (1958). Intercorrelations and factor analysis of tests given to teaching candidates. *Journal of Experimental Education, 27,* 1–22.

Groth-Marnat, G. (1996). *Handbook of psychological assessment* (3rd ed.). New York: John Wiley & Sons.

Guilford, J. P. (1967). *The nature of human intelligence.* New York: McGraw-Hill.

Guilford, J. P., Guilford, J. S., & Zimmerman, W. S. (1978). *The Guilford-Zimmerman Temperament Survey: Manual.* Orange, CA: Sheridan Psychological Services.

Guilford, J. P., & Zimmerman, W. S. (1949). *The Guilford-Zimmerman Temperament Survey: Manual.* Beverly Hills, CA: Sheridan Supply.

Guilford, J. S., Zimmerman, W. S., & Guilford, J. P. (1976). *The Guilford-Zimmerman Temperament Survey handbook.* San Diego, CA: Educational and Industrial Testing Service.

Guttman, L. (1968). A general nonmetric technique for finding the coordinate space for a configuration of points. *Psychometrika, 33,* 469–506.

Guttman, L. (1982). Facet theory, smallest space analysis, and factor analysis. *Perceptual and Motor Skills, 54,* 491–493.

Hakstian, A. R., & Farrell, S. (2001). An openness scale for the California Psychological Inventory. *Journal of Personality Assessment, 76,* 107–134.

Hakstian, A. R., Scratchley, L. S., MacLeod, A. A., Tweed, R. G., & Siddarth, S. (1997). Selection of telemarketing employees by standardized assessment procedures. *Psychology and Marketing, 14,* 703–726.

Hall, W. B., & MacKinnon, D. W. (1969). Personality inventory correlates of creativity among architects. *Journal of Applied Psychology, 53,* 322–326.

Hansen, J. C. (1984). *User's guide for the SVIB-SCII.* Mountain View, CA: CPP, Inc.

Harker, L., & Keltner, D. (2001). Expressions of emotion in women's college yearbook pictures and their relationship to personality and life outcomes across adulthood. *Journal of Personality and Social Psychology, 80,* 112–124.

Harker, L., & Solomon, M. (1996). Change in goals and values of men and women from early to mature adulthood. *Journal of Adult Development, 3,* 133–143.

Harmon, L. W., Hansen, J. C., Borgen, F. H., & Hammer, A. L. (1994). *Strong Interest Inventory: Applications and technical guide.* Mountain View, CA: CPP, Inc.

Hartshorne, H., & May, M. A. (1928). *Studies in deceit.* New York: Macmillan.

Hathaway, S. R., & McKinley, J. C. (1940). A multiphasic personality schedule (Minnesota): I. Construction of the schedule. *Journal of Psychology, 10,* 249–254.

Hathaway, S. R., & McKinley, J. C. (1943). *Minnesota Multiphasic Personality Inventory.* Minneapolis: University of Minnesota Press.

Heilbrun, A. B., Jr. (1996). Criminal dangerousness and the risk of violence. Lanham, NY: University Press of America.

Heist, P., & Yonge, G. (1968). *Manual for the Omnibus Personality Inventory.* New York: The Psychological Corporation.

Helson, R. (1996). Personality change in women and their adult development. Polish *Quarterly of Developmental Psychology, 2,* 269–273.

Helson, R., & Klohnen, E. C. (1998). Affective coloring of personality from young adulthood to midlife. *Personality and Social Psychology Bulletin, 24,* 241–252.

Helson, R., & Moane, G. (1987). Personality and change in women from college to midlife. *Journal of Personality and Social Psychology, 53,* 176–186.

Helson, R., & Pals, J. L. (2000). Creative potential, creative achievement, and personal growth. *Journal of Personality, 68,* 1–27

Helson, R., & Picano, J. (1990). Is the traditional role bad for women? *Journal of Personality and Social Psychology, 59,* 311–320.

Helson, R., & Roberts, B. W. (1994). Ego development and personality change in adulthood. *Journal of Personality and Social Psychology, 66,* 911–920.

Helson, R., Roberts, B. W., & Agronick, G. (1995). Enduringness and change in creative personality and the prediction of occupational creativity. *Journal of Personality and Social Psychology, 69,* 1173–1183.

Helson, R., Stewart, A. J., & Ostrove, J. (1995). Identity in three cohorts of midlife women. *Journal of Personality and Social Psychology, 69,* 544–557.

Helson, R., & Wink, P. (1987). Two conceptions of maturity examined in the findings of a longitudinal study. *Journal of Personality and Social Psychology, 53,* 531–541.

Helson, R., & Wink, P. (1992). Personality change in women from the early 40s to the early 50s. *Psychology and Aging, 7,* 46–55.

Hirschfeld, R. M. A., Klerman, G. L., Gough, H. G., Barrett, J., Korchin, S. J., & Chodoff, P. (1977). A measure of interpersonal dependency. *Journal of Personality Assessment, 41,* 610–618.

Hogan, R. T. (1967). *Moral development: An assessment approach.* Unpublished doctoral dissertation, University of California, Berkeley.

Hogan, R. (1969). Development of an empathy scale. *Journal of Consulting and Clinical Psychology, 33,* 307–316.

Hogan, R. (1970). A dimension of moral judgment. *Journal of Consulting and Clinical Psychology, 35,* 205–212.

Hogan, R. (1986). *Hogan Personality Inventory manual.* Minneapolis: National Computer Systems.

Hogan, R., & Dickstein, E. (1972). A measure of moral values. *Journal of Consulting and Clinical Psychology, 39,* 210–220.

Hogan, R., & Mankin, D. (1970). Determinants of interpersonal attraction: A clarification. *Psychological Reports, 26,* 235–238.

Hogan, R., Mankin, D., Conway, J., & Fox, S. (1970). Personality correlates of undergraduate marijuana use. *Journal of Consulting and Clinical Psychology, 35,* 58–63.

Holland, J. L. (1973). *Making vocational choices: A theory of careers.* Englewood Cliffs, NJ: Prentice-Hall.

Holland, J. L. (1985). *Making vocational choices* (2nd ed.). Englewood Cliffs, NJ: Prentice-Hall.

Holliman, N. B., & Guthrie, P. C. (1989). A comparison of the Millon Clinical Multiaxial Inventory and the California Psychological Inventory in assessment of a nonclinical population. *Journal of Clinical Psychology, 45,* 373–382.

Holliman, N. B., & Montross, J. (1984). The effects of depression upon responses to the California Psychological Inventory. *Journal of Clinical Psychology, 40,* 1373–1378.

Horn, J. M., Plomin, R., & Rosenman, R. (1976). Heritability of personality traits in male adult twins. *Behavior Genetics, 6,* 17–30.

Humm, D. G., & Wadsworth, G. W. (1934). The Humm-Wadsworth Temperament Scale, *Personnel Journal, 12,* 314–323.

Jackson, D. N. (1967). *Personality Research Form manual.* Goshen, NY: Research Psychologists Press.

Jacobs, R. L. (1992). Moving up the corporate ladder: A longitudinal study of motivation, personality, and managerial success in women and men. Unpublished doctoral dissertation, Boston University.

James, W. (1907). *Pragmatism.* New York: Longmans, Green and Company.

Johnson, J. A. (1981). The "self-disclosure" and "self-presentation" views of item response dynamics and personality scale validity. *Journal of Personality and Social Psychology, 40,* 761–769.

Johnson, J. A. (1997). Seven social performance scales for the California Psychological Inventory. *Human Performance, 10,* 1–30.

Johnson, J. A., Cheek, J. M., & Smither, R. (1983). The structure of empathy. *Journal of Personality and Social Psychology, 45,* 1299–1312.

Johnson, R. P. (1957). *The isolation of personality dimensions through a factor analysis of the California Psychological Inventory.* Unpublished doctoral dissertation, University of North Carolina, Chapel Hill.

Kadden, R. M., Cooney, N. L., Getter, H., & Litt, M. D. (1989). Matching alcoholics to coping skills or interactional therapies: Posttreatment results. *Journal of Consulting and Clinical Psychology, 57,* 698–704.

Kadden, R. M., Litt, M. D., Donovan, D., & Cooney, N. L. (1996). Psychometric properties of the CPI socialization scale in treatment-seeking alcoholics. *Psychology of Addictive Behaviors, 10,* 131–146.

Kanner, A. D. (1976). Femininity and masculinity: Their relationship to creativity in male architects and their independence from each other. *Journal of Consulting and Clinical Psychology, 44,* 802–805.

Karni, E., & Levin, J. (1972). The use of smallest space analysis in studying scale structure: An application to the California Psychological Inventory. *Journal of Applied Psychology, 56,* 341–346.

Kassebaum, G. K., Couch, A. S., & Slater, P. E. (1959). The factorial dimensions of the MMPI. *Journal of Consulting Psychology, 23,* 226–236.

Kegel-Flom, P. (1992). What kinds of leaders are entering optometry schools? *Optometry and Vision Science, 69,* 991–996.

Kegel-Flom, P., & Fort, D. C. (1995). Dr. Sandra Davis on leadership. *American Women in Science Magazine, 24*(1), 12–13, 18.

Kelly, E. L., Miles, C. C., & Terman, L. M. (1936). Ability to influence one's score on a typical pencil and paper test of personality. *Character and Personality, 4,* 206–215.

Klohnen, E. C. (1996a). Conceptual analysis and measurement of the construct of ego resiliency. *Journal of Personality and Social Psychology, 70,* 1067–1079.

Klohnen, E. C. (1996b). Negotiating the midlife years: Ego resiliency and successful midlife adjustment in women. *Psychology and Aging, 11,* 431–442.

Kohlberg, L. (1981). *The meaning and measurement of moral development.* Worcester, MA: Clark University Press.

Kosson, D. S., Kelly, J. C., & White, J. W. (1997). Psychopathy-related traits predict self-reported sexual aggression among college men. *Journal of Interpersonal Violence, 12,* 241–254.

Kosson, D. S., Steuerwald, B. L., Newman, J. P., & Widom, C. S. (1994). The relation between socialization, antisocial behavior, substance abuse, and family conflict in college students. *Journal of Personality Assessment, 63,* 473–488.

Kubicka, L., Matejcek, Z., David, H. P., Dytrych, Z., Miller, W. B., & Roth, Z. (1995). Children from unwanted pregnancies in Prague, Czech Republic, revisited at age thirty. *Acta Psychiatrica Scandinavica, 91,* 361–369.

Kuhlman, F., & Anderson, R. G. (1940). *Kuhlman-Anderson Intelligence Test* (5th ed.). Minneapolis: Educational Test Bureau.

Kuhlman, F., & Anderson, R. G. (1985). *Kuhlman-Anderson technical manual* (8th ed.). Bensenville, IL: Scholastic Testing Service.

Kurtines, W. M., Hogan, R., & Weiss, D. S. (1975). Personality dynamics of heroin use. *Journal of Abnormal Psychology, 84,* 87–89.

Labouvie-Vief, G., Diehl, M., Tarnowski, A., & Shen, J. (2000). Age differences in personality: Findings from the United States and China. *Journal of Gerontology, 55*(B), 4–17.

Lanning, K. (1989). Detection of invalid response patterns on the California Psychological Inventory. *Applied Psychological Measurement, 13,* 45–56.

Lazare, A., Klerman, G. L., & Armor, D. (1966). Oral, obsessive, and hysterical personality patterns: An investigation of psychoanalytic concepts by means of factor analysis. *Archives of General Psychiatry, 14,* 624–630.

Lazare, A., Klerman, G. L., & Armor, D. (1970). Oral, obsessive, and hysterical personality patterns: Replication of factor analysis in an independent sample. *Journal of Psychiatric Research, 7,* 275–290.

Leary, T. (1957). *Interpersonal diagnosis of personality.* New York: Ronald Press.

Leventhal, A. M. (1966). An anxiety scale for the CPI. *Journal of Clinical Psychology, 22,* 459–461.

Leventhal, A. M. (1968). Additional data on the CPI anxiety scale. *Journal of Counseling Psychology, 15,* 479–480.

Levin, J. (1971). Spherical model of vector extension for determining the factor pattern of the California Psychological Inventory. *Journal of Counseling Psychology, 18,* 579–582.

Levin, J., & Karni, E. S. (1970). Demonstration of cross-cultural invariance of the California Psychological Inventory in America and Israel by the Guttman-Lindoes smallest space analysis. *Journal of Cross-Cultural Psychology, 1,* 253–260.

Levin, J., & Karni, E. S. (1971). A comparative study of the CPI femininity scale: Validation in Israel. *Journal of Cross-Cultural Psychology, 2,* 387–391.

Levin, J., & Karni, E. (1981). A note on the interpretation of the factor pattern of the CPI. *Journal of Personality Assessment, 45,* 430–432.

Levinson, D. J., & Sanford, R. N. (1944). A scale for the measurement of anti-Semitism. *Journal of Psychology, 17,* 339–370.

Loevinger, J. (1979). Construct validity of the sentence completion test of ego development. *Applied Psychological Measurement, 3,* 281–311.

Lorr, M., & Burger, G. K. (1981). Personality types in data from the California Psychological Inventory as defined by cluster analysis. *Psychological Reports, 48,* 115–118.

Lykken, D. T. (1971). Multiple factor analysis and personality research. *Journal of Experimental Research in Personality, 5,* 161–170.

MacKinnon, D. W. (1962). The personality correlates of creativity: A study of American architects. In G. S. Nielson (Ed.), *Proceedings of the XIV International Congress of Applied Psychology, Copenhagen, 1961* (Vol. 2, pp. 11–39). Copenhagen: Munksgaard.

Maslach, C. M., & Jackson, S. E. (1986). *Maslach Burnout Inventory* (2nd ed.). Mountain View, CA: CPP, Inc.

Mazen, A. M., & Lemkau, J. P. (1990). Personality profiles of women in traditional and nontraditional occupations. *Journal of Vocational Behavior, 37,* 46–59.

McAllister, L. W. (1996). *A practical guide to CPI interpretation* (3rd ed.). Mountain View, CA: CPP, Inc.

McClosky, H. (1969). *Political inquiry.* New York: Macmillan.

McKinley, J. C., Hathaway, S. R., & Meehl, P. E. (1948). The MMPI: VI. The K scale. *Journal of Consulting Psychology, 12,* 20–31.

Meehl, P. E. (1993). Four queries about factor reality. *History and Philosophy of Psychology Bulletin, 5*(2), 4–5.

Meehl, P. E. (1954). *Clinical versus statistical prediction*. Minneapolis: University of Minnesota Press.

Mees, H. L., Gocka, E. F., & Holloway, H. (1964). Social desirability values of California Psychological Inventory items. *Psychological Reports, 15*, 147–158.

Megargee, E. I. (1969). Influence of sex roles on the manifestation of leadership. *Journal of Applied Psychology, 53*, 377–382.

Megargee, E. I. (1972). *The California Psychological Inventory handbook*. San Francisco: Jossey-Bass.

Megargee, E. I., Bogart, P., & Anderson, D. J. (1966). The prediction of leadership in a simulated industrial task. *Journal of Applied Psychology, 50*, 292–295.

Meyer, P., & Davis, S. (1992). *The CPI applications guide*. Mountain View, CA: CPP, Inc.

Miller, W. S. (1970). *Manual for the Miller Analogies Test*. New York: The Psychological Corporation.

Millon, T. (1983). *Millon Clinical Multiaxial Inventory, manual* (3rd ed.). Minneapolis: National Computer Systems.

Mills, J. K., & Taricone, P. F. (1991). Interpersonal dependency and locus of control as personality correlates among adult male alcoholics undergoing residential treatment. *Psychological Reports, 68*, 1107–1112.

Mitchell, J. V., Jr., & Pierce-Jones, J. (1960). A factor analysis of Gough's California Psychological Inventory. *Journal of Consulting Psychology, 24*, 453–456.

Mongtomery, R. L., & Mathis, B. (1992, April). *The effect of self-rated attractiveness on personal and interpersonal functioning*. Paper presented at the meeting of the Southwestern Psychological Association, Austin, TX.

Myers, E. B., & McCaulley, M. H. (1985). *Manual: A guide to the development and use of the Myers-Briggs Type Indicator*. Mountain View, CA: CPP, Inc.

Nichols, R. C., & Schell, R. R. (1963). Factor scales for the California Psychological Inventory. *Journal of Consulting Psychology, 27*, 228–235.

Nishiyama, T. (1975). Validation of the CPI femininity scale in Japan. *Journal of Cross-Cultural Psychology, 6*, 482–489.

Otis, A. S., & Lennon, R. T. (1979). *Otis-Lennon School Ability Test*. Cleveland, OH: The Psychological Corporation.

Park, J. H., Meyers, L. S., & Czar, G. C. (1998). Religiosity and spirituality: An exploratory analysis using the CPI 3-vector model. *Journal of Social Behavior and Personality, 13*, 541–552.

Parloff, M. B., Datta, L. E., Kleman, M., & Handlon, J. H. (1968). Personality characteristics which differentiate creative male adolescents and adults. *Journal of Personality, 36*, 528–552.

Peskin, H., Jones, C. J., & Livson, N. (1997). Personal warmth and psychological health at midlife. *Journal of Adult Development, 4*, 71–83.

Pfeiffer, C. M., Jr., & Sedlacek, W. E. (1974). Predicting black student grades with non-intellectual measures. *Journal of Negro Education, 43*, 67–76.

Picano, J. J. (1989). Development and validation of a life history index of adult adjustment for women. *Journal of Personality Assessment, 53*, 308–318.

Pierce-Jones, J. (1961). Social mobility orientations and interests of adolescents. *Journal of Counseling Psychology, 8*, 75–78.

Pitariu, H. (1981). Validation of the CPI femininity scale in Romania. *Journal of Cross-Cultural Psychology, 12*, 111–117.

Pitariu, H. D., Pitariu, H. A., & Ali Al Mutairi, M. (1998). Psychological assessment of managers in Romania: Validation of a test battery. Paper given at the 1998 meetings of the American Psychological Association, San Francisco, CA, August 13–18, 1998.

Raskin, R. N., & Hall, C. S. (1979). A narcissistic personality inventory. *Psychology Reports, 45*, 159–162.

Repapi, M., Gough, H. G., Lanning, K., & Stefanis, C. (1983). Predicting academic achievement of Greek secondary school students from family background and California Psychological Inventory scores. *Contemporary Educational Psychology, 8*, 181–188.

Roberts, B. W. (1997). Plaster or plasticity: Are adult work experiences associated with personality change in women? *Journal of Personality, 65*, 205–232.

Roberts, B. W., & Friend, W. (1998). Career momentum in midlife women: Life context, identity, and personality correlates. *Journal of Occupational Health Psychology, 3*, 195–208.

Roberts, B. W., & Helson, R. (1997). Changes in culture, changes in personality: The influence of individualism in a longitudinal study of women. *Journal of Personality and Social Psychology, 72*, 641–651.

Roberts, M. D. (1995a). Personal communication. Los Gatos, CA: Law Enforcement Psychological Services, Inc.

Roberts, M. D. (1995b). *Police and public safety selection report: California Psychological Inventory—434*. Los Gatos, CA: Law Enforcement Psychological Services.

Rogers, M. S., & Shure, G. H. (1965). An empirical evaluation of the effect of item overlap on factorial stability. *Journal of Psychology, 60*, 221–233.

Rokeach, M. (1960). *The open and closed mind*. New York: Basic Books.

Rosen, A. (1977). On the dimensionality of the California Psychological Inventory socialization scale. *Journal of Consulting and Clinical Psychology, 45*, 583–591.

Rotter, J. B. (1966). Generalized expectancies for internal vs. external control of reinforcement. *Psychological Monographs, 80*, 1 (Whole No. 609).

Ruch, F. L. (1942). A technique for detecting attempts to fake performance on the self-inventory type of personality test. In Q. McNemar & M. A. Merrill (Eds.), *Studies in personality* (pp. 229–234). New York: McGraw-Hill.

Sandoval, J. (1993). Personality and burnout among school psychologists. *Psychology in the Schools, 30,* 321–326.

Schaie, K. W. (1996). The sequential development of personality traits and attitudes. In K. W. Schaie, *Intellectual development in adulthood: The Seattle longitudinal study* (pp. 278–295). New York: Cambridge University Press.

Schalling, D. (1978). Psychopathy-related personality variables and the psychophysiology of socialization. In R. D. Hare & D. Schalling (Eds.), *Psychopathic behavior: Approaches to research* (pp. 85–106). Chichester, Great Britain: Wiley.

Schinka, J. A., & Borum, R. (1994). Readability of normal personality inventories. *Journal of Personality Assessment, 62,* 95–101.

Seisdedos, N. (1992). *Inventario Psicologio de California de H. G. Gough.* Madrid: TEA Ediciones, S.A.

Shostrum, E. L. (1963). *The Personal Orientation Inventory.* San Diego, CA: Educational and Industrial Testing Service.

Shujaat, R., Zehra, F., & Anila (1996). Personality characteristics of executives in business organizations as revealed through selected scales of the California Psychological Inventory. *Pakistan Journal of Psychological Research, 11,* 65–80.

Shure, G. H., & Rogers, M. S. (1963). Personality factor stability for three ability levels. *Journal of Psychology, 55,* 445–456.

Siegelman, M. (1972). Adjustment of male homosexuals and heterosexuals. *Archives of Sexual Behavior, 2,* 9–25.

Siegelman, M. (1978). Psychological adjustment of homosexual and heterosexual men: A cross-cultural replication. *Archives of Sexual Behavior, 7,* 1–11.

Solomon, M. F. (2000). The fruits of their labors: A longitudinal exploration of parent personality and adjustment in adult children. *Journal of Personality, 68,* 281–308.

Spence, J. T., & Helmreich, R. L. (1979). *Masculinity and femininity: Their psychological dimensions, correlates, and antecedents.* Austin, TX: University of Texas Press.

Spencer, D. (1938). The frankness of subjects on personality measures. *Journal of Educational Psychology, 29,* 26–35.

Spielberger, C. D., Gorsuch, R. L., Lushene, R., Vagg, P. R., & Jacobs, G. A. (1983). *Manual for the State-Trait Anxiety Inventory.* Mountain View, CA: CPP, Inc.

Springob, H. K., & Streuning, E. L. (1964). A factor analysis of the California Psychological Inventory on a high school population. *Journal of Counseling Psychology, 11,* 173–179.

Stein, K. B., Gough, H. G., & Sarbin, T. R. (1966). The dimensionality of the CPI socialization scale and an empirically developed typology among delinquent and nondelinquent boys. *Multivariate Behavioral Research, 1,* 192–208.

Stewart, A. J., & Vandewater, E. A. (1998). The course of generativity. In D. P. McAdams & E. de St. Aubin (Eds.), *Generativity and adult development: How and why we care for the next generation* (pp. 75–100). Washington, DC: American Psychological Association

Strong, E. K., Jr. (1943). *The vocational interests of men and women.* Stanford, CA: Stanford University Press.

Sullaway, M., & Dunbar, E. (1996). Clinical manifestations of prejudice in psychotherapy: Toward a strategy of assessment and treatment. *Clinical Psychology: Science and Practice, 3,* 296–309.

Taub, J. M., & Hawkins, D. R. (1979). Aspects of personality associated with irregular sleep habits in young adults. *Journal of Clinical Psychology, 35,* 296–304.

Taylor, J., McGue, M., Iacono, W. G., & Lykken, D. T. (2000). A behavioral genetic analysis of the relationship between the socialization scale and self-reported delinquency. *Journal of Personality, 68,* 29–50.

Tellegen, A. (1985). Structures of mood and personality and their relevance to assessing anxiety with an emphasis on self-report. In A. H. Tuma & J. D. Masser (Eds.), *Anxiety and anxiety disorders* (pp. 681–706). Hillsdale, NJ: Erlbaum.

Torki, M. A. (1988). The CPI femininity scale in Kuwait and Egypt. *Journal of Personality Assessment, 52,* 247–253.

Twisk, J. W. R., Snel, J., Kemper, H. C. G., & van Mechelen, W. (1998). Relation between the longitudinal development of personality characteristics and biological and lifestyle risk factors for coronary heart disease. *Psychosomatic Medicine, 60,* 372–377.

Vandewater, E. A., Ostrove, J. M., & Stewart, A. J. (1997). Predicting women's well-being in midlife: The importance of personality development and social role involvements. *Journal of Personality and Social Psychology, 72,* 1147–1160.

Vandewater, E. A., & Stewart, A. J. (1997). Women's career commitment patterns and personality development. In M. E. Lachman & J. B. James (Eds.), *Multiple paths of midlife development* (pp. 375–410). Chicago, IL: University of Chicago Press.

Vandewater, E. A., & Stewart, A. J. (1998). Making commitments, creating lives: Linking women's career roles and personality at midlife. *Psychology of Women Quarterly, 22,* 717–738.

Veblen, T. (1914). *The instinct of workmanship and the state of the industrial arts.* New York: Macmillan.

Veldman, D., & Pierce-Jones, J. (1964). Sex differences in factor structure for the California Psychological Inventory. *Journal of Consulting Psychology, 28,* 93.

Vernon, P. E. (1934). The attitude of subjects in personality testing. *Journal of Applied Psychology, 18,* 165–177.

Vernon, P. E. (1953). *Personality tests and assessments.* London: Methuen & Co.

Weber, M. (1930). *The Protestant ethic and the spirit of capitalism.* New York: Scribner. (Originally published in 1904 as *Die protestantische Ethic und der Geist des Kapitalismus*)

Wechsler, D. (1939). *The measurement of adult intelligence.* Baltimore, MD: Williams and Wilkins.

Wechsler, D. (1955). *Manual for the Wechsler Adult Intelligence Scale.* New York: The Psychological Corporation.

Weekes, B. S. (1993). Criterion-oriented validity of the responsibility scale of the California Psychological Inventory. *Psychological Reports, 73,* 315–320.

Weiser, N. L., & Meyers, L. S. (1993). Validity and reliability of the revised California Psychological Inventory Vector 3 scale. *Educational and Psychological Measurement, 53,* 1045–1054.

Welsh, G. S. (1956). Factor dimensions A and R. In G. S. Welsh & W. G. Dahlstrom (Eds.), *Basic readings on the MMPI in psychology and medicine* (pp. 264–281). Minneapolis: University of Minnesota Press.

Welsh, G. S. (1975). *Creativity and intelligence: A personality approach.* Chapel Hill, NC: University of North Carolina, Institute for Research in Social Science.

Werner, P. D. (1988). Personality correlates of reproductive knowledge. *Journal of Sex Research, 25,* 219–234.

Wiggins, J. S. (1979). A psychological taxonomy of trait-descriptive terms: The interpersonal domain. *Journal of Personality and Social Psychology, 37,* 395–412.

Wiggins, J. S. (1995). *Interpersonal Adjective Scales professional manual.* Odessa, FL: Psychological Assessment Resources.

Williams, J. E., & Best, D. L. (1982). *Measuring sex stereotypes: A thirty-nation study.* Beverly Hills, CA: Sage.

Williams, J. E., & Best, D. L. (1990). *Sex and psyche: Gender and self viewed cross-culturally.* Newbury Park, CA: Sage.

Wilson, M. L., & Greene, R. L. (1971). Personality characteristics of female homosexuals. *Psychological Reports, 28,* 407–412.

Wink, P. (1996). Transition from early 40s to the early 50s in self-directed women. *Journal of Personality, 64,* 49–69.

Wink, P., & Gough, H. G. (1990). New narcissism scales for the California Psychological Inventory and MMPI. *Journal of Personality Assessment, 54,* 446–462.

Wink, P., & Helson, R. (1997). Practical and transcendent wisdom: Their nature and some longitudinal findings. *Journal of Adult Development, 4,* 1–15.

Woychyshyn, C. A., McElheran, W. G., & Romney, D. M. (1992). MMPI validity measures: A comparative study of original with alternative indices. *Journal of Personality Assessment, 58,* 138–148.

Yang, J., & Gong, X. (1993). Revising of the California Psychological Inventory in China. *Chinese Journal of Clinical Psychology, 1,* 11–15. (In Mandarin)

Yang, J., McCrae, R. R., & Costa, P. T., Jr. (1998). Adult age differences in personality traits in the United States and the People's Republic of China. *Journal of Gerontology: Psychological Sciences, 53*(B), 375–383.

Ying, Y. (1991). Validation of the California Psychological Inventory femininity scale in Taiwan college graduates. *Journal of Multicultural Counseling and Development, 19,* 166–172.

Zuckerman, M. (1971). Dimensions of sensation-seeking. *Journal of Consulting and Clinical Psychology, 36,* 45–52.

Zuckerman, M., Kolin, E. A., Price, L., & Zoob, I. (1964). Development of a sensation-seeking scale. *Journal of Consulting and Clinical Psychology, 28,* 477–482.

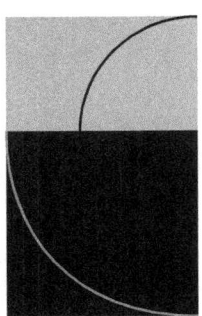

Index

Note: Page number followed by *t* locate tables.